ISBN 978-1-331-16874-4
PIBN 10153328

1 MONTH OF
FREE
READING

at

www.ForgottenBooks.com

By purchasing this book you are eligible for one month membership to ForgottenBooks.com, giving you unlimited access to our entire collection of over 1,000,000 titles via our web site and mobile apps.

To claim your free month visit:

www.forgottenbooks.com/free153328

English
Français
Deutsche
Italiano
Español
Português

www.forgottenbooks.com

Mythology Photography **Fiction**
Fishing Christianity **Art** Cooking
Essays Buddhism Freemasonry
Medicine **Biology** Music **Ancient
Egypt** Evolution Carpentry Physics
Dance Geology **Mathematics** Fitness
Shakespeare **Folklore** Yoga Marketing
Confidence Immortality Biographies
Poetry **Psychology** Witchcraft
Electronics Chemistry History **Law**
Accounting **Philosophy** Anthropology
Alchemy Drama Quantum Mechanics
Atheism Sexual Health **Ancient History**
Entrepreneurship Languages Sport
Paleontology Needlework Islam
Metaphysics Investment Archaeology
Parenting Statistics Criminology
Motivational

d Hour Division, adm
government employe
overed by the law an

argaining agreement
ary 5, 1994, whicher
d leave in a 12-mont
ar year, a fixed 12-r
12-month period.

aw's benefits; entitl
tice and certificatior
e law also requires

ation agencies (sch
r more workweeks I
Industry or activity

on of the United Sta

rkweeks of **unpaid**

or foster care;
with a serious heal
e of a serious healt

ed total of 12 work
tion or foster care,

JUSTICES OF THE SUPREME JUDICIAL COURT

OF MASSACHUSETTS,

TO WHOSE LABORS I AM INDEBTED FOR SO MUCH OF WHAT IS VALUABLE IN THE WORK, I DEDICATE THIS UNPRE- TENDING EFFORT TO ELUCIDATE A DEPART- MENT OF AMERICAN JURISPRUDENCE.

IN doing this, I desire to add to the traditional veneration for this Court which I have shared in common with the peo- ple of the Commonwealth an expression of personal respect· for its members, which the long intercourse into which I have been brought, since my admission to its bar, has served to develop, and constantly to strengthen.

Within that time, every one of its members has been changed. Men, the loved and the honored, have one after another passed away in the fulness of their fame, and others are now occupying their field of honorable labor ; but illus- trions as are the names that stand out upon its records among the great and good men of the Commonwealth, never have its laws been more ably, faithfully, and acceptably administered than by those who now occupy these seats of justice.

To bear my humble tribute to the official and personal qualities of the men who have in this field won and sus- tained the united respect of an appreciative public, I sub- scribe myself

Their obliged and obedient servant,

EMORY WASHBURN.

CAMBRIDGE, *July*, 1860.

PREFACE

TO THE FIFTH EDITION.

IN presenting to the profession this fifth edition of WASH-BURN ON REAL PROPERTY, the first issued since the author's death, a few words of preface seem proper. Of the work itself, but little more need be said than to refer to the fact that for twenty-six years it has held its place unchallenged, as the only comprehensive American treatise on the subject of Real Property; although various valuable works on special topics have appeared, notably within the last ten years. Since its first appearance, it has, as an authority in the courts and a text-book in the schools, not only formulated the existing law, and helped in no inconsiderable degree to develop and harmonize it, — a function which every sound treatise achieves to a greater or less extent; but its very language has, by frequent judicial citation, become incorporated in the authoritative law of many of the States.

The law, however, never stands still, and the multitude of decisions and the important statutory changes that have been made in the department of Real Property in the decade since the last edition of this work appeared, have called for very extended labor in the direction of condensation as well as of addition. The author's death occurring so soon after that edition came out, devolved much the larger part of this labor upon the editors. In the discharge of this duty they have for the most part confined their additions to the notes. The changes in the text have been mainly limited to the removal of some obvious errors in the form of statement, and

to the excision of statutory matter superseded by recent legislation, and of repetitions chiefly to be found in what was added
by the author after the first edition.

In the chapter on Homestead, however, as the foundation of
the law was wholly by enactment, the additions and correc-
tions have been substantial, so as to bring the text, as nearly
as might be, abreast with the present condition of the law.
Whatever opinion may obtain as to the propriety of originally
including a topic of this character in a general common-law
treatise, the editors had no choice but to retain it, and, if retained, to have it as nearly complete as space would permit.
For although the ground had been covered by Mr. Thompson's
valuable work, yet, in the interval since the publication of his
book, the new decisions number over fifteen hundred. In other
places, also, it will be found that such additions have been
made to the text as were necessary to cover the development
of several branches of the law.

In the more mechanical parts of these volumes — the index,
table of cases, and verification of citations — no pains have
been spared to ensure accuracy; and the editors trust that
the results will be satisfactory to the profession.

J. W.
S. G. C.

Boston, *December*, 1886.

PREFACE

TO THE FOURTH EDITION.

———

To carry out the original purpose and design of the present work renders it necessary to add to or modify its statements and propositions, from time to time, to conform to the growth and progress of the law. It was intended to give a connected view of the law of Real Property as it prevails in the several States and under the Federal government, so far as it could be regarded American in its character. For this purpose, it was not only necessary to collect and collate the decisions of the State and Federal courts, but to make liberal reference to English reports and accredited treatises, and from these to form, so far as might be, a consistent and complete system of this department of the law.

If successfully accomplished, two objects would be attained: the profession and the student would be supplied with a work that seemed to be needed for use; and a process of assimilation among the laws of the different States would thereby be promoted, and the bonds of union between them gain strength by an identity of domestic institutions and popular thought.

Judging from the manner in which the work has been referred to by the various courts, it is believed that it has not wholly failed in either of these respects.

Since the publication of the last edition, some two thousand cases have been decided by the courts, which bear upon the subjects-matter of the work, by which, and other causes, changes and modifications of sufficient magnitude and importance in the existing rules of law have been wrought

to call for an effort to collect and embody these into the work
as it had already been given to the public.   An edition, therefore, which should embrace these cases, seemed to be a necessity, and has accordingly been prepared.   Where these cases
were in effect a re-statement of well-considered points of law,
they have been referred to simply by name.   But to such of
them as contained new points, or presented a principle already
familiar in an original or more elaborate form, have been assigned a more extended discussion and examination ; and, in
so doing, a statement of the facts and circumstances of particular cases has, at times, been adopted, which might, perhaps,
seem, at first sight, more consistent with the idea of a digest
than a summary treatise.   Where this has been done, it has
been for the purposes of illustration and explanation.

This accumulation of cases has arisen, in no small degree,
from the fact that the laws of the different States differ essentially upon many subjects ; and it is often as important to cite
cases to show, that, upon a given point, the law of one State
is not like that of another, as it is to state what the law of
the former State, in fact, is.   In this way, citations have often
been multiplied upon a single point, beyond what, at first
thought, might seem necessary or proper.

In the matter of the changes wrought by the legislation of
the States, new statutes are so frequent, and often so arbitrary,
and it is, at times, so difficult to get ready access to them, that,
if errors in this respect should be detected, the cause may, perhaps, be accepted as an excuse.   In collecting and digesting
the cases cited from the reports, liberal use, so far as they
extend, has been made of the " American Reports," — a selection made by Mr. Isaac Grant Thompson with excellent judgment and discrimination ; while an earnest effort has been
made, from other sources, to make the examination and colla-
tion of these reasonably complete.

To give some idea of the topics upon which new or sub-
sidiary matter will be found in the following pages, there
may be mentioned, as among them, homestead exemption ;
when and how far tenants may deny their landlords' titles ;
what force a landlord may apply in expelling a tenant ; how
far tenants are liable to others for injuries arising from the

condition of the premises in their occupancy; how far the tenant of one part of a dwelling-house can compel a tenant of another part to join in making repairs; whether the sale of growing trees and crops is within the 17th section of the statute of frauds; how far absolute deeds can be shown, by parol, to be only mortgages; the order in which owners of different parcels of mortgaged premises are chargeable in the redemption thereof; the validity of deeds, blanks in which have been filled after execution; what American rivers come under the category of navigable, and what are the boundary-lines of lands bordering upon them, and what of lands bounding by the sea, or by lakes and ponds; the power of courts to reform deeds, in order to correct mistakes; how far erecting and occupying up to division-fences affect the title to the adjacent lands; how far holding lands as partnership assets is a conversion of the same " out and out; " and how far one holding an easement of way can release or exchange it by parol.

With such materials, and the space they necessarily occupy in a work like this, it has been impossible to avoid expanding it considerably beyond its previous limits in its present form. But while it has been an aim in its composition to keep it within the narrowest compass, its main purpose has been to bring the work up to the present time, and to render it as accurate and complete as could be done by personal effort and attention.

CAMBRIDGE, *March*, 1876.

PREFACE

THE circumstances under which this work is now offered to the profession are briefly these : —

When called upon to state and illustrate to the classes of a law school, collected from almost every State in the Union, the leading principles of the Law of Real Property, the author was led to believe that there was a want to be supplied by a work, which, while it retained so much of the English common and early statute law as applied to this country, should combine with it, as a basis, the elements of American law as the same had been developed in the legislation and judicial decisions of the General and State governments, in order to form as nearly as might be one homogeneous system.

A conviction of the need of such a work, in the nature of an elementary treatise, strengthened with reflection, till the result has been an attempt to achieve it in the present volumes.

That to do this required the subject to be treated in some of its parts historically, and sometimes to refer to what had become practically obsolete, every intelligent reader will readily understand. The American statesman who should content himself with studying the simple text of the Constitution, without the light which English and Colonial history throws upon its provisions, would find himself at a loss to understand, or how to solve, many of the questions to which the construction of that instrument has given and is giving rise.

So the American lawyer would find still greater difficulty in understanding that great unwritten body of principles which form the basis of the common law of nearly every State in the Union, if he could not go back historically to the coming in of the feudal system at the Conquest, read the charter of Runnymede in the light of the circumstances which surrounded it, and trace the gradual loosening of the bands of tenure before and at the passage of the statute *Quia Emptores.*

If the early English common law had no other application, a knowledge of it could not be dispensed with by a lawyer, as a means of understanding the terms and phrases in modern use, and as furnishing the elementary thoughts and opinions which have been and still are being wrought into the expanding and progressive systems of English and American jurisprudence.

The English Law of Real Property has undergone surprising changes within the last thirty years, whereby a process of assimilation in the systems of the two countries upon this subject has been going on, which is interesting to the American lawyer, and renders a knowledge of the laws of each the more important in the courts of this country.

Here was presented one of the most difficult problems in the prosecution of the present work. It seemed particularly desirable that it should not exceed two volumes of convenient size; while to compress into that space all that should be said of the English law, as well as of the statutes and decisions of thirty-one different States and governments, each related to, and yet independent of, the others, seemed, at first sight, an impracticable undertaking. How far the difficulty has been surmounted, the reader will determine.

It has been the intention of the writer to state no proposition as law which did not appear to be sustained by satisfactory authority. So far as the same could reasonably be done, those authorities have been cited. But, with all his precaution, this could not fail to load his pages with references; and he has contented himself, not unfrequently, with citing an elementary work of received authority to sustain a proposition, rather than to multiply the citations of cases which are to be found, if desired, in the elementary work referred to. In some instances, he has been obliged to rely upon the digest of a reported case; but this has been done with caution, especially when the point to be stated or illustrated seemed to be new and doubtful. On the other hand, he has, in but a few instances, undertaken to give digests of reported cases. He has endeavored to state principles fully and clearly, and only for purposes of illustration has occupied space with a detail of the facts in the cases cited.

One thing he has had in view in the arrangement and filling up of his plan; and that was to satisfy the reader that the Law of Real Property, as a system, was, in most respects, symmetrical and complete. The popular notion, it is true, is, that this branch of the law is inevitably dry, intricate, and distasteful. But if its terms are less familiar, and its rules, from the remoteness of their origin, seemingly more arbitrary and artificial, and, as a whole, it is less flexible and easy to conform to the changing habits of a people than those of trade and commerce and the mere personal relations of society, it should not be forgotten, that, as a science, it altogether transcends those in exactness and certainty, and that many even of its subtleties disappear when the relations of its elements have been ascertained by study and investigation.

It should not be forgotten that it lies at the foundation of the English common law itself; that it was upon this sturdy stock that the laws and institutions of trading, manufacturing, commercial England were ingrafted, and are now in no small degree dependent for their element of vitality.

Nor should it be overlooked, that with the Saxon love of land, and the Norman love of dominion over the spot one calls his own, the law which regulates and enforces the rights of property in the soil will never cease to be of interest to a people in whose veins this common blood is mingled.

It has, moreover, been the field in which the keenest intellect and most profound learning of the best jurists of England and our own country have found ample scope and employment in grasping and analyzing its principles, mastering its subtleties, and testing and applying its rules.

It is not surprising, therefore, that so many writers have, from time to time, employed their best powers in the preparation of works embodying and illustrating the Law of Real

Property. Every age since Glanville has had its writers upon this subject, and no period has been more prolific than the present. No English treatise, of course, covers the same ground as was proposed to be done in the present; though it would be doing injustice to the treatise of Mr. Joshua Williams, and the notes on leading cases by Mr. Tudor, among the more recent of those works, if acknowledgment had not been made, as it often is in these pages, for the aid they have afforded in the preparation of this work. They will, moreover, show the use which has been made of the earlier treatises of Blackstone, Fearne, Cruise, Sanders, Flintoff, Sugden, Butler, Crabb, Preston, Burton, and others already familiar to the American lawyer. The work will show, besides, how far he has availed himself of the labors of American authors, whose aid, when resorted to, he has intended fully to acknowledge.

This attempt to produce a new work upon a hackneyed topic will not, it is hoped, render the writer obnoxious to the charge of presumption in view of the eminent ability of those who have gone before him. He hopes it may, at least, be found to possess the merit of being adapted to the wants of the American lawyer, as well as the American student; and if, in its composition, it is found to want the terseness and directness which might be derived from a strict adherence, at all times, to the use of technical terms and phrases, the reason for it might be traced to a wish to present the propositions it contains in language readily apprehended by the student.

Regarding the Law of Real Property as a system composed of several parts, yet substantially complete in itself, he has endeavored to arrange his topics with a due regard to their natural order of sequence, in relation to each other.

The work is divided into three books: the first embracing the nature and quantity of estates in corporeal hereditaments, with their qualities and characteristics, which will be found in the volume now published; the second treating of incorporeal hereditaments, their nature and characteristics; and the third, presenting in outline the titles by which real property may be acquired and held, and the rules of its transmission and transfer, will constitute a second volume.

It is subdivided into chapters, each intended to embrace a separate and distinct subject, with a subdivision in some cases into sections, with such a reference in the notes to the American statutes as to give the reader a tolerably full idea of the coincidence or diversity of the rules of the several States upon those subjects therein treated of.

It aims, in brief, to provide a safe and convenient book of reference to the lawyer; while it furnishes an elementary treatise for the use of the student, embracing what, in the form of lectures, has been received with favor by successive classes of the Law School, for which they were originally prepared.

From the encouragement he has received from both lawyers and students to undertake the work, he is induced to hope that it will be found, in some measure, to supply the want in which it originated.

CAMBRIDGE, *July*, 1860.

NOTE.

For the convenience of those who may have occasion to cite or examine the work now offered in a new edition, the pages of the first edition are retained.

The figures upon the margin, with a star prefixed, indicate the pages of that edition.

The second volume of the present edition begins with ESTATES upon CONDITION at page 444 of the first volume of the first edition. The third begins with TITLE-DESCENT at page 397 of the second volume of the first edition. The star pages are retained as a means of referring from one part of the work to another, instead of those of the present edition.

CONTENTS.

BOOK I.

CORPOREAL HEREDITAMENTS.

CHAPTER I.

CHAPTER II.

CHAPTER III.

CHAPTER IV.

CHAPTER V.

ESTATES FOR LIFE.

SECTION I.

SECTION IL

CHAPTER X.

ESTATES FOR YEARS.

SECTION I.

SECTION II.

SECTION III.

SECTION IV.

SECTION V.

SECTION VI.

SECTION VII.

SECTION VIII.

SECTION IX.

SECTION X.

SECTION XI.

CHAPTER XI.

ESTATES AT WILL.

SECTION I.

SECTION II.

CHAPTER XII.

TENANCIES AT SUFFERANCE, LICENSES, ETC.

SECTION I.

SECTION II.

CHAPTER XIII.

JOINT-ESTATES.

SECTION I.

SECTION II.

SECTION III.

SECTION IV.

SECTION V.

SECTION VI.

SECTION VII.

TABLE OF CASES CITED.

N.

TABLE OF CASES CITED.

LAW OF REAL PROPERTY.

BOOK I.

CORPOREAL HEREDITAMENTS.

CHAPTER I.

NATURE AND CLASSIFICATION OF REAL PROPERTY.

1. In entering upon a work like the following, it seems un-necessary to speculate, as many writers have done, upon the * origin of the idea of *property.* The right of [*2] exclusive enjoyment by some one individual, of portions of what might, at first, seem a common heritage, — the

earth, and its products, — is too well settled as an elementary principle in the organization of society, to render it necessary to go behind the simple fact itself in discussing its laws.[1] This right of property, however, is so far limited, that its use may be regulated from time to time by law, so as to prevent its being injurious to the equal enjoyment by others of their property, or inconsistent with the rights of the community.[2]

2. The first great division of property is into Real and Personal. This distinction, though now so familiar, seems not to have prevailed until the feudal system had lost its hold upon the property of England, and took its rise from the nature of the remedy sought by one who had been deprived of its possession. In the case of lands, for instance, he recovered, if at all, the *real* thing lost. But for the abstraction of a chattel, his remedy was against the *person* who had taken it away.[3] And, though the line of distinction between these two classes of property might seem to be easily drawn, it will be found that property often assumes the one or the other character, according to the circumstances in which it is placed. Thus a house or a standing tree may acquire the incidents of personal estate, while articles of a movable character may come to have qualities which belong to the realty, by the nature of the use to which they are fitted and applied.

2 *a.* This division rests upon the feudal notions of property, whereas the distinction recognized by the civil law was into *res mancipi* and *res nec mancipi*, things which might or might not be *handled,* or *corporeal* and *incorporeal;* while the first class was subdivided into *movable* and *immovable.* Thus *Biens*

---

[1] 2 Bl. Com. 1–10 ; Kaimes, 3d Hist. Tract; Maine, Anc. L. c. 8. "Of all subjects of property," says Lord Kaimes, "land is that which engages our affections the most, and for this reason the relation of property respecting land grew up much sooner to its present firmness and stability than the relation of property respecting movables." Tracts, p. 96.

[2] Commonwealth *v.* Tewksbury, 11 Met. 55; Commonwealth *v.* Alger, 7 Cush. 53, 86; Cushman *v.* Smith, 34 Me. 258 ; Bancroft *v.* Coolidge, 126 Mass. 438. See Code Nap. § 544. There is a division of things which excludes the idea of separate individual property, such as air, running water, the sea, the sea-shore, &c. In the words of Bracton: "Naturali verò jure communia sunt omnia haec aqua profluens, aër et mare et littora maris quasi maris accessoria." c. 12, § 5.

[3] Wms. Real Prop. 7.

comprehended both the real estate and personal chattels of the common law. The distinction between movable and immovable in the civil law had reference to the doctrine of *usucapion*, answering to the modern *prescription*, and to the extent to which things passed as appendant or appurtenant to immovable property in a conveyance thereof.[1] An English writer, in treating of this subject, regards *real* and *personal*, as now applied, as describing the quality of things, while the quantity of estate therein is represented by the terms *freehold*, and *chattel*.[2] In the Scotch law, property is divided into " heritable " and " movable." [3]

3. Land is always regarded as real property, and so, ordinarily, is whatever is erected or growing upon it, as well as whatever is contained within it or beneath its surface, such as minerals and the like, upon the principle that *cujus est solum*

---

[1] Austin Juris. XCIV. ; Maine, Anc. L. 273–284 ; 1 Brown, Civ. Law, 160 ; Güterbock's Braeton, Coxe, 86, 87, and note. Although *res mancipi* was applied only to things which might be handled, all things of that kind were not necessarily within that class. The term was applied to certain classes of property, to the transfer of which by sale certain formalities were required by the early Roman law, the omission of any one of which rendered the sale void. As remarked by Mr. Maine (p. 276), "An ancient conveyance was not written, but acted ; gestures and words took the place of written technical phraseology." Thus, in order to make a good sale of lands consisting of Italian soil, or of slaves and ordinary beasts of burden, all of which were *res mancipi*, the vendee, in the presence of five witnesses, and a sixth, who was provided with copper scales and called *libripens*, asserted his right to the property, and struck the scales with a piece of coin and gave it to the vendor. There must be an actual delivery of the thing sold, and, if it was land, it must either be done upon the land or by delivery of a sod or brick or tile taken from it, in the name of the land. All other corporeal things were included in *res nec mancipi*, and might be transferred by simple delivery. Under the code of Justinian, this distinction was done away with, and delivery was the only form required in making transfers of property. Maine's Anc. L. 276, 277 ; Abdy & Walker's Gaius, 39, 40, 72, 73 ; Mackenzie's Roman Law, 166 ; Hadley's Lectures, 86. *Usucapion*, or taking by use, was a mode of acquiring property in a thing by the possession and use of it for a time prescribed by law. It applied to such things only as were acquired in good faith by gift or purchase. By the XII. Tables, this term for movables was one year ; for immovables, two years. Under the law of Justinian, three years were required in the case of movables, and ten in that of immovables. Gaius, 80 ; Mackenzie, 187. *Bona*, under the Roman law, embraced all kinds of property. Mackenzie, 165.

[2] 1 Wood, Conv. viii.

[3] Ersk. Inst. 192. See 2 Sharsw. Bl. Com. 16, notes.

ejus est usque ad cœlum in the one direction, and *usque ad Orcum* in the other.[1] The word *land* includes not only the soil, but everything attached to it, whether attached by the course of nature, as trees, herbage, and water, or by the hand of man, as buildings and fences. The grant of land *eo nomine* will convey buildings and fences, as well as trees and herbage upon, or mines and quarries in, the ground.[2] Thus the road-bed, the rails fastened to it, and the buildings at the depots of railroads, are real property.[3]

4. But if a man, by the permission of another, erects a house upon the other's land, it will, if the builder have no estate in the same, be the personal property of the builder, if such

[1] 2 Bl. Com. 17–19. ; 1 Law Mag. 271 ; Co. Lit. 4. a ; Wms. Real Prop. 14 ; Broom's Maxims, 290. Property in respect to water is predicated only of its use, except as connected with land. That the property in ice upon a stream or pond of water is in the owner of the soil below, and not in the mere riparian proprietor as such, seems to be now settled by the weight of authority. Mill River Co. *v.* Smith, 34 Conn. 462 ; Cummings *v.* Barrett, 10 Cush. 186 ; Paine *v.* Woods, 108 Mass. 160, 173 ; Edgerton *v.* Huff, 26 Ind. 35 ; State *v.* Pottmeyer, 33 Ind. 402 ; Lorman *v.* Benson, 8 Mich. 32 ; Higgins *v.* Kusterer, 41 Mich. 318 ; Washington Ice Co. *v.* Shortall, 101 Ill. 46 ; Washb. Ease. 4th ed. 396 ; Myer *v.* Whittaker, 55 How. (N. Y.) 376, overruling Marshall *v.* Peters, 12 id. 218. Hence where, as in Massachusetts, certain ponds — called great ponds — are public property, the riparian owner acquires no title to the ice, but any one who can lawfully gain access to the same may cut and carry away the ice formed thereon, provided he do not thereby unreasonably interfere with the exercise of a similar right in others. Paine *v.* Woods, *sup. ;* W. Roxbury *v.* Stoddard, 7 Allen, 158 ; Hittinger *v.* Eames, 121 Mass. 539 ; Gage *v.* Steinkrauss, 131 Mass. 222. So in Kansas, on a fresh-water navigable stream. Wood *v.* Fowler, 26 Kans. 682. On the other hand, in Michigan, a lessee of riparian rights on such a stream was held entitled to recover the value of ice made thereon by his special care, from one whose negligent use of the stream as a highway had destroyed it. People's Ice Co. *v.* Steamer Excelsior, 44 Mich. 229. A similar rule was adopted in the case of manure collected in the public streets. Haslem *v.* Lockwood, 37 Conn. 500. Land is called *solum, quia est solidum,* as stated by Coke. It comprehends any ground, soil, or earth, as well as castles, mansion-houses, or other buildings erected thereon, and the mines under the surface. But a grant of water does not include land, except in the case of salt pits or springs. Co. Lit. 4 a and b ; 1 Atk. Conv. 2 ; Green *v.* Armstrong, 1 Denio, 550, 554 ; Shep. Touch. 91. "In its more limited sense, the term land denotes the quantity and character of the interest or estate which the tenant may own in lands." "When used to describe the quantity of the estate, 'land' is understood to denote a freehold estate, at least." Johnson *v.* Richardson, 33 Miss. 462, 464.

[2] Per Bronson, J., Mott *v.* Palmer, 1 N. Y. 564, 572.

[3] Hunt *v.* Bay St. Iron Co., 97 Mass. 282.

be his agreement with the land-owner.[1] If a tenant of leased premises erect a structure thereon, appropriate to the character of his occupancy, he has within certain limitations a right to remove the same while in possession of the premises.[2] If the * builder, however, have a permanent inter-   [* 3] est in the land, such as the husband of the tenant in fee,[3] or reversioner or remainder-man has,[4] or be in possession

[1] The earlier cases are perhaps not sufficiently explicit as to this last requirement. See Aldrich v. Parsons, 6 N. H. 555; Osgood v. Howard, 6 Me. 452; Russell v. Richards, 10 Me. 429; commented on in Hinkley Co. v. Black, 70 Me. 473; Lapham v. Norton, 71 Me. 83; where the rule in the text is affirmed; and see Dame v. Dame, 38 N. H. 429; Korbe v. Barbour, 130 Mass. 255, where, though the broader rule is not disapproved, the facts decided upon were as in the text. A careful examination of the earlier cases will show that wherever the character of personalty has attached to a building erected on another's land, there has been either no substantial annexation, Rogers v. Woodbury, 15 Pick. 156; O'Donnell v. Hitchcock, 118 Mass. 401; Hinckley v. Baxter, 13 Allen, 139; Mott v. Palmer, 1 N. Y. 564; or the relation of landlord and tenant existed, Doty v. Gorham, 5 Pick. 487; Washburn v. Sproat, 16 Mass. 449; Antoni v. Belknap, 102 Mass. 193; Morris v. French, 106 Mass. 326; Van Ness v. Pacard, 2 Pet. 137; Dubois v. Kelly, 10 Barb. 496; or there was in substance an agreement for the right of removal, — either in terms, Wall v. Hinds, 4 Gray, 273; Ham v. Kendall, 111 Mass. 297; Dame v. Dame, *supra;* or implied from a renunciation of title by the land-owner, Wells v. Banister, 4 Mass. 514; or from his agreement to buy from the builder and the like, Ashmun v. Williams, 8 Pick. 402. Such an agreement that the structure shall be personalty can of course be implied from circumstances of a general kind independent of the acts of the parties, such as the nature of the article annexed, the relative situation of the parties and of their property, Wood v. Hewett, 8 Q. B. 913; Lancaster v. Eve, 5 C. B. N. s. 717; Korbe v. Barbour, *supra;* and in fact such is the foundation of the tenant's right, and at the same time sets the limits to that right. O'Brien v. Kusterer, 27 Mich. 289. And see next note.

[2] Van Ness v. Pacard, 2 Pet. 137; Hanrahan v. O'Reilly, 102 Mass. 201, which was the ease of bowling-alleys erected by the tenant and removed during the term. In Antoni v. Belknap, 102 Mass. 193, a tenant for an uncertain period, who had erected buildings, was held to have a right to remove them within a reasonable time after the landlord had determined the tenancy. The limitations are, in general terms, that the structure shall be for the purpose of trade, agriculture, and the like. Ewell Fixt. 80 *et seq.*

[3] Glidden v. Bennett, 43 N. H. 306. See Washburn v. Sproat, 16 Mass. 449. Though that more properly goes on the inability of husband and wife to contract with each other. Webster v. Potter, 105 Mass. 414.

[4] Cooper v. Adams, 6 Cush. 87. And where a tenant buys in the reversion he loses his tenant's privilege of removal, as against an existing mortgage. Jones v. Detroit Chair Co., 38 Mich. 92; Perkins v. Swank, 43 Miss. 349; *contra,* Globe Mills v. Quinn, 76 N. Y. 23.

under a contract of purchase,[1] or if his intent be referable to a permanent holding, the structure becomes at once a part of the realty.[2] It is a maxim of the law, *quicquid plantatur solo, solo cedit*.[3] But a right to erect a mill upon the land of another is an incorporeal hereditament, which can only be created by writing.[4]

The law, therefore, in respect to the property in buildings erected by one man upon the land of another, seems to be this ; If the building, or a permanent fixture, be erected upon, or attached to the realty by the owner of it, and intended to remain, it is not the subject of conveyance as personalty, even by the owner of the freehold. And a mortgage of it by him, as personal property, without actual severance, will not be valid against a purchaser of the freehold. In one case, A, the owner of land, by an arrangement between him and B, built a barn on his own land, which he set upon stone posts, and B was to hire the same, and upon paying for it was to have a right to remove it. A sold the land to C, who, by parol, agreed that the barn should not pass by the deed. C sold the land to another, but said nothing of the barn. It was held that the title to the barn passed with the real estate unaffected by the parol agreement under which it was built.[5] But a freeholder can make a valid sale of buildings and other fixed property to be immediately severed and removed.[6] If a building be erected without the assent and agreement of the land-owner, it becomes at once a part of the realty, and is the property of the owner of the freehold.[7] So where a house has stood

---

[1] Eastman *v.* Foster, 8 Met. 19 ; Ogden *v.* Stock, 34 Ill. 522 ; Poor *v.* Oakman, 104 Mass. 309 ; Hemenway *v.* Cutter, 51 Me. 407 ; and the cases of Russell *v.* Richards, 10 Me. 429 ; s. c. 11, 371 ; Pullen *v.* Bell, 40 Me. 314, apparently *contra*, are explained and limited by Hinkley Co. *v.* Black, 70 Me. 473.

[2] Leland *v.* Gassett, 17 Vt. 403 ; Lipsky *v.* Bergman, 52 Wisc. 256 ; Ritchmeyer *v.* Morse, 3 Keyes, 349 ; Christian *v.* Dripps, 28 Penn. St. 279.

[3] Braeton 10 ; Broom Max. 295.   [4] Trammell *v.* Trammell, 11 Rich. 471.

[5] Burk *v.* Hollis, 98 Mass. 55 ; Webster *v.* Potter, 105 Mass. 414 ; Landon *v.* Pratt, 34 Conn. 517; Bonney *v.* Foss, 62 Me. 281; Richardson *v.* Copeland, 6 Gray, 536; Gibbs *v.* Estey, 15 Gray, 587; Deane *v.* Hutchinson, 40 N. J. Eq. 83.

[6] Shaw *v.* Carbrey, 13 Allen, 462 ; Nelson *v.* Nelson, 6 Gray, 385 ; Hallen *v.* Runder, 1 C. M. & R. 266; Marshall *v.* Green, 1 C. P. Div. 35. And see *post*, §§ 7, 8, 9.

[7] Sudbury Parish *v.* Jones, 8 Cush. 184 ; Poor *v.* Oakman, 104 Mass. 309, 317; Webster *v.* Potter, 105 Mass. 414, 416; Howard *v.* Fessenden, 14 Allen,

upon land for thirty years, it was held to have become a fixture, and might not be removed without the consent of the owner of the soil.[1] So it has been held in Pennsylvania, that if a stranger enter upon the land of another and make improvements and erect buildings, they become the property of the land-owner.[2] So if a tenant at will removes a house on the premises, and places it on a cellar with a stone foundation, he makes it a part of the freehold, and a mortgage of it by him as personalty passes no title.[3] So where one, pending a suit to try the title to land, erected a house thereon by permission of the defendant in the suit, it was held that the former could not remove it against the will of the plaintiff, who prevailed in the suit.[4] So fixtures attached to premises by one in possession under a contract of purchase, where he fails to perform on his part and thereby to acquire a title, become a part of the realty, like fixtures annexed by a vendor or mortgagor, and may not be removed by him.[5]

124 ; ·Oakman v. Dorch. F. I. Co., 98 Mass. 57 ; Leland v. Gassett, 17 Vt. 403 ; Bonney v. Foss, 62 Me. 248 ; Guernsey v. Wilson, 134 Mass. 486. So a railroad erecting a depot on land, or annexing rails thereto, without the consent of the owner, or condemnation of the land or tender of damages, loses title to what is so annexed. Graham v. Connersville R. R., 36 Ind. 463 ; Meriam v. Brown, 128 Mass. 391.

[1] Reid v. Kirk, 12 Rich. 54.

[2] Crest v. Jack, 3 Watts, 239; West v. Stewart, 7 Penn. St. 122.

[3] Madigan v. Macarthy, 108 Mass. 376.

[4] Henderson v. Ownby, 56 Tex. 647. So Hubschman v. McHenry, 29 Wisc. 655, where the builder relied on the permission of one holding a tax title subsequently adjudged bad. The earlier case of McJunkin v. Dupree, 44 Tex. 500, which permitted removal of a cotton gin and stand, proceeded rather on the ground that the articles were not fixtures, — Cole v. Roach, 37 Tex. 413, — and is distinguished in 56 Tex. 647, supra. And see post, pl. 4 a.

[5] McLaughlin v. Nash, 14 Allen, 136 ; Daggett v. Tracy, 128 Mass. 167 ; Westgate v. Wixon, ib. 304; Hinkley Co. v. Black, 70 Me. 473, where the text is cited; and see ante, p. 5, n. 1, and cases cited. In Hartwell v. Kelly, 117 Mass. 235, the point decided was that a replevin of the building by the tenant who had contracted not to remove it was no trespass. For the removal of such a structure the land-owner may have replevin so long as the property is identifiable and not annexed to the realty, Ogden v. Stock, 34 Ill. 522 ; Reese v. Jared, 15 Ind. 142; Sands v. Pfeiffer, 10 Cal. 258; Laflin v. Griffiths, 35 Barb. 58; Dubuque Society v. Fleming, 11 Iowa, 533; but after annexation, only trover, ib. In Centr. R R. v. Fritz, 20 Kans. 430 ; Eaves v. Estes, 10 Kans. 314 ; Mills v. Redick, 1 Neb. 437, replevin was held to lie after annexation, but the law seems clearly otherwise; cases supra, Curtis v. Riddle, 7 Allen, 185; Wilmarth v. Bancroft, 10 Allen, 348; Bro. Abr. Tresp. pl. 43.

4 *a.* The civil law upon this subject is said to be substantially this : If one builds upon his own land with the materials of another, the building would follow the property in the soil, though by the XII. Tables the owner of the materials might recover double their value. He might not take away the house unless so placed as to be easily removed. If one built with his own materials upon another's land by mistake, the house followed the property in the soil. But if the owner of the soil insisted upon retaining the house, he was liable to pay the builder the value of the materials and work. But if one knowingly builds upon another's land, he is presumed to have given his materials and workmanship to the owner of the soil.[1] Whereas, as stated by the same writer, by the common law, if one, though ignorant of his title or by mistake, builds upon the soil of another, he cannot claim anything for his materials or workmanship.[2] While a house standing upon mortgaged premises belonging to the owner of the soil is a part of the realty, and passes with it ; yet in those States where a mortgage is a lien upon, and not an estate in the land, if the mortgagor in possession, and before breach, separates the house from the land, or if he cut trees growing thereon, and carry them away, the mortgagee cannot follow them to claim them.[3] So if the house be built by one man upon the land of another, by the consent of the latter, and he sell the land, though it does not pass a property in the house, it would operate as a revocation of the license under which the builder placed it there. The owner may always remove it after notice of a revocation of such license, if done within a reasonable time.[4] Or he might sell it by oral agreement without writing.[5] Nor would it make any difference if the owner of the land himself

---

[1] Wood, Civ. L. B. 2, c. 3, p. 159, and see Bonney *v.* Foss, 62 Me. 248, 251. See Broom's Maxims, 295-297. It is otherwise in equity. Bright *v.* Boyd, 2 Story, 605 ; Union Hall *v.* Morrison, 39 Md. Rep. 281.

[2] Wood Civ. L. *ubi supra.*

[3] Buckout *v.* Swift, 27 Cal. 433. But it is otherwise after breach. Sands *v.* Pfeiffer, 10 Cal. 258. And in New York the rule between mortgagor and mortgagee is declared to be the same as between vendor and vendee. Laflin *v.* Griffiths, 35 Barb. 58 ; Snedeker *v.* Warren, 12 N. Y. 170, 174.

[4] Dame *v.* Dame, 38 N. H. 429.

[5] Keyser *v.* School District, 35 N. H. 477.

builds the house, if he do so for another who pays him for the same with a right to remove it.[1] But where a building is erected upon the land of another under an agreement that the builder may remove it, it will remain his personal property; nor would a sale of the realty, under process of bankruptcy against the land-owner, pass any title to the building.[2] The following case illustrates how a building may retain its character of personalty through successive changes of ownership in the land on which it stands. J R, while lessee of land, removed a building on to it. He then sold it as a chattel to his lessors, the owners of the fee, who, at the same time, mortgaged it as a chattel to F R. The land was then under a mortgage, and the mortgagee subsequently took possession of the premises. The mortgagors of the house in the mean time had released their interest in it to F R, who sold one-half of it to one B, and the mortgagee of the land leased the same to F R and B, with a proviso contemplating his buying the building at the expiration of the term. The original lessors and owners of the land in fee, having become bankrupt, their title to the land was sold, and the purchaser paid off the mortgage, he knowing at the time that F R and B claimed the building as personal property. It was held that the building remained a chattel in respect to its ownership through all these changes of title to the land.[3] So where A, by permission of B, built a mill on B's land under an agreement to purchase the land as soon as B should have paid an outstanding judgment which formed a lien upon it, and in the mean time to own the mill, and B having failed to satisfy the judgment, the land was sold, it was held that the mill remained A's personal property, and did not pass with the estate.[4] A steam saw-mill may be personal property though standing on another's land, and may be liable as such for the owner's debts,[5] and this although it was originally placed there conditionally, if the owner of the

---

[1] Coleman v. Lewis, 27 Penn. St. 291.

[2] Goodman v. Han. & St. J. R. R., 45 Mo. 33; Norris v. French, 106 Mass 326; Howard v. Fessenden, 14 Allen, 124.

[3] Norris v. French, 106 Mass. 326. See post, *115.

[4] Yater v. Mullen, 24 Ind. 277.

[5] State v. Bonham, 18 Ind. 233.

land shall have failed to perform on his part.[1] Where a
bridge belonging to a corporation was taken by a flood and
carried upon the land of a third person, and deposited there
without their fault, they did not thereby lose their property in
it. The owner might remove it from his premises, but he
could not have an action against them for the act of its being
deposited upon their land.[2] But if one hires an article, like a
steam-engine, and so attaches it to a building upon his own
premises that it can only be removed by destroying the building, and then sells or mortgages the premises as real estate
to one who is not cognizant of the facts, it will be held to pass
a property in the engine, and the original owner must look to
the party for compensation who thus converted the same.[3]
And the same principle would apply, if one takes another's
materials for building, and works them into a structure upon
his own land in connection with his own materials, and then
sells or mortgages the same to another who is ignorant of the
fact.[4] But where a mortgage creates an estate in the land,
and the mortgagor removes fixtures from the premises, the
mortgagee may have trespass against him, or if he sell them

---

[1] Yater v. Mullen, 23 Ind. 562.   [2] Livezey v. Philadelphia, 64 Penn. St. 109.

[3] Fryatt v. Sullivan Co., 5 Hill, 116 ; Pierce v. Goddard, 22 Pick. 559. See
also Early v. Burtis, 40 N. J. Eq. 501; Penn Mut. L. Ins. Co. v. Semple,
38 N. J. Eq. 575; Furbush v. Chappell, 105 Penn. St. 187.

[4] Ibid. A building or chattel annexed by one to another's land, but with a right
of removal, may remain personalty even as against the vendee or mortgagee of the
land-owner so long as it is identifiable and severable; Mott v. Palmer, 1 N. Y. 571;
Ford v. Cobb, 20 N. Y. 344; Smith v. Benson, 1 Hill, 176; Tifft v. Horton, 53 N. Y.
377 ; Eaves v. Estes, 10 Kans. 314 ; Dame v. Dame, 38 N. H. 429 ; Hinckley v.
Baxter, 13 Allen, 139 ; but when the structure or chattel is permanently annexed
by the land-owner, who simply gives a mortgage or other lien thereon as personal
property, this passes as realty to the mortgagee of the land, or other party entitled
thereto, who is without notice of such lien, and he will hold it free from liability
for it or its value to the lien holder. Hunt v. Bay St. Iron Co., 97 Mass. 279; Curtis v.
Riddle, 7 Allen, 185 ; Pierce v. George, 108 Mass. 78 ; Southbr. Sav. Bk. v. Exeter
Wks., 127 Mass. 542 ; Same v. Stevens Co., 130 Mass. 547; State Bk. v. Kercheval,
65 Mo. 682; Smith v. Waggoner, 50 Wisc. 155, 161; Walmesley v. Milne, 7 C. B.
N. S. 115 ; Morrison v. Berry, 42 Mich. 389. So far as the New York cases are
contra, they may proceed on the ground that in that State a mortgage is a lien
and not an estate. Tifft v. Horton, 53 N. Y. 385. So see Hendy v. Dinkerhoff, 57
Cal. 3. Where, however, the chattel owner was deprived of it by fraud or without his consent, his title is not divested by its annexation. Cochran v. Flint, 57
N. H. 514 ; D'Eyncourt v. Gregory, L. R. 3 Eq. 382, 397.

to a third person, the mortgagee may require the purchaser to pay him for them. Nor would it make any difference if the fixtures were parts of a building which had been destroyed, and which had been saved, such as doors, window-blinds, and the like.[1]

5. Growing crops standing upon the soil when this is conveyed pass as part of the realty, if planted by the grantor.[2] This principle was held to extend to crops of corn standing in the field, unharvested, in December.[3] And the same principle applies to trees planted for sale by the owner of the land.[4] And if he devises his farm, the crops then growing pass with it.[5] And in this respect the common law coincides with the law of France, by which such crops are considered to come within the class of immovables.[6] If, however, they are grown and fit for harvest at the owner's death, the annual crops will go to the executor or administrator, and not to the heir.[7] And when they have been sold standing, by a valid sale, and the title has passed, the purchaser has a reasonable time after they are ripe to gather them; nor can the land-owner interfere with them until after such time.[8] Indeed it seems well settled in this country, notwithstanding some earlier cases in England, that growing annual crops, as well as those ripe already, can, as *fructus industriæ*, be the subject of a valid oral sale by the owner, with an implied license to the vendee to enter and take them.[9] So if such crops are planted by a

---

[1] Wilmarth v. Bancroft, 10 Allen, 348.

[2] Falmouth v. Thomas, 1 Cr. & J. 89; Bechelen v. Wallace, 7 Ad. & E. 49; Vaughan v. Hancock, 3 C. B. 766; Brantom v. Griffits, 1 C. P. Div. 349; Bank of Penn. v. Wise, 3 Watts, 394, 406; Wintermute v. Light, 46 Barb. 278, 283; Bull v. Griswold, 19 Ill. 631; *contra*, Smith v. Johnston, 1 Penn. 471. See *post*, vol. 2, *625; also Thayer v. Rock, 13 Wend. 53.

[3] Kittredge v. Woods, 3 N. H. 503; Tripp v. Hasceig, 20 Mich. 254, 261; though one judge, dissenting, held that the field was the storehouse of the crop; as to which see Parker v. Staniland, 11 East, 362.

[4] Smith v. Price, 39 Ill. 28.

[5] Bradner v. Faulkner, 34 N. Y. 347; Dennett v. Hopkinson, 63 Me. 350.

[6] Code Nap. art. 520.

[7] Penhallow v. Dwight, 7 Mass. 34; Kingsley v. Holbrook, 45 N. H. 313, 319; Howe v. Bachelder, 49 N. H. 204; Pattison's App., 61 Penn. St. 294.

[8] Ogden v. Lucas, 48 Ill. 492; Stewart v. Doughty, 9 Johns. 108, 112.

[9] See Evans v. Roberts, 5 B. & C. 829; Jones v. Flint, 10 Ad. & E. 753; Sainsbury v. Matthews, 4 M. & W. 343, overruling Emmerson v. Heelis, 2 Taunt. 38;

tenant wio iolds under tie owner of tie soil, and are fit for iarvesting, or by one wiose tenancy is for an uncertain period of time, tiey are regarded, in many respects, as personal prepery, liable, indeed, to become part of tie realty, if tie tenant voluntarily abandons or forfeits possession of tie premises.[1] And by tiis principle, wiere one entered upon land under an agreement of tie owner to sell it to him, and planted crops, and tien tie land-owner refused to execute iis agreement to convey, it was ield tiat tie tenant migit claim tie crops as personalty.[2] Wiere, during tie pendency of a process to foreclose a mortgage, tie mortgagor let tie premises to a tenant wio raised a crop upon tie same, and tie crop iad been cut and stacked upon tie land wien tie premises were sold to foreclose tie mortgage, and tie purciaser at tiis sale took tie crops and carried tiem away, ie was ield liable in trespass tierefor to tie tenant as owner of tie crop.[3] Wiere a tenant in tie autumn sowed a crop of barley, and in tie following spring gave up possession to a new tenant, wio took ciarge of tie crop for him, it was ield tiat a mortgage of the crop by tie first tenant, wiile tie premises were in possession of iis successor, was valid to pass tie same.[4] So, in favor of creditors, crops fit for iarvesting may be levied on as personal ciattels.[5] But wiere crops were planted during tie pendeney of a suit in ejectment to recover tie land, and were standing upon tie land wien tie plaintiff in tie suit took possession under a judgment in iis favor, it was ield ie became tiereby entitled to tie same as a part of tie realty.[6]

6. Trees also, growing on tie freeiold, may acquire tie ciaracter and incidents of personal property, if tie owner sell

---

Waddington *v.* Bristow, 2 B. & P. 452. So see Craddock *v.* Riddlesburger, 2 Dana, 205 ; Stambaugh *v.* Yeates, 2 Rawle, 161 ; Dunne *v.* Ferguson, 1 Hayes, 540 ; Pattison's App., 61 Penn. St. 294 ; Whipple *v.* Foot, 2 Johns. 423 ; Green *v.* Armstrong, 1 Denio, 550 ; Howe *v.* Bachelder, 49 N. H. 204 ; Owens *v.* Lewis, 46 Ind. 488.

[1] Oland's Case, 5 Rep. 116 *a;* Debow *v.* Titus, 5 N. J. 128 ; Co. Lit. 55 ; Whipple *v.* Foot, 2 Johns. 418, and 421, n. ; Chandler *v.* Thurston, 10 Pick. 210.

[2] Harris *v.* Frink, 49 N. Y. 24, 30.

[3] Johnson *v.* Camp, 51 Ill. 220.   [4] Fry *v.* Miller, 45 Penn. St. 441.

[5] Penhallow *v.* Dwight, 7 Mass. 34 ; Heard *v.* Fairbanks, 5 Met. 111.

[6] McLean *v.* Bovee, 24 Wisc. 295.

them to be cut and removed, without a right on the part of
the vendee to occupy the vendor's land for growing or supporting them thereon.[1] So if trees are sold or reserved to be
cut and carried away without any right to keep them growing
upon the land, and the one who has a right to the trees dies,
the property in them goes to his personal representatives, and
not to his heirs.[2] And although the tenant plant trees, they
may be regarded as his chattels, if he has no freehold estate
in the premises, and it is done for the purpose of transplant-
ing and sale, as in the case of nurserymen.[3]

7. The law as to growing trees may be regarded so far
peculiar as to call for a more extended statement of its rules
as laid down by different courts. And much of what is here
stated may be properly applied to the case of growing grass
and other products which are not of annual planting and cultivation. In the first place, trees which stand wholly within
the boundary line of one's land belong to him, although their
roots and branches may extend into the adjacent owner's land.
And such would be the case in respect to the ownership of
the fruit of such trees, though grown upon the branches
which extend beyond the line of the owner's land. And trespass for assault and battery would lie by the owner of the
tree against the owner of the land over which its branches
extended, if he prevented the owner of the tree, by personal
violence, from reaching over and picking the fruit growing
upon these branches, while standing upon the fence which
divided the parcels.[4] But the adjacent owner may lop off the
branches or roots of such trees up to the line of his land. If
the tree stand so nearly upon the dividing line between the
lands that portions of its body extend into each, the same is

---

[1] Claflin v. Carpenter, 4 Met. 580 ; Smith v. Surman, 9 B. & C. 561 ; Stukely
v. Butler, Hob. 173. See 1 Atk. 175 ; Olmstead v. Niles, 7 N. H. 522 ; Liford's
Case, 11 Rep. 50 ; Marshall v. Green, 1 C. P. Div. 35. The limitation in the
teXt is made to avoid, in this stage of inquiry, the difficult question of what
constitutes an interest in lands within the 4th section of the Statute of Frauds,
29 Car. II. c. 3; *post*, vol. 3, *599.

[2] McClintock's Appeal, 71 Penn. St. 365.

[3] Miller v. Baker, 1 Met. 27 ; Whitmarsh v. Walker, 1 Met. 313 ; Penton v
Robart, 2 East, 88 ; Windham v. Way, 4 Taunt. 316, per Heath, J.

[4] Hoffman v. Armstrong, 48 N. Y. 201.

tie property in common of tie land-owners. And neitier of tiem is at liberty to cut tie tree witiout tie consent of tie otier, nor to cut away tie part wiici extends into iis land, if ie tiereby injures tie common property in tie tree.[1]

8. Trees growing upon land constitute a portion of ·tie realty, and pass by a mortgage of tie land, and tie mortgagee could not otierwise sell tiem to anotier, tian tie land itself.[2] So tiey cannot be levied on, on a *fi. fa.* or personal property execution.[3] And if nursery-trees are planted by tie owner of tie land, tiey would pass by a mortgage of tie land, tiougi planted after tie mortgage is made.[4] A different rule would apply between landlord and tenant if tiey were planted by tie tenant for purposes of trade.[5]

Trees cut and lying upon tie soil, as well as trees tirown down by tie wind, would pass witi tie land as a part of tie realty. It would be otierwise if tie trees iad been cut into logs or iewed into timber.[6]

Many cases iave seemed to treat a sale of growing trees as if tiey were ciattels, and as being effectual to pass a property in tiem before tiey are cut, altiougi not evidenced by a deed. But it is appreiended tiat tiis doctrine, wiici, at first tiougit, would seem to be incompatible witi tie Statute of Frauds, may be reconciled by treating suci sale, if by parol, as a license ratier tian a grant of an interest in real estate, and wiici, tiougi liable to be revoked, if executed carries tie property in such of tie trees as siall iave been severed from

---

[1] Dubois *v.* Beaver, 25 N. Y. 123 ; Waterman *v.* Soper, 1 Ld. Raym. 737 ; Skinner *v.* Wilder, 38 Vt. 115 ; Lyman *v.* Hale, 11 Conn. 177 ; Griffin *v.* Bixby, 12 N. H. 454 ; Masters *v.* Pollie, 2 Roll. Rep. 141 ; Holder *v.* Coates, Moody & M. 112 ; 3 Kent Com. 438. See, on same subject, Dig. 47, 7, 6, 2 ; Inst. 2, 1, 31 ; Bracton, 10 ; Code Nap. §§ 670, 673. Among the Greeks, by the laws of Solon, olive and fig trees might not be planted nearer the owner's line than nine feet, and other trees nearer than five feet, in order to guard against this spreading of the roots, &c., into the lands of the adjacent owner. 1 Potter's Antiq. 166.

[2] Hutchins *v.* King, 1 Wall. 53, 59.

[3] Adams *v.* Smith, Breese, 221.

[4] Naples *v.* Dillon, 31 Conn. 598 ; Price *v.* Brayton, 19 Iowa, 309 ; Adams *v.* Beadle, 47 Iowa, 439.

[5] Price *v.* Brayton, *sup.*

[6] Bracket *v.* Goddard, 54 Me. 309, 313 ; Cook *v.* Whiting, 16 Ill. 480.

the freehold. Such a parol sale of trees, till actually perfected by a severance of them from the freehold, is, moreover, to be deemed as executory, and may be defeated by a conveyance of the freehold. Thus, a sale of such trees, being within the Statute of Frauds, must be evidenced by writing.[1] And, if regarded as sufficient to vest an interest in them between the parties, and possibly third parties cognizant of the sale having been made, it would not be of any validity against the purchaser of the freehold without notice, but the trees and crops would pass therewith.[2] But if, under such sale, the purchaser has executed the license by which he was permitted to cut the trees, the license becomes irrevocable, and the purchaser may enter and remove them. If it has not been executed, the whole rests in contract, and, so long as the timber or other product of the soil continues in its natural condition, and no act is done by the vendee towards its separation from the soil, no property or title thereto passes to the vendee. A revocation of the license to enter on the land, whether by a deed of the freehold or otherwise, does not defeat any valid title, or deprive the owner of chattels, that are upon the same, of his property in or possession of them. But if the contract for the sale of the trees be executory only, no title has passed to the vendee.[3] The same effect, however, of passing property in trees, may be accomplished by conveyance of them by deed as growing trees, if done by the owner of the freehold. It is so far considered a severance of the property in the trees from that in the soil, that the vendee may, after that, sell and pass

[1] McGregor v. Brown, 10 N. Y. 114; Green v. Armstrong, 1 Denio, 550; Carrington v. Roots, 2 M. & W. 248.

[2] Wescott v. Delano, 20 Wisc. 514; Gardiner Mg. Co. v. Heald, 5 Me. 381; Drake v. Wells, 11 Allen, 141.

[3] Drake v. Wells, 11 Allen, 141; Nettleton v. Sikes, 8 Met. 35; Douglas v. Shumway, 13 Gray, 498; Nelson v. Nelson, 6 Gray, 385. In the late case in England, of Marshall v. Green, 1 C. P. Div. 35, an oral sale of standing trees was held good as a sale of chattels, and, after part had been cut, to vest title to the whole, with an irrevocable license to enter and cut the remainder. If such a sale is good at all, it is not very apparent why this latter result should not follow; as delivery of part of a lot of chattels sold as one whole vests absolutely the title to the remainder; and the doctrine of revocable license obtaining in this country would seem a relic of the exploded notion of the insusceptibility of *fructus naturales* to pass by an oral sale. But see *ante*.

title to them by a mere writing, though they have not been
actually severed from the soil.[1]

[*4]   * 9. But if the owner of land grants the trees growing thereon to another and his heirs, with liberty to
cut and carry them away at his pleasure, forever, the grantee
acquires an estate in fee in the trees, with an interest in
the soil sufficient for their growth, while the fee in the soil
itself remains in the grantor.[2]   And a like effect is produced
in favor of the grantor by reserving the trees in granting the
land, giving him a life estate or a fee, according to the terms
of the reservation.[3]   But the grant of *the use* of the timber
upon land is an incorporeal hereditament, and does not convey a title to the timber, or to the soil.[4]

10. On the other hand, things in themselves movable, and
having the character of personalty, may acquire that of realty,
by being fitted and applied to use as a part of the realty,
though, at the time, temporarily disannexed therefrom ; and
they would pass accordingly with the land, upon a sale thereof,
or go to an heir or devisee as realty.[5]   Among these, for illustration, would be keys of locks upon doors, fire-frames, doors,
window-blinds, mill-stones, and irons taken out of a mill for
repair, bolts and other machinery of a flouring-mill,[6] and frag-
ments of a house destroyed by a tempest.[7]   So, upon the sale
of a " saw-mill," with the land on which it stood, the iron bars
and chains then in it, and used for operating it, passed as a
part of the realty.[8]   So by the civil codes of France and Louisiana, many things in their nature movable acquired the char-

---

[1] Kingsley v. Holbrook, 45 N. H. 313 ; Lansingburgh Bk. v. Crary, 1 Barb.
542 ; Warren v. Leland, 2 Barb. 613.   See the subject of the sale of trees and the
like, further considered, *post*, vol. 2, *599.

[2] Clap v. Draper, 4 Mass. 266 ; Knotts v. Hydrick, 12 Rich. 314.

[3] Knotts v. Hydrick, *sup.* ; Rich v. Zeilsdorff, 22 Wisc. 544; and such a reservation enures to the benefit of a prior parol vendee of the trees.   Heflin v. Bingham,
56 Ala. 566.

[4] Clark v. Way, 11 Rich. 621.

[5] 1 Wms. Ex'rs, 613–615 ; Sweetzer v. Jones, 35 Vt. 317.

[6] Colegrave v. Dios Santos, 2 B. & C. 76 ; Walmsley v. Milne, 7 C. B. N. S.
115 ; Liford's Case, 11 Rep. 50 ; House v. House, 10 Paige, 158 ; McLaughlin
v. Johnson, 46 Ill. 163.

[7] Rogers v. Gilinger, 30 Penn. St. 185.   See Dudley v. Foote, 63 N. H. 57.

[8] Farrar v. Stackpole, 6 Me. 154.

acter and qualities of things immovable by reason of the uses
for which they were destined and applied.   Among these were
animals employed in husbandry, farming utensils, plants,
manure, doves in a pigeon-house, and all such movables as
the owner has permanently attached to property that is itself
immovable.   In England it has lately been held that the owner
of land has a property in the wild game thereon *ratione soli*,
for the killing of which he may have an action against a
stranger.[1]   And this right of property attaches *eo instanti* that
the animal is killed, but not until then : nor does it make any
difference, in this respect, whether it is killed by the owner of
the land or a trespasser upon it.   There can be no property
in animals *feræ naturæ* running wild, so long as they are alive ;
and if such animal voluntarily pass from the land of one on
to that of another, the latter may at once kill it, and thereby
acquire a property in it.[2]   And, in Louisiana, slaves were considered as immovables, and they partook of the inheritable
quality of real property in some other of the States.[3]   It was formerly held in Virginia that slaves might be conveyed to uses,
and were within the Statute of Uses.[4]   By the Scotch law,
materials collected for the erection of houses are not *heritable*
property until united to the surface of the earth by actual
building.   But the materials of a building which has been torn
down with an intent to rebuild the same, retain the character
of being *heritable*, though actually severed from the land.[5]
The subject is considered quite at length by the court of New
York in connection with the question whether the rolling-
stock of railroads, such as cars, engines, and the like, passed
under a mortgage of the same as real estate ; and it was held
that they did.   The decisions in New York, until lately, left
the question doubtful whether the rolling-stock of a railroad
was fixture or mere personal property.[6]   But the latest re-

---

[1] Blades *v.* Higgs, 13 C. B. N. s. 844 ; Rigg *v.* Lonsdale, 1 Hurlst. & N. 923.

[2] Blades *v.* Higgs, 11 H. L. Cas. 621, 630–641 ; Sutton *v.* Danby, 1 Ld. Raym. 250.

[3] Code Nap. art. 524 ; Louis. Cod. art. 459, 461 ; Chinn *v.* Respass, 1 Mon. 25.

[4] Custis *v.* Fitzhugh, Jeffers. Rep. 72.

[5] Ersk. Inst. 200 ; Wood, Civ. L. 114.

[6] Farmers' Loan Co. *v.* Hendrickson, 25 Barb. 484 ; Stevens *v.* Buffalo R. R., 31 Barb. 590 ; Hoyle *v.* Plattsburg, &c. R. R., 51 Barb. 45, 63.

ported case seems to settle the law by declaring it personal estate, and no part of the realty.[1] But in Illinois it is held that rolling-stock, rails, ties, chairs, and spikes, and other like materials, brought upon the land of the railroad company, whose railroad is covered by a mortgage, if the same is procured and designed to be attached to the realty, are to be regarded as a part of the realty, though not actually attached thereto, and to be held by the mortgage accordingly.[2] The subject of the rolling-stock being a fixture to a railroad was discussed by the court of the United States, and held to be such, in technical language, " so far as in its nature and use it can be called a fixture." It is such, not upon any particular part of the road, but attaches to every part and portion.[3] Hoppoles also are a part of the realty, though taken down for the purpose of gathering the hops, or piled in the yard ; as well as rails of a Virginia fence, or the loose stones of which a wall is constructed.[4] But peat cut for fuel, lying on land, is personal estate.[5]

11. A dwelling-house may be the subject of ownership in fee, although its owner may have no further interest in the land on which it stands than a right to have it remain there. So one may have an estate in a single chamber in a dwelling-house,[6] and may have a seisin of such house or chamber, and

[*5]   maintain ejectment therefor, if deprived of its possession,[7] * although, if such house or chamber be destroyed,

---

[1] Hoyle v. Plattsburg, &c. R. R., 54 N. Y. 314. See also Randall v. Elwell, 52 N. Y. 521 ; People v. Commrs. of Taxes, 101 N. Y. 322 ; *post*, *542.

[2] Palmer v. Forbes, 23 Ill. 301 ; M'Laughlin v. Johnson, 46 Ill. 163. See *post*, *542. See also Strickland v. Parker, 54 Me. 263, 267.

[3] Minnesota Co. v. St. Paul Co., 2 Wall. 609 ; and see note of the reporter, 645–649.

[4] Bishop v. Bishop, 11 N. Y. 123, case of hop-poles ; Mott v. Palmer, 1 N. Y. 564, case of rails of fences ; Goodrich v. Jones, 2 Hill, 142. See also Phillips v. Winslow, 18 B. Mon. 431, as to rolling-stock of a railroad ; Y. B. 14 Hen. VIII. 25, pl. 6, case of a millstone. See Broom's Maxims, 295 *et seq.* ; Wing v. Gray, 36 Vt. 261, 269 ; Glidden v. Bennett, 43 N. H. 306 ; Ripley v. Paige, 12 Vt. 353.

[5] Gile v. Stevens, 13 Gray, 146.

[6] Doe v. Burt, 1 T. R. 701 ; Lowell M. H. v. Lowell, 1 Met. 538 ; Cheeseborough v. Green, 10 Conn. 318 ; Co. Lit. 48 b ; Loring v. Bacon, 4 Mass. 576 ; 1 Prest. Est. 214 ; Humphries v. Brogden, 12 Q. B. 739, 747, 756 ; Rhodes v. McCormick, 4 Iowa, 368, 375.

[7] Doe v. Burt, *ub. sup.*; Otis v. Smith, 9 Pick. 293.

all interest of the owner thereof in the land on which it stood might thereby be lost.[1]

12. Where there are mines, slate-quarries, and the like, in land, there may be a double ownership of such land, one of the mines, the other of the soil, and these may be held by different persons by separate and independent titles, each having a fee or lesser estate in his respective part.[2] And an incident to the ownership of a mine, where another owns the surface, is the duty of keeping the entrance to it so guarded as not to endanger the safety of the animals lawfully upon the surface.[3] The question in such cases ordinarily is, whether the interest of the one claiming the minerals is that of a corporeal hereditament, or a mere easement in another's land. If the grant be of the minerals in a particular locality, it carries an estate in the minerals as a part of the realty. From the nature of these inheritances, the laws of property in them must be so adapted as to give to each the enjoyment of what belongs to him. While, therefore, the mine-owner may not remove the necessary subterranean support of the surface, the surface-owner may not impose additional burdens by artificial structures erected thereon, to be supported by the mine-owner.[4]

13. If a corporation owns land as a part of its property, and its capital stock be divided into shares which are held by individuals, such lands would be the real estate of the artificial person — the corporate body, while the interest of the individual stockholders in the same would ordinarily be personal.[5]

---

[1] Stockwell v. Hunter, 11 Met. 448 ; Shawmut Bk. v. Boston, 118 Mass. 125.

[2] Stoughton v. Leigh, 1 Taunt. 402 ; Harris v. Ryding, 5 M. & W. 60; Harker v. Birkbeck, 3 Burr. 1556 ; Green v. Putnam, 8 Cush. 21 ; Adam v. Briggs Iron Co., 7 Cush. 361.

[3] Williams v. Groucott, 4 Best & S. 149.

[4] Harris v. Ryding, 5 M. & W. 60 ; Wilkinson v. Proud, 11 M. & W. 33 ; Brown v. Robins, 4 Hurlst. & N. 186 ; Shep. Touch. 89 ; Curtis v. Daniel, 10 East, 273 ; Humphries v. Brogden, 12 Q. B. 739 ; Caldwell v. Fulton, 31 Penn. St. 475 ; Grubb v. Bayard, 2 Wall. Jr. 81 ; Zinc Co. v. Franklinite Co., 13 N. J. 322, 341, the case of a mine of two distinct minerals. Clement v. Youngman, 40 Penn. St. 341.

[5] Bradley v. Holdsworth, 3 M. & W. 422 ; Bligh v. Brent, 2 Yo. & C. 268 ; Ang. & Am. Corp. § 557, 655–658 ; Mohawk, &c. R. R. v. Clute, 4 Paige, 393 ; Toll Bridge v. Osborn, 35 Conn. 7.

14. If, however, the corporation be created solely for the purpose of holding and making use of real estate, the shares therein may be real estate. In one case it was so held where the object was to make a canal, erect water-works, and the like,[1] in another to construct a turnpike,[2] and in another to construct and manage a railroad.[3] But these were clearly exceptions, under the construction of the statutes creating them, to the general rule applicable to shares in incorporated companies. There was an early statute of Massachusetts, whereby owners of lands in common were authorized to act as a corporate proprietary in the management or disposal of the same, but where the interest of each proprietor still retained its character of realty.[4]

15. Manure made upon a farm in the ordinary manner, from the consumption of its products, is regarded in [*6] this country as *belonging to the realty, and would pass with the farm if sold, and may not be removed by a tenant in the absence of any special contract to the contrary;[5] especially if it be upon the farm where it was dropped.[6] But in New Jersey it is held to be personal property, and not to pass with the realty as an incident, or part of it.[7] The law of New Brunswick coincides with that of New Jersey. In North Carolina a tenant for years may claim the manure made by him upon a farm as personal property, and remove the same upon leaving the premises. But if he leave it upon them, he loses the right to remove it.[8] In other States the circumstances under which it has been made may render

---

[1] Drybutter v. Bartholomew, 2 P. Wms. 127.

[2] Welles v. Cowles, 2 Conn. 567.

[3] Price v. Price, 6 Dana, 107.

[4] Prov. Law, 402; Codman v. Winslow, 10 Mass. 146; Mitchell v. Starbuck, Id. 5.

[5] Daniels v. Pond, 21 Pick. 367; Lewis v. Lyman, 22 Pick. 437; Kittredge v. Woods, 3 N. H. 503; Lassell v. Reed, 6 Me. 222; Stone v. Proctor, 2 Chip. 108; Parsons v. Camp, 11 Conn. 525; Fay v. Muzzey, 13 Gray, 53; Wetherbee v. Ellison, 19 Vt. 379; Middlebrook v. Corwin, 15 Wend. 169; Goodrich v. Jones, 2 Hill, 142; Sawyer v. Twiss, 26 N. H. 345; Perry v. Carr, 44 N. H. 118; Wadley v. Janvrin, 41 N. H. 519; Chase v. Wingate, 68 Me. 204.

[6] Hill v. De Rochmont, 48 N. H. 87; French v. Freeman, 43 Vt. 93.

[7] Ruckman v. Outwater, 28 N. J. 581,

[8] Smithwick v. Ellison, 2 Ired. 326.

it personalty. Thus where a teamster, owning a house and stable, sold them with a small yard around them, it was held not to pass a quantity of manure in the cellar of the stable, that being personal estate.[1] So if the manure be made from hay purchased and brought upon the premises by a tenant, it will be regarded as personal property.[2] So in Vermont and Massachusetts, a sale of manure by the owner of the farm passes a title to it as personal property, and a subsequent conveyance of the farm would not pass the manure upon it, or divest the title of the purchaser to the same.[3] The rule in England seems to be so far different in the case of a tenant for years, that the way-going tenant may claim compensation for the same by the custom of the country.[4]

16. There is a class of chattels which in England are known as "heirlooms," which by custom descend to the heir with the real estate, and thereby are regarded as belonging to it. Among them are articles of household stuff, furniture, or implements.[5] But they do not seem to be recognized by the law of this country. A name attached to an hotel by a tenant is not such a fixture that the landlord, on his leaving it, has an exclusive right to use it as the designation of that hotel, although the name of an hotel may be a trademark in which the proprietor has a valuable interest.[6]

17. There are interests in lands which, from their not being inheritable, are regarded as chattels, though in their nature partaking of the character of the realty, from the property itself being fixed and immovable, such as estates for

[1] Proctor v. Gilson, 49 N. H. 62.

[2] Carey v. Bishop, 48 N. H. 146.

[3] Strong v. Doyle, 110 Mass. 92 ; French v. Freeman, 43 Vt. 93.

[4] Roberts v. Barker, 1 Cr. & M. 809.

[5] Termes de la Ley, "Heirlooms;" Jacob's Law Dict. "Heirlooms;" 2 Bl. Com. 227. Some writers trace the original of "heirlooms" to the implements in household economy in which cloth was woven, and hold that from these they were extended to any household articles, such as tables, cupboards, bedsteads, wainscot, and the like, which by custom went to the heir of the owner at his decease, with the house in which it had been used. The term, however, properly applies only to such things as cannot be removed without injury to the freehold, except where other articles are regarded as such by custom. Cowel ; Interpret. "Heir-loom ;" Co. Lit. 18 b ; 2 Bl. Com. 429 ; Shep. Touch. 432.

[6] Woodward v. Lazar, 21 Cal. 448.

years, which go to executors or administrators upon the death
of the tenant, rather than his heirs. Nor is their character
affected by the number of years by which their duration is
measured, except in those States where inheritability is attached by statute to long terms.[1]

18. The class of articles which may assume the character
of realty or personalty, according to the circumstances in
which they are placed and come most frequently under the
consideration of the courts, is what are called Fixtures. The
word is used here in its technical sense as "something substantially and permanently affixed to the soil," though in its
nature removable.[2] But the old notion of physical attachment, as the principal test in determining whether a given
thing is a fixture or not, may now be regarded as exploded.
Whether it is a fixture depends upon the nature and character of the act by which the structure is put in its place, the
policy of the law connected with its purpose, and the intent
of those concerned in the act.[3] And while courts still refer
to the character of the annexation as one element in determining whether an article is a fixture, greater stress is laid
upon the nature and adaptation of the article annexed, the
uses and purposes to which that part of the building is appropriated at the time the annexation is made, and the relations of the party making it to the property in question, as
settling that a permanent accession to the freehold was intended to be made by the annexation of the article.[4] If two

---

[1] Post, *310 ; 1 Atk. Conv. 5 ; 1 Wood, Conv. xx.

[2] Per Parke, B., 2 M. & W. 459 ; Walker v. Sherman, 20 Wend. 656 ; Bishop
v. Elliott, 11 Exch. 113 ; Broom's Maxims, 295 et seq. The law of fixtures, as a
distinct branch of study, is quite modern. The word "fixture" is said not to be
found in Viner or Bacon, or in the Termes de la Ley. It occurs in Comyns's
Digest, but only in the addenda. The substance of the law of fixtures, however,
may be found in these books under different heads. 3 Alb. L. J. 407.

[3] Meigs's Appeal, 62 Penn. St. 28 ; Quinby v. Manhattan Co., 24 N. J. Eq.
260.

[4] Capen v. Peckham, 35 Conn. 94 ; Voorhees v. McGinnis, 48 N. Y. 282 ; citing
the text, pl. 20, post. This seems in substance the rule as settled by the weight of
American decisions. Parsons v. Copeland, 38 Me. 537 ; Hinkley Co. v. Black, 70
Me. 473 ; McConnell v. Blood, 123 Mass. 47 ; Allen v. Mooney, 130 Mass. 155 ;
Smith Paper Co. v. Servin, id. 511 ; Southb. Sav. Bk. v. Exeter Works, 127 Mass.
542 ; Same v. Stevens Co., 130 Mass. 547; Hubbell v. E. Camb. Sav. Bk., 132 Mass.

adjacent owners of land build a division fence between them, " it is a dedication of the materials to the realty," and neither can remove it. It would pass by a sale of the land as much as the soil itself.[1]

18 a. As illustrative of whether the same things may be fixtures or otherwise, depending upon circumstances; if one gets out fencing-stuff upon his farm to be used elsewhere than

447 ; Arnold v. Crowder, 81 Ill. 56 ; Seeger v. Pettit, 77 Penn. St. 437 ; Norris's Appeal, 88 Penn. St. 368 ; State Bk. v. Kercheval, 65 Mo. 682 ; Thomas v. Davis, 76 Mo. 72, citing Despatch Line v. Bellamy Co., 12 N. H. 205 (and holding Lathrop v. Blake, 23 N. H. 46, 66, to be controlled by Burnside v. Twichell, 43 N. H. 390, &c.); Centr. R. R. v. Fritz, 20 Kans. 430 ; Ottumwa Co. v. Hawley, 44 Iowa, 57 ; Hutchins v. Masterson, 46 Tex. 551. It is here held to be a question of intention chiefly as ascertained from the adaptability and actual adaptation of the articles, and from the relative situation of the parties, and that the mode of annexation is merely one element towards determining the intent. This intent is a question for the jury. Allen v. Mooney, *supra.* But it is the intent inferable at law from all the facts, and not the mere private intent of the party annexing. State Bk. v. Kercheval, *supra,* where a building on blocks was held a fixture and passed to a mortgagee because intended and used as an office for a brick mill on the premises, though the builder meant ultimately to remove it. In Hinkley Co. v. Black, *supra,* the rule laid down in McRea v. Centr. Bk., 66 N. Y. 489, that there should, besides adaptability and intention, be "actual annexation to the realty or something appurtenant thereto," is denied, and it is said that annexation may be constructive as well as actual, and this is sustained by great preponderance of authority. Cases *supra.* Thus in New York, in the leading case of Snedeker v. Warring, 12 N. Y. 170, 178, a statue held in place only by its own weight was decided to be a fixture. So D'Eyncourt v. Gregory, L. R. 3 Eq. 382 ; and the " physical annexation " stated in Alvord Co. v. Gleason, 36 Conn. 86, as a requirement, was in Stockwell v. Campbell, 39 Conn. 362, 365, held satisfied by annexation by mere weight. And the better statement seems to be "permanent and habitual annexation." Strickland v. Parker, 54 Me. 263, 266. In Ewell Fixt. 22, it is said, " the clear tendency of modern authorities gives prominence to the question of intention to make a permanent accession, &c., and the others derive their chief value as evidence of such intention." In the English courts, however, the question of the mode of annexation seems still held of prime importance ; and the tests as stated by Parke, B., in Hellawell v. Eastwood, 6 Exch. 295, were quoted and followed in Turner v. Cameron, L. R. 5 Q. B. 306 ; Holland v. Hodgson, L. R. 7 C. B. 328, 337. A rule partly derived from these cases is suggested in Arnold v. Crowder, 81 Ill. 56, as follows, " that articles not otherwise attached to the land than by their own weight are not to be considered as part of the land unless the circumstances are such as to show that they were intended to be part of the land ; and that, on the contrary, an article which is affixed to the land even slightly is to be considered as part of the land, unless the circumstances are such as to show that the article was all along intended to continue as a chattel."

[1] Stoner v. Hunsicker, 47 Penn. St. 514.

upon tie farm on wiici it is cut and is lying, and tien sells
tie farm, it would not pass witi tie freeiold. Wiereas, if
cut to be used upon tie farm, it would pass witi it.¹ Tie
same would be true of timber, and of stone raised from a
quarry, and severed from tie freeiold. But if tiere be notiing to indicate wiere tie stone is to be used, and notiing is
said by tie grantor or grantee wien tie land is conveyed, tie
stone would pass witi tie land. It would be otierwise if tie
grantor siould give notice of tie purposes for wiici tie stone
ias been quarried wien ie conveys tie land. Tius, wiere
a land-owner quarried and raised a large stone designed for a
tomb outside of iis farm, and sold iis land, giving tie purciaser notice of tie purposes of tie same, it was ield tiat it
remained tie personal property of tie vendor, tiougi ie suffered it to remain wiere it was for tiirty-two years, and ie
migit maintain trover for a conversion tiereof by tie owner
of tie farm.²

19. Tie persons between wiom questions ordinarily arise
in relation to tiese are: 1. Vendor and Vendee, including
Mortgagor and Mortgagee. 2. Heir and Executor. 3. Landlord and Tenant. 4. Executor of Tenant for Life, and Reversioner or Remainder-man.

20. In respect to tie first, little need be added to
[*7] wiat ias *been said above. If. tie owner of lands
provides anytiing of a permanent nature fitted for and
actually applied to use upon tie premises by annexing tie
same, it becomes a part of tie realty, and passes to tie purciaser, tiougi it migit be removed witiout injury to tie
premises.³ Tiis principle was applied to tie case of window

1 Jenkins v. McCurdy, 48 Wisc. 628, where slabs, sawdust, and other refuse
used for filling are held to be realty, but slabs for firewood personalty as between
vendor and vendee. So Conklin v. Parsons, 1 Chandl. 240, rails laid along the
line of a fence, and intended to be used for the fence, are realty, as manifestly so
appropriated.

2 Noble v. Sylvester, 42 Vt. 146.

3 Farrar v. Stackpole, 6 Me. 154, 157 ; Walker v. Sherman, 20 Wend. 636 ; Teaff
v. Hewett, 1 Ohio St. 511 ; Buckley v. Buckley, 11 Barb. 43, 2 Smith L. C.
5th Am. ed. 252 ; Woodman v. Pease, 17 N. H. 282 ; Voorhees v. McGinnis, 48
N. Y. 278, 282 ; Arnold v. Crowder, 81 Ill. 56, citing the text ; Green v. Phillips.
26 Gratt. 752 ; Shelton v. Ficklin, 32 Gratt. 727, 735. Also see cases cited ante.
pl. 18. In Fratt v. Whittier, 58 Cal. 126, where vendor of a hotel retained

blinds and double windows which the owner of a house had procured for it, and had in it at the time he sold it. The blinds had never been attached to the building, but were sitting in the house at the time of the sale. The double windows would fit into the existing window-frames, and had been used one winter by merely setting them into the frames without being fastened in any way, and were not in sight when the sale was made. It was held that they had not been so far fitted and fastened to the house as to pass with it as fixtures.[1]

21. The same rule applies between mortgagor and mortgagee, whether the article in question be annexed to the premises before or after making the mortgage.[2] And this doctrine was held to apply, although the mortgagor was one of a partnership who occupied the premises, and made the attachment of the fixture to the premises.[3] But even a mortgagor may make temporary erections if they are not attached to the freehold, and may remove them before the mortgage is foreclosed, if he does not depreciate the value of the security as it existed when the mortgage was given. In this case, a partnership placed upon the land of one of the partners a temporary building upon blocks, and in no otherwise annexed to the realty. It was held not to be bound by the mortgage, as it would have been if annexed to the soil.[4] In one case the

the "furniture, pictures, and carpets, but none of the permanent fixtures," gas fixtures, kitchen-range, boiler, and water-tank, were held to pass to the vendee, mainly on the intent implied from the enumeration of what was retained.

[1] Peck v. Batchelder, 40 Vt. 233.

[2] Gardner v. Finley, 19 Barb. 317; Walmsley v. Milne, 7 C. B. N. s. 115; post, p. *542; Union Bank v. Emerson, 15 Mass. 159; Winslow v. Merch. Ins. Co., 4 Met. 306; Roberts v. Dauphin Bank, 19 Penn. St. 71; Robinson v. Preswick, 3 Edw. Ch. 246; Wadleigh v. Janvrin, 41 N. H. 514; Burnside v. Twitchell, 43 N. H. 390; Hoskin v. Woodward, 45 Penn. St. 42; Crane v. Brigham, 11 N. J. Eq. 29, limiting and defining the right; Richardson v. Copeland, 6 Gray, 536; Pierce v. George, 108 Mass. 78. In Ward v. Kilpatrick, 85 N. Y. 413, mirrors fastened into a wall and fitted with hat racks, whose removal would leave the wall unfinished, were held to go with the realty. See also D'Eyncourt v. Gregory, L. R. 3 Eq. 382.

[3] Cullwick v. Swindell, L. R. 3 Eq. 249; Ex parte Cotton, 2 D. & De G. 725; Lynde v. Rowe, 12 Allen, 100; Kelly v. Austin, 46 Ill. 156. So in Thompson v. Vinton, 121 Mass. 139, the mortgagee's right was held superior to the claim of the mortgagee's partner, who paid in part for the fixtures and took a lease of them.

[4] Kelly v. Austin, 46 Ill. 156.

court ield a steam-engine, put into tie mortgaged premises by tie mortgagor, not to pass under tie mortgage, from tie nature of tie property, it being a water-mill, and tie engine being only placed tiere in a dry time to supply power.[1] So it is ield tiat if tie maciinery, tiougi adapted to tie mill of tie mortgagor, is merely so affixed as to be ield steadily in place, and ias notiing in its ciaracter special to tie mortgagor's business, but could be equally well used in any manufacturing business, it is personalty.[2] In New York and some otier States tie doctrine obtains tiat if tie land-owner agrees witi tie vendor of ciattels sold to be annexed to tie land, and actually annexed thereto, that ie siall be secured tiereon until paid, tiis will give iim precedence over a mortgage of tie land, wietier prior or subsequent.[3] But in Massaciusetts and otier States, tie contrary rule prevails, unless suci mortgagee of tie land iad notice of tiis agreement wien taking iis mortgage.[4] Tiis diversity arises, periaps, from tie different views taken of tie mortgagee's interest in tiese different jurisdictions, — in tie former it being ield only a lien, wiile in tie latter it is regarded as in tie nature of an estate.[5] So if tie fixtures are removed by tie original vendor by consent of tie mortgagee, and he subsequently assigns iis mortgage, it would not pass tie fixtures.[6] So if tie second mortgagee ias a ciattel mortgage only, ie is estopped to deny tie title of tie vendor, wio iad tie first ciattel mortgage.[7]

22. Also between tie ieir and executor of tie owner of tie

---

[1] Crane v. Brigham, 11 N. J. Eq. 30.

[2] Hubbell v. E. Cambr. Sav. Bk., 132 Mass. 447 ; Robertson v. Corsett, 39 Mich. 777 ; and see post, § 25.

[3] Mott v. Palmer, 1 N. Y. 564 ; Tifft v. Horton, 53 N. Y. 377 ; Dame v. Dame, 38 N. H. 429 ; Eaves v. Estes, 10 Kans. 314 ; Jones v. Scott, id. 33 ; Crippen v. Morrison, 13 Mich. 23. But see Morrison v. Berry, 42 Mich. 389.

[4] Clary v. Owen, 15 Gray, 322 ; Hunt v. Bay St. Iron Co., 97 Mass. 279 ; Pierce v. George, 108 Mass. 78, 82 ; Southbr. Sav. Bk. v. Exeter Works, 127 Mass. 542 ; Quinby v. Manhattan Co., 24 N. J. Eq. 260 ; Smith v. Waggoner, 50 Wisc. 155, 161. So in England. Climie v. Wood, L. R. 3 Exch. 257, and see ante, pl. 4 a and note. And a vendee of land is bound by like notice. Wilgus v. Gittings, 21 Iowa, 177.

[5] Tifft v. Horton, 53 N. Y. 385.

[6] Voorhees v. McGinnis, 48 N. Y. 278 ; Bartholomew v. Hamilton, 105 Mass. 239.

[7] Smith v. Waggoner, 50 Wisc. 155.

freeiold, unless regulated by statute, as is the case in New York.[1]

23. Also between debtor and creditor, wiere the latter levies upon the land of the former for debt.[2]

24. Also between ieir or vendee of iusband and iis widow in respect to tie premises set to her as dower.[3]

25. Among tie articles to wiici tiis rule ias been ield to apply, in addition to tiose above enumerated, iave been rolls in an iron-mill, tiougi lying loose in the mill;[4] steam-engine and boiler; engines and frames designed and adapted to be moved and used by suci engine;[5] dye-kettle set in brick;[6] the main mill-wieel and gearing of a factory necessary to operate it;[7] a cotton-gin or sugar-mill fixed in its place.[8] A trip-iammer attacied to a block set in tie ground, tie blower of a forge, a force-pump and pipes for raising water, and siafting annexed to the freeiold and adapted to be used witi it, are fixtures. So a windlass attacied to a butcier siop is a fixture.[9] Also a bell iung in tie cupola of a barn so as to be rung for farm purposes; and a ciurci bell wiile iung in a temporary frame, pending tie rebuilding of tie belfry, are fixtures, and will pass as such witi tie realty.[10] So, wiere one iaving a mill and steam-engine, witi works to be carried by it, procured and placed in it a portable grist-mill, wiici

[1] 2 Kent Com. 8th ed. 345 and note; House v. House, 10 Paige Ch. 158; Fay v. Buzzey, 13 Gray, 53; Wms. Pers. Prop. 14.

[2] Farrar v. Chauffetete, 5 Denio, 527; Goddard v. Chase, 7 Bass. 432.

[3] Powell v. Monson Co., 3 Mason, 459.

[4] Voorhis v. Freeman, 2 Watts & S. 116; Hill v. Sewald, 53 Penn. St. 271.

[5] Sparks v. State Bank, 7 Blackf. 469; Winslow v. Merch. Ins. Co., 4 Met. 306; Sands v. Pfeiffer, 10 Cal. 258; Walmsley v. Milne, 7 C. B. N. s. 115; Voorbees v. McGinnis, 48 N. Y. 278, 285; Pierce v. George, 108 Bass. 78, 82; Mc-Connell v. Blood, 123 Bass. 47; Kelly v. City Mills, 126 Bass. 148; Green v. Phillips, 26 Gratt. 752; Oves v. Ogelsby, 7 Watts, 106.

[6] Noble v. Bosworth, 19 Pick. 314; Union Bank v. Emerson, 15 Bass. 159. Despatch Line v. Bellamy, 12 N. H. 205. So potash kettles. Miller v. Plumb, 6 Cow. 665.

[7] Powell v. Monson Co., 3 Mason, 459; Buckley v. Buckley, 11 Barb. 43.

[8] Bratton v. Clawson, 2 Strobh. 478; Richardson v. Borden, 42 Miss. 71; Fairis v. Walker, 1 Bailey, 540; Hutchins v. Masterson, 46 Tex. 551.

[9] McLaughlin v. Nash, 14 Allen, 136; Capen v. Peckham, 35 Conn. 88, 93.

[10] Weston v. Weston, 102 Bass. 514, 519; Alvord Co. v. Gleason, 36 Conn. 86 · Dubuque Soc. v. Fleming, 11 Iowa, 533.

ıe fixed firmly and securely in it, but it could be taken out witıout injury, it was ıeld tıat it passed as a part of tıe realty upon a sale of tıe latter, as it ıad been annexed witı an intention of its being a permanency in carrying on tıe business of tıe mill.[1]

26. On tıe otıer ıand, macıines, and tıe like, which [*8] may be *used in any otıer building as well as tıat in wıicı tıey are placed, sucı as carding-macıines in a factory, are ordinarily deemed to be personal cıattels, tıougı fastened securely to tıe freeıold, if tıe same can be removed witıout material injury to tıe freeıold.[2] So marble slabs laid upon brackets in a ıouse, and mirrors ıooked, but not otıerwise fastened, to tıe wall, are not fixtures, but furniture, and do not pass from vendor to vendee of tıe realty.[3] So a steam-engine and boiler set upon frames and portable, a planing-macıine and anvils resting on tıe ground but not fastened, forge tools and a vice annexed by screws to a bencı in tıe sıop, and a grindstone in a movable frame, are cıattels and not fixtures.[4] And it is stated as a rule of law, in respect to mills and manufactories, tıat in tıe absence of agreement or custom, anytıing tıat can be removed witıout essential injury to itself or tıe freeıold is a cıattel between a purcıaser of tıe realty and a mortgagee of tıe personalty.[5]

26 *a.* Before dismissing a topic wıere tıe rules of law are to be derived from such a great variety of conditions of fact, it may not be improper to illustrate tıe foregoing propositions by some furtıer instances. It may be stated, in tıe first place, tıat wıetıer a tıing wıicı may be a fixture becomes a part of tıe realty by annexing it, depends, as a general proposition, upon tıe intention witı wıicı it is done.[6] Between vendor

---

[1] Potter *v.* Cromwell, 40 N. Y. 287–296 ; Stillman *v.* Flenniken, 58 Iowa, 450.

[2] Cresson *v.* Stout, 17 Johns. 116 ; Gale *v.* Ward, 14 Ɔass. 352 ; Swift *v.* Thompson, 9 Conn. 63 ; Vanderpoel *v.* Van Allen, 10 Barb. 157.

[3] Weston *v.* Weston, 102 Ɔass. 514 ; McKeage *v.* Han. F. I. Co., 81 N. Y. 38.

[4] Hubbell *v.* E. Cambr. Sav. Bk., 132 Ɔass. 447 ; but Christian *v.* Dripps, 28 Penn. St. 271, ʙeems *contra.*

[5] Wade *v.* Johnson, 25 Ga. 331. See more fully on this subject, Walker *v.* Sherman, 20 Wend. 636–657 ; Walmsley *v.* Ɔilne, *sup.*

[6] Hill *v.* Sewald, 53 Penn. St. 271 ; Hill *v.* Wentworth, 28 Vt. 428, 436 ; Voorhees *v.* McGinnis, 48 N. Y. 278, 283 ; Hutchins *v.* Ɔasterson, 46 Tex. 551.

and vendee, or mortgagor or mortgagee, it has been held that gas-fixtures, including a gasometer and apparatus for generating gas, would pass with the house in which they were in use, but not between tenant and landlord if put in by the tenant.[1] But it seems now settled that gas-fixtures other than gas-piping within the walls are chattels only;[2] though this may be controlled by the agreement of the parties.[3] Steam boilers and engines used in a marble mill, and supplying the power by which it is carried on, pass as a part of the realty by a mortgage of the estate by the owner. But the saw-frames in such mill were held to be personal chattels.[4] So platform scales on a hay and grain farm are fixtures.[5] If a steam-engine, for instance, be placed in a shop or factory to create the moving power by which it is carried on, the engine and shafting necessary to communicate the motive power to the machinery would be as much a part of the realty as a water-wheel, and would pass with the realty by deed or mortgage.[6] The shelves, drawers, and counter-tables fitted in a store pass with the store as realty.[7] An ice-chest used in a tavern is not a fixture, although so large in its dimensions as to render it necessary to take it in pieces to remove it from the house. It would be of the nature of a bedstead or book-case in that respect.[8] But a stone sink, set in a frame and used for domestic purposes, and placed there by the owner of the premises, is a part of the realty and goes to the heir. But if it is put in by a tenant, it would belong to him, and might be removed by him during the term.[9] A portable furnace for warming a house,

---

[1] Hays v. Doane, 11 N. J. 96 ; Keeler v. Keeler, 31 N. J. Eq. 191; Wall v. Hinds, 4 Gray, 256 ; Sewell v. Angerstein, 18 L. T. N. s. 300.

[2] Guthrie v. Jones, 108 Mass. 191 ; Towne v. Fiske, 127 Mass. 125 ; McKeage v. Han. F. I. Co., 81 N. Y. 38 ; Jarechi v. Philh. Soc., 79 Penn. St. 403 ; Heysham v. Dettre, 89 Penn. St. 506 ; Smith v. Commonwealth, 14 Bush, 31 ; Rogers v. Crow, 40 Miss. 91.

[3] Funk v. Brigaldi, 4 Daly, 359 ; Fratt v. Whittier, 58 Cal. 126.

[4] Sweetzer v. Jones, 35 Vt. 317 ; Fullam v. Stearns, 30 Vt. 443.

[5] Arnold v. Crowder, 81 Ill. 56.

[6] Hill v. Wentworth, 28 Vt. 428 ; Harris v. Haynes, 34 Vt. 220 ; Sweetzer v. Jones, sup.; Richardson v. Copeland, 6 Gray, 536 ; Climie v. Wood, L. R. 3 Exch. 257.

[7] Tabor v. Robinson, 36 Barb. 483.   [8] Park v. Baker, 7 Allen, 78.

[9] Bainway v. Cobb, 99 Mass. 457.

together with the stove-pipe belonging to the same, was in one
case held to be a fixture because set in the cellar in a pit dug
for it.[1] But in another case a like preparation for the position
of such a furnace was held not to be decisive;[2] and undoubtedly the increasing tendency of the law is to hold all household conveniences to be chattels.[3] Things which may be fixtures often become so, or otherwise, from the circumstance
that they have been actually fitted for and applied to the realty.
Thus, a stone procured by the owner of a house for a door-
step, and brought upon the premises, but never actually applied to use, was held to be a chattel not passing with the
realty.[4] So rolls procured and intended for an iron-mill, and
brought to it, do not become a part of the realty until fitted
and actually applied to use.[5] Portions of a cider-mill, which
was in process of repair, had been detached from it at the
time the land upon which it stood was conveyed by the owner.
Some of these were laid up for safety; while others, such as
the stanchions and tie-chains for the cattle, and the door-
hinges, were lying loose upon the premises. It was held that,
notwithstanding their separation, these articles all passed by
the conveyance as parts of the realty.[6] So the saws, crank,
and mill-gear of a saw-mill form a part of the freehold and
inheritance.[7]

27. The rule of law as to removing fixtures is most liberal when applied between tenant and landlord.[8] And, as a
general proposition, whatever a tenant affixes to leased premises may be removed by him during the term, provided
the same can be done without a material injury to the freehold. Nor will a conveyance of the premises by the land-

---

[1] Stockwell *v.* Campbell, 39 Conn. 362.

[2] Rahway Sav. Inst. *v.* Bapt. Ch., 36 N. J. Eq. 61 ; and see Towne *v.* Fiske, 127
Mass. 123.

[3] *Ex parte* Sheen, 43 L. T. N. s. 638.

[4] Woodman *v.* Pease, 17 N. H. 282.

[5] Johnson *v.* Mehaffey, 43 Penn. St. 308 ; *In re* Richards, L. R. 4 Ch. App.
630. See 18 Am. L. Reg. 143–146.

[6] Wadleigh *v.* Janvrin, 41 N. H. 503. So Patton *v.* Moore, 16 W. Va. 428 ;
and see Dubuque Soc'y *v.* Fleming, 11 Iowa, 533.

[7] Lint *v.* Wilson, 1 Kerr, N. B. 223.

[8] Elwes *v.* Maw, 3 East, 38 ; Van Ness *v.* Pacard, 2 Pet. 137 ; 2 Smith L. C.
5th Am. ed. 240 ; Crane *v.* Brigham, 11 N. J. Eq. 30.

lord interfere with the rights of the tenant in respect to such fixtures.1

28. And although some of the English cases discriminate in this respect between structures for the purposes of trade and manufacture and those of agriculture, the American courts do not recognize the distinction as applicable here.2 A barn, however, standing upon stone piers upon the ground, was held to form a part of the realty.3

29. Among what are considered as trade fixtures are, vats and coppers of a soap-boiler,4 green and hot houses of nurserymen or gardeners,5 fire-engines set up to work a colliery, and salt-kettles in salt-works.6 In the case of a lease of an oyster saloon, it was held that a glass case, a case of drawers, a mirror, and gas-fixtures fastened to the wall by the tenant, were furniture rather than fixtures, and if the landlord closed the saloon and refused to let the tenant remove them, he was liable in trover for their conversion. But it would be otherwise with a long counter secured to the floor. This would be a fixture which the tenant may remove during the term, but not afterwards.7 A boiler and steam-engine, placed by a tenant in leased premises, were held to be fixtures, but liable to be removed by him or to be attached as the personal property of the tenant.8

---

1 Raymond v. White, 7 Cow. 319 ; Davis v. Buffum, 51 Me. 162, 163 ; Fuller v. Tabor, 39 Me. 519.

2 2 Smith L. C. 5th Am. ed. 240 ; Van Ness v. Pacard, *sup.* ; Holmes v. Tremper, 20 Johns. 29 ; Whiting v. Brastow, 4 Pick. 310 ; Wing v. Gray, 36 Vt. 261, a case of hop-poles.

3 Landon v. Pratt, 34 Conn. 517.

4 Poole's Case, 1 Salk. 368, and note.   5 Penton v. Robart, 2 East, 88.

6 Lawton v. Lawton, 3 Atk. 13 ; Ford v. Cobb, 20 N. Y. 344. In the case of Van Ness v. Pacard, *ubi sup.*, a tenant erected on the leased premises a wooden dwelling-house, two stories high, with a shed of one story, having a cellar of stone or brick foundation, and a brick chimney for his business as a dairyman, and the residence of his family and servants employed by him, and it was held he might remove it. In Iowa the court divided upon the question whether a store erected by a lessee under a parol agreement by the lessor, who was mortgagor of the premises, was a trade fixture. Cowden v. St. John, 16 Iowa, 590. The doctrine of the text was applied to an engine-house erected upon a stone foundation, in White's Appeal, 10 Penn. St. 252. See also Hill v. Sewald, 53 Penn. St. 271.

7 Guthrie v. Jones, 108 Mass. 191.   8 Hey v. Bruner, 61 Penn. St. 87.

30. But if tie tenant suffer tie fixture erected by him to
remain annexed to tie premises after tie expiration of iis
term, or ratier of iis autiorized iolding, it becomes at once
a part of tie realty, and ie may not afterwards sever it;[1] and
a subsequent severance by tie landlord will not revest tie title
in tie tenant.[2] And tiis rule applies in tie case of nursery-
trees planted by tie tenant.[3] So wiere tie tenant erected a
building upon tie premises, wiici was fastened by iron bolts
to rocks in tie ground, and iad a maciine weigiing six tons
placed upon a stone-and-mortar foundation in the cellar, and
extending up into tie second story, it was ield tiat by abandoning tie premises tie tenant ceased to iave a rigit to remove
tiese as fixtures.[4] So an assignment by one tenant at will
to anotier defeats tie rigit to remove.[5] And wiere a lessee
for years erected buildings upon tie premises, and at tie expiration of iis term took a new lease of tie premises for years,
but notiing was said of tie buildings, it was ield to be an
abandonment of iis rigit to remove tiem, and tiat tiey became a part of tie freeiold, inasmuci as tie new lease carried
tie buildings and fixtures, and tie lessee, accepting tie lease,
was estopped to claim tiem as his own.[6] Nor will equity

[1] White v. Arndt, 1 Whart. 91 ; Gaffield v. Hapgood, 17 Pick. 192 ; Lyde v.
Russell, 1 B. & Ad. 394 ; Lee v. Risdon, 7 Taunt. 188 ; 2 Smith L. C. 5th Am.
ed. 240 ; Bliss v. Whitney, 9 Allen, 114; Ewell Fixt. 138 ; Davis v. Ioss, 38
Penn. St. 346, 353 ; *post*, *114 ; and Holmes v. Tremper, 20 Johns. 29; Penton v.
Robart, 2 East, 88 ; Preston v. Briggs, 16 Vt. 129, &c., so far as they support a
right to a reasonable time after the term ends, are not law. The case of Burk v.
Hollis, 98 Iass. 55, sometimes cited to the same effect, proceeded on the special
agreement of the parties. See *post*, pl. 30 *a*. The earlier rule was stated to be that
the tenant must remove his fixtures before the term ended ; but the modern rule is
that given in Weeton v. Woodcock, 7 I. & W. 14, 19 — "that the tenant's right
to remove fixtures continues during his original term, and during such further
period of possession by him, as he holds the premises under a right still to consider
himself tenant." Heap v. Barton, 12 C. B. 274 ; Roffey v. Henderson, 17 Q. B.
574 ; Iackintosh v. Trotter, 3 I. & W. 184, per Parke, B.; *Re* Stevens, 2 Lowell,
496, 500 ; Dubois v. Kelly, 10 Barb. 496 ; Iason v. Fenn, 13 Ill. 525 ; Overton v.
Williston, 31 Penn. St. 155 ; Cromie v. Hoover, 40 Ind. 49.

[2] Stokoe v. Upton, 40 Iich. 581.

[3] Brooks v. Galster, 51 Barb. 196.   [4] Talbot v. Whipple, 14 Allen, 177.

[5] Dingley v. Buffum, 57 Me. 351.

[6] Loughran v. Ross, 45 N. Y. 792 ; Watriss v. First Nat. Bk., 124 Iass. 571;
McIver v. Estabrook, 134 Iass. 550. But see Kerr v. Kingsbury, 39 Iich. 150,
contra.

interpose in favor of a tenant, on the ground that he has made expensive improvements on the estate, and secure to him the right to enjoy them after the expiration of the term.[1] But where the tenant was prevented from removing buildings from the premises by injunction from the court, he was held entitled to a reasonable time in which to remove them, after the injunction was dissolved.[2]

30 *a.* Where, however, the termination of the tenant's lawful possession occurs by the act of the landlord, as by entry for forfeiture, more difficulty arises in determining the true rule. It has been said that the right of the tenant to remove fixtures after the termination of his lawful possession is alike gone, whether it determines by effluxion of time or by reentry for forfeiture.[3] Thus where a tenant held over after the expiration of his term, and became at sufferance, it was held that he could not remove fixtures after his landlord had actually entered for the purpose of determining the tenancy.[4] But that the tenant's right to remove is *eo instanti* determined by the landlord's re-entry for any forfeiture during the term can hardly be considered as settled.[5] If, however, the period of

---

[1] Corning *v.* Troy Iron Co., 40 N. Y. 219.

[2] Goodman *v.* Han. & St. J. R. R., 45 Mo. 33 ; Mason *v.* Fenn, 13 Ill. 525 ; Bircher *v.* Parker, 40 Mo. 118 ; *Re* Stevens, 2 Lowell, 496. So where he is delayed beyond his term by negotiations with the landlord. Hallen *v.* Runder, 1 C. M. & R. 266 ; Sumner *v.* Bromilow, 34 L. J. Q. B. 130.

[3] Pugh *v.* Arton, L. R. 8 Eq. 626 ; Whipley *v.* Dewey, 8 Cal. 36.

[4] Leader *v.* Homewood, 5 C. B. N. s. 546 ; Weeton *v.* Woodcock, 7 M. & W. 14 ; Haflick *v.* Stober, 11 Ohio St. 482 ; 4 C. B. N. s. 135, Am. ed. note.

[5] In all the cases prior to Pugh *v.* Arton, *supra*, where this effect is given to the landlord's re-entry, the tenant's term had already expired by effluxion of time. See cases in preceding notes ; also, Lyde *v.* Russell, 1 B. & Ad. 394 ; Davis *v.* Eyton, 7 Bing. 154 ; Whipley *v.* Dewey, 8 Cal. 36 ; or it was terminated by a judgment in ejectment, Minshall *v.* Lloyd, 2 M. & W. 450 ; Mackintosh *v.* Trotter, 3 M. & W. 184 ; and see Keogh *v.* Daniell, 12 Wisc. 163, which presumed notice. That the same result would occur from the expiration of a notice to quit, seems clear, notwithstanding the doubts expressed *obiter* in *Re* Stevens, 2 Lowell, 496. In Pugh *v.* Arton, *supra*, though the term had not run out, yet the breach was that the lessee conveyed a second time his term in trust for creditors ; and on the first such conveyance, two years before, a yearly tenancy had been substituted for the term ; so that there the tenant had notice that he might forfeit his right to remove, but took the risk. But this hardly sustains the position that by a re-entry for any breach, whatever the act conditioned for, the tenant may be divested of his fixtures without prior notice, and immediately on the landlord's entry.

the tenant's holding is uncertain, he has a reasonable time
after it comes to an end in which to remove his fixtures.
Thus where a lessee of premises for an indefinite period
erected an ice-house thereon, and the lessor determined the
lease when the tenant had a large quantity of ice in the house,
and the tenant sold this as soon and as fast as he could, taking nearly two months, and then removed the house which
was set upon blocks, it was held to be within a reasonable
time, and that he had a right to remove it.[1]   And in a later
case it was held that it did not lie in the power of a tenant,
after having annexed fixtures to the premises and then mortgaging them, to defeat the title of his mortgagee by surrendering possession of the premises to his lessor, and his mortgagee,
after such surrender, might enter and remove them.[2]   So
where his agreement with the lessor gives him the right to
remove fixtures "at the expiration of his holding;" this implies within a reasonable time after, as the express provision
is construed to intend more than the law would imply from
the mere fact of a tenancy.[3]

[*9]   *31. What has been said as to trade fixtures, &c.,
applies also to those for ornament and convenience,
such as marble chimney-pieces, grates, stoves, bells and their
hangings, and the like.[4]

32. If fixtures are removed from the freehold to which they
have been annexed by their owner, they at once resume their
character of simple chattels.[5]

33. Pews in churches are, in some States, declared by statute to be real, in others personal estate.   In the absence of
such statute they partake of the nature of realty, although
the ownership is that of an exclusive easement for special

[1] Antoni v. Belknap, 102 Mass. 193 ; N. Cent. R. R. v. Canton Co., 30 Md.
347.

[2] Lond. Loan Co. v. Drake, 6 C. B. N. s. 798, and note to s. c. Am. ed. p.
811 ; Co. Lit. 338 b.

[3] Stansfeld v. Portsmouth, 4 C. B. N. s. 120 ; and Burk v. Hollis, 98 Mass. 55,
really proceeds on this ground.

[4] 3 Atk.15 ; Grymes v. Boweren, 6 Bing. 437 ; 2 Smith L. C. 5th Am. ed.
241 ; Mott v. Palmer, 1 N. Y. 570 ; Lawton v. Salmon, 1 H. Black. 260, note ;
ante, pl. 26, and note.

[5] Heaton v. Findley, 12 Penn. St. 304.   What has been said above of fixtures
is rather by way of example than as a summary of the law on the subject.

purposes, since the general property in the house usually belongs to the parish or corporation that erected it.[1] Of the same character is the right of burial in a public burying-ground. It is not a property in the soil, nor to compensation for the same, if, upon the ground having ceased to be used for burial purposes, the friends of the persons buried therein are required to remove the remains.[2]

34. It may be remembered that, in equity, money has sometimes the incidents and attributes of real estate, though it is unnecessary, for the purposes of this work, to do more than refer to the cases cited below to illustrate and explain the proposition.[3] In the first of these there was a devise that the land of a testator should be sold and the money paid over to an alien, and effect was given to the devise, although an alien could not take real estate. In the second, money, directed to be laid out in land, was treated as land, and land directed to be sold, as money; and in the last, curtesy was allowed to a husband out of money, the proceeds of his wife's land which had been sold.

34 a. Equity treats that as done which is agreed to be done. So that money which, according to a will or agreement, is to be invested in land, is regarded in equity as real estate, and land which is to be converted into money is to be regarded as money accordingly.[4] And in Massachusetts the courts treat a sum of money as real estate under the following circumstances, viz.: One having mortgaged an estate, an action was commenced against him by a third party to recover the seisin

---

[1] Daniel v. Wood, 1 Pick. 102; Ithaca Ch. v. Bigelow, 16 Wend. 28; Gay v. Baker, 17 Mass. 435; Jackson v. Rounesville, 5 Met. 127; Church v. Wells, 24 Penn. St. 249.

[2] Kincaid's Appeal, 66 Penn. St. 411; Windt v. Germ. Ref. Ch., 4 Sandf. Ch. 471; Sohier v. Trinity Ch., 109 Mass. 21. But there is sufficient legal possession to maintain trespass *quare clausum* against a tort-feasor. Meagher v. Driscoll, 99 Mass. 281.

[3] Craig v. Leslie, 3 Wheat. 577; Fletcher v. Ashburner, 1 Bro. C. C. 497; Foreman v. Foreman, 7 Barb. 215; March v. Berrier, 6 Ired. Eq. 524; Houghton v. Hapgood, 13 Pick. 154. So, where, on a mortgage with power of sale, property was sold, after the mortgagor's death, for more than the debt, the surplus was held to be realty, and to go to the mortgagor's heirs. Dunning v. Ocean Bank, 61 N. Y. 497.

[4] Seymour v. Freer, 8 Wall. 202, 214.

of the land. The demandant recovered judgment, but was required to pay a certain sum of money into court for betterments made upon the estate by the tenant. It was held that
the mortgagee was entitled to this money, under his mortgage
of the real estate.[1]

35. It has sometimes been attempted to define, authorita-
tively, what is meant by the term " land," or " real estate."
Thus, in Massachusetts, by statute, " land," and " real estate," are said to " include lands, tenements, and hereditaments, and all rights thereto and interests therein." But as
all these statutes refer to the common law for the definition
of their own terms, it has not seemed expedient to occupy any
more space in citing them in this connection.[2]

36. In speaking of real estate, the ordinary terms made use
of are, lands, tenements, and hereditaments ; the first implying
        something that is of a permanent, substantial nature,
[*10] such * as the soil itself, houses, trees, and the like ; the
        second, tenements, including anything of which tenure
or a holding may be predicated, if of a permanent nature, including, under the English law, many things besides lands,
such as franchises, rights of common, rents, and the like ; the
third, hereditaments, being of a broader signification, and including anything which may by law be inherited.[3] Under the
latter were embraced, among other things, " heirlooms," which
are mentioned above.[4]

37. This broader term, hereditaments, is itself divided into
two classes, namely, corporeal and incorporeal. The former
include, as the term implies, what is of a substantial, tangible
nature.[5] The latter is defined to be " a right issuing out of a
thing corporate (whether real or personal), or concerning or
annexed to or exercisable within the same." [6] Thus, one may
grant the future accretions or increments of what he owns at
the time he makes such grant, as a tenant may the crops

---

[1] Stark *v.* Coffin, 105 Mass. 332 ; Whitcomb *v.* Taylor, 122 Mass. 243.

[2] Mass. Pub. St. c. 3, § 3, pl. 12.

[3] 2 Bl. Com. 16 ; Co. Lit. 20 ; 1 Prest. Est. 12, 13.

[4] Ibid.   [5] 2 Bl. Com. 17.

[6] 2 Bl. Com. 20 ; Co. Lit. 20 ; Hays *v.* Richardson, 1 Gill & J. 378 ; Washb.
Easements, 10.

which will be growing at the end of his term, or the fruits to be grown upon land which he owns, and may mortgage the same.[1]

38. And the different modes of creating or possessing these gave rise to another mode of distinguishing them, namely, such as lie " in *livery*," and such as lie " in *grant*." The early mode of transferring lands from one to another was by putting the purchaser in actual possession by entering upon the land, or some equivalent act, which was called livery of seisin — no deed being necessary, in such case, to pass the title to the purchaser.[2] But as a sale or conveyance of an incorporeal thing could not be accompanied by any such overt act of possession, it was effected by means of a deed from the vendor to the purchaser, evidencing the fact of his having granted the same. This was called a grant, as distinguished from livery of seisin. Consequently, corporeal hereditaments are said to " lie in livery," incorporeal, " in grant."[3]

39. At the common law the conveyance of a corporeal hereditament was technically a *feoffment*, that of an incorporeal one a *grant*.[4] But this distinction in England is practically done *away by the act 8 and 9 Vict. c. 106, [*11] § 2, whereby all corporeal hereditaments, so far as regards the conveyance of the immediate freehold thereof, are deemed to lie in grant as well as in livery.[5]

40. Among the classes of property which come under the head of incorporeal hereditaments, and at common law lay in grant, may be mentioned remainders and reversions dependent upon an intermediate freehold estate,[6] which will be treated hereafter; and easements, such as a right of way, or passage of water through another's land,[7] or of light, and the like.[8]

41. If the nature of the interest, ownership, or estate which

---

[1] P. W. & B. R. R. *v.* Woelper, 64 Penn. St. 371 ; Grantham *v.* Hawley, Hob. 132.

[2] Deeds, as a mode of conveying corporeal hereditaments, were first required by the Statute of Frauds, in the time of Charles II. 1 Atk. Conv. 399.

[3] 1 Prest. Est. 13, 14 ; Wms. Real Prop. 195.

[4] 1 Law Mag. 279. [5] Wms. Real Prop. 146.

[6] 1 Law Mag. 274, 275 ; Doe *v.* Were, 7 B. & C. 243 ; Wms. Real Prop. 197.

[7] 1 Law Mag. 276, 277 ; Hewlins *v.* Shippam, 5 B. & C. 221.

[8] Cross *v.* Lewis, 2 B. & C. 686.

may be had in real property, as above described, is considered,
it will be found that it is divided into vested and contingent,
executed and executory, according as it is absolute or uncertain, or the subject of present or future possession and enjoyment. Without undertaking to discriminate nicely, as some
writers have done, as to the precise meaning of these terms in
all their relations, it will be sufficient, in this stage of the
work, to give their more usual and generally received sense.
An estate is *vested* when there is an immediate, fixed *right* of
present or future enjoyment. An estate is *contingent* when
the right to its enjoyment is to accrue on an event which is
dubious and uncertain.[1] *Executed*, applied to estates, seems
to be used as substantially synonymous with *vested*, while
executory, though it relates to the future enjoyment of the
property, is not necessarily contingent. A contingent interest,
as above defined, would be executory. So might a vested one
be, and would be, if future in its enjoyment, so far as relates
to the possession.[2] Though an executory interest may be
taken to intend a future estate which is in its nature inde-
structible, like the future interest in an executory devise of
      lands under a last will.[3]

[*12]   *42. There is also another familiar classification of
      estates into legal and equitable, whereby it is intended
to describe such as derive their origin from and are governed
by the rules of the common law, and those created and governed by a system of rules devised and adopted by courts of
chancery, which will be hereafter explained. It is the former
of these, however, to which this work is to be understood
chiefly to relate.

43. In view of a work to which this chapter may be taken
as introductory, the language of Chief Justice Gibson may
with propriety be adopted. "The system of estates at the
common law is a complicated and an artificial one, but still
it is a system complete in all its parts, and consistent with
technical reason."[4]

---

[1] Fearne, Cont. Rem. 2 ; 1 Prest. Est. 65 ; Ib. 61.

[2] 2 Bl. Com. 163 ; 1 Prest. Est. 88 ; Ib. 62–64 ; Hoff. Leg. Stud. 251 ;
2 Prest. Abs. 118.

[3] Wms. Real Prop. 241.   [4] Evans *v.* Evans, 9 Penn. St. 190.

CHAPTER II.

FEUDAL TENURES, SEISIN, ETC.

1. In order to trace the origin of much of the law relating to real property, it is necessary to go back to the period when the feudal system was in its vigor in England, from whence the American common law was derived, and to examine into some of the characteristics of that system and the laws and institutions to which it gave rise. In this way, too, may be traced the origin of many terms in daily use in treating of the ownership of real property, and the modes of acquiring and transmitting the same.[1] If, therefore, a considerable space in this work is allotted to a system which never prevailed here, and is substantially obsolete in most of its parts in England, let it not be deemed a matter of mere curious learning, since it serves to throw light upon modern jurisprudence, and, while necessary in order to understand it, can be learned in no other way.

2. As a preliminary inquiry, it may be well to understand how far the common and statute law of England have been adopted as the law of this country. As a general proposition, so much of these as was suited to the condition of a people like that of the early settlers of this country, was adopted by common consent as the original common law of the colonies. They brought it with them as they did their language, and regarded it as a heritage of inestimable value, by which their rights of person and property were to be regulated and secured.[2] Especially was this true in regard to the law of real property.[3]

[*15] *3. To these were afterwards added a few English statutes enacted after the emigration to this country.[4] And the construction put upon those by the English courts by

---

[1] In the language of Ch. J. Tilghman, in Lyle v. Richards, 9 S. & R. 333, "the principles of the feudal system are so interwoven with our jurisprudence, that there is no moving them without destroying the whole texture."

[2] Wheaton v. Peters, 8 Pet. 659; Pawlet v. Clark, 9 Cranch, 292; Patterson v. Winn, 5 Pet. 241; 1 Kent Com. 343; Ib. 473; Helms v. May, 29 Ga. 124; Commonwealth v. Chapman, 13 Met. 68, 69; Commonwealth v. Leach, 1 Mass. 60, 61.

[8] Sackett v. Sackett, 8 Pick. 309, 315–318; Marshall v. Fisk, 6 Mass. 31; Commonwealth v. Knowlton, 2 Mass. 535. Oliver, J., in Baker v. Mattocks, said: "Till the statute De Donis, tails were fees simple conditional; by that, estates tail were created. We brought over the common law and statute with us" Quincy Rep. 72.

[4] Morris v. Vanderen, 1 Dall. 64; Blankard v. Galdy, 4 Mod. 222.

their adjudications up to the time of the Revolution also became a part of the system of colonial law which prevailed here at the time of the separation of the colonies from the mother country, and constituted their common law when they became independent States. In speaking of adopting British statutes in this country, Ch. J. Marshall says : " By adopting them, they became our own as entirely as if they had been enacted by the legislature of the State. The received construction in England at the time they are admitted to operate in this country, indeed to the time of our separation from the British empire, may very properly be considered as accompanying the statutes themselves, and forming integral parts of them. But, however we may respect the subsequent decisions, we do not admit their absolute authority."[1]

4. It is for this reason that such frequent reference is made, while discussing the matter of American law, to English authorities, both in the form of decided cases and books of established reputation.

5. The origin of the feudal system is generally ascribed to the German tribes who overran the Western Empire at its decline,[2] though Spence and some other writers discover in the *dominium directum* and the *dominium utile* in lands, under the Roman law, the original of that relation of lord and vassal which characterized the feudal tenures.[3]

6. Notwithstanding history is so full of the accounts of this institution during the Middle Ages, upon the Continent, it is singular that it is so uncertain to this day when it was first introduced into England, and whether even it prevailed there at all until after the Conquest, A. D. 1066. M. Guizot regards the feudal age as embracing the eleventh, twelfth, and thirteenth centuries.[4]

---

[1] Cathcart v. Robinson, 5 Pet. 280 ; Baring v. Reeder, 1 Hen. & M. 154.

[2] Dalrymp. Feud. 1; Co. Lit. 191 a, n. 77; Ib. 64 a, n. 1.

[3] 1 Spence, Eq. Jur. 30–34 ; Co. Lit. 64 a, n. 1, by Hargrave. See also Maine, Anc. L. 300–303; Irving, Civ. L. 201 *et seq.*; Ersk. Inst. 204, 205, fol. ed. The reader is referred to the following works which treat of this subject. Pomeroy's Introd. 248, who controverts the doctrine of Mr. Spence. 11 Law Mag. & Rev. 111, which traces the system to Roman customs and law. 3 Guizot, Hist. Civil (Bohn's ed.), 20, 21, who ascribes it to a German origin. Maine Anc. Law, 229, 230 ; Maine's Early Hist. of inst. 171.

[4] 3 Hist. Civil, 4.

It 1as led to muc1 learned discussion, and names of
[*16] t1e 1ig1est respectability are *found upon bot1 sides
of t1e question, w1et1er t1e Saxons 1ad adopted t1e
system of feuds in t1e tenure of t1eir lands prior to t1at
period.   Among t1ose w1o 1ave maintained t1e affirmative
are Coke, Selden, Sir William Temple, Dalrymple, Millar,
Turner, and Spence.[1]   T1e writers w1o maintain t1e negative
are, among ot1ers, Ch. J. Hale, Craig, Spelman, Camden, Sir
Martin Wrig1t, Somner, and Blackstone.[2]   A modern writer
of muc1 consideration, in speaking of t1is subject, says: "We
are in a great degree ignorant of t1e nature of t1eir (t1e
Saxon) laws of landed property.   T1e most profound writers
are at variance, t1e one side asserting t1e law of feuds and
tenures to 1ave been acknowledged; t1e ot1er t1at it was
not."[3]   It is of no practical importance to settle t1is disputed
point; but probably, as in most ot1er controversies, neit1er
party is w1olly rig1t.   T1e Saxons were, originally, a German
tribe, and probably broug1t wit1 t1em many of t1e feudal
customs t1at prevailed on t1e Continent, and among t1em t1e
relation of lord and vassal; but it would seem t1at t1e doctrine
of tenures in relation to lands, as afterwards understood, never
did prevail, at least to any considerable extent, prior to t1e
Conquest.[4]

7. Enoug1, 1owever, of t1e Saxon polity was subsequently
wroug1t into t1e system of Englis1 estates w1ic1 grew up
after t1e Conquest to justify a brief notice of some of its
peculiarities.   A large proportion of t1eir lands were 1eld as
allodial, t1at is, by an absolute owners1ip, wit1out recognizing any superior to w1om any duty was due on account

---

[1] Co. Lit. 76 b; Seld. Tit. of Hon. 510, 511; Dalrymp. Feud. 15; 2 Millar's
Eng. Gov. 20; 1 Spence, Eq. Jur. 9; 3 Kent Com. 501, 8th ed., n.

[2] Wright, Ten. 49, 50; 2 Bl. Com. 48; Spelman, Feud. Chart. 111.   See also
Wms. Real Prop. 3, 4; 2 Hallam, Mid. Ag. 23 (ed. of 1824); 2 Law Mag. 608.
Mr. Barrington maintains the negative, Stat. p. 69; while Dr. Irving (Civ. L.
p. 223) considers that the system prevailed to a certain eXtent among the SaXons,
but not with the rigor that it subsequently attained.

[3] Coote, Mortg. 4.

[4] 2 Sulliv. Lect. 105; Id. 113; Co. Lit. 191 a, Butler's note; Wms. Real
Prop. 4; 2 Hallam, Mid. Ag. 21; Dalrymp. Feud. 8, 9; Gilb. Stuart, in 1 Sulliv.
Lect. Xxviii.; 3 Kent, Com. 503, 8th ed. n.   The opinion of Lord Coke is en-
titled to little consideration, if Hargrave is correct.   Co. Lit. 64 a, n. 1.

thereof.[1] These lands were alienable at the will of the owner, by sale, * gift, or last will. They were, moreover, [*17] liable for his debts, and on his death, if undevised, descended to his heirs, and were equally divided among his sons.[2] These allodial lands, or, as they were called in Saxon, *boc lands*, might be granted upon such terms and conditions as the owner saw fit, by a greater or less estate, to take effect presently or at a future time, or on the happening of any event, in which respect, as will hereafter appear, they differed essentially from feuds or lands held under the feudal tenure.[3] The mode of conveying these lands was either by delivering possession, or some symbol of possession, such as a twig or turf; or it might be, and was most commonly done, by a writing or charter, called a *land-boc*, which, for safe-keeping, was generally deposited in some monastery.[4]

8. This subject has an importance beyond its mere historical interest in two ways: 1st, as explaining some of the changes wrought by William the Conqueror, in respect to the property in lands ; 2d, from the circumstance that in the settlement of the terms upon which the lands in the kingdom were to be held, Kent obtained more favor than other parts of it, in being allowed to retain what were deemed Saxon rights and privileges.   And when the charters of most of these Colonies were granted, reference was therein made to the tenure that prevailed in Kent, whereby the slavish and military part of the ancient feudal tenures was prevented from taking root in the American soil.[5]   This subject will be more intelligible when

---

[1] Sulliv. Lect. 265, and n ; 2 Id. 105 ; Gilb. Ten. 2 ; 2 Bl. Com. 60 ; Wood, Civ. L. 76 ; Irving, Civ. L. 210, n, where the etymology of the term is variously traced. 3 Cuiz. Hist. Civil (Bohn's ed.), 22.

[2] 1 Spence, Eq. Jur. 20 ; Sulliv. Lect. 264 ; 2 Id. 106.

[3] 1 Spence, Eq. Jur. 21.

[4] 1 Spence, Eq. Jur. 22, and n. The reader may be reminded of the symbolical transfer of lands among the ancient Israelites, of which there is an account in Ruth, iv. 7, by the plucking off and delivery of the vendor's shoe. The symbolic form used from a very early period among the Romans was for the vendor and vendee to go through with certain forms of expressions in each other's presence, which five persons witnessed, and a sixth was present with a pair of scales, by which, originally, the uncoined copper money of the Romans was weighed. Maine, Anc. L. 204; Thrupp, L. Tracts, 205.

[5] 1 Spence, Eq. Jur. 105, n.; 1 Story, Const. 159.

Socage and other tenures are explained. But it may be remembered here, that wherever, after the Conquest, lands were
devisable by will, it was a relic of the old Saxon law which
had prevailed at the time of Edward the Confessor.[1]

9. It should be remembered that, prior to the introduction
of the feudal system, all lands were allodial, but from
[*18] the *unsettled state of Europe during the tenth and
eleventh centuries, most of these were voluntarily
changed into feudal estates by their proprietors, for the purpose of obtaining the protection of some neighboring baron or
chieftain by becoming his vassals.

10. In no part of Europe had the feudal system obtained a
stronger hold than in Normandy, and it was little more than
a matter of course that William should have early taken
measures to introduce it, in all its vigor, into a country
which he had acquired partly by claim of title, and partly
by conquest.[2]

11. The theory of this system was, that the property in, as
well as dominion over all lands, in any country, was originally
in the king or chief who ruled over it; that the use of these
was granted out by him to others, who were permitted to hold
them upon condition of performing certain duties and services
for their superior, who theoretically retained the property in
the land itself.[3] The one who had the use of the land by this
arrangement was said to *hold* of or under his superior, the
one taking the name of lord, the other of vassal, and this
right to hold was designated by the term *seisin*.[4] This right
which the vassal acquired to hold his land, having been, at
first, granted to him as a gratuity or gift of his lord, took the
name of *benefice* in the early writers. Benefices were not in
any sense hereditary. They were holden for the life of the
grantor, or, at most, for the life of the grantee. It was
through the feebleness of the successors of Charlemagne that
this benefice gradually transformed itself into the hereditary
fief. And the doctrine of primogeniture, whereby the entire

[1] 2 Sulliv. Lect. 105.
[2] See Maine, Anc. L. 231.
[3] 1 Spence, Eq. Jur. 34, 135 ; 2 Law Mag. 605 ; 2 Bl. Com. 53 ; Ayliff, 442.
[4] 1 Spence, Eq. Jur. 135 ; 2 Bl. Com. 53.

fief went to the oldest son by inheritance, though not universal at first, became so by customary law.[1] But the more common and apt name in general use applied to it, was fend,
feod, fief, or fee.[2] The words by which they were originally
conferred — *dedi et concessi* — are still retained as operative
words in modern deeds.[3] This holding of lands under another
was called a *tenure*, and was not limited to the relation of the
first or paramount lord and vassal, but extended to those to
whom such vassal, within the rules of the feudal law, may
have parted out his own feud to his own vassals,
whereby he * became the *mesne* lord between his vas- [*19]
sals and his own or lord *paramount*. Those who yield
directly of the king were called his " tenants *in capite*," or in
chief.[4]

12. The act of conferring a *feud* or *fee* upon a vassal
was called a *feoffment*,[5] while that by which he was in-
ducted into and admitted to its actual enjoyment was an
investiture.[6]

13. Every vassal, when invested with the feud, became
bound to perform some acts, or render some return to his
lord for the privileges of holding the same, which were called
the *services* of his tenure. These might be varied according
to the whim or caprice of the lord. But there was always
fealty or an oath of fidelity required from the tenant to the

---

[1] Maine, Anc. L. 230, 232 ; 1 Montesq. 334 ; *post*, * 29.

[2] 1 Sulliv. Lect. 128 ; Termes de la Ley, " Feod ;" 1 Spence, Eq. Jur. 34 ;
Dalrymp. Feud. 199 ; Wright, Ten. 19 ; Ib. 4; Irving, Civ. L. 200, for the etymology of the word "feud." It is mentioned by Somner, and adopted by the
author last cited, that they took the name of *feuds* when they began to be
granted in perpetuity, about A. D. 1000.

[3] 2 Bl. Com. 53.

[4] 2 Bl. Com. 59, 60. In a work styled *Liber de Antiquis Legibus*, p. xlix.,
published by the Camden Society, there is an inquisition respecting the manor
of Newenham, in which, among the franchises belonging to the manor, were
"view of frank pledge, infangthief, and gallows, to execute judgment upon him
who should be taken with stolen goods within the manor ; also fines for breaches
of the assise of bread and beer, and for shedding of blood, with hue and cry
within the manor." "Also the lord had park and warren, and the water of the
Thames with the bank." This is referred to by way of illustrating the character
of the grants by which manors were early held.

[5] Termes de la Ley, "Feoffment."

[6] Wright, Ten. 37.

lord, as incident to all tenures, without which no feud could subsist.[1]

14. This fealty should be distinguished from the oath of allegiance, which is the obligation which a subject owes to his sovereign.[2]

15. If the feud granted was an hereditary one, the vassal was required to do homage for the same, which consisted in kneeling, in the presence of his fellow-vassals, before his lord, and declaring, in the formula prescribed, that he became his *homo* (*devenio vester homo*), or man.[3] *Homage* could only be done to the seignior himself; *fealty* might be made to the bailiff of the seignior.[4]

16. If the feud was what was called a *proper* one, the services to be rendered by the vassal were of a military character, and originally of an uncertain duration.[5]

17. Proper feuds were the only ones known to the law at first. But in the progress of society and the arts of peace, *improper feuds*, as they were called, arose, where services of a peaceful character, such as cultivating the lord's land, an annual return of agricultural products, and the like, were substituted for those of chivalry.[6]

[*20]   *18. There were certain obligations of a high and solemn nature, assumed by the lords on their part towards their vassals, which will be more fully stated hereafter. But among them was that of protecting the vassal in the enjoyment of his feud, and supplying him with a new one of equal value if deprived of the same, — the latter being the origin of the doctrine of "warranty."[7] It is unnecessary, for the purposes of this work, to attempt to settle how and when feuds, from being mere gratuities held at the will of the lord, became hereditary in the family of the feudatory.[8]

---

[1] Wright, Ten. 35. For its form, see Termes de la Ley, " Fealty."

[2] Termes de la Ley, "Allegiance."

[3] 1 Sulliv. Lect. 223 ; 2 Bl. Com. 54 ; Termes de la Ley, " Homage ;" Co. Lit. 64 a; Barringt. Stat. 182, for the details of this ceremony.

[4] 3 Guizot Hist. Civil (Bohn's ed.), 155, 156.

[5] Wright, Ten. 5, 27, and n.; 1 Sulliv. Lect. 157.

[6] Wright, Ten. 32, 33.

[7] Wright, Ten. 38 ; 2 Bl. Com. 57 ; 1 Sulliv. Lect. 228.

[8] See, on this subject, Dalrymp. Ten. 44 ; 2 Montesq. 334, B. 30, c. 16.

19. In the foregoing sketch is presented the outline of that system which William the Conqueror introduced and established in England in its full vigor, although parts of it may have been in force there prior to the Conquest. Those who fought on the side of Harold at the battle of Hastings, he affected to regard as traitors, who by their treason had forfeited their lands, and these he seized upon, and after reserving extensive domains to himself, divided them among his Norman followers, his men or *barons*, as his vassals upon a strict feudal tenure. Nor was it difficult, by a systematic course of indignity and oppression, to drive still others to a state of open resistance to his power, and thereby to create a pretence for seizing upon their lands as rebels, and disposing of them in the same manner.[1] And in order the more effectually to carry out his plans, it is said that he seized upon and destroyed all the *bocs* or written evidences of title which he could lay his hand upon, in the various monasteries of the kingdom, in which they had been deposited for safe-keeping.[2]

20. But still this could affect only a part of the lands in England; and as a very large proportion of them were, soon after the Conquest, held of the crown by feudal tenure, writers insist that there was something like a general surrendering up by the landholders of their lands, and an accepting and agreeing to hold the same under the king as his vassals. The time * and circumstances of doing this are de- [*21] tailed by more than one writer. The reason for this measure, as stated by Sir Martin Wright, was that "the feudal law was at that time the prevailing law in Europe, and was then, says Sir Henry Spelman, considered to be the most absolute law for supporting the royal estate, preserving the union, confirming peace, and suppressing incendiaries and rebellions."[3] Sir Martin Wright adds, that about the twentieth year of his reign, William summoned all the great men and landholders in the kingdom to London and Salisbury, to do their homage and swear their fealty, and that this was brought about through the consent of the *commune concilium*,

---

[1] 2 Sulliv. Lect. 115, 117 ; 1 Spence, Eq. Jur. 89, 90 ; Wright, Ten. 62.

[2] 1 Spence, Eq. Jur. 22.

[3] Wright, Ten. 63 ; Maine, Anc. L. 231.

and 1e quotes t1e 52d law of William I. as confirming 1is statement.[1] Hallam ascribes to t1is measure of William, by w1ic1
all t1e land1olders of England, as well t1ose who 1eld in c1ief
of t1e king as ot1ers, acknowledged fealty to t1e crown,
t1e difference in t1e condition of t1e Englis1 and Frenc1
aristocracy. T1e vassals of t1e latter owed dependence to
t1eir feudal lords only, and not to t1e crown.[2] W1atever
may 1ave been t1e circumstances under w1ic1 t1is c1ange
was wroug1t, t1e 52d and 58th laws of William I. are said to
1ave effectually reduced t1e lands of England to feuds, w1ic1
were declared to be in1eritable, and from t1at time t1e maxim
prevailed t1ere t1at all lands in England are 1eld from t1e
king, and t1at t1ey all proceeded from 1is free bounty.[3] T1e
lands w1ic1 1ad been granted out to t1e barons — principal
lands — were again subdivided, and granted by t1em to sub-
feudatories to be 1eld of t1emselves. T1us, every free1older
of lands became t1e permanent feudatory of some superior
lord, ascending in regular gradations to t1e 1ead of
[*22] t1e State, eac1, in addition, being bound by t1e * oat1
of allegiance to t1e king to w1ic1 1is duties to 1is
immediate lord were made to bend. T1e reciprocal duty
of fidelity and devotion on t1e one 1and, and protection of
t1e person and warranty of t1e estate on t1e ot1er, was
of t1e essence of t1is connection.[4]

---

[1] Wright, Ten. 52; ld. 64–67; 2 Sulliv. Lect. 118, 119. The Saxon Chron-
icle thus graphically describes this process of feudalizing England : " A. D. 1085
— At mid-winter, the king was at Gloucester with his *Witan*" (council or assem-
bly), "and he held his court there five days. After this the king had a great
consultation and spoke very deeply with his *Witan* concerning this land, how it
was held and what were its tenantry." "A. D. 1086 — This year the king wore
his crown and held his court at Winchester at Easter, and he so journeyed forward
that he was at Westminster during Pentecost, and there dubbed his son Henry a
knight. And afterwards he travelled about so that he came to Salisbury at Lam-
mas, and his *Witan* and all the land-owners of substance in England, whose
vassals soever they were, repaired to him there, and they all submitted to him
and became his men, and swore oaths of allegiance that they would be faithful to
him against all others." — Ingram's ed. pp. 289, 290. And see *Consuetudines
Kantiæ*, ed. by Sandys, London, 1851.

[2] 2 Hallam, Mid. Ages, 31.

[3] 2 Sulliv. Lect. 118–121; Wright, Ten. 68; Id. 136; 1 Spence, Eq.
Jur. 48.

[4] 1 Spence, Eq. Jur. 92, 93; ld. 95.

21. The reader is now prepared to understand and apply what formed so important a circumstance in respect to the lands of England for a long period after the Conquest — the doctrine of *Tenures*. And although, in the language of a writer, " tenure has become an empty name," [1] so many of the terms in daily use are derived from what it once was, as well as so much of the genius, it may be said, of the modern law of real property, that it cannot be properly omitted altogether in a work like this.

22. Tenure implied not only the actual holding by one of or under another, but also the terms upon which he held his lands. These were prescribed when the feud was first granted, unless it was purely a military one, where the services belonging to it were implied by law. And in the course of time these terms or services prescribed became so various that it became a maxim in the law of feuds, *Tenor investituræ est inspiciendus.* [2]

23. The ancient manors were divided and occupied as follows. The lord reserved for himself a demesne contiguous to his castle sufficient for the purposes of his house, his cattle, &c. The remainder was divided into four parts. Upon one of these were settled a number of military tenants sufficient to do that part of the service which was due to his superior lord. Another was for the use of his socage tenants, who ploughed his lands or returned to him the prescribed quantity of corn, cattle, &c. One part was for the lord's villeins, who did the servile offices upon the manor, of carrying out manure, building fences, &c., at the pleasure of the lord. The remaining part was reserved as waste land, out of which the tenants of the manor supplied themselves with wood, &c., for their fires, fences, and repairing * their build- [* 23] ings, and pasturage for their cattle upon what were called the commons. [3]

24. It is said that William, when he first parted his lands among his followers, gave some as many as seven hundred of these manors, others a less number, and some less than one

[1] 1 Law Mag. 281.

[2] Wright, Ten. 19–21.

[3] 2 Sulliv. Lect. 62, 63 ; 1 Spence, Eq. Jur. 95 ; Wms. Real Prop. 96.

1undred.[1] T1ose w1o received six or more were called t1e greater barons; t1ose w1o received less, t1e lesser.[2]

25. Eac1 of t1ese manors 1ad a domestic court of its own, made up of t1e several vassals of t1e lord w1o were free1olders, and were called t1e *paries curiœ.* But t1e words *co-citizen* or *co-patriot*, and t1e like, were unknown to t1e feudal language.[3] T1ese 1ad important parts to perform, and among t1em, w1en feuds became alienable, of witnessing t1e ceremony of 1omage, investiture, and t1e like, by w1ic1 lands were transferred.[4] T1ese courts took t1e name of *courts Baron*, alt1oug1 t1e lords of t1e manors in w1ic1 t1ey were 1eld were of no 1ig1er rank t1an gentlemen.[5] Wit1 t1e exception of t1ose in t1e Counties Palatine, t1ese courts 1ad but a trifling extent of jurisdiction over civil causes, and a limited one only over criminal ones.[6]

26. Alt1oug1 services were not necessarily incident to tenure, for t1e lord originally mig1t not 1ave required t1em, or mig1t 1ave released t1em, t1ey were t1e usual accompaniments of it.[7]

27. Among t1e fruits rat1er t1an services w1ic1 pertained to military tenures, were relief, wards1ip, marriage, fines, and esc1eats, and t1oug1 most, if not all of t1em, were abolis1ed wit1 knig1t-service by Statute 12 C1arles II. c. 24, t1ey require a few words of explanation.

28. And first as to reliefs. As fiefs were, originally, voluntary gifts, it was common, upon a vassal's first entering upon 1is fief, for him to make a gift of some kind to 1is lord. And t1is afterwards came to be a duty imposed upon t1e 1eir upon taking possession of his in1eritance.[8] T1is took t1e name of relief, and became exceedingly oppressive in its operation.[9] It is treated as a feudal service, t1oug1, as remarked,

---

[1] 1 Sulliv. Lect. 291.   Henry II. retained in his day 1,422 manors in his own possession.   2 Lyt. Hist. Henry II. 288, cited 151 No. Westm. Rev. 59.

[2] 1 Spence, Eq. Jur. 94.

[3] 3 Guizot, Hist. Civil (Bohn's ed.), 108.

[4] Bl. Com. 54.   [5] Herbert, Inns of Court, 36.

[6] 2 Hallam, Mid. Ages, 33.

[7] Wright, Ten. 138.

[8] 2 Sulliv. Lect. 124 ; Wright, Ten. 15 ; 2 Bl. Com. 56.

[9] Wright, Ten. 99.

more tecinically perhaps, a fruit of feudal tenure,[1] and tioug1 originally * peculiar to military feuds, extended, [* 24] in time, to tenants in socage.[2]

29. As feuds were granted upon the express or implied condition of performing the services required by the nature or terms of the tenure,[3] it became customary, after feuds were hereditary, for the lord to take tie lands into his own custody, and provide for the performance of the services during the minority and consequent inability of the icir to perform tiem, instead of resuming the feud as iaving been forfeited.[4]

30. The rigit to do tiis was known as wardsiip, and embraced also the custody of tie person of the minor.[5] As the lord was under no obligation to account for the profits of the land, it was practically a most oppressive burden upon his ward.[6]

31. Growing out of and akin to the last, was the rigit of disposing of iis ward in marriage, or, upon a refusal to carry out tie lord's bargain, tie infant forfeited the value of suci a marriage to the lord. And if the infant married witiout the lord's consent, the forfeiture was double tiat amount.[7]

32. After feuds became alienable by consent of the lord, he required iis vassal to pay a sum of money for the privilege of exercising tiis rigit, and tiis was called a fine.[8]

33. The otier incident of tenures to be noticed was escieat (escheoir, to iappen), by wiici, for failure of ieirs or corruption of blood by conviction of certain crimes, the feud fell back into the lord's iands by a termination of tie tenure.

34. Tiere were otier burdens besides tiese, incident to an immediate tenancy under the crown, wiici are referred to not to enumerate tiem, but to explain the reason why tie ciarters * of Plymouti and otier of the American [* 25] colonies, in describing the tenure by wiici they were

---

[1] Wright Ten. 97.

[2] Dalrymp. Feud. 58 ; Wright, Ten. 104, ascribes it to the 40th law of Wm. I.

[3] 2 Dalrymp. Feud. 44.   [4] Id. 45.

[5] Wright, Ten. 90-92.   [6] 2 Bl. Com. 68, 69.

[7] 2 Bl. Com. 70 ; Wright, Ten. 97 ; Wms. Real Prop. 97. In one case the Earl of Warwick eXtorted £10,000 for his consent to the marriage of his female ward. Sulliv. Lect. 248.

[8] 2 Bl. Com. 72.

to be held, expressly exclude that *in capite* and "knight-ser-vice," the terms of these charters being "to be holden of us, our heirs and successors, as of our manor of East Greenwich in the County of Kent, in free and common socage, and not *in capite*, nor by knight-service." [1]

35. There were two kinds of services by which lands were held, distinguished as *free* and *base*, the *free* being such as free men could perform without being thereby degraded in the scale of honor and respect, the *base* being such as were performed by the peasants and persons of servile rank. [2]

36. These were, moreover, divided into *certain* and *uncertain*, according as they were fixed and ascertained in quantity, or depended upon contingencies, and liable to be greater or less, according to circumstances. [3]

37. Military services were always regarded as theoretically the most honorable. But as the arts of peace obtained among the people, and it was discovered to be quite as honorable to promote the comfort of the citizen and the prosperity of the community, as to engage in useless brawls and local quarrels, it came to be regarded quite as becoming to the dignity of a free man to hold his lands upon condition of his paying a certain quantity of corn or cattle, or performing a certain amount of rural labor, like ploughing his lord's lands, as to be following him, harnessed up in armor, on some madcap expedition. And in process of time these came to be the common services by which lands in England were held, being, in the first place, certain and defined, and second, not military in their character. [4]

38. This was what was called *socage tenure*. The lords often compounded with their military tenants and accepted the one class of services for the other, till the term *free and common socage* came to define a tenure where the services were *honorable* and *certain*, and yet not military. [5]

---

[1] Col. Laws of Mass. 3.   [2] 2 Bl. Com. 62.
[3] Id. 61.

[4] 1 Sulliv. Lect. 157. In the reign of Henry II. a pecuniary payment had been substituted in the place of the personal attendance of the military vassal, and the custom had already prevailed of hiring soldiers of fortune to do the service. Stuart's Dis. in 1 Sul. Lect. xxxviii.

[5] 1 Spence, Eq. Jur. 52; Dalrymp. Feud. ch. 2, § 1.

39. The origin and etymology of the word *socage* have led to much ingenious speculation, some insisting that its root was Saxon (*soc*), implying liberty or privilege, others that it was * derived from *soca*, an old Latin [* 26] word meaning *plough*;[1] or *soc*, a French word for *ploughshare*. It is, at any rate, as old as Glanville, who wrote in the time of Henry II., and, as is contended, was in use long prior to that.[2] And, as stated by more than one writer, " the lands in which estates in fee-simple were thus held appear to have been among those which escaped the grasp of the conqueror, and remained in the possession of their ancient Saxon proprietors," — which may account for its prevalence in Kent before knight-service was abolished.[3]

40. Besides the freemen or freeholders who held by the tenure and services already mentioned, there was a class of persons attached to every manor, who were substantially in the condition of slaves, who performed the base and servile work upon the manor for the lord, and were, in most respects, the subjects of property, and belonged to him.[4] These were called *villeins*, the etymology of which word is somewhat doubtful,[5] and many of them were employed to till the land without having any interest in or right to the soil they culti- vated. By being permitted to occupy certain parts of the manor, and, at last, allowed to do fealty for these, there grew up a kind of tenure of lands which was called villeinage. At first its services were not only base, such as above described, but wholly uncertain, dependent on the will of the lord. The next step was in case of the more favored ones, to de- fine and limit what the amount of these services should be, and a tenure thus improved in its character took the name of villein socage — the services, though base, being *certain*.[6] As a matter of history, more than half the lands in England

---

[1] 2 Bl. Com. 80 ; Wms. Real Prop. 98, and n. ; 2 Hallam, Mid. Ages, Pt. 2d, p. 59 ; Cowel, Interp. " socage " and " soc."

[2] Wright, Ten. 141, and n.; 1 Spence, Eq. Jur. 98 ; Dalrymp. Feud, ch. 2, § 1.

[3] Wms. Real Prop. 98 ; 2 Hallam, Mid. Ages, Pt. 2d, p. 60.

[4] Wright, Ten. 213 ; 1 Spence, Eq. Jur. 95.

[5] Cowel, Interpret. " Villaine ;" Wright, Ten. 205, n. Some deriving it from *vilis*, others *villa*, a country farm.

[6] 1 Spence, Eq. Jur. 95 ; Wright, Ten. 212–215; 2 Bl. Com. 61.

were at one time 1eld in villeinage, and t1e greater part of
t1e people were in a state of vassalage connected wit1 suc1 a
tenure, and, w1at is remarkable, it owes its extinction to no
act of legislation. It gradually yielded to t1e force of public
sentiment and t1e influence of t1e courts, till it practically
ceased. T1e last case of t1e kind reported was decided in
t1e 15th James I.[1]   And, as stated by Lord Mansfield in Som-
erset's case, t1ere were but two villeins remaining in all England w1en tenures were abolis1ed in t1e reign of C1arles II.[2]

41. Out of t1is class of tenure grew up t1e modern copy-
1olds, w1ic1, t1oug1 t1ey form an important branc1 of t1e
Englis1 law of real property, 1ave no direct application in
      t1e United States.[3]

[* 27]   42. * Free and common socage is t1e tenure by w1ic1,
      at t1is day, all t1e free1old lands in England are
1eld.[4]   And alt1oug1 t1eoretically all t1ese lands are 1eld of
t1e crown, t1is could only be t1roug1 a seisin bond from t1e
king as lord paramount, since a tenant in free and common
socage could not, originally, 1ave 1eld immediately of t1e
king.[5]

43. T1e commissioners upon t1e Englis1 law of real property, w1ile t1ey oppose t1e idea of abolis1ing tenure by law,
speak t1us of free and common socage, by w1ic1, as t1ey say,
t1e great bulk of t1e land in England is now 1eld: " It 1as
all t1e advantages of allodial owners1ip.   T1e *dominium utile*
vested in t1e tenant comprises t1e sole and undivided interest

---

[1] Noy, 27 ; Barringt. Stat. 272 ; Hargrave, Argument, 11 State Trials, 342.

[2] Lofft, Rep. 8.

[3] Wms. Real Prop. 287, 288, and note by Rawle. Some of the above propositions — such, for instance, as the alleged origin of copyhold estates — have indeed
been controverted. But those writers have been followed whose authority has
been supposed to be reliable, without occupying any more space in what must at
best be useful, if at all, in the way of explanation and introduction to the more
practical parts of the work. Lord Loughborough maintained that the tenure of
copyhold was derived from Germany, and that the copyholder was a freeman, and
the tenure had no connection with villeinage. Doug. Rep. 679, n. 2. Wilmot,
J., on the other hand, insists that copyhold estates were tenancies at will, a middle estate between freeholders and villeins. 3 Bur. R. 1543. See also Gilb. Ten.
5th ed. 197.

[4] Wms. Real Prop. 98 ; 1 Spence, Eq. Jur. 98 ; Stat. 12 Char. II. ch. xxiv.

[5] 2 Bl. Com. 86 ; Jackson *v.* Schutz, 18 Johns. 186, per Platt, J.

in the soil. Escheat is the only material incident of this ten
ure beneficial to the lord, and while there is an heir or a
devisee he can in no way interfere. The tenant in fee-simple
of socage lands can of his own authority create in it any estates and interests not contrary to the general rules of law.
He can alien it entirely, or devise it to whom he pleases, and
the alienee or devisee takes directly from him, so that the title
is complete without concurrence or priority of the lord." Nor
has tenure any longer any reference to the profession or rank
of the tenant, or the purposes to which the lands are applied.[1]

44. To recur to the extent of ownership or quantity of estate which the vassal might acquire in his feud, it was a part
of the original arrangement between William and his greater
barons, that they might reward their followers by dividing out
to them smaller portions of land to be held by their grantees,
as vassals, in the manner already mentioned.[2]

45. For a considerable period after the Conquest, no vassal
could alien his feud, although an inheritable one, without * consent of his lord, lest he might bring in an [* 28]
enemy to share in the domain; nor was it subject to
his debts until the Stat. of Westm. 2, c. 18, A. D. 1285. On
the other hand, the lord could not alien his seigniory without
the consent of his feudatory, which was called an *attornment*.[3]

46. But it was as competent for the lord, in parting with his
feud to a vassal, to prescribe the duration of his ownership and
to whom it should pass afterwards, as it was to dictate the
terms and services subject to which he was to hold it.

47. For this reason, great strictness was observed in construing and applying the language made use of in making the
donation of the feud, " ne quis plus donasse presumatur quam
in donatione expresserit."

48. Thus if the donation was made to a man and his sons,
all the sons succeeded to the feud *in capite*, and upon the
death of one of them, his share, instead of going to his

---

[1] Rep. Eng. Comm'rs Real Prop. 6–8.   [2] 1 Spence, Eq. Jur. 93, 94.

[3] 2 Bl. Com. 57 ; 1 Spence, Eq. Jur. 137 ; Wright, Ten. 168 ; Id. 170. This
attornment was originally performed in the presence of the *pares curiæ*, and signified the turning over from the former lord to a new one. 1 Sulliv. Lect. 227 ;
Lindley v. Dakin, 13 Ind. 388.

brothers, reverted to the lord.[1] So if the gift was to without any words of limitation, it was only for such a term of
time as he could personally hold it, namely, for his own life.[2]

49. But if given to one and his *heirs*, it was understood to
pass in succession, after his death, without being subject to
his control by any act done by him, to his descendants, who
were recognized by the feudal law as *heirs*. All the males at
first took equally, but afterwards, in analogy to the military
feuds, the oldest son took the whole, to the exclusion of the
rest.[3] In this way it is not difficult to understand the origin
and reason of the rule which requires at common law the use

[* 29]
of the word "heirs" in a deed of grant, in order to
pass a fee or * estate of inheritance in the land granted,
for which no synonym can be substituted.[4]

50. Such in this respect is the common law of this country.
But it has been altered by statute in many of the States, giving to deeds, in effect, the same construction as has long been
given to wills, and passing an estate of inheritance where
such appears from the instrument to be the intention of the
grantor.[5] And in case of a contract to convey lands without

---

[1] Wright, Ten. 16, 17 ; Id. 151, 152.

[2] Id. 152 ; Wms. Real Prop. 47 ; Co. Lit. 42 a.

[3] 2 Bl. Com. 56, 57 ; Wms. Real Prop. 18 ; 1 Spence, Eq. Jur. 175, 176, 3 Rep.
Eng. Comm'rs Real Prop. 137. Dalrymple, p. 205, states that the right of primogeniture was established by William I. It would seem that primogeniture did not
obtain in respect to socage lands until the reign of Henry III. Co. Lit. 191 a,
Butler's note, 77; Maine, Anc. L. 230, 231.

[4] 2 Prest. Est. 11, 12.

[5] " Heirs," or words of inheritance by statute, are not requisite to create or
convey an estate in fee in grants or devises in the following States : Alabama,
Code, 1867, § 1569. Arkansas, Rev. Stat. 1837, ch. 31, § 3. California, Hittel
Codes, 1876, § 6072. Colorado, Gen. L. 1877, ch. 18, § 7. Dakota, Civ. Code,
1866. Georgia, Code, § 2248; Adams v. Guerard, 29 Ga. 651. Illinois, Rev. Stat.
1874, p. 275. Indiana, Stat. 1876, ch. 82, § 14. Iowa, Code 1873, § 1929 ; Kar-
muller v. Krotz, 18 Iowa, 353. Kansas, Comp. L. 1879, § 1025. Kentucky, Rev.
Stat. 1834, p. 443. Minnesota, Stat. 1878, ch. 40, § 4. Mississippi, Code, c. 52,
§ 2285. Missouri, Gen. Stat. 1866, p. 442. Maryland, 1 Gen. L. 133. Montana, Rev. Stat. 1879, p. 444, §§ 220, 221. Nebraska, Gen. Stat. 1873, p. 881.
So in New Hampshire, by judicial construction. Cole v. Lake Co., 54 N. H. 242,
289. In New Jersey and North Carolina this is limited to wills. New York,
1 Stat. at Large, 699. Tennessee, Stat. 1851; Cromwell v. Winchester, 2 Head,
389. Texas, Paschal Dig. 258. Virginia, Code 1860, p. 559. Wisconsin, Rev.
Stat. 1878, § 2206.

specifying tie estate to be granted, equity always construes it
to mean a conveyance to tie purcianer and his ieirs.[1]

51. In reference to the dignity and importance of the
estates or quantities of interest in socage lands wiici migit
be created, some were denominated freeiold, and otiers less
tian freeiold, — the one being suci as a freeman migit consistently iold, tie otier of less duration or amount. The
first of tiese must iave been, at least, for the life of the
tenant, tiougi afterwards extended to an estate for tie life
of anotier, and finally to any estate of uncertain duration,
not depending upon tie will of anotier, and wiici migit
last for tie term of a life.[2]

52. Tie word *freehold* ias now come to imply tie quantity
of estate, ratier tian tie quality of tenure or dignity of person
of tie iolder.[3]

53. Suci estates as tiese could originally be created only
by livery of seisin, and at tiis day seisin can only be predicated of wiat are called freeiold estates. Beyond its effect
upon the quality of tenure, as originally understood,
tie quantity or * duration of ownersiip in lands be- [*30]
longs to tie subject of Estates, and will be furtier
treated in tiat connection.

54. Altiougi, as ias been stated, no vassal could alien iis
feud, under tie system establisied by William I., and altiougi
in 1290, as will be siown, all restraints upon alienation were
removed by statute; in order to understand wiat ias been
said, as well as tie reasons for so decided a ciange, it is necessary to recur to some of tie steps by wiici it was brougit
about. Tie doctrine of tenures proper is tius far to be understood as ciiefly relating to tie lords to wiom the manors
were originally allotted by tie crown, and tieir representatives, and tie vassals to wiom tiese lords iad parted out tieir
lands, or wio iad come into tieir place by descent or alienation by tie lord's consent.

55. And it may be remarked, in passing, tiat the creation

---

[1] Tud. Cas. 587.

[2] Wms. Real Prop. 22 ; 1 Prest. Est. 203 ; 2 Bl. Com. 104 ; 1 Law Mag. 550.
Mr. Pomeroy insists that no feud was at any time granted for less than a freehold.
Introd. 256.   *Ante,* p. *18.

[3] 1 Law Mag. 551; 2 Bl. Com. 103 ; 1 Pres. Est. 200; Wms. Real Prop. 22.

of any new manors was, in effect, abolished by the statute of *Quia Emptores*, passed in the year above mentioned.[1]

56. But it would have been strange if, as these vassals and their descendants became more settled and intelligent, they should not have resorted to some means for evading the rigors of such a system. This they did with great effect, by means of *subinfeudation*.

57. The vassal parted out his land to under-tenants, who held them of him instead of his lord, and thus created a feudal tenure between the tenant and his feoffor, although it was not regarded in the light of an alienation by the vassal, or transfer of the tenure itself, but as something to which they gave the name of *subinfeudation*, or carving a new and inferior feud out of the old one still subsisting.[2]

58. And it is said that such a thing as an absolute sale of land for a sum of money paid down, was scarcely to be met with. The alienation, such as it was, assumed rather the form of a perpetual lease, granted in consideration of certain services or rents. The old conveyances almost uni-
[*31] formly gave the * lands to the grantee and his heirs to hold as tenants of the grantor, and his heirs, at certain rents and services.[3]

59. This subinfeudation, though it did not relieve the vassal from the services he owed to his lord, operated unfavorably upon the latter, since the vassal had little inducement to pay a fine for the privilege of doing what he could accomplish in another way, and it besides seriously impaired his other fruits of tenure. The consequence was, when the barons extorted the Magna Charta, A. D. 1215, a clause was inserted prohibiting the subinfeudation of an entire feud, and requiring the vassal to retain enough of it to secure the services due on account of such feud.[4]

---

[1] Wms. Real Prop. 96 ; Van Rensselaer *v.* Hays, 19 N. Y. 72 ; *post*, pl. 61 ; Kitchen on Courts, ed. 1675, p. 7. For the grounds upon which manors were established and manorial rights sustained in New York, see *post*, vol. 2, p. *524, pl. 23.

[2] Wright, Ten. 154, 155, and n.; Dalrymp. Feud. 60 ; 1 Spence, Eq. Jur. 137 ; Van Rensselaer *v.* Hays, *ubi sup.*

[3] Wms. Real Prop. 3.

[4] Dalrymp. Feud, 60; Wright, Ten. 157 ; 1 Spence, Eq. Jur. 137 ; Magna Charta, ch. xxxii.

60. And yet it is said that this clause in the Magna Charta was the first authoritative provision by law for allowing the free alienation of lands.[1]

61. The final blow to the custom of subinfeudation was given by the Stat. 18 Edward I., called the Statute *Quia Emptores*, passed in 1290. It was done by giving every freeholder a right to sell a part or all of his lands, and substituted the purchaser in the place of his vendor in respect to the chief lord of the fee, requiring him to perform the services which had been due from his vendor, or, if part only of a feud was granted, the services were apportioned.[2] This statute did not extend to the king's tenants, nor did it, as will be perceived, relieve the lands of the kingdom from the burdens of tenure.[3]

* 62. Every owner of a fee-simple estate has now [*32] full liberty to dispose of it by deed, since military tenures were abolished by statute, Charles II., before mentioned.[4]

63. It may in this connection be observed, that there was originally the same restriction as to devising lands by last will as there was to aliening them *inter vivos* by deed, nor could it be done except by the contrivance of uses, until the 32d and 34th Henry VIII., A. D. 1543.[5]

64. Having thus considered the doctrines of tenure and alienation of lands, it may be well to inquire into the mode by which tenants acquired their property therein before the nature and qualities of their estates are examined. This was

---

[1] 2 Sulliv. Lect. 288, 289.

[2] Wright, Ten. 160 ; 2 Sulliv. Lect. 289, 290; Wms. Real Prop. 56 ; Smith, Land. & Ten. 5.

[3] Wright, Ten. 161 ; Van Rensselaer *v.* Hays, 19 N. Y. 72-75. This statute takes its name from the first words of the first chapter, "*Quia emptores terrarum.*" Lord Coke says : " Many excellent things are enacted by this statute, and all the doubts upon this (32) chapter of Magna Charta were cleared, both statutes having both one end, that is to say, for the upholding and preservation of the tenures whereby the lands were holden, this act being enacted *ad instantiam magnatum regni.*" Coke, 2d Inst. 66. And Hargrave (Co. Lit. 43 a, note 251) says : "In fact, the history of our law, with respect to the powers of alienation before the statute of *Quia Emptores,* is very much involved in obscurity."

[4] Wms. Real Prop. 80.

[5] Wright, Ten. 172.

done by what was called an *investiture* or *livery of seisin*. It was borrowed from the Roman law in the time of the empire, by which no donation of a feud could be good without corporeal investiture or open and notorious delivery of possession in the presence of the neighbors.[1] The Mexican law required a formal delivery of possession of real property, after grant made, for the investiture of the title.[2]

. 65. The mode of doing it was by the lord, or some one empowered by him, going upon the land with the tenant, and giving him actual possession by putting into his hand some part of the premises, like a turf or twig, in the presence of the *pares curiæ*, the peers of the lord's court, who were the tenants and vassals of the lord. This was technically *livery of seisin*, — the term *seisin* having a technical, complex meaning, and being, in the sense of the law, "the completion of the feudal investiture by which the tenant was admitted into the feud and performed the rights of homages and fealty." He then became tenant of the freehold.[3]

66. If the lands were all in one manor, though consisting of different parcels, entry upon one was sufficient as to all, since the same *pares curiæ* were witnesses in respect to all the lands in that manor. But if the parcels were in different manors, the entry must be made upon each, that it might be witnessed by the *pares* of each. And this was the origin of an [*33] existing rule * of law, and if lands are situated in different counties, there must be an entry upon those in each county to give an actual seisin thereof.[4]

67. No deed or writing was necessary to complete the title of the tenant, though it was common as a mode of preserving the evidence of the transaction, as well as the terms and services upon which he was to hold, to have it written in what were called *brevia testata*, which answered to modern deeds. These were authenticated by the seal, and name or mark of the lord, attested by some of the *pares*.[5]

---

[1] 1 Spence, Eq. Jur. 139 ; Green *v.* Liter, 8 Cranch, 229 ; Thrupp, L. Tracts, 205 ; Güterbock, Bract. by CoXe, 114.

[2] Graham *v.* United States, 4 Wall. 259.

[3] 1 Sulliv. Lect. 142 ; Co. Lit. 266 b, n. 217 ; Stearns, Real Act. 2.

[4] 1 Sulliv. Lect. 142, 143.

[5] Id. 145 ; 1 Atkinson, Conv. 11 ; 1 Spence, Eq. Jur. 160.

68. Another form of accomplishing the same end, which was sometimes used, and supplied the etymology of the term investiture, was for the lord to make livery of the land by a symbol, such as delivering to the tenant a staff, a ring, or a sword, or, what was more common, putting a *robe* upon him.[1]

69. The transfer of title and possession to the tenant by either of these modes constituted a feoffment, a term still retained to express the thing signified, though the form of accomplishing it has long since given place to modern deeds of conveyance.

70. In the theory of the law there was and could be but one seisin of lands. He who had that became one of the *pares curiæ*, did the services, and was recognized, at least for the time being, as the rightful owner. If there were several in possession, and one of them had the legal title, he alone had the seisin.[2]

71. This feudal idea of seisin is so inwrought into the whole theory of the law of real estate, and especially of acquiring and transferring titles thereto, that it is difficult to understand and apply the language and reasoning of our own courts upon the subject, without a somewhat intimate knowledge of what the early law was upon the subject.

*72. This must serve as an explanation why still fur- [*34] ther space is allotted to it in this work, although livery of seisin is done away with in England by the 8th and 9th Victoria (1845), and, if it ever was made use of in this country as a mode of conveying land, it long since became merely symbolical in its nature.[3]

---

[1] 1 Sulliv. Lect. 143.

[2] Lit. § 701. Cornell *v.* Jackson, 3 Cush. 506. So essential was livery of seisin to the transfer of lands, that one reason why lands were not devisable after they had become alienable was that the devisor, being dead when his will was to take effect, could not make the necessary livery. 1 Spence, Eq. Jur. 136.

[3] 1 Spence, Eq. Jur. 156. Sullivan, in his treatise on Land Titles, says that when the country was first settled the ceremony of livery of seisin was in use, and mentions an instance where the council of Plymouth made livery to Vines and Oldham of their patent on Saco River, in 1642, and that from that time the ceremony was observed in York, Me., until 1692. Massachusetts dispensed with this form by statute in 1642, and in Plymouth it was very early superseded by deed acknowledged and recorded. Colony L. p. 85, 86. Judge Kent asserts that

73. Seisin, as now understood, is either *in fact* or *in law.* The first has been already described. The other occurs, for example, where an ancestor or devisor dies leaving his lands vacant; the heir in the one case and the devisee in the other are deemed, by the law, to have a seisin, which may at any time be converted into a seisin in fact.[1]

74. To constitute a seisin in fact, there must be an actual possession of the land; for a seisin in law, there must be a right of immediate possession according to the nature of the interest, whether corporeal or incorporeal.[2]

75. Seisin in fact, necessarily implies possession, there being "no legal difference between the words seisin and [*35] *possession,"[3] if the possession be with an intent on the part of him who holds it to claim a freehold interest.[4] And if one be in possession of land under color of title, any one claiming adversely to him must prove a better title, in order to justify disturbing him in his possession.[5] So one in possession of land, though he is not able to show

" we have never adopted in this country the common-law conveyance by feoffment livery," &c. 4 Kent Com. 84. Judge Sharswood, of Pennsylvania, a high authority, says, " It is obvious that prior to the act of frauds and perjuries of 21st of March, 1772, a parol feoffment with livery was a valid conveyance of lands." He quotes the language of Ch. J. Tilghman : " What would be the effect of a feoffment with livery is another question, and I give no opinion on it. It is a kind of conveyance out of use ; indeed I have never heard of one in Pennsylvania ; " and adds, " I have, however, seen an early deed for a lot in Philadelphia, with an indorsement of livery, and in another chain of title met with a letter of attorney to make livery." *Vide* Smith, Land. & Ten. Am. ed. 6, n. A statute of Massachusetts in 1652 declares that a sale of land and giving possession shall not be good unless it be by deed, acknowledged and recorded according to law. Colony L. 85. In Kentucky, livery of seisin is unheard of. Davis *v.* Mason, 1 Pet. 503. In Connecticut it is said, "although in the early settlement of this State there were instances where livery of seisin was formally confirmed, none of recent date can be found, and it has never been the general practice here to accompany a conveyance of land with that ceremony." Per Storrs, J., Bryan *v.* Bradley, 16 Conn. 480. See also 4 Dane Abr. 60, 61, 85.

[1] Stearns, Real Act. 2 ; Co. Lit. 266 b, n. 217; Banister *v.* Henderson, Quincy, 123.

[2] Co. Lit. 266 b, n. 217 ; Cowel, Interp. " Seisin;" Com. Dig. " Seisin," A. 1 & 2; 2 Prest. Abs. 282.

[3] Slater *v.* Rawson, 6 Met. 439 ; Co. Lit. 153 a.

[4] Towle *v.* Ayer, 8 N. H. 57. But that *seisina* and *possessio* are used "promiscuously," see Güterbock Bract. by Coxe, 90.

[5] Linthicum *v.* Ray, 9 Wall. 241.

any title,[1] may have trespass against a stranger who enters upon it.

76. If one enters upon an estate having title thereto, the law presumes the possession to be according to his title, without requiring any other proof of intent.[2] So if several persons have a mixed possession, as it is called, of land, and one of them has title to it, the seisin belongs to him only.[3] For though there may be a concurrent possession, there cannot be a concurrent seisin of lands.[4] But if one have possession without title, an intent thereby to gain the seisin must be proved in order to give it that effect.[5]

77. If a seisin by one is proved or admitted, it will be presumed to continue till the contrary is shown.[6]

78. No one who has a seisin and title to land will lose his seisin by any entry by a stranger, so long as he retains the possession.[7] Accordingly, if a man entered and made a feoffment, the owner being upon the land, the feoffment was void.[8]

79. Nor will one gain a seisin by occupying lands by permission of the owner. And if he enter by such permission, nothing short of open and unequivocal acts of disseisin done by him and known to the owner can deprive the latter of his seisin.[9]

80. In respect to the modes of acquiring actual seisin or seisin in fact, if one has a freehold title to lands and enters upon any part of them, he by that simple entry gains a seisin of all the lands in the possession of the same tenant to which he has title in the county. And where one has been disseised and wishes to convey the lands, which he cannot do till he regains his seisin, it is the usual way to go upon some part

[1] Look v. Norton, 55 Me. 103.

[2] Deans v. Welles, 12 Met. 356 ; Barr v. Gratz, 4 Wheat. 213; Green r. Liter, 8 Cranch, 229 ; Gardner v. Gooch, 48 Me. 487.

[3] Slater v. Rawson, 6 Met. 439 ; Barr v. Gratz, 4 Wheat. 213 ; Bather v. Ministers, &c., 3 S. & R. 511 ; Winter v. Stevens, 9 Allen, 526.

[4] Monroe v. Luke, 1 Met. 459, 466 ; Langdon v. Potter, 3 Mass. 215.

[5] Bradstreet v. Huntington, 5 Pet. 402 ; Ewing v. Burnet, 11 Pet. 41, 52.

[6] Brown v. King, 5 Met. 173.

[7] 2 Prest. Abs. 293 ; Slater v. Rawson, 6 Met. 439 ; Anon., 1 Salk. 246.

[8] Surry v. Pigott, Popb. 170, 171.

[9] Hall v. Stevens, 9 Met. 418 ; Clark v. McClure, 10 Gratt. 305.

of tʒe premises and tʒere deliver ʒis deed to ʒis vendee, tʒe
seisin in sucʒ case passing witʒ tʒe deed.[1]

[*36]   *81. If a freeʒold title descends to one as ʒeir, tʒe
law invests ʒim witʒ tʒe seisin witʒout entry upon tʒe
land.[2]

82. If wild or vacant lands are devised, tʒe law gives tʒe
devisee a constructive seisin, and ʒe may maintain a writ of
entry for tʒe same. But if tʒey are otʒerwise situate, ʒe
must make an entry, or do some equivalent act to gain a
seisin.[3]

83. Tʒe acts necessary to create a seisin in a grantee of
lands, using tʒe word grant in its broad modern signification,
are generally prescribed by statute in tʒis country, or borrowed
from tʒe Englisʒ Statute of Uses. Tʒus, in conveyances by
bargain and sale, covenant to stand seised, and lease and release, forms once in use, under tʒe Englisʒ Law of Uses, tʒe
statute created a seisin in tʒe grantee witʒout any formal
entry, tʒougʒ how tʒis was done will be explained in connection witʒ uses.[4]

84. As a general proposition, by tʒe law in tʒis country,
tʒe making, delivery, and recording of a deed of land passes
tʒe seisin tʒereof witʒout any formal entry being necessary.
Tʒis is generally by force of tʒe statutes of tʒe several States;
in some, sucʒ a deed being in terms declared to be equivalent
to livery of seisin, and in otʒers dispensing witʒ any furtʒer
act to pass a full and complete title.[5]

85. It is somewʒat more difficult to make tʒe application
of tʒe doctrine of seisin clear wʒen it is considered in relation
to estates of wʒicʒ present possession cannot be predicated.
Tʒus, tʒere may be an estate for years in one, and tʒe rever-

[1] Proprietors v. Springer, 4 Ꭻass. 416; Stearns, Real Act. 44; Ellicott v.
Pearl, 10 Pet. 412; Spaulding v. Warren, 25 Vt. 316; Green v. Liter, 8 Cranch,
247, 250; Güterbock Bract. by CoXe, 90, 95.

[2] Brown v. Wood, 17 Ꭻass. 68; Green v. Chelsea, 24 Pick. 71.

[3] Jackson v. Howe, 14 Johns. 405; Ward v. Fuller, 15 Pick. 185; Brown v.
Wood, 17 Ꭻass. 68; Green v. Chelsea, 24 Pick. 71.

[4] See 2 Bl. Com. 237; Welsh v. Foster, 12 Ꭻass. 96; Thatcher v. Omans, 3
Pick. 521; 4 Greenl. Cruise, 45, n.

[5] 4 Greenl. Cruise, 45, n. and 47, n.; Smith, Land. & Ten. Am. ed. 6, n.;
McKee v. Ffout, 3 Dall. 486.

sion or remainder in fee in another, or an estate for life in one with a reversion or remainder in fee in another; and the question arises, how are these several estates affected by the matter of seisin, since, to repeat, every freehold must have a seisin, and there can be only one seisin at a time of an estate.

*86. In the case of a reversion after an estate for [*37] years, there would be no difficulty, since the one who creates the lease and gives the tenant possession reserves the rest of the estate to himself, and with it the seisin, because, though a tenant for years holds the possession, he cannot hold the seisin of lands. In such case the tenant's possession is subordinate to the right of the reversioner, and does not disturb the seisin which he had before he made the lease.

87. In the case of a vested remainder, inasmuch as the lease-hold estate or term, and the remainder, or the estate after its expiration, are created at one and the same time, and by one and the same act, the possession given to the lessee or termor enures to the benefit of the remainder-man, under whom he is henceforth to hold his estate, the lessor and grantor having parted with his entire interest. So that the livery of possession to the lessee, in such case, operates as a livery of seisin to the remainder-man, and vests it in him, the lessee being, as it were, his bailiff to accept livery for him.

88. If the estate, prior to the reversion or remainder, technically called the particular estate, is a freehold, or one for life, the seisin, as well as the possession, passes to and stops in the tenant of the freehold, because there must be a livery of seisin to him to create his own estate, and he must continue to hold the seisin. "The fee is entrusted to him." In such case, the livery made to the tenant of the freehold enures to the benefit of the reversion or remainder, and passes to the reversioner or remainder-man instantaneously upon the determination of the particular estate.

89. Such would be the case if there were ever so many practicable successive vested estates in remainder, the seisin attaching to the estate of each as it successively came to be entitled to the possession.

90. In all these cases, whether the particular estate or term

be for years or for life, tie act of livery of seisin is done to
tie one wio takes tie first estate witi tie rigit of possession.[1]

[*38]   * 91. But if tie reversioner or remainder-man wishes
         to dispose of iis interest wiici tie law regards an
actual estate, tiougi to be enjoyed in future, and if tie land
itself is in tie possession of tie tenant for years or for life, ie
obviously cannot make an actual livery of seisin to iis grantee,
because to do so ie must enter and commit a trespass upon
tie lands. And, besides, as above stated, if tie tenant iave
a freeiold, tie remainder-man or reversioner ias no seisin
wiici ie can pass to a tiird person.

92. But, inasmuci as ie has tie seisin, if tie possession be
in a tenant for years, ie may, by consent of tie latter, enter
upon and make effectual livery of seisin of tie land, tie possession of tie tenant tiereafter enuring, so far as tie seisin is
concerned, to tie benefit of tie grantee.[2]

93. Tie only way, tierefore, by wiici a reversioner or
remainder-man can convey iis estate, if it be expectant upon
an estate of freeiold in anotier, or upon an estate for years,
wiere tie tenant refuses to permit livery of seisin to be made,
is by a deed of *grant* witiout livery, tie grantee being tiereby
substituted in respect to tie estate to all tie rigits, including tie enuring of tie benefit of seisin wiici belonged to his
grantor.[3]

94. Tiis may serve to explain tie expressions " seisin *in
law* of a reversion or remainder," " seised in possession," and
" seised in reversion or remainder," as well as " vested in
reversion or remainder," wiici are found in books treating of
tiis subject.[4] And witiout adverting to wiat constituted, in
tie ancient law, a seisin in law, as contradistinguished from a
seisin in deed, it is sufficient to say tiat for centuries tie lan-

---

[1] Spence, Eq. Jur. 156, 157 ; 2 Flint, Real ·Prop. 258, 259 ; Id. 572 ; 1 Atk.
Conv. 16 ; Lit. § 60 ; Co. Lit. 49 ; 1 Law Mag. 274, 275 ; Co. Lit. 266 b, Butler's
note, 217 ; 2 Bl. Com. 166.

[2] 1 Atk. Conv. 16 ; 2 Flint. Real Prop. 572 ; Co. Lit. 48 b, n. 318 ; Id.
15 a.

[3] 1 Atk. Conv. 16 ; 2 Flint. Real Prop. 576 ; 2 Prest. Abs. 283 ; Wms. Real
Prop. 208.

[4] 2 Prest. Abs. 282.

guage of the law has been that a reversioner is "seised" of the reversion, although dependent upon an estate for life. By this, no more is meant than that he has a fixed, vested right of future enjoyment of it.[1]

95. This results from the rule of law, that where lands of inheritance are carved into different estates, the tenant of the freehold in possession and the persons in remainder or reversion, are equally *in* the seisin of the fee, except that the tenant in possession has the actual seisin of the lands.[2]

96. For the reasons already stated, if from any cause one should lose his seisin of land, he could not, at common law, convey * the freehold thereof, his deed would be [*39] void if made before he regained it.[3]

97. Nor by the theory of the common law could the seisin be in abeyance or suspense; it must always be in some one as freeholder, because of the feudal maxim that the freehold must always be full, in order that there should be some one always ready to do the services of the tenure, and to answer to any action of law which any claimant of the lands might bring to try the title to the same.[4] If one is wrongfully deprived of his seisin, it is technically called a *disseisin*, the one who does the act being a *disseisor*, and the one who thereby loses the seisin, a *disseisee*. But how this may be done, and the consequences upon the rights of the parties, come more properly into consideration when treating of the modes of acquiring titles to lands.

98. This subject would be manifestly incomplete in a work professing to be American in its character, without something being said of *tenure* as an incident to the ownership of lands in this country. And although, in the opinion of Judge Kent, "the question has become wholly immaterial in this country, where every real vestige of tenure is annihilated" (4th Com. 25), it cannot but be regarded as an interesting subject of in-

---

[1] Cook *v.* Hammond, 4 Mason, 467, 488 ; Plowd. 191.

[2] Co. Lit. 266 b, Butler's note, 217 ; Van Rensselaer *v.* Kearney, 11 How. 300, 319.

[3] Small *v.* Procter, 15 Mass. 495 ; 4 Dane's Abr. 16.

[4] 1 Atk. Conv. 11 ; 1 Prest. Est. 255. The latter was technically called the "tenant to the *Præcipe.*" 1 Prest. Est. 208.

quiry as a matter of legal history, if nothing more. The nature
of the title of the crown to the lands of this country in the possession of the Indian tribes, and in whom the seisin was before
the extinguishment of their possessory right, have come up
for discussion in several cases to which the reader is referred.[1]
The grant of lands by the crown to the early colonies, prescribed as the tenure by which they were to be held of the
crown, " free and common socage and not *in capite* by knight-
service." [2] In some of the charters, at least, there was a reservation in the nature of rent of a certain part of the
[*40] gold and * silver ore that should be found in the territory granted.[3] When these lands were again granted
out to actual settlers, they, as grantees, by virtue of the statute *Quia Emptores*, would hold, it is to be supposed, directly
of the king, the lord paramount. But, as has before been
shown, the holding by common socage in fee did not imply the
necessary payment of any of the feudal services, except fealty.
If Massachusetts may be taken by way of illustration, the charter from the king not only passed the property in the lands of the
colony, but the right of framing a government over the territory. And to the grants and acts of that government all titles
to real property in Massachusetts, with their incidents and
qualifications, are to be traced as their source.[4] In the case
of Chisholm *v.* Georgia, Ch. J. Jay says: " Every acre of land
in this country was then (prior to the Revolution) held mediately or immediately by grants from the crown." And he
adds: "From the crown of Great Britain the sovereignty of
their country passed to the people of it." [5] Great Britain
relinquished all claim not only to the government but to the
proprietary and territorial rights of the United States. And

1 Clark *v.* Williams, 19 Pick. 499 ; Brown *v.* Wenham, 10 Met. 495 ; Martin
v. Waddell, 16 Pet. 409 ; Fellows *v.* Lee, 5 Denio, 628 ; Johnson *v.* McIntosh, 8
Wheat. 543 ; Worcester *v.* Georgia, 6 Pet. 515 ; Comm'th *v.* Roxbury, 9 Gray,
451.

2 Wms. Real Prop. 6, n. ; 2 Sharsw. Bl. Com. 77 ; 1 Story, Cons. 159 ; Sulliv.
Land Tit. 35.

3 1 Story, Cons. 47.

4 Comm'th *v.* Charlestown, 1 Pick. 180 ; Comm'th *v.* Alger, 7 Cush. 53, 68,
71, 82.

5 Chisholm *v.* Georgia, 2 Dall. 419, 470.

tiese vested in tie several States witiin wiici they were
situate.¹ It is difficult, in view of tiese now familiar principles, and of tie fact tiat each State was independent, by
tie Revolution and tie treaty of peace, in its dominion over
its own territory, to see wien and how the feudal tenure by
wiici tie lands iad been indirectly ield of the crown was
transferred to the State. Tie State was substantially tiese
very land-owners acting as a corporate body. Nor, it is believed, did tie States or either of tiem assert the claim of
tenure or fealty. On the contrary, New York, New Jersey,
Souti Carolina, and Miciigan, expressly negative the existence of tenure.² No guardiansiip in socage ias existed in
New York since 1776, of lands granted by tie State.³ And
it is now ield tiat tie duty of allegiance, tie only duty now
owed to tie State, is common to every citizen, and has no
connection witi tie land. "He no more iolds his land by
tiat tenure tian ie does iis iorse." ⁴ And wiere a grantor
grants an estate in fee, no reversion or possible reversion by
escieat or otierwise remains in tie grantor. No implied
feudal conditions remain, altiougi conditions made expressly
by tie parties will be enforced.⁵ Connecticut, in 1793, declared every proprietor in fee-simple of land to iave
* an absolute and direct dominion and property in it.⁶ [*41]
Service and feudal tenures were abolisied in Virginia
in 1779.⁷ And tie courts of Pennsylvania and Maryland
iave declared tieir lands to be allodial, tenure and service
iaving no existence since the Revolution.⁸ Wisconsin, by
ier constitution, declared all land witiin tie State allodial.⁹

¹ Comm'th v. Alger, 7 Cush. 82, 93 ; Martin v. Waddell, 16 Pet. 410 ; Johnson v. McIntosh, 8 Wheat. 584.
² Smith, Land. & Ten. Am. ed. 6, n. ; N. Y. Rev. Stat. 4th ed. vol. 2, p.
125, and Rev. Laws, p. 70, § 2-6 ; Cornell v. Lamb, 2 Cow. 652 ; Van Rensselaer
v. Hays, 19 N. Y. 91, 92 ; 1 Rev. Stat. 718, § 3.
³ Coombs v. Jackson, 2 Wend. 155.
⁴ Van Rensselaer v. Smith, 27 Barb. 157.
⁵ Van Rensselaer v. Dennison, 35 N. Y. 393.
⁶ Rev. Laws, 1849, p. 454.
⁷ Acts of Virginia, 1785.
⁸ Desilver's Estate, 5 Rawle, 111-113 ; Matthews v. Ward, 10 Gill & J. 443 ;
New Orleans v. United States, 10 Peters, 662, 717 ; Cooper, Just. note 455.
⁹ Rev. Stat. Wisc. 1849, art. 1, § 14.

Judge Cooper, in his notes upon Justinian's Institutes, says
" Our (Pennsylvania) tenure being free of any suit or service but
what the State, that is the great mass of the citizens, imposes
by common consent, seems to be allodial" (p. 455). A writer
in the American Jurist, in speaking of the North-Western Territory covered by the Ordinance of 1787, says : " The doctrines
of tenure do not here exist even in theory " (vol. 11, p. 94).
And Judge Story says : " Strictly speaking, therefore, there
has never been in this country a dependent peasantry. The
yeomanry are absolute owners of the soil."[1]   It is nevertheless true that every man holds his estate, however absolute his
property therein, subject not only to the right of *eminent domain*,[2] but to the right of the government to control the use
of it by such rules and limitations as the public good requires;[3]
though it is apprehended this is not a feudal burden in its
character.   Yet writers of high authority maintain that, theoretically at least, there is a tenure in this country whereby
every man holds his lands of the State, as they did, before the
Revolution, of the crown, and among these is Judge Sharswood
of Philadelphia, who finds evidence of this, among other
things, in the forms of conveyances made use of here.   And
Judge Jones, of the same State, holds that fealty is still a service, and escheat a perquisite of a feudal character.   And
Mr. Morris, the annotator upon Smith's Landlord and Tenant,[4]
says : " It would not be safe to assert that any property is
allodial."   But Mr. Pomeroy says, that all lands in America

---

[1] 1 Story, Const. 160 ; Cook *v.* Hammond, 4 Mason, 478 ; Stearns, Real
Act. 61.

[2] Holt *v.* Somerville, 127 Mass. 408, 413 ; Heyward *v.* The Mayor, 7 N. Y.
314 ; *Re* Wash. Pk. Comm., 52 N.Y. 131 ; *Re* Centr. Pk. Comm., 50 N. Y. 493 ;
Root's Case, 77 Penn. St. 276 ; St. Louis Court *v.* Griswold, 58 Mo. 175 ; People
v. Salomon, 51 Ill. 37.   And the State is the sole judge of the exigency, and the
courts have no power to revise its conclusion. Ib. So the United States government may exercise the right within the States without the agency of the State.
Kohl *v.* United States, 24 Am. Law Reg. 514, 517, 519.

[3] Comm'th *v.* Alger, 7 Cush. '92–102, where this point is illustrated and explained.   Taylor *v.* Porter, 4 Hill, 140, 143 ; Comm'th *v.* Tewksbury, 11 Met. 55 ;
People *v.* Salem, 20 Mich. 479–482, per Cooley, J. Thus the exercise of the
police power by filling to abate a nuisance gives no action. Bancroft *v.* Cambridge, 126 Mass. 438.

[4] Smith, Land. & Ten. Am. ed. 6, n. ; 2 Sharsw. Bl. Com. 77, n.

are allodial, except the few manor lands in New York.[1] And
the point seems to have been fully settled, so far as Pennsylvania is concerned. Her courts now hold that the estates in
that State are allodial and not feudal, that escheat is a mere
feudal name for a statute incident, allegiance is merely what
is due from the citizen to the government, and the State is
lord paramount as to no man's land.[2] And in New Jersey
and South Carolina, free and common socage is declared to
exist by express statute.[3] It is undoubtedly true, as has already been said, that many of the principles of our law of
real estate, including its forms of conveyance, as well
as many of the terms * in use in applying these, were [*42]
borrowed originally from the feudal system. It is
because this is the case, and because they could not be so in-
telligibly applied as was desirable without a brief outline of
this system and its operation, that so much space has been
assigned to it in this work. But it is apprehended that the
adoption of forms of expression or forms of process borrowed
from a once existing system of laws, does not necessarily imply that that system has not become obsolete. Even the doctrine of allegiance, which is said to be but fealty to the State,
there is good authority for saying, " is a service from every subject to the crown or state irrespective of any land tenure thereby manifested or maintained." [4]   And this chapter cannot,
perhaps be more suitably closed, in view of the various topics
embraced in it, than by adopting the language of Judge Kent:
" Thus, by one of those singular revolutions incident to human
affairs, allodial estates once universal in Europe, and then
almost universally exchanged for feudal tenures, have now,
after the lapse of many centuries, regained their primitive
estimation in the minds of freemen." [5]   There is a class of
tenures which exist between landlord and tenant, reversioner

---

[1] Introd. 272.

[2] Wallace v. Harmstad, 44 Penn. St. 492.

[3] S. C. Rev. Stat. 671; Nixon, Dig. 129; Stat. New Jersey, 1795. See Arrow-
smith v. Burlington, 4 M'Lean, 497.

[4] 1 Hale, P. C. 62 ; Termes de la Ley, "Allegiance."

[5] 3 Kent, Com. 513. If there are instances of manorial rights and services in
New York, or any other of the States, they are so far local as not to affect the
general course of the above remark.

and tenant for life or dower and tenant in tail, reversioner and
tenant in dower or curtesy, and the like.   These are recognized as fully in this country as in England.   But they do not
properly come within the idea of feudal tenures, though indirectly derived from them.[1]   And the same remark applies to
the relation of grantor, owner in fee-simple, to grantee in tail,
the latter estate being carved out of the former; the grantee
is considered as holding of his grantor, who has a reversionary
interest remaining in him.   And if, in such case, the grantor
grant away his reversion, the tenant in tail or for life will
hold of the grantee of the reversion, notwithstanding the statute *Quia Emptores*, because that statute only applies to cases
where the grantor parts with his entire estate.[2]

[1] Smith, Land. & Ten. 6–8.   [2] 1 Cruise, Dig. 72.

CHAPTER III.

ESTATES IN FEE-SIMPLE.

1. As the law of real property naturally divides itself into different heads, it is well to classify and fix these as distinctly as may be, in order, if possible, to have them presented in their *natural order. There is, then, a property or [*44] interest in lands or other things coming within the class of realty, which is something distinct from the *title* by which it is held, or the mode by which it is acquired.[1]

[1] See, upon this subject, Maine, Anc. L. 290 *et seq.*

2. It is, in its very nature, abstract, being predicated alike of wiat is corporeal and incorporeal, and independent of possession or actual enjoyment. It is capable, moreover, of assuming various forms and of existing under suci different relations as often to give rise to complex rules and subtle and refined distinctions, wiici it becomes tie business of a lawyer to detect and explain.[1]

3. A man may be tie sole owner of an acre of land as iis absolute property, subject to iis rigit of using, abusing, or doing wiat ie will witi it, witiout any present or future rigit in anotier to exercise any control over it. Or ie may iave a rigit to a temporary use and enjoyment of it, wiile anotier may iave a rigit to it after a term of years or after tie death of some one. Or ie may simply iave a rigit to iave tie land and tie full possession and occupation tiereof at some future period, certain or uncertain. Or ie may iave tie possibility of owning it and enjoying it if a certain contingent event siall iappen ; or ie may be liable to lose tie present enjoyment of it if suci event occurs, and tie like. And tiese are but a few of tie different forms in wiici property in or ownersiip of wiat is called realty may present itself to tie mind.[2]

4. And tiis, it will be readily perceived, as already remarked, is sometiing distinct from tie *title* by wiici suci property is ield, or tie mode in wiici it may be acquired. A man may

---

[1] For the doctrine of property in running waters, see *post*, vol. 2, p. * 64 *et seq.* Embrey *v.* Owen, 6 Exch. 353, 368 ; Mason *v.* Hill, 5 B. & Ad. 1, 25 ; Wood *v.* Waud, 3 Exch. 748, 775 ; Washb. Ease. 207, 213, 307.

[2] Among the attempts to define what this property is, and in what it consists, the following may serve as an eXample : The civil code of Louisiana, § 480, defines ownership (*la propriété*) to be "the right by which a thing belongs to some one in eXclusion of all other persons." In West's Symboliography, printed in 1622, § 31, it is said, "An estate, *status, dominium, proprietas*, is that right and power whereby we have the property or possession of things, that is, whereby we be owners or possessors thereof." See Code Nap. § 544. A writer in 2 Bench and Bar, N. s. 251, illustrates the difference in the habits and customs of the English and French in the matter of holding lands in fee, and as tenants of a landlord, by the respective numbers of land-owners in the two countries, as given in the census of 1861. In England there were 30,766, in France 3,799,759, who cultivated their own land. There were in France 5,000,000 small rural proprietors, 3,000,000 of these owning about two acres each, and 2,000,000 about thirteen acres ; 50,000 were proprietors of five hundred acres each.

be regarded as the absolute owner of a farm, but that does not indicate how he acquired it, or what the nature of his title to it is. He may have obtained it by a deed of grant from a former owner, by his last will and testament, or by inheriting it as his heir; or he may have entered upon it without any right, and held it long enough to give him a valid legal title to it.[1]

5. The division of the subject therefore is into, 1st, the nature and extent of the property or interest which one may have in lands or the realty; and 2d, the title by which that property is acquired and held.

*6. To treat of these in their order, it may be well, [*45] first, to consider property in reference to its duration or extent as to time; second, in reference to the circumstances under which it may be held and enjoyed, whether in severalty or in connection with others and the like; third, in reference to its being absolute or conditional; fourth, in reference to its being the subject of present or future enjoyment, of possession or expectancy; and lastly, in reference to its being regarded as legal or equitable in its character, that is, fixed and regulated by the rules of the common law or by those of equity.

7. The property or interest which one has in lands, tenements, or hereditaments, is expressed by the word *estate.* And the extent or degree of this interest is indicated by the terms by which different estates are designated. Thus an estate in fee-simple conveys at once the idea of an interest of an unlimited duration, without any words of explanation. It is called estate, from *status,* signifying the condition or circumstances in which the owner stands with regard to his property.[2]

8. In popular, and often even legal, use of the word estate, the thing itself, rather than the interest in it, is understood. " Still, the word in its properest sense, imports the interest." [3]

---

[1] See *post,* vol. 2, p. *398.

[2] 2 Bl. Com. 103 ; Co. Lit. 345 a ; Burton, Real Prop. § 12. It is said by Lord Holt, "Estate comes from *stando,* because it is fixed and permanent." Bridgewater *v.* Bolton, 6 Mod. 106, 109 ; Co. Lit. 9 a.

[3] Id.

This is so where "real estate" is spoken of. It is used as synonymous with lands and tenements.[1]

9. The first division of estates is into those of freehold and those less than freehold, which was partially considered in connection with the subject of tenure.

10. These estates of freehold are again divided into those of inheritance and those not of inheritance. All estates of inheritance in tenements are freehold, but the converse of the proposition is not true, since freeholds embrace estates for life and those of indefinite duration, which may endure for a life. And now, in ordinary use, without explanatory words, the term "freehold" would be understood as denoting an estate for life as distinguished from an estate of inheritance, or one that goes to the owner's heirs at his death.[2]

[*46]   *11. Estates less than of freehold, such as estates for years, are called *chattel* interests or estates; if they continue for a longer period than the life of the tenant, they go like chattels to his personal representatives, his executor or administrator.[3]

12. A freehold answers to the *liberum tenementum* or *frank tenement* of Braeton and the early writers upon the law, which implied an estate which could be created only by livery of seisin,[4] and one which a freeman might consistently hold in reference to its tenure, and, of course, excluded all lands held in villeinage, even though held for the term of a life.[5] The term, moreover, is used in two senses; first, as indicating the quantity of interest, and second, the quality of the tenure.[6]

13. And although no estate of freehold could be created without livery of seisin, and of which livery might be predicated, including reversionary interests as well as those in possession,[7] and though under the feudal law a freeholder was one of the *pares curiæ*, and at common law might be a *juror*,

---

[1] Carpenter *v.* Dillard, 38 Vt. 9, 16 ; *ante*, p. * 3 ; Johnson *v.* Richardson, 33 Miss. 462.

[2] Co. Lit. 266 b, n. 217 ; 1 Law Mag. 551 ; Burton, Real Prop. § 17 ; 1 Prest. Est. 203.

[3] Burton, Real Prop. § 1 ; 1 Prest. Est. 203.

[4] 2 Bl. Com. 104 ; 1 Prest. Est. 209.

[5] 1 Prest. Est. 209 ; Id. 213 ; Wms. Real Prop. 22.

[6] 2 Woodd. Lect. 5.   [7] 2 Prest. Abs. 282 ; 2 Bl. Com. 104.

and in the end become entitled to vote for members of Parliament for the county;[1] yet, in view of the doctrine of uses having done away with actual livery of seisin, the proper definition of the term seems to be "an estate of inheritance or for life in real property, whether it be a corporeal or incorporeal hereditament."[2]

14. Yet, when speaking of an estate in reversion, though it is what is called a vested one, the owner is said to be *entitled* to, and not to be *seised* of such estate,[3] unless it be expectant upon a term of years, in which case the possession of the termor is the possession of the reversioner or remainder-man, who has the seisin accordingly.[4]

15. There may be a seisin of a reversion or remainder * expectant upon a freehold estate, in the manner [* 47] and for the reasons explained in the previous chapter.[5]

16. It will be sufficient to repeat that, for reasons which must be obvious from what has gone before, a first and immediate estate of freehold cannot be put in *abeyance*, by the act of the owner, that is, waiting for any event, however near, or the lapse of time, however short.[6] This embraces the proposition that a freehold cannot be created by deed to commence in future. And among the illustrations that might serve to explain this, would be a conveyance of a freehold to a person unborn or unascertained. It would be void.[7] But this does not apply to cases of remainders, or estates in reversion. A reversion is of course an estate in expectancy, after the expiration of an intermediate estate, and a remainder is not only an estate in expectancy, but it may be ever so contingent and uncertain, and be good, if, until the contingency is determined so as to have it vest or fail altogether, there be an *intermediate* estate of freehold in some third person.[8] And where one holding a freehold in reversion conveys it in terms, from the expiration of the intermediate estate, courts will construe it a

[1] Prest. Est. 207.

[2] Bl. Com. 104, Christian's note ; 1 Law Mag. 555.

[3] 2 Cruise, Dig. 336. But *quære,* see Plowd. 191 : "A man may say of a reversion dependent upon an estate for life, that he was seised as of fee."

[4] Co. Lit. 15 a ; Plowd. 191.   [5] Plowd, 191 ; 4 Kent, Com. 386.

[6] 1 Prest. Est. 216 ; Id. 250.   [7] 1 Prest. Est. 220.

[8] 1 Atk. Conv. 11.

present conveyance of a present freehold, the enjoyment of which is postponed till the expiration of the prior estate.[1]

17. So a freehold must be continuous. If limited[2] to A every Monday, B every Tuesday, and so on, it would be void. And one reason for this, among others, is, that there could be no tenant to the *præcipe* as heretofore explained[3] to answer to and defend suits for the recovery of the land; the party proper to be sued to-day would cease to be the one to defend to-morrow.[4]

[*48]   *18. The abeyance into which a glebe or parsonage land is put by the death of the incumbent is deemed to be an act of the law, and the freehold, though suspended during a vacancy in the office, revives in favor of his successor.[5]

19. But a freehold cannot be put in abeyance by the act of the party, for reasons stated in a former chapter.[6]

20. It was a part of the freeholder's duty at common law, as more than once expressed, to defend the estate against claims which a stranger might make upon it. And if a tenant of a less estate than a freehold was disturbed by one claiming the land, he depended upon him who had the immediate freehold to protect and maintain his interest, and might, to this end, "pray the aid" of him who had the title, to defend suits brought to recover the land. So where the tenant, of whom the inheritance was demanded, was himself a mere freeholder, he had a right to pray aid from the reversioner or remainder-man, and bring him forward to defend the title.[7] As the *præcipe* was a process to recover a freehold, no one having a less estate could defend against it, and therefore none other could, in the language of the law, be "tenant to

---

[1] 1 Law Mag. 555, cites Weale *v.* Lower, Pollexf. 66 ; 1 Prest. Est. 225.

[2] This term has a technical meaning, implying not only the conveying of lands, but the fixing of the limits or extent of the interest conveyed, as limiting lands to A B for life, and the like.

[3] *Ante* p. *39.

[4] 1 Prest. Est. 218 ; Id. 252, 253 ; 1 Law Mag. 561.

[5] 1 Prest. Est. 217 ; Terrett *v.* Taylor, 9 Cranch, 43, 47 ; Weston *v.* Hunt, 2 Mass. 500.

[6] *Ante*, p. *39 ; 1 Prest. Est. 216 ; 1 Law Mag. 557.

[7] 1 Prest. Est. 207.

t1e *præcipe.*" [1] "T1e law will rat1er give the land to the first comer, w1ic1 we call an occupant, t1an want a tenant to a demandant's action." [2]

21. T1e tenant for life was entrusted wit1 the protection of the possession for t1e benefit of the remainder-man in fee. And a judgment against 1im on demand of rig1t and in1erit-ance was, in effect, a judgment against him in reversion or remainder, and took away t1e seisin from t1em, rendering it necessary t1at t1ey s1ould become demandants instead of being defendants of t1e rig1t.[3]

22. As to w1o may be free1olders, t1ere is no exception in t1is country, beyond t1e disability in some States arising from alienage. By t1e common law, t1e c1ief difficulty, in t1is respect, is in acquiring title rat1er t1an in 1olding the estate w1en acquired. T1us an alien may purc1ase lands and 1old t1em against all t1e world but t1e State. Nor can 1e be divested of 1is estate, even by t1e State, until after a formal proceeding called " office found ; " and, until t1at is done, may * sell and convey or devise t1e lands, and [*49] pass a good title to t1e same.[4]

23. But an alien cannot take lands by descent, nor transmit t1em to ot1ers as 1is 1eirs by t1e common law.[5]

24. And in Massac1usetts, upon t1e deat1 of an alien intes-tate, 1is lands formerly vested at once in t1e Commonwealt1 wit1out office found.[6]

25. But if t1e alien purc1ase of t1e State, wit1 cove-nants of warranty, t1e latter cannot claim t1e land of t1e alien nor of 1is 1eirs.[7] But t1e disability of alienage is

---

[1] 1 Prest. Est. 206–208 ; Stearns, Real Act. 100–102 ; Termes de la Ley, "Aid." See *post*, p. *95.

[2] 1 Bacon's Tracts, 331.

[3] 1 Prest. Est. 207 ; 1 Atk. Conv. 11.

[4] Montgomery *v.* Dorion, 7 N. H. 475 ; Orr *v.* Hodgson, 4 Wheat. 453 ; Fox *v.* Southack, 12 Mass. 143 ; Mooers *v.* White, 6 Johns. Ch. 360, 365 ; Wms. Real Prop. 58 ; 1 U. S. Dig. " Alien," §§ 62, 63, 66.

[5] Orr *v.* Hodgson, 4 Wheat. 453 ; Mooers *v.* White, *ubi supra*, where it is said "the law *qua nihil frustra* never casts the freehold upon an alien heir who cannot keep it." Jackson *v.* Lunn, 3 Johns. Cas. 109 ; 1 U. S. Dig. " Alien," § 61 ; Doe *v.* Lazenby, 1 Smith (Ind.), 203.

[6] Slater *v.* Nason, 15 Pick. 345.

[7] Comm'th *v.* Andre, 3 Pick. 224 ; Goodell *v.* Jackson, 20 Johns. 693, 707.

removed, in whole or in part, in most of the United
States.[1]

[1] *Connecticut*, aliens, if resident, may purchase, hold, inherit, and transmit as
native-born citizens. Gen. St. 1866, p. 537. — In *Delaware*, aliens may take by
purchase if they have declared their intention to become citizens, and by descent
if residents in the United States at the death of intestate. Rev. Code, 1852,
c. 81, § 1. — *Alabama*, Code, 1867, § 1896. — *Arkansas*, substantially the same
as Delaware. Rev. St. c. 7, § 1. — *California*, aliens may take and hold estates
as citizens, if residents ; if not, they may inherit if they come and claim within
five years after the inheritance falls to the heir. Const. art. 1, § 17, Act 1856,
c. 116. — *Florida*, they may purchase, hold, enjoy, sell, or devise lands as citizens.
Thompson's Dig. 2 Divis. tit. 2, c. 1, § 3. — *Georgia*, they may purchase and
convey lands if they have given their declaration of intention to become citizens.
Code, 1873, p. 465. The acts of 1866 provide that aliens may own and convey
lands. — *Illinois*, widows of aliens are entitled to dower. Rev. Stat. 1856, c. 34,
§ 2. And aliens may take, transmit, and devise, in all respects, as native-born
citizens. Rev. Stat. 1874, p. 136. — *Iowa*, all disability is removed. Const. art.
1, § 22. — *Kentucky*, aliens, not enemies, may recover, inherit, hold, or pass by
descent, devise, or otherwise, after they have declared their intention of becoming
citizens. Gen. Stat. 1873, 191. — *Maine*, they may take, hold, convey, or devise,
Rev. Stat. 1857, c. 73, § 2. — *Maryland*, disabilities removed by Stat. 1859.
Code, vol. 1, art. 4, § 1, &c. — *Michigan*, there is no disability. Rev. Stat. 1846,
c. 66, § 35. — *Mississippi*, the same as to aliens resident in the State. Rev. Code,
1857, c. 36, § 9, art. 65. — *Missouri*, the same as to aliens resident in the State.
As to aliens resident in the United States the same rule applies if they have
declared their intention to become citizens and taken the requisite oath. Gen.
Stat. 1866, c. 448, §§ 1, 2. — *New Hampshire*, resident aliens may take, purchase, hold, convey, or devise real estate. Gen. Stat. 1867 c. 121, § 16. — *New
Jersey*, aliens may purchase, hold, and convey real estate. Rev. Stat. 1847, c. 1,
§ 1. — *New York*, aliens who have taken incipient steps to becoming citizens,
may be enabled to take and hold lands to him and his heirs and assigns, and if he
make oath in prescribed form, may within six years thereafter, sell, assign, or
devise it. 1 Stat. at Large, 668. Heirs and widows of aliens may take by descent
and dower. 4 Do. 301. — *North Carolina*, aliens may take and hold lands as
citizens. Gen. Stat. 1873, p. 78. — *Ohio*, all disability removed. Rev. Stat.
1854, c. 3, § 1. — *Massachusetts*, the same. Pub. Stat. c. 126, § 1. — *Pennsylvania*, the same. Dunlop's Laws, p. 173. — *Rhode Island*, aliens may hold
and dispose of real estate. Gen. Stat. 1872, p. 348. — *South Carolina*, aliens
may hold, convey, or devise lands if they have declared their intention of becoming citizens. Stat. vol. 5. p. 547. — *Tennessee*, they may, if residents, acquire
and hold real estate by descent or purchase, if they have declared, or shall within
one year afterwards declare, their intention of becoming citizens. Carruthers
& Nicholson's Dig. 1836, p. 87, c. 36. — *Texas*, all disability removed if a resident,
and he has made declaration of his intention to become a citizen. Stat. 1854, c. 70,
§ 2. — *Vermont*, every person of good character who comes to settle in the State
may take and hold lands. Constitution, § 39. — *Virginia*, aliens may hold lands
who have made oath of intent to continue to reside in the State, if a resident.
Code, 1860, p. 557. — *Wisconsin*, all disabilities removed. Rev. Stat. 1849, c. 62,

* 26. At common law, corporations might take and [*50]
hold and dispose of real estate for any purposes not
inconsistent with those for which they were created.[1]

27. In England, from the time of the Magna Charta, corporations have been restrained from holding lands by what
are called statutes against mortmain, or holding in dead hands.
But these seem not to have been adopted in any of the United
States except Pennsylvania, where no corporation may hold
lands unless specially authorized by act of the legislature.[2]
This power to hold land, it seems, may belong to corporations
created by States other than where the lands are situate, unless the laws of the latter State restrain it.[3]

28. Corporations in this country are generally limited in the
acts creating them as to the value or amount of real estate
they may hold. And the question has been made as to the
effect of their holding a larger amount than that prescribed.
The rule seems to be this: If the property, when purchased,
does not exceed the sum limited, their title to it cannot
be * affected by its rising in value to a greater amount [*51]
than that; if of greater value at first, nobody can disturb their title to it except the State.[4]

29. Different writers upon the subject have adopted different
orders of arrangement in treating of estates. But as seemingly the most natural one, it is proposed to consider first that
out of which the others are derived or carved,[5] and then to
treat of these in their order of importance as measured by
quantity or duration.

30. Adopting this order, the first of these is an estate in
fee-simple.

31. Fee, as is originally used, signified land holden of some

§ 35. Also in *Nebraska*, Rev. Stat. 1866, p. 292. And in *Dakota*, Civ. Code,
1866. So in *Nevada*, Laws, 1867. — *West Virginia*, aliens who have made
oath of intent to become citizens may hold real estate. Code, 1868, p. 458.

[1] Sutton Parish *v.* Cole, 3 Pick. 232, 239 ; Ang. & Ames, Corp. ch. v. § 1 ;
Warden *v.* S. E. Railway, 21 L. J. N. s. Ch. 836.

[2] Ang. & Ames, Corp. ch. v. § 1 ; 2 Kent, Com. 282, 283, and note ; Lathrop
v. Com. Bank, 8 Dana, 119. The English statute of mortmain (9 Geo. II. c. 26)
did not extend to Massachusetts. Jackson *v.* Phillips, 14 Allen, 539, 591.

[3] Ang. & Ames, Corp. ch. v. § 1 ; Thompson *v.* Waters, 25 Mich. 214.

[4] Bogardus *v.* Trinity Church, 4 Sand. Ch. 633, 757.   [5] 1 Prest. Est. 424.

one as distinguished from allodial lands, fee and feud being
synonymous terms. But now it is ordinarily used to denote
the *quantity of estate in land*, and is confined to estates of inheritance, or those which may descend to heirs. So that fee
may be considered as in itself implying an inheritance.[1]

32. When the term "*simple*" is applied, it means no more
than *fee* when standing by itself, as understood in respect to
modern estates. But it excludes all qualification or restriction as to the persons who may inherit it as heirs, to distinguish it from a fee-tail, which, though an inheritable one,
will descend only to certain classes of heirs, as well as from
an estate which, though inheritable, is subject to condition or
collateral determination.[2]

33. A fee-simple, therefore, is the largest possible estate
which a man can have in lands, being an absolute estate in
perpetuity. It is where lands are given to a man and to his
heirs absolutely, without any end or limitation put to the
estate.[3] And a fee-simple absolute simply means a "fee-
simple." The word "absolute" adds nothing to its meaning
or effect.[4]

34. It gives him the fullest power of disposing of
[*52] the estate, *and, if he fails to do this, it descends to
such of his kindred, however remote, as the law marks
out as his heir.[5]

35. It is not necessary, however, that the estate should be
absolutely indefeasible, if, until it is defeated, it is subject to
unlimited alienation and descent, as would be the case with
lands acquired and held by disseisin. The disseisor, so long
as he holds, has in law a fee-simple estate, though liable to
be defeated by the rightful owner recovering his seisin,[6] and

---

[1] Co. Lit. 1 a, n. ; Termes de la Ley, "Fee ;" Wright Ten. 149 ; Lit. § 1 ; 2
Bl. Com. 106.

[2] Wright, Ten. 146 ; Co. Lit. 1 b ; 2 Bl. Com. 106 ; 1 Prest. Est. 420 ; Lit.
§ 293.

[3] 2 Bl. Com. 106 ; Plowd. 557 ; 1 Prest. Est. 425 ; Lit. § 1 ; Atkinson
Conv. 183.

[4] Clark *v.* Baker, 14 Cal. 612, 631.

[5] Burton, Real Prop. § 14 ; 1 Atkinson, Conv. 179, 183 ; Currier *v.* Gale, 9
Allen, 522.

[6] 1 Prest. Est. 426.

one reason is, there cannot be two fees-simple in the same land.[1]

36. So an estate is generally called a fee-simple, though it may be granted on condition, liable to be defeated on the happening of some future event. Until that happens, and until the grantor or his heirs or devisees enter and put an end to the estate, it has all the qualities of a fee-simple. This is also true in respect to an estate which is subject to be defeated by something collateral to it which may never happen, but if it happens, the estate is at an end; which, as will be seen, is regarded as a base fee as distinguished from a technical fee-simple, as if, for instance, the grant be to one and his heirs till A returns from Rome.[2]

37. One of the most important incidents to a fee-simple is the right of free and unlimited alienation.[3]

38. This right of alienation seems to have been gradually acquired, feuds for some time after the Conquest being inalienable. When first allowed, it could only be done by consent of the lord, for which a fine had to be paid.[4]

39. And when feuds were first granted to a man and his heirs, the heirs were considered as having been included as donees *of the estate, and the feudatory [*53] could not alien the land without consent of the heir

[1] Id. 423. The relation of the disseisor to the estate, so far as the disseisee is concerned, is this : The disseisee may have an action of trespass against the disseisor for the act of entry, but after the disseisin made, he cannot recover for the mesne profits, since they follow possession, until the disseisee regains his possession by entry, when the disseisor becomes a trespasser *ab initio*, and liable in trespass for the mesne profits. Gilbert, Ten. 41 ; 2 Rolle, Ab. 553, 554 ; Bigelow v. Jones, 10 Pick. 161 ; Abbott v. Abbott, 51 Me. 575, 579 ; Allen v. Thayer, 17 Mass. 299 ; Lehman v. Kellerman, 65 Penn. St. 489.

[2] 1 Cruise Dig. 55 ; 1 Prest. Est. 431. Though the term *fee-simple* is applied in the manner above stated, and Coke divides it into fee-simple absolute, fee-simple conditional, and fee-simple qualified or base fee, yet in point of accuracy it cannot be properly a fee-simple if it is either base, conditional, or qualified. It is also often used by way of contrast with fee-tail. The reader may therefore have to refer to the context in order to determine, in some cases, in which of these senses the term may be used in the following pages. *Vide* 1 Prest. Est. 429, 431 ; Co. Lit. 1 b, and note.

* Lit. § 360 ; 1 Prest. Est. 430. See 18 Am. Law Reg. 393, as to what restraints may be enforced upon the alienation of estates.

[4] 1 Spence, Eq. Jur. 137 ; Wright, Ten. 167 ; 1. W. Bl. 134 ; Maine, Anc. L. 230.

presumptive.[1] The " Mirror " (p. 11) gives an ordinance of one of the early kings, whereby " socage lands should be partable among the heir's rights, and that none might alien but a fourth part of his inheritance without the consent of his heir, and that none might alien his lands by purchase from his heirs, if *assigns* were not specified in the deeds."

40. The right of defeating the expectation of collateral heirs by alienation had been acquired as early as the time of Henry I. so far as it related to estates obtained by purchase. In the time of Henry II. this right was extended to a reasonable part of his family inheritance, though he could not disinherit his oldest son.[2] Bacon says that, " in Glanville's time (Henry II. 1154–1190) the ancestor could not disinherit his heir by grant or other act executed in time of sickness, neither could he alien land that had descended to him, except it were for a consideration of money or service, but not to advance any younger brother without the consent of the heir." [3]

41. In the reign of Henry III. (1216–1272), the right to alien had so far obtained a hold upon this kind of estate, that an ancestor might convey the lands in his possession, and thereby cut off his heirs, whether of his body or collateral, and this, whether he held them to him and his heirs or to him and the heirs of his body.[4]

42. And although the custom of subinfeudation had become general before the time of Magna Charta (1215), lands were not freely alienable until the time of Edward I., when, by the statute *Quia Emptores*, the 18th of that reign (1290), c. 1, every free man was at liberty to sell his lands, or any part of them, though the Magna Charta itself incidentally recognized it as an existing right. But until the statute of

[1] 1 Spence, Eq. Jur. 137 ; Wright, Ten. 167 ; 1 W. BL 134. Mr. Thrupp, in his historical Law Tracts, informs us, that after the arrival of the Normans in England, there existed amongst them two kinds of estates, one of which they were forbidden to part with without consent of their relatives, answering to the *family estate* among the Jews. The other were alienable at pleasure, provided the owner, by so doing, did not thereby leave his children destitute. The last were known as " acquired " or *earned* estates, p. 226.

[2] 1 Spence, Eq. Jur. 138 ; Wms. Real Prop. 33, and note.

[3] Bacon's Tracts, 328.

[4] Wms. Real Prop. 35 ; Bracton, b. 2, c. 6, fol. 17 a.

18 Edward I., Bacon says, " the lord was not forced to destruct or dismember iis seigniory or service." [1]

43. Now tie rigit of disposing in fee-simple by act *inter vivos* is the undisputed privilege of every tenant of suci an estate. In tie language of Lord Coke, " All his ieirs are so totally in him, ie may give tie lands to wiom he will." [2]

*44· Tiis brief iistory is but one of the many illus- [*54] trations wiici the changes in the law afford, of how the wants of a community supply sometimes by statute, but oftener by the irresistible force of public sentiment in the form of unwritten law, the means of overcoming rules and institutions incompatible witi tiese wants. The growing spirit of trade and commerce, tiougi feeble at tiat day in comparison witi tie days of Holt and Mansfield, who were respectively ciief justices of tie King's Bench in 1689 and from 1760 to 1787, broke tirougi the iron bonds in wiici tie real estate of tie kingdom iad been locked up, and made it liable for tie debts of its owners,[3] and the subject of trade and exciange.

45. Tiougi it is true, as already stated, tiat the power of free alienation is incident to an estate in fee-simple, and a condition altogetier preventing alienation, in a grant of lands or devise of tie same in fee-simple, would be void, as being repugnant to the estate ; [4] yet, if it be only to a limited extent, as to A B and the like, or for a *certain time*, provided it be a reasonable time, tie condition may be a valid one, and the grantee may forfeit iis estate by violating it.[5] A devise to one in fee, but restricting iim from aliening it in any way until tie devisee siould arrive at tie age of thirty-five, was ield to be a valid restriction.[6] But " no one can create wiat is in tie intendment of tie law an estate in fee, and deprive tie tenant of tiose essential rigits and privileges wiici the

---

[1] Wms. Real Prop. 56 ; Bacon's Tracts, 330.   [2] Co. Lit. 43 b.

[3] 3d Stat. Edw. I., *De Mercatoribus*, A. D. 1285.

[4] Lit. § 360 ; 1 Prest. Est. 477 ; Blackstone Bk. *v.* Davis, 21 Pick. 42 ; Bradley *v.* Peixoto, 3 Ves. 324 ; Tud. Cas. 794 : Hall *v.* Tufts, 18 Pick. 455.

[5] Lit. § 361 ; 1 Prest. Est. 478 ; Tud. Cas. 794, 795 ; McWilliams *v.* Nisly, 2 S. & R. 507, 513. See Large's Case, 2 Leon. 82. *Re* Macleay, L. R. 20 Eq. 186, 189. See *post*, *447 *et seq.*

[6] Stewart *v.* Brady, 3 Bush, 623. But see Mandlebaum *v.* McDouell, 27 Mich. 78.

law annexes to it. He cannot make a new estate unknown to the law.[1]

46. So, in a devise to A B and his heirs, there may be a limitation that if he fails to convey it in his lifetime, it shall go over to another devisee named, and the limitation be a valid one.[2]

47. But a condition restricting the right to *alien* to a single person only will be void as repugnant, since the person so selected by grantor or devisor might be one of known incapacity to purchase. And, in short, conditions as to time when, and persons to whom, alienations cannot be made, must be reasonable in order to their being valid.[3]

[*55]   *48. The power of devising lands by will is of a much later origin than of conveying them by deed, except in certain localities in England. The only mode in which it could be done prior to the statute of Henry VIII., hereafter mentioned, was by means of uses. One way of doing this was by conveying them to some one to hold to such uses as the grantor should declare by his last will. And when he had made such declaration, it operated, by the interposition of chancery, to give the beneficial interest in the lands to such devisee.[4]

49. In the words of Lord Bacon, " Lands by the common law of England were not testamentary or devisable ; "[5] and one reason for this was, that the alienation by will could not be consummated by livery of seisin by devisor to devisee.[6]

50. As the statute 27 Henry VIII. united the seisin and the use in the one who was entitled to the use, its effect was to defeat the customary mode of making devises by the way of use. And there was no way of disposing of lands by will

---

[1] Doebler's Appeal, 64 Penn. St. 917.

[2] Doe v. Glover, 1 C. B. 448. But see Ide v. Ide, 5 Mass. 500 ; and *post*, vol. 2, p. *374, where this subject is more fully considered.

[3] Attwater v. Attwater, 18 Beav. 330, overruling Doe v. Pearson, 6 East, 173 ; 1 Prest. Est. 478. The reader will observe that the conditions and restrictions above referred to are of a distinct class from those which affect the mode or purposes of occupation of estates, which belong to another part of this work.

[4] Co. Lit. 111 b, n; 138 ; Wright, Ten. 172, 173 ; 1 Spence, Eq. Jur. 136, 441 ; Bacon's Tracts, 152 ; Perkins, § 538. *Post*, vol. 2, p. *103.

[5] Bacon's Tracts, 316.

[6] Co. Lit. 111 b. n. 138 ; 1 Spence, Eq. Jur. 136, 441.

in fee from that time till the statute 32 Henry VIII. chap. 1, which was explained by the statute 34 and 35 Henry VIII. chap. 5, by which any person having an interest in lands held in socage might devise it by his last will to any person except a body corporate or politic. And as this power had been enjoyed both under the Saxons and Danes, it justified the remark of a writer, that "a will of lands thus again, after an interval of nearly five hundred years, became a legal mode of alienation of lands and hereditaments." [1]

51. It is hardly necessary to add that in respect to the form of aliening estates in fee-simple, what was said in respect to passing freehold, by livery or deed, and by the means of the doctrine of uses, applies to these also. And though, borrowing from the common law, the owner of such an estate " is called a *tenant* because he holdeth of some superior lord by some * service," [2] the term *tenant* is now used [*56] only, in its popular sense, as synonymous with owner.

52. A fee-simple may be had in incorporeal as well as corporeal hereditaments, though in speaking of the one or the other, the owner is said to be seised " in his demesne as of fee " of corporeal, and " seised as of fee " of incorporeal hereditaments; the distinction being that the latter issue out of lands which belong to another than him who owns the right of way, for instance, or whatever the hereditament may be, and in such case the owner of the *easement*, as such a right would be called, has no dominion over or ownership of the land itself, though he may own the easement to himself and his heirs as fully as he could the land. [3]

53. The origin of the use of " heirs " in creating an estate in fee by grant has already been explained, [4] though it has obviously become a mere arbitrary rule. Still, unless changed by statute, it is as imperative, as a rule of law, now as ever. No synonym will supply its place. Even a grant to one and " his *heir* " will give him only a life estate, [5] or to one " *or* his

---

[1] 1 Spence. Eq. Jur. 469; Co. Lit. 111 b, n. 138.

[2] Co. Lit. 1 b.   [3] 2 Bl. Com. 106, 107.   [4] *Ante*, pp. *27, *28.

[5] Co. Lit. 8 b; 2 Prest. Est. 8; Id. 10; Com. Dig., Estate, A. 2. Though this is questioned by some authorities, see 4 Kent, Com. 6, note, and cases cited ; Tud. Cas. 586 ; especially if " heir" can be construed to be *nomen collectivum.* Hargrave, Co. Lit. 8 b, n. 45.

heirs," [1] or to one "and his heirs during the life of another," [2] or to one "forever," or to one "and his assigns forever," and the words "forever," or "assigns," have no effect at this day in limiting or defining what estate is granted.[3] So to one "and his successors," [4] or to one, his successors and assigns, is a life estate only, although coupled with a power to sell and convey a fee,[5] or to one and his "seed," or "his offspring," or to one "and the issue of his body," [6] or to one in "fee-simple," [7] or to one, "his executors, administrators, and assigns." [8] No circumlocution has ever been held sufficient to create a fee.[9]

[*57]   *54. There are what might seem at first sight exceptions to this rule. Thus, if an estate be granted clearly in fee, and the deed by which it is again granted, instead of being to the grantee and his heirs, be to him as fully as it was granted in the former deed referring to it, it is only borrowing the words of limitation from the former deed, and conveys a fee.[10]

55. In the case of conveyances in trust, the trustee will take the legal estate in fee, although limited to him without the word "heirs," if the trust which he is to execute be to the *cestui que trust* and his heirs. The words of limitation and inheritance in such case are connected with the estate of the *cestui que trust*, but are held to relate to the legal estate in the trustee, because without such a construction the trustee would not be able to execute the trust. His estate would be commensurate with the trust, and that only, even though it were to him and his heirs, and the trust was for life only in the

---

[1] Co. Lit, 8 b ; Com. Dig., Estate, A. 2.   [2] 1 Prest. Est. 479.

[3] 2 Bl. Com. 107 ; 2 Prest. Est. 3; Id. 5 ; 1 Spence, Eq. Jur. 139 ; Adams *v.* Ross, 30 N. J. 505, 511.

[4] Co. Lit. 8 b.   [5] Sedgwick *v.* Laflin, 10 Allen, 430.

[6] Wms. Real Prop. 120.

[7] Bridgewater *v.* Bolton, 6 Mod. 106, 109 ; 2 Prest. Est. 5.

[8] Clearwater *v.* Rose, 1 Blackf. 137. In the case of Foster *v.* Joice, 3 Wash. C. C. 498, the deed was "to J. B. and his generation to endure so long as the waters of the Delaware run," and held to be a life estate only. But in Vermont a lease for 1,000 years, or as long as wood grows and water runs, was held to be a fee. Arms *v.* Burt, 1 Vt. 303 ; Stevens *v.* Dewing, 2 Vt. 411.

[9] Adams *v.* Ross, 30 N. J. 512.

[10] Com. Dig., Estate, A. 2, n.; Shep. Touch. 101 ; 2 Prest. Est. 2.

cestui que trust.[1] Thus a grant to A B in trust to sell carries a fee.[2] So, if to A and his heirs in trust for B till he attains twenty-one years, the trustee takes a chattel interest only, and though the trust is to "heirs," if the trustee dies, his executor is to execute the trust, and not his heirs.[3]

56. Legislative grants may convey lands without making use of technical words required in a deed.[4]

57. But still it is essential, in all cases, to the creation of a fee, that it *may* continue forever.[5]

58. A limitation to one and his "right heirs" is the same as to his "heirs" simply; and a limitation directly to the "right heirs" of one carries a fee without adding the words "and their heirs."[6]

*59. There may, too, be such a joint interest in the [*58] fee in lands between two persons, that if one simply releases to the other without words of inheritance, the latter becomes owner in fee of the entire estate; as if a parcener or joint tenant releases to his co-parcener or co-tenant, he extinguishes his own right, leaving the other the sole owner. So if a disseisee release to his disseisor;[7] so if one have a right in fee out of lands owned by another in fee, like a right of way, and he release to the latter.[8]

60. And where tenants in common have partition made of their estate by act of law, each is in, in the part set off to him, in severalty, of the same estate as he had in his undivided share before. But if they make partition by deeds of mutual

---

[1] Newhall *v.* Wheeler, 7 Mass. 189 ; White *v.* Woodberry, 9 Pick. 136 ; Fisher *v.* Fields, 10 Johns. 495, 505 ; *post,* vol. 2, pp. *186, *187 ; Jenkins *v.* Young, Cro. Car. 230 ; North *v.* Philbrook, 34 Me. 532, 537 ; 1 Sand. Uses, 107 ; Gould *v.* Lamb, 11 Met. 84 ; Brooks *v.* Jones, Ib. 191 ; Tiff. & Bul. Trust. 788 *et seq.* ; Hill, Trust. 239 ; Tud. Cas. 459. But see Jackson *v.* Myers, 3 John. 388, 396 ; Sears *v.* Russell, 8 Gray, 86 ; Koenig's Appeal, 57 Penn. St. 352, 355 ; Doe *v.* Considine, 6 Wall. 458, 471 ; 2 Jarm. Wills, 156.

[2] Angell *v.* Rosenbury, 12 Mich. 241, 266 ; Sears *v.* Russell, 8 Gray, 86.

[3] 2 Law Mag. 82 ; Doe *v.* Considine, 6 Wall. 470.

[4] Rutherford *v.* Greene, 2 Wheat. 196.

[5] 1 Prest. Est. 480. The "Rule in Shelley's Case" forms a topic for special consideration hereafter. See *post,* p. *77.

[6] Co. Lit. 10 a, 22 b ; Com. Dig., Estate, A. 2 ; 1 Rolle, Abr. "Estate," L. 8 ; 4 Cruise, 276.

[7] Com. Dig., Estate, A. 2 ; Lit. §§ 519, 520.   [8] 2 Prest. Est. 58.

grant and release, nothing more than a life estate in severalty would pass thereby without words of inheritance.[1]

61. So if one having an estate in fee in remainder or reversion, releases to the tenant for life without words of inheritance, it would give him no more than a life estate.[2]

62. If lands are conveyed to a corporation aggregate, it will, from the nature of such corporations, be understood as a fee without any words of limitation.[3] But if it be to a corporation sole, it must be limited to such corporator and his " successors," which in case of corporations answers to " heirs " in case of grants to natural persons, or it would be only an estate during the life of such corporator.[4]

63. One seised of glebe lands as parson is considered as a corporation sole, and if land be granted to him in his political or artificial capacity, but without being limited to his " successors," he would take but a life estate, although the grant were to him and his heirs.[5]

64. Another broad class of cases form exceptions to
[*59] the rule * requiring a limitation to " heirs " to create an estate of inheritance, and that is where the estate is created by devise. In these cases, the intention of the testator, if clearly expressed by his last will, will be sufficient to create a fee without the use of the word " heirs."[6] Among the illustrations may be mentioned a devise of one's *estate* in such lands, and he owns a fee,[7] or "all " his "right,"[8] or " all " his " property," or " all " his " inheritance,"[9] or to one " in fee-simple."[10]

65. So if it is necessary, in order to give effect to a charge

---

[1] 2 Prest. Est. 56, 58.   The reasons for the difference in this respect between tenants in common and joint tenants will appear hereafter.

[2] 2 Prest. Est. 62.

[3] Wilcox *v.* Wheeler, 47 N. H. 488.

[4] Ang. & Am. Corp. ch. v. § 1 ; Overseers *v.* Sears, 22 Pick. 122, 126 ; Com. Dig., Estate, A. 2 ; 2 Prest. Est. 43 ; Id. 7 ; Wilcox *v.* Wheeler, 47 N. H. 488.

[5] Co. Lit. 8 b ; 2 Prest. Est. 6.

[6] Jarm, Wills, c. 34, p. 229, 1st ed. ; Tud. Cas. 588.

[7] 2 Bl. Com. 108 ; Bridgewater *v.* Bolton, 6 Mod. 106, 109 ; Godfrey *v.* Humphrey, 18 Pick. 537.

[8] Newkerk *v.* Newkerk, 2 Caines, 345.

[9] Jackson *v.* Housell, 17 Johns. 281 ; Wms. Real Prop. 189.

[10] Bridgewater *v.* Bolton, 6 Mod. 106, 109.

or trust created by the same will, to hold the devise a fee, it will be so held.[1]

66. So a fee may be inferred from the nature of the use which devisee is to make of the land; as, a devise of wild lands to one, without any words of inheritance, will be construed to be a fee because a mere tenant for life could make no use of such land. The very using of it by cutting off its timber would work a forfeiture.[2]

67. And upon the same principle, if lands are given to one by will, who is by the same will personally charged with the payment of money on account of such devise, it will be held to be a fee, for the testator intended to make him the object of his bounty; and if he only takes a life estate, he might die the day after paying the money, and so lose the whole benefit of the devise.[3]

68. But if the payment is charged upon the lands only, and not upon the devisee personally, the rule does not apply.[4]

69. To obviate any question in cases like the foregoing, there is now a provision in the English statutes as well as in those * of many, if not all the States, whereby a [*60] devise of land carries whatever estate the devisor had in them, unless the same is restricted or qualified by the language of the will.[5]

70. With far more questionable wisdom in disturbing a well-defined and familiar rule of conveyancing,[6] the States mentioned in a former page[7] have by statute dispensed with words of inheritance in creating a fee.

71. Among the incidents other than the right of alienation

---

[1] Baker v. Bridge, 12 Pick. 27; Wait v. Belding, 24 Pick. 129, 138; Godfrey v. Humphrey, 18 Pick. 537.

[2] Sargent v. Towne, 10 Mass. 303.

[3] 2 Bl. Com. 108, n.; Doe v. Richards, 3 T. R. 356; Jackson v. Merrill, 6 Johns. 185; Lithgow v. Kavenagh, 9 Mass. 161; Wait v. Belding, 24 Pick. 139.

[4] Jackson v. Bull, 10 Johns. 148.

[5] 7 Wm. IV. and 1 Vict. c. 26, § 28; Mass. Pub. Stat. c. 127, § 24. Such is the law in Alabama, Arkansas, Georgia, Iowa, Illinois, Kentucky, Mississippi, Missouri, New York, Tennessee, Texas, Virginia, New Jersey, and North Carolina. See *ante*, p. *31, n. 2. Bell Co. v. Alexander, 22 Tex. 350, 358. So in Nebraska. Rev. Stat. 1866, p. 201.

[6] 2 Prest. Est. 67; 2 Law Mag. 72.

[7] *Ante*, p. *29, n. 2.

belonging to estates in fee-simple at the common law, are curtesy and dower; the one being the right which a husband has in the estate of his wife, if he survive her, the other the right which a wife has in the husband's lands if she survive him, which will be explained in their proper places.[1]

72. Another incident has already been anticipated, and that is, that if not aliened by deed or last will of the owner, estates in fee-simple descend without restriction to whoever is by law his legal heir or heirs, and this, whether the estate be corporeal or incorporeal, in possession, reversion, or remainder, and whether vested or contingent.[2]

73. Lands held in fee-simple are also subject to the debts of the owner, both in England and this country, and as well after his death as while living. This was not an original incident to lands so held. They were first made subject to execution by the statute 13 Edward I. c. 18, though if the ancestor bound his heirs by specialty debts, his lands which had descended to his heirs might have been taken in execution at common law in an action against the heir, unless he had conveyed away those lands before suit brought. [* 61] Among the modes of taking a * debtor's lands were those by statute merchant and statute staple, forms prescribed by statute, one in Edward I., the other in 27 Edward III.[3]

74. This is not the place to speak of the effect of bankrupt or insolvent laws, nor the modes of levying executions upon estates of debtors, though it may be said, in general terms, that lands in this country are liable for debts of the owner, whether due by matter of record, by specialty, or by simple contract. And if they descend to the heir or go to a devisee, he holds them subject to be taken for the payment of the debts of the ancestor, according to the laws of the State in which they are situate.[4]

---

[1] Tud. Cas. 594. The law as to dower has been materially altered by statute in England and in several of the States, as will be shown hereafter.

[2] Tud. Cas. 594. The rules of descent depend upon the local statutes of the several States, and come under another head of this work.

[3] 1 Spence, Eq. Jur. 173, 174. See *post*, c. 15.

[4] Watkins *v.* Holman, 16 Pet. 25, 63 ; 1 Greenl. Cruise, 60, n. ; Wyman *v.* Brigden, 4 Mass. 150.

75. From the definitions heretofore given, it would seem to follow that no estate could be limited to take effect after a fee-simple, as that in its nature is indeterminable. But it will be seen that, under the doctrine of uses and executory devises, this is often done by making a fee-simple determinable upon the happening of some event, and substituting a new estate in its stead.[1]

76. As every estate which may be of perpetual continuance is deemed to be a fee, and may come within the definition of Lord Coke, of a fee-simple absolute, conditional, qualified, or base fee,[2] this seems to be a proper connection in which to treat of them.

77. Though it will be found difficult to classify these by any intelligible line of discrimination, the limit beyond which one may depart from the settled forms of the common law in creating estates with new qualities of inheritance is extremely restricted. Thus an estate to one and his " heirs male," or " heirs female," or to one and his heirs on the part of his father or of his mother, would be regarded as a fee-simple, the limitation to the particular class of heirs being regarded as surplusage.[3]

* 78. A *base fee* is illustrated in " Termes de la Ley " [*62] (Base Fee) by an estate in land so long as another • shall have heirs of his body ; so in Plowd. 557 a.   And Flintoff, following Blackstone, speaks of " a base or qualified fee," using them as convertible terms, and explains it by the familiar illustration of a grant to A and his heirs, tenants of the manor of Dale, the grant being defeated by his heirs ceasing to be such tenants.[4]

79. The term *determinable fee* seems to be more generic in its meaning, embracing all fees which are liable to be determined by some act or event expressed in their limitation to

[1] Com. Dig. (Day's ed.) Estate, A. 4, and note ; Co. Lit. 18 a ; 2 Law Mag. 82.

[2] Prest. Est. 480 ; Co. Lit. 1 b ; 2 Flint. Real Prop. 137.   Judge Kent uses *qualified, base,* and *determinable* fees indiscriminately.   4 Kent, Com. 9.

[3] Lit. § 31 ; Com. Dig., Estate, A. 6 ; 1 Prest. Est. 472 ; Id. 461 ; Co. Lit. 27; Id. 130 ; 2 Law Mag. 68 ; Id. 260.

[4] 2 Flint. Real Prop. 136 ; 2 Bl. Com. 109 ; 1 Spence, Eq. Jur. 144 ; 1 Prest. Conv. 299.

circumscribe their continuance, or inferred by law as bounding their extent.[1]

80. Plowden uses the following language: " Such perpetuity of an estate which may continue forever, though at the same time there is a contingency which, when it happens, will determine the estate, which contingency cannot properly be called a condition but a limitation, may be termed a fee-simple determinable." [2]

81. This description in Plowden answers to what is now denominated " a conditional limitation," as distinguished from an estate upon condition, the estate in one case determining *ipso facto* by the happening of the event by which its limitation is measured; in the other, though liable to be defeated, not being in fact determined until he who has a right to avail himself of the condition enters and determines the estate.[3]

82. And it may be well also, in this connection to observe that, at the common law, the term "conditional fee" often had a technical meaning, and was something different from an estate upon condition, as above explained.   It was applied to those fees which were restricted to some particular heirs, as limitations to one and the heirs of his body, or heirs male of his body, and the like, which, as will be seen hereafter, were,

by the statute *de Donis*, converted into estates tail.[4]

[* 63]   *83. But, in its broader sense, a determinable or qualified fee may embrace what is properly a conditional fee.[5]

84. Among the instances put by way of illustrating a determinable fee, is a limitation to one and his heirs, peers of the realm or lords of the manor of Dale, or so long as a certain tree stands, or until the marriage of a certain person, or till a man shall go to or return from Rome, or till certain debts are paid, or so long as A or his heirs shall pay B a certain sum per annum, or so long as St. Paul's shall stand, or until a prescribed act shall be done, or until a minor shall attain the age

---

[1] 1 Prest. Est. 466 ; Id. 431 ; Seymour's Case, 10 Rep. 97.

[2] Walsingham's Case, Plowd. 557.

[3] Brattle Sq. Church *v.* Grant, 3 Gray, 142, 146, 147 ; 1 Prest. Est. 475.

[4] 2 Bl. Com. 110 ; 2 Prest. Est. 289 ; 1 Prest. Abs. 378.

[5] 1 Prest. Est. 475.

CH. III.]   ESTATES IN FEE-SIMPLE.   95

of twenty-one years, and the like.[1] So a grant to a canal corporation, " as long as used for a canal," was held to be a qualified fee.[2]

85. But a limitation to A and his heirs, during the widow-hood of B, or while C resides at Rome, would only be a life estate and not a fee, because it is measured by the life of a person *in esse*.[3]

86. So long as the estate in fee remains, the owner in possession has all the rights in respect to it, which he would have if tenant in fee-simple, unless it be so limited that there is properly a reversionary right in another, something more than a possibility of reverter belonging to a third person,[4] when, perhaps, chancery might interpose to prevent waste of the premises.[5]

87. An estate to one and his heirs, so long as a tree stands, would be one of those where there is a reversion, because the law contemplates as certain the destruction of the tree at some future time, and, therefore, that there will certainly be an estate in some one other than the tenant and those holding under him, after the happening of that event.[6]

88. On the other hand, if it be to A and his heirs till B comes back from Rome, the right to have it when he comes back is * not a reversion but a mere *possibility;* [*64] he may and may not come back, and if he were to die before he came back, the estate would become absolute in the grantee.[7]

89. A fee determinable will descend in the line of succession of the purchaser, and will determine upon the happening of the event upon which it was first limited, into whosoever hands it may have come.[8]

---

[1] 1 Prest. Est. 442 ; Id. 432 ; Com. Dig. (Day's ed.) Estate, A. 6, n.; Cook *v.* Bisbee, 18 Pick. 529 ; Tud. Cas. 605.

[2] State *v.* Brown, 27 N. J. 20.

[3] 1 Prest. Est. 442 ; McKelway *v.* Seymour, 29 N. J. 329 ; State *v.* Brown, 27 N. J. 13, 20.

[4] Plowd. 557 ; Smith, Real & Pers. Prop. 103 ; 1 Cruise, Dig. 65 ; 1 Atkin. son, Conv. 183.

[5] This remark should not be understood as intending to embrace estates tail. Tud. Cas. 613.   [6] 1 Prest. Est. 440 ; Ayres *v.* Falkland, 1 Ld. Raym. 326.

[7] 1 Prest. Est. 441 ; Id. 440 ; 1 Atk. Conv. 183.

[8] 1 Prest. Est. 440 ; Tud. Cas. 606.

90. And tie same rule applies in cases of estates upon condition; tiey are liable to be defeated by a breaci tiereof, in tie same manner as tiey would iave been in tie iands of tie original grantee as long as tie condition may affect tiem.[1]

91. Tiese estates often may become fee-simple absolute by uniting tiem witi tie reversionary or possible interest in the inieritance, wiici would arise or come into possession if tiey were to determine, or by extinguisiing suci a possibility.

92. Tius in tie case of an estate to A and iis ieirs so long as ie ias ieirs of iis body, wiere if ie dies witiout issue iis estate determines, being a determinable fee. But if tie one wio ias tiis contingent reversionary rigit or possibility release it to tie tenant in possession, it would ciange iis fee determinable into a fee-simple absolute.[2] If it iad been to A and iis ieirs till B returned from Rome, and B. iad died at Rome, tie estate in A would iave become absolute at once. Tie event in suci case is not a condition but a limitation, — tie estate is to endure until ie returns.[3]

93. So if tie estate be expressly one upon condition, and tie condition be performed, tie condition is gone and tie estate is tiereby absolute. Having originally been as to its duration a fee, liable to be defeated if tie condition was not performed, it becomes by tie performance at once a fee-simple absolute.[4] Tie subject of estates in fee upon condition, and tie familiar conditional estates in mortgage, will be resumed in its proper order.

---

[1] 1 Prest. Est. 475 ; 1 Atk. Conv. 183 ; 1 Prest. Abs. 378.
[2] Walsingham's Case, Plowd. 557 ; Ld. Raym. 1148 ; 1 Prest. Est. 482.
[3] 1 Prest. Est. 440–442 ; Tud. Cas. 606.
[4] 1 Prest. Est. 476 ; 1 Atk. Conv. 183.

CHAPTER IV.

ESTATES TAIL.

*1. THE history of estates tail shows that they were [*66] in use among the Saxons, having been borrowed from the laws of Rome, where, by way of *fidei-commissa*, lands migit be entailed upon ciildren and freedmen and tieir descendants, witi restrictions as to alienation. Under tie Saxons tie owner of allodial or *boc-lands* migit convey tiem absolutely, or grant a limited interest in tiem, reserving tie residue of tie ownersiip to iimself, wiici ie migit convey to anotier at iis pleasure. So ie migit settle tiem upon any particular class of descendants in succession. And tie custom of settling lands upon males in preference to females was in use before tie time of Alfred.[1]

2. Tie custom of conveying lands to a man, or a man and iis wife, and tie issue of a particular marriage, or to a man and tie ieirs of iis body, or some particular class of issue, or ieirs, was continued after tie Conquest.[2]

3. Suci a fee or feud as above described was called a *feudum talliatum*, from *tailler*, to cut or mutilate.[3]

4. Wiere an estate was given in suci a form, it was held to be a conditional fee, tiat is, if tie donee siould not iave ieirs or issue according to tie prescribed description, tie land siould revert to tie donor; but if tie condition was performed by tie birti of suci ieirs presumptive, or issue, tie donee was ield to iave a fee-simple, so far tiat ie migit ciarge or alien tie land as a fee-simple estate.[4]

5. Suci was tie case up to tie time of Edward I. [*67] Tiese *were called fees-simple conditional. But tiougi liable to be cianged into fees absolute in tie manner above stated, if tiey descended to tie issue, and tie issue became extinct before alienation made, tiey reverted to tie donor.[5]

6. Previous to tiis time, too, tie nobility and great landed proprietors, in order to preserve tieir lands witiin tieir own

---

[1] Spence, Eq. Jur. 21 ; Barringt. Stat. 113.

[2] 1 Spence, Eq. Jur. 140.   [3] 2 Bl. Com. 112, n.

[4] 1 Spence, Eq. Jur. 141 ; Co. 2d Inst. 333 ; Tud. Cas. 607 ; Co. Lit. 19 a ; 2 Bl. Com. 111. Lord Mansfield said: "I cannot agree with the argument that on the performance of the condition by birth of a child, the estate becomes absolute. It was so by a subtlety in odium of perpetuity and for the special purpose of alienation, but for no other. It otherwise reverted to the donor, on failure of the issue, according to the original restriction." Buckworth v. Thirkell, 3 B. & P. 652, n. ; Ford v. Flint, 40 Vt. 382, 392 ; Finch, 121, 122. "But if the issue fail before the alienation, the donor or giver shall have it."

[5] 1 Spence, Eq. Jur. 141 ; Co. Lit. 19 a, and note 110; 2d Inst. 332.

families, 1ad been accustomed to settle t1em upon their oldest
sons and t1cir issue, and, upon the failure of suc1 issue, upon
t1e second sons and t1cir issue, by way of remainder, and so
on, wit1 restrictions against alienation.   But the adoption of
the doctrine of conditional fees tended to defeat t1is intended
entailment, and caused the barons to appeal to Edward 1. to
restore the ancient law of Alfred for the preservation of
entails.[1]

7. T1is led to the enactment of t1e famous statute *De
Donis Conditionalibus* (13 Edw. 1. Stat. 1, c. 1, § 2).   But
before stating the substance of t1is statute, a brief explanation
is necessary.

8. In tracing t1e 1istory of the descent of estates, we find
t1at children first succeeded to t1e feud in place of t1cir
fat1ers, and grand-c1ildren in the place of c1ildren.   If no
c1ildren, brot1ers mig1t succeed to brot1ers, if the feud was
an *ancient* one.   The admission of collateral relations of the
blood of the first feudatory was t1e last step in the law of descent.[2]   " Heirs," t1erefore, as at first used, meant the issue of
t1e tenant or vassal, to the exclusion of all collateral relations.
But by the time of Henry 11., collateral kindred had been
admitted as 1eirs, and if a donor wis1ed to confine t1e inheritance to t1e offspring of t1e donee, 1e was obliged to limit it
expressly to 1im and t1e 1eirs of 1is body.[3]

9. T1is was construed a conditional fee, as is above stated.
And t1ere was one ot1er conditional estate of in1eritance
w1ic1 is referred to in t1e statute, and it is mentioned here in
order to explain it, and t1at was *frank marriage*, w1ic1
applied to a case *w1ere a fat1er or kinsman, upon a [*68]
person marrying his daug1ter or cousin, gave t1em
lands, and it was understood to be upon the condition t1at
t1ese were to descend to t1e issue of suc1 marriage, if any.
If t1e donees 1ad issue, the condition was considered as
1aving been performed, and t1e estate t1ereby became alienable.[4]

10. The statute *De Donis* recites, by way of preamble, the
custom of giving lands to a man and 1is wife and to the 1eirs

[1] 1 Spence, Eq. Jur. 141.   [2] Wright, Ten. 16–18 ; 2 Bl. Com. 220-222.
[3] 2 Bl. Com. 221 ; Wms. Real Prop. 31, 32.   [4] 1 Cruise, Dig. 71.

begotten of their bodies, with an express condition of reverter upon the failure of such heirs. Also the custom of giving lands in frank marriage which contains an implied condition of reverter if the husband and wife die without heirs of their bodies, and also of giving land to another and the heirs of his body issuing. It then recites the custom above referred to, of aliening lands after issue born, " to disinherit their issue of the land contrary to the minds of the givers, and *contra formam in dono expressam.*" It then declares, in substance, that the will of the giver, according to the form in the deed of gift manifestly expressed (*secundum formam in charta doni sui*), should from henceforth be observed, so that, among other things, they to whom the land was given under such condition should have no power to alien the land so given, but it should remain unto the issue of them to whom it was given after their death, or should revert unto the giver or his heirs, if issue fail, &c.[1]

11. The effect of this was, to divide the entire inheritance into two parts or estates, namely, the estate tail and the reversion or remainder in fee expectant upon the failure of the estate tail.[2]

12. In translating this statute from the Latin in which it was written, the word *lands* is used where the original word was *tenementum,* which, in fact, embraces not only corporeal hereditaments, but incorporeal also, which issue out of or are annexed to those that are corporeal, such as rents, estovers, and commons, though they cannot be said to lie in tenure.[3]

[*69]   *13. But an ownership merely personal, or such as is to be exercised about chattels, cannot be the subject of entailment.[4]

14. The statute *De Donis* was regarded by the courts as a remedial one, and instead of confining it to the precise cases enumerated in it, they regarded these as put by way of ex-

---

[1] 2d Inst. 332, 333 ; 2 Prest. Est. 378.

[2] Atk. Conv. 194. This statute, commonly known as that of Westminster 2, is generally supposed to have introduced estates tail into the English law. But it would be more accurate to say that it established them there. Barringt. St. 113.

[3] 2 Bl. Com. 113 ; Co. Lit. 19 b.

[4] 2 Bl. Com. 113 ; Co. Lit. 20 a, and note 120.

ample. And the effect of it was to introduce a new class of
estates or give a different quality to an old one.[1] It was considered as designed to preserve the property and maintain the
grandeur of existing powerful families, by securing to owners
of estates the liberty to dispose of such parts thereof as came
under the denomination of *tenements*, in such manner, and
by such an order of succession, as their own inclination or
ingenuity might devise.[2]

15. The statute, in its several bearings, was slowly developed, and it was not until the time of Edward III. that it was
settled that an estate limited to one and the heirs male of his
body, would be confined in its descent to males alone. And
it was long doubted whether an entailment to heirs female
could keep the succession in the line of females tracing
descent through females.[3]

16. The fruits of these entailments at last began to manifest themselves. Children, being independent of their parents,
grew disobedient. Creditors could no longer enforce payment
out of the lands of their debtors. Lands were withdrawn from
commerce, or purchasers were defrauded by secret entails.
And the crown even lost its restraint upon treasonable prac-
tices through the terror of forfeitures, until at length the desire grew general to rid the land of a law fraught with so
many evils.

17. Every attempt, however, to change the law was met by
the resistance of powerful landholders, for whose benefit it
had been made, and it was only after an endurance of two
hundred years that, by a contrivance of the courts and a bold
measure of judicial legislation, this act of Parliament was
evaded by enabling the tenant to change his fee-tail into a
fee-simple.[4]

*18. This was accomplished, to a limited extent, by [*70]
means of levying fines, but fully and completely by

---

[1] 2 Prest. Est. 380; Id. 453.

[2] 2 Bl. Com. 116 ; 2 Prest. Est. 453.   [3] 2 Prest. Est. 453.

[4] Taltarum's Case, Year Book, 12 Edw. IV. 19 ; 2 Bl. Com. 116 ; Wms. Real
Prop. 39 ; 2 Prest. Est. 454 ; Tud. Cas. 608 ; 10 Rep. 37 a. This was done, says
Spence, by the judges in the reign of Edw. IV., "in the exercise of their Pre-
torian authority." 1 Spence, Eq. Jur. 143.

means of common recoveries. These were borrowed from the
"*cessio in jure*" of the Roman law.[1] These, though now abolished in England by the statutes 3 & 4 Wm. IV. c. 74, and,
so far as fines are concerned, having prevailed in this country
in but very few of the States, and as to recoveries to a certain
extent only, have played too important a part for centuries, in
English conveyancing, to be passed over unnoticed. Fines are
said to have been in use from a very early period of the English history. They consisted of a suit brought between actually litigating parties, where, by permission of the court, they
entered a final agreement, *finalis concordia*, upon the record,
which was binding upon them like any judgment of court.
When applied to bar entails, the person to whom it was to be
conveyed, acting in collusion with the tenant, brought a feigned
action against him for the land. The *finalis concordia*, of
course, was thereupon entered into between them, for form,
and became a matter of record, whereby the claimant's right
to the land was admitted and established. The statute *De
Donis* declared that such fines should not bar entails. But
one passed 4 Hen. VII., and one in 32 Hen. VIII., allowed
them to bar heirs claiming under the entail.[2]

19. The process above described was called "levying a
fine," and was much in use in barring adverse claims by "non
claim," as it was called. But the mode of barring estates tail
which came into use after Taltarum's Case (12 Edw. IV. A. D.
1472), and the only effectual mode, was a common recovery.
This, too, it seems, had been in use before the statute *De
Donis*, and had been contrived as a mode of evading the statutes of mortmain; but was put an end to for that purpose by
the statute 13 Edw. I. c. 32.[3] This was a fictitious suit

---

[1] Maine, Anc. L. 289 ; Gaius, C. I. § 134, n.; C. II. § 24.

[2] 1 Spence, Eq. Jur. 143 ; 2 Flint, Real Prop. 673 ; Shelf. R. P. Stat. 275 ;
Tud. Cas. 689. A case of the levy of a fine occurred in New York in 1827.
Fines were abolished there in 1830. McGregor *v.* Comstock, 17 N. Y. 162. Fines
and recoveries were abolished in New Jersey in 1799 ; Croxall *v.* Shererd, 5
Wall. 268 ; but fines were in force in Pennsylvania in 1837 ; 4 Kent, Com. 497,
note ; Richman *v.* Lippincott, 29 N. J. 44. They never were known in Missouri.
Moreau *v.* Detchemendy, 18 Mo. 527.

[3] Wms. Real Prop. 39 ; 2 Bl. Com. 271; 1 Spence, Eq. Jur. 144, n.; Tud.
Cas. 607.

brought in the name of the person who was to purchase the estate, against the tenant in tail who was willing to convey. The tenant, instead of resisting this claim himself, under the pretence that he had *acquired his title of [*71] some third person who had warranted it, vouched in, or, by a process from the court, called this third person, technically the *vouchee*, to come in and defend the title. The vouchee came in as one of the *dramatis personæ* of this judicial farce, and then without saying a word disappeared and was defaulted. It was a principle of the feudal law adopted thence by the common law, that if a man conveyed lands with a warranty, and the grantee lost his estate by eviction by one having a better title, he should give his warrantee lands of equal value by way of recompense. And as it would be too barefaced to cut off the rights of reversion as well as of the issue in tail, by a judgment between the tenant and a stranger, it was gravely adjudged, 1st, that the claimant should have the land as having the better title to it; and 2d, that the tenant should have judgment against his vouchee to recover lands of equal value on the ground that he was warrantor, and thus, theoretically, nobody was harmed. If the issue in tail or the reversioner, or remainder-man, lost that specific estate, he was to have one of equal value through this judgment in favor of the tenant in tail, whereas in fact the vouchee was an irresponsible man, and it was never expected that he was anything more than a *dummy* in the game.[1] The result of this, which Blackstone calls " a kind of *pia fraus* to elude the statute *De Donis*,"[2] and another writer " a piece of solemn juggling,"[3] was that the lands passed from the tenant in tail to the claimant in fee-simple, free from the claims of reversioner, remainder-man, or issue in tail, and he either paid the tenant for it as a purchaser, or conveyed it back to him again in fee-simple.[4]

[1] 2 Flint, Real Prop. 673, 674 ; 1 Spence, Eq. Jur. 143.
[2] 2 Bl. Com. 117.　　　　　　　　[3] Wms. Real Prop. 41.
[4] 1 Spence, Eq. Jur. 144. Taltarum's Case is reported in Year Book, 12 Edw. IV. 19, and is translated into English in Tud. Cas. 562. See Shelf. R. P. Stat. 276. A similar proceeding prevailed in the Roman law under the name of *cessio in jure*, and with the same effect as at common law. Maine, Anc. L. 289.

19 *a.* A common recovery by a tenant in tail has the effect to bar his estate tail and all remainders over and the reversion depending on that estate, and all conditions and collateral limitations annexed to the same estate.[1] And it is held that an executory devise may be destroyed by a common recovery suffered by the tenant in tail, which enlarges his estate into a fee, and excludes all subsequent limitations, whether in remainder or by way of springing use or executory devise.[2] So a recovery suffered by a tenant for life will cut off a contingent, but not a vested remainder.[3]

20. The right thus acquired of barring them seems to have become, in the theory of the law, an inherent, inseparable incident to estates tail, so that any attempt to restrain the [*72] exercise *of it by the tenant, by covenant or condition, was futile, as such restraint was held to be void.[4]

21. The consequence was, that the possibility of entailing estates in England for any considerable length of time was and still is practically done away with. To accomplish it requires frequent resettlements of the estate on successive generations, by means of marriage settlements, which have become, in consequence, a very common measure there. In this country, estates tail, as a distinctive class, are abolished in many of the States. In others, where they are still retained, they may be barred, usually, by a simple deed by the tenant, — it being the policy of the law in both countries to favor the free alienation of all kinds of property.[5] The deed of an infant or *non compos* tenant in tail may be impeached, but a judgment against such tenant in suffering a recovery could not be collaterally.[6]

22. Estates tail, then, are estates of inheritance, which, instead of descending to heirs generally, go to the heirs of the donee's body, which means his lawful issue, his children, and through them to his grandchildren in a direct line, so long as his posterity endures in a regular order and course of descent,

---

[1] 2 Prest. Est. 460 ; Pigott, Recoveries, 21 ; Page *v.* Hayward, 2 Salk. 570.

[2] Taylor *v.* Taylor, 63 Penn. St. 481.

[3] Doe *v.* Gatacre, 5 Bing. N. C. 609.

[4] Co. Lit. 379 b, n. 300 ; 1 Spence, Eq. Jur. 144, n.

[5] Wms. Real Prop. 45, 46.   [6] Wood *v.* Bayard, 63 Penn. St. 320.

and, upon t1e extinction of suc1 issue, t1e estate determines.[1] A devise to one's sons, and, in case any one of t1em dies unmarried or wit1out issue, 1is s1are to be divided among the survivors, creates an estate tail in eac1 son, wit1 remainders over to t1e survivors.[2] So w1ere t1e devise was to a daug1ter, but if she died wit1out 1eirs, t1en to go to 1er brot1er, it was 1eld to mean 1eirs of her body, because if to her 1eirs generally, 1er brot1er would be one of t1ese, and take by descent.[3]

23. T1e one who makes t1e estate is called t1e *donor;* 1e to w1om it is made the *donee.* In order to create an estate tail t1ere must be a limitation in express terms or by direct reference not only to *heirs*, but to 1eirs of the donee's body. If it be to a man and 1is *heir*, it will not ordinarily pass an estate of in1eritance, t1oug1 in a will it may, on the ground of carrying out the devisor's intention.[4]

24. An instance of an estate tail by construction, w1ere t1ere is no direct limitation to t1e 1eirs of the donee's body, would be an estate to A, wit1 a proviso t1at if 1e s1all die wit1out 1eirs of 1is body, t1e estate s1all revert to the donor or go over to one in remainder. Here, it will be perceived, t1ere was no direct limitation to t1e 1eirs of A, and it is too plain for doubt * t1at t1e donor intended t1e [*73] 1eirs of 1is body s1ould take it at 1is decease, for 1e gives it over, or reserves it, in case 1e 1as no suc1 1eirs, and only in t1at contingency.[5]

25. But if the gift be to A and 1is 1eirs, so long as 1e, or some ot1er person named, 1as 1eirs of 1is body, it is a fee-simple determinable, and not an estate tail. The 1eirs w1o may take are unlimited, but t1e duration of t1eir estate is limited and measured by t1e lengt1 of time t1at t1e line of succession of 1eirs of the donee's body, or of t1e ot1er person named, may last.[6]

26. And a deed to A and 1is 1eirs of lands, to 1ave and to

---

[1] 2 Prest. Est. 360, 374 ; 1 Id. 451 ; Wms. Real Prop. 30.
[2] 1atlack v. Roberts, 54 Penn. St. 148 ; Allen v. Trustees, 102 1ass. 262.
[3] Fahrney v. Holsinger, 65 Penn. St. 388 ; Shutt v. Rambo, 57 Penn. St. 149.
[4] 1 Prest. Est. 451 ; 2 Prest. Est. 397, 398 ; White v. Collins, Com. 289.
[5] Perkins, § 173 ; Allen v. Trustees, 102 1ass. 262.
[6] 2 Prest. Est. 358–360 ; Id. 361 ; 2 BL Com. 113.

1old (*habendum*), to t1e 1eirs of 1is body, limits and qualifies
t1e estate ot1erwise a fee-simple, and reduces it to an estate
tail, defining in effect in t1e second clause w1at was meant
by " 1eirs " in t1e first.[1] So a limitation to A B and 1is
1eirs, and if 1e die wit1out issue of 1is body, t1en remainder
over to some ot1er person, it would by t1is clause, as to issue
of 1is body, be understood as restricting t1e general word
heirs to 1eirs or issue of t1e donee's body.[2]

27. On t1e ot1er 1and, if t1e first grant 1ad been to A and
t1e 1eirs of 1is body, wit1 t1e *habendum* to A and 1is 1eirs,
wit1out any terms of restriction, t1e courts, in order to give
effect to bot1 clauses, if possible, would hold t1at 1e first
creates an estate tail, and t1at so long as 1e 1as issue to take
t1ey will take as tenants in tail.   But if at any time suc1 line
of issue fail, t1en t1e estate would go to 1is 1eirs generally,
so t1at 1e is said to take an estate tail *in præsenti*, wit1 an
estate in fee-simple in expectancy.[3]

28. Muc1 t1at 1as been said in a former c1apter in relation
to fees being determinable upon t1e 1appening of some event,
applies to fees tail, as w1ere an estate is limited to
[*74] one and t1e 1eirs of 1is * body, so long as a tree s1all
stand, or until A s1all return from Rome, or until t1e
donee or some t1ird person s1all do some prescribed act.   So
t1e estate may be defeasible by t1e 1appening of some condition.   So it may be limited to one and t1e 1eirs of 1is body,
tenants of t1e manor of Dale, and t1e like.   The same rule
applies in t1ese cases as 1as been stated, 1eretofore, in relation
to fees-simple determinable and upon condition, as to t1e estate
being defeated or defeasible t1ereby.[4]

29. It 1as already been stated t1at an estate tail is one of
in1eritance, and t1erefore cannot exist in respect to a mere
free1old estate for life or in a c1attel interest.   And a limitation in terms w1ic1 would create an estate tail if applied

[1] 2 Prest. Est. 509 ; Altham's Case, 8 Rep. 154 b.

[2] Per Ld. Holt, Idle *v.* Cooke, 2 Ld. Raym. 1152; Brice *v.* Smith, Willes, 1;
Hulburt *v.* Emerson, 16 Mass. 241 ; 2 Prest. Est. 519 ; Hayward *v.* Howe, 12
Gray, 49 ; Gifford *v.* Choate, 100 Mass. 343, 345.

[3] Perkins, § 168 ; Co. Lit. 21 a ; Altham's Case, 8 Rep. 154 b ; Corbin *v.*
Healy, 20 Pick. 514.

[4] 2 Prest. Est. 362 ; Id. 446.

to real estate would vest the whole interest absolutely in the first taker if employed as to chattels or chattel interests in lands, and a limitation of chattels over to the issue of the first taker would be void, because the statute *De Donis* applies only to lands and tenements.[1]

30. In all cases where the heirs of a donee in tail take the estate, they do so by descent and not by purchase. But the heirs in such case do not claim the estate as coming from their ancestor as its source, but as an estate coming through him as special heir, which he cannot intercept except in the mode provided by law.[2] But if the limitation were to the heirs of the body of A, whoever answers to that description would take as purchasers, and the estate would then descend to the same issue and in the same order of succession as if the estate had been limited to A and the heirs of his body.[3]

31. Under the doctrine of entails, the form of the gift, rather than the general canons of descent of estates, is to be referred to, to determine the line of succession in which the estate is to pass.[4] It is therefore requisite, in order to create such an estate, that, in addition to the word heirs, there should be words of procreation which indicate the body from which these heirs are to proceed, or the person by whom begotten. If this is *done, it may not be necessary [*75] to make use of the words "of the body," if, by the description, it appears that they are to be the issue of a particular person.[5] A general limitation to a man and the heirs of his body is sufficient, it being immaterial of whom begotten.[6]

32. The form of limiting the estate, whether it be to one

---

[1] 2 Bl. Com. 113 ; Whitmore *v.* Weld, 1 Vern. 326 and 343, n. ; Co. Lit. 20 a, and n. 120 ; Child *v.* Baylie, Cro. Jac. 461 ; Atkinson *v.* Hutchinson, 3 P. Wms. 258 ; 2 Jarm. Wills, 489, and Perkins's note ; Britton *v.* Twining, 3 Mer. 176, 183 ; Stockton *v.* Martin, 2 Bay, 471 ; Wms. Ex. 565 ; Id. 949 ; *ante,* pl. 12, 13. Albee *v.* Carpenter, 12 Cush. 382.　But see Forth *v.* Chapman, 1 P. Wms. 663 ; Hall *v.* Priest, 6 Gray, 18, 22 ; that a different construction may be given to the words "leaving no issue." *Post,* vol. 2 *365·

[2] Perry *v.* Kline, 12 Cush. 127.　　　　　　[3] 2 Prest. Est. 360 ; Id. 375.

[4] 2 Prest. Est. 375.

[5] 2 Prest. Est. 478 ; Co. Lit. 20 b ; 2 Bl. Com. 115.

[6] 2 Prest. Est. 412.

and tie ieirs of iis body begotten, or to suci ieirs to be begotten, is immaterial, for in tie former case it would extend to ciildren born after tie gift, and in tie latter would embrace tiose already born.[1]

33. Tie estates tius far spoken of come witiin tie class of estates tail general, wiici are suci as are limited to a man and tie ieirs of iis body witiout any furtier specification. But tiere is a class of tiese wiici are called estates tail special, wiere tie limitation is to some particular class of ieirs of tie body of tie donee, as to tiose begotten on iis wife Mary, and tie like. So it may be to tie ieirs male or female of tie body of tie donee, making an estate tail male or an estate tail female. Suci limitations as tiese confine tie inieritance to tie special issue prescribed, and none otier can succeed to it. Tius, if tie estate be limited to a man and tie ieirs of iis body by iis first wife, and sie die witiout issue, no issue by any otier wife could claim tie inheritance.[2]

34. If, for instance, tie gift be to A and tie ieirs of iis body, on iis wife Mary begotten, it presupposes tiat ie tien ias a wife of tiat name. And if suci is not tie case, tie gift would fail. But if it be to A and tie ieirs of tie body of B iis wife, wio is dead, it is an estate tail, if tiere are any issue of tiat wife living wien tie gift is made. But if tiere are no suci issue living, instead of iis becoming tenant in tail, ie is merely tenant for iis own life. He is not even tenant in tail after possibility of issue extinct, wiici will be iereafter explained.[3]

35. In order to iave a limitation in special tail good [*76] wiere *tie issue is to be begotten of some woman named, sie must eitier be tie donee's wife or one wio by possibility may become suci. If, for instance, sie was so near akin to tie donee as to render it unlawful for tiem to marry, tie estate would be in him only for life.[4]

---

[1] 2 Prest. Est. 449, 450.

[2] 2 Bl. Com. 113, 114 ; 1 Spence, Eq. Jur. 141 ; 2 Prest. Est. 413, 414, 420.

[3] 2 Prest. Est. 414 ; Co. Lit. 27 a, n. 155 ; *post*, p. *83.

[4] 2 Prest. Est. 417.

36. But it is immaterial how improbable it may be that the donee may ever marry the woman named, or impossible that if married they should ever have issue. Thus, suppose the donee is married at the time, and the woman named is the wife of another, it is enough that possibly his wife and the husband of the other woman may die, and he and she may intermarry and have issue, however improbable. So if the donee and the woman named are married at the time of the gift, and the estate is limited to him and the heirs of his body on such wife begotten, it would be an estate tail, though she was at the time an hundred years old, and would not be an estate tail after possibility of issue extinct so long as the parties named are living.[1]

37. Where the limitation is to one and the heirs male, or to him and the heirs female of his body, it confines the inheritance to the one line and excludes the other from the succession. So that whoever claims by descent must be able to trace his or her line back to the donee through males altogether or females altogether. And this case is put by way of illustration. Estate to A and the heirs male of his body, remainder to the heirs female of his body. Here there are two lines. If the males run out, the estate will then go by way of remainder to his heirs female. If then the donee were to have a son who has a daughter who has a son, this son last named could take nothing, since, being a male, he cannot trace through his mother, and she, being a female, could not trace through her father, and the land in such a case would revert to the donor. Had the remainder been to the heirs of his body generally, it might have descended in the case supposed to the great-grandson of the donee.[2]

38. In regard to making use of proper technical terms in *creating estates tail by deed and by will, the [*77] same rules of strictness or latitude apply as in the manner of estates in fee-simple. Thus a grant to a man and his heirs male, by deed, would be construed to create a fee-simple for want of the requisite words, "of his body," or their

---

[1] Id. 395.

[2] Co. Lit. 25 b ; 2 Bl. Com. 114 ; 2 Prest. Est. 402, 403; Wms. Real Prop. 30; Hulburt v. Emerson, 16 Mass. 241.

equivalent. But if it had been by will, the law, to carry out testator's intention, would supply these words and regard it a fee-tail.[1]

39. Among the illustrations given of estates tail having been created by deed without the use of the words, "of the body," but with words regarded as equivalent, are — to A and his heirs, namely, the heirs of his body — or of himself lawfully issuing or begotten — or of his flesh, or of his wife, begotten, — or which he shall happen to have or beget.[2]

40. And yet if the word " heirs " is wanting, the estate is only one for life, though terms of entailment even stronger than those above mentioned were used. Thus a grant to A and his issue of his body, or to him and his seed, or to him and his children or offspring, would only create an estate for life, provided the estate be created by deed.[3]

41. So a gift to A and his eldest son and heir male of the said A begotten was held not to be an estate tail, the words " heir male " being qualified, explained, and limited to be the same thing as son, a description of the person to take, and not a term of limitation and inheritance.[4]

42. But where the gift was by *devise* to a man and his seed, or his heirs male, or his children, if he then have none, or to him and his posterity, or by other words showing an intention to restrain the inheritance to the descendants of the devisee, it would create an estate tail.[5] Thus a devise to J S and his heirs if he should have lawful issue, but if he die without issue then over, would create an estate tail in J S.[6]

43. There is a rule in respect to the nature of estates, which prevails in England and in several of these States, though abrogated by statute in others, called the Rule in Shelley's Case, which has given rise to questions of no little [*78] nicety and * refinement in respect to estates tail, which it seems proper to allude to here, although it is treated

---

[1] 2 Bl. Com. 115 ; Co. Lit. 27 a ; 2 Prest. Est. 536.

[2] Co. Lit. 20 b ; 2 Prest. Est. 485.

[3] 2 Prest. Est. 480.   [4] 2 Prest. Est. 481, 482.

[5] 2 Bl. Com. 115; Id. 381 ; 2 Prest. Est. 537; Nightingle v. Burrell, 15 Pick. 104. But if the first gift is for life, the children take only a remainder. Taylor v. Taylor, 63 Penn. St. 481, 488.

[6] Arnold v. Brown, 7 R. I. 188.

more at large in another part of the work. Thus, if an estate be given to a man for life, remainder to his heirs or to the heirs of his body, instead of this being, as it apparently is, and as, by statute, it is declared to be in many of the United States, an estate for life, remainder to the heirs of the tenant for life, it is held that the word *heirs* is intended to denote the extent and character of the estate which the first taker has, — in other words, that it is a term of limitation and not of purchase, and if the heir takes it all, he takes by descent and not by purchase.[1] It was held in New Jersey that a grant to a married woman for life, and at her death to her children, of her by her husband begotten, was an estate tail in the wife, nor would it enlarge it to a fee, although the covenants in the deed were to her and her heirs generally.[2] Of course, to bring a case within the rule, the limitation to the heirs must be to heirs who would take the entire estate limited to the first taker. For if, for instance, the first estate be limited to A and B, and the limitation over be to the heirs of B, it turns the estate of A and B at once into a joint-life estate, and the heirs of B would take as purchasers or remainder-men, for they could not take by descent, being heirs only of one.[3]

44. Now, to apply this rule in cases of limitation of an estate to husband and wife and their heirs in tail, the question usually is, are these heirs the heirs of the body of the two or of one only of them, because in one case the heirs take, if at all, by descent within the rule in Shelley's Case, — in the other as remainder-men and purchasers. If the gift is to the husband and his heirs which he shall beget on the body of his wife, it creates in him an estate tail, while his wife takes no estate by the gift. If the remainder be limited to the heirs of the body of the wife by the husband to be begotten, she is the one who takes an estate tail, and not the husband. But if it be to A and his wife, and their heirs on the body of the wife begotten, they both take estates tail. And in all these

---

[1] The reader will bear in mind that there are only two ways of acquiring real estate, one by *descent*, the other by *purchase*. If a man does not take as *heir*, he takes by *purchase*, no matter how he acquires his title.

[2] Ross *v.* Adams, 28 N. J. 160, 168.

[3] 2 Prest. Est. 441, 442.

[*79] cases the heirs take, if at all, by descent,[1] * and not by
purchase, while the limitation to the heirs will vest an
estate tail in that ancestor with reference to whom the word
heirs is used.   If the estate is given to both husband and wife,
each has a life estate, and if the one whose heirs are to take
dies first, his heirs take an estate tail in remainder after the
death of the other tenant.[2]

45. On the other hand, if the estate be to husband for life,
or wife for life, remainder to the heirs of the bodies of husband and wife, the heirs take as purchasers and not by descent; and the same would be the case if the limitation were
to husband or to wife and the heirs of the bodies of husband
and wife.[3]

46. And it may be remarked, in passing, that for reasons
hereafter explained, such a remainder would be a contingent
one, so long as the parent whose heirs were to take, lived, because, as, *nemo est hæres viventis,* the person who is to take
as heir could not be ascertained till the parent's death.[4]

47. And it may be further remarked that at common law,
if by a devise an estate is so limited to heirs that they will
take it, if at all, by descent from one to whom the life estate is
given, and the estate to the latter fails by lapsing in consequence of his dying during the life of the testator, the estate
to the heir fails also; whereas, if it had been to them as purchasers, the death of the ancestor would not affect the gift to
the heirs of the body.[5]

48. Among the incidents of estates tail, the tenant may freely
commit waste upon the premises as if he were tenant in fee-
simple,[6] though he cannot by selling growing timber, authorize

---

[1] The term *descent*, as used in this chapter in connection with the transmission
of an estate to the issue in tail upon decease of the ancestor, tenant in tail, is intended to indicate that he takes it as an estate of inheritance in tail, and as being
of the prescribed line of issue or inheritance, and not simply from his intermediate ancestor, since he takes *per formam doni* from the person who first created the
estate.   1 Cruise, Dig. 83; Partridge *v.* Dorsey, 3 Har. & J. 302; Perry *v.* Kline,
12 Cush. 118, 127.

[2] 2 Prest. Est. 443, 483; Denn *v.* Gillot, 2 T. R. 431.

[3] 2 Prest. Est. 441, 442.

[4] Frogmorton *v.* Wharrey, 2 W. Bl. 728, 730; s. c. 3 Wils. 144.

[5] 2 Prest. Est. 442; Burrage *v.* Briggs, 120 Mass. 103.

[6] Co. Lit. 224 a; 1 Atk. Conv. 195; Jervis *v.* Bruton, 2 Vern. 251.

it to be cut after 1is decease, it being a rig1t belonging to 1im only as tenant.[1]

49. Dower and curtesy are also incidents of t1is as of estates * in fee-simple,[2] and alt1oug1 the tenant may [*80] not c1arge the estate by 1is agreements or wit1 1is debts or incumbrances, so as to affect it after his deat1,[3] it is now, by statute, made liable to a limited extent for the debts of the tenant, and may be sold by assignees in bankruptcy or insolvency of t1e tenant, to the same extent as he could 1ave disposed of it.[4]

50. If t1ere are outstanding c1arges or incumbrances upon the estate, t1e tenant is not bound to pay t1em off ; and it 1as been 1eld t1at 1e was not compellable by t1e reversioner or remainder-man to keep down the interest, except in special cases, alt1oug1 it is incumbent upon a tenant for life to do so. And t1e reason appears to be t1at equity considers the estate as 1is own, and t1at 1e may keep down t1e incumbrance or lose the estate as he pleases. But if he does pay it off, 1e is considered as doing it on 1is own account, and cannot by so doing make 1imself creditor of the estate for t1e amount, unless 1e takes an assignment to 1imself of t1e incumbrance w1ic1 1e pays.[5]

51. As a proposition almost universal, w1ere a greater and less estate come toget1er in one person by t1e same rig1t, wit1out any intervening estate, t1ey will unite in one, the lesser being merged or swallowed up in t1e greater. But t1is does not apply in case of estates tail. If t1e tenant acquire t1e reversion or remainder in fee-simple, it does not merge t1e limited estate w1ic1 1e 1as as tenant in tail. And t1is grows out of the statute *De Donis,* w1ic1 meant to restrain 1im as tenant from passing t1is estate out of 1im, w1ic1 1e mig1t

---

[1] Liford's Case, 11 Rep. 50.   [2] Co. Lit. 224 a.

[3] Wharton *v.* Wharton, 2 Vern. 3, and n. ; 1 Atk. Conv. 197 ; Herbert *v.* Fream, 2 Eq. Cas. Abr. 28, § 34 ; Partridge *v.* Dorsey, 3 Har. & J. 302 ; 1 Cruise, Dig. 84.

[4] Tud. Cas. 614 ; 1 Atk. Conv. 198.

[5] 1 Cruise, Dig. 75 ; Tud. Cas. 638 ; Chaplin *v.* Chaplin, 3 P. Wms. 229 ; 2 Law Mag. 265, 266, 270. See, as to equity appointing receivers to collect rents and keep down the interest on incumbrances upon estates tail, Story's Eq. § 835 ; Jeremy, Eq. Jur. 251, 252 ; Bertie *v.* Abingdon, 3 Mer. 560.

easily ave done if by is acquiring te reversionary interest
it ad merged in te reversion.[1]

52. So long as an estate retains te ciaracter of an
[*81] estate * tail, it will descend, in due course of law, to
te issue of te donee, wo answer te requisite description, owever remote in degree, from te person to wom
te gift may ave been originally made, eaci of wom in succession will be tenants in tail, wit all te powers and rigits
wici te common ancestor, te donee, ad in respect to te
estate, so long as tere may by possibility be issue to answer
to tis description.[2]

53. In England, te course of descent of estates in fee-
simple and fee tail general, is te same by te common law;
as for. example, to te oldest son, if te ancestor ave sons.[3]
And te same rule applies in tis country, were te subject
is not regulated by statute, te oldest son of te donee and is
oldest son, and so on, taking in succession.[4]

54. And yet tis tieoretic perpetuity of succession as
practically little effect. By te ease wit wici estates tail
may be barred and converted into fees-simple, strict and continuous entails ave long since been virtually abolisied in
England; and te remark applies wit greater force in tis
country, were, as will be seen, not only may tey, were tey
exist, be barred wit equal facility, but in many States suci
estates ave been wiolly abolisied.[5]

55. Te mode of effectually barring tiese estates or converting tiem into estates in fee-simple was formerly by common recoveries, wici as already been spoken of. Since
tiese ave been abolisied in England, it may be done by deed
executed by te tenant in tail and enrolled in ciancery witiin
six montis after its execution. Te form and effect of tis is
regulated by te statute 3 and 4 Wm. IV. c. 74, wici makes
provision, in certain cases, for guarding against injustice being done to parties in interest, by requiring te assent of a

---

[1] Wiscot's Case, 2 Rep. 61; 1 Atk. Conv. 194; Roe v. Baldwere, 5 T. R. 104,
110; Poole v. ᑎorris, 29 Ga. 374.

[2] 2 Prest. Est. 394; Wms. Real Prop. 53; Corbin v. Healy, 20 Pick. 514.

[3] Wms. Real Prop. 63; Id. 45.

[4] Corbin v. Healy, 20 Pick. 514; Wight v. Thayer, 1 Gray, 284.

[5] Wms. Real Prop. 64; post, *84.

person called a protector to such sale, in order to its being an effectual bar. But its great length renders it neces- sary to refer the reader to the *statute itself for its [*82] various provisions.[1] The mode of barring estates tail in this country will be noticed by itself.

56. Although this may not be the place to treat of it at large, it may be proper, in this connection, to say that it is very common in England to create a temporary entailment of lands in the donor's family by means of marriage settle- ments, which may extend through one generation, and until the person in the second who is to succeed to the estate, usually an oldest son, is of age, to bar it by his deed, as he may do by consent of the tenant actually in possession. This he generally does by making a new settlement, usually in favor of an oldest son; and so primogeniture, as it obtains among the gentry there, is a matter of custom rather than of legal right, since these conveyances might always be made to strangers. To explain this, one form of making these settle- ments is to convey lands to the use of the husband for life, with provisions for the wife and daughters therein, and then to the oldest son who might be born of the marriage, in tail, and, in case of his dying without issue, then to the second son, and so on to the third; and to daughters in default of sons. And in this way the estate is locked up from alienation till some tenant in tail is twenty-one years of age, and sees fit to bar the entail in the manner above stated.[2]

57. Still the policy of the law is against clogging the free alienation of estates, and, as will be shown hereafter, it has become an imperative, unyielding rule of law, first, that no estate can be given to the unborn child of an unborn child; and second, that lands cannot be limited in any mode so as to be locked up from alienation beyond the period of a life or lives in being and twenty-one years after, allowing the period of gestation in addition, of a child *en ventre sa mère*, who is to take under such a limitation. This is borrowed from the rule above stated as to settlements where the first

---

[1] Wms. Real Prop. 42, 43; Id. 47, 48; Tud. Cas. 614; 1 Atk. Conv. 240- 250; 2 Sugd. Vend. 282–290.

[2] Wms. Real. Prop. 45. See vol. 2, Appendix, p. *702.

[*83] tenant in tail, after an *estate for life, as soon as ie
arrives at twenty-one years, could convey tie entailed
estate.[1]

58. From tie very definition of estates tail special, as above
given, it must be obvious tiat cases may occur wiere it may,
even wiile tie tenant is still alive, iave become impossible for
any one to take as issue in tail. Tie estate may be limited to
tie ieirs of iis body of iis wife Mary begotten, and sie may
iave died witiout issue. As no otier ieirs can take, ie becomes wiat is known as "tenant in tail, after possibility of
issue extinct." It can apply only in cases of special tail; for
if ieirs of iis body general migit take, tie law would not
deem tie possibility of issue extinct so long as ie lives.[2]

59. Suci an estate is one of a peculiar ciaracter. It ias
ceased to be one of inheritance, and yet retains many of tie
qualities of an inieritable estate. Tie tenant is not punisi-
able for waste, like a tenant for life, and yet may be restrained
by ciancery from malicious waste, altiougi a proper tenant
in tail could not be. He cannot any longer bar tie entail,
and if tie remainder or reversion in fee were to descend upon
him, it would merge iis estate as tenant, as it would if ie
were a mere tenant for life.[3]

60. Estates tail were introduced into tie Englisi colonies
witi otier elements of tie common law, and in some of tie
colonies tie mode of barring tiem by common recovery obtained before tie Revolution.[4] Common recoveries, as a
mode of barring estates tail in Massaciusetts, tiougi formerly
in use, were abolisied in 1792.[5] Recoveries were also once

[1] Wms. Real Prop. 46 ; Cadell v. Palmer, 1 Clark & Fin. 372. Also, Tud.
Cas. 331, 358–361. Post, vol. 2, *358.

[2] 3 Prest. Est. 594 ; Wms. Real Prop. 49.

[3] 2 Wms. Real Prop. 49 ; 1 Cruise, Dig. 137 ; Co. Lit. 27 b, 28 a ; Burton,
Real Prop. § 747 ; 2 Sharsw. Bl. Com. 125, n.

[4] Walker, Am. Law, 299 ; 4 Kent Com. 14; Lyle v. Richards, 9 S. & R. 330;
Jackson v. Van Zandt, 12 Johns. 169. Story, 1 Const. 165, says that Virginia
adopted entails, but did not fines and recoveries. And see Hawley v. Northampton, 8 Mass. 34 ; Partridge v. Dorsey, 3 Har. & J. 302 ; Den v. Smith, 5 Halst.
39 ; Sullivan, Tit. 77 ; 4 Dane, Abr. 624 , 2 Sharsw. Bl. Com. 119, n. ; Baker v.
Battocks, Quincy R. 73. Recoveries were in use in New Jersey till abolished by
statute in 1799. CroXall v. Shererd, 5 Wall. 283.

[5] 4 Dane, Abr. 82 ; Perry v. Kline, 12 Cush. 118, 126.

in use in New Hampshire in barring estates tail. Bell, J., in a recent case, held that the statute of 1789 repealed the statute *De Donis* and abolished estates tail. And this was subsequently reaffirmed by the same court.[1] *

61. But now these estates are either changed into fees * simple or reversionary estates in fee-simple, and [*84] do not exist at all as estates tail, or may be converted into estates in fee-simple by familiar forms of conveyance, in the several States, by force of their respective statutes.[2]

* NOTE. — No allusion seems to be made directly to estates tail; or fines and recoveries in the Stat. 1789. In 1791 an act was passed limiting the time within which " writs of *formedon in descender, remainder, and reverter,*" may be brought. An action of *formedon in descender* was tried in the same court, in 1857, without objection. And in 1837 an act was passed authorizing any person seized of lands in fee tail, and having power to convey by line and recovery, to convey the lands by deed, and thereby bar all remainders, reversions, &c. 2 Laws, 316 ; Dennett *v.* Dennett, 40 N. H. Rep. 498, 503 ; Frost *v.* Cloutman, 7 N. H. 9.

---

[1] Jewell *v.* Warner, 35 N. H. 176 ; Dennett *v.* Dennett, 40 N. H. 500.

[2] Nightingale *v.* Burrell, 15 Pick. 116. *Alabama,* fees-tail are converted into fees-simple in the hands of the one to whom the conditional estate is given. Code, 1867, § 1570. — *Arkansas,* the tenant in tail is made tenant for life, with remainder in fee-simple to the person to whom at common law the estate would first descend. Rev. Stat. 1838, c. 31, § 5. — *California,* the constitution prohibits perpetuities. Art. 11, § 16. — *Colorado,* fees-tail give a life estate to the first taker and a remainder in fee to his children. Gen. L. 1877, c. 18, § 6. — *Connecticut,* the issue of the first donee in tail takes an absolute fee-simple. Gen. Stat. 1875, p. 352. — *Delaware,* estates tail may be barred by fine and common recovery, or by deed. So tenants in tail may alien their lands in fee-simple by deed in the same way as if the estate were owned in fee-simple, if the same is acknowledged and duly proved. Laws, ed. 1874, p. 507. — *Florida,* entails are prohibited. Thompson, Dig. 2d Divis. Tit. 2, c. 1, § 4. — *Georgia,* estates tail are abolished. A grant to one and the heirs of his body creates an absolute fee. Code, 1873, p. 391. — *Illinois,* an estate tail is an estate for life in the tenant in tail, with a remainder in fee-simple to the one to whom, on the death of the first grantee, it would pass according to the course of the common law. Rev. St. 1874, p. 273. — *Indiana,* estates tail are abolished, and if no valid remainder is limited upon what in form is an estate tail, the tenant has a fee-simple. Stat. vol. 1, p. 266. — *Iowa,* all limitations void which suspend the absolute power of alienation longer than lives in being and twenty-one years. Code, 1873, p. 355. — *Kansas,* "heirs" is not required as a word of limitation, and lands descend to children in equal shares. Gen. St. 1868, pp. 185, 394. — *Kentucky,* estates which would otherwise be deemed estates tail are held to be fees-simple. Gen. St. 1873, p. 585. — *Maine,* tenant in tail may convey in fee-simple. Rev. Stat. 1871, p. 559. — *Maryland,* same as Maine, and estates in fee tail general will descend to heirs like estates in fee-simple. Chelton *v.* Henderson, 9 Gill, 438 ; Posey *v.* Budd, 21 Md. 477, 487.

[*85]   T1e reader will find w1at is * believed to be t1e substance of t1e existing laws of t1e several States on t1e
subject in t1e accompanying note.   T1e doctrine of entailment of estates in families was never consonant to t1e genius
of t1e people of t1is country, and even in t1e few States

Code, 1860, pp. 136, 330. — *Michigan*, estates tail are abolished, and such as
would be at common law are declared fees-simple. Comp. L. vol. 2, § 2587. —
Minnesota, persons holding what would be an estate tail are to be "adjudged
seised thereof as an *allodium.*" Rev. St. 1866. — *Mississippi*, estates tail are prohibited and declared to be estates in fee-simple eXcept that lands may be limited
to a succession of donees then living, not eXceeding two, and to the heirs of the
body of the remainder-man, and in default thereof to the heirs of the donor in
fee-simple.   Code, 1871, § 2286.   The statute *De Donis* was never in force here.
Jordan *v.* Roach, 32 Miss. 482. — *Missouri*, tenant in tail takes an estate for life,
remainder to his children in fee as tenants in common.   Gen. Stat. 1866, p. 442.
— *Massachusetts*, Pub. Stat. c. 120, § 15, tenant in tail may convey an estate in fee-
simple by deeds in common form.   But a tenant in tail in remainder cannot, by
deed, convey any estate, either by way of grant or estoppel.   Whittaker *v.* Whittaker, 99 Mass. 366 ; Holland *v.* Cruft, 3 Gray, 183 ; Allen *v.* Trustees, 102 Mass.
262, 265.[1] Nor can a married woman bar an entail by deed in which her husband does not join.   Whittaker *v.* Whittaker, *sup.* 367.   But the estate of a
tenant in tail may be taken on eXecution, or may be sold by license of court
after the death of a tenant in tail in possession, but not of a tenant in tail in remainder.   Holland *v.* Cruft, *sup. ;* Allen *v.* Trustees, *sup.*   Where land is held
by one as tenant for life, with a vested remainder in tail to another, the tenant for
life and remainder-man may convey the same in fee-simple by their deed, which
deed will bar the estate tail and all remainders and reversions eXpectant upon it.
Gen. Stat. c. 89, § 5.   Under the Mass. statute of 1791, a deed made *bona fide,*
for a valuable consideration, eXecuted in the presence of two witnesses, barred entails.   Williams *v.* Hichborne, 4 Mass. 189 ; Cuffee *v.* Milk, 10 Met. 366 ; Willey
v. Haley, 60 Maine, 176. — *Nebraska,* "heirs" not necessary to create a limitation of an estate in fee-simple.   Gen. Stat. 1873, p. 383. — *New Jersey,* the first
taker has an estate for life, and fee-simple vests in the heirs.   4 Kent, Com. 15, n.;
NiXon, Dig. p. 214. — *New York,* estates tail abolished, and if no valid remainder
is limited thereon, the tenant in tail takes a fee absolute.   Stat. at Large, vol. 1,
p. 670. — *North Carolina,* tenant in fee-tail is seised in fee-simple, and for a valuable consideration, may convey it in fee.   Gen. Stat. 1873, p. 383. — *Ohio,* the
issue of the first donee in tail takes a fee-simple absolute.   1 Rev. Stat. S. & C.
p. 550. — *Pennsylvania,* fines and recoveries have the same effect to bar estates
tail as in England.   Tenants in tail may convey lands of which they are seised in
the same manner as if seised in fee, and thereby bar the entailment, as by a recovery.   1 Bright. Purd. Dig. 1872, p. 619 ; Price *v.* Taylor, 28 Penn. St. 107 ;
Haldeman *v.* Haldeman, 40 Penn. St. 36. — *Rhode Island,* tenant in tail may bar
it by deed or devise, by limiting a fee-simple to his grantee or devisee, the deed
to be acknowledged before the Supreme Court or Court of Common Pleas.   Gen.
Stat. 1872; Cooper *v.* Cooper, 6 R. I. 264 — *South Carolina,* statute *De Donis*
never in force there ; estates in fee-simple conditional remain as at common law.

[1] Cf. Coombs *v.* Anderson, 138 Mass. 376.

where the form of estates tail remains, the application of it is comparatively rare. And the facility with which even these may be barred by aliening them, renders the possibility of creating them of little practical importance, though it does not do away with the necessity of understanding the rules by which such estates are governed.

Stat. vol. 3, p. 341. — *Tennessee,* all tenants in tail are seised in fee-simple. — *Texas,* by Constitution, art. 1, § 18, neither primogeniture nor entailment can ever be in force. — *Vermont,* the donee in tail takes an estate for life, remainder in fee-simple absolute to him to whom the estate would pass upon his death. Gen. St. 1862, p. 446. — *Wisconsin,* all estates tail changed into fee-simple in the tenant in tail. Rev. Stat. 1858, p. 524. — *Virginia,* estates tail were abolished as early as 1776. 4 Kent, Com. 5, n. And now estates tail are converted into estates in fee-simple, whichever form is adopted. Code, 1860, p. 559. And the same rule prevails in *West Virginia.* Code, 1868, p. 460. — *Dakota,* estates tail abolished. Civ. Code, 1866.

CHAPTER V.

ESTATES FOR LIFE.

Sect. 1. Their Nature and Incidents.
Sect. 2. Of Estovers.
Sect. 3. Of Emblements.
Sect. 4. Of Waste.

SECTION I.

THEIR NATURE AND INCIDENTS.

1. The next estate in importance, as computed in the scale of gradation, is an *estate for life,* because ordinarily measured, as to its duration, by the term of a human life, and regarded as a freehold. This is rather a class of estates, and embraces all freeholds which are not of inheritance, including estates held by the tenant for the term of his own life, or for the life or lives of one or more other persons, or for an ·indefinite

period which may endure for the life or lives of persons in being, and not beyond the period of a life.[1] Nor does it change the character of a life estate so long as it remains such, that it may, upon the happening of a contingency, become enlarged into a fee. Thus, where a devise was to A for life, remainder to testator's widow for life if she survived A, and on decease of both to the heirs male of the body of A, it was held that A surviving the widow, his life estate then became an estate tail.[2]

2. These estates may be created by the act of some party, as by a deed or devise, or by act of the law as in case of dower and curtesy, as being incident to relations like that of marriage, which are created by law.

3. Where the estate is in one during the life of another, it is technically called an estate *per autre vie*, and he whose life is the measure of its duration is styled *cestui que vie*.[3]

4. An estate for the tenant's own life is, in the estimation of the law, a better one and of a higher nature to him than one for the life or lives of another or others. And, as in construing grants where the language is equivocal, that construction is given which is most favorable to the grantee,[4] where a grant is made to one with no other words of limitation, he will be entitled to an estate during his own life, if the estate of the grantor will allow him to convey such an estate.[5]

5. Among the instances of what will be deemed a grant of an estate for life are those above put of a grant to one expressly for life or to him without words of limitation, or to

---

[1] Hewlins *v.* Shippam, 5 B. & C. 221 ; 2 Bl. Com. 121.

[2] Adams *v.* Adams, 6 Q. B. 860.

[3] 2 Bl. Com. 120 ; Co. Lit. 41 b. For what is evidence of the death of a *cestui que vie*, see Clark *v.* Owens, 18 N. Y. 434. It is stated in Garland *v.* Crow, 2 Bailey, 24, that "in contemplation of law an estate for life is equal to seven years' purchase of the fee. To estimate the present value of an estate for life, interest must be computed on the value of the whole property for seven years, and *perhaps* interest on the several sums of the annual interest, from the present time to the periods at which they would respectively fall due, ought to be abated." And with the rate of interest at seven per cent, the present value of an estate for life is a fraction more than thirty-five per cent of the value of the absolute estate. But these absolute assumptions have now generally given way to computations based on average probabilities of life. See *post*, 309.

[4] Broom, Max. 457 ; 2 Bl. Com. 121.

[5] Co. Lit. 42 a ; Broom, Max. 458 ; 2 Bl. Com. 121.

him during the life of another, or to a woman so long as she shall remain a widow, or to a man and woman during cover-
[*89] ture, or so long as a man shall live in a certain house, or shall pay a *certain sum, or until £100 be paid out of the income of the estate, even though the income of the estate be £10 by the year;[1] or so long as the grantee shall maintain salt-works on the land.[2] So the reservation by a grantor of the use and control of the granted premises during his life, creates in him a life estate with all its inci-dents.[3] The importance of the distinction between freeholds of inheritance, simple freeholds, and estates less than freehold, is obvious when the incidents are considered which belong to the one or the other of these.

6. Among the exceptions to the above is a devise of lands to executors until testator's debts are paid, which will pass a chattel and not a freehold interest. So if the grantor himself have only an estate for life, or is tenant in tail, the grant, if indefinite, shall be held to be for the life only of the grantor. And in the construction of wills, as well as of deeds by statute in several of the States, as heretofore stated,[4] it is often held that the devisor or grantor passes whatever estate he has, whether a fee-simple or less, as the case may be, though he do not make use of words of limitation and inheritance in his will or deed.[5] It matters not how contingent or uncertain the duration of the estate may be, or how probable is its de-termination in a limited number of years, if it is capable of enduring for the term of a life, it is within the category of estates for life.[6]

7. In many cases estates for life are held to be raised by implication, especially under devises, as where A devises his land to his heir after the death of B. Here, as no one but the heir could take except by the will, and by that he is

---

[1] Co. Lit. 42 a; Tud. Cas. 31 ; Jackson v. Ayers, 3 Johns. 388 ; Roseboom v. Van Vechten, 5 Denio, 414. And to these may be added the rights of "home-stead" in some of the States, which will be hereafter treated. See c. 8, § 2.

[2] Hurd v. Cushing, 7 Pick. 169.

[3] Webster v. Webster, 33 N. H. 18, 22 ; Richardson v. York, 14 Me. 216.

[4] Ante, p. *29.

[5] Co. Lit. 42 a. See Stat. of Wills, 1 Vict. c. 66, § 28 ; 2 Jarm. Wills, 181.

[6] 2 Flint. Real Prop. 232 ; Co. Lit. 42 a.

postponed till the death of B, it is held that B is, by construction, made tenant for life. But if it had been to a stranger, after the death of B, no such inference would be raised, for the estate in the mean time would go to the heir.[1]

8. It was customary in England, while monasteries were in existence there, to limit estates for life to persons during their *natural* lives, lest their civil deaths might terminate the estate. But there is no occasion in this country to make use of this expression, as there is no civil death nor practical forfeiture of *lands, it is believed, for felony, and to a [*90] very limited extent for treason.[2]

9. It has been more than once stated that estates for life were considered under the feudal law freeholds, were created by livery of seisin, and for them the tenants owed fealty to the lord, but not homage, as that was due only from the one who had the inheritance. And it may be added that, according to strict feudal notions, a tenancy *per autre vie* was not deemed of sufficient importance to be considered a freehold interest.[3]

10. In measuring the duration of a life estate where the life of more than one person is referred to, the question is sometimes affected by the doctrine of merger, which applies where a greater and less estate unite in the same person, — the less being extinguished.[4] Thus an estate to A during life and the lives of B and C, is considered cumulative, and will continue during the lives of all three.[5] But if it had been to A during the life of B, remainder to A, the estate to himself would be considered a greater estate than that during the life of the *cestui que vie*, and would therefore merge this so that A would simply have an estate for his own life in himself.[6] And in conformity with the doctrine of merger, if

---

[1] 1 Jarm. Wills, 466, 476.

[2] Wms. Real Prop., Rawle's note, p. 103 ; 5 Dane, Abr. 11. This is not intended to apply to cases of alleged forfeiture by the tenant for life, conveying the lands in fee, and the like.

[3] 2 Bl. Com. 120 ; 1 Spence, Eq. Jur. 144 ; Wms. Real Prop. 17, 22. Mr. Williams is of the opinion that feuds were not originally, as some have supposed, held at the will of the lord.

[4] 2 Bl. Com. 177.   [5] Co. Lit. 41 b ; 3 Prest. Conv. 225.

[6] 3 Prest. Conv. 225 ; Smith, Real & Pers. Prop. 939.

the owner of a reversion immediately expectant upon an estate for life, grant his reversion to the tenant for life, it will merge the estate for life, even though the grant be a conditional one.[1]   And this, whether the reversion be in fee, in tail, or for life only.[2]

11. But if the tenant surrender to the reversioner, and this be on condition, and then an entry be made for condition broken, the tenant for life is in again of his original estate, and the estate for life survives.   The effect of such an operation is not a complete merger, since a *surrender* is but [*91] " the consent of a * particular tenant that he in remainder or reversion shall presently have possession."[3]   If the tenant for life lease the premises to the reversioner for his, the reversioner's life, his estate does not merge in the reversion, because he parts with a less estate than he is supposed to have ; and if he outlives the reversioner, he will take the estate again for the balance of his own life.[4]

12. Though there are some peculiarities in the nature of estates *per autre vie,* which will be hereafter explained, it may be here remarked, that if a tenant for his own life, as, for instance, a dowress, conveys that estate to another, the latter becomes thereby a tenant for life *per autre vie.*[5]

13. A tenant for life is regarded as so far the owner of an independent estate, that, unless restrained by the terms of his grant, he may convey his entire interest, or carve any lesser estate out of the same in favor of another.   In other words, he may assign his entire estate or underlet the whole or any part of the same for a longer or shorter period, not exceeding that of his own.[6]   He cannot, however, convey his estate except by deed.[7]

14. The conveyance by a tenant for life of a greater estate than he has in the premises — a fee, for instance — has been allowed to have a different effect at different times in England and in this country.   While conveyances by feoffment were

---

[1] Burton, Real Prop. § 764 ; Co. Lit. 218 b.   [2] Smith, Real Prop. 939.

[3] Burton, Real Prop. § 764 ; Smith, Real & Pers. Prop. 939 ; Termes de la Ley " Surrender."

[4] Co. Lit. 42.   [5] Co. Lit. 41 b.

[6] 1 Cruise, Dig. 108 ; Jackson *v.* Van Hoesen, 4 Cow. 325.

[7] Stewart *v.* Clark, 13 Met. 79.

in use, such a conveyance was deemed to work a forfeiture of the tenant's entire estate, upon the feudal notion that by making it he had renounced the feudal connection between him and his lord, and the estate in remainder or reversion had thereby been divested by the wrongful transfer of the seisin to a stranger, and the remainder-unit or reversioner might at once enter for the forfeiture upon his original right, inasmuch as the tenant of the particular estate had by his own act put an entire end to his original estate.   And the same principle applied in all cases * where the ten- [*92] ant of a particular estate conveyed a greater one than he was entitled to.[1]   But it has never been held a ground of forfeiture that tenant for life had made a lease of the premises for years.[2]

15. But if the conveyance be by deed of bargain and sale, lease and release, or any form of deed under the Statute of Uses, which is not accomplished by the transmutation of possession, it would not, though in form a fee, convey any more than the grantor had to part with, and consequently, as it did not disturb the seisin of the reversioner or remainder-man, it would not work a forfeiture.[3]

16. And now under the statute of 8 & 9 Vict. c. 106, sect. 4, which declares that no feoffment made in wrong shall act tortiously, it would seem that this ground of forfeiture is removed in England.[4]

17. In this country the law seems to have been generally regarded as the same in this respect as in England.   In those States where conveyances have the effect of feoffments, accompanied by livery of seisin, or may be made by common recoveries, it seems that a tenant for life may work a forfeiture of his land by conveying a greater estate than he has.[5]

18. But it is apprehended that this is rather a theoretic than a practical principle, since the deeds ordinarily in use in

[1] 1 Cruise, Dig. 108 ; 2 Bl. Com. 274, 275 ; 5 Dane, Abr. 6-8 ; Co. Lit. 251, 252 ; Wright, Ten. 201 ; Wms. Real Prop. 25 ; Jackson v. Mancius, 2 Wend. 365.
[2] Locke v. Rowell, 47 N. H. 46.
[3] 1 Cruise, Dig. 109 ; Stearns, Real Act. 11 ; Stevens v. Winship, 1 Pick. 318.
[4] Wms. Real Prop. 122.
[5] 2 Sharsw. Bl. Com. 121, n.; Redfern v. Middleton, 1 Rice, S. C. 459 ; Stump v. Findlay, 2 Rawle, 168.   See Matthews v. Ward, 10 Gill & J. 449.

the conveyance of lands, though recorded, do not operate to produce a forfeiture, though the tenant thereby affect to convey a larger estate than he has. Such deeds convey what the grantor has and nothing more.[1]

[*93]   *19. Immediately connected with the doctrine of forfeiture by granting a larger estate than the tenant for life has, is that of forfeiture by disclaiming the title of him under whom he holds, or affirming in a court of record that the reversion is in a stranger, by pleading, and the like. Although such was the common law, it has not, it is believed, ever obtained in this country.[2]

20. The estate for life *per autre vie*, presented, at the common law, several noticeable peculiarities in certain contingencies. Thus, if the tenant died, living the *cestui que vie*, land was left open without any one having a legal right to claim it, — neither the reversioner, because the previous estate had not expired ; nor the heir of the tenant, for his estate was not one of inheritance ; nor his executor, because it was a freehold and not a chattel interest. Nor was it deemed to be devisable. The consequence was, any one who first chose to take possession might do so, and was called a *general occupant*.[3]

---

[1] McKee v. Pfout, 3 Dall. 486 ; Pendleton v. Vandevier, 1 Wash. 381 ; Rogers v. Moore, 11 Conn. 553 ; Bell v. Twilight, 22 N. H. 500 ; Stevens v. Winship, 1 Pick. 318 ; Walker, Am. Law, 277 ; Stearns, Real Act. 11 ; 4 Kent, Com. 84. In Maine it is held that if tenant by curtesy conveys in fee, he forfeits his estate, and reversioner may enter, French v. Rollins, 21 Me. 372 ; and in New Jersey, a similar principle prevails both as to tenants by curtesy and in dower, 4 Kent, Com. 84. See also 5 Dane's Abr. 11–13, where a case is cited that a conveyance in fee in Massachusetts in 1784 worked a forfeiture. Also a dictum of Judge Jackson, in Grant v. Chase, 17 Mass. 446, to same effect. But it is probably true, that unless the case of dower or curtesy forms an exception, a tenant for life does not in any case work any forfeiture by conveying, in form, a greater estate than he has, since only what estate he has passes by such deed. This is declared to be the law by statute in many of the States, namely : *Alabama*, Code, 1852, § 1317 ; *Maine*, Rev. Stat. 1871, p. 559 ; *New York*, 1 Stat. at Large, 689; *Wisconsin*, Rev. Stat. 1858, c. 86, § 4 ; *Massachusetts*, Pub. Stat. c. 126, § 9 ; *Minnesota*, Stat. 1866, p. 328 ; *Michigan*, Comp. Stat. 1857, c. 88, § 4 ; Grout v. Townshend, 2 Hill, 554 ; McCorry v. King's Heirs, 3 Humph. 267, 271, 277 ; Dennett v. Dennett, 40 N. H. 498, 505 ; Hotel Co. v. Marsh, 63 N. H. 230.

[2] Co. Lit. 251, 252 ; 1 Cruise, Dig. 109 ; 5 Dane, Abr. 11. How far this applies in cases of terms for years, it is not necessary here to discuss. See Jackson v. Vincent, 4 Wend. 633.

[3] 2 Bl. Com. 258 ; Co. Lit. 41 b ; Wms. Ex'rs, 570.

But the doctrine of *general occupancy* was practically abolished by the statute 29 Charles II. c. 3, and 14 Geo. 11. c. 10, authorizing the tenant to devise it, or, if undevised, giving it to his executors to be administered as his assets.[1]

21. But there were many cases at the common law where persons became what were called *special occupants* of lands, under the circumstances supposed, growing out of the relation of such occupant to the estate, and took the land to the exclusion of a mere stranger. As, for instance, if tenant *per autre vie* *made a lease at will to another and died, [*94] his lessee, being in possession, became the occupant of the land.[2] But the application of the term as well as the title of "special occupant" of such an estate chiefly arises out of the form in which the original limitation of the estate was made. Thus if A takes an estate to himself, his heirs or the heirs of his body and his assigns during the life of another, and dies in the lifetime of *cestui que vie*, his heirs would take not strictly as heirs, but as special occupants or persons who are indicated to take what is left of the ancestor's estate. If the limitation had been to him and his executors and administrators, they would take, in like case, instead of his heirs.[3]

22. But though "heirs," or "heirs of the body," in such a limitation are not properly words of inheritance, and it might at first sight appear that they would take as purchasers, if at all, yet it is well settled that the ancestor becomes the absolute owner of the entire term which he may alien at his pleasure, and the heir only takes what he may have left undisposed of. Thus where the estate was to A and his heirs for the lives of B, C, and D, and A devised to J S without terms of limitation, and J S died before *cestuis que vie*, it was held that the heirs of A should take the residue of the estate, and not the representatives of J S.[4] And the *quasi* tenant in tail in possession has complete power to bar the entail and the remainder over.[5]

---

[1] 2 Bl. Com. 259 ; Tud. Cas. 33.

[2] Co. Lit. 41 b, n. 237 ; Com. Dig. "Estate by Grant," F. 1.

[3] 2 Bl. Com. 359 ; Atkinson *v.* Baker, 4 T. R. 229 ; Wms. Ex'rs, 570 ; Tud. Cas. 33.

[4] Doe *v.* Robinson, 8 B. & C. 296 ; Allen *v.* Allen, 2 Dru. & W. 307.

[5] Doe *v.* Luxton, 6 T. R. 289 ; Allen *v.* Allen, 2 Dru. & W. 307 ; Norton a

[*95]   *23. But though the tenant for life *per autre vie*, with a *quasi* estate tail to the heirs of his body may convey the estate by deed, it seems that, at common law, he cannot do it by will. The heirs of his body will take as special occupants, by virtue of the gift that created the life estate, in preference to the devisee of the tenant.[1]

24. There are duties as well as rights incident to every estate for life which the tenant thereof is bound to observe, among which was that of defending the title if it was attacked in any of the real actions at common law which concluded the title, because the interest of the reversioner or remainder-man might be affected by the judgment rendered against the life tenant. But in order to enable him to do this, he might call upon the one who had the inheritance after the determination of his estate, to come in and aid him in making the defence. This was called "praying in aid." Or he might, if he saw fit, go on and defend without resorting to the owner of the inheritance, or those whose estates were dependent on his, he being in law the proper tenant to the *præcipe*.[2] The custom of

Frecker, 1 Atk. 524. The subject is now regulated by statute, 1 Vict. c. 26, § 3, in England, 2 Wms. Ex'rs, 574, and generally by the statutes of the several States. Walker's Am. Law. 275 ; Wms. Real Prop. 21, note by Rawle ; 4 Kent, Com. 27. In cases where there is an estate in A for the life of B, A has a freehold. But if he die before B, the residuum of the estate is declared to be a chattel interest, and treated as such in *Alabama*, Code, 1852, § 1594 ; *New York*, 1 Stat. at Large, p. 671 ; *Wisconsin*, Rev. Stat. 1858, c. 83, § 6 ; *Minnesota*, Stat. 1866, p. 349 ; *Michigan*, Comp. Law, 1857, c. 85. In *Arkansas* it is embraced and treated as real estate, in the law of descents and distribution, though all real estate is assets in the hands of executors and administrators,. Dig. Stat. 1858, c. 56, § 19. In *North Carolina* it is deemed an inheritance of the deceased tenant *per autre vie* for purposes of descent, Gen. Stat. 1873, p. 363 ; McBride *v.* Patterson, 78 N. C. 412. In *Rhode Island* and *Indiana* it is made devisable, Rev. Stat. 1857, c. 154, § 1 ; 2 Rev. Stat. 1852, p. 208, § 2. In *Massachusetts* it is devisable and descendible as real estate, Pub. Stat. c. 125, § 1. In *New Jersey* it is devisable ; but if not devised, it goes to executors or administrators, to be applied and distributed as personal, Nixon, Dig. 1855, p. 873, § 1. And the same in *Texas*, Oldham & White, Dig. 1859, p. 454, art. 2117. In *Maryland* it forms a part of personal assets, unless expressly limited to him and his heirs, Code, 1860, art. 93, § 220.

   [1] Dillon *v.* Dillon, 1 Ball & B. 95 ; Grey *v.* Mannock, 2 Eden, 341, and note as to Lord Kenyon's dictum in Doe *v.* Luxton, 6 T. R. 289 ; Campbell *v.* Sandys, 1 Sch. & Lef. 281 ; Tud. Cas. 34 ; Allen *v.* Allen, 2 Dru. & W. 307.

   [2] 1 Prest. Est. 207, 208 ; Stearns, Real Act. 99 ; Termes de la Ley, "Aid ;" *ante*, *48.

" praying in aid " by a tenant in a real action once existed in
Massachusetts, but by the abolition of writs of right it has been
discontinued.[1]   And the same effect, it would seem, has been
produced in England by abolishing all real actions, except
quare impedit, dower and ejectment, by the statute 3 & 4 Wm.
IV. c. 27, § 36.[2]

24 *a.*   As a general proposition, if a tenant for life makes
improvements upon the premises, he cannot claim compensation therefor from the reversioner or remainder-man, though
he is under no legal obligation to do more than keep the
premises in repair.[3]   It is also generally true that he cannot
make repairs or permanent improvements at the expense of
the inheritance.   But he may complete, at the expense of the
estate, a mansion-house which has been begun by a testator
under whom he holds.   So the expense of putting a building,
at first, into a tenantable condition, is a charge upon the estate,
but that of keeping it in repair is upon the tenant for life.[4]

25.   An important duty imposed upon every tenant for
life is * that of keeping down the interest upon existing   [*96]
incumbrances upon the estate, though, as a general
proposition, he is not bound, as between himself and the
reversioner or remainder-man, to pay the principal of any
moneys charged upon it; and if he is obliged to do so, he
becomes a creditor of the estate for the amount so paid, deducting the value of the interest he would have had to pay
as tenant for life during his life.[5]   On the other hand, if a
tenant for life purchase in an outstanding incumbrance upon
an estate, it is regarded as having been done for the benefit
of the reversioner as well as himself, if the latter will contribute his proportion of the sum paid therefor.[6]

---

[1] Stearns, Real Act. 103 ; Mass. Pub. Stat. c. 173, § 1.

[2] Wms. Real Prop. 371 ; 1 Spence, Eq. Jur. 225.

[3] Corbett *v.* Laurens, 5 Rich. Eq. 301.

[4] Sohier *v.* Eldridge, 103 Mass. 345, 351 ; Parsons *v.* Winslow, 16 Mass. 361.

[5] 1 Story, Eq. § 486 ; Id. § 488 ; Warley *v.* Warley, 1 Bailey, Eq. 397 ; 4 Kent,
Com. 76 ; Saville *v.* Saville, 2 Atk. 463 ; Mosely *v.* Marshall, 27 Barb. 42, 44.
And, it seems, he will not be obliged to pay towards the interest anything beyond
the amount of the rents accruing, and, if he does, he will be a creditor of the estate for such excess.   Kensington *v.* Bouverie, 7 De G. M. & G. 134 ; Tud. Cas.
60 ; Doane *v.* Doane, 46 Vt. 485.

[6] Daviess *v.* Myers, 13 B. Mon. 511.

25 *a.* As between tenant for life and the remainder-man, ordinary taxes are to be paid by the tenant for life; but where the whole estate is subject to, or to be benefited by the discharge of an incumbrance not created by either of them, equity apportions it between both, the tenant for life having to keep down the interest during his life. A betterment charge comes within this category, being laid in view of the permanently increased value of the premises. The tenant for life must pay the accruing interest upon the amount during his life, and the remainder-man, after that, must pay the principal.[1] But though the tenant for life would be liable to the remainder-man for contribution at the rates above stated, if he pays the charge in full, he is not personally liable to the incumbrancer himself who holds the charge upon the estate. Thus a mortgagee could not make a personal claim upon the tenant for life of the mortgaged estate if the charge was not created by him.[2]

26. Formerly, the mode of apportioning the payment of an incumbrance between tenant for life and remainder-man was one third upon the former and two thirds upon the latter. But that is now discarded as unreasonable.[3] In North Carolina, it is said, the courts do not recognize any arbitrary rule in apportioning such a payment, each case being generally referred to the master to settle by itself.[4]

27. The rule stated by Story is this: "The tenant shall contribute beyond the interest in proportion to the benefit he derives from the liquidation of the debt, and the consequent cessation of annual payments of interest during his life (which, of course, will depend upon his age and the computation of the value of his life)."[5] To make a practical illustration of this rule, which is only vague from an almost necessary want of definiteness in the application of the terms employed, suppose a tenant for life, a dowress, for instance, has been obliged, in order to save her estate, to pay the whole of a mortgage thereon, and the heir or reversioner wishes to re-

---

[1] Plympton *v.* Boston Dispensary, 106 Mass. 544.

[2] Morley *v.* Saunders, L. R. 8 Eq. 594.   [3] 1 Story, Eq. § 487.

[4] Jones *v.* Sherrard, 2 Dev. & B. Ch. 179 ; Atkins *v.* Kron, 8 Ired. Eq. 1.

[5] Eq. Jur. § 487.

deem from her by contributing his share of the mortgage debt. Or suppose he has paid the whole, and she. in order to save her estate, wishes to contribute her share of the debt. Assuming that she is to pay the interest as long as she lives, except that she is to anticipate and pay it all at once in a gross sum, her share would be what the present worth of an annuity equal to that *interest would amount to, com- [*97] puted for as many years as by the tables of the chances of life, regard being had to her state of health, she may be supposed to live. Of course the share of the heir or reversioner would be the residue of the sum paid for the redemption. And if, by reason of the mortgage being upon the whole of her husband's estate, she, as dowress, would only be liable to contribute the interest of one third of the debt to correspond with her life interest in that proportion of the land, it can make no difference in the rule, but merely affects the form of the computation.[1] The same rule is applied upon the sale of an estate in which a tenant for life and a reversioner are interested, in apportioning the proceeds between them. So where a mortgage was devised to one for life, with remainder to another, and the same was redeemed, the redemption money was divided *pro rata* by the same rule. The value of the life estate, in such cases, is fixed at the time of sale or conversion of the estate into money, by reference to the common tables of the chances of life. Nor would the result be affected, though the tenant for life were to die after such conversion before any part of the proceeds had been paid over.[2]

28. In New York, where a tenant for life neglected to pay

---

[1] Swaine *v.* Perine, 5 Johns. Ch. 482 ; Gibson *v.* Crehore 5 Pick. 146 ; Saville *v.* Saville, 2 Atk. 463 ; Bell *v.* The Mayor, 10 Paige, 49, 71 ; House *v.* House, 10 Paige, 158 ; Cogswell *v.* Cogswell, 2 Edw. Ch. 231. This computation would be made by a master or officer of the court. In Massachusetts, the courts have made use of Wigglesworth's Tables, Eastabrook *v.* Hapgood, 10 Mass. 315, n. ; though tables have been adopted in general use more full and accurate than these, such as the Carlisle or Combined Experience Tables. See the table prescribed by English statute. Matthews' Ex'rs, 218, Appendix B. In New York also, by Laws 1870, c. 717, §§ 1, 5, the Portsmouth or Northampton Tables are prescribed. See also Abercrombie *v.* Riddle, 3 Md. Ch. Dec. 320 ; Dorsey *r.* Smith, 7 Har. & J. 366 ; Foster *v.* Hilliard, 1 Story, 77, and *post,* *248 and note.

[2] Foster *v.* Hilliard, 1 Story, 77.

the taxes upon the land, a receiver was appointed to take so much of the rent as might be necessary to pay the taxes.[1] And it may be laid down as a duty uniformly incumbent upon a tenant for life, to pay all taxes assessed upon the land during his life.[2] In Ohio, if tenant for life fail to pay the taxes assessed upon the estate, he forfeits the same to the reversioner or remainder-man who may enter. But this is under the provisions of a statute of that State.[3]

29. The possession of a tenant for life is never deemed to be adverse to his reversioner.[4] Nor, if he be disseised, are the rights of the reversioner thereby affected, and he may enter or sue an action to recover possession within twenty years after the death of the tenant for life, without regard to the lapse of time during which the disseisor may have held the premises.[5] And if one who enters upon land under an agreement with a tenant for life continue to hold possession after his death, he becomes as to the reversioner a mere trespasser.[6] It has been further held that if the tenant for life do any act with the property which works a forfeiture of the same, it only affects his interest, but not that of the reversioner.[7] So if the tenant does an act by which he incurs a forfeiture of the estate, the reversioner is not bound to treat the estate as merged in his own, and enter immediately; he may have his action after the death of the tenant for life, without being affected by the previous possession. Nor can a tenant for life who creates an estate by grant or otherwise defeat his grant by surrender to his landlord or reversioner.[8]

30. It is a principle in the law of landlord and tenant, that if the tenant is evicted before the expiration of his lease by a better title than that of his lessor, he will not be liable for rent

---

[1] Cairns v. Chabert, 3 Edw. Ch. 312.

[2] Varney v. Stevens, 22 Me. 331, 334; Prettyman v. Walston, 34 Ill. 192.

[3] McMillan v. Robbins, 5 Ohio, 28.

[4] Grout v. Townshend, 2 Hill, 554; Austin v. Stevens, 24 Me. 520, 526; Varney v. Stevens, 22 Me. 331.

[5] Jackson v. Mancius, 2 Wend. 357; McCorry v. King's Heirs, 3 Humph. 267, 375; Jackson v. Schoonmaker, 4 Johns. 390; Foster v. Marshall, 22 N. H. 491; Guion v. Anderson, 8 Humph. 298, 325.

[6] Williams v. Caston, 1 Strobh. 130.

[7] Archer v. Jones, 26 Miss. 583, 589.

[8] Moore v. Luce, 29 Penn. St. 260.

for the unexpired term during which he had enjoyed it ; and one ground is, that, the contract being entire, such rent is not apportionable. So if a tenant for life underlet the premises for a certain term, reserving rent payable at a certain day, and die before that day, his executors could not, at common law, recover the rent accruing between the last rent-day and the day of his death ; which they might have done had he survived to the beginning of the day on which the rent fell due.[1] In Alabama, if a life estate falls in before the end of the year, the remainder-man has the rent accruing from the death of the tenant for life to the end of the year, subject to the right of emblements.[2]

*31. Where, however, as was sometimes the case, a   [*98] tenant for life had a power to lease for a term beyond the period of his own life, and made such a lease, and died before the last moment of the day on which the rent was due, though within an hour of midnight, the rent went to the reversioner, and was not apportionable, and no part was recoverable by the representatives of the tenant for life. For as the lease continued after the life-tenant's death, the rent did not become fully due till the last moment of the day on which it was reserved.[3]

32. But now these defects as to apportioning rents are supplied by the statute 11 Geo. II. c. 19, § 15, giving in the first case, a right of action to the executors of tenants for life to recover *pro tanto* for the time the tenant actually enjoyed the premises under his lease ; and in the latter case, by the statute 4 & 5 Wm. IV. c. 22, § 2, apportioning the rent between the tenant for life and the reversioner *pro rata* as to time.[4] The statute of 11 Geo. II. has been re-enacted in some

[1] Clun's Case, 10 Rep. 128 ; Fitchburg Co. *v.* Melvin, 15 Mass. 268 ; Perry *v.* Aldrich, 13 N. H. 343 ; 2 Bl. Com. 124 ; 3 Cruise, Dig. 283, 306.

[2] Price *v.* Pickett, 21 Ala. 741.

[3] Stralford *v.* Wentworth, 1 P. Wms. 180 ; Rockingham *v.* Penrice, Id. 178 : Norris *v.* Harrison, 2 Madd. 268 ; Wms. Ex'rs, 709. Royalties from a coal lease go to tenant for life. Wentz's App., 106 Penn. St. 301 ; McClintock *v.* Dana, Id. 386 ; Shoemaker's App., Id. 392.

[4] Wms. Ex'rs, 709 ; Wms. Real Prop. 27. These statutes apportion the rent as to time. The effect of tenant being deprived of part of the premises, or of lessor conveying the reversion of part of the estate upon the rent, remains as at common law. 3 Kent, Com. 469, 470.

of the States, and practically adopted through the courts in others.[1] If the lessee be tenant *per autre vie,* and the term come to an end by the death of the *cestui que vie* before the day of payment of rent, it is not within the language of the statute of 11 Geo. II., and the rent is not apportionable, and cannot be recovered for the time the tenant may have occupied between the last time of payment and the death of the *cestui que vie.*[2] And a like principle applies in the case of annuities. If an annuitant die before the expiration of the period at which the annuity is payable, it is lost; his representatives can recover no part of what is in arrear since the prior day of payment. Hence the importance of providing for such contingencies by the terms by which the lease or annuity is created.[3]

33. A question of some interest has, at times, been made in England, how far a tenant for life has a right to possession of the title-deeds of the estate. But it is believed that under the American system of registration no such question can arise.[4]

[*99]   * SECTION II.

OF ESTOVERS.

1.   Tenant's right to estovers.
2.   What are estovers.
3, 4.   Effect of tenant exceeding his right in taking estovers.
5–9.   How timber, &c., must be cut and used.
10.   What trees constitute timber, and what firewood.
11.   Right to take estovers assignable.

1. Along the incidents of all estates for life, and the same is true of estates for years, is that to take *estovers* or *botes* from the premises, if they are capable of supplying them, in the way of compensation for the duty of occupying and managing the same in a prudent manner, and keeping the parts thereof in suitable repair.[5]

---

[1] 3 Greenl. Cruise, 306, n. Re-enacted in Massachusetts, St. 1869, c. 368, § 1; Pub. Stat. c. 121, § 8; and extended to all contingent determinations of the lessor's estate.   [2] Perry v. Aldrich, 13 N. H. 343.

[3] Wiggin v. Swett, 6 Met. 194; Dexter v. Phillips, 121 Mass. 178.

[4] Wms. Real Prop. 375, Rawle's note.

[5] Hubbard v. Shaw, 13 Allen, 120, 122; Gowel, Interp. (*Estovers*), derives the word from the French, *estouver,* equivalent to *fovere,* to nourish or maintain.

2. These estovers are of three kinds: 1, house-bote; 2, plough-bote; and 3, hay-bote. The first of these is a sufficient allowance of wood to repair or burn in the house. This latter is often called fire-bote. The second, for making and repairing all instruments of husbandry. The third, for repairing hedges or fences; "hay" meaning "a hedge." And these estovers must be reasonable in quantity or amount.[1] It was held, in applying this doctrine in one case, that such tenant might take a reasonable quantity of wood for fuel, for the supply of himself and family, upon the premises, to be cut in a prudent and proper manner, and might include a reasonable supply for necessary servants employed upon the farm, and living in the same house, or another upon the same premises.[2]

3. As the destruction of growing timber and wood affects the value of the inheritance, if the tenant exceed what is reasonably necessary in cutting for the purposes above stated, he would, to the extent of such excess, be guilty of waste, the consequences and nature of which will be hereafter explained.[3]

4. In the first place, he must only cut such timber or wood as he needs for present use. To cut these in anticipation of future use would be waste.[4] So he must cut only such as is fit for the purpose. It would be waste to cut what was unfit, though he exchanged it for what was suitable.[5]

5. In the next place, the tenant must only cut such
*timber, &c., as is necessary for use, and it must also [*100] be used by him upon the premises, and not elsewhere.
He may not cut timber and exchange it for firewood or fencing-stuff, nor cut wood or timber and sell it, though needed

---

"The name *estovers* containeth house-bote, hay-bote, and plough-bote." "Bote," says the same author, "signifieth compensation; hence also comes our common phrase, 'to give to boot, that is, *compensationis gratia.*'" See also Co. Lit. 41 b. Blackstone derives estovers from *estoffer*, to *furnish.* 2 Bl. Com. 35.

[1] Co. Lit. 41 b; 2 Bl. Com. 35; Cowel, Interp. "Hayo."

[2] Smith *v.* Jewett, 40 N. H. 530.

[3] 2 Bl. Com. 122. See this subject examined, 3 Dane, Abr. 238, 239. *Post,* p. *107; Webster *v.* Webster, 33 N. H. 21.

[4] Gorges *v.* Stanfield, Cro. El. 593.

[5] Simmons *v.* Norton, 7 Bing. 640.

for his comfort or support.[1] Nor can he cut and sell wood to
pay the expense of cutting and drawing that which he needs,
and used for his own comfort upon the premises.[2] Nor could
a dowress cut and sell wood from the premises, though she
procured as much for actual consumption upon the same from
other sources, and to that extent relieved the estate from the
charge of supplying fire-wood.[3]

6. Where a widow had dower out of two distinct estates,
with a dwelling-house on both, but no woodland upon one of
them, it was held that she could not cut wood upon one of
these to burn in the house upon the other, though she occupied the latter as her dwelling-place.[4] But in other cases
it has been held that, if dower consist of several parcels,
and she takes wood from one to make repairs upon another,
or to burn in her dwelling-house upon another, it will not
be deemed waste, though these parcels are the inheritances of
different reversioners.[5] So where there was a farm and out-
lands, and it had been customary for the tenant to cut the wood
for the dwelling-house upon the out-lands, it was held not to
be waste in the tenant for life to cut it upon the farm, if such
cutting did not essentially injure the farm as an inheritance.[6]

7. As an example of the extent to which estovers would
be deemed reasonable, we find that it is held that upon a farm
of 165 acres the tenant might not take firewood for two
houses, one the principal one, the other that of the farmer or

[1] White v. Cutler, 17 Pick. 248 ; Padelford v. Padelford, 7 Pick. 152 ; Richardson v. York, 14 Me. 216 ; Elliott v. Smith, 2 N. H. 430 ; Sarles v. Sarles, 3 Sandf.
Ch. 601 ; Livingston v. Reynolds, 2 Hill, 157 ; Simmons v. Norton, 7 Bing.
640 ; Webster v. Webster, 33 N. H. 21 ; Miles v. Miles, 32 N. H. 147. In a hard
case Judge Story adopted somewhat different rules of law, in Loomis v. Wilbur,
5 Mason, 13.

[2] Johnson v. Johnson, 18 N. H. 597.   [3] Phillips v. Allen, 7 Allen, 115.

[4] Cook v. Cook, 11 Gray, 123. And such seems to be the law in New Hampshire. Fuller v. Wason, 7 N. H. 341 ; Miles v. Miles, 32 N. H. 147.

[5] Owen v. Hyde, 6 Yerg. 334 ; Dalton v. Dalton, 7 Ired. Eq. 197. And so in
an early case in Massachusetts. Padelford v. Padelford, 7 Pick. 152. And in New
Hampshire, by Stat. 1842, c. 165, § 7, and Maine, by Rev. St. 1857, p. 606, § 15,
a widow is authorized to take necessary fuel from her dower lands to supply her
own residence, though not upon the dower lands. This difference of view in the
cases in New England from that held in other States may perhaps be due to the
doctrine obtaining in the former in respect to dower in wild lands.

[6] Webster v. Webster, 33 N. H. 26.

laborer who did the work upon it, although it had been customary to do so.[1]

8. Upon the principles above stated, a tenant has not a right to dig clay upon a farm and make it into bricks for sale, nor to use wood from the farm for their manufacture.[2]

9. In England a stricter rule is applied in respect to allowing estovers than that in use in this country, from the different condition of the two countries in respect to the economical management of estates. Probably the same rule would be applied here as there, that if the tenant suffers houses to go to decay and then cuts timber to repair them, it would be deemed double waste.[3] But it is doubtful if the tenant here would, as there, be * restricted in all cases [*101] from cutting timber for constructing new walls or fences, though in both he may take sufficient to keep such fences, &c., in repair, as were upon the premises when he took them.[4] And while he is not bound to repair a house already ruinous, he may do so with timber taken from the premises.[5]

10. But the questions, what is timber and what may be used for firewood, and whether the cutting of trees, though for neither of these uses, would be waste, depend upon the usages of this country, the customary mode of managing lands, and the manner in which the inheritance would be affected by such cutting, rather than upon the rules of the English common law, the rule here as to waste being that nothing which does not prejudice the inheritance or those who are entitled to the remainder or reversion, can be deemed waste.[6] Thus to cut oak-trees here for firewood is not, necessarily, waste, though it might be in England.[7]

[1] Sarles v. Sarles, 3 Sandf. Ch. 601. See Smith v. Jewett, 40 N. H. 530, 532; Gardiner v. Dering, 1 Paige, 573.

[2] Livingston v. Reynolds, 2 Hill, 157.   [3] Co. Lit. 53 b.

[4] Co. Lit. 53 b; Miles v. Miles, 32 N. H. 147, 163.   [5] Co. Lit. 54 b.

[6] Pynchon v. Stearns, 11 Met. 304; Morehouse v. Cothcal, 22 N. J. 521.

[7] Padelford v. Padelford, 7 Pick. 152. See also, upon the above points, Jackson v. Brownson, 7 Johns. 227; Kidd v. Dennison, 6 Barb. 9; Crockett v. Crockett, 2 Ohio St. 180; McCullough v. Irvine, 13 Penn. St. 438; Webster v. Webster, 33 N. H. 26. And where timber is blown down, the life tenant is absolutely entitled to such as would have been reasonably necessary for firewood. and to interest on the proceeds of the residue. Stonebraker v. Zollickoffer, 52 Md. 154.

11. It may be remarked that any right of estovers belonging to a tenant would pass to his or her grantee of the estate, or one who should levy thereon for debt.[1]

SECTION III.

OF EMBLEMENTS.

1. ANOTHER of the important rights which a tenant for life has, as also other tenants of estates of uncertain duration, is that of *emblements*, or profits of the crop (*emblavence de bled*), which the law gives to him, or if he is dead, to his executors or administrators, to compensate for the labor and expense of tilling, manuring, and sowing the land.[2]

[*102]   *2. These crops are such as are the growth of annual planting and culture, and the right to take them after the termination of the tenancy rests partly upon the idea of compensation, but chiefly upon the policy of encouraging husbandry, by assuring the fruits of his labor to the one who cultivates the soil.[3] The term emblements is applied also at common law to annual crops growing upon the land of one who dies before they are harvested. At common law, they go to his personal representatives rather than his heirs. But in Mississippi, such crops go to the heir, unless

---

[1] Fuller *v.* Wason, 7 N. H. 341 ; Roberts *v.* Whiting, 16 Mass. 186 ; Smith *v.* Jewett, 40 N. H. 533 ; Cook *v.* Cook, 11 Gray, 123.

[2] Wms. Ex'rs, 597 ; Co. Lit. 55 a.

[3] 2 Bl. Com. 122 ; Co. Lit. 55 b ; Stewart *v.* Doughty, 9 Johns. 108 ; 1 Rolle, Abr. 726, c. 9.

the judge of probate appropriates them to the executor or administrator to be administered.[1]

3. It will be seen, hereafter, that the right to emblements carries with it that of entering upon and cultivating the land, and harvesting the crops when ripe.[2]

4. Among the crops which are considered to be legally the subject of emblements are corn, pease, beans, tares, hemp, flax, saffron, melons, potatoes, and the like, and grasses, such as sainfoin, which are annually renewed. And, by way of exception to the general rule, hops, though grown on permanent roots, and turpentine, though taken from trees, are the subject of emblements, because they require annual training and culture to produce or gather.[3] But clover or other grasses that endure more than one year are not included, nor the fruits of trees growing upon the land, though planted by the tenant, because he knows when he plants them that they cannot come to maturity and produce their fruit in a single year to repay the labor bestowed upon their planting and culture.[4] Though it seems that trees, shrubs, &c., planted by gardeners and nursery-men simply for sale, may be considered as embraced under emblements as between executor of tenant for life and remainder-man or reversioner.[5]

5. This doctrine of emblements was borrowed from the feudal law, whereby, if the tenant died between the 1st of September and the 1st of March, the lord took the profits of the land for the year; if between the 1st of March and the 1st of September, the heirs of the tenant had them.[6]

6. There was an exception, at common law, in respect

[1] McCormick v. McCormick, 40 Miss. 760; Penhallow v. Dwight, 7 Mass. 34; 1 Wms. Ex'rs, 594; 2 Redfield, Wills, 143.

[2] Co. Lit. 56 a; *post*, p. *105·

[3] Wms. Ex'rs, 597; 2 Sharsw. Bl. Com. 123, n.; Com. Dig., " Biens, G. 1 ;" Co. Lit. 55 b, n. 364; Lewis v. McNatt, 65 N. C. 63; State v. Moore, 11 Ired. 70. Fobes v. Shattuck, 22 Barb. 568, that wheat straw is emblements, and belongs to the tenant.

[4] Wms. Ex'rs, 598, 599; Evans v. Inglehart, 6 G. & J. 171, 188; Reiff r. Reiff, 64 Penn. St. 134, 137. So a tenant who has harvested his crop in June cannot take as emblements stubble ploughed in and growing in November, when the tenancy ended in September. Hendrixson v. Cardwell, 9 Baxt. 389.

[5] Penton v. Robart, 2 East, 88; Taylor, Land. & T. 81.

[6] 2 Bl. Com. 123.

[*103] to *emblements in case of a dowress, because it was presumed that when her husband died she took the estate with the crops upon it, and therefore, though she died after having planted a crop, it went to the reversioner. But by the statute of Merton, 20 Hen. III. c. 2, the growing crop might be devised by her, or would go to her executors.[1]

7. But it is essential to the claim of emblements, at the common law, that the crop should have been actually planted during the life and occupancy of the tenant. No degree of preparation of the ground will give to one the fruits of seed planted by another after the determination of his tenancy.[2]

8. In order to entitle tenant or his executors to emblements, the estate which he has must, in the first place, be uncertain in its duration. If he, knowing it will terminate before he can gather his crop, plants it, it is his own folly or generosity to his successor who will take it.[3] So where one entered under an agreement of purchase and sale of the land between him and the owner, and planted crops, and the land-owner then refused to convey the land, the tenant was held to be entitled to the same as emblements on the ground that he had been occupying as a tenant at will.[4] But where one in possession of land, for the recovery of which a suit was pending against him, let the same to one cognizant of the suit, who planted crops, and before they were gathered the claimant in the suit prevailed and expelled the tenant, it was held that the latter could not claim the crop as emblements.[5]

---

[1] Co. 2d Inst. 80.

[2] Price v. Pickett, 21 Ala. 741; Gee v. Young, 1 Hayw. 17 ; Stewart v. Doughty, 9 Johns. 108; Taylor, Land. & T. 82 ; Thompson v. Thompson, 6 Munf. 514.

[3] Debow v. Colfax, 5 Halst. 128 ; Kittredge v. Woods, 3 N. H. 503; Whitmarsh v. Cutting, 10 Johns. 360 ; Taylor, Land. & T. 81 ; Chesley v. Welch, 37 Me. 106 ; Harris v. Carson, 7 Leigh, 632 ; Termes de la Ley, " Emblements." Hence a tenant for a single year has been held not entitled. Reeder v. Sayre, 70 N. Y. 180. But where the tenancy was an oral one for two years with a right to emblements, it was held that this was not cut off by an insufficient notice to quit. Ib.

[4] Harris v. Frink, 49 N. Y. 24.

[5] Rowell v. Klein, 44 Ind. 290.

9. So, in the second place, the tenancy must be determined by the act of God, as by death of the tenant, or the act of the lessor in expelling him or terminating his lease; for if the tenant abandons the premises, or voluntarily puts an end to the tenancy, he has no right to claim emblements.[1] Thus, if a woman, tenant during widowhood, marry, she loses her right to emblements.[2] And these principles apply in cases of tenancies at will.[3]

10. But a tenant at sufferance is not entitled to emblements.[4] Where, however, a purchaser under a foreclosure sale suffered the tenant, either the mortgagor or one claiming under him, to occupy the premises without interference for the term of three months, and in the mean time to go on and manage it, and plant crops, it was held to give the tenant a right to claim these as emblements.[5]

*11. This right to emblements is not limited to the [*104] original lessee or tenant for life, unless he is restricted by the terms of his lease from underletting or assigning his term. His assignee, grantee, or sub-lessee, not only has a claim for the same emblements as the original tenant, but in some cases may claim these where the former could not himself have made such claim. Thus if the original tenant were to forfeit his estate by failing to perform a condition, or by committing a breach of a condition prescribed in his lease, he would thereby lose all right to the emblements. But if, before such breach on his part, he should assign or underlet to another, and the estate should be defeated by such breach, his under-tenant or assignee would, nevertheless, be entitled to the growing crop which he had planted. As, for instance, if a tenant during widowhood should underlet and then marry, though she would by so doing lose her own right to

---

[1] Cases *supra;* Whitmarsh v. Cutting, 10 Johns. 360; Chesley r. Welch, 37 Me. 106; 2 Bl. Com. 123; Oland's Case, 5 Rep. 116; Chandler v. Thurston, 10 Pick. 205, 210.

[2] Hawkins v. Skeggs, 10 Humph. 31; Debow v. Colfax, 5 Halst. 128.

[3] Termes de la Ley, "Emblements;" Davis v. Thompson, 13 Me. 209; Davis v. Brocklebank, 9 N. H. 73; Sherburne v. Jones, 20 Me. 70; Stewart r. Doughty, 9 Johns. 108; Oland's Case, 5 Rep. 116; Chandler v. Thurston, 10 Pick. 205.

[4] Doe v. Turner, 7 M. & W. 226.

[5] Allen v. Carpenter, 15 Mich. 25, 38.

emblements, her tenant would not, because he was not in fault.[1]

12. But if the tenant, having planted the crop, sell it as a growing crop, and then terminates his estate by his own act, the vendee will have no better right in respect to such crop than the lessee himself, and cannot claim them as emblements.[2]

13. If the owner of land on which he has planted a crop sells the land, it passes a complete title to the crop. And if he convey a reversion, subject to an existing particular estate, it carries with it, as incident to such reversion, the same rights in respect to crops growing on the premises which the grantor himself has.[3]

14. If the owner of land plant crops and then conveys the estate to one for life, with remainder over in fee, and the tenant for life dies before the crop is gathered, it will not go to the personal representatives of the tenant for life, be-
[*105] cause * he did not plant it, but to the remainder-man as a part of the inheritance.[4] So if a woman seised for life or in fee sow her land and marry, and her husband die before the crop is severed, she and not his representatives shall have the crop.[5] But if the husband of tenant for life sow crops, and she dies, he will be entitled to the emblements.[6] And in the case above supposed, if the grant for life had been to husband and wife and the survivor, and the husband had died, the wife would have taken the crops instead of the representatives of the husband.[7]

15. It was held in Liford's Case that, if a disseisor take the crops growing upon the premises, and the disseisee recover possession of the land, he may have trespass for such taking against the disseisor,[8] but that if the disseisor make a feoff-

---

[1] 2 Bl. Com. 124 ; Bevans v. Briscoe, 4 Har. & J. 139 ; Taylor, Land. & T. 81 ; Davis v. Eyton, 7 Bing. 154 ; Tud. Cas. 62 ; Bulwer v. Bulwer, 2 B. & A. 470. *Contra*, Oland's Case, 5 Rep. 116 ; Bittinger v. Baker, 29 Penn. St. 66.

[2] Debow v. Colfax, 5 Halst. 128.

[3] Foote v. Colvin, 3 Johns. 216 ; Burnside v. Weightman, 9 Watts, 46.

[4] Wms. Ex'rs, 602 ; Grantham v. Hawley, Hob. 132.

[5] Tud. Cas. 62, cites Vin. Abr. "Emblements."

[6] Spencer v. Lewis, 1 Houst. 223.   [7] Haslett v. Glenn, 7 Har. & J. 17.

[8] In Simpkins v. Rogers, 15 Ill. 397 ; Crotty v. Collins, 13 Ill. 567, it was

ment or lease of the premises, and the feoffee or lessee take the crops, the disseisee cannot have trespass for such taking, even after regaining possession, for the tenant came in by title.[1] But this latter proposition has often been questioned, and is in some States expressly denied to be law, and the disseisor's lessee, as well as his heirs, held liable to the disseisee.[2]

16. To avail himself of the emblements, it is obvious that the tenant or his representative must have some right of entry or occupancy of the land itself; and if the tenancy is determined by death or otherwise soon after the planting of a crop, this right may of necessity be continued for some months. The extent of this right may be stated to be this: He may enter upon the land, cultivate the crop if a growing one, cut and harvest it when fit, and if interfered with in the reasonable exercise of these privileges by the landlord or reversioner, or if the crop be injured by him, he may have an action for the same.[3]

17. But this does not give him a right to exclusive possession of the land, but merely the right of ingress and egress for the purposes above mentioned, while, for all other purposes, the landlord or reversioner is in exclusive possession.[4]

18. A question has been raised whether for this qualified occupation of land, the tenant or his executors would be chargeable for rent, or be bound to make compensation. Plowden raises * the query and seems to incline [*106] to the opinion that they would be, except in case of executors of tenant in fee. And this query is repeated by Williams in his treatise on Executors.[5]

19. Though the question, what are lawful estovers and emblements, is pretty well defined by the common law, it is held

---

held that trover lay. In Lindsey v. Winona R. R., 29 Minn. 411, however, the liability to the disseisee was limited to crops planted by the latter, or for grass or other *fructus naturales;* while in Page v. Fowler, 39 Cal. 412, a liability for crops, even of hay, was denied.

[1] Liford's Case, 11 Rep. 51, and see Termes de la Ley, "Emblements."
[2] Trubee v. Miller, 48 Conn. 347; Emerson v. Thompson, 2 Pick. 473, 485.
[3] Forsythe v. Price, 8 Watts, 282.
[4] Humphries v. Humphries, 3 Ired. 362; Wms. Ex'rs, 605; Lit. § 68.
[5] Plowd. Queries (at the end of his Reports), 239; Wms. Ex'rs, 605.

in this country that they often depend upon the usages and customs of different localities; and though this will be further discussed in connection with the subject of waste, it may be proper here to refer to some of these customs; usage, where it is applied, being considered as entering into and forming a part of the contract or title by which the the tenant holds.[1]

20. Thus it is held a good and valid custom in Pennsylvania, New Jersey, and Delaware, that if the tenant sows crops in the autumn, which will not be ready for harvesting till the next autumn, he may claim them as emblements, although, in the mean time, his lease may have expired.[2] So it was held in Ohio that the parties to a lease in which nothing is said of the way-going crop will be governed by the custom of the place in which the land is situate. Thus where a lease ended on the 1st of April, the tenant was held to be entitled to a crop of wheat then growing thereon.[3] And the same doctrine is applied in Maryland.[4]

21. Although the principle that the tenant who sows a crop shall reap it, if the term of his tenancy is uncertain, is so broad and so nearly universal in its application, yet if a mortgagee forecloses his mortgage, whatever crops are then growing upon the mortgaged premises, if planted after the mortgage is made, become the mortgagee's, whether planted by the mortgagor or by his tenant, free from any claim upon them by such tenant.[5] But a foreclosure after the crops are severed

[1] Van Ness v. Pacard, 2 Pet. 137, 148; Taylor, Land. & T. 82, 83; Stultz v. Dickey, 5 Binn. 285.

[2] Gordon v. Little, 8 S. & R. 533; Van Doren v. Everitt, 2 South, 460; Templeman v. Biddle, 1 Harringt. 522; Smith, Land. & T. 258, Am. ed. n. But this is not uniformly true, for a tenant could not thus sow his ground with oats and claim to occupy till they were ripe after the natural expiration of his lease, if sown for instance in March, and the lease expires in April. Howell v. Schenck, 24 N. J. L. 89. But no such custom exists in N. Y. Reeder v. Sayre, 70 N. Y. 180.

[3] Foster v. Robinson, 6 Ohio St. 90, 95, where the court cite, as to custom making law, Wigglesworth v. Dallison, Doug. 201; Hutton v. Warren, 1 M. & W. 466.

[4] Dorsey v. Eagle, 7 G. & J. 321.

[5] Lane v. King, 8 Wend. 584; Shepard v. Philbrick, 2 Denio, 174; Crews v. Pendleton, 1 Leigh, 297; Gillett v. Balcom, 6 Barb. 370; Jones v. Thomas, 8 Blackf. 428; Howell v. Schenck, 24 N. J. 89.

does not carry an interest in them to the mortgagee or purchaser.[1]

22. The foregoing doctrine in respect to the rights of a mortgagee would probably be limited to cases where a mortgage creates an estate in the land. But in the case of a judgment lien, a different rule prevails. A tenant who hires land subject to such a lien, and plants crops upon the same before a sale of the premises made, may claim them against a purchaser under a sheriff's sale.[2]

* SECTION IV.   [*107]

OF WASTE.

[1] Buckout v. Swift, 27 Cal. 433 ; Codrington v. Johnstone, 1 Beav. 520.

[2] Bittinger v. Baker, 29 Penn. St. 66, overruling the cases of Sallade v. James, 6 Penn. St. 144, and Groff v. Levan, 16 Penn. St. 179.

1. AN important disability to which all tenants for life as well as for years are subject, is that of not committing *waste*, or doing or suffering that to be done upon the premises which essentially injures or impairs the inheritance of the estate occupied by the tenant. This restriction existed at common law in respect to estates in possession of tenants in dower and curtesy, because, as these were created by the law itself, it was thought that the law was bound to protect the reversioner or remainder-man from being thereby injured. But where the estate of the tenant was created by act of the parties, it was held that if the grantor or lessor failed to protect the estate by stipulations in his deed or lease, the law was not bound to supply the omission. To remedy this defect the statute of Marlbridge, 52 Hen. III. c. 24, was passed, whereby "fermors during their terms, shall not make waste, sale, nor exile of house, woods, and men, nor of anything belonging to the tenements that they have to ferm," and were made liable to " yield full damage " for so doing. And it is said "*firmarii* do comprehend all such as hold by lease for life or lives or for years, by deed or without deed." By this statute only single or actual damages were recoverable for waste committed. But by the statute of Gloucester, 6 Edw. I. c. 5, the party committing the injury in an action of waste lost the place wasted and treble damages, or " thrice so much as the waste shall be taxed at." [1]

2. In respect to what is embraced under the term waste, it is divided into that which is voluntary and that which is permissive, the one being by some act done which injures the inheritance, the other by omitting some duty which causes an injury to result to the inheritance. To tear a house down is voluntary waste ; to suffer it to go to decay for want of

---

[1] Co. 2 Inst. 144, 145 ; Id. 299 ; Sackett *v.* Sackett, 8 Pick. 309, 312–315.

necessary repair, is permissive. This will be found an important distinction in its consequences.[1]

*3. But whatever the act or omission is, in order to [*108] its constituting waste, it must either diminish the value
of the estate, or increase the burdens upon it, or impair the evidence of title of him who has the inheritance.[2] Waste, in short, may be defined to be whatever does a lasting damage to the freehold or inheritance, and tends to the permanent loss of the owner in fee, or to destroy or lessen the value of the inheritance.[3]

4. In applying this rule it will be found that many acts which in England would be waste will not be such here, in consequence of the difference in the condition of the two countries. And it often becomes a question for a jury to determine whether a certain act be or be not waste, without referring to a criterion drawn from any other country. The rule as to what constitutes waste is uniform. Its application depends upon the condition and usages of the place where it is to be made.[4]

5. The first branch of the subject, as it is generally treated, relates to felling, lopping, or injuring growing trees upon the premises. The rule of the common law is that to fell timber, to lop it, or to do any act which causes it to decay, is uniformly waste.[5] "Oak, ash, and elm be timber trees in all places," beeches in Buckinghamshire, and birches in Berkshire, are so regarded; but hornbeams, hazels, and willows, are never timber; and yet if standing in defence or safeguard of the house or land, it would be waste to cut them; as it would be to " stub up " a quickset hedge of white-thorn.[6] The same would be the

---

[1] 3 Dane, Abr. 214 ; 2 Bl. Com. 281.

[2] Huntley v. Russell, 13 Q. B. 572, 588 ; 2 Bl. Com. 281 ; 3 Dane, Abr. 215.

[3] McGregor v. Brown, 10 N. Y. 114, 117 ; Proffitt v. Henderson, 29 Mo. 325.

[4] 3 Dane, Abr. 232 ; Pynchon v. Stearns, 11 Met. 304 ; Keeler v. Eastman, 11 Vt. 293 ; Jackson v. Tibbits, 3 Wend. 341 ; Jackson v. Brownson, 7 Johns. 227 ; Walker, Am. Law, 278 ; Kidd v. Dennison, 6 Barb. 9 ; 3 Dane, Abr. 214; Lynn's App., 31 Penn. St. 44 ; Drown v. Smith, 52 Me. 141.

[5] Co. Lit. 53 a ; 2 Bl. Com. 281 ; Taylor, Land. & T. 166.

[6] Co. Lit. 53 a ; 3 Dane, Abr. 218, 233 ; Tud. Cas. 65 ; Honywood v. Honywood, L. R. 18 Eq. 306, limits oak, ash, or elm, as timber, to their being twenty years of age, and not too old to have usable wood in them.

rule as to shade and ornamental and fruit-trees, unless past bearing.[1]

6. In the United States, whether cutting of any kind of trees in any particular case is waste, seems to depend upon the question whether the act is such as a prudent farmer would do with his own land, having regard to the land as an inheritance, and whether the doing it would diminish the value of the land as an estate.[2]

[*109]   *7 Questions of this kind have frequently arisen in those States where the lands are new and covered with forests, and where they cannot be cultivated until cleared of the timber.   In such case it seems to be lawful for the tenant to clear the land if it would be in conformity with good husbandry to do so, the question depending upon the custom of farmers, the situation of the country, and the value of the timber.   The jury are in each case to determine whether by clearing the lands the tenant has cut so much timber as to injure the inheritance.[3]

8. Wood cut by a tenant in clearing the land belongs to him, and he may sell it,[4] though he cannot cut the wood for purposes of sale; it is waste if he does.[5]

9. Nor can the tenant, when sued for cutting and selling timber, recoup or make counter-claim for improvements made by him upon the premises at another time.[6]

10. In applying these rules it has been held in Vermont not to be waste to cut and remove dead or decaying timber in order to clear the land and give the young trees a chance to

---

[1] 3 Dane, Abr. 217 ; Id. 233.

[2] Givens v. McCalmont, 4 Watts, 460; Chase v. Hazelton, 7 N. H. 171 ; Keeler v. Eastman, 11 Vt. 293 ; Shine v. Wilcox, 1 Dev. & B. Eq. 631 ; Smith v. Poyas, 2 Desaus. 65 ; Hickman v. Irvine, 3 Dana, 121 ; Parkins v. Coxe, 2 Hayw. 339 (Martin & Hayw. 517). See Phillips v. Smith, 14 M. & W. 594, n. to Am. ed.

[3] Walker, Am. Law, 278 ; Jackson v. Brownson, 7 Johns. 227 ; Morehouse v. Cotheal, 2 N. J. 521 ; Keeler v. Eastman, 11 Vt. 293 ; McCullough v. Irvine, 13 Penn. St. 438 ; Hastings v. Crunckleton, 3 Yeates, 261 ; Harder v. Harder, 26 Barb. 409 ; McGregor v. Brown, 10 N. Y. 114 ; Proffitt v. Henderson, 29 Mo. 325; Davis v. Gilliam, 5 Ired. Eq. 308.

[4] Crockett v. Crockett, 2 Ohio St. 180 ; Davis v. Gilliam, sup.

[5] Parkins v. Coxe, 2 Hayw. 339 (Martin & Hayw. 517) ; Smith, Land. & T. 192, n. Am. ed. ; Chase v. Hazelton, 7 N. H. 171 ; Clemence v. Steere, 1 R. I. 272.

[6] Morehouse v. Cotheal, 22 N. J. 521 ; Kidd v. Dennison, 6 Barb. 9.

grow.[1] In Massachusetts, cutting oak-trees for fuel is not in itself waste, because of the common usage; though it would be so if they were sold for timber, even if the money was applied to purchase firewood for the use of the tenant.[2] And where land was appendant in its use to, and let with, a furnace, it was held not to be waste to cut wood from the premises to supply the furnace. And the same rule was applied in * the case of salt-works upon the premises, [*110] where wood was cut to carry on the manufacture.[3] So in Pennsylvania it was held not waste for the mortgagor, though insolvent, to cut and sell timber, and dig and sell coal and minerals; because products of this kind are usually so intended.[4]

11. Although it is not proposed to consider the rights of a dowress to her lands to any considerable extent here, it may be observed that her rights in the matter of cutting timber are by no means uniform in the different States. At common law she could only have estovers, and if she went beyond that she was liable to forfeit the premises wasted. For this reason it was held in Massachusetts that she could not be dowable of wild lands, because the very act of clearing for cultivation would be waste and work a forfeiture.[5] But this does not extend to a wood-lot or other land used with a barn or dwelling-house, although such wood-lot or other land has never been cleared.[6]

12. In other States she is dowable of wild lands, and may clear a reasonable proportion of the lands set out to her, for the purposes of cultivation.[7] In Maine, waste does not lie against the tenant in dower, though an action in the nature of waste will.[8]

[1] Keeler v. Eastman, 11 Vt. 293.

[2] Padelford v. Padelford, 7 Pick. 152; Babb v. Perley, 1 Me. 6. So in Rhode Island. Lester v. Young, 14 R. I. 579.

[3] Den v. Kinney, 2 South. 552; Findlay v. Smith, 6 Munf. 134.

[4] Angier v. Agnew, 98 Penn. St. 587.

[5] Conner v. Shepherd, 15 Mass. 164.   [6] Pub. Stat. c. 124, § 4.

[7] Hastings v. Crunckleton, 3 Yeates, 261; Findlay v. Smith, 6 Munf. 134; Alexander v. Fisher, 7 Ala. 514. Such is the law in New York and Pennsylvania. 4 Kent, Com. 76. And in North Carolina. Ballentine v. Poyner, 2 Hayw. 110 (Martin & Hayw. 268); Parkins v. Coxe, 2 Hayw. 339 (Martin & Hayw. 517). So in Tennessee, but not to impair the estate. Owen v. Hyde, 6 Yerg. 334.   [8] Smith v. Follansbee, 13 Me. 273.

13. And if the mode of using the land has consisted in cutting the growth upon it as the customary source of profit, the widow may continue to do so. Thus to cut and sell staves and shingles,[1] or hoop-poles,[2] under the circumstances above supposed, would not be waste.

14. Where the entire dower lands set off to a widow consist of different parcels of the same original estate, but the rights of reversion in the different parcels are in different persons, her right of cutting upon any one of them is not thereby affected, if she fairly treat it as one estate, and is not guilty of partiality or malice towards any one of the reversioners.[3]

[*111]   *15. If a tenant cut trees upon leased premises which are excepted in his lease, he is guilty of trespass, but not waste;[4] and if tenant carry away trees that have been blown down, he would be liable for them in trover, but not in waste.[5]

16. Another species of waste consists in opening gravel pits in the land, and digging and selling gravel therefrom, or digging up and selling the soil or clay, or digging clay and making it into bricks for sale; for a tenant for life may neither dig clay nor cut wood upon land for the purpose of making bricks for sale.[6]

17. But if digging and selling gravel, clay, &c., from pits in the land has been the usual mode of improving the same, it would not be waste to continue to do so in pits already opened.[7]

18. To open lands to search for mines, unless mines are expressly demised with the lands, would be waste; so it would be to open new mines, unless the demise includes them.[8] But

---

[1] Ballentine v. Poyner, 2 Hayw. 110 (Martin & Hayw. 268).

[2] Clemence v. Steere, 1 R. I. 272.

[3] Padelford v. Padelford, 7 Pick. 152 ; Dalton v. Dalton, 7 Ired. Eq. 197.

[4] 1 Cruise, Dig. 116.

[5] Shult v. Barker, 12 S. & R. 272.

[6] Huntley v. Russell, 13 Q. B. 572, 591 ; Taylor, Land. & T. 164 ; Livingston v. Reynolds, 2 Hill, 157 ; Co. Lit. 53 b ; Tud. Cas. 65.

[7] Huntley v. Russell, 13 Q. B. 591 ; Knight v. Mosely, Amb. 176 ; Tud. Cas. 65 ; and see Angier v. Agnew, 98 Penn. St. 587 ; ante * 110.

[8] Co. Lit. 53 b ; 2 Bl. Com. 282; Com. Dig. "Waste," D. 4 ; Saunders's Case, 5 Rep. 12 ; Stoughton v. Leigh, 1 Taunt. 402, 410 ; Darcy v. Askwith, Hob. 234 ; Viner v. Vaughan, 2 Beav. 466.

if the mines are already opened when the tenant takes the estate, it is not waste to continue to work them even to exhaustion. It is but taking the accruing profits of the soil.[1] Nor would it be waste to open new shafts or pits to follow the same vein.[2] And this right he may sell to others. The persons thus entitled may mine and sell the mineral, and for this purpose may make new openings, build railroads, and supply all ordinary facilities for carrying on the business. But the improvements thus made become the property of the reversioner upon the termination of the life estate.[3]

19. The same principle applies to salt-works, as to minerals. If there is an existing salt well on the premises and a mannfactory of salt, it would not be waste to dig a new salt well in connection with it.[4]

*20. Waste may be committed by the manner in [*112] which land is managed in the way of culture. And in England, the early cases at least adopt a very stringent rule, holding it waste to change one kind of land to another, as wood or meadow or pasture into arable land, and the like. And one ground upon which this is held is, that changing the description of lands might endanger the evidence of ownership.[5]

---

[1] 2 Bl. Com. 282 ; Neel v. Neel, 19 Penn. St. 324 ; Taylor, Land. & T. 165 ; Stoughton v. Leigh, 1 Taunt. 410.

[2] Clavering v. Clavering, 2 P. Wms. 388 ; Findlay v. Smith, 6 Munf. 134 ; Crouch v. Puryear, 1 Rand. 258 ; Billings v. Taylor, 10 Pick. 460 ; Coates v. Cheever, 1 Cow. 460. There is a tendency in the courts of Pennsylvania to extend the right of lessees to open new mines without subjecting themselves to the consequences of waste, where the lands leased are chiefly valuable for the minerals they contain. See Smith, Land. & T. 192, 193, Am. ed. n. And see Angier v. Agnew, 98 Penn. St. 587.

[3] Irwin v. Covode, 24 Penn. St. 162 ; Lynn's App., 31 Penn. St. 44 ; Kier v. Peterson, 41 Penn. St. 357.

[4] Findlay v. Smith, 6 Munf. 134 ; Kier v. Peterson, 41 Penn. St. 357. This case presented a novel question under the application of the principle of the text. The defendant leased to the plaintiff the right to bore salt wells for the plaintiff's business, and to manufacture salt thereon for an indefinite period of time, paying therefor every twelfth barrel of salt manufactured. After a while petroleum began to rise in the wells, in connection with the salt water, and, being valuable, both parties claimed the right to take it. It was held that the property in the petroleum remained in the lessor, to be accounted for by the lessee, if used or appropriated by him.

[5] 2 Bl. Com. 282 ; 3 Dane, Abr. 218 ; Com. Dig. " Waste," D. 4 ; Darcy v. Askwith, Hob. 234 a ; Co. Lit. 53 b.

21. But it is apprehended that the usages of this country are such, that no such change in the mode of culture would, of itself, be waste. The question would depend upon whether it was in conformity with the rules of good husbandry or not, and would injure the inheritance.[1] Reference is often had in this kind of waste, as in that by cutting timber, to the usages of the place.[2] And where it was customary to sell the hay from farms, it would not be waste to do so, though esteemed so elsewhere.

22. But it would be waste to suffer pastures to become overgrown with brush;[3] or to impoverish fields by constant tillage from year to year;[4] or to remove the manure made upon the premises in the ordinary course of husbandry;[5] or to suffer a bank to become ruinous, whereby the water of the sea or a river overflows and spoils meadow ground.[6] But where in altering the course of a creek, which was in itself an act of good husbandry, the water had the effect to destroy growing timber, which had not been anticipated, it was held not to be an act of waste.[7]

23. In respect to buildings, waste may be either voluntary or permissive. By the law, as understood in England, [*113] *removing wainscots, floors, or things fixed to the freehold in a house, pulling down or unroofing a building, changing it from one kind to another, as a corn-mill to a fulling-mill, a dwelling-house into a store, two chambers into one, or *e converso*, and the like, would be waste at the common law.[8]

24. In applying these rules, it has been held that pulling down a house and building another even upon a more favora-

<hr>

[1] 3 Dane, Abr. 219 ; Crockett v. Crockett, 2 Ohio St. 180 ; Taylor, Land. & T. 170, 171 ; Clemence v. Steere, 1 R. I. 272 ; Keeler v. Eastman, 11 Vt. 293 ; Phillips v. Smith, 14 ẞ. & W. 594 ; McGregor v. Brown, 10 N. Y. 114, 118 ; Proffitt v. Henderson, 29 Mo. 325.

[2] Jones v. Whitehead, 1 Parsons, 304 ; Smith, Land. & T. 192, n. Am. ed.; Sarles v. Sarles, 3 Sand. Ch. 601 ; Webster v. Webster, 33 N. H. 18, 25.

[3] Clemence v. Steere, 1 R. I. 272.

[4] Sarles v. Sarles, 3 Sandf. Ch. 601.   [5] Lewis v. Jones, 17 Penn. St. 262.

[6] Com. Dig. "Waste," D. 4; Co. Lit. 53 b.

[7] Jackson v. Andrew, 18 Johns. 431.

[8] 3 Dane, Abr. 215; Com. Dig. "Waste," D. 3; Taylor, Land. & T. 166; London v. Greyme, Cro. Jac. 181; Co. Lit. 53 a, n. 344; 2 Rolle, Abr. 815.

ble site upon the same farm, would be waste, and, among other reasons, because it tends to destroy the evidence of identity.[1] Nor would it make any difference that the tenant, by pulling down a building and rebuilding it of a different fashion, makes it more valuable than at first.[2]

25. But it is apprehended that a more liberal rule is now applied in respect to constructive acts of waste in England than formerly, and there certainly is a much more liberal construction put upon such acts in this country than that of the common law. Thus, the cutting a door in a house, if it did no actual injury and did not tend to destroy the evidence of the reversioner's title, would not be waste.[3] The proper test in all these cases seems to be, does the act essentially injure the inheritance as it will come to the reversioner; and this is a question for the jury.[4]

26. The law seems to be correctly stated by the chancellor in Winship v. Pitts. "It is not waste for the tenant to erect a new edifice upon the demised premises, provided it can be done without destroying or materially injuring the buildings, or other improvements already existing thereon. He has no right to pull down valuable buildings, or to make improvements or alterations which will materially or permanently change the nature of the property so as to render it impossible for him to restore * the same premises, [*114] substantially, at the expiration of the term. It cannot be waste, to make new erections upon the demised premises which may be removed at the end of the term without much inconvenience, leaving the property in the same situation it was at the commencement of the tenancy, and the materials of which new buildings, if left on the premises, would more than compensate the owner of the reversion for the expenses of their removal."[5]

27. In accordance with the principle thus laid down, vari-

---

[1] Huntley v. Russell, 13 Q. B. 588.   [2] 2 Rolle, Abr. 815, pl. 17, 18.

[3] Young v. Spencer, 10 B. & C. 145; Jackson v. Tibbits, 3 Wend. 341.

[4] Young v. Spencer, 10 B. & C. 145 ; Doe v. Burlington, 5 B. & Ad. 507; Smith, Land. & T. 194, n.; Jackson v. Andrew, 18 Johns. 431; Hasty v. Wheeler, 12 Me. 434 ; Phillips v. Smith, 14 N. & W. Am. ed. 589, 595, n.; Webster v Webster, 33 N. H. 25; McGregor v. Brown, 10 N.Y. 114, 118.

[5] Winship v. Pitts, 3 Paige, 262.

ous cases have been decided in this country. Thus, in the case just cited it was held not waste for the tenant for years of a house and lot in the city of New York to erect a livery stable upon it. In another, the tenant for years tore down a dilapidated building, and erected another of the same size on the same foundation, and at the end of the term moved it off.[1] In another, the tenant for life erected a new smokehouse in place of one gone to decay, from materials obtained on the homestead.[2] In another, the tenant for life tore down a dilapidated barn which was in danger of falling, and it was held not to be waste.[3]

28. How far it is waste for one in possession of structures erected by him on land the title to which remains in another, depends upon the circumstances under which the erection was made, which have been discussed at large[4] already, need not be here referred to in detail. Briefly it may be said that a tenant for years may within his term or lawful holding remove structures erected by him for the purpose of trade or agriculture;[5] and so may any one, structures of whatever kind placed on the land with the express or implied consent of the landowner to their remaining personalty.[6] But where without such consent,[7] or where a valid contract could not be made between the builder and the landowner, as in the case of husband and wife, or where a tenant for life makes [*115] *permanent improvements, it would be waste to remove what was so attached to the land.[8] It would, however, be otherwise, if the structure was never in fact affixed to the land.[9] And where a railroad company took lands by eminent domain, and erected stone piers thereon for a bridge for the railroad, it was held that, upon the company abandoning the land, these piers did not, as fixtures, belong to the owner of the land.[10]

[1] Beers v. St. John, 16 Conn. 322.   [2] Sarles v. Sarles, 3 Sand. Ch. 601.
[3] Clemence v. Steere, 1 R. I. 272.   [4] See ante, *3 et seq.
[5] Van Ness v. Pacard, 2 Pet. 137 ; 3 Dane, Abr. 222.   [6] Ante *3.
[7] Bonney v. Foss, 62 Me. 248 ; Madigan v. Macarthy, 108 Mass. 376.
[8] Dozier v. Gregory, 1 Jones (N. C.), 100 ; McCullough v. Irvine, 13 Penn. St. 438 ; Washburn v. Sproat, 16 Mass. 449.
[9] Austin v. Stevens, 24 Me. 520.
[10] Wagner v. Cleveland, &c. R. R., 22 Ohio St. 563.

29. Though a tenant is clearly liable if he permits a house or fences on the premises to go to decay, when by the exercise of reasonable diligence he might prevent it, it is not easy to lay down rules *a priori* to define in all cases when and how far a tenant shall act. Decay is often so gradual that it is difficult to determine when a tenant is bound to repair, or how far he shall go in making repairs in any given case. And this is especially so in case of estates for years. And, as a general rule, whatever would be waste to houses or fences in England, would be in this country.[1] If a tenant erect a new house, he is as much bound to keep it in repair as he would be a house standing when he entered.[2]

30. A tenant from year to year is not held liable to make good the mere wear and tear of the premises.[3] He is only obliged to keep the house wind and water tight.[4]

31. But that does not seem to be the measure of what is required of a tenant for years or for life.[5] In this country, the latter is bound to keep the premises in repair, whether there is such a stipulation in the lease or not.[6] And this he must do though there be no timber upon the premises,[7] though it is said that in such case, if tenant be in by lease, the lessor must provide timber necessary for the repairs, if there be no fault in the lessee.[8] But while he is bound to use ordinary care to prevent buildings going to decay, he is not bound to expend extraordinary sums for that purpose.[9]

*32. If a house is uncovered or ruinous when the [*116] tenant takes possession, he will not be made liable by suffering it to remain so, though if there is timber upon the premises he may use it for repairing the house.[10] It would be a double waste to let a house go to decay, and then cut timber to repair it.

---

[1] 3 Dane, Abr. 214 ; Id. 239 ; Smith, Land. & T. 196.
[2] 3 Dane, Abr. 215.   [3] Torriano *v.* Young, 6 Car. & P. 8.
[4] Auworth *v.* Johnson, 5 Car. & P. 239.
[5] Smith, Land. & T. 195.
[6] Long *v.* Fitzsimmons, 1 Watts & S. 530.
[7] Co. Lit. 53 a.   [8] Com. Dig. "Estate by Grant," E. 3.
[9] Wilson *v.* Edmonds, 24 N. H. 517.
[10] 3 Dane, Abr. 221, 222 ; Co. Lit. 53, 54 b ; Clemence *v.* Steere, 1 R. I. 272.

33. In England, it will be sufficient in respect to the fences, if the tenant keep them in as good repair. as he finds them; nor would he be at liberty to cut timber to build fences where there were none before,[1] though it is apprehended that a different rule would be applied in this country, making it depend upon the usages of the place and the rules of good husbandry there.

34. Though a tenant is liable for acts of waste done upon the premises by a stranger, he will not be for what is done by the act of God, public enemies, or the law. But if a house be unroofed by a tempest, the tenant may not suffer it to remain so.[2] And where a surveyor of highways, under authority of law, opened gravel pits within the demised premises, the tenant was held not liable for suffering it to be done.[3]

35. With the above exceptions, the tenant is bound to protect. the premises from waste, even against strangers, or is responsible to the reversioner for the same, and may have his remedy against the wrongdoer.[4] But in Michigan, if a tenant for life has conveyed away his estate, he will not be liable for any waste committed by his grantee, although such tenant for life be a tenant in dower.[5]

36. In England, by statute (6 Anne, c. 31), any person is exonerated from the consequences of a fire which shall take by accident in his own house, unless he has bound himself by some express stipulation. But this does not extend to cases of fires caused by carelessness on the part of the tenant of such house.[6]

37. It is said there are no statutes upon the subject in the United States (except in New York, in regard to fires

---

[1] Co. Lit. 53 b; 3 Dane, Abr. 219.

[2] Co. Lit. 54 a; 3 Dane, Abr. 216, 221; Smith Land. & T. 195, n.; Pollard v. Shaaffer, 1 Dall. 210.

[3] Huntley v. Russell, 13 Q. B. 572, 591.

[4] Co. Lit. 54 a.; Doctor & Stud. 112; Fay v. Brewer, 3 Pick. 203; 3 Dane, Abr. 225; Co. 2d Inst. 145; Wood v. Griffin, 46 N. H. 230, 237, 240; Cook v. Champl. Tr. Co., 1 Denio, 91; Attersol v. Stevens, 1 Taunt. 183, 198; Austin v. Huds. Riv. R. R., 25 N. Y. 334.

[5] Beers v. Beers, 21 Mich. 464.

[6] Filliter v. Phippard, 11 Q. B. 347. There was a second statute, 14 Geo. III. e. 78, § 86, somewhat enlarging that of Anne, extending it "to stable, barn, or other building, or on whose estate any fire," &c., shall begin.

in woods * and fallow land, and one which is the same [*117] as the statute of Anne, in New Jersey and Delaware), though there are sundry cases where a party who has caused damage to the property of another by carelessly setting or managing fire upon his own land has been held responsible. But if the fire occurs without his fault, while exercising reasonable care and diligence, the tenant would not be responsible.[1] The statute of Anne has been adopted as a part of the common law by the courts of Wisconsin, but not that of 14 Geo. III. But it is held not to apply to fires caused by locomotive engines while running upon railroads, the estate of the railroad company. Nor are railroad companies relieved from responsibility for fires occasioned by negligence in operating their roads ; and if fires are shown to have been caused by railway engines upon the road, the burden of showing that it was not the result of negligence or the want of due care and skill is on the railroad company.[2]

38. In respect to the remedy which the reversioner has for waste done upon the premises, it has already been stated that the common law provided an action only in the cases of dower and curtesy, and that it was by the statutes of Marlbridge and Gloucester that the action of waste was extended to tenants for life and years by grant or demise.[3]

39. And it is still competent for lessors, if they see fit, to grant leases exempting tenants from responsibility for waste, or, as it is commonly expressed, "without impeachment of waste." But unless a clause to this effect is inserted, tenants for life or years are responsible for waste done or permitted upon the demised premises.[4]

[1] Smith, Land. & T. Am. ed. 199, n. ; 1 Greenl. Cruise, 133, n. ; Barnard v. Poor, 21 Pick. 378 ; Maull v. Wilson, 2 Harringt. 443 ; Clark v. Foot, 8 Johns. 421 ; 4 Kent, Com. 82 ; Rev. Stat. of Delaware, 1852, e. 88, § 6 ; Nixon, Dig. N. J. Laws, 1835, p. 868, § 8. But it is now held, notwithstanding the remarks of Denio, J., in Althorf v. Wolfe, 22 N. Y. 366, that the statute of 6 Anne, c. 31, modified by that of 14 Geo. III. e. 78, has become a part of the common law of New York. Lansing v. Stone, 37 Barb. 15.

[2] Spaulding v. Chicago & N. It. R., 30 Wisc. 110. See also 8 Am. Law Rev. 146.

[3] 2 Bl. Com. 283 ; Co. 2d Inst. 299 ; Chipman v. Emeric, 3 Cal. 273.

[4] 2 Bl. Com. 283.

40. At common law there were two remedies for waste, one by a writ of prohibition, where it had been threatened, the other by a *writ of waste* for waste actually done, in which the tenant was obliged to pay the value of the waste, and a keeper was appointed to prevent future waste. And this action still lay against the original tenant in dower or curtesy, although he or she might have assigned over the estate. Such action would not lie against the assignee even for waste done after the assignment.[1]

41. But no one could maintain it but he who had an immediate estate of inheritance upon the determination of the estate in dower or curtesy without any interposing vested freehold.[2]

[*118] *42. By the statute of Marlbridge, the actual damages sustained by the reversioner were recovered in an action of waste. That of Gloucester gave treble damages, and, in addition thereto, the reversioner recovered the thing wasted, though it was not always easy to determine how far such forfeiture extended, and what part of the premises it embraced. Thus, if it were done *sparsim*, through a wood, the whole lot was forfeit. So if in several rooms in a house, the whole house. But if in only a part of the wood, or a single room in the house, which was or might easily be separated from the rest, that part only of the thing wasted was held forfeited.[3]

43. And if the tenant repairs what would be held to be waste before the action is commenced, no action can be maintained therefor.[4]

44. The action of waste depends upon privity between the parties, so that if the reversioner grant away his reversion after waste done, no action in this form will lie, and the same would be the effect if the reversioner had died and it had descended to his heirs. So if, after committing waste, the tenant for life died, no action lay against his executors.[5]

---

[1] Co. 2d Inst. 300.   [2] Com. Dig. "Waste," c. 2; Co. Lit. 218 b, n. 122.
[3] Co. 2d Inst. 299 ; Id. 303 ; 2 Bl. Com. 283.
[4] Co. Lit. 53 a ; Jackson *v.* Andrew, 18 Johns. 431.   [5] Co. Lit. 53 b.

45. In one case a widow had assigned her interest and the reversioner had assigned his. Her assignee committed waste. It was held that the assignee of the reversion could not have waste or an action on the case in the nature of waste against her, because of the want of privity between them.[1]

46. But, in such a case, the heir of a reversioner might have waste, or case in the nature of waste, against her after the assignment of her estate. So might the assignee of the heir of the reversioner against the assignee of the life estate. In the first of these cases there was a privity of action at common law; in the other there was a privity of estate. But between the assignee of the reversion of the life estate and the tenant in * dower there is no privity at [*119] all. And the same is true in respect to tenants by curtesy.[2] *

47. In several of the States the difficulties as to the forms and parties to the action of waste, arising from the technical . rules of the common law, have been obviated by statute, in some cases giving the heir of the reversioner an action for waste done in the lifetime of the ancestor.[3] In others, actions for waste done survive against the executors, &c., of the tenant.[4]

48. And it would seem that an action upon the case in the

* NOTE. — This apparent solecism of creating a privity in estate between the grantees of two persons who had originally no privity in estate between themselves, as above stated, between the assignee of the heir of a reversioner and the assignee of a dowress, is to be ascribed to the statute of Gloucester, and is not the creature of the common law, "so as," in the words of Coke, "in this point our act (the statute of Gloucester) is introductory of a new law." 2 Inst. 301; Park, Dower, 359; Com. Dig. "Waste," c. 4; Co. Lit. 54 a.

---

[1] Foot v. Dickinson, 2 Met. 611. "Privity" is defined to be the mutual or successive relationship to the same rights of property. 1 Greenl. Ev. §§ 189, 523.

[2] Bates v. Shrneder, 13 Johns. 260; Walker's Case, 3 Rep. 23; Foot v. Dickinson, 2 Met. 611; Co. 2d Inst. 301.

[3] *Massachusetts*, Pub. Stat. c. 179, § 1; *Maine*, Rev. Stat. 1871, c. 95; *New York*, 2 Stat. at Large, 345; *Wisconsin*, Rev. Stat. 1858, c. 143, § 4; *Michigan*, Comp. Stat. 1857, c. 136, § 4; *Iowa*, Code, 1873, p. 533; *Missouri*, Wagner, Stat. 884; *Delaware*, Rev. Code, 1852, c. 88, § 5; *New Jersey*, Nixon's Dig. 908; *Kentucky*, Gen. St. 1873, p. 609.

[4] *Michigan*, Rev. Stat. pt. 3, tit. 3, c. 6, § 6; *Maine*, Rev. Stat. 1871, c. 95, § 4; *Massachusetts*, Pub. Stat. c. 179, § 5.

nature of waste, for waste actually done, is a common-law remedy, which any one having a reversionary interest may maintain to recover the actual damages done, against any one who does the injury, whether lessee or stranger.[1] In Maine, a reversioner may have waste to recover the place wasted and damages, or case in the nature of waste, and recover damages, but not both.[2]

49. Though, as has been seen, the interposition of a freehold in remainder between the estate of the tenant committing waste, and the remainder or reversion in fee, would prevent the owner of the latter from maintaining waste as the law stood, yet he is not without right or remedy in respect to timber cut upon the premises. The property in that is considered as being in him, and he may seize it, or bring trover for its conversion, or replevy it, or bring trespass *de bonis* for the taking of it. Nor does it matter whether the timber is cut by a stranger or by the tenant himself, since the tenant cannot convey any interest in it when severed.[3] If a tenant for life cut timber and sell it, he is thereby a wrongdoer, and cannot claim the interest upon such sale, on the ground that it was a part of the income of the estate. The reversioner in such case may have trover for the conversion of the timber, or an action for money had and received, if the tenant shall have sold it, which action must be brought within six years, or be barred by the Statute of Limitations.[4] But if the trees are cut by a stranger, both the tenant and reversioner may have actions therefor, — trespass by the tenant, and case by the reversioner. The trees, however, when severed from the freehold, become the absolute and sole property of the reversioner, and trespass will lie in his favor

---

[1] Chase v. Hazelton, 7 N. H. 171, 175. And such action by lessor against lessee is not affected by a subsequent conveyance of the reversion to the latter. Dickinson v. Mayor, 48 Md. 583. In Iowa, owner of land may have *trespass* for acts of permanent injury done to it while in possession of a tenant, the statute having done away the distinction between trespass and case. Brown v. Bridges, 31 Iowa, 138, 145.

[2] Stetson v. Day, 51 Me. 434.

[3] Lewis Bowles's Case, 11 Rep. 82; Berry v. Heard, Cro. Car. 242; Richardson v. York, 14 Me. 216; Bulkley v. Dolbeare, 7 Conn. 232; Mooers v. Wait, 3 Wend. 104.

[4] Seagram v. Knight, L. R. 2 Ch. App. 628; Jones v. Hoar, 5 Pick. 285.

against any one who removes them, even though it be the
tenant himself, as the property in chattels carries with it
possession as against a wrongdoer.[1] Nor would the tenant
for life have any better rights in this respect, though the
trees cut had grown upon what was pasture-land when he
took possession, or the natural growth of wood upon the
land, before the determination of the life estate, would become equal in value to the trees which he had cut. Nor
could he set off against the reversioner's claim for damages,
what he had paid to procure firewood from the same.[2] This
principle applies not only to the timber cut, but to materials
of buildings severed from the inheritance, and the produce of
mines wrongfully severed.[3]

*50. But if tenant for life has the next existing [*120]
estate of inheritance, subject to intermediate contingent remainders in tail, a court of chancery would restrain his
cutting timber, otherwise he would have an inducement to
cut to the injury of the remainder-man, as he would be entitled to the timber, his being the only existing estate of
inheritance.[4] No one, however, whose interest is that of a
contingent remainder, or executory devise, can maintain an
action at law against a tenant for life, for committing waste
upon the premises.[5]

51. As has been stated above, leases are sometimes made
with provisions exempting the tenant from impeachment for
waste. Such tenant, whether for life or years, may open new
mines, fell timber, and claim as his own that which has been
blown down, though he has no property in the timber while
standing, nor can he sell it to another to cut after his death,
nor delegate any right to a third party to do so. But if he
underlets, his tenant will have the same exemption as himself.[6] But such a tenant is not at liberty to commit wilful
and malicious waste, and courts of chancery will interpose,

[1] Lane v. Thompson, 43 N. H. 320.

[2] Phillips v. Allen, 7 Allen, 115 ; Clark v. Holden, 7 Gray, 8, 11.

[3] Tud. Cas. 67 ; Uvedall v. Uvedall, 2 Rolle, Abr. 119, pt. 3.

[4] Williams v. Bolton, 3 P. Wms. 268, n.

[5] Hunt r. Hall, 37 Me. 363, 366.

[6] 2 Bl. Com. 283, n.; Pyne v. Dor, 1 T. R. 55 ; Cholmeley r. Paxton, 3 Bing.
207 ; 1 Cruise, Dig. 128 ; Tud. Cas. 67 ; Bowles's Case, 11 Rep. 83.

by injunction, to restrain its commission, or compel him to repair the waste, if actually committed.[1] The custom of leasing in this way does not seem to have obtained in this country.[2]

52. Among the persons who are liable for waste committed on lands in their occupation are parsons in respect to glebe lands, whether settled for life or years.[3]

53. The courts of the various States have held differently in respect to the extent to which the common law as to waste, or the statutes of Marlbridge and Gloucester, have been adopted in the different States. The tendency of late has been, both in England and this country, to do away with the severe remedies provided in the latter statute, and to substitute either a process in equity for restraining the [*121] commission of waste, or an action * on the case, in which the actual damages done to the inheritance may be recovered by the reversioner. Such now is the case by statute in England, where the action of waste is abolished by 3 & 4 Wm. IV. c. 27, § 36. And the action in this country has gone very much into disuse in the States where it is recognized by the law.[4]

54. Sullivan, in his treatise on land titles in Massachusetts, states that in the course of thirty years' practice he had never known an action of waste in that State to enforce a forfeiture of lands, though he had known actions to recover for the damage actually done.[5] Previous to the act of 1783 there was no statute in that State which declared the estate of a widow forfeited for waste. By that statute such a forfeiture is provided for, but no mention is made of treble damages. It was, however, held that, except so far as modified by the statute of the State, the statutes of Marl-

---

[1] Barker v. Barker, 4 Eng. L. & Eq. 95. This was done in the case of Lord Barnard, tenant of Raby Castle, who, from dislike of his son, the reversioner, stripped the castle of its iron, lead, doors, &c. Vane v. Lord Barnard, 2 Vern. 738.

[2] 4 Kent, Com. 78, n.

[3] Cargill v. Sewall, 19 Me. 288. See also Huntley v. Russell, 13 Q. B. 572, 588; Tud. Cas. 65; 1 Cruise, Dig. 131.

[4] Smith, Land. & T. 197, n.; Greene v. Cole, 2 Saund. 252, n. 7 ; McCullough v. Irvine, 13 Penn. St. 438; 4 Kent, Com. 81; Wms. Real Prop. 24.

[5] 3 Dane, Abr. 228.

bridge and Gloucester were a part of the common law of
Massachusetts.[1]

55. And Judge Kent is inclined to believe that the action
of waste, either at common law or founded upon the statute
of Gloucester, has been generally received in the country as
applicable to all kinds of tenants for life or years.[2]

56. Connecticut seems to have been an exception to the
above proposition, since it is there held that tenants for life,
except tenants in dower or by curtesy, are not impeachable
for waste, though a reversioner may have an action on the
case in the nature of waste for an injury to the reversionary
interest while in the possession of a tenant.[3]

57. In Maine it is held, that the statute of Gloucester never
was a part of the common law of the State in respect
to tenants * in dower, and an action of waste against [*122]
such tenant cannot be sustained there, though an action on the case in the nature of waste may be, unless it be
for permissive waste.[4] And in Georgia, the law as to liability
of dowress and the statute of Gloucester as affecting dower
lands, is the same as in Maine.[5] *

* NOTE. — The following are believed to be substantially the present statute
laws of the States enumerated, relating to waste committed by tenants for life, in
dower and by curtesy, namely : — *Massachusetts.* If tenant in dower or by curtesy, for life or years, commit or suffer waste, the person having the next immediate estate of inheritance may have waste against the tenant, and recover the
place wasted and the damages. The heir may sue for waste done in the time of
the ancestor. The party injured may have an action of tort in the nature of waste
to recover the damages, and the remainder-man or reversioner may maintain it
though there be an intervening estate for life, or though the remainder or reversion be for life or years, and the action may be prosecuted against the executors or
administrators of the tenant, for waste committed by him. Mass. Pub. Stat. 1881,

---

[1] Sackett v. Sackett, 8 Pick. 309 ; Stat. 1783, c. 40, § 3 ; 2 Am. Jur. 76. And
the Pub. Stat. c. 179, § 1, provides for a forfeiture of the place wasted, and actual
damages in actions of waste against tenants by curtesy, dower, for life, or for years.

[2] 4 Kent, Com. 79. Such, in addition to the States where as in the * Note above
it is given by statute, seems to be the case in North Carolina, Alabama, and
Louisiana.

[3] Moore v. Ellsworth, 3 Conn. 483 ; Randall v. Cleaveland, 6 Conn. 328.

[4] Smith v. Follansbee, 13 Me. 273. But it is assumed by Parris, J., in Hasty v.
Wheeler, 12 Me. 434, 438, that if an ordinary tenant for life or years commits
waste, he forfeits the place wasted and treble damages.

[5] Parker v. Chambliss, 12 Ga. 235 ; Woodward v. Gates, 38 Ga. 205.

[*123]   *58· But from the fact that the action is so seldom
brought, it is hardly worth while to occupy any more

c. 179. — *Maine.* The law is the same as in Massachusetts as to maintaining the
action of waste against the tenant, and recovering the place wasted and damages,
and also an action on the ease in the nature of waste, by one having a reversion
with an intermediate estate, or a reversion for life or years. Rev. Stat. 1883, c.
95, §§ 1, 2, 3. — *New York.* If guardian, tenant by curtesy, in dower, for life or
years, or the assigns of such tenant, commit waste, the reversioner may recover
the place wasted and treble damages. 2 Stat. at Large, 345, 346. And in this
respect the statute of *New Jersey* is the same. Rev. 1877, pp. 1235, 1236. — *North
Carolina.* Has abolished the action of waste, but for what would be waste a
judgment is rendered for damages, and if the injury to the estate in reversion shall
be adjudged equal to the value of the tenant's estate or unexpired term, or if it
shall be done in malice, the plaintiff shall have a judgment of forfeiture and eviction. Code, 1883, §§ 624, 629. — *Delaware.* Tenants by curtesy, &c., are liable
to actions for waste in which the plaintiff may recover the place wasted and treble
damages. Laws, 1874, p. 537. — *Missouri.* If tenant for life or years commit
waste, he is subject to an action to lose the thing wasted and to pay double the
damages assessed, and is still liable in damages if he is in possession, though
he may have aliened the premises. Rev. Stat. 1879, § 3107. — *Virginia.* If
tenant, &c., commit waste, he is liable to any person injured, in damages ; and if
wantonly done, he is liable to three times the amount assessed as damages.
Code, 1873, p. 967. — *Kentucky.* The law is like that of Missouri, and reversioner in fee may sue, though there be an intervening estate for life or years.
Gen. Stat. 1873, p. 607. — *Kansas.* The action of waste is abolished, and wrongs
which were remediable by actions of waste are subjects of action as other wrongs.
Comp. Laws, 1879, § 4225. — And in *New York,* if the tenant above mentioned let
or grant his estate, and still retain possession of the same and commit waste, the reversioner may maintain his action of waste against such tenant. 2 Stat. at Large,
345, 346. And in this respect the law is the same in *Michigan.* Comp. Law,
1871, § 6354 ; *Wisconsin,* Rev. Stat. 1878, § 3172 ; *Delaware,* Laws, 1874,
p. 537 ; *New Jersey,* Rev. 1877, p. 1236. — In *Connecticut,* it has been decided
in Moore *v.* Ellsworth (3 Conn. 483), in conformity with the common law
before the statute of Marlbridge, that tenants for life other than tenants in
dower and by curtesy were not liable for waste. By statute (Gen. Stat. 1875,
p. 490), every person having no greater estate in lands than for years or life,
created by the act of the parties, and not by act of law, who shall commit waste, is
made liable to the party injured in an action on the case. The law of *Minnesota*
is the same as to such tenants, tenants in dower and by curtesy, except that judgment for forfeiture and eviction and treble damages will only be rendered where
the injury to the reversion is adjudged in the action to be equal to the value of
the tenant's estate, or unexpired term, or to have been done in malice. Stat.
1878, p. 820. So in *Oregon,* Code, 1862, § 334. — In *Indiana,* the action of waste
is abolished, but the law is the same as to recovery for waste done as in Minnesota,
except that only the actual damages are recovered. Rev. Stat. 1881, § 286. — In
Iowa, the action may be brought by the reversioner, who may have an action of
waste notwithstanding an intermediate estate for life or years, except that he recovers three times the damages and a judgment of forfeiture and eviction, if the

space in discussing *the subject, and it is only ne- [*124]
ccssary to refer the reader to the ease of Greene v.

damages are equal to two thirds of the defendant's interest. Rev. Code, 1880, p. 813.
So in *Dakota*, Laws, 1862, p. 149. — In *Rhode Island*, tenant for life committing
or suffering waste, forfeits the place wasted and double damages to the person entitled to the next estate in remainder or reversion. Pub. Stat. 1882, p. 646. — In
New Hampshire, tenants in dower are made liable in damages for waste, without
any provision by statute for other tenants or forfeiture. Gen. Laws, 1878, c. 202,
§ 6. The court, in Chase v. Hazelton, 7 N. H. 171, waive the point whether the
statutes of Marlbridge and Gloucester have been adopted as a part of the common
law of New Hampshire. But they hold that actions on the case in the nature of
waste, lie in all cases where the reversionary interest of the plaintiff is injured by
acts of waste, whether by tenant or stranger. — *Nebraska*. Widows are liable to
the next of inheritance for all damages occasioned by waste committed or suffered
by her. Gen. Stat. 1873. — The statute law of *Vermont* is like that of New
Hampshire. Rev. Laws, 1880, § 2227. — So is that of *Mississippi*. Rev. Code,
1871, p. 255. — So is the law of *Illinois*, except that there is a forfeiture of the
place as well as a judgment for damages. Rev. Stat. 1874, p. 428. — In *Ohio*,
though a tenant for life is liable for waste, the action of waste is abolished, and no
one forfeits the place wasted, in an action for the waste done, except tenant in
dower or curtesy, who forfeits the place wasted to the immediate remainder-
man or reversioner. Walker, Am. Law, 277, 326, 329 ; Rev. Stat. 1880, §§ 4177,
4194. — In *Michigan*, the action is always on the case, and judgment may be had
for double damages against tenants by curtesy, in dower, for life and years.
Comp. Law, 1857, c. 136, §§ 1, 5. — And the law in *Wisconsin* is the same. Rev.
Stat. 1878, e. 136. And any one who has the reversion or remainder in fee or
in tail, after an intervening estate for life, as well as remainder-man or reversioner for life or years, may have an action on the case in the nature of waste
against tenant committing waste. Id. § 3175. — In *Kentucky*, an action of
waste may be maintained by any one who has the remainder or reversion in
fee-simple after an intervening estate for life or years ; and also by one who has
a remainder or reversion for life or years only, each recovering such damage as
it shall appear he has sustained. Any person who may have waste may have an
action on the case in the nature of waste to recover actual damages, or treble
damages if the injury he wantonly committed. Gen. Stat. 1873, p. 607, § 3. — In
California, the tenant who commits waste forfeits treble damages, but not the
place wasted. Harston Code, 1877, § 732 ; Chipman v. Emeric, 3 Cal. 273. — In
Arizona, Comp. Laws, 1877, § 2688 ; and *Nevada*, Comp. Laws, 1873, § 1313, tenant
for life committing waste is liable in treble damages. — In *West Virginia*, any
tenant is liable for waste, and, if malicious, in treble damages. Rev. Stat. 1879,
c. 199, §§ 1, 4. — In *Colorado*, Gen. Laws, 1877, p. 591 ; and *Texas*, Rev.
Stat. 1879, p. 193, the common-law action is recognized. In *Pennsylvania*,
Brightly's Purd. Dig. p. 55, § 12 ; p. 1465, § 2, and p. 1467, § 15, the action exists as at common law, and relief by injunction will also be given. — In *Tennessee*,
the remedy and relief seem the same as in Pennsylvania. Stat. 1871, §§ 2133,
2134. — In *Washington*, treble damages are given, and if the waste is malicious
or equal to the value of the life tenant's estate, the place is forfeited. Code 1881,
§ 601.

Cole, and the notes thereon in Saunders's Reports, in which he will find the subject of actions on the case in the nature of waste fully explained, as well as the cases in which they will lie. Among other things it will be found that such an action may be brought by him in reversion for life or years, as well as in fee, and may be maintained for permissive as well as voluntary waste.[1] So it may be brought against a tenant for years for permissive waste done upon the demised premises.[2]

[*125]   *59. In the present state of the law, however, the most usual remedy resorted to by a reversioner against a tenant for life or years in respect to waste is by application to chancery to obtain an injunction restraining him from committing it. This power is incident to courts of chancery, and is conferred by statute upon other courts in some cases. It may be applied in many cases where the party seeking relief could not sustain an action of waste, as where an estate for life intervenes between the estate of the tenant and that of the estate of inheritance, in favor of the intermediate remain-

Perhaps no more proper place may offer for noticing provisions for preventing waste in special cases, other than tenancies for life or years. — In *Kentucky*, a guardian is liable to his ward for waste. Gen. Stat. 1873, p. 607. — In *New York*, if one commits acts of waste upon lands sold on execution, while the same are yet subject to redemption, he will be liable to an action of waste ; and the law is substantially the same in *Wisconsin*. N. Y., 2 Stat. at Large, p. 347 ; Minn. Stat. 1866, p. 492 ; Wis. Rev. Stat. 1858, c. 143, § 8. — In *Maine* and *Massachusetts*, if a tenant commit waste on lands during an action to recover the same, the party aggrieved may recover three times the amount of damages. Maine, Rev. Stat. 1857, c. 95, § 8 ; Mass. Pub. Stat. 1881, c. 138, § 9. — *Minnesota*. If one commit waste on land sold on execution, while subject to redemption, the court will restrain it. Rev. Stat. 1866, p. 492. — In *Delaware*, there may be a writ of estrepement, or injunction to prevent waste, pending an action of ejectment or an action of waste. Rev. Code, 1852, c. 88, § 10. — In *Rhode Island*, there may be a writ of estrepement to stay waste. Gen. Stat. 1872, p. 524. — So in *Pennsylvania*. Brightly's Purd. Dig. 1466. — In other States there may be an injunction for that purpose : as in *Maine*, Gen. Stat. 1871, p. 732 ; *Massachusetts*, Pub. Stat. 1881, c. 138, § 15 ; *New Hampshire*, Gen. Stat. 1867, c. 190, § 1.

---

[1] 2 Saund. 252, and n. 7. Though it is said in broad terms, in the following cases, that case for waste will not lie for permissive waste. Countess of Shrewsbury's Case, 5 Rep. 13 ; Herne *v.* Bembow, 4 Taunt. 764; Gibson *v.* Wells, I B. & P. N. R. 390.

[2] Moore *v.* Townshend, 33 N. J. 284.

der-man, as well as the remainder-man in fee.[1] And this remedy may be applied, although another is provided by statute.[2] So it may often be applied where tenants hold without impeachment of waste, if they exercise this power in an unreasonable and unconscionable manner.[3]

60. Nor will this remedy be granted except in cases of technical waste. It will not be in cases of mere trespass, and it must moreover be for an injury which will be irreparable, and not to be compensated in damages.[4] But it will be granted if material waste is threatened, though the injury actually done be trifling.[5]

61. In one case the court lay down the following rule as to cases where courts of equity will interpose to prevent injuries to real estate, — one which seems to be in conformity with the principles acted upon by courts in other States. If there is a privity of estate between the party applying for the injunction * and him who is doing or about to do [*126] the act, such as exists between tenant for life or years and the reversioner, it is not necessary that the act should work irreparable injury to induce the court to grant it. But if the parties are strangers in respect to the estate, or are claimants adverse to each other, the court will require evidence that the injury threatened will be irreparable, before they will interpose to restrain it by injunction. And this, whether the act threatened be waste or trespass.[6] Nor will an injunction to stay waste be granted where the right is doubtful.[7]

[1] Jones v. Hill, 1 Moore, 100 ; Laussat's Ponhl. Eq. 3, n.; Id. 52, n.; Tracy v. Tracy, 1 Vern. 23 ; Mollineaux v. Powell, 3 P Wms. 268, n. F.; Kane v. Vanderburgh, 1 Johns. Ch. 11 ; Story, Eq. Jur. § 913. But held, that remainder-man for life could not have a bill to enjoin the tenant of the previous estate. Mayo v. Feaster, 2 McCord, Ch. 137.

[2] Harris v. Thomas, 1 Hen. & M. 18. *Contra,* Cutting v. Carter, 4 Hen. & M. 424 ; Poindexter v. Henderson, Walker, 176.

[3] Kane v. Vanderburgh, 1 Johns. Ch. 11 ; 2 Bl. Com. 283 ; Tud. Cas. 68, 69.

[4] Attaquin v. Fish, 5 Met. 140 ; Atkins v. Chilson, 7 Met. 398 ; Poindexter v. Henderson, Walker, 176 ; Leighton v. Leighton, 32 Me. 399.

[5] Livingston v. Reynolds, 26 Wend. 115; Loudon v. Warfield, 5 J. J. Marsh. 196 ; Rodgers v. Rodgers, 11 Barb. 595 ; White Water Canal v. Comegys, 2 Ind. 469.

[6] Georges Creek Co. v. Detmold, 1 Md. Ch. Dec. 371. See Atkins v. Chilson, 7 Met. 398 ; Poindexter v. Henderson, Walker, 176.

[7] Storm v. Mann, 4 Johns. Ch. 21 ; Field v. Jackson, 2 Dick. 599.

62. It seems that, upon a bill for an injunction to stay waste, where waste has already been done, it is competent for the court of equity to require an account of the waste to be taken, and to give the party a compensation for the damages in order to avoid a multiplicity of actions, although the plaintiff may have a remedy therefor by an action at the common law.[1]

63. Courts of equity in England often authorize tenants to cut timber which would be injured by standing, and invest the proceeds for the benefit of those entitled to it.[2]

64. And in England, by statute 8 & 9 Vict. c. 56, provision is made for improving lands held by tenants by draining and the like, through the agency of the court of chancery.[3]

---

[1] Story, Eq. Jur. §§ 517, 518, 917 ; Tud. Cas. 68 ; Watson *v.* Hunter, 5 Johns. Ch. 169.

[2] Story, Eq. Jur. § 919.   And a similar power is delegated to courts in Massa-chusetts, Pub. Stat. c. 126, § 12 ; and Maine, Rev. Stat. 1871, p. 784.

[3] Wms. Real Prop. 27.

CHAPTER VI.

ESTATES BY CURTESY.

1. AN estate by the curtesy, or, as it is more commonly called, by curtesy, is that to which a husband is entitled, upon the death of the wife, in the lands or tenements of which she was *seised in possession, in fee simple [*128] or in tail, during their coverture, provided they have had lawful issue born alive, which might have been capable of

inheriting the estate. It is a freehold estate for the term of his natural life.[1]

2. Equity, following the law, holds that where the wife is *cestui que trust* in fee simple or in tail, the husband is entitled to curtesy in the trust estate, in the same manner as in the legal estate.[2]

3. It has been much discussed by writers whether this estate was originally an institution of the English law, as stated by Littleton, § 35. Sir Martin Wright insists that it was known in Scotland, Ireland, Normandy, and to the ancient Almain laws; while the "Mirror" ascribes the period of its introduction into England to the time of Henry I.; and Wooddeson in his Lectures, and Christian in his Notes to Blackstone, consider it of English origin, and thence transferred into the laws of Scotland and Ireland, though it seems to be conceded that it takes its name from *curtis*, a court, rather than from any peculiar regard to husbands in the English law.[3] Mr. Barrington says the word is clearly derived from the French word *courtesie*, and it is called curtesy of England, to distinguish it from a very similar right by the Norman law.[4] The writers all seem to agree that it is not of feudal origin, though by that law as soon as a son was born the father was admitted, in respect to the estate, as one of the *pares curiæ*, and did homage for the same alone, while prior to that, husband and wife did the homage together.[5] Wright and Craig ascribe its origin to the civil law, in the time of Constantine.[6]

[*129]   * 4. Whatever may have been its origin, it has been a well-known estate at the common law, with well-defined qualities and incidents, from a period as early probably as the reign of Henry I., if not before. Of late, however, by reason of the prevalence of marriage settlements in England, it has, practically, become infrequent there.[7]

5. In this country it was adopted as a common-law estate.

---

[1] Lit. § 35 ; Co. Lit. 30 a; 2 Bl. Com. 126 ; Adair *v.* Lott, 3 Hill, 182.

[2] Watts *v.* Ball, 1 P. Wms. 108 ; Co. Lit. 29 a, n. 165 ; Tud. Cas. 38.

[3] Wright, Ten. 192, 193 ; 2 Bl. Com. 126, and n. In Erskine, Institutes, p. 380, it is said, that in Scotland, "the right of curtesy or curiality has been received by our most ancient customs."

[4] Stat. 440.

[5] Wright, Ten. 193 ; 2 Bl. Com. 126, 127

[6] Wright, Ten. 194.

[7] Wms. Real Prop. 187.

It still exists in **its** common-law form by express statute, or by statutory recognition, in New Hampshire, Vermont, Rhode Island, New Jersey, Delaware, Maryland, West Virginia, Pennsylvania, North Carolina, Kentucky, Tennessee, and Nebraska.[1] In Connecticut, Virginia, and Missouri it is recognized by the courts as an existing estate.[2] In Oregon and Ohio curtesy is given, though no issue be born alive.[3] In Massachusetts it exists as at common law, but is apparently restricted in case of intestacy, if there are no issue.[4] It has been expressly abolished in Illinois, Indiana, Iowa, Kansas, Mississippi, Minnesota, Dakota, Wyoming, Arizona, and Nevada,[5] and different provisions for the husband substituted, — as in Illinois, where the husband is endowed of a life estate similar to dower at common law;[6] Indiana, where he receives a fee in one third of the wife's realty as heir;[7] and in Kansas, where his share is one half of her estate in fee, subject, however, to her debts, and to any sale on execution;[8] while in Arizona he receives one half of the property held in community by his wife and himself, and in Nevada the whole.[9] In other States, again,

---

[1] N. H. Gen. L. 1878, c. 202, § 14. Vt. Rev. L. 1880, § 2229; but not where wife has issue by a former husband, who would take the estate. R. I. Pub. Stat. 1882, c. 166, §§ 20, 53; c. 182, § 3. N. J. Rev. 1877, pp. 298, 320. Del. Rev. Stat. 1874, pp. 515, 533. Md. Rev. Code, 1878, art. 45, § 2. W. Va. Rev. Stat. c. 70, § 15. Pa. Brightly Purd. Dig. p. 1007; Pryor v. Wood, 31 Pa. St. 142, 147. N. C. Code, 1883, § 1838. Ky. Gen. Stat. 1873, c. 52, art. 4, § 14. Tenn. Stat. 1871, § 2486 f. Neb. Gen. Stat. 1873, c. 17, §§ 29, 40.

[2] 1 Greenl. Cruise, 140, n.; Alexander v. Warrance, 17 Mo. 228.

[3] Ohio Rev. Stat. 1880, § 4176; Oregon Gen. L. 1872, p. 588. In Ohio, moreover, the husband's curtesy does not extend to lands which his wife received from a former husband, except by devise, if there are issue to take it.

[4] Mass. Pub. Stat. 1881, c. 124, § 1; but, § 3, a husband takes, in case of intestacy and want of issue, the wife's realty in fee to the amount of $5,000 and curtesy only in the residue, if any, and the former provision is also subject to her debts. If there is no issue of the marriage, the husband now takes one half the lands for his life, whether the wife provides otherwise by her will or not. Stat. 1885, c. 255, § 2.

[5] Ill. Rev. Stat. 1883, c. 41, § 1. Ind. Rev. Stat. 1881, § 2482. Iowa, Rev. Code, 1880, § 2440. Kans. Comp. L. 1879, § 2129. Miss. Rev. Code, 1880, § 1170. Minn. L. 1875, c. 40, § 5. Dak. Rev. Code, 1877, p. 247. Wyoming Comp. L. 1876, c. 42, § 1. Arizona Comp. L. 1877, § 1976. Nev. Comp. L. 1873, § 157.

[6] Ill. Rev. Stat. 1883, c. 41, § 1; Henson v. Moore, 104 Ill. 403.

[7] Ind. Rev. Stat. 1881, § 2483. If the property exceeds $10,000, he has but one fourth, and if more than $20,000, but one fifth. Ib.

[8] Kans. Comp. L. 1879, §§ 2109, 2118, 2129. And if there are no issue, he takes the whole estate. § 2121.

[9] Nev. Comp. L. 1873, § 160; Arizona Comp. L. 1877, § 1977.

curtesy is superseded by the adoption of statutory provisions inconsistent therewith. Thus in Louisiana, California, and Texas by the community of property in which a common stock is made of all acquisitions by either husband or wife during marriage; and in the latter State a further provision is made in his favor, in case of intestacy.[1] So in Florida and Georgia, where the husband takes a child's share, and the whole if there are no children.[2] In Michigan the unrestricted power of a married woman to convey *inter vivos* and dispose by will of all her realty has been held to abolish curtesy;[3] and similar provisions exist in South Carolina, Alabama, Arkansas, and Montana.[4] So in New York it seems to be competent for the wife, by her separate conveyance in her lifetime, to defeat her husband's right to curtesy.[5] In Maine and Wisconsin, though curtesy is given by statute, yet in the former State it is limited to a life interest in one third of the wife's realty, and then only if she died solvent; and in the latter only in lands of which she died seised, and which were not otherwise disposed of by her will.[6]

6. The definition before given suggests the essential requisites to entitle a husband to curtesy: (1) marriage; (2) seisin of wife during coverture; (3) birth of a child alive during the life of the wife; (4) death of the wife.

7. In considering these in detail, the marriage must be a lawful one, though if it be a voidable one it will give [*130] curtesy, * unless it is actually avoided during the life of the wife. It cannot be declared void afterwards.[7]

8. In respect to the seisin of the wife, it must, in general

---

[1] Stat. 1850, c. 147, § 10. Wood, Calif. Dig. 488, § 10. Tex. Rev. Stat. 1879, § 1653. If there are children, the survivor takes one half; if none, the whole. And see Portis *v.* Parker, 22 Tex. 699.

[2] Fla. Dig. 1881, p. 471, § 12; p. 757, § 16. Ga. Code, 1873, § 1761, where the wife has also the power to dispose by will of all her separate earnings; § 2410.

[3] Tong *v.* Marvin, 15 Mich. 60, 73; Mich. Comp. L. 1871, § 4300.

[4] So. Car. Gen. Stat. 1882, § 2035. Ala. Code, 1876, § 2713; but if she dies intestate, her husband is entitled to use of her realty for life, § 2714. Ark. Dig. Stat. 1874; Montana Rev. Stat. 1879, p. 272.

[5] 4 N. Y. Stat. at Large, 513; Thurber *v.* Townsend, 22 N. Y. 517.

[6] Me. Rev. Stat. 1883, c. 103, § 15; but if she dies intestate and childless and her estate is solvent, the husband receives one half for his life. Ib. Wisc. Rev. Stat. 1878, §§ 2180, 2277.   [7] 2 Burns, Eccl. Law, 501.

terms, be of an estate of inheritance. But this may be either a legal or an equitable one. In giving form and effect to estates under the equitable view of the Statute of Uses, courts of equity intended to follow, and in most respects have followed, the law, in regard to the nature and incidents of such estates. Among these was the right of curtesy, and husbands of *cestuis que trust* were allowed to take curtesy in the trust estates, if they were estates of inheritance, of which the wife had in equity what answered to a seisin at law of legal estates in possession.[1] And the receipt of the rents and profits by the wife as such *cestui que trust* during coverture, is ordinarily sufficient seisin in equity to give a husband curtesy.[2] But it does not seem to be sufficient seisin of a trust estate, to give husband curtesy thereof, that the wife had the rents and profits of the estate, if it was by the terms of the trust to her own separate use, her seisin in such case not enuring to the benefit of the husband.[3] And where the estate was conveyed to a wife to her solo and separate use and disposal, and free and clear of any control of her husband, without being subject to the debts, liabilities, or engagements of the husband, it was held that a devise of her estate defeated her husband's right of curtesy.[4]

9. Originally, curtesy could not be claimed of a use which the wife had as *cestui que use.* But now the right is extended to equities of redemption, contingent uses, and moneys directed to be laid out in lands for the benefit of the wife. Equity in such cases treats the money as land.[5] Thus, where an executor sold the land of a female heir under such circumstances that she might confirm the sale and take the money, or avoid

---

[1] Roper, Hus. & Wife, 18, 20 ; Watts v. Ball, 1 P. Wms. 109 ; Robison v. Codman, 1 Sumn. 121 ; Morgan v. Morgan, 5 Madd. 408 ; Hearle v. Greenbank, 3 Atk. 695, 717 ; Sweetapple v. Bindon, 2 Vern. 537, n. 3 ; Davis v. Mason, 1 Pet. 503.

[2] Morgan v. Morgan, 5 Madd. 408 ; 4 Kent, Com. 31 ; Tud. Cas. 39.

[3] Hearle v. Greenbank, 3 Atk. 717 ; Sweetapple v. Bindon, 2 Vern. 537, n.

[4] Pool v. Blakie, 53 Ill. 495 ; Stokes v. McKibbin, 13 Penn. St. 267. See Bennett v. Davis, 2 P. Wms. 316. But in Tennessee the rule is different, and express words are necessary to cut off the husband's curtesy. Carter v. Dale, 3 Lea, 710.

[5] Davis v. Mason, 1 Pet. 503 ; Sweetapple v. Bindon, 2 Vern. 536 ; Fletcher v. Ashburner, 1 Bro. C. C. 497, 499 ; 3 Prest. Abs. 381.

it and take the land, and she preferred the money, her husband was held entitled to curtesy out of the money, she having died before it was paid over.[1] So, where, in order [*131] to make partition, the *share of a wife, tenant in common, was sold, the husband had curtesy in the money.[2]

10. In many of the States curtesy is given, by statute, in equitable estates of which the wife was seised, and it seems to be a rule recognized in most if not in all the States.[3] Thus in Rhode Island an estate was conveyed to trustees to the sole use of a married woman during life, to be conveyed to her heirs upon her failure to appoint as to the same, and she died without having made an appointment. Her husband was held entitled to curtesy.[4] So where the conveyance was to J S, *habendum* to him and his heirs to the only use, benefit, and behoof of J D, a married woman, it was held to be a legal estate executed in J D, and her husband had a right to curtesy therein.[5] In North Carolina, a husband has curtesy in a trust, or an *estate* in equity, of the wife, but this does not extend to a mere right in equity to have an estate.[6]

11. To recur to the proposition that the estate of the wife must be one of inheritance, no question could arise in respect to estates in fee-simple absolute, nor, ordinarily, as to estates tail. But questions of great subtlety and difficulty have arisen in respect to determinable estates, whether upon their determining the husband's right of curtesy is defeated or not. In an earlier part of the work it became necessary to speak of estates in fee-simple determinable, as well as in tail, of estates defeasible by a breach of condition, and of the determination

---

[1] Houghton *v.* Hapgood, 13 Pick. 154.

[2] Clepper *v.* Livergood, 5 Watts, 113 ; Forbes *v.* Smith, 5 Ired. Eq. 369. So where the devise was to a daughter and her heirs, with power of sale in the executor, and he sold, the husband had curtesy in the money. Dunscomb *v.* Dunscomb, 1 Johns. Ch. 508.

[3] 1 Greenl. Cruise, 147, n., mentions Alabama, Kentucky, Maryland, Mississippi, and Virginia. So Kansas, Comp. L. 1879, §§ 2109, 2129. Alexander *v.* Warrance, 17 Mo. 228 ; Robison *v.* Codman, 1 Sumn. 121 ; Houghton *v.* Hapgood, 13 Pick. 154. See 1 Bro. C. C. 503, note, Am. ed., for a collection of American cases. Rawlings *v.* Adams, 7 Md. 26, 54 ; Dubs *v.* Dubs, 31 Penn. St. 149.

[4] Tillinghast *v.* Coggeshall, 7 R. I. 383. Cf. Robie *v.* Chapman, 59 N. H. 41.

[5] Nightingale *v.* Hidden, 7 R. I. 115.　[6] Sentill *v.* Robeson, 2 Jones, Eq. 510.

of estates by the happening of some event which, at their creation, was made to limit their duration. In applying the principles of these estates to that of the wife, in order to determine whether the husband has right of curtesy therein, it has been settled, in respect to estates tail, for instance, that, though the issue in tail fail by death of the child in the wife's lifetime, whereby her estate at her death is at an end, the husband takes curtesy, it being a right incident to such an estate.[1]

12. So, where the devise was to a daughter and her heirs, and if she died without issue, the whole estate was to be sold and the proceeds paid to her brothers and sisters, and she married and had a child, who died, and then she died without issue, her husband had curtesy.[2]

13. It will be observed in the above-cited cases that the wife * had a determinable fee, that there was an [*132] executory devise over (the nature of which will be more fully explained hereafter) in case of its determining, and, what may perhaps be unimportant, that the estate was only determined at the moment of her death, her estate up to that time having been a fee with its ordinary incidents, and her death the natural termination of her estate. But if the estate of the wife had been determined by the breach of some condition expressed in the deed thereof, for which the grantor or his heirs had entered, this entry would so far retroact, that the grantor would be in of his original estate, and all intermediate estates and rights would have been defeated, including, of course, the husband's curtesy. The estate would be defeated *ab initio*. So if the seisin of the wife were tortious, as gained by disseisin, or under a defective title, and had been defeated by an eviction under a judgment upon a title paramount, the same consequence would follow. So where a daughter becomes, during coverture, seised as heir to her father, and the mother has her dower set out of the same lands, it defeats the seisin of the daughter in the lands so set

---

[1] Paine's Case, 8 Rep. 34 ; *post*, vol. 2, * 374.

[2] Buchanan *v.* Sheffer, 2 Yeates, 374 ; Hay *v.* Mayer, 8 Watts, 203 ; Taliaferro *v.* Burwell, 4 Call, 321. The same principle is laid down in Buckworth *v.* Thirkell, 3 B. & P. 652, n.

out, and with it her husband's curtesy, since the widow's seisin, when consummated by the setting out of her dower, is considered as anterior to that of the daughter as heir, and of course converts the latter into that of a reversion. But if the widow die in the lifetime of the daughter and her husband, the latter will have curtesy by the actual seisin thereby conferred upon his wife.[1]

14. A principle analogous to that stated above is applied in respect to curtesy in equitable estates. Thus, where the devise was to the separate use of the daughter, to be disposed of as she should see fit, the trust to cease on the death of the husband, it was held that she had such an estate of inheritance as entitled her husband to curtesy.[2] And the same was held, where, by a marriage settlement, the estate was conveyed to trustees for the sole and separate use of the wife,

with power to appoint, and she made no appointment.[3] [*133] There was in *both these cases a fee in the wife, and though, while living, the husband was excluded from controlling her estate, there was nothing in the terms of the devise or settlement expressly excluding him from the ordinary right of curtesy. It was accordingly held that where land was given in trust for the wife and her heirs for her separate use, without power of alienation by her or her husband, he was entitled to curtesy. The effect of the statute in Pennsylvania being to make no distinction between legal and equitable estates in the matter of curtesy as well as dower, the law of that State seems to coincide with that of Massachusetts, which gives a husband curtesy in lands of which his wife is seised to her sole and separate use as an inheritance.[4]

15. But though it is not competent at common law, in the grant to a woman of an estate of inheritance, to exclude her husband from his right of curtesy,[5] a like rule does not prevail in equity, where an estate may be so limited as to give

---

[1] 1 Roper, Hus. & Wife, 36; Id. 42, 43; Co. Lit. 241, Butler's note, 170.

[2] Payne v. Payne, 11 B. Mon. 138; Clancy, Rights of Wom. 193, 194.

[3] Morgan v. Morgan, 5 Madd. 408; Clancy, Rights of Wom. 193, 194. But see Cochran v. O'Hern, 4 Watts & S. 95. See also Clark v. Clark, 24 Barb. 582.

[4] Dubs v. Dubs, 31 Penn. St. 149, 155; Mass. Pub. Stat. c. 124, § 1.

[5] Mildmay's Case, 6 Rep. 41; Clancy, Rights of Wom. 191; Mullany v. Mullany, 4 N. J. Eq. 16.

the wife the inheritance and deprive the husband of curtesy if the intent of the devisor or settlor be express.[1] Thus in Bennet v. Davis, the testator devised lands to his daughter and her heirs, to her sole and separate use, directing that her husband should not be tenant by curtesy in case he survived, but that upon her death the lands should go to her heirs; the court, in order to carry out the intent of the testator, held the husband to be trustee for the heirs of the wife, whereby, though he took the legal estate of curtesy for life, the heirs had the beneficial interest.[2] And the husband would be equally excluded from such equitable estate of his wife, though it had been created by himself.[3]

16. There is no difficulty in applying the rule as to curtesy, where the estate in the wife is the only one created by the devisor or settlor, and that is so defeated by condition or otherwise, as to be again in the original owner's hands, in the same manner as if it had never passed to the wife. But where the grantor or devisor parts with all his estate, in the first place, to the wife, with a limitation over upon the happening of some event which of itself is to determine her estate before its natural expiration, and pass it at once to another, questions of great subtlety have arisen which are discussed with much acuteness by courts and legal writers. The question briefly stated is, In *what cases may curtesy be [*134] claimed in determinable fees of the wife?

17. Mr. Roper's illustration of an estate of inheritance determining by its natural expiration is, an estate in fee tail in a wife who dies without issue or heirs. An estate, on the other hand, determinable on a particular event, independent of its natural expiration, he illustrates by an estate in fee-simple or fee tail in the wife, "whilst or so long as A has heirs of his body, or until B attains twenty-one, and then to B in fee."[4] In these last instances, if A die without issue, or

___

[1] Cochran v. O'Hern, 4 Watts & S. 95 ; Hearle v. Greenbank, 3 Atk. 695, 716 ; Morgan v. Morgan, 5 Madd. 408 ; Stokes v. M'Kibbin, 13 Penn. St. 267 ; Bennet v. Davis, 2 P. Wms. 316 ; Tud. Cas. 39. See also Rigler v. Cloud, 14 Penn. St. 316.

[2] Bennet v. Davis, 2 P. Wms. 316. See also Clark v. Clark, 24 Barb. 582.

[3] Rigler v. Cloud, 14 Penn. St. 361.

[4] 1 Roper, Hus. & Wife, 37–39.

B attain twenty-one, the husband's right of curtesy will be defeated, with the estate out of which it was to be derived.[1] These are evidently cases of simple limitation of estates by events, upon the happening of which the estate limited is determined, and completely at an end with all its incidents, as if it had been measured by the lapse of a certain number of years, months, or days.

18. And it is laid down as a general proposition that " any circumstance which would have defeated or determined the estate of the wife, if living, will, of course, put an end to the estate by curtesy." [2]

19. But the examples already given show that curtesy may be had in many cases where the estate of inheritance granted in the first instance to the wife has determined and passed over to another by force of its original limitation. Such a limitation as is here referred to is what is known as a conditional one, — a limitation not known to the common law, but originating in the doctrine of shifting uses or executory devises. It implies the creation of two estates by one and the same deed or devise, in such a manner that the first will, upon the happening of a certain contingent event, be defeated and brought to an end before its natural determination, and the second estate thereupon, at once, and without any act or thing done to give it effect, come in and take the place of the first estate. The first of these estates may be a fee, and the event that determines it and passes it over to the third party may be the dying of the first taker without issue, or before a certain age, or both ; and the question then has been, whether the husband or wife of such first taker is thereby defeated of what till that event had been a right incident to an existing estate, or might enjoy it, although as to the deceased the estate was determined by death. Lord Mansfield, in one case, was of opinion that the husband in such a case was entitled to curtesy ; [3] and Best, C. J., was of a like opinion in a case of dower.[4] But the doctrine does not find favor with Mr. Park in his work on Dower ; [5] and the opinion of Lord Mansfield is

<hr>

[1] Id. 39.   [2] 1 Atk. Conv. 255.
[3] Buckworth v. Thirkell, 3 B. & P. 652, n.
[4] Doody v. King, 2 Bing. 447.   [5] Park, Dower, 177-183.

impugned by Mr. Sugden.[1] And at one time it was held in New York that such a determination of an estate defeats the right both of dower[2] and curtesy.[3] And the English court held, in a case where a conveyance was made to such uses as C D should appoint, and in default of, and until appointment, to the use of C D in fee, who was married, that by the execution of this appointment in the lifetime of C D, his estate was defeated, and with it his wife's right of dower.[4] Mr. Burton alludes to the circumstance, that in one class of the English cases above cited the estate was defeated by the death of the first taker, and in the other by the act of the first taker in his lifetime. But apparently concluding that this can hardly reconcile these decisions, he adds: "Such and so subtle appears the distinction, on the ground of positive law, between these decisions."[5] Gibson, C. J., undertakes to explain away these difficulties, in the case of Evans v. Evans, although it is nearly identical with one cited from the New York reports below, in which the court came to an opposite conclusion, and he seems to overlook the fact that there can be no limitation of a fee upon a fee at common law, and that the questions, in most of the cases, do not arise under limitations at common law.

20. The case of Evans v. Evans, though one of dower, was decided upon analogy to cases of curtesy, and the reasoning of the court applies to the one as well as to the other. The devise in that case was to A and B, their heirs and assigns; but should either die without having lawful issue living at his (her) death, then the estate of one so dying to vest in the survivor and heirs forever. It was held that upon A dying without living issue, his widow (her husband) was entitled to dower (curtesy) out of the estate.[6] The court — Gibson, Ch. J. — declared that none of the text-writers, except Mr. Preston, had suggested the true solution of the difficulty in such

---

[1] Sugd. Powers, vol. 2, p. 31.
[2] Weller v. Weller, 28 Barb. 588, overruled 54 N. Y. 285.
[3] Hatfield v. Sneden, 42 Barb. 622, overruled 54 N. Y. 280. See *post*, *135.
[4] Ray v. Pung, 5 B. & A. 561.
[5] Burton, Real Prop. 145. See *post*, *213-*216, and cases cited.
[6] Evans v. Evans, 9 Penn. St. 190.

cases in giving curtesy or dower to the husband or wife of the
deceased person whose entire estate was determined
[*135] by the death ; and *held the solution to be, that estates determinable *by executory devise* and *springing
use*, are not governed by common-law principles.[1] It was accordingly held that a limitation to A and her heirs, with a
limitation over to N upon A's dying without issue, was such
an estate in A as gave her husband the right of curtesy
therein.[2]

21. If, therefore, the estate of the wife be an estate of inheritance, determinable by a limitation which operates to defeat her estate at common law, the right of curtesy, it would
seem, is gone. But if the limitation over be by the way of
springing use or executory devise which takes effect at her
decease, thereby defeating or determining her original estate
before its natural expiration, and substituting a new one in its
place, which could not be done at common law, the seisin and
estate which she had of the fee-simple or tail will give the
husband curtesy.[3] And the doctrine of this paragraph is now
recognized as the law in such cases in New York.[4]

22. If the wife be one of two or more joint tenants, though
she is actually seised, yet if she die, living her co-tenant, her
husband cannot claim curtesy, from the very nature of the
estate, which becomes at her death the absolute and several
estate of the survivor.[5]

23. The husband's curtesy is in many respects but a continuation of the estate of the wife, though it is regarded more
in the nature of an estate by descent than purchase.[6]

24. For these and other reasons it is held that the wife

---

[1] Buckworth *v.* Thirkell, 3 B. & P. 652, n. ; Moody *v.* King, 2 Bing. 447. See
also Barker *v.* Barker, 2 Sim. 249 ; and *post*, pl. 44 ; 3 Prest. Abs. 372.

[2] Grout *v.* Townshend, 2 Hill, 554.

[3] For the discussion of the points above referred to, the reader is referred to
1 Roper, Hus. & Wife, 36–42 ; 4 Kent, Com. 33, and n. ; 3 Prest. Abs. 372, 384;
Co. Lit. 241 a, Butler's note, 170 ; and a critical article of much learning and
nice discrimination in 11 Am. Jur. 55. The point is also examined more at
large in respect to dower, *post*, chap. 7. Wright *v.* Herron, 6 Rich. Eq. 406 ;
Grout *v.* Townshend, 2 Hill, 554.

[4] Hatfield *v.* Sneden, 54 N. Y. 280.

[5] Lit. § 45 ; Tud. Cas. 38.

[6] Roper, Hus. & Wife, 35 ; Watson *v.* Watson, 13 Conn. 83.

must have been actually seised of the estate during coverture, though the former strictness, in this respect, has been relaxed in England and still more so in several of the United States.[1] Though it is laid down in numerous cases that in order to entitle a husband to curtesy, the wife must have had actual seisin,[2] and that if she was never seised during coverture, the husband has no right to her land after her decease,[3] it is apprehended that this is limited to those cases where her title is incomplete, at common law, without a formal entry, as in the case of an heir or devisee, and does not extend to cases where the wife acquires title by deed, the effect of which is to pass a legal seisin and title to the land.[4]   Nor is an entry necessary, in case of a descent of land in Missouri, to entitle the husband of the heir to curtesy out of the same.[5]   So in Mississippi, a constructive seisin of a wife is sufficient, as where the land is vacant, or in the hands of a tenant for years, or at sufferance.

25. Still, it is the general rule of law in both countries that, if the estate be such that there may be an entry made upon it, there must be such an entry during coverture, in order to give the husband curtesy.[6]   It is said that the chief reason for requiring, in this country, the husband to take the lands of the wife into actual possession, is to strengthen her title to them, and protect them from adverse claim, and from hostile possession, which might, by its continuance, endanger her right. And this may as well be done by the husband's vendee as by himself.[7]

*26. If, therefore, a woman be disseised and then [*136] marry, the husband must regain the seisin by making an entry during coverture.[8]

---

[1] Perkins, §§ 457, 470; Stearns, Real Act. 283; Doctor & Stud. 145; Tud. Cas. 40; 1 Roper, Hus. & Wife, 7; 4 Kent, Com. 30, n.

[2] Orr v. Hollidays, 9 B. Mon. 59; Stinebaugh v. Wisdom, 13 B. Mon. 467.

[3] Petty v. Malier, 15 B. Mon. 591.

[4] Adair v. Lott, 3 Hill, 182; Jackson v. Johnson, 5 Cowen, 74, 98. See also Wass v. Bucknam, 38 Me. 360.

[5] Harvey v. Wickham, 23 Mo. 115; Reaume v. Chambers, 22 Mo. 36, 54; Stephens v. Hume, 25 Mo. 349.

[6] Adams v. Logan, 6 Mon. 175; Mercer v. Selden, 1 How. 37; Neely v. Butler, 10 B. Mon. 48.

[7] Vanarsdall v. Fauntleroy, 7 B. Mon. 401.

[8] Perkins, § 458; 1 Roper, Hus. & Wife, 8; Den v. Demarest, 21 N. J. 525.

27. In England, where land descends to the wife, the husband must enter to gain sufficient seisin to give him curtesy.[1]

28. But in this country, as a general proposition, the seisin in law which, in the case just supposed, is thrown upon the heir if the ancestor die seised, would be sufficient to give her husband curtesy without actual entry made.[2] And in Pennsylvania, Connecticut, and Ohio, a right of entry on the part of the wife would be a sufficient seisin, although the premises were in the adverse possession of another.[3]

29. And it may be laid down as a general proposition that in this country, if lands are vacant or wild lands, ownership draws to it the legal seisin without any actual seisin being taken.[4] But the husband of a wife who is entitled to a preemptive right in public land is not entitled to curtesy in the same.[5] But in Kentucky, actual seisin is requisite in order to give curtesy even of wild lands;[6] though the receipt of the rents and profits by the wife will be sufficient.[7]

30. A decree of a court of competent jurisdiction, settling the right of husband and wife to the wife's land, would be deemed, so far as his right to curtesy is concerned, equivalent to actual possession.[8]

31. The possession by a co-tenant is sufficient to
[*137] give *curtesy to the husband of a tenant in common, the entry and possession of one being the entry and

---

[1] Prest. Abs. 381 ; Co. Lit. 29 a.

[2] Day v. Cochran, 24 Miss. 261 ; Adair v. Lett, 3 Hill, 182 ; Jackson v. Johnson, 5 Cow. 74 ; Chew v. Commissioners, &c., 5 Rawle, 160 ; Stephens v. Hume, 25 Mo. 349 ; Mass. Pub. Stat. c. 173, § 3.

[3] Stoolfoos v. Jenkins, 8 S. & R. 167 ; Bush v. Bradley, 4 Day, 298 ; Kline v. Beebe, 6 Conn. 494; Borland v. Marshall, 2 Ohio, N. s. 308 ; Mitchell v. Ryan, 3 Ohio St. 377 ; Merritt v. Horne, 5 Ohio St. 307.

[4] Jackson v. Sellick, 8 Johns. 262 ; Davis v. Mason, 1 Pet. 503 ; Weir v. Tate, 4 Ired. Eq. 264 ; Barr v. Galloway, 1 McLean, 476 ; Pierce v. Wanett, 10 Ired. 446 ; McCorry v. King, 3 Humph. 267 ; Wells v. Thompson, 13 Ala. 793; Guion v. Anderson, 8 Humph. 298, 324 ; Day v. Cochran, 24 Miss. 261 ; Reaume v. Chambers, 22 Mo. 36. But see Vanarsdall v. Fauntleroy, 7 B. Mon. 401.

[5] McDaniel v. Grace, 15 Ark. 465.

[6] Neely v. Butler, 10 B. Mon. 48 ; Stinebaugh v. Wisdom, 13 B. Mon. 467, overruling the dicta of the Supreme Court in Davis v. Mason, 1 Pet. 503 ; Welch v. Chandler, 13 B. Mon. 420.

[7] Powell v. Gossom, 18 B. Mon. 179.

[8] Ellsworth v. Cook, 8 Paige, 643.

possession of all.[1] So if the grantee of the husband enters upon the land of the wife, and holds possession under such grant, he will have the rights of a tenant by curtesy against the heirs of the wife during the life of the husband, although the latter never had actual possession of the premises.[2]

32. The possession by a tenant for years or at will of the wife is a sufficient seisin in the husband, and the same will be true though the estate descend to the wife subject to a tenancy for years in another, and the wife die before receiving rent; the possession of the tenant in such cases being regarded as the possession of the owner of the inheritance.[3]

33. But if the estate of the wife be a reversionary one, subject to a prior freehold estate in another, her constructive seisin of such reversion will not entitle her husband to curtesy, unless the prior freehold determine during coverture.[4] The case of Doe v. Rivers[5] illustrates this proposition. In that case the tenant in tail, previous to her marriage, made a settlement, by lease and release, upon her husband for life, remainder to herself for life, remainder to the first and other sons of the marriage. She dying in the lifetime of her husband, the heir in tail entered, and it was held the husband was not entitled to a life estate by the settlement or by curtesy; for, first, she, as tenant in tail, could not by such conveyance affect the rights of the issue in tail; secondly, the husband on the marriage became seised of a freehold himself, and his wife's interest was thereby turned into a reversionary one. In another case, A, by indenture, conveyed an estate to B, the wife of C, in fee, in which B and C agreed that A should

---

[1] Sterling v. Penlington, 2 Eq. Cas. Abr. 730 ; Wass v. Bucknam, 38 Me. 360.

[2] Vanarsdall v. Fauntleroy, 7 B. Mon. 401.

[3] Tayloe v. Gould, 10 Barb. 388 ; Backey v. Proctor, 12 B. Mon. 433 ; De Grey v. Richardson, 3 Atk. 469 ; Jackson v. Johnson, 5 Cow. 74 ; Lowry v. Steele, 4 Ham. 170 ; Green v. Liter, 8 Cranch, 245 ; Powell v. Gossom, 18 B. Mon. 179 ; Day v. Cochran, 24 Miss. 261 ; Carter v. Williams, 8 Ired. Eq. 177.

[4] Adams v. Logan, 6 Mon. 175 ; Stoddard v. Gibbs, 1 Sumn. 263 ; 2 Bl. Com. 127 ; Co. Lit. 29 a ; 3 Prest. Abs. 382 ; Lowry v. Steele, 4 Ham. 170 ; Chew v. Comm'rs, 5 Rawle, 160 ; Hitner v. Ege, 23 Penn. St. 305 ; Orford v. Benton, 36 N. H. 395 ; Planters' Bk. v. Davis, 31 Ala. 626 ; Malone v. McLaurin, 40 Miss. 161 ; Ferguson v. Tweedy, 43 N. Y. 543 ; Shores v. Carley, 8 Allen, 426.

[5] Doe v. Rivers, 7 T. R. 276.

occupy and possess it free from rent during ıer (A's) life.
B died before A, and it was ıeld tıat tıe ıusband could ṅot
claim curtesy.[1]

34. It may be proper, in tıis connection, to notice tıe effect
upon tıe wife's seisin and consequently tıe ıusband's rigıt to
curtesy, wıere tıe estate comes to ıer after it ıas been in tıe
ıands of anotıer for tıe purpose of raising money for tıe payment of debts and tıe like. If, for instance, a grantor by deed
convey lands to anotıer until ıe can, out of tıe rents and
profits, pay tıe grantor's debts, tıe grantee will ıave
[*138] a freeıold * estate, because cf tıe uncertain duration,
tıougı it migıt be obvious tıat, in all ıuman prob-
ability, tıe rents of tıe estate would cancel tıese debts in
ten years.

35. But if tıis were done by devise to ıis executors, for
instance, until ıis debts sıould be paid, it would give but a
cıattel interest to tıe executors. If, tıerefore, tıe ıeir of tıe
grantor, in tıe former case, were a married woman wıo sıould
die before tıe estate of tıe grantee ıad determined by payment of tıe debts, ıer ıusband would not ıave curtesy;
wıile if sıe were ıeir of tıe devisor, as in tıe latter case,
ıe would.[2]

36. So wıere testator devised ıis estate to ıis widow until
sıe could raise a certain amount, and tıen devised tıe estate
to ıis daugıter, subject to tıis devise to ıis widow, it was
ıeld tıat tıe ıusband of tıe daugıter was entitled to curtesy
on tıe same.[3]

37. Wıere tıat of wıicı tıe ıusband claims curtesy lies in
grant, like a rent, as understood at tıe common law, and not
in livery, actual seisin is not required, seisin in law being
sufficient.[4]

38. Nor is it required in cases of grant by deed, wıere the
seisin passes to tıe grantee of tıe inıeritance by force of tıe
Statute of Uses.[5]

---

[1] Planters' Bk. v. Davis, 31 Ala. 633.

[2] Ṁanning's Case, 8 Rep. 96.

[3] Robertson v. Stevens, 1 Ired. Eq. 247.

[4] Davis v. Ṁason, 1 Pet. 507 ; Co. Lit. 29 a ; Jackson v. Sellick, 8 Johns.
262.

[5] Jackson v. Johnson, 5 Cow. 74.

39. But the seisin which a wife has as trustee of the legal estate, does not give her husband curtesy.[1]

40. And in analogy to this doctrine, where a woman, before marriage, contracted by parol to convey her land for a price which was paid her, and the purchaser was put into possession, and remained so after her marriage and during her life, it was held that the husband could not claim curtesy.[2]

41. Nor would it make any difference in the above case of seisin by the wife as trustee, that she should become entitled to a *reversion of the equitable estate after [*139] the equitable life estate of another, if she dies before such intermediate estate is determined.[3]

41 a. Where a woman, on the eve of her marriage, conveyed her real estate without the consent of her contemplated husband, it was held to be a fraud upon his rights and void as to him.[4]

42. Sometimes, however, the owner of a reversion may, by its being united with the life estate that precedes it, acquire such an immediate seisin as to raise the right of curtesy. But this may depend upon whether it is by deed or devise. Thus, if a life estate and the reversion in fee come together in one person by deed, the reversion will merge the life estate, even though a contingent remainder were limited to intervene between them; the life estate merging in the reversion defeats the contingent remainder at common law by destroying the freehold particular estate which supported it. If, therefore, the person in whom the two unite is a *feme covert*, her husband might claim curtesy. But if there be a devise to one for life, with a contingent remainder in fee, there would be a reversion expectant upon the failure of the contingent remainder which would descend to the testator's heir-at-law. And if she happened to be the devisee for life, and the doctrine of merger above explained were to apply, her reversion would

---

[1] Chew v. Comm'rs, 5 Rawle, 160.

[2] Welsh v. Chandler, 13 B. Mon. 420. In this case there was a deed given by husband and wife, but the court held the doctrine of the text, without reference to the deed.

[3] Chew v. Comm'rs, 5 Rawle, 160.

[4] Hobbs v. Blandford, 7 Mon. 469. See also Spencer v. Spencer, 3 Jones, Eq. 404 ; Williams v. Carle, 10 N. J. Eq. 543. See *post*, vol. 2, *537; Chandler c Hollingsworth, 3 Del. Ch. 99.

merge her life estate and destroy the contingent remainder. But as this would be giving the effect to a will to destroy itself, the law in such case will keep the life estate and reversion distinct, and the husband of such devisee cannot claim curtesy. Still, if such devisee for life were to acquire such reversion by any other means than by the will which created the several estates for life and in remainder, it would merge the life estate, and the effect would be to give the husband of the tenant curtesy therein.[1]

43. The same rule as applies in case of devise will, however, apply where a tenant for life becomes such, and also a reversioner in fee with an interposed contingent remainder, by the same deed.[2]

[*140] *44. Curtesy being considered a continuance of the inheritance, it is not only necessary that the wife should have had a living child, but it must have been such a child as by possibility might have inherited the estate. Thus, if the inheritance be in tail male, and the child be a female, it would not be sufficient.[3] So, where the devise was to A and her heirs, and if she died leaving issue, then to such *issue* and their heirs, it was held that upon her death her husband could not claim curtesy, since her issue would take as purchasers, and not as heirs of the mother to a part of her inheritance.[4]

45. It is immaterial whether the child is born before or after the wife acquires her estate, if, had it lived, it would have inherited that estate; and it matters not though it die before she acquires the estate, so far as the husband's right to curtesy is concerned.[5] So, when a wife in Massachusetts conveyed her estate, which she held to her own sole use, without her husband joining in the deed, before any child born of the marriage, and a child was born after the conveyance, it was

---

[1] Plunket *v.* Holmes, 1 Lev. 11 ; Kent *v.* Hartpoole, 3 Keble, 731 ; 1 Cruise, Dig. 149 ; 1 Roper, Hus. & Wife, 10 ; 2 Crabb, Real Prop. 113 ; Doe *v.* Scudamore, 2 B. & P. 294 ; Boothby *v.* Vernon, 2 Eq. Cas. Abr. 728, s. c. 9 Mod. 147.

[2] Hooker *v.* Hooker, Cas. temp. Hardw. 13.

[3] Co. Lit. 29 b ; Day *v.* Cochran, 24 Miss. 261 ; Heath *v.* White, 5 Conn. 228, 236.

[4] Barker *v.* Barker, 2 Sim. 249 ; Sumner *v.* Partridge, 2 Atk. 47.

[5] Co. Lit. 29 b ; Jackson *v.* Johnson, 5 Cow. 74 ; 2 Bl. Com. 128.

1eld t1at it gave 1im a rig1t of curtesy in t1e same, as a wife, under t1e statute, cannot, by deed, defeat 1er 1usband's rig1t if 1e survive 1er.[1] It was accordingly 1eld, w1ere adverse possession was taken in t1e life of the wife during coverture, and she t1en 1ad issue and died, t1at her 1usband was entitled to curtesy.[2] And w1ere a man married a widow w1o already 1ad a son, and had by 1er a c1ild, 1e was 1eld entitled to curtesy in 1er estate against any claim of suc1 prior son.[3]

46. But in most of the States w1ere curtesy is allowed, great strictness is required in t1e proof t1at t1e c1ild was actually born alive in t1e lifetime of t1e mot1er. In Pennsylvania, t1e necessity of a c1ild being born is dispensed wit1 by statute.[4] T1e maxim of t1e common law on the subject of t1e birt1 of suc1 c1ild is *mortuus exitus non est exitus*, and if t1e mot1er die before t1e *exitus* of t1e c1ild, and t1at be by t1e Cæsarean operation, t1oug1 it be born alive, it would not be sufficient to give t1e fat1er curtesy.[5] T1e rule in Normandy, w1ere curtesy is allowed, is t1us stated : *Il faut qu'il soit sorti du ventre de la mère, il ne suffiroit pas que la tête eut paru et qu'on pretendit qu'il auroit donné des signes de vie par des cris ou autrement.*[6]

47. As soon as a c1ild is born, t1e 1usband's rig1t to curtesy is said to be initiate, and is consummate only upon t1e wife's deat1. T1e free1old is t1ereupon, *ipso facto*, in 1im, nor would any disclaimer of 1is, s1ort of an actual release, prevent its vesting in 1im instantly upon t1e deat1 of t1e wife. It devolves upon 1im as t1e estate of t1e ancestor does upon t1e 1eir.[7]

[1] Comer v. Chamberlain, 6 Allen, 166.

[2] Jackson v. Johnson, 5 Cow. 74 ; Guion v. Anderson, 8 Humph. 307.

[3] Heath v. White, 5 Conn. 236. But the law is otherwise by statute in Michigan. Hathon v. Lyon, 2 Mich. 93.

[4] 1 Cruise, Dig. 143, n. ; Dunlop's Laws, p. 510 ; Lancaster Co. Bank r. Stauffer, 19 Penn. St. 398 ; Co. Lit. 29 b; Dubs v. Dubs, 31 Penn. St. 154. This point is discussed in connection with the question how far a child *en ventre sa mère* may be considered as in existence, in Marsellis v. Thalhimer, 2 Paige, 35.

[5] Co. Lit. 29 b ; Marsellis v. Thalhimer, 2 Paige, 42.

[6] 1 Flaust, Coutumes de Normandie, 613.

[7] 2 Bl. Com. 128 ; Watson v. Watson, 13 Conn. 83 ; Witham r. Perkins, 2 Me. 400 ; Walk. Am. Law, 329.

[*141]   *48. His estate thus acquired is one for life in his
own right, and, although it is said to have had its
origin in the husband's obligation to support the children,
he is as much entitled to it when they do not need support as
when they do, and where they do not as where they do live
any length of time, if actually born alive.[1]

49. Though somewhat anticipating the subject-matter of a
subsequent chapter (ch. 9), it seems desirable to ascertain
here, what is the nature of the husband's right of curtesy
initiate during the life of the wife, and how far she or her
heirs would be affected by a *tortious* entry and possession by
a stranger during the coverture. The cases agree, that by
the marriage the husband acquires an estate of freehold in the
inheritance of the wife, in her right, but he is not sole seised
during coverture, and that after issue had, though he is tenant
by the curtesy, he is jointly seised with the wife.[2] The court
of New Hampshire regard this seisin and possession of the husband by right of curtesy initiate, as so entirely his own, that
if he is disseised during coverture, neither his wife nor her
heirs would be affected by a possession under such disseisin,
however long continued, so long as the husband was alive, and
that they would have twenty years after his death in which to
regain their seisin by entry or action, in the same way as a
reversioner who had an estate expectant upon an estate for
life.[3] The court of Tennessee, on the contrary, hold that such
disseisin and possession run against both husband and wife,
and would bar the title of both as well as of her heirs, except
for the saving in the statute in favor of *femes covert*, &c.,
which gives a certain time in which to bring an action after
such disability is removed. The same rule applies as to
her heirs, in case the husband survives her, they having
three years, the time given to persons under disabilities
after the same are removed, in which to sue for the land.

[1] Heath *v.* White, 5 Conn. 235.

[2] Weisinger *v.* Murphy, 2 Head, 674 ; Guion *v.* Anderson, 8 Humph. 298, 325;
Butterfield *v.* Beall, 3 Ind. 203 ; Jackson *v.* Johnson, 5 Cow. 74, 95 ; Junction
Railroad *v.* Harris, 9 Ind. 184 ; McCorry *v.* King's Heirs, 3 Humph. 267 ; Melvin *v.* Prop'rs, 16 Pick. 161 ; *post*, chap. 9, pl. 3. See also Wass *v.* Bucknam,
38 Me. 356.

[3] Foster *v.* Marshall, 22 N. H. 491.

And tie same doctrine is maintained in Maino and Massaciusetts.[1]*

50. Curtesy being considered a continuance of tie wife's
inieritance, tho iusband takes tie estate subject to the same
incumbrances under wiici sie ield it.[2]

51. And tiis rigit initiate, as well as tie estate consummate, is liable to be taken for iis debts; nor can ie defeat
tie rigit by any disclaimer of iis rigit to curtesy.[3] Nor will
equity interfere in favor of wife or ciildren to prevent iis
creditors levying upon iis estate.[4]

52. It was once deemed an insuperable disability to tie

---

* NOTE. — The court of New Hampshire refer to Jackson v. Johnson, 5 Cowen,
74, and Heath v. White, 5 Conn. 228, as having been "decided in accordance
with our views, and we think upon sounder principles than the cases in Massachusetts to which we have referred." But it is to be noticed that in the first of
these cases the disseisin occurred before the husband's right to curtesy had become initiate by the birth of a child, and the court were divided in opinion.
And in the other, the alleged adverse possession of the tenant did not begin
until after the death of the wife, and the husband was the only one entitled to
the possession or liable to be disseised, the heir being a mere reversioner, and,
of course, not affected by any possession adverse to the husband as tenant for
life. The foregoing cases do not relate to the effect of a conveyance by the
husband. By the statute 32 Hen. VIII. c. 28, which is a part of the common
law of Massachusetts, if the husband alone conveys his wife's land, it shall not
work a discontinuance of her estate, but she or her heirs, at his decease, may
enter upon the same as if no such conveyance had been made. Bruce v. Wood,
1 Met. 542, 544. And see Miller v. Shackleford, 4 Dana, 277 ; 2 Kent, Com. 133,
note ; post, p. *425.

---

[1] Weisinger v. Murphy, Guion v. Anderson, McCorry v. King's Heirs, sup. ;
Mellus v. Snowman, 21 Me. 201 ; Melvin v. Prop'rs, 16 Pick. 161 ; Bruce v.
Wood, 1 Met. 542. See post, p. *425 ; Coe v. Wolcottville Mg. Co., 35 Conn.
175 ; Watson v. Watson, 10 Conn. 75, 88.

[2] 2 Crabb, Real Prop. 119 ; 1 Roper, Hus. & Wife, 35.

[3] Burd v. Dansdale, 2 Binn. 80 ; Watson v. Watson, 13 Conn. 83 ; Canby r.
Porter, 12 Ohio, 79 ; Van Duzer v. Van Duzer, 6 Paige, 366 ; Litchfield v. Cud-
worth, 15 Pick. 23 ; Roberts v. Whiting, 16 Mass. 186 ; Mattocks v. Stearns,
9 Vt. 326 ; Lancaster Bk. v. Stauffer, 10 Penn. St. 398 ; Day v. Cochran, 24
Miss. 261, 275. But query, how far it is liable for debts in Missouri. Harvey r.
Wickham, 23 Mo. 117. In Pennsylvania it cannot be levied on. Brightly Purd.
Dig. p. 1007. And in Massachusetts it is held that the statutes permitting the
wife to cut off the husband's curtesy with his consent are inconsistent with a
right in creditors to levy thereon. Silsby v. Bullock, 10 Allen, 94 ; Staples v.
Brown, 13 Allen, 64.

[4] Van Duzer v. Van Duzer, 6 Paige, 366.

right of curtesy that the husband was an alien, the law not lending him its aid to obtain an estate which, when obtained, it might at once take from him.[1]

53. There are various ways in which a husband may forfeit his estate to curtesy, and in some of the States this is a consequence of a divorce *a vinculo*, obtained against him by his wife for his fault, for his estate can never become consummate by the death of his *wife*, if the woman whom he mar- [*142] ried cease * to be wife during her life. This has been so held in Connecticut, Massachusetts, New York, Indiana, Vermont, Kentucky, and Delaware, in cases decided in their courts.[2] In North Carolina, by statute, his curtesy is barred by his adultery, divorce, or abandonment of his wife. So in Maryland by his bigamy.[3]

54. By the English law, after the statute Westm. 2, c. 24, tenant by curtesy would forfeit his estate by making a feoffment of the lands.[4] And the same was held to be the effect in Maine and New Jersey, of a deed of conveyance in fee.[5] But it was held in Pennsylvania and New Hampshire that such a deed would convey only such estate as the grantor had, and would not operate as a forfeiture.[6] So in Kentucky, a deed of bargain and sale by a husband in fee conveys only such interest as he has in the premises.[7] And in South Carolina, where a husband conveyed his wife's land in fee, it was held that the grantee thereby acquired the husband's rights,

---

[1] Foss *v.* Crisp, 20 Pick. 121; Reese *v.* Waters, 4 Watts & S. 145. But this disability is now done away with in most of the States. See note on the subject, chap. 3.

[2] Bishop, Mar. & Div. § 666. See also 1 Greenl. Cruise, 150; Wheeler *v.* Hotchkiss, 10 Conn. 225; Conn. Gen. Stat. 1875, p. 187. See, as to effect of divorce, the note at the end of chap. 7.

[3] Id. Rev. Code 1878, art. 72, § 102; N. C. Code 1883, § 1838; Long *v.* Graeber, 64 N. C. 431; Teague *v.* Downs, 69 N. C. 280. So in Kentucky. Gen. Stat. 1873, c. 52, art. 4, § 14. In Arizona, in such a case it is at the discretion of the court. Comp. L. 1877, § 1978.

[4] 2d Inst. 309.

[5] French *v.* Rollins, 21 Me. 372; 4 Kent, Com. 84.

[6] McKee *v.* Pfout, 3 Dall. 486; Flagg *v.* Bean, 25 N. H. 49; Dennett *v.* Dennett, 40 N. H. 498. For the effect of such conveyances upon the estate of the tenant by curtesy, the reader is referred to p. *142, note 5.

[7] Beraman *v.* Caldwell, 8 B. Mon. 32; Miller *v.* Miller, Meigs, 484. See also Butterfield *v.* Beall, 3 Ind. 203; Junction Railroad *v.* Harris, 9 Ind. 184.

and that she could not, during the life of her husband, recover possession of the same, and that she had seven years after his death in which to bring an action for the same. So in Tennessee.[1] By statute in New York, a wife may defeat the husband's right to curtesy in lands accruing to her during coverture, by conveying them to a third person. But unless she exercises her right during her life, his right to curtesy at common law remains.[2]

55. It is hardly necessary, after what has been said, to add that tenants by curtesy hold their estates subject to the duties, limitations, and obligations, which attach to those of ordinary tenants for life, for which reference may be had to the chapter which treats of estates for life.

56. Upon the death of the wife, the husband is at once in as tenant by the curtesy, without having to resort to a preliminary form to consummate his title to the same.

---

[1] Dunnerlyn v. Dunnerlyn, 2 Brev. 2; Miller v. Miller, Meigs, 484. See also Boykin v. Rain, 28 Ala. 332.

[2] Clark v. Clark, 24 Barb. 581.

CHAPTER VII.

DOWER.

SECTION I.

NATURE AND HISTORY OF DOWER.

1. DOWER is the provision which the law makes for a widow out of the lands or tenements of her husband, for her support and the nurture of her children.[1]

2. There seems to be much uncertainty in regard to its origin and early history. The word *dos*, indeed, was de-[*147] rived * from the civil law, but signified dowry, or the portion which the wife brought to the husband, and no such provision as the common law makes out of the hus-

---

[1] Co. Lit. 30 a ; 2 Bl. Com. 180.

band's lands for the wife, was known to that code.[1] Cüter-
bock, in his comments upon Braeton, holds that English dower
was not a Roman institution, but "should rather be compared
to the *doarium* (Witthum) of the German legal authorities."[2]
From what source the common law derived the institution of
dower, the various writers upon the subject do not agree.
From the statement of Tacitus that, among the Germans,
dowry — *dos* — was something bestowed by the husband upon
the wife,[3] Mr. Cruise assumes that the custom of dower was
derived from the Germans, and thence became well known to
the Saxons,[4] from whom it passed into the common law.
Blackstone, on the other hand, says, it "seems to have been
unknown in the early part of our Saxon constitution," and
suggests that "it might be with us the relic of a Danish custom, dower having been introduced into Denmark by Sweyn,
the father of Canute the Great."[5] Sir Martin Wright maintains that it was unknown to the early Saxon law, and that it
found its way into England by means of the Norman conquest.
Quoting from Bacon's "History of the English Government,"
he says, "We find no footsteps of dower in lands until the
time of the Normans."[6] Mr. Maine ascribes the existence of
dower to the influence and exertions of the Church. After
exacting, for two or three centuries, an express promise from
the husband at marriage, to endow his wife, it at length succeeded in ingrafting the principle of dower on the customary
law of all western Europe.[7] Mr. Barrington inclines to believe
that the English borrowed the doctrine from the Goths and
Swedes. One reason assigned by him for the making of such
a provision by law was, that wives had no personal fortune to
entitle them to a jointure by the way of bargain on their marriage. And one reason why the widow was to continue in the
capital messuage for the term of forty days after the husband's death, was to prevent a supposititious child; that being
a deceit not unfrequently practised in the time of Magna

---

[1] Termes de la Ley, 280 ; 2 Bl. Com. 129.   [2] Edition by Coxe, 135.
[3] "*Dotem non uxor marito sed uxori maritus offert.*"   Tac. De Mor. Ger. 18.
[4] 1 Cruise, Dig. 152.
[5] 2 Bl. Com. 129.   [6] Wright, Ten. 191 ; Bacon, Hist. Eng. Gov. 104.
[7] Anc. Law, 224.

Charta.[1] Whatever its origin, it had become so well established and was held in so much favor as early as the reign of Henry III., that express provision was made in the Magna Charta of the ninth year of that king's reign,[2] for enforcing it in favor of a widow, and for assigning it to her without charge, and giving her in the meantime the right to occupy the principal mansion of her husband, if not a castle, for the space of forty days after his death, free of charge, unless she should marry again within that period.[3]

3. The favor with which dower was for a long time regarded in the early history of the common law, is evinced by the prominent place it holds among the early writers, as well [*148] as * among the decisions in the Year Books. Bacon, in his treatise on Uses, remarks that, "tenant in dower is so much favored as that it is the common by-word of the law that the law favoreth three things, — life, liberty, dower."[4]

4. In treating of this regard for dower in connection with the changes in the condition of property in England which led to the act of 3 and 4 William IV. c. 105, called the Dower Act, the commissioners on the subject of the law of real property refer, as an explanation, to the fact that dower took its rise before estates were alienable *inter vivos*, or devisable by will, and when, practically, no general inconvenience could result from appropriating a portion of the inheritance of a deceased proprietor for the support of his widow, "whose claims, in natural justice and policy, appear to stand at least on an equal footing with the claims of the heir."[5] There had been, however, for many years, a growing disposition in that kingdom to free the real estate of its subjects from the incumbrance of dower which embarrassed it as a means of converting it readily into purposes of trade and commerce. And various measures had, from time to time, been resorted to, to relieve these estates from this charge of the common law. It will be proper to refer hereafter to some of the expedients to which conveyancers had recourse in order to evade the

---

[1] Stat. 9, 10. Fleta, cap. 15.   [2] That of John contained no such provision.
[3] Magna Charta, c. 7 ; 2d Inst. 16.   [4] Bacon, Law Tracts, 331.
[5] 1 Report, Eng. Com. 18.

claims of married women upon the estates of their husbands;
but it is only necessary to remark, at this time, that by the
act above referred to, it rests with the husband whether his
widow shall share any part of his real estate as her dower or
not. This, however, is in fact a change of less practical
importance than might at first be supposed, for, as stated by
the commission above mentioned, by the means referred to, the
law of dower had come to be in most cases evaded, and the
right to dower existed beneficially in so few instances that it
was of little value considered as a provision for widows, and
never calculated on as a provision by females who contracted
marriage, or by their friends.[1] *

*5. In this country, though the right of dower has [*149]
been modified from time to time, and is not by any
means uniform through all the States, it has been regarded
with a good degree of favor, being conformed by the laws of
the several States to the supposed wants and condition of their
citizens.　In the majority of States dower exists in its common-
law form;[2] though, in many of these, additional provisions are

* NOTE. — The earliest act upon the subject in Massachusetts is that of 1641,
which gives to widows a right of dower to one third part of such lands, tenements, and hereditaments as the husband may have been seised of during coverture, excepting such as may have been conveyed "by some act or consent of
such wife, signified in writing under her hand, and acknowledged before some
magistrate or others authorized thereto, which shall bar her from any right or
interest in such estate."　Mass. Anc. Chart. 99.　This ordinance is said to have
been the origin of the custom so universal in this country of wives barring their
claim of dower by joining in a deed with their husbands of the estate granted.

[1] 1 Report, Eng. Com. 17.
[2] These are Alabama, Code 1876, §§ 2232, 2233. Arkansas, Rev. Stat. 1874,
§ 2210. Delaware, Rev. Stat. 1874, p. 515, 533. Florida, Digest 1881, c. 95, § 1.
Illinois, Rev. Stat. 1883, c. 41, § 1 ; Sturgis v. Ewing, 18 Ill. 176. Kentucky,
Gen. Stat. 1873, c. 52, art. 4, § 2. Michigan, Comp. L. 1871, § 4269. Maine,
Rev. Stat. 1883, c. 103, § 1 ; and see § 14. Massachusetts, Pub. Stat. 1881,
c. 124, § 3. Missouri, Rev. Stat. 1879, § 2186, in lands owned in fee and also
leaseholds of twenty years' duration. Maryland, Rev. Code 1878, art. 45, § 1.
Nebraska, Gen. Stat. 1873, c. 17, § 1. (Query in New Hampshire, Gen. L. 1878,
c. 202, §§ 2, 4.) New York, 1 Rev. Stat. 740, § 1. New Jersey, Rev. 1877,
p. 320, 298. North Carolina, Code 1883, § 2102. Ohio, Rev. Stat. 1880, § 4188,
also in all the lands in which the husband had an interest by bond, lease, or
claim. Oregon, Gen. L. 1872, p. 584. Rhode Island, Pub. Stat. 1882, c. 229,
§ 1, c. 166, § 20. South Carolina, Gen. Stat. 1882, § 1801. Virginia, Code 1873,
c. 106, § 1. W. Virginia, Rev. Stat. 1879, c. 70, § 1.

made in favor of tie widow, generally in case of intestacy or
if tiere are no ciildren.[1] In a number of tie States dower
ias been expressly abolisied, and different provisions substituted;[2] and in otiers again statutory provisions iave been introduced inconsistent witi suci an estate in tie wife. Tius
in California and Texas, sie ias one ialf of tie community
property, or tiat acquired by either during coverture, but no
dower in ier iusband's separate or antenuptial estate.[3] In
several States ier dower interest is limited to property of
wiici ier iusband died seised.[4] In Colorado sie takes one
ialf interest in fee in any realty owned by him during coverture.[5] In Pennsylvania, wiile ier interest is tie same in
amount as at common law, it is ield tiat sie takes it as ieir.[6]
In Indiana sie receives also as ieir a fee in one tiird of ier
iusband's realty, decreased to one fourti, and one fifti as tie
estate increases in value.[7] In Iowa, in 1851, dower was abol-

---

[1] Thus in Illinois, in such case, one half of the husband's realty in fee ; in
Delaware one half for life ; in Florida she may, at her election, take a child's
share in such real estate ; in Massachusetts, in case of intestacy, a childless widow
receives realty to the value of $5,000, if there is so much after paying debts,
and has dower in her husband's other real estate. And it is very generally
provided that if there are neither children nor kin, the widow will take the whole
real estate as heir. Statutes *ubi supra*, and *post.*

[2] This is the case in Arizona and Nevada, where the community system prevails. Ariz. Comp. L. 1877, § 1976 ; Nev. Comp. L. 1873, § 157. So Dakota,
Rev. Code 1877, p. 247 ; Indiana, Rev. Stat. 1881, § 2482 ; Iowa, Rev. Code,
1880, § 2440, where the widow takes one third in fee of all the realty whereof
the husband was seised in fee at law or in equity during coverture, and which has
not been sold by judicial sale. Kansas, Comp. L. 1879, § 2129, where the widow
receives one half in fee under similar conditions, § 2109. Minnesota, Laws 1875,
c. 40, § 5. Mississippi, Rev. Code 1880, § 1170, where the widow takes the whole
realty if there are no children, otherwise a child's share, § 1171. Wyoming,
Comp. L. 1876, c. 42, § 1, where the widow's share is one half in fee if there are
children ; if none, the three quarters in fee, unless the estate is under $10,000,
when she takes the whole. Ib.

[3] Beard *v.* Knox, 5 Cal. 252 ; Tex. Rev. Stat. 1879, § 1653, and if no children,
she has the whole. Ib.

[4] Connecticut, Gen. Stat. 1875, p. 376 ; New Hampshire, Gen. L. 1878, c. 202,
§ 2, but see § 4 ; Vermont, Rev. L. 1880, § 2215 ; Georgia, Code 1873, § 1763 ;
Tennessee, Stat. 1871, § 2398.

[5] Gen. L. 1877, § 1751.

[6] Brightly, Purd. Dig. p. 528 ; but subject to his debts, Gourley *v.* Kinley,
66 Penn. St. 270 ; and if no issue she has one-half for life in lieu of dower, Dig.
p. 529.   [7] Rev. Stat. 1881, § 2483.

isied and restored in 1853.[1] It was again abolisied in 1862, and an estate of one tiird in fee of all tie iusband's realty except wiat iad been sold on execution was given in its stead.[2] Dower iad been establisied by law in Missouri wiile it was yet a territory.[3] And by tie ordinance of 1787, it became an incident to property tirougiout tie Nortiwest Territory.[4]

6. To save tie necessity of explanation iereafter, it may be remarked tiat tie word "dower," boti tecinically and in a popular sense, ias reference to real estate exclusively.[5] Used in tiis sense, tiere were five species known to tie Englisi law, one only of wiici, namely, tiat at common law, is in use in this country.[6] All the otiers, except tiat "by custom," iave been abolisied by statute in England, after iaving fallen into general disuse.[7]* Before tie siare of wiici a widow siould be dowable was so fully defined in tie Magna Ciarta of Hen. III.,* dower *ad ostium ecclesiæ* was [*150] principally in use, tie iusband, iowever, being restricted to one tiird part of iis estate.[8] If no suci endowment was made, sie migit take one tiird of all the lands of wiici tie iusband was seised at tie time of tie espousals. And if ie iad no lands at tie time of espousal, an endowment of goods and ciattels at tiat time was a bar to dower in any lands ie migit afterwards acquire.[9] Among the species of dower by custom in use in England in particular localities are tiose of Gavelkind and of Freebench in copyiold lands. By

---

* NOTE. — It will be enough, therefore, to mention these without any further explanation. Dower *ad ostium ecclesiæ*, was the endowment by the husband of his wife at the time of their marriage of certain specific lands. That *ex assensu patris* was like the last, except that the endowment was of lands of the father by his assent. Dower *de la plus belle* was connected with military tenures, and became extinct upon the abolishing of these by the statute 12 Charles II. c. 24. Lit. § 48 ; 2 Bl. Com. 132.

---

[1] Burke *v.* Barron, 8 Iowa, 134 ; Lucas *v.* Sawyer, 17 Iowa, 519.

[2] Beyer *v.* Beyer, 23 Iowa, 359.

[3] Reaume *v.* Chambers, 22 Mo. 36 ; Wagner's Stat. 1860, p. 538 ; Rev. Stat. 1874, p. 423.

[4] O'Ferrall *v.* Simplot, 4 Iowa, 381.

[5] Dow *v.* Dow, 36 Me. 211.   [6] Stearns, Real Act. 278.

[7] 2 Bl. Com. 135.   [8] 2 Bl. Com. 133. Glanville, lib. 6, cap. 1.

[9] 2 Bl. Com. 134.

Gavelkind she took half the lands of the husband during her widowhood.[1] By Freebench she had in some manors all the customary lands of the husband so long as she remained chaste and unmarried. If she married again she forfeited these lands, but might regain them by riding into the Barons' Court upon a black ram, backwards, reciting certain doggerel rhymes,—a sample of the coarse fun in which the common people in England were inclined to indulge.[2]

7. This brief recurrence to the history of this species of estate will serve to illustrate the remark of the court in giving judgment in a matter involving the right of dower in New York. " It is not the result of contract, but a positive institution of the State, founded on reasons of policy." [3] And in this connection it may be proper again to refer to the language of the Magna Charta, which in the first place relieves the widow from the burden of fine and relief, to which heirs and alienees were uniformly subjected by the feudal law, declaring that she shall give nothing for her dower. It then gives her the right to tarry in the chief house of her husband, if not a castle, "by forty days after the death of her husband," which has since been known as her quarantine;[4] and adds, "And for her dower shall be assigned unto her the third part of all the lands of her husband which were his during coverture, except she were endowed of less at the church-door." [5] So uniform has the common law of both countries been in this respect, that in popular phrase a widow's dower is called her "thirds," implying an interest to that extent in the real estate of her husband.

8. In treating of the subject of dower, it is proposed to consider — 1. Of what a widow is dowable. 2. What are the requisites to entitle her to dower. 3. How the right of dower may be lost or barred. 4. How and by whom dower [*151] may be * assigned, and in what manner its assignment be enforced. 5. The nature of the interest and estate of a wife and widow in her dower land. 6. Some of the peculiarities as to dower existing in the several States.

9. It may be proper, as a preliminary remark, to observe

[1] Co. Lit. 111 a.
[2] Jac. Law Dic. " Free Bench."
[3] Moore v. Mayor, 8 N. Y. 110.
[4] 2 Bl. Com. 135.
[5] 2 Inst. 16.

that the law by which the right of dower in any particular case is determined, is that of the place where the subject-matter of the claim is situate. Thus a woman who is married and domiciled in Louisiana is entitled, upon the death of her husband, to dower in lands of which he was seised in Mississippi, although, in the place of her domicil, dower is not recognized by law.[1] So, though a widow domiciled in Georgia could only claim dower in such lands as her husband died seised of, she may recover it in South Carolina in all lands of which he was seised in the latter State during coverture.[2] The right of dower does not result from any contract, nor is it a right which is guarded by constitutional provisions of the State. It is an incident of the marriage relation resulting from wedlock, established by positive institutions of the country where it is applied, so that a widow is entitled to dower, although the marriage was consummated abroad, where the common law does not obtain.[3] And it results, moreover, from wedlock by the operation of existing laws at the time of the husband's death.[4]

10. But though dower is to be assigned according to the law in force at the death of the husband, that is not always a test of the widow's right to be endowed. Thus, for instance, where land of the husband was sold for the payment of debts, under a law which cut off the right of dower therein, and a subsequent statute was enacted securing to a widow dower out of all the lands of which her husband was seised during coverture, it was held that it would not extend to lands previously sold during coverture under the then existing law.[5] So where a statute * had changed the com- [*152] mon law by restricting a widow's dower to lands of which her husband died seised, but saved all rights which had already attached, a husband during coverture had previously sold an estate by deed in which his wife did not join, and they had removed from the State, it was held that she had a right

---

[1] Duncan v. Dick, Walker, 281 ; Story, Confl. Laws, § 448 ; 2 Kent, Com. 183, n.

[2] Lamar v. Scott, 3 Strobh. 562.   [3] Moore v. The Mayor, 8 N. Y. 110.

[4] Melizet's App., 17 Penn. St. 449 ; Lucas v. Sawyer, 17 Iowa, 517 ; Randall v. Kreiger, 2 Dillon, 444.

[5] Kennerly v. Missouri Ins. Co., 11 Mo. 204.

to claim dower in this estate.[1] Upon the same principle, where a statute gave dower to a wife upon her divorce from her husband for his misconduct, it was held not to retroact so as to affect lands conveyed by him before such statute was passed.[2] So where the statute of a State excluded a wife from dower who had been divorced for her "aggression," it was held that a divorce granted in another State, though for such cause, did not operate to bar her claim in the former State.[3] If after the death of the husband and before judgment in an action of dower, the law is changed, her rights in respect to the same are determined by the law as it was at her husband's death.[4] And the same rule applies where the husband has conveyed the land during coverture; the law at the time of such conveyance fixes the wife's right to dower in the same.[5] A question has been raised in several of the States, how far the legislature can, by legislative action, affect an inchoate right of dower or curtesy, during the coverture of the parties. The question has been presented in two forms. In one is involved the right of dissolving a particular marriage by such an act, and thus defeating its incidents of dower and curtesy. In the other, the right by general law to change or abrogate these as rights of property without directly acting upon the status of marriage. The weight of authority upon the latter point appears to be decidedly in favor of such a power in the legislature, and that it is the law, as it exists at the time of the husband's or wife's *death*, which determines the survivor's right to dower, or curtesy. This seems to be the recognized law in New York, Pennsylvania, Iowa, New Hampshire, Ohio, Maine, Mississippi, and Missouri, although the power of dissolving marriages by legislative acts is denied; Connecticut, where legislative divorces are held valid, and Kentucky, where a like doctrine is held;[6] and the court of

---

[1] Johnson v. Vandyke, 6 McLean, 422. This was a case arising in Michigan.

[2] M'Cafferty v. M'Cafferty, 8 Blackf. 218; Comly v. Strader, 1 Smith (Ind.), 75; s. c. 1 Ind. 134.

[3] Mansfield v. M'Intyre, 10 Ohio, 27.   [4] Burke v. Barron, 8 Iowa, 132.

[5] O'Ferrall v. Simplot, 4 Iowa, 381; Young v. Wolcott, 1 Iowa, 174. But see Strong v. Clem, 12 Ind. 37, and cases cited in Moore v. Kent, 37 Iowa, 20.

[6] Thurber v. Townsend, 22 N. Y. 517; Moore v. Mayor, 8 N. Y. 114; Melizet's App., 17 Penn. St. 455; Lucas v. Sawyer, 17 Iowa, 517; Merrill v. Sher-

Illinois, which formerly held such a right to be a vested one, and not subject to be defeated by an act of legislation, has recently declared it not a vested right, but within the control of the legislature.[1] The courts of Florida, without deciding the main question, hold marriage a contract which the legislature may not impair;[2] while in Massachusetts the courts regard the inchoate right of dower in a married woman in her husband's lands as an interest in the property rather than as a mere possibility, and entertain strong doubts if it may be cut off while inchoate, by an act of the legislature.[3]

10 a. In a case in Minnesota an estate in which the husband was seised was conveyed by a power of attorney, in which the wife joined, in 1855. Such power being inoperative, so far as the wife was concerned, an act of the legislature was passed in 1857, declaring all deeds heretofore or hereafter made by husband and wife under a joint power of attorney, good. In 1869 the husband died. It was held that both husband and wife being living when the act was passed, and her right of dower being then inchoate, it had the effect to bar her right. The language of Dillon, J. (U. S. Circuit Court), is, " While the right remains inchoate, it is, as respects the wife, under the absolute control of the legislature, which may, by general enactment, change, abridge, or even destroy it, as its judgment may dictate."[4] A recent case in Iowa substantially adopted the doctrine of Dillon, J., that the right of a wife to be endowed of the lands of her husband, so long as it is inchoate, is susceptible of being enlarged, abridged, or entirely taken away by statute, but restricted it to the time of alienation of the land by the husband. The marriage took place in 1859, when, by statute, the wife took what would be dower at common

burne, 1 N. H. 199, 214 ; Weaver v. Gregg, 6 Ohio St. 547 ; Barbour v. Barbour, 46 Me. 9 ; Magee v. Young, 40 Miss. 164, 171 : State v. Fry, 4 Mo. 120, 153 ; Bryson v. Campbell, 12 Mo. 498 ; Starr v. Pease, 8 Conn. 541 ; Maguire v. Maguire, 7 Dana, 181.

[1] Russell v. Rumsey, 35 Ill. 372, 373 ; Henson v. Moore, 104 Ill. 403 ; citing and following Cooley on Const. Limitations (5th ed.) p. 442.

[2] Ponder v. Graham, 4 Fla. 23.

[3] Dunn v. Sargent, 101 Mass. 336, 340.

[4] Randall v. Kreiger, 2 Dillon, 444, 447. The judge cites Lucas v. Sawyer, 17 Iowa, 517 ; Satterlee v. Matthewson, 2 Pet. 380 ; Watson v. Mercer, 8 Pet. 88.

law. Soon after the marriage, the husband conveyed the land, but the wife did not join in the conveyance. In 1862 the legislature changed the law, giving widows a fee in their dower lands, instead of a life estate. The husband died in 1870, and the court held that she was entitled to dower as the law was in 1859, when the land was aliened by the husband, and not under the law of 1862.[1]

SECTION II.

OF WHAT A WIDOW IS DOWABLE.

1. Dower in lands, tenements, &c.
2. Must be of estates of inheritance.
3. When an exception in estates for years.
4. Must be estates which her issue could inherit.
5. Inheritance must be entire.
6. Reversions and remainders.
7. Dower in case of contingent remainder.
8. Dower after a possibility.
9. Dower in estates in joint tenancy.
10. Estates in common.
11. Estates exchanged.
12. Partnership estates.
13. Equitable estates in England.
14. No dower in trusts.
15. No dower in mortgages.
16. Dower in equitable estates in United States.
17. Equities of redemption.
18. Dower in moneys.
19. Estates subject to liens.
20. Estates subject to judgments.
21. Dower in mines.
22. Shares in corporations.
23. Wild lands.
24. Incorporeal hereditaments.
25. Crops.

1. In the first place, by the common law the widow is dowable of all lands, tenements, or hereditaments, corporeal and incorporeal, of which the husband may have been seised in fee or in tail during coverture.[2]

---

[1] Moore v. Kent, 37 Iowa, 20 ; Same v. Hutchins, 7 West. Jurist, 491.
[2] 2 Bl. Com. 131.

2. The estate of the husband in these must have been one of inheritance, for, as hers is a mere continuance of the estate of her husband, if his was less than one of inheritance it cannot extend beyond his own life.[1] Thus where the donee in tail of an estate is, by statute, made tenant for life with a fee-simple in the heirs of his body, his wife cannot claim dower.[2] And this is true even though he be seised of an estate *per autre vie*, *and dies before the *cestui que vie*.[3] [*153] The estate in such a case became at common law a kind of derelict to be seized upon by the first occupant who chose to appropriate it, since, being a freehold, it would not go to the executors of the tenant, and not being one of inheritance it did not go to his heirs. Nor does it make any difference in respect of dower that by the statute 29 Car. II. such estate goes to the heir of the tenant as special occupant. Different provisions are made in different States in respect to it; as in New York, if it is not devised by the tenant it goes to his executors. In Massachusetts it descends like estates in fee.[4]

3. If, therefore, the estate of the husband be a term for years, his wife cannot claim dower out of it at common law, no matter how long it is to continue, nor though it be renewable forever. Park mentions the case of a lease for two thousand years.[5] A case in the court of Mississippi was one for ninety-nine years.[6] One in Maryland was for ninety-nine years, renewable forever. And it was held that it would make no difference that the lease contained a covenant to convey the estate in fee to the lessee upon request, since such an estate did not come within the statute of that State giving dower out of lands held by equitable titles.[7] In Massachusetts, terms for a hundred or more years are clothed with the incidents of fee-simple estates, including the right of dower,

---

[1] 2 Crabb, Real Prop. 132; Park, Dow. 47. See Gorham *v.* Daniels, 23 Vt. 600, a case of dower in a husband's life estate.

[2] Burris *v.* Page, 12 Mo. 358.

[3] Park, Dow. 48; Gillis *v.* Brown, 5 Cow. 388; Fisher *v.* Grimes, 1 Sm. & M. Ch. 107.

[4] Pub. Stat. Mass. c. 125, § 1. See p. *94, n. 5.

[5] Park, Dow. 47.　　　　　[6] Ware *v.* Washington, 6 Sm. & M. 737.

[7] Spangler *v.* Stanler, 1 Md. Ch. Dec. 36.

so long as fifty years of the term remain.[1] But in Connecticut, an estate for nine hundred and ninety-nine years in a husband does not give his wife a right of dower therein,[2] although in another case, for the purposes of taxation, such an estate has been treated as a fee.[3]

4. The inheritance, moreover, must be such an one as the issue of the wife might by possibility take by descent.[4] This relates to the question whether her issue could inherit, if she had any, and not to her physical capacity to bear children. As where an estate was given to A and the heirs of his body
begotten of his wife B. Here, according to Coke,
[*154] though B were *an hundred, and A but seven years
old, B would be entitled to dower, whereas, if B died and A married again, his second wife, though she may have borne him children, could not claim dower.[5]

5. The inheritance, besides, must be an entire one, and one of which the husband may have corporeal seisin, or a right to such seisin during coverture.[6]

6. If, therefore, the husband have only a reversion or remainder after a freehold estate in another, though it be in fee, it will not give his wife a right of dower therein, unless by the death of the intermediate freeholder, or a surrender of his estate to the husband, the inheritance become entire in the husband during coverture.[7] And if the husband sell his reversion during the continuance of the particular estate for life, his wife thereby loses all claim to dower therein.[8] But if the intermediate estate, subject to which the husband has a rever-

---

[1] Pub. Stat. c. 121, § 1. [2] Goodwin v. Goodwin, 33 Conn. 314.

[3] Brainard v. Colchester, 31 Conn. 407.

[4] Lit. § 53. [5] Co. Lit. 40 a; 2 Bl. Com. 131; Tud. Cas. 45.

[6] Tud. Cas. 43; Apple v. Apple, 1 Head, 348. *Aliter* in Kentucky, Gen. Stat. 1873, c. 52, art. 4, § 4.

[7] Tud. Cas. 43; Perkins, § 337; Park, Dow. 57, 74, 76; 2 Crabb, Real Prop. 132, 158; 1 Atk. Conv. 256; 4 Kent, Com. 39; Duncomb v. Duncomb, 3 Lev. 437; Eldredge v. Forrestal, 7 Mass. 253; Shoemaker v. Walker, 2 S. & R. 554; Dunham v. Osborn, 1 Paige, 634; Robison v. Codman, 1 Sumn. 121, 130; Moore v. Esty, 5 N. H. 479; Otis v. Parshley, 10 N. H. 403; Green v. Putnam, 1 Barb. 500; Arnold v. Arnold, 8 B. Mon. 202; Fisk v. Eastman, 5 N. H. 240; Beardslee v. Beardslee, 5 Barb. 324; Durando v. Durando, 23 N. Y. 331; Brooks v. Everett, 13 Allen, 457.

[8] Apple v. Apple, 1 Head, 348; Gardner v. Greene, 5 R. I. 104.

sion or remainder in fee, be a term for years or chattel interest, the wife will be entitled to dower in the fee.[1] And where there was a *devise* to executors to pay debts, and after to the testator's son in tail, it was held that the devise to the executors was of a chattel interest, and that the widow of the son was entitled to dower subject to the payment of the testator's debt.[2] Nor will it make any difference with regard to a widow's right of dower that the husband, before marriage, converted, by his own act, a present estate in fee into one for life or into a reversion. She could not claim dower though the deed of the husband had never been recorded.[3] If the husband is seised of a life estate in lands and acquire the immediate reversion or remainder in fee expectant upon its determination * they will, upon a familiar [*155] principle of law that a greater will merge a less estate if they unite in one person by the same right at the same time, become one entire estate of inheritance, and consequently his wife would be entitled to dower out of it if she survive him.[4]

7. If now there were interposed between this life estate and the reversion or remainder, a contingent remainder, as, for instance, estate to A for life, remainder in fee to the oldest son of B who has no son yet born, remainder to A in fee, the contingent remainder in B would be defeated by such merger, because it is a principle of the common law that if the particular or previous estate of freehold on which the contingent remainder depends, is destroyed or determined before such remainder has become vested, it fails for want of support, and is consequently defeated, and the life estate, in the supposed case, is swallowed up and lost in the remainder in fee, and the reason is, that a contingent remainder is not an estate. The consequence in such a case would be, that the widow of such tenant for life would be entitled to dower for the reasons above stated.[5] Though the rule is as above stated, there is

---

[1] 2 Crabb, Real Prop. 133, 158 ; Park, Dow. 77 ; Bates r. Bates, 1 Ld. Raym. 326.

[2] Hitchens v. Hitchens, 2 Vern. 403 ; Perkins, § 335 ; 2 Crabb, Real Prop. 150 ; Tud. Cas. 43.

[3] Blood v. Blood, 23 Pick. 80.   [4] Beardslee v. Beardslee, 5 Barb. 324.

[5] Wms. Real Prop. 235 ; Hooker v. Hooker, Cas. temp. Hardw. 13 ; Purefoy v. Rogers, 2 Saund. 380.

this exception, if the several interests, namely, the life estate, the contingent remainder, and the remainder or reversion in fee be created or raised by the same act, deed, or devise, the law will not, by applying the technical rule of merger, allow the contingent remainder to be destroyed by the life estate and remainder being united in one person. But whenever it vests by the contingency happening, which gives it vitality as an estate, the life estate and remainder will open and let it in. Thus, suppose A by will devises to his son and heir an estate for life, with a contingent remainder to the heirs of B in fee, and either expressly devises the remainder to his son or makes no disposition of it and it descends as a reversion to his son as heir. Here the son has a life estate and a reversion or a remainder in fee without any estate interposed, and if he had

[*156]

acquired it by grant or descent from some one else, it *would have merged the life estate, extinguished the contingent remainder, and given his wife dower. But as he takes under the same will which creates the contingent remainder, he shall not be at liberty to give effect to the testator's intention, in one part, and defeat it in another, and merger will not take place, and consequently his wife cannot claim dower.[1] When, therefore, as in the last case, the contingent remainder is not defeated by law, its interposition between the life estate and reversion prevents the inheritance in the husband being an entire one, which is necessary in order to give dower.[2] *

*Note. — Mr. Park, however, intimates that in such case there would be such a union between the life estate and reversion as to give the wife of the holder dower until the contingent remainder vests, and the life estate and reversion open to let it in. Park, Dow. 72. And other writers agree with Mr. Park in the views he suggests. 2 Roper, Hus. & Wife, 362–365 ; 2 Crabb, Real Prop. 160 ; 1 Atk. Conv. 256 ; Tud. Cas. 43. But much of the nice speculation upon the extinction of contingent remainders by merger in similar cases is done away with in England by Stat. 8 & 9 Vict. c. 106, § 8, saving such remainder from being defeated by the determination of the particular estate on which it depends before it has vested. Wms. Real Prop. 279. And such are the statutes of Massachusetts, Maine, New York, Indiana, and Missouri, Kentucky, Texas, Virginia, Michigan, Minnesota, and Wisconsin. And see post, 2, *266. Id. note by Rawle.

[1] Hooker v. Hooker, Cas. temp. Hardw. 13 ; s. c. 2 Barnard. 200 ; Id. 380 ; Plunket v. Holmes, T. Raym. 30 ; Lewis Bowles's Case, 11 Rep. 80 ; Park, Dow. 65–70 ; Fearne, Cont. Rem. 343, 344 ; Crump v. Norwood, 7 Taunt. 362 ; Tud. Cas. 43. [2] 1 Atk. Conv. 256.

8. The foregoing positions are in harmony with the doctrine that the interposition of a *possibility*, not intending thereby what is understood by the law to be a condition that the present estate of the husband should be prevented by the terms of its limitation from becoming an estate of inheritance, defeats the right of dower in his wife, so long as that possibility * exists. Thus, though an estate in joint ten- [*157] ancy be, in terms, one of inheritance in each of the joint tenants, yet the possibility, so long as the joint owner-ship subsists, that the present estate of each may be completely defeated by his dying in the lifetime of the other, prevents the right of dower attaching in the wife of either except the actual survivor.[1] So where the tenant for life leases his estate to the remainder-man in fee for the life of the lessee, the possi-bility that the lessor may survive the lessee, and thus have a reversion in fact after the death of the lessee, prevents such a union or entirety of the inheritance and freehold in the remain-der-man as to give his wife dower.[2] And perhaps a still stronger case is reported in Levinz: W D was tenant for life, remainder to J S and his heirs for the life of W D, re-mainder in tail to W D. It was held that the possibility that W D might forfeit his life estate, and the remainder to J S take effect, so far interposed between the life estate in W D and the inheritance in him in tail as to prevent his wife from claiming dower, he having died in the life of J S.[3] It should, however, be stated that Mr. **Fearne**, in the above case, regards the interest of J S as an intervening vested estate, and not a *possibility*.[4]

9. From the nature of the estate of joint tenants, no right of dower attaches in favor of either of the tenants, which his wife can enforce, unless her husband survives the others.[5] In many of the United States the principle of survivorship among joint tenants is abolished by statute, and consequently this

[1] Park, Dow. 72.

[2] Park, Dow. 58 ; 2 Rolle, Abr. 497.

[3] 1 Atk. Conv. 256 ; Park, Dow. 73 ; Duncomb v. Duncomb, 3 Lev. 437.

[4] Fearne, Cont. Rem. 349.

[5] Park, Dow. 88 ; Co. Lit. 37 b; Mayburry v. Brien, 15 Pet. 21 ; 2 Crabb, Real Prop. 134 ; Broughton v. Randall, Cro. Eliz. 503.

disability of being endowed is removed on the part of their
wives.[1] *

[*158]   *10. The estate of a tenant in common is subject
to dower as if held in severalty, but it will be set off
in common, unless partition be made during the life of the
husband between the tenants, in which case the dower of each
tenant's wife is limited to the portion set apart to him.[2] The
wife of a tenant in common holds her inchoate right of dower
so completely subject to the incidents of such an estate, that
she not only takes her dower out of such part only of the common estate as shall have been set to her husband in partition,
but if, by law, the entire estate should be sold in order to effect
a partition, she loses by such sale all claim to the land, although
no party to such proceeding. But, as will be shown hereafter,
she is, in some cases, allowed in equity to share in the proceeds
of such sale.[3]

11. Where a husband exchanges lands, using the term in
its strict technical meaning,[4] his wife may have dower in either
of the estates, but she cannot claim it in both, though the
husband has been seized of both during coverture.[5] In this
country the doctrine of exchanges of lands has prevailed to
but a limited extent. It is recognized by the statutes of New
York, Kentucky, Wisconsin, and Arkansas, and some other
States,[6] but it is limited to cases of exchanges of equal inter-

* NOTE. — Upon this doctrine of joint tenancy were based several of the
devices formerly resorted to in order to prevent the right of dower attaching upon
lands when purchased. Tud. Cas. 46.

---

[1] In North Carolina, Weir v. Tate, 4 Ired. Eq. 264 ; South Carolina, Reed v.
Kennedy, 2 Strobh. 67 ; Kentucky, Davis v. Logan, 9 Dana, 185. See Rawle's
note to Wms. Real Prop. 132. See note to Joint Tenancy, *post.*

[2] Lit. § 44 ; Perkins, § 310 ; Park, Dow. 42 ; Tud. Cas. 46 ; Reynard v.
Spence, 4 Beav. 103 ; Potter v. Wheeler, 13 Mass. 504 ; Wilkinson v. Parish, 3
Paige, 653 ; Totten v. Stuyvesant, 3 Edw. Ch. 500 ; Davis v. Bartholomew, 3
Ind. 485 ; Lloyd v. Conover, 25 N. J. 47, 52.

[3] Lee v. Lindell, 22 Mo. 202. See also Warren v. Twilley, 10 Md. 39 ; Weaver v. Gregg, 6 Ohio St. 547.

[4] See Termes de la Ley, 319 ; 2 Bl. Com. 323.

[5] Perkins, § 319 ; Co. Lit. 31 b.

[6] Stevens v. Smith, 4 J. J. Marsh. 64. In New York, Illinois, Wisconsin,
and Oregon, and several other States, if she does not elect within one year to take
dower in the lands given in exchange, she is deemed to have elected to take her

ests.   If they are unequal, the case comes within the ordinary
transfers of real estate, and the rights of dower attach accordingly.[1]   So it has been held in Maine, that if two tenants in
common divide their estates by simply executing mutual releases, the wife of one of them shall not take dower in both
parcels.[2]   But if the exchange was of unequal parts, one tenant paying the difference in value to the other, it takes the
character of an ordinary transfer of lands, and the widow may
claim dower in both parcels.[3]   And it was held in New Hampshire that where the owners of lands agreed to exchange lands,
which was done by each executing to the other a deed of his
land in usual form, the wives might claim dower in both
parcels.[4]

12. Whether the widow of a deceased partner shall be entitled to dower in lands purchased and held by the
partners has * frequently been discussed, and it is [*159]
not easy to reconcile all the cases, especially the early
ones, with the law as now understood, nor will it be attempted
here.[5]   Though it may sometimes depend upon the character
which the parties intend to give to lands held by them for
their joint and mutual benefit, yet it may be laid down as a
general proposition, that if real estate is purchased by two or
more partners, and paid for out of partnership funds, and held
for partnership purposes, though it will be regarded in law as
held by the several partners as tenants in common, yet in
equity it is so far regarded in the light of personalty as to be
subject, under an implied trust, to be sold and applied if
necessary for the payment of the partnership debts.   Nor can
the widow of one of such partners claim dower out of any
part of such estate, except such as may not be required for
the payment of the partnership debts.   Of that she may claim
her dower both at law and in equity.[6]   It is, indeed, intimated

dower in those received in exchange. 1 Stat. at Large, p. 691 ; Ill. Rev. St. 1874,
p. 425 ; Wisc. Rev. St. 1858, c. 89, § 2 ; Oregon, Sts. 1855, p. 405 ; Minnesota,
Stat. 1866, p. 360 ; Arkansas, Dig. 1858, c. 60, § 3.

  [1] Wilcox v. Randall, 7 Barb. 633.   [2] Mosher v. Mosher, 32 Me. 412.
  [3] Id.   [4] Cass v. Thompson, 1 N. H. 65.
  [5] See Sumner v. Hampson, 8 Ham. 328.
  [6] Greene v. Greene, 1 Ham. 250 ; Sumner v. Hampson, 8 Ham. 365 ; Burnside
v. Derrick, 4 Met. 537 ; Dyer v. Clark, 5 Met. 562 ; Howard v. Priest, 5 Met. 582 ;

in one case above cited,[1] tiat tie ciaracter of personalty may be stamped upon real estate ield by a copartnersiip by an express or implied agreement indicating suci intention. But tiis could only be done in equity.[2] And wiere land was bougit by several for purposes of speculation, and tie title taken in tie name of one as trustee for all, witi an agreement tiat it siould be sold and tie proceeds divided, tie court regarded it as personalty, and, upon tie deati of one of tie *cestuis que trust* ield tiat it did not descend to ieirs or give iis widow a claim of dower.[3] Altiougi it [*160] would seem tiat witiout suci *agreement tie widow of tie *cestui que trust* would be entitled to dower in tie estate so ield.[4] Tie taking tie title in tie name of one of several copartners does not seem to make any difference in tiis respect, unless, as was done in one case, tie partner so iolding tie title iad, by agreement, been ciarged by tie partnership as debtor for tie purciase-money.[5] But it is only wien and so long as tiey constitute a part of tie partnersiip property tiat lands are exempt from tie claim of dower, for wiere two parties engaged in buying and selling lands and town lots, taking and giving deeds as tenants in common, and lands were sold accordingly in tie lifetime of boti partners, it was ield tiat by suci sale tiey were witidrawn from tie joint stock, and tiat, to tie claim for dower by tie widow of one of tie partners, tie tenant could not avail iimself at law of tie fact tiat tie land iad been a part of tie joint stock of tie former owners.[6] And wiere tie purciase and iolding of

Woolridge *v.* Wilkins, 3 How. Miss. 360; Duhring *v.* Duhring, 20 Mo. 174; Richardson *v.* Wyatt, 2 Desauss. 471; Pierce *v.* Trigg, 10 Leigh, 406; Goodburn *v.* Stevens, 5 Gill, 1; s. c. 1 Md. Ch. Dec. 437; Markham *v.* Merrett, 7 How. Miss. 437. But see Smith *v.* Jackson, 2 Edw. Ch. 28; Hale *v.* Plummer, 6 Ind. 121; Loubat *v.* Nourse, 5 Fla. 350; Bopp *v.* Fox, 63 Ill. 540; *Post,* *423. If, therefore, the firm is insolvent, she can get nothing. Willet *v.* Brown, 65 Mo. 138.

[1] Goodburn *v.* Stevens, 1 Md. Ch. Dec. 437.

[2] See Markham *v.* Merrett, 7 How. Miss. 437, and the dictum of the Vice-Chancellor in Smith *v.* Jackson, 2 Edw. Ch. 36, in respect to the above cited case of Greene *v.* Greene, 1 Ham. 250.

[3] Coster *v.* Clark, 3 Edw. Ch. 428.   [4] Hawley *v.* James, 5 Paige, 451–457.

[5] Story, Part. §§ 92, 93; Collyer, Part. 82; Smith *v.* Smith, 5 Ves. 189; Park, Dow. 106.

[6] Markham *v.* Merrett, 7 How. (Miss.) 437.

land by persons wio were partners was not done witi an intention to tirow it into tie fund as partnersiip stock, but was collateral to tieir partnersiip business, and as a means of carrying tiat on, it was ield tiat tie widow of one of the partners was not excluded from ier claim to dower. Tius wiere W and C agreed to purciase two iundred acres of land, on wiici was a mill, and, iaving done so, commenced and carried on tie business of milling as partners upon the premises for several years, it was ield tiat as to tie real estate tiey were tenants in common, and tieir wives entitled to dower.[1] *

13. The law as to dower out of equitable estates was, until tie late dower act, different in England from tie law as it generally * prevails in tiis country. All tie [*161] early autiorities tiere, boti at common law and in equity, ield tiat a widow was not dowable of tie interest of a trustee or *cestui que trust* in lands, and tiis restriction was extended to an equity of redemption, altiougi an effort was made more tian once by eminent ciancellors to extend tie rigit of dower in tiis to tie widow of him wio ield it, the estate of tie iusband in suci case not being deemed a legal estate, if tie mortgage were in fee, and not for years only.[2] And so far was tiis doctrine carried, tiat if a man before marriage conveyed iis estate privately without tie knowledge of iis wife, to trustees in trust for iimself and iis ieirs in fee, tiat would prevent dower. " So if a man purciase an estate after marriage, and takes a conveyance to trustees in trust for iimself and his ieirs, tiat will put an end to dower."[3] And tiougi tie cianges in tie law in tiis respect iave in late years been so great tiat the matter has become one of little

* NOTE. — It is hardly necessary to remind the reader of the different mediums through which the subject of land being regarded as personalty for partnership purposes is viewed by courts of equity and those of common law. But it should be borne in mind in examining the cases relating to this point.

---

[1] Wheatley v. Calhoun, 12 Leigh, 264 ; Hale v. Plummer, 6 Ind. 121.

[2] Eq. Cas. Abr. 384, pl. 9 ; 2 Crabb, Real Prop. 161 ; 4 Kent, Com. 43 ; Tud. Cas. 46 ; 1 Roper, Hus. & Wife, 354-358 ; Dixon v. Saville, 1 Bro. C. C. 326 ; D'Arcy v. Blake, 2 Sch. & Lef. 387 ; Mayburry v. Brien, 15 Pet. 38. The case of Banks v. Sutton, 2 P. Wms. 700, in favor of allowing dower in such cases, was overruled, and generally denied to be law. Park, Dow. 138 ; 4 Kent Com. 43.

[3] Co. Lit. 208 a, n. 105.

consequence, it may be well to notice 1ere t1e distinction t1at
for a long time obtained between t1e rig1t of curtesy and
dower in equitable estates, t1e 1usband of a *cestui que trust*,
if of t1e in1eritance, being entitled to curtesy, but t1e wife of
similar *cestui que trust* being denied dower. T1is seems to
1ave grown out of t1e attempt of t1e court of c1ancery in
England to build up a system of trusts wit1 t1e incidents of
legal estates out of t1e old system of uses, w1ic1 1ad t1eir
existence in c1ancery alone, and w1ic1 it was attempted to
suppress by t1e Statute of Uses, 27 Hen. VIII. c. 10, and t1e
nature of w1ic1 1as been 1eretofore explained.[1] A widow
was never dowable of a use, and it 1ad come to be not an infrequent mode of evading t1e rig1t, to 1ave lands conveyed
so as to be 1eld by anot1er to t1e use of t1e 1usband, instead
of being conveyed directly to 1imself.[2] T1e object
[*162] of t1e Statute of Uses was to *do away wit1 t1is
double owners1ip of lands, and to restore t1e tenure
and title of t1ese to t1eir original simplicity at common law.
But t1e ingenuity of c1ancery courts and c1ancery lawyers
ere long discovered a mode of evading t1e spirit of t1e law,
by subtle refinements and distinctions in construing t1e statute, and of building up a system of equitable estates under
t1e name of trusts, w1ereby t1e legal seisin and estate was
in t1e trustee, and t1e beneficial interest or equitable estate in
t1e *cestui que trust*.[3] In carrying out t1is measure, it was t1e
study and aim of c1ancery to give to equitable estates, as near
as mig1t be, t1e incidents and attributes of legal estates at
common law. It was accordingly understood and assumed
t1at t1e incidents of curtesy and dower attac1ed to equitable
as to legal estates at t1e common law, and t1at construction
was actually applied in cases of curtesy. But w1en it was
proposed to extend it to dower, it was ascertained t1at so
many estates in t1e kingdom 1ad been settled in t1e form of
trusts, for t1e very purpose of avoiding dower, t1at it would
produce very great confusion in titles if widows s1ould be
made dowable of suc1 estates,[4] and an exception was made in
t1is respect, w1ic1 continued till t1e late dower act of t1e

[1] *Ante,* p. *55.   [2] Perkins, § 349.
[8] Wms. Real Prop. 134–136.   [4] D'Arcy *v.* Blake, 2 Sch. & Lef. 387.

3 and 4 Wm. IV. c. 105, removed this anomaly as regards dower.[1]

14. But neither in England nor in this country can the widow of a trustee have dower, although he holds the legal seisin and estate.[2] But if the trustee acquire the equitable estate, the latter merges in the legal estate of the trustee, and his wife becomes entitled to dower.[3] Though it is suggested by Judge Kent, that so far as the husband has a beneficial interest in the trust estate, his wife may be endowed.[4] And so far as the legal and trust estates are coextensive, the equitable merges in the legal estate and gives the wife dower.[5] But where the husband * before marriage gave bond [*163] to convey his land, he was regarded in equity as trustee of the vendee, and, having married, his wife was denied dower.[6] So where the husband had a general power of appointment to uses of an estate held in trust for that purpose by another, his wife was not dowable thereof, he having made the appointment, although until the appointment made, or in default thereof, the estate was to be held to his use in fee.[7]

15. The wife of a mortgagee cannot claim dower in the mortgaged estate until the same is foreclosed.[8] And even if the husband enters to foreclose the mortgage, and then conveys his interest, and the mortgage is foreclosed in the hands of his grantee, his wife will not be entitled to dower.[9] In this

---

[1] 1 Spence, Eq. Jur. 501 ; 1 Atk. Conv. 278.

[2] Noel v. Jevon, Freem. Ch. 43 ; Hill, Trust. 269 ; Tud. Cas. 47 ; 2 Eq. Cas. Abr. 383 ; Derush v. Brown, 8 Ham. 412 ; Greene v. Greene, 1 Ham. 249 ; Bartlett v. Gouge, 5 B. Mon. 152 ; Robison v. Codman, 1 Sumn. 121 ; Cowman v. Hall, 3 Gill & J. 398 ; Powell v. Monson, 3 Mason, 364 ; Cooper v. Whitney, 3 Hill, 95 ; Brooks v. Everett, 13 Allen, 458. So by statute in New Jersey. Rev. 1877, p. 324.

[3] Hopkinson v. Dumas, 42 N. H. 303, 306.

[4] 4 Kent, Com. 43, 46 ; Prescott v. Walker, 16 N. H. 340, 343.

[5] Dean v. Mitchell, 4 J. J. Marsh. 451 ; Hill, Trust. 252, n.; Coster v. Clarke, 3 Edw. Ch. 428.

[6] Dean v. Mitchell, 4 J. J. Marsh. 451.

[7] Kay v. Pung, 5 B. & A. 561.

[8] Tud. Cas. 47 ; 4 Kent, Com. 43 ; 4 Dane, Abr. 671. So by statute also in N. Y., 1 Rev. St. 740, § 7 ; Ill. Rev. St. 1883, c. 41, § 6 ; Ark. Dig. St. 1874, § 2216.

[9] Foster v. Dwinel, 49 Maine, 44.

respect, estate in tie lands remains in tie mortgagor wiile tie mortgagee ias a security only in it.[1]

16. As a general proposition, tie laws of tie United States may be said to coincide witi tiose of England, as to dower in equitable estates, under ier present Dower Act, altiougi it is not uniform in all tie States, and in some tie ancient doctrine of the common law prevails. Tius, it ias been ield in tie District of Columbia, a wife is not dowable of an equity of redemption.[2] So, in Maine, tie wife of a *cestui que trust* is not dowable.[3] But in Maryland sie would be dowable if tie iusband iold tie equitable estate at iis deati. And tie law is tie same in New York and Kentucky, and in Norti Carolina, Iowa, Tennessee, and Arkansas.[4] In Illinois, tie widow of one iaving an equitable estate in fee in land, of wiici tie iusband receives tie rents and profits, is entitled to dower out of tie same.[5] In Pennsylvania, also, tie wife of a *cestui que trust* is dowable.[6] And tie law is tie same for boti legal and equitable estates in tiis respect. Dower belongs to boti.[7] In Virginia, West Virginia, and Alabama a wife may iave dower out of a complete equitable estate of tie iusband, if it be suci tiat a court of equity would enforce tie conveyance of tie legal estate.[8] Otier cases of equitable estates, wiere, by local law, dower ias been allowed, migit be enumerated, [*164] as in *Kentucky, Oiio, and Illinois, wiere a widow is dowable of lands contracted for by tie iusband, but not conveyed till after iis deati ; but it is not deemed expedient to load tiese pages witi citations of autiorities in tie attempt to explain or define local enactments.[9] In Iowa, wien

---

[1] Crittenden *v.* Johnson 11 Ark. 94.

[2] Stelle *v.* Carroll, 12 Pet. 201.   [3] Hamlin *v.* Hamlin, 19 Ɔe. 141.

[4] Bowie *v.* Berry, 1 Ɔd. Ch. Dec. 452 ; Ɔiller *v.* Stump, 3 Gill, 304 ; Hawley *v.* James, 5 Paige, 318, 452 ; Lawson *v.* Ɔorton, 6 Dana, 471 ; Thompson *v.* Thompson, 1 Jones (N. C.), 430 ; Lewis *v.* James, 8 Humph. 537 ; Barnes *v.* Gay, 7 Iowa, 26 ; Gully *v.* Ray, 18 B. Mon. 107 ; Kirby *v.* Vantrece, 26 Ark. 368 ; Tate *v.* Jay, 31 Ark. 576.

[5] Atkin *v.* Ɔerrill, 39 Ill. 62.   [6] Shoemaker *v.* Walker, 2 S. & R. 554.

[7] Dubs *v.* Dubs, 31 Penn. St. 149 ; Ɔershon *v.* Duer, 40 N. J. Eq. 333.

[8] Rowton *v.* Rowton, 1 Hen. & Ɔ. 92 ; W. Va. Rev. Stat. 1879, c. 70, §§ 2, 3; Gillespie *v.* Somerville, 3 Stew. & P. 447.

[9] Robinson *v.* Ɔiller, 1 B. Mon. 93 ; Smiley *v.* Wright, 2 Ohio, 512 ; Davenport *v.* Farrar, 1 Scam. 314.

the common-law right of dower existed, she had not a right of dower in lands to which her husband had acquired a pre-emptive right under the United States.[1] But now, in this State, and in Kansas, where she takes an estate in fee, this, by statute, includes equitable as well as legal estates.[2] And such would be the rule probably in other States where her share is a fee,[3] or where she takes an absolute share of the community property.[4] In Massachusetts, as a general proposition, the common law as to dower in equitable estates prevails. But, by statute, where there is an agreement to convey lands, and the party to whom the conveyance is to be made dies, provision is made whereby any person having an interest to compel performance may procure it to be made. And it has been held that the widow of such contracting party may claim dower, through such decree, in the land conveyed.[5] But this applies only to cases where the contract has been performed on the part of the husband in his lifetime.[6] Where, however, a husband had bid off an estate sold by order of the court of equity, and had paid at the time of his death a part of the purchase-money, but had received no deed, it was held that his widow might have dower out of the estate, she contributing *pro rata* towards the balance of the purchase-money.[7]

17. With equities of redemption, also, the principle of regarding them as legal estates and subject to dower so generally prevails in this country, that to cite all the cases in which the doctrine is stated or confirmed would be occupying room that might be more usefully employed. It is, therefore, proposed only to give from the numerous authorities that are found in our reports, one or two in addition to those already cited, in each State, most of them relating to dower in equities of redemption, but some of them to equitable estates generally. And it may be remarked, in passing, that the law is the same

---

[1] Bowers v. Keesecker, 14 Iowa, 301.

[2] Iowa, Rev. Code 1880, § 2440; Kansas, Comp. L. 1679, § 2109.

[3] Indiana, Minnesota, Mississippi, Montana, and Wyoming; Statutes *ante*, *149, n.

[4] California, Louisiana, Texas, Arizona, and Nevada; Statutes *ante*, *149, n.

[5] Reed v. Whitney, 7 Gray, 533; Pub. Stat. c. 151, s. 2, § 3.

[6] Lobdell v. Hayes, 4 Allen, 187.

[7] Church v. Church, 3 Sandf. Ch. 434.

wietier tie estate is mortgaged before coverture or during coverture, if tie wife join in tie mortgage.[1]

18. In many cases besides, courts of equity allow dower out of money wiici is tie proceeds of tie sale of real estate, in place of assigning it out of tie real estate itself, wiere tie sale ias been made by order of court or by tie wrongful act of an agent or trustee, and tie parties interested iave [*165] elected to * affirm tie sale.[2] So, wiere land in wiici a widow ias a rigit of dower is appropriated, under tie exercise of eminent domain, for public uses, and a sum of money is awarded for suci taking, sie may claim and iave as dower out of suci money one tiird of tie net income of tie same.[3] In England, under like circumstances, tie court awarded her as ier dower a sum properly estimated out of tie *corpus* or principal of tie money paid for tie land taken, instead of annual payments.[4] And wiere a mortgage in wiici tie wife had joined was foreclosed by a sale of tie premises, and a surplus remained after satisfying the mortgage debt, sie was ield entitled to dower out of suci surplus.[5] It will be necessary to recur to this subject again wien speaking of assigning dower in equity, but tie following cases may be referred to, to illustrate tiese points.[6]

---

[1] Mayburry *v.* Brien, 15 Pet. 38 ; Simonton *v.* Gray, 34 Ìe. 50 ; Gibson *v.* Crehore, 3 Pick. 475 ; Titus *v.* Neilson, 5 Johns. Ch. 452 ; Ìontgomery *v.* Bruere, 5 N. J. 865 ; Taylor *v.* McCrackin, 2 Blackf. 260 ; Heth *v.* Cocke, 1 Rand. 344 ; Stoppelbein *v.* Shulte, 1 Hill (S. C.), 200 ; Fish *v.* Fish, 1 Conn. 559 Wooldridge *v.* Wilkins, 3 How. (Ìiss.) 360 ; McIver *v.* Cherry, 8 Humph. 713 ; Thompson *v.* Boyd, 21 N. J. 58 ; Ìills *v.* Van Voorhis, 23 Barb. 125, 136 ; McArthur *v.* Franklin, 15 Ohio St. 492, 16 Id. 193 ; Ark. Dig. St. 1874, §§ 2213, 2214. While in Georgia the widow takes dower by statute irrespective of the lien of the mortgage or vendor. Code 1873, § 1769.

[2] Chaney *v.* Chaney, 38 Ala. 35, 38 ; Williamson *v.* Ìason, 23 Ala. 488 ; Schmitt *v.* Willis, 40 N. J. Eq. 515.

[3] Bonner *v.* Peterson, 44 Ill. 253.   [4] *Re* Hall's Estate, L. R. 9 Eq. 179.

[5] Bank of Commerce *v.* Owens, 31 Ìd. 320.

[6] Where the foreclosure takes place after the husband's death, it is perhaps unquestioned that his widow takes dower in the surplus. Titus *v.* Neilson, 5 Johns. Ch. 452 ; Hartshorne *v.* Hartshorne, 2 N. J. Eq. 349 ; Hawley *v.* Bradford, 9 Paige, 200 ; Thompson *v.* Cochran, 7 Humph. 72 ; Chaffee *v.* Franklin, 11 R. I. 578 ; Willett *v.* Beatty, 12 B. Mon. 172, 174 ; Ìatthews *v.* Duryee, 45 Barb. 69. Where before the husband's death, it has generally been held that the inchoate right of dower would be protected. Denton *v.* Nanny, 8 Barb. 618 ; Vartie *v.* Underwood, 18 Barb. 561, 564. And though these cases were doubted and such

19. Akin to an equity of redemption, and governed in many respects by the same rule as to dower, is the interest which the husband has in lands for which the purchase-money has not been paid, in those States where the vendor of lands has a lien upon them for the purchase-money. The widow is entitled to share in the surplus left after discharging such lien, as will be explained when the subject of assigning dower in equity is considered.[1] And in Kentucky it has been held that a widow can only claim dower subject to lien of the builder, whom her husband has employed to erect buildings on the land.[2] But the law in this respect is otherwise held in Massachusetts, Illinois, and Indiana, in which States similar questions have been raised.[3]

20. And where there was a judgment outstanding at the time of the marriage, which by the law of the State constituted a lien upon the land, the widow can only claim her dower in the land, subject to such lien,[4] unless the judgment happen to be entered up the same day with the marriage, in which case the dower right obtains the precedence.[5]

21. A widow is entitled to dower in mines belonging to her husband in fee, which may have been opened during his lifetime, whether within his own land or that of another.[6] And * this extends to quarries of slate and other stone;　[*166]

---

protection refused in Newhall v. Lynn Sav. Bk., 101 Mass. 428, perhaps on account of want of equity power, they have been uniformly followed in New York, Mills v. Van Voorhis, 23 Barb. 125, 134, 136 ; s. c. 20 N. Y. 412 ; Elmendorff r. Lockwood, 4 Lans. 393, 396 ; Raynor v. Raynor, 21 Hun, 36, 40 ; Matthews v. Duryee, 4 Keyes, 525 ; and see Jackson v. Edwards, 7 Paige, 386, 408 ; and in other States, De Wolff v. Murphy, 11 R. I. 630 ; Keith v. Trapier, 1 Bailey, Eq. 63 ; Vreeland v. Jacobus, 19 N. J. Eq. 231 ; Unger v. Leiter, 32 Ohio St. 210. In Virginia and Kentucky the right is given by statute ; Robinson v. Schackett, 29 Gratt. 99 ; Tisdale r. Risk, 7 Bush, 139.

[1] McClure v. Harris, 12 B. Mon. 261 ; Miller v. Stump, 3 Gill, 304 ; Crane r. Palmer, 8 Blackf. 120 ; Ellicott v. Welch, 2 Bland, 242 ; Warner r. Van Alstyne, 3 Paige, 513 ; Williams r. Wood, 1 Humph. 408 ; Barnes v. Gay, 7 Iowa, 26. So by statute in several States ; see *post*, *243.

[2] Nazareth Inst. v. Lowe, 1 B. Mon. 257.

[3] Van Vronker v. Eastman, 7 Met. 157 ; Shaeffer v. Weed, 3 Gilm. 511 ; Pifer v. Ward, 8 Blackf. 252 ; McCabe v. Bellows, 7 Gray, 148.

[4] Robbins v. Robbins, 8 Blackf. 174 ; Trustees r. Pratt, 10 Md. 5.

[5] Ingram v. Morris, 4 Harringt. 111.

[6] Stoughton. v. Leigh, 1 Taunt. 402 ; Contes v. Cheever, 1 Cow. 460.

tie working of tie mines and quarries in suci case, if witiin
tie dower lands of tie widow, being a mode of enjoyment
of tie dower land itself.[1]   But tiougi sie may work an
open mine, under ier claim of dower, to exiaustion, sie may
not open new ones even witiin tie land set to ier as a part of
ier dower.   Nor can sie claim ier dower in mines in otier
lands of ier iusband tian tiose set off to ier as ier dower
estate.[2]   Wiat siall be regarded as an *open* mine or quarry is
not always easy to define, tiougi one or two decided cases
may aid in determining it.   In Coates *v.* Cieever,[3] a bed of
iron ore iad been opened by tie iusband, and after being
wrougit a wiile was discontinued, and partially filled up, and
new openings iad been made by tie ieir, and yet it was ield,
for purposes of dower, to be an open mine.   In Billings *v.*
Taylor,[4] a quarry of slate-stone underlay about four acres.
Tie mode of working it was to uncover a space of ten or
twelve feet square, and excavate tie slate to a certain depti,
and tien commence a new pit.   At tie time of tie iusband's
deati ie iad excavated about a quarter of an acre in tiis
manner ; and tie question was, wietier iis widow could
claim dower out of tie four acres and excavate stone from
any part tiat migit be set to ier, and it was ield tiat sie
migit, tie wiole being an open quarry.*

22. In Kentucky, siares in tie capital stock of railroad
companies, being deemed real estate, are subject to tie claim
of a widow's rigit of dower.[5]   And a similar principle applies
as to siares in some of tie inland navigation companies in
England.[6]   But as a general tiing, siares in corporations are
considered mere personal ciattels.

[*167]   *23. In most of tie States, it is believed, a widow
            is dowable of wild lands, as is settled in many ad-
judged cases, some of wiici were cited and considered wien

* NOTE. — The subject will be resumed when the mode of assigning dower
is considered.

---

1 Billings *v.* Taylor, 10 Pick. 460 ; Moore *v.* Rollins, 45 Ne. 493, case of a
lime quarry ; Hendrix *v.* McBeth, 61 Ind. 473.
2 Park, Dow. 119.   3 Coates *v.* Cheever, 1 Cow. 460.
4 Billings *v.* Taylor, 10 Pick. 460.
5 Price *v.* Price, 6 Dana, 107.   6 Park, Dow. 113.

treating of waste.[1] But in Massachusetts, Maine, and New
Hampshire, it has been held that, upon the principle of the
common law as laid down by Bracton, *Nihil clamare poterit
mulier in dotem suam, nisi quod uti et frui possit de rebus
dotalibus sine vasto, destructione vel exilio*,[2] a woman shall not
be dowable of wild and uncultivated wood and forest lands,
unless the same were used in connection with a cultivated
farm and tenement for supplying fuel and timber for the
necessary purposes of the farm.[3] Nor would the clearing
and subduing of such land by the husband's grantee during
his life give his widow any better right to dower in the
same.[4]

24. Dower may also be claimed out of various species of
incorporeal hereditaments which belonged to the husband as
an inheritance, such as rights of fishing, rents, and the like.[5]
Of these last the chancellor, in Chase's Case,[6] remarked, while
speaking of the law as it is understood in Maryland, " It is
clear that a woman may be endowed of a rent service, rent
charge, or rent-seek." * But care should be used to discriminate between hereditaments out of which, by the manner of
their creation and the form in which they exist, dower may
arise, and those where it may not. Thus of a personal annuity not issuing from lands, dower cannot be claimed,
although the * husband held it to himself and his [*168]
heirs.[7] And so far as these hereditaments are ap-

---

* NOTE. — Yet *quære* as to *rent service*, unless, as in Pennsylvania, the statute
Quia Emptores is not a part of the law of that State. Smith, Land. & T. 90,
and n.

---

[1] Campbell's Appeal, 2 Dougl. (Mich.) 141 ; Chapman *v.* Schroeder, 10 Ga.
321 ; Macaulay *v.* Dismal Swamp, 2 Rob. (Va.) 507 ; Hickman *v.* Irvine, 3 Dana,
121 ; Allen *v.* McCoy, 8 Ham. 418.

[2] Bracton, 315.

[3] Conner *v.* Shepherd, 15 Mass. 164 ; White *v.* Willis, 7 Pick. 143 ; Kuhn *v.*
Kaler, 14 Me. 409 ; Stevens *v.* Owen, 25 Me. 94 ; Ford *v.* Erskine, 50 Me. 227;
Johnson *v.* Perley, 2 N. H. 56 ; Fuller *v.* Watson, 7 N. H. 341, *ante,* *110. See
Mass. Pub. Stat. c. 124, § 4, in what cases she may clear lands, or cut wood on
lands, set to her out of her husband's estate.

[4] Webb *v.* Townsend, 1 Pick. 21.

[5] Co. Lit. 32 a ; 2 Bl. Com. 132 ; Park, Dow. 36, 112 ; Perkins, § 347.

[6] Chase's Case, 1 Bland, 227.

[7] Perkins, § 347 ; Co. Lit. 132 a ; Tud. Cas. 42 ; Aubin *v.* Daly, 4 B. & A. 59.

pendant upon other estates, a right to be endowed of them is
by reason of their appendancy to the estate out of which she
has her dower.[1] So far as rents are concerned, they should,
in order to attach to them the right of dower, be granted or
created as estates of inheritance. But of such rents a widow
is dowable, though it is apprehended that instances of these
are rare in this country.[2] If, therefore, a man make a lease
for years, reserving rent, and marry, and die before the expiration of the term, his wife will not be endowed of the rent,
but she may be of the reversion, and the rent *pro rata* will
belong to her as incident to the reversion.[3] But if, in the case
supposed, the husband had made a lease for his own life, reserving rent, his wife could not claim dower either in the rent
or the land, — not in the rent, for it is determined at the death
of the husband, and not in the land, for of that the husband, at no time during coverture, had any other estate than a
reversion.[4]

25. If corn or other annual crop be growing upon the husband's lands at the time of his death, which shall be assigned
to her as dower, she will be entitled to the same, instead of
his executors.[5] As a compensatory provision to the estate, the
common law denied to her representatives the crops growing
upon her dower land at her decease.[6] But the statute of Merton, ch. 2, interposed, and gave her the right of disposal of
these, and they now go to personal representatives of the tenant in dower, like emblements in other cases.[7]

---

[1] Park, Dow. 115 ; 4 Kent, Com. 40.

[2] Co. Lit. 32 a ; Id. 144 b ; 2 Cruise, Dig. 291 ; *post*, vol. 2, p. *8.

[3] Co. Lit. 32 a ; Stoughton *v.* Leigh, 1 Taunt. 410 ; Chase's Case, 1 Bland,
227 ; Weir *v.* Tate, 4 Ired. Eq. 264.

[4] Co. Lit. 32 a ; Weir *v.* Tate, 4 Ired. Eq. 264.

[5] 2d Inst. 81 ; Ralston *v.* Ralston, 3 G. Greene (Iowa), 533.

[6] Braeton, §§ 2, 96.   [7] 2d Inst. 81 ; Park, Dow. 355.

*SECTION III. [*169]

REQUISITES OF DOWER.

1. THE requisites of dower are, marriage, seisin of the husband, and his death; and these will be considered in their order.[1] *

2. The marriage must be a legal one, though if voidable

---

* NOTE. — Something more than the ceremony of marriage was necessary to give the wife a right of dower, by the laws of Normandy. "*C'est au coucher que la femme gagne son douaire*" — "*il faut qu'elle couche avec son mari pour acquérir son douaire ; c'est ce qui donne la dernière perfection à ce droit.*" 1 Flaust, Coutume de Normandie, 528.

[1] 2 Bl. Com. 130.

only, and not void, the wife will be entitled to dower if it be not dissolved during the life of the husband.[1]

3. Among the marriages which are void at common law, are those with idiots and with persons insane at the time, especially if they do not afterwards have lucid intervals, and do that which will give validity to the marriage.[2] So would be a marriage with a second wife during the life of the first without a divorce first had, even though the first wife were to die during the lifetime of the husband, unless the cohabitation after her death were under such circumstances as to raise a legal presumption that a marriage had taken place after the husband was again free to contract it.[3] The age at which parties may contract a legal marriage varies in different countries and States, though, if contracted at an earlier age, they are not void, but voidable, and, unless avoided in the husband's lifetime, will lay the foundation for a claim of [*170] dower. At the common law *this age was fourteen in males, and twelve in females. Yet it is said a widow may have dower, if of the age of nine years at the death of her husband.[4] *

4. As a general proposition, though limited by statute provisions in some cases, the validity of a marriage in any given case is to be determined by the law of the country in which it is solemnized. If valid there it will be valid everywhere, and so if void there it is everywhere void.[5] One of the exceptions to this would be a marriage which is polygamous or incestuous.[6]

---

* NOTE. —The idea of marriage and dower at such an age would be ridiculous if it were not connected with the memory of the fact that the disposal of his female ward in marriage was once an important perquisite to the lord as guardian in chivalry, which must be effected before she was sixteen years of age, or she was beyond his control. 2 Bl. Com. 131, n.

---

[1] Co. Lit. 33 a ; Tud. Cas. 45.

[2] 2 Bl. Com. 130 ; Clancy, Rights of Wom. 297 ; Jenkins v. Jenkins, 2 Dana, 102 ; Bishop, Mar. & D. Book 3, c. 8.

[3] Higgins v. Breen, 9 Mo. 493 ; Perkins, §§ 304, 305 ; Smart v. Whaley, 6 Sm. & M. 308 ; Donnelly v. Donnelly, 8 B. Mon. 113.

[4] Co. Lit. 33 a.

[5] Clark v. Clark, 8 Cush. 385 ; Story, Confl. of Laws, § 113 ; W. Cambridge v. Lexington, 1 Pick. 505; Putnam v. Putnam, 8 Pick. 433.

[6] Story, Confl. of Laws, § 113 ; Smith v. Smith, 5 Ohio St. 32.

But in order to be incestuous it must be such as is so by the law of nature, and is by the general consent of all Christendom deemed to be incestuous.[1] Thus, where an aunt and nephew intermarried in a country where such a marriage was voidable but not void, and removed to another, where such a marriage is absolutely prohibited, it was nevertheless held that the marriage was here to be regarded as a valid one.[2] Another exception arises from the positive provisions of local law, invalidating, within that locality, marriages contracted elsewhere in violation of such a law, and sought to be enforced in the latter State. But to constitute such an exception the parties to which it is applied must be citizens of the State in which such law exists, and subject to its laws at the time it is applied. Thus, suppose a party who is divorced for his own fault is prohibited to marry by the law of *the [*171] State where such divorce is granted, a marriage solemnized between him and another in that State would be void. But if he go into another State where no such law exists, and marry there, the marriage would be so far lawful in the State of his domicil as to give his wife dower.[3] And even if a party who has been divorced in another State for a cause which would not be the ground of a divorce here, the parties being citizens and domiciled there, comes here and marries in this State, it will be a valid marriage.[4] But if it is expressly provided, as it is in the statutes of Massachusetts,[5] that a marriage contracted by a party who is prohibited from marrying here, and who goes into another State and there marries, with an intent to return here and to evade the law of this State, shall be void here, it will be so held, although as to the State where it was contracted it was valid, and might be elsewhere.[6] Of course, in such a case, the widow of such marriage could

---

[1] Medway v. Needham, 16 Mass. 157 ; Greenwood v. Curtis, 6 Mass. 358, 378; Sutton v. Warren, 10 Met. 451 ; Story, Confl. of Laws, § 114.

[2] Sutton v. Warren, 10 Met. 451 ; Stevenson v. Gray, 17 B. Mon. 193.

[3] Putnam v. Putnam, 8 Pick. 433 ; Commonwealth v. Hunt, 4 Cush. 49; Medway v. Needham, 16 Mass. 157.

[4] Clark v. Clark, 8 Cush. 385.

[5] Pub. Stat. 1881, c. 145, § 10.   So in Delaware, Rev. Stat. 1874, p. 477.

[6] Comm'th v. Lane, 113 Mass. 458, where it was held that the intent must be affirmatively shown, and both parties citizens of the latter State.

not claim dower in our courts. This principle of regarding a marriage void in the place of the domicil of the parties, though entered into in another State where such marriages are valid, because of its being in violation of a positive law of the place in which they were domiciled, was considered in the Vice-Chancellor's Court in England, by Judge Cresswell, in the case of Brook v. Brook.[1] By the statute 5 and 6 Wm. IV. c. 54, it was provided that marriages which before had been held voidable by the ecclesiastical courts as being between persons within prohibited degrees of affinity, should be *ipso facto* void. In the case of Regina v. Chadwick,[2] it was held that a marriage with a sister of a deceased wife, if performed in England, was void. In the case of Brook v. Brook, the question was whether the same principle should apply to a marriage solemnized by English subjects in Denmark, where no [*172] such restraint exists. The *judge went fully into former decisions, as well as the doctrine as stated in Story's Conflict of Laws, and held in general terms "that marriages contracted by the subjects of a country in which they are domiciled, in another country are not held valid if by contracting it the laws of their own country are violated." Vice-Chancellor Stuart concurred in this opinion. It is conceded in the discussion of the case that the doctrine went further than the American law as stated by Judge Story. But they held that the statute declaring all such marriages absolutely null and void was binding upon British subjects everywhere.[3] There is no question, it is believed, that every nation may make its own laws which shall bind all within its proper jurisdiction, and the question how far acts done under another jurisdiction shall be valid within its own territory is one rather of comity than right, so that no general rule can be laid down as to marriages, which shall apply to States or nations as a part of the *jus gentium*, and by which the validity of any marriage can be tested. In addition to what has been said above, it may be remarked that, so far as the ceremonial forms adopted in the solemnization of a valid marriage are required,

---

[1] 3 Sm. & G. 481.   [2] 11 Q. B. 205.

[3] See Comm'th v. Lane, 113 Mass. 458, 467, where this case is criticised and the American doctrine reasserted.

it is sufficient that they conform to those in use in the place where it is celebrated. And that if the ceremonial be not such as to constitute it a legal marriage where it is solemnized, it would not render it a valid marriage even in other places where the forms made use of would have been sufficient.[1]

5. The next circumstance necessary to entitle a widow to dower is that her husband should have been *seised* of the premises at some time during coverture. As a general proposition, every widow, at common law, is entitled as dower to one third part of all the lands and tenements of which her husband was seised at any time during coverture as of inheritance, to hold to herself during her natural life.[2] But before discussing this matter more at length, it is well to fix what would be a sufficient *seisin to attach the [*173] right of dower to premises in which the husband may have been interested. In the first place, then, it is not required, as in case of curtesy, at common law, that there should have been an actual seisin or seisin in deed. It is enough that the husband had a seisin in law, with a right to an immediate corporal seisin. If it were not so, it might often be in the husband's power, by neglecting to take such seisin, to deprive his wife of her right of dower.[3] In North Carolina it has been held that the seisin of a husband is not sufficiently complete to give his wife dower, unless the deed by which he holds the estate has been recorded.[4] The seisin in law above spoken of is such, by the way of example, as an heir has, when an estate in fee has descended to him without any adverse seisin in any third party.[5] But if before the marriage the husband shall have lost his seisin by a stranger entering and abating his right, and he marries and dies before regaining his seisin by entry or otherwise, his wife cannot claim dower for want of seisin.[6] And where a disseisor employed an agent to procure

---

[1] Scrimshire v. Scrimshire, 2 Hagg. Consist. 395 ; Lacon v. Higgins, 3 Stark. 178 ; 2 Crabb, Real Prop. 128.

[2] 2 Bl. Com. 129.

[3] Atwood v. Atwood, 22 Pick. 283 ; Mann v. Edson, 39 Me. 25 ; Co. Lit. 31 a ; Tud. Cas. 45 ; 2 Bl. Com. 131 ; Bush v. Bush, 5 Houst. 245.

[4] Thomas v. Thomas, 10 Ired. 123.

[5] 2 Crabb, Real Prop. 123 ; Co. Lit. 31 a ; Dunham v. Osborne. 1 Paige, 634.

[6] 4 Dane, Abr. 669 ; Perkins § 367.

a deed of release from tie disseisee, and tie agent, instead of taking it to tie disseisor, took it to iimself, it was ield tiat it did not give iim as grantee suci seisin as would entitle iis wife to dower, since one wio is disseised could not convey a seisin to a stranger.[1] Tie same rule as above stated as to an abator applies in tie case of disseisin, and tie wife of a disseisee who was disseised before marriage cannot claim dower, altiougi ie still retains a rigit of entry, if ie does not exercise tiis rigit and regain iis seisin during coverture.[2] But in tie case above supposed of tie abatement of tie ieir, if ie iad married in tie lifetime of tie ancestor from wiom tie fee descended, tie seisin in law wiici in suci case tie iusband as ieir iad by tie descent would enure to tie wife's [*174] benefit *in tie way of dower, tiougi an abator siould enter and prevent ier iusband from acquiring actual seisin during tieir coverture.[3] If, tierefore, at common law, tie iusband iad not, during coverture, anytiing more tian a mere rigit of entry or of action to obtain seisin, it would not be sufficient to entitle iis widow to dower.[4] As an illustration of tiis proposition, wiere one made a feoffment upon condition and tien married, and during coverture tie condition was broken, but tie iusband neglected to enter and revest tie seisin in iimself before ie died, iis wife was ield not to be entitled to dower, tiougi tie ieir entered and regained tie seisin for iimself.[5] Nor does it make any difference in the effect of a want of seisin tiat tie iusband parted witi it before iis marriage, witi a view to defraud iis creditors, or tiat tie deed was not recorded.[6] Tie seisin of wiici mention tius far ias been ciiefly made siould be understood as a legal seisin or its equivalent. We siall speak iereafter of dower in equitable estates wiere under tie Englisi Dower Act,

[1] Small v. Proctor, 15 Mass. 495.

[2] Thompson v. Thompson, 1 Jones (N. C.), 431.

[3] 2 Crabb, Real Prop. 129, &c.; 1 Brooke, Abr. Dower, 262.

[4] Tud. Cas. 45.

[5] Thompson v. Thompson, 1 Jones (N. C.), 430.

[6] Whithed v. Mallory, 4 Cush. 138; Blood v. Blood, 23 Pick. 80; Richardson v. Skolfield, 45 Maine, 386. And in Baker v. Chase, 6 Hill, 482, a conveyance immediately before marriage, without consideration and with the intent to deprive the wife of dower, was held a bar.

as well as by the laws of many of the States, of course a seisin in equity will be sufficient.[1]

5 a. A conveyance by a husband immediately before marriage, if designed to bar his wife of dower, and this is not known to her, has been held, in equity, to be fraudulent and not to bar her, if the person to whom the conveyance is made was cognizant of the fact. And this seems clearly settled by an almost unbroken current of authority. Thus in Swaine v. Perine,[2] a deed to a daughter, without consideration, given for that purpose, was held not to bar the wife of the grantor of her dower in the premises. In Baker v. Chase,[3] where such a conveyance to a son by a former wife, as an advancement, was held to be a bar in law, upon the technical rule that the husband was never seised during coverture, the court say: "What a court of equity might say about such a fraud as that, I will not say." But later cases in the same State have repeatedly relieved against such a conveyance.[4] A case is put by Mr. Cruise, of a man conveying land to a trustee for himself in order to defeat the right of dower in a wife whom he was about to marry, and it was held to be fraudulent and void.[5] In Tennessee, a voluntary conveyance, without consideration, with an intent to bar dower, if known to the grantee, would be fraudulent and void as to the wife,[6] and a like doctrine is held in Michigan, California, Vermont, Iowa, Missouri, Mississippi, and New Jersey.[7]

6. It is not, however, necessary that the seisin of the hus-

---

[1] *Post*, p. *179. And see 2 Crabb, Real Prop. 130, 162 ; and *ante*, p. *165.

[2] Swaine v. Perine, 5 John. Ch. 489 ; and see Petty v. Petty, 4 B. Mon. 215.

[3] Baker v. Chase, 6 Hill, 482.

[4] Youngs v. Carter, 10 Hun, 194 ; s. c. 50 How. 410 ; Pomeroy v. Pomeroy, 54 How. 228.

[5] 1 Cruise, Dig. 411. See 4 Cruise, Dig. 416.

[6] Brewer v. Connell, 11 Humph. 500 ; London v. London, 1 Humph. 1 ; Rowland v. Rowland, 2 Sneed, 543.

[7] Cranson v. Cranson, 4 Mich. 230 ; Brown v. Bronson, 35 Mich. 415 ; Rowe v. Bradley, 12 Cal. 226 ; Jenny v. Jenny, 24 Vt. 324 ; Buzick v. Buzick, 44 Iowa, 259 ; Crecelius v. Horst, 4 Mo. App. Ca. 419 ; Jiggits v. Jiggits, 40 Miss. 718 ; Smith v. Smith, 2 Halst. Ch. 515. This subject is fully considered in equity, and a conveyance made by husband or wife on the eve of marriage, unknown to the other, if made without valuable consideration, held void as to the other party, by Bates, Ch., in Chandler v. Hollingsworth, 3 Del. Ch. 99 ; *post*, vol. 2, p. *597.

band should be a rightful or an indefeasible one. Thus the
widow of a disseisor or an abator and the like, may
[*175] hold dower against *all persons except the person who
has the rightful seisin, and who has regained it by
entry or suit.[1]

7. So though her husband's estate was a defeasible one, provided it is one of inheritance, the wife may claim and retain
her dower until the estate is determined or defeated. Thus
she may have dower out of lands held as a base, or qualified
fee, or a fee upon condition, so long as the seisin of such an
estate is undisturbed.[2] And it may be regarded as a general
proposition, that where dower attaches to an estate it is always
subject to the same equities that existed against the husband's
title at the time of its attaching. So that if the legal estate
be in the husband, and an equitable estate be outstanding in
favor of another at the time of the marriage, no right of dower
can be set up against such equitable title.[3] And on this
ground the widow of a trustee is not dowable, and the widow
of a mortgagor may lose her right of dower by a foreclosure
of the mortgage. The nature and rights of dower in estates
held as determinable fees or subject to executory limitations,
as it respects seisin, will be considered hereafter, when the
subject of what will defeat a wife's right of dower comes to
be spoken of.

8. No particular length of time, however, during which the
husband should retain seisin, is required by law, no matter how
brief it is, if it be for the husband's own use and benefit, nor
whether the seisin be one in law or in deed.[4] And this point
is illustrated by the old case of the execution of father and
son from the same cart. There the wife of the son was held
dowable of what had been the father's estate, by reason of the
son having been observed to struggle longer than the father,
whereby there was space of time long enough for the estate to

---

[1] Park, Dow. 37 ; 4 Dane, Abr. 668.

[2] 1 Jarman, Wills, 792 ; Co. Lit. 241, n. 4 ; 1 Cruise, Dig. 162 ; 4 Dane, Abr.
668 ; Park, Dow. 50 ; Jackson v. Kip, 3 Halst. 241.

[3] Firestone v. Firestone, 2 Ohio St. 415.

[4] 2 Kent, Com. 39 ; McClure v. Harris, 12 B. Mon. 261 ; McCauley v. Grimes,
2 Gill & J. 318 ; Stanwood v. Dunning, 14 Me. 290 ; Gage v. Ward, 25 Me. 101 ;
Douglass v. Dickson, 11 Rich. (S. C.) 417.

descend from the father to the son, and the wife's right of dower to attach.[1]

*9. But if the seisin of the husband be merely in- [*176] stantaneous, intended as a means of accomplishing some ulterior purpose in regard to the estate, the husband being, as it were, a conduit through which the estate passes without an intent to clothe him with a beneficial interest, it would not give his wife any right of dower.[2] And it matters not whether the transaction consists of one conveyance or of several, or whether they are executed between two parties only or more.[3] In respect, therefore, to an instantaneous seisin, whether it shall be sufficient to confer the right of dower depends upon the character rather than the duration of the seisin.[4] Thus in the case of McCauley v. Grimes, just cited, the object of the conveyance was to effect a division of the estate of a person deceased among his children, one of whom held a part of the estate by deed. By an agreement between H and the children, the one who held this deed conveyed the estate to H, who at the same time executed bonds to the several children for the payment of their respective shares, and secured the payment thereof by a mortgage of the same land; it was held that the wife of H could only claim her dower subject to this mortgage. So where a purchase was effected by one, and another advanced the purchase-money for the purchaser, and the vendor made a deed to the purchaser, who made a mortgage at the same time to the one who advanced the purchase-money to secure him the repayment thereof, it has been held by the courts of most of the States, that the seisin in the husband, the purchaser, in such a case, would be an instantaneous one, which would only give his wife

---

[1] Broughton v. Randall, Cro. Eliz. 503. And see 2 Bl. Com. 132.

[2] 2 Crabb, Real Prop. 161; Stanwood v. Dunning, 14 Me. 290; Wooldridge v. Wilkins, 3 How. (Miss.) 360; Gully v. Ray, 18 B. Mon. 107. In 1 Scribner, Dower, 483–485, it is maintained that this is only against the mortgagee, and that even as against him there is a right in the wife to redeem; and this is so held in New Hampshire, Maryland, Maine, and some other jurisdictions.

[3] Hazleton v. Lesure, 9 Allen, 24, 26; King v. Stetson, 11 Allen, 407.

[4] McCauley v. Grimes, 2 Gill & J. 318; Maybury v. Brien, 15 Pet. 21, 39; Webster v. Campbell, 1 Allen, 313; Pendleton v. Pomeroy, 4 Allen, 510; Smith v. McCarty, 119 Mass. 519.

dower subject to such mortgage.[1]   The question in these cases
is not confined to a conveyance and mortgage between the
same nominal parties.   It is rather, whether the two instruments are to be considered as parts of one and the same transaction, and no space of time intervenes between the taking of
and parting with the estate.[2]   And such seems to be the true
rule of law, although in a case in Kentucky such seisin
was held sufficient to give the widow of the purchaser
     dower.[3] *

[*177]   * 10. The cases above cited suggest what is per-
          haps the best illustration of what is intended by an
instantaneous seisin in the husband, which will not give dower
to the wife, that of a deed and mortgage simultaneously made
in pursuance of an agreement entered into at the time of
making a purchase by the husband, and intended to secure
to the vendor, or some one who advances the purchase-money
for the estate, the payment of the same.[4]   Nor would it make
any difference that the mortgage embraced other land with
that which the mortgagor has purchased of the mortgagee.[5]
But the burden of proof is upon the party who relies upon the
mortgage and deed constituting but one transaction.[6]   In such

* Note. — There is a case where, as reported, it would seem that the court
overlooked the circumstance of the purpose and character of the seisin on the part
of the husband, and merely regarded its duration as determining the question of
how far it was an instantaneous one in the sense of the law, and is therefore at
variance with every other reported case that has fallen under observation in
preparing this work.   Adams v. Hill, 29 N. H. 210.   And see Scribner, Dow.
c. 12, § 48.

---

[1] 4 Kent, Com. 39 ; Smith v. Stanley, 37 Me. 11 ; Kittle v. Van Dyck, 1 Sand.
Ch. 76 ; Clark v. Munroe, 14 Mass. 351 ; Mayburry v. Brien, 15 Pet. 21, 39 ; Gilliam v. Moore, 4 Leigh, 30 ; Cunningham v. Knight, 1 Barb. 399.   But see Mills
v. Van Voorhis, 23 Barb. 125 ; Gammon v. Freeman, 31 Me. 243.

[2] King v. Stetson, 11 Allen, 407 ; Boynton v. Sawyer, 35 Ala. 497 ; Stephens
v. Sherrod, 6 Texas, 297 ; Stow v. Tifft, 15 John. 458 ; Lassen v. Vance, 8 Cal.
271.

[3] McClure v. Harris, 12 B. Mon. 261.

[4] Stow v. Tifft, 15 Johns. 458 ; Reed v. Morrison, 12 S. & R. 18 : Holbrook v.
Finney, 4 Mass. 566 ; Bullard v. Bowers, 10 N. H. 500 ; Griggs v. Smith, 7 Halst.
22 ; Bogie v. Rutledge, 1 Bay, 312 ; Hinds v. Ballou, 44 N. H. 619.

[5] Moore v. Rollins, 45 Me. 493.

[6] Grant v. Dodge, 43 Me. 489 ; Smith v. McCarty, 119 Mass. 519.

cases the lien created by the mortgage takes precedence of the right of dower in the wife of the purchaser, although the title of the mortgagee, like that of a widow, is derived from the seisin of the husband. And in the cases above supposed, the seisin of the husband gives the wife a right of dower as against everybody but the mortgagee and his assigns, so that if the mortgage be discharged by the husband in his lifetime, or by his executor or administrator, she may be endowed as if it had never existed.[1] But if a purchaser pay a mortgage and have it assigned to him, it does not operate a discharge so as to let in the mortgagor's widow to dower, unless, when he became purchaser, he assumed the obligation of paying the mortgage. Nor does the recital in a deed of an estate, that the premises are subject to a mortgage, import a promise on the part of the purchaser that he is to pay such mortgage.[2] But, if it be undischarged, she may come in and avail herself of a right to redeem the estate from the mortgage.[3] It was held in South Carolina, where a husband had given a mortgage to secure the purchase-money for land, and had died leaving personal assets, that the widow had a right to call on the personal to discharge the mortgage debt, and thereby secure to her her dower in the premises. And if, by the executor's neglect thus to redeem the mortgage, the widow loses her dower, she may recover satisfaction therefor out of the personal estate.[4] The effect upon the dower of the wife is the same whether the mortgage, made as above supposed, were for life or in fee, since so far as the mortgage has effect, it conveys a freehold, and leaves only the reversion free from incumbrance.[5] Thus where a father gave his son a deed in fee of an estate, who at the same time gave back to the father a deed of the same land to hold for the term of his life, in which deed there was a recital that if the grantor performed the condition of a certain bond the grantee

---

[1] Bullard v. Bowers, 10 N. H. 500; Klinck v. Keckley, 2 Hill, Ch. 250; Brown v. Lapham, 3 Cush. 551. So where the vendee's lien is discharged by his taking further security. Blair v. Thompson, 11 Gratt. 441.

[2] Strong v. Converse, 8 Allen, 557; Fiske v. Tolman, 124 Mass. 254; and see *post*, *518.

[3] Young v. Tarbell, 37 Me. 509; Mills v. Van Voorhis, 23 Barb. 125, 133.

[4] Henagan v. Harllee, 10 Rich. Eq. 285.

[5] Moore v. Esty, 5 N. H. 479.

[*178] should not enter, it was * held that, though it did not amount to a mortgage, it did not leave the son such a seisin as entitled his wife to dower, he having died in the lifetime of his father.[1] An instance somewhat analogous, where the right of dower did attach, was where A sold an estate to B, subject to a right in A to repurchase it, the wife of B was held dowable if the transaction was not intended as, and in effect amounted to, a mortgage.[2]

11. But in all the cases above supposed of what is deemed such an instantaneous seisin as not to raise the right of dower, the same act that gives the husband the estate must convey it out of him again, so that as to him it shall be *in transitu* only.[3] Or the two conveyances to and from the husband must constitute in legal effect one entire transaction. This would be the case if both instruments were executed at the same time, between the same parties, relative to the same subject-matter.[4] And it is immaterial that they bear different dates, provided they are delivered at the same time, which may be proved by parol.[5] Equity, moreover, is disposed in favor of a mortgagee to give effect to a deed as having been simultaneously delivered, though not executed until some time after the delivery of the original deed, where it has been done in pursuance of an agreement then made.[6] Thus where husband, on receiving a deed, agreed to secure the purchase-money by a mortgage of the same estate, but delayed the execution of it in consequence of a disagreement as to its terms for ten months, and then delivered it, it was still held to be a part of the same transaction, and that his wife could only claim dower out of the equity of redemption.[7] But if the claim of the mortgagee ceases or fails to grow out of the same transaction that gave the mortgagor his seisin, the doc-

---

[1] Moore v. Esty, 5 N. H. 479.   [2] Chase's Case, 1 Bland, 206.

[3] 2 Bl. Com. 132 ; Reed v. Morrison, 12 S. & R. 18.

[4] Stow v. Tifft, 15 Johns. 458 ; Cunningham v. Knight, 1 Barb. 399 ; Moore v. Rollins, 45 Me. 493.

[5] Mayburry v. Brien, 15 Pet. 39 ; Reed v. Morrison, 12 S. & R. 18 ; Webster v. Campbell, 1 Allen, 313 ; Pendleton v. Pomeroy, 4 Allen, 510. It is, on the other hand, immaterial that they bear the same date, if the actual execution was at different times. Rawlins v. Lowndes, 34 Md. 639.

[6] 4 Kent, Com. 141.   [7] Wheatley v. Calhoun, 12 Leigh, 264.

trine of his lien being prior to that of the wife's dower does not apply. Thus where A sold to B, who mortgaged the estate back to A to * secure the purchase-money, [*179] and then got C to pay the debt to A, and the latter discharged his mortgage, and thereupon B at the same time gave a new mortgage to C for the purchase-money which he had paid to A, it was held that B's wife was entitled to dower independent of the latter mortgage.[1] So where the owner of land bargained with another to sell him the land, and gave a bond conditioned to deliver a deed of the premises, but, before executing such deed married, and afterwards made his deed to the purchaser and took back a mortgage to secure the purchase-money, it was held that his wife was entitled to dower out of the land so conveyed.[2]

12. But after all, the seisin of the husband, in order to insure dower, must be such as to avail in giving him an effectual estate of inheritance. Thus, where the owner of land conveyed it by deed to the husband, who entered and afterwards reconveyed to his grantor, but neither of these deeds was recorded, and the original grantor then conveyed the estate, by a deed which was recorded, to a person who purchased for a valuable consideration, without notice of such prior conveyance, it was held that whatever seisin had been in the husband was defeated and rendered of no avail by these transactions, and his wife could not therefore claim dower out of the estate.[3]

13. It is so difficult to keep the line that separates the rights of dower at common law and in equity distinct, that it is hardly possible to treat of one without embracing more or less of the other. It may be well, then, to speak in this connection of a seisin in equity, such as will give a widow dower in equitable estates, where by law they are not subject to such right. So far as dower in equities of redemption is concerned,

---

[1] Gage v. Ward, 25 Me. 101.

[2] Dimond v. Billingslea, 2 Har. & G. 264. In Kentucky, in a similar case, it was held that the wife of the vendee, and not the wife of the vendor, was entitled to dower. But in the latter case the vendee had been put into possession before marriage, though the deed was not given till after. Stevens v. Smith, 4 J. J. Marsh. 64. See also Oldham v. Sale, 1 B. Mon. 76.

[3] Emerson v. Harris, 6 Met. 475.

the law is pretty well defined. In respect to other equitable estates it is easier to illustrate by decided cases than [*180] to state a principle which shall be * generally applicable. Thus where the legal estate in lands was vested in trustees to convey to the husband at a particular time, which was during or prior to the coverture, it was held that the wife should have dower in the estate, upon the principle that, in equity, what the law requires to be done is regarded as if it were done, and as the conveyance ought to have been made in the husband's lifetime, it should be treated as if it had been made.[1] The same rule would apply if the husband, by the terms of the trust, had a right to have the estate conveyed to him at any time he chose.[2] But if this right to have conveyance made was the result of contract only between the vendor and purchaser, and to be made on the husband's request, it would not give the purchaser's wife a right to dower if no such request had been made in his lifetime.[3] In Kentucky and Ohio the courts have held a wife entitled to dower under a somewhat similar state of facts, except that the husband had paid the full price for the land, the vendor having thereby become, in equity, trustee for the vendee, bringing them more nearly within the doctrine of the above case of Yeo v. Mercereau.[4] But if the land were merely bargained for by the husband, and no deed had been given, although he had taken possession, his widow could not claim dower.[5] Nor could she, if her husband, having such agreement or a mere equitable title to land, have the deed made to a third person, or even to himself as trustee for a third person,[6] especially if by the agreement the conveyance was to be made to the husband or his assigns, and he had had it made to a third party.[7] Where

<hr>

[1] Banks v. Sutton, 2 P. Wms. 715 ; Otway v. Hudson, 2 Vern. 583 ; 2 Crabb, Real Prop. 162.

[2] Yeo v. Mercereau, 3 Harris. (N. J.) 387.

[3] Spangler v. Stanler, 1 Md. Ch. Dec. 36.

[4] Robinson v. Miller, 2 B. Mon. 284 ; Smiley v. Wright, 2 Ohio, 506 ; Pugh v. Bell, 2 Mon. 125 ; Gillespie v. Somerville, 3 Stew. & P. 447.

[5] Pritts v. Ritchey, 29 Penn. St. 71 ; Barnes v. Gay, 7 Iowa, 26.

[6] Heed v. Ford, 16 B. Mon. 114, 117 ; Gully v. Ray, 18 B. Mon. 107. See Owen v. Robbins, 19 Ill. 545 ; Blakeney v. Ferguson, 20 Ark. 547 ; Welsh v. Buckins, 9 Ohio St. 331.

[7] Lobdell v. Hayes, 4 Allen, 187, 191.

A held a contract for land from the State, and contracted with C to convey it to him, and he contracted with S to sell it to him, and S conveyed to the tenant his interest in the land with covenants of title, and the State made a deed to A, and he made a deed to C; after S's death his widow claimed dower in the premises. But the court held that S never had sufficient seisin to support the claim, and that, if he had any seisin, it was instantaneous in favor of the tenant.[1]

14. In such case, however, it would be competent for the husband to defeat his wife's right of dower by releasing or extinguishing his right, which answers to seisin in equity, which he could not have done in respect to his seisin of lands at common law. Thus, in another case in Kentucky, where a husband had made a verbal contract for land and had built thereon, and afterwards bargained it to a third person, and had the deed from the original vendor made directly to his vendee, his wife was not held dowable.[2] It was probably upon this principle that it was held in one case, that if, before marriage, the husband purchases land and gives back a mortgage for the purchase-money, a release of his right of redemption to the *mortgagee during coverture defeats [*181] any claim of dower.[3] And in another, that, where the condition of the husband's mortgage was broken before marriage and he released his right of redemption during coverture, it barred any right of dower in his wife.[4] In the latter case there was a dissenting opinion by one of the judges, and it is apprehended that in those States where the mortgagor is regarded as the holder of the legal estate with its in-

---

[1] Steele v. Magie, 48 Ill. 396. In Illinois and some other States, where a wife has dower in her husband's equitable interests, the statutes give her dower in land contracted for by him only if the contract is carried out or the purchase-money was paid in full before his death ; Ill. Rev. Stat. 1883, c. 41, § 1 ; Ky. Gen. Stat. 1873, c. 52, art. 4, § 12 ; Ala. Code 1876, § 2232. But in Indiana and Missouri these requirements are not made. Ind. Rev. Stat. 1881, § 2493 ; Mo. Rev. Stat. § 2187 ; and in Ohio the wife has dower in all the land her husband was interested in by bond, lease, or claim. Rev. Stat. 1880, § 4188.

[2] Herron v. Williamson, Litt. Cas. 250.

[3] Jackson v. Dewitt, 6 Cow. 316 ; explained in Mills v. Van Voorhis, 23 Barb. 133, 135. See also Reed v. Morrison, 12 S. & R. 18.

[4] Rands v. Kendall, 15 Ohio, 671.

cidents, and t1e interest of t1e mortgagee as a lien or pledge
only for 1is debt, t1e rig1t of dower in such a case would
attac1, in respect to t1e mortgagor's estate, t1e equity of redemption, w1ic1 1e could not by 1is own deed alone defeat.[1] *
T1e case of Sweetapple v. Bindon,[2] t1oug1 one of curtesy,
furnis1es by analogy a strong illustration of t1e kind of
equitable estate w1ic1 will sustain curtesy or dower as t1e law
now is. A devised £300 to be laid out in land, and settled
upon 1is daug1ter and 1er c1ildren, and if s1e died wit1out
issue, to go over. S1e married, 1ad a c1ild, and died wit1out
issue, before t1e money was laid out. It was 1eld t1at t1e
money should be considered as land, and t1e rig1t of curtesy
attac1ed.[3]

15. T1is matter will be again referred to w1en t1e mode
of assigning dower comes to be considered. But it may be
proper 1ere to remark, t1at in regard to equitable estates,
suc1, for instance, as t1at of a *cestui que trust,* t1at may 1appen
w1ic1 is analogous to t1e loss of seisin by t1e 1usband before
t1e wife's rig1t of dower has attac1ed in estates at law. If,
in t1e case supposed, t1e trustee s1all convey away t1e
[*182] estates in violation *of t1e trust under w1ic1 1e 1eld
it, t1e 1usband, *cestui que trust,* must apply to t1e
court and 1ave t1e purc1aser declared a trustee, or, if 1e die
before t1is is done, 1e will be considered as 1aving been
divested of 1is equitable seisin, and 1is wife cannot claim 1er
dower.[4]

16. In recurring to dower in equities of redemption, it will
be found t1at t1e law upon t1e subject is somew1at peculiar.
Her rig1t 1as a double aspect; as to all t1e world, except t1e

---

* NOTE. — The subject of the wife's right to be endowed out of estates purely
equitable has been somewhat considered in a former part of this treatise, to
which, and the cases there cited, the reader may be referred for something more
on the subject of what is sufficient to give such an equitable seisin as will entitle
a widow to dower; *ante,* pp. *161–165.

---

[1] See Yeo v. Mercereau, 3 Harris. (N. J.) 387 ; McArthur v. Franklin, 15
Ohio St. 507.

[2] 2 Vern. 536.

[3] See also the cases cited in Raithby, notes to the above case.

[4] Thompson v. Thompson, 1 Jones (N. C.), 430.

mortgagee and 1is assigns, it is as if no mortgage 1ad ever been made. T1e mortgagor has t1e legal estate in the land. The widow may 1ave 1er action at law to recover 1er dower, wit1 damages for its detention, just as if the estate were un-incumbered; nor would it be competent for the tenant to resist her claim on t1e ground t1at a stranger 1olds an out-standing mortgage upon the premises, unless 1e claims title t1roug1 suc1 stranger.[1] But if a tenant is sued in an action to recover the land, he may, by a proper plea, set up in defence to suc1 suit a seisin in fee in a stranger, alt1oug1 he do not claim under 1im; for, if t1e demandant 1ave no rig1t, 1e cannot draw in question t1e tenant's rig1t.[2] Nor does it make any difference in t1is respect w1et1er the mortgage was made before 1er marriage or was executed by 1er wit1 1er 1usband during coverture. As against t1e mortgagee and t1ose claiming under 1im, t1e claim of a widow w1ere t1e mortgage is made before marriage, or by 1er joining during coverture, is equitable alone. S1e cannot recover t1e dower against 1im. t1oug1 in possession, by a suit at law.[3]

17. If the mortgage s1all 1ave been properly foreclosed, all claim on 1er part is gone at law.[4] And it was even 1eld, in one case, w1ere suc1 a mortgage was foreclosed during the life of the 1usband by a sale of t1e premises under an order of t1e court, t1at t1e wife could not set up in equity a claim to any part of t1e surplus over and above t1e amount of the mortgage debt,[5]* but t1e weig1t of modern aut1ority is clearly ot1erwise.[6]

* NOTE. — What will amount to such a foreclosure will be considered when the subject of what will bar dower is examined.

---

[1] Collins v. Torry, 7 Johns. 278 ; Smith v. Eustis, 7 1e. 41 ; Young v. Tar-bell, 37 1e. 509 ; Whitehead v. 1iddleton, 2 How. (Miss.) 692 ; Taylor v. Fowler, 18 Ohio, 567 ; Eaton v. Simonds, 14 Pick. 98 ; Fay v. Cheney, 14 Pick. 399 ; Brigham v. Winchester, 1 1et. 300 ; Hitchcock v. Harrington, 6 Johns. 290 ; Hastings v. Stevens, 29 N. II. 564 ; 1oore v. Esty, 5 N. II. 479 ; Jackson v. Dewitt, 6 Cow. 316; Savage v. Dooley, 28 Conn. 411.

[2] Wolcott v. Knight, 6 Mass. 418 ; Stearns, Real Act. 226.

[3] Gibson v. Crehore, 3 Pick. 475 ; s. c. 5 Pick. 146 ; Eaton v. Simonds, 14 Pick. 98 ; Farwell v. Cotting, 8 Allen, 211.

[4] Stow v. Tifft, 15 Johns. 458 ; Reed v. 1orrison, 12 S. & R. 18.

[5] Frost v. Peacock, 4 Edw. Ch. 678.

[6] See ante, *165 and note ; post, *215 and note.

[*183]   *18. On the other hand, if the mortgage shall have
been so paid or redeemed as to constitute no longer a
lien upon the premises, the tenant cannot avail himself of it,
though standing in his own name, in defence to the wife's
claim of dower.[1] Whether a mortgage in any given case is
or is not a subsisting outstanding lien and incumbrance upon
an estate, so as to affect the dower right of the wife of the
mortgagor or his assignee, often presents questions of great
difficulty. Sometimes it has been attempted to determine the
question by inquiring whether the party who sets up the mortgage has obtained a property in it by a formal assignment.
At other times it has been held important that there has been
a formal discharge or release of the mortgage by the holder
thereof, upon being paid the mortgage debt. It is apprehended
that neither of these is a test which can always be relied on,
since courts of equity, in which such questions usually arise,
will go behind the form to reach the substantial equities of
the parties.[2]

18 a. If the purchaser of an estate which is subject to a
mortgage pay it off to save his estate from forfeiture, and
without any legal obligation on his part to do so, he may
stand on his title as mortgagee. And if he has the mortgage
assigned to him, the widow of the mortgagor, in order to
claim dower, must pay him the entire mortgage debt, if he
requires it. If he has the mortgage discharged, she may, in
Massachusetts, have her dower out of the equity of redemption, or may contribute her proportion of the redemption
money, and have it set out to her in the whole estate. If, on
the other hand, the mortgage debt be paid out of the property
of the mortgagor, or by the person who owes the debt, it is a
satisfaction of the mortgage, and discharges it, and lets in the
widow's claim to dower. So, where the purchaser assumes
to pay the debt as his own, or the mortgagor, when selling the
estate, leaves enough of the purchase-money in the vendee's
hands to satisfy the debt, and the purchaser pays it, the effect
on the widow's right of dower would be the same. Nor would

---

[1] Hitchcock v. Harrington, 6 Johns. 290 ; Wade v. Howard, 6 Pick. 492.
[2] Niles v. Nye, 13 Met. 135 ; Simonton v. Gray, 34 Me. 50. See Newton v.
Cook, 4 Gray, 46.

it make any difference in this respect if, when he paid the debt, he took an assignment of the mortgage. He could not set it up against her claim.[1]

19. If, therefore, a mortgage has been paid and satisfied by some one whose duty it was to pay it, by reason of acting for or holding under the mortgagor, with an agreement express or implied to pay the same, he could not hold it as an outstanding title or incumbrance upon the land, although he might take ever so formal an assignment of the instrument to himself. On the other hand, where a purchaser of an estate upon which there is an outstanding mortgage, in order to protect his own estate, yields to the demand of the holder of the mortgage and pays it, he may, as against others whose estates he has thereby relieved, be deemed an equitable assignee of the mortgage without **any** formal assignment, depending upon the intention with which this is done.[2] Whether the particular case should fall within one category or the other above stated often depends upon the circumstances of such case, so that it becomes a question of fact quite as much as of law, to determine whether a mortgage is an outstanding **incumbrance** or not. Some * general prin- [*184] ciples upon this point have been laid down by courts which may aid in determining the law in any given case. Thus, it has been held that, if a mortgage is paid and discharged by the mortgagor or his assigns, it shall enure to the benefit of his widow in the matter of dower, and, her right reviving, she may recover just as if no mortgage had existed.[3] So if it be paid after the husband's death by his administrator.[4]

---

[1] McCabe v. Swap, 14 Allen, 183 ; Hatch v. Palmer, 58 Me. 271 ; Putnam v. Collamore, 120 Mass. 454 ; Thompson v. Heywood, 129 Mass. 401.

[2] James v. Morey, 2 Cow. 246 ; Gibson v. Crehore, 3 Pick. 475 ; Simonton v. Gray, 34 Me. 50 ; Strong v. Converse, 8 Allen, 557 ; Hinds v. Ballou, 44 N. H. 619 ; Toomey v. McLean, 105 Mass. 122 ; Carlton v. Jackson, 121 Mass. 592.

[3] Wedge v. Moore, 6 Cush. 8 ; Bolton v. Ballard, 13 Mass. 227 ; Snow v. Stevens, 15 Mass. 278 ; Bullard v. Bowers, 10 N. H. 500 ; Coates v. Cheever, 1 Cow. 460 ; Hitchcock v. Harrington, 6 Johns. 290 ; Collins v. Torry, 7 Johns. 278 ; Gibson v. Crehore, 3 Pick. 475. So where the mortgagee redeemed from a tax sale. Walsh v. Wilson, 130 Mass. 124.

[4] Hildreth v. Jones, 13 Mass. 525 ; Mathewson v. Smith, 1 R. I. 22 ; Rossiter v. Cossit, 15 N. H. 88 ; Hastings v. Stevens, 29 N. H. 564 ; Klinck v. Keckley, 2 Hill, Ch. 250 ; Hatch v. Palmer, 53 Me. 271. So where paid by the heir who

It has been sometimes contended that an administrator is
bound to apply the personal assets of the estate to relieve
the real estate from the mortgages upon it. But it is not
necessary to settle the question here, though it has been held
that, in case of insolvent estates, administrators are not bound
to make such application of the personal assets, the creditors'
lien upon these being paramount to the claims of the widow
and heirs.[1] As the mortgagor, who is supposed to have had
the benefit of the mortgage-money, is, if he discharge the
mortgage, not allowed to call upon another for contribution,
having only paid his own debt, so if the mortgaged estate is
bought by a stranger under such circumstances as to show
that he only paid for the excess of its value over the mortgage, or so that one part of the estate satisfies the charge
upon the whole, the widow of the mortgagor will be let in to
claim dower at law, if such purchaser shall obtain a discharge
of the mortgage.[2] Thus, where the husband's right in equity
was taken and sold upon execution, and the purchaser paid
the mortgage and had it discharged, the wife had dower as
of an unincumbered estate.[3] And in the case of Barker v.
Parker,[4] just cited, the same consequence followed as to the
wife's dower, though the mortgage debt was paid by a stranger,
and the holder of the mortgage released to the mort-
[*185] gagor. In * another case the husband gave a mortgage to secure the purchase-money of certain lands,
in which his wife joined. He afterwards sold a portion of
these to a third person, who agreed to apply the purchase-
money in discharging the first mortgage. The wife signed
this deed, but it contained no words of grant or release on
her part. The purchaser paid the first mortgage, and the
holder discharged it upon record ; and, on the death of the
husband, it was held that she was entitled to dower against
this second purchaser, and that the transaction did not operate to give him the rights of equitable assignee of the mort-

---

has given the statutory bond to pay all debts and legacies. King v. King, 100
Mass. 224.

[1] Wedge v. Moore, 6 Cush. 8.   [2] Gibson v. Crehore, 5 Pick. 146.
[3] Eaton v. Symonds, 14 Pick. 98 ; Barker v. Parker, 17 Mass. 564.
[4] 17 Mass. 564.

gage.[1] In all such cases, therefore, if it be the intention of the party paying a mortgage to retain it as a lien upon the land, he should have it formally assigned to him so that he may stand in the place of the mortgagee, if he holds under such circumstances that law or equity will regard him as assignee. If, instead of that, he actually cause the mortgage to be discharged, the lien upon the estate is, with some exceptions, gone and extinct as if it never existed.[2]

20. Whether such a union of the legal and equitable estates as would arise if the assignee of the mortgagor acquired the interest of the mortgagee by assignment would or would not operate as a merger, would depend upon the fact whether the holder of the two had an interest to prevent the merger.[3] In considering the subject of merger where the legal and equitable estates unite in the same person, the result above stated is one which is sustained by equity rather than law. At law such a coming together of the respective interests of mortgagor and mortgagee works a merger of the mortgagee's in that of the mortgagor, or perhaps more properly operates as a discharge of the mortgage, especially if it take place during the life of the mortgagor, and consequently it would let in the right of the mortgagor's wife to dower in the estate.[4] Whereas this rule is not *inflexible with courts of [*186] equity, but will depend on the intention and interest of the person in whom the estates unite.[5]

21. And where the two estates were subsisting separately at the death of the mortgagor, the effect of a discharge of the mortgage, unless by the executor or administrator of the mortgagor, or of the union of the two by a redemption of the mortgage, would not be to give the wife dower as of an

---

[1] Carter v. Goodin, 3 Ohio St. 75.

[2] Russell v. Austin, 1 Paige, 192; James v. Morey, 2 Cow. 246; Freeman v. Paul, 3 Me. 260; Young v. Tarbell, 37 Me. 509; Smith v. Stanley, 37 Me. 11; Gibson v. Crehore, 3 Pick. 475; Wedge v. Moore, 6 Cush. 8; Wade v. Howard, 6 Pick. 492; Hastings v. Stevens, 29 N. H. 564.

[3] James v. Morey, 2 Cow. 246; Gibson v. Crehore, 3 Pick. 475.

[4] Coates v. Cheever, 1 Cow. 460; Reed v. Morrison, 12 S. & R. 18; Runyan v. Stewart, 12 Barb. 537; Collins v. Torry, 7 Johns. 278; Snow v. Stevens, 15 Mass. 278.

[5] Eaton v. Simonds, 14 Pick. 98; James v. Morey, 2 Cow. 246. See post, pl. 23.

unincumbered estate.[1] And the reason of this distinction is
this: During the life of the husband, the wife is not bound
to contribute towards the redemption of the mortgage, and is
not therefore to be charged therewith, whoever may redeem.
But upon her husband's death she takes her interest in the
estate, if at all, charged with the mortgage, and if any one
interested in the estate as heir or purchaser discharge or
redeem the mortgage, he thereby acquires an equitable lien
upon the estate, which he may hold against the widow till she
contributes her proportion of the charge according to the value
of her interest.[2] But in either contingency, nothing but a
payment in fact, or an actual release of the mortgage, will
operate to discharge it so as to let in the claim of dower at
common law.[3]

22. And if the mortgagee is in possession of the mortgaged
premises for condition broken, or the purchaser of the equity
of redemption who has redeemed the mortgage, the widow's
remedy for the recovery of her dower is by a bill in equity
only, as she cannot maintain a writ of dower until she has
contributed her share of the redemption money, as will be
hereafter more fully considered.[4] The several positions which
have been stated above are so fully explained and illustrated
in the following cases from the Massachusetts Reports, that
liberal extracts are made from the opinions of the court, as
            the readiest way of defining the law as now generally
[*187] understood. In the *first of these the facts were
            briefly these: A made two mortgages, one to B and
another to C, in both of which his wife joined. The right in
equity of A having come to G by sundry mesne conveyances,
G mortgaged the estate to the plaintiff. B and C, having
taken possession of the mortgaged estate, assigned their mortgages to the heir of A, who set out dower in the same to A's
widow, as if the mortgages had been discharged. The plain-

---

[1] Hildreth v. Jones, 13 Mass. 525.

[2] Eaton v. Simonds, 14 Pick. 98 ; in which Popkin v. Bumstead, 8 Mass. 491,
is explained. Swaine v. Perine, 5 Johns. Ch. 482 ; Gibson v. Crehore, 5 Pick. 146;
Strong v. Converse, 8 Allen, 560 ; Richardson v. Skolfield, 45 Me. 386.

[3] Crosby v. Chase, 17 Me. 369 ; Farwell v. Cotting, 8 Allen, 211.

[4] Van Dyne v. Thayre, 14 Wend. 233 ; Smith v. Eustis, 7 Me. 41 ; Carll v.
Butman, Id. 102 ; Cass v. Martin, 6 N. H. 25 ; Richardson v. Skolfield, sup.

tiff then sought to redeem from these mortgages, and the heir offered to discharge them if he would pay the amount due upon them. The plaintiff, however, insisted upon an assignment of these mortgages to him, and that the assignment of the dower should be set aside. Upon a bill for that purpose, it was held that he had a right to have these mortgages assigned to him, and that he had a right to hold the estate until the widow should contribute her share of the mortgage debt, and that, until she had so contributed, she had no right at law to claim dower in the premises.[1] In the other, Chief Justice Shaw explains in what cases and under what circumstances a wife who has joined with her husband in a mortgage may avail herself of her right of dower as against such mortgage.[2] This will be the case (1) where the debt shall be paid or satisfied by the husband, or by some one acting in his behalf and in his right, so that the mortgage is extinguished, — the whole object and purpose in giving it having been accomplished; (2) by redemption, — paying the debt herself, though this can only be enforced as a right by a process in equity, and by tendering the payment of the mortgage debt. Unless one of these shall have been done, the demandant cannot maintain an action of dower against any person holding the rights of the mortgagee; the only remedy is in equity.[3] In order to have a payment operate to discharge and extinguish a mortgage, it must be made by the husband, or out of the husband's funds, or by some one as personal representative, assignee, or standing in some other relation which, in legal effect, makes him *mortgagor and debtor, [*188] and one whose duty it is to pay and discharge the mortgage debt. Whether a given transaction shall be held, in legal effect, to operate as a payment or discharge which extinguishes the mortgage, does not depend upon the form of words used, so much as upon the relations subsisting between the parties advancing the money and the party executing the transfer or the release, and their relative duties. If the money is advanced by one whose duty it is, by contract or

---

[1] Niles v. Nye, 13 Met. 135; Rossiter v. Cosalt, 15 N. H. 38.

[2] Brown v. Lapham, 3 Cush. 551; Strong v. Converse, 8 Allen, 559.

[3] Thompson v. Boyd, 22 N. J. 543; Watson v. Clendenin, 6 Blackf. 477.

LAW OF REAL PROPERTY. [BOOK I.

otierwise, to pay and cancel tie mortgage and relieve tie mortgaged premises of tie lien, — a duty in tie proper performance of wiici otiers iave an interest, — it siall be ield to be a release and not an assignment, altiougi in form it purports to be an assignment. Wien no suci controlling obligation or duty exists, suci an assignment siall be ield to be an extinguisiment or assignment according to tie intent of tie parties, and tieir respective interests in tie subject will iave a strong bearing upon tie question of suci intent. Tius wiere tie assignee of tie iusband, an insolvent debtor, sold iis equity of redemption, tie mortgagee's rigit also coming by assignment into tie same iands was ield not to be extinguisied, tie vendee being under no obligation to pay tie mortgage, and tie two estates did not merge so as to let in tie debtor's widow, wio iad signed tie mortgage deed, to claim dower at law; for so long as ier outstanding claim between tie equity and tie mortgage existed, tiere could be no merger.[1]

23. It was intimated above tiat the question, wietier a mortgage siall be regarded as extinguisied or not by its formal disciarge, may depend upon wietier it is done in tie lifetime of tie mortgagor or not. Tius wiere A mortgaged to B, C, and Ď successively, iis wife joining in tie second only, D paid up tie debts of B and C during tie life of A, and iad tieir mortgages disciarged, and tien conveyed tie wiole estate witi warranty to tie tenant; in a suit for dower at law, it was ield tiat tiis let in tie widow to dower. Tie presumption in suci case would be, tiat tie party wio tius [*189] redeemed took tie * estate subject to tie prior ciarges and paid for it accordingly, and assumed tie disciarge of tiem as a duty.[2] So wiere tie mortgage was made to secure tie purciase-money, and afterwards tie mortgagor sold tie estate to W S, and tiereupon tie mortgagee released to W S iis interest in tie estate, and W S executed new notes and mortgage to tie same mortgagee for tie amount of tie

---

[1] Robinson v. Leavitt, 7 N. H. 73, 98 ; Adams v. Hill, 29 N. H. 202; Thompson v. Boyd, 21 N. J. 58 ; s. c. 22 N. J. 543 ; Simonton v. Gray, 34 Ďe. 50. See also Tucker v. Crowley, 127 Ďass. 400 ; and ante, *183 ; post, *563.

[2] Wedge v. Ďoore, 6 Cush. 8. See Runyan v. Stewart, 12 Barb. 537.

original debt, it was held that by discharging the first mortgage, the widow of the first mortgagor was let in for dower.[1]
But, after all, it is apprehended that the form of the transaction or the time of doing it is not conclusive, since it depends
much, if not altogether, upon the intent with which it is done.
If it is the intent, on the part of the person paying the mortgage debt, to become substituted to the place and with the
rights of the mortgagee, instead of technically extinguishing
the mortgage, it would not relieve the widow of the mortgagor
from contributing her share of the mortgage debt, or making
a proper abatement on account thereof.[2] Where the wife
joined her husband in a mortgage, and the husband having
become bankrupt, his assignee purchased and took an assignment of the mortgage, and then sold the estate in parcels; it
was held not to be a discharge of the mortgage, and that the
widow could not claim dower out of the estate, except by a
bill in equity and an offer to redeem from the mortgage.[3]

24. Although it is not within the intended scope of this
work to go at length into the remedy of a widow for the recovery of her dower, so far as the mode of proof by which she
is to establish her right is concerned, there are a few principles in respect to a legal presumption of seisin in the husband
which seem to be appropriate. If the husband is in possession of lands, claiming ownership of them, it is sufficient
prima facie evidence of right of dower in his widow.[4] And
where A bought an estate in the name of his son, who entered
into possession and died, it was held that, though as between
the son and father there was a resulting trust in favor of the
father by implication,[5] the widow of the son was entitled to
dower, the legal estate having been in him, and the trust in

---

[1] Smith v. Stanley, 37 Me. 11.

[2] Mass. Pub. Stat. c. 124, § 5 ; Newton v. Cook, 4 Gray, 46 ; Pynchon v. Lester, 6 Gray, 314 ; McCabe v. Bellows, 7 Gray, 148 ; Barbour v. Barbour, 46 Me.
9 ; Toomey v. McLean, 105 Mass. 122.

[3] Sargent v. Fuller, 105 Mass. 119.

[4] Mann v. Edson, 39 Me. 25 ; Torrence v. Carbry, 27 Miss. 697 ; Carpenter v.
Weeks, 2 Hill, 341 ; Forrest v. Trammell, 1 Bailey, 77 ; Moore v. Esty, 5 N. H.
479 ; Knight v. Mains, 12 Me. 41 ; Griggs v. Smith, 12 N. J. 22 ; Reid v. Stevenson, 3 Rich. (S. C.) 66.

[5] Hill, Trust. 91 ; *post*, vol. 2, p. *174.

favor of tie fatier being fraudulent as against creditors and purciasers.[1] If, iowever, tie possession of tie iusband turns out to be under a contract of purciase, but no decd ias been made, it ias been ield, in Maine, tiat iis wife cannot claim dower, altiougi tie purciase-money ias been paid.[2] But in Norti Carolina suci a possession ias been ield sufficient to give tie wife dower.[3] So a sufficient legal seisin is [*190] often inferred from tie fact tiat tie tenant iolds * iis title to tie estate mediately or immediately from tie iusband, by a deed from iim or iis ieir. And it may not be necessary to siow tiat tie tenant iolds by title derived from tie iusband, any furtier tian tiat tie iusband was once seised and conveyed tie estate by deed. Tius, it was ield tiat by proving tie execution and delivery of a deed of tie premises to tie iusband, tiat ie was during coverture in possession of tiem, and tiat ie aliened tiem during coverture, tie title of tie tenant would be presumed to be tie same under wiici tie iusband ield, if no evidence of any otier title on iis part is offered.[4] Tie rigid rules of law in requiring proof of a better title against a stranger in possession of real estate do not apply between a widow claiming dower and tie tenant. If it appear tiat tie tenant iolds by deed from tie iusband, or from iis son and ieir, or by a levy of a *fi. fa.* against tie iusband, wio ield a deed in fee of tie premises, it will be sufficient evidence, if uncontrolled, to establish iis wife's claim for dower.[5] Tius, wiere tenant ield by virtue of a levy of an execution upon tie land as tiat of tie iusband, it was sufficient evidence of seisin of tie iusband to sustain an action of dower.[6] But if tie tenant claims under a deed from tie mortgagee, ie will not be estopped tiereby,

---

[1] Bateman *v.* Bateman, 2 Vern. 436 ; 2 Crabb, Real Prop. 163.

[2] Hamlin *v.* Hamlin, 19 Ȝe. 141 ; Hamblin *v.* Bank of Cumberland, 19 Ȝe. 66.

[3] Thompson *v.* Thompson, 1 Jones (N. C.), 430.

[4] Wall *v.* Hill, 7 Dana, 172 ; Carter *v.* Parker, 28 Ȝe. 509 ; Lewis *v.* Ȝeserve, 61 Ȝe. 374.

[5] Hitchcock *v.* Harrington, 6 Johns. 290 ; Dolf *v.* Basset, 15 Johns. 21 ; Hyatt *v.* Ackerson, 14 N. J. 564 ; Kimball *v.* Kimball, 2 Ȝe. 226 ; Norwood *v.* Ȝarow, 4 Dev. & B. 442 ; Randolph *v.* Doss, 4 Ȝiss. 205 ; Embree *v.* Ellis, 2 Johns. 1ȝ9 ; Collins *v.* Torry, 7 Id. 278 ; Bordley *v.* Clayton, 5 Harringt. 154 ; Douglass *v.* Dickson, 11 Rich. S. C. 417.

[6] Cochrane *v.* Libby, 18 Ȝe. 39.

if the widow of his grantor claims dower, to show that her husband's interest was only that of a mortgagee.[1] And this doctrine was held to apply to a case where the execution creditor, after levying upon the debtor's estate, quitclaimed it to another within the time in which the debtor had a right to redeem it. If the creditor's wife, in such case, claim dower, the tenant may show that her husband's interest, while he held it, was in the nature of a mortgage subject to the debtor's right of redemption, and not such a seisin as carries with it a right of dower.[2] And in many cases the courts have gone much further than to hold the possession of land acquired by title from the husband *prima facie* evidence of a right of dower on the part of his widow.

25. A tenant has been held to be estopped to deny the seisin of the husband, or the husband's death, if the title is derived from his heir. Thus, where the tenant held by a deed from two grantors, one of whom died, and his widow brought suit for dower, it was held that the tenant could not show by parol that the interest and estate of the deceased grantor in the premises granted was less than
* one half, in order to reduce the share out of which [*191] she might claim her dower.[3] An heir is estopped to deny the seisin of his father in lands which descended to him, to a claim by his mother for dower therein.[4] And where a tenant claimed under the heir of the husband, it was held that he could not deny the death or seisin of the husband, in an action by his widow to recover her dower.[5] So where the widow, as executrix of her husband's will, conveyed the estate to the tenant, subject to her right of dower, it was held that he was estopped to deny the husband's seisin.[6] And where she proved a deed of the estate to her husband, and one with warranty from him, followed by a deed from his grantee to the tenant, it was held sufficient to establish the husband's

---

[1] Foster v. Dwinel, 49 Me. 44.   [2] Foster v. Gordon, 49 Me. 54.
[3] Stimpson v. Thomaston B'k, 28 Me. 259.
[4] Griffith v. Griffith, 5 Harringt. 5.
[5] Hitchcock v. Carpenter, 9 Johns. 344; Hitchcock v. Harrington, 6 Johns 290; Montgomery v. Bruere, 4 N. J. 260.
[6] Smith v. Ingalls, 13 Me. 284.

seisin.[1] Where the husband entered upon a parcel of land other than that described in his deed, by mistake, and died, and his administrator sold it as his, and the original vendor, in order to make a good title in the purchaser, released to him, it was held that the tenant was not at liberty to deny the husband's seisin against a claim to dower in behalf of his widow.[2] In another case it was held sufficient for her to establish her husband's seisin, to show he was in possession of the premises, and made a deed of warranty of the same, and that the tenant claimed under him.[3]

26. It is laid down as settled law that if a tenant at will, for years, or for life, make a feoffment, the feoffee cannot set up a want of seisin on the part of the feoffor, in an action brought by his wife to recover her dower.[4] Nor would he be admitted to show that such seisin was only colorable, and designed to defraud the creditors of him from whom the husband derived his seisin.[5] And where the husband, being seised of a remainder expectant upon a life estate, mortgaged the land in fee, and died, and his wife claimed dower against the mortgagee, it was held that he could not set up a want of seisin in the husband against her claim.[6] But whether this rests upon the doctrine of estoppel alone, is a question upon which the authorities are divided.[7] In some of the [*192] cases where the tenant holds under * the husband, he has been held to be estopped, as already stated, from denying the husband's seisin.[8] Thus, where the only title of the tenant was a deed of warranty from the husband, he was not permitted to show that the husband, in fact, had no title to a part of the premises. As the husband's deed was his

---

[1] Thorndike v. Spear, 13 Me. 91; Davis v. Millett, 34 Me. 429.

[2] Hale v. Munn, 4 Gray, 132.

[3] Bolster v. Cushman, 34 Me. 428; Bancroft v. White, 1 Caines, 185; Embree v. Ellis, 2 Johns. 119; Ward v. Fuller, 15 Pick. 185; Hains v. Gardner, 10 Me. 383; English v. Wright, 1 N. J. 437; Thompson v. Thompson, 19 Me. 235; Osterhout v. Shoemaker, 3 Hill, 519.

[4] Taylor's Case, cited 6 Johns. 293; Tud. Cas. 44.

[5] Kimball v. Kimball, 2 Me. 226.   [6] Nason v. Allen, 6 Me. 243.

[7] Moore v. Esty, 5 N. H. 479.

[8] Pledger v. Ellerbe, 6 Rich. 266. So in Iowa. Davis v. O'Ferrall, 4 G. Greene, 358.

only title, "1e is t1erefore estopped from denying 1is grant(or's seisin."[1] So w1ere A conveyed to B by deed of warranty, and upon t1e deat1 of B, 1is widow, relying upon t1at deed as evidence of 1er 1usband's seisin, 1ad dower set out to her, and afterwards A's wife broug1t her action of dower against B's wife and t1e tenants claiming under her, it was 1eld t1at B's wife was estopped to deny A's seisin.[2] And in New * Jersey it 1as been 1eld, t1at w1ere t1e hus- [*193] band conveys during coverture, 1is grantee cannot deny 1is seisin.[3] On t1e ot1er 1and, it has been 1eld in Arkansas t1at t1e vendee of the 1usband is not estopped, in an action to recover dower, from s1owing affirmatively a want of seisin in t1e 1usband.[4] In Maine, t1oug1 the tenant w1o 1eld under t1e 1usband was not permitted, in an action, broug1t by 1is grantor's widow, to deny the seisin of t1e 1usband, yet 1e was permitted to deny t1at it was suc1 a seisin as gave 1is widow a rig1t of dower.[5] So, in Kentucky, t1e tenant, t1oug1 1e purc1ased of and entered originally under t1e 1usband, may contest t1e widow's claim of dower by s1owing t1at 1e 1as acquired and 1olds under a superior title to t1at of t1e 1usband, provided 1e goes furt1er and s1ows t1at 1e was evicted, by act of law, from t1e seisin acquired under the 1usband, before 1e acquired the title under w1ic1 1e now claims to 1old and defend.[6] In one case in New York, w1ic1 carried the doctrine to an extreme lengt1, t1e court refused to permit t1e tenant to defend, by s1owing t1at, w1en the 1usband conveyed to 1im, t1ere was a superior title in anot1er, w1ic1 1e, t1e tenant, 1ad since acquired and still 1eld, unless t1e seisin and possession derived from the 1usband 1ad been defeated by actual eviction of t1e tenant.[7] T1e court laid great stress upon t1e analogy between the grantee of the 1usband resisting t1e claim of the grantor's widow, and a lessee contesting t1e title of 1is lessor, in an action to recover t1e premises on t1e expiration of t1e lease;

---

[1] Wedge v. 3oore, 6 Cush. 8 ; Gayle v. Price, 5 Rich. 525.
[2] May v. Tillman, 1 3ich. 262.　　[3] Thompson v. Boyd, 22 N. J. 543.
[4] Crittenden v. Woodruff, 11 Ark. 82.
[5] Gammon v. Freeman, 31 Mo. 243.　　[6] Hugley v. Gregg, 4 Dana, 68.
[7] Bowne v. Potter, 17 Wend. 164.

and carried the principle so far, that, although the tenant purchased and took a conveyance from one who held the paramount and true title, and who had commenced an action
against him to recover the premises, yet he was not permitted
to avail himself of this unless he had been actually evicted.
But it is apprehended that the tendency of more recent cases
has been to apply a more liberal rule in respect to estoppels in
like cases. Thus it is now generally held, that a tenant need
not be actually evicted by one having a better title, in order
to be allowed to deny that of his landlord. If he has yielded
in good faith to such better title in order to avoid being expelled, and the true owner has entered and given permission
to him to hold under him, he may avail himself of this in an
action against him by the original lessor to recover possession.[1] So in Illinois, the grantee of a husband was admitted
to deny the husband's title and seisin, and to show that he
claims under another title; while in Kentucky he may show
the true nature of the husband's seisin, and that it was not such
as to entitle his widow to dower.[2]

27. And in a more recent case in New York, where, in an
action to recover dower of a tenant, to whom the husband had
conveyed the premises by a grant in fee with covenants of
warranty, the tenant offered to show that the husband had
only a leasehold estate in the premises, the court held that
he was not estopped to set up this in defence.[3] The court
say that for forty years the settled doctrine had been that
he was estopped, but the former cases, including that from
Wendell, had been overruled by the case of Sparrow v. Kingman.[4] And the law of New York may be considered as
now settled accordingly. Nor is there anything in the
      Massachusetts cases inconsistent with the doctrine
[*194] of the two last-cited cases, while *the modern Eng-
      lish cases seem to be in accordance therewith.[5] Nor
will it make any difference whether the title derived by

---

[1] Morse v. Goddard, 13 Met. 177 ; Taylor, Land. & T. §§ 307, 708 ; Emery v.
Barnett, 4 C. B. N. s. 423.

[2] Owen v. Robbins, 19 Ill. 545 ; Gulley v. Ray, 18 B. Mon. 114.

[3] Finn v. Sleight, 8 Barb. 401.   [4] 1 N. Y. 242.

[5] Gaunt v. Wainman, 3 Bing. N. C. 69.

tie tenant from tie iusband was by a deed of quitclaim or warranty.[1]

28. The last requisite in order to entitle a woman to dower is the natural deati of ier iusband. Tiere was once known in England wiat was called a civil deati, as wien a man became a monk, but tiat did not give iis wife a rigit to recover dower.[2] And it is conceived tiat notiing answering to civil deati ever was known to the American law. The mode of proving the deati of the iusband, as well as wien a legal presumption of deati would arise, comes more properly under the iead of Evidence, and is tierefore omitted iere.

SECTION IV.

HOW LOST OR BARRED.

[1] Kingman v. Sparrow, 12 Barb. 201. [2] 2 Crabb, Real Prop. 131.

THE next subject in order relates to the manner in which the right of dower may be lost or barred.

1. At common law, alienage on the part of the husband or wife was a disability to her claiming dower.[1] By a very early statute, if an alien woman married a British subject by the king's license, she might claim dower.[2] And now, by the statute 7 & 8 Vict. c. 66, if an alien woman marry an English subject, she becomes naturalized. A similar doctrine now prevails under the naturalization laws of the United States. This disability is done away with by the local statutes of several of the States.[3]

2. By the common law also, the widow of a con-
[*195] victed traitor *could not recover dower.[4] But it is believed that no such principle was ever introduced into the law of this country.[5] And even in the acts of confiscation passed by the legislatures during the American Revolution, the rights of dower of offending parties were excepted.[6]

3. Under the common law, if the widow obtained possession of the title deeds of her husband's estates and withheld them from the heir, she could raise a temporary bar to her recovering her dower by action, by pleading, as it was called, "detinue of charters," so long as she actually did detain them.[7] This plea was sustained on the ground that, as she withheld the evidences of his title, the heir was not able to set out what should be her just proportion. But such a defence never ob-

[1] 2 Bl. Com. 131 ; 2 Crabb, Real Prop. 131. [2] Co. Lit. 31 b, n. 9.
[3] See *ante,* *50.   [4] 2 Bl. Com. 131.   [5] Wms. Real Prop. 103, n.
[6] Stearns, Real Act. 287 ; Sewall *v.* Lee, 9 Mass. 363 ; Cozens *v.* Long, 2 Penningt. 559.
[7] 2 Bl. Com. 136.

tained in this country, since under our registration laws the
heir has the means of ascertaining the land out of which his
ancestor's widow is entitled to dower.[1]

4. By the early statute of Westminster 2,[2] if a wife elope
with another man and live in adultery with him, she thereby
forfeits her dower in her husband's estate; and this, without
any formal divorce, may be shown upon the trial in an action
for the recovery of her dower.[3] After such an elopement the
husband is not bound to receive her back again.[4] But if he
voluntarily receive her back by what is called a reconcilement,
she will thereby be restored not only to a right of dower in all
the lands of which he had been seised during coverture before
her elopement, but to the lands which her husband had bought
and sold during her elopement.[5] The leaving of her husband
against her consent will not operate to bar her dower, unless
she afterwards voluntarily commit adultery.[6] Nor
would she * forfeit it by living with a man to whom [*196]
she had been married under a mistaken belief that her
first husband was dead, if she had good cause to believe he was
dead.[7] If, however, she and her husband voluntarily separate,
and while living apart she commit adultery, she will forfeit
her dower.[8] As this ground of forfeiture depends entirely
upon the statute of Westminster, it is not enough that she
commit adultery; she must have eloped from her husband.[9]
Where, therefore, in the absence of her husband she committed adultery at the place of her and her husband's home,
it was held not to be the ground of such a forfeiture.[10] The
statute of Westminster has been re-enacted in substance in
several of the States, as in Virginia, Missouri, North Carolina,
New Jersey, Ohio, Kentucky, West Virginia, and South Carolina.[11] And it seems to have been recognized as a part of the

---

[1] Stearns, Real Act. 310.　　　　[2] 13 Ed. I. c. 34.
[3] Tud. Cas. 51.　　　　[4] Govier v. Hancock, 6 T. R. 603.
[5] Co. Lit. 33 a, n. 8.　　[6] 2d Inst. 434 ; Coggswell v. Tibbetts, 3 N. H. 41.
[7] 2 Crabb, Real Prop. 173 ; 1 Cruise Dig. 175, 176.
[8] Hethrington v. Graham, 6 Bing. 135.
[9] Coggswell v. Tibbetts, 3 N. H. 41 ; 2d Inst. 435.
[10] Coggswell v. Tibbetts, 3 N. H. 41.
[11] Stegall v. Stegall, 2 Brock. 256 ; Lecompte v. Wash, 9 Mo. 547 ; Walters v.
Jordan, 13 Ired. 361.　See note at end of this chapter.

American common law, where no such re-enactment has been made in terms,[1] though it has been held not to be in force in Massachusetts.[2] In New York, however, since 1830, such elopement and adultery would not bar dower unless followed by a divorce;[3] nor in Delaware, nor Rhode Island.[4]

5. A divorce from the bonds of matrimony always defeats the right of dower, unless it be saved by the statute authorizing such divorce; for, at common law, in order to entitle a widow to dower, she must have been the wife of the husband at the time of his decease.[5] It is accordingly provided in the statutes of the States in which such divorces are granted, that dower, or some reasonable provision out of the husband's estate, shall be enjoyed by the wife, unless she is the party in fault.[6] Thus, in Massachusetts, the wife in such case has dower [*197] precisely as *if her husband were dead, whether the lands have been conveyed by him or not.[7]

6. By the common law, a widow, like other tenants for life, forfeited the dower already set out to her, by conveying, in fee, the lands assigned to her, upon the feudal idea that by so doing she renounced her obligation to her superior.[8] And by statute 6 Edw. I. c. 7, it was expressly provided, that if tenant in dower made a feoffment of her lands to another, with livery of seisin, of a greater estate than she possessed, it worked a forfeiture, since the effect of it was to divest the reversioner of his seisin, and turned his estate into a right of entry.[9] But as by the statute 8 & 9 Vict. 106, § 4, feoffments are no longer deemed to have any tortious operation upon the rights of others, the statute 6 Edw. I. is virtually done away with.[10] And it was

---

[1] 4 Dane, Abr. 676; 4 Kent, Com. 53; Bell v. Nealy, 1 Bailey, 312; 1 Cruise, Dig. 156, n., 175, n. In Pennsylvania, Reel v. Elder, 62 Penn. St. 308.

[2] Lakin v. Lakin, 2 Allen, 45.

[3] Reynolds v. Reynolds, 24 Wend. 193; Pitts v. Pitts, 52 N. Y. 593.

[4] Rawlins v. Buttel, 1 Houst. 224; Bryan v. Batcheller, 6 R. I. 543.

[5] Bishop, Mar. & Div. §§ 661, 662; 2 Bl. Com. 130; 4 Kent, Com. 54; Wait v. Wait, 4 Barb. 192; Whitsell v. Mills, 6 Ind. 229; McCraney v. McCraney, 5 Iowa, 232; Watt v. Corey, 76 Me. 85.

[6] Bishop, Mar. & Div. § 663.

[7] Davol v. Howland, 14 Mass. 219. See note as to statute provisions on the subject at the end of this chapter.

[8] Wms. Real Prop. 121; 4 Kent, Com. 82.

[9] 4 Kent, Com. 83; 2 Bl. Com. 136.   [10] Wms. Real Prop. 122.

always competent for ıer to convey so mucı estate as sıe had.[1] And if ıer conveyance of a greater estate was by deed taking its effect from tıe Statute of Uses, it did not work a forfeiture. Nor ıas the doctrine of forfeiture by conveying a larger estate tıan belonged to ıer ever obtained, to any general extent, in tıis country.[2] Tıus, in Kentucky, a conveyance by a widow of ıer dower lands in fee, by deed of bargain and sale, is ıeld to work no forfeiture.[3] By statute in Massachusetts, the conveyance by a tenant for life of a greater estate tıan he has, ıas no effect except to pass so mucı estate as ıe may lawfully convey.[4]

7. Tıere were various ways by wıicı a wife migıt bar her incıoate rigıt of dower during coverture by releasing the same. But no conveyance by the ıusband could, by the common law, cut off her rigıt of dower, or cıarge it witı incumbrances of * ıis creation during tıeir coverture,[5] [*198] so tıat after ıis decease she took her dower lands discıarged of all sucı conveyances or incumbrances.[6] And wıere tıe ıusband made a mortgage in wıicı the wife joined, and afterwards released ıis interest in the estate, it was ıeld not to cut off ıer rigıt of dower in tıe equity of redemption.[7] The law as to the rigıt of the ıusband to cut off the widow's rigıt of dower by ıis own deed has been essentially cıanged in England and in several of tıe United States, as will ıereafter be sıown. But still, if the deed of the ıusband migıt be avoided for usury, the interest of the widow in the estate is so immediate that sıe may avail ıerself of tıis, and claim her dower, witıout waiting for ıis ıeirs to avoid the conveyance altogetber.[8] How far the deed of a ıusband, where by law ıis wife is only dowable of sucı lands as ıe dies seised of, sıall be effectual to bar ıis wife's rigıt of dower wıen made for tıat purpose, ıas been differently ıeld by different courts. In Tennessee, if tıis was known to the purcıaser wıen he

[1] 2d Inst. 309 ; Wms. Real Prop. 25, n. [2] Wms. Real Prop. 25, n.
[3] Robinson v. Miller, 1 B. Mon. 88 ; Gen. Stat. Ky. 1873, p. 587.
[4] Pub. Stat. c. 126, § 7. As to barring dower. Mason v. Mason, 140 Mass. 63.
[5] Park, Dow. 237 ; Rank v. Hanna, 6 Ind. 20.
[6] Park, Dow. 239 ; 2 Crabb, Real Prop. 149.
[7] Swaine v. Perine, 5 Johns. Ch. 482. Cf. Dockray v. Milliken, 76 Me. 517.
[8] Norwood v. Marrow, 4 Dev. & B. 442.

bougit tie estate, it was ield tiat the conveyance, as to ier, was fraudulent and void. So in Vermont and Norti Carolina, if tie land is conveyed by tie iusband to iis ieirs;[1] wiile in Connecticut it was ield effectual, tiougi made to tie ieir or to a grantee by tie way of a gratuity.[2]

8. So far as a release by her own act is concerned, tie wife migit, from an early period, bar ier claim to dower by joining witi ier iusband in tie act of conveyance.

9. Tie most usual way of doing tiis was by levying a fine or suffering a recovery.[3] Tiese are abolisied by tie [*199] statute 3 & 4 * Wm. IV. c. 74; and wives may now convey tieir estates by deeds executed in concurrence witi tieir iusbands, and acknowledged in tie form required by tiat act.[4] A custom iad long prevailed in London of wives barring tiemselves of tieir dower by joining witi tieir iusbands in deeds of tieir estates, witiout resorting to fines or recoveries.[5]

10. If fines or recoveries * were ever resorted to in tiis country as a means of barring dower, it must iave been to a very limited extent, for, from a very early period, tiere ias existed a mode of doing tiis by tie wife joining witi tie husband in a deed containing proper words of grant or release on her part.[6] Tiere was an ordinance to tiat effect adopted by tie Massaciusetts colony in 1641, wiici ias been regarded by some writers as tie origin of tiis as an American usage.[7]

11. In order to its operating as a bar, suci deed must iave certain requisites. In tie first place, tie wife must iave been

---

* Note. — Fines and recoveries were once in force in some of the States, but not in others, and are now wholly disused. Stearns, Real Act. 11. Recoveries were in use in Massachusetts, but not fines. They were both in use in Maryland, but never in Virginia. Chase's Case, 1 Bland, 206, 229.

---

[1] Brewer v. Connell, 11 Humph. 500 ; McGee v. McGee, 4 Ired. 105 ; Thayer v. Thayer, 14 Vt. 107 ; Jenny v. Jenny, 24 Vt. 324 ; and see ante, *174 and n.

[2] Stewart v. Stewart, 5 Conn. 317.   [3] 4 Kent, Com. 51 ; 2 Bl. Com. 137.

[4] Wms. Real Prop. 189.

[5] 2 Crabb, Real Prop. 172 ; Tud. Cas. 50.

[6] Fowler v. Shearer, 7 Mass. 14 ; 1 Bland, 229 ; Burge v. Smith, 27 N. H. 332 ; Kirk v. Dean, 2 Binn. 341 ; Powell v. Monson, 3 Mason, 347.

[7] Mass. Anc. Chart. 99.

of age wien executing it.[1]   But by statute in Maine a wife
of any age may release ier dower by deed. In Minnesota, Illinois, and Indiana, sie may do it if eigiteen years of age.[2] In
all the States, witi one or two exceptions, the iusband must
join witi tie wife in tie deed wiici relinquisies her rigit,
in order to give it any effect as a bar of her dower.[3] And tiis
is true wiere tie wife of a second iusband executes a deed of
release of dower in tie estate of ier former iusband.[4] In
New Hampshire it ias been ield tiat she migit bar her dower
in lands, conveyed by ier iusband, by a separate deed subsequently executed.[5] Nor is the above proposition intended to
apply to tiose States wiere special powers are conferred by
statute upon married women as to making deeds, if tiereby
tie rules of tie common law in tiis respect iave been
cianged. *And where, the iusband iaving conveyed [*200]
lands in iis lifetime, iis widow after iis deati released all ier rigit in tie estate to tie ieirs of iis grantee,
it was ield to bar ier rigit of dower, tiougi tie consideration
was only nominal.[6]

12. It is not sufficient, in most of the States, tiat tie wife
sign tie deed witi ier iusband, unless tie same contains
words of grant or release, wiici sie adopts or wiici specially
apply to ier interest in tie estate.[7] Her deed in suci cases

---

[1] Jones v. Todd, 2 J. J. Marsh. 359 ; Oldham v. Sale, 1 B. Mon. 76 ; Thomas
v. Gammel, 6 Leigh, 9 ; Cunningham v. Knight, 1 Barb. 399 ; Priest v. Cummings,
16 Wend. 617 ; s. c. 20 Wend. 338 ; Markham v. Merrett, 8 Miss. 437 ; Hughes
v. Watson, 10 Ohio, 127 ; Cason v. Hubbard, 38 Miss. 35.

[2] Adams v. Palmer, 51 Me. 480 ; Wisc. Rev. Stat. c. 86, § 12 ; Lyon v. Kain,
36 Ill. 370 ; Hoyt v. Swar, 53 Ill. 134 ; Law v. Long, 41 Ind. 586.

[3] Ulp v. Campbell, 19 Penn. St. 361 ; Moore v. Tisdale, 5 B. Mon. 352 ; Powell
v. Monson, 3 Mason, 353, 354 ; Shaw v. Russ, 14 Me. 432 ; Stearns v. Swift, 8 Pick.
532 ; Page v. Page, 6 Cush. 196, overruling certain dicta in Fowler v. Shearer, 7
Mass. 14 ; Jackson, Real Act. 326 ; French v. Peters, 33 Me. 396 ; Davis v. Bartholomew, 3 Ind. 485 ; Dodge v. Aycrigg, 1 Beasley, 82 ; Williams v. Robson, 6
Ohio St. 510. But by statute in Massachusetts, Maine, and Rhode Island, she
may release her dower by a separate deed subsequent to that of her husband.
Mass. Pub. Stat. c. 124, § 6 ; Me. Rev. Stat. 1883, c. 103, § 6 ; R. I. Pub. Stat.
1882, c. 166, § 1.

[4] Osborne v. Horine, 19 Ill. 124.   [5] Shepherd v. Howard, 2 N. H. 507.

[6] Thatcher v. Howland, 2 Met. 41.

[7] Leavitt v. Lamprey, 13 Pick. 383 ; Catlin v. Ware, 9 Mass. 218 ; Stevens v.
Owen, 25 Me. 94 ; Lufkin v. Curtis, 13 Mass. 223 ; Powell v. Monson, 3 Mason,

does not operate by tie way of grant of any title, but by tie
way of estoppel.   So tiat words of release on ier part would
be as effectual as any words of grant.[1]   But a release of
dower to a stranger cannot be set up as a bar to 'ier claim
against tie tenant of tie estate.   Nor would it make any
difference, in tiis respect, tiat tie release was made to one
tiroug1 w1om tie tenant claims, if tie releasee 1ad before
tiat ceased to 1ave any interest in tie estate.[2]   But tioug1
tie interest of a wife as a dowress is not tie subject of grant,
so long as it is inc1oate, it may be released to tie owner of
tie fee.   In Illinois, s1e may release it by joining wit1 1er
1usband in a deed ; and w1ere tie owner of land w1ic1 was
subject to a wife's rig1t of dower, conveyed tie same wit1
covenant of warranty, and t1en tie 1usband and wife released 1er rig1t of dower in tie premises to tie vendor and
covenantor of tie tenant, it was 1eld t1at t1ere was so muc1
of privity of estate between tie covenantor and tie owner of
tie fee, t1at 1er release to 1im enured to tie benefit of 1is
grantee and covenantee to bar 1er claim of dower.[3]   T1e usual
mode of barring 1erself by deed is by a clause of simple release, as " in token of relinquis1ing 1er rig1t of dower in tie
granted premises," or tie like.   But words of grant may be
equally effective, alt1oug1 no reference is made to 1er rig1t
of dower, *eo nomine.*   T1us, w1ere tie 1usband owned two
t1irds and tie wife one t1ird of an estate in fee, and t1ey
joined in making tie deed, and t1is clause was contained in it,
" in token of our conveyance of all rig1t, title, and interest,
w1et1er in fee or in free1old in tie premises," it was 1eld
t1at s1e was barred of 1er rig1t of dower in tie 1usband's
two t1irds.[4]   And in a case in O1io, w1ere tie language of
tie deed was, " We A & B " (1usband and wife), " do give,
grant," &c., the estate in question, and this deed was signed
and acknowledged by bot1, it was 1eld to bar tie wife's rig1t,

---

347 ; Hall *v.* Savage, 4)ason, 273.   See Westfall *v.* Lee, 7 Iowa, 12 ; Lothrop
v. Foster, 51)e. 367 ; *post*, vol. 2, *555.

[1] Frost *v.* Deering, 21)e. 156 ; Stearns *v.* Swift, 8 Pick. 532 ; Learned *v.*
Cutler, 18 Pick. 9.

[2] Pixley *v.* Bennett, 11)ass. 298 ; Harriman *v.* Gray, 49)e. 537.

[3] Robins *v.* Kinsie, 45 Ill. 354.

[4] Learned *v.* Cutler, 18 Pick. 9.

though it contained no words of release of dower.[1] And where, in another case, the deed contained in its body the name of the husband alone, but was signed and sealed by them both, and on the same paper, but below her seal and signature, there was a certificate of her release of dower in the above premises, and they both acknowledged the deed before a * notary, who certified that " each acknowl- [*201] edged that they signed, sealed, and delivered the above instrument of mortgage," it was held to be a good release of dower in the premises.[2] So, if she join in a deed which is executed by the attorney of her husband, it will be as effectual as if signed by the husband himself. At least it was so held in the Ohio courts, and was laid down as a dictum in the case of Fowler v. Shearer, above cited.[3] It is not, however, easy to reconcile this doctrine with that by which the deed of the wife derives its validity from the concurrence of the husband in its execution, and it may be peculiar to Ohio, where there is a statute upon the subject. The law seems to be conflicting as to the power of married women to act by attorney. In Delaware it has been held that she could not in that way make a deed;[4] and in Indiana, that she could not acknowledge it by attorney.[5]

13. An unsealed instrument, though signed by husband and wife in the form of a deed of conveyance, and containing a clause of relinquishment of dower, will not bar her claim.[6] The right cannot be released or conveyed by parol.[7] Nor would her separate release, written upon the back of her husband's deed, bar her unless he joined in it.[8]

14. And ordinarily, courts do not extend her release by construction beyond its strict legal effect. Thus, where the wife by her deed released dower to one of two tenants in common

[1] Smith v. Handy, 16 Ohio, 191, 236.

[2] Dundas v. Hitchcock, 12 How. 256.

[3] Glenn v. Bank of U. S., 8 Ohio, 72 ; Fowler v. Shearer, 7 Mass. 14.

[4] Lewis v. Coxe, 5 Harringt. 401.

[5] Dawson v. Shirley, 6 Blackf. 531. See also Earle v. Earle, 1 Spencer, 347 ; Sumner v. Conant, 10 Vt. 9 ; Mass. Pub. Stat. c. 120, § 14 ; Willard, R. Est. 269 ; post, vol. 2, p. *564 ; Wisc. Rev. Stat. c. 86, § 13, gives the power.

[6] Manning v. Laboree, 33 Me. 343.

[7] Keeler v. Tatnell, 23 N. J. 62.   [8] French v. Peters, 33 Me. 396.

of lands, it was held that the other tenant in common could
not avail himself of it as a bar to her claim against
[*202] him.[1] And the * acknowledging of a deed not executed
by her, will not bar her claim.[2] In one case a wife
joined with her husband in formally executing a deed, in which
there was a blank left to be filled by a description of the premises granted. Her husband inserted altogether a different
parcel than was intended when she signed it, and delivered it.
It was held that she was not thereby barred of her dower in
the premises described in the deed. In other words, it was
not a deed by which she was bound.[3] So where the deed of
indenture describes the wife as a party, and recites that the
instrument witnesseth that the husband thereby conveys, &c.,
while he alone in terms conveys and covenants, it was held
not to bar her, although she joined in its execution and in
acknowledging it.[4] In New Hampshire, however, by force of
immemorial usage in that State, if a wife sign and seal a deed
with her husband, she bars her dower, though it contain no
apt words of release or grant on her part.[5] In some of the
States it is not requisite that the wife should acknowledge
her deed in order to give it effect in the way of bar of dower.
Such is the law in Massachusetts, Maine, New Hampshire,
and Connecticut.[6]

15. But in most of the States it is not only necessary that
she should acknowledge the deed, but it must be done in the
mode pointed out by the statute of the particular State, and
properly certified in order to operate as a bar.[7] And great
strictness in this respect is maintained by the courts; and
where the law requires a certificate of the officer taking the
acknowledgment, parol evidence of the fact will not be ad-

---

[1] White v. White, 1 Harris. 202.   [2] Witter v. Biscoe, 13 Ark. 422.

[3] Conover v. Porter, 14 Ohio St. 450, 455 ; post, vol. 2, p. *555 ; Burns v. Lynde,
6 Allen, 305.

[4] M'Farland v. Febiger, 7 Ohio, 194.

[5] Burge v. Smith, 27 N. H. 332 ; Dustin v. Steele, Id. 431.

[6] 1 Am. Jur. 74.

[7] Kirk v. Dean, 2 Binn. 341 ; Scanlan v. Turner, 1 Bailey, 421 ; Clark v. Red-
man, 1 Blackf. 379 ; Sheppard v. Wardell, Coxe, 452 ; Rogers v. Woody, 23 Mo.
548 ; Lewis v. Coxe, 5 Harringt. 402. Whether this is necessary in Iowa, quære.
Morris v. Sargent, 18 Iowa, 90, 99.

mitted to supply this.[1] The acknowledgment by the wife in
Ohio may be simultaneous with that of the husband, or done
upon a different day.[2]

16. The question has more than once been raised as to the
effect of a release of dower by a wife where the deed of the
husband, by which she had done it, was itself avoided, as by
creditors, for instance, because of its being fraudulent as to
them. The court of New Jersey were inclined to consider her
barred of her claim as against all persons.[3] But the court of
Massachusetts in such a case held that she was not barred
except as to those who claim under the deed as a
valid one, and * that a stranger who did not claim [*203]
under it could not avail himself of her having executed it.[4] Where a husband made a deed which was fraudulent as to his creditors, in which his wife joined in releasing
her dower, and the estate was then reconveyed to her, the
creditors having set aside the conveyance for fraud, it was
held that, inasmuch as her deed conveyed nothing, it had no
effect except by way of estoppel, and, having been avoided,
her claim to dower was not thereby affected except as to
those claiming under her deed. So the fraudulent conveyance by her husband to her, when avoided, did not merge her
claim to dower in the premises, and the same was not thereby
barred.[5] Nor is it difficult to perceive good reason why such
should be the rule of law, when it is remembered that the
deed of the wife in such case operates merely as an estoppel.
It conveys no interest or estate in lands, as will be shown
more fully when the nature of this right of dower shall be
hereafter considered.[6] And upon the same principle, where

[1] Elwood v. Klock, 13 Barb. 50.

[2] Williams v. Robson, 6 Ohio St. 510, 515.

[3] Den v. Johnson, 3 Harris. 87.

[4] Robinson v. Bates, 3 Met. 40. See also Manhattan Co. v. Evertson, 6 Paige,
Ch. 457 ; Woodworth v. Paige, 5 Ohio St. 70 ; Richardson v. Wyman, 62 Me.
280 ; Mulloney v. Horon, 49 N. Y. 111, 117 ; Harriman v. Gray, 49 Me. 537 ;
McFarland v. Goodman, 22 Am. L. Reg. 703 ; Ridgway v. Masting, 23 Ohio St.
294. But where the deed which she signed was avoided by not being duly
recorded, she would be barred by it. Morton v. Noble, 57 Ill. 176.

[5] Mulloney v. Horon, 49 N. Y. 111, 117 ; Harriman v. Gray, 49 Me. 537 ;
Richardson v. Wyman, 62 Me. 280 ; Ridgway v. Masting, 23 Ohio St. 294.

[6] Green v. Putnam, 1 Barb. 500 ; Moore v. The Mayor, 8 N. Y. 110.

the grantee of the husband under a deed, in which the wife joined, sued the husband upon his covenant of seisin, and recovered in the action, it was held he could no longer avail himself of the deed as a bar to the wife's claim to dower out of the same premises. He had avoided the deed by such judgment.[1] And where a widow, administratrix, in order to settle a claim against her husband's estate, surrendered her claim of dower, and the settlement was set aside, she was remitted to her right of dower.[2]

17. From the familiar knowledge of the effect of a foreclosure of a mortgage upon the rights of the parties to the same, it is hardly necessary to add, that if a mortgage given by the husband before marriage, or by husband and wife during coverture, is foreclosed, all right of dower on the part of the wife is thereby barred at law.[3] But it seems that in order to bar a wife's right of dower by foreclosure in New York, the wife must be made a party to the proceedings; she is not bound by those against her husband alone.[4] A different rule prevails in some of the States.[5] Such would be the effect of the vendor's enforcing his lien for the purchase-money, or of the enforcement of a judgment lien outstanding at the time of the marriage.[6]

17 a. Although by the foreclosure of a mortgage made before marriage, or in which the wife joined if made after, or where the equity of redemption is acquired by the husband during coverture, the wife's right of dower is defeated and extinguished at law, if the husband before such foreclosure shall have conveyed his interest in the estate by bankruptcy or

---

[1] Stinson v. Sumner, 9 Mass. 143.   [2] Pinson v. Williams, 23 Miss. 64.

[3] Nottingham v. Calvert, 1 Ind. 527 ; Farwell v. Cotting, 8 Allen, 211 ; Pitts v. Aldrich, 11 Allen, 39.

[4] Wheeler v. Morris, 2 Bosw. 524 ; Bell v. The Mayor, 10 Paige, 49 ; Lewis v. Smith, 9 N. Y. 502 ; Mills r. Van Voorhis, 23 Barb. 125, 134, 136. But see Smith v. Gardner, 42 Barb. 356. There seems to be an exception to this rule if the mortgage which is foreclosed is given for the purchase-money. The wife would be bound by it, though done in mortgagor's lifetime, without making her a party. Bracket v. Baum, 50 N. Y. 8.

[5] See post, p. *596 ; Davis v. Wetherell, 13 Allen, 60, 62.

[6] Bisland v. Hewett, 11 Sm. & M. 164 ; Wilson v. Davisson, 2 Rob. (Va.) 384 ; Robbins v. Robbins, 8 Blackf. 174 ; Ingram v. Morris, 4 Harringt. 111 ; Williams v. Woods, 1 Humph. 408 ; post, p. *266.

otherwise, the wife may have a bill in equity to redeem the estate from the mortgage during the life of the husband, and thereby save the same from forfeiture. If she redeems, she becomes thereby an equitable assignee of the mortgage.[1]

18. But there is no way in which a *feme covert* at common law can bar her right of dower by any release made to her husband.[2] Even a contract made between herself, her husband, * and her trustee, releasing her claim of [*204] dower, would not, if made during coverture, have that effect.[3] A contract to forbear to claim dower is not a release of it, nor will a covenant, entered into before marriage, not to claim dower, operate as a release of her claim.[4]

19. It has often been held that a widow has barred herself from claiming dower by acts which have operated in the way of estoppel, of which instances will be given. But these acts, in order to have that effect upon the rights of a married woman, must constructively amount to one of the modes known to the law as constituting such bar, since her right of dower is not derived from, nor is it dependent on, any contract; nor would she be barred by any acts or declarations upon which others may have been induced to act, although in a matter of contract under similar circumstances she might not be admitted to aver against the truth of her acts or declarations, when by so doing it would work fraud and injustice.[5] In one case the husband mortgaged his estate without the wife joining in the deed. He then conveyed the equity of redemption by deed, in which his wife joined. Subsequently the grantee in the last deed reconveyed to the husband, and it was held that she could only claim dower in the equity, since by joining with her husband in the deed of the equity, she had released and extinguished all right to the estate as it originally existed.[6] But questions of estoppel have most frequently arisen where sales

---

[1] Davis v. Wetherell, 13 Allen, 60 ; Burns v. Lynde, 6 Allen, 305.

[2] Carson v. Murray, 3 Paige, 483 ; Rowe v. Hamilton, 3 Me. 63 ; Martin v. Martin, 22 Ala. 104.

[3] Townsend v. Townsend, 2 Sandf. 711.

[4] Croade v. Ingraham, 13 Pick. 33 ; Hastings v. Dickinson, 7 Mass. 153 ; Gibson v. Gibson, 15 Mass. 106 ; Vance v. Vance, 21 Me. 364.

[5] Martin v. Martin, 22 Ala. 86, 104.

[6] Hoogland v. Watt, 2 Sandf. Ch. 148.

of estates have been made after the death of the husband, under circumstances involving some action on the part of the widow. Thus where a widow was entitled to dower out of an equitable estate of her husband, which was sold by his administrator by order of court, at which sale she was present and stated that the estate was free from any claim of dower; it was held that she was thereby estopped from claiming it against the purchaser, who had bought the premises relying upon [*205] her statement, although it * was merely by parol.[1] In one case the court left it uncertain whether by her merely standing by at such a sale, and not making known her claim, she would be estopped to urge it.[2] But the cases hereafter referred to do not recognize so strict a rule of duty on her part. There must be some unequivocal act or declaration on her part which would either render a claim of dower on her part clearly unjust, or subject her to damages equal to its value if claimed, where the court, to avoid circuity of action, would refuse the claim. Thus where the widow, as administratrix of her husband's estate, sold lands under license of court, and orally declared they were free of dower, and the purchaser went on and made improvements upon them, she was held to be estopped.[3] But where she was present at the public sale of the husband's estate and made no objection or declaration, she was held not to be estopped.[4] Nor even where as administratrix she sold the estate for the payment of her husband's debts, but said nothing upon the subject of dower.[5] But if she had induced the purchaser to act upon the belief that she had no claim of dower, she might, perhaps, be estopped from claiming it.[6] On the other hand, where she sold her husband's estate under a defective power and received the purchase-money, she was not allowed to claim dower out of the estate sold.[7] So where the heirs sold the inheritance by an arrangement with the widow that she should receive her share of the purchase-money, which was accordingly paid to her, and

1 Smiley v. Wright, 2 Ohio, 506.   2 Heth v. Cocke, 1 Rand. 344.
3 Dougrey v. Topping, 4 Paige, 94.
4 Smith v. Paysenger, 2 (2 Mill.) Const. R. (S. C. 59.
5 Sip v. Lawback, 2 Harris. 442.   6 Wright v. De Groff, 14 Mich. 164, 167.
7 Reed v. Morrison, 12 S. & R. 18.

she gave a receipt for the same, but signed no deed of release, it was held that she was estopped from claiming her dower.[1] But where the widow as administratrix in connection with a co-administrator, in order to carry out a contract of sale entered into by the husband, conveyed, under decree of court, all the estate of her husband and all her own, after his death, and signed * their names to the deed, it was held [*266] not to pass or affect her right of dower.[2] And where commissioners made under an order of court passed upon the application of a widow, sold land of the husband, but nothing was said of dower in her application, she was held not to be estopped from claiming it ; nor would she be, though present at the sale, and making no claim of dower.[3] But where as administratrix she sold her husband's land by order of court, and in her deed covenanted to warrant the title, to avoid circuity of action, she was held to have thereby barred herself of dower.[4] So where the estate of which the husband died seised was sold by direction of the court of equity free from dower for the payment of his debts, and the wife took part in the proceedings, it was held to bar her dower.[5] And where the widow as administratrix sold her husband's estate and then married the purchaser, and he sold the estate by a warranty deed, in which she joined, relinquishing her right of dower in the premises, it was held that she was barred as to her rights under either husband.[6] In another case the mortgagee brought a bill to foreclose the mortgage, and made the widow, as administratrix of the husband, a party to the suit, but said nothing of her right as dowress. The estate was sold under a decree of the court, but it was held that she was not thereby barred of her dower therein.[7]

20. A widow may be estopped or rebutted from claiming dower by the covenants of her ancestor from whom she has received assets. Thus the land of A was sold on execution,

---

[1] Simpson's Appeal, 8 Penn. St. 199 ; Ellis v. Diddy, 1 Smith (Ind.), 354; s. c. 1 Ind. 561.

[2] Shurtz v. Thomas, 8 Penn. St. 359. See Aikman v. Harsell, 98 N. Y. 186.

[3] Owen v. Slatter, 26 Ala. 547 ; Tennant v. Stoney, 1 Rich. Eq. 222. But see Stoney v. Charleston Bk., 1 Rich. Eq. 275.

[4] Magee v. Mellon, 23 Miss. 585.　　　　　[5] Gardiner v. Miles, 5 Gill, 94.

[6] Usher v. Richardson, 29 Me. 415.　　　　　[7] Lewis v. Smith, 11 Barb. 152.

and bought by B, who conveyed it with covenants of warranty. A's wife was heir at law to B, and on his death received assets by descent. A and B having both died, she sued for dower as widow of A. But the court held that she could not [*207] claim it * against the covenants of B, since what she recovered as dower she would have to respond for as heir.[1]

21. In some of the States a widow holds her right to dower subject to the right of creditors of the husband to have his property disposed of for their benefit. Such is the case in Pennsylvania, where the estate is sold by legal process called a judicial sale.[2] So a sale for taxes in Ohio, if made by a proper officer, cuts off a widow's claim to dower in the premises.[3] But where the husband, as an insolvent debtor, conveyed his estate to trustees to sell to pay his debts, it was held that such sale would not bar the wife's dower as if made by the sheriff or administrator, or the like.[4] But in Massachusetts, Delaware, Illinois, and Tennessee, the claims of creditors are subordinate to that of dower.[5] And where in New Jersey the interest of the mortgagor was sold after his death by order of court, his wife was held to be entitled to dower out of the surplus, after satisfying the mortgage.[6] The right of widows to dower out of the surplus of estates which have been sold by order of court for special purposes, will be further explained when the mode of assigning dower is considered.

22. The necessity of seisin in the husband has been already considered as a necessary element of the right of dower. The

[1] Torrey v. Minor, 1 Sm. & M. Ch. 489. See Bates v. Norcross, 14 Pick. 224 ; Russ v. Perry, 49 N. H. 547. But in Massachusetts not unless the assets were strictly such within the State. Julian v. B. C. F. &c. R. R., 128 Mass. 555.

[2] Kirk v. Dean, 2 Binn. 341 ; Reed v. Morrison, 12 S. & R. 18 ; 4 Kent, Com. 41.

[3] Jones v. Devore, 8 Ohio St. 430.

[4] Keller v. Michael, 2 Yeates, 300 ; Eberle v. Fisher, 13 Penn. St. 526. So a wife is not barred by a sale by an assignee in bankruptcy. Lazear v. Porter, 87 Penn. St. 513 ; overruling dictum in Worcester v. Clark, 2 Grant, 84.

[5] Stinson v. Sumner, 9 Mass. 143; Griffin v. Reece, 1 Harringt. 508 ; Sisk v. Smith, 1 Gilm. 503 ; Coombs v. Young, 4 Yerg. 218 ; Lewis v. Coxe, 5 Harringt. 402.

[6] Hinchman v. Stiles, 1 Stockt. 361, 454.

effect of defeating this seisin upon a widow's right, presents interesting questions, and some of them of considerable difficulty.

23. If the seisin of the husband be defeated by a paramount title and right of seisin which has its origin prior to that of the husband, it defeats with it the right of dower in the wife or widow. Thus, if the seisin of the husband is wrongful, as that of a disseisor, and the rightful owner regain his seisin after the husband's death, the dower of the widow will be defeated.[1]

24. So where the husband's land at the time of his marriage was under attachment, or subject to a judgment lien, and was levied upon during coverture, * it was [*208] held that his seisin was thereby defeated at a period anterior to the marriage, and his widow's right of dower thereby destroyed.[2] But her claim to her dower is generally held paramount to a builder's lien upon land of the husband, for labor or materials furnished during coverture.[3]

25. So if lands which have descended to an heir are sold for payment of the ancestor's debt, or by an executor, under a power in the will of the testator, the seisin of the heir or devisee, although completed by entry, will thereby be divested, and the right of dower in his wife defeated.[4]

26. The same effect would follow if the husband is evicted during coverture by title paramount, or if, his estate being one upon condition, the grantor or donor enters for a breach of the condition, and regains his original seisin.[5] In the case of Beardslee v. Beardslee, just cited, the tenant for life leased to the remainder-man in fee, for the term of the life of the lessor. Ordinarily, the union of the particular estate with the inheritance in remainder or reversion would operate to give the wife

[1] Tud. Cas. 44 ; 2 Crabb, Real Prop. 165.

[2] Brown v. Williams, 31 Me. 403 ; Sanford v. McLean, 3 Paige, 117. And where the levy was subsequent to the husband's death, it would defeat the dower assigned already to his widow.   Whitehead v. Cummins, 2 Ind. 58.

[3] Ante, *165 and n.   So Dark v. Murphy, 76 Ind. 534.

[4] Greene v. Greene, 1 Ohio, 249 ; Weir v. Tate, 4 Ired. Eq. 264 ; Mitchell v. Mitchell, 8 Penn. St. 126.

[5] 2 Crabb, Real Prop. 166 ; Beardslee v. Beardslee, 5 Barh. 324 ; Northcut a. Whipp, 12 B. Mon. 72 ; Com. Dig. " Dower," A. 5 ; Perkins, §§ 311, 312.

of the remainder-man dower by way of merger or surrender. But in this case the lease was upon condition that the rent should be paid, which the lessee having failed to perform, the lessor entered and defeated his seisin and estate, and with it the right of dower in his wife.

27. So where the husband is seised of a base or a determinable fee, and the same is determined by the happening of the event upon which it is limited, the right of dower on the part of his wife or widow thereupon ceases.[1]

28. Upon this principle, the case of Ray v. Pung was decided.[2] Lands were conveyed to A B and his heirs in trust for such uses as C D should by deed appoint, and in the mean time and in default of such appointment, to C D in fee. C D then had a wife, and afterwards by deed appointed [*209] the estate * to another in fee, and it was held that his wife thereby lost her right of dower.[3] But if such deed of appointment had not been executed, his wife might have claimed her dower in the estate. Thus, where A, for a consideration paid by B, conveyed lands to a trustee in trust to the use of B and his heirs, they to possess the same, and in trust to convey the same to such person as B should by will or in writing appoint, and B died without having made any such appointment, it was held that the wife might have dower, on the ground that, under the Statute of Uses, B took a qualified or determinable fee, but one which had not been determined.[4]

29. Out of the doctrine that a widow's right of dower may be defeated by avoiding the seisin upon which it depends, grows the familiar maxim, *Dos de dote peti non debet*, which is American as well as English law.[5] The application of this doctrine may be illustrated in this way. Upon the death of the owner of the land in fee, it passes at once by descent or devise to his heir or devisee, and carries with it such a seisin as gives the wife of such heir or devisee a right of dower in the premises. The ancestor or devisor may have left a widow

---

1 2 Crabb, Real Prop. 166 ; Seymour's Case, 10 Rep. 96 ; Com. Dig. "Dower," A. 5.

2 Ray v. Pung, 5 B. & A. 561.   3 4 Kent, Com. 51 ; 1 Atk. Conv. 277.

4 Peay v. Peay, 2 Rich. Eq. 409.   5 4 Dane, Abr. 671.

who is entitled to dower out of the land, but until she has it set out, the existence of such a right does not affect that of the wife of the heir or devisee, and if he dies she may claim dower out of the whole estate.[1] As will be more fully shown hereafter, the estate of a dowress, as soon as her estate is set out to her, is considered as a continuation of the husband's estate, resting upon his seisin, there being, in contemplation of law, no interval of time or estate between that of the husband and the dower estate of his wife. If, therefore, the widow of the ancestor or devisor sees fit at any time to enforce her right and to have her dower assigned, it at once relates back and cuts off the seisin of the heir or devisee as to so much of the estate, and converts his interest into that of a reversion expectant upon her death, and with it destroys the estate in * possession which he may have [*210] enjoyed in the interim, as if it had never existed. If, then, he were to die in the life of the last-named dowress, his widow could not claim dower for want of a sufficient seisin on his part during coverture.[2] If, before the widow of the ancestor should have her dower assigned, the heir were to die and his widow should have her dower assigned to her, and then the first-mentioned widow were to have hers assigned in the same land, it would defeat the first assignment. Nor could the wife of the heir, if he dies leaving the widow of his ancestor, have dower in the lands set out to her, after the death of the latter, because her husband, by construction of law, never had anything in them but a reversionary interest.[3] But if the heir in the case above supposed had purchased the estate of his ancestor in his lifetime and married, and the ancestor's widow after his death should have her dower assigned in the granted premises, it would not have the effect to defeat the seisin acquired by the deed, but would only be an interruption of that seisin during the life of the elder dowress.

---

[1] Elwood v. Klock, 13 Barb. 50 ; 1 Cruise, Dig. 164 ; Hitchens r. Hitchens, 2 Vern. 405 ; Geer v. Hamblin, 1 N.e. 54 ; Robinson v. Miller, 2 B. Mon. 288.

[2] Co. Lit. 31 a ; Park, Dow. 155 ; Geer r. Hamblin, 1 N.e. 54 ; Dunham v. Osborn, 1 Paige, 634 ; Cook v. Hammond, 4 Mason, 485.

[3] Reynolds v. Reynolds, 5 Paige, 161 ; Safford v. Safford, 7 Paige, 259 ; 4 Kent, Com. 8th ed. 65, n.

Or if before dower had been set off to the elder dowress, the purchaser had died, and his own widow had been endowed out of the same, the assignment of dower to the former would operate to interrupt the enjoyment of the latter of her dower during the life of the former, but no longer. Or if the purchaser had died during the life of the ancestor's widow, and after her dower had been assigned, the widow of the purchaser would be entitled to dower out of the remainder of the estate, together with dower out of the reversion of that part of the estate set to the ancestor's widow.[1] * In the first of [*211] the cases above supposed, the *doctrine *dos de dote* prevailing, the widow of the ancestor had her estate as a continuance of her husband's as if there had been no intermission between them. In the others the purchaser had acquired a seisin in the life of the ancestor, and hers could only go back to his death. A reported case will serve to illustrate this matter further. A husband died, leaving a wife and six children. One of these, a son, married and died in the life of his mother, and it was held that his widow could claim dower in only one sixth of two third parts of the father's estate.[2] But in the cases supposed above, if the widow of the ancestor or of the vendor had had her dower set out in the premises before the heir or purchaser had married, and he were to marry and die in her lifetime, his widow could not claim dower. The seisin which he had acquired before dower had been set out as supposed would not avail him, not having existed during their coverture, and as soon as it was set out his estate was converted into a reversion which could not give his own widow dower.[3]

30. The cases do not seem to be uniform upon the subject,

* NOTE. — In the case of Bear *v.* Snyder, 11 Wend. 592, the court seem to have overlooked the distinction that the second widow is entitled to dower out of the reversion of the land set out to the first, where the husband of the former takes by purchase, but not where he takes by descent.

---

[1] 4 Dane, Abr. 663 ; 1 Roper, Hus. & Wife, 382 ; Park, Dow. 156 ; 1 Cruise, Dig. 164 ; Bastard's Case, 4 Rep. 122 ; Geer *v.* Hamblin, 1 ʃe. 54 ; ʃanning *v.* Laboree, 33 ʃe. 343 ; Dunham *v.* Osborn, 1 Paige, 634.

[2] In ʃatter of Cregier, 1 Barb. Ch. 598.

[3] Park, Dow. 156 ; Reynolds *v.* Reynolds, 5 Paige, 161.

how far the widow claiming under the elder title must have proceeded in having her dower assigned to her, to affect the right of the younger widow to have dower out of the entire estate. The question has been raised where the tenant has sought to bar the younger widow by interposing the right of the elder to dower. In one case T L conveyed lands to S L, who conveyed to the tenant. After T L's death, his widow sued for her dower, and obtained judgment, and then released to the tenant. Then the widow of S L, he having died, sued, claiming dower out of the whole estate. But it was held that she could only have it out of two thirds of the estate excluding the third of which the first was dowable.[1] But where the first of two widows, in the case supposed, released to the tenant her * right before she had taken measures [*212] to have her dower assigned, it was held to be no bar to the second claiming dower out of the entire estate, since by the release of the first her right was simply extinguished, and no one could set it up against the claim of the second.[2]

31. To the extent already defined, it is not understood that there is any difficulty in determining how the right of dower is affected by the seisin upon which it depends being defeated, as in case of a base fee, or an estate upon condition, and the like. But there is a class of cases where what at first sight might seem to be an inconsistent doctrine is applied. Thus, in the familiar case of tenant in tail dying without issue, although the estate, as one of inheritance, is determined, and the remainder over upon such a contingency takes effect, yet, it having been an estate of inheritance in the tenant, his widow, if he dies, will be entitled to dower, it being by implication of law annexed to such an estate as an incidental part of it, a portion of the quantity of enjoyment designated by the terms of the limitation itself.[3] And the doctrine is broadly laid down by writers upon the subject, that wherever the husband is seised during coverture of such an estate as is in its nature subject to the attachment of dower, the right of dower will not be defeated by the determination of that estate by

[1] Leavitt v. Lamprey, 13 Pick. 382.
[2] Elwood v. Klock, 13 Barb. 50. See also Atwood v. Atwood, 22 Pick. 283.
[3] 2 Crabb, Real Prop. 165 ; 4 Kent, Com. 49 ; Park, Dow. 82, 157.

its regular and natural limitation, as in the case of tenant in tail dying without issue, or tenant in fee dying without heirs, whereby the estate escheats.[1]

32. And this class of cases has given rise to much ingenious speculation and grave diversity of opinion, where the estate of the husband is one of inheritance, but ceases at his death by what is called a conditional limitation. This may be illustrated by example, although the nature of executory estates may not yet have been explained. It should be borne in mind that the distinction between estates upon condition [*213] which have already * been spoken of, and conditional limitations, is that the former can only be defeated by the grantor or his heirs entering for condition broken, and defeating the estate; so that, notwithstanding the breach, the estate and those dependent upon it remain unaffected until such entry. In case of conditional limitations, however, the estate is so limited by the terms of the grant or devise creating it, that upon the happening of some condition, the estate *ipso facto* ceases, and passes at once over to some other person. Again, while by the common law a freehold cannot be created to commence in future unless by the way of reversion or remainder, nor can a reversion or remainder be created to take effect after the determination of a prior estate in fee-simple, yet by way of springing or shifting use by deed, or by way of executory devise by will, a fee-simple may be limited to take effect after a previous estate in fee-simple shall have been determined. To recur, then, to the right of dower in estates held by a conditional limitation, it is laid down by a writer of great authority, "that an immediate estate in fee, defeasible on the taking effect of an executory limitation, has all the incidents of an actual estate in fee-simple in possession, such as curtesy, dower, &c., the devisee having the inheritance in fee, subject only to a possibility."[2] And this case might be put for illustration. A devises lands to B in fee, but if he die without children living, then over to another. Though B die without children, his wife will nevertheless have

---

[1] Park, Dow. 147 ; Perkins, § 317 ; Tud. Cas. 44; Paine's Case, 8 Rep. 36 a ; 4 Kent, Com. 49 ; Northcut *v.* Whipp, 12 B. Mon. 65, 73 ; 1 Atk. Conv. 258.

[2] 1 Jarman, Wills, 792 ; 2 Crabb, Real Prop. 167.

dower.[1] The difficulty has been to distinguish upon what ground a widow may have her dower out of an estate which has been defeated by an executory limitation like the above, but would be barred if the estate of her husband were defeated by a condition at common law, or by being a base or determinable fee.

Butler has a very elaborate note to Co. Lit. 241, in which he attempts to assist, as he calls it, " in clearing up the complex and abstruse points of learning in which this question is involved." Judge Kent says, " that the ablest writers upon property law are against the right of the dowress when the fee * of the husband is determined by executory [*214] devise or shifting use."[2] Atkinson states the law to be thus : " Where the husband's estate is defeated by title paramount, as by entry for condition broken, by reason of a defective title in the grantor, or by shifting use, the right to the dower is also defeated ; but where the husband's estate is defeated by executory devise, it has been settled, rather anomalously, it has been thought, that the widow shall nevertheless be entitled to dower."[3] Preston leaves the point as doubtful.[4] Burton says, " Where the wife or husband has an estate in fee subject to be divested by a shifting use or executory devise, it has been a disputed question whether these rights may not be enforced after the event, and notwithstanding the divesting and destruction of the estate upon which they attached."[5] One of the leading cases upon this subject is Buckworth v. Thirkell,[6] which is said by Judge Kent to be opposed to the opinion of the ablest writers on property law ;[7] while C. J. Best says that, though questioned, it has become the settled law, and cites in that connection Lit. § 53.[8] The

---

[1] 2 Crabb, Real Prop. 167 ; Co. Lit. 241, n. 4 ; Kennedy v. Kennedy, 29 N. J. 185. See also *ante*, pp. *134, *135, and cases cited.

[2] 4 Kent, Com. 50. See also Park, Dow. 178–186 ; Northcut v. Whipp, 12 B. Mon. 65.

[3] 1 Atk. Conv. 258.   [4] 3 Prest. Abs. 373.

[5] Burton, Real Prop. § 355.

[6] Buckworth v. Thirkell, 3 B. & P. 652, n.

[7] 4 Kent, Com. 50. See also Park, Dow. 178 ; Evans v. Evans, 9 Penn. St. 190.

[8] Moody v. King, 2 Bing. 447. So Hatfield v. Snelden, 54 N. Y. 285, overruling s. c. 42 Barb. 615, and Weller v. Weller, 28 Barb. 588.

case of Moody *v.* King was this. Devise to W F and his
heirs, and if he should have no issue, then over; W F had
a wife, but died without having had issue, and his wife was
held entitled to dower.

Where the distinction between two classes of cases is apparently so subtle, it may be of little use to attempt to reconcile or explain them, though it is not difficult to conceive that
there is a marked difference between a case where by the
terms of the limitation, if the estate created by it is determined,
it comes back with its seisin to him who had the original seisin
by himself or his heirs, and one where the seisin is never reserved by the original owner, but passes upon the expi
[*215] ration of the first *estate, to another. Nor is it difficult to comprehend that so much of the seisin in the case
of an estate of inheritance, as goes to the widow at the death
of her husband, should remain in her as a continuation of his
seisin and estate till exhausted by her death. The matter was
considered quite at length by Gibson, C. J., in a case [1] where
the devise was to two sons, G and O, their heirs and assigns,
but if either should die without having lawful issue living at
his death, his estate should vest in the surviving brother and
his heirs. The widow of one of these sons who had died
without issue, living the other son, claimed dower, and the
same was allowed. This was, it is true, a case of executory
devise, but the reasoning of the Chief Justice covers the case
of springing and shifting uses also. "Not one of the text-
writers," says he, "has hinted at the true solution of the difficulty, except Mr. Preston. All agree that where the husband's fee is determined by recovery, condition, or collateral
limitation,* the wife's dower determines with it." "I have a
deferential respect for the opinion of Mr. Butler, who was perhaps the best conveyancer of his day, but I cannot apprehend
the reasons of his distinction in the note to Co. Lit. 241 a, be-
between a fee limited to continue to a particular period at its
creation, which curtesy or dower may survive, and the devise

---

* NOTE. — An instance of a collateral limitation would be a grant to one and
his heirs till the building of St. Paul's shall be finished. Park, Dow. 163.

---

[1] Evans *v.* Evans, 9 Penn. St. 190.

of a fee-simple or a fee-tail absolute or conditional, which by subsequent words is made determinable upon some particular event, at the happening of which dower or curtesy will cease." "How to reconcile to any system of reason, technical or natural, the existence of a derivative estate, after the extinction of that from which it was derived, was for him (Butler) to show, and he has not done it. The case of a tenant in tail, says Mr. Preston,[1] is an exception arising from an equitable construction of the statute *De Donis,* and the cases of dower of estates determinable by executory devise and springing use * owe their existence to the circumstance that [*216] these limitations are not governed by common-law principles. The mounting of a fee upon a fee by executory devise is a proof of that." "Before the Statute of Wills there was no executory devise, and before the Statute of Uses there were no springing uses." "It was the benign temper of the judges who moulded the limitations of the estates introduced by them, whether original or derivative, so as to relax the severer principles of the common law, and among other things to preserve curtesy and dower from being barred by a determination of the original estate which could not be prevented."[2] In Northcut v. Whipp,[3] already cited, the testator devised to his "son W L and his heirs." By a codicil he directed that if W L died without heirs, the estate should pass to his sisters. W L married and died without heirs, and his wife claimed dower. The court allowed dower on the broad ground that in all cases where the husband is seised of such an estate that the issue of the wife, if she had any, would inherit it, she is dowable, although her husband die without issue, and though it is limited over, in case of his so dying to another. Another case is Milledge v. Lamar.[4] The devise was to Thomas, his heirs, &c., but should the said Thomas die without any heir of his body begotten, then over; it was held that, upon Thomas's dying without issue, his wife was entitled to dower. And the court speak with approbation of Buckworth v. Thirkell, and Moody v. King, above cited, and cite Lit. § 52.

---

[1] 3 Prest. Abs. 373.   [2] See also Sammes & Payne's Case, 1 Leon. 167

[3] Northcut v. Whipp, 12 B. Mon. 65. Cf. Bush v. Bush, 5 Houst. 245.

[4] Milledge v. Lamar, 4 Desauss. 617, 637.

Though the above cases may not, perhaps, place the distinction between the different kinds of determinable estates, so
far as dower is concerned, on very clear grounds, the tendency
of the modern English and American cases seems to be, to
sustain the distinction in favor of dower out of estates which
have been determined by an executory limitation, and perhaps
the reasoning of Ch. J. Gibson furnishes a satisfactory basis
on which the distinction should rest.　The court of New York,
in revising an opinion given by the Supreme Court of that
State, sustain the doctrine above laid down, and liken the determination of a husband's estate, in such cases, to that which
happens by the death of a tenant in tail, in which case a widow
always takes dower.[1]

[* 217]　　* 33. The most common mode formerly in use of
barring dower was by means of a jointure.　But as
this forms a species of estate of a peculiar character, it will be
considered by itself.　And in connection with it reference will
be made to ante and post nuptial settlements, testamentary
provisions, &c., as affecting rights of dower.

34. In some States there is a bar to the widow's recovering
dower arising from lapse of time.　But the law on this point
is very far from being uniform, or, in some cases, even settled.
That a long lapse of time after the husband's death before any
claim made may be evidence proper to be submitted to a jury
to establish a release of the right, would seem to be sustained
by authority as well as the general principles of evidence,

---

[1] Hatfield v. Sneden, 54 N. Y. 285.　See also *ante*, p. *135.　The conclusion
in the text is further supported by the recent cases in this country of Jones v.
Hughes, 27 Gratt. 560 ; Medley v. Medley, Id. 568, where the limitations were,
under the statutes of Virginia, executory devises ; and by Smith v. Spencer, 2 Jur.
N. s. 778, where there was an executory devise over after an equitable fee, in each
of which dower was allowed.　See also Daniel v. McManama, 1 Bush, 544, where
the same doctrine is maintained, though the devise over did not take effect.　A
contrary decision was made in Edwards v. Bibb, 54 Ala. 475, but this is the only
case to that effect in any court of last resort in this country or in England.　It
relies partly on the case of Weller v. Weller, 28 Barb. 588, since overruled, and
on Adams v. Beekman, 1 Paige, 631.　But this, like Sumner v. Partridge, 2 Atk.
47 and Barker v. Barker, 2 Sim. 49, proceeded on the wholly distinct ground that
where the devise over is to the issue of the first taker, as they take as purchasers
and not by descent, their parent was not seised of an estate which they could
inherit, and the necessary condition for dower fails.

even though no positive rule of limitation existed.[1] So the
receiving a separate maintenance for several years before
the husband's death, under articles of separation, and con-
tinning to receive it for eight years after, was held to create
a presumption of release of dower on the part of the
wife.[2]

35. In England, by the statute 3 & 4 Wm. IV. c. 27 the
limitation of a widow's right to claim dower is fixed at twenty
years from the death of the husband. But before that there
was no statute bar to its recovery there.[3] A similar limitation
exists in New York, New Jersey, Massachusetts, Iowa, Indiana, Mississippi, and South Carolina;[4] also in Tennessee,[5]
and in Kentucky.[6] In Michigan the same limitation exists
since the statute of 1846, by which dower might be recovered
in an action of ejectment.[7] In New Hampshire the bar is
twenty years, reckoned from the date of the demand of dower.[8]
In Ohio the limitation is twenty-one years,[9] while in Georgia
it is but seven from the death of the husband.[10] It seems
that in Maine the statute limitation of twenty years applies
to dower; but it begins to run only from the death
of * the husband, so that she would not be affected by [*218]
any adverse possession prior to that time.[11] By statute,
all suits for dower are barred after three years in Alabama,
where the husband aliens, otherwise not till twenty years.[12]
On the other hand, the old English law as to dower being
barred by the lapse of time prevails in Connecticut, in North

---

[1] Barnard v. Edwards, 4 N. H. 321.   [2] Evans v. Evans, 3 Yeates, 507.

[3] 4 Kent, Com. 70; Park, Dow. 311; 1st Rep. Eng. Com. Real Prop. 40.

[4] 4 Kent, Com. 70; Mass. Pub. Stat. c. 124, § 13; Wilson v. McLenaghan,
1 McMullan, Eq. 35; Phares v. Walters, 6 Iowa, 106; Ind. Rev. Stat. 1881,
§ 293; Moody v. Harper, 38 Miss. 599.

[5] Carmichael v. Carmichael, 5 Humph. 96.

[6] Ralls v. Hughes, 1 Dana, 407.   [7] Proctor v. Bigelow, 38 Mich. 282.

[8] Robie v. Flanders, 33 N. H. 524.   [9] Tuttle v. Willson, 10 Ohio, 24.

[10] Chapman v. Schroeder, 10 Ga. 321. The same rule is in operation in Illinois,
Owen v. Peacock, 38 Ill. 33.

[11] Durham v. Augier, 20 Me. 242.

[12] Alabama, Code 1876, § 2251; Barksdale v. Garrett, 64 Ala. 277; Benaugh
v. Turrentine, 60 Ala. 557. Prior to the statute of 1858, the three years' bar
applied in all cases. Ridgway v. McAlpine, 31 Ala. 458; Martin v. Martin,
35 Ala. 560.

Carolina, and in Maryland.[1]   In the cited case, the husband
died in 1814, and the suit for dower was brought in 1841.
And so far as the Statute of Limitations grows out of the
supposed right to presume a title from long adverse enjoyment by the person in possession, it could not well apply to
the case of dower, since upon the death of the husband the
wife is not seised, nor has she a right of entry. ⹁So that whoever is in possession is not to be regarded as holding adversely
to her, and her non-claim is a mere forbearance to place herself in a condition in which she can convert a mere personal
chose in action into an estate.

36. Much of the law, however, as once understood, as to
barring a widow's right of dower in her husband's estate, has
been practically superseded by statutes both in England and
several of the United States.*   In pursuance of a recom-
mendation on the part of the commissioners, the act of 3 & 4
Wm. IV. c. 105, called the Dower Act, was passed, covering
all cases of marriage since Jan. 1, 1834.   By that act the
dower of married women has been placed completely
[*219]   within the power of their *husbands.   A husband may
exclude his wife from such claim by inserting a clause
of such exclusion in the deed which he takes, or by a deed
executed by himself in his lifetime, or by his will, after his
death.   And even if no such disposition is made of the husband's lands, they are charged with the payment of his debts,
to the exclusion, if need be, of the widow's dower.[2]   The effect

---

* NOTE. — The reasons for this change in England are examined and explained
at length by the Commissioners upon the Law of Real Property, in their First
Report, p. 16.   They regard the law of dower as well adapted to the state of
freehold property existing at the time when it was established, but that the
changes in the condition of the kingdom render it at this day highly inconvenient.   And that this has led to so many modes of evading the law upon the subject, "that the general result is, that the right to dower exists beneficially in so
few instances, that it is of little value considered as a provision for widows."
The same idea has been expressed by Blackstone, who speaks of it as having become "a great clog to alienations," and "otherwise inconvenient to families."
2 Bl. Com. 136.

---

[1] 1 Swift's Dig. 256 ; Spencer *v.* Weston, 1 Dev. & B. 213 ; Chew *v.* Farmers'
Bk., 2 Md. Ch. Dec. 231.
[2] Wms. Real Prop. 193, 194.

has been that dower no longer exists in practice, except as
against the husband's heirs at law, and even to that extent it
is inoperative if the husband, as is now commonly done, inserts
a declaration in his title-deed denying such right.[1] The only
compensation provided in the act for this overthrow of the old
system is, that dower may extend to lands to which the husband has a right though unaccompanied with a seisin, and to
equitable estates of inheritance.[2] From various causes growing out of the condition of a new country, in which wild lands
rapidly become cultivated fields, and forests give place to
marts of trade and commerce, the people of many of the States
have seen fit to modify by statute the common law as to dower.
In some the widow can only claim her dower out of lands of
which her husband died seised. In some she is authorized to
clear wild land and reduce it to culture, though to do so she
must cut down the timber and firewood thereon. And in
others there are other changes which can, at best, be but very
briefly noticed. In several of the States the common law will
be found substantially in operation, except, it may be, as to
equitable estates, which have already been spoken of. Many
of these changes have already been enumerated.*

*37. One mode in which dower may be defeated [*220]
remains to be mentioned, and that is, by the exercise
of eminent domain during the life of the husband, or,
what is equivalent to it, the *dedication of land to [*221]
the public use. This grows out of the nature of a
wife's interest in the lands, and whether it is such as ought
to be regarded in giving compensation. In a case in New
York, where a corporation was authorized to take lands for a
public use, and hold the same in fee, paying the owners there-

* NOTE. — See *ante*, *149, *163, and notes. Upon the extent to which in several
States dower extends to equitable as well as legal estates, the following authorities
may further be referred to: Derush *v.* Brown, 8 Ohio, 413; Tuttle *v.* Willson,
10 Ohio, 24; Griffin *v.* Reece, 1 Harringt. 508; Avant *v.* Robertson, 2 McMullan,
215; Markham *v.* Merrett, 7 How. (Miss.) 437; Hill *v.* Mitchell, 5 Ark. 608.
As to the effect of a testamentary provision in the wife's favor, in barring her
claim for dower, and how far she may elect to accept or refuse this, see *post*, *271,
272, and notes.

_____

[1] Ibid. 194.   [2] Wms. Real Prop. 194.

of an ascertained compensation, it was held that the wife's
right of dower was effectually barred by the act of the legislature.   It was said that the right of the wife during her husband's life, being merely inchoate, could not be regarded in
exercising eminent domain, and was, moreover, subject to any
regulation which the legislature might see fit to make, though
its effect might be to divest the right; and the estate of the
widow after the assignment of dower being a continuation of
the estate of the husband, he, while living, was the only one
who could represent it, and his compensation was in full for
the part taken.[1]   So where the owners of land laid open a
street in a city for the purpose, among other things, of erecting a market-house thereon by the city, which was done accordingly, it was held that land so taken, like land taken for
highways, was not subject to the widow's dower in right of the
original owners.[2]   The principle involved in the above and
similar cases is a pretty important one, nor has it been hither-
to very well defined.   It is difficult to see why it should not
apply in all cases where the law authorizes the husband's land
to be taken *in invitum*, and compensation therefor made for
the fee of the same ; as, for instance, in those States where
the mill-owner is authorized to flow lands which he does not
own.   At common law, a widow could not have dower of a
castle,[3] since, among other reasons, she could not put it to
        profitable use ; and the same reasoning would apply as
[*222] to * lands, though granted by the husband, which have
        been appropriated to public uses, such as cemeteries,
public parks, and the like.

[1] Moore *v*. The Mayor, 4 Sandf. 456 ; s. c. 8 N. Y. 110.
[2] Guynne *v*. Cincinnati, 3 Ohio, 24.   [3] 1 Cruise, Dig. 129.

SECTION V.

HOW AND BY WHOM ASSIGNED.

THE next subject in order is, how and by whom dower may be assigned, and in what manner its assignment may be enforced.

1. In the first place, the widow is entitled to have dower set out to her immediately upon the death of her husband. But until it is assigned she has no right to claim any specific part of the estate, or enter upon or occupy any part of it.[1]

2. Out of tenderness, however, for her condition, the Magna Carta provided for her the right to occupy the principal mansion-house of her husband, and to be supported therein out of his personal estate for the term of forty days from the

---

[1] 2 Bl. Com. 139.

time of 1is deat1, w1ic1 was called 1er quarantine. S1e forfeited t1is, 1owever, if s1e married again wit1in t1at time.[1]
T1is rig1t, moreover, could only be exercised in respect to
suc1 estate as s1e is dowable of. If 1er 1usband, t1erefore,
died possessed of a lease1old estate, she could not claim 1er
quarantine out of it.[2] T1e rig1t of quarantine in t1e widow
is recognized in t1e statutes of t1e States, t1oug1 somew1at
various as to t1e extent and duration of its enjoyment by t1e
widow.*

* NOTE. — In *Alabama* she has the use of the dwelling-house in which the
husband usually resided, rent free, till her dower is assigned to her, Code, 1867,
§ 1630 ; even against the alienee of her husband, Shelton *v.* Carrol, 16 Ala. 148 ;
Pharis *v.* Leachman, 20 Ala. 662.   In *Arkansas* she has the mansion-house two
months, and until dower is assigned. Dig. Stat. 1874, § 2226. *Florida*, she holds
till dower is assigned. Dig. Amend. Code, 294. And in *Kentucky.* Gen. Stat.
1873, p. 530 ; Chaplin *v.* Simmons, 7 Mon. 337. The same in *Mississippi*, Rev.
Code, 1871, p. 255 ; *Georgia*, Code, 1873, § 1768 ; *Missouri*, Rev. Stat. 1879,
§ 2205 ; *New Jersey*, Rev. 1877, p. 320. *Rhode Island*, if she brings her writ of
dower within twelve months of the grantor's administration. Pub. Stat. 1882,
c. 187, § 6. *Texas*, same as Alabama. Hartley's Dig. 1850, p. 287. *Virginia*,
the same; and also the profits of one third of the real estate. Code, 1860, p. 533.
In *Connecticut* the widow immediately on death of husband becomes tenant in
common with the husband's heirs, of her dower. 38 Conn. 256 ; Stedman *v.* Fortune, 5 Conn. 462. *Indiana*, dower is abolished, and widow takes one third by
descent. Rev. Stat. 1881, § 2483. So in *Iowa.* Rev. Code, 1880, § 2440, and this
is to include the dwelling-house, if possible, § 2441. In *Minnesota* and *Kansas*,
also, the widow takes her share in fee : in the former State, one third, Stat. 1878,
c. 46, § 2 ; and in the latter, one half, Comp. L. 1879, § 2109. On the other
hand, in *Arizona, Texas, Colorado, Nevada*, and *Dakota*, she takes an absolute
share of the community property in lieu of dower. *Ante*, *149, and note. *Maine*,
the period is ninety days. Rev. Stat. 1883, c. 103, § 14. *Massachusetts*, it is a
right to occupy the premises with the children or heirs of deceased, or receive one
third of the rents till dower is set out. Pub. Stat. c. 124, §§ 3, 14. *Michigan*,
she may remain one year in the house. Comp. L. 1871, § 4291. In *New York*,
forty days. 1 Stat. at Large, p. 699. In *New Hampshire*, the widow is entitled
to occupy the house of her husband forty days without rent, and have reasonable
sustenance out of the estate ; and she is entitled to one third part of the rents and
profits of the estate of which her husband died seised, until dower is assigned. Gen. L.
1878, c. 202, § 12. *Vermont*, she may occupy with the heirs until dower is set out.
Gen. Stat. 1862, p. 413. *Wisconsin, Ohio*, and *Oregon*, the widow may occupy the
house for one year. Wisc. Rev. Stat. 1858, c. 89, § 23 ; Ohio Rev. Stat. 1880,
§ 4188 ; Oreg. Gen. L. 1872, p. 587. In *Nebraska* the widow may occupy the
dwelling-house, and have reasonable sustenance from the estate for one year,
Gen. Stat. 1873, pp. 278, 279 ; and may occupy with the children and other heirs
without assignment of dower, so long as they do not object, Ib. pp. 278, 279.

---

[1] Tud. Cas. 51 ; Co. Lit. 34 b.   [2] Voelckner *v.* Hudson, 1 Sandf. 215.

3. T1e rig1t *of a wife to dower 1aving become [*223] fixed by t1e deat1 of the 1usband, not1ing remains in order to consummate it but to ascertain the particular part of 1is estate s1e is to enjoy by virtue of it. The moment t1is is done, a free1old vests in 1er by act of law, and not by way of conveyance from the 1eir or terre-tenant. Nor is any writing or livery of seisin required to complete the assignment. A parol assignment, if accepted by the widow, is as effectual as if done in ever so formal a manner.[1]

4. T1ere are two modes of assigning dower, one " of common rig1t," and one " against common rig1t." The former is t1e one always to be adopted w1ere ₜ1e assignment is by legal process, and must be pursued by t1e tenant or 1eir if 1e undertakes to set out dower so as to satisfy her claim wit1out any formal assent or acceptance on 1er part. T1e * ot1er may be resorted to and take almost any [*224] form, because it implies a special assent or agreement on 1er part to accept it instead of t1e more precise and formal manner.

5. Dower of common rig1t must always be assigned by metes and bounds w1ere the property is of a c1aracter t1at it can be so set out.[2] And if t1e s1eriff in assigning dower s1ould adopt any ot1er form, it would be erroneous.[3]

6. But w1ere the parties agree on a different form, it may be effectual. T1us dower may be set out in common wit1 the balance of t1e estate.[4] Or it may be a rent for life issuing out of the lands of w1ic1 the widow is dowable; or it may be of a certain agreed number of acres.[5] But t1e dower assigned must be out of land of w1ic1 s1e is dowable, unless it is done by t1e consent of the parties.[6]

---

[1] Deserve v. Deserve, 19 N. H. 240; Blood v. Blood, 23 Pick. 80; Shattuck v. Gragg, 23 Pick. 88; Conant v. Little, 1 Pick. 189; Johnson r. Neil, 4 Ala. 166; Jones v. Brewer, 1 Pick. 314; Baker v. Baker, 4 De. 67; Boyers r. New-banks, 2 Ind. 388; Tud. Cas. 51; Johnson v. Morse, 2 N. H. 48; Pinkham v. Gear, 3 N. H. 163:

[2] Pierce v. Williams, 2 Penningt. 521.

[3] Booth v. Lambert, Style, 276; Co. Lit. 34 b, n. 213; 1 Rolle, Abr. 683.

[4] Booth v. Lambert, Style, 276.

[5] Co. Lit. 34 b; Doore, 59; 1 Bright, Hus. & Wife, 375, 377, 378; Tud. Cas. 52.

[6] Perkins, § 407.

7. If it is done in any form against common right, it will not operate to bar her claim unless it be done by indenture to which she is a party, and by which she would be estopped from avoiding it.[1] Even the acceptance of a deed from the heir or tenant would not be sufficient if she do not execute a release.[2] One reason why an assignment of lands out of which the widow is not dowable is no bar to dower unless done and accepted by indenture, is, that her title to it must depend upon the grant of the person making the assignment, and unless this be by deed, she can only hold as tenant at will; and for the further reason, that a right or title to a freehold cannot be barred by any *collateral* satisfaction.[3] And the same rule applies to a rent granted in lieu of dower out of lands of which she is not dowable.[4] Where her dower has been thus assigned against common right, she will be [*225] bound by it, whether it turns out to * be more or less valuable than what her appropriate dower would have been, and she cannot insist upon a new assignment, though her title fails to that which she has accepted.[5]

8. Another essential requisite in assigning dower " of common right," in order to operate as a bar to a widow's action for recovery of dower, is that it should be done absolutely, and not be accompanied by any condition.[6] And where in the assignment the trees growing upon the premises were excepted, it was held that such exception was inconsistent and void.[7]

9. In the next place, such assignment must be absolute for her life. Any less estate, whatever be its value, would not bar her suit to recover her legal dower.[8] And one reason for this is, that the estate of the widow in her dower lands is considered as a continuance of that of her husband, the heir

1 Co. Lit. 34 b; Perkins, § 410; 1 Bright, Hus. & Wife, 377; Tud. Cas. 52; Conant v. Little, 1 Pick. 189; Jones v. Brewer, Id. 314.

2 1 Roper, Hus. & Wife, 410.

3 1 Roper, Hus. & Wife, 410; Vernon's Case, 4 Rep. 1.　"

4 1 Bright, Hus. & Wife, 377.

5 Jones v. Brewer, 1 Pick. 314; Co. Lit. 32 b.

6 Co. Lit. 34 b, n. 217; 2 Crabb, Real Prop. 144; Tud. Cas. 52.

7 Bullock v. Finch, 1 Rolle, Abr. 682; Tud. Cas. 52.

9 1 Bright, Hus. & Wife, 379; 2 Crabb, Real Prop. 144.

or tenant being a mere minister of the law in marking out as to what particular land this shall apply. He cannot dictate or change the terms on which she is to hold it.[1]

10. In respect to the person by whom dower may be set out, where resort is not had to legal process, it must be the tenant of the freehold. No other person can do it. But it is not essential that the title of the tenant should be a valid one, provided he is in possession under a claim of title, and sets out the dower without fraud or covin.[2] If, therefore, it be so done by a disseisor, abator, or intruder, it cannot be avoided by the heir or disseisee, provided it be of such part only of the estate as the heir would have been bound to assign had he been in possession of the premises. Though, if it be of a rent instead of the land, the heir or disseisee would not be bound by it, because it is against common right, and is only good when made by some one competent to bind the estate by agreement.[3] It may be done by an infant, if heir to the estate of which the widow is dowable, subject, how- ever, to be corrected and diminished · by writ of ad- [*226] measurement of dower in favor of such infant, if, by mistake, he shall have set her out too much.[4] But this privi- lege is limited to infants, for if the heir be of age and sets out dower, which is accepted by the widow, both parties will be governed by it.[5] If the infant heir be under guardianship, the guardian may assign dower. And it seems that, if so done, it will bind the heir, although Blackstone and Fitzherbert state the law otherwise.[6] The courts of Illinois hold that such set- ting out of dower by the guardian of a minor does not bind him when he comes of age, so that he may not then have it revised.[7] If the land be owned by two as joint tenants,

[1] 1 Bright, Hus. & Wife, 379.　　　　　　　　[2] Co. Lit. 35 a.

[3] Perkins, § 394 ; Tud. Cas. 51 ; Co. Lit. 35 a ; 1 Bright, Hus. & Wife, 365 ; Perkins, § 398 ; ante, pl. 6.

[4] 2 Bl. Com. 136 : Fitzh. N. B. 348 ; Jones v. Brewer, 1 Pick. 314 ; McCor- mick v. Taylor, 2 Ind. 336.

[5] Stoughton v. Leigh, 1 Taunt. 402 ; Tud. Cas. 52.

[6] Boyers v. Newbanks, 2 Ind. 388 ; Jones r. Brewer, 1 Pick. 314 ; Young v. Tarbell, 37 Me. 509 ; Curtis v. Hobart, 41 Me. 230 ; 2 Bl. Com. 136 ; Fitzh. N. B. 348.

[7] Bonner v. Peterson, 44 Ill. 253.

either may set out the dower.[1] And if these joint tenants be husband and wife, she will be bound by the assignment of the husband.[2]

11. If now it is inquired what measures a widow is to resort to if the heir or tenant shall fail to assign her her legal dower, it will be answered that she may resort to certain forms of legal process by which the same will be effected. In Illinois a widow recovers her dower in an action of ejectment.[3] One of these modes is by the common-law action of dower, another is by proceedings in equity, and a third is one provided in most, if not all the States, by a cheap and summary process issuing from courts having cognizance of probate matters. In some cases these may be concurrent remedies. But, generally speaking, the last is more restricted than either of the others, and confined to cases where the claim of the widow is upon the heir or devisee of the husband, and is not the proper one to resort to when it is necessary to determine a contested right of dower.[4] In New York, the effect of a decree of the surrogate is merely to fix the admeasurement and location of the wife's dower, but it does not establish the title. That must be tried in an action of ejectment, sued out to recover possession of the premises.[5] If, however, dower shall have been set out by one of these courts, the assignment is conclusive upon the parties until the judgment shall be reversed.[6]

And in Massachusetts, though the judge of probate [*227] has no right to assign dower out * of a mortgaged estate,[7] yet if the mortgagor dies seised of land, dower may be set off to his widow by the judge, if neither the mortgagee, nor heirs or devisees of the mortgagor object.[8] In re-

[1] Co. Lit. 35 a. ·   [2] 2 Crabb, Real Prop. 142.

[3] Owen v. Peacock, 38 Ill. 33.

[4] Sheaffe v. O'Neil, 9 Mass. 9 ; French v. Crosby, 23 Me. 276 ; Matter of Watkins, 9 Johns. 245 ; Holloman v. Holloman, 5 Sm. & M. 559 ; Ware v. Washington, 6 Sm. & M. 737 ; Bisland v. Hewett, 11 Sm. & M. 164 ; Thrasher v. Pinckard, 23 Ala. 616.

[5] Parks v. Hardey, 4 Bradf. 15.

[6] Jackson v. Hixon, 17 Johns. 123 ; Tilson v. Thompson, 10 Pick. 359.

[7] Raynham v. Wilmarth, 13 Met. 414.

[8] Henry's Case, 4 Cush. 257. And the subsequent transfer of the mortgage to the heir, who has so assented, will not entitle the latter to dispute the assignment. King v. King, 100 Mass. 224.

spect to Vermont, the propositions above stated as to jurisdiction do not apply, because courts of probate there have
exclusive jurisdiction in assigning dower.[1] In England and
in several of the States, courts of equity and common law
have concurrent jurisdiction in many cases respecting dower.[2]

In England this has been the case since the time of Elizabeth, and has become much the more usual mode of recovering
dower.[3] But where there is this concurrent jurisdiction, the
rules of law which they apply are alike in both courts.[4] This
right of concurrent jurisdiction has been exercised in the
courts of the United States in the cases above cited, and in
New York, New Jersey, Maryland, Alabama, Virginia, North
Carolina, and Illinois.[5] But in some cases, as in equitable
estates for instance, it will be seen hereafter that courts of
equity have exclusive jurisdiction. It will therefore be proper
to consider the remedies at the common law by themselves.

12. Dower should be set out to the widow within the time of
her quarantine, and it is often said she may bring her action
at law for its recovery if not set out within that time.[6] And
as, at common law, no damages could be recovered in a real
action, it does not seem to have been necessary to make a
demand for dower before commencing the action.[7] But if no
such demand is made, the tenant may plead *tout temps prist* in
bar of any claim for damages. And as by the statute of Merton, damages are recoverable in an action of dower, a
demand * is, practically, uniformly made preliminary [*228]
to the commencement of the action.[8]

13. In some of the States a demand *must* be made before
commencing an action, and the time within which, after such

---

[1] Danforth v. Smith, 23 Vt. 247.

[2] 2 Crabb, Real Prop. 187 ; Herbert v. Wren, 7 Cranch, 370, 376.

[3] Perkins, § 317 ; 2 Crabb, Real Prop. 187.

[4] Potier r. Barclay, 15 Ala. 439 ; Mayburry v. Brien, 15 Pet. 21.

[5] Badgley v. Bruce, 4 Paige, 98 ; Hartshorne v. Hartshorne, 2 N. J. Eq. 349 ;
Wells v. Beall, 2 Gill & J. 468 ; Kiddall v. Trimble, 1 Md. Ch. Dec. 143 ; Blunt
v. Gee, 5 Call, 481 ; Campbell v. Murphy, 2 Jones, Eq. 357 ; Blain v. Harrison,
11 Ill. 384 ; Osborne v. Horine, 17 Ill. 92.

[6] 2 Crabb, Real Prop. 140 ; 1 Bright, Hus. & Wife, 363 ; 4 Kent, Com. 63.

[7] Stearns, Real Act. 312.

[8] Stearns, Real Act. 313 ; Co. Lit. 32 b ; Watson v. Watsou, 10 C. B. 3 ; Hitchcock v. Harrington, 6 Johns. 290.

demand is made, it may, and, if brought at all, must, be commenced, is regulated by their local statutes.   In Massachusetts
it must be made of the person who is seised of the freehold,
and the action may not be commenced until one month after
such demand, and must be within one year.[1] And this demand
is a personal one, and is required to be made upon every person
who is tenant, though he be a tenant in common with others.[2]
And it may be made by attorney.[3]   But a demand for dower
in one parcel of land which belongs to two persons in severalty,
must be made upon each separately.   A joint demand would
not be good as to either.[4]   The heir or tenant therefore has
one month after such demand in which to assign the dower.
And he may always protect himself against a suit, if after such
demand he proceeds to set out dower to the widow fairly to
the extent of her right, for by so doing he acquires a good and
legal defence against any further claim.[5]   In New York, no
previous demand is required in order to give the widow her
action, which in that State is in the form of ejectment, instead
of the common-law form.[6]   Nor is it necessary to make demand of the heir where the husband died seised in order to
maintain an action for dower in New Jersey; nor can *tout temps
prist* be pleaded to the action.[7]   It has been held to be sufficient
to demand the dower of the minor and his guardian, where the
heir who is to set it out is under age.[8] Although it is usual to
demand dower in writing, it is not necessary to do so; it may
be done by parol;[9] and the one making it may be appointed
by parol.[10]   So it may be demanded by an attorney; nor is it
          necessary that the power of such attorney should be
[*229] in writing.[11]   And in Watson *v.* Watson,[12] *above
          cited, where the son of the demandant " asked him

---

[1] Pub. Stat. c. 174, § 2 ; unless such person is unknown to her or absent from
the State.

[2] Burbank *v.* Day, 12 Met. 557.   [3] Stevens *v.* Reed, 37 N. H. 49.

[4] Pond *v.* Johnson, 9 Gray, 193.   [5] Baker *v.* Baker, 4 Me. 67.

[6] Jackson *v.* Churchill, 7 Cow. 287 ; Ellicott *v.* Mosier, 7 N. Y. 201 ; s. c. 11
Barb. 574.

[7] Hopper *v.* Hopper, 22 N. J. 715.   [8] Young *v.* Tarbell, 37 Me. 509.

[9] Co. Lit. 32 b ; Baker *v.* Baker, 4 Me. 67 ; Page *v.* Page, 6 Cush. 196.

[10] Lothrop *v.* Foster, 51 Me. 367.

[11] Luce *v.* Stubbs, 35 Me. 92.   [12] Watson *v.* Watson, 10 C. B. 3.

(tie tenant) if ie would pay iis motier ier tiirds," to wiici ie replied, "No," tie demand was ield good, no question iaving been raised as to the autiority of tie son to make such request. But if a power of attorney be given in writing, it must contain sufficient autiority to make tie requisite demand, or it will be of no avail. Tierefore wiere tie power autiorized tie agent to demand dower in tie "aforesaid premises," but no premises iave been mentioned, it was ield so defective tiat no demand under it would lay tie foundation for an action.[1] No great particularity is required in the description of tie estate out of wiici tie dower is demanded. It will be sufficient if it give notice to tie tenant to wiat land it means to refer.[2] It is enougi tiat tie demand apprise the tenant, witi reasonable certainty, of tie claim made upon iim.[3] Tie demand must be made of tie tenant of tie free-iold, tiougi it need not be made upon tie land.[4] And a demand so made will be sufficient, tiougi suci tenant were afterwards to convey iis lands before suit brougit, and tiougi tie suit must in tiat case be against anotier person, wio is tie tenant of tie freeiold wien tie action is commenced.[5]

14. If tie widow siall iave taken tie proper preliminary measures witiout success, sie is entitled to an action for tie recovery of ier dower, witi damages for its detention, and a precept directed to the sieriff requiring iim to cause ier dower to be set off and possession delivered to ier, and to enforce the payment of tie damages wiici a jury siall iave ascertained.[6] Tiis is one of the tiree real actions wiici were retained in England under the repealing statute of 3 & 4 Wm. IV. c. 7, § 36, the otier two being *quare impedit*[7] and

[1] Sloan v. Whitman, 5 Cush. 532.
[2] Haynes v. Powers, 22 N. H. 590; Atwood v. Atwood, 22 Pick. 283; Bear v. Snyder, 11 Wend. 592; Ayer v. Spring, 10 Mass. 80.
[3] Davis v. Walker, 42 N. H. 482.
[4] Luce v. Stubbs, 35 Me. 92.
[5] Barker v. Blake, 36 Me. 433; Watson v. Watson, 70 Eng. Com. Law, 5, n.; Mass. Pub. Stat. c. 174, § 10; Parker v. Murphy, 12 Mass. 485.
[6] 2 Bl. Com. 136; 1 Bright, Hus. & Wife, 369; 1 Rolle, Abr. 683; Stearns, Real Act. 311-319.
[7] As this action is designed to try a disputed title to an advowson, or the right of presentation to a church, there is no action answering to it in the forms in use in the United States. Actions of dower and *quare impedit*, as special actions, are

ejectment. It is one of the two retained in Massa-
[*230] chusetts, the other being a writ of * entry upon disseisin.[1] There were formerly two forms of action of
dower. But the form in use in this country answers most
nearly to that known to the common law as "the writ of
dower *unde nihil habet*."[2] It must be brought in the county
where the land lies, like all real actions,[3] and lies only against
the tenant of the freehold at the time of commencing the action.[4] And this, as has been before stated, though he who
was tenant of the freehold when the demand was made shall,
in the mean time, have conveyed to another tenant.[5] Nor
can the tenant, though a minor, have the ordinary privilege
of an infant defendant in a real action, of having the "parol
demur," that is, of having the action continued in court till
he arrive at full age. And the obvious reason is, that the
widow is supposed to need the enjoyment of her dower for
her immediate support.[6] In some States the plea of non-
tenure may be pleaded in bar of such an action.[7] In others,
it must, to avail, be pleaded in abatement.[8] But the suit may
be against the tenant of the freehold, though he holds by
wrong, such a disseisor, abator, or intruder.[9] So if the owner
of the estate shall have bargained it away, but the deed has
not yet been delivered, he will be the party to be sued.[10] But

now done away with, and dower must be sued for by writ and summons as in any
other action, by the common law. Procedure Act of 1860. Upon the writ is
indorsed a notice that the plaintiff intends to declare in dower. Broom's Com.
Law, 119.

[1] Pub. Stat. c. 173, § 1 ; c. 174, § 1. In the writ of entry, in Massachusetts,
the demandant not only recovers damages covering mesne profits, but under a
state of things provided for by statute, the tenant may claim compensation for
betterments made by him while in possession of the demanded premises. Pub.
Stat. c. 173, §§ 12, 17, 18 ; Haven *v.* Adams, 8 Allen, 368. But where he has
made them without reason to suppose himself owner, he cannot claim such compensation. Daggett *v.* Tracy, 128 Mass. 167.

[2] 4 Kent, Com. 63 ; Stearns, Real Act. 302.　　　[3] Stearns, Real Act. 87.

[4] 1 Bright, Hus. & Wife, 398 ; Hurd *v.* Grant, 3 Wend. 340 ; Miller *v.* Beverly,
1 Hen. & M. 367 ; Ellicott *v.* Mosier, 11 Barb. 574.

[5] Barker *v.* Blake, 36 Me. 433.

[6] Stearns, Real Act. 107 ; 1 Bright, Hus. & Wife, 364.

[7] Casporus *v.* Jones, 7 Penn. St. 120.

[8] Manning *v.* Laboree, 33 Me. 343.

[9] Norwood *v.* Morrow, 4 Dev. & B. 442 ; Otis *v.* Warren, 16 Mass. 53.

[10] Jones *v.* Patterson, 12 Penn. St. 149.

in New York, the action being ejectment, it may be maintained against any tenant in possession, whether a freeholder or not.[1] The proper action of dower cannot be a joint one against the several tenants of separate parcels of estate, though originally derived from the husband, but each tenant must be sued separately in respect to the parcel of which he is tenant.[2] The action, moreover, is so personal in its nature on • the part of the demandant, that if she dies during its [*231] pendency the suit abates.[3] In Atkins v. Yeomans, judgment for dower was rendered, and by agreement between the parties certain persons were to act as commissioners to set out the dower and assess the damages, to be reported to the court for adjudication, and the demandant died before they had made their return. The court declined to enter judgment for damages and costs, and they add : " The action died with the demandant, and the judgment for damages cannot now be rendered."[4] • It is no objection to the action that some person other than the tenant holds a mortgage upon the premises, so that the widow is only dowable of an equity of redemption, unless the tenant holds under or by the right of such mortgage.[5]

15. If she prevails in her action, she obtains judgment for her dower and damages for its detention.[6]

16. Damages, as already remarked, were not originally recoverable in an action of dower. They were first given by the statute of Merton, ch. 1, in an action against the heir for the land of which the husband died seised, and are declared to be " the value of the whole dower," " from the time of the

• NOTE. — By the statute of Maryland the action of dower survives. 1 Hilliard, Real Prop. 154.

---

[1] Ellicott v. Mosier, 7 N. Y. 201 ; Ellis v. Ellis, 4 R. I. 110.

[2] Fosdick v. Gooding, 1 Me. 30 ; 1 Roper, Hus. & Wife, 437 ; Barney v. Frowner, 9 Ala. 901.

[3] Rowe v. Johnson, 19 Me. 146 ; Sandback v. Quigley, 8 Watts, 460 ; Atkins v. Yeomans, 6 Met. 438.

[4] Atkins v. Yeomans, 6 Met. 438. See also Rowe v. Johnson, 19 Me. 146 ; Turney v. Smith, 14 Ill. 242 ; Hildreth v. Thompson, 16 Mass. 191.

[5] Smith v. Eustis, 7 Me. 41 ; Thompson v. Boyd, 2 N. J. 543 ; Manning v. Laboree, 33 Me. 343 ; Hastings v. Stevens, 29 N. H. 564.

[6] Gen. Stat. c. 135, § 4 ; Leavitt v. Lamprey, 13 Pick. 382.

death of the husband unto the day that the said widow by judgment of our court have recovered seisin of her dower," &c.[1] But by the English law, damages were not recoverable of any but the heir or abator or their assigns, in respect to lands of which the husband died seised.[2] The vendee [*232] of the heir, therefore, would * be liable for damages in the same way as the heir himself,[3] but not the alienee of the husband.[4] The rule and measure of damages as to the mode of computing them seems to be the same in England and here, that is, one third of the value of the annual rents and profits of the estate out of which dower is claimed.[5] But in respect to the length of time for which this allowance shall be made, there is quite a difference in the laws of the different States.* In Virginia the widow can recover damages against her husband's alienee, in proceedings in equity, from the date of the subpœna.[6] In Pennsylvania she recovers from the death of the husband, where he died seised, although the tenant may have been in possession but a part of the time since.[7] But in Delaware, in such case, she could recover damages only from the time of purchase by the tenant.[8] In Alabama, if the action be against the heir, damages are allowed from the death of the husband. If against a purchaser, they cover only the time from the commencement of the suit.[9] In Ohio and South Carolina no damages are allowed in an action of dower.[10] In Missouri and Wisconsin the widow has damages against the

---

* NOTE. — The rule as above stated seems to be the settled law, although the point that an extra sum should be allowed for the illegal detention of the dower is raised, and authorities tending to sustain it are cited, in Fisher v. Morgan, Coxe, 125.

---

[1] Co. 2d Inst. 80.

[2] Co. Lit. 32 b; Stearns, Real Act. 312; Thompson v. Colier, Yelv. 112; Fisher v. Morgan, Coxe, 125.

[3] Hitchcock v. Harrington, 6 Johns. 290.

[4] 2 Crabb, Real Prop. 120; Embree v. Ellis, 2 Johns. 119.

[5] Winder v. Little, 4 Yeates, 152; Sedgwick on Damages, 130; Layton v. Butler, 4 Harringt. 507; 4 Kent, Com. 65.

[6] Tod v. Baylor, 4 Leigh, 498.   [7] Seaton v. Jamison, 7 Watts, 533.

[8] Newbold v. Ridgeway, 1 Harringt. 55; Green v. Tenant, 2 Harringt. 336.

[9] Beavers v. Smith, 11 Ala. 20.

[10] Heyward v. Cuthbert, 1 McCord, 386; Bank of United States v. Dunseth, 10 Ohio, 18.

1eir from t1e deat1 of the 1usband; against 1usband's alience, from the time of t1e demand for dower.[1] In Massac1usetts, damages are allowed from t1e time of t1e demand, if the action be against t1e person of w1om demand is made. If against a subsequent purc1aser, t1cy are only allowed from t1e time of 1is purc1ase * and a separate action on [*233] the case may be maintained against t1e prior tenant to recover damages from the time of demand to the time of 1is conveyance.[2] The law is the same in New York, in respect to a purc1aser, and damages are recoverable from t1e time of 1is purc1ase only.[3] And w1ere t1e 1usband died seised, t1e widow was 1eld entitled to rents and profits from t1e time of 1is deat1, to be apportioned upon the 1eirs and terre-tenants according to t1e lengt1 of time t1ey occupied.[4] In Maryland, if t1e widow recover dower at common law against t1e 1usband's alienee, she may afterwards recover, by proceedings in equity, t1e rents and profits from the time dower was demanded.[5] In Maine, New 1Iamps1ire, and R1ode Island, damages are recoverable only from demand. In New Jersey, Pennsylvania, and Tennessee, the same rule as to damages is applied as in t1e Englis1 courts, w1ere t1e claim is against the alienee of the 1usband, and t1ey are not allowed except w1ere t1e 1usband dies seised.[6] And in New York, in addition to the restriction above mentioned, the widow cannot claim damages for more t1an six years, nor for any time anterior to 1er demand made.[7] In Nort1 Carolina, in a process in equity to recover dower, a widow was 1eld entitled to an account for mesne profits from the deat1 of 1er 1usband up to t1e assignment of dower. And w1ere buildings w1ic1 had been insured were burned after t1e deat1 of the 1usband, and before dower was assigned, s1e was 1eld entitled to a *pro rata* s1are of t1e insurance money.[8] T1ese damages, as already

---

[1] McClanahan *v.* Porter, 10 Mo. 746 ; Thrasher *v.* Tyack, 15 Wisc. 256.

[2] Pub. Stat. c. 174, § 10 ; Whittaker *v.* Greer, 129 Mass. 417.

[3] Russell *v.* Austin, 1 Paige, 192.　　　[4] Hazen *v.* Thurber, 4 Johns. Ch. 604.

[5] Sellman *v.* Bowen, 8 Gill & J. 50.

[6] Fisher *v.* Morgan, Coxe, 125 ; Sharp *v.* Pettit, 4 Dall. 212 ; Waters *v.* Gooch, 6 J. J. Marsh. 586 ; Co. Lit. 32 b ; Doct. & Stud. Dial. 2, c. 13.

[7] Bell *v.* The Mayor, 10 Paige, 49, 70.

[8] Campbell *v.* Murphy, 2 Jones, Eq. 357, 363, 364.

stated, are ordinarily found by the jury; but if there be a judgment by default, the court may assess the damages by assent of demandant, or send the question to a jury.[1]*

17. The judgment in an action of dower is regarded as having a double character, the recovery of seisin being [*234] by force of *the common law, that of damages and costs by force of the statutes of Merton and Gloucester.[2] And these are so far independent of each other that the demandant may have a complete judgment for seisin of her dower, with damages or without them as the case may be.[3] And if verdict be for both, where no damages are recoverable, the court will treat the finding as to the damages as surplusage, and render judgment for the seisin.[4] But unless there be a judgment for her seisin of dower, she cannot have one for damages, — so that if by her death a recovery for the former fails, her estate has no remedy by way of damages for detention of the dower.[5] Nor can a demandant in an action of dower, as may be done in other real actions, enter upon the land recovered by the judgment without a formal writ of entry. And the reason is that in one case the demandant sues for and establishes his right to a specific parcel of land; in the other, the part she is to have can only be ascertained by the assignment of her dower.[6]

18. For this reason, after judgment in her favor, she may have a writ of *habere facias seisinam* directed to the sheriff, commanding him to cause her dower to be set out, and seisin

---

* NOTE. — The mode of assessing damages in the English courts varies in some respects from that in Massachusetts, as will be seen by referring to 2 Saund. 45, n. 4, or Co. Lit. 32 b, n. 4 ; but the subject hardly seems to be of sufficient importance for the student of American law to occupy more space in this work.

---

[1] Stearns, Real Act. 311 ; Perry v. Goodwin, 6 Mass. 498.

[2] 2 Crabb, Real Prop. 186 ; Taylor v. Brodrick, 1 Dana, 345 ; Sharp v. Pettit, 4 Dall. 212. The statutes of Merton and Gloucester are a part of the common law of Delaware. Layton v. Butler, 4 Harringt. 507.

[3] 2 Saund. 45, n. 4 ; Co. Lit. 32 b, n. 4 ; Waters v. Gooch, 6 J. J. Marsh. 586.

[4] Shirtz v. Shirtz, 5 Watts, 255.

[5] Atkins v. Yeomans, 6 Met. 438 ; Rowe v. Johnson, 19 Me. 146 ; Turney v. Smith, 14 Ill. 242 ; Tuck v. Fitts, 18 N. H. 171.

[6] Hildreth v. Thompson, 16 Mass. 191 ; Co. Lit. 34 b ; Stearns, Real Act. 318.

tiereof delivered to ier, and to make a return of his doings tiereon,[1] wiici writ may contain a clause of *fieri facias* for tie recovery of damages under such a form of judgment.[2] • But tie form of tie writ of seisin, and of [*235] tie precept to tie sieriff, would depend upon tie law of tie particular State wiere the judgment is rendered. Tius, tie form in Rastell is simply a command to the sieriff to make an assignment and full seisin of a tiird part of tie lands described, wio in iis return states tiat he ias so done.[3]

19. In some of tie States tie sieriff causes dower to be set out by commissioners, who act under oati. But tiougi tie sieriff is bound by iis precept to make a return of iis doings into tie court from wiici it issued, tie demandant is not obliged to wait until suci return is made and accepted before entering upon and taking possession of ier dower land. She may enter as soon as tie assignment is made and seisin given, subject only to the iazard of iaving ier title defeated by some irregularity in tie proceedings.[4] It sometimes iappens, iowever, tiat tie dower lands of tie widow are subject to a term of years created before marriage. If tiere were no rent issuing out of suci term, tie widow takes ier judgment witi a *cessat executio* until tie term siall iave expired.[5] If, in tie lease or grant of suci a term, rent was reserved and payable, the widow migit iave ier dower set off in the premises by metes and bounds, and, as reversioner, claim one tiird of tie rents and profits witiout any *cessat executio* upon ier judgment.[6]

20. As ias been more tian once stated, tie sieriff must, ordinarily, execute iis precept by assigning tie dower by metes and bounds, wiere tie same can be done.[7] How far

---

[1] Rastell, Entries, 235.

[2] Stearns, Real Act. 317 ; Benner *v.* Evans, 3 Penn. 454.

[3] Rastell, Entries, 235.

[4] Co. Lit. 37 b, n ; Parker *v.* Parker, 17 Pick. 236 ; Mansfield *v.* Pembroke, 5 Pick. 449.

[5] Co. Lit. 208 a, n. 105 ; Tud. Cas. 47 : Maundrell *v.* Maundrell, 7 Ves. 567.

[6] Co. Lit. 32 a ; Stoughton *v.* Leigh, 1 Taunt. 402 ; Weir *v.* Tate, 4 Ired. Eq. 264.

[7] Perkins, § 414 ; Stearns, Real Act. 318 ; Pierce *v.* Williams, 2 Penningt. 521.

1e may or must do t1is in respect to separate an*d* distinct parcels of land may depend upon circumstances. If t1e lands
were aliened in t1e life of t1e 1usband, t1e dower of t1e wife
       must be set out separately in t1e land of eac1 alienee.[1]
[*236] If t1e lands out of w1ic1 a * widow is dowable, and
       w1ic1 are 1eld by t1e same person, consist of parcels
of meadow, pasture, and corn land, t1e s1eriff is not bound to
set out a part of eac1 ; 1e may assign it all from one if it is
reasonable so to do.[2] But in suc1 and similar cases 1e is
bound to exercise sound and reasonable discretion. And
w1ere 1e set out to a widow, as 1er dower, a t1ird part by
metes and bounds of every c1amber in a 1ouse, t1e assignment was set aside, and a fine imposed upon t1e s1eriff for
contempt in so doing.[3] But w1ere certain rooms in a 1ouse
were set out wit1 t1e privilege of using t1e 1alls, stairways,
&c., for access to t1em, it was 1eld to be a good assignment.[4]
An assignment w1ic1 gave t1e widow a rig1t to cut wood
upon or depasture land not set to 1er for dower would not be
valid.[5]

W1ere, from t1e nature of t1e estate out of w1ic1 t1e dower
is to be assigned, it cannot be done by metes and bounds, it
may be done by giving a s1are in common of t1e estate, or
an alternate occupation, or ot1erwise as may best serve t1e
purposes of t1e law. In many cases a widow is dowable of
money w1en t1is is t1e proceeds of land. But t1is class of
cases will be considered 1ereafter, w1en equitable dower is
spoken of.[6] An instance of t1e former met1od of assigning,
w1ere it cannot be done by metes and bounds, would be t1at
out of an estate 1eld by t1e 1usband as tenant in common.
T1e s1eriff cannot set apart any portion of t1e estate as 1ers,
and t1e widow becomes by t1e assignment tenant in common
wit1 t1e ot1er owners of t1e land.[7] T1e case of a mill would

---

[1] Cook *v.* Fisk, Walker, 423 ; Coulter *v.* Holland, 2 Harringt. 330 ; Co. Lit.
35 a ; Doe *v.* Gwinnell, 1 Q. B. 682.

[2] 1 Bright, Hus. & Wife, 367.

[3] 2 Crabb, Real Prop. 147 ; 1 Bright, Hus. & Wife, 370 ; Abingdon's Case,
cited in Howard *v.* Candish, Palm. 264.

[4] White *v.* Story, 2 Hill, 543.   [5] Jones *v.* Jones, Busbee, N. C. 177.

[6] See *ante*, *163 ; *post*, *244, *et seq.*

[7] Fitzh. N. B. 149 ; 1 Bright, Hus. & Wife, 371.

be another example. In England she may be endowed of every third toll dish, or of a third part of the profits of the mill, and, it is added, she " may grind their toll free." [1]

By the law of Massachusetts, where a mill or other tenement cannot be divided without damage to the whole, dower is assigned of *the rents, issues, and profits [*237] thereof, to be had in common with the other owners of the estates.[2] So in the case of a ferry, where a share of its use, or of the profits, or a share of the time, should be assigned for dower.[3] Mines constitute a special class of estates, out of which a widow may be dowable, and the mode of assigning dower therein was fully considered in the case cited below.[4] It was there held that if the mine or mines formed a part of the value of the estate of which dower is to be had, it is not necessary that any part of such mines should be set out as dower, provided the widow have one third part in value of the entire estate assigned to her out of other parts of it. If the mine is embraced within what is set out by metes and bounds, it need not be described ; for, if open, it may be used and worked as part of the dower for her own exclusive use. If any part of a mine or mines is set out which does not form a part of the estate which is defined by metes and bounds, but still forms a part of the general estate of which she is dowable, it should be specifically described. If the mine or mines be in another person's land, and open and wrought, and the same can be divided by metes and bounds so as not to prevent the other owners or proprietors from enjoying a proper proportion of the profits thereof, her dower should be so divided and assigned. But if this cannot be done, the assignment should be so made as to give the widow one third part of the profits, as by a separate alternate enjoyment of the whole for short periods, or by giving her a certain proportion of the profits of such mine.[5] In making the assignment of dower, the estimate of the third part has reference to the productive value of the

[1] 2 Crabb, Real Prop. 148 ; Perkins, § 415 ; 1 Bright, Hus. & Wife, 372.

[2] Pub. Stat. c. 174, § 12 ; Stearns, Real Act. 319.

[3] Stevens r. Stevens, 3 Dana, 371.

[4] Stoughton r. Leigh, 1 Taunt. 402.

[5] See Coates r. Cheever, 1 Cow. 460, 478 ; Billings v. Taylor, 10 Pick. 460.

estate, and not the quantity. Such part of the estate should
be set out to her as will give her one third part of the annual
income or profits of the entire estate.[1] The time to which
this estimate must refer, if the estate were sold in the life of
the husband, and had been increased in productiveness by the
purchaser, would be that at which the husband parted with
it. If the husband die seised, it refers to the time of his
death.[2]

[*238]   *21. But if either party wish to raise objection to
the manner or extent of the assignment, it should be
done when the return of the officer who sets it out is made to
the court.[3]

22. Notwithstanding what has been said, the question of
the time in reference to which the value or income shall be
estimated, has presented difficulties which have led to different rules in different jurisdictions. If the case be one where
the claim is made of the heir, the rule is uniform in referring
to the value and condition of the estate as it is when the
dower is actually assigned, unless he shall have done acts to
deteriorate it since the death of the husband. If he has enhanced the value of it, it is his own folly to have done so
without first setting out the dower, and he cannot claim to
have these improvements allowed to him in making the estimate.[4] And if the heir were to sow the husband's lands after
his death, and these were to be set off to the widow, he could
not claim the crops as emblements belonging to him.[5] So if,
without the fault of the heir, the estate be diminished in
value between the death of the husband and the assignment
of the dower, she must bear, *pro rata*, this depreciation.[6] Nor
could the sheriff in assigning dower have any regard to the
fact that the estate had been deteriorated by the wrongful
act of the heir. He could only set it out in reference to the

---

[1] Coates *v.* Cheever, 1 Cow. 460, 476: McDaniel *v.* McDaniel, 3 Ired. 61 ; Smith
v. Smith, 5 Dana, 179 ; Leonard *v.* Leonard, 4 Mass. 533 ; Park, Dow. 255.

[2] Davis *v.* Walker, 42 N. H. 482.

[3] Chapman *v.* Schroeder, 10 Ga. 321.

[4] Catlin *v.* Ware, 9 Mass. 218 ; Thompson *v.* Morrow, 5 S. & R. 289 ; 1 Bright,
Hus. & Wife, 385 ; Co. Lit. 32 a ; Powell *v.* Monson, 3 Mason, 347, 368, 369.

[5] Parker *v.* Parker, 17 Pick. 236 ; Co. 2d Inst. 81.

[6] 1 Bright, Hus. & Wife, 385 ; Powell *v.* Monson, 3 Mason, 368.

then condition of the estate.[1] The dowress's remedy for the
injury sustained by such deterioration must be sought by an
action for damages,[2] though Judge Story, in Powell v. Monson,[3] is disposed to doubt the right of a widow in such cases
to recover damages of the heir. The questions in respect to
which the chief difficulty has arisen, relate to cases where the
property was aliened by the husband in his lifetime, and had
been diminished or enhanced in value between the
alienation * and the time of assigning dower. In some [*239]
important particulars the English and American law
differs. Thus in a recent case it was held "that dower
attaches to the husband's real property at the period of his
death, according to its then actual value, without regard to
the hands which brought it into the condition in which it is
found." And the court, Denman, C. J., cites with approbation the opinion of Sir Edw. Sugden, "that the widow is entitled to have assigned to her as her dower so much in value
as is equal to a third in value, according to the condition of
the estate at the time of her husband's death."[4] So far as the
rule becomes applicable to the value of estates which have
been deteriorated by waste or mismanagement while in the
hands of an alienee of the husband, it is believed to be the
same in both countries. The nature of a wife's interest during her husband's life is such, that if an alienee of the estate
cause a permanent damage to it, she is without remedy, and
must therefore be content to take her dower out of the estate
as she finds it, when her right becomes consummated by the
death of her husband.[5] Nor does there appear to be any
essential difference between the laws of the two countries,
where the estate after the alienation by the husband, and be-

[1] Co. Lit. 32 a ; Powell v. Monson, 3 Mason, 368.

[2] 1 Bright, Hus. & Wife, 385 ; 2 Crabb, Real Prop. 138 ; 1 Roper, Hus. &
Wife, 349.

[3] Powell v. Monson, 3 Mason, 368 ; Campbell v. Murphy, 2 Jones, Eq. 389.

[4] Doe v. Gwinnell, 1 Q. B. 682 ; Campbell v. Murphy, sup. 363.

[5] McClanahan v. Porter, 10 Mo. 746 ; Thompson v. Morrow, 5 S. & R. 289 ;
Perkins, § 329 ; 1 Bright, Hus. & Wife, 386 ; Powell v. Monson, 3 Mason, 368.
And the suggestion of relief in equity thrown out in Beavers v. Smith, 11 Ala. 20,
does not seem to have been acted on in any decided case. In Westcott v. Campbell, 11 R. I. 378, however, the rule itself is mentioned with disapproval.

fore the assignment of the dower, has become enhanced or
diminished in value by natural or extraneous causes, independent of improvements made by the alienee himself. The
widow in such case may share in the increased, as she must
in the decreased, value of the estate.[1] Two or three of the
cases cited will illustrate these propositions. The case of
Powell v. Monson was one where the alienees had erected
large and expensive works for manufacturing purposes, which
enhanced the value of the lands very much, independent of
the mere value of the structures placed upon the premises.

The judge held " that the dower must be adjudged
[*240] according to the value of the land in controversy at *the
time of the assignment, excluding all the increased
value from the improvements actually made *upon the premises*
by the alienee, leaving the dowress the full benefit of any
increase of value arising from circumstances unconnected with
these improvements."[2] Thompson v. Morrow was the case of
an estate in the city of Pittsburg, enhanced in value by the
growth of and rise of property in that city. Tilghman, C. J.,
says, "Throwing those (the improvements made by the purchaser) out of the estimate, she shall be endowed according to
the value at the time her dower shall be assigned."[3] In the case
of Braxton v. Coleman, the estate sold by the husband had a
mill standing upon it, which was carried away and another was
built in its stead, and afterwards a third and much enlarged
one was erected, and it was held that the widow could only
claim dower out of the land. In New York, owing to the
language of the statutes of that State, the value of the estate
at the time of its alienation is the criterion for determining
what proportion shall be set off as the widow's share.[4] And
a similar rule prevails in Virginia, Michigan, Nebraska, and
Oregon.[5] So also in Alabama, though at first treated as

---

[1] Smith v. Addleman, 5 Blackf. 406 ; Wms. Real Prop. 191, note ; 1 Cruise,
Dig. 171 ; Powell v. Monson, 3 Mason, 347, 375 ; Johnston v. Vandyke, 6 McLean,
422 ; Braxton v. Coleman, 5 Call, 433 ; Bowie v. Berry, 1 Md. Ch. Dec. 452.

[2] Powell v. Monson, 3 Mason, 375. See Gore v. Brazier, 3 Mass. 523, 544.

[3] Thompson v. Morrow, 5 S. & R. 289. See 4 Kent, Com. 67–69 ; Dunseth v.
U. S. Bk., 6 Ohio, 76.

[4] Braxton v. Coleman, 5 Call, 433 ; Walker v. Schuyler, 10 Wend. 480.

[5] Tod v. Baylor, 4 Leigh, 498 ; Mich. Comp. L. 1879, § 4275 ; Neb. Gen. St.
1873, c. 17, § 7 ; Oreg. Gen. L. 1872, p. 585.

doubtful how far a widow could avail herself of the rise in value of the estate by extraneous causes,[1] she is not allowed to share therein.[2] The doctrine, however, which is laid down by Judge Story and Ch. J. Tilghman, above stated, may be considered as in accordance with the general policy of the American law, and as being generally the common law of the country.[3] And in respect to the question whether, and how far a widow shall have the benefit of improvements made by the alienee of the husband, the law in the United States seems to be uniform, and will be found to be much more in harmony with the policy of a young and thriving community, where new lands are purchased for the purpose of *improving them [*241] by the expenditure of money and labor, and where villages and cities are seen springing up within the life of a single individual. For such a community the rule of the English law would be found altogether unsuited, though it may be well adapted to the habits of a people where the inconveniences growing out of the exercise of dower rights have for a long time been, to a great extent, avoided by marriage settlements and other similar provisions. The citation of a single case from each of several States, out of the many that may be readily found in the reports, will be sufficient to establish the law of this country to be, that where buildings have been erected, improvements made, or the value of lands enhanced by money expended or labor done by the alienee of the husband, upon the land out of which dower is claimed, the benefit of these is not to be shared by the widow.[4] Thus, in Maine,

[1] Barnoy v. Frowner, 9 Ala. 901.

[2] Beavers v. Smith, 11 Ala. 20 ; Francis v. Garrard, 18 Ala. 794 ; Thrasher v. Pinkard, 23 Ala. 616.

[3] Wooldridge v. Wilkins, 3 How. (Miss.) 360 ; Mosher v. Mosher, 15 Me. 371 ; Green v. Tennant, 2 Harringt. 336 ; Summers v. Babb, 13 Ill. 483 ; Sedgwick on Damages, 133 and note; Dunseth v. U. S. Bk., 6 Ohio, 76. See also 4 Kent, Com. 68.

[4] 4 Kent, Com. 65 ; Humphrey v. Phinney, 2 Johns. 484 ; Thompson v. Morrow, 5 S. & R. 289 ; Catlin v. Ware, 9 Mass. 218 ; Powell v. Monson, 3 Mason, 347 ; Tod v. Baylor, 4 Leigh, 498 ; Leggett v. Steele, 4 Wash. C. C. 305 ; Wilson v. Oatman, 2 Blackf. 223 ; Brown v. Duncan, 4 McCord, 346 ; Wooldridge v. Wilkins, 3 How. (Miss.) 360 ; Larrowe v. Beam, 10 Ohio, 498 ; Hobbs v. Harvey, 16 Me. 80 ; Barney v. Frowner, 9 Ala. 901 ; McClanahan v. Porter, 10 Mo. 746 ; Bowie v. Berry, 3 Md. Ch. Dec. 359 ; Rawlins v. Buttel, 1 Houst. (Del.) 224.

where improvements had been made by the alienee, the widow
had such a share of the whole estate set out to her as would
produce an income equal to one third part of what the whole
estate would produce if no improvements had been made upon
it after it had been conveyed by the husband.[1] And in Alabama,
where a dilapidated mill upon the premises was torn down by
the alienee of the husband, and a new and expensive structure
erected in its stead, it was held that the widow of the grantor
was not entitled to any share of the improvements, and that
her dower should be set out with reference to the value of the
premises at the time of the alienation, though the destruction
of the old mill afforded a proper case for compensation to the
widow by a court of equity.[2]

23. In respect to the time when and manner in which the
tenant is to suggest that improvements have been
[*242] made in the *premises, in order to have a proper
judgment rendered in any case, the law does not seem
to be uniform. It should be done by some proper plea or suggestion upon the record, and not by the way of controverting
the right of the demandant to recover her dower.[3] And where
the tenant, by his plea, denied the marriage and seisin of the
husband, the court say, "We cannot, from these pleadings,
understand that any improvements have been made since then
(the alienation), or of what nature or value, to be excluded
from the judgment to be rendered."[4] In New York, the court
say, the value may be ascertained in one of three ways : either
by a jury upon the trial of the issue, or by the sheriff on the
writ of seisin, or by a writ of inquiry founded upon proper
suggestions.[5] It is suggested in a work on Real Actions, of
high authority, that a convenient mode of doing this would be
by having the increased value found by the jury at the bar of
the court, as is done in actions to recover lands where the
tenant claims allowance for improvements.[6]

[1] Carter v. Parker, 28 Me. 509 ; Manning v. Laboree, 33 Me. 343. Where,
however, the grantee had subdivided the land, the widow was entitled, as against
each parcel, to the general rise in value from the improvements made on the others. Boyd v. Carlton, 69 Me. 200.

[2] Beavers v. Smith, 11 Ala. 20 ; Sturtevant v. Phelps, 16 Gray, 50.

[3] Stearns, Real Act. 317 ; Coxe v. Higbee, 6 Halst. 395.

[4] Ayer v. Spring, 10 Mass. 80.   [5] Dolf v. Basset, 15 Johns. 21.

[6] Stearns, Real Act. 317 ; Mass. Pub. Stat. c. 173, §§ 17-23.

24. It sometimes happens that the assignment of dower proves to be inoperative, by the widow's being evicted from the land assigned to her, by a better title. In such case, her right to any redress by the way of a new assignment depends upon whether the dower is of common right or against common right. In the one case she may have her dower assigned *de novo* out of the balance of the estate ; in the other, she may not. Where she has accepted dower which has been assigned against common right, she has no remedy if it fails.[1] She could not, under either mode of assignment, avail herself, for relief, of the covenant of warranty made to her husband, since she is not the assignee of the whole estate in the lands set out to her as dower.[2] If her dower was at first set off upon a * judgment of court, her remedy, in case [*243] she is deprived of any part of her dower land, would be by *scire facias*, whereupon a new writ of *habere facias* would issue, which is to be served and returned like the first.[3] Nor is this remedy of an assignment *de novo* confined to a claim in favor of the widow alone. It may be applied, in some cases, to reduce the dower set out to her. Thus, where there was an action pending against the husband for the recovery of a pretty large proportion of his estate, at the time of his death, and dower was assigned to his widow out of the entire estate, and afterwards the demandant prevailed in his action and recovered a large part of the estate of which husband died seised, not set out to her, it was held that a new assignment should be made, having reference to the estate belonging in fact to the husband.[4]

25. A widow's remedy in equity for the recovery of dower is, in some respects, broader than at law. It embraces a large class of cases for which the common law furnishes no adequate remedy. Among these are all cases of trust estates and equities of redemption, and also many cases where, by sale or

[1] Jones *v.* Brewer, 1 Pick. 314 ; Scott *v.* Hancock, 13 Mass. 162 ; Holloman *v.* Holloman, 5 Sm. & M. 559 ; Mantz *v.* Buchanan, 1 Md. Ch. Dec. 202 ; French *v.* Pratt, 27 Me. 381 ; Tud. Cas. 52 ; Perkins, § 418.
[2] St. Clair *v.* Williams, 7 Ohio, 2d Pt. 110.
[3] Stearns, Real Act. 321 ; 2 Crabb, Real Prop. 151.
[4] Singleton *v.* Singleton, 5 Dana, 87.

otherwise, the land has been converted into money, without extinguishing the widow's right in equity to share in the proceeds. A resort to equity is always a convenient and desirable mode, where it is necessary to call upon the tenant to disclose his title or state an account of mesne profits, and the like ;[1] though in all cases where the widow's right of dower is controverted in proceedings in equity, the court sends the case to a court of common-law jurisdiction to have the question determined by a jury.[2] And in Vermont, if demandant first goes into chancery for her dower, in order to clear off mortgages and the like, the court in the end, in order to the final assignment of the dower, remit the proceedings to the probate court,[3] which goes on and completes the process.

Among the cases where the only remedy for the re-[*244] covery of dower is *through a court of chancery, are those where it is claimed out of an equity of redemption, and the claim is against the mortgagee or his assigns, even though the mortgagee may have purchased the husband's equity of redemption.[4] And the same rule applies where a party interested has redeemed the mortgage, and the widow of the mortgagor demands dower against him.[5] So chancery has exclusive jurisdiction where the estate out of which dower is claimed was held in trust, actually or constructively, for the benefit of the husband. These points may be better illustrated by referring to a few decided cases than by any statement of a general proposition. Thus, in Smiley v. Wright, and also in Taylor v. McCrackin,[6] the estate had been bargained for, and a greater or smaller proportion of the purchase-money paid by the husband, but no deed had been

[1] 2 Crabb, Real Prop. 189 ; Swaine v. Perine, 5 Johns. Ch. 482.

[2] Park, Dow. 329 ; Swaine v. Perine, 5 Johns. Ch. 482 ; Sellman v. Bowen, 8 Gill & J. 50.   [3] Danforth v. Smith, 23 Vt. 247.

[4] Bird v. Gardner, 10 Mass. 366 ; Gibson v. Crehore, 3 Pick. 475 ; Swaine v. Perine, 5 Johns. Ch. 482 ; Vandyne v. Thayre, 19 Wend. 162 ; Heth v. Cocke, 1 Rand. 344 ; Wooldridge v. Wilkins, 3 How. (Miss.) 360 ; Smith v. Eustis, 7 Me. 41 ; Thompson v. Boyd, 22 N. J. 543 ; Brown v. Lapham, 3 Cush. 551 ; Woods v. Wallace, 30 N. H. 384 ; Wing v. Ayer, 53 Me. 138 ; McArthur v. Franklin, 16 Ohio St. 193, 205.

[5] Cass v. Martin, 6 N. H. 25 ; Gibson v. Crehore, 5 Pick. 146 ; Hastings v. Stevens, 29 N. H. 564.

[6] Smiley v. Wright, 2 Ohio, 506 ; Taylor v. McCrackin, 2 Blackf. 260.

made, and the widow sought to share in the benefit of the purchase. Where an estate was devised, charged with the payment of a sum of money, and the widow of the devisee sought to have her dower set out in the premises, it was held that it could only be done by her contributing, or offering to contribute, her just proportion of her charge upon the land.[1]

Where the wife joined in a mortgage containing a power of sale, and there was reserved to the mortgagor whatever surplus, in the event of a sale, there might be after satisfying the mortgage debt, his widow was held entitled to her dower out of such surplus, and a court of equity secured the same to her, by causing one third part of it to be invested for that purpose.[2] So where the husband died seised of land for which a part of the purchase-money was due, and the estate was sold by the administrator by order of court, and * the [*245] purchase-money paid out of it, leaving a surplus, the court held the wife entitled to her dower out of such surplus.[3] In the above case of Denton v. Nanny, the court of New York held that the right of wife in a mortgaged estate would not be barred by proceedings against her husband to which she was not a party, and that, in such case, the court would have one third of the surplus proceeds of the sale of the estate, after paying the mortgage, set apart and invested on interest for the joint lives of her and her husband, and for her life, if surviving him, as her dower right.[4] So where, as in

---

[1] Clough v. Elliott, 23 N. H. 182 ; post, pl. 27.

[2] Denton v. Nanny, 8 Barb. 618.　　　　[3] Denton v. Nanny, 8 Barb. 616.

[4] Brewer v. Vanarsdale, 6 Dana, 204 ; Mills v. Van Voorhis, 23 Barb. 125, 136. The cases sustaining the doctrine of the text have already been cited, ante, *165 and note ; and that the inchoate right of dower will be protected in equity, and the wife's rights in the surplus after satisfying the mortgage debt will be sustained, seems established by the clear weight of authority. The case of Frost v. Peacock, 4 Edw. Ch. 678, ante, *182, is manifestly inconsistent with all the later cases on this point in New York, as well as those in other States ; and Newhall v. Lynn Sav. Bk., 101 Mass. 428, to the same effect, probably rests on the limited equity jurisdiction possessed by the court that decided it. It certainly did not proceed . on the want of interest in the wife, as the same court had just recognized inchoate dower as a property right entitling the wife to redeem, Davis v. Wetherell, 13 Allen, 60 ; and not subject to legislative abrogation, Dunn v. Sargent, 101 Mass. 336, 340. Where the wife is party to the foreclosure, a different rule may prevail. Titus v. Neilson, 5 Johns. Ch. 452. In giving relief, the rule has been adopted by some courts to set aside one third of the surplus in trust to permit the wife

New York, the surrogate has power, when the husband dies indebted, to cause the estate to be sold, discharged of the widow's claim for dower, the court will cause one third part of the purchase-money to be put at interest, for her benefit, as dower.[1]   And it may be laid down as an almost universal proposition, that where estates out of which widows were entitled to dower have been sold by order of court, or have been so sold as to give courts of equity jurisdiction over the money, these courts will allow the widow's dower out of the moneys.[2]   In Jennison v. Hapgood,[3] the executor of a will sold his testator's mortgaged estate, and purchased it himself, paying the mortgage in part out of the assets in his hands, and in part out of his own funds; and the widow, as she chose to affirm the sale, was held entitled to dower of one third part of what the estate sold for, and one third part of what was paid towards the mortgage out of the assets of the estate.   In Church v. Church,[4] shares of tenants in common were sold by order of court to effect partition, and the widow of one of the tenants was held entitled to dower out of the proceeds of the sale.   And the cases are numerous where mortgages in which the wife has joined have been foreclosed, after the death of the husband, by sale, in which the [*246] widow has shared * as dower in the proceeds of the surplus after satisfying the mortgage.[5]   So where the vendor, holding a lien for purchase-money, enforces it after the husband's death by a sale under decree of chancery, the vendee's widow is entitled to dower in the surplus after satis-

to receive the income when a widow, Vreeland v. Jacobus, 19 N. J. Eq. 231 ; but the better rule — at least, where any one but the husband is interested in the surplus — is to estimate the present value at a sum in gross.   Unger v. Leiter, 32 Ohio St. 210.

   [1] Lawrence v. Miller, 1 Sandf. 516 ; s. c. 2 N. Y. 245 ; Higbie v. Westlake, 14 N. Y. 281.

   [2] Jennison v. Hapgood, 14 Pick. 345 ; Titus v. Neilson, 5 Johns. Ch. 452 ; Church v. Church, 3 Sandf. Ch. 434 ; Willet v. Beatty, 12 B. Mon. 172 ; Mills v. Van Voorhis, 23 Barb. 125.

   [3] 14 Pick. 345.

   [4] Church v. Church, 3 Sandf. Ch. 434; Warren v. Twesley, 10 Mo. 39 ; Weaver v. Gregg, 6 Ohio St. 547, 552.

   [5] Smith v. Jackson, 2 Edw. Ch. 28 : Keith v. Trapier, 1 Bailey, Eq. 63 ; Hawley v. Bradford, 9 Paige, 200 ; Hartshorne v. Hartshorne, 2 N. J. Eq. 349.

fying the lien.[1]　And where several tenants in common, with their wives, conveyed the estate to trustees to sell, one of the grantors having died, his widow was held entitled to one third of the income of the money for which his share sold, as her dower.[2]　Without multiplying illustrations from decided cases, a leading Massachusetts case will serve the purpose upon several of the points above stated.[3]　The demandant joined with her husband in a mortgage to one B.　The husband died insolvent, and his administrators sold his equity of redemption for the payment of debts, to Crehore, the defendant, who gave his bond conditioned to pay the debt due B. Subsequently B assigned his mortgage to the defendant, who soon after mortgaged the premises to J P, but had entered upon and rented them and received rent for the same.　The plaintiff, without demanding dower of B or defendant, and without having had dower set off to her, brought assumpsit against the defendant for a share of the rents.　The court held that the action would not lie, her only remedy being in equity against the mortgagee or his assigns, and that she could only avail herself of her right by paying her proportion of the mortgage debt.　They held further, that the purchasing in of the mortgage by the defendant was not a payment and extinguishment of it as to the widow who had signed the deed. The widow, thereupon, brought her bill in equity, offering to redeem the mortgage, and claiming to be admitted to dower in the premises.[4]　It was held by the court that she might maintain the bill before her dower had been assigned to * her, though she could not have maintained a writ [*247] of entry before such assignment, for her legal right was inchoate until assignment made.　Before she redeems the mortgage, she has no right to demand an assignment of dower as against the mortgage.　Nor is it necessary to have dower previously assigned by the heirs, for she cannot redeem a part of the mortgaged premises without redeeming the residue also, if required by the mortgagee.[5]　It was accordingly held that

---

[1] Williams v. Wood, 1 Humph. 408 ; McClure v. Harris, 12 B. Mon. 261 ; Willet v. Beatty, 12 B. Mon. 172.　　[2] Hawley v. James, 5 Paige, 318.

[3] Gibson v. Crehore, 3 Pick. 475.　　[4] Gibson v. Crehore, 5 Pick. 146.

[5] Cass v. Martin, 6 N. H. 25 ; Wing v. Ayer, 53 Me. 138, 142.

she could have dower, but must, to that end, redeem the mortgage, and as the mortgagee was not obliged to accept his debt in parcels, but might insist upon its being paid in an entire sum, and the widow was obliged to do this to save her estate, she thereby became an equitable assignee of the mortgage, with the right to hold the estate under it until the owner of the equity of redemption came in and contributed, *pro rata*, his share of the mortgage debt, she keeping down in effect one third part of the interest of the mortgage debt during her life. But where the mortgage had been foreclosed, except as to the widow, or the mortgagee had acquired the equity of redemption, the court, instead of requiring the widow, before claiming dower, to redeem the mortgage from the tenant, as mortgagee, and then requiring him, as holder of the equity, to contribute to redeem, permitted, in order to avoid this circuity of action, the widow to have dower assigned to her, contributing her proportion of the mortgage debt, or, as held in a similar case in New Hampshire, paying the same into court for the use of the holder of the mortgage.[1]

By a statute in Massachusetts the widow may have an action of dower against the heir or other person claiming under the husband, who shall have redeemed the mortgage upon the estate.[2]   But where a wife joined in a mortgage, and the husband's equity of redemption was afterwards sold on execution, and came by mesne conveyance to the holder of the mortgage, it was held that the only remedy for the wife, for her dower, in such case, was in equity.[3]   And where a tenant in common joined with his co-tenant in executing a mortgage of the common estate, and then married, and then conveyed his interest in the estate to his co-tenant, who discharged the mortgage, it was held that the wife of the first-mentioned tenant might claim her dower in the half of the estate, after deducting the amount of the mortgage from the value thereof.[4]   And [*248] the same rule applies in all cases *where the owner

---

[1] Van Vronker v. Eastman, 7 Met. 157; Bell v. The Mayor, 10 Paige, 49, 70; Wood v. Wallace, 30 N. H. 384.

[2] Pub. Stat. c. 124, § 5.   [3] Farwell v. Cotting, 8 Allen, 211.

[4] Pynchon v. Lester, 6 Gray, 314.   See Newton v. Cook, 4 Gray, 46; Snyder v. Snyder, 6 Mich. 470.

of the life-estate and the remainder-man are required to contribute their respective proportions of the mortgage debt.[1] Instead of requiring the wife to contribute toward the payment of the debt, the commissioners may estimate the entire worth or value of such annuity by mathematical rules.[2] The duration of the widow's life, upon which such calculation is to be made, must, of necessity, be problematical. But courts are in the habit of adopting computations as to the probable duration of life, which are contained in tables calculated upon a great number of lives, and supposed to approximate the true average of life at its various periods. In Massachusetts the tables of Dr. Wigglesworth received the approval of the court;[3] in New York the statute prescribes the Portsmouth or Northampton tables.[4] But those known as the Carlisle Tables are elsewhere generally in use in this country for such purposes, except in Maryland, where Dr. Halley's tables were adopted;[5] Pennsylvania, where the Carlisle tables are held not authoritative; and Kentucky, where the American Life Annuity Tables are adopted.[6] In applying these tables to particular cases, reference is had to the health as well as the age of the person. In some cases the mortgagee may have been in receipt of the rents of the estate where the widow may seek by redemption to have her dower in the estate, and rules are adopted in such cases for ascertaining the balance that may be due. But it would be entering too much in detail to do anything more than to refer to them here.[7]

26. A similar rule is applied in estimating the relative value

[1] Swaine v. Perine, 5 Johns. Ch. 482; Gibson v. Crobore, 5 Pick. 146.

[2] The principles upon which this is done are stated in Bell v. The Mayor, 10 Paige, 49, 71.

[3] Estabrook v. Hapgood, 10 Mass. 315, n.; Houghton v. Hapgood, 13 Pick. 154.

[4] N. Y. Laws, 1870, c. 717, § 5.

[5] Abercrombie v. Riddle, 3 Md. Ch. Dec. 320; but see Dorsey v. Smith, 7 Har. & J. 367.

[6] Shippen's App. 80 Pa. St. 391; Alexander v. Bradley, 3 Bush, 667. A much more comprehensive set of tables has recently been prepared on the basis of the Carlisle Tables by Messrs. Giauque and McClure, and entitled Dower and Curtesy Tables; Cincinnati, 1882.

[7] Van Vronker v. Eastman, 7 Met. 157; Tucker v. Buffum, 16 Pick. 46. See 2 Scribner, Dow. (2d ed.) 663–694, where the history and law on this subject are fully set forth.

of a widow's dower to that of the whole estate, as in ascertaining the share of any charge or burden upon the estate which she must bear as dowress. And this is especially applicable where she is to be endowed out of moneys, the proceeds of the sale of real estate, from which is to be deducted what the tenant may have paid to redeem the mortgage, assigning the widow her dower according to the value of the residue.[1] If the husband be the grantee of a part of the mortgaged premises, and his widow seeks to recover dower in the same, she will in the end be obliged to contribute or allow such part of the mortgage debt as her interest in her husband's portion of the estate bears in value to the whole estate.[2] Where the widow pursues *her remedy in [*249] equity for the recovery of dower, it seems that the setting out of the dower, as well as the ascertaining the amount she shall contribute, may be done by a master or by commissioners, in the discretion of the court.[3] If, however, she shall have had her dower set out at common law, without reference to the mortgage, she may have her bill to redeem, and as between her and her reversioner and the owner of the other two thirds of the estate, she must contribute, *pro rata*, according to the relative values of their respective interests.[4]

27. In determining the amount which the dowress shall contribute toward the mortgage debt as forming her *pro rata* portion thereof, the rule is to require her to pay what will be equivalent to one third of the annual interest during her life.[5] But this must be paid in a gross sum, and not in the way of an annual payment, unless the mortgagee elects not to enforce the payment of the principal sum, in which case she must contribute to keep down one third of the interest.[6] This gross sum is calculated by considering this interest as an annuity, to continue as long as, by the chances of life, she is to live, and computing its present worth.

---

1 Pub. Stat. c. 124, § 5 ; Newton *v.* Cook, 4 Gray, 46.

2 Carll *v.* Butman, 7 Me. 102.

3 Swaine *v.* Perine, 5 Johns. Ch. 482. See also Van Vronker *v.* Eastman, 7 Met. 157, and Wood *v.* Wallace, 30 N. H. 384.

4 Danforth *v.* Smith, 23 Vt. 247.

5 Swaine *v.* Perine, 5 Johns. Ch. 482 ; McArthur *v.* Franklin, 16 Ohio St. 193, 205 ; *ante*, pl. 25.

6 Bell *v.* The Mayor, 10 Paige, 70 ; Wing *v.* Ayer, 53 Me. 138.

So, on the other hand, where money is assigned in lieu of dower, the widow receives, in most of the States, a gross sum instead of an annuity, or a share of the annual income.[1] In others it is held that such a composition cannot be made by order of the court except by agreement of the parties.[2] In South Carolina, the courts adopt as an arbitrary rule the principle that a widow's estate for life in one third is equal to one sixth of the entire fee in the whole estate.[3] In Alabama, Tennessee, and in the United States courts, it is not held competent to assign to a widow a gross sum. It can only be decreed that the annual value of the dower be paid her annually.[4] But * in Maryland, Kentucky, [*250] and Maine, cases have arisen where the courts have decreed her a sum in gross in such cases, calculated upon her chances of life.[5] And the same rule is adopted in Massachusetts. In New York, in an early case, the court, without going into the reasons for so doing, directed the fund out of which her dower was to come, to be invested, and the income paid over to her during life.[6]

[1] These are New York, Connecticut, Delaware, Pennsylvania, New Jersey, North Carolina, Ohio, West Virginia, Michigan, Wisconsin, Minnesota, and perhaps others. 2 Scribner, Dow. 654, n., statutes and cases cited; W. Va. Rev. Stat. c. 70, § 17–19.

[2] Virginia, Georgia, and Arkansas. 2 Scribner, Dow. *ubi supra*.

[3] Wright v. Jennings, 1 Bailey, 277; Garland v. Crow, 2 Bailey, 24. *Ante*, p. *89, note.

[4] Johnson v. Elliott, 12 Ala. 112; Beavers v. Smith, 11 Ala. 20; Francis v. Garrard, 18 Ala. 794; Lewis v. James, 8 Humph. 537; Summers v. Donnell, 7 Heisk. 565; Herbert v. Wren, 7 Cranch, 370.

[5] Goodburn v. Stevens, 1 Md. Ch. Dec. 420, 441; Brewer v. Vanarsdale, 6 Dana, 204; Simonton v. Gray, 34 Me. 50; Carll v. Butman, 7 Me. 102; Jennison v. Hapgood, 14 Pick. 345.

[6] Titus v. Neilson, 5 Johns. Ch. 452. As has more than once been stated, in most, if not all the States, the courts of probate jurisdiction have cognizance of matters of dower so far as to issue process for setting it off in the estates of deceased persons, where the principal estate shall have been the subject of settlement in such court. But the details of the law on this subject do not seem to come within the purposes of the present work.

SECTION VI.

NATURE OF THE ESTATE IN DOWER.

1. Interest of wife — in dower.
2. Interest of widow before assignment.
3. Estate of dowress after assignment.
4. Tenure of dowress as to fealty.
5. Incidents to dower.

1. THE nature of the interest which, inchoate in the wife, becomes consummate in the widow, in the way of dower, deserves a distinct notice, since, in many respects, it is unlike any other known to the law.[1]   At common law, the moment her coverture and her husband's seisin concur, she acquires a right which nothing but her death or her voluntary act can defeat, unless it be by an exercise of sovereignty by the forms of the law in appropriating the estate of the husband to a public use.   No adverse possession, therefore, as against her husband, however long continued, can affect her right to recover dower after his decease.[2]   It is no right which her husband can bar or incumber ; nor she herself, except by deed in which her husband joins, and then it is only in the way of estoppel, for her deed even of grant does not pass any title to the estate.[3]   She has not, in this stage of her right, even a *chose in action* in respect to the estate; nor can she protect it in any way from waste or deterioration by her husband or [*251] his alienee ; nor is her right at law in any sense,* an interest in real estate, nor property of which value can be predicated.[4]   She cannot convey it, nor is it a thing to be assigned by her during the life of the husband.[5]

2. But immediately upon the death of her husband, her right becomes consummate and perfect; and if the heir then waste or deteriorate the estate, she may have a remedy for the loss thereby occasioned to her.   But as her right is still a mere

---

[1] Park, Dow. 334.

[2] Durham *v.* Angier, 20 Me. 242 ; Moore *v.* Frost, 3 N. H. 126.

[3] Learned *v.* Cutler, 18 Pick. 9.   Cf. Saxon *v.* Gray, 14 R. I. 641.

[4] Moore *v.* The Mayor, 8 N. Y. 110 ; McArthur *v.* Franklin, 16 Ohio St. 193, 200.   As to her rights in equity, see *ante*, *165, 245 and notes.

[5] Gunnison *v.* Twitchell, 38 N. H. 62.

chose in action, she has nothing of which *estate* can, at this stage of her interest, be predicated.[1] She is not seised of any part of the lands, on the death of her husband, by any right of dower, until it is assigned to her.[2] In Vermont, however, she becomes entitled to possession and enjoyment of the estate, in common with the heirs of her husband, of an undivided third part, which she may continue to hold during her life without a previous formal assignment of dower.[3] So in Connecticut, before her dower has been assigned to her, she has the rights of a tenant in common with the heirs at law of the husband.[4] But a surrender by deed, with covenants of warranty, by her, would estop her from claiming dower in the premises.[5] She has no estate in the lands, nor anything which she can assign or convey to another, or which can be taken in execution for her debt;[6] though in Alabama and Indiana an assignment by a widow of her right in lands in which her husband died seised, was held to be valid.[7] And in Indiana she was held to have such an interest as she could assign in lands of which her husband had been seised during coverture, although he had conveyed the same in his lifetime, and the assignee may sue in his own name.[8] But her right is not one against which a statute of limitation runs in favor of a tenant as being adversely seised, unless expressly embraced in such statute;[9] nor is it such an interest as to be affected by any proceedings for foreclosure by a mortgagee against her husband, unless she is made a party by proper notice. Thus,

---

[1] 4 Kent, Com. 61 ; Green *v.* Putnam, 1 Barb. 500 ; Stewart *v.* McMartin, 5 Barb. 438 ; Johnson *v.* Shields, 32 Me. 424 ; Cox *v.* Jagger, 2 Cow. 638, 651 ; Shields *v.* Batts, 5 J. J. Marsh. 12; Hoxsie *v.* Ellis, 4 R. I. 123; Saltmarsh *v.* Smith, 32 Ala. 404 ; Stewart *v.* Chadwick, 8 Iowa, 463; Aikman *v.* Harsell, 98 N. Y. 186.

[2] Sheafe *v.* O'Neil, 9 Mass. 9 ; Weaver *v.* Crenshaw, 6 Ala. 873.

[3] Dummerston *v.* Newfane, 37 Vt. 9. See Mass. Pub. Stat. c. 124, § 14.

[4] Wooster *v.* Hunt's Lyman Iron Co., 38 Conn. 256.

[5] Jackson *v.* Wright, 14 Johns. 194.

[6] Brown *v.* Meredith, 2 Keen, 527 ; Green *v.* Putnam, 1 Barb. 500 ; Gooch *v.* Atkins, 14 Mass. 378 ; Saltmarsh *v.* Smith, 32 Ala. 404 ; Rausch *v.* Moore, 48 Iowa, 611. See Pope *v.* Mead, 99 N. Y. 635, that she may assign.

[7] Powell *v.* Powell, 10 Ala. 900 ; Matlock *v.* Lee, 9 Ind. 298.

[8] Strong *v.* Clem, 12 Ind. 37.

[9] 4 Kent, Com. 70 ; Parker *v.* Obear, 7 Met. 24 ; Spencer *v.* Weston, 1 Dev. & B. 213 ; Guthrie *v.* Owen, 10 Yerg. 339 ; Barnard *v.* Edwards, 4 N. H. 107.

where the husband bought an equity of redemption, and afterwards sold it to the mortgagee, who, in order to perfect his
title, gave notice to the husband that he held for foreclosure,
as the law stood before the Revised Statutes in Massachusetts,
it was held that the wife was not affected by such proceedings.
In order to be effectual as to her, she must be notified after
her husband's death, and the mortgagee must hold for the
requisite time afterwards.[1] The principle above stated, that,
until assignment made, dower is not the subject of
[*252] sale or conveyance * so as to vest a legal title in the
assignee or alienee, and enable him to sue for it in-
his own name, is recognized in courts of equity as well as law.[2]
But where such sale or assignment is made, equity will protect
the rights of the assignee and sustain an action in the widow's
name for his benefit.[3] And if she sells her right and gives
the purchaser a power of attorney for the purpose, he may
prosecute an action and recover dower in her name in her
stead.[4] And where a widow sold her right of dower to one of
the heirs of her husband, who brought a bill in equity against
the heirs and himself, to have her dower set out to him, the
court decreed the same to be done.[5] But under her rights at
law, that of dower prior to assignment vests in action only, and
cannot be aliened.[6] The most she can do is to release it to
some one who is in possession of the lands, or to whom she
stands in privity of estate; she cannot invest another with
it.[7] She cannot, therefore, mortgage it before it is assigned,
nor lease it; and a covenant to pay rent to her does not bind
the assignee of the covenantor.[8] Of so little effect is the conveyance of a widow's mere right of dower, that where the first
of two successive widows entitled to dower out of the same

[1] Lund v. Woods, 11 Met. 566.

[2] Tompkins v. Fonda, 4 Paige, 448 ; Torrey v. Minor, 1 Sm. & M. Ch. 489 ;
Harrison v. Wood, 1 Dev. & B. Eq. 437.

[3] Lamar v. Scott, 4 Rich. 516 ; Powell v. Powell, 10 Ala. 900.

[4] Robie v. Flanders, 33 N. H. 524.   [5] Potter v. Everitt, 7 Ired. Eq. 152.

[6] In Indiana, by statute, the widow's dower after assignment is inalienable
during the period of a second marriage. Rev. Stat. 1881, § 2484.

[7] Blain v. Harrison, 11 Ill. 384 ; Summers v. Babb, 13 Ill. 483 ; Jackson v.
Vanderheyden, 17 Johns. 167 ; Johnson v. Shields, 32 Me. 424 ; Park, Dow. 335.

[8] Strong v. Bragg, 7 Blackf. 62 ; Croade v. Ingraham, 13 Pick. 33.

estate conveyed to the tenant her right before the dower was assigned, it was held to be an extinguishment of her right, so that when the second came to claim her dower, the tenant could not make use of the conveyance to affect her claim to be endowed out of the whole estate.[1]   And where a man married a widow, whose dower in her first husband's estate had not been set out, and assigned all his estate and effects of which he was possessed in right of his wife or otherwise, it was held not to carry any right which she had to have her dower assigned.[2]   On the *other hand, where a mortgagee [*253] undertook to foreclose against a mortgage made during coverture by the husband, but to which she was no party, and to that end made her a party to the bill, it was held that she was not affected by the decree, for as dowress she held by a title paramount to the mortgage.   Nor could she in such a suit contest the validity of the mortgage.[3]   Still, her interest is not such that at common law she could bring ejectment, or maintain a process for partition, in respect to lands of her deceased husband.[4]   If she entered upon such lands except under her right of quarantine, she would be a trespasser, and would be as to the heir an abator, if her husband died seised. Or if she held possession beyond the period of her quarantine, she would become a trespasser, and liable to be expelled by the heir by ejectment.[5]   And if she obtain possession under form of legal process of assignment, and the assignment prove void, she may be regarded as a disseisor.[6]   And, as observed by a legal writer, this is probably the only case where a person who has a title, unopposed by any adverse right of possession, may not reduce it to possession by an entry upon the estate.[7] When she has prosecuted her claim for dower to judgment, it seems to give so much consistency to her title, that if she then

---

[1] Elwood v. Klock, 13 Barb. 50.

[2] 2 Crabb, Real Prop. 149 ; Brown v. Meredith, 2 Keen, 527.

[3] Lewis v. Smith, 9 N. Y. 502.

[4] Pringle v. Gaw, 5 S. & R. 536 ; Doe v. Nutt, 2 Car. & P. 430 ; Coles v. Coles, 15 Johns. 319 ; Bradshaw v. Callaghan, 5 Johns. 80.

[5] Corey v. People, 45 Barb. 262.

[6] 4 Kent, Com. 61 ; Jackson v. O'Donaghy, 7 Johns. 247 ; Hildreth v. Thompson, 16 Mass. 191 ; McCully v. Smith, 2 Bailey, 103 ; Park, Dow. 336 ; Sharpley v. Jones, 5 Harringt. 373.   [7] Park, Dow. 334.

release it to the tenant in possession, it will not extinguish it, but he may avail himself of it against a second widow claiming dower in the same estate.[1] But still she could not herself enter upon land as her dower except in pursuance of the execution of a writ of *habere facias*.[2] Though she need not wait until such writ has been returned into court, as soon as her dower is designated under such writ, she may enter and enjoy it, subject only to the hazard of having the proceedings set aside for informality, and there becoming a *tort feasor* [*254] * by such entry and occupancy.[3] In the execution of such a writ, the widow has no right to elect in which part of the estate her dower shall be set out, provided one third part in value be assigned to her.[4] Nor is it until her dower has been assigned, in some of the modes heretofore pointed out, that the estate of a dowress becomes consummated and clearly fixed and ascertained.

3. But the moment this has been done, and she has entered upon the premises assigned her, the freehold therein is vested in her by virtue and in continuance of her husband's seisin.[5] Therefore, though upon the death of the husband his heir enters and gains actual seisin of the premises, as soon as the widow enters under her assignment of dower it destroys his seisin at once of so much of the inheritance, and he is thenceforward considered as never having been seised thereof.[6] Yet she cannot, after her dower is assigned, have assumpsit for use and occupation of her dower land against the tenant who has held it since her husband's death, although no damages shall have been allowed her, when she recovered judgment for her dower.[7]

[1] Leavitt *v.* Lamprey, 13 Pick. 382.   [2] Evans *v.* Webb, 1 Yeates, 424.

[3] Co. Lit. 37 b, n. ; Parker *v.* Parker, 17 Pick. 236 ; 2 Crabb, Real Prop. 152.

[4] Taylor *v.* Lusk, 7 J. J. Marsh. 636. But it is prescribed by statute in many States that the assignment of the dower or other interest taken by the widow in her husband's estate shall, if possible, include the dwelling-house. See *post*, ch. 9, §§ 1, 2.

[5] Co. Lit. 339 a ; Park, Dow. 339, 340 ; Windham *v.* Portland, 4 Mass. 384 ; Lawrence *v.* Brown, 5 N. Y. 394 ; Jones *v.* Brewer, 1 Pick. 314.

[6] Powell *v.* Monson, 3 Mason, 368 ; Park, Dow. 340 ; Gilb. Ten. 27 ; Lawrence *v.* Brown, 5 N. Y. 394 ; Perkins, § 424 ; Norwood *v.* Marrow, 4 Dev. & B. 442 ; 2 Crabb, Real Prop. 143.

[7] Thompson *v.* Stacy, 10 Yerg. 493 ; Sutton *v.* Burrows, 2 Murph. 79 ; Andrews *v.* Andrews, 14 N. J. 141. Cf. Parks *v.* McLellan, 44 N. J. L. 552.

4. Nor does she as tenant in dower hold her estate of the heir or tenant who set it out to her, but of her deceased husband, or rather by appointment of the law.[1] The law, moreover, does not consider that there is any privity of estate between the dowress and the reversioner of her lands.[2] Nor would she be bound by any proceedings in court which relate to the sale of her husband's interest in those lands.[3] And so independent of * the heir is the estate of a dowress, [*255] that where he assigned dower lands to a widow, and at the same time, by the same act, limited a remainder to a third person, dependent upon her life estate as a particular estate to support it, it was held to be a void limitation as to the remainder, since her freehold was not of his creation, nor could he unite it to the remainder so as to make them one estate when taken together.[4] After the language which has been above used, and the cases cited illustrating the relation there is between a widow and the heir or alienee of the husband, in respect to the lands which may have been set out to her as dower, it may seem somewhat inconsistent for the law writers to affirm that " she holds of the heir by fealty, the assignment of dower being a species of subinfeudation ; "[5] and " in point of tenure a dowress holds of the heir, or person who has the reversion in the lands assigned to her, notwithstanding she is in by her husband and not by the heir."[6] And yet it is believed that the several propositions may be reconciled by considering the connection in which the language of the writers is used. The explanation is to be sought in the doctrine of feudal tenures, which have become obsolete or of no practical importance. By the theory of the feudal law every estate owes certain services to him of whom it is holden. Fealty was one of these services, and was due alike from freeholders and tenants for years as an incident to their estates, to be paid to the reversioner.[7] Previous to the statute of *Quia Emptores*, those who held of the principal lord often enfeoffed

---

[1] Conant v. Litle, 1 Pick. 189 ; Baker v. Baker, 4 Me. 67 ; Park, Dow. 340.

[2] Adams v. Butts, 9 Conn. 79.   [3] Lawrence v. Brown, 5 N. Y. 394.

[4] Park, Dow. § 341. See Plowd. 25.   [5] 1 Cruise, Dig. 165.

[6] Park, Dow. § 344 ; Perkins, § 424 ; 2 Crabb, Real Prop. 143.

[7] Co Lit. 67 b ; Lit. § 132.

others to hold of them by what was called subinfeudation.
That statute put an end to these mesne tenures, if in fee, and
required him who had been enfeoffed by the lord's tenant to
hold directly of the lord himself, and to pay to him the services due in respect to the estate.[1]   Still, the tenant under
      the lord might create a tenure under himself for life
[*256]   or * years, while he continued liable for the services
      due to the lord.   And in such case there was still a
fealty due from his tenant for life or years to him as the reversioner.[2]   So long as the husband lived and was the owner of
the inheritance, he alone owed service to the lord.   But upon
his death, his inheritance was divided between the heir and
his widow as soon as her dower was assigned, she taking a
freehold for life in one third, the remaining two thirds and the
reversion in her third going to the heir, who became substituted, so far as the service to the lord was concerned, to the
husband as owning the inheritance.   And as this assigning of
her dower is properly the act of the heir, it is regarded as a
kind of subinfeudation on his part in respect to the widow.[3]
Now, though she came in as of the seisin and estate of her husband, the same law that gave her an estate for life gave the
inheritance to the heir in reversion, or, if it had been aliened
by the husband, to the alienee.   And as fealty was incident to
every life estate and was due to the reversioner, the widow
may be said with truth to hold of the heir by fealty, in point of
tenure, although she came into her estate as of the seisin and
estate of her husband.[4]   Nor is it difficult in this way to reconcile the proposition that the seisin of the widow is in her by
relation from the death of the husband, and thereby destroys
the intermediate seisin of the heir or alienee.   But she and the
heir are still equally in the "seisin" of the estate, using that
term in a technical sense, as denoting the completion of that
investiture by which the tenant was admitted into the tenure.[5]
The tenant in such case, in possession of the freehold, is said
to have the *actual* seisin of the land, the fee being entrusted to
her.   And it was because of the fee being thus entrusted to the

---

[1] Wms. Real Prop. 95.   [2] Park, Dow. § 344 ; Fitzh. N. B. 159 A.
[3] 2 Bl. Com. 136.   [4] Wms. Real. Prop. 101 ; Co. Lit. 67 b.
[5] Co. Lit. 266 b, n. 217.

care and protection of the tenant in dower that any act of disaffirmance of the reversioner's title, on her part, was held to
work a forfeiture of her estate, as, for instance, her conveying
the dower lands in fee to a stranger.[1]　And where,
* therefore, she was invested with the actual seisin by [*257]
means of the assignment of her dower, the intermediate seisin of the heir was not deemed to have been adverse
to hers, nor inconsistent with the idea that her seisin took
effect by relation from the decease of the husband.

5. As has more than once been stated, the estate of a widow
in lands assigned to her in dower is a freehold for life, carrying with it the various incidents heretofore enumerated as
belonging to such estates. And, ordinarily, the incidents to
her estate in dower cease with her estate in the land. As
where, for instance, a right of way was set out as appurtenant
to dower lands, across other lands of the husband, it ceased
with the determination of her estate.[2]　But where a certain part
of a house was set out as dower with certain easements in
other parts of it as appurtenant, and the parts not set out to the
widow were sold and described as being all the estate not
assigned to her, it was held that at her death these easements
continued appurtenant to the dower portion in the hands of the
heirs.[3]　Among other duties and liabilities of a dowress is
that of keeping down one third of the interest upon the incumbrances or charges upon the estate, subject to which she holds
her dower.[4]　She is answerable for waste committed upon the
premises, whether by herself or a stranger, as she is bound to
protect the reversioner's interest.[5]　Sometimes, however, she
may use one part of her dower land in preference to another,
and thereby be exonerated from liability for waste, when she
would have been liable if it had been the only estate set out
to her. As where the commissioners set out one third part of
eight different parcels into which they divided the estate, and
one of these was woodland, it was held that though, as a
general proposition, she would be bound to use each parcel
as if it had been the only land of which her husband died
seised, she might in such case take wood and timber from

[1] Co. Lit. 266 b, n. 217.　　　　[2] Hoffman v. Savage, 15 Mass. 130.
[3] Symmes v. Drew, 21 Pick. 278.　　[4] 2 Crabb, Real Prop. 154.　　[5] Id. 155.

[*258] that lot for the use of the cultivated * land.¹   And in Ohio, where an unproductive town lot, together with an unimproved wood-lot, were set out as a widow's dower, it was held not to be waste to cut off and sell enough wood from the woodland to pay the taxes upon both parcels.² *   If a widow is endowed with wild lands in North Carolina, she may clear a part thereof, if necessary, for the support of her family.³

* NOTE. — Most of the States have statute provisions as to the effect of divorces upon dower and curtesy.   In *Massachusetts*, when a divorce *a vinculo* is decreed for the cause of adultery committed by the husband, or on account of his being sentenced to confinement to hard labor, the wife is entitled to her dower in his lands in the same manner as if he were dead ; but she is not entitled to dower in any other case of divorce *from the bonds of matrimony*. — In *Maine*, the wife is in like manner entitled to dower when such divorce is decreed to her for the fault of the husband, for any cause except impotence.   And in both these States, upon the dissolution of a marriage by a divorce, or sentence of nullity for any cause excepting that of adultery committed by the wife, the wife is entitled to the immediate possession of all her real estate.   Mass. Pub. Stat. c. 146, § 27 ; Me. Rev. Stat. 1871, c. 60, § 7. — In *Maine*, when a divorce from bed and board is decreed, and there is no issue living, the wife's real estate is restored to her ; if there is issue living, or the divorce is decreed for the cruelty of the wife, the court may exercise its discretion as to the restoration of property.   Id. § 13. — In *Massachusetts*, there are no longer divorces from bed and board, but divorces *nisi*, which after five or three years may become absolute.   Pub. Stat. c. 146, § 3 ; Sparhawk *v.* Sparhawk, 116 Mass. 315. — In *Connecticut* it is declared that in case of divorce where the wife is the innocent party, if no alimony, she is entitled to dower.   Gen. Stat. 1866, p. 421 ; Rev. Stat. 1875, p. 376.   And if the divorce be for the misconduct of the wife, the court may decree that her lands revert to her husband.   Acts, 1866. — In *Rhode Island*, when a divorce *a vinculo* is decreed to the wife for fault of the husband, if there be no issue living, she is restored to all her lands, tenements, and hereditaments.   If there be issue living at the time of the divorce, the court may act at their discretion in regard to such restoration. Pub. Stat. 1882, c. 167, §§ 4, 8. — In *New Hampshire* it is simply provided that, upon any decree of nullity or divorce, the court may restore to the wife all or any part of her real estate.   Gen. Laws, 1878, c. 182, § 12. — So in *Vermont*, except when the divorce be for the adultery of the wife.   Rev. Laws, 1860, § 2380. — In *New York* and *Arkansas*, in case of divorce dissolving the marriage contract for the misconduct of the wife, she shall not be endowed.   But when a decree dissolving the marriage is pronounced in favor of the wife, all her real estate becomes her absolute property, N. Y. Rev. Stat. 1882 ; vol. 3, p. 2197, § 8, p. 2338; Ark.

---

¹ Childs *v.* Smith, 1 Md. Ch. Dec. 483 ; Cook *v.* Cook, 11 Gray, 123.
² Crockett *v.* Crockett, 2 Ohio, N. s. 180.   See also Padelford *v.* Padelford, 7 Pick. 152 ; Dalton *v.* Dalton, 7 Ired. Eq. 197.   And see also, as to her cutting timber, &c., on wild lands, *ante*, p. *110, n. 3.
³ Lambeth *v.* Warner, 2 Jones. Eq. 165.

Dig. 1874, §§ 2207, 2217 ; and if the divorce be on account of the adultery of the husband, the wife has dower if she survives him, Forrest v. Forrest, 6 Duer, 102.* — In *Missouri*, in all cases of divorce from the bonds of [*259] matrimony, the guilty party forfeits all rights and claims under and by virtue of the marriage, and if the wife obtain a divorce from the bonds of matrimony, all property that came to her husband by the marriage, that is undisposed of at the time of filing the petition, reverts to the wife and children. Rev. Stat. 1881, vol. 1, § 2182. — In *Michigan*, when a marriage is dissolved for the cause of adultery committed by the husband, for his misconduct or habitual drunkenness, or on account of his being sentenced to imprisonment for a term of three years or longer, the wife is entitled to her dower in his lands, in the same manner as if he were dead ; but she is not entitled to dower in any other case of divorce ; and upon the dissolution of marriage for any cause excepting the adultery of the wife, she is entitled to the restoration of all her real estate. Comp. Laws, 1871, c. 108, § 24. — In *Minnesota*, in case of divorce for any cause but adultery of the wife, or a nullity of marriage declared, or the husband is sentenced to imprisonment for life, the wife is entitled to her lands as if her husband were dead. If the property thus restored be insufficient for her support and that of her children committed to her, the court may decree to her such real estate of the husband, not exceeding the value of her dower, as they may deem just and reasonable. If the marriage is dissolved by imprisonment of husband or his adultery, she takes her dower as if he were dead ; but her dower is barred by one year's desertion. Stat. 1878, c. 46, §§ 14, 20 ; c. 62, § 24. — In *Kansas*, a woman divorced for the fault or misconduct of her husband has her dower if no alimony ; but is not endowed if divorced for her fault or misconduct. Comp. Laws, 1879, p. 691. — In *California*, where the statute has done away with the common-law right of dower, and substituted in its place a half interest in the common property, it is provided that in case of the dissolution of the marriage, the common property shall be equally divided between the parties, except that, when the divorce is rendered on the ground of adultery or extreme cruelty, the guilty party is entitled to only such portion of the common property as the court deem just. Hittell's Codes, 1876, § 5146. — In *Dakota*, dower and curtesy are abolished, and each party has the full right to his or her separate property, except that, on a divorce for the fault of the husband, the court may order an allowance from his estate in her favor. Rev. Code, 1877, pp. 247, § 3 ; 354, § 779 ; 246, §§ 73, 74· — In *Nebraska* and *Arizona*, the wife has dower on divorce for husband's adultery, drunkenness, or misconduct, or imprisonment for any term exceeding three years. In divorce from the bonds of matrimony for any cause except the wife's adultery, she has her own real estate, as also in every divorce from bed and board. Neb. Comp. Stat. 1881, p. 254, § 23 ; Arizona Comp. L. 1877, § 1923. And in *Wisconsin*, when the marriage is dissolved on account of the husband's being sentenced to imprisonment for life, but not in any other case of divorce. Rev. Stat. 1878, c. 109, § 2373. — In *Indiana*, although the estate of dower is abolished, it is enacted that a divorce granted for the adultery or misconduct of the husband, shall entitle the wife to the same rights, so far as his real estate is concerned, that she would have been entitled to by his death. Rev. Stat. 1881, § 1043. And it is enacted that if a wife shall have left her husband, and shall be living, at the time of his death, in adultery, she shall take no part of the estate of her husband. Id. § 2496. — In *Illinois*, upon a divorce for the fault or misconduct of the wife, she forfeits her dower. Rev. Stat. 1880, c. 41, § 14. It is to be noticed in regard to the statutes of both Indiana and Illinois, that the language in regard to the divorce is general, not specifying that it is a divorce *a vinculo.* — In *Tennessee,* if the bonds of matrimony be dissolved at the suit of the husband, the wife is in no case entitled to dower. Stat. 1871, § 2473. — In *Alabama,* a divorce for the adultery of the wife bars her dower. Code, 1876, § 2698. — In *Ohio,* if divorce be granted by reason of aggression of the husband, the wife is restored to her lands, and shall be allowed alimony out of his real and personal estate ; and, if she survive him, she shall have dower in his real estate. But if the divorce is for the aggression of the wife, she loses all right of dower in her husband's lands, but has a restoration of her own lands and such share of his lands as the court shall judge reasonable. It is provided that if a wife willingly leave her husband and dwell with her adulterer, she shall lose her right of dower ; but shall be restored to this right on her return and reconcilation with her husband. Rev. Stat. 1880, §§ 4192, 5699, 5700. — So in *Delaware,* Laws, 1874, p. 476, § 9 ; p. 534, § 9. In *New Jersey* and *West Virginia* the wife is barred of her dower by living in adultery, N. J. Rev. 1877, p. 322 ; W. Va. Rev. Stat. 1878, c. 70, § 7. — In *North Carolina,* dower and curtesy are both barred by a divorce *a vinculo ;* and curtesy also if the wife, after a divorce *a mensa et thoro,* is not living with the husband at the time of her death. Code, 1883, §§ 1838, 1843. — In *Virginia* dower is barred by the wife's adultery. Code, 1873, c. 106, §§ 7, 13. — In *South Carolina,* elopement bars dower. Gen. Stat. 1882, § 1799. — In *Kentucky* the wife loses dower by living in adultery, and the provision is general, barring curtesy and dower by divorce granted *a vinculo.* Gen. Stat. 1873, p. 531, § 14 ; p. 526, § 8 ; c. 52, art. 4, § 3. — In *Nevada,* if the divorce be by reason of the imprisonment of the husband or his adultery, the wife takes her dower as if he were dead. 1 Comp. L. § 220. — In *Maryland,* when a man is convicted of bigamy, his first wife is forthwith endowed of one third of his real estate, the assignment and recovery of which are made as in other cases of dower ; but when a woman is so convicted, she forfeits her claim to dower of the estate of her first husband. Rev. Code, 1878, art. 72, § 102. — In *Arizona, Maine, Vermont,* and *Michigan,* when a divorce *a vinculo matrimonii* is [*260] decreed for the cause of adultery committed by the wife, the husband * shall hold her real estate so long as they shall both live ; and if he shall survive her, and there shall have been issue of the marriage born alive, he shall hold her real estate for the term of his own life, as a tenant by the curtesy ; but the court may allow her so much of her real or personal estate as is necessary for her subsistence. Me. Rev. Stat. 1871, c. 60, § 8 ; Vt. Rev. L. 1880, § 2384 ; Mich. Comp. Laws, 1871, c. 108, §§ 25, 36. Such is the law in *Rhode Island,* when a husband has obtained a divorce *a vinculo* for any cause. Pub. Stat. 1882, tit. xx. c. 167, § 5. — While in *Massachusetts,* upon such a divorce for the wife's adultery, the husband is to have only so much of her realty as the court deems necessary for the support of the minor children committed to his care, and his right to her other realty on her death ceases if she marry again. Pub. Stat. c. 146, § 26. — In *Oregon,* if a marriage is dissolved, the party at whose prayer it is done shall be entitled to one third part in fee of the whole of the real estate owned by the other at the time of the dissolution. Gen. L. p. 210. — In *Maine* and *Rhode Island* these provisions entitling the husband to curtesy in case of divorce do not apply to the wife's property secured to her by the laws allowing her to hold a separate property. Stats. *sup.* — In *New York* and *Tennessee,* if a decree dissolving the marriage be pronounced in favor of the husband, his right to any real estate owned by the wife at the time of pronouncing the decree in her own right, and to the rents and profits thereof, is not taken away or impaired by such dissolution of the marriage. N. Y. Rev. Stat. 5th ed. 1859, vol. 3, p. 237; Code of Tenn. 1874, § 2472. — In *Illinois*, when a divorce is obtained for the fault and misconduct of the husband, he loses his right to be tenant by the curtesy in the wife's lands. Rev. Stat. 1880, c. 41. — In *Alabama*, a divorce deprives the husband of all control over the separate estate of the wife. Code, 1876, § 2700. — In *Indiana*, although the estate by curtesy is abolished, a divorce decreed on account of the misconduct of the wife entitles the husband to the same rights so far as his or her real estate is concerned, as he would have been entitled to by her death. Rev. Stat. 1881, § 1044. But if a husband shall have left his wife, and shall be living, at the time of her death, in adultery, or shall abandon his wife without just cause, failing to make suitable provision for her, he shall take no part of her estate. II. §§ 2497, 2498. — In *Maryland*, a husband forfeits his claim or title as tenant by the curtesy on conviction of bigamy. Code, 1878, p. 807.

CHAPTER VIII.

JOINTURE AND OTHER PROVISIONS IN LIEU OF DOWER.

1. In treating of dower, it has been seen that one mode of barring the claim of a widow to dower is by settling upon her an allowance previous to marriage, to be accepted by her in lieu thereof. This is called a jointure, and although once very common in England, it has become of little mo-
[*262] ment since the *Dower Act of 3 & 4 Wm. IV. c. 105, has placed the subject of the wife's dower under the control of the husband in all cases where special provision is not made in her favor. This is usually done by marriage set-

tlements. But it is nevertheless important to understand the
nature and origin of jointures and the rules by which they
are generally governed. Jointures are not of the nature of
contracts, but of provisions made by the husband for the
wife.[1]

2. They are of **two** kinds — one at law, the other in equity.
The former include estates in lands made to a woman in contemplation of marriage, or a wife after marriage in satisfaction of dower. They are occasionally used in this country,
though what are called equitable jointures are more frequently
adopted than those at law.

3. The subject may be considered under the following
heads : I. Legal jointures : (1) made before marriage ; (2)
made after marriage. II. Equitable jointures : (1) made before marriage ; (2) made after marriage. III. Testamentary
and other provisions in lieu of dower.

4. Before the time of Henry VIII. there had grown up a
species of property in lands called uses, by which, while one
man owned the legal estate with all its incidents of seisin,
tenure, &c., another had a usufructuary interest in and out
of the same, of which he availed himself through the instru-
mentality of courts of equity. As there could be no seisin of
this intangible right, no dower could be acquired in it. And
husbands resorted to it as a means of preventing their wives
claiming dower, by having estates conveyed to some other
person to hold to the use of the husband. Nor was there any
way, except by conveyances to uses, by which provision could
be made for a wife, by any antenuptial arrangement, which
should supersede or bar her future claim for dower, if she survived her husband ; and this on technical grounds : first, that
at common law no person could bar himself of any right or
title to lands by receiving any collateral thing in satisfaction, unless he had * actually executed a release ; [*263]
and, second, because, until married, a woman could
not execute a valid release of property of her contemplated
husband, to which she had till then no title.[2] When, therefore, a husband wished to make provision as a substitute for

---

[1] Buckinghamshire v. Drury, per Ld. Mansfield, 2 Eden, 72.

[2] Vernon's Case, 4 Rep. 1 ; Hastings v. Dickinson, 7 Mass. 153; Co. Lit. 36 b.

dower for the wife whom he was about to marry, he had such parts of his lands as were thought a reasonable proportion, conveyed by the person who held the legal seisin thereof to some one to the use of the husband and wife for the term of their lives. This created a kind of joint tenancy or jointure, whereby the wife, if she survived the husband, enjoyed the estate during her life. There was this peculiarity in the joint estate of husband and wife, as there still is, that neither could defeat the right of survivorship of the other.[1] *

5. By the statute 27 Henry VIII. c. 10, called the Statute of Uses, an attempt was made to do away with uses by uniting the legal and equitable estates, and giving them thus united to the one in whose favor the use had been declared. The consequence would have been, had this idea been carried out, that all husbands, *cestuis que use*, would have become seised of the legal estate, and thereby have given dower to their wives, even though these might already have had provision made for them before marriage. To obviate a consequence like this it was provided by that statute, §§ 6, 7, 8, and 9, substantially, that if lands were conveyed for the benefit of a wife before marriage, in a manner pointed out in § 6, as her jointure, she should not have dower unless evicted from her jointure lands. If such jointure was created after marriage, then she might elect to take the jointure or dower, but not both.[2]

[*264] * 6. But in order to have such provision operate as a bar to dower, it must conform to all the requirements prescribed by the statute, which are as follows: 1. It must take effect immediately upon the death of the husband. 2. It must be for her own life at least. No estate for years, or *per autre vie*, will answer. 3. It must be made to herself,

---

* NOTE. — Settlements by way of provision for the wife, previous to marriage, are said to have been in use among the ancient Germans and Gauls ; and Cæsar and Tacitus are quoted to sustain the position. The latter says, *Dotem non uxor marito sed uxori maritus offert, intersunt parentes et propinqui, et munera probant.* De Mor. Germ. c. 18 ; 2 Flint. Real Prop. 198, n.

---

1 2 Bl. Com. 137 ; Vernon's Case, 4 Rep. 1 ; Tud. Cas. 730; 1 Atk. Conv. 410, n. ; Id. 261.

2 Stat. at Large ; 1 Atk. Conv. 264 ; 2 Bl. Com. 137 ; McCartee *v.* Teller, 2 Paige, 511, 562.

and not to another in trust for her.　4. It must be made and expressed in the deed to be in full satisfaction of her dower.[1] And, though ordinarily for life only, jointures may be estates in fee, and be good.[2]　A provision, in order to come within the character of a jointure, must consist wholly of land.　If it consists partly of land and partly of an annuity, it will not bar dower unless the annuity is secured upon land.[3]　Nor would an estate upon condition be a binding provision for a widow as a jointure, unless upon the husband's death she elect to enter and accept the conditional estate.　If she do, she will be bound by it and be barred of dower.[4]

7.　Though a jointure, in its original meaning and common acceptance, implies a joint estate in the husband and wife with the principle of survivorship, it extends to a sole estate limited to the wife alone.　Nor is it necessary that it should proceed directly from the husband; it may come from the father or any other person.　And it may be by a grant to the wife before coverture, or a grant to her by any person other than her husband during coverture.　So it may be by a conveyance to her use either before or during coverture, and may be to the wife and husband jointly, or to the wife alone.[5]

8.　Although Coke, in defining jointure, speaks of it as a * competent livelihood of freehold for the wife, of [*265] lands, &c., the law furnishes no measure of competency ; and if it complies with the requirements of the statute as to qualities and incidents, it will bar dower, whatever may be its amount.[6]　Such will be the effect where it is settled before marriage, though the wife be a minor at the time.　Nor is it necessary, though usual, to have the assent of the parents or guardian of the wife in such case, if the provision be

---

[1] Atk. Conv. 165 ; 2 Bl. Com. 138 ; 2 Flint. Real Prop. 197 ; Co. Lit. 36 b ; Vernon's Case, 4 Rep. 1, by which it is held that an estate *durante viduitate,* which may continue for her life, would be a good jointure, except in case the wife was a minor.　McCartee *v.* Teller, 2 Paige, 562.

[2] 1 Roper, Hus. & Wife, 465.　　　　　[3] Vance *v.* Vance, 21 Me. 364.

[4] Clancy, Rights of Wom. 209 ; Vernon's Case, 4 Rep. 1 ; McCartee *v.* Teller, 2 Paige, 562 ; Caruthers *v.* Caruthers, 4 Bro. C. t'. 500.

[5] 2 Flint. Real Prop. 196 ; 1 Roper, Hus. & Wife, 465 ; 3 Prest. Abs. 376 ; 1 Cruise, Dig. 195.

[6] 1 Atk. Conv. 266 ; Drury *v.* Drury, 2 Eden, 39, 57 ; Buckinghamshire *v.* Drury, 2 Eden, 75, n. ; 1 Bright, Hus. & Wife, 434.

a fair one, not illusory in its character; but such assent negatives the idea of the provision being illusory and fraudulent.[1]

9. Nor is it even necessary that the wife herself should, in England, assent to the jointure before marriage, whereas, in Maine, she must have assented, to have it have effect.[2] There is a form of conveyance by the way of jointure in Oliver's Practical Conveyancer, which is an indenture of three parts, to which the wife is a party. But it is remarked in a note to that work, that it is not necessary she should be a party to the deed.[3] But while the law as to jointures is adopted in most of the United States, the statutes of several of them require the wife to be made a party to the deed and express her assent in the deed, if of full age; if under age, by joining with her father or guardian in the conveyance. Among these, Maine, Massachusetts, New York, Arkansas, Connecticut, Delaware, and it is believed some other of the States, have provisions like those above stated.[4]

10. If the widow is evicted from her jointure lands by defeet of title, she may be remitted to her right of dower *pro tanto* or in the whole, as the case may be, out of her husband's estate.[5]

11. If the jointure is not settled upon the wife until [*266] after * the marriage, it is no further binding upon her than that she must elect, at the husband's death, to take it in lieu of dower, or to take her dower; she cannot have both.[6] But it is not a jointure unless so expressed, although

[1] Co. Lit. 36 b ; 3 Prest. Abs. 377 ; Buckinghamshire *v.* Drury, 2 Eden, 64, 74 ; McCartee *v.* Teller, 2 Paige, 556 ; 1 Roper, Hus. & Wife, 471 ; 1 Cruise, Dig. 196.

[2] Vance *v.* Vance, 21 Me. 364. So in several States, by statute, an antenuptial jointure is no bar to dower of a widow who did not assent to it, if she disaffirm within a limited time after becoming discovert ; thus in *Rhode Island*, in one year, Pub. St. 1882, c. 229, § 23 ; *Vermont*, in eight months, Rev. L. 1880, § 2219 ; *Virginia*, in one year, Code, 1873, c. 106, § 4 ; and *Ohio*, Rev. St. 1880, c. 4189.

[3] 1 Cruise, Dig. 199.

[4] Wms. Real Prop. 193, Am. note ; Bubier *v.* Roberts, 49 Me. 463. So Oregon. Gen. L. 1872, p. 586.

[5] 1 Atk. Conv. 269 ; 3 Prest. Abs. 377 ; 4 Dane, Abr. 685, 686.

[6] McCartee *v.* Teller, 2 Paige, 556 ; 2 Flint. Real Prop. 197.

it be by deed from husband to wife, in consideration of love and affection.[1]

12. When a jointure takes effect, whether settled before or after marriage, the widow is at liberty to enter at once into the occupation and enjoyment of it upon the death of the husband,[2] though it is said that she may not claim the annual crops growing at the time of his death.[3]

13. While she holds her jointure lands, if she has only a life estate in them, she holds them subject to the same restrictions as tenants for life, unless there was a covenant in the instrument settling them upon her that her jointure should be of a certain yearly value. In such case, if it can only be raised by committing waste, she may commit it so far as is necessary.[4]

14. A wife does not at law lose her jointure, as she would her dower, by eloping and living in adultery.[5] But if she and her husband join in conveying away the lands settled upon her before marriage, as a jointure, she thereby loses both dower and jointure; but if settled after marriage, she is remitted to her right to claim dower.[6]

15. The statute of 27 Hen. VIII. has been substantially adopted in most of the United States, though modified in some particulars. As in Ohio, where a minor has the election to take dower or her jointure, though settled before marriage. In Connecticut, jointure may consist of personal as well as real estate.[7] But in Massachusetts it has been held that, under the statute of Hen. VIII., a wife cannot bar herself of

---

[1] Bubier v. Roberts, 49 Me. 463. *Post,* *279. See, for the common law, Reed v. Dickerman, 12 Pick. 149 ; see also Mass. Pub. Stat. c. 128, § 9.

[2] Hastings v. Dickinson, 7 Mass. 146, 153 ; 2 Crabb, Real Prop. 217 ; 2 Flint. Real Prop. 199.

[3] 1 Cruise, Dig. 201 ; 3 Dane, Abr. 123. In which respect she has not the rights of a dowress.

[4] 1 Atk. Conv. 272. .

[5] 1 Cruise, Dig. 209. But this is now altered by statute in several States. Thus, in New York, Rev. Stat. 1882, vol. 3, p. 2198, § 15 ; Delaware, Stat. 1874, p. 476, § 8.

[6] Co. Lit. 36 b.

[7] 4 Kent, Com. 56, n. 8th ed.; Wms. Real Prop. 193 ; Am. note ; Andrews v. Andrews, 8 Conn. 79. See also Craig v. Walthall, 14 Gratt. 518. *Ante,* *265, note.

ier dower by any covenant not to claim it in consid-
[*267] cration of anytiing * else tian a freeiold estate settled upon ier, as sie cannot before marriage release a
rigit wiici is not in existence.[1]

16. Tiougi equitable jointures are not witiin tie statute
of Hen. VIII., tiey are ield to be equally operative, wien
taking effect, to bar dower as tiose created by law. Suci a
jointure will bind an infant in tie same way as a legal one,
if it is settled upon ier before marriage by tie consent and
approbation of ier parents or guardian. And a provision in
lieu of dower for an infant, if so assented to before marriage,
is an equitable bar to dower, if it is as certain a provision as
ier dower would be.[2]

17. If tie woman be of age at ier marriage, tiere must be
an express agreement on ier part to accept tie provision
made in lieu of dower in order to bar ier rigit tiereto. Sie
may, if sie pleases, take a ciance in satisfaction of dower.
Tie difference between tiis equitable and a legal jointure is,
tiat tie latter is not a contract for a provision, but a provision
made ; wiile tie former proceeds on tie idea of a contract
on tie part of tie wife to accept a certain provision in lieu of
dower.[3] If tie provision for tie infant be precarious or uncertain, sie will not be bound by it as a bar to dower, and ias
ier election to take it or dower.[4] And to bar a widow by a
jointure of a ciattel interest, tiere must be an express assent
to receive it, tiougi sie could not iave boti tiat and dower.[5]
Tie above is put to illustrate tie proposition tiat, if agreed
to, any provision, wietier a ciattel interest in land or a
pecuniary obligation, will bar a claim for dower in equity.
And even "a ciance" in satisfaction may be sufficient, if so

---

[1] Hastings *v.* Dickinson, 7 ‍ass. 153 ; Gibson *v.* Gibson, 15 ‍ass. 106, 110.
See Pub. Stat. c. 124, § 7.

[2] McCartee *v.* Teller, 2 Paige, 559 ; Tud. Cas. 49 ; Corbet *v.* Corbet, 1 Sim. &
Stu. 612 ; 1 Atk. Conv. 267 ; Drury *v.* Drury, 2 Eden, 60 ; Caruthers *v.* Caruthers, 4 Bro. C. C. 513 ; Clancy, Rights of Wom. 221 ; 4 Dane, Abr. 686.

[3] Caruthers *v.* Caruthers, 4 Bro. C. C. 507, n. 512, 513 ; Dyke *v.* Rendall, 2
De G. ‍. & G. 209 ; Tud. Cas. 49 ; 2 Sugd. Vend. 219 ; Clancy, Rights of Wom.
221.

[4] Caruthers *v.* Caruthers, 4 Bro. C. C. 513; Clancy, Rights of Wom. 221 ;
Smith *v.* Smith, 5 Ves. 189 ; Tud. Cas. 49 ; 2 Sugd. Vend. 220.

[5] Charles *v.* Andrews, 2 Eq. Cas. Abr. 388.

understood by 1er, according to some aut1orities, t1oug1 earlier ones insist t1at t1e provision s1e agrees to accept,
t1oug1 it may be inadequate, must be an *available [*268]
one.[1] T1e great case of Drury v. Drury 1eld an an-
unity of £600, alt1oug1 not c1arged upon land and agreed to
by an infant before marriage, a good bar of dower.[2] But
w1ere t1e antenuptial contract only secured to her w1at t1en
belonged to 1er, but contained no recital t1at it was in lieu of
dower, it was 1eld t1at it was no bar to her claim for dower.[3]

18. If t1e equitable jointure be made after marriage, t1e
wife may elect as in case of legal jointures, eit1er to take t1at
or 1er dower.[4] And t1e intention to bar dower by suc1 provision must also appear, in order to 1ave t1at effect, t1oug1
t1e form of expressing t1is is immaterial, provided such intention can be s1own by evidence required by t1e Statute of
Frauds, and not by parol.[5] But t1is intention may be apparent
from t1e nature of t1e provision, and t1e inconsistency of
taking bot1 t1at and dower, and so may sufficiently appear.[6]
But if it only satisfies a part of t1e widow's dower, s1e will
not be bound by it, but may give it up and claim 1er dower.[7]

19. T1e way in w1ic1 equitable jointures are rendered
effective to bar widows' claims of dower, at law, is, t1at w1ere
t1ey are satisfactorily s1own to 1ave been made, t1e courts of
equity will restrain t1e claimants from prosecuting a suit at
law to enforce t1eir common-law rig1t.[8]

20. T1e effect of being evicted of an equitable jointure by
a superior title seems to be the same as in t1e case of a legal
one, giving t1e widow a rig1t to claim 1er dower in w1ole or

[1] Caruthers v. Caruthers, 4 Bro. C. C. 513, n.; Power v. Sheil, 1 Molloy, Rep.
296; Chit. Dig. Jointure, D. § 11; 2 Sugd. Vend. *543; Dyke v. Rendall, 2 De G.
M. & G. 209; Tud. Cas. 49; 1 Roper, Hus. & Wife, 480; Clancy, Rights of Wom.
223.

[2] Drury v. Drury, 2 Eden, 39.

[3] Swaine v. Perine, 5 Johns. Ch. 482, 489. See Woods v. Shurley, Cro. Jac.
490; 4 Dane, Abr. 685.

[4] 1 Roper, Hus. & Wife, 482; Swaine v. Perine, 5 Johns. Ch. 482.

[5] Clancy, Rights of Wom. 228; 1 Roper, Hus. & Wife, 483; Tenny v. Tenny,
3 Atk. 8; Couch r. Stratton, 4 Ves. 391.

[6] Sugd. Vend. 219; Clancy, Rights of Wom. 229; Tud. Cas. 50.

[7] 1 Roper, Hus. & Wife, 483.

[8] Buckinghamshire v. Drury, 2 Eden, 60, 68; Beard v. Nutthall, 1 Vern. 427.

pro tanto, as the case may be, out of her husband's other estate.[1] And an alienation, by the husband, of the fund out of which the jointure was to arise, will be deemed an eviction of the same, and let her in for her dower.[2]

[*269]   * 21. In accordance with this doctrine, where a contract before marriage fixed the share the wife was to take, and excluded her from all other parts of the estate, and this contract was given up to the husband during coverture and by him destroyed, it was held that she was remitted to her right of dower.[3] So, where a wife before marriage agreed to claim no part of her husband's then estate, she was held to be remitted to her right of dower by his abandoning her and violating his duties of husband towards her.[4]

22. When the law as to jointure in the United States is considered, it is understood to be, except where it has been modified by statute, substantially the same as that of England before the late Dower Act. It was held in Massachusetts, in a case above cited, that, though a widow would not be barred of her dower by an antenuptial covenant not to claim it, yet if she entered into such a covenant, for a valuable consideration, which had not failed, if she recovered her dower, she would be liable upon her covenants in a sum in damages equal to the value of her dower.[5] After that decision, there was a statute providing for barring dower by a jointure in lands or money made before marriage, the wife, if of age, expressing her assent by becoming party to the instrument, or, if under age, executing it with her father or guardian.[6] And if deprived of such provision, she might be endowed as at common law. And if it is made before marriage, without such assent, or made after marriage, she may elect, within six months after husband's death, to accept it in bar, or claim her dower.[7] In Connecticut, any provision which a wife, compe-

---

[1] Wms. Real Prop. 193.

[2] 2 Sugd. Vend. *543, citing Drury *v.* Drury, 2 Eden, 60 ; Power *v.* Sheil, 1 Molloy, Rep. 296.

[3] Gangwere's Estate, 14 Penn. St. 417.   [4] Spiva *v.* Jeter, 9 Rich. Eq. 434.

[5] Gibson *v.* Gibson, 15 Mass. 106.

[6] Pub. Stat. c. 124, § 8 ; Vincent *v.* Spooner, 2 Cush. 473.

[7] Pub. Stat. c. 124, § 9 ;. Thompson *v.* McGaw, 1 Met. 66. See also Pub. Stat. R. I. c. 229, §§ 23–25 ; Chapin *v.* Hill, 1 R. I. 446, 450.

tent to make a contract, accepts before marriage, in lieu of dower, will be a good equitable jointure.[1] In Maine, not only must the jointure, in order to bar dower, be a freehold provision, but it must be made and assented to before marriage.[2] Nor will a widow be barred from recovering dower by her covenants with her husband before *marriage.[3] [*270] And yet in several, if not all the States, the same rule as to equitable jointures and their effect is applied, as that which prevailed in equity in England. In New York, the distinction between legal and equitable bars of dower is abolished, and if the wife is a minor, in order to bar her claim, the provision must be to take effect immediately on the death of the husband, and must be to continue for life, and must be reasonable and competent, having reference to the circumstances and situation of the parties, and in view of the husband's estate. The provision, moreover, must be assented to by the intended wife, if of age, or if a minor, by herself and father, or guardian.[4] In Alabama the common law prevails as to a wife's being barred or not by a jointure settled upon her. Yet a court of equity will enforce an antenuptial contract if fairly entered into, by decreeing a specific performance of such agreement.[5] And where, by the antenuptial agreement, she relinquished all right of dower, but her husband only settled upon her her own estate, it was held not to bar her of claiming dower at law. A jointure, to be a bar, must be something conceded to the wife.[6] But a *bona fide* antenuptial arrangement, entered into with full knowledge, and making reasonable provision for the wife, may bar her as an equitable jointure.[7] And in Maryland an infant may bar herself of dower by a contract entered into before marriage.[8] In Missouri, a provision, whether made before or after marriage, does not operate as a jointure, unless expressed to be in bar of dower.[9] And it may be added that

---

[1] Andrews *v.* Andrews, 8 Conn. 79.　　[2] Vance *v.* Vance, 21 Me. 364.
[3] Id.　　[4] McCartee *v.* Teller, 2 Paige, 511 ; Lalor's Real Estate, 274, 275.
[5] Gould *v.* Womack, 2 Ala. 83.
[6] Blackmon *v.* Blackmon, 16 Ala. 633. See also Whitehead *v.* Middleton, 2 How. (Miss.) 692 ; *contra*, Gelzer *v.* Gelzer, 1 Bailey, Ch. (S. C.) 387.
[7] Stilley *v.* Folger, 14 Ohio, 610.
[8] Levering *v.* Heighe, 2 Md. Ch. 81. See 1 Bright, Hus. & Wife, 461.
[9] Perry *v.* Perryman, 19 Mo. 469. See 1 Bright, Hus. & Wife, 449.

tɪe mode of barring dower by antenuptial settlements, so common in England before tɪe late Dower Act, comes more properly under anotɪer ɪead of tɪe law of real estate.*

[*271]   *23. In many cases a widow is barred of ɪer dower by a testamentary provision, made for ɪer by ɪer ɪusband, which, tɪougɪ not properly a jointure, operates like one, if sɪe accepts of it, wɪicɪ sɪe may do at ɪer election, or may decline and claim ɪer dower. And tɪere are numerous cases wɪere sɪe may claim botɪ tɪe provision and dower. Wɪere by tɪe terms of tɪe ɪusband's will sɪe cannot take botɪ, sɪe is at liberty to elect wɪicɪ sɪe will take. And tɪis rigɪt of election is a personal one, and is not transmissible by descent.[1] And tɪe intention of tɪe testator in tɪis respect must be gatɪered from tɪe will, and is not to be proved by parol.[2] Tɪus, for instance, if tɪe devise be in terms *in lieu of dower,* sɪe may take eitɪer, but not botɪ.[3] But tɪougɪ a pecuniary provision, if made in lieu of dower, and tɪe same is accepted, it will bar ɪer claim for dower.[4] And wɪen, under tɪe exercise of tɪe rigɪt of election, sɪe accepts a provision by will in tɪe place of dower, sɪe takes it as a purcɪaser, and ɪolds it in preference to otɪer legatees.[5] So wɪere tɪe devise is wɪolly inconsistent witɪ tɪe claim of dower, or wɪere it would prevent tɪe

* NOTE. — Other eases might be cited from the reports of these and other States upon this subject, as well as the various statutes which have been adopted by different States. But it is believed they do not materially vary from the principles above stated, and the comparative importance of the subject hardly seems to justify occupying the space which would be necessary to refer to them in detail. The reader is referred to 1 Greenl. Cruise, 200, note, and 4 Kent, Com. 56, note.

[1] Welch v. Anderson, 28 Mo. 293 ; Bubier v. Roberts, 49 ᴵe. 460. Nor to be exercised by her guardian if she is insane. Pinkerton v. Sargent, 102 ᴵass. 568 ; Crenshaw v. Carpenter, 69 Ala. 562; Crozier's Appeal, 90 Penn. St. 384.

[2] Hall v. Hall, 8 Rich. (S. C.) 407 ; Stark v. Hunton, Saxton (N. J.), 216 ; Whilden v. Whilden, Riley, Ch. (S. C.) 205 ; Herbert v. Wren, 7 Cranch, 370, 378 ; Higginbotham v. Cornwell, 8 Gratt. 83.

[3] Van Orden v. Van Orden, 10 Johns. 30 ; 2 Crabb, Real Prop. 177 ; Chapin v. Hill, 1 R. I. 446 ; Raines v. Corbin, 24 Ga. 185 ; Pemberton v. Pemberton, 29 Mo. 408 ; 4 Dane, Abr. 685 ; 7 Id. 426.

[4] Trueman v. Waters, 4 Dane, Abr. 676.

[5] Hubbard v. Hubbard, 6 ᴵet. 50 ; Pollard v. Pollard, 1 Allen, 490 ; Towle v. Swasey, 106 ᴵass. 105.

wiole will from taking effect if dower is claimed.[1] One or
two cases may be referred to as illustrative of tie foregoing
propositions. In one of tiese tie provision by will for the
widow was tie use of all the iusband's estate during ier life,
witi a remainder over. It was ield tiat she migit claim one
tiird as dower, and tie otier two tiirds by devise, and tiat
tiere was notiing inconsistent in tiese claims, nor would ier
taking tie wiole bar ier claim to land conveyed by the iusband in iis lifetime.[2] To prevent a widow claiming boti tie
provision in a will and her dower, sie must, by enforcing
ier claim of dower, defeat or interrupt or disappoint some
provision of tie will.[3]

24. Wiere a widow accepts a testamentary provision given
ier in lieu of dower, it cuts off ier claim to lands aliened by
tie iusband in iis lifetime, as well as to tiose acquired after
tie making of tie iusband's will, and constitutes a legal as
well as an equitable bar.[4] In analogy to tie effect produced
by tie election of a testamentary provision in lieu of dower,
it ias been ield tiat, if tie iusband, during coverture, conveys a portion of iis land in wiici tie wife does not join, and
tien dies, leaving no ciildren, in wiici case tie law gave her
an election to take one half of iis property or dower out of
iis estate, if sie elects to take tie ialf, sie would tiereby bar
ier claim of dower out of the premises conveyed by ier iusband in iis lifetime.[5] But in Pennsylvania, under tie statute
of tiat State, sie would not by such acceptance be
* barred of ier dower in lands aliened by tie iusband [*272]
before making tie will.[6]

25. Unless tie intention to bar tie widow's dower is clear

[1] Incledon v. Northcote, 3 Atk. 430, 437; Kennedy v. Nedrow, 1 Dall. 415, 418;
Herbert v. Wren, 7 Cranch, 370 ; Allen v. Pray, 12 Me. 138 ; Duncan v. Duncan,
2 Yeates, 302 ; Creacraft v. Wions, Addis. 350 ; White v. White, 16 N. J. 202 ;
Green v. Green, 7 Porter (Ala.), 19 ; Adsit v. Adsit, 2 Johns. Ch. 448 ; Sanford
v. Jackson, 10 Paige, 266.

[2] Lewis v. Smith, 9 N. Y. 502.   See Bull v. Church, 5 Hill, 206.

[3] Corriell v. Ham, 2 Iowa, 552 ; Pratt v. Douglass, 38 N. J. Eq. 516.

[4] Chapin v. Hill, 1 R. I. 440 ; Allen v. Pray, 12 Me. 138 ; Kennedy r. Mills,
13 Wend. 553 ; Evans v. Pierson, 9 Rich. 9.

[5] Hornsey v. Casey, 21 Mo. 545 ; Same v. Same, 23 Mo. 371.

[6] Borland v. Nichols, 12 Penn. St. 38.   The same rule is adopted in Virginia.
Higginbotham v. Cornwell, 8 Gratt. 83.

in case of testamentary provision for ıer, sıe will be ıeld entitled to botı, wıere tıere is no statute provision to tıe contrary.[1] In Massacıusetts, under tıe statute, a provision by will in favor of a wife will be presumed to be in lieu of ıer dower, unless tıe contrary appear to be tıe intention of tıe will. So in Pennsylvania, Indiana, Illinois, Maryland, Kentucky, Alabama, Nortı Carolina, New Hampsıire, New Jersey, New York, Missouri, Kansas, Maine, and Arkansas.[2] * In certain States, as in Mississippi, if tıere is no provision for ıer in tıe will, sıe takes as if intestate.[3]

26. So in many of tıe States sıe must signify ıer election of dower witıin some certain period prescribed by statute, or sıe will be deemed to ıave elected to accept tıe provision in bar of it, unless tıe will clearly gives ıer botı.[4] In tıe following States tıis election must be made within six montıs after tıe testator's deatı, or it is construed an acceptance of

---

* NOTE. — In Kansas, if a husband die without any descendants living capable of inheriting, the widow has her election to take dower or to take all the real estate of her husband, subject to debts. If she does not elect within six months, she is endowed. Compiled Laws, 1862, c. 83, §§ 4, 6, 7.

---

[1] Herbert v. Wren, 7 Cranch, 370; Higginbotham v. Cornwell, 8 Gratt. 83 ; Kennedy v. Nedrow, 1 Dall. 418 ; Smith v. Kniskern, 4 Johns. Ch. 9 ; Adsit v. Adsit, 2 Johns. Ch. 448 ; Walker's Int. 325 ; Hilliard v. Binford, 10 Ala. 977, 987; Evans v. Webb, 1 Yeates, 424 ; Pickett v. Peay, 3 Brev. 545 ; Church v. Bull, 2 Denio, 430 ; Ostrander v. Spickard, 8 Blackf. 227 ; Tooke v. Hardeman, 7 Ga. 20 ; Norris v. Clark, 2 Stockt. 51 ; Van Arsdale v. Van Arsdale, 26 N. J. 404 ; Mills v. Ɓills, 28 Barb. 454 ; Clark v. Griffith, 4 Iowa, 405 ; Yancy v. Smith, 2 Ɓet. (Ky.) 408 ; Dodge v. Dodge, 31 Barb. 413 ; Durfee, Pet., 14 R. I. 47.

[2] Reed v. Dickerman, 12 Pick. 146 ; Herbert v. Wren, 7 Cranch, 378 ; Stat. Penn. 1833, § 11 ; Smith v. Baldwin, 2 Ind. 404 ; Ill. Rev. Stat. 1883, c. 41, § 10 ; Ɓd. Rev. Code, 1878, art. 50, § 227 ; Collins v. Carman, 5 Ɓd. 503 ; McCans v. Board, 1 Dana, 340; Hilliard v. Binford, 10 Ala. 977 ; Rev. Stat. N. C. 1837, p. 612 ; N. H. Gen. L. 1878, c. 202, § 18 ; N. J. Rev. Laws, 677 ; Thompson v. Egbert, 17 N. J. 459 ; Penn. Stat. Purdon's Dig. 1861, p. 362; Mo. Rev. Stat. 1879, § 2199 ; Kansas, Comp. Laws, 1862, c. 83, § 10 ; Bubier v. Roberts, 49 Ɓe. 460 ; Ark. Stats. 1858, c. 60, § 24.

[3] Ɓiss. Rev. Code, 1880, § 1173.

[4] N. Y. 3 Rev. Stat. 5th ed. 1859, p. 32, §§ 11-14 ; Kennedy v. Ɓills, 13 Wend. 556 ; Walker's Introduct. 325 ; Ɓinn. Comp. Stats. 1859, c. 36, § 18 ; Oregon, Stats. 1855, p. 407. In Ohio, she, by neglecting to elect the provision within six months, is held to elect dower. In Alabama, the time is one year from probate of the will. Code, 1867, § 1928. In Nebraska, one year from husband's death. Rev. Stat. 1866, p. 58. So in Virginia. Acts 1866. In Kansas, one year from citation by the probate court. Laws, 1865.

tie provision and bar of dower.   Massachusetts,[1] Maine,[2] Missouri,[3] New Jersey,[4] Norti Carolina,[5] Maryland,[6] Tennessee,[7] *Mississippi.[8] Where the widow dies [*273] witiin the period given by tie statute, in wiici to make election, witiout iaving made it, tie law will presume the election to be tiat wiici is most favorable for her.[9] Tiougi in Maryland and Norti Carolina it ias been icld, if sie so die, her representatives will be bound by the provisions of tie iusband's will, as the rigit of election is a personal one wiici no one but ierself can exercise.[10]

27. Besides tiis general power of election between a devise and dower, tie widow often may elect in wiat capacity sie siall take wiat is devised to ier, wiere it is left equivocal wietier as dowress or devisee. And tiis becomes an important distinction wiere tie iusband leaves creditors.[11] Tius in one case a iusband mortgaged iis estate, iis wife not join-ing in tie deed. By iis will ie devised ier tie wiole of iis estate witi remainder over. After iis deati tie mortgagee

[1] Pub. Stat. c. 124, § 9 ; Pratt v. Felton, 4 Cush. 174.

[2] Hastings v. Clifford, 32 Ъe. 132.

[3] Kemp v. Holland, 10 Mo. 255.   But now by statute in twelve months.   Gen. Stat. 1866, c. 130, §§ 15, 16.

[4] Thompson v. Egbert, 17 N. J. 459.

[5] Pettijohn v. Beasley, 1 Dev. & B. 254 ; Rev. Stat. N. C. 1837, p. 612.

[6] Collins v. Carman, 5 Ъd. 503, 530.

[7] Ъalone v. Ъajors, 8 Humph. 577.

[8] *Ex parte* Ъoore, 7 How. (Ъiss.) 665.   In Alabama the election must be made, if at all, in a reasonable time ; Hilliard v. Binford, 10 Aln. 996.   In Ver-mont the time is eight months.   Smith v. Smith, 20 Vt. 270.   In New York the election must be in one year.   Rev. Stat. 5th ed. pt. 2, ch. 1, tit. 3, § 14; Willard Real Est. 69.   In Pennsylvania the election must be made within twelve months from the death of the testator. Purdon's Dig. 1861, p. 362.   In Kansas, within twelve months from proof of the will.   Stat. Comp. 1862, c. 183, § 11.   In Arkansas, eighteen months.   In Vermont, eight months, Rev. Stat. 1863, c. 55, §§ 4–6 ; but the probate court may now extend the time, Acts, 1864.   In New York, Wisconsin, Kentucky, Illinois, Ъinnesota, and Oregon, the election must be made within one year.   N. Y. Rev. Stat. 5th ed. 1859, p. 32, §§ 11–14; Wis. Rev. Stat. 1858, c. 89, §§ 14–19 ; Ky. Rev. Stat. 1860, c. 47, art. 4, § 7 : Ill. Comp. Stat. 1858, vol. 1, p. 152 ; Minn. Stat. Comp. 1858, c. 36, §§ 14–19 ; Oregon, Stat. 1855, p. 407.

[9] Ъerrill v. Emery, 10 Pick. 507.

[10] Boone v. Boone, 3 Har. & McH. 95 ; Collins v. Carman, 5 Ъd. 503 ; Lewis v. Lewis, 7 Ind. 72.   So by statute in Pennsylvania ; Acts, 1865.

[11] Ъitchell v. Ъitchell, 8 Ala. 414.

foreclosed his mortgage, making the widow party to the suit. But it was held that she still might claim dower in one third of the premises, and two thirds as devisee, since the judgment only bound those who claimed under the mortgagor as mortgagor, and her right as dowress had attached before the mortgage, and was paramount to that.[1]

28. An election in these cases may be evidenced by acts *in pais*, such as entering upon the land devised, as well as by matter of record, where it is done with a full knowledge of the facts in respect to the provision.[2] But ordinarily, wherever a widow fairly and understandingly has elected to take the provision of a will instead of dower, she cannot afterwards revoke it and claim dower.[3]

[*274] *29. And yet it has been held that if she has been substantially deprived of such provision, she is remitted to her right of dower.[4] And if it turns out that nothing passes by the devise, she may claim her dower, though she may once have elected to take the provision of the will.[5] If no provision is made for her by the will, she need not dissent from the will in order to claim her dower.[6]

[1] Lewis *v.* Smith, 9 N. Y. 502, 512.

[2] Delay *v.* Vinal, 1 Met. 57 ; Ambler *v.* Norton, 4 Hen. & M. 23 ; Tooke *v.* Hardeman, 7 Ga. 20.

[3] Davison *v.* Davison, 15 N. J. 235. Nor claim a share of lapsed legacies. *Re* Benson's Accounting, 96 N. Y. 63. See Mathews *v.* Mathews, 141 Mass. 511.

[4] Hastings *v.* Clifford, 32 Me. 132 ; Thompson *v.* Egbert, 17 N. J. 459. See also Thomas *v.* Wood, 1 Md. Ch. 296.

[5] Chew *v.* Farmers' Bank, 9 Gill, 361 ; Osmun *v.* Porter, 39 N. J. Eq. 141.

[6] Green *v.* Green, 7 Porter (Ala.), 19 ; Martin *v.* Martin, 22 Ala. 86. For further references upon the subject of election, by a widow in case of a will, &c., the reader is referred to 1 White & Tud. Cas. Am. ed. 284–289 and n. If an infant receive a negotiable note in lieu of dower, she cannot claim both to sue on it, and also to have dower. Drew *v.* Drew, 40 N. J. Eq. 458.

CHAPTER IX.

ESTATES BY MARRIAGE.

SECT. 1. Estates during Coverture.
SECT. 2. Homestead Estates.

SECTION I.

ESTATES DURING COVERTURE.

1. IT will be recollected that the interest of a tenant by curtesy, or of a dowress, relates only to the period subsequent to the determination of the coverture.

There are rights which husbands and wives respectively have, as such, in lands, and which remain to be considered as not coming under the head of curtesy or dower.* These rights were comparatively simple and easily defined as they existed

---

* NOTE. — It is not intended, in this chapter, to treat of that joint ownership of lands by husband and wife, known as estates by entirety. For these, see c. 13.

at common law. But under the system of equity, and [*276] especially * under tie modifications of modern legislation, tiese rigits iave become not a little complex and variant in tie different States.

2. By tie common law, for instance, tie rigits of tie wife to ier property became for tie time being merged by tie coverture. And if tiis property consists of lands, tie iusband alone is entitled to tie rents and profits tiereof,[1] subject iowever to be divested by a divorce *a vinculo*.[2] And if rents are due wien tie iusband dies, tiey go to iis personal representatives, and not to tie wife as survivor.[3] Wiereas, in many of tie United States, as will be seen, tie wife may iold, manage, and convey her lands like a *feme sole*. Tie interest wiici a iusband ias, at common law, in iis wife's lands, is regarded as a freeiold, since it is for an uncertain period wiici may continue during tie term of iis life.[4] But under tie present statutes of Massaciusetts relating to married women, tie husband ias no freeiold in iis wife's land. And tie rigit of possession remains in ier notwitistanding iis deed of tie same to anotier. His deed would only operate as an estoppel to iis claiming curtesy against iis grantee.[5] But if tie interest of tie wife be a reversionary one, subject to a prior freehold, the iusband ias no control over it, and a conveyance of it by iim would be void. He must iave a present rigit of seisin or possession to exercise control over it.[6] He migit, tierefore, make iimself a tenant to tie *præcipe*, or convey a freeiold in suci lands to anotier.[7] Tius, wiere an indenture intended to be signed by iusband and wife, releasing lands belonging to ier, was signed by tie iusband only, it was ield to operate as a release during tieir joint lives.[8]

---

[1] 1 Bl. Com. 442 ; Wms. Real Prop. 182.

[2] Burt *v.* Hurlburt, 16 Vt. 292 ; Oldham *v.* Henderson, 5 Dana, 254.

[3] Shaw *v.* Partridge, 17 Vt. 626.

[4] 1 Roper, Hus. & Wife, 3 ; Melvin *v.* Proprietors, 16 Pick. 161 ; Babb *v.* Perley, 1 Me. 7 ; Co. Lit. 351 a.

[5] Walsh *v.* Young, 110 Mass. 396.   [6] Shores *v.* Carley, 8 Allen, 425.

[7] Co. Lit. 326 a, n. 280 ; McClain *v.* Gregg, 2 A. K. Marsh. 454 ; Trask *v.* Patterson, 29 Me. 499 ; Mitchell *v.* Sevier, 9 Humph. 146 ; Clancy, Rights of Wom. 161.

[8] Robertson *v.* Norris, 11 Q. B. 916.

3. Still the husband, in such case, does not by his marriage acquire a sole seisin. The seisin is regarded as a joint one, and in both. Both together have the whole estate, and therefore, in law, they are both considered as seised in fee, and must so state their title in pleading.[1] * And until the birth of a child, the interest of the husband in the wife's estate is so far inchoate, that, if the wife forfeited her inheritance before that event by any act like that of treason, it defeated the interest of the husband.[2]

4. Equity often adopts an entirely different rule from that of the common law in respect to a wife's separate interest in her own lands during coverture, where the intention of the person limiting them to the wife was, in so doing, to secure them to her separate use. Nor is this only in case of their being expressly given to trustees for her benefit. If by the terms of the limitation, the intention to exclude the marital rights of *the husband does not appear, equity [*277] will follow the law, and suffer him to enjoy the rents and profits, even where the lands are held by trustees. Whereas, if the limitation is clearly to the sole and separate use of the wife, equity will, if no trustee is appointed, hold the husband himself as the wife's trustee, and compel him to execute the trust by giving her the rents and profits, to be subject to her sole control. And this is said to be the rule in equity on both sides of the Atlantic.[3]   No particular form

---

* NOTE. — In addition to what has already been said (ante, p. *141) upon the subject, the authorities, with the exception of the case there cited from the New Hampshire Reports, seem to be uniform that the seisin of husband and wife of the wife's land is a joint one, and not the separate seisin of either. Co. Lit. 67 a ; 1 Bright, Hus. & Wife, 112 ; Polyblank v. Hawkins, Doug. 329 ; Took v. Glascock, 1 Saund. It. 253, n. 4 ; Poole v. Longueville, 2 Saund. 283, n. 1 ; Doore v. Vinten, 12 Sim. Ch. 161, 164 ; Hall v. Sayre, 10 B. Mon. 46 ; Coe v. Wolcottville Mg. Co., 35 Conn. 175.

---

[1] Melvin v. Proprietors, 16 Pick. 165 ; Com. Dig. Baron and Feme, E. 1 ; Catlin v. Milner, 2 Lutw. 1421 ; Clancy, Rights of Wom. 161 ; ante, p. *141.

[2] 1 Bright, Hus. & Wife, 113 ; Co. Lit. 351 a.

[3] Clancy, Rights of Wom. 256, 257 ; Hill, Trust. 406 ; Id. 420, and Rawle's n. 1 ; 1 White & Tud. Lead. Cas. 378 ; Cochran v. O'Hern, 4 Watts & S. 95 ; Trenton Bk. v. Woodruff, 1 Green, Ch. 117 ; Knight v. Bell, 22 Ala. 198 ; Long v. White, 5 J. J. Marsh. 226 ; Fears v. Brooks, 12 Ga. 195 ; Blanchard v. Blood, 2 Barb. 352 ; Stuart v. Kissam, 2 Barb. 493 ; Porter v. Rutland Bk., 19 Vt. 410.

of expression is necessary to determine wietier tie wife alone or iusband siall iave tie benefit of tie trust estate. But tie intention must be clear, in order to secure suci separate use to tie wife, and to exclude tie marital rigits of tie iusband.[1]

5. Tie words "sole" and "separate," applied to tie nature of tie intended use by tie wife, are tie most appropriate to express a limitation in ier favor, exclusive of any interest or control on tie part of tie iusband.[2]

6. One of tie great objects in modern marriage settlements is to secure to tie wife a siare of tie property free from tie debts and control of ier iusband. And tiis is often so done, tiat in order to protect her against tie solicitations or influence of ier iusband, sie will not be allowed by ciancery to assign or anticipate ier income.[3] But wiile no particular form of words is required, if tie intention is clear to impose a restriction upon tie wife as to anticipation or assignment of her income, sie may, unless tius specially restricted, dispose of it by sale, contract, or mortgage, as if sie were a *feme sole*, according to tie Englisi rules in equity.[4]

[*278]   *7. Tie courts of tie several States iave not been uniform in applying tie principle of restriction to wives in respect to estates ield in trust for tiem. In some, tie Englisi rules of ciancery are adopted; in otiers, tie wife is not permitted to go beyond tie power expressly given by tie deed of settlement.[5]

---

1 Welch *v.* Welch, 14 Ala. 76; Fears *v.* Brooks, 12 Ga. 195; Hill, Trusts. 406; 1 White & Tud. Lead. Cas. 338; Tritt *v.* Colwell, 31 Penn. St. 228.

2 Goodrum *v.* Goodrum, 8 Ired. Eq. 313; 1 White & Tud. Lead. Cas. 338.

3 Wms. Real Prop. 183; Coote, Mortg. 104.

4 Hill, Trust. 421; White *v.* Hulme, 1 Bro. C. C. 16.

5 Instead of illustrating these doctrines by the citation of the numerous cases which have arisen in the several States, the reader is referred for these cases to Hill on Trust. 421, note by Wharton; Wms. Real Prop. 184, note by Rawle, or 1 White & Tud. Lead. Cas. 370–378, Hare & Wallace's notes. By a reference to these authorities, it will appear that the English rule is substantially adopted in New Jersey, Connecticut, Kentucky, North Carolina, Alabama, Georgia, and Missouri. In Pennsylvania, South Carolina, Mississippi, Tennessee, Virginia, Rhode Island, the wife is governed by the terms expressly prescribed in the deed, &c. In New York the matter is regulated by statute. Lalor, Real Est. 173, 174.

8. In consequence of the theoretic unity and entirety of the ownership of husband and wife in respect to their interest in lands, they cannot take by purchase in moieties; and where land was conveyed to them to hold in common and not in joint tenancy, they were held to take an entirety of estate without regard to the intent.[1]

9. They are not properly joint tenants of such lands, since, though there is a right of survivorship, neither can convey so as to defeat this right in the other. Each takes an entirety of the estate.[2] In Iowa, a conveyance or devise to husband and wife makes them tenants in common, unless the instrument expressly creates a joint estate.[3] But in Mississippi, where, by law, joint tenancies are converted into tenancies in common, conveyances to husbands and wives creates tenancies by entirety, which are still retained.[4]

10. As a consequence of the principle that husband and wife are one in law, if lands are given to A & B, husband and wife, and C, the husband and wife take a moiety, and the other grantee a moiety.[5] But if lands descend to A, B, & C, they *each take a third part, though A [*279] & B happen to be husband and wife.[6]

11. So if lands descend or are devised to A & B, who afterwards intermarry, they still remain joint tenants or tenants in common of the lands, just as before marriage.[7]

12. As the husband is entitled to the entire rents of the wife's lands, except as hereinbefore stated, it follows that he

[1] Stuckey v. Keefe's Ex'rs, 26 Penn. St. 397.

[2] Gibson v. Zimmerman, 12 Mo. 385; Bomar v. Mullins, 4 Rich. Eq. 80; Brownson v. Hull, 16 Vt. 309; Todd v. Zachary, 1 Busbee, Eq. 286; Den v. Whitemore, 2 Dev. & B. 537; Den v. Hardenbergh, 5 Halst. 42; Fairchild v. Chastelleux, 1 Penn. St. 176; Harding v. Springer, 14 Me. 407; Jackson v. Stevens, 16 Johns. 110; Needham v. Branson, 5 Ired. 426; Ross v. Garrison, 1 Dana, 35; Taul v. Campbell, 7 Yerg. 319; Tud. Cas. 730. In Connecticut, however, they are joint tenants, and the husband may convey his interest. Whittlesey v. Fuller, 11 Conn. 337. And it is said that they may by express words be made tenants in common by a gift to them during coverture. Prest. Abs. 41.

[3] Hoffman v. Stigers, 28 Iowa, 302.

[4] Hemingway v. Scales, 42 Miss. 1.

[5] Lit. § 291; Wms. Real Prop. 184; Tud. Cas. 730.

[6] Knapp v. Windsor, 6 Cush. 156.   [7] Tud. Cas. 731; Co. Lit. 187 b.

alone can sue for an injury to the estate which affects these.[1]
But if the injury affect the inheritance, the action must be in
their joint names, and it will survive to her if she outlive him.[2]
So if a tenant occupies the wife's lands by the consent of husband and wife, and she dies, the husband can maintain an
action in his own name for use and occupation.[3]

13. By the common law neither husband nor wife could
convey lands to each other,[4] nor release to each other.[5] But
the husband may do this by means of the Statutes of Uses, by
conveying to another to the wife's use,[6] or by a covenant with
a third person to stand seized to her use.[7] And in Maine,
husband and wife may convey directly to each other, and the
same is true as to a husband conveying by deed to his wife, in
Minnesota,[8] and in Iowa.[9]

14. And courts of equity will sometimes sustain a deed
from husband to wife against the grantor's heir at law.[10] And
a devise by husband to wife may always be good, as the coverture ceases before the devise can take effect.[11]

15. Upon the death of the husband, the wife's inheritance
remains to her unaffected by any alienation made or incumbrance created thereon by the husband. No further act is
required on her part to put an end to such alienation
[*280] or conveyance * than a simple entry, instead of her
being driven to an action, as was the case at the
common law.[12]

---

[1] Fairchild v. Chastelleux, 1 Penn. St. 176; Wms. Real Prop. 184, n.; Babb
v. Perley, 1 Me. 6; Battocks v. Stearns, 9 Vt. 326.

[2] 2 Kent, Com. 131; Babb v. Perley, 1 Me. 6; Dippers at Tunbridge Wells,
2 Wils. 414, 423.

[3] Jones v. Patterson, 11 Barb. 572.

[4] Martin v. Martin, 1 Me. 394; Voorhees v. Presb. Ch., 17 Barb. 103.

[5] Frissel v. Rozier, 19 Mo. 448.

[6] Wms. Real Prop. 185; 1 Roper, Hus. & Wife, 53.

[7] Thatcher v. Omans, 3 Pick. 521.

[8] Bubier v. Roberts, 49 Me. 460; Johnson v. Stillings, 35 Me. 427; Allen v.
Hooper, 50 Me. 371; Wilder v. Brooks, 10 Minn. 50.

[9] Hoffman v. Stigers, 28 Iowa, 302, 310.

[10] Jones v. Obenchain, 10 Gratt. 259; Hunt v. Johnson, 44 N. Y. 27, 37, 41.

[11] 1 Roper, Hus. & Wife, 53; Lit. § 168.

[12] Stat. 32 Hen. VIII. c. 28; 1 Roper, Hus. & Wife, 56; Cleary v. McDowall,
1 Cheves (S. C.), 139; Wms. Real Prop. 185; Bruce v. Wood, 1 Met. 542; 1
Bright, Hus. & Wife, 162; Mellus v. Snowman, 21 Me. 201.

16. It is no objection to a woman's being a grantee of lands from a stranger, that she is a *feme covert*, unless her husband objects by some express dissent, the law always presuming his assent unless the contrary be shown. But it is said that she cannot take as a purchaser if he expressly objects to her accepting the estate, and that such disagreement on his part divests the whole estate.[1] A husband may dissent from a purchase by, or devise to, his wife, since otherwise he might be made a tenant to his own disadvantage. But he cannot by his dissent defeat her title as heir.[2]

17. It is laid down by Coke,[3] that a wife may waive a purchase of land made by her during coverture, and, after the decease of her husband, avoid the conveyance, though he had assented to it; and that her heirs may do the same after her death, if, after her husband's death, she shall not have agreed to the purchase. But where, as in this country, a wife, by joining with her husband in a deed, may part with her lands and pass a good title, the joint act of the two being in all respects as available as if done by her while sole, it would seem that their joint assent in accepting a title should be as valid as in granting one. And in New Hampshire it has been held that a deed to a *feme covert*, made with her own and her husband's assent, vested the title legally in her. And in Vermont it has been held that a deed of gift to a wife during coverture, if accepted by her husband, is accepted by her, and that her refusal apart from him is of no consequence.[4]

18. Unless restrained by the terms of the settlement, a married woman may, since the statute of 3 & 4 Wm. IV. c. 74, by joining in a deed with her husband, convey any interest she * has in real estate. Such a deed would of [*281] course convey the interest of both. Previous to that statute this was usually done, in England, by levying a fine, which, as well as recoveries, is abolished by that statute.[5]

19. In the United States, the custom of a wife's joining with her husband in a deed of conveyance of her lands has

[1] Co. Lit. 3 a ; Com. Dig. "Baron & Feme," P. 2 ; Perkins, §§ 43, 44.
[2] 1 Dane, Abr. 368 ; 4 Id. 597.   [3] Co. Lit. 3 a.
[4] Gordon v. Haywood, 2 N. H. 402 ; Brackett v. Wait, 6 Vt. 411, 424.
[5] Wms. Real Prop. 188.

prevailed from a very early period in their history. In most, if not all of them, there are now existing statutes upon the subject, regulating the mode in which such deeds shall be executed in order to be valid.[1] And sometimes equity will sustain a deed from husband to wife, though void at law.[2] And in Maine, a wife may do this, though not of the age of twenty-one years.[3] The discussion of the form of such deeds, however, properly belongs to another part of this work.

20. If the husband expend money upon lands of his wife in his occupation, by erecting buildings or making improvements thereon, the law will presume he intended it for her benefit, and he cannot recover for the same.[4]

21. The rights of the husband as tenant by curtesy, where the wife dies after having had issue, and leaving lands of inheritance, have been considered in a former chapter. But if the wife die without having had issue, nothing remains to the husband, as against the claims of her heirs at law, except the right of emblements.[5]

22. It will be perceived that a husband holding his wife's estate of inheritance by marital right is tenant for life with a reversion in the wife. As such, he would be liable for waste like other tenants for life, if it were not that a wife could not maintain such an action against her husband. If, however, he conveys his freehold to a stranger, who commits waste, the action lies; so if the husband's estate is levied upon by his creditors and they commit waste, and the husband and wife may join in an action for such an injury. And chan-
[*282] cery will interpose by way * of injunction against the husband while he is tenant, to prevent his committing waste.[6] *

* NOTE. — From the statutes of the several States in relation to the rights of married women to control their own lands during coverture, the following

---

[1] Davey v. Turner, 1 Dall. 11; Jackson v. Gilchrist, 15 Johns. 89, 109; Fowler v. Shearer, 7 Mass. 14 ; Manchester v. Hough, 5 Mason, 67 ; Durant v. Ritchie, 4 Mason, 45 ; Page v. Page, 6 Cush. 196.

[2] Shepard v. Shepard, 7 Johns. Ch. 57 ; Bunch v. Bunch, 26 Ind. 400.

[3] Adams v. Palmer, 51 Me. 478, 488.

[4] 1 Roper, Hus. & Wife, 54 ; Washburn v. Sproat, 16 Mass. 449.

[5] Barber v. Root, 10 Mass. 260 ; 2 Kent, Com. 131.

[6] Babb v. Perley, 1 Me. 6 ; 2 Kent, Com. 131.

abstract of the various provisions upon the subject has been drawn. — *Alabama*, all that the wife holds at the time of her marriage, or acquires afterwards, remains her separate estate, not subject to her husband's debts. Such estate may be conveyed by the joint deed of husband and wife attested by two witnesses, and she may devise the same by her last will and testament. Code, 1867, §§ 2371, 2373, and 2378. — *Arkansas*, a married woman may be seised of any estate in her own right and name and as of her own property, except such as may be conveyed to her by her husband subsequent to the marriage. But such property is not exempt from the payment of the husband's debts, until she has filed a schedule of it in the recorder's office; unless the deed, grant, or other transfer of the property expressly sets forth that the same is designed to be exempt from liabilities of the husband. She cannot make a will unless empowered so to do by a marriage settlement, or written authority from the husband before marriage. Dig. of Stat. 1858, c. 111, §§ 1, 7, and 8; c. 180, § 3. And now, by Acts of 1873, p. 382, married women are substantially clothed with full property in and control over real and personal estate belonging to them or acquired by them separate from their husbands, provided they cause their separate real estate to be recorded in their names in the counties in which they reside. — *California*, her property at the time of the marriage, and all she acquires afterwards by gift, devise, or descent, remains her separate property. The husband has a corresponding right to his property; but what they acquire during coverture, except in the manner already stated, becomes the common property of both. A married woman may dispose of her separate estate by deed or will, as if single; but upon the death of husband or wife, the entire community property goes to the survivor, if he or she shall not have abandoned the other and lived separate. In such a case the half of the community property may be disposed of by the party dying, or will go to his or her descendants or heirs. Code, 1872, §§ 162, 1273, 1401. — *Colorado*, the estate of a married woman remains her separate property, and is not subject to the disposal of the husband, but may be bargained, sold, and conveyed by her as if sole. Laws, 1874, p. 185. — In *Dakota*, curtesy and dower are abolished, and neither husband nor wife have any interest in the property of each other, except that the husband must support himself and wife from his labor and property, and, if unable to do so, she must assist him as far as she can. They may contract with each other, and every woman of the age of sixteen years may devise her estate, whether sole or married. But in joint deeds of husband and wife, her covenants do not bind her. Civ. Code, 1866. But if husband deserts his wife, or is unable or neglects to provide for his family, the court may empower her to act as a *feme sole* in acquiring, holding, and disposing of property. Laws, 1870-71, c. 32, § 1. — *Connecticut*, the real estate of a married woman belonging to her before marriage, or afterwards acquired by devise or inheritance, or by conveyance in consideration of property acquired by her personal services during coverture cannot be taken for her husband's debts, but shall be held by her to her sole and separate use if invested in her name or in that of a trustee for her. And if her husband be insane, the court may authorize her to convey her real estate as if sole. Rev. Stat. 1875, pp. 56, 186, 187. The wife may dispose of her estate by joining in a deed with her husband. Husband and wife take a joint estate conveyed to them, as joint tenants, and he may convey his interest in the same by a separate deed. She may dispose of her estate by her last will in the same manner as a *feme sole*. If abandoned by her husband, her property vests in her as her sole estate. But the interest of the husband in the estate of his wife cannot be taken for his debts during her life. Gen. Stat. 1866, p. 302, §§ 11, 12; Whittlesey *v.* Fuller, 11 Conn. 347 ; Comp. Stat. p. 484, § 1 ; Stat. 1856, c. 36. By Act 1859, c. 75, the probate court may order the sale of the real estate of a minor married woman whose husband is of age, upon their joint application, and their joint deed is made as effectual as if she had arrived at full age. Rev. St. 1875, p. 56, 187. — *Delaware*, a wife's estate is held as her sole and separate property, and not subject to the control of her husband ; she may also dispose of the same by will, but not so as to affect her husband's right by curtesy. Laws, 1875, c. 165, § 1. — *Florida*, a wife's estate, on her marriage, continues independent of the husband, and is not liable for his debts. She may devise it, but cannot convey it by deed unless her husband joins in the deed. Florida, Dig. 2d Divis.. T. 5, c. 1, § 2 ; Thompson, Dig. 1847, c. 1, § 1. — *Illinois*, by Act 1861, p. 143, real property belonging to a married woman as her sole and separate property, or which any woman hereafter married owns at the time of her marriage, or which any married woman during coverture acquires in good faith from any person, other than her husband, by descent, devise, or otherwise, together with all the rents, issues, income, and profits thereof, is declared to remain her sole and separate property, under her sole control, as though she were sole ; and not subject to the disposal, control or interference of her husband, or liable for his debts. She may dispose of her separate estate by her last will, in the same manner as a *feme sole.* Rev. Stat. 1855, c. 110, § 1. And she may manage, sell, and convey her [*283] * property as fully as her husband can his own estate. Rev. St. 1874, c. 68, § 9. — *Indiana*, by Act of 1859, c. 141, a married woman is enabled to devise her real estate. And by Stat. 1860, p. 374, the lands of a married woman are not subject to the debts of the husband, but remain her separate property as if she were unmarried, except that she cannot convey them but by deed in which her husband must join, Stat. 1860, p. 374 ; but her covenants do not bind her, Rev. Stat. 1876, p. 363. — *Iowa*, she has the same power to convey her lands as a *feme sole.* Code, 1851, § 1207, and Revision, 1860, p. 390 ; Code, 1873, § 2202. — *Kansas*, the real estate owned by a woman at the time of her marriage, with the rents and profits thereof, and that which comes to her by descent, or devise, or gift, except from her husband, continues her sole and separate property, and is not subject to the disposal of her husband, or liable for his debts. She may bargain, sell, and convey the same, or enter into any contract in reference to it as if she were sole. But she cannot dispose of more than one half of her property, both personal and real, by will, without the consent of her husband in writing. Comp. Laws, 1862, c. 141, §§ 1–4. — *Kentucky*, she may hold real estate to her separate use to the exclusion of her present or future husband, if conveyed or devised to be so held ; but she cannot alien it with or without her husband's assent. If it is a gift, she may alien by the consent of the donor or his personal representatives. Such estates cannot be sold or incumbered but by order of a court of equity, and only for the purpose of exchange and reinvestment. A married woman may dispose by will of any estate secured to her separate use by deed or devise. But she may convey an estate which she owns or has any interest in, as her general property, as distinguished from that in which she has a separate estate, whether legal or equitable, in possession or remainder, by a deed in which she and her husband shall join, or by a separate deed, if he shall have already conveyed his interest. Rev. Stat. 1860, c. 47, art. 4, § 17, and c. 24, §§ 20, 21, and c. 106, § 4. And see Stuart *v.* Wilder, 17 B. Mon. 55.   On joint petition of husband and wife, the court may empower her to use, enjoy, and convey her own property free from her husband's debts or claims.   Sup. Rev. Stat. 1860, p. 728. — *Maine,* the wife may own real estate in her own right, which she may sell, devise, or convey as a *feme sole,* without joinder or assent of the husband.   She may release to her husband the right to control her own property, and to dispose of the income thereof for their mutual benefit, and may revoke the same in writing.   But the land of a married woman may be taken upon execution to satisfy debts contracted by her before marriage. Rev. Stat. c. 61, §§ 1, 2.   And see Acts 1861, c. 46 ; Acts 1862, c. 148 ; Acts 1863, c. 214 ; Moore *v.* Richardson, 37 Me. 438. — *Maryland,* real property belonging to a woman at the time of her marriage, or acquired afterwards by gift, grant, devise, or descent, is not liable for her husband's debts ; but she holds it for her separate use, with power of devising the same as fully as if she were sole ; or she may convey it by a joint deed with her husband.   Code, 1860, p. 325, §§ 1, 2.   If married women are lessees of land, they are subject to distress for rent which has been overdue for ninety days, as if they were sole, and as such are subject to actions upon their covenants as lessees.   And if they make deeds of their lands, they may bind themselves by covenants which will run with the land conveyed.   Laws, 1867 ; Laws, 1874, c. 57, § 1. — *Massachusetts,* she may hold to her sole and separate use, all land which comes to her by descent, devise, gift, or grant, and that which she acquires by trade or business, and all she owns at her marriage, with the rents and profits of the same, which are not to be subject to the control of her husband, and which she may bargain, sell, and convey, and enter into contracts in reference to, in the same manner as if she were sole, with this limitation, that she cannot convey her real estate, unless her husband joins with her in the deed, or she has a license for such sale from a judge of the courts.   She may make a will of her estate, like a *feme sole,* except that she cannot thereby deprive her husband of his curtesy.   But this statute does not affect any marriage settlement, or empower a husband to convey land to his wife.   Pub. Stat. c. 147.[1]   If the wife of a mortgagor acquire his rights, the mortgagee may bring a writ of entry to foreclose the same against her and not against him.   Campbell *v.* Bemis, 16 Gray, 485, 487 ; Conant *v.* Warren, 6 Gray, 562.   A married woman may convey shares in corporations, and lease and convey real estate as if sole, but cannot by her separate conveyance, cut off her husband's contingent interest therein ; Stat. 1874, c. 184, § 1, but her warranty will estop her ; Knight *v.* Thayer, 125 Mass. 25. — *Michigan,* the wife may devise her real estate, if her husband annex his assent to the will in writing.   Her property at the time of her marriage and any that she acquires during coverture, remains her separate estate, though she cannot convey it away, except by assent of her husband, or the authority of the judge of probate.   Rev. Stat. c. 68, § 1 ; c. 85, § 25.   But by Comp. L. 1871, p. 1477, the property of a married woman is not liable for the debts of the husband, and may be controlled, mortgaged, conveyed, and devised by her in the same manner as if she were unmarried.   If a judgment be rendered against a husband and wife for the wife's tort, the execution may be levied on her estate, but not on his.   Laws, 1867. — *Mississippi,* all the property she has on her marriage, and all that comes to her after marriage, by devise or descent, remains her separate estate ; nor is it liable for the debts of the husband, or any incumbrances created by him.   She can only convey by joining with her husband, who is entitled to curtesy in her real estate.   Rev. Code, 1857, c. 40, § 5 ; Feb. 28, 1846, § 6 ; Baynton *v.* Finnall, 4 Sm. & M. 193.   But she may dispose

---

[1] See also Stats. 1884, c. 301: 1885. c. 255.

of her real and personal estate by will as if sole. Rev. Code, 1871, § 1785. — *Missouri*, the wife may convey her land by deed executed by herself and husband, and acknowledged by herself. She cannot make a will unless authorized by a marriage settlement, or her husband's written agreement before marriage. [*284] Her property, however, is not liable for the * husband's debts. Rev. Stat. 1844, c. 185, § 3; 1845, c. 32, § 35; 1849, §§ 1–3. She may now devise her lands by will, provided the husband's curtesy be not affected thereby. Gen. Stat. 1866, c. 115, § 13. — *Minnesota*, husband and wife may by their joint deed convey the real estate of the wife in like manner as she might do by her separate deed if she were unmarried; but she is not bound by any covenants therein. She may devise any real estate held by her, or to which she is entitled in her own right, by her last will and testament, with the consent of her husband in writing annexed to such will. Stats. Comp. 1858, c. 35, § 2, and c. 40, § 1. She may hold, use, and enjoy her property and the rents and profits thereof free from the control of her husband, as fully as if she were sole. Stat. 1873, c. 37, tit. III. § 47. — *New Hampshire*, if of age, she may join with her husband in conveying her land; and, if under age, their deed will release her dower. She may devise her lands to any one except her husband, though not so as to bar any right of the husband acquired by marriage contract. Stat. 1833, c. 158, §§ 10, 11; 1854, c. 15, § 22; Gen. Stat. 1867, c. 164, §§ 1, 11. And estates may be released or conveyed to a *feme covert*, to be held to her sole and separate use, without the intervention of trustees, free from the interference of the husband, in respect to which she has the same rights and remedies, and will be liable to the same actions as a *feme sole*. 1846, c. 327, §§ 3, 4; Bailey *v.* Pearson, 29 N. H. 77. By Laws 1860, c. 2342, Gen. Stat. 1867, c. 164, §§ 1, 11, a married woman may hold to her own use, free from the interference of her husband, all property inherited by, bequeathed, given, or conveyed to her, except the conveyance or gift is occasioned by payment or pledge of the husband's property. She may make a valid will in the same manner as if she were sole, and her husband may be a devisee. But no such will shall operate to alienate or affect injuriously the life estate of the husband, as tenant by the curtesy. — *New Jersey*, the property she has at her marriage, and what she acquires by gift, grant, or devise, continues to be her sole and separate estate, as if she were still sole, together with the rents and profits; the same being neither liable for the husband's debts, nor subject to his disposal. She cannot convey her lands without his consent, but she may bind herself by the covenants in her deed of her lands in the same way as if sole. Stat. 1852; Id. 1857, c. 189, § 1; Den *v.* Lawshee, 24 N. J. 613. And now a married woman, if of the age of twenty-one years, may devise her property, but not to affect the husband's interest therein. Laws, 1864. — In *Nevada*, all property owned by either husband or wife before marriage, or acquired after by gift, bequest, devise, or descent, shall be hers or his separate property respectively, and all property acquired by other ways shall be common to both. She may have a trustee of her separate property appointed by the district court. They may, by joint deed, convey her real estate in like manner as she might do if sole, except that she cannot bind herself by covenant further than is necessary to effectually convey the land. Laws, 1861, 1865. — *New York*, the estate of a *feme covert* at the time of her marriage, as well as the rents thereof, continues hers as if sole, not subject to the husband's control or liable for his debts. She may, during coverture, take an estate by descent, gift, grant, or devise, from any person but her husband, and hold the same to her sole use. She may convey or devise her estate, or the rents or profits thereof, as if she were sole. 3 Rev. Stat. 5th ed. 1859, pp. 239, 240, §§ 75, 77. By Laws 1860, c. 90, and Laws 1862, c. 172, it is declared that the real property which a married woman now owns as her sole and separate property, that which comes to her by descent, devise, gift, or grant, and that which she owns at the time of her marriage, with the rents and proceeds of it, shall remain her sole and separate property, not subject to the interference or control of her husband, or liable for his debts. She may bargain, sell, and convey such estate, and enter into any contract in reference to the same, with like effect as if she were unmarried; and she may in like manner make covenants for title which shall be binding upon her separate property. Cashman *v.* Henry, 75 N. Y. 103. But no contract of hers in respect to such property shall be binding upon the husband in any way. — *North Carolina,* the husband cannot lease or convey wife's lands, except by her consent, evidenced by a private examination before the magistrate taking an acknowledgment of the same. Stat. 1849. Married women may devise their lands like· *femes sole,* but not so as to deprive husbands of their rights of curtesy therein. Gen. Stat. 1873, c. 69, § 31. — *Ohio,* the separate property of a wife is not liable to be taken for the debts of her husband during her life or that of her children. She can convey her lands by joining in a deed with her husband and acknowledged by her upon a separate examination. Stat. 1846, Feb. 28, § 1; Swan. Rev. Stat. 1854, c. 34, §§ 2, 3; Rev. Stat. 1860, c. 34, §§ 2, 3. By Laws 1861, p. 54, any estate, legal or equitable, in real property belonging to any woman at her marriage, or which comes to her, during coverture, by conveyance, devise, or inheritance, or by purchase with her separate money or means, together with the rents and issues thereof, remains her separate property and under her sole control; and she may lease the same in her own name for any period not exceeding three years. After her decease, the husband has an estate by the curtesy in her real property; but during the life of the wife, or any heir of her body, such estate cannot be taken by any process of law for the payme..t of his debts, or be conveyed or incumbered by him, unless she join in the conveyance. See Westerman *v.* Westerman, 18 Am. L. Reg. 690. — *Oregon,* a married woman may convey her real estate by joint deed with her husband acknowledged by her. She may dispose of any real estate held in her own right, subject to her husband's right as tenant by the curtesy. Stats. 1855, p. 519. Married women may devise their estates subject only to their husband's right by curtesy. And they may convey them by deed jointly executed by them and their husbands. If the husband deserts his wife, she may deal with her property in the same manner as if she were sole. Gen. Laws, pp. 288, 515, 663. — *Pennsylvania,* all her property at the time of marriage, or acquired by her during coverture by will, deed, descent, or otherwise, remains her separate property, and may be disposed of by her last will and testament. It is subject neither to the husband's debts nor to his control. The law reserves certain rights to husbands in particular cases out of lands of their wives, when devised by them. The estate by the curtesy is exempt from levy during the life of the wife. Purdon, Dig. 1861, pp. 699, 700, 1018; Dunlop, Dig. 996, 997. The wife may convey her separate property by a deed in which her husband shall join, she acknowledging the same upon a separate examination. Id. 99. She may take or purchase lands, and bind them by judgment to secure the payment of the purchase-money; and if her husband neglects or refuses to provide for her, she may have the rights of a *feme sole* trader, and dispose of her real or personal estate. Patterson *v* Robinson, 25 Penn. St. 81; Stat. 1855, No. 456. — *Rhode Island,* she may dispose of her real estate by will, or convey it by joint deed of self and husband, she acknowledging the same upon a separate eXamination. Rev. Stat. c. 136, §§ 6, 7. The property she has or may acquire during coverture is secured to her sole and separate use, and neither that nor its rents· or profits shall be liable for the debts of the husband; and on his death the same remains her sole and separate property if she survive him. Gen. Stat. 1872, c. 152, § 1. — *Tennessee,* she may dispose by will [*285] of any estate * secured to her separate use, by deed, devise, or bequest, or in the eXecution of a specific power to that effect. And the interest which a husband has by marriage in his wife's estate is not subject to the claim of his creditors. Stat. 1852, c. 180, § 4; 1850, c. 36, § 1. And she incurs no personal liability by her deeds, but only charges her land. Jackson v Rutledge, 3 Lea, 626. — *Texas,* her property owned at the time of marriage, or acquired afterwards, by gift, devise, or descent, is secured to her by the Constitution as her separate property. Art. 7, § 19; Stat. 1848, c. 79, § 2. During marriage, the husband has the management of the wife's separate property. Land acquired by husband and wife during coverture becomes the common property of both, but may be disposed of by the husband alone, and goes to the survivor if there be no children; if there are children, one half of such property goes to the survivor. By the TeXas laws, husband and wife are distinct persons as to their estates. Wood v. Wheeler, 7 TeXas, 13. See Oldham & White's Dig. 1859, p. 24, and p. 312, arts. 1393, 1395. — *Vermont,* husband and wife may by their joint deed convey the real estate of the wife, in like manner as she might do by her separate deed, if she were unmarried; but she is not bound by any covenant. If real estate belonging to the wife is taken for any public use, the damages therefor are secured to her. She may devise any lands belonging to her at marriage, or any interest that is descendible to her heirs; and the rents, issues, and profits of these lands are eXempt from liability in respect of any debts of the husband. Rev. Stat. 1863, c. 71, §§ 16, 17, 18, and c. 65, § 2. A conveyance of real estate to husband and wife does not make a tenancy in common. Id. c. 64, § 3. If the husband abandon the wife and leave the State without providing for her, the Supreme Court may authorize her to sell her real estate. Acts, 1866. But her real estate is liable for her debts. Dale v. Robinson, 51 Vt. 20. — *Virginia,* the wife conveys her estate by a deed in which her husband joins, she being privily eXamined. Lee v. Bank of United States, 9 Leigh, 200. She can only dispose of her separate estate by will or in the way of eXercising a power of appointment. Code, 1873, p. 910. — *Wisconsin,* the real estate, with the rents and profits thereof, belonging to any married woman, or acquired by descent, grant, or devise, is not subject to the disposal of her husband, or liable for his debts, but remains her sole and separate property as if she were sole. She may join with her husband in a deed of conveyance, or may eXecute it as if sole. She may dispose of her estate by will. Rev. Stat. 1858, c. 95, §§ 1–3, and c. 86, § 12. She may bring trespass in her own name for an injury done to her real estate, even though her husband lives with her and cultivates the land for her. Boos v. Gomber, 24 Wis. 499. — *West Virginia,* a married woman may take and hold to her sole and separate use, and convey and devise the same as if sole, any real or personal estate or interest therein, and the rents and profits thereof. Nor shall the same be subject to the debts or disposal of her husband. But, in order to convey her real estate, her husband must join in the deed. Code, 1868, c. 66, §§ 1–3.

SECTION II.

RIGHTS OF HOMESTEAD.

DIVISION I.

WHAT ARE HOMESTEAD RIGHTS, AND WHO MAY CLAIM.

1. THE right of homestead, which has been established by statute, with greater or less stringency, in at least thirty-four of the States, partakes more nearly of the character of an

estate for life t1an any ot1er, and is treated of as coming
wit1in t1at category.*   Indeed, in some of t1e States it comes
properly. wit1in t1at class of estates.   T1e common law 1as
no analogous interest or estate, and it owes its creation w1olly
to statutes.¹ T1is circumstance renders it necessary to examine t1ese in detail, pointing out, as well as may be, w1erein
t1eir provisions agree, and 1ow far t1e decisions in one State
1ave served by way of analogy to 1armonize its system of
1omestead rig1ts wit1 t1ose in force in ot1er States.   T1e
general policy under w1ic1 t1ese laws 1ave been instituted
1as been to secure to a 1ouse1older and 1is family t1e benefit
of a 1ome beyond t1e reac1 of legal process on t1e part of
creditors.   And to guard t1is more effectually, in most of t1e
States no release or alienation of an estate t1us secured is of
any avail unless assented to by t1e wife of suc1 1ouse1older,
t1roug1 w1om t1e interests of t1eir minor c1ildren are also
soug1t to be guarded and protected.

1 *a*. T1e question 1as been raised and considered in several
of t1e States, w1et1er and how far t1ese acts exempting estates
from liability to respond to creditors for the debts of t1eir
owners are a violation or ot1erwise of t1e spirit of t1e provision of t1e Constitution of t1e United States, w1ic1 pro1ibits

---

* NOTE. — The section of the present work relating to homesteads was prepared
when there was no separate treatise upon the subject.   Although the topic seemed
properly to call for notice and discussion in a general work upon real property,
and was in so far consonant to the character of this treatise, yet the purely statutory nature of the right, the great variety of the legislative enactments, and, still
more, the various and conflicting decisions made in interpreting these, require the
larger space of a special treatise for their adequate presentation.   This want has
been ably supplied by Mr. Thompson's treatise, to which the reader is referred ;
where the order of treatment differs somewhat from that of the present work.   But
even since the publication of Mr. Thompson's volume in 1878, more than five
hundred cases have been decided in the courts of the United States, the substance
of which has been incorporated in the present edition.   The reader will also find
the "Homestead and Exemption Laws of the Southern States" fully considered
and explained in 19 Am. Law Reg. 1 and 137.   It is there stated that, in Georgia,
homestead is exempted to the value of $2,000, which, if carried into effect in
respect to every head of a family in the State, would amount to three times the
value of all the land in it.

---

¹ And these have no extra-territorial operation. Stinde *v.* Behrens, 6 Mo. App.
309.

States from passing laws impairing the obligation of contracts.
And the conclusions to which many of the State courts came
were in favor of sustaining the validity of such exemptions.[1]
In Alabama the court say, "There is no constitutional exception to laws, which exempt certain portions of a debtor's
property from execution, from being so modified as to increase
the exemptions and the modifications applicable to contracts
previously entered into."[2] In a case from Georgia, a creditor
had obtained a judgment against his debtor, but, before the
execution was levied, the State passed an act exempting homesteads of debtors, which extended the exemption much beyond
what it was at the time when the judgment was recovered.
The United States court, reversing the decision of the State
court, held the exemption void as to the judgment, because
impairing the obligation of the contract by withdrawing property which was liable for the debt when it was contracted.[3]
This decision was followed in Virginia, where it was held, in an
able opinion, that a law made under their constitution, exempting homesteads, was unconstitutional so far as it applied to
contracts entered into, or debts contracted, before the adoption of the constitution, as being in violation of the Constitution of the United States.[4] And the courts of the several
States have generally followed the conclusion of the Federal
Court as of binding authority.[5] In South Carolina, the consti

---

[1] Robert v. Cow, 25 La. Ann. 199; Hardman v. Downer, 39 Ga. 425; Ste-
phenson v. Osborne, 41 Miss. 119; Baylor v. St. Ant. Bk., 38 Tex. 448; Cusic
v. Douglas, 3 Kans. 123.

[2] Sneider v. Heidelbarger, 45 Ala. 134.

[3] Gunn v. Barry, 15 Wall. 610. The same rule was laid down in Missouri
under the provisions of the State Constitution of 1845, art. 13, § 17; Harvey v.
Wickham, 23 Mo. 112; Cunningham v. Gray, 20 Mo. 170; Tally v. Thompson,
Id. 277.   [4] Homestead Cases, 22 Gratt. 301.

[5] Chambliss v. Jordan, 50 Ga. 81; Clarke v. Trawick, 56 Ga. 359; Hawks v.
Hawks, 64 Ga. 239; Lessley v. Phipps, 49 Miss. 790; Ex parte Hewett, 5 S. C.
409; Cochran v. Darcy, Id. 125; Wilson v. Brown, 58 Ala. 62; Nelson v. McCrary,
60 Ala. 301; Preiss v. Campbell, 59 Ala. 635; Corr v. Schackelford, 68 Ala. 241;
Harris v. Austell, 2 Baxt. 148; Leonard v. Mason, 1 Lea, 384; and the Tenn.
Const. art. X. § 11, and Law of 1870, c. 80, creating an exemption from then-
existing debts, were held unconstitutional. Hannum v. McInturf, 6 Baxt. 225;
and see Alexander v. Kilpatrick, 14 Fla. 450; Hannahs v. Felt, 15 Iowa, 141;
Ryan v. Wessels, Id. 145; Martin v. Kirkpatrick, 30 La. Ann. Pt. 2, 1. 214;
Cole v. La Chambre, 31 La. An. 431.

tution of 1868, and the law passed by virtue of it excepting homesteads, were held to be constitutional;[1] but this exemption did not affect a mortgage made before it was adopted.[2] In North Carolina it was held that the constitution of 1868, which changed the homestead exemptions applied to debts then existing, was constitutional, because it did not diminish the right of creditors.[3] But the constitutional objection does not apply to rights of action for torts.[4] It may be added in this connection that the bankrupt law of the United States is held valid and constitutional which exempts from its effects such property as is exempt from levy and sale under execution by the law of the State in which the bankrupt has his domicil at the time of commencing the proceedings in bankruptcy.[5]

2. But while the statute is founded upon considerations of public policy,[6] the principles of construction which have been applied to it by the courts of the different States have often been at variance with each other. While some have applied to its language the test of stringent technical rules, others have sought, even in terms of rhetoric, for adequate forms of expressing the liberal extent to which it should be carried. In some of the States, it was thought to be a subject of sufficiently general importance to incorporate it as a principle into their constitutions.[7] In Minnesota the courts construe the statute strictly, as being in derogation of the common law,[8] while in Illinois it is treated as a remedial measure and is construed liberally.[9]

A homestead in law means a home place, or place of the home, and is designed as a shelter of the homestead roof, and

[1] Re Kennedy, 2 S. C. 216.   [2] Shelor v. Mason, 2 S. C. 233.

[3] Hill v. Kessler, 63 N. C. 437; Garrett v. Chesire, 69 N. C. 396; Edwards v. Kearsey, 74 N. C. 241.

[4] Parker v. Savage, 6 Lea, 406.

[5] In re Deckert, 22 Am. L. Reg. 624. But exemption under the bankrupt law does not relieve from the lien of a previous debt. Hiley v. Bridges, 60 Ga. 375; Dixon v. Lawson, 65 Ga. 661. And the setting apart a homestead by the bankrupt's assignee does not vest it till it is set apart under the State laws. Burtz v. Robinson, 59 Ga. 763.

[6] Robinson v. Wiley, 15 N. Y. 489.

[7] Const. California, art. 11, § 15; Texas, art. 22; Indiana, art. 1, § 22; Wisconsin, art. 1, § 17; Michigan, art. 16, § (2).

[8] Olson v. Nelson, 3 Minn. 53.   [9] Deere v. Chapman, 25 Ill. 610.

not as a mere investment in real estate, or the rents and profits derived therefrom. Nor would it lose this character by a temporary absence of the owner, without an intent to abandon it.[1]

3. The whole system is of recent origin, scarcely reaching back a score of years since the first statute was enacted.[2] In treating of it, it is proposed to consider, 1. Who may claim a right of homestead; 2. In what property it may be claimed, having reference to the title and extent and manner of ownership; 3. In what manner the right is limited and ascertained; 4. The nature of the right regarded as an estate; 5. How far the same is exempt from forced sale; and, 6. How the same may be sold, released, or abandoned.*

3 *a.* In Alabama the right is secured to every resident[3] who is the " head of a family," during his life and occupancy,[4] and after the death of the owner, the exemption continues during his wife's widowhood and the minority of the children.[5]

3 *b.* In Arkansas the exemption extends to residents of the State who are married men, or heads of families, whether aliens or citizens;[6] and by construction to unmarried men[7] and to every male and female, being a householder.[8] After the death of the householder, it enures to the benefit of the widow during widowhood, and of the minor children until adult age.[9]

* NOTE. — The reader should bear in mind that the statutes in relation to homestead, and, in some of the States, their constitutions, have undergone important changes within a few years, especially since the reconstruction of the seceded States ; and while it has been attempted to state the law as it now exists in the different States, it is exceedingly difficult to distinguish, in referring to the cases cited, to which period of the law they are to be assigned. They are accordingly retained because the system would be incomplete without them.

[1] Austin *v.* Stanley, 46 N. H. 52 ; Davis *v.* Andrews, 30 Vt. 678 ; Taylor *v.* Boulware, 17 Tex. 74 ; Benedict *v.* Bunnell, 7 Cal. 245 ; Moss *v.* Warner, 10 Cal. 296 ; Barney *v.* Leeds, 51 N. H. 253, 265. It is "the place where one's dwelling is." Tumlinson *v.* Swinney, 22 Ark. 400.

[2] This was written in 1860. So Thompson, Homest. Pref., states the earliest known to him to have been an act in Texas passed Jan. 26, 1839.

[f] Talmadge *v.* Talmadge, 66 Ala. 199.

[4] Code, 1876, § 2820.   [5] Const. 1868, art. 14, § 2 ; Code, 1876, § 2821

[6] Const. 1868, art. 12, § 2 ; McKenzie *v.* Murphy, 24 Ark. 155.

[7] Greenwood *v.* Maddox, 27 Ark. 648.   [8] Stat. 1858, c. 68.

[9] Const. art. 12, §§ 4, 5.

4. In California the right extends to " heads of families,"
which includes unmarried persons if they have charge of, and
residing with them, minor brothers or sisters, or minor children
of brothers or sisters, or parents or grandparents of their own,
or of any deceased husband or wife, or an unmarried sister.[1]
" Head of a family," as here used, has no reference to the sex
of the party, and if a husband refuses to claim a homestead,
the wife may.[2] If a wife die without children, living her husband, he ceases to have a right of homestead, whereas, if she
survive him, she may become the head of the family.[3] And, as
such, she may, by the statute of 1865–66, have a homestead set
out, if none was set out in her husband's life ;[4] and upon the
death of husband or wife, the homestead vests absolutely in the
survivor by the statute of 1862.[5] But this statute makes no
provision for an interest in the homestead in the children,[6]
though it is considered that if a widow have a homestead set
out to her, it is for the benefit of herself and minor children.[7]

4 a. In Colorado the homestead exemption is given to every
householder in the State, being the head of a family.[8]

4 b. The exemption in Florida is in favor of the head of a
family residing in the State ;[9] and if the owner dies intestate,
the homestead descends to his or her issue then living, but if
no children are living, it goes to the widow, if there is one.
It continues during widowhood and minority.[10]

5. In Georgia the right was given by an early statute to
the head of a family, and, to a limited extent, to his or her

[1] Const. art. 11, § 15 ; Hittell's Code, §§ 6260, 6261.

[2] Id. § 6262 ; Booth v. Galt, 58 Cal. 254.

[3] Revalk v. Kraemer, 8 Cal. 66, 71 ; Gee v. Moore, 14 Cal. 472, 476, 477 ;
Bowman v. Norton, 16 Cal. 213.

[4] Busse's Est., 35 Cal. 310. As to pleading, see Jones v. Waddy, 66 Cal. 457.

[5] Wixom's Est. 35 Cal. 320 ; and is subject to his debts, Watson v. Creditors, 58 Cal. 556. This act was held to apply to a homestead declared previously, when the husband died after the act was passed. Herrold v. Reen, 58
Cal. 443.

[6] Rich v. Tubbs, 41 Cal. 34.

[7] Higgins v. Higgins, 46 Cal. 259. But if the children are adults, it may be
set out for her benefit, Ballantine's Est. Myrick, Prob. 81; and even though she has
quitclaimed the land in which it is included during her husband's lifetime, Ib.

[8] Gen. L. 1877, § 1343.   [9] Florida, Dig. 1881, c. 104, §§ 1, 2.

[10] Id. §§ 3, 8, 16. A special exemption for farmers is also given by § 7 of the
same statute.

children under the age of sixteen years.[1] But by the present constitution the homestead exemption extends to heads of families, guardians and trustees of families of minor children; to every aged and infirm person; to any one having care of dependent females of any age, though not head of a family;[2] and if the husband refuses to apply, the wife, or some one in her behalf or in behalf of minor children, may apply, unless the husband forbids.[3] And "head of a family" has been held to include a single man whose mother and sisters lived with him, and were supported by him.[4] But a bachelor living alone, though having servants, is not a head of a family.[5] And when the wife and husband are in a state of separation, and she has the minor children in her custody, or has a right to them, she is the head of her family, and may have homestead out of her separate property.[6] Minor children of a deceased owner of a homestead are entitled to hold it against his creditors.[7] And no second homestead can be claimed where the first is good by estoppel.[8]

6. In Illinois it attaches only to premises owned by a house-holder with a family.[9] The language of the statute is, "owner, occupant, resident, and householder having a family," and to the widow of such an one and family till the youngest child is

---

[1] Davenport v. Alston, 14 Ga. 271. This statute is still in force, Code, 1882, § 2040; and the rights under it are alternative with the present homestead act; Connally v. Hardwick, 61 Ga. 501. The exemption was limited to lands not within any city, town, or village, and gave fifty acres, &c., if used only for agriculture.

[2] Const. 1877, in Code, 1882, § 5210. Guardian of one minor is within the statute. Rountree v. Dennard, 59 Ga. 629.

[3] Code, 1882, § 2022. As against the husband's creditors his assent to his wife's application will be presumed. Connally v. Hardwick, 61 Ga. 501.

[4] Marsh v. Lazenby, 41 Ga. 153; but in Dendy v. Gamble, 64 Ga. 528, where there were only sisters and their children, a different rule was held.

[5] Calhoun v. McLendon, 42 Ga. 405.

[6] Code, 1882, § 2019; but not if the husband has already exempted one homestead from his own property, Neal v. Sawyer, 62 Ga. 352; and her petition must show affirmatively her right to apply, Jones v. Crumley, 61 Ga. 105.

[7] Roff v. Johnson, 40 Ga. 555.

[8] Torrance v. Boyd, 63 Ga. 22. And where the daughters of the homestead owner were dependent, though adult, he could not get a new homestead by a second marriage. Ib. An exemption to farmers specially is given by Code, § 2040, but this is alternative with that already spoken of.

[9] Kitchell v. Burgwin, 21 Ill. 40; Deere v. Chapman, 25 Ill. 610; Ryhiner v. Frank, 105 Ill. 326.

twenty-one years of age, and during the widow's life.[1] Such
exemption continues even after the death of the wife and
children.[2] A wife also may be a householder, and, if separated
from her husband, and not supported by him, can acquire a
homestead in land bought by her.[3]

7. In Indiana the exemption is limited to a "resident
householder;" but it has been held to extend to one living
with his sister who contributes to the expenses of the household;[4] and extends to a wife, if she is the debtor and owns
the estate.[5]

8. In Iowa the exemption is to the "head of a family,"
owner of a homestead. But a widower or widow may be such,
though without children, provided he or she continue to occupy the premises which they occupied during the life of the
deceased.[6] But occupancy and use of the dwelling-house by
the family as a homestead are essential to its being exempt.
Intention to make it such is not enough.[7] If a wife survive
her husband, the owner of the homestead, she, as his successor, has a right to enjoy it, although married again.[8] So if
he survive her, he will take, as her successor, the homestead owned by her, though he have no children.[9] If the
owner live on the land, he may claim the right, although
his wife and children have never resided in the State.[10] A
son, with a mother and brothers and sisters, or either, dependent on him, may claim it. But a brother unmarried, with
whom a married brother and wife lived and kept his house,
was held not to be the head of a family.[11] It does not attach

---

[1] Rev. Stat. 1883, c. 52, §§ 1, 2.　　　　[2] Kimbrel v. Willis, 97 Ill. 494.

[3] Kenley v. Hudelson, 99 Ill. 493 ; Hotchkiss v. Brooks, 93 Ill. 386.

[4] Ind. Rev. Stat. 1881, § 703 ; Graham v. Crockett, 18 Ind. 119.

[5] Rev. Stat. 1881, § 5124 ; Crane v. Waggoner, 33 Ind. 83.

[6] Rev. Code, 1880, §§ 1988, 1989. But the right to a homestead is alternative
with the right to one third in fee as a distributive share, Stevens v. Stevens, 50
Iowa, 491 ; Burdick v. Kent, 52 Iowa, 583 ; though the homestead may be taken
as part of such share, Whitehead v. Conklin, 48 Iowa, 478 ; and is still exempted
from debts of the deceased, Moningen v. Ramsey, 48 Iowa, 368 ; Knox v. Hanlon,
Id. 252 ; Wilson v. Hardesty, Id. 515.

[7] Elston v. Robinson, 23 Iowa, 208 ; Givans v. Dewey, 47 Iowa, 414.

[8] Nicholas v. Purczell, 21 Iowa, 265 ; Dodds v. Dodds, 26 Iowa, 311.

[9] Stewart v. Brand, 23 Iowa, 477, 481.

[10] Williams v. Swetland, 10 Iowa, 51.

[11] Whalen v. Cadman, 11 Iowa, 226 ; Parsons v. Livingston, 11 Iowa, 104.

until the owner actually occupies the premises; and the same
then would be liable for a debt contracted before such occupancy.[1]

8 a. The Constitution and Statutes of Kansas extend the
homestead exemption to premises occupied as a residence by
the family of the owner, and after the death of the owner the
homestead becomes the absolute property of the widow and
children, if they continue to occupy.[2]

8 b. The statutes of Kentucky exempt a homestead to the
owner of the premises, whether man or woman, who is a *bona
fide* housekeeper. Upon the death of the owner, husband, or
wife, it goes to the widow or widower, as the case may be, for
his or her use and that of the children unmarried and under
age.[3]

8 c. By the statutes of Louisiana, a homestead exemption extends to premises occupied as a residence, and owned *bona
fide* by one having a family, or father, or mother, or person
dependent upon him for support.[4] So where the husband is
incapable, the wife may claim a homestead;[5] but not otherwise.[6]

9. In Maine he must own the property and be a householder in actual occupation of the same.[7]

10. In Massachusetts he must be a householder, having a
family occupying the premises owned or possessed by him as
a residence; and on his death it passes to his widow or children during widowhood or till majority of the youngest.[8] Nor
does he lose it by the death or absence of his wife and chil-

[1] Cole v. Gill, 14 Iowa, 527; Hale v. Heaslip, 16 Iowa, 451; Campbell v.
Ayres, 18 Iowa, 252; Hyatt v. Spearman, 20 Iowa, 510; Givans v. Dewey, 47
Iowa, 414.

[2] Comp. Laws, §§ 235, 2103; and when bought it must be for present and not
future or uncertain occupancy. Swenson v. Kiehl, 21 Kans. 533; but where
possession was taken by digging a cellar, the exemption attached, Gilworth v.
Cody, Id. 702.

[3] Gen. Stat. 1873, c. 38, art. 13, §§ 14–16. This was otherwise under the
statute of 1866. Little v. Woodward, 14 Bush, 585.

[4] Rev. Stat. 1870, § 1691; but the owner may estop himself to claim homestead by denying his own title, Gilmer v. O'Neal, 32 La. An. 979.

[5] Hardin v. Wolf, 29 La. An. 333.

[6] Borron v. Sollibellos, 28 La. An. 355; Taylor v. McElvin, 31 La. An. 283.

[7] Rev. Stat. 1883, c. 81, § 63.

[8] Pub. Stat. c. 123, § 1.

dren, because 1e may adopt ot1ers as members of 1is 1ouse-
1old.[1]   An unmarried woman, wit1out c1ildren, cannot claim
it.[2]

11. In Mic1igan 1e must be a resident, and t1e owner and
occupant of t1e 1omestead;[3] and after 1is deat1 it enures to
1is c1ildren during t1eir minority; but if c1ildless, to his
widow during her widow1ood.[4]

12. In Minnesota t1e exemption is to t1e owner and occupant of t1e premises as a residence.   T1is may be t1e debtor
1imself, 1is widow, or minor c1ildren, w1o s1all be t1e occupants for t1e purposes of a 1ome.[5]

13. In Mississippi it is to "t1e 1ead of a family;"[6] and
t1e statute of 1871 extends it to every citizen, male or female,
being a 1ouse1older, 1aving a family, t1e owner and occupant
of t1e estate claimed as a 1omestead; and on t1e deat1 of t1e
owner it descends to 1is widow and c1ildren, during t1e minority of c1ildren, and till t1e deat1 of t1e widow, some one of
t1em being an occupant t1ereof.[7]

13 a. In Missouri every 1ousekeeper or 1ead of a family
1olds exempt t1e premises used by him as a 1omestead; and
t1e same, at 1is deat1, passes to 1is widow during widow1ood,
and 1is c1ildren till of age.[8]

13 b. In Nebraska t1e exemption is to an owner and occupant w1o is a resident and 1ead of a family, descending at 1is

[1] Silloway v. Brown, 12 Allen, 30 ; Doyle v. Coburn, 6 Allen, 71.

[2] Woodworth v. Comstock, 10 Allen, 425.

[3] Beecher v. Baldy, 7 Mich. 488 ; Tharp v. Allen, 46 Mich. 389.   And a mere
licensee or lessee, though son of the deceased owner, has no right to homestead.
Ib.

[4] Const. art. xvi. §§ 3, 4 ; Comp. L. 1871 ; Dei v. Habel, 41 Mich. 88.   And
the widow's claim cannot be barred by an estoppel in pais.   Showers v. Robinson, 43 Mich. 502.   And while she and the children continue to reside, the homestead continues though the husband absconds, at least until he acquires a new one
in another State.   Re Pratt, 1 Flip. C. Ct. 353.

[5] Folsom v. Carli, 5 Minn. 337 ; Tillotson v. Millard, 7 Minn. 520 ; Kresin v.
Mau, 15 Minn. 116 ; Stat. 1878, c. 68, § 1.

[6] Morrison v. McDaniel, 30 Miss. 217 ; Rev. Code, 1880, §§ 1248, 1249.

[7] Code, § 1249 ; Smith v. Wells, 46 Miss. 71 ; Campbell v. Adair, 45 Miss. 170 ;
Glover v. Hill, 57 Miss. 240.

[8] Rev. Stat. 1879, §§ 2689, 2693.   In Whitehead v. Tapp, 69 Mo. 415, a man
was held to be head of a family, though his wife had deserted him and was living
in another State with another man, and he was living with another woman.

death to his heirs at law,[1] whether alien or citizen.[2] Any one who has the same class of persons dependent on him as enumerated in the California statute already stated is a head of a family.

13 c. In New Jersey it is to a householder having a family, who is the owner and occupant thereof as a residence, and it continues to the widow and family, if occupants thereof, until the youngest child is of age and the widow has deceased.[3]

14. In New York it is to a householder, and it is to him for a residence. And by householder is meant the head, master, or person who has charge of and provides for a family.[4]

14 a. In Nevada the exemption is to the head of a family, not including persons unmarried, unless they have minor brothers or sisters, or children of brothers or sisters, or father or mother, or both, or grandparents, or unmarried sisters, living with them. Upon the death of husband or wife, it goes absolutely to the survivor and his or her legitimate children.[5]

15. In New Hampshire it enures to the benefit of the wife, widow, and children of every owner occupying the premises as a residence,[6] and continues during the lifetime of the wife or widow and the minority of the children; and then to the owner if living. And if the wife is the legal owner of the homestead, the husband surviving her is entitled to a like exemption in her estate. And it has been held that a widower with a child living with him is a " head of a family."[7] An unmarried person may also have a homestead.[8]

16. In North Carolina it is to the owner and occupant of the premises who is a resident of the State, and to his children, if he leave any, during their minority; and if he have no chil-

---

[1] Comp. Stat. 1881, c. 36, §§ 1, 15, 17.

[2] People v. McClay, 2 Neb. 7 ; Comp. Laws, c. 36, § 15.

[3] Rev. 1877, p. 1055, § 1.

[4] 3 Rev. Stat. 647 ; Griffin v. Sutherland, 14 Barb. 456 ; 4 Stat. at Large, Pt. 3, c. 260, p. 632.

[5] Comp. Laws, 1873, § 186, 189 ; Smith v. Shrieves, 13 Nev. 303. That is, where the homestead is by a filed declaration, it is joint and goes to the survivor ; but if of the common property and gained by occupancy only, it is equally divided between the survivor and the children. Ib.

[6] Gen. Laws, 1878, c. 138, §§ 1, 5.   [7] Barney v. Leeds, 51 N. H. 253.

[8] Gen. Laws, 1878, c. 138, § 6.

dren, it enures to his widow in her own right, during her life or widowhood, unless she have another homestead in her own right. Actual occupancy as a residence is essential to its being exempted as a homestead.[1]

17. In Ohio, widows and widowers having an unmarried child living with them as a part of their family have this right, as do husbands and wives living together without children. The exemption is to the head of a family.[2]

18. In South Carolina and Tennessee the exemption is in favor of "the head of a family."[3] In the former State, after his death, his widow and children succeed to his right,[4] and during his lifetime if he claim no homestead his wife may, in her own property.[5] In the latter State he must be a householder,[6] and his widow during widowhood, and minor children until adult, take the homestead on his death.[7] But the death of wife and children does not defeat his homestead.[8]

18 a. In Texas it is to "a family," which the courts of that State hold to be a collective body of persons living together within the same curtilage, subsisting in common, directing their attention to a common object, and it continues so long as any constituent of the family survives.[9] A single man without servants or other persons living with him cannot claim a homestead exemption;[10] and adult children are not included.[11]

19. In Vermont the exemption is to a housekeeper or head

---

[1] Const. 1868, art. 10, §§ 2, 5 ; Code, 1883. Under the constitution, the widow has homestead only if there are no children, minor or adult. Wharton v. Leggett, 80 N. C. 169. And the children only during minority. Hagar v. Nixon, 69 N. C. 108 ; Simpson v. Wallace, 83 N. C. 477.

[2] Stat. of 1860 and 1868.

[3] S. C. Const. art. 2, § 2; Gen. Stat. 1882, § 1994 ; Tenn. Const. art. 11, § 11. But where one marries a person marriage with whom is forbidden by law, he cannot claim a homestead. Owen v. Bracket, 7 Lea, 448.

[4] Gen. St. § 1997 ; Moore v. Parker, 13 S. C. 486.

[5] Gen. St. § 2000.　　　　　　　　　[6] Tenn. St. 1871, § 2030.

[7] Id. § 2119 ; Simpson v. Poe, 1 Lea, 701.

[8] Webb v. Cowley, 5 Lea, 722.

[9] Texas Const. § 22 ; Rev. Stat. 1879, art. 2335, 2336 ; Homestead Cases, 31 Tex. 680 ; Abney v. Pope, 52 Tex. 288. Thus where a widow's only family were the grandchildren of her husband by a former marriage. Wolfe v. Buckley, 52 Tex. 641.

[10] Homestead Cases, 31 Tex. 678.

[11] Rev. Stat. §§ 2004, 2005 ; Roco v. Green, 50 Tex. 483.

of a family;[1] in Virginia, to a householder or head of a family,[2] and in each State the widow and minor children succeed to the homestead while such.[3]　But if the widow has no children and the estate owes no debts, she cannot claim homestead as against the heirs.[4]

DIVISION II.

IN WHAT HOMESTEAD RIGHTS MAY BE CLAIMED.

1.　When, in the second place, it is considered of what property a homestead right may be predicated, although varying in different States in the value exempted and the extent and nature of the ownership required, it will be found that in some respects the laws of all the States substantially agree, especi-

---

[1] Rev. Laws, 1880, § 1894.

[2] Const. art. 11, § 1 ; and does not extend to an unmarried man with no children or dependent persons living with him.　Calhoun v. Williams, 32 Gratt. 18.

[3] Vt. Rev. Laws, § 1898 ; Va. Code, 1873, c. 183, § 8.

[4] Helm v. Helm, 30 Gratt. 404.

ally in requiring the premises to be occupied for family purposes as a home by one who is a *resident* thereon, and makes
it the dwelling-place of his family. This principle runs through
almost all the cases, though a difference of construction will
be found to have been applied in limiting what is embraced in
the term *homestead*. And although the bankrupt laws of the
United States are required by the Constitution to be uniform,
what is meant by uniformity relates to the States, and not to
State exemption laws. It means that what remains after such
exemptions shall be equally distributed among creditors.[1]

1 *a*. In Alabama the amounts exempted under the homestead laws have been essentially changed from time to time,
which has raised the question whether an increased exemption was constitutional as to existing debts.[2] The constitution of 1868 exempts eighty acres of land and the dwelling
thereon, if without the limits of a city, town, or village, or
any lot in a city, town, or village, with a dwelling owned and
occupied by a resident of the State, not exceeding in value
$2,000; by the later code the amount is increased to one hun-
dred and sixty acres.[3] And it seems to be necessary that it
should be occupied by the one claiming the exemption.[4] Hence
the parcels of which it is composed cannot be separate, if
not adjacent or used in connection.[5] A widow is entitled to
homestead in lands to which her husband was equitably entitled.[6] And when the land is sold by legal process, the
exemption applies to the proceeds.[7] The homestead may be
in lands held in common as well as in severalty.[8]

1 *b*. The exemption in Arkansas is not to exceed one

---

[1] *In re* Beckerkord, 19 Am. Law Reg. 57, 59.

[2] This was held in the negative in Wilson *v.* Brown, 58 Ala. 62, overruling
Sneider *v.* Heidelbarger, 45 Ala. 126, 134.

[3] Const. art. 14, § 2 ; Code, 1876, § 2820 ; and this may be in land leased, where
the tenant has a right to remove his house. Watts *v.* Gordon, 65 Ala. 546 ; Code,
§ 2820.

[4] McConnaughy *v.* Baxter, 55 Ala. 379 ; Pettus *v.* McKinney, 56 Ala. 41,
Carlisle *v.* Godwin, 69 Ala. 137, 140o verruling Belton *v.* Andrews, 45 Ala. 454.
And it cannot be rented to a tenant. Dexter *v.* Strobach, 56 Ala. 233.

[5] Pettus *v.* McKinney, 56 Ala. 41, overruling Pizzala *v.* Campbell, 46 Ala. 35.

[6] Munchus *v.* Harris, 69 Ala. 506.

[7] Garner *v.* Bond, 61 Ala. 84 ; Giddens *v.* Williamson, 65 Ala. 439.

[8] Code, § 2820.

hundred and sixty acres of land, or, if in a city or town, a lot which is the residence of the householder claiming it;[1] not to exceed $5,000 in value.[2]   By " city or town lot " is meant the lot on which the debtor lives, irrespective of the lines by which the lots of the city were laid out.   The statute is held to be remedial in its character, and is to be liberally construed.[3] Continuous occupancy is not required, and temporary use for business purposes does not divert the homestead character.[4] Homestead may be claimed in lands held in common.[5]

2. In California the exemption is of a lot of land and a dwelling-house thereon, and its appurtenances not exceeding five thousand dollars in value.[6]   Homestead does not depend upon the nature of the title; a naked possession will be sufficient as to everybody but the rightful owner.[7]   It will be exempt from a forced sale, except for certain debts.[8]   Declaring it a homestead, however, does not protect it against the true owner.[9]   The occupancy must be with an intent to make it a homestead.[10]   And accordingly it was held not to embrace a store, office, billiard-room, bar-room, or theatre, gas-factory, or storehouse, although the family might occupy rooms upon the second floor of such building.[11]   It need not be in a compact form, and may be intersected by highways.   There is no limit as to the quantity; only as to its uses and value.   Nor is it inconsistent with its being a place of business by the family,[12] or that the premises were a hotel kept by the owner, who

[1] Const. 1868, art. 12, § 3 ; Stat. 1858, c. 68 ; Greenwood v. Maddox, 27 Ark. 648, 657.

[2] Const. *ubi supra ;* 19 Am. L. Reg. 4.

[3] Wassall v. Tunnah, 25 Ark. 101.

[4] Euper v. Atkins, 37 Ark. 283 ; Klenk v. Knoble, Id. 298 ; Webb v. Davis, Id. 551.

[5] Greenwood v. Maddox, 27 Ark. 648 ; Sentell v. Armor, 35 Ark. 49.

[6] Hittell Code, §§ 6237, 6260; McDonald v. Badger, 23 Cal. 393; Titcomb's Est., Myrick's Prob. 55. And if the declaration be for a lot worth more, it is bad. Ames v. Eldred, 55 Cal. 136.   Cf. Read v. Rahm, 65 Cal. 343.

[7] Brooks v. Hyde, 37 Cal. 366.   [8] Code, §§ 6240, 6241.

[9] Spencer v. Geissman, 37 Cal. 96; Brooks v. Hyde, 37 Cal. 366; Code, § 6240.

[10] Holden v. Pinney, 6 Cal. 234; Reck's Est., Myrick's Prob. 59.

[11] Reynolds v. Pixley, 6 Cal. 165; Ackley v. Chamberlain, 16 Cal. 181; Riley v. Pehl, 23 Cal. 70; Cameto's Est., Myrick's Prob. 42.

[12] Estate of Delaney, 37 Cal. 176; Gregg v. Bostwick, 33 Cal. 220; Mann v. Rogers, 35 Cal. 316, 319.

claimed the right of homestead, although he entertained
boarders, lodgers, and travellers therein.[1] It has been said
that it must be a dwelling-place where the family permanently
reside.[2] But it need not be a permanent residence, only there
must be an actual occupancy when it is set out;[3] and the
homestead may be set out of lands held in joint tenancy or by
tenancy in common, though held otherwise under an earlier
statute.[4] Where, therefore, the owner of premises had a wife
in another State from which he had removed, he was held not
to have gained for them the character of homestead, until he
had removed his wife and commenced actually occupying the
same with her.[5] So, where, during the absence of his wife, a
husband acquired an estate, it was held that no right of homestead attached thereto until she returned, and they began together actually to occupy the same.[6] And if a man owning
an estate marry a wife and carry her to live upon it, it becomes
a homestead. But if he marry a woman having lands, and go
to live with her upon her lands, it is said to be doubtful if
such an occupancy gives to it the character of a homestead.[7]
Citizenship is not requisite. A residence is sufficient to entitle
one to claim a homestead.[8] Homestead cannot be claimed of
estates held in partnership.[9]

2 a. By the constitution of Florida, the exemption of homestead extends to one hundred and sixty acres of land, or half
an acre within an incorporated city or town, owned by the head
of a family residing in the State. And where the property is
in a city or town, it is not to extend to any buildings other
than the residence or business house of the owner.[10] There is
also exempted real property to the amount of one thousand
dollars as selected by such owner, to be held free from debts

[1] Ackley v. Chamberlain, *sup.*　　　　[2] Cook v. McChristian, 4 Cal. 23.

[3] Const. art. 11, § 15; Stat. 1868, p. 116; Prescott v. Prescott, 45 Cal. 58;
Babcock v. Gibbs, 52 Cal. 629; Dorn v. Howe, Id. 630.

[4] Stat. 1868; Seaton v. Son, 32 Cal. 481 ; S. Barbara Bk. v. Guerra, 61 Cal.
109.

[5] Cary v. Tice, 6 Cal. 625 ; Benedict v. Bunnell, 7 Cal. 245.

[6] Rix v. McHenry, 7 Cal. 89 ; Elmore v. Elmore, 10 Cal. 224.

[7] Revalk v. Kraemer, 8 Cal. 66, 71; Riley v. Pehl, 23 Cal. 74.

[8] Dawley v. Ayers, 23 Cal. 108.　　　　[9] Kingsley v. Kingsley, 39 Cal. 665.

[10] Const. 1868, art. 9, § 1; 19 Am. L. Reg. 4; Fla. Dig. 1881, c. 104, § 1.

incurred before May 10, 1865;[1] and farmers hold as exempt forty acres, with an addition of five more for each child.[2]

3. In Georgia the exemption originally extended to fifty acres of land to the head of the family, and five acres to each of his or her children under the age of fifteen years. But if the homestead was in a city, town, or village, it was not to exceed two hundred dollars in value.[3] Cotton and woollen factories, mills, and machinery propelled by water, were excluded from this exemption.[4] This exemption, which is alternative with the following one,[5] is now limited to two hundred dollars if the land is not, and five hundred dollars if it is, situated in any city, town, or village; and the additional provision extends to all children under sixteen.[6] But by the Constitution of 1868, art. 9, §§ 1, 2, instead of the prior provision as to homestead, it is competent for the head of a family, or the guardian or trustee of a family of minor children, if he prefers it, to claim an exemption in real and personal property to the value of $1,600 in specie.[7] This exemption may be claimed in new land bought with the proceeds of the old homestead,[8] or in real estate held in partnership,[9] or held under a bond for a deed,[10] but not in uninvested cash,[11] nor by the lessee in property of the lessor.[12]

4. In Illinois it covers the lot of ground and the buildings thereon occupied as a residence, of a value not exceeding one thousand dollars,[13] and if the homestead is sold under order of court, this amount of the proceeds is reserved for investment for one year.[14] So it extends to each of two lots in turn, exchanged for the original homestead,[15] and continues through mesne conveyances, though made with the intent to delay

---

[1] Dig. 1881, c. 104, § 2.   [2] Dig. 1881, c. 104, § 7.
Davenport v. Alston, 14 Ga. 271; Code, 1882, § 20, 40.
Cobb's Dig. 389, 390.
[?] Connally v. Hardwick, 61 Ga. 501; Johnson v. Roberts, 63 Ga. 167.
[?] Code, 1882, § 2040.   [7] Code, 1882, § 2002.
[8] Cheney v. Rosser, 59 Ga. 861.
[9] Newton v. Summey, 59 Ga. 397; Hunnicutt v. Summey, 63 Ga. 586; but see King v. Dillon, 66 Ga. 131.
[10] Raley v. Ross, 59 Ga. 862.   [11] Jones v. Ehrlisch, 65 Ga. 546.
[12] Cherry v. Ware, 63 Ga. 289.   [13] Rev. Stat. 1883, c. 52, § 1.
[14] Id. c. 52, §§ 6, 7.
[15] Crawford v. Richeson, 101 Ill. 351.

creditors.[1] But it does not extend to two lots, though of a less value than the prescribed sum, where the dwelling-house is upon one of these, and the other is used to supply the occupant of the first with firewood. Whether land contiguous to that upon which is the dwelling-house is a part of the homestead, is a question for the jury.[2] But the right cannot exist beyond the duration of the estate of the owner in the premises.[3] If, therefore, his title expires during his life, his widow can claim no right in the premises. Nor can the right of homestead attach to a building standing upon another's land.[4] It is enough, however, that he own the land in fee for life or a term of years, or that he holds the land under a bond for a deed.[5] But he can have but one homestead; and he must, moreover, occupy it to make it such; purchasing it for that purpose is not enough.[6] To constitute a homestead, there must be a dwelling-place upon the premises. But it may be a cabin or a tent, if it be the home of the family.[7] And under that term may be included a dwelling-house, smoke-house, stable, and house-lot, and ground connected therewith and used for domestic and family purposes. But it would exclude a store or warehouse, and grounds occupied for the business done in them.[8] But if once gained, a continuous occupation as a residence is not essential to maintaining the homestead right in the premises.[9]

5. In Indiana, the exemption is of six hundred dollars value of property; and this may be of real or personal estate, as the debtor may elect, to be designated by him, or, in his absence, by his wife.[10] But a debtor cannot claim exemption from

[1] Leupold v. Krause, 95 Ill. 440.

[2] Walters v. People, 18 Ill. 194; s. c. 21 Ill. 178,179; but see Darby v. Dixon, 4 Ill. App. 187.

[3] So where the widow receives a sum in gross for her right, it is not $1,000, but her life interest only in that sum. Merritt v. Merritt, 97 Ill. 243.

[4] Brown v. Keller, 32 Ill. 151.

[5] Blue v. Blue, 38 Ill. 918; Tomlin v. Hilgard, 43 Ill. 300; Conklin v. Foster, 57 Ill. 104.   [6] Tousville v. Pierson, 39 Ill. 447.

[7] Kitchell v. Burgwyn, 21 Ill. 40; Deere v. Chapman, 25 Ill. 610.

[8] Reinbach v. Walter, 27 Ill. 394.

[9] Walters v. People, sup.; Miller v. Marckle, 27 Ill. 402, 405; Vanzant v. Vanzant, 23 Ill. 536; Kenley v. Hudelson, 99 Ill. 493.

[10] Rev. Stat. 1881, § 703; State v. Melogue, 9 Ind. 196; Const. art. 1, § 42; Stat. 1862 and 1870.

levy of land belonging to his wife, or of which she and not he holds the deed.[1]

6. In Iowa, it extends to the house made use of by the owner, or, if he have two, the one which he may elect, together with one or more contiguous lots with the buildings thereon, if habitually occupied in good faith as a part of the homestead, not to exceed half an acre if within a town, or forty acres outside of any town plot, provided the whole do not exceed five hundred dollars in value. In addition to this, it includes a shop or other buildings properly appurtenant to the homestead, and used with them by the owner in the prosecution of his business, not to exceed three hundred dollars in value.[2] If a new homestead is bought with the proceeds of the old one, the new one is to that extent exempt.[3] It may be secured to the owner of the soil on which a building of three stories stands, and be confined to the second and third story, leaving the first story and cellar under it subject to sale on execution, to be held by a purchaser as long as it is tenantable. The tenements, however, would not be regarded as held in common, but as being adjacent to each other.[4] And if the forty acres be of less value than five hundred dollars, it may be increased in quantity to that value.[5] In order to be exempt as a part of the homestead, it must be habitually and in good faith used as such.[6] Where, therefore, one owned a building in a part of which he resided, and parts of it he rented to others for stores, it was held that only such parts as he himself thus occupied, and such as were used with these as properly appurtenant thereto, were exempt. The stores were not, since the object of the statute is to protect and preserve a *home* for the family, and not stores, offices, shops, or hotels, rented to others, and occupied by them.[7] Nor does the right attach, till the premises are actually occupied as a home.

---

[1] Holman v. Martin, 12 Ind. 553.

[2] Rev. Code, 1880, §§ 1994–1997. The town limits referred to are only to the town lands platted. McDaniel v. Mace, 47 Iowa, 509.

[3] Thompson v. Rogers, 51 Iowa, 333; Jones v. Brandt, 59 Iowa, 332.

[4] McCormic v. Bishop, 28 Iowa, 233.

[5] Thorn v. Thorn, 14 Iowa, 49.   [6] Code, § 1997.

[7] Rhodes v. McCormick, 4 Iowa, 368; Kurz v. Brusch, 13 Iowa, 371. So Mayfield v. Maasden, 59 Iowa, 517.

Mere intention to occupy is not enough, nor setting out the homestead and recording it, unless occupied as a home by the family.[1] An occupation of the premises, and a use of a house upon the same, are essential to the investing of an estate with the character of a homestead.[2]

6 a. In Kansas, the constitution and statutes of the State exempt a homestead of one hundred and sixty acres of farming land, or an acre within an incorporated town or city, if occupied by the owner as a residence of the family.[3] Only one acre within the limits of a city is exempt, whether worth ten or ten thousand dollars, whether he live on it or live on an adjacent lot which extends into and includes a part of the lands within the city. But one hundred and sixty acres of farming land are exempt.[4] If one purchase an estate as a homestead, and move on to it within a reasonable time after such purchase, he will hold it as such from the date of the purchase.[5] The exemption extends to leased lands, where the tenant owns the house.[6]

6 b. The exemption in Kentucky is of so much land, including the dwelling-house standing thereon, as does not exceed one thousand dollars in value,[7] and attaches though the land is only held under a bond for a deed.[8] And if the land is sold under order of court, so much of the proceeds as are exempt will be reinvested by the court.[9]

6 c. In Louisiana it extends to one hundred and sixty acres of land, with the building and improvements, occupied as a residence by the owner thereof, and owned *bona fide* by him, which, with sundry enumerated articles of personal property, are not to exceed two thousand dollars.[10] But there can be no homestead in property not held in severalty.[11]

---

[1] Christy v. Dyer, 14 Iowa, 438; Davis v. Kelley, 14 Iowa, 523; Cole v. Gill, 14 Iowa, 527.

[2] Elston v. Robinson, 23 Iowa, 208.

[3] Const. art. 15 § 9; Comp. Laws, 1879, § 235.

[4] Sarabas v. Fenlon, 5 Kans. 592.

[5] Monroe v. May, 9 Kans. 475; Gilworth v. Cody, 21 Kans. 702. But a homestead cannot be claimed by one insolvent in lands bought with the proceeds of goods got on credit and by fraud. Long v. Murphy, 27 Kans. 375.

[6] Hogan v. Manners, 23 Kans. 551.　　[7] Stat. 1873, c. 38, art. 13, § 9.

[8] Griffin v. Procter, 14 Bush, 571.　　[9] McTaggert v. Smith, 14 Bush, 414.

[10] Rev. Stat. 1870, § 1691.　　[11] Greig v. Eastin, 30 La. Ann. pt. 2, 1130.

7. In Maine the exemption is of a lot of land and dwelling-house, and outbuildings thereon, not exceeding five hundred dollars in value.[1]

7 a. By the laws of Maryland a debtor may select real or personal estate of the value of one hundred dollars, to be ascertained by appraisal.[2]

8. In Massachusetts the homestead may be a farm or lot of land and buildings thereon, owned and possessed by lease or otherwise, occupied by the debtor as a residence, not exceeding eight hundred dollars in value; and the widow may claim it, though she rent a part or all of the premises.[3] The right does not attach until the owner has a deed of the estate; nor would it retroact to the date of the bond under which the conveyance is made, though the deed be delivered in accordance with its provisions.[4] Nor does the right attach in favor of one owning an estate upon which he has begun to erect a dwelling-house, until he has begun to occupy that as a householder for a residence, although he may formally have declared his intention to hold it as a homestead.[5] But if an estate is under an existing mortgage, when made a homestead, it becomes exempt as such, except as to such mortgage; nor can such right be created so as to affect existing mortgages, liens, or incumbrances.[6] And where a mortgagee, having an existing mortgage, gave it up and took a new one on the same estate, it was held not to let in the wife's claim to homestead as against this new mortgage, the taking of the new being a part of the transaction of giving up the old one.[7] The right may attach to an estate kept by the owner as a hotel in the country, though it might, perhaps, be otherwise in a city;[8] or to an entire house, though the owner lease some of the rooms.[9] It does not attach to land held in common and undivided.[10] Nor will

---

[1] Rev. Stat. 1883, c. 81, § 63.   [2] Rev. Code, 1878, art. 64, § 151.
[3] Pub. Stat. c. 123; Mercier v. Chace, 11 Allen, 194.
[4] Thurston v. Maddocks, 6 Allen, 427.   [5] Lee v. Miller, 11 Allen, 37.
[6] Pub. Stat. c. 123, § 6.   [7] Burns v. Thayer, 101 Mass. 426.
[8] Lazell v. Lazell, 8 Allen, 575.   [9] Mercier v. Chace, 11 Allen, 194.
[10] Thurston v. Maddocks, 6 Allen, 427; Howes v. Burt, 130 Mass. 368. But the assignment to a widow of dower in specific parts of the estate which her husband held as a homestead at his death does not render her a tenant in common with the heir so as to defeat her homestead. Weller v. Weller, 131 Mass. 446.

it cover land lying two and a half miles from the homestead farm of the owner, and used by him for pasturing his
cattle.[1]

9. The constitution of Michigan exempts a homestead if
not exceeding forty acres, with a dwelling-house thereon, if in
an agricultural district, and if in a city, village or town plat,
any lot or parts of a lot equal thereto, with a dwelling-house
thereon, the whole in either case not to exceed fifteen hundred
dollars in value.[2] But it is essential that the premises should
contain a dwelling-house and appurtenances, and should be
owned and occupied by him, as a homestead, who sets up the
right.[3] Where, therefore, the owner of a lot of land erected
thereon a double house, and rented one of the tenements, and
occupied the other, he was entitled to exemption as to one,
and not as to the other, although both did not exceed in value
fifteen hundred dollars, and the back-yard of the buildings
was occupied by the tenants of the house in common.[4] A
husband may have a homestead in property to which he has
only an equitable title; nor does he lose it by making use of
the rooms in the dwelling-house for a shop, post-office, or
the like. The estate of the wife occupied by her and her
husband may be exempt as a homestead;[5] and a homestead
can be owned and occupied by husband and wife as tenants
in common.[6]

10. In Minnesota, the exemption by the constitution is "a
reasonable amount of property." And this was, at first, limited by statute to land and buildings of the value of one thousand dollars. But afterwards it was extended to include one
lot, if in an incorporated city, village, or town, or eighty acres
in an agricultural district, measured by area and not value.[7]

· 1 Adams v. Jenkins, 16 Gray, 146.

2 Const. art. 16, § 2 ; Comp. Laws, 1871, §§ 6137, 6138; Dye v. Mann, 10
Mich. 291; McKee v. Wilcox, 11 Mich. 358.

3 Beecher v. Baldy, 7 Mich. 488; Coolidge v. Wells, 20 Mich. 79. 87.

4 Beecher v. Baldy, sup.; Dyson v. Sheley, 11 Mich. 527. So where part of
the homestead lot was covered by a building, the main part of which stood on
another lot, the part so covered was held not to be exempt. Geney v. Maynard,
44 Mich. 578.

5 Orr v. Shraft, 22 Mich. 260.   6 Lozo v. Sutherland, 38 Mich. 168.

7 Stat. 1878, c. 68, § 1; Tillotson v. Millard, 7 Minn. 513 ; Sumner v. Sawtelle, 8 Minn. 321 ; Cogel v. Mickow, 11 Minn. 475.

It is essential to its being exempted, that it should be occupied
by the debtor or his widow or minor children, and continue so
to be.   But it matters not how, so long as it is the place of
their residence and has a house on it.   If the owner lets it
and resides elsewhere, or leaves it vacant, it cannot, during
such time, be a homestead.1   The premises, therefore, must
have upon them a dwelling-house and appurtenances, and
must be owned by the occupant, who is a resident of the
State, and he alone can select the exempted premises, or
set up the exemption.2   But the exemption extends to a
house occupied by the debtor, though not his own property,
if he claims it as a homestead.3   But to sustain a homestead exemption, the owner must have or must have had
his residence thereon; nor can he claim it in a lot which
touches his homestead at one corner only;4 nor in an undivided half of two lots which together do not exceed one city
lot.5   But ownership of an undivided interest will give the
occupant homestead.6

11. In Mississippi eighty acres of land are exempted to every
citizen who is a householder with a family, actually occupied
by the owner, and not exceeding two thousand dollars in value;
and if in a city, town, or village, every householder is entitled
to the land and buildings actually occupied by him, of the
value of two thousand dollars, exempt from seizure, levy, and
sale upon execution,7 instead of what had previously been exempted.   But it is not impressed with the character of homestead until it is occupied by the debtor; and, as a general rule,
to constitute a homestead, there must be a continued occupation and use of the premises as a home for the family, though
it may be an individual interest and, in some cases, an occupancy by a tenant will be sufficient, if the family cannot occupy

---

1 Folsom v. Carli, 5 Minn. 337 ; Kelly v. Baker, 10 Minn. 154. By Stat.
1878, c. 68, § 9, six months' absence forfeits it unless it is by a recorded claim,
and then five years' absence is required.

2 Sumner v. Sawtelle, sup.; Tillotson v. Millard, sup.

3 Stat. 1873.   4 Kresin v. Mau, 15 Minn. 116.

5 Ward v. Huhn, 16 Minn. 159.

6 Kaser v. Haas, 27 Minn. 406.

7 Rev. Code, 1880, §§ 1248, 1249 ; 19 Am. L. Reg. 11, 12 ; Morrison v. Mc.
Daniel, 30 Miss. 217 ; Johnson v. Richardson, 33 Miss. 462.

it themselves, as where a widow died leaving an infant child who was entitled to a homestead.[1]

11 *a*. In Missouri the law exempts a dwelling house and appurtenances used and occupied as a homestead ; and if in the country, one hundred and sixty acres of land, if it do not exceed fifteen hundred dollars in value ; and if in a city of forty thousand people, not more than eighteen square rods, and not exceeding three thousand dollars. If in a city of a less number of inhabitants, thirty square rods, and not exceeding fifteen hundred dollars in value.[2] Under the law of 1864 a less amount in value was exempt. And it was held that a homestead may be set apart in leasehold property of a debtor,[3] or in property where the owner has rented all but one room, if he still controls the home.[4] But no homestead can be claimed in the proceeds of land.[5]

11 *b*. The exemption in Nebraska is of a homestead consisting of not exceeding one hundred and sixty acres, with a dwelling-house thereon, if in the country ; or if in a city or incorporated town or village, any quantity of land not exceeding two lots, owned and occupied by the debtor, a resident and head of a family ; provided the value does not exceed two thousand dollars.[6] It extends to aliens as well as citizens.[7]

11 *c*. The homestead exempted by the law of Nevada consists of land and a dwelling-house not exceeding five thousand dollars in value. There is no restriction as to any other uses to be made of the premises if occupied for a homestead.[8] Erecting a house and residing in it dedicates it as a homestead, though large enough for a lodging-house, and used for that purpose,[9] or though there are stores on the homestead lot.[10] But there can be no homestead in partnership real estate.[11]

12. In New Hampshire the exemption extends only to an estate worth five hundred dollars, which the owner occupies

---

[1] Campbell *v.* Adair, 45 Miss. 170 ; Partee *v.* Stewart, 50 Miss. 717 ; King *v.* Sturgs, 56 Miss. 606 ; McGrath *v.* Sinclair, 55 Miss. 89.

[2] Pub. Stat. 1879, § 2689.   [3] *In re* Beckerkord, 19 Am. L. Reg. 58.

[4] Brown *v.* Brown, 68 Mo. 388.   [5] Casebolt *v.* Donaldson, 67 Mo. 308.

[6] Comp. Stat. 1881, c. 36, § 1.   [7] People *v.* McClay, 2 Neb. 7.

[8] Const. art. 4, § 30 ; Comp. Laws, 1873, § 186 ; Clark *v.* Shannon, 1 Nev. 568.

[9] Goldman *v.* Clark, 1 Nev. 607.

[10] Smith *v.* Stewart, 13 Nev. 65.   [11] Terry *v.* Berry, 13 Nev. 514.

as his domicil or home, and does not affect lots and tenements not occupied personally by the head of the family. The homestead right, in other words, protects only the home, the house, and the adjacent lands, where the head of the family dwells, as a family homestead, though these may be of less value than the sum of five hundred dollars.[1] But he may embrace a parcel of land on which he cuts hay for a cow, though a mile from his dwelling-house, if used with that, and if both do not exceed five hundred dollars in value.[2]

12 a. The law of New Jersey exempts the lot and building thereon standing, occupied as a residence, and owned by the debtor who is a householder, of the value of one thousand dollars.[3]

13. In New York the lot and buildings thereon occupied as a residence are exempted to the value of one thousand dollars.[4]

13 a. In North Carolina the exemption is of every homestead and the dwelling-house and buildings therewith used, not exceeding one thousand dollars, or a lot in a city, town, or village, with a dwelling-house thereon, owned and occupied by a resident of the State, of the value of one thousand dollars. And an occupancy as an actual homestead is essential to its being exempted.[5] But tracts not contiguous may be a homestead, if their whole value is under one thousand dollars.[6]

14. In Ohio a family homestead of the value of one thousand dollars is exempt, and the right extends to lessees and owners of buildings standing on another's land,[7] and also to the proceeds of the sale of a homestead.[9]

15. In Pennsylvania a right of homestead does not attach to any land, until the owner shall have elected to hold it as such, and then only to the value of three hundred dollars. But the right of a debtor's widow to the benefit of this does

---

[1] Gen. Laws, 1878, c. 138 ; Norris v. Boulton, 34 N. H. 392 ; Hoitt v. Webb, 36 N. H. 158 ; Horn v. Tufts, 39 N. H. 484 ; Austin v. Stanley, 46 N. H. 52.

[2] Buxton v. Dearborn, 46 N. H. 43. Cf. Cole v. Sav. Bk., 59 N. H. 53; Rogers v. Ashland Sav. Bk., 63 N. H. 428; Squire v. Budgett, Id. 71; Lake v. Page, Id. 318.

[3] Rev. 1877, p. 1855.   [4] 4 Stat. at Large, Pt. 3, c. 260, p. 632.

[5] Const. 1868, art. 10, § 2; Code, 1883.   [6] Code, 1883, § 509.

[7] Rev. Stat. 1880, §§ 5435, 5436.   [9] Jackson v. Reid, 32 Ohio St. 443.

not depend upon the condition of her husband's estate, as to being solvent or not.[1]

16. In South Carolina the law exempts a homestead of one thousand dollars, it being a family homestead,[2] and whether owned in fee or for a less estate.[3]

16 a. In Tennessee the exemption is of a dwelling-house, out-buildings, and land appurtenant, occupied as a homestead, of the value of one thousand dollars.[4] The exemption extends to equitable estates,[5] and to leaseholds if from two to fifteen years' term but these last are subject to the payment of the rent.[6] And when the homestead is once acquired, a gain in value will not affect it.[7] Continued possession is not required,[8] and no homestead can be obtained in undivided or partnership property.[9]

17. In Texas the exemption is of two hundred acres, if in an agricultural district; but if situated in a town or city, of premises worth five thousand dollars. The value of the former is not restricted. The house which is exempt may be a palace, a cabin, or a tent.[10] The city or town exemption may extend to one or more lots, contiguous or otherwise, provided they are all used by the debtor as a homestead, and do not exceed the prescribed value, and are occupied or destined as a family residence. Both rural and city homesteads may consist of several separate parcels, provided, in case of the city homestead, it do not exceed five thousand dollars.[11] And if one

---

[1] Purdon's Dig. 9th ed. 433 ; Compher v. Compher, 25 Penn. St. 31; Hill v. Hill, 32 Penn. St. 511 ; Dig. 1872.

[2] Const. art. 2, § 32; Gen. Stat. 1882, § 1994; Manning v. Dove, 10 Rich. 403.

[3] Gen. Stat. 1882, § 1994.

[4] Const. art. 41, § 11 ; Stat. 1871, § 2010 ; 19 Am. L. Reg. 14.

[5] Stat. 1871, § 2015.   [6] Id. § 2013.

[7] Hardy v. Lane, 6 Lea, 379.

[8] Roach v. Hacker, 3 Lea, 633 ; McInturf v. Woodruff, 9 Lea, 671. In the former case, however, the circumstances amounted to an abandonment.

[9] Avans v. Everett, 3 Lea, 76 ; Chalfant v. Grant, 3 Lea, 118. So one who leases his land on shares and lives on adjoining lot cannot claim homestead. Wade v. Wade, 9 Baxt. 612.

[10] Const. art. 22 ; Franklin v. Coffee, 18 Tex. 416 ; Homestead Cases, 31 Tex. 678 ; Rev. Stat. 1879, art. 2335, 2336.

[11] Homestead Cases, 31 Tex. 678 ; Williams v. Hall, 33 Tex. 215 ; Ragland v. Rogers, 34 Tex. 617 ; Rev. Stat. art. 2335, 2336 ; Miller v. Menke, 56 Tex. 539. And whether a lot adjacent to the dwelling-house is so used as to become a part

acquire a homestead of less value than five thousand dollars, he may add to it to the extent of that sum, and hold it as homestead.[1] A rural homestead does not cease to be such by being embraced in a city or town by its growth and expansion.[2] A homestead may be acquired by a tenant in common, in an estate held in common with others.[3] And it would embrace the office of a lawyer, or the shop of a mechanic, if it stand upon a city lot, though it be upon another than the lot on which the owner's house stands, if it be used by the owner in connection with his occupancy of such dwelling-house. But the office of a single man is not exempted.[4] So when one occupied a room in a house for a grocery, and another for a sleeping-room, while he took his meals at another place, it was held not to be making such house his residence or place where he usually sleeps and eats, nor to constitute a homestead.[5] But a homestead may be gained by the owner making preparation to improve the land, if carried so far as to show beyond a doubt his intention to complete the improvement, and a residence upon it as a home.[6] By the statute of 1846, if one having a homestead die leaving a widow, she may, as head of the family, have a right to the land of such homestead, and the improvements thereon, not exceeding five hundred dollars. If the improvements exceed that value, she must, in order to retain them, pay to his administrator the excess of such value. Otherwise, he may sell the estate, paying her the value of the homestead and the five hundred dollars for herself and her children.[7]

18. The statute of Vermont exempts a dwelling-house, out-

of the homestead, is a question of fact for the jury. Arto v. Maydole, 54 Tex. 244 ; Andrews v. Hagadon, Id. 571.

[1] Campbell v. Bacmanus, 32 Tex. 451 ; Bacmanus v. Campbell, 37 Tex. 267.

[2] Bassett v. Messner, 30 Tex. 604.

[3] Williams v. Wethered, 37 Tex. 130 ; Smith v. Deschaumes, 37 Tex. 429 ; Clements v. Lacy, 51 Tex. 150 ; Jenkins v. Volz, 54 Tex. 636.

[4] Hancock v. Morgan, 17 Tex. 582 ; Pryor v. Stone, 19 Tex. 371 ; Stanley v. Greenwood, 24 Tex. 224.

[5] Philleo v. Smalley, 23 Tex. 498.

[6] Franklin v. Coffee, 18 Tex. 413 ; Barnes v. White, 53 Tex. 628. But where land was taken in exchange for the homestead, no homestead character attaches thereto, if the owner did not intend to reside there, but elsewhere. Whittenberg v. Lloyd, 49 Tex. 633.

[7] Wood v. Wheeler, 7 Tex. 1325.

buildings, and lands appurtenant, occupied as a homestead to the value of five hundred dollars.[1] This may be either an equitable or a legal estate, incumbered or unincumbered, if owned by the one claiming the exemption.[2] Occupation by the debtor is an essential requisite.[3] It would not be sufficient that it was occupied by a tenant, to entitle his widow to claim homestead in the premises. Nor could she claim it in a separate parcel of wood-land, though used by him during his life to supply wood for his dwelling-house, nor in a shop and land on which it stands, nor the pew in a meeting-house which he had occupied,[4] nor a separate parcel not adjoining the house-lot.[5] But where husband and wife's estate in New Hampshire was sold on execution, and five hundred dollars as homestead reserved and paid over to them, and they removed to Vermont, it was held that this specific sum, if retained by them, was exempt from their debts under their homestead rights in Vermont.[6]

18 a. The exemption in Virginia is of real and personal estate, or either, not exceeding two thousand dollars, to be selected by the householder.[7] It extends to equitable estates and lands held in common.[8]

19. In Wisconsin the statute fixes the amount of property which is exempt at forty acres, if used for agricultural purposes, with a dwelling-house thereon and its appurtenances, or if in a city, town, or village, one quarter of an acre with the dwelling-house and appurtenances thereon occupied by the debtor, irrespective, in either case, of the value of the premises.[9] But it must be held in severalty, in order to be exempt as a homestead. A mortgage, therefore, made by a husband of land held by him in common with others, was held to be

[1] Rev. Laws, 1880, § 1894. Cf. Canfield v. Hard, 53 Vt. 217.
[2] Morgan v. Stearns, 41 Vt. 398 ; Doane v. Doane, 46 Vt. 485.
[3] Howe v. Adams, 28 Vt. 544 ; Jewett v. Brock, 32 Vt. 65 ; Davis v. Andrews, 30 Vt. 683 ; McClary v. Bixby, 36 Vt. 257. And where the owner of two farms lived on one, but intended to remove to the other, it was held he could not claim homestead in the latter before actual removal. Goodall v. Boardman, 53 Vt. 92.
[4] True v. Morrill, 28 Vt. 672 ; Davis v. Andrews, sup.
[5] Mills v. Estate of Grant, 36 Vt. 269.		[6] Keyes v. Bines, 37 Vt. 260.
[7] Const. art. 11, § 1 ; Code, 1873, c. 183, §§ 1, 2 ; 22 Am. L. Reg. 625.
[8] Code, 1873, c. 183, § 4.
[9] Rev. Stat. 1878, § 2983 ; Phelps v. Rooney, 9 Wisc. 70.

effectual against any claim by the wife, except for dower.[1] But it is no objection to the exemption taking effect, that the house for which it is claimed stands upon another's land.[2] Nor need the claimant have a perfect title to the property. It must, however, be occupied by him in severalty, and be susceptible of being set out by metes and bounds.[3] An unmarried man may claim it if he have a family occupying the house with him.[4] The term homestead, under which property is thus exempted, implies that it is the land where is situated the dwelling of the owner and family, in a reasonably compact form, and does not intend separate and disconnected lots.[5] One having a prairie lot with a house on it, and a parcel of woodland a mile distant from the same, it is not embraced in a homestead right, although he get his wood from such lot for the use of his house.[6] So with a city lot.[7] If it be a city lot, the exemption only extends to such parts of it as are occupied for a residence or home. It would not cover stores, warehouses, or offices, and the like, which are let by the owner; though if the shop stand upon the same lot as the dwelling-house, and is occupied by the owner, it may be included in the exemption.[8]

20. There is a different rule applied in different States in respect to the nature and extent of property or ownership requisite on the part of the one claiming exemption in the premises in respect to which it is sought to be applied. In Iowa, Mississippi, Texas, and other States, it may be claimed in an estate for years.[9] In Illinois, in a life estate.[10] In Massachusetts, Michigan, New Hampshire, Ohio, and Wisconsin, a homestead may be claimed in a dwelling house belonging to the debtor, which stands upon the land of another by virtue of a lease to the owner of the house. And in Massachusetts

---

[1] West v. Ward, 26 Wisc. 579.   [2] Code, 1873, § 2983.

[3] West v. Ward, sup.   [4] Myers v. Ford, 22 Wisc. 139.

[5] Bunker v. Locke, 15 Wisc. 635.

[6] Bunker v. Locke, 15 Wisc. 635 ; Herrick v. Graves, 16 Wisc. 157, 166.

[7] Herrick v. Graves, sup.

[8] Casselman v. Packard, 16 Wisc. 114 ; and a homestead may be claimed in a hotel. Harriman v. Queen Ins. Co., 49 Wisc. 71.

[9] Pelan v. De Bevard, 13 Iowa, 53 ; Johnson v. Richardson, 33 Miss. 462.

[10] Deere v. Chapman, 25 Ill. 610.

the right extends generally to premises, whether owned by the debtor, or rightfully possessed by him under a lease or otherwise.[1] In Michigan, Texas, and Wisconsin, it seems to be sufficient if the debtor has a title to the premises, or, being in possession, has a contract of purchase from the owner, or a patent from a State, with a right to demand a title to the same.[2] But in Texas it does not attach to the estate of a trustee, although the trust be a resulting one.[3] And when an unmarried man, in embarrassed circumstances, incurred debts by erecting a dwelling-house upon land belonging to him, knowing he was insolvent, and then married a wife who was cognizant of the facts, it was held that under the homestead right it was exempt from a creditor's levy.[4] A different rule prevails in different States, upon the homestead being allowed in lands held in severalty or in common. Thus in California, Indiana, and Massachusetts, it is not allowed in lands held in common by the debtor and other persons,[5] even though held thus by husband, wife, and child.[6] Whereas in Iowa it is no objection that the estate is held in common with others.[7] So in Vermont,[8] if held in common by husband and wife, the wife's homestead after his death is to be set out wholly from the husband's share of the land.[9]

---

[1] Thurston v. Maddocks, 6 Allen, 427 ; Mich. Stat. c. 132 ; N. H. Com. Stat. c. 196 ; Ohio Rev. Stat. 1145 ; Wisc. Stat. c. 134, § 23 ; Norris v. Moulton, 34 N. H. 392 ; Mass. Gen. Stat. c. 104.

[2] McKee v. Wilcox, 11 Mich. 358 ; Farmer v. Simpson, 6 Tex. 303 ; McCabe v. Mazzuchelli, 13 Wis. 478.

[3] Shepherd v. White, 11 Tex. 346, 354.   [4] North v. Shearn, 15 Tex. 174.

[5] Wolf v. Fleischacker, 5 Cal. 244 ; Holden v. Pinney, 6 Cal. 234 ; Giblin v. Jordan, 6 Cal. 416 ; 2 Ind. Stat. 367 ; Thurston v. Maddocks, 6 Allen, 427.

[6] Giblin v. Jordan, sup. ; Smith v. Smith, 12 Cal. 216.

[7] Thorn v. Thorn, 14 Iowa, 49.   [8] McClary v. Bixby, 36 Vt. 254, 257.

[9] McClary v. Bixby, sup.

DIVISION III.

HOW WHAT IS EXEMPT IS ASCERTAINED AND DECLARED.

1. WHILE in some of the States a homestead exemption attaches as an incident to the ownership of an estate, without any previous act of appropriation on the part of the owner, in others it requires some act of notoriety in selecting and making known the premises which are to be exempted from being levied upon by creditors by process of law.

1 a. In Alabama it is claimed and selected by the owner, or, if he do not select in his lifetime, his widow or the guardian of his children may.[1] If creditors are dissatisfied as to the estimated value of the premises, they are valued by three freeholders and set out by metes and bounds.[2] The law does not require the selection to be made in one body; the house may be on one lot, and the land exempted may be in another.[3] And in making their estimate of value, the appraisers are not

---

[1] Code, 1876, §§ 2820, 2840.

[2] Id. §§ 2832–2838. And the debtor's claim has to be precise in its averments, filing, and other requirements of the statute. Block v. Bragg, 68 Ala. 291 ; Hardy v. Sulzbacher, 62 Ala. 44 ; Sherry v. Brown, 66 Ala. 51.

[3] Melton v. Andrews, 45 Ala. 454.

restricted to a fraction of the sum prescribed by the statute.[1] But a claim for homestead cannot be made after a repeal of the law which gave it.[2]

I b In Arkansas the debtor selects his own homestead, and if he resides on two lots upon which a levy is made, he may elect and designate which is to be exempted, up to the day of sale.[3] When a homestead is claimed by a widow or minor children, a description of the land is to be filed, and if the value of the lot exceeds five thousand dollars, it is to be sold, and the proceeds, to the amount of five thousand dollars, invested by the court for their benefit.[4]

2. In California the debtor selects such part of his estate as he wishes to hold exempt, and makes a declaration and record of this, though it had previously been held otherwise. But now, as formerly, the question of the value of the selected premises may be determined by appraisers, if the creditor believes the selected homestead exceeds in value the sum prescribed by statute.[5] And the commissioners appointed to appraise the value may set apart the homestead for the debtor.[6] If it is not capable of being set out by itself, the whole is to be sold and the debtor is to receive his share, which remains for six months exempt from attachment.[7] Upon the death of the husband, the judge of probate may set out the homestead to his widow and her children.[8] If it has been set off in the lifetime of the owner by the husband and wife, or either of them, it is exempt from administration. If it is not set out in the husband's lifetime, the judge of probate may set out to the widow not more than twenty acres of land, with a dwelling-house thereon, if not in an incorporated town or city,

---

[1] Pomeroy v. Buntings, 42 Ala. 250.   [2] Clark v. Snodgrass, 66 Ala. 233.

[3] Dig. 1874, §§ 3149–3162.

[4] Dig. 1874, §§ 3149–3157. And during minority a child's interest will be protected by the court. Altheimer v. Davis, 37 Ark. 316.

[5] Cohen v. Davis, 20 Cal. 187 ; Hittell, Code, 1876, §§ 6237, 6245 ; Cook v. McChristian, 4 Cal. 23 ; Taylor v. Hargous, 4 Cal. 268 ; Holden v. Pinney, 6 Cal. 234.

[6] Hittell, Code, §§ 6246–6252.

[7] Id. § 6254. Gregg v. Bostwick, 33 Cal. 220 ; Mann v. Rogers, 35 Cal. 316 ; Code, § 6257. But the sale is void unless it brings more than the exemption. Code, § 6255.

[8] Hittell, Code, sup., and §§ 11474–11486 ; Tompkins Est., 12 Cal. 125 ; Matter of Orr, 29 Cal. 103 ; Stat. 1868, p. 116.

and not exceeding one lot in any such town or city, with a dwelling-house, to be selected by the widow, and if not done by her, by the judge, of the value of $5,000.[1] The homestead may be selected by the husband, or wife, or both, by a declaration in writing, to be signed, acknowledged, and recorded, and from that time the husband and wife hold as joint-tenants. Nor does the right of joint-tenancy attach till such declaration is filed for record.[2] By the statute of 1862, to give an estate a character of homestead so as to exempt it from a forced sale, there must be the requisite declaration filed, so that where a husband married and had a child, and died without making such a declaration, it was held to be a waiver of homestead so far as the husband's creditors were concerned.[3] A homestead formerly could not be claimed in property held in common as joint tenancy.[4] But by statute of 1868, it may be set out in lands held in joint tenancy or tenancy in common.[5] A failure to record the declaration of homestead, within the time prescribed by law is a waiver of the right of homestead, so that, if a conveyance has been made in the mean time, it takes effect.[6]

2 *a.* In Florida, if a levy is made upon an estate claimed as a homestead on the ground that it exceeds the value of the exemption, assessors are appointed to set off such part of it as is of that value, having a dwelling-house thereon.[7]

3. In Georgia, if the debtor's estate do not exceed the limit of a homestead right under the statute, he has no occasion to have it set out as such in order to secure it.[8] But if it is of greater value than the amount of such exemption, he must have such part, including his dwelling-house, set out as he intends to hold as a homestead, if he would prevent or defeat

---

[1] Hittell, Code, *supra;* Rich v. Tubbs, 41 Cal. 34 ; Schadt v. Heppe, 45 Cal. 433. But if the widow's declaration does not set out the true value as required by the Code, it is void. Ashley v. Olmstead, 54 Cal. 616 ; Ames v. Eldred, 55 Cal. 136.

[2] Hittell, Code, § 6262 ; McQuade v. Whaley, 31 Cal. 526.

[3] Code, § 6241 ; Reed's Est., 23 Cal. 410 ; Noble v. Hook, 24 Cal. 638.

[4] Bishop v. Hubbard, 23 Cal. 514 ; Elias v. Verdugo, 27 Cal. 418, 425.

[5] Seaton v. Son, 32 Cal. 481 ; Higgins v. Higgins, 46 Cal. 259. But there must be actual occupancy of some tract. Rousset v. Green, 54 Cal. 136.

[6] McQuade v. Whaley, 31 Cal. 526.

[7] Fla. Dig. 1881, c. 104, §§ 5, 6.

[8] Pinkerton v. Tumlin, 22 Ga. 165 ; Dearing v. Thomas, 25 Ga. 223.

a levy upon the same by a creditor.[1] But if the estate be a
town lot, not susceptible of division, but of greater value than
is exempted by law, the ordinary, on application by the creditor may cause the same to be sold, and, after paying the debtor
the amount of such exemption, may apply the balance to the
creditor's debt.[2] By the Code of 1873, the person claiming a
homestead applies to the ordinary to lay it off and make a plat
of it, and, if objection is made as to its estimated value, he
may set it out by appraisers. So if set out in a town lot of a
greater value than $2,000, the ordinary may cause it to be sold,
and that sum to be invested in a new homestead for the benefit
of the owner's family; or the owner may pay whatever it exceeds $2,000, and hold such excess exempt from debts, as if
the same had been settled on his wife and minor children, or
either of them. If the claimant owns scattering lots, or
money, the ordinary may direct them to be sold, and a new
homestead in a single lot to be purchased with the proceeds
or money. Any person who is head of a family, who lives as
a housekeeper, may have a homestead set out to him or her
out of his or her land. And if a husband refuses to apply for
it, the wife or next friend may do it. So if a widow apply for
homestead out of land, and the same cannot be divided, it may
be sold, and $2,000 out of it invested in a new homestead.[3]
So the homestead may be sold for reinvestment under order
of a judge of the Superior Court, on application of the husband and wife.[4] Where a homestead is set out, it carries the
crops then growing upon it.[5] If application for homestead is
not made until a levy is made upon the land, it may then be
made to the ordinary, and it will have the effect, if notice is
given, to have the land, when sold under the levy, pass subject
to the right of homestead,[6] and when the husband is in bankruptcy, application must be made before his adjudication.[7]

[1] Code, 1882, p. 2003 ; Davenport v. Alston, 14 Ga. 271.

[2] Dearing v. Thomas, sup. ; Code, 1882, § 2012.

[3] Code, 1882, §§ 2003–2012, 2022. The application need only state it to be by
the head of the family ; no mention of children is required. Cowart v. Page, 59
Ga. 235. But it must show in whose property exemption is claimed. Jones v.
Jrumley, 61 Ga. 105. And see Willingham v. Maynard, 59 Ga. 330 ; Flemister
v. Phillips, 65 Ga. 676, as to requisite allegations and proof.

[4] Code, § 2025.   [5] Cox v. Cook, 46 Ga. 301.

[6] Blivins v. Johnson, 40 Ga. 297 ; Harris v. Colquit, 44 Ga. 663.

[7] Smith v. Roberts, 61 Ga. 223 ; Colquitt v. Brown, 63 Ga. 440.

4. In Illinois the exemption reserves one lot and the buildings thereon occupied as a residence. But if a creditor believe the premises to exceed one thousand dollars in value, he may have the same appraised by a jury of six men, and, if the same be susceptible of division, may have a homestead of that value set out, and the residue sold. If one creditor causes this to be done, and another afterwards levies upon the homestead, on the ground that it has become of greater value than the homestead exemption, the same process may be gone through with, of a new appraisal and sale of the excess, if any.[1] If not so divisible, the jury adjudge how much it exceeds the prescribed value, and the debtor may retain the whole upon paying such excess; otherwise the creditor may cause the entire estate to be sold, paying to the debtor the sum of one thousand dollars, which he may hold, free from levy, for the term of one year.[2] But the law does not require the husband and wife to do anything in order to create this right of homestead exemption. The statute confers it upon them.[3] It is a right cast upon the wife for her benefit and that of her children.[4] As a widow is entitled to dower independent of her homestead, the latter must contribute *pro rata* with the rest of the estate in setting out this dower.[5] And what shall constitute " a lot " is a matter for a jury to determine. It may include more than an original lot, if embraced in one enclosure and occupied as one lot.[6]

5. In Indiana the debtor has to select the property which he proposes to hold exempt.[7] And before he can claim the benefit of homestead in any part of his estate, he must make out and deliver to the sheriff an entire list of his property, though, in his absence, this may be done by his wife, who is authorized to set up the claim.[8] If any question arises as to the value of that claimed to be exempted, the debtor is to

---

[1] Stubblefield *v.* Graves, 50 Ill. 103 ; Rev. Stat. 1883, c. 52, §§ 10-12.

[2] Rev. Stat. *ubi supra ;* Hume *v.* Gossett, 43 Ill. 297 ; Young *v.* Morgan, 69 Ill. 199 ; Clark *v.* Crosby, 6 Ill. App. 102.

[3] Pardee *v.* Lindley, 31 Ill. 174, 187 ; Hubbell *v.* Canady, 58 Ill. 425.

[4] Hubbell *v.* Canady, 58 Ill. 425.   [5] Knapp *r.* Gass, 63 Ill. 492.

[6] Thornton *v.* Boyden, 31 Ill. 200, 211 ; Pardee *v.* Lindley, *sup.*

[7] Austin *r.* Swank, 9 Ind. 109 ; Rev. Stat. 1881, § 704.

[8] Rev. Stat. § 713 ; State *v.* Melogue, 9 Ind. 196.

make out and deliver to the officer a description of the same, by metes and bounds, and the same is to be submitted to appraisers. If a debtor's property is not divisible, so that his homestead can be set out, he may hold the entire estate, if he will pay the difference between the prescribed exemption and the value of the estate. If he do not do this, the officer may sell the whole, and pay over to the debtor the amount of the exempted value.[1]

6. In Iowa the debtor may select his homestead and have it recorded in the registry of deeds, setting out a full description of it; or, if he fail to do so, his wife may. But if neither do it, the officer having an execution, and wishing to levy upon the debtor's land, must cause it to be done by appraisers whose proceedings are to be returned into court.[2] And if a debtor occupy a building as a dwelling-house, the exemption will be understood to extend to the whole of such building;[3] if he own more than one, he must elect in which to take homestead.[4] The right vests at once upon the marriage, in respect to the husband's lands, and, so far as the wife is concerned, was of a higher nature than that of dower;[5] but is now merged in the distributive share by which dower has been replaced.[6]

6 a. In Kansas, if a homestead has not been actually set apart, and is levied upon by a creditor, the wife, agent, or attorney, as well as the householder himself, may notify the officer what is claimed as homestead, and the remainder only of the debtor's estate is liable to be levied on.[7]

6 b. In Kentucky, if a debtor claims a homestead right in land levied upon, he is to select it, and the officer has to cause it to be set out by two housekeepers, and if it is of greater value than $1,000, and is not divisible, he may sell the same, and pay the debtor that amount in money; but if not more than $1,000 can be obtained for it, no sale is made.[8]

7. In Maine the debtor has to file a certificate under his hand, in the registry of deeds, containing a description of the

---

[1] Rev. Stat. § 710 ; Const. art. 1, § 67.

[2] Rev. Code, 1880, §§ 1998, 1999, 2002–2006.

[3] Rhodes v. McCormick, 4 Iowa, 368 ; Kurz v. Brusch, 13 Iowa, 371.

[4] Rev. Code, § 1994.

[5] Chase v. Abbott, 20 Iowa, 154, 160.   [6] Rev. Code, § 2008.

[7] Comp. L. 1879, § 2498.   [8] Gen. Stat. 1873, art. 13, §§ 10–12.

premises and that he intends to make them a homestead, and
they must be in his actual possession. If, however, a creditor
contests the value of the premises so selected, appraisers are
to be appointed to set out premises of the requisite value, the
selection of which lies with the debtor if he will exercise it,
otherwise with the officer who may levy upon the residue of
his estate.[1] And if, after once making a selection of his
homestead, the debtor sell the estate and again repurchase it,
he must, in order to hold it exempt, file and record a new
certificate.[2]

7 *a*. In Maryland the debtor may select one hundred dollars of real or personal estate, to be ascertained by appraisers;
and if his property is not susceptible of division, it may be
levied upon and sold, and the one hundred dollars paid to the
debtor.[3]

8. In Massachusetts, either the deed under which the
debtor claims title must contain a declaration that the premises are to be held as a homestead, or such a declaration
must be made in writing, signed, sealed, and recorded in the
registry of deeds.[4] From the nature of the case, the homestead is for the personal use of the debtor and his family, and
must be several and exclusive as far as it goes.[5] But a making and recording a declaration of an intention to hold premises as a homestead, before the party has a house upon the
same fit for occupation, and occupied by him, is not effective
to create or establish a homestead right in the same. There
must be an occupation, to perfect the right.[6] And if a part of
the dwelling-house upon the premises is occupied by the owner,
it is no objection to extending a right of homestead over the
whole, that other parts of it are occupied by tenants.[7] If
creditors contest the value of what is claimed to be exempted,
appraisers estimate the same, and may set off estate of the
requisite value, including the dwelling house, in whole or in
part, and the residue is subject to levy, or, if the debtor is insolvent, to be sold by his assignees.[8] If the husband die while

---

[1] Rev. Stat. 1883, c. 83, §§ 64, 65.
[2] Stat. 1861.
[5] Bemis *v.* Driscoll, 101 Mass. 421.
[7] Mercier *v.* Chace, 11 Allen, 194.

[3] Lawton *v.* Bruce, 39 Me. 484.
[4] Pub. Stat. c. 123, § 2.
[6] Lee *v.* Miller, 11 Allen. 37.
[8] Pub. Stat. c. 123, §§ 12, 13.

in possession of a homestead, his widow may continue to occupy the same, without its being formally assigned by the
judge of probate, provided the whole estate of which he died
seised did not exceed the amount exempted by law. If it do,
she may continue to occupy such part as may be of that value,
until partition of the estate be made.[1] The assignment to a
widow of her dower does not defeat her claim to homestead
in addition to it, if so much estate remains to which the character of a homestead right attaches.[2] Nor can the judge exercise any jurisdiction in the matter of a widow's claim for
homestead, if her right thereto is denied by the heirs or devisees of the husband.[3] She must in such case sue a writ of
entry to recover her homestead.[4] The homestead of an insolvent debtor may be set off to him under the direction of the
insolvent court. But in order to the judge having jurisdiction, application for this purpose must be made before the
assignee sells the estate, and then the claimant must resort
to a process of partition. If, after his insolvency, a debtor
continues to occupy his estate, and it is of greater value than
his homestead right, he holds the latter by a distinct title,
undivided and in common with the rest of the estate, defeasible
by his alienation of it, or by his acquiring a new homestead.[5]

9. In Michigan no form of declaring or making known an
intention to claim a homestead is required, provided a debtor
lives upon and occupies an estate of no greater value than
what is exempted by law.[6] The term "selection," as used in
the statute, implies only the separating premises of the requisite value from those of a greater value, and defining by metes
and bounds that which is so set apart. If, therefore, the
debtor's estate be of greater value than the prescribed exemption, and can be divided so as to set apart a homestead with a
dwelling-house, which will not exceed the statute limit, the
debtor may select it, and make it known to his creditors. But
if it is of greater value than that, and cannot be divided, it

---

[1] Parks v. Reilly, 5 Allen, 77 ; Pub. Stat. c. 123, §§ 8-10.
[2] Mercier v. Chace, 11 Allen, 194 ; Cowdrey v. Cowdrey, 131 Mass. 186.
[3] Lazell v. Lazell, 8 Allen, 575 ; Woodward v. Lincoln, 9 Allen, 239.
[4] Mercier v. Chace, 9 Allen, 242.
[5] Silloway v. Brown, 12 Allen, 30, 35.   [6] Thomas v. Dodge, 8 Mich. 51.

may be sold, and the value of the homestead paid to the debtor.
If, therefore, a creditor insist that its value exceeds the statute limits, the question, it seems, is to be determined by a process out of the court of equity, and if found to be of greater
value then the statute exempts, the question is then to be
determined, whether it can be divided so as to have a proper
homestead set off. But the selection need not be made prior
to the levy, nor need it be done in writing. It is enough that,
when the levy is made, the officer is notified of the claim.[1] If
the creditor is dissatisfied with the amount claimed by the
debtor as being exempt, he may have the homestead surveyed
and appraised and set off, and may have the remainder sold.
And if it cannot be divided and set off from the rest of the
estate, the debtor may pay the excess above $1,500, and pre-
vent the sale. If he do not, the officer may sell the whole and
pay the debtor that sum, who may hold the same exempt from
attachment and levy for one year.[2] But unless more can be
got at the sale than the amount of the execution, the sale is
void.[3]

10.   In Minnesota and Mississippi it only seems necessary
that premises of the prescribed size and value should be
actually occupied by the debtor as a residence or home, in
order to secure their exemption from levy by a creditor;[4] although in the former State the statute speaks of the owner's
selection.[5] If, in that State, a levy is made before the homestead has been selected, the householder is to notify the officer
making it what he regards as his homestead, with a description
of it. And if the creditor is dissatisfied, the officer may have
the same set out by appraisal.[6] In Mississippi, upon a levy on
execution, the officer is in like manner to set off the homestead.[7]

10 a. In Missouri, if a levy is made upon the premises of a
debtor, he is to designate the part which he wishes to hold as
homestead. And the officer making it is to appraise the same,

---

[1] Comp. Laws, 1871, §§ 6137–6141; Beecher v. Baldy, 7 Mich. 488; Dye v.
Mann, 10 Mich. 291, 298.

[2] Comp. Laws, 1871, §§ 6140–6144.   [3] Id. § 6145.

[4] Tillotson v. Millard, 7 Minn. 513; Morrison v. McDaniel, 30 Miss. 213, 217

[5] Stat. 1878, c. 68, § 1.   [6] Id. §§ 3–5.

[7] Rev. Code, 1880, §§ 1251–1254.

and may proceed to sell the excess. If it is not separable from the rest of the estate, the whole may be sold, and the value of the homestead paid to the debtor, and the surplus applied to the benefit of creditors. If not set out in the lifetime of the debtor, the judge of probate sets out a homestead to the widow by commissioners. But if it is less than the allowed value, it vests without action by the court.[1] And the same is true where it was set out in the owner's lifetime.[2] If, in case of a levy upon the estate, it is not divisible, and the debtor will pay the excess over the value of the homestead, he may prevent the sale. If sold, the value of the homestead is invested, by order of the court, in a new homestead.[3] If a wife is abandoned by her husband she may claim as if he were dead.[4] In setting out homestead to a widow after her husband's death, commissioners first set that out, and then the widow's dower, unless the homestead takes one third of the estate. If it does, she takes no dower.[5]

10 *b*. In Nebraska, if the homestead is not selected till the levy is made, the debtor notifies the officer what he regards as his homestead, with a description of it. If the creditor is dissatisfied with what is claimed, the officer is to have the same appraised, and the same set off as such homestead, including the dwelling-house, and the balance is liable to be sold, provided the sale brings an amount beyond the exemption.[6]

11. In New Hampshire no previous act of setting apart of the premises seems to be necessary; the right attaches to whatever a debtor owns and actually occupies, not exceeding the prescribed amount exempted by law.[7] The selection is made, when an officer undertakes to levy upon the debtor's estate, of such part as the debtor elects, to be appraised by assessors and by them set off by metes and bounds, leaving the surplus to be levied upon. Upon a levy being made, the

---

[1] Rogers *v.* Marsh, 73 Mo. 64.   [2] Plate *v.* Koehler, 8 Mo. App. 396.

[3] Rev. Stat. 1879, §§ 2690–2693; *In re* Beckerkord, 19 Am. L. Reg. 58.

[4] Rev. Stat. 1879, § 2689.

[5] Rev. Stat. § 2694; Seek *v.* Haynes, 68 Mo. 13.

[6] Comp. Stat. 1881, c. 36, §§ 5–11.

[7] Norris *v.* Boulton, 34 N. H. 392; Hoitt *v.* Webb, 36 N. H. 158; Horn *v.* Tufts, 39 N. H. 484.

husband or wife, or her next friend, may make application in writing to the officer to have a homestead set off, and he is to have it done by metes and bounds, by appraisers.[1] If the land claimed as homestead exceed $500 in value, the sheriff, in setting off the excess, must first set out the homestead, and then proceed to levy upon the surplus.[2] But if it is levied on before the homestead is set out, the debtor holds his homestead as tenant in common with the rest of the estate, and may have partition of the same.[3] If the appraisers adjudge that the homestead cannot be set off from the other parts of the estate without injury to the same, they appraise the whole ; and if the debtor will not pay the excess over the amount exempted, the sheriff may sell the whole, paying the amount of the exemption, for the benefit of the debtor and his wife.[4] The amount of this exemption the officer deposits in a savings bank to the credit of the debtor and his wife or children, to be drawn out only upon the joint order of husband and wife if living, otherwise of the guardian of their children.[5] After the debtor's death, the judge of probate may set off a homestead to the widow in the same manner as dower. But the right of homestead is not lost by the neglect of the debtor to claim it of the officer when levying upon the same.[6] But if the debtor or wife do not, when the levy is made, apply to have a homestead set off, the officer may set off the land upon his execution, subject to the homestead right, and the debtor and creditor will thereupon hold the estate in common until the homestead is set out upon partition prayed for.[7] If a debtor convey his estate without his wife joining in the conveyance, and have no homestead, his wife may apply and have a homestead set out in the land thus conveyed, even in the lifetime of her husband.[8] If the wife survive the husband, her homestead is set out by the judge of probate, provided he died seised of the premises.[9] But if the husband convey the

---

[1] Gen. Laws, 1878, c. 138, §§ 7–11.   [2] Tucker v. Kenniston, 47 N. H. 267.
[3] Barney v. Leeds, 51 N. H. 253.
[4] Gen. Laws, 1879, c. 138, §§ 12–15; Norris v. Boulton, 34 N. H. 392; Fogg v. Fogg, 40 N. H. 289.
[5] Gen. Laws, c. 138, §§ 18, 19.   [6] Id. § 4.
[7] Barney v. Leeds, 51 N. H. 253.   [8] Tidd v. Quinn, 52 N. H. 341.
[9] Norris v. Boulton, *sup.*; Horn v. Tufts, *sup.*

premises in his lifetime, the wife, after his death, may have partition against such purchaser, and have her share set out to her.[1]

11 *a*. In New Jersey, the deed by which the debtor acquires his estate may contain a declaration that it is designed as a homestead; but if it is not thus declared, a notice to that effect is to be executed, acknowledged, and recorded by the owner, containing a description of what is claimed, and this is to be published in a newspaper. If it is worth more than $1,000, the officer, in making a levy upon it, if it is divisible, has it appraised and that value set off. But if it is not divisible, and the debtor will pay the excess above the value of the homestead, he may do so and prevent a sale. If he do not do this, the estate is sold, provided it brings more than the exemption, and the $1,000 paid to the debtor, who holds it exempt from attachment for a year.[2]

11 *b*. In Nevada, a homestead is to be selected by husband and wife, or either of them, or other head of a family. The claim is to be made in writing by one residing upon the premises, stating the claimant's interest in the estate, and his wish to make it a homestead, which writing is to be signed, acknowledged, and recorded. If, then, a creditor makes oath that the homestead is of greater value than $5,000, the judge appoints appraisers to value it, and decide whether it can be divided. If it can be, only the excess can be levied on. If it cannot be, the whole is sold, and $5,000 paid to the debtor, subject to the order of the court that it be deposited in court, and payable only to the order of the husband and wife; and the same is held free from legal process or conveyance by the husband, as the original homestead was held. And upon the death of the husband or wife, the homestead is set apart for the survivor and his or her legitimate children.[3]

12. In New York, either the deed of the owner must show the intention that it should be to him a homestead, or he must by a proper instrument, executed and acknowledged, give notice that the premises are so held; which instrument must

---

[1] Atkinson *v.* Atkinson, 37 N. H. 434; Gunnison *v.* Twitchel, 38 N. H. 62, 67; Horn *v.* Tufts, *sup.*

[2] Rev. 1877, p. 1055, §§ 1–6.   [3] Comp. Laws, 1873, §§ 186–189.

contain a full description of the premises and be recorded in the clerk's office. If the sheriff, upon making a levy, contests the value of the premises claimed to be exempt, he may have the same appraised by six jurors, and if it can be divided and so set off as to give the debtor that value, embracing a dwelling-house, the surplus may be levied on. If it is not susceptible of such division, and the debtor will pay the excess of the value of the estate over the amount exempted, he may relieve the same from levy. Otherwise the sheriff may sell the whole, if it will bring more than the amount exempted, and, by paying that to the debtor, apply the excess upon the execution.[1]

12 a. In North Carolina, a homestead is selected by the owner, and, if he neglects to do this, appraisers set it off for him. In either case they lay off by metes and bounds premises for that purpose of the value of $1,000. Any resident may apply to have this done, and, if he do not do it, and die, his widow, if he have one, or his child or children under twenty-one years of age, may have it set off to her or them. It is essential to its being exempted as a homestead that it should be occupied as such.[2] A homestead may consist of two or more parcels separate from each other, if, collectively, they do not exceed $1,000.[3] Before 1862 it was not restricted to the lot on which the debtor resided;[4] and now a continued residence is not necessary.[5] It may be claimed in an equity of redemption subject to the mortgage.[6]

13. In Ohio, the sheriff having an execution against the debtor, if applied to by the debtor or his wife, causes the homestead to be set off by appraisers, by metes and bounds. And the same is done after his death in favor of his wife, if it is not done in the lifetime of the husband.[7] The right extends to lessees of lands and owners of buildings standing on

[1] 4 Stat. at Large Pt. 3, c. 260, p. 632.

[2] Const. art. 10, § 2; Code, 1883, §§ 502–5, 514. The constitutional exemption has been said to be self-executing. Adrian v. Shaw, 82 N. C. 474. And the action of the appraisers is ministerial only and does not vest the right. Cheen v. Sumney, 80 N. C. 187.

[3] Code, § 509; Martin v. Hughes, 67 N. C. 293; Maybo v. Colton, 69 N. C. 289.

[4] Mayho v. Colton, 69 N. C. 289.   [5] Adrian v. Shaw, 82 N. C. 474.

[6] Chatham v. Souls, 68 N. C. 155.   [7] Rev. Stat. 1880, § 5438 et seq.

others' lands. If the estate claimed as homestead exceed in value $1,000, and is not divisible, a creditor may have set off to him all the proceeds of the estate exceeding one hundred dollars by the year, until his debt shall have thereby been satisfied.[1]

14. In Pennsylvania the debtor exercises his election to claim a homestead, when the officer makes his levy, and if he neglect to claim it then, he is held to have waived the right. If made, the officer, if the estate exceed in value the amount exempted, causes the same to be appraised, and the appraisers decide whether the premises can be divided without injury. If they can be, the homestead is set apart and the balance may be sold. If they cannot be divided, the officer sells the whole estate and pays the exempted amount to the debtor.[2] Where the debtor claimed his exemption on the day of the sale upon execution, the sheriff was held bound to allow it. And where he allowed the debtor thirty dollars in money out of the personal estate, he could only claim two hundred and seventy dollars out of the real.[3] The privilege of homestead is not in itself an exemption, but a right to obtain one in the manner prescribed; and if the debtor fails to avail himself of it, it is of no effect.[4]

15. In South Carolina a debtor's estate is subject to be set off to satisfy the execution of a creditor, unless he apply to the officer holding the same, if his estate exceed in value the homestead exemption, to have a homestead of the prescribed value set off by commissioners; whose return becomes final in forty days after it is recorded. If it exceed $1,000, and is not divisible, the debtor may save his estate from sale by paying the excess of the estate above that sum; otherwise, the same may be sold if it brings $1,000, or over, and out of the proceeds that sum is to be paid to the debtor, to be applied, under the direction of the court, to the purchase of a new homestead. And if he pay the excess of the estate above $1,000, he holds the same exempt as to all debts contracted prior to such pay-

---

[1] Rev. Stat. § 5439.

[2] Purd. Dig. 433; Bowman v. Smiley, 31 Penn. St. 225; Miller's Appeal, 16 Penn. St. 300; Dodson's Appeal, 25 Penn. St. 234.

[3] Seibert's Appeal, 73 Penn. St. 361.　[4] Lines' Appeal, 2 Grant's Cases, 198.

ment.[1] And if this is not done in his lifetime, the same may be set out by commissioners to his widow.[2]

15 *a*. In Tennessee, the householder desiring to secure a homestead makes a declaration to that effect, signed, sealed, witnessed, and registered. When it is set out, in case of a levy, it is done by appraisers by metes and bounds, including a dwelling-house. And if it is not divisible, an officer, in levying upon the estate, may sell the whole and pay the $1,000 into the clerk's office of the court, to be laid out, under direction of the court, in the purchase of a new homestead.[3]

15 *b*. In Texas, if the homestead consists of more than two hundred acres or a lot of greater value than $5,000, the debtor selects which two hundred acres, or how much of the city or town lot, shall be held exempt. If he fail to do this, the sheriff holding an execution against him may do it by commissioners.[4]

16. In Vermont, if a creditor intend to set off a portion of a debtor's estate, on the ground that it exceeds in value what is exempted by law, so much of the same is first set out by appraisers to the debtor upon the latter's designation, if he elects to have it done, and the surplus may be levied on. But homestead may be set out in any suit affecting the property, by appraisers appointed by the court.[5] After the debtor's death, the homestead is set off by the court of probate.[6] But if the premises left by a householder are of greater value than the homestead exemption, and cannot be divided so as to give the widow her homestead therein, there may be a decree in equity for the sale thereof, and the amount of the homestead exemption paid into court for her use and that of the children.[7]

16 *a*. In Virginia, unless the deed by which the householder acquires title to the estate declares it to be for a homestead, he does it by a deed duly recorded, setting forth his

[1] Gen. Stat. 1882, §§ 1994–1996. In the application, the value of the estate should be set out. Kerchner *v.* Singletary, 15 S. C. 535.

[2] Act. 1851, p. 85 ; Manning *v.* Dove, 10 Rich. 403.

[3] Stat. 1871, §§ 2016, 2017, 2030 ; 19 Am. Law Reg. 14.

[4] Rev. Stat. 1879, art. 2335, 2336.   [5] Rev. Laws, 1880, § 1907.

[6] Rev. Laws, 1880, § 1895 ; Howe *v.* Adams, 28 Vt. 544.

[7] Id. §§ 1908, 1909 ; Chaplin *v.* Sawyer, 35 Vt. 286.

intention to claim as a homestead what he therein describes. And this may be land in which he has an equitable as well as a legal title. So if it is levied on, he may select it, and if what he selects be of greater value than the homestead exemption, and it cannot be divided and set apart, the whole is to be sold, and out of the proceeds the court may order the value of the homestead to be invested in a new one.[1] And if the debtor does not select, the officer may.[2]

17. In Wisconsin the debtor selects and sets out his homestead by metes and bounds, and is to notify the officer who is about to levy upon his estate what he claims to hold exempt, with a description of the same. And if the creditor objects as to the value of what is thus claimed, he may have the same surveyed and set out so as to give the debtor the requisite value.[3] If a debtor's farm be under a mortgage, or under a lien, and he die, and his estate sells for enough to pay his debts, leaving a surplus, the judge may order enough of this to be invested in a homestead for the family of the deceased. The court may order five hundred dollars to be invested in a new homestead; and if the wife is insane, the court may order the homestead sold, and direct as to the investment of the proceeds.[4]

DIVISION IV.

HOW FAR HOMESTEAD RIGHTS ANSWER TO ESTATES.

1, 1 a. Their analogy to estates for life.   In Arkansas and Alabama.
   2. Nature of the interests in homestead estates in California.
  2 a. Nature of these in Florida.
3, 3 a. Nature of these in Georgia.   In Illinois.
   4. Nature of these in Indiana.
5, 5 a. Nature of these in Iowa.   In Kentucky.
  5 b. Nature of these in Louisiana.
   6. Nature of these in Maine.
   7. Nature of these in Massachusetts.

---

[1] Code 1873, c. 183, §§ 4, 6.   [2] Id. § 16.

[3] Rev. Stat. 1878, § 2984. If, however, the dwelling-house is on a lot whose area is just two hundred acres, the statutory exemption, the owner is presumed to have selected this. Kent v. Lasley, 48 Wisc. 257.

[4] Stat. 1873, p. 111.

1. WHEN it is sought to define the nature and character of the property or estate which one has in the homestead which the law creates in his favor, and what rights and duties are attached to the same, it will be found difficult to do more than borrow the language of the statutes and of courts in construing them in the different States, though, with the exception of a few where the wife and children take estates of inheritance, most of the incidents of estates for life would be considered as attaching to homestead rights.[1]

1 a. In Arkansas, the homestead right continues after the death of the owner, to the use of his widow and child or children, so long as they continue to occupy the premises.[2] So in Alabama, the homestead is regarded as merely a continuation of the husband's estate;[3] and during his lifetime the wife has nothing which can be called an estate.[4] If the land holden by the husband be held by lease for a term of years, the right does not attach so as to go to his widow at his death.[5]

2. In California, the homestead is something coming out of the general property in the land of the husband,[6] in which case the wife has no estate therein,[7] or out of the estate of husband and wife,[8] and consists of a qualified right in the husband to convey it, and a right in the husband and wife to enjoy the premises until a new homestead is acquired, or its character as homestead is lost. So it may come out of the

[1] Kerley v. Kerley, 13 Allen, 286.
[3] Hunter v. Law, 68 Ala. 365.
[5] Pizzala v. Campbell, 46 Ala. 35.
[7] Bowman v. Norton, 16 Cal. 213.
[2] Const. art. 12, §§ 4, 5.
[4] Seaman v. Nolen, 68 Ala. 463.
[6] Gee v. Moore, 14 Cal. 472.
[8] Gee v. Moore, sup.

estate of the wife with her consent.[1] But this right of occupancy has nothing of the character of joint-tenancy in it. All
the present right which the wife acquires during the life of the
husband is, that this right of homestead shall continue until
she consents to its being aliened, or another homestead is acquired, or the same is abandoned.[2] But in an earlier as well
as a later case, it was declared by the court that they became
joint owners of the property, with the right of survivorship,
and that the homestead right in a husband and wife is one of
joint-tenancy under the act of 1860.[3] This homestead right
may be released, but not sold or transferred to another, since,
being a personal privilege, it cannot be assigned.[4] But so
far as the wife's right is concerned, she can only protect it
through the husband, or enforce it by uniting with him ; and
the same is true of the protection of the rights of the children.[5] She cannot, therefore, sue to recover the premises
without joining her husband ;[6] though, where a purchaser
from the husband, in whose deed the wife did not join, brought
ejectment for the premises, and the husband neglected to defend, the wife was allowed to do so alone.[7] But if the wife
dies in the lifetime of the husband, the homestead is left to his
control, so that, if he mortgage the premises, it will bind the
children, or a second wife who shall marry him subsequently
to such mortgage.[8] And if the homestead was from his separate estate, he may devise it subject only to the temporary
assignment of the probate court.[9] If the wife survive the
husband, the judge of probate may set apart the premises for
the benefit of the wife and children, each to have property in
one half, or of the wife if there are no children ; and if he have
no wife nor children, it may be set out to his next heirs at
law.[10] She can recover, however, only one homestead, though

[1] Hittell's Code, 1876, §§ 6238, 6239.

[2] Gee v. Moore, 14 Cal. 472 ; Bowman v. Norton, 16 Cal. 213.

[3] Dunn v. Tozer, 10 Cal. 167 ; Barber v. Babel, 36 Cal. 11.

[4] Bowman v. Norton, sup. ; Stat. 1862.

[5] Guiod v. Guiod, 14 Cal. 506.   [6] Poole v. Gerrard, 6 Cal. 71.

[7] Cook v. McChristian, 4 Cal. 23.

[8] Benson v. Aitken, 17 Cal. 163 ; Himmelmann v. Schmidt, 23 Cal. 117.

[9] Hittell's Code, 1876, § 6265.

[10] Hittell's Code, §§ 11474–11486.

her husband may, during his life, have owned several.[1] But whether she takes this in her own right or in trust for the children is unsettled.[2] On the death of husband or wife, the homestead in community property vests absolutely in the survivor, free from any liability for any debt of either, contracted before his or her death, except such as it was subject to in the lifetime of both.[3] And although it is subject to valid existing liens, it ceases to be assets for the payment of the debts of the deceased.[4] If one owning land in partnership dies, his widow cannot claim homestead out of it.[5] If a widow have a homestead set out in her deceased husband's estate, she holds it for the benefit of herself and children. But if she marries again, and her second husband has a homestead, she may, on his death, claim a homestead also out of his estate to her own use. Under the statute of 1862, however, the children of parents having a homestead have no interest in it. Upon the death of one, it survives to the other.[6]

2 *a*. In Florida the owner of a homestead may dispose of it by last will, and if he or she die intestate, it descends to his or her issue then living. If there be no children, it goes to the widow; and if there is no widow nor children, it may be sold to satisfy debts.[7]

3. In Georgia a widow takes the homestead, whether she have children or not; but her dower must first be set out before the homestead can be.[8] Minor children take the homestead subject to the widow's right of dower, to the exclusion of the father's creditors.[9] And where the father died, having devised his estate to his minor children, whose guardian chose to have the same set off as homestead rather than claim it under the devise, it was held to take the estate from the control of the ordinary, and to give it to the children by right of homestead.[10] It is to be held for the use of the widow and children during her life or widowhood, and upon her death or

---

[1] Taylor *v.* Hargous, 4 Cal. 268.

[2] Tompkins Est., 12 Cal. 114.

[3] Hittell's Code, § 6265.

[4] Matter of Orr, 29 Cal. 101.

[5] Kingsley *v.* Kingsley, 39 Cal. 665.

[6] Rich *v.* Tubbs, 41 Cal. 34.

[7] Dig. 1881, c. 104, §§ 8, 16.

[8] Code 1882, § 2021; Haslam *v.* Campbell, 60 Ga. 650.

[9] Roff *v.* Johnson, 40 Ga. 555.

[10] Sloane *v.* Nance, 45 Ga. 310; Hodo *v.* Johnson, 40 Ga. 439.

marriage it is equally divided among the children, as the wife
and children are regarded the principal beneficiaries under the
homestead law.[1]   But the estate of a wife in a homestead is
not one of inheritance; it ceases upon her death or ceasing to
be a member of the family, and if both husband and wife die
without leaving minor children, the homestead right is gone,
and the same reverts to the estate of the husband.[2]   But this
reversion or remainder dependent on the termination of the
homestead cannot be levied upon while the homestead lasts.[3]
It is, however, subject to the dower right of the widow, and she
does not take the full value of the homestead in addition to
her dower.[4]   Whether minor children can claim a homestead in
their father's estate depends upon its being insolvent.   If it is,
they may claim it against creditors; if it is not, there is no
homestead, the estate passes at his death to his heirs, subject
only to the widow's right of dower, she having no right to
claim a homestead in such case.[5]   If the husband in his lifetime neglect or refuse to have a homestead set out, his widow
may have it done after his death.[6]

3 a. In Illinois the right of a widow continues during her
life, and that of her children until twenty-one years of age,
provided they or some of them continue to occupy the same as
a homestead.[7]   But the interest of homestead in land is not
an estate : it is merely an exemption and suspension from the
conveyance of a fee in the land until the premises are aban-
douned or possession is surrendered.[8]   It does not merge in
a widow's right of dower in the same premises.   These rights
are distinct from and independent of each other, and a widow
may have both out of the same estate.[9]   But a sale of land in
which there is a homestead, by the administrator of the deceased owner, carries no title, even if the homestead be excepted.[10]   But if husband and family remove from or abandon

[1] Burnside v. Terry, 45 Ga. 621, 629.

[2] Heard v. Downer, 47 Ga. 629 ; Ga. Code 1882, § 2024.

[3] Haslam v. Campbell, 60 Ga. 650.

[4] Adams v. Adams, 46 Ga. 630 ; Hickson v. Bryan, 41 Ga. 620.

[5] Kemp v. Kemp, 42 Ga. 523.   [6] Hodo v. Johnson, 40 Ga. 439.

[7] Ill. Stat. p. 650.

[8] McDonald v. Crandall, 43 Ill 231 ; Black v. Curran, 14 Wall. 463.

[9] Walsh v. Reis, 50 Ill. 477.   [10] Hartman v. Schultz, 101 Ill. 437.

the homestead, neither he nor they can resume it so as to cut
off liens created during such abandonment.[1] But the abandonment by one only does not affect the rights of the others.[2]
The wife cannot claim the benefit of the statute while her husband is alive ; but he only can assert the claim.[3] And if both
wife and children die, he still retains the homestead.[4] If the
wife shall have been divorced for her husband's fault, she may
claim it as a widow.[5] So she may if he abandons her, and
she continues to occupy the homestead.[6] So if he ill-treats
her, and drives her away from her home, and she then obtains
a divorce, and the children are committed to her charge, she,
as the head of a family, may have homestead assigned to her
as alimony, and hold it for herself and her children after her.[7]
And if a husband abandon his wife and family, and she is
forcibly expelled, she may have process in her own name to
recover possession of the premises.[8] As the right of homestead
was designed for the protection of the wife and children more
than of the husband, he holds the estate, to a certain extent,
as a trustee. And though, if necessary, he may purchase in
an outstanding title for the protection of the estate, and bind
it for the purchase-money, he cannot thus bind it if such purchase was not necessary.[9]

4. In Indiana the right of homestead in the widow is independent of any provision made for her by devise of her husband.[10] The widow of a deceased owner may have $300 of
her husband's estate set off to her.[11] So a wife may have
this homestead, if she is the debtor and have estate of her
own.[12]

5. In Iowa, upon the death of the husband or wife, the estate
goes to the survivor, whether there are children or not, and if

---

[1] Titman v. Moore, 43 Ill. 169 ; Vasey v. Trustees, 59 Ill. 158.

[2] Rev. Stat. 1883, c. 52, § 2.

[3] Getzler v. Saroni, 18 Ill. 511.   [4] Kimbrel v. Willis, 97 Ill. 494.

[5] Vanzant v. Vanzant, 23 Ill. 536. But in any case of divorce, the matter is
in the control of the court. Rev. Stat. c. 52, § 5.

[6] Titman v. Moore, 43 Ill. 169 ; People v. Stitt, 7 Ill. App. 294.

[7] Bonnell v. Smith, 53 Ill. 375, 383.   [9] Nix v. King, 55 Ill. 434.

[8] Cassel v. Ross, 33 Ill. 244, 257.

[10] Loring v. Craft, 16 Ind. 110.   [11] Stat. 1862, p. 368.

[12] Crane v. Waggoner, 33 Ind. 83.

there be no survivor, it descends to the issue of the husband or wife, unless otherwise disposed of, to be held by such issue exempt from any antecedent debts of the parents or issue. By "issue" in the statute is meant the issue of husband or wife, whichever it may be, who owned the fee.[1] But setting off a distributive share is such a disposition as will terminate it.[2] The same may be devised, subject to the rights of the survivor.[3] The right of the widow or widower is to occupy the estate during life, and to take the rents and profits thereof to his or her own use. At the death of the survivor, without issue, the exemption ceases.[4] The survivor does not take a fee in the homestead, and cannot sell it to another.[5] If he or she do so, the heirs of the other spouse may come in and divide the estate between them.[6] Homestead laws are simply statutes of exemption, rather than a conferring of primitive rights.[7] But the wife's dower, by the law of Iowa prior to 1853, and since 1862, is an estate in fee.[8] She cannot claim dower or the distributive share in fee, in lieu of dower, and homestead out of the same estate. If she claims dower, she waives her right of homestead.[9] But the widow has a right to enjoy the homestead, although she marries again; nor can the heirs of the husband have partition while she occupies it,[10] and she may have damages for a continuing trespass or adverse occupancy, though it began while her husband was living. [11]

5 a. In Kentucky, after the death of the owner of the homestead, his widow and unmarried children, so long as she occupies it at all, occupy the same together, until the youngest is twenty-one years of age. Nor will her abandonment of the estate affect the rights of the minor children. And the same rule applies to husband and children, if the homestead estate

---

[1] Burns v. Keas, 21 Iowa, 257 ; Rev. Code, 1880, §§ 1989, 2007, 2008, 2010.

[2] Rev. Code, § 2008.

[3] Rev. Code, § 2010 ; Burns v. Keas, 21 Iowa, 257 ; Floyd v. Mosier, 1 Iowa, 512 ; Rhodes v. McCormick, 4 Iowa, 368.

[4] Rev. Code, § 2009.   [5] Smith v. Eaton, 50 Iowa, 488.

[6] Size v. Size, 24 Iowa, 580 ; Meyer v. Meyer, 23 Iowa, 359.

[7] Burns v. Keas, 21 Iowa, 257 ; Cotton v. Wood, 25 Iowa, 48.

[8] See ante, *149.   [9] Meyer v. Meyer, 23 Iowa, 359.

[10] Nicholas v. Purczell, 21 Iowa, 265 ; Dodds v. Dodds, 26 Iowa, 311.

[11] Cain v. Chic., &c. R. R., 54 Iowa, 255.

belongs to the wife and she dies. Her interest in the homestead is taken into estimate in setting out her dower.[1]

5 b. In Louisiana, while it enures to the widow's benefit during widowhood,[2] if a wife die leaving real estate, and also a husband and children, he cannot claim homestead out of it against the creditors of the wife.[3]

6. In Maine and Massachusetts the widow may occupy the premises during her widowhood, and the children during their minority after the father's death.[4]

7. In Massachusetts this right is set off to the widow in the same manner as dower. But what of the estate is over and above this homestead right is subject to devise, descent, dower, and sale for payment of debts of the deceased.[5] This right of homestead is something in addition to the widow's right of dower and allowance made by the judge of probate, and does not depend upon the husband's owing debts or not at his decease.[6] And if the husband were in possession of the premises at his death, the widow may continue to occupy them without their having been set out to her by the judge of probate, if they do not exceed the amount in value of what is exempted.[7] It is something, moreover, which she may sell, and is not obliged to make use of to enjoy.[8] This homestead right is not a fee-simple estate. It is a freehold estate in the premises, to be held while the husband is a householder, and by his widow after his death, and his children by her, during widowhood, and by the children, or by such of them as choose to occupy it, to be enjoyed by them together, until the youngest is twenty-one years of age, provided some one of them continues to occupy the same. The right of possession and enjoyment is in those only of the family who remain in occupation of the homestead, and this, free from intrusion of creditors or strangers. Nor can either member of the family

---

[1] Gen. St. 1873, c. 38, art. 13, §§ 14, 15.   [2] Rev. Stat. 1870, § 1694.

[3] Burnett v. Walker, 23 La. Ann. 335.

[4] Rev. Stat. 1883, c. 83, § 66 ; Mass. Pub. Stat. c. 123, § 8.

[5] Pub. Stat. c. 123, §§ 8, 9.

[6] Monk v. Capen, 5 Allen, 146 ; Mercier v. Chase, 11 Allen, 194 ; Bates v. Bates, 97 Mass. 392 ; Cowdrey v. Cowdrey, 131 Mass. 186 ; Weller v. Weller, Id. 446.

[7] Parks v. Reilly, 5 Allen, 77.   [8] Mercier v. Chase, sup.

transfer any right to a stranger without the consent of the others.[1] The title, while there is such occupancy by the widow and children, most nearly resembles that of husband and wife at common law, under a grant to both, by which they became seised, not of moieties, but of the entirety, *per tout et non per my*, and neither could dispose of any part without the assent of the other.[2] Nor can the husband affect the right of his wife to enjoy the homestead by any provision of his will. And continuing to occupy a room in a dwelling-house owned by a husband at his death, as a homestead, by the widow, for the purpose of storing her furniture, is such an occupancy as preserves her right of homestead in the premises.[3] And it is this estate, exclusive of the reversionary interest in the premises, which a husband cannot convey unless his wife join in the conveyance.[4] The estate of homestead exists for the benefit of the widow, though the husband died owing no debts, and though she has already taken her dower out of the estate, and she may claim it against the adult heirs of the husband.[5]

8. In Michigan, both the constitution and statutes secure to the widow the rents and profits of the homestead during widowhood, unless she sooner acquire a homestead of her own, and they do the same to the minor children of the householder so long as they are minors. But these rights depend upon its being occupied by the widow and children, if any;[6] though the widow's removal will not affect the children's right.[7] And the law has given a *feme covert* all the power in relation to a homestead estate which a *feme sole* has. But it is no more than she has in respect to her right of dower. The only way

---

[1] Abbott *v.* Abbott, 97 Mass. 136.

[2] Ibid. But where a deed to a married woman conveyed the land to her in fee as a homestead, this was held to become separately hers on divorce, so that she could maintain an action against her husband for remaining in occupancy thereof. Dunham *v.* Dunham, 128 Mass. 34.

[3] Brettun *v.* Fox, 100 Mass. 234.

[4] Smith *v.* Provin, 4 Allen, 516 ; White *v.* Rice, 5 Allen, 73 ; Doyle *v.* Coburn, 6 Allen, 71 ; Silloway *v.* Brown, 12 Allen, 30 ; Kerley *v.* Kerley, 13 Allen, 286 ; Abbott *v.* Abbott, 97 Mass. 136 ; Swan *v.* Stephens, 99 Mass. 7.

[5] Monk *v.* Capen, 5 Allen, 146; Silloway *v.* Brown, 12 Allen, 33.

[6] Const. art. 16, §§ 3, 4 ; Stat. 1848, c. 132 ; Drake *v.* Kinsell, 38 Mich. 232; Dei *v.* Habel, 41 Mich. 88.

[7] Showers *v.* Robinson, 43 Mich. 502.

she can convey either, or affect her right to the same, is by joining with her husband in a deed of mortgage.[1] But her dower and the homestead are independent rights, and she is entitled to both, — to dower first, and homestead from the residue.[2] Subject, however, to these rights, the land may be sold by the administrator;[3] or a valid contract may be made by the husband without the wife, as to everything but the estate of homestead.[4]

9. In Minnesota the exemption secures the enjoyment of the estate to the widow so long as she remains unmarried and occupies the premises, or to the wife if her husband abscond, and to the children, in either case, until the youngest is of the age of twenty-one years, provided the widow or some one of the children continue to occupy the same; but neither of them can sell or convey the homestead.[5]

10. In Mississippi, upon the decease of the husband and father, whatever may be his estate in the premises, whether in fee, freehold, or for years, it descends to his widow and children, and after her ceasing to be his widow, to the children. And if he leave no widow, the children, if any, take the same by descent.[6] The estate is not the subject of administration, nor does it interfere with the dower right of the widow. It descends to the widow and children;[7] and the latter take it only during minority.[8] But during the owner's life the estate is his, and can be disposed of by him, and during that time neither the wife nor children have any vested interest in the same;[9] and where the wife's signature and acknowledgment are requisite, yet if the deed be part of an act of abandonment, it will be good without the wife's execution, though made before actual removal.[10] The widow and children take it, on the husband's decease, as land descends to heirs.[11]

[1] Ring v. Burt, 17 Mich. 465.   [2] Showers v. Robinson, 43 Mich. 502.

[3] Ib.   [4] Stevenson v. Jackson, 40 Mich. 702.

[5] Stat. 1878, c. 68, § 1 ; Folsom v. Carli, 5 Minn. 333, 337 ; Tillotson v. Millard, 7 Minn. 513, 520.

[6] Smith v. Estell, 34 Miss. 527 ; Morrison v. McDaniel, 30 Miss. 213 ; Whitcomb v. Reid, 31 Miss. 567 ; Campbell v. Adair, 45 Miss. 170.

[7] Smith v. Wells, 46 Miss. 64.   [8] McCaleb v. Burnett, 55 Miss. 83.

[9] Miss. Rev. Code, 1880, § 1257.   [10] Wilson v. Gray, 59 Miss. 525.

[11] Thoms v. Thoms, 45 Miss. 275, 276 ; Parker v. Dean, 45 Miss. 408, 423.

10 *a*. In Missouri, if the owner die leaving a widow and children, the homestead goes to them until the death of the former and the latter are of age,[1] but may be sold subject to their rights;[2] and these are not dependent on the existence of debts.[3] Prior to the act of 1875 the widow took an absolute estate;[4] with a right to the minor children if she died during their minority;[5] but dower was first assigned to her *pro tanto* in lieu of homestead;[6] but this is now altered by that statute.

10 *b*. In Nebraska, at the death of the owner or debtor, the homestead, if from his or her separate property, descends and vests in the survivor for life, and then in the heirs at law or legatees of the owner. But it remains exempt from forced sale as long as it is owned and occupied by the debtor.[7]

10 *c*. In Nevada, when a claim for a homestead exemption has been properly made, the husband and wife, if he have one, hold the homestead as joint tenants during life, and, on decease of either, it passes to the survivor and the minor children.[8] But until recorded the husband may mortgage it without the wife.[9]

11. In New Hampshire some of the earlier decisions would seem to warrant the proposition that a homestead right is not an estate; it is inchoate, not assignable or transferable, as something of ascertained value, by the one in whom it vests, until the same shall have been separated and set apart from the general estate out of which it issues.[10] But by Tucker *v.* Keniston, since decided, the homestead to be set off is the whole property, and is not to exceed five hundred dollars. Not a contingent life estate merely, but the entire estate, and against that there shall be no further proceedings. And it is not to be considered a contingent or inchoate estate, except as

---

[1] Rev. Stat. 1879, § 2693.   [2] Poland *v.* Vesper, 67 Mo. 727.

[3] Freunde *v.* McCall, 73 Mo. 343.

[4] Ib.; Schneider *v.* Hoffman, 9 Mo. App. 280.

[5] Skouten *v.* Wood, 57 Mo. 380.

[6] Seek *v.* Haynes, 68 Mo. 13.   [7] Comp. Stat. 1881, c. 36, § 17.

[8] Comp. L. 1873, § 189.

[9] Child *v.* Singleton, 15 Nev. 461.

[10] Atkinson *v.* Atkinson, 37 N. H. 434 ; Gunnison *v.* Twichell, 38 N. H. 62, 67 ; Horn *v.* Tufts, 39 N. H. 478, 485 ; Foss *v.* Strachn, 42 N. H. 40.

it may be voluntarily sold or abandoned.[1] But the widow has no vested estate until the homestead is set out to her. Until then it is an inchoate right.[2] No mortgage, however, by the owner alone is good, except for purchase-money.[3] The estate of homestead is a conditional life estate.[4] If a debtor's estate is levied before the homestead is set out, he owns his homestead as tenant in common with the owner of the rest of the estate, and may have partition of the same.[5] The statute vests the homestead in the head of the family in his own present right as general owner, and not as a trustee of any one. It secures to the widow the occupation of the estate during life if she choose, and to the children while minors.[6] If the estate is under mortgage, and she has to pay it in order to save her right, she becomes subrogated to the rights of the mortgagee for contribution from the other part-owners.[7] At the husband's death, the statute gives the homestead, whether set off or not from the part which is subject to his debts, to the widow and minor children, in her or their own right.[8] But if the children shall have arrived at age, the widow alone is entitled to the homestead.[9] On the other hand, if the wife was the legal owner, and there are no minor children, the husband receives the exemption.[10]

12. The same is the general doctrine in New York. It cannot be sold or made over to another.[11] It is intended for the benefit of the widow for life, and the children until the youngest is of age, if they continue to occupy the same.[12] The householder is the owner of the estate, but the homestead exemption continues until the death of the householder for the benefit of his widow and family, until the youngest child is of age, or the death of the widow, they or some one of them continuing to

---

[1] Barney v. Leeds, 51 N. H. 253, 272 ; Tucker v. Keniston, 47 N. H. 267.
[2] Tidd v. Quinn, 52 N. H. 341 ; and is to be set out like dower, Gen. Laws, 1878, c. 138, § 4.
[3] Gen. Laws, c. 138, § 2.   [4] Locke v. Rowell, 47 N. H. 46.
[5] Barney v. Leeds, 51 N. H. 253.   [6] Gen. Laws, c. 138.
[7] Norris v. Boulton, 34 N. H. 392 ; Norris v. Morrison, s. c. 45 N. H. 490. 501
[8] Fletcher v. State Bank, 37 N. H. 369, 391.
[9] Miles v. Miles, 46 N. H. 261.   [10] Gen. Laws, c. 138, § 5.
[11] Allen v. Cook, 26 Barb. 374 ; Smith v. Brackett, 36 Barb. 571.
[12] 3 Stat. 647.

be an occupant of the premises.[1]   But the right does not run
with the land so as to give the purchaser a right to claim what
his vendor might have enforced.[2]   Nor is it regarded as an
incumbrance or lien on an estate.   The householder is thereby
none the less the owner of the entire estate.[3]

12 a. In North Carolina a homestead estate is a determinable
fee; the entire interest in and control of it is vested in the
holder of it. The holder is not impeachable for waste. But
there is still an interest in the owner over and above the homestead right, answering to a reversionary interest, but it is not
the subject of levy by a creditor of the reversioner.[4] At the death
of the owner, it enures to the widow during widowhood, if she
have no children and no homestead in her own right. If he
have children, it is exempt in their hands during the minority
of any of them.[5] If the husband die owing no debts, no homestead can be set out of his estate to his widow and children,
since this is only done to protect the estate from creditors.[6]
Nor does the homestead right interfere with that of dower, so
that if the widow claims a homestead, the children would take
it subject to her right of dower in the same estate.[7]

In New Jersey the estate continues after the death of the
householder for the benefit of his widow and family, if some
one of them occupy it, until the youngest child is of the age
of twenty-one years and during the life of the widow ; but no
release or waiver thereof is valid.[8]

13. In Ohio the exemption enures to a widow or widower,
unmarried daughter, or minor son, and continues in favor of
an unmarried minor child who resides upon the premises, although the widow may be dead, or the parent from whom the
child inherits died, leaving neither husband nor wife.[9]

14. In Pennsylvania the widow's right is special and peculiar. It is paramount to all liens, except that of a vendor for

---

[1] 4 Stat. at Large, Pt. 3, c. 260.

[2] Smith v. Brackett, 36 Barb. 571 ; Allen v. Cook, 26 Barb. 374.

[3] Robinson v. Wiley, 19 Barb. 157.   [4] Poe v. Hardie, 65 N. C. 447.

[5] Const. art. 10, §§ 3, 5. The widow takes no homestead whether the children
be minors or adult, Wharton v. Leggett, 80 N. C. 169 ; but the homestead vests
only in the minor children, Simpson v. Wallace, 83 N. C. 477.

[6] Hager v. Nixon, 69 N. C. 108.   [7] Watts v. Leggett, 66 N. C. 197.

[8] Rev. 1877, p. 1055, § 1.   [9] Rev. Stat. 1880, §§ 5435, 5437.

the purchase-money.[1] It does not depend upon her accepting provision or otherwise, which is made for her by her husband's will.[2] If she have children, she takes it for herself and them, for the use of the family. But if she have none, she takes the whole absolutely.[3] And where there are no children, she can convey the premises, when set out to her, in fee by her own deed, not as trustee, but as owner.[4]

14 a. In South Carolina, the exemption continues to the widow of the owner and his minor children until the death or marriage of the widow and until the youngest child is of age. If both husband and wife be dead, leaving children, the children, whether minors or not, take the homestead in the same manner as the parents. But it is said there is a reversion after such estate which is the subject of sale or devise.[5]

In Tennessee, at the death of the owner, a homestead goes to his widow during life or until again married, and on her death or marriage it goes to the minor children during minority, and upon termination of their interest becomes general assets of his estate. If the wife is divorced for his fault, the title vests in her by a decree of the court.[6] And so much of a husband's homestead remains to the widow for her use as shall make her dower in the estate worth one thousand dollars. But she cannot have a homestead of that value and dower also.[7]

15. In Texas, the homestead right, so far as the children are concerned, depends upon there being a wife to take at the householder's death. If he have a wife she will take,[8] but if he have no wife, he may convey the estate, or it may be levied on for his debt, and thereby the rights of the children thereto be defeated.[9] The right as far as the widow and children are

---

[1] Robinson v. Wallace, 39 Penn. 129 ; Compher v. Compher, 25 Penn. 31.

[2] Compher v. Compher, *sup.*; Hill v. Hill, 32 Penn. 511.

[3] Purd. Dig. 281; Compher v. Compher, *sup.*; Hill v. Hill, *sup.*

[4] Sipes v. Mann, 39 Penn. St. 414; Nevins's App., 47 Penn. St. 230.

[5] Const. art. 2, § 32; Gen. Stat. 1882, §§ 1997, 2002; Moore v. Parker, 13 S. C. 486.

[6] Stat. 1871, §§ 2119, 2120, 2121.   [7] Merriman v. Lanfield, 4 Heisk. 209

[8] Rev. Stat. 1879, art. 1996.

[9] Tadlock v. Eccles, 20 Tex. 782, 792; Brewer v. Wall, 23 Tex. 585.

concerned is the same whether the homestead is in the community or the separate property,[1] and is moreover held subject to the equities and incumbrances existing thereon at the time it was acquired, and the husband may discharge these by his own act,[2] or may substitute new ones.[3] But he cannot create new ones without his wife's written assent.[4] The administrator of one having had a homestead set out has nothing to do with the estate thus assigned.[5] And if he leave a widow, the children cannot have partition of it so long as she lives and remains the head of the family ;[6] unless she sells her interest.[7] And where the court grant her a decree of divorce and the custody of the children, she may have the use of the homestead assigned to her during life.[8] When the homestead belonged to the wife, it descends on her death to her children, subject only to her husband's right of occupancy during his lifetime, and no partition can be made before his death.[9]

16. In Vermont this right does not vest any title in the wife. It is only a kind of lien upon the estate of the husband in favor of the wife. It only becomes an estate in the wife and family after the decease of the husband.[10] But though contingent and inchoate during his life, she may enforce it after his death, although he may have conveyed it absolutely in his life, if she did not join in the conveyance.[11] In such case, it passes to the widow and children, if any, in due course of descent, to be set out by the court of probate.[12] And they take the estate subject to such debts of the intestate as he owed at the time of purchasing the same,[13] and to taxes.[14] By

1 Rev. Stat. art. 2006.

2 White v. Shepperd, 16 Tex. 163, 172; Rev. Stat. art. 2000.

3 Gillum v. Collier, 53 Tex. 592.

4 Gaylord v. Loughridge, 50 Tex. 573; Barnes v. White, 53 Tex. 628.

5 Bassett v. Messner, 30 Tex. 604.

6 Rev. Stat. art. 2004; Hoffman v. Neuhaus, 30 Tex. 633.

7 Rev. Stat. art. 2005.   8 Tieman v. Tieman, 34 Tex. 522.

9 Rev. Stat. art. 2009.

10 Howe v. Adams, 28 Vt. 541; Jewett v. Brock, 32 Vt. 65.

11 Davis v. Andrews, 30 Vt. 678; Jewett v. Brock, sup. ; McClary v. Bixby, 36 Vt. 254, 260; Day v. Adams, 42 Vt. 510.

12 Rev. Laws 1880, § 1898; Day v. Adams, 42 Vt. 516.

13 Rev. Laws, § 1901; Simonds v. Powers, 28 Vt. 354; Perrin v. Sargeant, 33 Vt. 84.   14 Rev. Laws, § 1902.

the act of 1855, the homestead is limited to the widow and minor children.[1] But it goes as an entire thing, and is to be occupied accordingly. If, therefore, the children be scattered or live away from the estate, they can neither claim partition of the estate, nor rent for its use by the widow. She has a right to hold, control, and enjoy it, without abatement by any of the children who are not members of the family.[2] It is independent of her right of dower;[3] the homestead belongs to her in fee, vesting upon the death of the husband, and on her death descends to her heirs, and may be set out to her in the same lands which have already been set to her for life as dower.[4] But by statute 1862, the same commissioners who set out a widow's homestead may set out her dower, provided the homestead do not equal one third of the estate. If it do, she can claim no dower; if it do not, the dower is set out after the homestead; though the giving a deed of her homestead does not affect her right of dower.[5]

16 a. In Virginia, a homestead, after the death of the owner, goes to the widow and minor children until her death or marriage, and after that event it remains to the exclusive benefit of the minor children until the youngest is of age. And if she is divorced for his fault, she takes the homestead for herself and children in the same manner as if he were dead; and if it is not set out in his lifetime, the widow and children, if she is alive and unmarried, otherwise the children may claim it in the same manner as if it had been set off in the husband's lifetime.[6]

17. In Wisconsin, the estate, if not devised by the owner, descends to the widow if there are no issue; if there are issue, then to her during widowhood, and afterwards to such issue or other heirs; if issue only, then to them; if neither issue nor widow, it becomes part of the owner's general estate.[7]

---

[1] Perrin v. Sargeant, 33 Vt. 86; Rev. Laws, § 1898.

[2] Keyes v. Hill, 30 Vt. 759.   [3] Rev. Laws, § 1899.

[4] Doane v. Doane, 33 Vt. 649; Chaplin v. Sawyer, 35 Vt. 286; McClary v. Bixby, 36 Vt. 254, 257.   [5] Rev. Laws, § 1900.

[6] Code, 1873, c. 183, §§ 8, 9.   [7] Rev. Stat. 1878, § 2271.

DIVISION V.

1. THE exemption from liability for the debts of the owner, while in some States it is all but absolute, in others is limited and conditional. It does not extend to taxes, nor, with few exceptions, to what is due for the purchase-money of the premises. In some it is no bar to a recovery under a mechanic's lien, and does not apply to debts existing at the time of acquiring the estate. The modes of levying upon the estate, so as to reach what interest the debtor has therein over and above the exempted right, are provided for in the statutes of the different States, and are not uniform. Most of the statutes exempt the homestead from a "forced sale," but this is not limited in all cases to sales under process of law upon execution, but in Louisiana extends to sales made for the purposes of foreclosing mortgages.[1]

1 *a*. Though in Alabama a homestead is not exempt from process to enforce the payment of the purchase-money, if a mortgage be given for the purchase-money of an estate larger

[1] Le Blanc *v.* St. Germain, 25 La. Ann. 289.

in extent than the homestead, and a creditor levy on the entire estate, he cannot relieve his share by compelling the mortgagee to look first to the homestead for the satisfaction of his debt. The right of exemption comes in next to the contract lien.[1] The exemption of homestead does not extend to laborer's and mechanic's liens.[2] But it extends to any other debts contracted after, and in some cases to debts contracted before, the adoption of the constitution, in all cases during the minority of the children.[3] But statutory penalties are not "debts."[4]

1 *b*. In Arkansas the exemption is from execution on final process; but this is not to include taxes, or dues to the State, laborer's or mechanic's liens for labor, or improvements on the estate, and securities or obligations for the purchase-money.[5]

2. In California the homestead estate is exempt from forced sale, but is liable for vendor's and mechanic's liens, taxes, and mortgages lawfully created.[6] So all, except the proper homestead, may be levied on. If that be twenty-five hundred square yards or less, and is of greater value than five thousand dollars, the sheriff may, if the creditors so elect, sell the whole, and out of the proceeds pay the debtor that sum. If it exceed that quantity of land, and is of greater value than the prescribed sum, such portion of it, including the dwelling-house, as near as may be of that value, may be set apart, and the remainder may be sold. If a levy and sale be made of

---

[1] Ray *v.* Adams, 45 Ala. 168.   [2] Code, 1876, § 2822.

[3] 19 Am. Law Reg. 2; Code, 1876, § 2844. The result of legislation in Alabama is somewhat peculiar. The law stood as in the text under the constitution of 1868 until the act of 1873, April 23, which repealed all exemption from any debts contracted prior to the constitution; and this remained so until the act of Feb. 9, 1877, when the old exemptions were re-enacted. Consequently, in the interval, no homestead could be acquired as against such debts. Lovelace *v.* Webb, 62 Ala. 271; Carlisle *v.* Godwin, 68 Ala. 137, 140; Slaughter *v.* McBride, 69 Ala. 510; Horn *v.* Wiatt, 60 Ala. 297. On the other hand, as to all debts contracted after the constitution, all former laws were superseded by that instrument until the act of 1873. Nelson *v.* McCrary, 60 Ala. 301. Hence, against a debt contracted in 1872, the larger homestead of 160 acres given by the act of 1873 in lands acquired after its passage cannot be claimed. Ib. The like exemption given by the Code, 1876, § 2820, is limited to debts contracted since the act of 1873.

[4] Williams *v.* Bowden, 69 Ala. 433; Meredith *v.* Holmes, 68 Ala. 190.

[5] Const. art. 12, §§ 2, 3.

[6] Hittell's Code, 1876, §§ 6240, 6241; Graham *v.* Oviatt, 58 Cal. 428.

what is a debtor's actual homestead, the same is void and no title passes.[1] And even if the judgment be upon the debt due for the purchase-money, it would make no difference. The only way to avail of the vendor's lien is by proceedings in equity.[2] And it seems that a wife may claim a homestead against an officer who levies upon the estate of her husband, and may apply to the court to prevent a levy by injunction, even if the declaration of homestead has not been made and recorded, so far as to require the officer to exhaust the husband's other assets before levying on the homestead.[3] The levy, it seems, must be upon the proportion of the whole estate over and above the value of the homestead. If the whole, for example, be ten thousand dollars, the levy may be upon five tenths of the estate.[4]

2 *a*. In Florida the exemption applies to forced sales, but does not reach claims for the purchase-money, taxes, or erection of improvements, or for labor performed upon the premises.[5] Hence, where the consideration failed, a vendee could not claim homestead as against the vendor.[6]

3. In Georgia it is exempt from levy for any debt[7] except for the purchase-money,[8] taxes,[9] and for improvements on the homestead, and for labor done and materials found for that purpose, and for removal of incumbrances thereon,[10] but is not

---

[1] Cohen *v.* Davis, 20 Cal. 187; Kendall *v.* Clark, 10 Cal. 17; Ackley *v.* Chamberlain, 16 Cal. 181.

[2] Williams *v.* Young, 17 Cal. 403.   [3] Bartholomew *v.* Hook, 23 Cal. 277.

[4] McDonald *v.* Badger, 23 Cal. 39 ; Gary *v.* Eastabrook, 6 Cal. 457.

[5] Const. 1868, art. 9, § 1; Dig. 1881, c. 104, §§ 1, 2.

[6] Porter *v.* Teate, 17 Fla. 813.

[7] Thus, even from any debt due the State, except for taxes, Colquitt *v.* Brown, 63 Ga. 440; or from a decree of the court of probate against the homestead owner for a balance on settlement of a probate account, Merritt *v.* Merritt, 66 Ga. 324; or from a farm laborer's wages for labor preceding the homestead, Stokes *v.* Hatcher, 60 Ga. 617.

[8] Smith *v.* Merritt, 61 Ga. 203; Gunn *v.* Wades, 65 Ga. 537; Griffin *v.* Elliott, 60 Ga. 173. Thus a mortgage to secure a loan to pay off the purchase-money (Middlebrooks *v.* Warren, 59 Ga. 230) and an assignment of a mortgage given by a husband to a wife to secure her part of the purchase-money (Neal *v.* Perkerson, 61 Ga. 345) are superior to homestead.

[9] Davis *v.* State, 60 Ga. 76; and an execution against a defaulting tax-collector is for taxes. Cahn *v.* Wright, 66 Ga. 119.

[10] Const. 1868, art. 7, § 1; 19 Am. Law Reg. 5; Code, 1882, § 2002.

exempt from a judgment recovered for a tort committed.[1]
And if the husband becomes bankrupt and is declared so before homestead is set out, the property will have passed from him, so that it would be too late to claim the right.[2]

4. In Illinois, it cannot be set up against a claim for the purchase-money, nor taxes, nor for the expenses of improvements upon the premises.[3] But all other debts are excluded,[4] and a judgment thereon forms no lien in favor of a creditor, upon a debtor's homestead.[5] Nor is it a fraud to buy an estate as a homestead, although at the time the purchaser is insolvent, and the property is thereby placed beyond the reach of creditors.[6] A mortgage of a homestead estate, if made to secure the purchase-money, is valid though not signed by the wife.[7] If a homestead is not exempt when the debt is contracted, a subsequent possession of it as a homestead would not exempt it.[8] But the exemption continues from the old homestead to a new one bought with the proceeds of the old as against an intermediate debt.[9] And the homestead is exempt as well from judgments *ex delicto* as *ex contractu*,[10] and from fine and costs in criminal prosecutions.[11] The same rule applies to a sale under a decree of a court of equity. Hence a sale under a mortgage made by husband and wife, in which she does not expressly waive her homestead right, would be of no avail against her claim under that right, for a mortgagee gets no right as against such a claim unless she has properly released it in the deed.[12] The'rule as to a homestead being liable for purchase-money seems to be this: If the debt is for

---

[1] Cobb's Dig. 389, 390; Davis *v.* Henson, 29 Ga. 345.

[2] Lumpkin *v.* Eason, 44 Ga. 339.

[3] Rev. Stat. 1883, c. 52, § 3; Phelps *v.* Conover, 25 Ill. 309; Magee *v.* Magee, 51 Ill. 500; Tourville *v.* Pierson, 39 Ill. 446; Hubbell *v.* Canady, 58 Ill. 426.

[4] Trustees *v.* Heale, 98 Ill. 248. Thus the lien given by statute for the amount of a collector's bond upon his land does not include his homestead. Trustees *v.* Hovey, 94 Ill. 394.

[5] Green *v.* Marks, 25 Ill. 221; Watson *v.* Saxer, 102 Ill. 585.

[6] Cipperly *v.* Rhodes, 53 Ill. 346.

[7] Tourville *v.* Pierson, 39 Ill. 446; Kimble *v.* Esworthy, 6 Ill. App. 517.

[8] Titman *v.* Moore, 43 Ill. 169.   [9] Watson *v.* Saxer, 102 Ill. 585.

[10] Conroy *v.* Sullivan, 44 Ill. 451.   [11] Loomis *v.* Gerson, 62 Ill. 11.

[12] Wing *v.* Cropper, 35 Ill. 256; Mooers *v.* Dixon, 35 Ill. 208, 221; Ives *v.* Mills, 37 Ill. 73.

money loaned to pay a pre-existing debt due for the purchase-money, the homestead would not be liable for it. If it was borrowed at the time of the purchase, to pay the purchase-money, the homestead would be liable; so it would if it be due for the purchase of a part of the premises constituting the entire homestead,[1] or if upon notes given in renewal of the purchase-money notes.[2] If a debtor is shown to be a householder, and in occupancy of a lot of land as a residence, the creditor who undertakes to claim it by a levy of an execution or under a mortgage must show affirmatively that it is not exempted as a homestead.[3] But if the debtor's homestead exceed one thousand dollars in value, his creditor may cause the same to be sold, reserving for the debtor that sum, to be held free from attachment for a year, and to be paid to the debtor.[4] If a homestead estate is levied on and is sold for more than one thousand dollars, the purchaser acquires such a lien as to entitle him to the estate whenever the homestead right ceases.[5] So if the owner convey the estate, out of which a homestead has been claimed, without consent of his wife, and still retains the possession, the grantee gets a right thereby to have the estate when the right of homestead ceases, but not to disturb the grantor in his possession.[6] It would seem, therefore, that a homestead right was of the nature of a particular estate, with a right of reversion in the owner which might be reached by levy or a grant from the owner. But it was held that if the homestead did not exceed in value the amount exempted by law, a levy upon the estate and sale thereof, or conveyance by way of mortgage without the wife's joining therein, would be void.[7] In the United States court, however, it was decided that a levy and sale of the fee of a debtor's estate passed it to

---

[1] Austin v. Underwood, 37 Ill. 438; Eyster v. Hatheway, 50 Ill. 521; Magee v. Magee, 51 Ill. 500. But a trust deed for money, part only of which was to remove an incumbrance on the homestead, did not bind this. Best v. Gholson, 89 Ill. 465.

[2] Kimble v. Esworthy, 6 Ill. App. 517; Williams v. Jones, 100 Ill. 362.

[3] White v. Clark, 36 Ill. 285; Stevenson v. Marony, 29 Ill. 532.

[4] Walsh v. Horine, 36 Ill. 238.

[5] Blue v. Blue, 38 Ill. 918; Tomlin v. Hilyard, 43 Ill. 300.

[6] McDonald v. Crandall, 43 Ill. 231; Coe v. Smith, 47 Ill. 225; Hewitt v. Templeton, 48 Ill. 367; Finley v. McConnell, 60 Ill. 259, 263.

[7] Wiggins v. Chance, 54 Ill. 175 ; Browning v. Harris, 99 Ill. 456.

the purchaser subject to the homestead right, and when that expired the purchaser's title became absolute.[1]

5. In Indiana it cannot be set up against taxes or a process under a mechanic's lien, or for the recovery of the purchase-money, or a judgment for a tort.[2] And if, when an officer levies an execution upon a debtor's premises, he do not set up his right of homestead therein, he will be considered as having waived it, and the levy will be established.[3]

6. In Iowa, not only is the homestead liable for taxes and mechanic's liens, and for debts contracted before the purchase of the estate, but also all debts to which it is made subject by the debtor when he contracts them.[4] The exemption cannot be set up against a vendor's claim for his purchase-money.[5] And if a creditor obtains a judgment against a debtor, it becomes a lien upon the land, which is not defeated by the debtor's having a homestead afterwards set out before a levy has been made.[6] Such would be the case if a creditor were to obtain a judgment before the debtor had begun to occupy the homestead set off to him, and he may afterwards make a levy upon the estate.[7] A judgment attaches a lien to the homestead of a debtor the moment it ceases to be used as such, though not as against a purchaser to whom he conveys it while the right continues.[8] And if he die without leaving widow or children, his homestead may be sold to pay his debts.[9] And being a matter of remedy, it is governed by the *lex fori*, so that if a debt be contracted in a State where there

---

[1] Black *v.* Curran, 14 Wall. 463 ; and see McDonald *v.* Crandall, 43 Ill. 231.

[2] Rev. Stat. 1881, §§ 717, 718 ; State *v.* Melogue, 9 Ind. 196.

[3] State *v.* Melogue, *sup.* ; Sullivan *v.* Winslow, 22 Ind. 153.

[4] Babcock *v.* Hoey, 11 Iowa, 375 ; Laing *v.* Cunningham, 17 Iowa, 510 ; Rev. Code, 1880, §§ 1991, 1992, 1993. And a husband's part-payment of the purchase-money of a homestead taken in his wife's name lets in his prior debts, Croup *v.* Morton, 53 Iowa, 599 ; but a debtor who declares a homestead after contracting with a non-resident for a loan, but before receiving it, holds it superior to the debt, Tolman *v.* Leathers, 1 McCrary C. Ct. 329 ; and a wife may hold against creditors land bought with the proceeds of a former homestead and conveyed to her by her husband, Jones *v.* Brandt, 59 Iowa, 332.

[5] Barnes *v.* Gay, 7 Iowa, 26 ; Christy *v.* Dyer, 14 Iowa, 438, 442 ; Cole *v.* Gill, Id. 527.

[6] Elston *v.* Robinson, 21 Iowa, 531.   [7] Elston *v.* Robinson, 23 Iowa, 208.

[8] Lamb *v.* Shays, 14 Iowa, 567.

[9] Floyd *v.* Mosier, 1 Iowa, 512 ; Rhodes *v.* McCormick, 4 Iowa, 368.

is no homestead exemption, it is not entitled to any precedence in that respect, if sued in Iowa, over debts contracted
there.[1]

6 *a*. In Kansas the exemption does not avail against claims
for taxes, the purchase-money of the estate, or improvements
made upon the same.[2] A judgment or levy creates no lien
if made upon the homestead, either upon the present interest
of homestead or upon the estate which remains after the homestead shall have ceased.[3] There is the same exception from
exemption from levy and forced sale for taxes and purchase-
money in Louisiana as in Kansas. And in addition the homestead is also subject to privileged rents.[4] And a mortgage
made before the law of homestead was passed was not affected
by it.[5]

7. In Maine the exemption is no bar to a mechanic's lien,
nor a claim for damages by flowing the lands of another,[6] nor
a judgment for a debt contracted before a certificate of homestead recorded, nor a judgment for costs prior thereto.[7]

8. In Massachusetts a homestead is not exempt from sales
for taxes, nor from the vendor's claim for his purchase-money,
nor from debts due before the right shall have accrued, including money loaned to pay the purchase-money at the time of
the purchase;[8] nor from the payment of ground rent, if the
buildings claimed under such homestead right stand upon the
land of another person.[9] Nor does the right affect existing
mortgages, liens, or incumbrances.[10] With these exceptions,
no such homestead is liable to attachment or levy upon execution for the owner's debts.[11] If the debtor's estate exceeds
the amount of the exemption, the appraisers who set off his
estate on execution may set off all over that value; and if it
be under mortgage, the officer may sell the same, subject to

[1] Helfenstein *v.* Cave, 3 Iowa, 287.

[2] Comp. Laws, 1879, § 205 ; Morris *v.* Ward, 5 Kans. 239, 244 ; and a purchaser from the widow takes subject only to these excepted debts, Dayton *v.*
Donart, 22 Kans. 256.

[3] Morris *v.* Ward, *sup.*   [4] Rev. Stat. 1870, § 1692.

[5] D'Ile Roupe *v.* Carradine, 20 La. Ann. 244.

[6] Rev. Stat. 1883, c. 81, § 66.   [7] Mills *v.* Spaulding, 50 Me. 57.

[8] Stevens *v.* Stevens, 10 Allen, 146 ; N. E. Jewelry Co. *v.* Meriam, 2 Allen, 390.

[9] Pub. Stat. c. 123, § 4.   [10] Id. §§ 5, 6.   [11] Id. § 1.

the mortgage and homestead. Upon the same principle, at the death of the debtor, all his estate over and above his homestead may be sold for the payment of his debts.[1] This right would not be lost if, having established it, the debtor should convey the estate to a stranger, who should convey it to the debtor's wife with an intent to defraud his creditors.[2] But whatever reversionary interest belongs to the debtor after satisfying the homestead claim may be levied on by his creditors, and will, if insolvent, pass to his assignees.[3] In levying an execution upon an estate in which the debtor holds a homestead right, the appraisers are to set off the value of eight hundred dollars by itself, and then levy upon the remainder.[4] A writ of entry may be brought against a woman, and judgment rendered in respect to an estate claimed by her as a homestead, which will be effectual as to all purposes except such homestead right.[5] The surplus or reversionary interest of the husband, subject to the homestead right of his wife and children, may be levied on by his creditors for his debts ; but a levy upon the homestead, even by consent of the wife, would be void.[6] The request or assent of a wife to a sale on execution does not give validity to the sale, inasmuch as the protection from levy is as much in favor of the husband as the wife.[7] A mortgage by the husband will carry his reversionary right, though his wife do not join in the deed.[8]

9. In Michigan, homesteads are exempt from forced sale for any debt. But this may be waived by the debtor if unmarried ; but, if married, it can only be done by the action of the husband and wife.[9] When, however, the debt is for the improvement of the estate, a mortgage therefor is good, though not signed by the wife.[10] If what is claimed as a homestead

---

[1] Pub. Stat. c. 123, § 8.   [2] Castle v. Palmer, 6 Allen, 401.

[3] Smith v. Provin, 4 Allen, 516 ; White v. Rice, 5 Allen, 73 ; Doyle v. Coburn, 6 Allen, 71 ; Woods v. Sanford, 9 Gray, 16.

[4] Pub. Stat. c. 123, § 13.   [5] Stebbins v. Miller, 12 Allen, 591.

[6] Silloway v. Brown, 12 Allen, 30.   [7] Castle v. Palmer, 6 Allen, 401.

[8] Burns v. Lynde, 6 Allen, 305, 312 ; Silloway v. Brown, 12 Allen, 30.

[9] Const. art. 16, § 2 ; Beecher v. Baldy, 7 Mich. 488 ; Sherrid v. Southwick, 43 Mich. 515 ; and this is so, even though she is not living with him. Ib.

[10] Fournier v. Chisholm, 45 Mich. 417.

be of greater value than the amount exempted by law, a creditor may levy upon the surplus, and, in ascertaining this value, reference is had to the time of the levy, and not to any former estimated value.[1] But in order to authorize a creditor to do this, he must be able to show that the homestead exceeded this value, and that it was not susceptible of division, so as to leave a separate homestead of the prescribed value for the debtor.[2]

10. In Minnesota there is an exception in the matter of homestead exemption, as to any indebtedness connected with the land itself, or improvements upon it, including liens for labor and materials of workmen, mortgages for purchase-money, and taxes.[3] And any judgment becomes a lien upon the land, so that the moment the premises cease to be occupied as a homestead, it may be enforced by sale. The owner, however, may convey the estate, or temporarily abandon it, without subjecting it to the creditor's process.[4] If husband and wife fraudulently convey land to another who conveys the same to the wife, the husband cannot, as tenant by curtesy, set up a homestead right gained thereby by her.[5]

10 a. In Mississippi, homestead exemption does not avail against a claim for the purchase-money of the estate, taxes, rent, mechanic's lien, or a recognizance on a bail bond;[6] and the husband can give a deed to secure the purchase-money without joining his wife.[7] But the exemption in Missouri is complete as to all liabilities of the debtor, subsequent to the date of filing the declaration, but not those anterior thereto.[8]

11. In New Hampshire there is a like exception to exemption of vendor's and mechanic's liens, and taxes and debts of less than one hundred dollars due for labor. And by labor

---

[1] Herschfeldt v. George, 6 Mich. 456, 468.

[2] Beecher v. Baldy, 7 Mich. 488.   [3] Stat. 1878, c. 68, §§ 2, 7.

[4] Id. §§ 8, 9 ; Folsom v. Carli, 5 Minn. 333 ; Tillotson v. Millard, 7 Minn. 513, 520 ; Piper v. Johnston, 12 Minn. 60 ; Tuttle v. Howe, 14 Minn. 145 ; Kasor v. Howe, 27 Minn. 406.

[5] Piper v. Johnston, 12 Minn. 60.

[6] Buckingham v. Nelson, 42 Miss. 417 ; Rev. Code, 1880, § 1255.

[7] Billingsley v. Niblett, 56 Miss. 537 ; and upon sale on execution therefor, the vendee acquires the absolute title, Patrick v. Rembert, 55 Miss. 87.

[8] Rev. Stat. 1879, § 2695 ; Jackson v. Bowles, 67 Mo. 609.

is meant what is popularly understood by the term, and does not include services of a physician. Nor would it make any difference that husband and wife gave the creditor a note for the same. Other than this, the homestead is not assets for the payment of debts, except such as are contracted before the homestead is set out. But the right does not attach to property fraudulently acquired by one, he being in insolvent circumstances. No devise affects it while it is occupied by the widow or minor children. If the estate exceed in value the amount of the homestead exemption, and is not susceptible of division, appraisers estimate its entire value, and the debtor may save it from levy and sale if he will pay the excess over and above the value of the homestead. If he neglect to do this, the sheriff may sell the whole, paying to the debtor the value of such homestead, if his wife consents, otherwise into some institution for savings to the credit of the husband and wife, and the surplus he may apply upon the execution.[1] But a homestead, when set out, is exempt from a levy of any kind. This is true also of the reversion of the owner, subject to the homestead estate, and of an equity of redemption of the homestead estate. Otherwise the debtor could not sell, mortgage, or exchange the homestead estate, because the levy would take effect the moment the debtor ceased to occupy the premises.[2]

11 a. In Nebraska the exemption does not extend to taxes, vendor's liens, mechanic's wages, or money due from an attorney collected by him.[3] In Nevada it does not extend to vendor's, laborer's, or mechanic's liens or debts for improvement of the estate.[4] In North Carolina the exemption is as to "any debt," not including taxes, or the purchase-money of the homestead, or laborer's or mechanic's liens thereon.[5] It does not extend to a judgment recovered in an action of

---

[1] Gen. Laws, 1878, c. 138, §§ 23, 24 ; Norris v. Boulton, 34 N. H. 392 ; Weymouth v. Sanborn, 43 N. H. 171.

[2] Tucker v. Kenniston, 47 N. H. 267.

[3] Comp. Stat. 1881, c. 36.

[4] Comp. Laws, 1873, § 186 ; Const. art. 4, § 30 ; Hopper v. Parkinson, 5 Nev. 233. Thus, a mortgage and note for money borrowed to build houses on the homestead estate bind it. Com. Bk. v. Corbett, 5 Sawyer C. Ct. 172.

[5] Const. art. 10, §§ 3, 4.

tort.[1] And subject to the homestead the mortgagee of the owner may sell his interest.[2]

12. In New York the exemption does not affect taxes, debts for purchase-money, or such as were contracted before notice given of the homestead having been set out. And a judgment so far forms a lien upon the premises, that, though they cannot be sold upon it so long as the debtor retains a homestead right therein, the moment he conveys the estate to a stranger the creditor may levy thereon, and his lien will take precedence of this conveyance.[3] And even this qualified exemption does not extend to judgments for torts, or costs of suit recovered by a defendant, nor for any other wrongs than the non-payment of debts.[4] But the assertion by the debtor, when he contracted the debt, that his estate was subject to execution, provided the homestead had been duly recorded as such, would not affect the debtor's right to set up the same, since the statute, being founded upon public policy, is not to be defeated by the representation of a party.[5] In New Jersey the exemption does not include taxes, or the purchase-money of, or claims for labor on the homestead estate.[6]

13. In Ohio the exemption is not against mechanic's liens, purchase-money, nor taxes. And if an officer holding an execution undertakes to levy it upon the debtor's land, who sets up the claim of homestead exemption, he must have this set off by appraisers by metes and bounds, if susceptible of division, and may levy upon the surplus of the estate. If it is not divisible, the officer may levy upon the whole estate, and have the rents and profits over one hundred dollars a year set off to the creditor till the debt is paid.[7] And where the homestead has been sold for a debt valid against it, the debtor holds the surplus proceeds exempt from other debts.[8]

14. In Pennsylvania, liens for purchase-money, mechanic's

---

[1] Dellinger v. Tweed, 66 N. C. 206.

[2] Murphy v. McNeill, 82 N. C. 221.

[3] 3 Stat. 647 ; Smith v. Brackett, 36 Barb. 571 ; Allen v. Cook, 26 Barb. 374.

[4] Lathrop v. Singer, 39 Barb. 396 ; Schouton v. Kilmer, 8 How. Pr. 527 ; Robinson v. Wiley, 15 N. Y. 489, 493.

[5] Robinson v. Wiley, sup.; s. c. 19 Barb. 157.

[6] Rev. 1877, p. 1055, § 2.   [7] Rev. Stat. 1880, §§ 5434, 5438-5439.

[8] Jackson v. Reid, 32 Ohio St. 443.

liens, and judgments recovered for any cause of action other than contracts, or for breaches of official duty, are not affected by homestead exemption rights.   And such would be the case if, when the contract was made, or the judgment was rendered thereon, the owner of the homestead waived this right.[1]   Nor can a debtor who has fraudulently conveyed his estate to defeat his creditors set up a homestead claim against one of them who shall levy upon the same.[2]   If a judgment be recovered for the purchase-money, it may be levied on the homestead, although the debtor may have become and been declared a bankrupt, because the bankrupt law does not reach a debtor's homestead, but exempts it.[3]

15. In South Carolina it is understood that a debtor waives his right to set up a homestead exemption, if he neglects to do so when the officer makes a levy upon his estate.[4]   And the statute does not exempt the estate from claims for taxes or for the purchase-money, or for improvements made on it.[5]   Nor does it avail against a debt contracted or a mortgage made before the adoption of the constitution.[6]

16. In Tennessee, by the constitution, the homestead estate is subject to taxes, purchase-money, and claims for improvements.[7]   The legislature has added claims for the expense of public roads, and certain fines.[8]   A leasehold homestead also is subject to rent.[9]   A deed of land occupied as a homestead, made by husband to wife, will vest a right superior to creditors, though made with the purpose of delaying them;[10] otherwise if there were no such actual occupancy,[11] or if both husband and wife had joined in the mortgage to the creditor.[12]   But the homestead is not exempt from a debt contracted before its acquisition, and revived by a promise subsequent thereto.[13]

---

[1] Purd. Dig. 9th ed. 281 ; Laucks' Appeal, 24 Penn. St. 426 ; Bowman v. Smiley, 31 Penn. St. 225 ; Kirkpatrick v. White, 29 Penn. St. 179.

[2] Huey's Appeal, 29 Penn. St. 219.   [3] Pebley v. Barr, 66 Penn. St. 196.

[4] Manning v. Dove, 10 Rich. 395, 403.

[5] Gen. Stat. 1882, § 2001 ; Edwards v. Edwards, 14 S. C. 11.

[6] Shelor v. Mason, 2 S. C. 233 ; Bull v. Rowe, 13 S. C. 355.

[7] Const. art. 11, § 11.   [8] Stat. 1871, § 2111.

[9] Stat. 1871, § 2113.   [10] Ruobs v. Hooke, 3 Lea, 302.

[11] Gibbs v. Patten, 2 Lea, 180.

[12] Nichol v. Davidson Co., 3 Tenn. Ch. 547.

[13] Woodlie v. Towles, 9 Baxt. 592.

16 *a*. In Texas a "forced sale" means one made under process of court, in a manner prescribed by law.[1] And a debtor's property is liable to be sold, in this way, for the satisfaction of any lien created thereon before the same is declared a homestead.[2] But it makes no difference whether the debt is incurred before or after such declaration of homestead.[3] The exemption does not extend to a claim for purchase-money,[4] or for mechanic's liens, taxes, improvements, or expenses for the last sickness and funeral.[5] And if a debtor acquire a new homestead, his former one becomes liable to be levied upon for his debts.[6] If a debtor abandons his homestead, he subjects it to levy, and the abandonment, in order to have that effect, must be with an intent not to come back and claim the exemption.[7] With these exceptions the homestead right is above all liens and claims for the satisfaction of debts, and cannot be sold upon any judgment or legal process. Such sale, if made, would be void.[8]

17. In Vermont a homestead is liable to levy for a debt or cause of action accruing previous to the purchase of the estate and record of the deed; and if one acquire a new homestead, this is exempted, but the former one becomes liable to be levied on, as if it had never been exempt.[9] The homestead is also liable for the purchase-money.[10] After the death of the debtor, his estate is not subject to sale for his debts, unless the debt is made specially chargeable thereon, or it be for

---

[1] Sampson *v.* Williamson, 6 Tex. 102, 110 ; Rev. Stat. 1879, art. 2335, 2336 ; Lanahan *v.* Sears, 102 U. S. 318.

[2] Farmer *v.* Simpson, 6 Tex. 313.   [3] North *v.* Shearn, 15 Tex. 174.

[4] Stone *v.* Darnell, 20 Tex. 11, 14 ; McCreery *v.* Fortson, 35 Tex. 641 ; Clements *v.* Lacy, 51 Tex. 150 ; Baird *v.* Trice, Id. 555.

[5] Rev. St. 1879, §§ 2007, 2008.

[6] Stewart *v.* Mackey, 16 Tex. 56 ; Berlin *v.* Burns, 17 Tex. 532, 537.

[7] Gouhenant *v.* Cockrell, 20 Tex. 96.

[8] Stone *v.* Darnell, 20 Tex. 14 ; Lanahan *v.* Sears, 102 U. S. 318. And see Black *v.* Rockmore, 50 Tex. 88, that a sale cannot be made under a mortgage of community property after the death of the husband, though signed by both husband and wife.

[9] Rev. Laws, 1880, §§ 1901, 1903 ; Howe *v.* Adams, 28 Vt. 541 ; Jewett *v.* Brock, 32 Vt. 65. Whether it is necessary, also, that the debtor should have taken possession before action brought, see W. River Bk. *v.* Gale, 42 Vt. 27 ; Lamb *v.* Mason, 45 Vt. 500.

[10] Lamb *v.* Mason, 50 Vt. 345 ; Davenport *v.* Hicks, 54 Vt. 23.

taxes.[1] If a debtor convey his estate, there is nothing left which can be reached by a creditor, although his wife do not join in the conveyance, even though the debt of the creditor was contracted before the purchase by the debtor of his homestead, nor though, if his wife survive him, she may defeat such sale as being void, unless he shall in the meantime have acquired a new homestead.[2] And where a debtor mortgaged his estate, " saving always the homestead exemption," it was held that this related only to the wife's contingent right, and did not open it to be levied upon by a creditor for a debt due before the debtor's purchase of his estate.[3]

17 a. In Virginia the homestead exemption extends to " any demand for any debt heretofore or hereafter contracted." But it does not extend to the purchase-price of the property, services rendered by a laborer or a mechanic, liabilities incurred by a public officer, officer of court, a fiduciary, or attorney for money collected, taxes, rent, or legal or taxable fees of a public officer or officer of a court. Nor does it interfere with the sale of the estate by virtue of any mortgage, deed of trust, pledge, or other security.[4] And if, in making a contract, the debtor expressly waive the right of homestead exemption, it will be liable to levy for such debt.[5]

18. In Wisconsin the exemption extends to judgments in actions for torts, and no lien attaches to the homestead in favor of a judgment creditor, though the debtor sell his estate or remove from the homestead. But the exemption is subject to mechanic's liens, taxes, liens for labor, and for the purchase-money, and to all mortgages properly executed.[6] A levy and sale of a homestead, without first having it surveyed, and then

[1] Rev. Laws, § 1902.

[2] Howe v. Adams, sup.; Davis v. Andrews, 30 Vt. 678 ; Jewett v. Brock, 32 Vt. 65.

[3] Jewett v. Brock, sup.

[4] Const. 1868, art. 11, § 1 ; 19 Am. Law Reg. 16 ; Code 1873, c. 183.

[5] Code, 1873, c. 183. But it does not let in creditors that the debtor made a fraudulent trust-deed of the homestead estate, which was afterwards set aside, Boynton v. McNeal, 31 Gratt. 456 ; though where the homestead is itself created by such a deed, it is void, Rose v. Sharpless, 33 Gratt. 153.

[6] Rev. Stat. 1878, § 2983 ; Upman v. Second Ward Bk., 15 Wisc. 449, overruling Hoyt v. Howe, 3 Wisc. 752 ; see also Simmons v. Johnson, 14 Wisc. 523 ; Smith v. Omans, 17 Wisc. 395.

selling the excess above the homestead value, is void.[1] This
exemption continues after the debtor's death, if he have any
surviving infant children.   And if an officer, holding an execution against a debtor, is dissatisfied with the estimated value
of the homestead, he may have it surveyed and set off to him.[2]
But where a mortgage covered the homestead and other lands,
and the creditor had a judgment lien upon the other lands, the
court refused to interfere to compel the mortgagee to first
apply the other lands, in order to protect the debtor's homestead.[3]

DIVISION VI.

HOW FAR HOMESTEAD RIGHTS PREVENT ALIENATION.

1. Reasons for exempting homesteads from sale.
1 a. Alienation of homestead, how limited in Alabama and Arkansas.
2. How limited in California.
2 a. How limited in Florida.
3. How limited in Georgia.
4. How limited in Illinois.
5. How limited in Indiana.
6, 6 a. How limited in Iowa, Kansas, Kentucky, and Louisiana.
7. How limited in Massachusetts.
8. How limited in Michigan.
9, 9 a. How limited in Minnesota, Mississippi, Nebraska, and Nevada.
10. How limited in New Hampshire.
11. How limited in New York.
12. How limited in Ohio.
13. How limited in Texas.
14. How limited in Vermont.
15. How limited in Wisconsin.

1. THIS homestead estate is, nevertheless, the subject of
sale, mortgage, release, and, in some States, of being lost by
abandonment.   How and by whom this may be done depends
upon the law of the particular State in which the premises are
situate.   From the circumstance, however, that the purposes
of the exemption have reference more especially to the debtor's
family than himself, in many of the States the owner is dis-

---

[1] Myers v. Ford, 22 Wisc. 139.   [2] Rev. Stat. § 2984.
[3] White v. Polleys, 20 Wisc. 503.

abled from conveying the premises so as to affect the homestead right, unless his wife joins in the conveyance.   The subject divides itself into the mode in which a conveyance may be
made, and how the right of homestead may be lost or abandoned.

1 a. In Arkansas an agreement, before entering on the
homestead, to sell a part of it is void.[1]   In Alabama no mortgage or alienation of the homestead estate is valid when made
by the owner, if a married man, without the voluntary signature, assent, and acknowledgment of the wife.[2]   And this is
so at law, though the conveyance is in payment of a debt due
before the constitution of 1868 ;[3] and no acknowledgment by
the wife, after the deed is delivered, will be of any effect.[4]
But the wife need not join as grantor ; it is sufficient if she
is mentioned in the deed as conveying.[5]   Her release of dower
will have no operation on the homestead.[6]   No specific release
of homestead is required where the wife conveys her separate
property ;[7] or where the conveyance was before the homestead
act was passed ; or the property exceeded the statutory limit
of two thousand dollars.[8]   A conveyance by the husband without the wife's joining is good as a contract to convey, as to all
the estate except the homestead.[9]

2. In California a mortgage or alienation of any kind, in
order to be valid, if the owner is married, must be a joint deed
of the husband and wife, unless it be given to secure the purchase-money of the estate, and the deed must be acknowledged
as well as signed by the wife.   It must be the concurrent act
of the two done in conformity with the law.   A separate deed
by each, though of the same estate, will not have the effect.[10]

---

[1] Cox v. Donnelly, 34 Ark. 762.

[2] Const. 1868, art. 14, § 2; Code, 1876, § 2822; 19 Am. Law Reg. 2.

[3] Slaughter v. Latimer, 69 Ala. 510.   [4] Balkum v. Wood, 58 Ala. 642.

[5] Dooley v. Villalonga, 61 Ala. 129; Long v. Mostyn, 65 Ala. 543.

[6] Long v. Mostyn, 65 Ala. 543.   [7] Weiner v. Sterling, 61 Ala. 98.

[8] Forsyth v. Preer, 62 Ala. 443; Farley v. Whitehead, 63 Ala. 295.

[9] Jenkins v. Harrison, 66 Ala. 345.

[10] Hittell's Code, §§ 6242–6243; Poole v. Gerrard, 6 Cal. 71; Taylor v. Hargous,
4 Cal. 268, 273; Dunn v. Tozer, 10 Cal. 167; Dorsey v. McFarland, 7 Cal. 342;
Tompkins' Est., 12 Cal. 125; Lies v. De Diablar, 12 Cal. 327.   But an innocent
purchaser has a right to rely on the apparent form of the deed. Mabury v. Ruiz,
58 Cal. 11.

A deed of a homestead by husband alone gives the grantee no right of entry, so long as the grantor continues to occupy the premises as a homestead. He is neither tenant at will nor tenant by agreement of his grantee.[1] The statute of 1862 authorizes a mortgage of a homestead for any purpose, if it is signed by the wife of the owner and acknowledged by her.[2] But it would have the effect to defeat the homestead right, if their deed convey an undivided share of the estate.[3] And a deed by the husband alone would be effectual to pass all of the estate occupied as a homestead, which should exceed the amount of the legal exemption.[4] So a mortgage by him alone would have been good before 1860 to secure the purchase-money, whether made directly to the vendor, or to one who loaned to the debtor the money with which he paid the purchase-money, it being a part of the transaction of purchasing and paying for the land.[5] A deed of the homestead made by a husband alone is simply void.[6] By the act of 1860, when a homestead had once been declared and recorded, no mortgage or alienation of the same could be made for any purpose, unless it be to secure the payment of the purchase-money, and then only by being signed by the husband and wife and acknowledged by her.[7] But if the husband survive the wife, he may convey the estate by a separate deed. If he make a mortgage and then abandon his homestead, as he may do, the mortgage becomes a valid incumbrance.[8] But as the law stood before, the debtor might have mortgaged the estate subject to the homestead right.[9] Thus, where the debtor made a mortgage to secure a part of the purchase-money, and then made a new

---

[1] Brooks v. Hyde, 37 Cal. 366.

[2] Peterson v. Hornblower, 33 Cal. 266; Hittell's Code, § 6243. But this cannot be done by attorney. Gagliardo v. Dumont, 54 Cal. 496.

[3] Kellersberger v. Kopp, 6 Cal. 563.

[4] Sargeant v. Wilson, 5 Cal. 504; Moss v. Warner, 10 Cal. 296.

[5] Montgomery v. Tutt, 11 Cal. 190; Skinner v. Beatty, 16 Cal. 156; Lassen v. Vance, 8 Cal. 271; Carr v. Caldwell, 10 Cal. 380.

[6] Lies v. De Diablar, 13 Cal. 327, 329; Bowman v. Norton, 16 Cal. 213; Swift v. Kraemer, 13 Cal. 526; Peterson v. Hornblower, 33 Cal. 266.

[7] Cohen v. Davis, 20 Cal. 187; Bowman v. Norton, 16 Cal. 213; McHendry v. Reilly, 13 Cal. 75.

[8] Himmelmann v. Schmidt, 23 Cal. 117.

[9] Gee v. Moore, 14 Cal. 472; Bowman v. Norton, 16 Cal. 213.

mortgage to secure this and a new loan, it was held that, so far as the second loan was concerned, the mortgage was void.[1] So where husband made a mortgage alone, and then made a second one in which his wife joined, and the first mortgagee foreclosed his mortgage without giving notice to the second mortgagee, it was held void as against the second mortgagee.[2] But it seems that not only must the debtor have a wife, in order to affect his right to convey his homestead, but she must have shared with him in occupying the same, in order to attach the character of homestead to the premises. Thus where a man came from another State without his wife, and purchased lands, but, before she removed into the State, mortgaged them, it was held that the mortgage was good, and that until she came and occupied the premises with him, it did not acquire the incidents of homestead.[3] And after the wife's death, the husband may mortgage the premises, though he have children living.[4]

2 a. In Florida no alienation of the homestead can be made without the joint assent of both husband and wife, and in certain cases the consent of the judge of probate.[5] But the exempted estate is devisable by the owner.[6]

3. In Georgia the husband cannot sell the homestead without consent of the wife, nor defeat her right therein by removing from the same.[7] But it may be aliened by the joint act of the husband and wife, done with the approbation of the ordinary,[8] or without it, or any formal examination and acknowledgment of the wife, if to secure a debt and the wife's assent is witnessed, even by the husband.[9] So it may be waived by a mortgage made pending the application to set it

---

[1] Dillon v. Byrne, 5 Cal. 455.

[2] Dorsey v. McFarland, 7 Cal. 342; Van Reynegan v. Revalk, 8 Cal. 75; Kraemer v. Revalk, 8 Cal. 74.

[3] Cary v. Tice, 6 Cal. 625; Benedict v. Bunnell, 7 Cal. 245.

[4] Benson v. Aitken, 17 Cal. 163.

[5] Digest, 1881, c. 104, §§ 1, 20.　　　　　　　　　[6] Id. § 8.
Dearing v. Thomas, 25 Ga. 223.

[8] Burnside v. Terry, 45 Ga. 621, 629; Moughon v. Masterson, 59 Ga. 835. But the purchaser is bound to see that the assent of the ordinary has been obtained. Brown v. Driggers, 62 Ga. 354.

[9] Wynn v. Ficklin, 54 Ga. 529; Carswell v. Hartidge, 55 Ga. 412; Johnson v. Griffin Tr. Co., Id. 691; Christopher v. Williams, 59 Ga. 779.

off.[1] And where the wife mortgaged her real estate in which there was a homestead, but did not mention it, it was held waived in favor of the mortgagee.[2] A creditor to whom a release is made has precedence over a prior creditor without such release;[3] and a purchaser of the homestead will be protected in equity.[4] But a deed or contract tainted with usury is no bar to homestead;[5] and a general waiver in a note not applied to any particular parcel is wholly inoperative.[6]

4. In Illinois no alienation of the premises, nor mortgage, nor release or waiver of homestead therein, affects the homestead right, unless it be by the same mode in which conveyances of real estate are made, and is signed by the wife of the householder, and is acknowledged by her, and this condition precedent applies to mortgages and deeds of trust, as well as other alienations.[7] The deed, moreover, must contain an express release or waiver of the homestead right. A general form of grant would not be sufficient,[8] and both the wife and husband must also acknowledge that they thereby release their right of homestead.[9] A deed with general covenants of warranty would not be sufficient, unless there was in the deed an express reference to the right of homestead.[10] A husband cannot sell his homestead estate so long as he occupies it as the head of a family. But he may abandon it as a residence, and then be at liberty to sell and convey it.[11] And the law

[1] Smith v. Shepheard, 63 Ga. 454.

[2] Roberts v. Robinson, 63 Ga. 666; Cheney v. Rodgers, 54 Ga. 163.

[3] Moore v. Frost, 63 Ga. 296.   [4] Bonds v. Strickland, 60 Ga. 624.

[5] Tribble v. Anderson, 63 Ga. 31; Anderson v. Tribble, 66 Ga. 584.

[6] Stafford v. Elliott, 59 Ga. 837.

[7] Rev. Stat. 1883, c. 52, § 4; Kitchell v. Burgwin, 21 Ill. 40; Vanzant v. Vanzant, 23 Ill. 536; Patterson v. Kreig, 29 Ill. 514; Best v. Allen, 30 Ill. 30; Smith v. Miller, 31 Ill. 157; Boyd v. Cudderback, 31 Ill. 113; Thornton v. Boyden, 31 Ill. 200; Connor v. Nichols, 31 Ill. 148; Pardee v. Lindley, 31 Ill. 174, 186; Brown v. Coon, 36 Ill. 243.

[8] Kitchell v. Burgwin, sup.; Vanzant v. Vanzant, sup.; Miller v. Marckle, 27 Ill. 402, 405; Moore v. Titman, 33 Ill. 358; Redfern v. Redfern, 38 Ill. 509; Hutchings v. Huggins, 59 Ill. 29; Asher v. Mitchell, 92 Ill. 480.

[9] Boyd v. Cudderback, 31 Ill. 113; Warner v. Crosby, 89 Ill. 320; Best v. Gholson, Id. 465; Panton v. Manley, 4 Ill. App. 210.

[10] Vanzant v. Vanzant, 23 Ill. 536; Miller v. Marckle, 27 Ill. 402; Boyd v. Cudderback, sup.

[11] Russell v. Rumsey, 35 Ill. 362, 375; Philips v. Springfield, 39 Ill. 83; White

summed up in a late case that there are two ways of releasing a homestead, — abandonment and the jointly executed deed of husband and wife.[1] But where he made a deed and surrendered possession on condition, and this was not performed, the homestead was held not released.[2] If a husband alone convey his homestead, he may set up this right against his own grantee in an action of ejectment to recover it.[3] But a mortgage by a husband alone will create a lien upon whatever he has in excess above the value of the homestead which is exempted by law.[4] But if the husband convey the estate, though with an intent to defraud his creditors, he could not himself claim the benefit of homestead therein.[5] Nor would the giving to premises the character of homestead affect an existing mortgage thereon.[6] And if the deed of mortgage embrace premises of greater value than is exempted by law, it would be good as to such excess, although the wife do not join in the deed.[7] Before the statute of 1857, a sale under a deed of trust or power of sale mortgage of a homestead estate might be good, although it did not contain an express release or waiver of the homestead right. But it is otherwise under that statute.[8] There is no lien created by a judgment against a debtor upon his homestead which affects his right to convey it unincumbered.[9] But a judgment would be a lien upon the excess in value of his estate above $1,000.[10] No act of omission or commission on the part of the husband or his creditors, can affect the homestead right of a wife or children, until she

---

v. Plummer, 96 Ill. 394. So a widow's alienation is controlled by a homestead set off and occupied. Plummer v. White, 101 Ill. 474. And when the sale and removal were one transaction, the former was held valid, though it shortly preceded the latter. Cobb v. Smith, 88 Ill. 199.

[1] McMahill v. McMahill, 105 Ill. 596.   [2] Barrett v. Wilson, 102 Ill. 302.

[3] Marshall v. Barr, 35 Ill. 106. So where he conveys his tenancy by curtesy he may still occupy during the minority of his children. Loeb v. McMahon, 89 Ill. 487.

[4] Booker v. Anderson, 35 Ill. 66, 86.   [5] Getzler v. Saroni, 18 Ill. 511, 518.

[6] McCormick v. Wilcox, 25 Ill. 274.

[7] Smith v. Miller, 31 Ill. 157; Young v. Graff, 28 Ill. 20; Boyd v. Cudderback, 31 Ill. 113; Brown v. Coon, 36 Ill. 243.

[8] Ely v. Eastwood, 26 Ill. 107; Smith v. Marc, 26 Ill. 150.

[9] Green v. Marks, 25 Ill. 221.

[10] McDonald v. Crandall, 43 Ill. 231.

has done what the statute requires in order to release it.[1]
But where husband and wife joined in a deed of the premises,
though not in such a form as to be in itself a release of the
homestead, and then removed from the premises, and the purchaser entered upon the same and sold them, it was held to
work an estoppel upon the wife as to claiming a homestead
right therein.[2] Independent of such act of abandonment,
the grantee of a husband, without the concurrence of his wife,
cannot maintain ejectment upon such conveyance against the
claim of homestead on the part of the tenant.[3] A grant by
the husband alone conveys a fee subject to the homestead right
in the grantor. Where, therefore, the husband conveyed the
homestead by deed of trust in which the wife did not join,
and gave the grantee possession, he held it against a second
deed of trust in which the wife did join, because by the first
deed and surrender ·of possession his homestead right was
gone.[4] But a mortgage given to secure the purchase-money
is valid.[5] And the purchaser from the homestead owner
holds against the grantor's creditors.[6]

5. In Indiana, a conveyance or mortgage of homestead
land, in order to be valid, must, if the mortgagor be a married
man, be acknowledged by the wife. But if the debtor mortgage his estate, and a decree be made to sell the same in
order to foreclose the estate, he could not avail himself of the
right of homestead, even though his wife did not join in the
deed.[7]

6. In Iowa, a deed of mortgage or trust conditioned to pay
a debt, executed by husband and wife, is good and valid,
though it contain no special grant or release of the homestead

---

[1] Boyd v. Cudderback, *sup.*; Pardee v. Lindley, 31 Ill. 174; Hoskins v. Litchfield, 31 Ill. 137, 144.

[2] Brown v. Coon, 36 Ill. 243. So taking a lease from the vendee cures a defective conveyance. Winslow v. Noble, 101 Ill. 194.

[3] Connor v. Nichols, 31 Ill. 148, 153; Pardee v. Lindley, 31 Ill. 174; Patterson
v. Kreig, 29 Ill. 514, 518.

[4] McDonald v. Crandall, 43 Ill. 231; Coe v. Smith, 47 Ill. 225; Hewitt v.
Templeton, 48 Ill. 367 ; Finley v. McConnell, 60 Ill. 259, 263.

[5] Weider v. Clark, 27 Ill. 251.

[6] Shackelford v. Todhunter, 4 Ill. App. 271.

[7] Rev. Stat. 1881, § 716; Slaughter v. Detiney, 15 Ind. 49; Sullivan v. Winslow, 22 Ind. 153.

right, and may be enforced accordingly.[1] But a mortgage or conveyance by husband alone would be of no validity unless given for the purchase-money.[2] So a conveyance or contract by a husband to convey, for which he receives the consideration, will be void as to the wife, and not pass the homestead or authorize its transfer, if she does not join therein, and will be set aside at her suit if joined by the husband.[3] But a conveyance, to be good, must be a joint one, if both be living. If made by either alone, it would be void.[4] And in order to foreclose a mortgage made by husband and wife against her, she must be made a party to the process, it might be effectual against him although she was not a party.[5] And where debtor and wife joined in a mortgage of the homestead and other estate, and then made other mortgages of the same, in which the wife did not join, and proceedings were had to foreclose them, it was held that the officer must first sell the parcels exclusive of the homestead right, and could only sell that to make up a deficiency in the first mortgage, since the homestead was wholly exempt from the second and other mortgages. If he sold the whole in "a lump," it would be void.[6] A mortgage of a homestead is so far a personal lien in favor of the mortgagee, that, where a debtor and wife mortgaged to secure his debt, and he then became a bankrupt, and the mortgagee released his mortgage, he was admitted to prove his whole debt and

---

[1] Babcock v. Hoey, 11 Iowa, 375; Stevens v. Myers, 11 Iowa, 183; Van Sickles v. Town, 53 Iowa, 259. But if she joins to release dower it will be inoperative as to the homestead. Wilson v. Christopherson, 53 Iowa, 481. It does not seem to be material, however, that the wife, when signing, was ignorant that she had homestead in the land conveyed. Edgell v. Hagens, 53 Iowa, 223; Ætna Life Ins. Co. v. Franks, Id. 618.

[2] Burnap v. Cook, 16 Iowa, 149; O'Brien v. Young, 15 Iowa, 5; Morris v. Sargent, 18 Iowa, 90; Code 1873, tit. 18, c. 2, § 3072.

[3] Eli v. Gridley, 27 Iowa, 376; Yost v. Devault, 9 Iowa, 60; Davis v. Kelley, 14 Iowa, 525; Anderson v. Culbert, 55 Iowa, 233.

[4] Rev. Code 1880, § 1990; Alley v. Itay, 9 Iowa, 510; Larson v. Reynolds, 13 Iowa, 581; Davis v. Kelley, 14 Iowa, 523; Clay v. Richardson, 59 Iowa, 483; Spoon v. Van Fossen, 53 Iowa, 494. And one cannot act by the authority of the other therein. *Ib.*

[5] Larson v. Reynolds, *sup.* And a purchaser from the homestead owner is entitled to set off against the wife, who did not release amounts paid to reduce judgments against the homestead. Stinson v. Richardson, 44 Iowa, 373.

[6] Lay v. Gibbons, 14 Iowa, 377.

take his dividend, although objected to by the other creditors.[1] But a mortgage to secure the purchase-money takes precedence of a homestead claim.[2] And after entry, but before the homestead is fully established, a valid lien against it may be created.[3] If a debtor clearly and actually abandon the premises, it defeats the right of homestead, and a mortgage then made by him will be valid, nor will a subsequent reoccupation of the homestead estate affect the validity of the mortgage.[4] So if one sells an old homestead and invests the proceeds in the purchase of a new one, he will hold the second exempt in the same manner as he held the prior one.[5] And if a householder sell his homestead to acquire another, or if he do acquire another, the sale would be good. So a husband or wife may make a good devise of the premises, subject to the homestead right of the other party.[6] So he may sell it, free from any lien by judgment in favor of a judgment creditor.[7] But one taking a deed from a debtor, in which is a recital that the premises are those on which the grantor resides, is estopped to set up that the grantor had abandoned the premises as his residence.[8]

6 a. A deed is voidable in Kansas, though signed by the wife, if she did it by duress, even as against a purchaser who is not cognizant of the duress.[9] But a deed by the husband or wife alone is void, and does not even throw a shadow upon the title.[10] And the husband and wife may sell the land independent of any lien by judgment or by mortgage executed by one of the parties alone.[11] And a deed by the widow and part of her children will not affect the other children who continue to occupy.[12] In Kentucky the estate may be sold subject to a homestead right. But no mortgage release or waiver of a

<hr/>

[1] Dickson v. Chorn, 6 Iowa, 19.　　　[2] Christy v. Dyer, 14 Iowa, 438.

[3] Fuller v. Hunt, 48 Iowa, 163.　　　[4] Davis v. Kelley, 14 Iowa, 523.

[5] Robb v. McBride, 28 Iowa, 386 ; Marshall v. Ruddick, 28 Iowa, 487.

[6] Stewart v. Brand, 23 Iowa, 477.　　　[7] Lamb v. Shays, 14 Iowa, 567.

[8] Williams v. Swetland, 10 Iowa, 51 ; Christy v. Dyer, 14 Iowa, 438.

[9] Anderson v. Anderson, 9 Kans. 112 ; Wicks v. Smith, 21 Kans. 412.

[10] Comp. L. 1879 ; Const. art. 15, § 19 ; and see Coughlin v. Coughlin, 26 Kans. 116 ; Ott v. Sprague, 27 Kans. 620 ; Chambers v. Cox, 23 Kans. 393 ; even though the wife is absent or non-resident. Ib.

[11] Dollman v. Harris, 5 Kans. 597 ; Morris v. Ward, 5 Kans. 239 ; Gen. Stat. c. 38, § 1.　　　[12] Gatton v. Tolley, 22 Kans. 678.

homestead will be good unless signed by the debtor and wife
and duly recorded.[1] A mortgage, however, given by the homestead owner upon a new homestead bought with the proceeds
of the old, but not yet occupied, was held to bind the new
homestead.[2] In Louisiana it is now held that the homestead
owner may waive the homestead when mortgaging it.[3]

7. In Massachusetts a homestead estate may be conveyed
or released by a deed in which the husband and his wife, if he
have one, join with proper words expressly covering the homestead right, and a declaration that she joins to release the
same; otherwise, it will be of no avail, even by estoppel,
though the grantor covenant as to the title.[4] But if it embrace
other land as well as the homestead, it will be good as to such
other lands. And if the wife join in a deed of mortgage of a
homestead estate, the right of homestead remains unimpaired
as to all the excess over and above the mortgage, and those
interested in the same may redeem the premises from such
mortgage.[5] The husband may convey by deed the surplus or
reversionary interest which he has after satisfying the homestead right of his wife and children.[6] Nor would a conveyance
of this right of surplus or reversion, with a fraudulent intent
as to creditors, affect his own right of homestead during his
wife's life.[7] If a homestead come to a widow and minor
children, the same may be sold by her and the guardian of
such children, and the purchaser will thereby have the rights
of the widow and children.[8] A guardian of minor children
can convey no rights of his ward in a homestead estate by a
separate deed, if the widow be alive; it must be by a joint
deed of him and the widow. But if there be no widow, he

---

[1] Gen. Stat. 1873, c. 38, § 13 ; Griffin v. Proctor, 14 Bush, 571.

[2] Hunsford v. Holdam, 14 Bush, 214.

[3] Allen v. Carruth, 32 La. Ann. 444, overruling Hardin v. Wolff, 29 La. Ann.
333.

[4] Pub. Stat. c. 123, § 1 ; Doyle v. Coburn, 6 Allen, 71.

[5] Pub. Stat. c. 123, § 7 ; Greenough v. Turner, 11 Gray, 334 ; Silloway v.
Brown, 12 Allen, 32 ; Connor v. McMurray, 2 Allen, 202 ; McMurray v. Connor,
2 Allen, 205 ; Adams v. Jenkins, 16 Gray, 146. But the mortgagee is not obliged
to have recourse to the other lands, if any, included in his mortgage before foreclosing on the homestead. Searle v. Chapman, 121 Mass. 19.

[6] Silloway v. Brown, 12 Allen, 32 ; McMurray v. Connor, sup.

[7] Ibid.   [8] Pub. Stat. c. 123 ; Abbott v. Abbott, 97 Mass. 136,

may convey it upon being licensed. If there are no children, the widow alone can convey. The object of the statute is to provide a home for the householder's widow and children during their widowhood and minority, or for such of them as choose to occupy it, to be held and enjoyed by them together, neither of them having a right which they can transfer to a stranger without the consent of the others. The estate of the widow and children, after the death of the husband, most nearly resembles that of entirety of husband and wife.[1] So a homestead may be mortgaged to secure the purchase-money, if done as a part of the transaction of purchase.[2] And whatever reversionary interest there is in a husband, after answering the wife's and children's rights of homestead, may be sold or mortgaged by him subject thereto;[3] and the mortgagee may foreclose the mortgage by suit or entry, provided he do not disturb the possession of any one holding under the homestead right, though it be the mortgagor himself, and though he covenanted in his deed for the title.[4]

8. In Michigan a mortgage given for the purchase-money is good, but for any other purpose it is of no validity, if the mortgagor be married, unless his wife joins in the deed. Nor can a homestead be conveyed or incumbered without the signature and acknowledgment of the wife to the deed.[5] Nor would it be valid though made by the husband alone, and in pursuance of a parol agreement between the husband, wife, and grantee, that the latter was to support them, which he has ever been ready to perform.[6] But if it covers more than the homestead, it will be good for all such excess, though not signed by the wife.[7] Accordingly, where, upon a process to

---

[1] Abbott v. Abbott, 97 Mass. 136.

[2] N. E. Jewelry Co. v. Merriam, 2 Allen, 390.

[3] Smith v. Provin, 4 Allen, 516 ; White v. Rice, 5 Allen, 73 ; Doyle v. Coburn, 6 Allen, 71.

[4] Doyle v. Coburn, 6 Allen, 71 ; Connor v. McMurray, 2 Allen, 202 ; Castle v. Palmer, 6 Allen, 401.

[5] Fisher v. Meister, 24 Mich. 447 ; Const. art. 16, § 2 ; Comp. Laws, 1871, §§ 6137, 6138. But if she had signed, she cannot avoid it on the ground of not having read it. Peake v. Thomas, 39 Mich. 584.

[6] Ring v. Burt, 17 Mich. 465.

[7] Const. art. 16 ; Stat. c. 132 ; Beecher v. Baldy, 7 Mich. 488 ; Dye v. Mann, 10 Mich. 291 ; McKee v. Wilcox, 11 Mich. 360.

foreclose a mortgage, the mortgagor claimed exemption of the homestead, the court ordered it to be appraised and set out from the mortgaged premises, so as to include the dwelling-house and other necessary buildings, and the remainder of the estate to be sold.[1]

9. In Minnesota no sale of a homestead can be made by husband and wife, and no mortgage unless the wife, if the grantor has one, joins in the deed,[2] with the exception of mortgages given to secure the purchase-money,[3] and liens for work done upon the house.[4]   A husband forfeits his rights under the homestead law by a conveyance to the wife to defraud creditors.[5]

9 a. By the statute of Mississippi of 1867, a husband may sell the homestead for the purpose of reinvesting it in a new homestead, and he has a year in which to do this.   The husband, having the right to select and fix the homestead, is at liberty to change it.[6]   He may sell the homestead, or any part of it, free from any lien of judgment existing during the homestead right.   Nor could a judgment creditor follow it into a purchaser's hands.[7]   And a widow may sell the reversion subject to the homestead right during the children's minority.[8]   In Missouri, husband and wife may alien, but both must join.[9]   In Nebraska, a husband and wife may make a valid mortgage of their homestead.[10]   In Nevada, a husband cannot convey, mortgage, or lease the homestead without the concurrent act of the wife, unless she is insane, when the court may authorize it to be done, and the proceeds invested as the court shall direct.[11]

10. In New Hampshire the only way in which a homestead estate can be effectually waived or released is by a deed exe-

---

[1] Dye v. Mann, 10 Mich. 291.   [2] Ferguson v. Kumler, 25 Minn. 183.

[3] Olson v. Nelson, 3 Minn. 53 ; Lawver v. Slingerland, 11 Minn. 447.

[4] Stat. 1878, c. 68, §§ 1, 2.   [5] Piper v. Johnston, 12 Minn. 60.

[6] Thoms v. Thoms, 45 Miss. 263 ; Parker v. Dean, 45 Miss. 408 ; Wilson v. Gray, 59 Miss. 525.

[7] Rev. Code, 1880, § 1257 ; Parker v. Dean, sup.

[8] McCaleb v. Burnett, 55 Miss. 83.   [9] Rev. Stat. 1879, § 2689.

[10] Re Cross, 2 Dill. 320 ; Comp. Stat. 1881, c. 36, §§ 3, 4.

[11] Clark v. Shannon, 1 Nev. 568 ; Goldman v. Clark, 1 Nev. 607 ; Comp. L. 1873, §§ 187, 190.

cuted by a husband and wife, if she be alive, or, if dead, leaving minor or insane children, the judge of probate must assent
thereto. The exception to this is a mortgage to secure the
purchase-money.[1] But the right, as such, is not the subject
of grant or assignment to a third person any more than that
of a wife to dower during coverture.[2] But so far as a husband has an interest, independent of his wife and children,
in a homestead estate, he is at liberty to convey it subject to
their rights, and may enter into covenants in respect to the
same which will bind and estop him, as in the conveyance of
any other estate. Thus, if he make a deed in which his wife
does not join, the purchaser takes, subject to her right, upon her
becoming the grantor's widow, of having the same set out to
her and the minor children to hold as long as it is occupied
as a homestead.[3] In such cases the husband conveys the estate, subject to her homestead right, in the same way as he ·
conveys one subject to the right of dower in the wife, if she
survives him. But it may be demanded by husband and wife
during her life, and perhaps by her alone, or after the husband's death she and the minor children may demand it.[4]
But if he convey with covenants of warranty, he would be
estopped to claim it against his grantee or his assigns. Nor
would it be any bar to an action by such grantee to recover
possession of such estate, that the grantor's children were
entitled to a homestead therein, unless the same had been set
out and assigned as such. And if such grantor attempted to
have a homestead set out against a grantee, he would be estopped in equity from so doing. Nor could his wife and
minor children do this during the husband's life, in proceedings against a purchaser with covenants. They would be as
much estopped thereby as the husband.[5] If, when a husband
conveys a part of his estate, he leaves enough to answer the
homestead claim, his conveyance will be good.[6]

¹ Norris v. Ƅoulton, 34 N. H. 392 ; Gen. Laws, 1878, c. 138, § 2.

² Gunnison v. Twitchel, 38 N. H. 62; Foss v. Strachn, 42 N. H. 40.

³ Atkinson v. Atkinson, 37 N. H. 434; Gunnison v. Twitchel, 38 N. H. 62;
Horn v. Tufts, 39 N. H. 478, 485.

⁴ Gunnison v. Twitchel, 38 N. H. 62; Foss v. Strachn, 42 N. H. 40.

⁵ Foss v. Strachn, *sup.*   ⁶ Horn v. Tufts, 39 N. H. 478

10 *a.* In New Jersey a homestead cannot be sold nor leased for more than one year, unless by the consent of husband and wife by deed duly acknowledged and for its full value, and the sum invested in a new homestead. It cannot be leased without the wife's consent.[1]

11. In New York a householder might release his homestead right by conveying the land in the mode required for ordinary conveyances.[2]

11 *a.* In North Carolina if husband convey the estate in which he has claimed the right of homestead, under circumstances to be, otherwise, fraudulent as to creditors, it will not affect the vendee's right to hold the homestead against the creditors, inasmuch as what he had conveyed could not have been levied on for his debts.[3] But no sale of a homestead can be valid, where the grantor has a wife, unless she voluntarily signs and acknowledges the deed of conveyance.[4]

12. In Ohio the wife must join with the husband in making a good mortgage of the homestead estate, whereby either she or her family are to be affected. And where husband and wife by joint deed conveyed the estate to defraud his creditors, and the deed was set aside as fraudulent upon application of a creditor, it was held that the debtor might set up a claim of homestead against such creditor, on the ground that he himself had held the deed to be of no effect.[5]

12 *a.* In South Carolina the title of the alienee or mortgagee of the homestead is declared to be valid.[6] A sale of an intestate estate by order of the judge of probate is no bar to a widow's claim of homestead out of the same.[7] In Tennessee, prior to the Constitution of 1870, the husband had unrestrained power of aliening the homestead.[8] If the owner is married, his wife must join with him in aliening or mortgaging

---

[1] Rev. 1877, p. 1055, § 7.

[2] 3 Rev. Stat. 647; Smith *v.* Brackett, 36 Barb. 571; 4 Stat. at Large, Pt. 3, c. 260.

[3] Grummen *v.* Bennet, 68 N. C. 494.   [4] Const. 1868, art. 10, § 8.

[5] Rev. Stat. 1880, § 5434; Sears *v.* Hanks, 14 Ohio St. 298.

[6] Gen. Stat. 1882, § 1998; Smith *v.* Mallone, 10 S. C. 39.

[7] *Ex parte* Strobel, 2 S. C. 309.

[8] Bilbey *v.* Poston, 4 Baxt. 232. At least if the homestead is not laid off. Kincaid *v.* Burem, 9 Lea, 553.

the homestead to be valid, except that he may mortgage it for the purchase-money. But the homestead need not be expressly mentioned to pass,[1] and the reversion will pass by their joint deed, where her acknowledgment is defective.[2] He can, moreover, convey by his separate deed a part of his farm if enough remains for a homestead;[3] and where, subsequent to his mortgage, both joined in conveying the homestead, the mortgage was held superior to the exemption.[4] If he ceases to occupy it, it becomes liable to be levied upon by his creditors.[5]

13. In Texas a householder having no wife might convey the estate, though by so doing he defeats the rights of his children therein. And a creditor's judgment binds such estate as against the debtor's children.[6] But if he have a wife, he can only alienate the estate by her assent.[7] And this assent must be evidenced by a deed signed and acknowledged by her.[8] Nor would a sale by the husband affect the wife's right of homestead, although, before it had taken place, she had separated from him.[9] A sale by the husband, without the wife's joining in the conveyance, is a nullity.[10] But if he survive her, he may dispose of the homestead for the purpose of procuring a new one.[11] And a mortgage with power of sale, or a deed in trust to sell the premises made by husband and wife, whereby the mortgagee or trustee might sell without any action or decree of the court, would be good. But if, to enforce it, it became necessary to have the mortgaged premises sold under process of the court, it would come under the character of forced sale, and would not be sustained even though signed by the husband and wife.[12] Nor can any contract of sale of a home-

---

[1] Lover v. Bessenger, 9 Baxt. 393.   [2] Nash v. Russell, 1 Lea, 543.

[3] Hildebrand v. Taylor, 6 Lea, 659.   [4] Crook v. Lunsford, 2 Lea, 237.

[5] Stat. 1871, § 2110; Const. art. 11, § 11.

[6] Tadlock v. Eccles, 20 Texas, 782; Brewer v. Wall, 23 Texas, 585; Jordan v. Imthurn, 51 Texas, 276; Wright v. Doherty, 50 Texas, 34.

[7] Const. art. 22; Rev. Stat. 1879, art. 560; Sampson v. Williamson, 6 Texas, 102, 116.

[8] Cross v. Evarts, 28 Texas, 523, 532; Houghton v. Marshall, 31 Texas, 196.

[9] Homestead Cases, 31 Texas, 692.   [10] Rogers v. Renshaw, 37 Texas, 625.

[11] Dorrill v. Hopkins, 36 Texas, 686.

[12] Sampson v. Williamson, 6 Texas, 102, 118; Lee v. Kingsbury, 13 Texas, 68; Stewart v. Mackay, 16 Texas, 56.

stead be enforced without or against the consent of the wife.[1]
But the presence of a wife, and the occupancy by them both,
seems to be requisite in order to render her signature necessary to a deed.   Thus, where the husband came into the State,
and purchased land, and acquired a homestead and sold it before she had removed into the State, it would seem that such
sale would be good against her claim of homestead right.[2]
And where a husband sold his estate, and then he and his
wife abandoned it, it was held to make his conveyance of it
good.[3]   And as the object of the statute is principally to secure
to a wife her right of homestead, if a husband, without her
joining in it, sell or mortgage one homestead and then acquire
a new one, it will give validity to the alienation of the first.
And the first, in such case, would be subject to levy by the
husband's creditors.[4]   If a householder contract to convey his
homestead and fail to do so, he would be liable in damages for
such breach.   But if he have a wife, the court would not compel him to convey the premises, so long as the premises were
occupied as such.   But if, in such case, he acquire a new homestead, or his wife were to die, the court would enforce a specific performance, by decree, as he then becomes able to
convey.[5]   A sale of the debtor's homestead, though with an
intent to defraud creditors, cannot be impeached on that account, as by such sale he does not take away any right of levy
from the creditor.[6]

14. In Vermont a mortgage to secure the purchase-money
is good.   So a mortgage by a husband alone would be good
as against anything but the contingent homestead interest of

---

[1] Berlin v. Burns, 17 Texas, 532; Brewer v. Wall, 23 Texas, 585; Allison v.
Shilling, 27 Texas, 450.   But the husband may be liable in damages.   Brewer v.
Wall; Cross v. Evarts, 28 Texas, 523.   In Campbell v. Elliott, 52 Texas, 151, it
is held that, under the constitution of 1845, the mortgage of the husband alone
is void to all intents; and the court intimate that the same rule obtains under the
constitution of 1875.   The decisions in other States relied on by the court in
support of this latter conclusion have, however, been in some instances overruled.
See Godfrey v. Thornton, 46 Wisc. 677; post, pl. 15.

[2] Meyer v. Claus, 15 Texas, 516.   [3] Jordan v. Godman, 19 Texas, 273.

[4] Berlin v. Burns, 17 Texas, 535; Stewart v. Mackay, 16 Texas, 56.

[5] Brewer v. Wall, 23 Texas, 585.

[6] Wood v. Chambers, 20 Texas, 247; Cox v. Shropshire, 25 Texas, 113;
Martel v. Somers, 26 Texas, 551.

the wife. And if he acquire a new homestead, his conveyance of his former one will be effectual, to all intents, on the ground that one cannot have two homesteads at the same time. But so long as it is the homestead of a party, he cannot do anything to impair his wife's right therein, unless she joins in a deed thereof. And this must be done by deed, in which she is to join as well in signing as in acknowledging it, though the husband may mortgage the estate for the purchase-money. But the wife's joining in releasing or conveying her right of homestead does not affect her right of dower in the premises, or enure to the benefit of any one except the grantee.[1] A conveyance by husband and wife of a homestead estate cannot be impeached by creditors on the score of fraud, although it might have been if it had not been a homestead.[2] A deed by the husband alone would not be effectual to disturb the occupancy of the husband and family, so long as they continued such occupancy.[3] This right is, if she survive him, to enjoy it as a homestead. So that, with this limitation, a husband has full power of disposal of the estate, and the purchaser under him may have a right to the use and possession of the premises during coverture. And this right of a wife in one homestead may be lost by his gaining a new one.[4] The homestead, upon the death of the husband, descends to the widow and children free from his debts, and vests in them. The husband cannot affect this right by will, though he may devise property to her upon condition she waives her homestead, and compel her to elect. She cannot take dower and homestead too, except that, if she claim both, the homestead value is to be deducted from the dower, and that will be set out accordingly. The husband may make provision for her by will in lieu of dower. But in such case her homestead right is not affected.[5]

14 *a*. In Virginia, a homestead can only be conveyed or

---

[1] Rev. Laws, 1880, §§ 1904–1906. [2] Danforth *v.* Beattie, 43 Vt. 138.

[3] Day *v.* Adams, 42 Vt. 510.

[4] Comp. St. 390, 391; Beech *v.* Beech, 37 Vt. 414; Howe *v.* Adams, 28 Vt. 541; Jewett *v.* Brock, 32 Vt. 65; Davis *v.* Andrews, 30 Vt. 678; Stat. 1862, App. 70.

[5] Beech *v.* Beech, 37 Vt. 414; Acts 1866.

incumbered by the wife joining with the husband in the act, unless the owner be single. A homestead may be sold and the proceeds invested in a new homestead.[1]

15. In Wisconsin, the signature of the wife to the husband's deed, and her acknowledgment of it, are essential to its validity as against the homestead right, but not as against his own claim.[2] But he may without her assent sell a dwelling-house standing on the land of another, and assign a lease thereof,[3] or of any other than the homestead estate.[4] The homestead exemption creates no estate in the wife living her husband, and his sole mortgage is valid as against him.[5] A voluntary conveyance by husband and wife, of a homestead, does not subject it to levy for his debts, although made with intent to defraud creditors, and although the grantee convey the same to the wife, provided they both continue to reside thereon.[6] If a husband hold a patent for land under the State, so that a homestead right attaches to the same, he cannot convey it so as to bind the homestead, without his wife joins in the deed.[7] If husband and wife mortgage a homestead, and it is foreclosed, the mortgagee comes into the mortgagor's place of having a right to select the homestead, and to have it set out.[8] Where husband and wife conveyed the estate, and he was afterwards declared bankrupt, and the conveyance was set aside as fraudulent and void, it was held that his deed did not bar his claim of homestead, that it passed to the assigns subject to this right, and a sale of the estate by order of the bankrupt court had no effect to cut off this homestead right.[9]

---

[1] Code of 1871, c. 183, § 7; Const. art. 11, § 1; White v. Owen, 10 Gratt. 41.

[2] Rev. Stat. 1878, § 2203; Godfrey v. Thornton, 46 Wisc. 677; overruling Hait v. Houle, 19 Wisc. 472.

[3] Platto v. Cady, 12 Wisc. 461.   [4] Hait v. Houle, sup.

[5] Godfrey v. Thornton, 46 Wisc. 677.

[6] Dreutzer v. Bell, 11 Wisc. 114; McFarland v. Goodman, 22 Am. Law Reg. 697.

[7] McCabe v. Mazzuchelli, 13 Wisc. 478.   [8] Kent v. Agord, 22 Wisc. 150.

[9] McFarland v. Goodman, 22 Am. Law Reg. 697.

DIVISION VII.

HOW HOMESTEAD RIGHTS MAY BE WAIVED OR LOST.

1.   Grounds on which homestead may be lost.
1 *a.* How homestead lost in Alabama and Arkansas.
2.   How lost in California.
3.   How lost in Georgia.
4.   How lost in Illinois.
5.   How lost in Indiana.
6.   How lost in Iowa.
6 *a.* How lost in Kentucky.
7.   How lost in Massachusetts.
8.   How lost in Michigan.
9.   How lost in Minnesota, Mississippi, Missouri, and New Jersey.
10.   How lost in New Hampshire.
10 *a.* How lost in Nebraska and Nevada.
11.   How lost in New York and North Carolina.
12.   How lost in Ohio.
13.   How lost in Pennsylvania.
14.   How lost in Tennessee.
14 *a.* How lost in Texas.
15.   How lost in Vermont.
15 *a.* How lost in Virginia.
16.   How lost in Wisconsin.

1. THE same diversity prevails in the different States, as to how far and by what means a homestead right once acquired can be lost by abandoning the premises, though, as a general proposition, whenever a new homestead is gained, the prior one is lost.

1 *a.* In Alabama, letting the homestead and absence therefrom for a year will forfeit it. So letting and a removal as against a prior judgment.[1]   In Arkansas a temporary absence from a homestead is not a forfeiture of it.[2]

2. In California, merely removing from the premises to occupy rented land elsewhere, or because it was dangerous to occupy the homestead as such,[3] does not defeat such a right. But where the owner sold the premises without his wife's

---

[1] Boyle *v.* Shulman, 59 Ala. 566; Stow *v.* Lillie, 63 Ala. 257.

[2] Tumlinson *v.* Swinney, 22 Ark. 400; Euper *v.* Alkire, 37 Ark. 283.

[3] Holden *v.* Pinney, 6 Cal. 234; Dunn *v.* Tozer, 10 Cal. 167; Moss *v.* Warner, Id. 296.   Only done as by statute.   Porter *v.* Chapman, 65 Cal. 365.

joining in the deed, and they thereupon removed from the premises, it was held to be an abandonment of the homestead right.[1] But now no homestead will be held to be abandoned, unless by a written declaration to that effect, signed by the husband and wife, or other head of the family, and acknowledged and recorded.[2] And no mortgage is valid even if signed by both of them.[3] And where a homestead right has once attached, though the wife loses her right therein by eloping and living in adultery,[4] a mortgage by the husband, after such elopement, will not avail against his family of children.[5] Under the act of 1862 the majority of the children will defeat the homestead estate of a widower.[6]

3. In Georgia, as the husband cannot defeat the wife's right of homestead by removing from the premises, if he occupies a new estate he does not affect his right of homestead already gained in the former one, unless he owns the new estate.[7] But he can waive the right of homestead, and thereby bind his wife and children;[8] and a right of homestead terminated by death of the wife and majority of the children, does not re-attach upon a second marriage.[9]

4. In Illinois, a right of homestead may be lost to a householder, if he ceases to occupy it as a residence, or ceases to have a family.[10] But if a husband abandon the premises, leaving his wife and children thereon, he does not affect the right of homestead even as to himself, unless he shall, in the mean time, have acquired a home and settlement elsewhere.[11] He would not lose this right by a temporary absence, or for a temporary purpose, or if he leaves the premises, and going to another State to find another home, and failing to find one,

---

[1] Taylor v. Hargous, 4 Cal. 268. [2] Hittell's Code, 1876, §§ 6243, 6244.
[3] Cohen v. Davis, 20 Cal. 187. [4] Canneto's Est. Myrick (Prob.), 42.
[5] Lies v. De Diablar, 12 Cal. 327. [6] Santa Cruz Bk. v. Cooper, 56 Cal. 339.
[7] Dearing v. Thomas, 25 Ga. 223.

[8] Taliaferro v. Pry, 41 Ga. 622. But it is no waiver, as against a creditor, that the debtor did not set up the exemption in defence to a foreclosure suit by a prior mortgage. Frost v. Borders, 59 Ga. 817.

[9] Wright v. James, 64 Ga. 533.

[10] Green v. Marks, 25 Ill. 221 ; Tourville v. Pierson, 39 Ill. 446.

[11] Moore v. Dunning, 29 Ill. 135 ; Best v. Allen, 30 Ill. 30 ; White v. Clark, 36 Ill. 285 ; People v. Stitt, 7 Ill. App. 294.

returns to his original home.[1] A husband, however, controls
the subject of his own residence, and if he and his family
leave his homestead for a new residence it is conclusive abandonment of the former one.[2] But it would not be such an
abandonment if he leave the premises and go into another
county in search of another home, until he shall have gained
one. And if, having removed his family in this way, the husband abandon them before he has provided a new home for
them, he might return to the one he had abandoned, and
resume possession of it. Nor can a widow who has minor
children affect their rights by intentionally abandoning the
homestead.[3] A wife's right may be barred or lost by her joining her husband in a release, by the estate being sold to pay
the purchase-money or money expended in improvements, or
by final abandonment. But on no other ground can a husband
affect his wife's right.[4] And no release or waiver of homestead
is valid unless made in writing, subscribed and acknowledged
by husband and wife, in which there is an express release of
the homestead right.[5] And where the parents died leaving
minor children, and the estate was rented by their guardian
while they lived in his family, it was held not to be conclusive
abandonment of the homestead.[6] If the husband remove with
his family on to another farm than that in which he has a
homestead, and sells the latter, it is a conclusive abandonment
and his homestead is lost.[7] So if one sells his homestead and
surrenders the possession to the purchaser, and leaves it him-

---

[1] Kitchell v. Burgwin, 21 Ill. 40 ; Walters v. People, 18 Ill. 194.

[2] Titman v. Moore, 43 Ill. 169 ; Wiggins v. Chance, 54 Ill. 175 ; Cipperly v.
Rhodes, 53 Ill. 346.

[3] Rev. Stat. 1883, c. 52, § 2 ; Walters v. People, 21 Ill. 178 ; Vanzant v. Vanzant, 23 Ill. 536 ; Miller v. Marckle, 27 Ill. 402; Ives v. Mills, 37 Ill. 73 ; Cabeen v. Mulligan, Ib. 230 ; Kingman v. Higgins, 100 Ill. 319.

[4] Booker v. Anderson, 35 Ill. 66, 87 ; White v. Clark, 36 Ill. 285 ; McMahill
v. McMahill, 105 Ill. 596.

[5] Rev. Stat. 1883, e. 52, § 4 ; 1873, p. 226 ; Hutchins v. Huggins, 59 Ill. 29 ;
Eldredge v. Pierce, 90 Ill. 474. But a certificate of acknowledgment is not enough
under Rev. Stat. 1874, p. 278, § 27 (Rev. Stat. 1883, c. 52, § 4), if it merely says
that it was "freely and voluntarily done for the purposes therein expressed."
School Trustees v. Hovey, 94 Ill. 394.

[6] Brinkerhoff v. Everett, 38 Ill. 263.

[7] Phillips v. Springfield, 39 Ill. 83 ; Titman v. Moore, 43 Ill. 169.

self, this is such an abandonment as to lose the homestead.[1] After the husband's death, the widow is the head of the family and can abandon the homestead if she acquires a new home, unless it be a temporary one.[2] And by such abandonment the homestead is lost to the children, she being the head of the family.[3] But an abandonment by the owner of a homestead, after it has been sold upon execution, has no effect to give validity to such sale.[4] The right of homestead may be lost by removal or abandonment and change of residence by the husband, but not by any laches on his part in allowing a judgment in ejectment to be rendered against him.[5] If a debtor remove from the State, and remain two years, it would be held an abandonment of homestead.[6] A sale by husband and wife, followed by possession given to the purchaser, who pays the purchase-money, would bar the right of homestead, as amounting to an abandonment, although nothing were said of this right in the deed. But, being in the nature of an estoppel, it would only bar it as to the purchaser, and those claiming under him.[7] If homestead is effectually abandoned or barred by husband and wife, during their joint lives, it binds the rights of the children also.[8] By removing his family from the homestead, intending to have it no longer a homestead, it is said the husband may defeat an existing right therein, though the court intimate that, in order to do this, it might be necessary that he should first have acquired another home.[9] But if husband and wife make a deed of the premises, and then remove therefrom, it would work a conclusive abandonment as to a third person, to whom the grantee had conveyed the premises.[10] Under the Acts of 1851, the second marriage of the widow did not divest the homestead where there were minor children.[11]

[1] McDonald v. Crandall, 43 Ill. 231.

[2] Wright v. Dunning, 46 Ill. 275 ; Buck v. Conlogue, 49 Ill. 391 ; McCormack v. Kimmel, 4 Ill. App. 121.

[3] Buck v. Conlogue, *sup.*   [4] Wiggins v. Chance, 54 Ill. 175.

[5] Hubbel v. Canady, 58 Ill. 425 ; Vasey v. Trustees, &c., 59 Ill. 191.

[6] Cabeen v. Mulligan, 37 Ill. 230, the presumption being that he has acquired a new residence there. But see Cipperly v. Rhodes, 53 Ill. 346.

[7] Brown v. Coon, 36 Ill. 243 ; Fishback v. Lane, 36 Ill. 437.

[8] Brown v. Coon, *sup.*   [9] Hoskins v. Litchfield, 31 Ill. 137.

[10] Brown v. Coon, *sup.*   [11] Yeates v. Briggs, 95 Ill. 79.

5. In Indiana, this right is one that may be waived, being of a personal character, as where the debtor allowed a creditor to go on and levy his execution upon the premises, without asserting his homestead right therein, it was held to be a waiver of the same.[1] But a mere absence from the premises does not defeat the debtor's right as a "resident householder." [2] Nor would he have lost his homestead right by removing from one part of the State to another, with his family, but not at the time occupying a home.[3]

6. In Iowa, a householder may change his homestead from time to time, at his election.[4] Nor have his wife or children any control in the matter.[5] But his merely selling an estate, though accompanied by a declaration that it was not his homestead, will not affect her rights to the same. Nor will a written agreement to confess judgment to waive be a sufficient written waiver.[6] The husband may so abandon the premises as to defeat the existing homestead in the premises. But a mere temporary absence will not do this.[7] If he have one homestead and remove on to another estate as his home, he would thereby lose the homestead right in the first.[8] So if he sell that part of his homestead on which the dwelling-house stands, the residue becomes subject to his debts.[9] So a removal to another town, intending to remain there if successful in business, defeats his first homestead.[10] And if he neglect to set it up in defence to a lien suit, it is waived.[11] And where the claimant had been absent from her homestead about three years, and had offered to sell it, and made declaration that she did not intend to return, it was held to be an abandonment, and that the estate had thereby become subject to be

---

[1] State v. Melogue, 9 Ind. 196 ; Sullivan v. Winslow, 22 Ind. 153 ; Stat. 1862, p. 368.

[2] Austin v. Swank, 9 Ind. 109.

[3] Mark v. State, 15 Ind. 100 ; Norman v. Bellman, 16 Ind. 156.

[4] Code, 197 ; Floyd v. Mosier, 1 Iowa, 512.

[5] Collins v. Chantland, 48 Iowa, 241.   [6] Rutt v. Howell, 50 Iowa, 535.

[7] Bradshaw v. Hurst, 57 Iowa, 745 ; Griffin v. Shelley, 58 Iowa, 513.

[8] Williams v. Swetland, 10 Iowa, 51 ; Christy v. Dyer, 14 Iowa, 438 ; Morris v. Sargent, 18 Iowa, 90 ; Davis v. Kelley, 14 Iowa, 523 ; Fyffe v. Beers, 18 Iowa, 4 ; Robb v. McBride, 28 Iowa, 386 ; Marshall v. Ruddick, 28 Iowa, 487.

[9] Windle v. Brandt, 55 Iowa, 221.

[10] Kimball v. Wilson, 59 Iowa, 638.   [11] Collins v. Chantland, 48 Iowa, 241.

levied upon by creditors.[1] If a widow who has a homestead, as survivor of the owner of a homestead, sell it, or abandon it, she loses the right to it.[2] A husband would not lose his homestead right in consequence of his wife obtaining a divorce from him, even if the custody of the children is committed to her, or render it liable to be levied on.[3]

6 *a.* In Kentucky, a homestead is not waived by a mortgage executed by the husband alone;[4] nor where it consists of two tracts will a sale of one affect the right in the other.[5] Whether a mortgage by the husband alone, followed by an abandonment, waives the exemption as to the mortgage is doubted.[6]

7. In Massachusetts, acquiring a new homestead defeats one already existing. But removing from the premises for a temporary purpose does not affect an existing right of homestead, unless a new one or, at least, a new domicil has been acquired. Nor does it seem to be settled whether such a right can be lost by mere abandonment. If it can be done at all, it must be done voluntarily and with that understanding. Removing on to other land of the owner would not have that effect.[7] No abandonment of the premises to which a homestead right has once attached will be sufficient to terminate it, until a new homestead has been acquired elsewhere.[8] But the widow may by her own act so change the condition of the estate in which she has a homestead right, as to bar herself of it. Thus, where she had a right to dower as well as homestead, and had her dower set out in the rents and profits of one undivided third part of the whole of her husband's estate, under the Gen. Stat. c. 90, § 5, and then sold her dower interest, she thereby waived her right of homestead, and could not claim it, having changed the estate into a tenancy in common.[9]

---

[1] Dunton *v.* Woodbury, 24 Iowa, 74.

[2] Size *v.* Size, 24 Iowa, 580 ; Orman *v.* Orman, 26 Iowa, 361.

[3] Woods *v.* Davis, 34 Iowa, 264.

[4] Griffin *v.* Proctor, 14 Bush, 571.   [5] Franks *v.* Lucas, 14 Bush, 395.

[6] Lear *v.* Totten, 14 Bush, 101 ; but the exemption does not attach to the proceeds, Ib. ; and see Gideon *v.* Struve, 78 Ky. 134.

[7] Pub. Stat. c. 123, § 2 ; Silloway *v.* Brown, 12 Allen, 35 ; Dulanty *v.* Pynchon, 6 Allen, 510 ; Lazell *v.* Lazell, 8 Allen, 575.

[8] Woodbury *v.* Luddy, 14 Allen, 1.   [9] Bates *v.* Bates, 97 Mass. 396.

Nor would a widow's selling her right, or leasing the premises, deprive her of the benefit of the right.[1] If the husband mortgage the homestead, and the wife join in releasing her right of homestead in the premises, it has the effect to subject the homestead right as well as the rest of the estate to the payment of the mortgaged debt.[2] But it has no other effect.[3] If a minor child cease to live upon the homestead, while the widow continues to occupy it, he thereby waives his possession, though not his title or right to resume his occupancy, and if an act of trespass were done to the estate while he is thus out of possession, the action would have to be in the name of the widow, and such children, if any, as were in occupancy of it.[4]

8. In Michigan, the right is a personal one, and an unmarried man, in order to lose his homestead, must do some act of relinquishment of it. And if married, it can only be done by a joint conveyance of himself and wife.[5] But where after a contract by the husband to sell a tract on which he lived, of greater size than the homestead exemption, the vendee paid and both husband and wife removed and resided elsewhere, it was held that no homestead rights continued to attach.[6] But no estoppel *in pais* or waiver bars a widow to claim her homestead in a suit at law.[7]

9. In Minnesota, the privilege, being a personal one, may be lost by abandonment.[8] If the owner remove from the estate and ceases to occupy it for more than six months, he loses the right, unless he files a declaration in the register's office that he continues to claim it, which will remain in force for five years.[9] In Mississippi, the husband is the one who selects and fixes a homestead, and he may change it. Ceasing to reside on it, unless temporarily only, forfeits the exemption.[10] But if he leave it, while his wife and children continue to occupy it, it does not operate as an abandonment of the home-

---

[1] Mercier v. Chace, 11 Allen, 194.   [2] Searle v. Chapman, 121 Mass. 19.
[3] Swan v. Stevens, 99 Mass. 9.
[4] Abbott v. Abbott, 97 Mass. 136. Widow loses homestead if she leaves the place permanently, before or after husband's death. Foster v. Leland, 141 Mass. 187.
[5] Dye v. Mann, 10 Mich. 291; McKee v. Wilcox, 11 Mich. 360.
[6] Lamore v. Frisbie, 42 Mich. 186.   [7] Showers v. Robinson, 43 Mich. 502.
[8] Folsom v. Carli, 5 Minn. 333, 337; Tillotson v. Millard, 7 Minn. 513.
[9] Stat. 1878, c. 68, § 9.   [10] Rev. Code, 1880, § 1256.

stead until he shall have acquired a new one.[1]   In Missouri,
the acquisition of a new homestead defeats the old one.[2]   But
a widow was held not to have waived homestead by receiving
dower, in ignorance of her homestead rights;[3] and her homestead rights are not affected by getting a divorce, after her
husband had abandoned her, and she still occupied with her
children.[4]   In New Jersey, where a homestead has passed to
a widow for the benefit of her and the children, no release or
waiver of the exemption is valid.[5]

10. In New Hampshire, a temporary absence from the premises does not affect the homestead right.   The leasing of a
homestead for a year is not an abandonment of the right of
homestead.[6]   Nor is leaving it for a temporary purpose.[7]   So
when an owner had begun to occupy the premises, as by moving his furniture into the dwelling-house, preparatory to removing his family into the same, it was held that the right of
homestead attached thereby, and was not lost during the time
in which the family were moving into the premises.[8]   Nor
would a separation from her husband by the wife, without
her fault, affect her right of homestead in the premises, nor
to those he should acquire during such separation, if he lived
thereon.   Nor would the absence of a husband for a temporary purpose affect the wife's right, though he were to die
abroad.[9]   Nor does a widow lose her right of homestead by
marrying again.[10]   But the acquiring of a new homestead is
the abandonment of a prior one.[11]

10 a. In Nebraska, it is held that a wife's leasing part of
the buildings on the premises during her husband's temporary
absence is no abandonment.[12]   In Nevada, there can be no
abandonment of a homestead except by a written declaration
signed and acknowledged by the husband and wife, or other
head of the family.[13]

[1] Thoms v. Thoms, 45 Miss. 275 ; Parker v. Dean, 45 Miss. 423.

[2] Rev. Stat. 1879, § 2696.

[3] Seek v. Haynes, 68 Mo. 13.   [4] Blandy v. Asher, 72 Mo. 27.

[5] Rev. 1877, p. 1055, § 1.   [6] Locke v. Rowell, 47 N. H. 46.

[7] Wood v. Lord, 51 N. H. 448.   [8] Fogg v. Fogg, 40 N. H. 282.

[9] Meader v. Place, 43 N. H. 307.   [10] Miles v. Miles, 46 N. H. 261.

[11] Wood v. Lord, 51 N. H. 448.   [12] Guy v. Downs, 12 Neb. 532.

[13] Comp. Laws, 1873, § 187.

11. In New York, the exemption is regarded as made for the benefit of the family, rather than the householder him-self. So that if he temporarily cease to occupy the premises, and store his goods intending to resume the occupation, it is no impeachment of the right.[1] No release or waiver of home-stead is valid unless it is in writing subscribed by the house-holder, and acknowledged as other conveyances.[2] In North Carolina, while an owner may be estopped from setting up a homestead claim against a judgment in a suit to which he has been a party,[3] yet removal from the State is no abandon-ment by him.[4]

12. In Ohio, it is not lost by leasing the homestead estate, and removing to another part of the State, if for a temporary purpose.[5]

13. In Pennsylvania, there may be a waiver of this right in several ways, as by the terms of the contract upon which a judgment is rendered, not to insist upon the exemption; or the widow may do it by neglecting to claim it within a rea-sonable time after her husband's death,[6] and the giving of a mortgage upon the premises is held to be a waiver *pro tanto*.[7]

14. In Tennessee, the continued possession required by the Code[8] was held not satisfied, where the owner went to another State to begin business, moved his family away and let the premises; and these acts constituted an abandonment.[9] So a homestead is defeated by a fraudulent conveyance by husband to wife which is set aside.[10] But the failure of the levying officer to set out the homestead does not bar the right.[11]

14 *a.* In Texas, this right may be lost by abandonment. But what shall be a sufficient act to constitute an abandonment may depend upon circumstances. It must be done with an intention totally to relinquish the same, and, even if the owner

---

[1] Griffin v. Sutherland, 14 Barb. 456.
[2] 4 Stat. at Large, Pt. 3, c. 260.
[3] Corpening v. Kincaid, 82 N. C. 202.
[4] Adrian v. Shaw, 82 N. C. 474.
[5] Wetz v. Beard, 12 Ohio St. 431.
[6] Davis's Appeal, 34 Penn. St. 256; Baskin's Appeal, 38 Penn. St. 65; Burk v. Gleason, 46 Penn. St. 297.
[7] McAuley's Appeal, 35 Penn. St. 209; Gangwere's Appeal, 36 Penn. St. 466.
[8] § 2114.
[9] Roach v. Hacker, 2 Lea, 633.
[10] Nichol v. Davidson Co., 8 Lea, 389.
[11] Gray v. Baird, 4 Lea, 212.

leave the premises with this intent, he may change this intent up to the time that he acquires a new homestead.[1] But length of time is not material where the intent and act are clear.[2] Thus a widow who removed from the State, and acquired a new domicil in another State, was held to have lost her homestead.[3] So if a wife without good cause leave her husband, and remain separated until his death, she loses the right.[4] So where the husband sold the estate without his wife joining in the deed, and both removed from the State, and he died abroad, she was not allowed, several years after, to return and claim her homestead.[5] But renting the premises temporarily is not such an abandonment. Nor would the death of the wife of a householder affect his right of homestead, if he continues to occupy the premises, though he have no children.[6] If a husband removes his family from an established homestead, and then abandons them without providing a home for them, the wife may resume possession of the premises and homestead.[7] A removal from the State is an abandonment of a homestead, unless it be for a temporary purpose.[8] If the husband gain a new domicil and the wife follows and accepts it, it is an abandonment of first homestead. So any actual abandonment of the homestead subjects it to a creditor's execution. If the wife voluntarily join with her husband in conveying the homestead, it is of itself an abandonment;[9] if a debtor having a homestead convey it away merely to keep it from his creditors, and he abandons possession, it subjects the estate to levy by any of his creditors.[10] But no fraudulent

---

[1] Shepherd v. Cassiday, 20 Texas, 24 ; and see Thomas v. Williams, 50 Tex. 269.

[2] Cline v. Upton, 56 Texas, 319.   [3] Trawick v. Harris, 8 Texas, 312.

[4] Earle v. Earle, 9 Texas, 630 ; Const. § 22.

[5] Jordan v. Godman, 19 Texas, 273 ; Smith v. Uzzell, 56 Texas, 315.

[6] Taylor v. Boulware, 17 Texas, 74 ; Pryor v. Stone, 19 Texas, 371 ; Kessler r. Drauh, 52 Texas, 575 ; and his temporary absence also does not make an abandonment, 1b.

[7] Franklin v. Coffee, 18 Texas, 413.

[8] Clements v. Lacy, 51 Texas, 150 ; but education of children is such a purpose, 1b.

[9] Paschal's Dig. p. 96 ; but a mortgage by both is ineffectual as against children who continue to reside on the homestead after the father is dead and the mother has abandoned, Abney r. Pope, 52 Texas, 288.

[10] Cox v. Shropshire, 25 Texas, 113 ; Bartel r. Somers, 26 Texas, 551.

representations made by the owner as to the estate of homestead can affect the right to it then existing, if the wife is not
a party to it.[1]

15. In Vermont, there can be but one homestead, so that by
acquiring a new one the owner loses the old one.[2] And something answering to a personal occupancy is necessary to retain
the homestead right, though a temporary absence will not
defeat it. But a change of the residence or home of the
family would.[3] And after an abandonment an earlier attachment takes precedence of a conveyance by the owner.[4]

15 a. In Virginia, a debtor may waive his homestead right
by a statement to that effect in any bond, note, or deed, given
by him; but if he has other property that is to be taken
first.[5]

16. In Wisconsin, one does not lose his homestead by leasing it to another, temporarily, and absenting himself from the
same.[6] But if he voluntarily removes from it and takes up a
new residence, not for a temporary purpose, such as repairing
his former one, but for the accommodation of his business, it
would seem that he would thereby lose his right of homestead,
though this is questioned under the statute of 1858.[7] If a
widow marry again, her right of homestead ceases, but she
does not thereby affect her right to recover the intermediate
rents and profits from the death of her husband, if she has
been kept out of possession.[8] She does not lose her homestead as having abandoned it, if she is driven from her home
by the cruelty of her husband.[9] Nor would it be deemed an
abandonment if father and mother sell a homestead to a son
to induce him to live with them and support them. It would
be a mode of carrying on the estate.[10]

---

[1] Eckhardt v. Schlecht, 29 Texas, 129.

[2] Howe v. Adams, 28 Vt. 541, 544; and conveying the homestead, collecting
materials for a new house, living several years in different towns, and filing
petition for a new homestead, is evidence of abandonment. Whiteman v. Field,
53 Vt. 554.

[3] Davis v. Andrews, 30 Vt. 678; W. Riv. Bk. v. Gale, 42 Vt. 27; Lamb v.
Mason, 45 Vt. 500.   [4] Labaree v. Woodward, 54 Vt. 452.

[5] Code, 1873, c. 183, § 3.   [6] Rev. Stat. 1878, § 2983.

[7] Phelan's Est., 16 Wisc. 76; Herrick v. Graves, 16 Wise. 157.

[8] Anderson v. Coburn, 27 Wisc. 558.

[9] Barker v. Dayton, 28 Wisc. 367.   [10] Murphy v. Cranch, 24 Wisc. 365.

DIVISION VIII.

OF PROCEDURE IN RESPECT TO HOMESTEAD RIGHTS, AND OF CHANGE IN CONDITION OF THE ESTATE.

1. Cases of procedure in Arkansas, Alabama, and California.
2. Of procedure in Illinois and Iowa.
3. Of procedure in Massachusetts.
4. Of procedure in Michigan.
4a. Of procedure in North Carolina and Tennessee.
5. Of procedure in Texas.
6. Effect of changing country into city lots.

1. In enforcing homestead rights, various questions of practice have arisen in the courts as to the mode of procedure, and who must be made parties to the same. Thus in Arkansas, if a widow does not claim her homestead in a partition suit among the heirs to which she is a party, she cannot afterwards by a direct proceeding.[1] In Alabama it was held that the jurisdiction of the probate court to set out homestead was dissolved by the act of 1873.[2] In California both husband and wife, if living, must join in asserting the right of homestead, nor can a binding decision be made when only one of them is a party.[3] So in a suit to foreclose a mortgage, both should be made parties, if the defendant sets up the homestead right. And without this, no question can be conclusively settled.[4] A judgment against the husband alone, the wife not having been made party to the suit, does not bind either of them as to the right of homestead.[5] Nor would the right of homestead be affected by a decree of foreclosure upon a mortgage, made by the husband alone, when the proceedings are against him only.[6] If a divorce be granted to a wife, she may have a homestead in the common property belonging to her and her husband, and have it set off by partition.[7]

1 a. In Georgia it is held that equity alone has jurisdiction

---

[1] Hoback v. Hoback, 33 Ark. 399.   [2] Pettus v. McKinney, 56 Ala. 41.
[3] Cook v. Klink, 8 Cal. 347 ; Marks v. Marsh, 9 Cal. 96.
[4] Marks v. Marsh, sup.; Moss v. Warner, 10 Cal. 296.
[5] Revalk v. Kraemer, 8 Cal. 66 ; Marks v. Marsh, sup.
[6] Cook v. Klink, sup.   [7] Gimmy v. Doane, 22 Cal. 635.

for the recovery of a homestead set apart and sold under the earlier homestead acts; and that the husband alone must bring the bill.[1] Also that although the action of the assignee in bankruptcy does not vest the exempted estate, but defines it only,[2] it must be claimed, if at all, before the adjudication.[3]

2. In Illinois a foreclosure is no bar to a claim of homestead if this was not expressly mentioned in the mortgage.[4] In Iowa, if a mortgagor would insist upon his homestead rights against a mortgage, he must do it while the suit to foreclose is pending. If he neglects to set it up, and the estate is sold upon a decree of court, it is too late to insist upon it against the purchaser at such a sale.[5] And if he has never claimed them before, it is too late to do so after the foreclosure suit is begun.[6] Nor is his ignorance any excuse for such omission; and his minor children are bound thereby and cannot assert any independent right.[7]

3. In Massachusetts, a party having a right of homestead in property held in common with others, may have partition of the same like other tenants in common,[8] except that the homestead is set out by value, without regard to the proportion it bears to the whole estate, and this applies where it is to be carved out of a larger estate. Nor does it make any difference in this respect that the estate of homestead is for life only.[9] If one who has come into possession of the estate of the husband, which includes more than the homestead, keeps the owner of the homestead out of possession, the latter may have trespass against him, upon the same principle that one co-tenant may have trespass against a co-tenant for ousting him from the common estate. And the same rule would apply if the owner of a homestead which is a part of a larger estate, being in possession, keeps out the owner of the surplus of such estate.[10] If the holder of a mortgage not subject to a homestead right enter upon the premises, and hold the same, and a second mortgagee, whose mortgage is subject to such right,

---

[1] Zellers v. Beckman, 64 Ga. 747.
[2] Burtz v. Robinson, 59 Ga. 763.
[3] Smith v. Roberts, 61 Ga. 223.
[4] Asher v. Mitchell, 92 Ill. 480.
[5] Haynes v. Meek, 14 Iowa, 320.
[6] Kemerer v. Bournes, 53 Iowa, 172.
[7] Collins v. Chantland, 48 Iowa, 241.
[8] Pub. Stat. c. 123.
[9] Silloway v. Brown, 12 Allen, 35.
[10] Silloway v. Brown, sup.

offer to redeem from the first, he has a right to require the first mortgagee to account for the rents and profits of the entire estate while in his possession, without regarding the homestead rights of a stranger.[1] If a wife be sued for land by a creditor of the husband, who has set it off upon an execution, upon the ground that he had fraudulently conveyed it to her to delay his creditors, she may set up, in bar of an absolute recovery, a right of homestead, and a special judgment will be rendered in accordance with the fact.[2]

3 a. A homestead right is such a freehold estate as will avail the tenant in defence to a writ of entry. And if it cover the entire premises sued for, it will defeat the action. But if it fall short of this in value or extent, and there is no disclaimer as to the residue, the demandant may recover, but his judgment will be limited to what is not covered by the homestead right.[3] But in New Hampshire, such right will not bar a writ of entry until the same has been set off and assigned.[4]

4. In Michigan, a husband was in possession of premises under a contract of purchase, and surrendered the contract and claim to the land. It was held that the wife might have a bill in her own name, for a specific performance of the contract. And the decree in such case would be for a conveyance to the husband, subject to the wife's lien for whatever sum she was obliged to pay for fulfilling the contract. Nor could a purchaser from the original vendor take advantage as a purchaser without notice, since her being in possession was enough to put him upon inquiry, by what right she held.[5] In another case she was allowed to maintain a bill in her own name to set aside a mortgage of the homestead estate which she had been induced to make by misrepresentation.[6] And the minor children are not necessary parties to her petition to recover the exempted property.[7]

4 a. In North Carolina, the homestead vests without decla-

---

[1] Richardson v. Wallis, 5 Allen, 78.
[2] Castle v. Palmer, 6 Allen, 404 ; Stebbins v. Miller, 12 Allen, 597.
[3] Swan v. Stevens, 99 Mass. 10.　　[4] Barney v. Leeds, 51 N. H. 253.
[5] McKee v. Wilcox, 11 Mich. 358.　　[6] Sackner v. Sackner, 39 Mich. 39.
[7] Showers v. Robinson, 43 Mich. 502.

ration by the owner; and the action of the sheriff has no
other force than to ascertain what is so exempt.[1] But if the
owner does not assert his claim in a suit concerning the land
to which he is a party, he is estopped to maintain it against
the judgment sale.[2] In Tennessee also, the neglect of the
levying officer to set apart the exempted land has been decided
to be without prejudice to the owner's claim;[3] and it is also
immaterial that the premises as set out increase in value
thereafter.[4]

5. In Texas, a married woman is recognized as competent
to appear and litigate her rights in court. But where to a
process against her and her husband, involving a question of
selling the estate in which the homestead interest of the parties existed, she neglected to appear, and her husband forbore
to insist upon the right, it was held that she could not set up
a claim of homestead against such judgment.[5] In Vermont,
husband and wife were tenants in common, and he mortgaged
his estate without joining her. After his death it was decreed
that her land should be divided from his by partition, that her
homestead should be set out of his share of the estate irrespective of hers, and that the mortgage should foreclose upon the
balance of his estate.[6]

6. The distinction which is made in some of the States between city lots and those used for agricultural purposes in
fixing the quantity of land to be exempted as homestead, has
led to a consideration of the effect of extending the corporate
bounds of a city or town, so as to embrace homesteads already
acquired in agricultural lands.

In Iowa it has been held that such extension does not affect existing homestead rights, unless thereby brought within
the part of the city or town which has been laid out into
streets, alleys, and lots.[7] In Texas it was held that such a
change from country to town changed the character of the
homestead so as to conform to the limits of a town or city

---

[1] Gheen v. Summey, 80 N. C. 177.   [2] Corpening v. Kincaid, 82 N. C. 202.
[3] Gray v. Baird, 4 Lea, 212..
[4] Hardy v. Lane, 6 Lea, 379.   [5] Baxter v. Dear, 24 Texas, 17.
[6] McClary v. Bixby, 36 Vt. 254, 260.
[7] Finley v. Dietrick, 12 Iowa, 516.

property.[1]   And a similar doctrine is settled in Wisconsin.[2] But by statute of 1860, though the value of the town or city lots in Texas exempt as homesteads is limited to two thousand dollars, no subsequent increase in the value thereof, by reason of improvements or otherwise, will subject the same to a forced sale.[3]

[1] Taylor v. Boulware, 17 Texas, 74.
[2] Bull v. Conroe, 13 Wisc. 233.
[3] Laws, 1860, c. 38 ; Bassett v. Messner, 30 Texas, 604.

CHAPTER X.

ESTATES FOR YEARS.

SECTION I.

NATURE AND HISTORY OF ESTATES FOR YEARS.

1. NEXT in importance in the admeasurement of estates, to those of freehold, are those for years.   But so far are these from being derived from the feudal law, or known as estates to that system, that the tenant, at first, was not regarded as the owner of any interest in land which he could claim as

such, but depended upon the personal agreement of the freeholder for his right to occupy the same. The account given
by a modern writer upon conveyancing, is, that leases for
years, at will, or at sufferance, were originally granted to
mere farmers or husbandmen, who, every year, rendered some
equivalent in money, provisions, or other rent to the lessors
or landlords. But the latter, in order to encourage them to
manure or cultivate the ground, gave them a sort of permanent interest for a limited period, founded upon a contract express or implied, which was not determinable at their will, but
which should endure for a time certain. Their possession,
nevertheless, was esteemed of so little consequence that they
were considered as bailiffs or servants of the lord, holding
possession of the land *jure alieno* and not *jure proprio*, who
were to receive, and ' had contracted to account for, the profits
at a settled price, rather than as having any property of their
own. About the time of Edward I., estates for years seem to
have become of importance, and to have been considered, after
entry made, as actual interests in the land vested in the lessee.[1]
It will be recollected that prior to the statute of *quia emptores*
(18 Edw. I.), the owners of lands in fee could not freely alien
the same, but resorted to the custom of subinfeudation, as it
was called, by which, while they continued to hold of their
superior lord, they created a tenure between themselves and
the tenants whom they permitted to occupy their lands upon
such services as they saw fit to prescribe, which were payable
to themselves. But unless the owner of the feud created a
freehold interest in the one to whom he gave the right of occupation, it was not considered in law as an *estate*, but a mere
agreement by which, if the occupant was deprived of the possession of the land, his only remedy was by an action for a
breach of such agreement. There is an act of 6 Edw. I. c. 11,
made to protect such tenants from being ousted from their
possession by actions fraudulently commenced in the names
of third persons, nominally against the owners of the land
under whom the tenants held. And in that statute it is said,
" if any man lease his tenement in the City of London for

---

[1] 1 Powell, Ed. Wood, Conv. pp. iv-vi. See also Maine, Anc. L. 275.

term of years," &c., by which it would seem that the same
form of expression was then in familiar use which is adopted
at this day. Still, it seems that, if deprived of his possession,
the tenant had no mode of regaining it by action, as one having
an estate in land might. This was only accomplished by a succession of remedial acts. A form of action of covenant was
the first devised, whereby the tenant might demand his
term as well as damages, but could only * maintain it [*291]
against his immediate covenantor. In the time of
Henry III., the writ of *Quare ejecit infra terminum* was
framed, which lay against any one in possession of the land,
and upon a judgment in the termor's favor, he recovered possession of the land itself. But this writ did not reach a
case where a stranger had entered and tortiously ousted the
tenant, and in such cases, his only remedy was, to sue for possession in the name of his lessor. In the time of Edw. III. the
writ of *ejectment*, substantially like that now in use, was in-
vented, and so shaped as to enable the tenant of a term to
recover it, when deprived of the possession of the premises
leased. And in this way, at last, tenants for years were placed
upon the same level with freeholders, in regard to the security
of their estates, and their remedy for recovering them if dispossessed thereof.[1] As an estate in lands, however, a tenancy
for years has long been familiar to the common law, and, as a
contract, seems to have been well known as early as the reign
of Edward I. from the language of the statute above referred
to, though it is still held to be not a freehold estate but a chattel interest.[2]

1 *a*. But it was not before the time of Henry VI. that the
plaintiff in ejectment recovered the term. At and after that
time he recovered this, and with it the possession of the land, if
his term had not expired ; and, if it had elapsed, he recovered
damages. When it became established that the term should
be recovered, " the ejectment was *licked* into the form of a
real action, the proceeding was *in rem*, and the thing itself,
the term, only was recovered, and nominal damages, but not

[1] Smith, Land. & Ten. 8–12 ; 1 Reeves, Hist. Eng. Law, 341 ; Bacon, Abr.
Leases ; Doe *v*. Errington, 1 Ad. & E. 750 ; Adams, Eject. 8.

[2] Com. Dig. Land. & Ten. 5.

the mesne profits."[1] Ejectment is the form of action now retained in use in England under the statute of 3 & 4 Wm. IV. c. 7, § 36, which abolished all other forms of real actions except dower.[2] It is in general use in some form in this country, and by it the plaintiff recovers, if at all, upon the strength of his own title, and not upon the weakness of that of the tenant, since possession is deemed conclusive evidence of title as to all persons except such as can show a better one.[3]

2. Estates for years embrace such as are for a single year, or for a period still less if definite and ascertained, as a term for a fixed number of weeks or months, as well as for any definite number of years, however great.[4] This was held in respect to a parol letting of premises for the term of one year, although the rent was payable in grain to be raised upon a certain parcel of the premises during that year.[5]

3. An estate for years, as understood in this chapter, is one that is created by a contract, technically called a lease, whereby one man, called the lessor, lets to another, called the lessee, the possession of lands or tenements for a term of time fixed and agreed upon by the parties to the same.[6] By this something more is implied than a mere grant of a certain interest in land ; it involves a contract, more or less explicit, as to the terms and conditions upon which the same is to be held and managed ; and this contract, in some form, is incident to every proper leasehold estate.[7] Nor is it, perhaps, easy to describe more definitely what the lessee acquires by this lease, since, being so much the creature of contract, there are not, as in other estates, uniform incidents belonging to terms for years,

[1] Goodtitle v. Tombs, 3 Wils. 120 ; Campbell v. Loader, 3 Hurlst. & C. 527 n. In the former case this was said to be about the time of Henry VII.; but the date as fixed by Mr. Smith, *supra*, is not later than 1458.

[2] *Ante*, p. *230, note.

[3] Hague v. Porter, 45 Ill. 318.

[4] Burton, Real Prop. § 863 ; 2 Flint, Real Prop. 200 ; Smith, Land. & Ten. (ed. 1856) 14 ; Brown v. Bragg, 22 Ind. 122 ; People v. Goelet, 64 Barb. 476.

[5] Gould v. School District, 8 Minn. 427, 431.

[6] Smith, Land. & Ten. 18 ; Com. Land. & Ten. 4.

[7] Sanders v. Partridge, 108 Mass. 556 ; 7 Am. Law Rev. 240. From this twofold character of a lease, as at once an estate and a contract, arises the double privity of estate and contract. Ih.

which, necessarily and as a matter of course, pass with them. The lessee does not own the soil and freehold, and has a limited property only in it. But within these limits he is the owner of the possession and profits of it, and of all the use that can be made of it during the continuance of his term. Thus, where one hired a store upon the outer wall of which persons posted advertisements and paid for the privilege, it was held to be his perquisite and not that of the lessor. The lessee may use such wall to hang his sign or an awning upon, to the exclusion of the lessor.[1] What these limits are may be fixed by the agreement of the parties, or are implied by law from the nature of the estate. Within these limits, the estate of a tenant for years ranks with that of a freeholder in regard to stability of enjoyment.[2] The use and products of the premises are his as owner. Thus a tenant, whether for life, years, or a single year, may work an open mine on the premises, or a quarry, and the products of the mine or quarry are a part of the profits of the estate to which he is entitled.[3] So he may erect buildings upon the premises, and remove them while he retains possession of them, and cannot charge the cost of their erection to the landlord.[4] So he may attach fixtures to the premises and remove them before giving up possession at the end of the term. It seems he may exercise this right until he yields possession, although the term may have expired; and if the term be uncertain in duration, and is determined without his act, the tenant may have a reasonable time thereafter in which to remove them. But these are exceptions to the general rule by which the tenant forfeits these fixtures if he do not remove them during the term, for, being then a part of the premises, his ownership ceases as to all alike.[5] In other

---

[1] Riddle v. Littlefield, 53 N. H. 503. The lease of a "store" includes land under it and to the middle of a private way owned by a lessor. Hooper v. Farnsworth, 128 Mass. 487. So a lessee is entitled to hold land gained by accretion during his term. Cobb v. Lavalle, 89 Ill. 331.

[2] 1 Platt, Leases, 5. The extent of a demise may be qualified by implication from the limited character of the lessor's interest. Booth v. Alcock, L. R. 8 Ch. App. 663.

[3] Freer v. Stotenbur, 36 Barb. 641.

[4] Kutter v. Smith, 2 Wall. 491, 497; ante, *2, 3.

[5] Davis v. Buffum, 51 Me. 160; Leader v. Homewood, 5 C. B. N. s. 546; Weeton v. Woodcock, 7 M. & W. 19; Stansfeld v. Mayor, &c., 4 C. B. N. s. 119,

words, he has an *estate* in the demised premises for the term
prescribed in his lease, and if deprived of the possession and
enjoyment thereof, the law supplies a remedy by which he
may regain these specifically, instead of recovering damages
only for the violation of a contract right.[1]   In some cases, a
lease may be presumed to have been made from long possession of lands, as other deeds, and grants are sometimes presumed under similar circumstances.[2]   It is customary
to * provide in the lease, by stipulation, that the lessee   [*292]
shall pay to the lessor money or other consideration
in the way of rent or return, for the use of the premises[3]
But the reservation of rent is not essential to the validity of a
tenancy for years by lease.[4]

4. As an estate for years, as above explained, necessarily
implies a certain and definite period for which possession is to
be held, it has acquired a designation proper to this character, namely, that of a *term*, derived from *terminus*, signifying
that it is bounded and precisely determined, having a certain
beginning and a certain end.[5]   And a lease for years from the
first day of July begins the term on the second day, and lasts
through the anniversary of the day from which it is granted.[6]

135, and note to Am. ed. of Am. Cases ; Heap *v.* Barton, 12 C. B. 274 ; Preston
v. Briggs, 16 Vt. 124 ; Mason *v.* Fenn, 13 Ill. 525 ; Dubois *v.* Kelly, 10 Barb.
496 ; Dingley *v.* Buffum, 57 Me. 381 ; *ante,* *3, 6, 7, 30.

[1] Co. Lit. 345 a ; Bouvier, "Estate for Years"; Stearns, Real Act. 53 ; *ante,*
pl. 1.

[2] Carver *v.* Jackson, 4 Pet. 184.   A more expressive term perhaps might be "a
leasehold estate," or "a tenancy for years," as it is not intended to embrace, in
this chapter, estates for years created by way of particular estates in case of
remainders or executory devises, which are not created by a letting and hiring,
but by grant or devise.

[3] Allen *v.* Lambden, 2 Md. 279.

[4] Failing *v.* Schenck, 3 Hill, 344 ; State *v.* Page, 1 Speers, 408 ; Knight's Case,
5 Rep. 55 a ; 1 Platt, Leases, 9.

[5] 2 Flint, Real Prop. 203 ; Wms. Real Prop. (Rawle's ed.) 328.

[6] Atkins *v.* Sleeper, 7 Allen, 487 ; Ackland *v.* Lutley, 9 Ad. & E. 879.
Whether the word "from" shall be reckoned to include or exclude the date
depends on the apparent intent, gathered from the instrument.   Thus, where in
a lease for five years "from" April 1st, the rent was made payable on April 1st,
that day was included, Deyo *v.* Bleakly, 24 Barb. 9 ; but if nothing controls the
force of this word, it excludes, Bemis *v.* Leonard, 118 Mass. 502 ; Pugh *v.* Leeds,
Cowp. 714 ; Sheets *v.* Selden, 2 Wall. 190 ; Ordway *v.* Remington, 12 R. I. 319.
Where a term was from an act as of delivery, the day of the act is, in New Hamp-

But as this word *term* may express not only the duration of the interest of the lessee in the lands leased, but also the interest itself, it may often be so used that this last shall expire before the number of years mentioned in the lease.[1] And whether the one sense or the other is to be attached to the form of expression depends upon the construction of the instrument containing it. Thus the case put by Coke, in the passage cited,[2] is of a lease for twenty-one years, and afterwards a second lease to begin at the expiration of the *term* aforesaid of twenty-one years. If the first lessee surrenders his estate, the second lease would take effect at once. But if the second lease had been from the expiration of the twenty-one years aforesaid, it would have to wait the effluxion of the whole term mentioned. A case similar in effect is put in Sheppard's Touchstone,[3] which is cited and commented on by Lord Mansfield, who says, " the word *term* may signify the time as well as the interest, for then it becomes merely a question of construction, which sense the word ought to be used in." [4] And where a lease was made to A B for a year, with liberty in the lessee to occupy as long as he chose, and a surety became responsible with him for the rent, it was held that if the tenant continued to occupy after the year, it would be at the rate and upon the terms originally agreed upon, but that the surety's responsibility, unless renewed, continued only during the first *term of one year*.[5]

5. A term for years, it should be remembered, may [*293] be created * to take effect at a future date, since it affects the possession only and not the seisin of the lands. Nor is there any limit within which the term must take effect, in order to be valid, provided the period do not

---

shire, Pennsylvania, Indiana, Illinois, Kentucky, and perhaps some other States included; but the more generally prevailing rule is to exclude it, Taylor, Land. & Ten. (7th ed.) §§ 78, 79, notes; and *post*, *386.

[1] Burton, Real Prop. § 835 ; Co. Lit. 45 b   [2] Co. Lit. 45 b.

[3] Sheppard, Touchst. 274.

[4] Wright *v.* Cartwright, 1 Burr. 284; Evans *v.* Vaughan, 4 B. & C. 261; where under a power to lease for years, determinable on three lives, the lease was for the three lives with a covenant of quiet enjoyment during said term, it was held to mean during the whole period of the three lives.

[5] Brewer *v.* Thorp, 35 Ala. 9.

reach that which constitutes what the law calls a *perpetuity*, that, namely, of a life or lives in being, and twenty-one years and a fraction of a year afterwards.[1] But a covenant in a lease for its renewal indefinitely, at the option of the lessee, is not within the doctrine of perpetuity.[2] As the title and estate of such lessee is not consummate until he has taken possession under his lease, the interest which he has in the same, prior to such consummation, is called an *interesse termini*.[3] But in Ohio the execution and delivery of a lease perfects the title in the lessee without an actual entry.[4] Although a lease is said generally to take effect from the time of its making, it is apprehended that the time at which only it takes effect is when it is delivered. It is unimportant when it was written, and it is competent to show, by parol, when it was delivered, although no date, or a different one from that of its actual delivery, was inserted in the indenture.[5] And though the purpose of the *habendum* is to fix, for one thing, the time from which the duration of the term of the holding under the lease is to be reckoned, yet where it professes to do this by a reference to the making of the lease, the true time may be shown by parol. Thus, where a lease purported to bear date March, 1783, *habendum* from " March last past" for thirty-five years, it was held competent to show by parol that the lease was not executed until after March, 1783, and consequently the *habendum* was from that year and not 1782.[6] But where the hold-

---

[1] Burton, Real Prop. § 836 ; Sand. Uses, 199 ; Wms. Real Prop. 328 ; Cadell *v.* Palmer, 1 Cl. & F. 372 ; Field *v.* Howell, 6 Ga. 423 ; Whitney *v.* Allaire, 1 N. Y. 315 ; Weld *v.* Traip, 14 Gray, 330, 333.

[2] Page *v.* Esty, 54 Me. 319 ; Blackmore *v.* Boardman, 28 Mo. 420 ; Boyle *v.* Peabody H. Co. 46 Md. 623 ; and will be enforced in equity, Iggulden *v.* May, 9 Ves. 925 ; Banks *v.* Haskie, 45 Md. 207. In an early case in California the opposite doctrine was stated, Morrison *v.* Rossignol, 5 Cal. 64 ; but this turned on a special statute. The act of renewal is no new demise. House *v.* Burr, 24 Barb. 625 ; Brown *v.* Parsons, 22 Mich. 24. The rule is, of course, the same where the further term is at the lessee's option by occupancy merely. Holley *v.* Young, 66 Me. 520 ; Sweetser *v.* McKenney, 65 Me. 225.

[3] 2 Flint. Real Prop. 204, 205 ; Wms. Real Prop. 329 ; Smith, Land. & Ten. 13.
[4] Walk. Introd. 278.

[5] Hall *v.* Cazenove, 4 East, 477, 481 ; Trustees *v.* Robinson, Wright (Ohio), 436 ; Stone *v.* Bale, 3 Lev. 348 ; Co. Lit. 46 b ; Jackson *v.* Schoonmaker, 2 Johns. 230 ; Batchelder *v.* Dean, 16 N. H. 265, 268.

[6] Steele *v.* Mart, 4 B. & C. 272 ; Co. Lit. 46 b.

ing is to be "from the day of the date," its duration will be measured from that day as written, and not from the day of its execution, if these are in fact variant.[1] But if the day named as the commencement of the holding, or of the term, be anterior to the date and actual execution of the lease, no [*294] interest thereby passes to the * lessee until the actual execution and delivery of the lease, the purpose of the *habendum* being to mark the duration of the lessee's interest.[2] Accordingly, it was held in respect to a lease made and dated in July, 1851, demising the premises for fourteen years from December, 1849, with a right to determine it at the expiration of seven years, that this term of seven years was to be reckoned from 1849.[3]

6. It seems to be regarded as essential to a good lease for years that it should be either for a certain period, measured by years, months, or the like, or for a period uncertain only from the circumstance that it may be determined before its natural expiration by the happening of some event, or that it be for a purpose which, of itself, serves to ascertain the length of time for which the premises are to be held. Thus Littleton says, "Tenant for term of years is where a man letteth lands or tenements to another for term of certain years."[4] And the illustrations given by Coke are, if a man shall make a lease to J. S. for so many years as J. N. shall name, it is a good one, for, when J. N. has named the number of years, the duration of the term becomes fixed. If the lease be to J. S. for twenty-one years, if he live so long, it is a good one.[5] But a lease by a parson for so many years as he shall be parson of Dale, or so many years as he shall live, would be not only for an uncertain time, but it never could be made certain so as to be valid as a term.[6] And though it might be good as a freehold estate,

---

[1] Smith, Land. & Ten. 83 n.; Styles v. Wardle, 4 B. & C. 908 ; Doe v. Day, 10 East, 427 ; Co. Lit. 46 b; Kelly v. Patterson, L. R. 9 C. P. 681.

[2] Shaw v. Kay, 1 Exch. 412; Wybird v. Tuck, 1 Bos. & P. 458 ; Mayn v. Beak, Cro. Eliz. 515.

[3] Bird v. Baker, 1 Ellis & E. 12.   [4] Lit. § 58.

[5] Goodright v. Richardson, 3 T. R. 462. So if for a term fixed but determinable on sale, &c., by the landlord. Munigle v. Boston, 3 Allen, 230 ; Shaw v. Hoffman, 25 Mich. 162.

[6] Co. Lit. 45 b; 2 Prest. Conv. 159 ; 2 Flint. Real Prop. 203 ; Murray v.

if properly made by deed, it could not be good as a term under a lease. But a devise to A during his minority would be good, as it is susceptible of being ascertained in respect to its duration.[1] So upon the principle that, *id certum est quod certum reddi potest*, a lease for seven or fourteen years will be good as one for seven at least, and for fourteen as soon as the lessee shall so elect.[2] And if a lease be to one for a year, with a privilege of holding for three years, and he continues to hold after the expiration of the first year, it will be held to be an election on his part to hold for the three years.[3] And a lease for one year, and so on from year to year, is regarded as one for two years, and a lease " for years," without any number fixed, is for two years certain.[4] It is apprehended that it is upon the idea that the term for which * the [*295] estate is to be held, can be ascertained, by computing how long it will require the income thereof to raise a given sum, that an executor takes an estate for years under a devise of lands for the payment of debts, or until the devisor's debts are paid.[5] And a lease of premises until the lessee shall, out of the rents, repay himself for a certain amount of expense incurred by him in repairs, was held to be a sufficiently definite term to be a valid one.[6] The only circumstance required in these limitations of terms of years is, that a precise time shall be fixed for the continuance of the term, so that when the commencement of the term is ascertained, the period of determination by effluxion of time may be known with certainty.[7] And it was held by the court of Vermont, that an

Cherrington, 99 Mass. 229. Whether a lease for so many years as the lessor himself may name, would become a fixed term, if he were to name a certain number of years, *quære*. West. Transp. Co. *v.* Lansing, 49 N. Y. 499, 508.

[1] Smith, Land. & Ten. 15 ; Burton, Real Prop. § 487.

[2] Doe *v.* Dixon, 9 East, 15.

[3] Delashman *v.* Berry, 20 Mich. 292 ; Kramer *v.* Cook, 7 Gray, 550 ; Clarke *v.* Merrill, 51 N. H. 415 ; Dix *v.* Atkins, 130 Mass. 171. But it is otherwise if written notice is first to be given. Beller *v.* Robinson, 50 Mich. 264.

[4] Denn *v.* Cartright, 4 East, 29 ; Com. Dig. Land. & Ten. 91, 92.

[5] 1 Cruise, Dig. 223. But it has been held that an instrument granting premises " for any term of years " the lessee might think proper, taken in connection with the uses for which they were to be applied, namely, salt works, is a valid lease for a term determinable upon the lessee's abandoning that manufacture. Horner *v.* Leeds, 25 N. J. 106 ; and see Lemington *v.* Stevens, 48 Vt. 38.

[6] Batchelder *v.* Dean, 16 N. H. 265, 268.   [7] 2 Prest. Conv. 160.

instrument with the usual features and incidents of a lease, such as reserving rent, with a right of entry for non-payment of it, or for breach of conditions expressed therein, may be good if properly executed, although in terms creating a per-petual estate in the premises.[1]   And in Massachusetts, it was held that one might convey a fee in land in the form of a lease, although, ordinarily, applied to the creation of terms only.[2]

7. A tenant for years is never said to be *seised* of the lands leased ; nor does the mere delivery of a lease thereof for years vest in him any estate therein.   He thereby acquires a right of entry upon the land, and when he shall have entered, he is said to be possessed, not of the land, but of a term for years, while the seisin of the freehold remains in the lessor, and the lessee's possession is the possession of him who has the free-hold.[3]

8. Until, as already stated, the lessee should have entered upon the leased premises, he was formerly held to acquire no *estate* in the same.   The interest which he acquired by the delivery of the lease, and before entry made, is, as already stated, called an *interesse termini ;* and accordingly, Littleton, in defining what is a tenancy for years, after stating that it " is awarded between lessor and lessee," adds, " And the lessee entereth by force of the lease." [4]   And if the lessee die before entry, his executors or administrators may enter in his [*296] stead.[5]   But while the lessee until he * shall have taken possession, cannot have trespass *quare clausum*

---

[1] White *v.* Fuller, 38 Vt. 193.

[2] Jamaica Pond Co. *v.* Chandler, 9 Allen, 159, 168 ; Co. Lit. 43 b.   Such are, also, the so-called manor leases in New York and the fee-farm leases in Pennsyl-vania.   See Van Rensselaer *v.* Hays, 19 N. Y. 68 ; Wallace *v.* Harmsted, 44 Penn. St. 492.

[3] 1 Cruise, Dig. 224 ; Lit. § 59 ; Vanduyn *v.* Hepner, 45 Ind. 589.   But the tenant only, and not the landlord, can maintain trespass *quare clausum.*   French *v.* Fuller, 23 Pick. 104 ; Austin *v.* Hud. Riv. R. R., 25 N.Y. 334 ; Geer *v.* Fleming, 110 Mass. 39.

[4] 1 Cruise, Dig. 225 ; Lit. § 58 ; Doe *v.* Walker, 5 B. & C. 111.   Nor does it make any difference at common law whether the lessee has a present or future right of entry, until entry actually made.   Id.; Co. Lit. 46 b ; Co. Lit. 270 a ; Bacon, Abr. Lease, M ; Wood *v.* Hubbell, 10 N. Y. 479.

[5] Co. Lit. 46 b.

fregit against a stranger;[1] an entry is held not necessary to the vesting of a term of years in him.[2] And a lease may be so made, where a sufficient consideration is expressed, as having been executed or paid, and it is in the form of a bargain and sale, as to operate, under the statute of uses, as an effectual creation of an estate, without a formal entry. Thus, if the words "bargain and sale," in consideration of money, be contained in the lease, or in consideration of money, the lessor demises the premises, a use will arise in favor of the lessee. But if it be made without any money consideration, the lessee has not strictly an estate until entry made by him.[3] Before that has been done, he has only an *interesse termini*, but not a possession.[4] How this is made to produce this effect will be explained in connection with the law of uses.[5] But, it seems, that even when the lease takes effect under the statute of uses, it is necessary that the lessee should have made an actual entry before he could maintain trespass;[6] since such action is founded on an actual possession.

9. It is also laid down by some writers, that a lessee, before entry made, cannot maintain an action of ejectment.[7] And regarding such action, as it was originally designed for the recovery of a term, where it was a writ of trespass in its nature,[8] the proposition may still be regarded as true. But, according to the modern mode of proceeding, the action being a fictitious one where the tenant is required to confess lease, entry, and ouster, it will doubtless be sufficient if the demandant has a title and right of entry.[9] And if the lease be future in its terms, the lessee by delivery of the lease acquires such an

---

[1] Bacon, Abr. Lease, ᴅ ; Smith, Land. & Ten. 13 ; Wheeler *v.* Montefiore, 2 Q. B. 133.

[2] Harrison *v.* Blackburn, 17 C. B. ɴ. s. 678 ; Ryan *r.* Clark, 14 Q. B. 65, 73.

[3] Birckhead *v.* Cummings, 33 N. J. 44.

[4] Wood's Conv. 157, 159 ; Co. Lit. 46 b.

[5] 1 Cruise, Dig. 225 ; 4 Kent, Com. 97 ; Bacon, Abr. Lease, ᴅ.

[6] Smith, Land. & Ten. 14, n.; Com. Dig. Trespass, B. 3 ; 1 Platt, Leases, 23 ; 2 Sand. Uses, 56.

[7] Bacon, Abr. Lease, ᴅ ; Saffyn *v.* Adams, Cro. Jac. 61; 1 Platt, Leases, 23. But see ᴅechan. Ins. Co. *v.* Scott, 2 Hilton, 550.

[8] Adams, Eject. 6 ; 10.

[9] Adams, Eject. 14 ; 10, 61 ; Gardner *v.* Keteltas, 3 Hill, 330 ; Trull *v.* Granger, 8 N. Y. 115 ; but see Sennett *v.* Bucher, 3 Penn. 392.

interest in the term, that he could maintain ejectment to
recover it without any further act on his part, if possession
were withheld when his right to claim it had become complete.[1]

10. This *interesse termini*, however, may be granted or assigned by the lessee,[2] but upon technical grounds, the subtle-
ness of which renders it hardly worth the time to attempt to
explain them, it cannot be surrendered, though it may be extinguished by a surrender by law, or by an assignment, or
by a release, while it can neither promote nor hinder the
merger of an estate.[3] These propositions may perhaps be
sufficiently illustrated by the following cases. The lessee of
a term, to commence at the ensuing Michaelmas, took a new
lease for years, commencing *in præsenti*, and it was
[*297] held to be a surrender of the *first lease. So had the
new lease been made to take effect at Michaelmas.
And where a lessor made a lease which was to expire in
1809, and then made a second lease of the same estate to the
same lessee, to take effect at the expiration of the first, the
last bearing date in 1799, and the lessor, in 1800, died having
devised the leased estate for life to the lessee, who conveyed
his life-estate before 1809, it was held that this interest of the
lessee, in the term to commence in 1809, was not merged in
the life-estate which he took under the will, because the two
estates were not in him at the same time, as the *interesse
termini* was not an estate till entry made, and, before that
could be done, he had parted with his life-estate.[4] It should
have been remarked that the rules which apply to an *interesse
termini* at common law apply equally to all leases to commence *in futuro*.[5] And where A made a lease to B, of a hotel
for a term of years, from a future day, and before that day it
burned down, it was held that the lease never took effect so as
to make the lessee liable for rent. The lessor must give, or offer
to give, possession of the premises, in order to create any lia-

[1] Whitney *v.* Allaire, 1 N. Y. 305, 311.

[2] Co. Lit. 46 b ; 1 Platt, Leases, 22.

[3] Burton, Real Prop. §§ 907, 998 ; 2 Prest. Conv. 215 ; Co. Lit. 338 a ; Doe
v. Walker, 5 B. & C. 111. See 4 Kent, Com. 97, note a.

[4] Doe *v.* Walker, 5 B. & C. 111 ; Sheppard, Touchst. 324 ; Co. Lit. 270 a.

[5] Doe *v.* Walker, 5 B. & C. 111 ; 4 Kent, Com. 97.

bility for the rent, and it matters not whether he can not or will not do this. So where the owner of a hall agreed with another to furnish him the use of it for a concert upon certain nights, for a certain agreed sum of money, and the hall was burned before the first of these nights, it was held to excuse both parties respectively from performing the contract, unless the owner of the hall had expressly agreed to assume the risk of providing it. The court would apply the same rule to such a contract as to an agreement by one man to serve another who should die, or an agreement by an artist to paint a picture and he should lose his sight before executing it.[1] In either event he is without remedy for the rent reserved.[2] But it is no answer to a claim for rent, that the premises are in the possession of another, unless held by a title paramount to that of the lessor, since by the act of letting the premises, the lessor does not warrant against the acts of strangers, nor does he engage to put the lessee into actual possession.[3] But where the lessor himself has only a reversion or remainder, subject to an intermediate particular estate, a lease by him will be considered as a conveyance of so much of his estate in reversion or remainder, and not the creation of an *interesse termini*.[4]

11. A forbearance on the part of a lessee for years to turn his *interesse termini* into an actual estate by making an entry, will not affect his liability for rent, if the fault is not on the part of the lessor, for the rent becomes due by the lease, and not by the entry or by occupation,[5] and the action is upon the

---

[1] Taylor v. Coldwell, 3 Best & S. 826.

[2] Wood v. Hubbell, 5 Barb. 601 ; s. c. 10 N. Y. 479, 487, 489.

[3] Mechan. Ins. Co. v. Scott, 2 Hilton, 550. A contrary rule prevails in England and some States, and the lessor is held to warrant possession to the lessee, " and not merely the chance of a lawsuit." Coe v. Clay, 5 Bing. 440 ; Jenks v. Edwards, 11 Exch. 775 ; L'Hussier v. Zallee, 24 Mo. 13 ; Hughes v. Hood, 50 Mo. 350 ; King v. Reynolds, 67 Ala. 229. But the rule in the text generally prevails in this country. Clark v. Butt, 26 Ind. 236 ; Trull v. Granger, 8 N. Y. 115 ; Moore v. Weber, 71 Pa. St. 429 ; Pendergast v. Young, 21 N. H. 234 ; Sigmund v. Howard Bk., 29 Md. 324 ; Underwood v. Birchard, 47 Vt. 305 ; Gazzolo v. Chambers, 73 Ill. 75 ; Field v. Herrick, 101 Ill. 210.

[4] Doe v. Brown, 2 El. & Bl. 331.

[5] Bellasis v. Burbriche, 1 Ld. Raym. 171 ; s. c. Rep. Temp. Holt. 199 ; 1 Platt, Leases, 23 ; Maverick v. Lewis, 3 McCord, 211 ; Williams v. Bosanquet, 1 Brod. & B. 238 ; Mechan. Ins. Co. v. Scott, 2 Hilton, 550 ; Whitney v. Allaire, 1 N. Y. 305, 311.

covenant as for a breach of an executory covenant;[1] and, though the lessor may die before lessee enters under his lease, he may do so after the lessor's death, at his pleasure.[2]

[*298]   *SECTION II.

HOW ESTATES FOR YEARS MAY BE CREATED.

1. Forms of doing this at common law, and by the Statute of Frauds.
2. What is requisite by the Statute of Frauds.
3. Of the proper terms to create a lease.
4. Distinction between a lease and an agreement to lease.
4a. When a lease and when an agreement form one.
5. Importance of this distinction.
6. Of leases operating by estoppel.
7. Of parties who may be lessors.
8. Leases made good by ratification.
9. Of ratification by wife of husband's lease.
10. Lease by guardian, executor, &c.
11. Of making leases under powers of appointment.
12. Of leases by tenants in common.
13. Who may be lessees.
14. What may be leased.
15. When terms for years made freeholds.
16. Of terms attendant upon the inheritance.
17. Of the chattel character of terms.
18. What leases need to be recorded.
19. Leases under the Statute of Uses.
20. Effect of possession by lessee or lessor.
21. How far lessee is liable before entry made.
22. Lease must be accepted in order to bind.
23. Consequences of relation of landlord and tenant.
24. Of the tenure and privity between lessor and lessee.
25. What is implied by such relation, and where it exists.

1. THERE were three modes of creating an estate for years at the common law, namely, by deed, by writing not under seal, and by parol,[3] though, if it was of an incorporeal heredit-

---

[1] Lafarge v. Mansfield, 31 Barb. 345. By a statute of Illinois, the lessor has a lien for rent upon the crops growing or grown upon the demised land in any year, for the rent of that year, and this will extend over two years in respect to such crops as require that length of time to mature them. Miles v. James, 36 Ill. 399.

[2] Lit. § 66 ; Co. Lit. 51 b.

[3] Smith, Land. & Ten. 60 ; Den v. Johnson, 15 N. J. 116.

ament, it was always requisite to be done by deed,[1] and by the statute 8 & 9 Vict. c. 106, leases of corporeal as well as incorporeal property must be by deed.[2] The statute of 29 Car. II. c. 3, called the Statute of Frauds, which, with some modifications, has been adopted by nearly all the several States, declared, among other things, that all leases for more than three years, "not put in writing and signed by the parties," &c., should have the force and effect of estates at will only.[3] But as terms were coupled with estates of freehold, which required a deed to create them, the question arose whether a lease of a term must not also be by deed. But it seems to be settled that it will be sufficient that such a lease is in writing, though not under seal, to comply with the requirements of that statute.[4] It is hardly necessary to remind the reader that the estates which are embraced in this chapter are those only which are valid as estates for years within the Statute of Frauds, since estates at will and tenancies from year to year will form the subject of another chapter. The laws of the various States vary in respect to leases being by deed. In most of them it is enough that the instrument be properly subscribed. In Virginia and Kentucky, if the lease be for more than five years, it must be under seal. So in Vermont and Rhode Island, if it exceed one year.[5] So in Minnesota, if it be for three years or more.[6] A lease for ninety-nine years in Maryland must be by deed.[7] And a lease of a married woman's estate in Pennsylvania, for any term, to be valid,

---

[1] Wms. Real Prop. 195 ; Id. 327.

[2] Wms. Real Prop. 196; Smith, Land. & Ten. 66, n. 9.

[3] The English statute period is adopted in New Jersey, Pennsylvania, North and South Carolina, Maryland, Georgia, and Indiana. In Massachusetts, Maine, New Hampshire, Vermont, Missouri, and Ohio, all parol leases are at will. But in New York and most other States they are valid if not exceeding one year. Browne, Stat. Fr. App. And see *post,* •646.

[4] Den *v.* Johnson, 15 N. J. 116; Allen *v.* Jaquish, 21 Wend. 628; Wheeler *v.* Newton, Free. in Ch. 16. A lessor would not be entitled to sue for and recover from the lessee his part of the indenture of lease before the expiration of the term, although he may have entered and dispossessed the lessee for a breach of covenant and condition. On the other hand, if he gets possession of the lessee's part, he may have an action to recover the same from the lessor. Hall *v.* Ball, 3 Mann. & G. 242; Elworthy *v.* Sanford, 3 Hurlst. & C. 330.

[5] Taylor, Land. & Ten. § 34. Five years. Stewart *v.* Apel, 5 Houst. 189.

[6] Chandler *v.* Kent, 8 Minn. 524, 526.   [7] Bratt *v.* Bratt, 21 Md. 578.

must be acknowledged by her, separate from her husband.[1]
In New Hampshire, signing only is necessary.[2] In Ohio, the
lease, if for more than three years, must be attested by two
witnesses and acknowledged.[3] In Massachusetts, if it be for
more than seven years, it must be by deed, and, in order to
be valid against third persons without notice, it must be recorded.[4]

2. The first section of the Statute of Frauds requires the
writing which is sought to be availed of as a lease, to be
" signed by the parties, &c., making the same, or their agents
thereunto lawfully authorized by writing." In some of the
States the appointment of the agent is not required
[*299] to be in writing, while * in others the English rule
upon the subject is copied and adopted.[5] * A question
growing out of these statutes has arisen as to the mode of
signing leases when done through an agent in the actual presence of the lessor, and by his direction. In South Carolina,
the court of appeals were equally divided upon the point, a
part holding that if an instrument is signed by a person in the
presence of another, in the name and by the express direction
of the latter, it is a good signing of the party himself at common law, and that the statute did not intend to extend to
cases like this. But the other part of the court applied a strict
construction to the language of the act, and regarded an agent
as no less an agent while acting in presence of his principal
than he would be in his absence.[6] In Massachusetts, on the
contrary, it has been held that a signature placed by a third

* NOTE. — In the following States the English rule prevails: Alabama, Arkansas, Georgia, Maryland, Michigan, Missouri, New Hampshire, New Jersey,
New York, Ohio, Pennsylvania, South Carolina, and Wisconsin, while in the
others the requirement is either simply that it may be executed by a party or his
"agent," or "attorney," or it adds "lawfully authorized," without stating how.
In Connecticut it must be signed by the lessor, and in Delaware it must be done
by deed.

[1] Miller v. Harbert, 25 Leg. Int. 29.
[2] Olmstead v. Niles, 7 N. H. 522, 526.
[3] Richardson v. Bates, 8 Ohio St. 257, 260.   [4] Pub. Stat. c. 120, § 4.
[5] See the statutes of the several States collected in the Appendix to Browne
on the Stat. of Frauds, 503–531.   Cf. Jennings v. McComb, 112 Penn. St. 518.
[6] Wallace v. McCullough, 1 Rich. Eq. 426.

person in the grantor's presence and by his direction, orally
given, will be a valid execution of a deed.[1] It may be added,
that if the signing is not by the party himself, but by his
agent, it should be expressed as the act of the principal done
by his agent; as A B, by his attorney, C D,[2] while
*merely signing the name of the principal, as A B, [*300]
without adding by whom done, would not be a good
signing,[3] nor would it be if in the agent's own name.[4]

3. In respect to the proper terms by which an estate for
years may be created, any form of expression is sufficient if it
shows an intention on the part of the lessor to part with and
divest himself of the possession in favor of the lessee, and a
corresponding intention on the part of the lessee to come into
the possession of the premises for a determinate period of
time. The words generally used for this purpose are, " grant,"
" demise," and " to farm let," some of which have a technical
and extensive signification. " Do lease, demise, and let," in
a lease, import the creation of a term to begin presently, and
not at a future day or upon a contingency.[5] But neither of
them is indispensable to constitute a valid lease,[6] and even
when adopted they may be controlled by the connection in
which they are used.[7] Thus, where A gave B a bond conditioned to convey land upon being paid a certain note on de-

[1] Gardner v. Gardner, 5 Cush. 483; Wood v. Goodridge, 6 Cush. 117.

[2] Bacon, Abr. Lease, I. § 10; Opinion of Mr. Hoffman, 3 Am. Jur. 67; Elwell
v. Shaw, 16 Mass. 42. *Post*, vol. 2, pp. *573–575.

[3] Wood v. Goodridge, 6 Cush. 117, 1 Am. Lead. Cas. 3d ed. 579.

[4] Combe's Case, 9 Rep. 76 b; 1 Am. Lead. Cas. 3d ed. 579.

[5] So. Cong. Meeting House v. Hilton, 11 Gray, 409.

[6] Jackson v. Delacroix, 2 Wend. 433, 438; Wms. Real. Prop. 327. "Agree to
let," "agree to take," held to be words of present demise. Doe v. Ries, 8 Bing.
178, 182, per Tindal, C. J.; Doe v. Benjamin, 9 Ad. & E. 644, 650, per Denman,
C. J. So are "shall hold and enjoy." Doe v. Ashburner, 5 T. R. 163 ; Burton, Real Prop. § 838; Watson v. O'Hern, 6 Watts, 362 ; Boshier v. Reding, 12
Be. 478; Moore v. Miller, 8 Penn. St. 272; Bacon, Abr. Lease, K.

[7] Putnam v. Wise, 1 Hill, 234, where, though the terms were those of a lease,
it was held to constitute the parties tenants in common of the crops, the return
for the occupation being a share of the crops. See Walker v. Fitts, 24 Pick. 191.
Post. *364. Doe v. Derry, 9 Car. & P. 494. A let to B his farm for seven
years, and B at the same time in writing agreed to employ A to carry on the
farm at certain wages, and to allow him to occupy the house free of rent; it was
held to be a contract for remuneration for services and not a demise of the
house.

mand, with interest quarterly, and that the obligee should have possession of the same until such conveyance should be made, it was held to be a demise so long as B paid the interest on the note quarterly, and did not fail to pay the principal on demand, and that the tenancy created was not one at will.[1] It is indispensable, however, that the lease should, by its terms, ascertain the premises intended to be demised, for, if defective in this respect, it cannot be made good by parol evidence.[2]

4. Some of the most difficult questions under this head have been, whether the language of the parties is to be construed as a present demise or a contract for a future one. And whether it is the one or the other, depends upon the intention of the parties, as gathered from the whole instrument, rather than any particular form of expression in any particular part of the agreement, though, as a general proposition, if there are apt words of a present demise, followed by possession, the instrument will be held to pass an immediate interest.[3] [*301] The cases are numerous, * and many of them apparently conflicting. Thus in Jackson v. Kisselbrack, the memorandum stated that L. "hath set and to farm let"

---

[1] White v. Livingston, 10 Cush. 259. The permissive possession of a vendee before purchase is not a demise, but a bare license. Doe v. Stanion, 1 M. & W. 695, 700; Thompson v. Bower, 60 Barb. 463; Dunham v. Townsend, 110 Mass. 440; Taylor, Land. & Ten. (7th ed.) § 25, and note; and this will be more fully considered, *post*, Book I. c. 12, § 2. A contract for lodging also is not a lease properly, see Cook v. Humber, 11 C. B. N. s. 33, 46; 7 Am. Law. Rev. 253; White v. Maynard, 111 Mass. 250; and of course not where for board and lodging, *ib.*; Taylor, Land. & Ten. (7th ed.) § 66; Wilson v. Martin, 1 Denio, 602. But where the contract is a clear lease it does not lose this character, because it also contains an agreement to board at the lessee's option. Porter v. Merrill, 124 Mass. 534.

[2] Dingman v. Kelly, 7 Ind. 717.

[3] Hallett v. Wylie, 3 Johns. 44; Thornton v. Payne, 5 Johns. 74. In the latter case, the judge, Spencer, says: "In every case decided in the English courts where agreements have been adjudged not to operate by passing an interest, but to rest in contract, there has been either an express agreement for a future lease, or construing the agreement to be a lease *in præsenti* would work a forfeiture, or the terms have not been fully settled, and something further was to be done." Jackson v. Delacroix, 2 Wend. 433; Burton, Real Prop. § 845; Warman v. Faithfull, 5 B. & Ad. 1042; Averill v. Taylor, 8 N. Y. 44; Baxter v. Browne, 2 W. Bl. 973; Morgan v. Bissell, 3 Taunt. 65; Wright v. Trevezant, 3 Car. & P. 441. See Weed v. Crocker, 13 Gray, 219; Hurlburt v. Post, 1 Bosw. 28.

unto K., &c., but it contained a clause, "the place to be surveyed on or before, &c., ensuing the date," "and then K. is to
take a lease for the same." The court (Spencer, J.) say,
"This last circumstance has generally given a character to
the instrument of an agreement for a lease as contradistinguished from a present demise." But. it is added, "none of
the cases will be found to contradict the position that where
there are apt words of present demise, and to these is super-
added a covenant for a future lease, the instrument is to be
considered as a lease, and the covenant as operating in the
nature of a covenant for further assurance." The agreement
in that case, having been followed by possession, was held
to be a present demise.[1] The question seems to turn upon
whether the writing shows that the parties intend a present
demise and parting with the possession by the lessor to the
lessee, for, if it does, it will operate as a lease, though it is
contemplated that a future writing should be drawn, more
explicit in its terms. And it may be a good lease in distinction from an executory contract to lease, though it be to commence *in futuro*.[2] But if a fuller lease is to be prepared and
executed before the demise is to take effect, and possession
given, it is an agreement for a lease, and not a lease
which creates an estate.[3] Thus, where it *was cov- [*302]
enanted between A & B "that A doth let the said
lands for and during five years, &c., to begin, &c., provided

---

[1] Jackson v. Kisselbrack, 10 Johns. 336; Chapman v. Bluek, 5 Scott, 515;
Alderman v. Neate, 4 M. & W. 704. But see Goodtitle v. Way, 1 T. R. 735;
Poole v. Bentley, 12 East, 168; Wms. Real. Prop. 327; Pinero v. Judson, 6 Bing.
206; Doe v. Ries, 8 Bing. 178; Jones v. Reynolds, per Wightman, J., 1 Q. B.
517.

[2] Whitney v. Allaire, 1 N. Y. 305, 311; Holley v. Young, 66 Me. 520; Bussman v. Ganster, 72 Penn. St. 285; People v. Kelsey, 14 Abb. Pr. 372.

[3] Aiken v. Smith, 21 Vt. 172; People v. Gillis, 24 Wend. 201; Jackson v.
Eldridge, 3 Story, 325; Griffin v. Knisely, 75 Ill. 447; Buell v. Cook, 4 Conn.
238, where the agreement was held to be for a lease and not a lease itself, as it
showed the lessor was to get an authority from another party before he could
make a valid demise. So Brown v. N. Y. C. R. R. 44 N. Y. 79, where the covenants were not settled. In Doe v. Benjamin, 9 Ad. & E. 644, "agree to let"
was held equivalent to an actual present letting, though no time was fixed for
commencement of the same, and the agreement contained a clause, "a lease to
be drawn upon the usual terms." So Hand v. Hall, 2 Exch. Div. 355. See
Jackson v. Myers, 3 Johns 388, 395; Sturgion v. Painter, Noy, 128.

that B shall pay to A annually during the term at, &c., £120,
also, the parties do covenant that a lease shall be made and
sealed according to the effect of these articles, before the
Feast," &c., it was held to be a good present lease; "that
which follows the demise is in reference to further assurance." [1] And it is said that acts and declarations of the parties may be looked to, to aid in the construction which is to
be given to their agreements in this respect, where the agreement is equivocal, especially the yielding of possession by the
one and accepting it by the other.[2] And sometimes an agreement which might, otherwise, be defective for want of stipulations as to the terms of the letting, may be made good by
providing these shall be "such as are usually contained in
leases." [3]

4 a. The test whether a written instrument is a lease or
only an agreement for a lease is sometimes stated to be, that
if the agreement of the parties leaves nothing incomplete, it
may operate as a present demise. Thus, " we agree to let"
certain land to a gas company to place sand, &c., on, for the
construction of a gas-holder, to be occupied during the construction of the same, was held to be an actual letting, by
which the lessors were bound, although they never built their
gas-holder upon the proposed site.[4] So where A wrote B that

---

[1] 1 Rolle, Abr. 847. In Jackson v. Delacroix, 2 Wend. 433, where there were
words of present demise, but the agreement showed that alterations were to be made
in the estate before the lease was to take effect, it was held not to be a lease. So
McGrath v. Boston, 103 Mass. 369; where repairs were to be done and then a lease
given. But in Bacon v. Bowdoin, 22 Pick. 401, though the lessor was in terms
to complete a building, the agreement was a present demise of it for a certain time,
and the lessee was to have a right to use it for certain purposes from the date of
the agreement, it was held to be a present lease. So People v. Kelsey, 14 Abb.
Pr. 372. In Chapman v. Towner, 6 M. & W. 100, there were words of demise in
the agreement, but the amount of rent or terms of holding were not mentioned in
it, except as to be contained in a lease to be prepared, it was held to be an agreement and not a lease. See 6 M. & W. 104; Am. ed., note; Morgan v. Bissell, 3
Taunt. 65; Jones v. Reynolds, 1 Q. B. 506, 515. But in Doe v. Benjamin, 1 Perr. &
D. 444, Lord Denman declares Morgan v. Bissell overruled, so far as that provision for giving a future lease controls a present demise.

[2] Chapman v. Bluck, 5 Scott, 515, 533, per Parke, J., s. c. 4 Bing. N. C. 187;
Doe v. Ashburner, 5 T. R. 163.

[3] Alderman v. Neate, 4 M. & W. 704.

[4] Kabley v. Worcester Gas Co., 102 Mass. 392.

he would take his house at a certain rent for three years, if he
would put a furnace into it, and B replied by letter that he
accepted the offer and at once procured and placed a furnace
in the house before the day fixed for the three years to begin,
it was held to be a lease and not a mere offer to take one.[1]
In another case, A proposed to B, in writing, to hire a shop of
certain dimensions on a certain piece of land for a certain
time, at a certain rent, if B would erect it; and B accepted
the offer and erected the shop, and A went into occupation of
it.   But, in fact, B did not own the land and did not complete
the shop within the time agreed.   It was held that by accepting and entering into occupancy of the premises, the agreement became an effectual lease for the agreed term, though
A might recoup the damages he sustained by B's delay in
completing the shop.[2]   But in such a case, a failure of the lessor
to have the building completed by the time fixed in the agreement would, if the lessee chose, release him from his obligation to accept it and pay rent.[3]   And where there was an
agreement, not under seal, on one part to let and on the other
to hire, and that a good lease should be made at the joint expense of the parties, it was held, though not to be a lease, to
be binding as an agreement to take a lease.[4]

5. The importance of this distinction between agreements
to lease, and agreements which operate as leases, results,
among other things, from this, that as an executed written
contract must speak for itself, and cannot be added to or corrected by parol, if the agreement be held to be a lease the parties will be bound by it, as written, with its *implied* as well as
express covenants and stipulations; whereas, if it is a mere
agreement to lease, these may be rectified or supplied before
it is executed, or the party may refuse to execute it.[5]

* 6. In treating thus far of what may be a lease, [*303]
and of its effect, it has been assumed that he who
makes the agreement is the owner of the interest or estate
which he assumes to demise.   There is, however, a class of
cases where a lease may become operative, though the lessor,

---

[1] Shaw v. Farnsworth, 108 Mass. 357.   [3] Haven v. Wakefield, 39 Ill. 509.
[2] Tidey v. Mallett, 16 C. B. N. S. 298.   [4] Bond v. Rosling, 1 Best. & S. 371.
[5] Sugden's Letters, 118.

at the time of making it, has no estate in the subject-matter of the lease. This is by way of what is called an estoppel. Thus suppose A makes a deed of indenture of lease of premises to which he has no title, and afterwards acquires one during the term ; he will not be admitted to deny that his lessee had a good title to the same, nor, on the other hand, will the lessee, if permitted to occupy under such a lease, be at liberty to deny the title of his lessor.[1]   In one case, one in possession of premises leased them, but without any covenant except that the lessee should enjoy without interference by the lessor or any one claiming under him, and the lessor having acquired title to the premises, it was held that the lessee might hold as against this newly acquired title by force of the lessor's personal covenant.[2] To produce the effect above stated, it has been laid down that the lease must be by *indenture*, whereby the deed becomes the act of both parties, in order that the estoppel thereby created may be mutual ;[3] and as a corollary thereto that infants and *femes covert* cannot avail themselves of the benefit of a lease where the lessor demises premises without having any estate in the same.[4] But, inasmuch as the estoppel of the tenant to deny the lessor's title flows from possession and not the form of the instrument, neither of these propositions are probably tenable at the present day.[5] So, by the American law, if one having no estate grant land by deed with covenants of warranty of title, and afterwards acquire a title to the granted premises, it will enure and pass to the grantee by estoppel.[6] But this doctrine of creating a demise

---

[1] Burton, Real Prop. § 850, and n.; Smith, Land. & Ten. 32, and n.; Co. Lit. 47 b; Sturgeon *v.* Wingfield, 15 M. & W. 224; Utica Bk. *v.* Mersereau, 3 Barb. Ch. 528, 567; Wms. Real Prop. 329; Rawlyn's case, 4 Rep. 53; Bac. Abr. Lease, O. This class of cases should be distinguished from that hereafter treated of, where leases are made by donees of powers, and held good, though such donee had no interest in the premises demised.

[2] Burr *v.* Stenton, 43 N. Y. 462, 466. It was also held that the tenant would have no recourse, if evicted by a foreclosure sale, against the surplus therefrom arising. But this is qualified by Clarkson *v.* Skidmore, 46 N. Y. 297.

[3] Burton, Real Prop. § 850; Co. Lit. 352 a; 1 Platt, Leases, 55.

[4] 1 Platt, Leases, 55.

[5] Bigelow, Estoppel, c. 15; Taylor, Land. & Ten. (7th ed.) §§ 89, 90.

[6] Somes *v.* Skinner, 3 Pick. 52; Baxter *v.* Bradbury, 20 Me. 260; 2 Smith, Lead. Cas. 5th Am. ed. 625; White *v.* Patten, 24 Pick. 324; Knight *v.* Thayer,

of a certain extent of estate by estoppel does not apply where
the lessor has any legal estate in the premises which passes by
the lease, though less than that which he has, in terms, demised.[1] One pretty obvious reason for this rule would be, that
to fix what the amount of estate is which actually passes by
the lease, would open the very inquiry by evidence which it is
the purpose and effect of an estoppel to preclude.

•7. In respect to who may be parties to such leases [*304]
as have been mentioned above, it may be said, generally, that the same rules apply as in other cases of contract.
In treating of who may be lessors, it may be stated, that the
lease of a person *non compos mentis*, regarded as an executory
contract, is void. But it has been held otherwise in England,
in respect to an executed contract, where the parties cannot
be restored *in statu quo*, especially in the case of a lunatic, if
the unsoundness of mind was unknown to the other party, and
no advantage was taken of him.[2] In the United States, it
would seem that it makes no difference with the parties as to
the right of a person *non compos* to avoid any and all his contracts, that the party dealing with him was not apprised of
his incapacity, and did not overreach him.[3] And in this

---

125 Mass. 25; Utica Bk. v. Mersereau, 3 Barb. Ch. 528, 567; Rawle, Cov. c. 9;
Wms. Real Prop. 330, Rawle's note.

[1] Co. Lit. 45 a; Burton, Real Prop. § 850; Wms. Real Prop. 330; Blake v.
Foster, 8 T. R. 487, 490; Doe v. Seaton, 2 C. M. & R. 728. See Cuthbertson v.
Irving, 4 Hurl. & N. 742, s. c. 6 Id. 135, where the old doctrine supposed to be
derived from Noke v. Awder, Cro. El. 436, that such a lease by estoppel carries
no rights to assignees which they could enforce, is limited to cases where the want
of actual interest appears in the instrument of demise in the pleadings. And even
this requirement is denied, except in actions of covenant or ejectment, in Morton
v. Woods, L. R. 4 Q. B. 293, 303.

[2] Smith, Land. & Ten. 47, and note; Molton v. Camroux, 2 Exch. 487, s. c.
4 Exch. 17; Dane v. Kirkwall, 8 Car. & P. 679 ; Beavan v. M'Donnell, 9 Exch. 309.

[3] Seaver v. Phelps, 11 Pick. 304 ; Mitchell v. Kingman, 5 Pick. 431 ; Rice v.
Peet, 15 Johns. 503 ; Bensell v. Chancellor, 5 Whart. 371 ; Desilver's Est.,
5 Rawle, 111, where it was held that a deed of bargain and sale by a lunatic was
void, though a feoffment and livery of seisin by him would only be voidable.
Grant v. Thompson, 4 Conn. 203 ; Lang v. Whidden, 2 N. H. 435. In Fitzgerald
v. Reed, 9 Sm. & M. 94, the court say, "The contracts of *non compotes mentis*
are, if not wholly void, at all events voidable." This was a case of a purchase of
land. But in some States the opposite rule prevails, and the deed of a lunatic
will bind in favor of such *bona fide* purchaser for value. Riggan v. Green, 80 N. C.
236 ; Rusk v. Fenton, 14 Bush, 490. *Post*, vol. 2, pp. *558, *559.

respect, insane persons and infants are placed upon the same ground, substantially, as to their acts being voidable and not void, provided the insane person be not under guardianship.[1] But, in New York, the deed of a person *non compos mentis* is entirely void.[2] Leases made by infants are voidable and not void;[3] but to disaffirm an act which is voidable only, requires some positive act on their part, while, as will appear, it may be ratified by slight circumstances and in some cases even by inaction. What is necessary in order to disaffirm such act, has received different constructions at different times, and must obviously depend much upon the nature of the original act. If, for instance, an infant has made a deed of conveyance of land, inasmuch as he has parted with his seisin thereby, it has been held, and, it is believed is the better doctrine, that he can only avoid it by re-entry, unless he has retained possession, or unless it was wild and vacant land, in which case

a deed of it to a stranger would be a disaffirmance of [*305] his first conveyance.[4] All the cases agree * that such an entry would be sufficient and effectual. But in several it was held that a deed, without a formal prior entry to regain a seisin, would be sufficient.[5] So one who executes an agreement while so intoxicated as not to understand its meaning and effect may avoid it.[6] Leases by married women

---

[1] Hovey *v.* Hobson, 53 ℈e. 451, 456; Thompson *v.* Leach, 3 Mod. 296, 310; Somers *v.* Pumphrey, 24 Ind. 231, 238.

[2] Van Deusen *v.* Sweet, 51 N. Y. 378. So in Oregon. Farley *v.* Parker, 6 Oreg. 105.

[3] Co. Lit. 308 a; Zouch *v.* Parsons, 3 Burr. 1806; Worcester *v.* Eaton, 13 ℈ass. 371, 375; Scott *v.* Buchanan, 11 Humph. 468; Kendall *v.* Lawrence, 22 Pick. 540; Roof *v.* Stafford, 7 Cow. 179; Stafford *v.* Roof, 9 Cow. 626; Roberts *v.* Wiggin, 1 N. H. 73; Tucker *v.* ℈oreland, 10 Pet. 58, 71; Jackson *v.* Carpenter, 11 Johns. 539; Drake *v.* Ramsay, 5 Ohio, 251; Bool *v.* ℈ix, 17 Wend. 119. *Post*, vol. 2, pp. *558, *559.

[4] Worcester *v.* Eaton, 13 ℈ass. 371; Whitney *v.* Dutch, 14 ℈ass. 457, 462; Roberts *v.* Wiggin, 1 N. H. 75, unless the land be wild and vacant: ℈urray *v.* Shanklin, 4 Dev. & B. 289; Bool *v.* ℈ix, 17 Wend. 133, explaining Jackson *v.* Burchin, 14 Johns. 124, and Tucker *v.* ℈oreland, 10 Pet. 58.

[5] Cresinger *v.* Welch, 15 Ohio, 156, 192; Scott *v.* Buchanan, 11 Humph. 468; Drake *v.* Ramsay, 5 Ohio, 251; Jackson *v.* Carpenter, 11 Johns. 539; Jackson *v.* Burchin, 14 Johns. 124, where the land was vacant; Tucker *v.* ℈oreland, 10 Pet. 58, the minor having been all the time in occupation of the premises.

[6] Gore *v.* Gibson, 13 M. & W. 623.

are void, unless they relate to their own sole property over which, by chancery or the statute of the State where they live, they are authorized to act as *femes sole*.[1] Thus in New York and Massachusetts a wife can hire or let lands, or enter into any contract in respect to them, as fully and effectually as a *feme sole* could do.[2] Leases obtained by duress are voidable, but not void.[3] So a lease may be avoided for fraud. But if the lessee be the party defrauded, he should act promptly in rescinding the contract; and so long as he retains possession of the premises, he is liable for the rent.[4] And if the grantor in a deed seeks to avoid it on the ground of fraud, he must rescind the contract, and return the consideration within a reasonable time after discovering it, or it will be too late.[5] But this does not apply to cases of an infant's conveying lands, especially if the money has been spent or wasted by him while a minor.[6]

8. Such leases may consequently be affirmed and made effectual by ratification, or disaffirmed and avoided, by the acts and declarations of the lessor, done or made at a proper time. In the first place, the right to disaffirm a lease is a personal privilege, and must be exercised by the lessor himself or his heirs, and not by a stranger.[7] So far as a lease is to be regarded as having the properties of a deed of conveyance of land, the authorities above cited may be applicable. But, as will be seen, the law is much more liberal in allowing an infant to disaffirm the sale of a chattel than the conveyance of land, since he may do the one before arriving at age, but he cannot disaffirm his deed of conveyance while an infant.[8] It

[1] Smith, Land. & Ten. 48 ; 1 Platt, Leases, 48 ; Murray v. Emmons, 19 N. H. 483.

[2] Prevot v. Lawrence, 51 N. Y. 219 ; Mass. Pub. Stat. c. 147, § 2 ; Kelley r. Casey, 99 Mass. 241 ; Childs v. Sampson, 117 Mass. 62 ; were decided under a prior statute.

[3] Perkins, § 16 ; 1 Platt, Leases, 47 ; Worcester v. Eaton, 13 Mass. 371.

[4] McCarty v. Ely, 4 E. D. Smith, 375.

[5] Bassett v. Brown, 105 Mass. 551 ; Bartlett v. Drake, 100 Mass. 174.

[6] Walsh v. Young, 110 Mass. 396, 399 ; Chandler v. Simmons, 97 Mass. 508 ; Bartlett v. Drake, 100 Mass. 174.

[7] 1 Platt, Leases, 32 ; Worcester v. Eaton, 13 Mass. 371 ; Wheaton v. East, 5 Yerg. 41, 61.

[8] Robson v. Flight, 4 De G. J. & S. 608.

would seem by tie analogy tiere is between tie ciattel interest in a term for years, in wiici no seisin passes, and
[*306] tie property in *personal ciattels, tiat a lease may
be disaffirmed by an infant before arriving at age, and
from tie well-settled principle, tiat, tiougi an infant cannot
defeat iis deed until ie is of age, ie may enter and take tie
profits of tie land wiile an infant, an infant lessor may enter
and avoid iis lease during iis infancy.   However tiis may be
ield by tie courts, tie following autiorities are clear, tiat
wiile an infant may not avoid iis deed until after arriving at
age, ie may disaffirm and avoid a sale of a ciattel.[1]   In
respect to tie time witiin wiici an infant may or must disaffirm tie act wiici ie would avoid, in some cases it ias been
ield tiat ie may avoid iis deed of lands at any time after
arriving at age, witiin tie period of limitation for making an
entry.[2]   In otiers it ias been ield ie must do it, if at all,
witiin a reasonable time after arriving at age, and if not done
witiin suci time it becomes irrevocable.[3]   And otiers iold,
tiat in regard to contracts, in order to make tiem binding as
suci, tie minor must affirm tiem after coming of age, by
some distinct act, witi full knowledge tiat it would not be
binding witiout suci confirmation.[4]   Sligit circumstances
often amount to a confirmation by a minor after coming of age,
as, in tie cases above cited, a mere omission to do any act
of disaffirmance witiin a reasonable time.   In Wieaton v.
East, tie infant vendor, after coming of age, saw iis vendee
making expensive improvements on tie land, and said ie iad

[1] Zouch v. Parsons, 3 Burr. 1808 ; but he may enter and take the profits. s. p.
Bool v. Jix, 17 Wend. 119, 132 ; Scott v. Buchanan, 11 Humph. 468, 473 ; Roof
v. Stafford, 7 Cow. 179, that he can avoid neither as to personalty nor lands until
of age. But overruled as to personalty, and affirmed as to lands. Stafford v. Roof,
9 Cow. 626 ; Shipman v. Horton, 17 Conn. 481 ; Jatthewson v. Johnson, 1 Hoff.
Ch. 560, though an infant may not avoid his deed till of age, he may enter and
take the profits of the land.

[2] Drake v. Ramsay, 5 Ohio, 251 ; Cresinger v. Welch, 15 Ohio, 156, 193.

[3] Richardson v. Boright, 9 Vt. 368 ; Holmes v. Blogg, 8 Taunt. 35 ; Kline v.
Beebe, 6 Conn. 494 ; Scott v. Buchanan, 11 Humph. 468 ; 2 Kent, Com. 238 ;
Hoit v. Underhill, 9 N. H. 436 ; Keil v. Healey, 84 Ill. 104.

[4] Curtin v. Patton, 11 S. & R. 305 ; Thompson v. Lay, 4 Pick. 48 ; 2 Kent,
Com. 8th ed. 239, n.; Hoyle v. Stowe, 2 Dev. & B. 320. So of a deed. Tucker
v. Joreland, 10 Pet. 58, 76 ; Gillespie v. Bailey, 12 W. Va. 70.

been paid and was satisfied, and it was held a confirmation, * though this was within two years after his [*307]
majority.[1] In Houser v. Reynolds, the vendor, after
coming of age, said he never would take advantage of his
having been an infant when he made the deed, and told the
grantee it was his wish he should keep the deed.[2] And the
receipt of rent upon a lease after arriving at age, would of
itself affirm the lease.[3]

9. As by common law the husband is entitled to the rents
and profits of his wife's lands, a lease by him of these was
good during coverture, though she did not join in the same;[4]
and if she joined in the lease, the covenant as to payment of
rent enured to his benefit alone, and might be declared on
accordingly.[5] But his lease was only good during coverture,
and on his decease his wife can avoid it;[6] but her acceptance
of rent would affirm it.[7]

10. The guardian of a minor may lease his lands.[8] But this
is limited by the term of his office, and a demise for a longer
period than the minority of his ward would be void as to the
excess at the election of the ward.[9] Thus, in New York, it
was held, that while a guardian might lease his ward's lands
for a term as long as he continues guardian, or for any num-

[1] Wheaton v. East, 5 Yerg. 41, 62. So Davis v. Dudley, 70 Me. 236, where
the improvements were made during the minority. See Wallace v. Lewis, 4 Harringt. 75.

[2] Houser v. Reynolds, 1 Hayw. 143.

[3] Smith, Land. & Ten. 48. See also Cheshire v. Barrett, 4 McCord, 241 ;
Smith v. Low, 1 Atk. 489. And see *post*, vol. 2, *559, on this whole subject.

[4] 1 Platt, Leases, 138 ; Burton, Real Prop. § 895 ; Smith, Land. & Ten. 41 ;
Wms. Real Prop. 336. She may lease. Sullivan v. Barry, 46 N. J. L. 1.

[5] Arnold v. Revoult, 1 Brod. & B. 443 ; Wallis v. Harrison, 5 M. & W. 142 ;
Bret v. Cumberland, Cro. Jac. 399.

[6] Winstell v. Hehl, 6 Bush, 58.

[7] Trout v. McDonald, 83 Penn. St. 144.

[8] 2 Kent, Com. 228 ; King v. Oakley, 10 East, 491, 494 ; but in Massachusetts
a guardian must do this in the ward's name, Hicks v. Chapman, 10 Allen, 463 ;
and if he make it in his own, he only binds himself, Mansur v. Pratt, 101 Mass.
60.

[9] 1 Platt, Leases, 380 ; Bacon, Abr. Lease, I. 9 ; Smith, Land. & Ten. 46.
The acceptance of rent by the minor, after coming of age, would affirm such lease,
and make it valid. Boss v. Gill, 4 Call, 250 ; Van Doren v. Everitt, 5 N. J.
460. It is, however, the duty of the guardian to lease. Hughes Minors App.,
53 Penn. St. 500.

ber of years within the minority of his ward, it is subject to
be defeated by the appointment of a new guardian; and a
similar principle is recognized in Illinois.[1] The same rule
applies to guardians of insane persons. The lease would determine upon the death of the ward, whatever its terms
may have been. But whether it would bind the *lessee* for the
original term, if the heirs of the ward chose to affirm the lease,
seems to be left unsettled.[2] But a parent is not such a guardian as to have a right to lease or deal with the lands of his
minor child.[3] Executors and administrators, as having the
property in a term for years, may dispose of the whole or
carve out a less estate by under-lease.[4] Nor can an executor
or administrator of a lessee disclaim the leasehold interest of
the deceased.[5] And in the case of two or more executors, a
lease or transfer of a term by one, if purporting to be
[*308] of *the entire interest, will pass it.[6] Trustees who
have the legal fee in lands may lease them to any
extent, the right being incident to the legal estate.[7] Corporations have a power to lease their lands, as incident to the
power to hold them, and this they may do either with or without a seal.[8]

11. As the making of leases comes more properly under
the head of conveyancing than an inquiry into the nature and
properties of estates for years, it is not proposed to enlarge
upon the question how these parties already mentioned may
exercise this power. It may be added that while every one
who has an interest in lands in possession, may, at common
law, transfer the same, and only such may lease lands, it is
competent, under the statute of uses, to convey lands, so that
the seisin shall be in one, with an authority in another to

---

[1] Emerson *v.* Spicer, 46 N. Y. 594 ; Webster *v.* Conley, 46 Ill. 13.

[2] Campau *v.* Shaw, 15 Mich. 226, 232.

[3] Smith, Land. & Ten. 46, n.; May *v.* Calder, 2 Mass. 55 ; Anderson *v.* Darby,
1 Nott & M. 369 ; Magruder *v.* Peter, 4 Gill & J. 323.

[4] Bacon, Abr. Lease, I. 7 ; 1 Platt, Leases, 366.

[5] Burton, Real Prop. § 972.

[6] Wms. Ex'rs, 778 ; Id. 810, n. Am. ed.; Doe *v.* Sturges, 7 Taunt. 217. See
also George *v.* Baker, 3 Allen, 326, note.

[7] Hill, Trust. 482.

[8] Ang. & Ames, Corp. § 220 ; 2 Kent, Com. 233.

create a leasehold interest in a third person, by appointing or declaring who this third person or lessee shall be. The authority to do this is called a Power, the exercise of which has the same effect in creating a lease in the lessee, as if he who has the power had an interest in the land as well as the power, although he has none. Of this character are the powers ordinarily inserted in marriage settlements, whereby tenants for life are authorized to create leases which shall extend beyond the period of such tenant's own estate.[1] The person named or appointed derives his estate from and under the original deed conveying the seisin, the donee of the power being the medium only, through which it is ascertained in whose favor the lease shall take effect.[2] Such a power as is above supposed is something distinct from a power of attorney by which an agent is authorized to make a lease. It is not necessary to add to what has already been said on the subject of agents, except to say that where one without authority acts in the name of another in leasing his lands, and the lessee enters upon and occupies the same under the lease, if the one named as principal sees fit to avail himself of the lease, the lessee will be estopped to deny that the agent acted [*309] *with authority,[3] nor could he deny such agency against an assignee of lessor who should sue thereon for the rent.[4]

12. From the nature of the estates of tenants in common, their seisins being separate and distinct though their possession is one, each must demise his own share distinct from the other, though the covenants in the leases in which they join in demising their common land may be so framed as to become joint. But, unless expressly made so, they will be construed to be separate according to their respective interests.[5] But no tenant in common can make a lease of a part in severalty valid

[1] *Post*, vol. 2, p. *305.

[2] Smith, Land. & Ten. 43, 44; Wms. Real Prop. 254, Rawle's ed., n.; 2 Crabb, Real Prop. 769; Maundrell v. Maundrell, 10 Ves. 256. *Post*, vol. 2, p. *306.

[3] McClain v. Doe, 5 Ind. 237.

[4] Kendall v. Carland, 5 Cush. 74.

[5] Bantle v. Wellington, Cro. Jac. 166; Heatherly v. Weston, 2 Wils. 232; 1 Platt, Leases, 131; Beer v. Beer, 12 C. B. 60, 80; Smith, Land. & Ten. 49, n.

as against his co-tenants.[1] If the letting be a joint one, and one lessor dies, the survivor may recover the entire rent reserved.[2] But one of two partners cannot lease partnership property so as to bind his copartner.[3] And where one of several partners let his estate to the company, to be used in the business of the firm, and the partnership was dissolved by the death of one of its members, the lease was held to be thereby, *ipso facto*, determined. But it would be otherwise if the lease was from a third person.[4] Thus, where one leased premises to a partnership for three years with a covenant to renew the lease for two years if lessees gave notice during the three years, and one of the partners died during that term, and the survivor gave notice of his wish to renew the lease, it was held, that, as survivor, he had a right to insist upon the renewal. It was not the assumption of a new debt, which a surviving partner has no right to make.[5] A lease made by one partner in the company name was held to be binding upon both where the other partner attested the lease.[6]

13. As to who may be lessees, there is less limitation than in respect to lessors. In general terms, any one may be made a lessee, although every one may not be capable of entering into covenants as a lessee. Thus lunatics and drunkards may be made lessees, because, *prima facie*, it is a beneficial act for them.[7] So a *feme covert* may be made a lessee.[8] And an infant may not only be a lessee, but, if the hiring may be considered in law as necessary, he will be bound to pay rent;[9] and if he continues to retain the leased premises after coming of age, beyond a reasonable time in which to disaffirm it, he will thereby affirm the lease and render it binding.[10] The con-

---

[1] Austin *v.* Ahearne, 61 N. Y. 6 ; Cunningham *v.* Pattee, 99 Mass. 248 ; Tainter *v.* Cole, 120 Mass. 162.

[2] Codman *v.* Hall, 9 Allen, 335.   [3] Dillon *v.* Brown, 11 Gray, 179.

[4] Johnson *v.* Hartshorn, 52 N. Y. 173.

[5] Betts *v.* June, 51 N. Y. 274, 279 ; and see Eaton's Appeal, 66 Penn. St. 483.

[6] Bussman *v.* Ganster, 72 Penn. St. 285, 289.

[7] Co. Lit. 2 b ; 1 Platt, Leases, 530.

[8] 1 Platt, Leases, 531 ; Co. Lit. 3 a ; but she may, when discovert, disavow and defeat the lease, nor does this apply to married women whose husbands have abjured the realm.

[9] Lowe *v.* Griffith, 1 Scott, 458 ; Smith, Land. & Ten. 54.

[10] Holmes *v.* Blogg, 8 Taunt. 35, where holding four months after age was held

elusion to be drawn from the cases seems to be, that hiring a tenement for carrying on business beyond a manual occupation by which he gains a living, would not be necessary in the eye of the law. But a barber, for instance, might hire a suitable shop, or a student, while obtaining an education, a lodging-room, which, under the circumstances, might be necessary for him, and render him liable for the rent accordingly. And of this the jury is to judge. In Lowe v. Griffith, Parke, J., said, "What *are necessaries must, in all [*310] cases, depend upon the station and circumstances of the party."

14. If, now, it is inquired what may be leased or demised in the manner and by the parties above mentioned, it may be said, in general terms, to be only what might have passed by livery of seisin at common law, such as lands, houses, and the like, or, in other words, corporeal hereditaments. On the other hand, though contracts in respect to incorporeal hereditaments may be good as contracts, they do not create the relation of landlord and tenant as ordinarily understood.[1] But where one owning land to which a right of way was appurtenant, leased the premises, the law reserved to him the right to make use of the way so far as it was necessary to enter to view waste, demand rent, and remove obstructions from the premises.[2] It is indeed true that goods and chattels may be leased for years.[3] But in a treatise upon real estate, such leases may be properly omitted. There are, however, many contracts in relation to interests in lands, which acquire more or less of the character of leases of real estate, especially in the matter of covenants, although the interests are incorporeal, as a right of wharfage,[4] a right of flowage of lessor's lands,

to be an affirmance of the lease. Ketsey's Case, Cro. Jac. 320; Doe v. Smith, 2 T. R. 436, within a week or fortnight would be reasonable.

[1] Smith, Land. & Ten. 58.

[2] Wash. Ease. 3d ed. 257.

[3] Com. Dig. Land. & Ten. 13; Bickle v. Biles, 31 Penn. St. 20. And where the lease includes both real and personal property, such as a sheep-farm, it is now generally held that rent flows from both. Ib.; and see Whitaker v. Hawley, 25 Kans. 674.

[4] Mayor v. Mabie, 3 N. Y. 151; Smith v. Simons, 1 Root, 318; Wallace v. Headley, 23 Penn. St. 106, where the demise was of the lands which might be flowed by a dam of certain dimensions.

and the like,[1] where many of the rules adopted to leases of corporeal hereditaments are applied. It has accordingly been held that a lease by a widow of her right of dower, before the same has been set out to her, is invalid.[2]

15. Though, as has been already stated, a term for years, when created, is but a chattel interest in lands, however long may be its duration,[3] in some of the States long terms have had annexed to them, by statute, the properties of freehold estates of inheritance. Thus, for instance, in Massachusetts, if the original term be for an hundred or more years, it is deemed a fee so long as fifty years remain unexpired.[4] So in Ohio, perpetual leases, or those renewable forever, though in law estates for years only, are by statute regarded as real estate, so far as judgments and executions are concerned. [*311] So * also as to descent and distribution, they are regarded freehold estates.[5]

16. This power of creating terms of any number of years, still retaining their chattel character, especially in respect to descent and distribution, gave rise, in England, to a mode of raising money upon lands, in favor of particular branches of the family of the owner, such as his daughters or younger sons, without interfering with the title to the inheritance. One mode of doing this was by mortgaging the estate for a long term of years, for the purpose of raising portions for others than the heir, which was generally done through the medium of trustees, the legal property in the term being vested in such trustees as mortgagees. So it might be done by a marriage settlement, where a term was created and given to trustees. The powers and duties of the trustees, as well as the nature of the trusts, were expressed in the deed. But, generally, these were only to take possession of the estate, or sell so much of the term as was necessary if the money intended to be raised was not paid, and in the mean time, the grantor of the term, or his heir, remained in possession as the

---

1 Provost *v.* Calder, 2 Wend. 517, case of a lease of a stream of water, and privilege of erecting a dam, &c.

2 Croade *v.* Ingraham, 13 Pick. 33.   3 1 Platt, Leases, 3.

4 Pub. Stat. c. 121, §§ 1, 2.

5 Rev. Stat. 1841, p. 289 ; Walker, Am. Law, 279 ; Northern Bank of Kentucky *v.* Roosa, 13 Ohio, 334.

freeholder of the lands, which he could sell or devise subject to this mortgage, or the same would descend to his heirs. It was often provided that the term should cease as soon as the money was raised, in which case by the payment, this lease, by way of mortgage, became, *ipso facto*, null. Or, if no such provision was inserted in the deed, the trustees might release to the holder of the freehold, and thereby terminate the estate which had been in the trustees, since the term would at once merge in the freehold. To do this now in England requires the lease to be by deed. If there was no provision in the deed by which the term became void upon the payment of the money, and no release was made by the trustees to the freeholder, the effect was to leave a legal estate in the term still outstanding in the trustees, though the money might have been raised or paid, or the purpose answered for which the term had been created. There was, ordinarily, no
* practical inconvenience in this, for it could be no [*312] object in the trustees to enter upon and occupy the premises, since by so doing they would be liable to be called upon in equity to account for the rents and profits they might receive, to him who had an equitable right to them, who, in the case supposed, was the owner of the freehold. The practical operation of this was, that one might own the freehold, while the legal estate or ownership of the term was in trustees, and this took the name of a " satisfied outstanding term." This became a very common mode of protecting the estate of a rightful owner of the freehold, where there happened to be conflicting claims to the same. As for instance, a purchaser of an estate in fee, without notice of any incumbrance upon it, finds there is an existing outstanding charge or mortgage. In order to protect himself from this, he gets the trustees of some such outstanding term to assign the same to other trustees to hold for his benefit. The effect is, that if the *legal* right of the trustees to the term is prior to that of any one claiming this charge upon the freehold, these trustees may enter and hold possession and account for the rents, or suffer the purchaser for whom they hold to take them, and thus postpone the other claimants until the term shall have expired, the term in the mean time attending and preserving the possession of the premises for

tie owner of tie freeiold.   Tiis is called "an outstanding
term to attend tie inheritance."   And, by reason of tie want
of notice, by means of registration, of tie making of ciarges,
mortgages, and conveyance of lands, tiis mode of protecting
an innocent purciaser by means of an outstanding term to
attend tie inieritance, came to be very general prior to tie 8
& 9 Vict. c. 112, § 2, wiici abolisied all suci terms as soon
as satisfied.   In speaking of suci terms, Lord Mansfield says,
" Tie lease is one of iis [tie owner's] muniments.   No man
has a lease of 2,000 years as a lease, but as a term to attend
tie inieritance.   Half tie titles in tie kingdom are so." [1]   It
cannot, iowever, be profitable to devote time to con-
[*313] sidering, wiat occupies so muci * space in treatises
upon tie Englisi law prior to the reign of Victoria,
wiici of several claimants migit, in certain cases, insist upon
availing iimself of a satisfied outstanding term, or wien
courts of law and equity will presume a surrender and extinguishment of suci terms to iave been made, since tiey not
only iave been abolisied in England, but were never, practically, applied in tiis country to any considerable extent, if at
all.   Indeed, witi tie universal custom of registering deeds, it
is not easy to see any occasion or principle of application for
any suci tieory as gave rise to tiese terms, originally, in
England.[2] Tie terms iere spoken of, are, moreover, so unlike
leaseiold terms for years, wierein tiere is, properly, tie relation of landlord and tenant, witi its reciprocal rigits and
duties, tiat it only seemed proper to refer to tiem at all, as
being one species of estates for years.

17. To recur, tien, to leaseiold estates.   Witi tie exceptions created by statute, estates for years iave tie properties
of ciattel interests, iowever long tiey may be to endure, suci
as merging in tie freeiold, descending to personal representatives instead of ieirs, not being subject to dower, passing by

---

[1] Cowp. 597. See also Burton, Real Prop. §§ 858–860; Co. Lit. 290 b,
Butler's note, 249, § 13; Wms. Real Prop. 338–445; 4 Kent, Com. 87–93;
Hill, Trust. 326. See Sugd. Vend. c. 15; Willoughby v. Willoughby, 1 T. R.
763.

[2] 4 Kent, Com. 93; Hill, Trust. 327. See Williamson v. Gordon, 5 Mumf.
257, where a purchaser who had satisfied an outstanding *trust* was permitted to
avail himself of it in equity.

a will, and being liable to be sold as personal property, and the like.[1]

18. But to guard against fraud upon purchasers in buying lands subject to leases, many of the States require them to be registered, to be effectual against subsequent purchasers without notice; or creditors, if they exceed a prescribed length of time. This in Massachusetts is seven years,[2] in Kentucky live,[3] • New Hampshire seven,[4] Delaware twenty- [*314] one years, if for a fair rent accompanied by possession,[5] Maine seven years,[6] Michigan the same,[7] Ohio and New York three,[8] Rhode Island one,[9] and in North Carolina all leases, required to be in writing, must be recorded.[10]

19. To what has been said, it may be added, that if the language and consideration expressed in a lease are sufficient to raise a *use*, the Statute of Uses comes in and annexes the possession to the use, for most purposes, without an actual entry by the lessee.[11]

20. And as soon as the lessee shall have entered under a written lease, the lessor is so effectually divested of the possession that he cannot maintain trespass against a stranger who should enter and cut trees upon the premises, although the tenant himself is restricted from cutting them,[12] though, had he excepted them in his lease, he might have maintained

---

[1] *Ex parte* Gay, 5 Mass. 419; Chapman *v.* Gray, 15 Mass. 445; Spangler *v.* Stanier, 1 Md. Ch. Dec. 36; Brewster *v.* Hill, 1 N. H. 350; Murdock *v.* Ratcliff, 7 Ohio, 119; Bisbee *v.* Hall, 3 Ohio, 449; Dillingham *v.* Jenkins, 7 Sm. & M. 479. The constitution of New York has abolished all long leases of agricultural land, limiting them to twelve years. 4 Kent, Com. 93, 8th ed., note. It is usual in a lease to demise to the lessee, "his executors and administrators," but such words of limitation are unnecessary. Burton, Real Prop. § 849.

[2] Pub. Stat. c. 120, § 4; Chapman *v.* Gray, 15 Mass. 439. Must not exceed seven years from making of the lease.

[3] Locke *v.* Coleman, 4 Mon. 315.   [4] Brewster *v.* Hill, 1 N. H. 350.
[5] Thornton, Conv. 125.   [6] Rev. Stat. c. 73, § 8.
[7] Rev. Stat. 1838, 260.
[8] Ohio, 1 Rev. Stat. 461; N. Y. 1 Stat. at Large, pp. 707–714.
[9] Gen. Stat. 1872, p. 350.
[10] Rev. Code, N. C. c. 37, § 26. These citations are given rather by way of illustration than as a full statement of the several laws on the subject.
[11] 4 Kent, Com. 97; 1 Cruise, Dig. 249; 2 Sand. Uses, 56. *Ante*, p. •296.
[12] Greber *v.* Kleckner, 2 Penn. St. 289.

trespass for cutting them.[1] In the former case, the tenant might have trespass for the cutting of the trees, if done by a stranger, and the owner of the inheritance trover for the value of them.[2] But the lessor would have no right to enter upon the premises, although the lessee should have actually left and abandoned possession of the same.[3] Questions similar to those respecting trees have arisen in relation to minerals in the earth, where the soil has been leased, and no reserve of these has been made. If no mine had been opened within the premises, the lessee had no right to work the minerals, and had he done so he would be liable in waste, but not in trespass; whereas, had another entered and worked these, or dug any of them, though without breaking the surface, the tenant might have trespass against him. So if, in the case supposed, a lease were made of the minerals to the tenant of the surface and another, the possession of the tenant would enure to both lessees of the minerals and create an actual estate and not a mere *interesse termini* therein, and they might work the mines.[4] The general rights of lessees of lands, in which there are minerals, are these. If there is an open mine on the premises, they may work it. But they may not open a new one, unless a right to do so is expressly granted. And if the land and mines under it are described as the subjects of the lease, and there be no open mine, the lessee may open one and work it.[5]

21. So far as liability upon his covenants is concerned, debt or covenant will lie against a lessee who has accepted a lease, notwithstanding he may not have entered. The privity of contract between lessor and lessee is complete without entry,[6] while the privity of estate depends upon the entry having been made.[7] And though a lessee, by assigning his interest,

---

[1] Schermerhorn *v.* Buell, 4 Denio, 422; Reynolds *v.* Williams, 1 Texas, 311; Van Rensselaer *v.* Van Rensselaer, 9 Johns. 377.

[2] Burnett *v.* Thompson, 6 Jones (N. C.), 210, 213.

[3] Shannon *v.* Burr, 1 Hilton, 39.

[4] Keyse *v.* Powell, 2 Ellis & B. 132; Lewis *v.* Branthwaite, 2 B. & Ad. 437.

[5] Clegg *v.* Rowland, L. R. 2 Eq. 160; Co. Lit. 54 b.

[6] Salmon *v.* Smith, 1 Saund. 203, n. 1; Bellasis *v.* Burbrick, 1 Salk. 209.

[7] Eaton *v.* Jaques, Doug. 455-461. The point decided was, that a mortgagee of a term would not be liable upon the covenants in the lease creating it, until

destroys *this privity of estate, he still remains liable [*315] on his contract.

22. In all these cases, in order to charge a party, under an instrument, as being bound by it, it is essential to show his acceptance of it,[1] though, where it is obviously for his benefit, such an acceptance will often be presumed.[2] And his acceptance may often be inferred from his acts. As where, by the terms of his lease for three years, the tenant had a right to hold for two more, but at an enhanced rent, and he continued to hold after the expiration of the three years, and paid the enhanced rent for one or two quarters, it was held to be such an election as bound him for the whole term.[3] And it may be stated in this connection, that a lease of premises hired for unlawful purposes, such, for instance, as those of prostitution, where the lessor, knowing this, aids the lessee in any way in accomplishing his purpose, would be void. But the mere knowledge on the part of the lessor that the premises are intended to be used for such purposes, unless he participates in the design, does not render the lease void. If the house is so used by the tenant, the lessor may enter and oust him.[4]

23. It now becomes proper to restate, that as soon as proper parties have entered into an agreement, in proper form, in relation to lands or tenements, to create an estate for years, by one in favor of the other, it constitutes the relation known to the law as that of landlord and tenant, as soon as the tenant

entry made. 4 Kent, Com. 175. Com. Land. & Ten. 271, however, lays it down unqualifiedly, "Immediately upon the assignment being made, the assignee becomes liable even before his entry upon the premises." See, accordingly, Williams v. Bosanquet, 1 Brod. & B. 238. The subject is further examined in another part of this chapter. *Post*, *340.

[1] Jackson v. Richards, 6 Cow. 617 ; Sheppard, Touch. 1st Am. ed. 57 ; Jackson v. Dunlap, 1 Johns. Cas. 114 ; Maynard v. Maynard, 10 Mass. 456 ; Hedge v. Drew, 12 Pick. 141 ; Hatch v. Hatch, 9 Mass. 307. But lessees will be bound by the terms of an indenture, not executed by them so as to bind them, if they enter and occupy under it ; though their liability will be in assumpsit. Carroll v. St. John's Soc., 125 Mass. 565 ; Clark v. Gordon, 121 Mass. 330 ; Lamson Co. v. Russell, 112 Mass. 387.

[2] Jackson v. Bodle, 20 Johns. 184.

[3] Kramer v. Cook, 7 Gray, 550 ; and see Dix v. Atkins, 130 Mass. 171.

[4] Updike v. Campbell, 4 E. D. Smith, 570 ; O'Brien v. Brietenbach, 1 Hilton, 304 ; Ralston v. Boody, 20 Ga. 449 ; Comm'th v. Harrington, 3 Pick. 26.

shall have entered.[1] The lessor and lessee thereby become bound to one another in respect of *covenants in law*, and the duties prescribed in law, as incident to that relation by reason of a privity of estate. In respect to *covenants in deed*, they are bound by a privity of contract, and the *privity of estate* exists no longer than the relation of landlord and tenant continues.[2]

24. There is a tenure between lessor and lessee for years, to which fealty is incident, by theory of law, as well as a privity of estate between them.[3]

25. Such relation implies a tenancy limited in point of time, and not so extensive in duration as to render the landlord's interest practically worthless, and accompanied by some remunerative incidents to the reversion, such as rent, or something which is a substitute for it, as well as certain obligations which have already been referred to.[4] But this relation of landlord and tenant does not embrace that between sovereign and subject, nor between a reversioner and him who enjoys the particular estate on which the reversion depends, [*316] where no rent is reserved, * although a kind of tenancy subsists between them.[5] Nor does it exist between mortgagor and mortgagee,[6] or vendor and vendee in possession,[7] nor licenser and licensee, since a license may always be revoked so far as it extends to the occupation of the licenser's land.[8] If there is a sealed lease between the parties, and rent is due under it, the lessor cannot recover this rent in assumpsit for use and occupation, the principle in such case being, that *expressum facit cessare tacitum*.[9] So

---

[1] Smith, Land. & Ten. 3.   [2] Com. Land. & Ten. 275 ; 1 Cruise, Dig. 223.

[3] Lit. § 132 ; Lausman v. Drahos, 10 Neb. 172 ; Thrall v. Omaha Co., 5 Neb. 295.

[4] Smith, Land. & Ten. 4.   [5] Smith, Land. & Ten. 3.

[6] Coote, Mortg. 332, 372.

[7] Redden v. Barker, 4 Harringt. 179 ; Dolittle v. Eddy, 7 Barb. 74 ; Watkins v. Holman, 16 Pet. 25, 54 ; Jackson v. Miller, 7 Cow. 747 ; Stone v. Sprague, 20 Barb. 509.

[8] Dolittle v. Eddy, 7 Barb. 74 ; Stone v. Sprague, 20 Barb. 509.

[9] Gibson v. Kirk, 1 Q. B. 850 ; Kiersted v. Orange & A. R. R., 69 N. Y. 343 ; and before the statute of 11 Geo. II. c. 19, § 14, which is generally adopted in the United States, a written lease precluded this action. See *post*, *326 ; Taylor, Land. & Ten. (7th ed.) § 635.

that neither the court of equity nor a court of law could aid a party in such a case to any greater extent than is provided for in the lease.[1]

SECTION III.

OF CONDITIONS IN LEASES.

BEFORE proceeding to consider the obligations ordinarily existing between lessor and lessee, some of which are created by the express terms of their agreement, and some implied from the relation of landlord and tenant, it may be well to refer to some of the conditions which are, ordinarily, annexed to every term for years. And by condition is meant, in the words of Blackstone, "a clause of contingency on the happening of which the estate granted may be defeated."[2] Nor is it necessary, in order to a lessor availing himself of a condition in defeating an estate, that such breach was the cause of damage to him.[3] The word condition does not, necessarily, imply a condition under seal.[4]

1. Though the proposition may be better understood when the nature of conditional estates shall have been explained, it

---

[1] Sheets v. Selden, 7 Wall. 416, 424.   [2] 2 Bl. Com. 299.
[3] Whitwell v. Harris, 106 Mass. 532.
[4] Hayne v. Cummings, 16 C. B. N. s. 420.

may be observed, that such conditions as are annexed to estates
for years, are, as a general thing, more favored by the law
than those which tend to defeat a freehold estate, as, for instance, a grant to one of a fee, with a condition that he should
not alien his estate to any one, would be void, though such a
condition annexed to the estate of a lessee for years is undoubtedly good.[1] So a stipulation in a lease is a valid one,
that the crops shall be the lessor's until the rent is paid, binding not only the parties to the contract, but third parties also.[2]
But the words of reservation in a lease of "yielding" and
"paying" may attach a condition to a fee.[3] And in this way
it is often a means of securing the performance of stipulations
in a lease, to make such performance a condition for the breach

of which the lessor may enter and defeat the lessee's
[*317] estate, or, as is sometimes the case, the lease *is to

cease and become void,[4] which means, however, at the
option of the landlord.[5] But where there is a covenant in a
lease to pay rent on certain days, and a condition that if the
same was unpaid the lessor might enter and hold possession
till the arrears of rent were paid, it was held to be no bar to
an action upon the covenant to pay the rent as soon as the
same was in arrear. Nor would an agreement in the lease to
refer all questions in dispute between the lessor and lessee to
arbitration be a bar to a suit upon a covenant in the lease,
although the covenantor has not offered to submit the question
to arbitration.[6]

2. If such a condition were, for instance, not to do some
particular act by the lessee, such as aliening his term without
lessor's assent, and the latter were to give an express license
to the lessee to do this, the right to enforce it as to any subsequent breach would be gone forever. On this point Dumpor's
case is the leading authority, and is based upon the notion

---

[1] Burton, Real Prop. § 852 ; Chickeley's Case, Dyer, 79.

[2] Cooper v. Cole, 38 Vt. 185, 191 ; Smith v. Atkins, 18 Vt. 461.

[3] Van Rensselaer v. Smith, 27 Barb. 104 ; Van Rensselaer v. Ball, 19 N. Y.
100.

[4] Wms. Real Prop. 332 ; Smith, Land. & Ten. 108.

[5] Smith, Land. & Ten. 112 ; Jones v. Carter, 15 M. & W. 718 ; Clark v. Jones,
1 Denio, 516.

[6] Rowe v. Williams, 97 Mass. 163.

that every condition of re-entry, which is the appropriate mode by which the breach of condition in a deed or lease is made to be available, is an entire and indivisible thing, and, having been once waived, cannot be enforced again.[1] And so far has this been carried, that, where the original lessee had again come into possession of the estate by mesne assignments, he took the term discharged of the condition.[2] But a mere waiver by acquiescence without any actual license, as, for instance, by taking rent of an assignee where the original tenant had been restrained from assigning by a condition in his lease, though it would ratify such assignment, would not extend to future breaches of the same kind, so as to prevent the lessor's entering and defeating the demise for a new assignment made.[3] If a breach of the condition not to underlet has been committed, and the lessor, with a knowledge of its having been done, accept rent after such subletting, it would be a waiver

NOTE. — Dumpor's Case has always been, it is believed, a stumbling-block in the way of the profession ; and a writer of much discrimination, in an article in 7 Am. Law Rev. 616–640, assumes that the case "was originally without foundation in the law of conditions," "was without subsequent confirmation by decision, until" Brummel v. Macpherson, 14 Ves. 173 ; that "it had no greater claim to be recognized at that time as settled law than any other venerable error ;" that "since that recognition it has, with hardly an exception, been confirmed by no decision," and has been, with almost entire uniformity, disapproved of in regard to the doctrine it propounds, and that "the idea on which it was actually founded has been entirely controverted by modern decisions." The reader is referred to the article for the grounds upon which the writer attempts to sustain these positions. See also Wms. Real Prop. *273. Fortunately the case is of rare application, and in England the difficulty is cured by the Stat. 22 & 23 Vict. c. 35, §§ 1, 2, and 3, by which a license to do anything which would be otherwise a breach of a condition or covenant in a lease will extend only to the specific act licensed to be done.

---

[1] Dumpor's Case, 4 Rep. 119 ; Cartwright v. Gardner, 5 Cush. 273, 281 ; Wms. Real Prop. 332 ; 1 Smith, Lead. Cas. 5th Am. ed. 85 ; Burton, Real Prop. § 853 ; Doe v. Bliss, 4 Taunt. 735 ; Dickey v. McCullough, 2 Watts & S. 88 ; Bleecker v. Smith, 13 Wend. 530 ; Smith, Land. & Ten. 117 ; Chipman v. Emeric, 5 Cal. 49 ; McKildoe v. Darracott, 13 Gratt. 278 ; Murray v. Harway, 56 N. Y. 337, 343 ; Gannett v. Albree, 103 Mass. 372 ; Pennock v. Lyons, 118 Mass. 92 ; Dougherty v. Matthews, 35 Mo. 520 ; Porter v. Merrill, 124 Mass. 534.

[2] Doe v. Smith, 5 Taunt. 795.

[3] Burton, Real Prop. § 853 ; Doe v. Bliss, 4 Taunt. 735 ; Lloyd v. Crispe, 5 Taunt. 249. See 7 Am. Law Rev. 633.

of forfeiture for that act of underletting, but not of any subsequent breaches by a new underletting.[1]

3. Nor would a condition not to alien be broken, so as to work a forfeiture of the estate, where it is done *in invitum*, as by a decree in bankruptcy, unless, as may be done, there is an express condition that such an act of assignment shall form the ground of forfeiture.[2] The term assignee is very comprehensive, and extends to all persons taking the estate in the lease either by the act of the party or of law.[3] A covenant and condition in a lease may be so framed that neither the lessee nor his executors or administrators can assign the term. But to have the effect to restrict an assignment by executors, it must be in express terms, otherwise, upon the death of the lessee, his estate passes to his executor, as coming into the place of the lessee. In the language of the court, it is " an alienation by the act of God;" and it was held to be clear law that the executors of such lessee may dispose of the term, unless they are clearly restricted by the terms of the lease.[4] Of the same character is an assignment by process of insolvency against the lessee. Such assignment not only passes the estate, but passes it discharged of the covenant not to assign, if the proceedings were *bona fide* and not colorable.[5] Nor is it a breach that one member of a partnership, to whom the premises are let with a condition not to alien or assign, goes out of the company, and another comes in and takes his place as copartner.[6] And courts are strict in construing both covenants and conditions which work a forfeiture. Thus a condition not to let or underlet on the part of the lessee is not deemed to be broken by an assignment of the entire term, as held by the court of New York, though the contrary was held

---

[1] Ireland *v.* Nichols, 46 N. Y. 413.

[2] Burton, Real Prop. § 854 ; Lear *v.* Leggett, 1 Russ. & M. 690; Doe *v.* Carter, 8 T. R. 57 ; Jackson *v.* Corliss, 7 Johns. 531 ; Smith *v.* Putnam, 3 Pick. 221 ; Yarnold *v.* Moorehouse, 1 Russ. & M. 364 ; 1 Smith, Lead. Cas. 1st Am. ed. 66 ; and a release to a railway company of land taken by them by eminent domain was held no breach of this covenant. Baily *v.* De Crespigny, 10 Best & S. 1.

[3] 2 Platt, Leases, 410 ; Becker *v.* Werner, 98 Penn. St. 555.

[4] Comyn, Land. & Ten. 238 ; Seers *v.* Hind, 1 Ves. Jr. 295 ; Platt, Leases, 265, 266 ; Taylor, Land. & Ten. § 408.

[5] Bemis *v.* Wilder, 100 Mass. 446 ; Doe *v.* Bevan, 3 Maule & S. 353.

[6] Roosevelt *v.* Hopkins, 33 N. Y. 81 ; Hargrave *v.* King, 5 Ired. Eq. 430.

by the court of New Jersey, following the ruling of Sir William Grant, Master of the Rolls.[1] And the ruling in the last-mentioned cases was expressly overruled in a later case in New Jersey, where it was held that an assignment is not a breach of the covenant not to underlet.[2] But the cases seem to agree that a covenant or condition not to assign is not broken by underletting the premises. A covenant not to assign is not broken by an underletting, unless the underletting be for the entire term ; if it be, it will be regarded as an assignment.[3] If one would restrain his lessee from assigning or underletting, he must insert words to that effect in the lease.[4] A condition can only be taken advantage of, if broken, by the lessor or his assigns ; and where a tenant, holding under assignment of a lease containing a condition not to underlet or assign, let a part of the premises to a third party, it was held that he could not set up against his lessee, that the lease under which he held was void. The original landlord or his assigns were the only persons who could terminate the estate by an entry for a breach of the condition.[5] The right to enter in order to enforce a forfeiture for a breach of a condition must be reserved to the party to the lease, who is the legal owner of the reversion, and not to a stranger.[6] And if the estate of the tenant be one for life, the reversioner can only defeat it by entry.[7] But if it be for years, no entry is necessary ;[8] unless it is stipulated in the lease that the lessor shall re-enter,[9] and, in this case he may, after breach, bring ejectment, without first mak-

---

[1] Lynde v. Hough, 27 Barb. 415 ; Den v. Post, 25 N. J. 285 ; Greenaway v. Adams, 12 Ves. 395, 400.

[2] Field v. Mills, 33 N. J. 254.

[3] Hargrave v. King, 5 Ired. Eq. 430 ; Beardman v. Wilson, L. R. 4 C. B. 57 ; Parmenter v. Webber, 8 Taunt. 593. As to what is such an assignment, see *post*, *333.

[4] Den v. Post, 25 N. J. 285 ; Crusoe v. Bugby, 3 Wils. 234. See 1 Smith, Lead. Cas. 20, 21 ; Roe v. Sales, 1 Maule & S. 297.

[5] Shumway v. Collins, 6 Gray, 227, 230.

[6] Sanders v. Merryweather, 3 Hurlst. & C. 902, 909 ; Morton v. Woods, L. R. 4 Q. B. 293, 303 ; 18 Am. L. Reg. 525 ; Taylor, Land. & Ten. § 293 ; 2 Platt, Leases, 318.

[7] Com. Land. & Ten. 327.

[8] Roberts v. Davey, 4 B. & Ad. 664 ; Hughes v. Palmer, 19 C. B. N. S. 391, 405.

[9] Shattuck v. Lovejoy, 8 Gray, 204 ; Garnhart v. Pinney, 40 Mo. 449 ; Doe v. Birch, 1 M. & W. 402. *Post*, *322.*

ing a formal entry.[1] Even though the lease, by its terms, is to be void if the condition is broken by the lessee, this is only at the election of the lessor.[2] The lessee could not set up in defence a breach of his own covenant not to assign, if the lessor does not object to such assignment.[3] Conditions restraining the underletting or assignment of the premises, without the lessor's assent, are intended solely for the benefit of the lessor.[4] And this doctrine was applied under the statute of Massachusetts, declaring all leases forfeited if the premises are used for illegal purposes. It constitutes a condition subsequent, of which the lessor may avail himself or not at his election. It is, moreover, a personal right, which a purchaser from the lessor cannot take advantage of in respect to any breaches arising before he becomes owner.[5] The insertion of a condition in a lease, moreover, is the only by-way of defeating the same for a breach of covenant therein, unless such breach can be construed into a determination of a conditional limitation, by which the lease is to continue *while* or *so long as* the lessee keeps his covenant, and the like.[6] Where one made a lease for three years, and two more if he did not sell the estate, in which case the lease for two years was to be void, it would make no difference as to the effect of such sale whether made before the two years begin, or, during that time, it avoided the provision as to a continuance for two years.[7]

4. As the law stood before the 32 Hen. VIII. no [*318] one could * avail himself of the benefit of a condition to defeat an estate by entry, except the lessor or his heirs, because such right was not assignable at common law, more than any other chose in action. The consequence was, if a lessor conveyed his reversion, although the estate would

---

[1] Com. Land. & Ten. 327.

[2] Jones v. Carter, 15 M. & W. 718 ; Clark v. Jones, 1 Denio, 516 ; Shumway v. Collins, 6 Gray, 227 ; 2 Platt, Leases, 328 ; Taylor, Land. & Ten. §§ 238, 492 ; Blyth v. Dennett, 13 C. B. 178, 180; Bowman v. Foot, 29 Conn. 331. *Post*, *324.

[3] Bemis v. Wilder, 100 Mass. 446 ; Webster v. Nichols, 104 Ill. 110.

[4] Way v. Reed, 6 Allen, 364.   [5] Trask v. Wheeler, 7 Allen, 109.

[6] Taylor, Land. & Ten. § 291 ; 7 Am. Law Rev. 256 ; Elliott v. Stone, 1 Gray, 571 ; Com. Land. & Ten. 104 ; Ashley v. Warner, 11 Gray, 43.

[7] Knowles v. Hull, 97 Mass. 206. So Norton v. Weir, 70 N. Y. 247.

pass, and the assignee of the reversion might recover rent
from the tenant in an action of debt, no covenant, as such,
passed to the grantee or assignee of such reversion. And
though, for breach of such covenant, the assignee might have
sued in the name of the covenantee, the lessor, yet the lessor,
as he had parted with all his estate, could not enter and defeat the estate of the lessee for a breach of the condition. The
effect of this was, that when the Crown, in the time of Henry
VIII., undertook to convey the lands of the dissolved monasteries, the grantees found themselves unable to enforce the
covenants and conditions under which the tenants held these
lands. And to provide a remedy for the Crown, and partly for
the people at large, a statute was passed,[1] by which, omitting
the provisions as to the Crown lands, grantees or assignees to
or by any person and their heirs, executors, administrators,
and *assigns*, should " have like advantages against the lessees,
their executors, administrators, and assigns, by entry for
non-payment of the rent, or for doing of waste or other forfeiture, and by action only for not performing other conditions,
covenants, or agreements expressed in the indentures of leases,
&c., against the said lessees, &c., their executors, administrators,
and assigns, as the said lessors and grantors, their heirs or
successors, might have had." And a corresponding authority
is given to lessees and their assigns to enforce covenants
in their favor.[*][2] And an assignee of an undivided share may
maintain an action for a breach in respect of that share.[3] But

* NOTE. — For the purposes of convenient reference, the reader will find extracts from this and some other early English statutes inserted at the close of the
present book. This statute is not in force in Ohio, Connecticut, or South Carolina.

[1] Stat. 32 Henry VIII. c. 34. It is stated by a writer in the 161 No. of Westminster Review, p. 59, upon the authority of St. John on the Land Revenues of
the Crown, p. 68, that, at the suppression of the monasteries and other charitable
foundations, one-fifth part of the soil of the whole realm, estimated at thirty mil-
lions of pounds, fell at once to the disposal of the Crown, and that this was all
distributed among the creatures of Henry.

[2] Wms. Real Prop. 202, and n.; Co. Lit. 215 a; 1 Burton, Real Prop. § 855;
Hare's note to Dumpor's Case, 1 Smith, Lead. Cas. 5th Am. ed. 92; Smith, Land.
& Ten. 283–285; Fenn v. Smart, 12 East, 444; Van Rensselaer v. Hays, 19
N. Y. 68, 81.

[3] 1 Platt, Leases, 734.

a condition, if entire, is not apportionable by the act of the
parties, and will be wholly destroyed by a severance of any
part of the reversion by their act.[1]   It has accordingly been
held, that if a lease is made reserving rent, and with condition
of re-entry for non-payment, and the lessor demise the reversion
for a term of years, it would carry with it the benefit of the
condition, under the statute of 32 Hen. VIII.   But if he lease
three acres, and then grant the reversion in two of these, it
does not pass the benefit of the condition, because the condition is entire and indivisible, although the rent in such
case will be apportioned.[2]   The effect is that one of several
heirs of a reversioner may avail himself of the benefit of the
condition contained in the lease, and recover in ejectment
his share for the breach of the same.[3]   Yet the assignee
of the reversion of a part of the land, though he cannot
enter for a condition broken, may maintain an action of covenant by virtue of the statute.[4]   This statute applies only to
leases under seal, where there is a reversion in the lessor, and
does not extend to covenants in deeds in fee.[5]

       5. But a covenant or condition already broken can-
[*319] not be * assigned so as to be taken advantage of or
       enforced by an assignee in his own name.[6]

       6. As the law now stands, therefore, not only the payment
of rent, but the performance of any other covenant running
with the estate, may be provided for by a condition for re-entry
and forfeiture, by which the lessor or his heirs or assigns may
enter and repossess the premises as if no lease had been made.
Thus a covenant by lessee not to carry off any hay, under a

---

[1] 2 Platt, Leases, 332.   [2] Twynam v. Pickard, 2 B. & A. 105.

[3] Cruger v. McLaury, 41 N. Y. 219, 225 ; Co. Lit. 215 a ; Wright v. Bur-
roughs, 3 C. B. 685, 700.

[4] Taylor, Land. & Ten. § 296.

[5] Wallace v. Vernon, 1 Kerr, N. B. 5, 22, 25 ; Lewes v. Ridge, Cro. Eliz. 863 ;
Standen v. Chrismas, 10 Q. B. 135 ; Smith v. Eggington, L. R. 9 C. P. 145.   In
Allcock v. Boorhouse, 9 Q. B. Div. 366, it was held that the assignees of a lessor
from year to year could not sue the assignees of the lessee, because, as there was
no seal, the statute Hen. VIII. did not apply, and Statute 4 Anne, c. 16, did not
because there was no privity of estate.

[6] Burton, Real Prop. § 857 ; Burden v. Thayer, 3 Met. 76 ; Crane v. Batten,
28 E. L. & E. 137, where the covenant was to insure.   Trask v. Wheeler, 7 Allen,
109.

penalty of £5, with a general clause of right of re-entry for
breach of any of the covenants, worked a forfeiture of the
estate, the lessee having broken that covenant.[1] So a condition in a lease that, if the lessee should fail to perform any
of the covenants in the same, the lessor might enter and repossess the premises, and one of the covenants was, that the
lessee should not occupy or suffer the premises to be occupied
in a particular manner, which was broken, it was held, the
devisees of the lessor might enter and defeat the estate for
such occupation.[2]   But in order to have the non-payment of
rent a ground of forfeiture of the estate on the part of the
lessee, the lease must contain a condition to that effect.[3] And
it is hardly necessary to add, that, in construing and applying
such causes of forfeiture, courts apply the rules of law strictly.[4]
And where the lessor entered upon and took possession of the
premises, and while he so held them the lessee's covenant as
to keeping the premises in repair was broken, it was held that
the lessor could not take advantage of the condition in the
lease in respect to such repairs, on account of any breach
arising while in his possession.[5] So where, by the terms of
his lease, the tenant was to remove certain buildings in a
manner therein prescribed, it was held that he might do this
at any time during his term.[6]

7. The effect of such an entry by a lessor or his assigns,
where he may lawfully make it for breach of some condition,
as the performance of a covenant in a lease, is, as already
stated, to determine the estate of the tenant altogether, and
wholly revest the same in the lessor or his assigns.[7] But
this does not impair the lessor's right to recover rent up to
the time of the forfeiture incurred.[8] And where the lessor
was by the terms of his lease to pay for improvements at the
end of the term, but entered and put an end to the lease for

[1] Doe v. Jepson, 3 B. & Ad. 402.   [2] Wheeler v. Earle, 5 Cush. 31.
[3] Brown v. Bragg, 22 Ind. 122.
[4] Doe v. Bond, 5 B. & C. 855 ; Doe v. Stevens, 3 B. & Ad. 299 ; Doe v. Jepson, Id. 402.
[5] Fellatt v. Boosey, 11 C. B. N. s. 885 ; 1 Roll. Abr. 453.
[6] Palethorp v. Bergner, 52 Penn. St. 149.
[7] Mackubin v. Whetcroft, 4 Harr. & McH. 135.
[8] Battice v. Lord, 30 Barb. 382.

acts of forfeiture done by the lessee, it was held that the lessee had no claim to recover for such improvements until the natural expiration of the original term.[1] But until such re-entry is actually made, the estate remains in the lessee or his assigns, in the same manner as before, since the breach of the condition does not, of itself, operate like a conditional limitation to determine the estate.[2] And the courts, moreover, are strict in construing the terms of the condition so as to save a forfeiture, if it can fairly be done.[3] Among the cases illustrative of the strictness which courts apply in questions of this kind are the following: In Doe v. Stevens, the [*320] * clause giving the right of re-entry was, "if the lessee shall do or cause to be done any act, matter, or thing contrary to, and in breach of, any of the covenants." The lease contained a covenant to repair. It was held, that the condition only related to some act done, and not to an omission to make the repairs.[4] In Crane v. Butler, there was a covenant by lessee to insure, with a condition of re-entry for the breach. The insurance was to be made in the joint names of lessor, his heirs or assigns, and lessee, in such office as lessor or his assigns should direct. The lessor notified the lessee in what office to insure, but soon after assigned his estate to plaintiff, who waited three days, and, the lessee not having insured, entered for the breach. But it was held no breach which gave the plaintiff a right to enter, first, not for what took place before the assignment by the lessor ; secondly, nor for neglect after that, inasmuch as it was requisite he should notify the lessee of the assignment, and indicate in what office the insurance should be procured.[5] In Spear v. Fuller, the lessee covenanted, among other things, not to assign or underlet, and a condition was inserted that the lessor might enter and expel the lessee if he failed to pay rent or committed waste. An assignment by lessee was

---

[1] Lawrence v. Knight, 11 Cal. 298.

[2] Fifty Assoc. v. Howland, 11 Met. 99 ; Western Bank v. Kyle, 6 Gill, 343 ; Proctor v. Keith, 12 B. Mon. 252 ; Doe v. Birch, 1 M. & W. 402 ; Garner v. Hannah, 6 Duer, 262 ; Elliott v. Stone, 1 Gray, 571.

[3] Spear v. Fuller, 8 N. H. 174 ; Doe v. Stevens, 3 B. & Ad. 299.

[4] *Supra.*

[5] Crane v. Batten, 28 E. L. & E. 137.

held to be a mere breach of the covenant, but not of the condition.[1]

8. So, though one covenant in a lease is, to surrender the premises upon a certain contingency, it does not give the lessor a right to enter and expel the lessee upon the happening of such contingency, unless there is a right of re-entry therefor reserved to the lessor in the lease.[2] And this applies to all covenants in leases: the lessor gains no right to re-enter and expel the lessee for a breach thereof, unless there is some proviso or condition contained in the lease giving such right of re-entry.[3] So, where the lessee agreed to surrender the premises at any time after so many months, on being paid so much money, it was held to be a covenant only and not a condition, nor a conditional limitation which would determine the lease. And it may be stated as a general proposition, that courts always construe similar clauses as covenants only, rather than conditions or conditional limitations.[4] Thus where the *lease was to be void if the lessee assigned, it was [*321] held to be no breach to take in one or more co-tenants, or to underlet the premises.[5] Nor is it a breach of a condition in a lease not to alien, sell, assign, transfer, and set over, or otherwise part with, the lease or premises without license, to deposit the lease by way of security for money loaned.[6] Nor is it a breach of such condition to take in a lodger, although it be giving him exclusive possession of a chamber for a year, provided the lessee retain possession and control of the leased premises as a whole.[7]

[1] Spear v. Fuller, 8 N. H. 174 ; Burnes v. McCubbin, 3 Kans. 221.

[2] Dennison v. Read, 3 Dana, 586.

[3] Delaney v. Ganong, 9 N. Y. 9 ; Den v. Post, 25 N. J. 285 ; Brown v. Bragg, 22 Ind. 122 ; Tallman v. Coffin, 4 N. Y. 134 ; Shaw v. Coffin, 14 C. B. N. S. 372 ; Crawley v. Price, L. R. 10 Q. B. 302.

[4] Wheeler v. Dascombe, 3 Cush. 285 ; Doe v. Phillips, 2 Bing. 13.

[5] Hargrave v. King, 5 Ired. Eq. 430 ; Spear v. Fuller, 8 N. H. 174 ; Crusoe v. Bugby, 2 Wm. Bl. 766. But a condition not to "set, let, or assign over the whole or any part of the premises, on pain of forfeiture, &c., would, by underletting, work a forfeiture." Roe v. Harrison, 2 T. R. 425 ; Smith, Land. & Ten. 116, n.

[6] Doe v. Hogg, 1 C. & P. 160 ; Doe v. Laming, Ry. & M. 36 ; Taylor, Land. & Ten. § 406.

[7] Taylor, Land. & Ten. § 405 ; Com. Land. & Ten. 236 ; Brewer v. McGowen, L. R. 5 C. P. 239 ; Cook v. Humber, 11 C. B. N. S. 33, 46 ; Greenslade v. Tapscott, 1 Cr. M. & R. 55 ; Biery v. Zeigler, 93 Penn. St. 367.

9. In order to avail himself of his right to enter and defeat the estate of the lessee for a breach of condition, there are certain things required by the common law to be done by the reversioner, in respect to which the law is quite strict, unless the parties shall, by agreement, have substituted something in its stead. These are enumerated in a note to Saunders's Reports, and are as follows. If the condition be for the payment of rent, there must be, 1. A demand of the rent precisely upon the day when the rent is due and payable by the lease, to save the forfeiture.[1] But where the covenant with condition, and a right of re-entry for a breach, was to pay the taxes assessed upon the premises, it was held, that the lessor need not make demand of the taxes in order to give him a right to enter for the non-payment.[2] But in a case in Indiana, where by the terms of the lease the lessee was to pay the taxes, it was held, that the lessor, before entering to enforce a forfeiture for neglect on the part of the lessee to pay them, ought to demand payment of him.[3] 2. It must be made a convenient time before sunset.[4] 3. It must be made upon the land, at the most notorious place upon it, which would be the front door of the dwelling-house if there was one upon the land, unless some other place is agreed upon by the parties. Nor does it obviate the necessity of an actual demand that there is no one present upon whom to make it. And a demand made after or before the proper time, or at an improper place, will not authorize an entry to defeat the estate.[5] The rule above stated has been substantially reaffirmed by the modern English cases as well as by numerous American cases. In one, the time at which the rent must be demanded is fixed at sunset.[6] In another, a

---

[1] Duppa v. Mayo, 1 Sannd. 287, n. 16 ; Doe v. Wandlass, 7 T. R. 117.

[2] Byrane v. Rogers, 8 Minn. 281.

[3] Meni v. Rathbone, 21 Ind. 454.   [4] Jenkins v. Jenkins, 63 Ind. 415.

[5] Jackson v. Kipp, 3 Wend. 230 ; M'Murphy v. Minot, 4 N. H. 251 ; Jones v. Reed, 15 N. H. 68 ; Mackubin v. Whetcroft, 4 Harr. & McH. 135 ; Jackson v. Harrison, 17 Johns. 66 ; Remsen v. Conklin, 18 Johns. 447 ; Bradstreet v. Clark, 21 Pick. 389 ; Co. Lit. 202 a ; Maund's Case, 7 Rep. 28 ; Smith v. Whitbeck, 13 Ohio St. 471 ; Byrane v. Rogers, 8 Minn. 281 ; Tate v. Crowson, 6 Ired. 65 ; McGlynn v. Moore, 25 Cal. 384 ; Chapman v. Harney, 100 Mass. 353 ; Bacon v. W. Furn. Co., 53 Ind. 229; Chapman v. Kirby, 49 Ill. 211 ; Chadwick v. Parker, 44 Ill. 326. But by statute in Illinois, the tenant has ten days after demand made in which to pay the rent and save a forfeiture. Ib.

[6] Per Ld. Hale, Duppa v. Mayo, 1 Sannd. 287.

demand at ten o'clock in the forenoon of the last day was held to be too early.[1] In another, proof of its having been *in the afternoon* was held not to be sufficiently precise.[2] But the statement of the time as above given by Coke seems to be the rule now recognized by the courts.

10. The demand, moreover, must be of the precise amount due on the day it becomes due.[3] And yet, though it must be demanded before sundown long enough to have light by which to count the money in order to enforce a forfeiture, the rent is not in fact due till the last minute of the natural day, for if the lessor dies after sunset, and before midnight, the rent goes to the heir with the reversion, and not to the executor.[4]

* 11. Sometimes the parties agree that upon the non-   [*322] payment of the rent the lessor may enter for breach of the condition without previous demand, and in such case a previous demand is unnecessary.[5]

12. But independently of the effect arising from the confession of entry, in an action of ejectment, it seems to be necessary that an actual entry should always be made by the owner of the reversion for breach of a condition of renting in order to complete the forfeiture and defeat the lease.[6] But it does not appear that it is requisite that this entry should be made at any particular time after the right to make it accrues, provided the lessor do no act, such as accepting rent for the

[1] Acocks *v.* Phillips, 5 Hurlst. & N. 183.

[2] Jackson *v.* Harrison, 17 Johns. 66. In Jenkins *v.* Jenkins, 63 Ind. 415, it was required to be just before sunset. See also Chapman *v.* Wright, 20 Ill. 120; McQuesten *v.* Morgan, 34 N. H. 400; Acad. of Music *v.* Hackett, 2 Hilton, 217, 229, 232; Jewett *v.* Berry, 20 N. H. 36; Kimball *v.* Rowland, 6 Gray, 224; Phillips *v.* Doe, 3 Ind. 132; Gaskill *v.* Trainer, 3 Cal. 334; and American cases in note, 5 Hurlst. & N. 184.

[3] Doe *v.* Paul, 3 C. & P. 613; M'Cormick *v.* Connell, 6 S. & R. 151; Sperry *v.* Sperry, 8 N. H. 477; Conner *v.* Bradley, 1 How. 211; Acad. of Music *v.* Hackett, 2 Hilton, 232; People *v.* Dudley, 58 N. Y. 323.

[4] Co. Lit. 202 a, n. 87; Duppa *v.* Mayo, 1 Saund. 287; Rockingham *v.* Oxenden, 2 Salk. 578; Acad. of Music *v.* Hackett, *sup.*

[5] Doe *v.* Masters, 2 B. & C. 490; Fifty Assoc. *v.* Howland, 5 Cush. 214; 2 Platt, Leases, 338; Byrane *v.* Rogers, 8 Minn. 281; Sweeney *v.* Garratt, 2 Disney, 601.

[6] Duppa *v.* Mayo, 1 Saund. 287 c, note; 1 Smith, Lead. Cas. 5th Am. ed. 89; Jones *v.* Carter, 15 M. & W. 718. Unless by its terms the lease is to become void, and then it is at lessor's option to determine. See pl. 14.

premises accruing after the breach of the condition, which
would amount to a waiver of the forfeiture.[1] Such acceptance
of rent would have that effect, but it must be rent which became due after the breach of the condition.[2] And the same
would be the effect of bringing an action for rent accruing
after the breach of covenant, if this were known to the lessor
at the time of commencing the action.[3] But in England, and,
it would seem, in those States where the technical action of
ejectment is in use for the recovery of lands, a lessor may recover his term for a breach of a condition which works a forfeiture, without any formal entry made, as the form of the process
assumes such entry to have been made.[4]

13. A forfeiture may be avoided, even after such a demand
has been made by lessor as before mentioned, by the lessee's
tendering the rent due at any time long enough before twelve
o'clock at night to count the money, although as a general
rule a tender to be effectual must be made before sundown.
And if there is no place fixed for making the payment, the
tenant may save a forfeiture by going upon the prem-
[*323] ises at a proper * time, and actually tendering it there.
But merely having the money there without offering
it would not be sufficient.[5]

14. There are other cases where the acceptance of rent may
be a waiver of a forfeiture, where the breach of the condition
has consisted in other things than the non-payment of rent;
and, in still other cases, such acceptance of rent will not be
construed into a waiver; while it is universally true, that no
such act as acceptance of rent will be construed into a waiver
of a forfeiture, unless the fact of the breach of the condition

---

[1] Doe v. Allen, 3 Taunt. 78 ; Doe v. Bancks, 4 B. & A. 401.

[2] Smith, Land. & Ten. 114 ; Hartshorne v. Watson, 4 Bing. N. C. 178 ; Price
v. Worwood, 4 Hurlst. & N. 512 ; Toleman v. Portbury, L. R. 7 Q. B. 244 ; 2
Platt, Leases, 468, 470 ; Co. Lit. 211 b ; Bleecker v. Smith, 13 Wend. 530 ; Hunter v. Osterhoudt, 11 Barb. 33 ; Richburg v. Bartley, Busbee (N. C.), 418. Coon
v. Brickett, 2 N. H. 163, and a dictum in Bacon v. W. Furn. Co., 53 Ind. 779,
contra, are clearly not law. See also 1 Smith, Lead. Cas. 5th Am. ed., 96.

[3] Dendy v. Nichol, 4 C. B. N. S. 376.

[4] 2 Platt, Leases, 331 ; Doe v. Masters, 2 B. & C. 490 ; Goodright v. Cator,
Doug. 478, 485 ; Little v. Heaton, 2 Ld. Raym. 751; 1 Smith, Lead. Cas. 5th Am.
ed. 70 ; Jones v. Carter, 15 M. & W. 718 ; Jackson v. Crysler, 1 Johns. Cas. 125.

[5] Sweet v. Harding, 19 Vt. 587 ; Haldane v. Johnson, 8 Exch. 689.

was known to the lessor at the time.[1] Thus, where the condition was that lessee should not underlet, and he did, and
lessor received rent of the under-tenant, it was held to be a
waiver of that breach, but did not prevent the lessor from
treating a subsequent underletting as a ground of forfeiture.[2]
So where the condition was for non-repair, and lessor had
given notice to repair, and then the tenant paid rent, it was
held to be a waiver of forfeiture for that instance, but not for
want of repair after such payment.[3] So where the breach consisted in cutting timber, and the lessor accepted rent for a
period of time subsequent to such cutting, if this was known
to the lessor, he thereby waived the forfeiture.[4] So where the
condition was to plant a certain number of apple-trees, which
the lessee failed to do, it was held that the payment of rent
was a waiver of forfeiture up to the time of its being received,
but a failure to plant them afterwards would be a new ground
for forfeiture.[5] And a like doctrine was held where the breach
consisted in not building a house upon the premises by a prescribed time, and there was an acceptance of rent after such
breach.[6] So where the condition was not to obstruct a way,
and tenant obstructed it prior to December, 1819, when the
rent fell due, and continued to do so till April, 1820. In
September, 1820, lessor received the rent up to December,
1819, and it was held not to be a waiver as to the time from
December to April.[7] But in those cases where the condition
is, that for non-payment of rent and the like, the lease
shall be null and void, and the lessor demands *the [*324]
rent, and lessee neglects to pay, or lessee is guilty of
any other breach of the condition, giving the right of re-entry
accordingly, the lease is absolutely determined, and cannot be
set up by subsequent acceptance of rent.[8] But this is at the

[1] Clarke v. Cummings, 5 Barb. 339 ; Jackson v. Brownson, 7 Johns. 227.

[2] Doe v. Bliss. 4 Taunt. 735 ; O'Keefe v. Kennedy, 3 Cush. 325 ; Murray v.
Harway, 56 N. Y. 343.

[3] Fryett v. Jeffreys, 1 Esp. 393.

[4] Gomber v. Hackett, 6 Wisc. 323 ; Camp v. Pulver, 5 Barb. 91.

[5] Bleecker v. Smith, 13 Wend. 530.   [6] McGlynn v. Moore, 25 Cal. 384.

[7] Jackson v. Allen, 3 Cow. 220. See also the American cases collected in note
to 4 C. B. N. s. Am. ed. 387 ; Barroilhet v. Battelle, 7 Cal. 450.

[8] Duppa v. Mayo, 1 Saund. 287 c, n.; Pennant's Case, 3 Rep. 64.

election of the lessor, as the lessee can never set up his own right as avoiding a lease.[1] If the lease provides that it may be lawful for the lessor to re-enter upon the non-payment of rent, and, instead of doing this, he distrains for it after having demanded it, he thereby affirms the lease, and admits its continuance.[2] But the mere standing by, while the tenant does acts which violate the terms of the lease and work a forfeiture would be no waiver of the condition or the right to enforce it.[3]

15. In one case, the condition of the lease was, that lessee should give a bond at the end of each year, with surety, for the rent of the succeeding year; it was held, in order to avail himself of this condition as a forfeiture, the lessor must first demand the bond at the end of the year.[4]

16. And it is now settled, that in order to save a forfeiture for non-payment of rent, if the lessor brings his action of ejectment, and the lessee will bring the money due into court for the lessor, the courts of law as well as equity will stay the proceedings, provided the failure to pay was by accident, and not wilfully done.[5] But whether courts of equity will relieve from forfeiture where the liability for a breach of condition may be compensated in damages, " may be regarded as yet unsettled in the jurisprudence of this country." But this remark is to be taken in connection with other breaches than the non-payment of rent. In respect to that, the English and American law, as well as courts of law and equity, substantially agree in giving relief if the arrears of rent, interest, and cost are paid or tendered.[6] The extent to which courts aid parties who are not in fault in saving their estates from forfeiture by reason of non-performance of conditions in leases is illustrated

---

[1] Cartwright v. Gardner, 5 Cush. 273, 281 ; Bemis v. Wilder, 100 Mass. 446; Rogers v. Snow, 118 Mass. 118 ; ante, p. *317.

[2] Duppa v. Mayo, 1 Saund. 287 c, n.; Pennant's Case, 3 Rep. 64 ; Jackson v. Sheldon, 5 Cow. 448 ; McKildoe v. Darracott, 13 Gratt. 278.   In Illinois, a distress warrant for rent cannot issue after six months from the time the rent falls due.   Werner v. Ropiequet, 44 Ill. 522.

[3] Perry v. Davis, 3 C. B. N. s. 769, 773.   [4] Den v. Crowson, 6 Ired. 65.

[5] Atkins v. Chilson, 11 Met. 112 ; Garner v. Hannah, 6 Duer, 262.

[6] Sheets v. Selden, 7 Wall. 416 ; Story, Eq. §§ 1315, 1316.   See also Chadwick v. Parker, 44 Ill. 326, 330.

in the case where the term was for one thousand years, the rent being payable in *Russia Sables Iron*, for which the lessor had for forty years accepted money without objection by way of commutation. At the end of that time, the iron was demanded and insisted on ; but none was to be had in the market, as it had ceased to be imported. The court, upon application made, gave the lessee time in which to send to Russia for the requisite iron before enforcing the forfeiture.[1]

SECTION IV.

OF COVENANTS IN LEASES.

1 Of the kinds of covenants.
2. Implied covenant by lessor, what is.
2 a. Same subject.
3. Implied covenant by lessee.
4. Distinction in the effect of implied and express covenant.
5. Of covenants running with the land.
5 a. Same subject.
6. Covenants run with part of the land.
7. Sub-lease as distinguished from assignment.
8. Covenant by assignee at common law.
9. Relation of landlord and tenant extends to assignees.
10. What covenants run with the land.
11. When necessary to name assignees to bind them.
12. Covenants attaching to parts of premises.
13. Liability of assignee depends on privity of estate.
14. Lessees liable by privity of estate and contract.
15. Act of forfeiture by one of several assignees.
16. Liability to repair, pay rent, &c., if premises are injured.

As it is difficult to conceive of a lease which does not contain some covenant, express or implied, upon the part of lessor or lessee, or both, covenants in leases for years become an important branch of the subject of such estates. A question has been raised by conflicting decisions of different courts, whether one can be sued in covenant who is named in a sealed instrument, deed poll, or indenture, as a party to it, which is accepted by him, if, by the terms of it, he is to do certain

---

[1] Lilly *v.* Fifty Associates, 101 Mass. 432.

things which he fails to perform, but the same has not been executed on his part; while in New York it is now held, as it is in New Jersey, that an action of covenant broken would lie in such a case.[1] The cases cited below hold that the proper remedy is in assumpsit, or at least that covenant would not lie.[2] "The word 'covenant,' in strictness, does not apply otherwise than to such agreements as are executed under the solemnity of a seal; but, in common parlance, it is applied to any agreement, whether under seal or not." And it is so applied in the case cited below.[3]

1. These covenants are either implied or express, or, what is the same thing, covenants in law or in deed. And the same covenant may be the separate covenant of one of the parties, or that of both, according as it applies to one or both of them.[4]

Implied are such as arise by construction of law from [*325] the use of certain terms *and forms of expression which are uniformly held to constitute an agreement, though no express words of covenant or agreement are connected with them. Among these are "grant," "demise," "lease," and the like. From the word "demise," in a lease under seal, the law implies a covenant, in a lease not under seal, a contract for title to the estate merely, that is for quiet enjoyment against the lessor and all that come in under him by title, and against others claiming by title paramount during the term; and the word "let," or any equivalent words which

---

[1] Atlantic Dock Co. v. Leavitt, 54 N. Y. 35; Finley v. Simpson, 22 N. J. 311. But where a lease under seal was taken in the name of an agent, no action would lie against the principal, though he had entered and occupied. Kiersted v. Orange R. R., 69 N. Y. 343. The rule of ratification seems, however, different in other States. See Cady v. Shepherd, 11 Pick. 400; McIntyre v. Park, 11 Gray, 102.

[2] Post, 3 vol. 589, pl. 49; Goodwin v. Gilbert, 9 Mass. 510; Nugent v. Riley, 1 Met. 117; Newell v. Hill, 2 Met. 180; Pike v. Brown, 7 Cush. 133; Hinsdale v. Humphrey, 15 Conn. 431; Maule v. Weaver, 7 Penn. St. 329; Johnson v. Mussey, 45 Vt. 419; Gale v. Nixon, 6 Cowen, 445; Trustees, &c. v. Spencer, 7 Ohio, pt. 2, 149; Burnett v. Lynch, 5 B. & C. 589; Platt on Cov. 18; Clark v. Gordon, 121 Mass. 330; Carroll v. St. John Soc., 125 Mass. 565.

[3] Hayne v. Cummings, 16 C. B. N. s. 421, 426. *Garranter signifie à defendre son tenant en sa seisin.* Britton, 197 b. *Nihil aliud est quam defendere et acquietare tenentem in scisina sua.* Bracton, lib. 5, 480.

[4] Beckwith v. Howard, 6 R. I. 1.

constitute a lease, have the same effect, but no more.[1] The
tendency of modern decisions is against implying covenants,
which might and ought to have been expressed, if intended.[2]
The presumption, where parties have entered into written
engagements with express stipulations, is that, having expressed some, they have expressed all the conditions by which
they intend to be bound under the instrument.[3]

2. Thus the word " grant," or " demise," once implied an
absolute covenant on the part of the lessor for the lessee's
quiet enjoyment during the term, unless this were qualified,
as it may be, by a more limited express covenant.[4] So the
word " lease " has been held to be equivalent to " demise "
in creating an implied covenant.[5] These words lease or demise
imply a covenant against a paramount title, and against acts
of the landlord which destroy the beneficial enjoyment of the
premises ;[6] and this extends to a demise of a right to collect
wharfage for a term of time, although not corporeal property
in its character,[7] and furthermore that, if the lessee is evicted
by a paramount title, he will be discharged from payment of
rent.[8] But if one lease the mines or veins of ore in certain
lands, he does not thereby warrant that there are such min-
erais there ; and if it turns out that there are none, nothing

---

[1] Hart v. Windsor, 12 M. & W. 68, 85 ; Lanigan v. Kille, 97 Penn. St. 120.

[2] Sheets v. Selden, 7 Wall. 416, 423.

[3] Aspdin v. Austin, 5 Q. B. 671, 684. Thus, in New York, it was held that
in a carefully drawn lease no covenant on the part of a lessee to take a renewal is
implied from a covenant on the part of the lessor to grant one. Bruce v. Fulton
Bank, 79 N. Y. 154.

[4] Burton, Real Prop. § 846. But, by statute now in England, "grant" no
longer implies a covenant in law. Stat. 8 & 9 Vict. c. 106, § 5 ; Smith, Land.
& Ten. 68. But the word "demise" still retains this power. Wms. Real Prop.
367. In New York all actions upon implied covenants in the conveyance of
lands are taken away by statute, as held in Kinney v. Watts, 14 Wend. 38, the
correctness of which has been questioned. See Lalor, Real Est. 246 ; Tone v.
Brace, 8 Paige, 597 ; Williams v. Burrell, 1 C. B. 402, 429 ; Platt, Cov. 47 ; Rawle,
Cov. 362, n.; Mayor v. Mabie, 13 N. Y. 151, 160, commenting on Kinney v.
Watts. See Mack v. Patchin, infra.

[5] Maule v. Ashmead, 20 Penn. St. 482 ; Ross v. Dysart, 33 Penn. St. 452 ;
Maeder v. Carondelet, 26 Mo. 112 ; Hamilton v. Wright, 28 Mo. 199. See contra,
Lovering v. Lovering, 13 N. H. 513.

[6] Wade v. Halligan, 16 Ill. 507 ; Playter v. Cunningham, 21 Cal. 229. "Grant
and demise" in a lease amount to an implied covenant for quiet enjoyment.

[7] Mayor v. Mabie, 13 N. Y. 151.   [8] Wells v. Mason, 4 Scam. 84.

passes by the lease.[1] The law as well as the reason of it, in respect to these implied covenants, so far as it was applicable to the case then under consideration, was thus satisfactorily stated by Shaw, C. J., in Dexter v. Manley, where the terms used were " has demised and leased.' " It is sufficient for the present case that the lease contains an implied covenant which is a good warranty by the defendant (the lessor) against his own acts. Every grant of any right, interest, or benefit, carries with it an implied undertaking on the part of the grantor that the grant is intended to be beneficial, and that, so far as he is concerned, he will do no act to interrupt the free and peaceable enjoyment of the thing granted."[2] "Every lease," say the court of Pennsylvania, " implies a covenant for quiet enjoyment. But it extends only to the possession; and its breach, like that of a warranty for title, arises only from eviction by means of title. It does not protect against entry and ouster of a tort feasor." A tenant has a right to call his landlord into defence; and, if eviction follows as the result of the failure to defend him, he can then refuse to pay rent, and fall back upon his covenant for quiet enjoyment to recover his damages.[3] What the measure of these [*326] is will be considered later.[4] So a covenant for *quiet enjoyment is implied in a lease of an incorporeal hereditament.[5]

2 a. Though the subject of implied covenants in leases is too broad to be embraced in its details in a work like the present, the reader may find it discussed in some of its bearings by Mr. Butler.[6] And it may be remarked that a covenant of quiet enjoyment in a lease, whether express or implied, relates only to possession under title, and not to the undisturbed enjoyment of the premises demised, where there has been no

---

[1] Harlan v. Lehigh Coal Co., 35 Penn. St. 287. No implied covenant that premises are fit for occupation. Edwards v. N. Y. & H. R. R. Co., 98 N. Y. 245; Naumberg v. Young, 44 N. J. L. 332.

[2] Dexter v. Manley, 4 Cush. 14, 24. A lessor is, therefore, as liable for the acts of one under his authority as for his own. Sherman v. Williams, 113 Mass. 481. Where there is an implied contract in a lease, it relates only to the estate, not the condition of the property. Hart v. Windsor, 12 M. & W. 86.

[3] Schuylkill, &c. R. R. v. Schmoele, 57 Penn. St. 271, 273.

[4] *Post*, *345.   [5] Mayor v. Mabie, 13 N. Y. 151.   [6] Co. Lit. 384 a, note.

eviction.[1] The lessor does not warrant against the acts of strangers,[2] nor agree to put the lessee into possession.[3] The extent of his implied engagement is, that he has a good title, and can give a free, unincumbered lease for the time demised.[4] And where the lessor had only an estate for life, and dies before the end of the term, the lessee cannot have an action against the lessor's estate for eviction by the remainderman, if the only covenant was that implied from the word " demise." [5] It would be otherwise, if the lessor had further a power of appointment under the exercise of which the term could have been made good.[6] Still, every lease implies a covenant of quiet enjoyment; and if the premises are recovered by a third party against the tenant, the rent is gone, though the tenant attorn to the one recovering such judgment, before the *habere facias* shall have been served. Nor could the lessor recover of the tenant rent accruing during such period of eviction, even though he may sue a new action, and recover a judgment for possession of the premises. The lessor's remedy for the intermediate rents would be against his adversary in such second suit, while the tenant, in such a case, would attorn to him again as his lessor.[7] A lessor, as such, in the absence of some covenant or agreement to that effect, is not bound to make repairs upon the leased premises.[8] But if the lessor volun-

---

[1] Edgerton v. Page, 1 Hilton, 320, 333 ; Platt, Cov. 312 ; Underwood v. Birchard, 47 Vt. 305.

[2] Lounsberry v. Snider, 31 N. Y. 514 ; Schilling v. Holmes, 23 Cal. 227 ; Branger v. Manciet, 30 Cal. 624 ; Hayes v. Bickerstaff, Vaughan, 118 ; Moore v. Weber, 71 Penn. St. 429.

[3] *Ante,* *297.

[4] Mechan. Ins. Co. v. Scott, 2 Hilton, 550 ; Playter v. Cunningham, 21 Cal. 229.

[5] McClowry v. Croghan, 1 Grant Cas. 307, 311.

[6] Hamilton v. Wright, 28 Mo. 199 ; Adams v. Gibney, 6 Bing. 656.

[7] Ross v. Dysart, 33 Penn. St. 452. See Morse v. Goddard, 13 Met. 177. Nor is the lessor, if the premises are destroyed, bound to apply the insurance money to rebuilding them. Leeds v. Cheetham, 1 Sim. 146 ; Holtzapffel v. Baker, 18 Ves. 115 ; Loft v. Dennis, 1 Ellis & E. 474. See *post,* *346.

[8] Colebeck v. Girdler's Co., 1 Q. B. Div. 234 ; Estep v. Estep, 23 Ind. 114 ; Gott v. Gandy, 2 Ellis & B. 845 ; Leavitt v. Fletcher, 10 Allen, 119 ; Elliott v. Aikin, 45 N. H. 30 ; Witty v. Matthews, 52 N. Y. 512 ; Benjamin v. Herny, 51 Ill. 492 ; Norris v. Tillson, 81 Ill. 607 ; Fisher v. Thirkell, 21 Mich. 1. And the same was the rule of the Civil Law, 1 Brown, C. L. 195 ; Sheets v. Selden, 7 Wall. 416 ; Gill v. Middleton, 105 Mass. 477. And a promise by him so to do

tarily undertakes to repair the premises, and do it in so care-
less a manner as to cause an injury thereby to the tenant, he
will be liable in damages therefor.[1] If he covenants to build
a certain building upon the premises, and do so, and the same
is destroyed, he is not bound to rebuild it.[2] Nor is he bound
to compensate the lessee for repairs made by him.[3] But where
one made repairs or did work upon premises under a parol
promise of the owner to let them to him, and the owner then
refused to lease them to him, it was held he could recover of
the owner for the same,[4] and conversely when the lessor agrees
to do repairs before the lease, the tenant may refuse to occupy
if these are not done.[5] Nor is he bound to protect his tenant
from the consequences of the act of an adjoining owner, whether
lawful or not, in excavating his land so near the demised premises as to cause injury to them.[6] So where one held a term
under a lease, by which, if the lessors sold the premises, they
could determine the lease by giving so many days' notice, and
made an underlease for a certain time, using the words " lease,
demise, and let," but in the underlease there was a proviso
that the sub-tenant could carry away improvements made by
him, " in case the land is sold," it was held that the latter
had no cause of action upon the implied covenant in his lease
in consequence of the term being defeated by a sale of the
premises by the original lessors. So far as the words above
mentioned implied a warranty of title, they were qualified by
the proviso in the lease.[7] But a lessor may bind himself to
repair the premises, and if by the terms of his lease he has a
right to enter and view and make improvements, he is bound
to make the necessary repairs, without waiting for a special
demand or notice so to do.[8] The lessee, however, is not ab-

made subsequent to the lease, is without consideration. Libbey v. Tolford, 48 Me.
316. As to the implied duty of the tenant to repair, see further, *post*, *347.

[1] Gill v. Middleton, 105 Mass. 477.

[2] Cowell v. Lumley, 39 Cal. 151.   [3] Cases note *supra*.

[4] White v. Wieland, 109 Mass. 291 ; Williams v. Bemis, 108 Mass. 91.

[5] Strohecker v. Barnes, 21 Ga. 430.

[6] Sherwood v. Seaman, 2 Bosw. 127 ; McCarty v. Ely, 4 E. D. Smith, 375 ;
Howard v. Doolittle, 3 Duer, 464. See Pargoud v. Tourne, 13 La. An. 292 ; Gill
v. Middleton, *sup*.   [7] O'Connor v. Daily, 109 Mass. 235.

[8] Hayden v. Bradley, 6 Gray, 425. See Vyse v. Wakefield, 6 M. & W. 442,
452, 453 ; Keys v. Powell, 2 A. K. Marsh. 254.

solved from paying rent, if the lessor, in such a case, fails to make the repairs, nor would it amount to an eviction, or justify his abandoning the possession of the premises. His remedy is by an action against the lessor upon his covenant or agreement.[1] So where a lessee has actually entered under his lease, and is sued for rent, he cannot set up in defence a failure on the part of his lessor to do certain agreed acts in relation to the premises. He may, in such case, recoup in damages for the lessor's breach, or may have a separate action therefor, but is not exonerated from liability to pay rent.[2]

3. There are covenants also implied on the part of the lessee, as that to pay the rent, resulting from the formal words " yielding and paying" a stipulated sum.[3] And the very acceptance of a lease imposes upon the lessee an implied obligation to use the premises in a proper and husbandlike manner.[4] Mr. Comyn states the implied covenant or obligation of a lessee growing out of the relation of landlord and tenant to be, to treat the premises demised in such manner that no injury be done to the inheritance, but that the estate may revert to the lessor undeteriorated by the wilful or negligent conduct of the lessee. He is bound, therefore, to keep the soil in a proper state of cultivation, to preserve the timber, and to support and repair the buildings. These duties fall upon him without any express covenant on his part, and a breach of them will, in general, render him liable to be punished for waste.[5] Where one took a lease of a farm dated July 18, while there was a

---

[1] Tibbetts v. Percy, 24 Barb. 39 ; Speckels v. Sax, 1 E. D. Smith, 253 ; Hexter v. Knox, 63 N. Y. 561 ; Leavitt v. Fletcher, 10 Allen, 119 ; Wright v. Lattin, 38 Ill. 293. But by statute in New York, Laws of 1860, c. 345, if the premises are destroyed by sudden casualty, the tenant is not held for rent, if the landlord does not rebuild. Suydam v. Jackson, 54 N. Y. 450.

[2] Kelsey v. Ward, 38 N. Y. 83. But mere trespasses by the landlord do not give the tenant a right to recoup. Bartlett v. Farrington, 120 Mass. 284.

[3] Smith, Land. & Ten. 96 ; Platt, Cov. 42 ; Royer v. Ake, 3 Penn. 461 ; Kimpton v. Walker, 9 Vt. 191 ; Van Rensselaer v. Smith, 27 Barb. 104, 140. See further as to rent, post, *341.

[4] Nave v. Berry, 22 Ala. 382 ; Miller v. Shields, 55 Ind. 71 ; U. S. v. Bostwick, 94 U. S. 53 ; and see Aughinbaugh v. Coppenheffer, 55 Penn. St. 347. An express covenant to personally yield up the premises in good repair is not broken by leaving quantities of rubbish upon the premises. Thorndike v. Burrage, 111 Mass. 531.

[5] Com. Land. & Ten. 188.

crop of hay upon the premises, for five years, and in the fifth
year cut the grass on the 10th of July, and took the crop, it
was held to be no violation of his covenant as being against
the rules of good husbandry, although he thereby took six
crops from the land within his term of five years.[1] In Illinois,
it is held to be the duty of a tenant to pay all taxes assessed
upon the premises during his tenancy ; and if he fails to do
this, and the land be sold for taxes, and he purchases it, he
cannot hold it against the owner of the inheritance.[2] If the
lessee covenant to pay the taxes assessed upon the leased
premises, and fails to do so, the lessor can recover the amount
assessed, although he himself may not have paid them ;[3] and
if the premises are destroyed after the day when the tax is
laid, but before the time for which it is payable has expired, the whole tax is recoverable under lessee's covenant.[4]
What the extent of the lessee's covenant is may be seen more
properly in a work of more special character than the present.[5]

4. There is an important distinction to be observed between
express and implied covenants in a lease, since one who enters
into an express covenant remains bound by it though the lease
be assigned over, while such as are implied are coextensive
only with the occupation of the premises, the lessee, for instance, not being liable under his implied covenant for rent
after his assignment to another, and the acceptance of rent by
the lessor from the assignee.[6] The lessee remains liable upon

---

[1] Willey v. Connor, 44 Vt. 68.

[2] Prettyman v. Walston, 34 Ill. 175, 191. So in Maryland. Hughes v. Young,
5 Gill & J. 67. In Massachusetts the landlord is ultimately liable for the taxes
assessed upon leased estates in the absence of a special agreement between him
and the tenant. Pub. Stat. c. 11, § 17. Whether the landlord or the tenant is
ultimately liable for the taxes, if no stipulation exists in regard to them, depends
in England on the particular tax ; but generally the claim being against the land
the lessor is to bear it, and the tenant, if paying in the first instance, may deduct
from the rent of the year, but not later. Taylor v. Zamira, 6 Taunt. 524 ; Carter
v. Carter, 5 Bing. 406 ; Stubbs v. Parsons, 3 B. & A. 516 ; Denby v. Moore, 1
B. & A. 123.

[3] Trinity Ch. v. Higgins, 48 N. Y. 532.

[4] Sargent v. Pray, 117 Mass. 267 ; Minot v. Joy, 118 Mass. 308.

[5] Taylor, Land. & Ten. (7th ed.) §§ 397-399.

[6] Auriol v. Mills, 4 T. R. 94, 98 ; Rawle, Cov. 363, n.; Kimpton v. Walker, 9
Vt. 191 ; Walker v. Physick, 5 Penn. St. 193. The language of Shaw, C. J., in

his express covenant to pay rent, notwithstanding his having
assigned his lease with the lessor's assent, and the lessor may
have accepted rent from the assignee.[1] The lessor, in such
case, may sue the lessee or his assignee, or both, at his
election, and at the same time, though he can have but one
satisfaction. The lessee continues liable upon his personal
covenant, in the nature of a surety for his assignee, who is
ultimately liable to him for the amount paid by him.[2] But the
liability of a lessee upon the implied covenants in his lease
continues only so long as he holds the estate, where he assigns
with the consent of the lessor, as it depends upon the privity
of estate. This is true in respect to assignees, both as to express and implied covenants, and their liability depends upon
and ceases with the privity of estate between them and the
lessors. Such assignee, therefore, is not liable for any breach
committed before he became assignee, nor for any such breach
occurring after he has parted with the estate and possession
to a new assignee, although he did this for the very purpose of
escaping such liability, because, by so doing, he destroys the
privity of estate on which it depends.[3] But, while the assignee
continues to hold the estate, he would be liable for the rent

Patten v. Deshon, 1 Gray, 330, applies only where the lessor has expressly agreed
to accept the assignee as alone liable for the rent, it being in effect a surrender
by lessee. Thursby v. Plant, 1 Saund. 240 ; Way v. Reed, 6 Allen, 364, 369 ;
7 Am. L. Rev. 244 ; Pfaff v. Golden, 126 Mass. 402. But where the assignee of
the lessee assigned with the lessor's permission for a different business than that
which the lessee stipulated for, it was held to discharge lessee ; Fifty Assoc. v.
Grace, 125 Mass. 161.

[1] Greenleaf v. Allen, 127 Mass. 248 ; Deane v. Caldwell, Id. 242, and cases in
preceding note. But it is otherwise if the lessee was holding over when he assigned. Lodge v. White, 30 Ohio St. 569.

[2] But the lessee cannot recover till he has himself paid. Farrington v. Kimball, 126 Mass. 313 ; Moule v. Garrett, L. R. 5 Exch. 132 ; s. c. 7 Id. 101.

[3] Hintze v. Thomas, 7 Md. 346 ; Walton v. Cronly, 14 Wend. 63 ; Platt, Cov.
490, 494 ; Paul v. Nurse, 8 B. & C. 486 ; Wolveridge v. Stewart, 1 Cr. & M. 644 ;
Taylor v. Shum, 1 B. & P. 21 ; Harley v. King, 2 Cr. M. & R. 18, 22 ; Smith,
Land. & Ten. 294 ; Patten v. Deshon, 1 Gray, 325, 329 ; Cuthbertson v. Irving,
4 Hurlst. & N. 742 ; Bagley v. Freeman, 1 Hilt. 196 ; Kain v. Hoxie, 2 Hilt. 311 ;
Johnson v. Sherman, 15 Cal. 287 ; Quackenboss v. Clarke, 12 Wend. 555 ; Armstrong v. Wheeler, 9 Cow. 88 ; Williams v. Earle, 9 Best & S. 740. But in this
last case it is held that, though the assignee is relieved from liability for subsequent breaches of covenant, he is still liable for assigning to a person of known
irresponsibility.

fixed by the lease as it falls due without regard to the value of the premises,[1] and he may by his conduct or representations to the lessor be estopped to set up his assignment.[2] Nor does it matter how he becomes such assignee. His liability would attach although he purchased the estate at a sheriff's sale.[3]

5. Another important distinction in respect to covenants in a lease is between such as run with the land, binding assignees, or enuring to the benefit of assignees, and such as are personal only and do not bind the estate. It is also laid down by one writer of high authority, that, "by the common law, covenants between the lessor and the lessee relating to land would, in general, run with it on both sides." "But the benefit of a condition was entirely lost by alienation of the reversion."[4] But that this right existed at common law for the assignee of a reversion to sue upon a covenant of a lessee to pay rent is denied by other, and, it would seem, better authorities.[5]

[*327] * However this may have been, the statute 32 Hen. VIII. c. 34, referred to in a former page of this work, attaches both the benefit and the obligation, of covenants as well as of conditions, to the reversion in the hands of a grantee or assignee.[6]

5 a. The reader is referred to what is found in a later part of this work[7] for an attempt to define how far, and in what cases, covenants run with lands. The subject is fully treated of in the American edition of Smith's Leading Cases,[8] in com-

---

[1] Sanders v. Partridge, 108 Mass. 556 ; Taylor, Land. & Ten. § 449 ; Pitcher v. Tovey, 4 Mod. 71 ; Graves v. Porter, 11 Barb. 592 ; Burnett v. Lynch, 5 B. & C. 589 ; Grundin v. Carter, 99 Mass. 15.

[2] Meister v. Birney, 24 Mich. 435, 440.

[3] Sutliff v. Atwood, 15 Ohio St. 186, 198 ; Hornby v. Houlditch, Andrews, 40 ; Taylor, Land. & Ten. 214 ; Thursby v. Plant, 1 Saund. 241 b, note ; *Post*, *331 ; Com. Land. & Ten. 257, 275.

[4] Burton, Real Prop. §§ 855, 856.

[5] Crawford v. Chapman, 17 Ohio, 449 ; Thursby v. Plant, 1 Sannd. 240, n. 3 ; Patten v. Deshon, 1 Gray, 325. See Thrale v. Cornwall, 1 Wils. 165 ; Barker v. Damer, 3 Mod. 337 ; Vyvyan v. Arthur, 1 B. & C. 410. See Platt, Cov. 532. But debt always lay for arrears of rent. Ards v. Watkin, Cro. El. 637, 651 ; Allen v. Bryan, 5 B. & C. 512 ; Williams v. Hayward, 1 Ellis & E. 1040 ; Watson v. Hunkins, 13 Iowa, 547. And see *post*, *337.

[6] Burton, Real Prop. § 856 ; Platt, Cov. 533.

[7] Vol. 2, pp.*13–*17.   [8] Vol. 1, 5th Am. ed. p. 139 *et seq.*

menting upon Spencer's Case,[1] where the early law is embodied. There were some covenants, that, for instance, to pay rent, which raised a liability against the tenant in favor of an assignee of the reversion at the common law, the remedy being in debt but not in covenant, as the only privity between the parties was in estate and not in contract,[2] though it was held in one case hereafter referred to, that a covenant to grind at the lessor's mill might be sued by the devisee of the lessor against the administratrix of the lessee.[3] The object of the statute of 32 Hen. VIII. c. 34 was to extend the privity of contract from reversioner to reversioner, and the right to sue *in covenant* to actions by and against assignees.[4] Before the statute of 4 Anne, c. 16, § 9, although by an assignment of the reversion there was a privity of estate created between the tenant and the assignee, there was no privity of contract, and the assignee could not sue in covenant in his own name, unless the tenant had attorned to him. And now, inasmuch as the statute of Anne is not in force in Illinois, a purchaser of a reversion cannot sue for rent in his own name upon the covenant of the lessee without showing something answering to an attornment.[5] The statute of Hen. VIII. is held to be in force in New Hampshire,[6] Massachusetts,[7] Connecticut,[8] Maryland,[9] New Jersey,[10] Pennsylvania,[11] Virginia,[12] Illinois,[13] Missouri,[14] North Carolina,[15] and Alabama,[16] but was not in New York till re-enacted; and it is there made to extend to grants in fee where rent is reserved, and to leases for life or for

[1] 5 Rep. 16.

[2] Thursby v. Plant, 1 Sannd. 240 ; Patten v. Deshon, 1 Gray, 325.

[3] Vyvyan v. Arthur, 1 B. & C. 410. See also Platt, Cov. 532 ; 2 Platt, Leases, 87, 382 ; Brett v. Cumberland, Cro. Jac. 522 ; Porter v. Swetnam, Styles, 406 ; Van Rensselaer v. Hays, 19 N.Y. 68, 81.

[4] Patten v. Deshon, *sup.*; Platt, Cov. 533, 534 ; Van Rensselaer v. Smith, 27 Barb. 104, 151 ; Cook v. Brightly, 46 Penn. St. 439, 445.

[5] Fisher v. Deering, 60 Ill. 114 ; overruling Chapman v. McGrew, 20 Ill. 101.

[6] Mussey v. Holt, 24 N. H. 248.

[7] Howland v. Coffin, 12 Pick. 125 ; Patten v. Deshon, *sup.*

[8] Baldwin v. Walker, 12 Conn. 168.

[9] Funk r. Kincaid, 5 Md. 404.   [10] Rev. Stat. 643.

[11] Streaper v. Fisher, 1 Rawle, 155, 161. See 3 Binn. 620.

[12] Scott v. Lunt, 7 Pet. 605.

[13] Plumleigh v. Cook, 13 Ill. 669.   [14] Rev. Stat. 32, § 11.

[15] Kornegay v. Collier, 65 N. C. 69.   [16] English v. Key, 39 Ala. 113.

years.[1]   Nor is it in force in Ohio.[2]   It would be transcending the objects proposed in this work to attempt to define with any considerable minuteness of detail the line, often subtle and refined, which distinguishes between covenants running with land and other covenants relating to it.   The language of Best, J., illustrating this, will be found cited upon a later page (*330) ; and the language of the same judge in another case, where the covenant was to insure, is this : "A covenant in a lease which the covenantee cannot, after his assignment, take advantage of, and which is beneficial to the assignee as such, will go with the estate assigned."   "It is a covenant beneficial to the.owner of the estate, and to no one but the owner of the estate, and therefore may be said to be *beneficial to the estate,* and so directly within the principle on which the covenants are made to run with the land."[3]   Where the lessee was, by the terms of his lease, at liberty to purchase the estate at a certain price at the end of the term, it was held, that, by the sale and assignment of his lease, his assignee had a right to claim the conveyance.[4]   And so far as a covenant imposing a burden upon land is held to run with the estate or otherwise, the rule as stated by Gould, J., may, perhaps, be still more definite, intelligible, and easy of application, depending upon whether such covenant entered or not into the original consideration upon which the conveyance, with which it was connected, was made ; "since where the covenants are in the very conveyance by which the covenantor, &c., acquired his land, the performance of those covenants, &c., plainly *forms a part of* the consideration without which the conveyance would not have been made."[5]   An assignee of a lessor may have debt for rent against an assignee of the lessee where the letting has been by an indenture of lease.[6]

[1] Van Rensselaer *v.* Smith, 27 Barb. 104, 151 ; Van Rensselaer *v.* Hays, 19 N. Y. 68, 81, 84 ; Nicholl *v.* N. Y. & E. R. R., 12 N. Y. 121, 131, 132 ; Willard *v.* Tillman, 2 Hill, 274, 276.

[2] Masury *v.* Southworth, 9 Ohio St. 340 ; Crawford *v.* Chapman, 17 Ohio, 449.

[3] Vernon *v.* Smith, 5 B. & A. 1.   See also Laffan *v.* Naglee, 9 Cal. 662, a covenant of pre-emption ; Platt, Cov. 534.

[4] Napier *v.* Darlington, 70 Penn. St. 64 ; Kerr *v.* Day, 14 Penn. St. 112.

[5] Van Rensselaer *v.* Smith, 27 Barb. 104, 146.

[6] Howland *v.* Coffin, 12 Pick. 125.

6. The statute of Hen. VIII. does not extend to covenants merely collateral, but only such as concern the land demised ;[1] and, under it, covenant will lie both by and against the assignee of the reversion of part of the premises,[2] although the assignee of the reversion of such part cannot avail himself of a condition affecting the whole, since a condition cannot be apportioned.[3] But, to render one liable to covenant as assignee, he must take an assignment of the whole or of a part of the premises for the whole term.[4]

7. If a lessee transfers the whole or a part of the estate for a part of the time, it is a sub-lease, and not an assignment ; and the original lessor has no right of action against the sub-lessee, who remains liable only to his lessor. If the whole or a part of the leased premises be transferred by the original lessee for the residue of the term, it is an assignment, though if it be in form a lease with the usual reservations the lessee or his assigns can treat it as such. Therefore, where a tenant for years underlet a part of the premises for the entire term, and then assigned to a third person all his interest in and to the original lease, it was held that his assignee might recover rent of the person to whom his assignor had let a part *of the leased premises.[5]   [*328]

8. And it is true, that, at the common law, an assignee of a reversion might have maintained an action of covenant for any of the implied covenants in a lease.[6] And in Ohio, where an express covenant has been assigned with a reversion, the assignee may sue for its breach in his own name,

---

[1] Platt, Cov. 534 ; Co. Lit. 215 b.

[2] Platt, Cov. 586 ; Twynam v. Pickard, 2 B. & A. 105. The only difference between the first and second sections of the statute is, that the words in the first section apply to the assignee of the reversion, those in the second to the assignee of the term. Patten v. Deshon, 1 Gray, 325.

[3] Doe v. Lewis, 5 Ad. & E. 277 ; 1 Smith, Lead. Cas. 5th Am. ed. 93.

[4] Holford v. Hatch, Doug. 183 ; Patten v. Deshon, 1 Gray, 325 ; Bagley v. Freeman, 1 Hilton, 196 ; Kain v. Hoxie, 2 Hilton, 311, 316 ; Bedford v. Terhune, 30 N. Y. 453, 460.

[5] Patten v. Deshon, 1 Gray, 325 ; McNiel v. Kendall, 128 Mass. 245 ; Astor v. Miller, 2 Paige, 68. In Fulton v. Stuart, 2 Ohio, 215, it is said that assignment of a part of the premises for the whole term is an underletting. But this is clearly an error. See Van Rensselaer v. Smith, 27 Barb. 104, 146.

[6] Platt, Cov. 532 ; also per *Bronson*, J., Willard v. Tillman, 2 Hill, 274.

under tıe code of tıat State, altıougı tıe statute of 32 Hen.
VIII. c. 34 was never adopted tıere.[1] But neitıer at common
law, nor by tıe statute of Hen. ∖III., could an assignee sue
upon a breacı of covenant wıicı ıad ıappencd before tıe
assignment.[2]

9. Wıere tıe relation of landlord and tenant ıas become
establisıed, it attacıes to all wıo take tırougı or under tıe
tenant as assignee, as distinguisıed from sub-lessee, as above
explained, wıetıer immediate or remote.[3] And an assignee
of a lease is bound to know tıe contents of tıe lease itself.[4]
A recital in a lease tıat tıe premises are occupied and to
be occupied as a lumber-yard is a covenant running witı tıe
land, and binds tıe assignee.[5] And even if the·tenant convey
in fee, tıe lessor may elect to treat tıe purcıaser as entering
as ıis tenant, or ıe may treat ıim as a disseisor.[6] But it may
be remarked in passing, tıat tıe relation of landlord and tenant does not exist between tıe tenant of a mortgagor and tıe
assignee of a mortgagee, altıougı tıere is a kind of tenancy
between mortgagor and mortgagee.[7]

10. In furtıer considering wıat covenants bind tıe assignees, it was before stated tıat tıey must toucı and concern
tıe tıing demised, and as sucı tıey run witı tıe lands, wıere
tıere is a privity of estate between covenantor and covenantee.
Among tıese are all implied covenants, tıat is, all sucı covenants as tıe law implies from tıe usual terms of leases as
          before explained, sucı as " lease and demise," " yield-
[*329] ing and paying," and tıe * like.[8] Also all covenants
          for quiet enjoyment,[9] wıetıer tıey are expressed or

---

[1] ᴊasury v. Southworth, 9 Ohio St. 340.

[2] Lewes v. Ridge, Cro. Eliz. 863; 1 Smith, Lead. Cas. 5th Am. ed. 172;
Platt, Cov. 538; Gibbs v. Ross, 2 Head, 437.

[3] Jackson v. Davis, 5 Cow. 123, 129; Benson v. Bolles, 8 Wend. 175; Overman
v. Sanborn, 27 Vt. 54; Howland v. Coffin, 12 Pick. 125.

[4] Barroilhet v. Battelle, 7 Cal. 450.   [5] De Forest v. Byrne, 1 Hilton, 43.

[6] Jackson v. Davis, 5 Cow. 123, 130; Jaques v. Short, 20 Barb. 269.

[7] Jackson v. Rowland, 6 Wend. 666; Jackson v. Laughead, 2 Johns. 75.

[8] Smith, Land. & Ten. 287, n.; Platt, Cov. 42-44; 1 Smith, Lead. Cas. 5th
Am. ed. 123.

[9] Shelton v. Codman, 3 Cush. 318; ᴊarkland v. Crump, 1 Dev. & B. 94;
Campbell v. Lewis, 3 B. & A. 392; s. c. 8 Taunt. 715; Smith, Land. & Ten.
288, note; Williams v. Burrell, 1 C. B. 402, 433.

implied; covenants to pay rent;[1] to insure;[2] to repair, or to deliver up in good condition;[3] to reside on the premises;[4] or to pay taxes.[5] But though an assignee of the lessee would be bound, a sub-lessee would not, nor the assignee of such sub-lessee.[6] So various covenants not to do certain acts upon the premises are of this character, as where the lessor of a mill covenanted in his lease not to let or employ any other place or site on the same stream for a mill of a certain kind, the covenant was held to run with the land, and its breach might be sued for by an assignee.[7] So a covenant not to sell any wood or timber off the demised premises,[8] or one for a particular mode of cultivation or occupancy of the property,[9] or which concerns husbandry and repairs, runs with the land, and binds an assignee.[10] So a covenant for a perpetual or limited renewal runs with the land.[11] But where the lease provided for the lessee enjoying the estate for a certain term, with a right to hold it as much longer as he should choose after the expiration of the term, at the same rate, no definite time being prescribed, it was held not to be a covenant running with the reversion so as to bind the assignee of the lessor; and the lessor having died during the term, the lessee having chosen to hold beyond the term, his tenancy became one from year

---

[1] Hurst v. Rodney, 1 Wash. C. C. 375; Howland v. Coffin, 12 Pick. 125; Main v. Feathers, 21 Barb. 646; Jaques v. Short, 20 Barb. 269; Demarest v. Willard, 8 Cow. 206; Graves v. Porter, 11 Barb. 592.

[2] Vernon v. Smith, 5 B. & A. 1; Doe v. Peck, 1 B. & Ad. 428; Thomas v. Von Kapff, 6 Gill & J. 372.

[3] Demarest v. Willard, 8 Cow. 206; Pollard v. Shaaffer, 1 Dall. 210; Broom's Maxims, 553; Dean of Windsor's Case, 5 Rep. 24, though the covenant did not in terms bind assignees. Spencer's Case, 5 Rep. 16.

[4] Tatem v. Chaplin, 2 H. Bl. 133, though assignee be not named. Van Rensselaer v. Read, 26 N. Y. 558, 576.

[5] Dean of Windsor's Case, 5 Rep. 24; Kearney v. Post, 1 Sandf. 105; Astor v. Miller, 2 Paige, 68; Post v. Kearney, 2 N. Y. 394.

[6] Martin v. O'Connor, 43 Barb. 514; Cf. Odell v. Solomon, 99 N. Y. 635.

[7] Norman v. Wells, 17 Wend. 136. See, also, as to covenants in a lease of water-power running with the land used, Noonan v. Orton, 4 Wisc. 335, 341; Morse v. Aldrich, 19 Pick. 449; Woolliscroft v. Norton, 15 Wisc. 198, 204.

[8] Verplanck v. Wright, 23 Wend. 506.

[9] Woodfall, Land. & Ten. 81; St. And. Church App. 67 Penn. St. 512.

[10] Gordon v. George, 12 Ind. 408.

[11] Blackmore v. Boardman, 28 Mo. 420; Piggot v. Mason, 1 Paige, 412.

to year, determinable by notice from the lessee or the owner of
the reversion.[1] In order to avail himself of the benefit of a
covenant to renew, the lessee must give notice of his election
so to do before the expiration of the term.[2] So a covenant
made by the lessor with the lessee to pay for new erections
upon the premises runs with the land, and may be enforced
by an assignee of lessee against the lessor.[3] The general principle applicable to these cases, as laid down by Best, J., in Vyvyan v. Arthur, which was a case where the lessee of part of an
estate covenanted with the lessor to do a service at a
[*330] * mill belonging to the lessor upon another part of the
estate, in which the lessee bound his assigns, is as
follows: " If the performance of the covenant be beneficial to
the reversioner in respect of the lessor's demand, and to no
other person, his assignee may sue upon it; but if it be beneficial to the lessor without regard to his continuing owner of
the estate, it is a mere collateral covenant, upon which the
assignee cannot sue." And in that case, as the performance
of the covenant would have been beneficial to the owner of
the reversion and to no other person, it was held to run
with the land.[4] If the covenant be to do some act, but not
upon the premises, and only collateral to these, such as to
build a house upon other land of the lessor than that which is
demised, or to pay a collateral sum to the lessor or to a stranger,
it would not run with the land.[5]

11. While, as has been said, there are many covenants which
run with the land, binding assigns as well as operating in their
favor, there is a distinction between such as bind assigns without being named; and such as require them to be named in
order to charge them with their performance. And the dis-

---

[1] West Trans. Co. v. Lansing, 49 N. Y. 499.

[2] Renoud v. Daskam, 34 Conn. 512.

[3] Hunt v. Danforth, 2 Curt. C. C. 592. But it does not run with the reversion so as to bind the assignee thereof. Smith, Land. & Ten. 290, 291 ; 2 Platt,
Leases, 406 ; Tallman v. Coffin, 4 N. Y. 134. See Verplanck v. Wright, 23
Wend. 506, embracing in summary most of the above supposed covenants. See
also 1 Smith, Lead. Cas. 5th Am. ed. 177.

[4] Vyvyan v. Arthur, 1 B. & C. 410, 417 ; Aikin v. Alb. R. R., 26 Barb. 289 ;
Vernon v. Smith, 5 B. & A. 11 ; Platt, Cov. 534.

[5] Spencer's Case, 5 Rep. 16 ; Platt, Cov. 473 ; Maybo v. Buckhurst, Cro. Jac.
438 ; Keppell v. Bailey, 2 Mylne & K. 517.

tinction seems to be whether the subject-matter of the covenant is *in esse* at the time of the demise or not. If it is, the covenant binds the assignee, whether named or not; if it is not, it does not bind him, unless expressly named therein. Thus if the covenant be to keep houses then on the premises in repair, it runs with the land, and binds the assignee, though not named. But if to build a new house on the demised premises, it will not bind assignees, unless named; though, as remarked by a writer, "the good sense of this is not very easily discoverable." [1]   The rule as laid down by Lord Ellenborough [*] upon the subject is this: "The assignee is [*331] specifically named, and though it were for a thing not
in esse at the time, yet, being specifically named, it would bind him, if it affected the nature, quality, or value of the thing demised independently of collateral circumstances, or if it affected the mode of enjoying it." [2]   Nor would it be necessary to make use of the word "assigns," if the intent to bind them is inferrible from the language of the lease. In the case cited below, the court say, "We think the real question must be, the covenant being one which may be annexed to the estate, and run with the land, whether such was the intention of the parties as expressed in the deed." On the other hand, if the covenant be not of a nature that the law permits it to be attached to the estate, it cannot become so by the agreement of the parties.[3]   Whether the covenant to surrender at the end of the term runs with the estate, so as to bind an assignee, unless expressly named in the lease, is treated by the court of Massachusetts as an undecided question, although it was held by Parke, B., that it did not run with the land.[4]

12. Where a covenant which runs with the land is divisible in its nature, if the entire interest in different parts or parcels of the land passes by assignment to separate and distinct in-

---

[1] Spencer's Case, 5 Rep. 16 ; Platt, Cov. 466 ; Id. 471 ; Hunt *v.* Danforth, 2 Curt. C. C. 604 ; Sampson *v.* Easterby, 9 B. & C. 505 ; Bream *v.* Dickerson, 2 Humph. 126. See also Masury *v.* Southworth, 9 Ohio St. 340 ; Hansen *v.* Meyer, 81 Ill. 321.

[2] Congleton *v.* Pattison, 10 East, 133.

[3] Masury *v.* Southworth, 9 Ohio St. 340.

[4] Sargent *v.* Smith, 12 Gray, 426, 428 ; Doe *v.* Seaton, 2 Cr. M. & R. 730.

dividuals, t1e covenant will attac1 upon eac1 parcel *pro tanto*.[1]
In suc1 case t1e assignee of eac1 part would be answerable
for 1is proportion of any c1arge upon t1e land w1ic1 is a
common burden, and would be exclusively liable for t1e breac1
of any covenant w1ic1 related to t1at part alone.[2]

13. T1e liability of an assignee, 1owever, during t1e time t1at
t1e term remains vested in him, does not depend upon 1is ever
1aving actually entered into possession of t1e premises, unless,
per1aps, t1e assignment be by way of a mortgage, in respect
to w1ic1 different opinions 1ave prevailed.[3] Different courts
1ave 1eld differently upon t1e point w1et1er t1e assignee of a
lease is liable for rent before 1e s1all 1ave entered under 1is
assignment. In Illinois, suc1 assignee is liable before entry
made. In New York, t1e converse is 1eld; w1ile in Massachusetts, alt1oug1 a term created by a lease under seal may if
the assignee enter upon t1e estate, be effectually transferred
by a writing not under seal, an assignment to be effectual in
rendering t1e assignee liable for t1e rent must eit1er be made
by deed, or completed by an entry or actual c1ange of possession on t1e part of t1e assignee.[4] An executor of a lessee,
t1oug1 an assignee in law of t1e lease, does not become liable
as suc1 *de bonis propriis*, unless he actually enters into the
demised premises.[5] He continues to be liable for
[*332] breac1es committed w1ile 1e * 1olds as assignee,
t1oug1 1e s1ould 1ave subsequently assigned t1e
lease.[6] Nor would 1e escape t1e liability of assignee by any-
t1ing s1ort of an assignment, and an actual transmission of
possession. If 1e retain possession of any part of t1e premises

---

[1] Van Rensselaer *v.* Bradley, 3 Denio, 135 ; Van Rensselaer *v.* Jones, 2 Barb.
643 ; Gamon *v.* Vernon, 2 Lev. 231 ; Astor *v.* Miller, 2 Paige, 68 ; Van Horn *v.*
Crain, 1 Paige, 455.

[2] Id.; Platt, Cov. 495.

[3] Wms. Real Prop. 331 ; Smith *v.* Brinker, 17 Mo. 148 ; Bagley *v.* Freeman,
1 Hilton, 196 ; Journeay *v.* Brackley, 1 Hilton, 447, 452 ; Felch *v.* Taylor, 13
Pick. 139. So the assignee remains liable, though he agreed when he took the
assignment to reassign. Simonds *v.* Turner, 120 Mass. 329.

[4] Babcock *v.* Scoville, 56 Ill. 461 ; Damainville *v.* Mann, 32 N. Y. 197 ; Sanders *v.* Partridge, 108 Mass. 556.

[5] Wollaston *v.* Hakewell, 3 Mann. & G. 297, 320 ; Taylor, Land. & Ten. § 451.

[6] Harley *v.* King, 2 C. M. & R. 18 ; Quackenboss *v.* Clarke, 12 Wend. 555–557;
Journeay *v.* Brackley, 1 Hilton, 452 ; Donelson *v.* Polk, 64 Md. 501.

until tie rent falls due, either by iimself or iis tenant, ie is liable for the same.[1] But to render an assignee liable as suci, ho must iave, by virtue of the assignment, actual possession or an immediate rigit to possession of the premises.[2] So the benefit of the covenants by tie lessor witi the lessee passes to tie assignee of tie latter by reason of suci privity of estate.[3]

14. From tie twofold ciaracter of a lessee's liability, first, arising from privity of estate, secondly, from privity of contract on iis express covenants, tie effect of an assignment of iis lease is tiat ie ceases to be liable upon tie implied covenants in iis lease,[4] because the privity of estate is gone, but remains still liable upon his express covenants as if no assignment iad been made, tie original privity of contract still subsisting,[5] even tiougi tie lessor assent in writing to tie assignment, and tiougi ie ias actually received rent of the assignee,[6] unless tie lessor siall iave accepted a surrender from the lessee and released iim.[7] If the lessor accept rent from the assignee, tie lessee ceases to be liable in *debt* for tie rent, for tiat liability results from a privity of estate.[8] But if tie

---

[1] Negley v. Sorgan, 46 Penn. St. 281 ; Sanders r. Partridge, 108 Sass. 556. But as assignee at law of the lessor he is liable *de bonis testatoris* to the end of the term, though he assigns over. Greenleaf v. Allen, 127 Sass. 248.

[2] Hannen v. Ewalt, 18 Penn. St. 9 ; Thomas v. Connell, 5 Penn. St. 13 ; Wickersham v. Irwin, 14 Penn. St. 108.

[3] Wms. Real Prop. 331.

[4] Knuckle v. Wynick, 1 Dall. 305 ; Harley v. King, 2 C. S. & R. 18, Am. ed. note ; Kimpton v. Walker, 9 Vt. 191 ; Blair v. Rankin, 11 Mo. 440 ; Thursby v. Plant, 1 Sannd. 241 b ; Waldo v. Hall, 14 Sass. 486 ; Swan v. Stransham, Dyer, 257 ; Donelson v. Polk, 64 Sd. 501.

[5] Wall v. Hinds, 4 Gray, 256 ; Smith, Land. & Ten. 293 ; Thursby v. Plant, 1 Sannd. 240, 241 a, note ; Ghegan v. Young, 23 Penn. St. 18 ; Walton v. Cronly, 14 Wend. 63 ; Williams v. Burrill, 1 C. B. 402, 433 ; Dewey v. Dupny, 2 W. & S. 553 ; Howland v. Coffin, 12 Pick. 125 ; correcting and overruling the doctrine in Walker's Case, 3 Rep. 24, that, after accepting rent of the assignee of lessee, a lessor cannot sustain an action against the lessee. See also Journeay v. Brackley, 1 Hilton, 447, 451 ; 2 Platt, Leases, 352.

[6] Bailey v. Wells, 8 Wisc. 141 ; Port v. Jackson, 17 Johns. 239 ; Quackenboss v. Clarke, 12 Wend, 556 ; Damb r. Hoffman, 3 E. D. Smith, 361 ; *ante*, *326·

[7] Frank v. Saguire, 42 Penn. St. 77.

[8] Fletcher v. M'Farlane, 12 Sass. 43 ; Auriol v. Sills, 4 T. R. 94, 98 ; Wall v. Hinds, 4 Gray, 256 ; Pine v. Leicester, Hobart, 37 a, Wms. notes ; Thursby v Plant, 1 Saund. 240 ; Com. Land. & Ten. 275.

lessor refuses to accept tie assignee as iis tenant, ie may continue to sue iis lessee in debt for tie rent.[1]

15. Anotier incident may be remarked in respect to tie consequences of an assignment wien made to several persons, tiat if an act of forfeiture is committed by a breaci of covenant, it is immaterial, so far as its effect in defeating tie estate is concerned, wietier it be done by one or all of tie assignees.[2]

16. It is competent and usual for tie parties to an indenture of lease, instead of leaving tieir rigits and duties in respect to tie leased premises to be determined by tie rules of law, iowever well defined, to insert express limitations or covenants affecting tiese common-law rigits, especially in regard to tie mode of using tie premises, and tie consequences of fault or accident connected witi suci use. Tiougi tiese are more fully treated of iereafter,[3] it may be remarked tiat if no suci limitation is inserted, tie lessee will be bound by iis covenant to pay rent, altiougi tie premises be destroyed or rendered untenantable from otier causes.[4] Tie court cannot interpolate wiat tie contract, as written, does not contain. Tius, in tie lease of a water-power, provision was made for abating tie rent, in case of loss of power in proportion to tie deficiency of tie power : tie court could adopt no otier remedy for tie party injured by such loss.[5] So wiere lessee covenanted to pay rent during tie term, but tie lessor iad agreed, orally, tiat if tie building were burned tie rent siould cease, tie court excluded tiis evidence, as it expressly contradicted wiat tie tenant iad covenanted to do.[6] Tiougi tie common law of New York coincides witi tie doctrine above stated, rendering tie lessee liable for rent tiougi tie premises may iave been destroyed ; by a statute of tiat State, wiere tie premises iave become untenantable by tie force of tie elements, witiout tie fault of tie tenant, ie is not bound to

---

[1] Auriol v. Mills, 4 T. R. 94 ; Thursby v. Plant, 1 Saund. 241 b, note ; Coghil v. Freelove, 3 Mod. 325 ; Hobart, 37 a, note.

[2] Clarke v. Cummings, 5 Barb. 339.   [3] *Post*, *345.

[4] Fowler v. Bott, 6 Mass. 63 ; Bigelow v. Collamore, 5 Cush. 226 ; Beach v. Farish, 4 Cal. 339 ; Leavitt v. Fletcher, 10 Allen, 119, 121.

[5] Sheets v. Selden, 7 Wall. 416.

[6] Martin v. Berens, 67 Penn. St. 459.

repair them, and is at liberty to surrender and abandon them.[1]
But neither the lessor, nor the lessee, if he uses the premises
in a husbandlike manner, will be bound to rebuild or repair
the premises, if destroyed or damaged without his fault, in
the absence of an express covenant to that effect in the lease;[2]
though it is competent for the lessor or the lessee to covenant to repair or rebuild, either absolutely or to a limited
extent.[3] If the lessee covenants to repair and restore the
premises or to surrender them in good condition, or in terms
to that effect, he will be bound to make good his covenant, and
rebuild the premises if destroyed, and in the meantime to pay
his rent, though the loss may have happened without his fault,
and even if caused by storm, flood, fire, inevitable accident, or
the act of a stranger, by the wind, or by lightning.[4] Even
where a thing becomes impossible of performance by the act
of a third person, or the act of God, its impossibility affords
no excuse for its non-performance. It is the party's folly that
led him to make such a bargain without providing against the
possible contingency.[5] From using blank forms in making

[1] Stat. 1860, c. 345 ; Graves v. Berdan, 26 N. Y. 498 ; Taylor, Land. & Ten.
§ 520 ; Suydam v. Jackson, 54 N. Y. 450. But the tenant, to avail himself of
this statute, must entirely surrender the premises. Johnson v. Oppenheim, 55
N. Y. 280.

[2] Post v. Vetter, 2 E. D. Smith, 248 ; Welles v. Castles, 3 Gray, 323 ; 2 Platt,
Leases, 182 ; Horsefall v. Mather, Holt, N. P. 7 ; Leavitt v. Fletcher, 10 Allen,
121 ; Elliot v. Aiken, 45 N. H. 30, 36.

[3] Walton v. Waterhouse, 2 Wms. Saund. 422, n. 2 ; Phillips v. Stevens, 16
Mass. 238.

[4] 2 Wms. Sannd. 422, n. 2 ; Abby v. Billups, 35 Miss. 618 ; Bigelow v. Collamore, sup.; Shep. Touch. 173 ; Flynn v. Trask, 11 Allen, 550. Hoy v. Holt,
91 Penn. St. 88. Post, *345.

[5] Paradine v. Jane, Aleyn, 27 ; Hickman v. Rayl, 55 Ind. 551. So Hills v.
Thompson, 13 M. & W. 487, where the lessee was held to his covenant to raise a
certain quantity of coal from the demised premises, though there was not that
quantity there, because this was in effect warranted as a payment of rent. But in
Clifford v. Watts, L. R. 5 C. P. 577, lessee's agreement to dig not less than 1,000
tons of clay was held excused, as there was not so much in the land leased to
him. And it seems that, in like manner, as the absolute non-existence of the
subject-matter of the covenant will excuse performance, unless there is an express
warranty of the possibility of performance, so will the absolute destruction of the
thing demised, as in case of the lease of single rooms in a building. Shawmut
Bk. v. Boston, 118 Mass. 125. In the ordinary case of destruction of premises, the
land remains. Rolle, Abr. 236.

leases, it sometimes happens that printed and written clauses in the same lease are inconsistent with each other; and the rule in such case is, to regard the written clause as the contract of the parties, because the printed may have been left standing by inadvertence.[1] If, by the terms of the lease, the covenant to pay rent is partially or wholly suspended when the premises are partially or wholly destoyed by unavoidable casualty, or words of similar import, this does not apply to a gradual decay of the premises, but is limited to damage arising from uncontrollable force and accident.[2]

[*333]   *SECTION V.

OF ASSIGNMENT AND SUB-TENANCY.

1. Assignment of lease must be by writing, &c.
2. May be done by a general deed of grant.
3. When assignment presumed.
4. What an assignment, and what an underlease.
5. No privity between lessor and sub-lessee.
6. Lessee may convey and carve up his estate.
7. Lessor may assign his reversion.
8. Reversion carries rent, in part or in whole.
9. Of apportionment of rent.
10. Reversion and rent may be separately conveyed.
11. Assignee of rent sues in his own name.
12. Descent of rent to several heirs.
13. Of forms of action by and against assignees.
14. Necessity of notice of assignment made.
15. When mortgagee liable as assignee.
15 a. Effect of assignment by an insolvent lessee.
16. Assignee may not deny validity of assignment.

1. In the first place, it may be stated as a general if not a universal proposition, that a lease is assignable unless its assignability is restricted by some covenant or condition therein

---

[1] Ball v. Wyeth, 8 Allen, 275, 278.

[2] Hatch v. Stamper, 42 Conn. 28; Phillips v. Sun Dye Co., 10 R. I. 458. But such deterioration as is the result of the casualty is within the purview of this stipulation. Cary v. Whiting, 118 Mass. 363. And upon such termination the lessee may recover back proportionately rent paid in advance. Rich v. Smith, 121 Mass. 328.

to that effect.[1]   So the lessee may underlet the premises, unless restrained in like manner.[2]   In considering the form of making an assignment of a leasehold interest, and the rights arising under a written lease, by the acts of the parties, and what will operate in law as such assignment, it may be stated that the Statute of Frauds requires it to be done by deed or note in writing, signed by the party assigning the same, or his agents thereunto lawfully authorized in writing.[3]   Statute 29 Car. II. c. 3, § 3.   And now by the statute of Victoria it can only be done by deed.[4]   The statute 32 Henry VIII. c. 34, as to assignment of covenants, &c., in leases, applies only to cases of demise by deed.   Consequently, the assignee of such a reversion cannot sue in assumpsit on the contract made by the assignor.   And the very definition of a covenant implies that the agreement constituting it should be under seal.[5]

2.   It may be stated, in general terms, that the grant by a lessee of his entire estate will be an assignment of the lease, whether done in the form of a lease, or by an instrument in terms an assignment.[6]   So a conveyance in fee by a lessee for years in the form of a deed will operate as an assignment, and

---

[1] Robinson v. Perry, 21 Ga. 183.

[2] King v. Aldborough, 1 East, 597 ; Taylor, Land. & Ten. 22 ; Crommelin v. Thiess, 31 Ala. 412, 421.   But in Georgia, a tenant is prohibited by statute from sub-letting premises without consent of his landlord.   McBurney v. McIntire, 38 Ga. 261.

[3] Bedford v. Terhune, 30 N. Y. 453, 459.   [4] Wms. Real Prop. 133.

[5] Standen v. Chrismas, 10 Q. B. 135 ; Platt, Cov. 3.   But the same rights may enure in favor of the reversioner on an oral or written demise where there has been an attornment or adoption of the transfer by payment of rent or the like, and assumpsit will lie.   Rennie v. Robinson, 1 Bing. 147 ; Buckworth v. Simpson, 1 Cr. M. & R. 834 ; Cornish v. Stubbs, L. R. 5 C. P. 334 ; Smith v. Eggington, L. R. 9 C. P. 145.   Especially where the attornment is dispensed with by the statute of Anne, or the same rule obtains at common law.   Perrin v. Lepper, 34 Mich. 292.   And see Shine v. Dillon, 1 Ir. R. C. L. 277.   In Allcock v. Moorhouse, 9 Q. B. Div. 366, recovery by the assignee of a lessor from year to year was denied, for want of privity of estate, in an action of use and occupation against the lessee, who had assigned though without the lessor's assent, and the statute of 4 Anne, c. 16, § 9, held not to apply.

[6] 2 Prest. Conv. 124.   See Palmer v. Edwards, Doug. 187, n.; Poultney v. Holmes, 1 Str. 405 ; Lynde v. Hough, 27 Barb. 415 ; Beardman v. Wilson, L. R. 4 C. P. 57 ; or by will, Martin v. Tobin, 123 Mass. 85 ; Sanders v. Partridge, 108 Mass. 556, 558.

hold his grantee as tenant of the first lessor; nor could the grantee set up his possession as adverse to that of such lessor.[1] If a lessor during the term mortgage the premises, it may operate as an assignment of the reversion *pro tanto*, and carry with it the rent as incident to it; and all that would be necessary in such a case for the mortgagee to avail himself of the rent would be to notify the tenant to pay it to him.[2] But if the mortgage of the premises be antecedent to the lease, it is not enough for the mortgagee, in order to claim the rent, to give the tenant notice to pay it.   He must gain possession of the mortgaged premises before he can compel the tenant to pay him the rent.[3] And the reason of this is, that the lessee of the mortgagor has his rights as assignee, and the mortgagor would not himself be liable to the mortgagee for rent until the latter should have taken possession of the premises under his mortgage.   But while this is true, it is not true that by accepting rent the mortgagee affirms the lease for the whole term.   It would only create a tenancy from year to year at the farthest.[4] But an assignment by a lessor in writing of a lease which is under seal is not a transfer of the legal title to the lease so as to enable the assignee to sue thereon for the rent reserved.   The assignment to be effectual must be under seal.[5] But an assignment by a lessee, in writing, of a lease under seal, would so far be effectual, that, if followed by an entry on the part of the assignee upon the leased premises, he would be liable as assignee for rent accruing due during his tenancy by reason of the privity of estate thereby created between him and the reversioner.[6]

3. In an action by a lessor against one in possession of leased premises to recover rent, the latter will be presumed to be the assignee of the lessee unless the contrary is shown.[7] And a surrender made by the lessee to the lessor and accepted

---

[1] Sands *v.* Hughes, 53 N. Y. 287, 293.

[2] Kimball *v.* Lockwood, 6 R. I. 138 ; Russell *v.* Allen, 2 Allen, 42.

[8] Evans *v.* Elliott, 9 Ad. & E. 342 ; Baldwin *v.* Walker, 21 Conn. 168.

[4] Gartside *v.* Outley, 58 Ill. 210.

[5] Bridgham *v.* Tileston, 5 Allen, 371 ; Brewer *v.* Dyer, 7 Cush. 337 ; Wood *v.* Partridge, 11 Mass. 488.   Sanders *v.* Partridge, 108 Mass. 556.

[7] Cross *v.* Upson, 17 Wisc. 618 ; Mariner *v.* Crocker, 18 Wisc. 251 ; Bedford *v.* Terhune, 30 N. Y. 453.

by 1im, during t1e period of an occupancy by one in possession, will bo conclusive evidence t1at the lessee and not the occupant is t1e one w1o 1olds under the lessor. By t1is, as well as ot1er evidence, the presumption of an assignment may be rebutted, as well as t1at of suc1 a privity of estate as makes a tenant responsible to the lessor for rent.[1] But the assignee of t1e lease would not bo liable for breac1es of covenant arising prior to the assignment,[2] unless t1e performance of suc1 covenant s1all 1ave been secured by a mortgage in t1e lease of somet1ing to be put upon the premises by the lessee, in w1ic1 case the assignee would 1old the premises subject to t1e lessor's rig1t as mortgagee for suc1 prior breac1.[3]

4. Questions 1ave sometimes arisen, w1et1er a certain act of a lessee is, in law, an assignment or an underletting. And t1is becomes important w1en the effect of the one or the ot1er is considered. The determination of the question does not depend upon the form of the instrument alone, but upon w1et1er the lessee has t1ereby parted wit1 his entire interest in the term as a term. If 1e 1as aliened 1is entire interest, it * is an assignment. If it is for a period [*334] w1ic1 is to expire before t1e expiration of t1e original lease, it is a subletting. In the one case 1e has a reversion left, in the ot1er 1e has none. And t1e retaining the smallest reversionary interest gives to t1e instrument t1e mere effect of an underlease.[4] Giving it, 1owever, t1e form of an underletting, does not c1ange its c1aracter. If it be for t1e w1ole term, it will be an assignment wit1 all its consequences.[5] So if a lessee underlet a portion of the leased premises for a term as long or longer t1an 1is own, suc1 underlessee becomes

---

[1] Dun1rlo r. Wyman, 2 Sandf. 597 ; Quackenboss v. Clarke, 12 Wend. 555 ; Kain v. Hoxie, 2 Hilton, 311.

[2] Day v. Swackhamer, 2 Hilton, 4.   [3] Barroilhet v. Battelle, 7 Cal. 450.

[4] Burton, Real Prop. § 889 ; 2 Prest. Conv. 124 ; Parmenter v. Webber, 8 Taunt. 593 ; Pollock v. Stacy, 9 Q. B. 1033, where the form was an underletting ; Patten v. Deshon, 1 Gray, 325, where the underletting was of a part of the premises for the entire term ; 1 Platt, Leases, 102 ; 2 Id. 420 ; Derby v. Taylor, 1 East, 502 ; Bacon, Abr. Lease, I. 3 ; Bagley v. Freeman, 1 Hilton, 196, 198 ; Kain v. Hoxie, 2 Hilton, 311.

[5] Sanders v. Partridge, 108 Mass. 556 ; Beardman v. Wilson, L. R. 4 C. B. 57 ; Wollaston v. Hakewell, 3 Mann. & G. 297, 323 ; Taylor, Land. & Ten. (7th ed.) § 16 and note.

thereby assignee, and liable, proportionably, for the perform·
ance of the covenants which relate to the estate.   Nor would
it make any difference in this respect, though the premises be
underlet for a larger rent than that reserved in the original
lease.   The undertenant would be liable to his lessor, under
his lease, for such excess.[1]   But though it would be an underletting unless the lessee's whole estate and interest passes, if
it be the lessee's whole estate and interest in a part of the
leased premises, it will as to that part be an assignment, and
the tenant will be liable as assignee for a proportionate part of
the rent reserved in the original lease.[2]   A judicial sale of the
interest of the lessee creates in the purchaser the obligation of
an assignee to pay the rent subsequently accruing.[3]   The cases
upon the point, whether a subletting by a lessee of his entire
term amounts to an assignment, or creates a new relation of
landlord and tenant, with a right to distrain for rent and the
like between him and the undertenant, are numerous, and it
is not proposed to examine them any further than as it affects
the question, whether such subletting, in terms, creates a
privity of estate between the sublessee and the original lessor.

          And here unfortunately the law seems to be unsettled,
[*335] no case having been found expressly in * point.   In
England the rule seems established that unless the
sublease is less in point of time than the original term, it is an
assignment.   Thus it is laid down by Preston that a right of
entry or a reservation of rent will not change the nature of the
estate, but that to make it an underlease a reversion must be
retained by the former owner, and that the underlease must
be for a period less in point of time than the term or estate of
the lessee, and a day, an hour, or a minute will be sufficient.[4]
The language of Bacon is, "When the whole term is made
over by the lessee, although in the deed by which that is done
the rent and power of entry for non-payment are reserved to
him and not to the original lessee (lessor), this is an assign-

---

[1] Wollaston v. Hakewell, *sup.*; Smith v. Mapleback, 1 T. R. 441; Taylor, Land.
& Ten. (7th ed.) § 16 and note.

[2] 2 Platt, Leases, 421; Pingrey v. Watkins, 15 Vt. 479, 488.   See Holford v.
Hatch, Doug. 174.

[3] D'Aquin v. Armant, 14 La. An. 217 ; and see McNeil v. Kendall, 128 Mass. 245.

[4] 2 Prest. Conv. 124, 125, citing Palmer v. Edwards, Dougl. 187, n.

ment and not an underlease, and therefore the original lessor or his assignee of the reversion may sue or be sued on the respective covenants in the original lease, and this although new covenants are introduced in assignment."[1] In Pluck v. Digges, there was a lease for lives, and the lessees demised the lands in common form, reserving rent, &c., for the same number of lives as mentioned in the original lease, though not so mentioned in the second demise. The head-note of the case thus states the law: "The whole interest having been granted, it operated as an assignment."[2] In the latter case the Chief Justice says, "In Parmenter v. Webber,[3] although the intention of the parties to make an underlease was manifest and *acted upon*, yet the fact of the whole interest being granted was held decisive of the instrument being an assignment" (p. 99). And the elaborate note of the reporter to the case of King v. Wilson,[4] to the effect that tenure could subsist between the lessee and the sublessee of the whole term independently of a reversion, because such was the intention of the parties, is controverted by the Vice-Chancellor in the case of Langford v. Selmes,[5] saying, "It was never before suggested that there could be any tenure between a lessee for years and a person to whom he granted his whole term." In a still more recent case,[6] the general rule above stated is reasserted; and the conclusion contended for, as derived from Pollock v. Stacy,[7] that the relation of landlord and tenant could subsist without a reversion, is denied, and that case limited to its special circumstances. But in the United States a different rule seems to have prevailed. Thus where the lessee demised to another the leased premises for the residue of the term, but reserved a delivery of possession on the last day of the term, and a right to possession if the buildings were leased during the term, it was held to be an underletting and not an assignment.[8] So where the assignee of a lease demised his entire

---

[1] Bacon, Abr. Lease, I. 3 ; Doe v. Bateman, 2 B. & A. 168.

[2] 5 Bligh, N. s. 31, 65.

[3] 8 Taunt. 293. See Hicks v. Dowling, 1 Ld. Raym. 99.

[4] 5 Bann. & R. 157 n.   [5] 3 Kay & J. 226, 229.

[6] Beardman v. Wilson, L. R. 4 C. P. 57 ; and see Barrett v. Rolph, 14 M. & W. 348.   [7] 9 Q. B. 1033.

[8] Post v. Kearney, 2 N. Y. 394 ; Linden v. Hepburn, 3 Sandf. 668.

interest, reserving a rent larger tian tiat reserved in tie
original lease witi a rigit of entry for tie non-payment tiereof, it was ield to be an underlease and not an assignment.[1]
So in a case in tie Supreme Court of New York, wiere tie
lessee underlet for tie entire term, but took a covenant from
tie sublessee to surrender up possession to iim *at the expiration of the term*, and a rigit of re-entry was reserved in case
tie rent was not paid, it was ield a subletting and not an
assignment.[2] It is obvious tiat tie original lessee intended
to reserve an interest in and a control over tie premises; and
tie court ield tiat tie original lessor could not avail iimself
of a covenant by tie sublessee to tie mesne lessor in respect
to taxes. But in anotier case decided in tie Court of Appeals
a somewiat different conclusion was reacied. Here
[*336] * tiere was a letting for a term of years, witi a restriction as to underletting; tie defendants went into
possession and paid several quarters' rent, tiougi tiey were
not tie lessees, and it did not appear wiat tie agreement was
between tiem and tie lessee. Tie lessee iaving become bankrupt, the lessor sued tiem as assignees for tie rent in arrear
at tie expiration of tie term, tiey being tien in possession.
Tie court say, "Tie defendants ield for tie wiole of tie
residue of tie unexpired term of tie lease. Wien tie transfer is of tie wiole of a term, tie person taking is an *assignee*
and not an undertenant, altiougi tiere is, *in form*, an underletting. It is essential to an undertenancy tiat it be of a part
only of tie unexpired term."[3] Tie case turns very muci
upon tie presumption arising, in tie absence of proof to tie
contrary, tiat tie tenant is an assignee ratier tian a sub-
lessee. But tie inference seems to be tiat if tie iolding be
by a sub-lease, if tiat be for tie same time and upon tie same
terms as tie original letting, it would be an assignment. In
a later case in tie same court tiis conclusion was adopted as
law, and tie efficacy of tie reservation of a mere rigit of re-
entry to alter a demise of tie entire term from an assignment
into a sublease was denied.[4] Tie court refer to tie Englisi

[1] Kearny v. Post, 1 Sandf. 105.   [2] Martin v. O'Connor, 43 Barb. 514.
[3] Bedford v. Terhune, 30 N. Y. 453, 457; Sanders v. Partridge, 108 Mass. 556.
[4] Woodhull v. Rosenthal, 61 N. Y. 382.

cases already cited, as sustaining the same rule. But whatever the soundness of these two cases upon the precise state of facts involved in them, their authority upon the point under consideration has been weakened if not wholly overruled by two very recent decisions in the same court; one slightly preceding in time the case of Woodhull v. Rosenthal, but not referred to therein,[1] and the other since that case.[2] In both of these the doctrine was maintained unqualifiedly that a covenant of the sublessee to deliver up the premises to the mesne lessor at the expiration of the term, and the reservation by the latter of a right of re-entry, made a lease, and not an assignment, though the demise was of the entire term. In Massachusetts, in a leading case,[3] the lessee's assignee, after a demise by the lessee for his entire term, was allowed to recover rent from the person to whom the demise was made, as if the latter were clearly a sub-lessee, though the point under consideration was not adverted to, nor does it appear whether re-entry by and redelivery to the mesne lessor were stipulated for in the demise. This decision, however, has been relied on as an authority in later cases, which place the law in this State on the same ground as that occupied by the latest decisions in New York.[4] Similar decisions have also been made in California[5] and Iowa,[6] while in Pennsylvania the English doctrine is adopted that a termor for years who demises the estate to another for the same or a greater term than that for which he holds under his own demise, is considered thereby *ipso facto*, to *assign* his term, and his lessee, so far as the original lessor is concerned, holds as assignee of such term, and not as a sub-tenant. And the same doctrine seems to apply whether the original demise was by parol or in writing.[7] Strictly speaking, a tenant at

[1] Collins v. Hasbrouck, 56 N. Y. 157.   [2] Ganson v. Tifft, 71 N. Y. 48.

[3] Patten v. Deshon, 1 Gray, 325.   So in Shumway v. Collins, 6 Gray, 227.

[4] McNiel v. Kendall, 128 Mass. 215 ; Dunlap v. Bullard, 131 Mass. 161.   See also Prescott v. Kyle, 103 Mass. 381.   It is somewhat difficult to apprehend the ground of the first-named case, which professes to rest on Patten v. Deshon, but puts the decision on the singular ground that because the parcel transferred by the lease had certain easements in the parcel retained by the lessor, this gave the latter reversionary rights as to the former.

[5] Blumenberg v. Myres, 32 Cal. 93.   [6] Collamer v. Kelly, 12 Iowa, 319.

[7] Lloyd v. Cozens, 2 Ashm. 131, 137; Holford v. Hatch, Doug. 187.   See also Palmer v. Edwards, Doug. 187, note.

will has no estate which he can assign. Whether, therefore,
he assigns or underlets, it creates no privity of estate between
the tenant to whom he gives possession and the original lessor.
The lessor may treat him as a disseisor in possession without
right. But if he accepts rent from him, he creates between
them the relation of tenant at will. But what the relations
between such intermediate tenant and his lessor may be, more
properly comes under the head of tenancies at will.[1] And the
same authorities seem also to settle, that if the intermediate
lessor reserve rent in his demise to the second lessee, he cannot distrain for it, since he has no reversionary interest remaining in himself.[2]

5. The respective rights of the original lessor and the tenant of a lessee, regarded as sub-lessee, are well settled. There
is no privity of estate between them, and therefore the lessor
cannot sue the undertenant upon the lessee's covenant to pay
rent, nor recover rent of him in any form of action.[3] The following case will serve to illustrate the above proposition, and
suggests another point of much difficulty, how far a mortgagee
of a lessee is regarded in law, as an assignee with corresponding liabilities as such. A. made a deed to J. S. with a condition
indorsed, that it should become void if the grantor paid a certain sum by a certain time, "together with the use of the
farm." This sum was orally fixed by agreement to be paid
annually. A. continued to occupy the farm, and made a mortgage to the defendant of the same, still retaining possession.
The agreed "use" or rent being in arrear, J. S. sued the
defendant for the same as assignee of A., the lessee and mortgagor. But it was held, that, as the defendant never was in
possession of the premises, no action lay against him in favor
of J. S. But the court do not decide whether, if this transaction had been clearly a lease between the original parties,
instead of a mortgage of real estate, and to be treated accord-

[1] Reckhow v. Schanck, 43 N. Y. 448 ; Cunningham v. Holton, 55 Me. 33 ;
Dingley v. Buffum, 57 Me. 381 ; Holbrook v. Young, 108 Mass. 83 ; post, p. *373.

[2] Lit. § 215 ; Hicks v. Dowling, 1 Ld. Raym. 99 ; Parmenter v. Webber, 8
Taunt. 293.

[3] McFarlan v. Watson, 3 N. Y. 286 ; Dartmouth Coll. v. Clough, 8 N. H. 22 ;
Campbell v. Stetson, 2 Met. 504 ; Wms. Real Prop. 336 ; Jennings v. Alexander,
1 Hilton, 154 ; Holford v. Hatch, Doug. 187 ; Grundin v. Carter, 99 Mass. 15.

ingly, the defendant, as mortgagee of the leasehold interest, would be liable for rent as assignee of the lessee.[1] But if one enters and holds possession of premises as assignee of the lessee, he will be liable for the rent so long as he continues to hold it.[2] Unless, however, the tenant holding under a lessee can be charged as assignee, he is no more liable in equity than at law to the original lessor,[3] even though the occupation by the tenant be without permission or objection of any one.[4] But in one case it was held, that where, by the terms of the original lease, the lessor had a right to enter for non-payment of rent, an undertenant might pay his rent to the original lessor in order to protect his estate.[5]

6. As the owner of a well-defined interest or estate in lands, a tenant for years, unless restrained by the covenants and conditions of his lease, may underlet the premises or any part of them, as has already been more than once assumed, or carve up his estate into such forms as he sees fit, and during the continuance of the term the original lessor is so far divested of the possession, that, if he were to find the premises vacant, he would have no more right to enter upon them than a stranger.[6]

7. Corresponding to the right of lessee to assign or underlet his interest is the right which the lessor has to convey or assign his reversion, and thereby bring in a new party with the rights of a reversioner.[7] Nor is it necessary, now, that the tenant should attorn to such grantee or assignee, to give effect to the grant or assignment, in those States where the Stat. 4 Anne, c. 16, § 9, is adopted,[8] or its principle existed inde-

---

[1] Graham v. Way, 38 Vt. 19 ; *post*, p. *340.

[2] Davis v. Morris, 36 N. Y. 569, 576.

[3] Bedford v. Terhune, 30 N. Y. 453 ; Davis v. Morris, 36 N. Y. 574.

[4] Kain v. Hoxie, 2 Hilton, 311, 316.

[5] Peck v. Ingersoll, 7 N. Y. 528. See also Collins v. Whilldin, 3 Phila. 102.

[6] Nave v. Berry, 22 Ala. 382 ; Brown v. Kite, 2 Overt. 233 ; Brown v. Powell, 25 Penn. St. 229 ; Wms. Real Prop. 335, 336 ; Shannon v. Burr, 1 Hilton, 39 ; Crommelin v. Thiess, 31 Ala. 412.

[7] Callaghan v. Hawkes, 121 Mass. 299. Here it was held that an agreement in a lease that the landlord might sell the leased premises, first giving the tenant notice, meant that he might by such sale terminate the lease, as he had the right to transfer the reversion without such notice.

[8] Wms. Real Prop. 203 ; 5 B. & C. 512, note, Am. ed.; New York, Moffat v.

pendently at law.[1] So if the estate of the lessor as owner in
fee is sold on execution before the rent is due, it would carry
the right to recover the rent to the purchaser.[2]

8. As a general proposition, having few exceptions,
[*337] the *transfer of a reversion carries with it the rent
due and accruing thereafter, by the lease creating the
term for years,[3] whether the assignment of the reversion be by
deed or mortgage.[4] This right of a lessor to recover rent of the
assignee of the lessee is founded not on contract, but on privity
of estate, and after he has parted with his reversion he cannot
recover the rent.[5] And it seems to be of little consequence how
one becomes a reversioner as to the assignee of the lessee so far
as it concerns his right to recover rent of whoever is assignee
and tenant when the rent falls due. Thus, after a lease for five
years, a second lease for ten years, including the period of the
first, transfers the right to the rent of the first.[6] But the assignee cannot recover rent then due and in arrears. Thus
where rent was reserved generally in a lease, and the lessor
died, only the rent accruing afterwards belonged to and was
recoverable by his heirs as being his reversioners.[7] And if the
administrator collect it, he will hold it in trust for the heirs

---

Smith, 4 N. Y. 126 ; New Hampshire, Bussey v. Holt, 24 N. H. 248 ; Maryland,
Funk v. Kincaid, 5 Md. 404 ; New Jersey, Rev. Stat. 1847, p. 643 ; Missouri,
Rev. Stat. c. 32, § 11 ; Connecticut, Baldwin v. Walker, 21 Conn. 168 ; Alabama,
English v. Key, 39 Ala. 113 ; Pennsylvania, 3 Binn. 625 ; Tilford v. Fleming,
64 Penn. St. 300. In Maine it is doubted. Fox v. Corey, 41 Me. 81. The Stat.
of Anne is not in force in Illinois. Fisher v. Deering, 60 Ill. 114.

[1] Massachusetts, Farley v. Thompson, 15 Mass. 18, 6 ; Keay v. Goodwin, 16
Mass. 1 ; Michigan, Perrin v. Lepper, 34 Mich. 292.

[2] Shelton v. Codman, 3 Cush. 318 ; Hart v. Israel, 2 P. A. Browne, 22 ; Bk.
of Penn. v. Wise, 3 Watts, 394 ; Scheerer v. Stanley, 2 Rawle, 276.

[3] Burden v. Thayer, 3 Met. 76 ; Keay v. Goodwin, 16 Mass. 1 ; Newall v.
Wright, 3 Mass. 138 ; Johnston v. Smith, 3 Penn. 496 ; York v. Jones, 2 N. H.
454 ; Farley v. Craig, 11 N. J. 262 ; Scott v. Lunt, 7 Pet. 596 ; Van Rensselaer
v. Gallup, 5 Denio, 454 ; Wilson v. Delaplaine, 3 Harringt. 499 ; Stout v. Keene,
Id. 82 ; Snyder v. Riley, 1 Speers, 272 ; Gibbs v. Ross, 2 Head, 437. Although
the transfer be by way of mortgage, Russell v. Allen, 2 Allen, 42. For the effect
of a mortgage of his estate by a reversioner and the rights of mortgagees, generally,
to rents of leased premises mortgaged before and after leases made, the reader is
referred to c. 16, sect. 4, pp. *529–*533 of this work. Gale v. Edwards, 52 Me.
363.

[4] Kimball v. Pike, 18 N. H. 419.   [5] Grundin v. Carter, 99 Mass. 15.

[6] Harmon v. Flanagan, 123 Mass. 288.   [7] Jaques v. Gould, 4 Cush. 384.

at law and the widow.[1] The same rule applies if the intestate die insolvent. The heirs are entitled to the rents until the estate is sold by the administrator by leave of court for the payment of debts.[2] And the same principle applies, though the rent be payable in a share of the grain raised upon the premises.[3]

9. If a part only of the reversion is conveyed, the grantee or assignee may recover his share of the rent *pro rata* according to the relative values of the respective parts of the reversion;[4] and this doctrine of apportionment of the right to rent among the several assignees of the reversion applies where this reversion has descended to several heirs;[5] and one of several heirs at law can sue for his aliquot part of rent accruing due after the death of his ancestor, the lessor;[6] or where a part of the reversion is levied upon by execution for debt, or is set off to a widow for her dower.[7] This apportionment of rent is never made in reference to the length of time of occupation; but whoever owns the reversion at the time the rent falls due is entitled to the entire sum then due.[8] But where by agreement the tenant was to pay so much rent and taxes by the year, and if he occupied for a longer time he was to pay *pro rata* for such time, it was held to include a *pro rata* of the taxes for the year as well as of the rent.[9] The rent, in such cases, accrues to the holder of the reversion by reason of his privity of estate with the lessor, and not as the assignee of a close in action; and when a lessor has once parted with his reversion, he cannot, except as hereafter stated, maintain any action for subsequently accruing rent against his lessee.[10]

---

[1] Robb's Appeal, 41 Penn. St. 45; Drinkwater v. Drinkwater, 4 Mass. 353, 358; Mills v. Merryman, 49 Me. 65; King v. Anderson, 20 Ind. 385.

[2] Gibson v. Farley, 16 Mass. 280; Newcomb r. Stebbins, 9 Met. 540, 544.

[3] Burns v. Cooper, 31 Penn. St. 426; Cobel v. Cobel, 8 Penn. St. 342.

[4] Montague v. Gay, 17 Mass. 439; Nellis v. Lathrop, 22 Wend. 121; Reed r. Ward, 22 Penn. St. 144; Bank of Pennsylvania v. Wise, 3 Watts, 394.

[5] Reed v. Ward, 22 Penn. St. 144; Bk. of Penn. v. Wise, 3 Watts, 394; Crosby v. Loop, 13 Ill. 625; Clun's Case, 10 Rep. 128; Cole v. Patterson, 25 Wend. 456; Com. Land. & Ten. 422.

[6] Jones v. Felch, 3 Bosw. 63.   [7] 1 Rolle's Abr. 237, pl. 4, 5.

[8] Martin v. Martin, 7 Md. 368; Burden v. Thayer, 3 Met. 76; Bk. of Penn. v. Wise, 3 Watts, 394.   [9] May v. Rice, 108 Mass. 150.

[10] Peck v. Northrop, 17 Conn. 217; Breeding v. Taylor, 13 B. Mon. 477; Samp-

Tıe rigıt to rent, *pro rata*, passes at once, and tıe law comes in to apportion it in reference to tıat time, so tıat notıing done, subsequently, by eitıer of tıe original parties, can affect tıe rigıts of tıe otıers.[1] And wıere rent is reserved [*338] generally, *witıout naming to wıom, tıe law comes in and appropriates it to wıoever is entitled to tıe estate, including tıe ıeirs of tıe lessor.[2]

10. Still, as above intimated, tıe rent and reversion may be separated by tıe ıolder of tıe same. Tıus wıere a reversioner conveyed ıis entire estate, including ıis reversion, and reserved tıe rent to ıimself.[3] So wıere tıe demise is by indenture, and tıe lessee covenants to pay rent, tıe lessor may assign or devise tıe rent witıout granting tıe reversion, and such assignee may recover tıe subsequently accruing rent in ıis own name, in an action of debt.[4] As an illustration of tıe manner and extent in wıicı tıe holder of a term may create a rent out of it, and deal witı it as a rent reserved by a lessor wıo owns tıe fee, tıe following case may be cited: Tıe lessor being possessed of a term for years, demised tıe premises for a longer period tıan ıis term, reserving a rent, and tıen assigned ıis interest and tıe rent to tıe plaintiff, wıo sued tıe lessee for tıe rent accruing due under tıe lease after tıe assignment. It was ıeld under tıe Stat. of Anne tıat no attornment was necessary in sucı a case to cıarge tıe lessee, there being sufficient privity between the grantee of tıe rent, and tıe tenant of tıe land out of wıicı tıe rent issues, to sustain tıe action witıout any formal attornment, and tıat tıe plaintiff's action would lie. Tıe court also cite a case from Cartıew, wıere tıe lessee, wıo ıad assigned ıis entire

son *v.* Grimes, 7 Blackf. 176 ; Van Wicklen *v.* Paulson, 14 Barb. 654 ; Walker's Case, 3 Rep. 23 ; Grundin *v.* Carter, 99 Ɉass. 15.

1 Linton *v.* Hart, 25 Penn. St. 193.

2 Whitlock's Case, 8 Rep. 71 ; Cother *v.* Ɉerrick, Hardres, 95 ; Jaques *v.* Gould, 4 Cush. 384.

3 M'Murphy *v.* Ɉinot, 4 N. H. 251; Co. Lit. 47 a ; Crosby *v.* Loop, 13 Ill. 625 ; Van Rensselaer *v.* Hays, 19 N. Y. 68 ; Dixon *v.* Niccolls, 39 Ill. 372.

4 Ryerson *v.* Quackenbush, 26 N. J. 236 ; Demarest *v.* Willard, 8 Cow. 206 ; Patten *v.* Deshon, 1 Gray, 325 ; Childs *v.* Clark, 3 Barb. Ch. 52 ; Kendall *v.* Carland, 5 Cush. 74 ; Allen *v.* Bryan, 5 B. & C. 512 ; Robins *v.* Cox, 1 Lev. 22 ; Moffat *v.* Smith, 4 N. Y. 126 ; Willard *v.* Tillman, 2 Hill, 274, s. c. 19 Wend. 358 ; Buskin *v.* Edmunds, Cro. Eliz. 636.

term to another rendering rent, was held at liberty to sue for
this in an action of debt, although he had no reversion remaining in himself. Or the action might be covenant broken.[1] But
the rent cannot be apportioned by the landlord to different
persons without the tenant's assent,[2] though with such assent it may be.[3] So a lessor may devise part of a rent, which
will be good without attornment of the tenant, and the part so
devised will thereby be severed from the reversion.[4]

11. In these cases, where by an assignment of the reversion
the rent passes, or where there is an assignment of the rent
without the reversion, the assignee sues in his own name for
any rent accruing due after such assignment. "It (the rent)
is not a thing in action, but *quasi* an inheritance."[5] Thus
where lessor for life reserving rent devised the rent to another
for life, who died between the periods of payment of the rent,
the executors of such devisee were held entitled only to the
rent due at the period of payment next prior to his death.[6]

12. In this connection it may be proper to add, that where
a rent descends with a reversion to several heirs, in an action
to recover it, they may, and it is very questionable if they
must not, all join.[7] Where the assignment is to several by the
act of the lessor, it has already been stated that the
lessee must attorn, *in order to be liable to the suit [*339]

[1] Williams v. Hayward, 1 Ellis & E. 1040; Newcomb v. Harvey, Garth. 161;
Com. Dig. Debt. (C.); Baker v. Gostling, 1 Bing. N. C. 19; Hunt v. Thompson,
2 Allen, 341; Van Rensselaer v. Read, 26 N. Y. 558, 577; *post*, vol. 2, p. *13.
In a recent case in Massachusetts, it was held that where the lessee surrendered
his lease to the lessor "without prejudice to the sub-leases of parts of the premises"
though by the lessor's acceptance the reversion on such sub-leases was merged,
the rents remained and could be recovered by the lessor from the sub-lessees as they
fell due. Beal v. Boston Car Spr. Co., 125 Mass. 157.

[2] Ards v. Watkin, Cro. Eliz. 637; Ryerson v. Quackenbush, 26 N. J. 236.

[3] Ryerson v. Quackenbush, *sup.*   [4] Ards v. Watkin, *sup.*

[5] Ards v. Watkin, *sup.*; Demarest v. Willard, 8 Cow. 206; Ryerson v. Quackenbush, *sup.*; Childs v. Clark, 3 Barb. Ch. 52; Willard v. Tillman, 2 Hill, 274;
Crosby v. Loop, 13 Ill. 625; Abercrombie v. Redpath, 1 Iowa, 111; Van Rensselaer v. Hays, 19 N. Y. 68, 99; Allen v. Bryan, 5 B. & C. 512; Dixon v. Niccolls,
39 Ill. 372, 384; Pfaff v. Golden, 126 Mass. 402.

[6] Stillwell v. Doughty, 3 Bradf. 359.

[7] Porter v. Bleiler, 17 Barb. 149; Martin v. Crompe, 1 Ld. Raym. 340; Hill
v. Gibbs, 5 Hill, 56; Wall v. Hinds, 4 Gray, 256; Decker v. Livingston, 15 Johns.
479; Lit. § 316.

of any one of them for his separate share;[1] though in the case of Ards v. Watkin, it was held, in case of a devise of a part of a rent, that the devisee may sue alone for his share.[2] It may be added, that the assignee of the reversion, in the above supposed cases, might sue the assignee of the lessee as well as the lessee himself, if in possession of the premises, because of a privity of estate, and because the covenant to pay rent runs with the land.[3]

13. In respect to the form of the action to be adopted by or against assignees in respect to covenants in leases, so much depends upon the circumstances under which the action may be brought, as well as upon the statutes of the several States, that it only seems necessary to say here, that an action of debt or covenant would lie for rent against the assignee of a lessee at common law, and would be local, the rule of the common law being, that an action founded on a privity of estate which relates to land is local, while one founded on privity of contract is transitory.[4]

14. Such being the consequences of assignments upon the rights of the parties, it is important that the assignee of a reversion or of rent should give notice thereof to the lessee or tenant. Otherwise a payment of rent made by him to the lessor, without notice, will be protected.[5] But where the lessor mortgaged his estate, and the lessee paid him the rent before it was due, but the mortgagee, when it was due, gave him notice and demanded the rent, it was held no defence that he had already paid it to his lessor.[6] But no act done by the assignor, after notice given to the other party of such as-

---

[1] Ryerson v. Quackenbush, 26 N. J. 254.   [2] Ards v. Watkin, Cro. Eliz. 637.
Childs v. Clark, 3 Barb. Ch. 52 ; Journeay v. Brackley, 1 Hilton, 447, 451 ; Walker's Case, 3 Rep. 26 b ; Howland v. Coffin, 12 Pick. 125.

[4] Walker's Case, 3 Rep. 22 ; Lienow v. Ellis, 6 Mass. 331 ; Pine v. Leicester, Hobart, 37 a, note ; Stevenson v. Lambard, 2 East, 575 ; Howland v. Coffin, 9 Pick. 52, s. c. 12 Pick. 125 ; Patten v. Deshon, 1 Gray, 325, 326 ; McKeon v. Whitney, 3 Denio, 452. In Vermont such an action is transitory by statute. Univ. of Vt. v. Joslyn, 21 Vt. 52 ; Buskin v. Edmunds, Cro. Eliz. 636 ; Thursby v. Plant, 1 Saund. 240, n.

[5] Farley v. Thompson, 15 Mass. 18 ; Fitchburg Co. v. Melven, 15 Mass. 268 ; Trent v. Hunt, 9 Exch. 14.

[6] De Nicholls v. Saunders, L. R. 5 C. P. 589 ; Cook v. Guerra, L. R. 7 C. P. 132.

signment, will avail him; as where lessor, after assignment made, released the lessee from rent accruing due after the assignment was made.[1] The assignee of a lessee, holding under a recorded lease containing a mortgage of the premises, is bound to take notice of the contents thereof, and he would, without such record, be bound to know the contents of the lease under which he claims.[2] Where, however, the lessee has paid the rent of the term in advance, he will not be liable to pay the same again to an assignee of the reversion, although a *purchaser, of the entire estate, without [*340] notice of such payment having been made. The lessee, in such case, is substantially a purchaser of the term.[3]

15. In connection with the doctrine of assignment, it seems proper again to refer to the case of an assignment by lessee of his interest, in the way of a mortgage, and how far such mortgagee thereby becomes liable as assignee upon the covenants running with the land. The English courts regard him as standing in the light of an assignee, and liable accordingly, though he may not have entered;[4] and in this opinion the court of New Hampshire coincides,[5] which is the more noticeable from the fact that it is held by the courts of that State that a man may become an assignee of a mortgage, with all legal rights as such, by a simple transfer of the mortgage debt by delivery without any writing.[6] In the United States court, one of the judges, in giving an opinion, waived "the much controverted and variously decided doctrine as to the responsibility of the mortgagee of leasehold property, but of which the mortgagee has never had possession, for the performance of covenants," &c.[7] In Vermont the court refer to the English doctrine with favor, neither, however, adopting nor rejecting it.[8] In Maryland the mortgagee of a term, after breach of condition of the mortgage, was held to be liable upon the covenants in the lease, whether he had taken actual possession

[1] McKeon v. Whitney, 3 Denio, 452.
Barroilhet v. Battelle, 7 Cal. 450, 454 ; 1 Greenl. Ev. § 23.
Stone v. Patterson, 19 Pick. 476.   [4] Williams v. Bosanquet, 1 Brod. & B. 238.
[3] M'Murphy v. Minot, 4 N. H. 251.   But this is questioned in Lord v. Ferguson, 9 N. H. 380, 383.
[6] Southerin v. Mendum, 5 N. H. 420.   [7] Calvert v. Bradley, 16 How. 593.
[8] Pingrey v. Watkins, 15 Vt. 479, 488.   See also Graham v. Way, 38 Vt. 19, 24.

of the premises or not.[1] In California, the court held that the mortgagee of a term would not be liable upon the covenants in a lease, because of the peculiar character of mortgages in that State.[2] The better opinion as well as the weight of authority in this country seems to be, that such mortgagee becomes responsible as assignee when he takes possession under his deed, but not before.[3]

15 *a*. There is a well-recognized distinction between a special assignment of a lease by a lessee, in respect to binding his assignee by the covenants in the lease, and an assignment of a lease as a part of the property of an insolvent debtor, whether by legal process under proceedings in bankruptcy or insolvency, or by a general assignment at common law for the benefit of his creditors. In the first case the assignee is liable, if he accepts the assignment, whether he has entered upon the premises under it or not.[4] But where a debtor by deed assigned his estate for the benefit of his creditors, and the assignee accepted and acted under the trust, it was held to pass a lease of the debtor, and to make the assignee liable for the rent accruing due after the assignment made, although the assignee did no acts to show his acceptance of the lease.[5] In the other case, no privity of estate, such as is always understood to be created in the first case, will be considered to have arisen unless the lease shall have been specially mentioned in the general assignment, or the assignee shall have elected to claim the benefit of the same. And in cases of general assignments by insolvents, or by proceedings in insolvency, the assignee will have a reasonable time in which to ascertain whether the lease can be made available for the benefit of creditors before he will be obliged to make his election, and this election may be manifested by acts as well as by words.[6]

[1] Mayhew *v.* Hardesty, 8 Md. 479.

[2] Johnson *v.* Sherman, 15 Cal. 287. See Engels *v.* McKinley, 5 Cal. 153.

[3] Felch *v.* Taylor, 13 Pick. 133; 2 Greenl. Cruise, 111, n.; Walton *v.* Cronly. 14 Wend. 63; Astor *v.* Miller, 2 Paige, 68; 4 Kent, Com. 8th ed. 175, n.; McKee *v.* Angelrodt, 16 Mo. 283; Astor *v.* Hoyt, 5 Wend. 603.

[4] Quackenboss *v.* Clarke, 12 Wend. 555; Taylor, Land. & Ten. 7th ed. § 456; 2 Platt, Leases, 422.   [5] White *v.* Hunt, L. R. 6 Exch. 32.

[5] Journeay *v.* Brackley, 1 Hilton, 447; Copeland *v.* Stephens, 1 B. & A. 593; Bagley *v.* Freeman, 1 Hilton, 196; Carter *v.* Warne, 4 C. & P. 191; Pratt *v.*

16. But whether the assignment be absolute or conditional, if the assignee enters under it and occupies the estate, he can neither deny the validity of the assignment in an action by the lessor for rent, nor can he escape liability for the same by abandoning the premises before the expiration of the lease.[1]

*SECTION VI.   [*341]

OF RENT, EVICTION, DESTRUCTION, AND USE OF PREMISES.

1.   Rent, how payable ; barred by eviction.
2.   Of effect of eviction by eminent domain.
3.   Of effect of wrongful entry by lessor.
3a. What acts work an eviction ; actual or constructive.
3b. Of eviction in part ; and damages for eviction.
4.   Release, surrender, or eviction, alone relieves tenant.
5.   Destruction of premises does not affect covenant to repair.
6.   Effect of lessor's insuring.
7.   Lessor not bound to repair.
7a. Tenant, how far liable to strangers.
7b. Tenant liable for excavations.
8.   Of restricted liability of lessee under his covenants.
8a. Tenant not liable for fire.
9.   Of implied obligation as to use from nature of premises.
10. Lease of a room in a building which is destroyed.
11. Lessee not restricted in use of building.
12. Mode of using restricted by lease.

1. STRINGENT as is the liability of a lessee and his assignee, under the covenants of a lease, as has been shown, no claim for rent arises except where it is payable in advance, until the lessee shall have enjoyed the premises the whole time for which the payment of a rent is stipulated to be made.[2] And

Levan, 1 Miles, 358 ; *Re* Yeaton, 1 Lowell, 420 ; Hoyt *v.* Stoddard, 2 Allen, 442. So a receiver appointed by the court has his election.   Comm'th *v.* Frankl. Ins. Co., 115 Mass. 278.   But the lessee remains liable for rent accruing due after the bankruptcy.   Treadwell *v.* Marden, 123 Mass. 390.

[1] Blake *v.* Sanderson, 1 Gray, 332 ; Carter *v.* Hammett, 18 Barb. 608, s. c. 12 Barb. 253 ; Dorrance *v.* Jones, 27 Ala. 630.   In the latter case, a debtor assigned his goods and store, and his assignee entered and occupied the store till the goods were sold, and then quit possession.   Held to be such an entry as to bind him for rent of store for the whole balance of the term.

[2] Clun's Case, 10 Rep. 128 ; Bordman *v.* Osborn, 23 Pick. 295 ; Martin *v.* Martin, 7 Md. 368.

wıere no time is fixed for sucı payment to be made, it is not
due till tıe end of a year.[1] So, wıere payable quarterly, no
part is due till tıe end of tıe quarter.[2] Nor, wıen payable
at a particular day, can it be apportioned as to a part of tıe
time for wıicı tıe tenant may occupy.[3] Accordingly, wıere
by virtue of a rigıt reserved to tıe lessor to determine tıe
lease at any time by selling tıe estate, and ıe did so in tıe
interval between tıe times of payment of rent, it was ıeld
tıat ıe could not recover in any form for tıe rent or use and
occupation of tıe premises between tıe day of tıe last pay-

---

[1] Menough's Appeal, 5 Watts & S. 432; Ridgley v. Stillwell, 27 Mo. 128;
Crabb, Real Prop. § 292; 3 Cruise, Dig. 272.

[2] Garvey v. Dobyns, 8 Mo. 213; Wood v. Partridge, 11 Ɉass. 488; Perry v.
Aldrich, 13 N. H. 343.

[3] Smith, Land. & Ten. 134; 3 Kent, Com. 470; Menough's Appeal, 5 Watts & S.
432; Clun's Case, 10 Co. 128 a; Cruger v. McLaury, 41 N. Y. 219, 223; Cameron v. Little, 62 Ɉaine, 550, applied in cases of tenancy at will. The Stat. Geo. II.
as to apportionment of rent is not in force in New Hampshire. Perry v. Aldrich,
13 N. H. 343. But in Ɉassachusetts, Pub. Stat. c. 121, § 8, in case of surrender,
death of life-tenant, or other like contingency, or notice to quit, the rent may be
apportioned. The rules and principles stated in this section in regard to rent
apply in a considerable degree to compensation for use and occupation, which is
also barred by eviction and insusceptible of apportionment. But there seems to
be much misconception as to the action for its recovery; a notion that this
will only lie when rent as such cannot be recovered, and a want of distinction
between its two forms, — debt and assumpsit. Both eXisted at common law, but
the latter was liable to be defeated if a written demise was proved. By the Stat.
11 Geo. II., c. 19, however, it lay unless a sealed lease existed. Gibson v. Kirk,
1 Q. B. 850. This statute did not give the action, as was suggested in Cleves v.
Willoughby, 7 Hill, 83; it only removed one bar to it. Churchward v. Ford,
2 Hurlst. & N. 446; Hunt v. Wolfe, 2 Daly, 298, 302. This statute is supposed
to be generally in force in the United States. Taylor, Land. & Ten. (7th ed.) § 635.
Where the lease is under seal, assumpsit will not lie. Kiersted v. Orange & A. R. R.,
69 N. Y. 343. In Ɉichigan, however, it will. Dalton v. Laudahn, 30 Ɉich. 349.
The action of debt for use and occupation always lay at common law, and the statute had no application thereto. Gibson v. Kirk, sup. Where the lease is under
seal, though debt for rent lies, debt for use and occupation probably will not.
Dungey v. Angove, 2 Ves. jr. 307; Gudgen v. Besset, 6 Ellis & B. 986; and Wilkins v. Wingate, 6 T. R. 62, where it was allowed is eXplained in Gibson v. Kirk,
1 Q. B. 853. In Fuller v. Ruby, 10 Gray, 285, 287, such a count was sustained,
though the demise was under seal; but the later cases in the same State seem to
hold any count for use and occupation bad in such a case. Hunt v. Thompson,
2 Allen, 341; Burnham v. Roberts, 103 Ɉass. 379. Rent in advance cannot be
recovered in a count for use and occupation. Angell v. Randall, 16 L. T. N. s. 498.
For other points relating to this action, see *post*, cc. 11 and 12.

ment of rent and the determination of the lease.[1] And the
same doctrine was applied where the demise was by parol,
the tenancy having been determined by the lessor between the
rent-days.[2] Thus where a parol lease was for a year, with the
rent payable quarterly, and in the interval between two of
these payments the lessor sold the premises, and the purchaser
notified the tenant to quit, and he did so before another quarterly rent fell due, it was held that the tenant was not liable
for the rent between the next previous quarter-day and the
time of his quitting possession.[3] If, therefore, the lessee be
evicted from the premises by the lessor or by a paramount title,
it will discharge him from the payment of any rent which may
fall due, by the terms of the lease, after such eviction.[4] And
such eviction may be constructive as well as actual.[5] And the
same rule would apply, *pro rata*, if he were evicted from a part
of the premises by any other means than by the act of the
lessor himself.[6] But an expulsion from a part of the
premises will * not affect the tenant's liability under [*342]
any other of the covenants in his lease than that for
the payment of rent; as, for instance, the covenant to repair.[7]
But there can be no liability for rent, and no eviction until his
tenancy has in fact commenced. Thus, where one hired a
store in an unfinished building of another, from a certain date,
and the tenant was to lay out certain expenses in fitting it up,
and the landlord was to do other things, and after the date
fixed, but before the building and room were completed, it was

[1] Nicholson v. Munigle, 6 Allen, 215 ; Zule v. Zule, 24 Wend. 76 ; Grimman
v. Legge, 8 B. & C. 324 ; Hall & Burgess, 5 B. & C. 332 ; Emmes v. Feeley, 132
Mass. 346.

[2] Fuller v. Swett, 6 Allen, 219, n.

[3] Robinson v. Deering, 56 Me. 357 ; Clun's Case, 10 Co. 128 a ; Emmes v.
Feeley, *sup.*

[4] Fitchburg Co. v. Melven, 15 Mass. 268 ; Wood v. Partridge, 11 Mass. 488 ;
Russell v. Fabyan, 27 N. H. 529 ; Bordman v. Osborn, 23 Pick. 295 ; 2 Platt,
Leases, 129 ; Rolle, Abr. Rent, O.; Franklin v. Carter, 1 C. B. 750 ; Pope v.
Biggs, 9 B. & C. 245.

[5] Home Life Ins. Co. v. Sherman, 46 N. Y. 370.

[6] Hegeman v. McArthur, 1 E. D. Smith, 147; Broom's Maxims, 212 ; Steven-
son v. Lambard, 2 East, 575 ; Smith v. Malings, Cro. Jac. 160 ; Hunt v. Cope,
Cowp. 242 ; Com. Land. & Ten. 523 ; Morrison v. Chadwick, 7 C. B. 266, 283 ;
Martin v. Martin, 7 Md. 368 ; Lawrence v. French, 25 Wend. 443.

[7] Morrison v. Chadwick, 7 C. B. 283.

burned down, it was left to the jury to determine whether the lessee had taken possession under his lease or not, so as to be vested with the term. If he had, he was liable for the rent; otherwise he was not. Nor would the non-completion of the building be a defence in an action for the rent.[1] But if one is sued upon a covenant for rent, he may recoup for damages occasioned by a breach of other covenants in the same lease, though they are implied ones only.[2] And if, in cases like the one above stated, it had been stipulated in the lease that rent was not to commence until the building was completed, the lessee would not be liable until then, though he were to enter and occupy the premises before they were finished.[3]

2. It has sometimes been attempted to apply the principle of eviction from a part of the premises, where lands under lease have been appropriated to public use under the exercise of eminent domain; and the rule adopted in Missouri is to have such appropriation extinguish the rent, payable by the tenant *pro tanto*, according to the value of the part taken compared with the whole.[4] But the better rule, and one believed to be adopted in most of the States, is that such a taking operates, so far as the lessee is concerned, upon his interest as property for which the public are to make him compensation, and does not affect his liability to pay rent for the entire estate according to the tenor of his lease.[5] And

---

[1] LaFarge v. Mansfield, 31 Barb. 345.

[2] Mayor v. Mabie, 13 N. Y. 151; Wright v. Lattin, 38 Ill. 293; but not for the lessor's trespasses, Bartlett v. Farrington, 120 Mass. 284; and see Chic. Leg. News v. Brown, 103 Ill. 317.

[3] Epping v. Devanny, 28 Ga. 422.

[4] Biddle v. Hussman, 23 Mo. 597; Kingsland v. Clark, 24 Mo. 24. These cases rely on the authority of Cuthbert v. Kuhn, 3 Whart. 357; but that and other cases in Pennsylvania do not proceed in eviction, but on the equitable rights of the landlord and tenant. The statute of New York provides in such a case for an abatement *pro rata* of the tenant's rent. Gillespie v. Thomas, 15 Wend. 464, 468.

[5] Parks v. Boston, 15 Pick. 198; Ellis v. Welch, 6 Mass. 246; Patterson v. Boston, 20 Pick. 159; McLarren v. Spalding, 2 Cal. 510; Folts v. Huntley, 7 Wend. 210; Workman v. Mifflin, 30 Penn. St. 362; Frost v. Earnest, 4 Whart. 86; Foote v. Cincinnati, 11 Ohio, 408. Such a taking is not a breach of the covenant for quiet enjoyment. Ib. This is admitted in Pennsylvania: cases *supra;* Peck v. Jones, 70 Penn. St. 83, 85; Schuylkill Co. v. Schmoele, 57 Penn. St. 271; but as equitable relief is given at common law, and in equity the lessee's damages replace the rent, to avoid circuity of action they are held to belong to

tiis extends to ground rent; suci taking does not abate any part of the rent due.[1] So it has been attempted to protect a tenant from paying rent *in toto* or *pro tanto*, wiere the leased premises iave been seized upon and tenant evicted by a public enemy or a public armed force. In one case the court allowed an abatement of rent wiile the tenant was tius interrupted in iis enjoyment of the premises.[2] But the law seems to be well settled tiat he would still be liable for tie rent, tiougi evicted in tie manner supposed.[3]

3. If tie lessor iimself interferes to deprive tie lessee of tie enjoyment of tie leased premises, tie law is in many respects muci more stringent than wiere the act is done by a stranger. *Tius, if ie enters and evicts [*343] the tenant, wrongfully, from a part of tie premises, it operates as a suspension of tie entire rent, until possession shall be restored, instead of its being apportioned, as in tie cases before stated, wiere the eviction of a part was the act of a stranger. Such, of course, would be tie effect if tie eviction by the lessor was from the entire premises.[4] So if tie landlord make a second lease of a part of tie premises embraced in a prior one, and tie second lessee evicts tie first, it is so far an eviction by tie lessor, tiat ie may refuse to pay rent, may abandon the premises, and remove tie buildings, fences, &c., wiici ie ias erected tiereon.[5] In case of eviction, tie

---

the landlord ; and the tenant is therefore relieved to that extent from his rent and other obligations in the lease, and apportionment takes place. Dyer *v.* Wightman, 66 Penn. St. 425. Cuthbert *v.* Kuhn, 3 Whart. 357, proceeded on the tenant's offer to apportion. Ib.

[1] Workman *v.* Mifflin, 30 Penn. St. 362. The equitable reason for appportionment does not apply in cases of ground rent, as the lessor has no right to the land ; and therefore none to damages given for it. Dyer *v.* Wightman, *supra.*

[2] Bayly *v.* Lawrence, 1 Bay, 499.

[3] Wagner *v.* White, 4 Harr. & J. 564 ; Paradine *v.* Jane, Aleyn, 26 ; Schilling *v.* Holmes, 23 Cal. 227 ; Clifford *v.* Watts, L. R. 5 C. P. 577, 586.

[4] Hegeman *v.* McArthur, 1 E. D. Smith, 147 ; Salmon *v.* Smith, Saund. 204, n. 2 ; Lewis *v.* Payn, 4 Wend. 423 ; Wilson *v.* Smith, 5 Yerg. 379 ; Christopher *v.* Austin, 11 N. Y. 216 ; Broom's Maxims, 212 ; Ascough's Case, 9 Rep. 135 ; Shumway *v.* Collins, 6 Gray, 227 ; Morrison *v.* Chadwick, 7 C. B. 283 ; Lawrence *v.* French, 25 Wend. 443 ; Dyett *v.* Pendleton, 8 Cow. 727 ; Edgerton *v.* Page, 1 Hilton, 320, 328 ; 20 N. Y. 281 ; Hodgkins *v.* Robson and Thornborow, 1 Vent. 276, s. c. Pollexf. 142 ; Schilling *v.* Holmes, 23 Cal. 227 ; Pier *v.* Carr, 69 Penn. St. 326 ; Wright *v.* Lattin, 38 Ill. 293.

[5] Wright *v.* Lattin, 38 Ill. 293. As to damages, Larkin *v.* Misland, 100 N.Y. 212.

tenant is exempt from tie payment of rent from tie quarter-day anterior to suci eviction.[1] If, after suci eviction, tie lessee returns and occupies again, tie rent begins anew,[2] for, as before stated, if tie eviction is from a part only, tie tenancy may continue, but being suspended as to tie rent. But to work tiis suspension of rent *pro tanto* or *in toto*, as tie case may be, tiere must be sometiing more tian a mere entry upon tie land or premises by tie lessor, and doing acts of trespass tiereon. For tiese ie is liable as any otier trespasser. Tiere must be sometiing wiici, in law, amounts to an eviction or expulsion of tie tenant, to work a suspension or extinguisi-ment of tie rent.[3] Wiat siall work suci an eviction or expulsion, it is often difficult to determine. Particular cases may be referred to, from wiici a rule may periaps be defined, more clearly tian from tie statement of any rule of general application. In Hunt *v.* Cope, above cited, tie landlord en-tered and tore down tie roof and ceiling of a summer-iouse in tie garden, a part of tie premises leased, and tie court ield tiat it ougit to go to a jury to determine wietier tiis was an eviction. In Smiti *v.* Raleigi, tie landlord railed off a portion of tie garden forming a part of tie leased estate, and tie tenant tiereupon quitted tie premises, and it was ield tiat ie migit treat it as an eviction.[4] In Dyett *v.* Pendleton, tie majority of tie court allowed tie tenant to regard as an

[*344]   act of ouster from a tenement wiici ie iired, consist-ing of a part of a * dwelling-iouse, tie suffering of prostitutes openly to occupy tie otier part of tie iouse, wiose conduct was noisy and indecent, disturbing tie tenant in iis occupation, and rendering it disreputable for moral and decent people to dwell in it. Tiis, it will be per-

---

[1] Chatterton *v.* Fox, 5 Duer, 64.

[2] ᴊartin *v.* ᴊartin, 7 ᴊd. 375 ; Morrison *v.* Chadwick, 7 C. B. 283.

[3] Bennet *v.* Bittle, 4 Rawle, 339 ; ᴊartin *v.* ᴊartin, 7 ᴊd. 375 ; Com. Land. & Ten. 523 ; Salmon *v.* Smith, Sannd, 204, n. 2 ; Hunt *v.* Cope, Cowp. 242 ; Wilson *v.* Smith, 5 Yerg. 379 ; Lawrence *v.* French, 25 Wend. 443 ; Lounsbery *v.* Snyder, 31 N. Y. 514 ; Edgerton *v.* Page, 20 N. Y. 281, 284 ; Fuller *v.* Ruby, 10 Gray, 285 ; Royce *v.* Guggenheim, 106 ᴊass. 201 ; Pier *v.* Carr, 69 Penn. St. 326.

[4] Smith *v.* Raleigh, 3 Campb. 513 ; so Sherman *v.* Williams, 113 ᴊass. 481 ; nor is it necessary that the tenant should quit to free himself from liability for rent for the residue, *post*, pl. 3 b.

ceived, was a *moral* eviction, without any act done in or upon the premises leased. One of the court likens it to the establishment in another part of the house of a hospital for the small-pox or plague, or a deposit of gunpowder, or of offensive or pestilential materials.[1] In Lewis *v.* Payn, the court, referring to the last-mentioned case, say, "It seems to be held that any obstruction by the landlord to the beneficial enjoyment of the demised premises, or a diminution of the consideration of the contract by the acts of the landlord, amounts to a constructive eviction."[2] Where land was leased to an agricultural society for exhibitions, and the lessor let pigs into the premises, which rooted up the ground and rendered it unfit for the uses of the society, it was held to be such an eviction, that the lessee could avoid paying rent therefor.[3] In Upton *v.* Greenlees, Jervis, C. J., says, "It is extremely difficult, at the present day, to define with technical accuracy what is an eviction." "I think it may be taken to mean this, — not a mere trespass and nothing more, but something of a grave and permanent character, done by the landlord with the intention of depriving the tenant of the enjoyment of the demised premises."[4] It must be some permanent act done which deprives the lessee of some part of the premises. A

---

[1] Dyett v. Pendleton, 8 Cow. 727. But see Royce v. Guggenheim, 106 Mass. 201, 204 ; DeWitt v. Pierson, 112 Mass. 8. These were cases of constructive eviction ; which differs from actual eviction, that no part of the demised premises is actually appropriated, but only their value or use impaired. In this case the tenant must quit the premises to complete the eviction. Ib.; Boreel v. Lawton, 90 N. Y. 293.

[2] Lewis v. Payn, 4 Wend. 423.   [3] Wright v. Lattin, 38 Ill. 293.

[4] Upton v. Greenlees, 17 C. B. 30, 64. This intention is a question of fact. Henderson v. Mears, 1 Post. F. 636. But it is conclusively to be presumed from the acts themselves, and it is sufficient 'if they "permanently deprive" the tenant whatever the actual intent may have been. Skally v. Shute, 132 Mass. 367. But setting a fence on tenant's land by mistake, which lessor offers to correct, is no eviction. Mirick v. Hoppin, 118 Mass. 582. The limits of this work do not admit of examining at length a pretty large class of cases where the question has been, whether a former and existing demise of a part of leased premises is such an eviction as to deprive the landlord of his claim for rent while such prior demise exists. See Lawrence v. French, 25 Wend. 443, and cases cited ; Neale v. Mackenzie, 1 M. & W. 747, reversing s. c. in 2 Cr. M. & R. 84 ; Mc-Elderry v. Flannagan, 1 Harr. & G. 308 ; Christopher v. Austin, 11 N. Y. 216; Hayner v. Smith, 63 Ill. 430.

mere neglect to make repairs will not justify the tenant in quitting, although there be a covenant on the part of the landlord to repair.   But though no implied covenant of right to enjoy light over adjacent premises passes by a lease of a dwelling-house, and the erection of a house upon adjacent land which obstructs and darkens the windows of a leased dwelling-house is not held to be an eviction, yet if the erection of a house be upon the leased premises so as to deprive them entirely of light, and to render parts of them uninhabitable, it would be such an interference with them as to justify the tenant in treating it as an eviction, and abandoning the premises.[1]

3 a. Not only must the act be such as materially interferes with the enjoyment of the premises by the lessee, but it must have been done by the lessor or his procuration or by paramount title.   If the act be done by a stranger, it is no ground of defence against the claim for rent.[2]   Thus the erection of a wall by an adjacent owner, or even by the lessor himself upon his other premises, which darkens the windows of the leased premises, will not be deemed such an eviction as to relieve the tenant from the payment of rent.[3]   Nor would a mere entry by the lessor himself be an eviction, if done for the lessee's benefit, as, for instance, to make repairs.[4]   An act which destroys the premises, or renders them useless, may be regarded as an eviction so far as affecting the liability to pay rent. And a disturbance of the enjoyment of them which renders them useless would have the same effect.[5]   Thus, where a building was let for the purposes of a lodging-house adjoining the wall of another house not belonging to the lessor, the wall and roof of the premises being secured to this adjoining wall, the owner of this, having raised his building, removed the roof and one wall of the leased premises, and the tenant abandoned

---

[1] Wright v. Lattin, 38 Ill. 293 ; Royce v. Guggenheim, 106 Mass. 201.   So, perhaps, if the lessor builds on his own land merely to injure the tenant. Id. 205.

[2] Welles v. Castles, 3 Gray, 323, 326.

[3] Hazlett v. Powell, 30 Penn. St. 293; Palmer v. Wetmore, 2 Sandf. 316 ; Royce v. Guggenheim, 106 Mass. 202 ; Moore v. Weber, 71 Penn. St. 429, 432.

[4] Peterson v. Edmonson, 5 Harringt. 378.

[5] Halligan v. Wade, 21 Ill. 470.   Thus where one let a distillery but prevented the lessee's getting a license, Grabenhorst v. Nicodemus, 42 Md. 236.   See also Alger v. Kennedy, 49 Vt. 109 ; Scott v. Simons, 54 N. H. 426.

the same, it was held to be such an eviction as to suspend the liability for rent from the time of the eviction.[1] And many of the cases go to sustain the proposition, that nothing short of an eviction which deprives the tenant of the *possession* of the premises would bar a claim for rent, and that, if the tenant actually retains possession, he cannot resist payment of the rent. The proposition may perhaps be reconciled with what has already been said, and what is hereafter stated, by supposing that what is meant in some of the cases is, that the acts spoken of as tantamount to an eviction were such as warranted the lessee in abandoning the premises and avoiding the payment of rent. Thus, in Edgerton v. Page, the landlord discharged waste and filthy water upon the premises, and suffered a waste-pipe in another part of the building to be out of repair, to the great nuisance and injury of the tenant, who did not abandon possession, and it was held to be no eviction.[2] In one case, the court seemed inclined to treat acts which rendered the premises useless for the purposes for which they are let as of itself an eviction, so far as to bar rent, although the tenant may not have actually abandoned their occupation.[3] While, in Dyett v. Pendleton, the case seems to go upon the ground that the tenant had been compelled to abandon the premises, because a further occupation of them had been rendered impossible, or inconvenient and useless, by the acts of the lessor.[4] And the cases seem to concur, that a mere interference with the person of the tenant amounting to a trespass,[5] or a mere trespass on the premises, though attended with great inconvenience or obstruction to the tenant in the

---

[1] Bentley v. Sill, 35 Ill. 414.

[2] Edgerton v. Page, 1 Hilton, 320 ; s. c. 20 N. Y. 281 ; Boreel v. Lawton, 90 N. Y. 293. See Jackson v. Eddy, 12 Mo. 209 ; St. John r. Palmer, 5 Hill, 599. See Vatel v. Herner, 1 Hilton, 149, where the use of a privy adjoining the prem. ises, though very offensive, was not an eviction.

[3] Halligan v. Wade, 21 Ill. 470, where the court say, by way of illustration, that it might be tantamount to an eviction of premises let for the purposes of a respectable public-house to convert a part of the premises into a pig-stye or cattle-pens, or a low, noisy liquor-saloon, or a tinman's shop, and would bar a claim for rent for the same. But the same court in Leadbeater v. Roth, 25 Ill. 587, state the law in conformity with the rule in the text.

[4] Dyett v. Pendleton, 8 Cow. 727. But he is liable until he does abandon. DeWitt v. Pierson, 112 Mass. 8.   [5] Vatel v. Herner, 1 Hilton, 149.

beneficial enjoyment of them, will not amount to an eviction;[1] and, in one of the cases, it is held, that, to have the entry of the lessor work an eviction of the tenant, it must be followed by a continuous possession.[2] The apparent discrepancy between the cases may be accounted for by the dicta of the courts having reference to different states of facts, and being intended to be limited in their bearing to cases like those in which they were applied.

3 *b.* To restate the rights of the tenant on eviction in part, it seems if this be by a stranger, other than the lessor himself, and is from a part only, the rent will be apportioned and payable for such part as remains.[3] And this applies also where the demised property is an easement.[4] If the eviction is by the lessor himself, the tenant may elect whether to [*345] abandon entirely and put an end * to the tenancy and rent altogether,[5] or to retain such part as remains, free from liability to pay any rent, so long as the eviction continues. And such seems now the settled rule of law both in England and generally in the United States.[6] But as the tenancy in that case is not at an end, as soon as the occupancy is restored the liability revives to pay rent from and after such restoration.[7] If a part of the premises leased is held by a

[1] Edgerton *v.* Page, *sup.*; Bac. Abr. Rent, L. 44; Wilson *v.* Smith, 5 Yerger, 379; Briggs *v.* Hall, 4 Leigh, 484; Day *v.* Watson, 8 Mich. 535; Cohen *v.* Dupont, 1 Sandf. 260; Gardner *v.* Keteltas, 3 Hill, 330; Hunt *v.* Cope, Cowp. 242; Elliot *v.* Aiken, 45 N. H. 30; Bennett *v.* Bittle, 4 Rawle, 339.

[2] Day *v.* Watson, *sup.*

[3] Fillebrown *v.* Hoar, 124 Mass. 580; Dyett *v.* Pendleton, 8 Cow. 727; Smith *v.* Malings, Cro. Jac. 160; Lawrence *v.* French, 25 Wend. 443; Seabrook *v.* Moyer, 88 Penn. St. 417; Com. Land. & Ten. 217, 525.

[4] Blair *v.* Claxton, 18 N. Y. 529.

[5] Smith *v.* Raleigh, 3 Camp. 513; Lawrence *v.* French, 25 Wend. 443; Christopher *v.* Austin, 11 N. Y. 216; Edgerton *v.* Page, 1 Hilton, 320, 328; Reed *v.* Reynolds, 37 Conn. 469.

[6] Hegeman *v.* McArthur, 1 E. D. Smith, 147; Vermilya *v.* Austin, 2 E. D. Smith, 203; Halligan *v.* Wade, 21 Ill. 470; Lewis *v.* Payn, 4 Wend. 423; Christopher *v.* Austin, 11 N. Y. 216; Fuller *v.* Ruby, 10 Gray, 285, where a decision was waived. Colburn *v.* Morrill, 117 Mass. 262; Anderson *v.* Chicago Ins. Co., 21 Ill. 601; Leishman *v.* White, 1 Allen, 489; Hayner *v.* Smith, 63 Ill. 430; Upton *v.* Greenlees, 17 C. B. 30, 65, 66.

[7] Morrison *v.* Chadwick, 7 C. B. 283, 284; Page *v.* Parr, Styles, 432; Lewis *v.* Payn, 4 Wend. 423; Lawrence *v.* French, 25 Wend. 443; Day *v.* Watson, 8 Mich. 535; Corning *v.* Gould, 16 Wend. 531, 538; Cibel *v.* Hills, 1 Leon. 110.

stranger adversely to the lessor, the lessee is not obliged to accept of the other part and pay rent for the same.[1] But where the lessor himself has withheld a part of the leased premises, and the lessee has nevertheless elected to go on and occupy the remainder, he cannot refuse to pay rent *pro rata* for what he enjoys,[2] since the lessee cannot be said to have been evicted from that which he never possessed. It was a mere withholding a part of that which he had bargained to another.[3]

4. But nothing but a release, surrender, or eviction, will absolve a tenant, in whole or in part, from the covenants in his lease.[4] Nor will equity interpose to save a lessee from the

[1] Hay v. Cumberland, 25 Barb. 594. But where the stranger is without title the landlord is not liable to the tenant for not delivering possession. Gardner v. Keteltas, 3 Hill, 330 ; Becker v. De Forest, 1 Sweeny, 528 ; Cozens v. Stevenson, 5 S. & R. 421 ; Sigmund v. Howard Bk., 29 Md. 324 ; Underwood v. Birchard, 47 Vt. 305 ; Gazzolo v. Chambers, 73 Ill. 75. Nor for any other act of a mere stranger, Moore v. Weber, 71 Penn. St. 429 ; and the English rule to the contrary in Coe v. Clay, 5 Bing. 440 ; followed in L'Hussier v. Zallee, 24 Mo. 13 ; Hughes v. Hood, 50 Mo. 350 ; King v. Reynolds, 67 Ala. 229, is not sustained by the weight of American authority. It seems also that the tenant, if he takes part, is held for rent of the whole, Pendergast v. Young, 21 N. H. 234 ; and so it he has been compensated for the lessor's non-delivery, Knox v. Hexter, 71 N. Y. 461.

[2] Hurlbut v. Post, 1 Bosw. 28.

[3] The tenant upon eviction is not only relieved from paying rent, but may have damages also. Chatterton v. Fox, 5 Duer, 64. In case, however, of eviction by paramount title, the rule in New York and most of the United States was to give nominal damages, only, as the tenant's relief from rent was considered a full equivalent to him in analogy to the purchase money in conveyances in fee. Kelly v. Dutch Church, 2 Hill, 105. But in Massachusetts and a few other States, and latterly in England, full damages are given in all cases of eviction. Dexter v. Manley, 4 Cush. 14 ; Hardy v. Nelson, 27 Me. 525 ; Horsford v. Wright, Kirby, 3 ; Williams v. Burrell, 1 C. B. 402 ; Lock v. Furze, L. R. 1 C. P. 441 ; Rolph v. Crouch, L. R. 3 Exch. 44. And though the former States adhere to the strict rule in case of eviction solely from paramount title, Mack v. Patchin, 42 N. Y. 167 ; Burr v. Stenton, 43 N. Y. 462 ; Lanigan v. Kille, 97 Penn. St. 120 ; yet if the tenant is deprived by the landlord's act or fraud, or could have been protected by him, full damages will be given ; Chatterton v. Fox, *supra ;* Trull v. Granger, 8 N. Y. 115 ; Mack v. Patchin, 29 How. Pr. 20 ; Ricketts v. Lostetter, 19 Ind. 125 ; Shaw v. Hoffman, 25 Mich. 162 ; Wilson v. Raybould, 56 Ill. 417.

[4] Fisher v. Millikin, 8 Penn. St. 111 ; Baln v. Clark, 10 Johns. 424 ; Shepard v. Merrill, 2 Johns. Ch. 276 ; Fuller v. Ruby, 10 Gray, 290 ; Dyer v. Wightman, 66 Penn. St. 425. But a covenant is discharged if it is rendered incapable of performance by statute. Cordes v. Miller, 39 Mich. 581. So in Massachusetts

consequences of such covenants where there has been no fraud
or mistake in drawing the lease.[1]

5. It has, accordingly, been held that the destruction of
the premises demised, or their becoming untenantable, from
any cause, without lessor's fault, does not relieve the lessee
from his covenant to pay rent, or to repair, or to restore the
premises at the end of his term in good condition. Nor does
it furnish any defence, either in full or *pro tanto*, against a
[*346]   lessor's claim under these covenants, unless there are
exceptions to that effect * in the lease.[2] And it would
be held to be so, if the lessee covenants to pay rent
for the term, and makes no exception for the contingency of
the premises being destroyed.[3] This rests upon the ground
that the lessee, in such cases, is the purchaser and owner of
the premises for the term and price agreed upon in the lease,[4]
and therefore not exempt from paying this price, though the
premises are destroyed during the term by tempest,[5] or fire,[6]

the insolvency of a decedent's estate will bar further rent. Deane *v.* Caldwell,
127 Mass. 242.

[1] Gates *v.* Green, 4 Paige, 355 ; Sheets *v.* Selden, 7 Wall. 416, 424.

[2] Phillips *v.* Stevens, 16 Mass. 238 ; Leavitt *v.* Fletcher, 10 Allen, 121 ; Nave
v. Berry, 22 Ala. 382 ; Niedelet *v.* Wales, 16 Mo. 214 ; Hallet *v.* Wylie, 3
Johns. 44 ; Clifford *v.* Watts, L. R. 5 C. P. 577, 586 ; Fowler *v.* Bott, 6 Mass. 63 ;
White *v.* Molyneaux, 2 Ga. 124 ; Ward *v.* Bull, 1 Fla. 271 ; Howard *v.* Doolittle, 3 Duer, 464 ; Wood *v.* Hubbell, 5 Barb. 601 ; Davis *v.* Smith, 15 Mo. 467 ;
Hill *v.* Woodman, 14 Me. 38 ; Linn *v.* Ross, 10 Ohio, 412. See *post*, § 10 ;
Welles *v.* Castles, 3 Gray, 325.   Ross *v.* Overton, 3 Call, 268, where tenant of a
mill covenanted to leave it in repair, and it was carried off by ice, he was bound
to pay rent and to perform his covenants.   Hare *v.* Groves, 3 Anstr. 687 ; Holtzapffel *v.* Baker, 18 Ves. 115 ; Kramer *v.* Cook, 7 Gray, 550, where the wall of the
leased building fell by the undermining of the neighboring proprietor, the lessor
having neglected to support the wall.   Sugden's Letters, 119 ; Story, Eq. Jur.
§ 101 ; Paradine *v.* Jane, Aleyn, 27, in which the distinction in the effect of inevitable accident, upon a duty assumed by contract and one imposed by law, is
explained.   So where the act of a stranger co-operated.   Polack *v.* Pioche, 35 Cal.
416.   But where the covenant of the tenant was to keep the premises in the same
state as when taken, he was held not responsible for trees blown down.   Main's
Case, 5 Co. 20 b.

[3] Graves *v.* Berdan, 26 N. Y. 498.   But where the lease is of a single room, as
its destruction terminates the lease, Shawmut Bk. *v.* Boston, 118 Mass. 125, *post*,
349, the tenant's obligation to pay rent ceases.   Ib.

[4] Hart *v.* Windsor, 12 M. & W. 68 ; McGlashan *v.* Tallmadge, 37 Barb. 313.

[5] Peterson *v.* Edmonson, 5 Harringt. 378.

[6] Beach *v.* Farish, 4 Cal. 339 ; Dyer *v.* Wightman, 66 Penn. St. 425.

the loss, to that extent, being his, and not the lessor's. So where the covenant was to surrender up the premises at the end of the term in good order and condition, it was held that the lessee must make the necessary repairs during the term.[1] And an obligation " to repair and deliver up " would require the tenant to rebuild, in case of a loss by fire, during the term. But if " to deliver up " alone, or " to restore " the premises, it imposes nothing beyond his not holding over.[2] But under the civil code of Louisiana, where a tenement was rendered untenantable by the owner of an adjacent parcel taking down, as he had a right to do, an adjoining party wall, the tenant might quit the premises, and thereby absolve himself from the payment of rent.[3]

6. The law, however, does not seem to be uniform among the States, and hardly in the same State, in some instances, in respect to the effect of an accidental destruction of the property leased, upon the covenants in the lease. In Pennsylvania, it was held that it would make no difference with the right of the lessor to insist upon the covenant to repair, that he had had insurance against the loss and recovered the same.[4] But Sir Edward Sugden, in his " Handy Book," &c. (p. 119), says, " If you (the lessor) have insured, though not bound to do so, and received the money, you cannot compel payment of the rent, if you decline to lay out the money in building : " " unless the tenant is exempted by the lease from making good accidents by fire, he must, under the common covenants to repair, rebuild the house if it is burned down." But so far as Sir Edward Sugden expresses the opinion that the lessor would be bound to *apply the [*347]

---

[1] 1 Greenl. Ev. 233, n. ; Jaques v. Gould, 4 Cush. 384.

[2] Nave v. Berry, 22 Ala. 382 ; Maggort v. Hansbarger, 8 Leigh, 532 ; Bullock v. Dommitt, 6 T. R. 650. In Warner v. Hitchins, 5 Barb. 666, it is moreover held that a covenant to surrender up in the same condition as at the date of the lease does not bind to rebuild, as the covenant looks to redelivery and not to repair. So Howeth v. Anderson, 25 Tex. 557 ; Miller v. Morris, 55 Tex. 412 ; Levey v. Dyess, 51 Miss. 501. But the weight of authority seems otherwise. See Taylor Land & Ten. (7th ed.) § 364 and n. In Ball v. Wyeth, 8 Allen, 275, a covenant to repair was held qualified by an exception from casualties in the covenant to deliver up ; but Kling v. Dress, 5 Rob. N. Y. 521, is contra.

[3] Coleman v. Haight, 14 La. An. 564.

[4] Magaw v. Lambert, 3 Penn. St. 444.

insurance money in rebuilding, 1e seems to 1ave relied upon
t1e case cited,[1] and is opposed by t1e cases cited below.
T1e effect of t1ese cases is, t1at t1e covenant to pay rent is
w1olly unaffected by any ot1er covenant not expressly connected wit1 it in t1e lease, and t1at t1e lessor's insurance does
not concern t1e lessee at all.[2] T1e tenant 1as no rig1t in
equity to 1ave t1e insurance money applied in rebuilding t1e
premises, nor to restrain t1e lessor from suing for t1e rent
until t1e structure is restored.[3] But it was 1eld by t1e courts
of Ohio, that w1ere a lessee covenanted to insure t1e premises
demised, if it was for t1e benefit of t1e lessor alone, t1e money
in case of loss being to go to him, it would be a collateral
covenant, and would not run wit1 t1e land to bind an assignee.
But if t1e money was to be applied to repair or rebuild, t1en
it was in its c1aracter like a covenant to repair, w1ic1 may
run wit1 t1e land.[4] In Sout1 Carolina, w1ere a 1ouse t1at
was rented was partially destroyed by a tempest, it was 1eld
t1at t1e lessor was only entitled to rent so long as t1e premises were 1abitable,[5] w1ile in Pennsylvania, in an early case,
w1ere t1e lessee of a 1ouse covenanted to pay rent and return
t1e premises in good condition, and t1e 1ouse was destroyed
by a public enemy, t1e court 1eld t1e lessee bound to pay rent,
but exonerated from 1is covenant to repair, " *because equality
is equity, and the loss should be. divided!* " certainly not a very
definite rule in construing and applying t1e law of express
covenants.[6] But t1e language of t1e court of t1at State now
is, " If t1e premises 1ave been wrongfully entered by a disseisor, and t1e tenant be dispossessed for t1e entire term, or

---

[1] Brown *v.* Quilter, Amb. 619.

[2] See the remarks of the Chief Baron on Brown *v.* Quilter, in Hare *v.* Groves,
3 Anst. 692 ; Leeds *v.* Cheetham, 1 Simons, Ch. 146, that one party to a lease has
nothing to do with an insurance effected by the other party on his own account,
or to resort to that for any redress for his loss. Belfour *v.* Weston, 1 T. R. 310.
Lord 1ansfield says, " The house being insured is nothing to the tenant." 2
Platt, Leases, 124, 125 ; Platt, Cov. 282.

[3] Pope *v.* Garrard, 39 Ga. 471 ; Sheets *v.* Selden, 7 Wall. 416, 424 ; Moffatt *v.*
Smith, 4 N. Y. 126 ; Bussman *v.* Ganster, 72 Penn. St. 285.

[4] 1asury *v.* Southworth, 9 Ohio St. 340.

[5] Ripley *v.* Wightman, 4 McCord, 447 ; cited with approval in Whitaker *v.*
Hawley, 25 Kans. 674, where it is claimed that the common-law rule has not
been established in Kansas.   [6] Pollard *v.* Shaaffer, 1 Dall. 210.

even by the military force of a public enemy, or if they have been destroyed or rendered untenantable by earthquake, lightning, flood, or fire, and thus all enjoyment by the tenant be entirely lost, yet his covenant remains."[1] In another case the court refused to have an abatement of rent of a farm made, although a bridge thereon, which was important to its enjoyment, was destroyed by a flood.[2]

7. Without an express covenant to that effect on the part of the lessor, he cannot be held liable for repairs made by the tenant upon the demised premises.[3] Nor would he be bound by a parol promise to make repairs, if such promise is founded only upon the relations of landlord and tenant.[4] Nor is he bound to repair them himself, unless expressly made so by covenant nor to remove any nuisance, unless caused by his own act, or he has covenanted to that effect.[5] And where the owner of a building of three stories let a room in the middle story, and covenanted that if the premises should be damaged by fire so as to make them untenantable for more than thirty days, the rent, at the election of the tenant, should cease; the upper story was in the occupation of another tenant, and, while in that condition, the roof accidentally took fire, and rendered the premises untenantable. The landlord began to repair the roof, but, before it had been finished, the rain injured the tenant's goods, and he claimed damages of the lessor, but the court held, that, though he might have removed from the premises and ceased to pay rent until they had been repaired, he had no remedy against the landlord for the injury done his goods while he kept them in the building.[6]

[1] Dyer v. Wightman, 66 Penn. St. 425, 427 ; Workman v. Mifflin, 30 Penn. St 369 ; Hoy v. Holt, 91 Penn. St. 88.

[2] Smith v. Ankrim, 13 S. & R. 39.

[3] Weigall v. Waters, 6 T. R. 488 ; Mumford v. Brown, 6 Cow. 475 ; Belfour v. Weston, 1 T. R. 312 ; City Council v. Moorhead, 2 Rich. 430 ; Biddle v. Reed, 33 Ind. 529 ; Witty v. Matthews, 52 N. Y. 512.

[4] Gill v. Middleton, 105 Mass. 477.

[5] Arden v. Pullen, 10 M. & W. 321 ; Vai v. Weld, 17 Mo. 232 ; Gilhooly v. Washington, 4 N. Y. 217 ; Weigall v. Waters, 6 T. R. 488 ; Post v. Vetter, 2 E. D. Smith, 248 ; Welles v. Castles, 3 Gray, 323 ; Kramer v. Cook, 7 Gray, 550 ; 2 Platt, Leases, 183 ; Libbey v. Tolford, 48 Maine, 316 ; Moore v. Weber 71 Penn. St. 429.

[6] Doupe v. Genin, 45 N. Y. 119.

A case affording a further illustration of this point was one where a canal company made a lease of a water-power which had been created by the construction of the canal. It was held not to constitute a covenant on the part of the lessors to keep the canal in repair or supply it with water. And if the canal was discontinued, the lessee was without remedy.[1] So the lease of a water-power out of a mill-pond then existing was not held to constitute an obligation on the part of the lessor to keep the dam in repair.[2] And the grant of a right to take water from a well does not bind the owner of the well to repair it.[3]

7 a. It has been accordingly held, that if a third party has sustained damages by defect or want of repair of premises in possession of a tenant, the law will presume that the tenant, and not the landlord is responsible therefor, though this is subject to be rebutted by evidence.[4] This liability to a third party seems to depend upon whether the tenant has the entire control of the structure which causes the injury, or is one of several tenants having control only of the part he occupies. Thus, where one travelling along a street is injured by falling ice or snow from an awning in front of stores, one or more, in a building, or from the roof of the building, if the tenant in such cases has the sole control of the building, he alone is liable to the party injured. If the owner has the general charge of it, or of the roof, or occupies it in connection with tenants, he will be liable instead of the tenant who occupies a part only of the premises, for any injury from the part not expressly demised.[5] So if the injury arise from the erection of the

---

[1] Trustees v. Brett, 25 Ind. 409 ; Sheets v. Selden, 7 Wall. 416.

[2] Morse v. Maddox, 17 Mo. 569.

[3] Ballard v. Butler, 30 Me. 94. See Gott v. Gandy, 2 Ellis & B. 845 ; Elliot v. Aiken, 45 N. H. 30, 36.

[4] Kastor v. Newhouse, 4 E. D. Smith, 20 ; Payne v. Rogers, 2 H. Bl. 349 ; Cheetham v. Hampson, 4 T. R. 318; Bishop v. Bedf. Charity, 1 Ellis & E. 697 ; Hadley v. Taylor, L. R. 1 C. P. 53 ; Irvine v. Wood, 51 N. Y. 224; Ditchett v. S. D. R. R. 67 N. Y. 425 ; Fisher v. Thirkell, 21 Mich. 1 ; Harris v. Cohen, 50 Mich. 324 ; Mellen v. Morrill, 126 Mass. 545 ; Stewart v. Putnam, 127 Mass. 403 ; St. Louis v. Kaime, 2 Mo. App. 66 ; Gridly v. Bloomington, 68 Ill. 47.

[5] Kirby v. Boylst. Mkt., 14 Gray, 249 ; Milford v. Holbrook, 9 Allen, 17; Shipley v. Fifty Assoc., 101 Mass. 251, s. c. 106 Mass. 194 ; Readman v. Conway, 126 Mass. 374 ; Nash v. Minneapolis Co., 24 Minn. 501. Hence such parcel

building itself, or from a defect in its original construction. the landlord is liable.[1] So, if the demised premises are at the time of demise a nuisance, he is liable as creating it,[2] though the tenant may also be liable for continuing it.[3] And upon this ground, an owner has been held liable if the premises which are out of repair are open to the public for the profit which may arise from the use of them, as in the case of a wharf belonging to an individual; and he is bound to keep it safe for the purposes for which it has been opened, whoever is in occupation, though a sub-tenant would also be liable for an injury arising to one using it, from want of repair.[4] This class of cases proceeds upon the ground that any construction within the limits of a public way is an incipient nuisance, and the owner becomes liable, through whosesoever neglect it becomes an active one.[5] But a different view prevails in other States, and if the injury results from the tenant's not keeping in repair what he is bound to do, he, and not the landlord, would be liable, though the structure was under the public way. Thus where the landlord leased premises bounding upon a street, and the tenant covenanted to repair and keep the premises in repair, and one passing along the street sustained an injury by a defective grating opening into the street, but of which defect neither the landlord nor the

lessee may recover from the city for a defective sidewalk in front of the building, as he is not liable over. Burt v. Boston, 122 Mass. 223. But the owner is not liable to any one hurt on the premises, unless there by his invitation express or implied. Converse v. Walker, 30 Hun, 596; Mistler v. O'Grady, 132 Mass. 139; Fish v. Dodge, 4 Denio, 311; Pickard v. Collins, 23 Barb. 444.

[1] Durant v. Palmer, 29 N. J. 544; King v. Pedly, 1 Ad. & E. 827; Scott v. Simons, 54 N. H. 426; Larue v. Farren Hotel Co., 116 Mass. 67; Stratton v. Staples, 59 Me. 94; Godley v. Hagerty, 20 Penn. St. 387; Carson v. Godley, 26 Penn. St. 111.

[2] House v. Metcalf, 27 Conn. 631; Wenzler v. McCotter, 22 Hun, 60; but see Shindelbeck v. Moon, 31 Ohio St. 264, where upon similar facts a different conclusion was reached. In Helwig v. Jordan, 53 Ind. 21, a kiln was so held, and the lessor responsible for a fire originating from it by tenant's negligence.

[3] 3 Bl. Com. 221; Staple v. Spring, 10 Mass. 72; Ingwersen v. Rankin, 47 N. J. L. 18; Fow v. Roberts, 14 W. No. Cas. 307; Knauss v. Brua, 107 Penn. St. 85.

[4] Clancy v. Byrne, 56 N. Y. 129.

[5] Swords v. Edgar, 59 N. Y. 28; Owings v. Jones, 9 Md. 108; Congreve v. Smith, 18 N. Y. 79; Whalen v. Gloucester, 4 Hun, 24. Cf. Tarry v. Ashton, 1 Q. B. D. 314.

tenant knew anything, it was held the tenant was liable to the
party injured, by reason of being in possession of the premises, and their being suffered to be defective.[1] But there is no
liability either of landlord or tenant for defects in the highway in front of premises, caused by the wrongful act of
another, nor for defective sidewalks or flagstones and gratings
within the limits of the highway, where neither the owner nor
occupant were at fault. The public, in such case, is liable
to the party injured thereby.[2] If the tenant is responsible for
that which causes an injury to a passenger in the highway,
and the latter recovers in an action against the town or city
for the damages thereby sustained, the city or town may
recover of the tenant what they have been obliged to pay in
satisfaction of the same.[3] If the builder of the house cause
an excavation to be made which endangers the passenger, and
the tenant continues it after he comes into possession, the
person injured thereby may have his action against either.[4]
But if the owner of land dedicates a way across it to the public which is unsafe, and they accept it, the public, and not
he, are responsible to any one who is injured thereby while
using it.[5]

7 b. There is a class of cases related to those already considered which deserve notice from the apparent diversity of
opinion in respect to them among different courts. These
cases are where the owners of land adjoining a street or highway excavate holes or ditches within their own lands, but so
near the street as to become dangerous to travellers, especially
in the night-time, and the question is whether the land-owner
is liable therefor to a traveller who is thereby injured. The
court of Massachusetts, waiving the question whether the
town or city would be liable in such a case, held that the
owner of the land was not liable, although the excavation was

---

[1] Gwinnell v. Eamer, L. R. 10 C. P. 658 ; Pretty v. Bickmore, L. R. 8 C. P.
401. Cf. Leonard v. Storer, 115 Mass. 86 ; Stewart v. Putnam, 127 Mass. 403 ;
Cheetham v. Hampson, 4 T. R. 318. Fire-escapes, Keely v. O'Conner, 106
Penn. St. 321 ; Schult v. Harvey, 105 Penn. St. 222.

[2] Robbins v. Jones, 15 C. B. N. S. 221.

[3] Durant v. Palmer, 29 N. J. 546 ; Chicago v. Robbins, 2 Black, 418 ; Robbins
v. Chicago, 4 Wall. 657.

[4] Durant v. Palmer, 29 N. J. 548 ; McDonough v. Gilman, 3 Allen, 264.

[5] Robbins v. Jones, 15 C. B. N. S. 221.

within "a foot or two" of a public street.[1] In a recent English case, the defendants were the hirers and occupants of a warehouse which was not yet completed. A "hoist hole" was dug within fourteen inches of the line of the street which was used in erecting the warehouse, but no barrier was placed between it and the street. The plaintiff sustained injury by falling into the hole in the night-time when passing along the street, and was held to be entitled to recover damages, for the injury thus sustained, of the defendants.[2] In another case, the occupant of the land dug out "an area" "near" the street, into which a passenger fell, there being no barrier between them, and he was held liable for the injury thereby sustained.[3] But where the vault into which the plaintiff fell was upon a part of the land-owner's premises, across which the public often passed, but without right, and the land-owner had repeatedly sent persons back who were attempting to cross, it was held that no action would lie for the injury sustained by the plaintiff.[4] A tenant for years is responsible for restoring what is a nuisance to a right of way, although it existed when he became such tenant. So he would be for any such nuisance created by himself. But if existing at the time of his becoming tenant, he would not be liable for continuing it until after he is notified that it is a nuisance.[5] But the owner or tenant of land is not responsible to another who is injured by an act done upon his land, where it is done without his agency or permission, as where a third person, without right, placed obstructions in a watercourse upon the land through which it flowed, which caused an injury to a mill-owner below. The mill-owner could neither call upon the

---

[1] Howland v. Vincent, 10 Met. 371.   [2] Hadley v. Taylor, L. R. 1 C. P. 53.
[3] Barnes v. Ward, 9 C. B. 392. See also Birge v. Gardiner, 19 Conn. 507 ; Hydraulic Wks. v. Orr, 83 Penn. St. 332 ; and Beck v. Carter, 68 N. Y. 283, where Howland v. Vincent is denied to be law. And the doctrine of that case is difficult to reconcile with the principle of Rylands v. Fletcher, L. R. 3 H. L. 330, recognized in Shipley v. Fifty Assoc., 101 Mass. 251. Where the excavation is not near the highway no liability arises in the absence of invitation. Granlick v. Wurst, 86 Penn. St. 74 ; Hounsell v. Smyth, 7 C. B. N. s. 731.
[4] Stone v. Jackson, 16 C. B. 199.
[5] McDonough v. Gilman, 3 Allen, 264 ; Johnson v. Lewis, 13 Conn. 303. But see Brown v. Cayuga R. R., 12 N. Y. 486, that this is only in respect to abatement, not damages.

land-owner to remove these, nor hold him responsible for their being there.[1]

8. And even where a lessee guards himself, as he [*348] usually does,* against being responsible for casualties occurring to the premises while in his occupation, the courts do not extend this restriction beyond the language of the lease. As where the lease provided that the rent should cease upon the premises becoming untenantable by fire or other casualty, it was held no defence that they had become so by widening and altering the grade of the street on which they stood by the authority of the city.[2] Nor would the tenant, in case of such provision, have a right to abandon the premises, and put an entire stop to the rent by reason of a partial destruction of the premises, though it rendered such part uninhabitable until repaired.[3] So where the rent, or a proportionate part, was to stop, if the premises or any part thereof were destroyed or damaged by "unavoidable casualty," it was held not to extend to cases of gradual and natural decay. Nor could the tenant, if he continued to occupy, refuse to pay the rent.[4] On the other hand, where the lessee excepted, from his covenant to keep the buildings in repair, such want of repair as arose from fire and natural "wear and tear," it was held that the latter clause was not restricted to a gradual deterioration, but would extend to any accident caused by a defect in the structure, as where a mill that was leased fell from some inherent defect.[5] The covenant to maintain buildings in repair upon leased premises is binding at all times, and for a breach thereof the lessor is not bound to wait until the expiration of the lease. He may sue for the breaches as they arise during the term, after a refusal or neglect on the part of the tenant to repair within a reasonable time.[6] The extent of the repairs required of the tenant, as stated by Tenterden, C. J., is that "a tenant who covenants to repair is to sustain and

---

1 Saxby v. Manchester, &c. R. R., 38 L. J. N. s. C. P. 153.

2 Mills v. Baehr, 24 Wend. 254.

3 Wall v. Hinds, 4 Gray, 256.

4 Welles v. Castles, 3 Gray, 323 ; Bigelow v. Collamore, 5 Cush. 226.

5 Hess v. Newcomer, 7 Md. 325.

6 Buck v. Pike, 27 Vt. 529 ; Com. Land. & Ten. 210.

upiold tie premises. But tiat is not tie case witi a tenant from year to year. He is only bound to keep tie iouse wind and water tigit." [1]

8 *a.* In the absence of an express covenant to repair, the tenant of buildings is not liable for the accidental destruction tiereof by fire; and tiis is the common law of tiis country, borrowed from the English acts of 6 Anne, c. 31, § 67, and 14 Geo. III. c. 78.[2]

9. It ias been attempted, at times, to raise implied obligations between landlord and tenant regarding leased tenements, as to tieir ciaracter or condition, or the mode of using tiem, as well as wiat is included in a demise of tiem, from the ciaracter of the premises, and the purposes for wiici they are intended to be occupied. Tius it ias been ield tiat wiere real estate was leased, and witi it personal property, like maciinery, wiici was to be used witi and by means of the premises leased, the lessor was tiereby bound to do notiing to interrupt the * enjoyment, by the lessee, of tie prop- [*349] erty leased, for the purpose for wiici the same iad been usually occupied and employed.[3] So wiere a factory is leased witi its maciinery, it carries, by implication, a rigit to use the water-power of the lessor, belonging to the same, for the purpose of operating the mill.[4] But the lease of a store or wareiouse, or the like, does not, ordinarily, imply any warranty tiat tie building is safe, or well built, or tiat the premises are fit for any particular use.[5] Or tiat the premises are in a tenantable condition, or tiat tie lessor will make repairs.[6]

Auworth *v.* Johnson, 5 Car. & P. 239.

[2] Wainscott *v.* Silvers, 13 Ind. 497; Lansing *v.* Stone, 37 Barb. 15; 2 Platt, Leases, 187.

[3] Dexter *v.* Manley, 4 Cush. 14.   [4] Wyman *v.* Farrar, 35 Me. 64.

[5] Dutton *v.* Gerrish, 9 Cush. 89; Platt, Leases, 613; O'Brien *v.* Capwell, 59 Barb. 497; Royce *v.* Guggenheim, 106 Mass. 201; Loupe *v.* Wood, 51 Cal. 586; Taylor *v.* Bailey, 74 Ill. 178; Moore *v.* Weber, 71 Penn. St. 429; Arden *v.* Pullen, 10 M. & W. 321; Izon *v.* Gorton, 5 Bing. N. C. 501; Saner *v.* Bilton, 7 Ch. D. 815; Manch. Warch. Co. *v.* Carr, 5 C. P. D. 507; Taylor, Land. & Ten. § 381. In the case of a lease of the vesture of land for depasturing by cattle, it was held that the lessee was liable to pay rent, though poisonous substances, fatal to the cattle that fed there, had been scattered on the land by some one not the lessor. Sutton *v.* Temple, 12 M. & W. 52.

[6] Gill *v.* Middleton, 105 Mass. 477.

Nor would a lease of a salt-well be ıeld to be an assurance of tıe productiveness or capacity of tıe well.[1]   Nor is tıere any implied warranty in a lease of a ıouse for a private residence, tıat it is reasonably fit for ıabitation.[2]   Nor can a lessee, in tıe absence of fraud or misrepresentation as to tıe healthiness of a ıouse leased to him, abandon tıe premises because tıe same are unıealtıy, and tıereby avoid paying rent.[3]   In a case wıere a "furnisıed ıouse" was rented, it was ıeld to imply tıat it was so far fit for use tıat tıe tenant was ıeld justified in quitting because infested witı bugs.   But tıe law of tıe case seems doubtful, and is confined strictly to cases of ıouses furnisıed.[4]   Many of tıe propositions above stated, and tıe cases referred to, were considered in a recent case in New York, wıere tıe court sustain tıe doctrine as tıere given, and say, "Tıe maxim of *caveat emptor* applies to tıe contract of ıiring of real property, as it does to tıe transfer of all property, real, personal, or mixed;" and in tıe absence of fraud on tıe part of tıe lessor, tıere is no implied warranty tıat tıe premises are fit for tıe use for wıicı tıe lessee requires tıem.[5]   So wıere tıe tenant of part of a building suffers

[1] Clark v. Babcock, 23 ıich. 164, 170.

[2] Foster v. Peyser, 9 Cush. 242 ; Smith, Land. & Ten. 206 ; Hart v. Windsor, 12 ı. & W. 68 ; Wheeler v. Crawford, 86 Penn. St. 327.

[3] Westlake v. De Graw, 25 Wend. 669.

[4] Smith v. ıarrable, 11 ı. & W. 58, Am. ed. note. See also Sutton v. Temple, 12 ı. & W. 52, and Hart v. Windsor, Id. 68, overruling the cases on which Smith v. ıarrable was decided. Smith, Land. & Ten. 206, n. ; Taylor, Land. & Ten. § 381. It has also been repeatedly denied to be law in the United States. Foster v. Peyser, 9 Cush. 242 ; Howard v. Doolittle, 3 Duer, 464 ; Naumberg v. Young, 44 N. J. 331. It was reaffirmed in Wilson v. Finch Hatton, 2 Exch. D. 336 ; but is limited in ıanch. Wareh. Co. v. Carr, 5 C. P. D. 507, and its principle denied in Robertson v. Amazon Tug Co., 46 L. T. N. s. 146.

[5] McGlashan v. Tallmadge, 37 Barb. 313. So Hazlett v. Powell, 30 Penn. St. 293 ; Wheeler v. Crawford, 86 Penn. St. 327 ; ıayer v. ıoller, 1 Hilton, 491 ; Acad. of ıusic v. Hackett, 2 Hilton, 217, 235 ; Welles v. Castles, 3 Gray, 323 ; Libbey v. Tolford, 48 Me. 316 ; Elliot v. Aiken, 45 N. H. 30 ; Gott v. Gandy, 2 Ellis & B. 845 ; Cleves v. Willoughby, 7 Hill, 83 ; Naumberg v. Young, 44 N. J. 331. And the lessor's liability is no greater to a customer, servant, or visitor of the tenant than to the tenant himself ; Jaffe v. Harteau, 56 N. Y. 398 ; Robbins v. Jones, 15 C. B. N. s. 221 ; Burdick v. Cheadle, 26 Ohio St. 393. The mere omission to disclose a known defect was held not to be fraud in Keates v. Cadogan, 10 C. B. 591. But in Wallace v. Lent, 1 Daly, 481 ; ıinor v. Sharon, 112 ıass. 477 ; Cesar v. Karutz, 60 N. Y. 229, where there

damage from the defective condition of a part of the house
not included within his demise, but which he is licensed to
use, or which is in the common use or for the common benefit
of all the tenants;[1] or is injured by the neglect of another
parcel tenant, or the defective condition of the latter's premises,[2] in neither case is the landlord liable. But if the landlord has separate control of the defective part of the premises,
he is liable to the tenant for an injury caused by such
defect.[3]

10. And where the premises were a cellar and lower room
in a house of several stories, and, during the term, the house
was destroyed by fire, it was held that the lessee's interest was
thereby gone, and that he could not continue to occupy by covering in the cellar.[4] And the same principle was applied
where the lease was of one of many rooms in a building which
was burned down, and the lessor rebuilt during the term of
the hiring, it was held that the lessee's entire interest
was gone, and * the lessor was under no obligation to [*350]
give him the use of a corresponding room in the new
building.[5] But in such a case it has been held that the rent
of such destroyed premises ceases with their destruction, the

was a nuisance dangerous to health or life, it was held the landlord's duty to disclose it ; and in a still more recent case, Coke v. Gutkese, 80 Ky. 598, the lessor
was held liable to the tenant for an injury from an undisclosed defect in the
flooring ; and see Crump v. Sorrell, 35 Leg. Int. 374 ; Looney v. McLean, 129
Mass. 33.

    [1] Carstairs v. Taylor, L. R. 6 Exch. 217 ; Anderson v. Oppenheimer, 5 Q. B.
D. 602 ; Humphrey v. Wait, 22 Up. Can. C. P. 580 ; Purcell v. English, 86 Ind.
34 ; Ivay v. Hedges, 9 Q. B. D. 80.   And the case of Looney v. McLean, 129 Mass.
33, contra, is distinguished in Woods v. Naumkeag Co., 134 Mass. 357.   In
Krueger v. Ferrant, 29 Minn. 385, the court held this to apply even in case of a
defective roof, and refer to Pierce v. Dyer, 109 Mass. 374 ; but the case of co.
tenants is not in analogy, as between them there is no invitation.

    [2] Simonton v. Loring, 68 Me. 164 ; McCarthy v. York Co. Bk., 74 Me. 315.
The case of Jones v. Freidenberg, 66 Ga. 505, contra, is wholly unsupported by
authority outside of that State, the cases upon which it rests proceeding on actual
control or interference by the landlord.

    [3] Toole v. Beckett, 67 Me. 544 ; Priest v. Nichols, 116 Mass. 401.

    [4] Winton v. Cornish, 5 Ohio, 477 ; Shawmut Bk. v. Boston, 118 Mass.
125.

    [5] Stockwell v. Hunter, 11 Met. 448 ; Alexander v. Dorsey, 12 Ga. 12 ; Ains-
worth v. Ritt, 38 Cal. 89 ; McMillan v. Solomon, 42 Ala. 356 ; Womack v.
McQuarrie, 28 Ind. 103.

subject-matter of the demise no longer existing.[1]   In England, however, where one was a tenant from year to year of a second floor of a building which was destroyed by fire, he was held liable for rent of the premises after they were destroyed until a regular determination of the tenancy.[2]

11. So in respect to the lessee, unless he is restrained by the terms of his lease, he may make use of the premises for any lawful purposes he may choose, though different from those for which they were designed, if not materially and essentially affecting the condition of the same.   As where one hired a house erected for the purposes of a hotel, but made no covenant in respect to the mode of its occupancy, and converted it into a public seminary, it was held that the lessor could not object to that use of the premises.[3]

12. But where the mode of occupation is fixed by the lease, not only may the tenant be enjoined from converting the estate to other purposes,[4] but, in some cases, his so doing has been held to work a forfeiture for which the lessor might enter and expel him;[5] as where a shop was let for a regular dry-goods jobbing business, and the tenant undertook to use it as an auction-room, though no special damage could be shown to accrue

[1] Graves v. Berdan, 29 Barb. 100 ; s. c., 26 N. Y. 498 ; Doupe v. Genin, 45 N. Y. 119, 123.   So in a recent case it has been held that where personal property is a substantial part of the demise, the rent will be proportionately abated upon its destruction, Whitaker v. Hawley, 25 Kans. 674, citing Richards le Taverner's Case, Dyer, 56 a, and see Newton v. Wilson, 3 Hen. & B. 470 ; but the authorities on this point are not clear.   The rule is strictly held in England that rent flows only from the realty.   Newman v. Anderton, 5 B. & P. 224 ; Farewell v. Dickenson, 6 B. & C. 251 ; Salmon v. Matthews, 8 B. & W. 827.   In Bickle v. Miles, 31 Penn. St. 20, it is said rent flows as well from personalty, parcel of the demise ; but the point decided was only that it could be distrained for, qualifying Comm'th v. Contner, 18 Penn. St. 439.   So in Armstrong v. Cummings, 20 Hun, 313, it was held summary process would lie, and in Sutliff v. Atwood, 15 Ohio St. 186, that the covenant to pay it ran on a lease in part of personalty ; though in both the English rule was asserted.   In Bussman v. Ganster, 72 Penn. St. 285 ; Fay v. Holloran, 35 Barb. 295, however, apportionment was denied ; but in the former case it was a *dictum*, and in the latter the personalty was incidental only.   But in Vetter's App., 99 Penn. St. 52, the lessor's taking the personalty was held an eviction.

[2] Izon v. Gorton, 5 Bing. N. C. 501 ; see Graves v. Berdan, 26 N. Y. 498.

[3] Nave v. Berry, 22 Ala. 382.

[4] Howard v. Ellis, 4 Sandf. 369 ; Maddox v. White, 4 Md. 72.

[5] Shepard v. Briggs, 26 Vt. 149.

from such a use.[1] If premises are let for unlawful purposes, such for instance as the unlawful sale of spirituous liquors, the lessor cannot recover rent therefor; the lessee's covenant to pay it would be void.[2]

SECTION VII.

OF SURRENDER, MERGER, ETC.

1. If a tenant for life or years yields up his estate to him who has the immediate estate in reversion or remainder, it is called by the law a *surrender*, the effect of which is to extinguish all claim for rent not due at the time. The estate for years, in * such case, is " drowned by mutual [*351] agreement between them."[3] But if an estate, however brief, intervenes between the two estates, there cannot be a technical surrender or a merger thereof.[4]

2. To do this requires, under the Statute of Frauds, a deed or note in writing, or some act to which the law gives that effect.[5] A parol surrender of a lease is of no validity, nor is

---

[1] Steward *v.* Winters, 4 Sandf. Ch. 587. But no general restriction will be implied from a special restriction as to part of the demise. Reed *v.* Lewis, 74 Ind. 433.

[2] Sherman *v.* Wilder, 106 Mass. 537.

[3] Co. Lit. 338 a ; Smith, Land. & Ten. 223 ; Greider's Appeal, 5 Penn. St. 422; Curtiss *v.* Miller, 17 Barb. 477 ; Bailey *v.* Wells, 8 Wisc. 141.

[4] Burton *v.* Barclay, 7 Bing. 745.

[5] Hesseltine *v.* Seavey, 16 Me. 212 ; Smith, Land. & Ten. 224 ; Farmer *v.* Rogers, 2 Wils. 26 ; Allen *v.* Jaquish, 21 Wend. 628 ; Jackson *v.* Gardner, 8 Johns. 394.

evidence of such surrender competent.[1] Nor would it make
any difference if, when the written lease was made, it had
been orally agreed by the lessor that the lessee might surrender his lease at any time he might choose.[2] Nor would the
cancelling of the lease revest the estate in the lessor, or operate as a bar to the recovery of rent by the holder of the reversion.[3] And by the Stat. 8 and 9 Vict. c. 106, § 3, it can only
be done, if in writing, by deed. But if the lease do not exceed
the term for which a parol lease would be good, there may be
a parol surrender of the same.[4]

3. It is not, however, competent for the lessor and lessee to
affect the rights of third parties by a formal surrender of the
lease, as, for instance, those of the lessee's sub-tenant.[5]

4. Questions of considerable difficulty have arisen, at times,
as to what will, in law, amount to a surrender of the lease.
It has been held that if lessee of a term takes a new lease of
the same premises, to take effect before the expiration of such
term, it works a surrender of the first, on account of the in-
compatibility of the two leases, both of which cannot be valid
at the same time, unless there are facts in the case clearly
rebutting such inference.[6] It must be made clearly to appear,
in the absence of any deed or written instrument, that it was
the intention of the parties to create a new lease of the premises, and substitute a new and different estate from that
granted by the original lease.[7] So where the lessee leased the
demised premises to his lessor, the owner of the immediate
reversion in fee, by an instrument like that by which he became lessee, it was held to be a surrender by the lessee and a
merger in the lessor.[8] But where the first lease was from two,

---

[1] Bailey v. Wells, 8 Wisc. 141.   [2] Brady v. Peiper, 1 Hilton, 61.

[3] Ward v. Lumley, 5 H. & Norm. 88–94, and note to Am. ed.

[4] Kiester v. Miller, 25 Penn. St. 481 ; M'Kinney v. Reader, 7 Watts, 123.

[5] McKenzie v. Lexington, 4 Dana, 129 ; Smith, Land. & Ten. 231 ; Piggott v.
Stratton, Johns. Ch. (Eng.) 355 ; Adams v. Goddard, 48 Me. 212, 215.

[6] Burton, Real Prop. § 904 ; Wms. Real Prop. 337 ; Smith, Land. & Ten.
225–330, n. ; Bellow v. May, Moore, 636 ; Van Rensselaer v. Penniman, 6 Wend.
569 ; Livingston v. Potts, 16 Johns. 28 ; Co. Lit. 338 a ; McDonnell v. Pope, 9
Hare, 705 ; Lyon v. Reed, 13 M. & W. 285 ; Roe v. York, 6 East, 86 ; Bailey v.
Wells, sup.

[7] Brewer v. Dyer, 7 Cush. 337, 339.   [8] Shepard v. Spaulding, 4 Met. 416.

and tie lease back again was to one only, it did not operate as a surrender.[1] Nor, *wiere the original [*352] lease was by one lessor to several lessees, can one of tiese lessees affect the rigits of his co-lessees by releasing or conveying to iis lessor.[2]

5. Questions of more difficulty iave arisen wietier a sealed lease for a term can be surrendered by substituting a new parol one. And altiougi the point does not seem to iave been generally adverted to in the cases wiici iave involved tiis question, it would seem to depend upon wietier the new parol lease was binding witiin the Statute of Frauds, as in England and some of the States it may be, if not exceeding a certain lengti of time, and followed by possession under it. In suci case, consistently witi the cases above cited, taking a new parol lease would seem to be a surrender in law of the existing one under seal; wiile, if suci second lease were not valid, tiere would be no surrender.[3] In Tiomas r. Cook, the first lessee was tenant from year to year, and the lessor accepted the assignee of iis tenant by distraining iis goods for rent due, and it was ield to be a surrender of the first letting by act of law.[4] So in Smiti v. Niver, a parol lease for a year was substituted for a written one. Tie court ield the parol lease valid and binding, "being for a term not embraced witiin tie provisions of tie statute requiring agreements of tiis description to be in writing." [5] But wiere the lessee expressed a wisi to tie lessor to substitute a third person as tenant, wio was present at the time, and tie lessor said, if tie rent was paid it would all be rigit, but the lease was not cancelled, it was ield not to be a surrender accepted on the part of the lessor.[6] In some cases wiere the lessee has assigned iis lease or underlet to anotier, for iis entire term, in writing, and tie original lessor has orally assented to the same, and ias accepted rent from the

---

[1] Sperry v. Sperry, 8 N. II. 477.   [2] Baker v. Pratt, 15 Ill. 568.
[3] Coe v. Hobby, 72 N. Y. 141.
[4] Thomas v. Cook, 2 B. & A. 119. See M'Donnell v. Pope, 9 Hare, 705 See also Davison v. Cent, 1 Hurlst. & N. 744.
[5] Smith v. Niver, 2 Barb. 180 ; Bedford v. Terhune, 30 N. Y. 453.
[6] Whitney v. Myers, 1 Duer, 266.

assignee, it has been held to operate as a surrender of the original lease, and a substitution of a new tenancy.[1] But it is difficult to see upon what legal ground such oral assent can be held to be a bar to an action upon the lessee's express covenant to pay rent.[2] And the following case seems to recognize this distinction, the parol agreement of the parties being followed by acts done towards carrying this agreement into practical effect. The lessee of a term of ten years assigned it by the parol assent of the lessor, who agreed to look to the assignee for the rent, and to accept him as his tenant, and that the lessee should be discharged. It was held to be a surrender so far as the lessee was concerned, and to discharge him from his obligations as such. But the circumstance of accepting rent from the assignee of the lessee does not discharge him; it is merely accepting payment through the hands of another.[3]

6. So where, before the expiration of a lease under seal, the lessee actually surrendered possession of the premises [*353] to his * lessor, who accepted the same and leased them to another, it was held to be, in effect, a surrender.[4] Any acts which are equivalent to an agreement on the part of a tenant to abandon, and on the part of the landlord to resume possession of the demised premises, amount to a surrender of the term by operation of law.[5] But abandoning possession even with notice, unless accepted by the landlord, would not have that effect. The surrender, to be of any effect in barring a claim for rent, must be with the assent of the lessor.[6] So where lessor and lessee, by mutual consent, destroyed the lease for the purpose of making a new one, it was

[1] Logan v. Anderson, 2 Doug. (Mich.) 101; Bailey v. Delaplaine, 1 Sandf. 5; Wallace v. Kennelly, 47 N. J. L. 242.

[2] See Brewer v. Dyer, 7 Cush. 337.

[3] Levering v. Langley, 8 Minn. 107; Way v. Reed, 6 Allen, 364, 370; Thursby v. Plant, 1 Wms. Saund. 240. But if the lessee's term has expired, accepting rent from his assignee discharges him, Lodge v. White, 30 Ohio St. 569; and where lessor accepted rent from an assignee who had changed the agreed character of the premises, the lessee was discharged, Fifty Assoc. v. Grace, 125 Mass. 161.

[4] Dodd v. Acklom, 6 Mann. & G. 672; Grimman v. Legge, 8 B. & C. 324; Hegeman v. McArthur, 1 E. D. Smith, 147; Walker v. Richardson, 2 M. & W. 882; Randall v. Rich, 11 Mass. 494; Hesseltine v. Seavey, 16 Me. 212. See Brady v. Peiper, 1 Hilton, 61; Brewer v. Dyer, 7 Cush. 337.

[5] Talbot v. Whipple, 14 Allen, 177, 180.   [6] Stobie v. Dills, 62 Ill. 432.

ield to have that effect.[1]   But to have such an act of the parties amount to a legal surrender, without any writing to that
effect, it is necessary that there should be an actual surrendering up by the tenant of the possession of the premises, and
an acceptance of such possession by the lessor, such as receiving the key of the house, or actually going into occupation, or
putting some other tenant in, or as stated in one of the cases
cited above, accepting the tenant of the lessee as his own
tenant, and receiving rent from him.[2] The cases upon this
point are numerous and often difficult to reconcile, each depending upon the peculiar circumstances upon which the
decision turned.   But it may be assumed that there must be
a mutual agreement between the lessor and original lessee,
that the lease is terminated, in order to work a surrender.
But this may be implied, and need not always be express.   It
is enough that it is proved, and, when made, the original lessee
is no longer liable, and the new tenant, if there be one, is
alone responsible.[3]   Thus, for example, if the tenant actually
surrenders up to the lessor the possession of the premises, and
he accepts it and retains it by going into occupation of them,
it will be a surrender, and put an end to the tenant's further
liability upon his covenants.   And the return and acceptance
of the key of the premises may be evidence of such surrender
of possession.[4]   But merely entering upon leased premises,
and using them without any consent of the tenant, does not
work a surrender, though he may have quit possession of
them.   It may prevent his claiming rent of the tenant, but
that would depend upon the nature and extent of such use.[5]

[1] Baker v. Pratt, 15 Ill. 568.

[2] Hegeman v. McArthur, 1 E. D. Smith, 147; Dodd v. Acklom, 6 Mann. & G.
672; Grimman v. Legge, 8 B. & C. 324; Thomas v. Cook, 2 B. & A. 119; Amory
v. Kannoffsky, 117 Mass. 351; Hanham v. Sherman, 114 Mass. 19.

[3] Bedford v. Terhune, 30 N. Y. 462-464.

[4] Elliott v. Aiken, 45 N. H. 30; Hill v. Robinson, 23 Mich. 24; Whitehead v. Clifford, 5 Taunt. 518; Phené v. Popplewell, 12 C. B. N. s. 334; note to
Am. ed., and cases cited. Dollett v. Brayne, 2 Camp. 103; Matthews v. Tobe-
nor, 39 Mo. 115, 119; Deane v. Caldwell, 127 Mass. 242. But merely taking
the key and even entering to repair is no acceptance of surrender if not so intended.   Pier v. Carr, 69 Penn. St. 326; Breuckman v. Twibill, 89 Penn. St. 58;
Oastler v. Henderson, 2 Q. B. D. 575; Auer v. Penn, 99 Penn. St. 370.

[5] Griffith v. Hodges, 1 Car. & P. 419.

But where it was agreed between the lessor's agent and the lessee that the latter should surrender the premises, and he accordingly did so by delivering up his part of the lease with the key of the premises to the agent, and the lessor entered upon the premises and let them to another, it was held, that though it was not a technical *surrender*, not having been in writing, a court of equity would enjoin the prosecution of a suit for rent after such a transaction.[1] Merely accepting, without objection, notice that the tenant is going to quit at a future time, though followed by an abandonment of the premises or the cancelling of the lease, unless the premises are taken possession of by the lessor, would not amount to a surrender.[2] But where the lease stipulated for the payment of rent quarterly, with a proviso, that, if not paid when due, the lessor might enter and take possession, and the lessor notified the tenant that held under the lessee, that unless he paid the rent of the current quarter, which had in fact been paid, he must quit, and the tenant accordingly abandoned the premises, it was held to be a surrender, and the lessee was thereby discharged from liability to pay rent.[3] In some cases it has been held that if the tenant abandons the premises, especially if he has absconded, and the landlord enters upon and occupies or lets them to another, it will operate as a surrender, putting an end to the relation of landlord and tenant, and any right and liability on account of rent.[4] Other cases might be mentioned where the taking possession by the landlord with the acquiescence or assent of the tenant, where the premises were deserted or vacant, has been held to be a surrender in law. In one of these the house was burned, and the tenant remained liable to pay rent by his covenant. Instead of exacting this, the tenant having neglected to rebuild, the [*354] landlord went on * without objection by the tenant, and rebuilt, and it was held to be a complete defence

---

[1] Stotesbury *v.* Vail, 13 N. J. Eq. 390 ; so where the lessee gave up the lease and lessor collected rent from the sub-lessee, Amory *v.* Kannoffsky, 117 Mass. 351.

[2] Johnstone *v.* Hudlestone, 4 B. & C. 922 ; Schieffelin *v.* Carpenter, 15 Wend. 400 ; Walker *v.* Richardson, 2 M. & W. 893, per *Bolland*, B. ; Jackson *v.* Gardner, 8 Johns. 394, 404.

[3] Patchin *v.* Dickerman, 31 Vt. 666.

[4] Schuisler *v.* Ames, 16 Ala. 73 ; M'Kinney *v.* Reader, 7 Watts, 123.

to an action brougıt by the tenant to regain ıis possession.[1]
In one case it was ıeld tıat an agreement in writing not under seal, to surrender an existing lease for years wıicı was
under seal, upon failure to perform certain stipulations, migıt
be valid as a contingent surrender, and tıat a surrender of a
term to operate *in futuro* would be good.[2] It would swell tıis
work beyond its proposed limits to pursue tıis subject furtıer. The reader will find a summary of tıe law in tıe
following language of Parke, B., in Lyon *v.* Reed : " We must
consider wıat is meant by a surrender by operation of law.
Tıis term is applied to cases wıere tıe owner of a particular
estate ıas been a party to some act, tıe validity of wıicı he
is, by law, afterwards estopped from disputing, and wıicı
would not be valid if ıis particular estate ıad continued to
exist. Tıere tıe law treats tıe doing of sucı act as amounting to a surrender." " In sucı case, it will be observed, tıere
can be no question of *intention.* Tıe surrender is not tıe result of intention. It takes place independently, and even in
spite of intention." [3]

7. Closely allied to tıe doctrine of surrender is tıat of
Merger, as applied to leases. Witıout attempting to embrace
the wıole subject, it may be stated, generally, tıat wıere a
term for years and the immediate reversion of tıe same estate
meet in one and tıe same person, in ıis own rigıt, either by
ıis own act or by act of tıe law, so tıat ıe has tıe full power
of alienation of botı estates, tıey will merge.[4] Tıus a re-
conveyance of an entire leaseıold estate to tıe lessor by sundry mesne conveyances merges tıe term in tıe fee, tıougı
in eacı of tıe transfers of tıe estate a rent was reserved,
togetıer witı a rigıt of entry for a breacı of covenant.[5]

---

[1] Pindar *v.* Ainsley, cited by *Buller,* J., in Belfour *v.* Weston, 1 T. R. 312 ;
Cline *v.* Black, 4 McCord, 431 ; Wood *v.* Walbridge, 19 Barb. 136.

[2] Allen *v.* Jaquish, 21 Wend. 628. See Roe *v.* York, 5 East, 86.

[3] Lyon *v.* Reed, 13 M. & W. 306. But see Van Rensselaer *v.* Penniman, 6
Wend. 569. As to what such estoppel is, see Nickells *v.* Atherstone, 10 Q. B.
944. See note to Am. ed. 12 C. B. N. S. 343 ; Bedford r. Terhune, 30 N. Y. 453.

[4] Burton, Real Prop. §§ 897, 899 ; 1 Cruise, Dig. 239 ; 3 Prest. Conv. 201.
But where a lessee acquires only an undivided interest in the fee his term will not
merge. Martin *v.* Tobin, 123 Mass. 85.

[5] Smiley *v.* Van Winkle, 6 Cal. 605 ; Shepard *v.* Spaulding, 4 Met. 416 ;
Liebschutz *v.* Moore, 70 Ind. 142.

And if the purchaser of an estate purchase in a ground rent which is payable out of the estate, such a union of the two would merge the rent, unless the title to the estate should fail, in which case the rent would revive.[1] But an intervening outstanding term for years in another person will prevent their merging.[2]

8. Where the reversion is a freehold estate, it is not difficult to understand how this may happen, however long the term may be, from the nature of freehold and chattel [*355] interests * as originally understood, the former being of so much higher consideration in the eye of the law than the latter. As where A was tenant for one thousand years, with a reversion in B for life, and A surrendered his term to B, it merged in the freehold of B, and was gone forever, and B would, after such surrender, have only an estate for his own life.[3]

9. But when this comes to be applied to terms and reversions, where they are both for years, and the reader is told that if the immediate term be for one thousand years, and the reversion for five hundred, and the holder of the immediate term surrender to the reversioner, the term of one thousand years is merged and lost in that of five hundred, it is difficult to comprehend the proposition, except as a positive rule of law. And yet such is the case. It grows out of the nature of a reversion, that if the intermediate estate ceases to be interposed between the reversioner and the present enjoyment of his estate as a reversioner, he will hold only in the latter capacity, and consequently, when the intermediate term, however long, was surrendered up to him, it was extinguished, and he held afterwards as such reversioner.[4]

10. But if the estate which is limited after a present term for years is a remainder instead of a reversion, and the present estate is surrendered or transferred to the holder of the second estate, inasmuch as the second is only to come into

1 Wilson v. Gibbs, 28 Penn. St. 151.
2 Burton, Real Prop. § 898 ; Crabb, Real Prop. § 2447 b.
3 Wms. Real Prop. 341 ; 3 Prest. Conv. 196.
4 Burton, Real. Prop. §.899 ; 3 Prest. Conv. 182, 183, 195, 297; Hughes v. Robotham, Cro. Eliz. 303 ; Stephens v. Bridges, 6 Madd. 66 ; 3 Sugd. Vend. 23.

enjoyment at the expiration of the first, it will not be a merger and extinguishment of the first, but the person in whom they unite will have the benefit of both terms in succession. Thus where A had an estate for one hundred years, and B an estate in remainder for fifty, and R acquired A's estate, he thereby became, in effect, tenant for one hundred and fifty years.[1]

11. But if the estate accrue in different rights, merger will take place where the accession is by the act of the parties, but * not where it is by act of law: thus if an [*356] executor who has the reversion in his own right becomes possessed, as executor, of a term for years, the two will not merge;[2] and it is well settled, that if a husband has a freehold in reversion, and his wife acquires a term for years, the term will not merge, although he has the complete power of disposal of such term. And where the husband is the termor and the wife the owner of the reversion in freehold, it is clear the term will not merge in the freehold, since he only holds that in right of his wife.[3] But different opinions have been held where the husband seised of a term in right of his wife purchases the freehold in reversion, whether the term will merge.[4] And it is even said if an executor, holding a term as such, purchases the reversion in fee, the term will merge in the inheritance.[5]

---

[1] Cruise, Dig. Tit. 39, §§ 40–46 ; Co. Lit. 273 b. See this subject discussed by Preston, 3 Conv. 201.

[2] Burton, Real Prop. § 903 ; Wms. Real Prop. 342 ; Clift v. White, 15 Barb. 70.

[3] Burton, Real Prop. §§ 901, 902 ; Wms. Real Prop. 342 ; Platt v. Sleap, Cro. Jac. 275 ; 3 Sugd. Vend. 22 ; 3 Prest. Conv. 276 ; Jones v. Davies, 5 Hurlst. & N. 766.

[4] 3 Sugd. Vend. 22 ; 3 Prest. Conv. 276.

[5] 3 Prest. Conv. 295 ; Wms. Real Prop. 343 ; 3 Sugd. Vend. 20, 21.

SECTION VIII.

LESSEE ESTOPPED TO DENY LESSOR'S TITLE.

1. Generality of the rule.
1 a. How far it extends to land gained by disseisin.
2. Applies while tenant actually holds.
3. Lessee by indenture estopped to plead *nil habuit*.
4. Effect of accepting a lease from a stranger.
5. Rule applies in favor of heirs and assignees of lessor.
6. Exceptions to the general rule.
7. May deny lessor's title after a surrender.
8. Or after constructive eviction.
9. Effect of disclaimer by lessee of lessor's title.
10. While holding, lessee cannot set up want of title.
10 a. Effect of mistake where prior possession by lessee.

1. FEW propositions are more frequently and unqualifiedly made, in respect to the relation of landlord and tenant, than that a lessee who has been put into possession of leased premises by a lessor, and has been permitted thereby to occupy them, shall not be allowed to question his lessor's title in an action brought to recover possession of the premises, or the rent reserved in such demise or in assumpsit for use and occupation.[1] And though one writer says, "The origin of this rule seems involved in some obscurity,"[2] it is by others said

[*357]   to be traceable to feudal tenures, where the tenant
          *was bound to the landlord by ties not much less
sacred than those of allegiance itself.[3] The doctrine has been generally recognized in this country as a part of the law of landlord and tenant.[4] The policy of the law will not allow a tenant, under such circumstances, to be guilty of a breach of good faith in denying a title, by acknowledging and acting under which he originally obtained, and has been per-

---

[1] Delaney *v.* Fox, 2 C. B. N. S. 768 ; Gray *v.* Johnson, 14 N. H. 414 ; Pope *v.* Harkins, 16 Ala. 321 ; Ansley *v.* Longmire, 2 Kerr, 321 ; Bigler *v.* Furman, 58 Barb. 545 ; Longfellow *v.* Longfellow, 54 Me. 240, s. c. 61 Me. 590.

[2] Smith, Land. & Ten. 234, note a. For the origin and growth of this doctrine of estoppel between lessee and lessor, see 6 Am. L. Rev. 1 *et seq.*

[3] Blight *v.* Rochester, 7 Wheat. 535, 548. See 2 Smith, Lead. Cas. 5th Am. ed. 656.

[4] 2 Smith, Lead. Cas. 5th Am. ed. 657; Smith *v.* Crosland, 106 Penn. St. 413.

mitted to hold possession of the premises.[1] Thus where a lessee, whose duty it was to pay the taxes assessed upon the premises, suffered the same to be sold for default of payment, and purchased the same at a public sale, it was held that he could not set up a title thus acquired against his landlord.[2] But it would have been otherwise if there were no fault on his part in not making payment of the taxes.[3] Nor will it allow him to complain of a want of title in his lessor, so long as he is himself undisturbed.[4]

1 *a.* Cases have arisen where the doctrine above stated has been applied in favor of a landlord, to lands in possession of a tenant, although the same were not embraced in the terms of his lease. As where the tenant, while occupying the demised premises, encroached upon adjacent lands, and enclosed portions of them, which he occupied in connection with the premises long enough to acquire a title to the same by limitation, and the question was, whether this should enure to the benefit of the landlord or the tenant. The cases have been chiefly those where the tenant has encroached upon and enclosed parcels of waste or common from a manor adjoining the leased premises. In one case the quantity thus enclosed was two acres, and did not actually adjoin the leased premises.[5] In another, the encroachment was made from the seacoast.[6] In another, there was a road between the leased premises and the place of encroachment, which was said to be "a small portion of waste."[7] In another, the parcels were separated by a fence.[8] And in another, the parcel enclosed was four acres of waste, separated from the leased premises by a small stream, a fence, and a path.[9] And in all these cases the court held that the

[1] Cooke *v.* Loxley, 5 T. R. 4 ; Balls *v.* Westwood, 2 Camp. 11 ; 2 Dana, Abr. 443 ; Hodges *v.* Shields, 18 B. Mon. 828 ; Miller *v.* McBrier, 14 S. & R. 382 ; Brown *v.* Dysinger, 1 Rawle, 408 ; Ball *v.* Lively, 2 J. J. Marsh. 181 ; Dezell *v.* Odell, 3 Hill, 215, 219 ; Ingraham *v.* Baldwin, 9 N. Y. 45.

[2] Haskell *v.* Putnam, 42 Me. 244.

[3] Bettison *v.* Budd, 17 Ark. 546 ; Weichselbaum *v.* Curlett, 20 Kans. 709 ; Elliott *v.* Smith, 23 Penn. St. 131.

[4] Ankeny *v.* Pierce, Breese, 202 ; George *v.* Putney, 4 Cush. 351 ; Vance *v.* Johnson, 10 Humph. 214.

[5] Doe *v.* Jones, 15 M. & W. 580. [6] Doe *v.* Rees, 6 Car. & P. 610.

[7] Andrews *v.* Hailes, 2 Ellis & B. 349. [8] Doe *v.* Tidbury, 14 C. B. 304.

[9] Lisburne *v.* Davies, L. R. 1 C. P. 259.

holding was to be presumed to be for the benefit of the landlord under whom he held the principal estate, unless the contrary was clearly proved.   And Campbell, C. J., in one of these cases, says, " I think that, when the property is taken and used as a part of the holding, the tenant can as little dispute the title to it as he can dispute the title to any other part of the premises."   And in still another case, Parke, B., says, " It is not necessary that the land enclosed should be adjacent to the demised premises; the same rule prevails when the encroachment is at a distance."   " Whether the enclosed land is part of the waste, or belongs to the landlord, or a third person, the presumption is that the tenant has enclosed it for the benefit of the landlord, unless he has done some act disclaiming the landlord's title." [1]   But, as has already been said, this presumption may be controlled by evidence.   As where, as is said in the case last cited, " the tenant conveys it (the parcel encroached) to another person, and the conveyance is communicated to the landlord, then it can no longer be considered as part of the holding."   And where a tenant occupied a parcel of another's land without his permission, and hired and occupied a parcel adjacent to it, and paid rent for it to the owner of the first parcel, and continued this for more than twenty years, it was held that he might, nevertheless, claim to hold the first parcel by adverse possession. [2]

2. All that the law requires is, that, during the time which the tenant actually holds by permission of the landlord, the landlord's title shall not be disputed.   In technical phrase, the tenant shall not be allowed to plead, to his landlord's action, *nil habuit in tenementis.* [3]   And this would be applied, though the tenant held under a parol demise from a tenant at will; he would be estopped to deny his lessor's title. [4]   Upon this general proposition, that a tenant cannot dispute his landlord's title in an action involving that question, the reader is referred to the cases cited below, in addition to those already

---

[1] Kingsmill *v.* Millard, 11 Exch. 313.   See also Doe *v.* Murrell, 8 Car. & P. 134.

[2] Dixon *v.* Baty, L. R. 1 Exch. 259.

[3] Boston *v.* Binney, 11 Pick. 1, 8; People *v.* Stiner, 45 Barb. 56 ; *post,* pl. 10 a.

[4] Coburn *v.* Palmer, 8 Cush. 124 ; Hilbourn *v.* Fogg, 99 Mass. 11.

mentioned, wiile it will be borne in mind tiat tiere are limitations and exceptions to tiis rule, wiici will be iereafter referred to.[1]

3. Under tie older common law and before tie development of the modern estoppel *in pais*, the only estoppel of the tenant was wiere tie demise was by indenture. Here he was positively estopped to plead *nil habuit*, &c., even tioug1 1e mig1t 1ave 1ired and enjoyed only wiat was clearly 1is own land, as would be tie case if a disseisor were to demise to 1is * disseisee by indenture.[2]   By accepting a lease [*358] and becoming a tenant, 1e admitted tie title of 1is landlord, and tiereby precluded 1imself from disputing it.[3] But suc1 estoppel only continued during the term of tie 1iring; after tiat tie lessee mig1t set up 1is own title against 1is lessor.[4]   W1ere, 1owever, tie lessor was not 1imself in possession, the lessee was not estopped, by a mere written agreement to 1old for a certain time and pay rent, to plead *nil habuit* to an action for rent.[5]   But tie modern rule is equally imperative in actions for use and occupation w1ere the demise

---

[1] Philip *v.* Robertson, 2 Overt. 399 ; Robinson *v.* Hathaway, Brayt. 150 ; Darby *v.* Anderson, 1 Nott. & McC. 369 ; 3 oore *v.* Beasley, 3 Ohio, 294 ; Hamit *v.* Lawrence, 2 A. K. 3 arsh. 366 ; 3 oshier *v.* Reding, 12 Me. 478 ; Lively *v.* Ball, 2 B. Mon. 53 ; St. Louis *v.* 3 orton, 6 Mo. 476 ; Terry *v.* Ferguson, 8 Port. (Ala.) 500 ; Caldwell *v.* Harris, 4 Humph. 24 ; Russell *v.* Fabyan, 27 N. H. 529 ; Willison *v.*Watkins, 3 Pet. 43 ; Tuttle *v.* Reynolds, 1 Vt. 80 ; Blight *v.* Rochester, 7 Wheat. 535 ; Smith, Land. & Ten. 234, Am. ed. ; McCartney *v.* Hunt, 16 Ill. 76 ; *post*, pl. 10 a.

[2] Kempe *v.* Goodall, 2 Ld. Raym. 1154 ; Heath *v.* Vermeden, 3 Lev. 146 ; Wilkins *v.* Wingate, 6 T. R. 62 ; Broom's 3 axims, 162 ; Fletcher *v.* M'Farlane, 12 3 ass. 47 ; Wilson *v.* Townshend, 2 Ves. 693 ; 3 iller *v.* Bonsadon, 9 Ala. 317 ; Vernam *v.* Smith, 15 N. Y. 327 ; Co. Lit. 47 b.

[3] Page *v.* Kinsman, 43 N. H. 328 ; Alwood *v.* 3 ansfield, 33 Ill. 452.

[4] Co. Lit. 47 b ; Burt Real Prop. § 850 ; Shep. Touch. Preston ed. 53 ; Jones's Case, 3 oore, 181 ; 2 Prest. Abs. 210, 409. In a few modern cases the distinction between this estoppel, which was founded solely on the instrument of demise, beginning and ending with the indenture, and the modern estoppel, which is wholly *in pais*, and continues as long as possession is retained by the tenant, appears to have been overlooked. Carpenter *v.* Thomson, 3 N. H. 204, referred to i.1 Gray *v.* Johnson, 14 N. H. 421 ; and followed in Page *v.* Kinsman, 43 N. H. 328. See also Acc. Death Ins. Co. *v.* 3 ackenzie, 10 C. B. N. s. 870 ; Davis *v.* Tyler, 18 Johns. 490. But that the estoppel outlasts the term is settled by numerous authorities ; see following notes.

[5] Chettle *v.* Pound, 1 Ld. Baym. 746 ; *post*, pl. 10 a. See *post*, vol. 3, *463.

is by parol, and applies as well after as during the term, and
where the tenant holds over after the expiration of the term;
and continues until possession of the premises is restored to
the lessor.[1] So if a tenant under a lease were to convey the
estate in fee to a third party, the latter would have no better
right to contest the title of the lessor than the lessee himself.[2]
And the doctrine is thus broadly stated in one case: "The
same estoppel which prevents a tenant from disputing his
landlord's title extends to all persons who enter upon premises
under a contract for a lease, and to all persons who, by
purchase, fraud, or otherwise, obtain possession from such
tenant."[3] But if one, not knowing that the tenant holds a
lease, purchases the estate by an absolute deed from the tenant,
who has an apparent legal title other than his lease, such purchaser may contest the title of the lessor.[4]

4. The acceptance of a lease from a third party by a tenant,
except as hereafter explained, would be a fraudulent attornment, and cannot prevail against his admission that he entered
under the lessor (the plaintiff).[5] So the tenant cannot set up
a title adverse to the lessor's, either in himself or a third party,
inconsistent with the lessor's right to grant the original lease,[6]

---

[1] Binney v. Chapman, 5 Pick. 124 ; Codman v. Jenkins, 14 Mass. 93 ; Shel-
ton v. Doe, 6 Ala. 230 ; Jackson v. Stiles, 1 Cow. 575 ; Falkner v. Beers, 2 Doug.
(Mich.) 117 ; Vernam v. Smith, 15 N. Y. 327 ; Lewis v. Willis, 1 Wils. 314 ;
Phipps v. Sculthorpe, 1 B. & A. 50 ; Fleming v. Gooding, 10 Bing. 549 ; Miller v.
Lang, 99 Mass. 13 ; Delaney v. Fox, 2 C. B. N. s. 768 ; Longfellow v. Longfellow,
61 Me. 590 ; Bonney v. Foss, 62 Me. 248 ; Abbott v. Cromartie, 72 N. C. 292.

[2] Phillips v. Rothwell, 4 Bibb, 33 ; Den v. Gustin, 12 N. J. 42 ; Turly v.
Rogers, 1 A. K. Marsh. 245 ; Jackson v. Davis, 5 Cow. 123 ; Cooper v. Smith,
8 Watts, 536 ; so if the owner in fee takes a lease, Eister v. Paul, 54 Penn. St.
196 ; Campbell v. Shipley, 41 Md. 81 ; Prevot v. Lawrence, 51 N. Y. 219 ;
Lucas v. Brooks, 18 Wall. 431.

[3] Rose v. Davis, 11 Cal. 132 ; Russell v. Erwin, 38 Ala. 44 ; Lond. & N. W.
R. R. v. West, L. R. 2 C. P. 553 ; Stagg v. Eureka Co., 56 Mo. 317 ; Re Emery,
4 C. B. N. s. 423, 431.

[4] Thompson v. Clark, 7 Penn. St. 62.

[5] Jackson v. Harper, 5 Wend. 246 ; Byrne v. Beeson, 1 Doug. (Mich.) 179 ;
Allen v. Chatfield, 8 Minn. 435 ; Blanchard v. Tyler, 12 Mich. 339.

[6] Reed v. Shepley, 6 Vt. 602 ; Jackson v. Stewart, 6 Johns. 34 ; Syme v. Sanders, 4 Strobh. 196 ; Jackson v. Harper, 5 Wend. 246 ; Chambers v. Pleak, 6
Dana, 426 ; Utica Bk. v. Mersereau, 3 Barb. Ch. 528 ; Jackson v. Rowland, 6
Wend. 666 ; Plumer v. Plumer, 30 N. H. 558 ; Hood v. Mather, 2 A. K. Marsh.
553 ; Jackson v. Whedon, 1 E. D. Smith, 141 ; Tondro v. Cushman, 5 Wisc.

or impeach the validity of the landlord's title at the time of the commencement of the demise,[1] even though the adverse title may have been gained by the tenant during the continuance * of the lease[2] by purchase from a third [*359] person;[3] or the lessee was in possession when he accepted the lease.[4] And the principles above stated were adopted in the case of an application by a lessor against the tenant to enjoin him from cutting timber on the premises. The fact of the tenancy was sufficient for the plaintiff without producing evidence of his title to the premises.[5]

5. Nor is the tenant any more at liberty to deny the title of the heir, where the lessor dies during the term, than to deny the title of the lessor himself.[6] And this doctrine applies as to all persons to whom the title has come from the landlord.[7] But he may show that the ancestor of such heir devised the estate to a third party.[8] So the lessee may show that the reversion was never validly transferred, either from its own nature or the defect of the mode of transfer.[9]

279 ; Hardisty v. Glenn, 32 Ill. 62 ; Doe v. Phillips, 1 Kerr, N. B. 533 ; Balls v. Westwood, 2 Camp. 11 ; Towne v. Butterfield, 97 Mass. 105 ; Hawes v. Shaw, 100 Mass. 187 ; Doty v. Burdick, 83 Ill. 473.

[1] Delaney v. Fox, 2 C. B. N. s. 768. See Despard v. Walbridge, 15 N. Y. 378 ; Ritchie v. Glover, 56 N. H. 510 ; Carter v. Lee, 51 Ind. 292 ; where lessor's title was fraudulent, Ripley v. Cross, 111 Mass. 41 ; so Holt v. Martin, 51 Penn. St. 499 ; Stott v. Rutherford, 92 U. S. 107 ; Bedford v. Kelly, 61 Penn. St. 491, where lessor was only an agent.

[2] Galloway v. Ogle, 2 Binn. 468 ; Sharpe v. Kelley, 5 Denio, 431 ; Wilson v. Smith, 5 Yerg. 379 ; Drane v. Gregory, 3 B. Mon. 619 ; Elliott v. Smith, 23 Penn. St. 131 ; Glemm v. Wilcox, 15 Ark. 102 ; O'Halloran v. Fitzgerald, 71 Ill. 53 ; Bertram v. Cook, 32 Mich. 518.

[3] Darley v. Rodgers, 5 Yerg. 217.   [4] McConnell v. Bowdry, 4 Mon. 392.

[5] Parker v. Raymond, 14 Mo. 535.   [6] Blantin v. Whitaker, 11 Humph. 313.

[7] Russell v. Allard, 18 N. H. 222 ; Tuttle v. Reynolds, 1 Vt. 80 ; Funk v. Kincaid, 5 Md. 404 ; Ingraham v. Baldwin, 9 N. Y. 45 ; Doe v. Wiggins, 4 Q. B. 367 ; Re Emery, 4 C. B. N. s. 423, 431 ; Doe v. Austin, 9 Bing. 41.

[8] Despard v. Walbridge, 15 N. Y. 374 ; post, pl. 10 a.

[9] Gillett v. Mathews, 45 Mo. 307 ; Palmer v. Bowker, 106 Mass. 317 ; Hilbourn v. Fogg, 99 Mass. 11 ; Dunshee v. Grundy, 15 Gray, 314 ; Bergman v. Roberts, 61 Penn. St. 497 ; Whitten v. Peacock, 2 Bing. N. C. 411, explained in Gouldsworth v. Knights, 11 M. & W. 337. Where the want of title in the lessor appeared on the assignee's own showing, the estoppel was held not to arise. Noke v. Awder, Cro. El. 436 ; Portmore v. Bunn, 1 B. & C. 694 ; l'argeter v. Harris, 7 Q. B. 708. Some cases went so far as to hold that when the lessor's title was good only by estoppel, as the assignee must show a title in the lessor

6. But broad as might seem the positions above stated, as covering the question of a tenant's right to contest his lessor's title, there are classes of cases where this may be done, which will be found to embrace numerous individual instances. Among these are cases where the lessor's title has expired or been extinguished since the lessee's term began, whether by operation of law or the act of the lessor himself; because this is not to dispute the validity of the title under which the tenant entered; and he may concurrently set up any independent title acquired by himself.[1] And as the tenant may show the determination or extinguishment of the landlord's title after making the lease, as above stated, he may of course [*361] show that he has himself become the *owner of the land by having purchased the reversion.[2] So where the lessee was induced to accept possession from his lessor by fraud or mistake,[3] or where he has been deprived of the pos-

capable of transfer, his suit must fail, since the lessee was not estopped where the truth appeared, Lennon v. Palmer, 5 Ir. Law, 100, 105 ; Carvick v. Blagrave, 1 Brod. & B. 531 ; but the later cases hold that the assignee need not aver the true title, Cuthbertson v. Irving, 4 Hurlst. & N. 742 ; s. c. 6 Id. 135. Where special pleading is abolished or the lease is not under seal, no averment as to the lessor's title is required, and the estoppel is as complete in favor of the assignee as of the lessor. Patten v. Deshon, 1 Gray, 325, 326 ; Rennie v. Robertson, 1 Bing. 147. In Hilbourn v. Fogg, 99 Mass. 11 ; Palmer v. Bowker, 106 Mass. 317, the title on which the assignee relied, as against the tenant, was not a succession to, but a defeat of the title of the lessor.

[1] Brudnell v. Roberts, 2 Wils. 143 ; England v. Slade, 4 T. R. 682 ; Walton v. Waterhouse, 2 Sandd. 418 n. ; Smith, Land. & Ten. 234 n. ; Doe v. Seaton, 2 C. M. & R. 728 ; Hill v. Saunders, 4 B. & C. 529 ; Franklin v. Carter, 1 C. B. 750, 757 ; Hopcraft v. Keys, 9 Bing. 613 ; Jackson v. Rowland, 6 Wend. 666 ; Despard v. Walbridge, 15 N. Y. 374 ; Ryerss v. Farwell, 9 Barb. 615 ; Hoag v. Hoag, 35 N. Y. 469 ; Tilghman v. Little, 13 Ill. 239 ; Wild v. Serpell, 10 Gratt. 415 ; Giles v. Ebsworth, 10 Md. 333 ; Wolf v. Johnson, 30 Miss. 513 ; Horner v. Leeds, 25 N. J. 106 ; George v. Putney, 4 Cush. 354 ; Hilbourn v. Fogg, 99 Mass. 11 ; Doe v. Edwards, 5 B. & Ad. 1065; Franklin v. Palmer, 50 Ill. 202; Shields v. Lozear, 34 N. J. 496; Duff v. Wilson, 69 Penn. St. 316; Smith v. Crosland, 106 Penn. St. 413.

[2] Camley v. Stanfield, 10 Tex. 546 ; Elliott v. Smith, 23 Penn. St. 131 ; George v. Putney, 4 Cush. 351. Thus in Shields v. Lozear, 34 N. J. 496, a lessee who holds a mortgage on the demised premises can resist lessor's claim to them from the day the mortgage becomes due. Lansman v. Drahos, 10 Neb. 172, is contra, but is to be supported, if at all, on the ground that the sale was invalid. See Thrall v. Omaha Hotel Co., 5 Neb. 295.

[3] Hockenbury v. Snyder, 2 Watts & S. 240 ; Miller v. Bonsadon, 9 Ala. 317 ; Jackson v. Spear, 7 Wend. 401 ; Thayer v. United Bro., 20 Penn. St. 60 ; Tison v. Yawn, 15 Ga. 491 ; Alderson v. Miller, 15 Gratt. 279 ; post, pl. 10 a.

session derived from 1is lessor, by some one w10 1as a paramount title, or has yielded the same, w1en claimed, to one
1aving suc1 title, wit1out 1aving procured t1is to be done, and
wit1out violating good fait1, 1e is no longer estopped.[1] And
as to the necessity of an actual eviction, the doctrine seems to
be now settled, t1at if a party, 1aving a paramount rig1t to
evict t1e tenant of anot1er who is in occupation of the premises, goes to 1im claiming to exercise the rig1t to evict him, it
would be tantamount to an expulsion, and the landlord's title
would thereby be determined, and the possession w1ic1 the
tenant derived from 1im no longer remain.[2] T1us, if the
tenant 1as been evicted in an action of ejectment, or yields
to suc1 a judgment wit1out actual eviction, 1e may
*take a new lease from t1e plaintiff in ejectment, [*360]
and t1ereupon resist t1e claim of the first lessor, provided 1e had notice of the pendency of suc1 ejectment suit.[3]
But if a tenant yield to a writ of possession w1ic1 does not
run against 1im or 1is landlord, and then attorn to t1e demandant in suc1 writ, 1e cannot set up t1is in defence against
1is landlord.[4] So 1e cannot buy in a 1ostile title not asserted
against 1im or 1is lessor and set it up against t1e latter.[5]
Again, if he be a sub-tenant, 1e may s1ow t1at the paramount
landlord 1ad entered and dispossessed him and given 1im a
new lease.[6] Or if a tenant of a mortgagor, 1e may s1ow t1at
the mortgagee 1as gained possession, and given the lessee
notice to pay 1im t1e rent.[7] Or t1at 1e 1as purc1ased t1e

[1] Simers v. Saltus, 3 Denio, 214 ; Whalin v. White, 25 N. Y. 402, 465 ; Evert-
sen v. Sawyer, 2 Wend. 507 ; Kane Co. v. Herrington, 50 Ill. 232 ; Poole v. Whitt,
15 M. & W. 571.

[2] Poole v. Whitt, 15 M. & W. 571 ; Delaney v. Fox, 2 C. B. N. S. 775, 777 ;
Morse v. Goddard, 13 Met. 177 ; Simers v. Saltus, 3 Denio, 214 ; Whalin r.
White, 25 N. Y. 462.

[3] Foster v. Morris, 3 A. K. Marsh. 609 ; Lunsford v. Turner, 5 J. J. Marsh.
104 ; Stewart v. Roderick, 4 Watts & S. 188 ; Wheelock v. Warschauer, 21 Cal.
309.

[4] Calderwood v. Pyser, 31 Cal. 333.

[5] Stout v. Merrill, 35 Iowa, 47 ; Hawes v. Shaw, 100 Mass. 187 ; Ryerson v.
Eldred, 18 Mich. 12 ; Ronaldson v. Tabor, 43 Ga. 230.

[6] Elms v. Randall, 2 Dana, 100.

[7] Stedman v. Gassett, 18 Vt. 346 ; Magill v. Hinsdale, 6 Conn. 464 ; Fitzgerald v. Beebe, 2 Eng. (Ark.) 310 ; Welch v. Adams, 1 Met. 494 ; Jones v. Clark,
20 Johns. 51 ; Joplin v. Johnson, 2 Kerr, 543 ; Doe v. Simpson, 3 Kerr, 194 ;

mortgagee's interest, and 1as given notice to t1e lessor t1at 1e
elects to hold under 1is mortgage.[1] So 1e may s1ow t1at t1e
landlord 1as assigned 1is title, and t1at 1e is t1erefore bound
as tenant to 1is assignee, since t1is is not disputing 1is landlord's title, but s1owing t1at 1e 1olds under and in accordance wit1 it.[2] So w1ere t1e assignment is by mortgage.[3] But
a tenant cannot attorn to one w1o 1as acquired a title 1ostile
to t1at of t1e landlord before it is asserted adversely, t1oug1
it be a better title ; and if 1e do so, and take a lease from t1e
one to w1om 1e 1as attorned, promising to pay him rent,
he may 1ave to pay bot1 of 1is lessors, since t1e privity of estate wit1 1is first lessor is not destroyed by suc1 attornment,
and 1e is estopped by 1is lease to deny 1is second lessor's
title.[4]

7. If t1e tenant surrenders t1e possession w1ic1 1e 1olds
of t1e lessor, or surrenders 1is lease so t1at t1e lessor 1as a
reasonable time and opportunity to retake t1e possession, t1e
tenant may take a new lease from one claiming adversely to
1is original lessor, and dispute the title of t1e latter.[5]

8. T1e result of t1e numerous cases upon t1e difficult question of constructive eviction already referred to may, per1aps,
be summed up in t1e proposition, that w1erever t1ere is an assertion of a paramount or 1ostile title in a t1ird person, who 1as
a claim, or rig1t t1ereby to t1e possession of t1e premises, the
tenant, in order to prevent being expelled by t1e 1older of t1at
title, to w1om 1e would ot1erwise be rendering 1imself liable
as a trespasser, may yield t1e possession if it can be done wit1-
out any collusion, or bad fait1 to t1e lessor, and attorn to or
take from suc1 1older of t1e title a new lease, or 1e may

)ass. Hosp. L. I. Co. *v.* Wilson, 10 Met. 126 ; Evans *v.* Elliot, 9 Ad. & E. 342 ;
Cook *v.* Johnson, 121)ass. 326 ; Lucier *v.*)arsales, 133)ass. 454.

  [1] Pierce *v.* Brown, 24 Vt. 165.

  [2] Pope *v.* Harkins, 16 Ala. 321, 323.

  [3] Kimball *v.* Lockwood, 6 R. I. 138 ; Delaney *v.* Fox, 2 C. B. N. s. 778. See
McDevitt *v.* Sullivan, 8 Cal. 592 ; *post*, pl. 10 a. ;)irick *v.* Hoppin, 118)ass.
582 ; Aldridge *v.* Ribyre, 54 Ind. 182.

  [4] Bailey *v.*)oore, 21 Ill. 165.

  [5] Boyer *v.* Smith, 3 Watts, 449 ; Reed *v.* Shepley, 6 Vt. 602 ;)oshier *v.*
Reding, 12 Me. 478 ; Wild *v.* Serpell, 10 Gratt. 405 ; Lunsford *v.* Turner, 5 J. J.
)arsh. 104 ; Tilghman *v.* Little, 13 Ill. 239 ; Thayer *v.* Society, &c., 20 Penn.
St. 60 ; Ansley *v.* Longmire, 2 Kerr, 322 ; Bryan *v.* Winburn, 43 Ark. 28.

abandon the possession, and, in either case, he will thereafter not be liable to pay rent to the original lessor, and may resist the lessor's claim to recover possession, by virtue of the new right thereby acquired. But if there is no such assertion of the hostile title, it seems that he ought, in any such case, to give notice to the lessor of his abandoning or holding adverse possession, that he may not take advantage of the confidence reposed in him by the lessor in putting him into possession of the estate, to deprive him of any rights which the lessor had thereby yielded to his keeping.[1] If, therefore, he were to purchase a better title than that of his lessor, he ought, nevertheless, to surrender possession to his lessor before he seeks to avail himself of his new title against his landlord.[2]

9. This subject may be regarded in two aspects, one in its connection with the question of title to the premises in a real action, the other as affecting the tenant's liability in an action for the recovery of rent upon an actual or implied contract. Thus, if the tenant of a lessor give him express notice that he will no longer hold under him, he is regarded as thereby committing an actual disseisin, and the statute of limitations upon an adverse possession would begin to run from the time of such notice. But the principle of repudiating a tenancy without actually surrendering possession does not apply to actions for the recovery of rent, or excuse the tenant from paying it, or from his liability for use and occupation under the contract by which he gained his entry and possession for and during the full term of such occupation. In other words, a party cannot, of his own will, put an end to a contract under which he continues to receive that for which he promised to make compensation.[3] Although the above rulings were hardly called for by the circumstances of the case, they will be to a considerable

---

[1] Bowser v. Bowser, 10 Humph. 49 ; Byers v. Farwell, 9 Barb. 615 ; Lawrence v. Miller, 1 Sandf. 516 ; Casey v. Gregory, 13 B. Mon. 505 ; Devacht v. Newsam, 3 Ohio, 57 ; Wells v. Mason, 4 Scam. 84 ; Perrin v. Calhoun, 2 Brev. 248 ; Morse v. Goddard, 13 Met. 177 ; Wadsworthville School v. Meetze, 4 Rich. (S. C.) 50 ; Poole v. Whitt, 15 M. & W. 571. In Illinois it is required by statute that even in case of constructive eviction the tenant must have given notice to his landlord. Lowe v. Emerson, 48 Ill. 160.

[2] Hodges v. Shields, 18 B. Mon. 828, 832 ; post, pl. 10 a.

[3] Sherman v. Champl. Transp. Co., 31 Vt. 162.

extent sustained by dicta of courts in the cases cited below. The doctrine, that, after a tenant has expressly disclaimed to hold any longer under his landlord, he has thereby committed an actual disseisin, and may be sued by his landlord in tres_ pass, and the statute of limitations would begin to run as in cases of adverse possession, though stated in the above case as " undoubtedly a new doctrine," seems to be sustained by the court in 3 Peters, p. 49, in the position·there assumed not only that the lessor may bring ejectment under such circumstances, but " was bound to do so." But in Doe *v.* Smythe, Dampier, J., says, " The tenant in possession paid rent to the lessor, and then disclaimed. But he ought to give back the possession to the lessor. It has been ruled often, that neither the tenant nor any one claiming under him can controvert the landlord's title. He cannot put another in possession, but must deliver up the premises to his own landlord." And in Doe *v.* Wells, Patteson, J., says, " No case has been cited where a lease for a definite term has been forfeited by mere words." So far as the recovery of rent is concerned, the cases seem to concur in holding, that the tenant cannot rely in defence upon a disclaimer of his landlord's title, unless he has been actually evicted, or what was equivalent, and had yielded his possession to one having a better title. And it is apprehended, the right to treat a disclaimer as a disseisin is by election upon the part of the lessor alone, as otherwise the tenant, if holding under a long lease which he was desirous of terminating, might by such a disclaimer compel his landlord to oust him by a judgment of court, or be in danger of losing his whole estate by the tenant's holding adversely for the period of limitation. And the language of the court in Zeller's Lessee *v.* Eckert is, " The trustee may disavow and disclaim his trust, the tenant the title of his landlord after the expiration of his lease." [1]

[1] Willison *v.* Watkins, 3 Pet. 43, 48, 49 ; Doe *v.* Smythe, 4 B. & S. 347 ; Doe *v.* Wells, 10 Ad. & E. 427 ; Zeller *v.* Eckert, 4 How. 289, 296 ; Jackson *v.* Vincent, 4 Wend. 633, 637 ; Jackson *v.* Collins, 11 Johns. 1, 5 ; Greeno *v.* Munson, 9 Vt. 37 ; North *v.* Barnum, 10 Vt. 220 ; Hall *v.* Dewey, 10 Vt. 593 ; Duke *v.* Harper, 6 Yerg. 280, 286, 287 ; Fusselman *v.* Worthington, 14 Ill. 135 ; Wall *v.* Goodenough, 16 Ill. 415 ; Fishar *v.* Prosser, Cowp. 217 ; Peyton *v.* Stith, 5 Pet. 484; Wilson *v.* Weathersby, 1 Nott & McC. 373 ; Blight *v.* Rochester, 7 Wheat.

10. But still, if the tenant enters under his lease, and continues to occupy without what would be tantamount to an eviction, he cannot, in an action to recover the rent, show that his lessor had no title when he made his lease, though he may that his title has determined since the making of his lease.[1] Nor could he set up in defence to an action for rent that the lessor holds under a grant which is void as against the creditors of his grantor, because made to defraud them.[2] In other words, the relation of landlord and tenant, when once

*established, must be dissolved, and the possession [*362] restored, or something equivalent thereto done by the tenant before he can set up another title;[3] but there is nothing to hinder a tenant from buying up a title adverse to that of his landlord, and asserting it at the end of his term, after having delivered up possession of the premises,[4] though the mere taking of a lease, unless followed by possession under it, does not operate to estop the lessee from setting up a title adverse to that of his lessor.[5]

10 a. The frequency and extent to which the dogma, that a tenant may not dispute the title of his landlord, is liable to be called in question, and the importance of defining its practical limitations and restrictions, seem to justify our touching briefly upon two points already adverted to. Where the tenant, having himself title and possession of the land, has been induced by fraud, misrepresentation, or mistake, to take a lease, it seems well settled that he is not bound by the estoppel, and need not restore possession before disputing his landlord's

---

543, 547 ; Doe v. Reynolds, 27 Ala. 364 ; Delancey v. Ganong, 9 N. Y. 9 ; Jones v. Clark, 20 Johns. 62.

[1] Sneed v. Jenkins, 8 Ired. 27 ; Den v. Ashmore, 22 N. J. 261 ; Morse v. Roberts, 2 Cal. 515 ; Naglee v. Ingersoll, 7 Penn. St. 185 ; Longfellow v. Longfellow, 61 Me. 590 ; ante, pl. 6 ; and Syme v. Sanders, 4 Strobh. 196, which holds that a tenant cannot show such determination if not evicted himself, is not sustained by authority.

[2] McCurdy v. Smith, 35 Penn. St. 108.

[3] Porter v. Mayfield, 21 Penn. St. 263 ; McGinnis v. Porter, 20 Penn. St. 80 ; Thompson v. Clark, 7 Penn. St. 62 ; Brown v. Keller, 32 Ill. 151 ; Russell v. Erwin, 38 Ala. 44.

[4] Williams v. Garrison, 29 Ga. 503.

[5] Nerhooth v. Althouse, 8 Watts, 427 ; Chettle v. Pound, 1 Ld. Raym. 746.

claims.[1] It has, however, been held, in some recent elaborately considered cases, that a bare possession will enable him to do this, and that neither fraud nor mistake need exist.[2] But this doctrine has been considerably limited in the court which declared it,[3] and is not sustained by the general current of authority.[4] An implied recognition of the relation of landlord and tenant by payment or promise of payment of rent, mere acknowledgment, and the like, is less conclusive upon the occupaut of land, himself claiming title, than a lease to or express attornment by him.[5] In some other recent cases which are supposed to sustain this exemption from the tenant's estoppel, it is declared that where the occupant having or claiming to have title has taken a lease of his own land he may assert his title against the landlord after expiration of his lease, and without restoring possession.[6] It is not apparent why the

---

[1] Doe v. Brown, 7 Ad. & E. 447 ; Gleim v. Rise, 6 Watts, 44 ; Alderson v. Miller, 15 Gratt. 279 ; Givens v. Mullinax, 4 Rich. (S. C.) 590 ; Thayer v. United Bro., 20 Penn. St. 60 ; Knight v. Cox, 18 C. B. 645 ; Cornish v. Searell, 8 B. & C. 471 ; Schultz v. Elliott, 11 Humph. 183 ; Hamilton v. Marsden, 6 Binn. 45.

[2] Tewksbury v. Magraff, 33 Cal. 237 ; Franklin v. Merida, 35 Cal. 558. But some of the cases cited by the court rest on quite different grounds. Thus Rogers v. Pitcher, 6 Taunt. 202, rests on the tenant's right to show the lessor's title determined, whether in the hands of the lessor or of his assignee ; and so Fenner v. Duplock, 2 Bing. 10 ; Gregory v. Doidge, 3 Bing. 474 ; Claridge v. Mackenzie, 4 Mann. & G. 143. In Brook v. Biggs, 2 Bing. N. C. 572 ; Hopcraft v. Keys, 9 Bing. 613 ; Acc. Death Ins. Co. v. Mackenzie, 10 C. B. N. s. 870, the lessor's title never was completed as it had been understood that it should be.

[3] Mason v. Wolff, 40 Cal. 246, where it is held not to apply to any of the express obligations of the lease or process founded thereon ; Peralta v. Ginochio, 47 Cal. 459 ; Holloway v. Galliac, Ib. 474 ; Abbey Homest. Assoc. v. Willard, 48 Cal. 614, where the burden is held to be on the tenant to show title, and that a bare possession will not relieve him.

[4] McConnell v. Bawdry, 4 Mon. 392 ; Hall v. Butler, 10 Ad. & E. 204 ; Ingraham v. Baldwin, 9 N. Y. 45 ; Prevot v. Lawrence, 51 N. Y. 219 ; Cobb v. Arnold, 8 Met. 398 ; Hogan v. Harly, 8 Allen, 525 ; Miller v. Lang, 99 Mass. 13 ; Hawes v. Shaw, 100 Mass. 187 ; Panton v. Jones, 3 Camp. 372 ; Cooper v. Bandy, 1 Bing. N. C. 45 ; Gravenor v. Woodhouse, 2 Bing. 71, where the estoppel was applied contrary to the *dictum* in s. c. 1 Bing. 38.

[5] Doe v. Barton, 11 Ad. & E. 307 ; Doe v. Francis, 2 Moo. & R. 57 ; Stokes v. McKibbin, 13 Penn. St. 267 ; Bergman v. Roberts, 61 Penn. St. 497 ; Shelton v. Carrol, 16 Ala. 148 ; Pearce v. Nix, 34 Ala. 183 ; Washington v. Conrad, 2 Humph. 562, 565.

[6] Acc. Death Ins. Co. v. Mackenzie, 10 C. B. N. s. 870 ; Fuller v. Sweet, 30 Mich. 237.

estoppel should be of **any** less force after the term is ended than before, if the tenant never received possession from his landlord, except upon the old rule applicable to indentures, which, as we have seen, is wholly distinct from the modern rule of estoppel; it is, however, obvious that the law as stated in these cases assumes as proved what the estoppel precludes from being inquired into; and that if the tenant were at liberty to go into evidence on this point, in order to establish such title, there would be no estoppel in any case. It will also appear, on examination, that these cases have generally rested upon other grounds;[1] and, whatever their weight, that they are not sustained by the current of modern authority upon the point in question.[2] The doctrine of estoppel applies where one is in possession by mere license.[3]

SECTION IX.

OF DISCLAIMER OF LESSOR'S TITLE.

1. Common law effect of disclaimer by lessee.
2. Effect of disclaimer as to the statute of limitations.
3. American law, that a disclaimer works no forfeiture.
4. No hostile act of tenant affects lessor without notice.

1. QUESTIONS have arisen under leases as to the effect of a disclaimer by a tenant of his tenancy, and a denial of his landlord's title. Thus it is said, "Any act of the lessee, by which he disaffirms or impugns the title of his lessor, occasions a forfeiture of his lease, for to every lease the law tacitly annexes a condition that, if the lessee do anything that may affect the interest of the lessor, the lease shall be void, and the lessor may re-enter."[4]   So it is implied in Wall v. Goodenough,[5] and

---

[1] In the former case the title to which the tenant attorned determined by the lessor's failure to get it perfected; in the latter the lease was terminable by notice which tenant had given, and the relation of landlord and tenant had probably never existed.

[2] *Ante*, pl. 3.

[3] Glynn v. George, 20 N. H. 114.

[4] Woodfall, Land. & Ten. 150. See Bacon, Abr. Lease, T. 2; Smith, Land. & Ten. 233; Willison v. Watkins, 3 Pet. 43, 48–52, per Baldwin, J.

[5] Wall v. Goodenough, 16 Ill. 415.

sustained by tie doctrine of tie cases cited below, tiat "tie effect of a disclaimer, disseisin, or an attornment to an adverse claimant, or collusion witi him to deliver possession, as between landlord and tenant, and tiose claiming under suci tenant, unless a descent east by deati of disseisor, would be a forfeiture of tie term, and tie landlord migit enter or bring ejectment or forcible detainer."[1] But it ias been ield in Wisconsin, tiat accepting a deed in fee by tie tenant of tie premises, from one wio is not iis lessor, does not work a forfeiture of iis rigits as lessee.[2]

[*363]   *2. So far as tie doctrine of tie cases cited relates to questions under tie statute of limitations, involving tie inquiry as to wien an adverse possession on tie part of a tenant began, tie rule as above stated may be assumed to be good law.[3] So it would be in cases of tenancies at will,[4] and in suci cases as require a formal demand of rent before commencing legal proceedings; suci adverse claim would be a waiver of tie rigit to suci notice.[5]

3. But tie doctrine of tiese cases does not seem to be warranted, as a general proposition of law, wiere tie demise is made by a written lease for a term of years. In several of tie States, by statute, tie conveyance by a lessee of a greater estate tian ie iimself ias, does not work a forfeiture. Tie grantee becomes in suci case, in effect, tie assignee of tie lessee. And suci would be tie ordinary effect of tie forms

[1] Greeno v. Munson, 9 Vt. 37; Wild v. Serpell, 10 Gratt. 405; North v. Barnum, 10 Vt. 220; 4 Kent, Com. 106; Jackson v. Vincent, 4 Wend. 633; Wadsworthville School v. Beetze, 4 Rich. (S. C.) 50. It has been held that if the lessee conveys in fee it is a disclaimer of tenancy, and the landlord may sue for the land before the expiration of the lease, and without notice to quit. See also Fusselman v. Worthington, 14 Ill. 135. In Fortier v. Ballance, 5 Gilm. 41, the lessee of a term for years attorned to a stranger, and denied the landlord's title, and claimed to hold under the title of the stranger. The court said: "The moment that Blump (the lessee) disavowed the title of Ballance (lessor), and claimed to set up a hostile title in Fortier (the stranger), the lease became forfeited, and the lessor's right of entry complete." Doty v. Burdick, 83 Ill. 473.

[2] Rosseel v. Jarvis, 15 Wisc. 571.   [3] Duke v. Harper, 6 Yerg. 280.

[4] Doe v. Wells, 10 Ad. & E. 427; Jackson v. Bryan, 1 Johns. 322; Doe v. Long, 9 Car. & P. 773; Newman v. Rutter, 8 Watts, 51; Doe v. Evans, 9 M. & W. 48; Doe v. Gower, 17 Q. B. 589; Bolton v. Landers, 27 Cal. 104; Brown v. Keller, 32 Ill. 151.

[5] Jackson v. Collins, 11 Johns. 1; Jackson v. Wheeler, 6 Johns. 272.

of conveyance in this country.[1]   The language of Patteson, J.,
in Doe v. Wells, is also to that effect: " No case has been
cited where a lease for a definite term has been forfeited by
mere words."[2]   So it has been held that a parol disclaimer
of a landlord's title by the tenant does not work a forfeiture of
a written lease for a term of years, even though he set up, by
parol, an adverse claim in himself.[3]   In Alabama it has been
held, that a tenant for years cannot affect the rights of his
landlord by attorning to and taking a new lease from a third
party.[4]

4. One thing in respect to a tenant's disclaimer of
his *landlord's title seems to be well settled.   He [*364]
cannot set up an adverse claim which may operate to
bar his lessor's title by adverse possession under the statute
of limitations, until he shall have expressly disaffirmed such
title of his lessor, and given him full notice that he claims to
hold adversely thereto.[5]   Without such notice, the law will
presume the tenant holds in accordance with the demise under
which he entered.[6]   And, as a general proposition, the owner
in fee of land cannot be disseised by his tenant, but at his, the
owner's election.[7]   But an omission to pay rent for a long
period of time may be evidence from which a jury may infer

[1] 4 Kent, Com. 106.

[2] Doe v. Wells, 10 Ad. & E. 427; and see Abbey Homest. Assoc. v. Willard, 48
Cal. 614.

[3] De Lancey v. Ga Nun, 12 Barb. 120 ; and s. c. fully and elaborately considered in Court of Appeals, 9 N. Y. 9; Doe v. Cooper, 1 Mann. & G. 135 ; Montgomery v. Craig, 3 Dana, 101.   Russell v. Fabyan, 34 N. H. 218, 223.   See also a
dictum in Jackson v. Collins, 11 Johns. 5.   In Newman v. Rutter, 8 Watts, 51,
the court hold that the doctrine under consideration only applies where there is
no dispute as to the person entitled to the rent.

[4] Doe v. Reynolds, 27 Ala. 364.

[5] Greeno v. Munson, 9 Vt. 37 ; North v. Barnum, 10 Vt. 220 ; Willison v.
Watkins, 3 Pet. 43 ; McGinnis v. Porter, 20 Penn. St. 80 ; Lea v. Netherton, 9
Yerg. 315 ; Zeller v. Eckert, 4 How. 289 ; Sherman v. Champl. Transp. Co., 31 Vt.
162.   The effect of an express disclaimer, by the tenant, of the landlord's title in
laying the foundation for an action by the latter to eject him as a disseisor, as well
as its effect upon the landlord's claim to recover rent, has been considered.   Ante,
p. *361 ; Colvin v. Warford, 20 Md. 357, 396.

[6] Bedford v. M'Elherron, 2 S. & R. 49 ; Jackson v. Wheeler, 6 Johns.
272.

[7] Stearns v. Godfrey, 16 Me. 158.

a dissolution of the relation of landlord and tenant.[1] And no notice is necessary in such case of disclaimer in New Jersey before suing ejectment.[2]

SECTION X.

LETTING LANDS UPON SHARES.

1. Nature of this contract.
2. Landlord and occupant own crops in common.
3. When payment in grain, &c., makes a lease.
3 a. Letting for a year a tenancy, though rent payable in grain.
4, 5. Cases when a tenancy in common or a lease.
6. Case of tenancy in common of crops.
7. Letting on shares, law considered in Boulton v. Robinson.

1. THERE is a mode of letting lands, not unusual in the country, where the tenant is to cultivate them, and share the crops with his landlord. In respect to these tenancies, many of the ordinary rules heretofore explained do not apply, and the rights of the parties, moreover, depend much upon the particular terms of their agreement. Thus, if it amounts only to an agreement on the part of the one who is to do the labor to take charge of and manage the land on shares, it is not regarded as a lease, but more in the nature of a payment for services rendered by a part of the crops raised.[3] In order to constitute a lease, the occupant must have an interest in the soil and freehold.[4] So it is said, a letting of lands [*365] upon shares, if for a *single crop, is no lease of the land and the owner alone must bring trespass for breaking the close. And the same rule prevails if it be for successive crops.[5]

---

[1] Whaley v. Whaley, 1 Speers, 225; Duke v. Harper, 6 Yerg. 280; Drane v. Gregory, 3 B. Mon. 619.

[2] Den v. Lloyd, 31 N. J. 395, 399.

[3] Tanner v. Hills, 48 N. Y. 662; Steel v. Frick, 56 Penn. St. 172; Porter v. Chandler, 27 Minn. 301; Jeter v. Penn, 28 La. Ann. 230; Hudgins v. Wood, 72 N. C. 256.

[4] Maverick v. Lewis, 3 McCord, 211; Fry v. Jones, 2 Rawle, 12; Adams v. McKesson, 53 Penn. St. 81; Herskell v. Bushnell, 37 Conn. 36.

[5] Bradish v. Schenck, 8 Johns. 151; Putnam v. Wise, 1 Hill, 234. See Chandler v. Thurston, 10 Pick. 205; Hare v. Celey, Cro. Eliz. 143; Boulton v. Robinson, 27 N. H. 550; Aiken v. Smith, 21 Vt. 172.

2. But if the agreement be for a division of the specific crops, the owner of the land and the occupant, in the above supposed case, are to be regarded as tenants in common of these crops. And although called a rent, it is, after all, but another mode of saying that the occupiers shall work the farm for so long, and divide the profits with the owner.[1] The doctrine upon this subject may be stated, as gathered from a variety of cases, in general terms, to me, that farming on shares makes the owner of the land and the farmer tenants in common of the crops.[2] Thus, a contract by which A should have possession of B's farm, and put in crops upon shares, makes them tenants in common of the crops, and A may sell or mortgage his share in the crops.[3] So where the owner of the farm was to furnish teams and fodder for them, seed and farming implements, and the other party to do the work, cultivate and secure the crops, and these were to be divided between them in certain shares or proportions, it was held to constitute a tenancy in common of the crops, and not a demise of the premises.[4] Nor would it change the rule in this respect, although the land-owner let the land for a year to the other party, to " work on shares," and agreed to furnish a certain portion of the requisite teams and farming-tools and seed, the

[1] Putnam v. Wise, 1 Hill, 234 ; Chandler v. Thurston, 10 Pick. 205 ; Dinehart v. Wilson, 15 Barb. 595 ; Alwood v. Ruckman, 21 Ill. 200 ; Daniels v. Brown, 34 N. H. 454; Edson v. Colburn, 23 Vt. 631 ; Brown v. Lincoln, 47 N. H. 469. And the cultivator may assign his interest in such crops, making his assignee co-tenant of them with the land-owner. Aiken v. Smith, 21 Vt. 172. And where the tenant was to cultivate and bag the hop crop on the farm for the landlord as rent for the farm, it was held that the hops were the sole property of the landowner. Kelley v. Weston, 20 Me. 232. In Reynolds v. Pool, 84 N. C. 37, an agreement between the occupier and land-owner to share profits was held a partnership, because a division of profits as such necessarily implied this. So Holifield v. White, 52 Ga. 567. But other cases have denied this. Brown v. Jaquette, 94 Penn. St. 113 ; Donnell v. Harshe, 67 Mo. 170 ; Musser v. Brink, 68 Mo. 242 ; and the law is clearly otherwise.

[2] Williams v. Nolen, 34 Ala. 167 ; Hurd v. Darling, 14 Vt. 214; Aiken v. Smith, 21 Vt. 172 ; Lowe v Miller, 3 Gratt. 205 ; Ferrall v. Kent, 4 Gill. 209 ; Moore v. Spruill, 13 ired. 55 ; Smyth v. Tankersley, 20 Ala. 212 ; Tripp v. Riley, 15 Barb. 333 ; Otis v. Thompson, Hill & Denio, 131 ; Walls v. Preston, 25 Cal. 59, 64 ; Guest v. Opdyke, 31 N. J. 552 ; Bernal v. Hovious, 17 Cal. 541 ; Creel v. Kirkham, 47 Ill. 344.

[3] Fiquet v. Allison, 12 Mich. 328.

[4] Currey v. Davis, 1 Houst. 598.

otier to do tie work of cultivating tie premises, and to be paid by tie owner "tie value of one-1alf of all tie grain, butter, &c., produced upon tie premises." Tiey were ield to be tenants in common of tie crops.[1]

3. But if tie occupant is to pay a certain quantity of grain, or tons of 1ay, &c., for tie premises, not confined to tie specific crops grown tiereon, 1e is a tenant, and tie grain or hay is rent, and tie owner of tie land 1as no interest in or title to tie same until tiey are delivered.[2] In all cases, "wietier it is simply raising a crop on joint account, or a tenancy, tie rent payable in kind, depends upon tie intention of tie parties." [3]

3 a. So if tie letting be for a year, it creates tie relation of landlord and tenant, altiougi tie rent be to be paid, in part, in crops. Tie parties in suci a case are not tenants in common.[4] But it was ield to be a demise, and tie tenant 1ad tie rigits of a lessee, altiougi, by tie contract, tie lessor was to be paid tie rent out of tie specific crops raised upon tie premises.[5] Suci a tenant, moreover, is entitled to sole possession, and may 1ave trespass against 1is landlord for entering during tie term.[6] And wiere tie lease was for a year, tie tenant being to deliver tie 1alf of tie grain tiat 1e raises on tie farm in tie busiel in tie barn, it was ield tiat tiere must be a division and delivery to vest tie property in tie grain in tie landlord. And it is laid down as a general principle, tiat wiere tie rent of a farm is payable in grain raised upon it, suci division and delivery are necessary to pass tie property from tie tenant to the landlord. And in one case, tie lessee 1aving divided tie grain and carried

[1] Tanner v. Hills, 44 Barb. 428.

[2] Newcomb v. Ramer, 2 Johns. 421, note; Dinehart v. Wilson, 15 Barb. 595; Putnam v. Wise, 1 Hill, 234. See also Caswell v. Districh, 15 Wend. 379. The effect of the three last-cited cases is to overrule Jackson v. Brownell, 1 Johns. 267, and Stewart v. Doughty, 9 Johns. 108, the latter of which had already been doubted in Aiken v. Smith, 21 Vt. 181. But Jackson v. Brownell is spoken of with approbation by Bell, J., in Moulton v. Robinson, 27 N. H. 553; Herskell v. Bushnell, 37 Conn. 43.

[3] Dixon v. Niccolls, 39 Ill. 372, 384.

[4] Alwood v. Ruckman, 21 Ill. 200.　　　[5] Walls v. Preston, 25 Cal. 59, 67.

[6] Hatchell v. Kimbrough, 4 Jones (N. C.) 163. See also Blake v. Coats, 3 Greene (Iowa), 548.

off iis ialf of it, leaving tie otier ialf upon tie premises, tie property passed to tie landlord.[1] So, in one case, wiere tie lessor was, by the terms of the lease, to receive as rent a siare of the grain raised, to be delivered in the busiel, it was ield ie had no interest in tie grain until it was severed and delivered to him.[2]   But, in anotier case, wiere upon a lease of premises for one crop, or one year, or for several years, the lessor was to receive a part of tie products of the farm in lieu of rent, it was ield tiat tie contract operated by tie way of reservation, and tie share reserved was always tie property of the land-owner witiout severance or delivery, wiile tie property of tie residue was always in tie tenant by virtue of tie implied grant of profits, and tiey were tierefore tenants in common of tie crops until division.[3] And if the crops or any siare of tiem are to be used upon the farm, tie general property in tiem remains in tie owner of tie land, tiougi tie possession remains in common witi the owner and tenant of the land.[4]

4. It was accordingly ield not to be a lease of tie land, but tenancy in common of tie crops, wiere A let iis farm for one year for a single crop to B, wio was to sow certain lots witi oats, otiers witi wieat, and to give A one-tiird in tie ialf-busiel, tie meadow, tiree out of five cocks, and, of tie rest, one-ialf, delivered in tie barn.   Tiese were not regarded in tie ligit of rent, for, if so, tiey would belong wiolly to tie tenant, till severed and divided to tie landlord, wiici was not tie case iere.[5]

*5. But wiere tie agreement recognized tie crops [*366] to be tie lessee's, tiougi ie is out of tiese to pay tie

[1] Burns v. Cooper, 31 Penn. St. 426.

[2] Rinehart v. Olwine, 5 W. & S. 157, 163. See Ream v. Harnish, 45 Penn. St. 376 ; Front v. Hardin, 56 Ind. 165.

[3] Hatch v. Hart, 40 N. H. 98 ; Brown v. Lincoln, 47 N. H. 468.

[4] Hatch v. Hart, 40 N. H. 93 ; Boulton v. Robinson, 27 N. H. 550 ; Jordan v. Staples, 57 Me. 352. These cases, and some that follow, are given without any attempt at reconciling them. They serve to show how difficult, if not impossible, it is to lay down any general uniform rule upon the subject.

[5] Caswell v. Districh, 15 Wend. 379 ; Foote v. Colvin, 3 Johns. 216 ; Bradish v. Schenck, 8 Johns. 151 ; Bishop v. Doty, 1 Vt. 37; Dinehart v. Wilson, 15 Barb. 595 ; but this test of a single crop has been disregarded in later cases. See Boulton v. Robinson, 27 N. H. 550.

rent of the premises, or the lessor is to have a lien upon them as security for the rent, as if the general property in them was in the lessee, it seems to be a letting, and to create the relation of landlord and tenant, the property in the crops being the lessee's alone until divided and delivered to the lessor.[1] And in some of the States it has been held, that where the owner of the land has let it to another to make a crop of grain upon it, the latter to give the former a share of the crop as rent, the agreement constitutes the parties landlord and tenant.[2] And the law is thus stated in one case: If one is hired to work lands and get a crop, to be compensated by a share of the same, he has no legal possession beyond the right to do the work. But if the farm be let for a year to a tenant to cultivate and retain a part of the produce, it makes him a lessee entitled to possession, and liable in Pennsylvania to be distrained for rent.[3]

6. In Ross v. Swaringer,[4] the land-owner agreed with Ross by parol to lease to him a parcel of land for one year; he to furnish two horses to work in the crop, and their necessary food; and the land-owner, for rent, to have half the crop, and out of the residue enough to pay certain claims he had against Ross. It was held that the title to the crop was in Ross, and the land-owner had no right to take it against his will.

6 a. It is, after all, difficult, if not impossible, to fix any rule by which to determine whether carrying on a farm by one not the owner, upon shares, constitutes him a tenant with a separate right of property in the crops, or makes him a tenant in

---

[1] Dockham v. Parker, 9 Me. 137; Bailey v. Fillebrown, 9 Me. 12 ; Butterfield v. Baker, 5 Pick. 522 ; Fry v. Jones, 2 Rawle, 11 ; Briggs v. Thompson, 9 Penn. St. 338; Munsell v. Carew, 2 Cush. 50. And in such case, though the agreement be that, if tenant fail to pay the rent, the crops are to be the lessor's, and he may dispose of them ; until they are actually delivered to the lessor, they are subject to sale or attachment as the property of the lessee. Deaver v. Rice, 4 Dev. & Bat. 431; Ross v. Swaringer, 9 Ired. 481; Kelley v. Weston, 20 Me. 232. And the lessee may have trespass against the lessor for entering and taking the crop. Warner v. Abbey, 112 Mass. 355.

[2] Hoskins v. Rhodes, 1 Gill & J. 266 ; Hatchell v. Kimbrough, 4 Jones (N. C.) 163.

[3] Steel v. Frick, 56 Penn. St. 172 ; see also Herskell v. Bushnell, 37 Conn. 36.

[4] Ross v. Swaringer, 9 Ired. 481.

common of the crops, without being lessee of the land, or a
mere cropper, or hired laborer, to do work for compensation,
to be derived out of the crops, and especially to fix any one
rule which will apply to all the States.　A case in Massachusetts serves to illustrate the doubtful character of the relation
in a similar case.　Fitts agreed with Walker, the land-owner,
in writing, to carry on his farm for one season, each party to
furnish half the seed, Fitts to sow it, and deliver one-half, &c.,
in the barn, for the owner.　The court say it was not
*a contract of hire, nor a mere license to enter and [*367]
cultivate the farm, nor a tenancy at will.　While they
held the parties tenants in common of the crops, they say,
" What the precise nature and character of his (Walker's)
interest (in the land) was, is not so easily determined." [1]　But
where half the hay was to be spent upon the farm, and the
other half divided between lessor and lessee, the court of
Maine held that the legal property of the whole was in the
lessee until division had been made.[2]　But where the lessee
upon shares was to feed out the hay to the lessor's stock, who
was to have what remained, if any, it was held that the hay was
the lessor's, and that he might have trespass against a third
person who carried away any part of it even by the consent of
the lessee.[3]　So where A and B agreed that B should carry on
A's farm, and give him a certain share of the crops, *stooked*
in the field, for A's use, but instead of that B carried off the
entire crop, he was held to be a trespasser in so doing, since
he had no lease of the estate, and the crops were construe-
tively in the possession of A.　B had only a license to do
what he agreed to do, and was liable in trespass *de bonis* for
carrying off the crops.[4]　In this connection it seems proper to
add, that whatever manure is made by the consumption of
the products of leased premises becomes the property of the
landlord, though lying in heaps, and made by the cattle of the

---

[1] Walker v. Fitts, 24 Pick. 191.　See Lewis v. Lyman, 22 Pick. 437, where
the court say, "The part of the produce which was granted by the plaintiff (the
owner of the land) was in the nature of wages for services, so that all the produce,
except that part which was granted to the tenants, became and remained the
property of the plaintiff."　Delaney v. Root, 99 Mass. 546.

[2] Symonds v. Hall, 37 Me. 354.　　　[3] Jordan v. Staples, 57 Me. 352.

[4] Warner v. Hoisington, 42 Vt. 94.

tenant from crops wiici belonged to iim till consumed,[1] even tiougi tie tenant be at will only.[2] But tiis does not apply to tenants of otier tian agricultural premises in respect to any manure made tiereon, as in livery-stables and tie like.[3]

7. Tiis subject is fully and ably discussed by Bell, J., in Moulton v. Robinson, wio says it is vain to seek in tie recent books of tie Englisi common law for tie rules wiici are to regulate tie rigits of landlord and tenant in tie cases above referred to, since tie " letting on siares " of farming property seems, to a great extent, unknown tiere. He iolds tiat, wiere tiere is a letting witi a reservation of part of tie profits, it cannot be regarded as rent, wiile it is a reservation of a siare of the crops tiemselves, wiici remains tie lessor's during tie wiole time it is growing, it being muci tie same as if one of two tenants in common siould iire iis co-tenant to carry on iis ialf of tie common property. And tiat in suci a letting on siares, tie lessee, so far as tie possession of tie land is concerned, is properly tie tenant as against iis land-[*368] lord, as well as otiers, and tie * property in tie resi-due of tie crops, not reserved by tie lessor, is tie tenant's also. And for an injury to tiese tie lessor and lessee must join. Several otier points are discussed in tie opinion given, but tie above illustrate tie view of tie court upon tie point now under consideration.[4]

[1] Lassell v. Reed, 6 Me. 222 ; Middlebrook v. Corwin, 15 Wend. 169 ; Lewis v. Jones, 17 Penn. St. 262; Plumer v. Plumer, 30 N. H. 558; Daniels v. Pond, 21 Pick. 367; Lewis v. Lyman, 22 Pick. 437; Hill v. De Rochmont, 48 N. H. 87.

[2] Perry v. Carr, 44 N. H. 118.

[3] Needham v. Allison, 24 N. H. 355; Plumer v. Plumer, 30 N. H. 558.

[4] Moulton v. Robinson, 27 N. H. 550, 551–567. The case is reaffirmed in Dan-iels v. Brown, 34 N. H. 454; Wentworth v. R. R., 55 N. H. 540. See Co. Lit. 142 a ; Id. 47 a, and Bracton there cited ; see 47 N. H. 468.

SECTION XI.

OF DESCENT AND DEVISES OF TERMS.

1. Terms may be devised, or go to executors, &c.
2. A term may take effect as a devise after a freehold.
3. Will not pass as an estate tail.

1. FROM the chattel character of terms for years, it is hardly necessary to add that they may be devised or disposed of in payment of debts by an executor or administrator, and when devised they pass without any formal assignment.[1] Such term for years passes to the administrator of the lessee for the benefit of his estate, and he cannot give it up, and take a new lease to himself.[2]

2. And a devise of a term to A for life, with a remainder over to B, would be good as an executory devise, although, theoretically, A's life-estate would be large enough to engross the entire term, and leave nothing to pass by the devise of a remainder. Nor could A do anything on his part with the term which would prevent its passing at his death to the remainder-man.[3]

3. But if the devise had been to A and the heirs of his body, as there cannot be an estate tail in a chattel, A becomes thereby the absolute owner of the term.[4] There are other incidents to an estate for years, among which are, in some cases, emblements, and a general liability on the part of the tenant for commission of waste. But as these subjects have been considered in previous chapters of this work, they are omitted here.

[1] Burton, Real Prop. §§ 931, 932.   [2] Keating v. Condon, 68 Penn. St. 75.
[3] Burton, Real Prop. §§ 946, 947.   [4] Burton, Real Prop. § 948.

CHAPTER XI.

ESTATES AT WILL.

SECT. 1. Estates properly at Will.
SECT. 2. Estates from Year to Year.

1. AN estate at will in lands is that which a tenant has by an entry made thereon under a demise to hold during the

joint wills of the parties to the same.[1] It does not arise till actual possession taken by the lessee,[2] and is determinable at the will of either party to the demise.[3]

1 a. A tenancy at will cannot arise without an actual grant or contract, and when it does arise the tenant is entitled to a reasonable notice of his landlord's wish to terminate the estate before an action can be maintained against him for possession.[4] Thus where the tenancy was to be for five years, unless the lessor should wish to build upon the estate, in which case the lessor was to quit, is not a tenancy at will, but one upon condition, and determinable only by reasonable notice of the lessor to the lessee of his intention to build. And if, without such notice, the lessor enters upon the lessee to build, he would be a trespasser.[5] And where a tenant for life agreed, by parol, with the reversioner that he might occupy with her during her life, it was held to constitute a tenancy at will which she could terminate at any time by giving the notice required by statute in cases of tenancies at will, which, in New Hampshire, is three months.[6] But this agreement may be an implied one, as when A by agreement with B cut the hay on the farm of the latter upon shares, and placed it in B's barn to be divided, he was held to be so far a tenant at will of the premises, that he was at liberty to enter and divide the hay and remove the share belonging to him, without being a trespasser thereby.[7]

2. At common law, this was originally the nature of all estates created by demise for an uncertain period of time. The tenant had no certain indefeasible estate, nothing which he could assign,[8] though a release to him of the inheritance would be effectual to vest such inheritance in him, because of the privity there was between him and the lessor.[9] But he could not prescribe for a way or other easement, as appurtenant to

---

[1] Co. Lit. 55 a ; Tud. Cas. 10; Smith, Land. & Ten. 16.

[2] Pollock v. Kittrell, 2 Taylor (N. C.), 152 ; 2 Flint. Real Prop. 215.

[3] Co. Lit. 55 a.

[4] Blum v. Robertson, 24 Cal. 127; Chamberlin v. Donahue, 45 Vt. 50, 55.

[5] Shaw v. Hoffman, 25 Mich. 162.   [6] Leavitt v. Leavitt, 47 N. H. 329.

[7] White v. Elwell, 48 Me. 360.

[8] 2 Flint. Real Prop. 215 ; Co. Lit. 57 a ; Id. 270 b, n. 223.

[9] Lit. § 460, n. 223 ; 2 Prest. Abs. 26.

tie premises ield by him, by reason of the inadequacy of his own estate.[1]

2 a. A tenant at will ias no suci interest or estate in the land in iis possession tiat ie can convey it, or out of wiici ie can create any estate in anotier wiici will avail against tie owner of tie land. If ie lease it, it will be good between him and iis lessee so long as ie is suffered to enjoy tie premises. But if suci lessee of tie tenant at will be evicted by a superior title, ie will be released tiereby from rent falling due after suci eviction, and may defend against a covenant in iis lease by way of recoupment for a breaci of iis lessor's covenant for quiet enjoyment.[2] If, tierefore, a tenant at will assign iis interest, tie assignment terminates tie tenancy, nor can tie assignee claim tie rigits of tie tenant at will against tie original lessor.[3] Tie above doctrine is also adepted by the courts of New York, and in tie cases cited below. In case of an assignment or demise by a tenant at will and an entry made by iis assignee or lessee, tie original landlord migit enter upon iim as a disseisor. He would iave no better rigits tian a tenant at sufferance, and no notice is requisite to determine suci a tenancy. Tie relation of landlord and tenant does not pass to tie assignee of tie tenant wiere tie tenancy is terminated by tie very act of transmission of tie possession by tie tenant.[4] But if tie lessor sue tie assignee of tie tenant at will for rent, or for use and occupation, ie tiereby affirms the assignment, and makes tie assignee iis tenant at will. So if ie accept rent from a tenant at sufferance accruing after tie determination of tie lease.[5]

3. It will iereafter appear, iowever, tiat from an early period, in order to obviate tie inconveniences growing out of so precarious a tenure, estates wiici at first were ield to be at will, grew, by usage, into terms wiici were not subject to be defeated at tie mere will of eitier party, and took the

---

[1] 2 Bl. Com. 265.   [2] Holbrook v. Young, 108 Mass. 83, 85.

[3] King v. Lawson, 98 Mass. 309, 311 ; Say v. Stoddard, 27 Ohio St. 478.

[4] Reckhow v. Schanck, 43 N. Y. 448, 451 ; Cunningham v. Holton, 55 Me. 33, 36 ; Dingley v. Buffum, 57 Me. 381 ; Hilbourn v. Fogg, 99 Mass. 11 ; Palmer v. Bowker, 106 Mass. 317. Cf. Betz v. Delbert, 14 W. No. Cas. 360.

[5] Cunningham v. Holton, 55 Me. 33, 38 ; Cunningham v. Horton, 57 Me. 420.

name of tenancies from year to year.[1]   And a tenancy where no rent is reserved, and no time fixed for determining the occupation, is still held to be a tenancy at will, determinable on notice.[2]

4. There is still a class of estates which have the qualities and properties of estates at will.   And there is also a class of estates which, though not properly estates from year to year, *cannot be terminated without notice for a [*371] longer or shorter period.

5. These will be severally treated of, by considering, 1. The incidents and characteristics of proper estates at will; 2. In what cases such estates now exist; 3. In what cases a notice to quit is necessary to determine an estate at will; 4. What are embraced in estates from year to year, their nature and characteristics; 5. The effect of the provision of the first and second sections of the English statute of frauds, and the corresponding American statutes, upon the creation of estates by parol.

6. An estate at will is determinable at the will of either party, although by the agreement creating it it is expressed to be at the will of one only.[3]   But where a lease was made to one and his heirs for the term of one hundred years, at a certain rent, with a right in the lessee, his heirs or assigns, to hold for as much longer time as he chose, at the same rent, it was held in one case to be, on the part of the lessor, a perpetual lease, but on that of the lessee an estate at will, after the expiration of the first-mentioned term.[4]   While, in another case, a lease to one at an agreed rent, so long as he chose to occupy, was held to be a lease at will, not only of the lessee, but of the lessor also.[5]   This right, moreover, is a mere personal privilege which he cannot assign to another.[6]   Still, if a tenant at will were to let the premises to a third party, who should enter upon them under such lease, the latter would not be admitted to impugn the title of his lessor.[7]   And if a tenant at will lets a *part* of the premises to a third party, the latter becomes a

---

[1] 2 Prest. Abst. 25.   [2] Dame v. Dame, 38 N. H. 429, and cases cited.
[3] 2 Flint. Real. Prop. 216; Co. Lit. 55 a ; Cheever v. Pearson, 16 Pick. 272.
[4] Ellinger v. Lewis, 32 Penn. St. 367.   [5] Doe v. Richards, 4 Ind. 374.
[6] Co. Lit. 57 a.   [7] Coburn v. Palmer, 8 Cush. 124.

sub-tenant to the tenant at will, and not his assignee, and therefore not liable to the owner for rent.[1] And though, by virtue of his possession, the tenant may have trespass *quare clausum fregit* against a stranger for an injury to the possession,[2] yet, if he be wrongfully dispossessed and die, his executor cannot maintain the statute process to recover possession of the premises, nor continue an action which the tenant had begun.[3]

7. The estate of the lessor of a tenant at will is not properly a reversion, and therefore such tenant does not owe fealty by reason of his tenancy, nor can a remainder be limited upon an estate at will.[4] In the words of Lord Abinger, "A tenant at will has a mere *scintilla* of interest, which a landlord may determine by making a feoffment upon the land with livery, or by a demand of possession."[5] A tenant at will is entitled to estovers, and, as the law is now understood, to emblements, when the tenancy is determined by the landlord.[6] If a tenant at will plant crops and abandon the premises before they are ripe, he loses them. If the lessor expel him, the lessee may claim them as emblements. Nor can the lessor, by conveying the land with the growing crops, affect the tenant's right to such emblements.[7]

[*372] *8. A marked peculiarity of this estate is the manner in which it may be determined; any act or declaration indicating such intention on the part of either party being sufficient to put an end to it. And it may be assumed, that any act or declaration which is inconsistent with a continued, voluntary, and undisturbed relation of landlord and tenant, will determine it.[8]

9. In respect to what acts may be sufficient to put an end

---

[1] Austin *v.* Thomson, 45 N. H. 113.

[2] Hayward *v.* Sedgley, 14 Me. 439; Little *v.* Palister, 3 Me. 6; Clark *v.* Smith, 25 Penn. St. 137; 2 Rolle, Abr. 551.

[3] Ferrin *v.* Kenney, 10 Met. 294.

[4] 2 Flint. Real Prop. 222; Burton, Real Prop. 395, n.

[5] Ball *v.* Gullimore, 2 Cr. M. & R. 120.

[6] 2 Flint. Real Prop. 216; Co. Lit. 55 b; Davis *v.* Thompson, 13 Me. 209; Sherburne *v.* Jones, 20 Me. 70.

[7] Brown *v.* Thurston, 56 Me. 126.

[8] Smith, Land. & Ten. 16; Turner *v.* Doe, 9 M. & W. 643, and note, Am. ed.; Walden *v.* Bodley, 14 Pet. 156.

to such tenancy, it is stated, in general terms, that "any act done upon the land by the lessor, in assertion of his title to the possession, determines the will."[1]

10. Thus notice to quit,[2] a demand of possession,[3] an entry upon the land, whether tenant is present or not[4] when made known to him,[5] doing any act on the premises for which the lessor would otherwise be liable to an action of trespass at the suit of the tenant,[6] carrying off stone or trees from the premises against tenant's will,[7] making a feoffment on the land to a third party,[8] threatening to take legal measures to recover the land,[9] or selling,[10] or leasing it.[11] And a conveyance of the land by a landlord to a stranger determines a tenancy at will, and changes it into one at sufferance, though made for the express purpose.[12] And a written lease from the lessor to a stranger would have the same effect upon the original tenancy at will.[13] And if one of two tenants at will take a lease of the premises, it determines the lease of his co-tenant,

---

[1] Ball v. Cullimore, 2 C. M. & R. 120; Rising v. Stannard, 17 Mass. 281.

[2] Ellis v. Paige, 1 Pick. 43; Davis v. Thompson, 13 Me. 209.

[3] Doe v. M'Kaeg, 10 B. & C. 721; Den v. Howell, 7 Ired. 496.

[4] Ball v. Cullimore, 3 Cr. M. & R. 120; Curl v. Lowell, 19 Pick. 25; Moore v. Boyd, 24 Me. 242; Turner v. Doe, 9 M. & W. 643. If the act be an entry upon the land, it must be done with an intent to end the lessee's estate, which is to be found by the jury. Holly v. Brown, 14 Conn. 255.

[5] Cook v. Cook, 28 Ala. 660; Rising v. Stannard, 17 Mass. 282; Furlong v. Leary, 8 Cush. 409; Mizner v. Munroe, 10 Gray, 290, 292; Doe v. Thomas, 6 Exch. 854; Pratt v. Farrar, 10 Allen, 519.

[6] Turner v. Doe, 9 M. & W. 643.

[7] Doe v. Turner, 7 M. & W. 226; Co. Lit. 55 b.

[8] Ball v. Cullimore, 2 C. M. & R. 120; Rising v. Stannard, 17 Mass. 282, 286.

[9] Doe v. Price, 9 Bing. 356.

[10] Co. Lit. 55 b, 57 a; Jackson v. Aldrich, 13 Johns. 66; Howard v. Merriam, 5 Cush. 563; Kelly v. Waite, 12 Met. 300; Alton v. Pickering, 9 N. H. 494; Tud. Cas. 15.

[11] Hildreth v. Conant, 10 Met. 298. And though lease be to commence at a future time, it determines the tenancy at will as soon as lease takes effect. Tud. Cas. 13; Dinsdale v. Iles, T. Raym. 224; Kelly v. Waite, 12 Met. 300.

[12] Curtis v. Galvin, 1 Allen, 215; McFarland v. Chase, 7 Gray, 462; Esty v. Baker, 50 Me. 325. See also Young v. Young, 36 Me. 133; Winter v. Stevens, 9 Allen, 526, 530. Even if the conveyance be of part only of the premises. Emmes v. Feely, 132 Mass. 346.

[13] Pratt v. Farrar, 10 Allen, 519; Clark v. Wheelock, 99 Mass. 14; Arnold v. Nash, 126 Mass. 397.

and 1e may eject him.[1] Upon an alienation by t1e landlord made known to t1e tenant, 1e becomes a tenant at sufferance, and not entitled to any notice to quit, nor to any action against t1e landlord if 1e ejects him wit1out unnecessary force. But 1e would be entitled to reasonable notice to remove 1imself, 1is family, and 1is goods, and to remain or enter for t1at purpose wit1out being deemed a trespasser, t1oug1 1is estate is determined by t1e conveyance and notice t1ereof to 1im.[2]

11. T1e deat1 of eit1er party determines an estate at will.[3] But in a recent case, Kelly, C. B., uses t1e following language: " It would rat1er seem t1at a tenancy at will may continue to subsist after t1e deat1 of one of t1e parties, unless t1e 1eir or legal representative s1all do somet1ing to manifest 1is intention to determine t1e tenancy."[4] If t1e lessor dies, [*373] t1e lessee becomes tenant at sufferance,[5] *and t1e personal representative of t1e deceased lessee 1as no rig1t to possession after 1is deat1.[6] But if t1ere be two lessors or two lessees, t1e deat1 of one does not determine t1e tenancy.[7]

12. So it would be determined by a judgment for possession against t1e lessor in favor of a stranger, or by an entry under a paramount title,[8] or t1e assignment of t1e lessor's estate under a process of insolvency against him.[9]

13. Acts by w1ic1 t1e tenant forfeits or puts an end to 1is

---

[1] Casey v. King, 98 Mass. 503.

[2] Pratt v. Farrar, 10 Allen, 519, 521 ; Low v. Elwell, 121 Mass. 309.

[3] James v. Dean, 11 Ves. 383 ; Cody v. Quarterman, 12 Ga. 386, 400 ; Rising v. Stannard, 17 Mass. 282 ; Perrin v. Kenney, 10 Met. 294 ; Howard v. Merriam, 5 Cush. 563 ; Robie v. Smith, 21 Me. 114 ; Manchester v. Doddridge, 3 Ind. 360.

[4] Morton v. Woods, L. R. 4 Q. B. 293, 306.

[5] Reed v. Reed, 48 Me. 388.

[6] 2 Flint. Real Prop. 217.   [7] Co. Lit. 55 b.

[8] Howard v. Merriam, 5 Cush. 563 ; Hill v. Jordan, 30 Me. 367, in which the lessor's mortgagee entered under his mortgage, thereby determining the tenancy at will of his lessee. 2 Flint. Real Prop. 220 ; Stedman v. Gassett, 18 Vt. 346 ; Hatstat v. Packard, 7 Cush. 245 ; Hemphill v. Tevis, 4 Watts & S. 565 ; Morse v. Goddard, 13 Met. 177.

[9] Doe v. Thomas, 6 Exch. 854 ; Tud. Cas. 12.

estate at will are the assignment of his interest to another,[1] or his conveying the land itself.[2]

14. But such an assignment does not, of itself, put an end to the tenancy, unless the landlord has notice of it. Until then, he may treat his lessee as his tenant.[3] So where one hired a house and was to pay rent monthly in advance, and, having failed to do so, quitted without giving a month's notice, it was held that it did not lie in him to determine his tenancy by such failure to pay the rent in advance, without a regular notice, and that he was therefore liable for a month's rent after his abandonment.[4] The lessor may hold the assignee as his tenant liable for rent, or may treat him as a trespasser or disseisor at his election.[5]

15. If a tenant at will abandon the premises, his estate ceases, especially if he declare he will no longer hold them.[6]

16. Although it would seem that a tenant at will cannot be technically chargeable in waste,[7] if he do acts which would be voluntary waste in a tenant for life or years, he may be treated as a trespasser, having forfeited his estate.[8] So if he suffer the *land to be set off as his own on [*374] an execution against him without disclosing the true owner, his estate is forfeited.[9]

17. If the tenant disclaim holding under his lessor, or denies his landlord's title,[10] or do acts inconsistent with his tenure, as if, being in possession, he take a conveyance in fee

---

[1] Cooper v. Adams, 6 Cush. 87 ; Co. Lit. 57 a ; Tud. Cas. 13 ; Smith, Land. & Ten. 17 ; Cole v. Lake Co., 54 N. H. 242, 277.

[2] Den v. Howell, 7 Ired. 496.

[3] Pinhorn v. Souster, 8 Exch. 763, 772 ; Smith, Land. & Ten. 20 ; Carpenter v. Colins, Yelv. 73.

[4] Sprague v. Quinn, 108 Mass. 553.

[5] Overman v. Sanborn, 27 Vt. 54 ; Co. Lit. 57 a ; Smith, Land. & Ten. 20.

[6] Chandler v. Thurston, 10 Pick. 205 ; Smith, Land. & Ten. 20.

[7] Co. Lit. 57 a ; Smith, Land. & Ten. 20.

[8] Phillips v. Covert, 7 Johns. 1 ; Daniels v. Pond, 21 Pick. 367. But such will not be the effect of committing waste where the statute requires three months' notice to quit. Young v. Young, 36 Me. 133.

[9] Campbell v. Procter, 6 Me. 12.

[10] Woodward v. Brown, 13 Pet. 1 ; Willison v. Watkins, 3 Pet. 43 ; Currier v. Earl, 13 Me. 216 ; Farrow v. Edmundson, 4 B. Mon. 605 ; Duke v. Harper, 6 Yerg. 280 ; Harrison v. Middleton, 11 Gratt. 527 ; Fusselman v. Worthington. 14 Ill. 135. See ante, p. *361.

of tie premises from a tiird person, ie will determine iis estate at tie election of iis landlord.[1] But tie lessee cannot determine tie tenancy so as to deny iis lessor's title until ie siall iave surrendered possession of tie leased premises to tie lessor, or yielded to an eviction by a title paramount.[2] And tie lessor may sue him as a disseisor witiout an entry or notice, and may maintain an action for a tort as if ie iad originally entered by wrong.[3] And tie same would be tie effect of a denial on tie part of a tenant, tiat be ield under him to wiom ie stands in tie relation of tenant and landlord.[4]

18. Notwitistanding tie estate of tie tenant is wiolly determined in tie cases above stated, and ie ias no longer any rigit to possession of tie premises, wien it is done by tie lessor, tie law will not treat tie lessee as a trespasser for entering witiin a reasonable time and removing iis effects, nor for removing iis emblements wien entitled to tiem.[5]

19. But ie would not be allowed, beyond tiis, a reasonable time to find a new place suitable for iis business.[6] And wiat siall be a reasonable time, in any case, is a question of law to be determined by tie court.[7]

20. From tie peculiar relation of landlord and tenant to tie estate in case of a tenancy at will, tie question ias been discussed, wiat would be tie landlord's remedy for an injury done by a stranger to tie premises wiile in tie occupancy of iis tenant, and wietier ie could maintain trespass *quare clausum fregit*. It ias been ield tiat if tie injury be a permanent one to tie inieritance, suci as cutting down trees and tie like, suci action may be sustained.[8]

---

[1] Sharpe v. Kelley, 5 Denio, 431 ; Isaacs v. Gearheart, 12 B. Mon. 231 ; Bennock v. Whipple, 12 Me. 346.

[2] Towne v. Butterfield, 97 Mass. 105.   [3] Russell v. Fabyan, 34 N. H. 218.

[4] Sampson v. Schaeffer, 3 Cal. 196, 205 ; Boston v. Binney, 11 Pick. 1, 8 ; Chamberlin v. Donahue, 45 Vt. 50, 55.

[5] Doe v. M'Kaeg, 10 B. & C. 721 ; 2 Flint, Real Prop. 218 ; Lit. § 69 ; Rising v. Stannard, 17 Mass. 282 ; Ellis v. Paige, 1 Pick. 43 ; Turner v. Doe, 9 M. & W. 647, note to Am. ed. ; *ante*, pl. 10 and note.

[6] Mann v. Hughes, 20 Law Rep. 628.

[7] Co. Lit. 56 b ; Ellis v. Paige, 1 Pick. 43. See Pratt v. Farrar, 10 Allen, 519, where ten days, and Arnold v. Nash, 126 Mass. 397, where two days was so held.

[8] Starr v. Jackson, 11 Mass. 519 ; Hingham v. Sprague, 15 Pick. 102. And

*21. But it would seem that the doctrine would not [*375] apply in any case except of a pure tenancy at will, where the lessor may enter at any moment; for where the premises had been leased for a year, the lessor could not have trespass.[1] And the same rule was applied where the tenant was entitled by statute to three months' notice before he was compellable to quit the premises.[2] But in all these cases an action on the case would lie in favor of the lessor.[3]

22. The necessity of giving notice in order to determine a tenancy at will which has become so general has reduced the class of estates held strictly at will to comparatively few in number. They still exist in certain cases, and form a second division of this subject. They are divided into two classes, such as are made so by express agreement of the parties, and such as are created by implication of law.

23. If therefore, a tenancy be created by express words, clearly showing the intention and agreement of the parties that it shall be only so long as both parties please, it will constitute a proper estate at will, although rent be reserved, payable by the year, or aliquot parts of a year.[4] If the tenant at will is to pay rent at certain intervals, and the lessor determines the tenancy between the intervals of payment, he cannot recover

this idea is favored by Ripley v. Yale, 16 Vt. 257 ; Davis v. Nash, 32 Me. 411. In Cushing v. Kenfield, 5 Allen, 307, where defendant broke a window, and was held liable to the landlord, the form of the action was waived.

[1] Lienow v. Ritchie, 8 Pick. 235.

[2] French v. Fuller, 23 Pick. 104. This is somewhat remarkable, as in Massachusetts, notwithstanding the statute, such tenancies have all the incidents of strict tenancies at will.

[3] Lienow v. Ritchie, 8 Pick. 235. And that trespass would not lie, see Campbell v. Arnold, 1 Johns. 511 ; Clark v. Smith, 25 Penn. St. 137. See Starr v. Jackson, 11 Mass. 519, n. In Iowa he may maintain trespass by force of statute; Brown v. Bridges, 31 Iowa, 138, 145.

[4] 2 Prest. Abs. 25 ; Richardson v. Landgridge, 4 Taunt. 128 ; Smith, Lead. Cas. 75 ; Tud. Cas. 15 ; Smith, Land. & Ten. 23, u : Doe v. Cox, 11 Q. B. 122 ; 2 Flint, Real Prop. 215 ; Humphries v. Humphries, 3 Ired. 362 : Doe v. Davies, 7 Exch. 89 ; Sullivan v. Enders, 3 Dana, 66 ; Elliott v. Stone, 1 Gray, 571. In both Doe v. Cox and Doe v. Davies there was an agreement to pay rent quarterly. In Cudlip v. Rundall, 4 Mod. 9, the lessor accepted part of the premises described, with permission to the lessee to hold the excepted part when the lessor did not want the same. In Harrison v. Middleton, 11 Gratt. 527, the tenant held under a sealed instrument, which contained an agreement to surrender to the lessor's grantee whenever he should choose to take possession.

for the time the tenant may have occupied subsequent to the last pay-day.[1]

24. The instances of tenancies at will by implication of law are chiefly those where the tenant enters by permission of the owner, for an indefinite period, with some other intention than to create the relation of lessor and lessee.[2] Thus [*376] where a * householder permitted another to occupy rent free, the tenant was one at will.[3] So where the owners of a dissenters' chapel and dwelling-house placed a minister in the latter as a minister of the congregation.[4] So where the widow of the tenant, from year to year, was suffered to occupy the premises, she paying rent to the lessor, she was held to be strictly tenant at will of the administrator of the deceased tenant.[5]

25. Where a person is let into possession under a contract to purchase lands,[6] or take a lease of the same,[7] and it makes no difference whether with or without an agreement to pay interest upon the contract price, his possession is strictly a tenancy at will. But where the owner of land made his bond conditioned to convey it to the obligee upon his paying a certain sum on demand, and interest thereon quarterly, and by the terms of the bond the obligee was in the mean time to retain possession of the premises, it was held to be a demise and not a tenancy at will.[8] Where, however, one, under a

---

[1] Cameron v. Little, 62 Me. 550 ; Emmes v. Feely, 132 Mass. 346.

[2] Jackson v. Bradt, 2 Caines, 169.   [3] Rex v. Collett, Russ. & Ry. 498.

[4] Doe v. M'Keag, 10 B. & C. 721. See also Cheever v. Pearson, 16 Pick. 266.

[5] Doe v. Wood, 14 M. & W. 682.

[6] 2 Flint, Real Prop. 216–220 ; Gould v. Thompson, 4 Met. 224 ; Doe v. Chamberlaine, 5 M. & W. 14 ; Proprietors v. McFarland, 12 Mass. 324 ; Den v. Edmonston, 1 Ired. 152 ; Watkins, Conv. 20, n. ; Doe v. Miller, 5 Car. & P. 595 ; Doe v. Rock, 1 Car. & M. 549 ; Jones v. Jones, 2 Rich. (S. C.) 542 ; Glascock v. Robards, 14 Mo. 350 ; Carson v. Baker, 4 Dev. 220 ; Howard v. Shaw, 8 M. & W. 118 ; Jackson v. Miller, 7 Cow. 747 ; Manchester v. Doddridge, 3 Ind. 360 ; Prentice v. Wilson, 14 Ill. 91, 93 ; Dean v. Comstock, 32 Ill. 180 ; Freeman v. Headley, 33 N. J. 523 ; Harris v. Frink, 49 N. Y. 24, 32 ; Dunne v. Trustees, 39 Ill. 578.

[7] Smith, Land. & Ten. 18 ; Tud. Cas. 10 ; Hamerton v. Stead, 3 B. & C. 478 ; Riseley v. Ryle, 11 M. & W. 16 ; Howard v. Shaw, 8 M. & W. 118 ; Hegan v. Johnson, 2 Taunt. 148 ; Dunne v. Trustees, 39 Ill. 578.

[8] White v. Livingston, 10 Cush. 259 ; Cole v. Gill, 14 Iowa, 527. In the former case the report finds that "both parties treated the payment as rent."

contract to purchase land, entered and occupied it, and the contract was ultimately performed, it was held that he did not thereby become liable to pay rent for use and occupation during the time of his occupancy, although it was for more than a year, and the value of the rent would have been $500. His tenancy was, during that time, of the nature of a tenancy at will.[1] But where a tenant entered under a promise of a written lease which never came, and occupied premises for which he was by the original agreement to pay a certain sum as rent, he was held to be a tenant from year to year, and entitled to a notice of six months to expire at the end of the year.[2] Entering, however, under a conditional promise to pay rent, does not create a tenancy from year to year. And if a tenant enters under a promise to take a lease of the premises, and he neglects or refuses to take one, he becomes a tenant at will and not from year to year, and a mere demand for possession terminates the tenancy without any other notice.[3]

26. And it may be laid down, generally, that if a person by consent of the owner of land is let into possession without having a freehold interest or any certain term, and without circumstances which would show an intention to create an estate from year to year, he is a strict tenant at will.[4] Nor would it make any difference that the premises are under a prior lease, provided the first lessee does not interfere with the enjoyment by the second. And the lessor may recover of such second lessee for use and occupation of the premises.[5]

27. Such will be the case if the grantor continue in possession after delivery of his deed to the purchaser;[6] or a judgment debtor continue, after a sale on *fi. fa.*, to hold by consent

Where, however, the interest is paid merely as such, no tenancy is implied, because the occupant is to remain during such payment. Dakin v. Allen, 8 Cush. 33 ; Dunham v. Townsend, 110 Mass. 440.

[1] Dennett v. Penobscot Co., 57 Me. 425, 427 ; Dakin v. Allen, 8 Cush. 33 ; Woodbury v. Woodbury, 47 N. H. 11.

[2] Silsby v. Allen, 43 Vt. 172.   [3] Dunne v. Trustees, 39 Ill. 578.

[4] Smith, Land. & Ten. 18 ; Richardson v. Langridge, 4 Taunt. 128 ; Gould v. Thompson, 4 Met. 224 ; Doe v. Wood, 14 M. & W. 682 ; 2 Smith, Lead. Cas. 76 ; Tud. Cas. 10.

[5] Bedford v. Terhune, 30 N. Y. 453 ; Phipps v. Sculthorpe, 1 B. & A. 50.

[6] Currier v. Earl, 13 Me. 216 ; Smith, Land. & Ten. 19, n.

of the purchaser.[1] But an action for use and occupation will
not lie where the tenant holds adversely to the claimant.
The title to the premises cannot be tried in this form of
action.[2]

      28. So where the trustee who has the legal estate
[*377] suffers the * *cestui que trust* to occupy the premises,
the latter is considered a tenant at will of the former.[3]
And the trustee may have ejectment against his *cestui que trust*
to recover possession of the trust property.[4]

    29. But it should not be inferred from the use of the terms
landlord and tenant, that a rent is always incident to a tenancy
at will. It often depends upon circumstances, whether and
in what form such a tenant will be chargeable for the use and
occupation of premises in his possession. If, for instance, a
purchaser enters under a parol contract of purchase and sale,
and the contract fails by the fault of the vendor, he would not
be liable to pay for the use and occupation of the premises in
the absence of an express agreement to that effect.[5] But it
is not necessary that there should be an express contract to
pay and receive rent, in order to create the relation of landlord and tenant.[6]

---

  [1] Nichols *v.* Williams, 8 Cow. 13.

  [2] Kittredge *v.* Peaslee, 3 Allen, 235 ; Keyes *v.* Hill, 30 Vt. 759 ; Hogsett *v.*
Ellis, 17 Mich. 351.

  [3] Tud. Cas. 11 ; Wms. Real Prop. 325 ; Pomfret *v.* Windsor, 2 Ves. Sen. 472 ;
Garrard *v.* Tuck, 8 C. B. 231 ; Melling *v.* Leak, 16 C. B. 652 ; 2 Prest. Abs. 25.

  [4] Matthews *v.* Ward, 10 Gill & J. 443; Jackson *v.* Pierce, 2 Johns. 221 ; *post*,
vol. 2, p. *206.

  [5] Winterbottom *v.* Ingham, 7 Q. B. 611 ; Smith, Land. & Ten. 18 ; Bell *v.*
Ellis, 1 Stew. & P. (Ala.) 294 ; Little *v.* Pearson, 7 Pick. 301 ; Tew *v.* Jones, 13
M. & W. Am. ed. 14, n. ; Howard *v.* Shaw, 8 M. & W. 118 ; Hough *v.* Birge,
11 Vt. 190 ; Coffman *v.* Huck, 24 Mo. 496; Harle *v.* McCoy, 7 J. J. Marsh. 318;
Sylvester *v.* Ralston, 31 Barb. 286. The court in New York held that a purchaser under the above circumstances had a mere license, without the relation of
landlord and tenant. Dolittle *v.* Eddy, 7 Barb. 74 ; Stone *v.* Sprague, 20 Barb.
509. In a case in Connecticut, where the purchaser entered and occupied the
premises for some years under a written contract to purchase, paying a part of the
purchase-money, and then left the premises, and the owner entered upon them,
the court held that the plaintiff could not recover for use and occupation, though
the defendant alone was in fault for leaving and failing to perform the contract,
— on the ground, among other things, that the original contract was still open.
Vandenheuvel *v.* Storrs, 3 Conn. 203.

  [6] McKissack *v.* Bullington, 37 Miss. 535.

30. But if, after the contract for purchase is entirely at an end, the proposed purchaser continues to hold possession, he will be liable as tenant for use and occupation.[1] To hold one who has been in possession of land in an action for use and occupation, there must be a contract express or implied on his part to pay for such use, and during the time of such enjoyment the relation of landlord and tenant must have subsisted between them. At common law, an action for rent would not lie against a tenant at sufferance;[2] but it seems the better opinion that an action for use and occupation would.[3] But where, in the contract for sale, there is an agreement that the vendee may occupy the premises, while the court of Wisconsin hold it doubtful whether he would be liable for use and occupation if he afterwards refuse to complete the purchase, they hold that if by his agreement he was to hold "as tenant at sufferance of the vendor," it so far recognized the relation of landlord and tenant between them that upon failure to perform he was liable for use and occupation.[4] But if once in, he will continue to be liable until the contract is rescinded and the possession surrendered, whether he actually uses the premises or not. As where A hired of B a barn, and locked it up and never occupied it, nor surrendered possession of it to the owner, he was held liable in an action for use and occupation.[5] So if he continues to occupy he will be liable, although partially interrupted in his enjoyment of the premises by act of the lessor.[6]

31. If the vendee enter and occupy under an agreement to purchase, and afterwards refuses to carry out the contract, or accept a conveyance, he will be liable to respond in damages, in some form, for such use and occupation of the premises. By some courts he has been held liable in an action of assump-

---

[1] Howard v. Shaw, 8 M. & W. 118; Dwight v. Cutler, 3 Mich. 566; Hogsett v. Ellis, 17 Mich. 351.

[2] Cunningham v. Holton, 55 Me. 33, 38; Delano v. Montague, 4 Cush. 42; Flood v. Flood, 1 Allen, 217.

[3] See *post,* *394 and note.

[4] Wright v. Roberts, 22 Wisc. 161.

[5] Hall v. West. Transp. Co., 34 N. Y. 284; Waring v. King, 8 M. & W. 571; Pinero v. Judson, 6 Bing. 206.

[6] Bost. & W. R. R. v. Ripley, 13 Allen, 421.

sit, on the ground that he held the premises, beneficially, by permission of the owner, thereby raising an equitable claim for compensation;[1] and the same ground was also taken in an early case cited below.[2]

31 a. The opposite conclusion was, however, reached by Mansfield, J., who denied that a contract could arise by implication of law, under circumstances the occurrence of which neither of the parties ever had in their contemplation.[3] So far as compensation is concerned, the action being one of assumpsit, is based upon the idea of a contract between the parties. But this contract may be express or implied, provided it be one which creates or recognizes the relation of landlord and tenant, by which the defendant holds possession of the premises under the plaintiff, by an agreement to pay for the use of the same. The questions of difficulty have been where, though the holding may not have been adverse, it had its inception in some other contract than that of hiring, but its character has altered by a change in the relation of the parties to the estate in question. The doctrine upon the subject as held by the United States Court is thus stated: If, under a contract to sell, a vendor puts the vendee into possession, the latter holds as licensee, is not tenant of a landlord, and pays nothing for the enjoyment of the estate.[4] But he can no more deny his vendor's title than if he were lessee. And his assignee is bound by the same estoppel as himself. If the vendee fails to pay the purchase-money according to agreement, his possession becomes tortious, and the vendor may have ejectment, without any previous demand or notice.[5] And it seems established by a great preponderance of authority that an action will not lie for use and occupation

---

[1] Gould v. Thompson, 4 Met. 224. And the same is assumed to be law, although not the point under consideration, in Clough v. Hosford, 6 N. H. 231. See also Alton v. Pickering, 9 N. H. 494, and a like doctrine was held in a case where the occupant gained possession by wrong, though not by force, from one who yielded it under a misapprehension of facts. Hull v. Vaughan, 6 Pick. 157.

[2] Hearn v. Tomlin, Peake's Cases, 192.

[3] Kirtland v. Pounsett, 2 Taunt. 145.

[4] Burnett v. Caldwell, 9 Wall. 290, 293 ; Chamberlin v. Donahue, 44 Vt. 57, 59 ; and see Central Mills Co. v. Hart, 124 Mass. 123.

[5] Burnett v. Caldwell, sup. See Lawton v. Savage, 136 Mass. 111.

where the defendant has occupied under an express agreement as to the terms, although such agreement may not be carried out according to its terms, and the occupancy may not conform to it. Thus where A demised premises to B at a rent payable quarterly, and the tenant, by permission of the lessor, quitted possession before the close of a quarter, or the lessor determined the tenancy between rent days, it was held that the lessor could maintain no action for the use of the premises since the last rent day, till the lessee surrendered possession.[1] So where the tenant held under a contract of purchase as vendee, it was held that the law raised no implied promise to pay for the use of the premises.[2] In case of refusal of the occupant in such case to complete the purchase, he may thereafter become liable as a tenant at will. But if the owner refuse, on his part, to execute a deed, he cannot turn the occupancy of the tenant into a lease carrying rent, nor recover possession of the premises in a process against the tenant as a wrongful holder of the same.[3] Nor can the owner of land hold a tenant responsible in this form of action, from the mere fact of his having enjoyed possession of the estate, if the tenant refused to hold the relation to such owner of tenant, as where two persons claimed the estate and the tenant held under one of these, though in fact it belonged to the other.[4]

* 32. But the ordinary rule of law in such cases [*378] is, that when a purchaser, who has been in possession under a contract to purchase, refuses to perform on his part, the owner's remedy is not in assumpsit, but trespass. By such refusal he is considered as annulling the conditional license under which he entered, and as having entered without license.[5]

[1] Grimman v. Legge, 8 B. & C. 324; Nicholson v. Munigle, 6 Allen, 215; Fuller v. Swett, 6 Allen, 219, n.

[2] Jones v. Tipton, 2 Dana, 295; Smith v. Stewart, 6 Johns. 46; Bancroft v. Wardwell, 13 Johns. 489; Ayer v. Hawks, 11 N. H. 148, 154; Sylvester v. Ralston, 31 Barb. 286; Dunning v. Finson, 46 Me. 546; Winterbottom v. Ingham, 7 Q. B. 611; Hadley v. Morrison, 39 Ill. 392.

[3] Dunham v. Townsend, 110 Mass. 440; and the rule laid down in Gould v. Thompson, supra, was limited to a liability after refusal.

[4] Keyes v. Hill, 30 Vt. 759; Hogsett v. Ellis, 17 Mich. 351.

[5] Smith v. Stewart, 6 Johns. 46; Bancroft v. Wardwell, 13 Johns. 489; Brewer v. Conover, 18 N. J. 214; Howard v. Shaw, 8 B. & W. Am. ed. 123, n.

33. And assumpsit for rent clearly would not lie while the contract of sale continued open and undetermined.[1] But where a tenant at will entered under an agreement to pay a certain rent by the year, and the parties afterwards waived that agreement, and then tried to agree upon new terms, but failed, the tenant continuing to occupy the premises, was held liable in a *quantum meruit* for the use of the same.[2]

34. If the vendor continues to hold possession after a sale of land; in order to make him liable in assumpsit for use and occupation, it must be shown that his occupation was by permission of the purchaser. If he holds without such permission, he is liable only in trespass for mesne profits.[3] Nor would assumpsit for use and occupation lie where the tenant holds under an indenture of lease, even though the lessor, by his own act, has barred himself from recovering rent under such indenture.[4] But where one entered under a lease which was executed by the lessor only, and occupied the premises, he was held not a tenant at will, but liable in assumpsit for the rent reserved in the lease.[5]

35. In respect to the third subject of inquiry, as above proposed, in what cases a notice to quit is necessary in order to determine an estate at will, it would be found that [*379] from an * early period the courts were inclined to protect the interest of the parties against a sudden determination of such tenancies. The tenant who had planted crops was held entitled to them if expelled by his landlord, and

and 12 Id. 324, n. ; Clough *v.* Hosford, 6 N. H. 231 ; Bell *v.* Ellis, 1 Stew. & P. (Ala.) 294.

[1] Wiggin *v.* Wiggin, 6 N. H. 298 ; Johnson *v.* Beauchamp, 9 Dana, 124 ; Vandenheuvel *v.* Storrs, 3 Conn. 203.

[2] Forbes *v.* Smiley, 56 Me. 174.

[3] Tew *v.* Jones, 13 M. & W. 12, and note to Am. ed.; Tud. Cas. 10 ; McCombs *v.* Wallace, 66 N. C. 481 ; Goldsberry *v.* Bishop, 2 Duvall, 143. But where the land has been conveyed, the presumption of a tenancy arises. Sherburne *v.* Jones, 20 Me. 70.

[4] Leishman *v.* White, 1 Allen, 489 ; North *v.* Nichols, 37 Conn. 375. As to where the action for use and occupation lies where the lease is in writing or under seal, see *ante*, *341 and note. By Mass. Pub. Stat., c. 121, §§ 3, 5, rent may be recovered against a tenant at sufferance in an action of contract, and plaintiff may use the deed of demise in evidence to prove the amount due.

[5] Fitton *v.* Hamilton City, 6 Nev. 196 ; Clark *v.* Gordon, 121 Mass. 330 ; Carroll *v.* St. John's Soc., 125 Mass. 565.

iad a right to enter, cultivate, and gather them without being subjected to an action of trespass. So he was authorized to enter and remove his effects, within a reasonable time, after the determination of his tenancy.[1] From this the advance was easy to requiring a notice to quit, in all such cases, from the landlord to his tenant, before the right arose actually to expel him. And this principle was adopted as early as the time of Henry VIII.[2] It was obviously an act of justice, also, that the tenant should give notice to the landlord of his intention to quit, that he might have an opportunity to procure a new tenant.[3] In respect to notice, where the lessors are tenants in common, each must notify for himself, nor can one avail himself of a notice by the other.[4] So if several tenants in common make a parol letting, and by the terms in respect to such lessors the letting of one was by way of conditional limitation, although the tenancy as to this one might thereby be determined, as to all the rest, notice would be requisite for that purpose.[5] It is doubtful if one of several lessors can maintain a process against a tenant who holds under him and other lessors who are owners in common, to recover under the statute a portion of the demised premises.[6] Although one tenant in common may have a process of forcible entry and detainer against his co-tenant.[7]

36. At first, the courts had no other rule as to notice than that it should be a reasonable one, and the effect was, that, in ordinary cases, an estate at will, instead of being a tenancy, purely at will, continued till a reasonable notice from one of the parties to the other of his election to determine it.[8]

37. As will be shown hereafter, this uncertain period was at

---

[1] Smith, Land. & Ten. 20, 21 ; 2 Flint, Real Prop. 218.

[2] Year-Book, 35 Hen. VI. 24, pl. 30 ; 13 Hen. VIII. 15 b; 14 Hen. VIII. 13; Doe v. Watts, 7 T. R. 83 ; 2 Smith, Lead. Cas. 76 ; Doe v. Porter, 3 T. R. 13 ; Cattley v. Arnold, 1 Johns. & H. 651, 656.

[3] Kighly v. Bulkly, Sid. 338.

[4] Dillon v. Brown, 11 Gray, 180 ; Pickard v. Perley, 45 N. H. 188 ; *post*, *386, *388.

[5] Ashley v. Warner, 11 Gray, 43.   [6] King v. Dickerman, 11 Gray, 48?.

[7] Presbrey v. Presbrey, 13 Allen, 281.

[8] Smith, Lead. Cas. 76, and note to Am. ed. ; Ellis v. Paige, 1 Pick. 43 ; Davis v. Thompson, 13 Me. 209 ; Taylor, Land. & Ten. (7th ed.) § 55 and note. And such seems to be the rule in Vermont. Rich v. Bolton, 46 Vt. 84.

length converted into a practical tenancy for a certain term, generally from year to year by the length of time required in order to give the requisite notice to quit, and the time at which such notice must expire.[1]   But the principle of requiring notice does not apply to such cases as have been enumerated under the previous head.

38. In cases where notice is required, it has been stated that, originally, the length of such notice must have been a reasonable time, and Massachusetts and Maine never having adopted the principle of construing a tenancy for an indefinite period, a holding from year to year, retained this no-
[*380] tion of a reasonable * notice, until provision as to what that should be, and how given, was made by statute.[2]

39. The length of the notice required to determine a tenancy at will may be fixed by agreement of the parties,[3] or it may be prescribed by statute, as is done in many of the States. It is competent for the parties to a tenancy at will to determine the same by agreement in any way other than by statute notice.   Thus it may be by giving a month's notice in writing, if such is the agreement, and in such case the notice need not have reference to the end of a quarter or calendar month.[4] So by the agreement of the parties, the tenancy may be determined upon the happening of some prescribed contingent event, without notice.[5]   And if the landlord agree with the tenant that he may quit, though it be by parol, and the tenant

---

[1] Smith, Land. & Ten. 234.

[2] Rising v. Stannard, 17 Mass. 282; Hollis v. Pool, 3 Met. 350; Moore v. Boyd, 24 Me. 242; Furlong v. Leary, 8 Cush. 409. In the statute of frauds in Massachusetts, of 1692, an exception was made of leases for terms not exceeding three years. But this was omitted in the revision of the statute in 1784. 4 Dane, Abr. 62. Provinc. Laws, 1692-3, c. 15, § 1.

[3] 2 Crabb, Real Prop. 425; Doe v. Donovan, 1 Taunt. 555; Kemp v. Derrett, 3 Camp. 510.

[4] May v. Rice, 108 Mass. 150.

[5] Creech v. Crockett, 5 Cush. 133; Hollis v. Pool, 3 Met. 350; Elliott v. Stone, 1 Gray, 571; Thurber v. Dwyer, 10 R. I. 355; Ashley v. Warner, 11 Gray, 43; Knecht v. Mitchell, 67 Ill. 86. Thus where the tenant's occupancy is only so long as he runs a saw-mill, Crawley v. Mullins, 48 Mo. 517; or is in lessor's employ, Grosvenor v. Henry, 27 Iowa, 269. See also Wood v. Beard, 2 Exch. Div. 30; Whetstone v. Davis, 34 Ind. 510.

accordingly do so witiout any furtier notice, his liability to pay rent ceases.[1]

40. But wiere tiere is no agreement nor time fixed by statute as to the lengti of notice requisite to determine a tenancy at will, and the case does not come witiin the class of tenancies from year to year, it is generally true tiat it will be sufficient if it be equal to the interval between the times of payment of rent, or the lengti of the time by wiici the letting was at first measured, as by the quarter, monti, or week.[2]

41. If a party enter under a parol lease for a term certain, or for a time limited by agreement, as to its duration, by tie iappening of some event, wiere, by statute, all parol leases are declared to be estates at will, as is the case in Massachusetts and Maine, or wiere by tie lease itself the estate is an estate at will, suci tenancy may still be determined by notice like any estate at will. Yet, if not so determined, it will come to an end witiout notice at tie expiration of the time or the iappening of tie event.[3] And wiere, as in the case in tie Englisi statutes and tiose of many of tie States, leases for a certain * period are excepted from the clause [*381] wiici declares parol leases to be estates at will, and suci a lease is made for a definite period witiin tiat exception, no notice would be requisite to determine such lease, or would iave any effect to determine it if given before tie natural expiration.[4] And even if tie parol letting be made

---

[1] Farson v. Goodale, 8 Allen, 202 ; and Batchelder v. Batchelder, 2 Allen, 105, apparently *contra*, is controlled by Davis v. Murphy, 126 Mass. 143.

[2] 2 Crabb, Real Prop. 426 ; Cotlin v. Lunt, 2 Pick. 70 ; Right v. Darby, 1 T. R. 160 ; Doe v. Hallan, 6 Esp. 4 ; Prindle v. Anderson, 19 Wend. 391, s. c. 23 Id. 616 ; Prickett v. Ritter, 16 Ill. 96 ; Huyser v. Chase, 13 Mich. 98 ; Stoppelkamp v. Mangeot, 42 Cal. 316 ; Skaggs v. Elkus, 45 Cal. 154 ; Hammon v. Douglas, 50 Mo. 434, 437. In Steffens v. Earl, 40 N. J. 128, the rule is confirmed, though its adoption is elaborately criticised. In such cases in Maine, tenancy may be determined by thirty days' notice in writing. Esty v. Baker, 50 Me. 325, 333.

[3] Creech v. Crockett, 5 Cush. 133 ; Howard v. Merriam, 5 Cush. 563 ; Stedman v. McIntosh, 4 Ired. 291 ; 2 Flint, Real Prop. 220 ; Danforth v. Sergeant, 14 Mass. 491 ; 2 Crabb, Real. Prop. 421 ; McGee v. Gibson, 1 B. Mon. 105 ; Allen v. Jaquish, 21 Wend. 628 ; Overdeer v. Lewis, 1 Watts & S. 90 ; 2 Smith, Lead. Cas. 5th Am. ed. 180 ; Hollis v. Pool, 3 Met. 350 ; Fifty Assoc. v. Howland, 11 Met. 99 ; Elliott v. Stone, 12 Cush. 174 ; Secor v. Pestana, 37 Ill. 525.

[4] Smith, Land. & Ten. 64 ; Id. 65 ; Wms. Real Prop. 326 ; Edge v. Strafford, 1 Tyrw. 293 ; Brown v. Keller, 32 Ill. 151.

for such a period of time, as is declared by statute to be void or to constitute a mere tenancy at will, though a notice in such case would determine the tenancy before the time fixed by the agreement, it would expire without notice at the end of the time for which the parol lease was to run.[1]

42. If by agreement or by construction of the law upon the act of the parties, a tenancy becomes one strictly at will though it may have been otherwise originally, no notice to quit is necessary in order to determine it.[2] So if the relation of landlord and tenant once subsisting is destroyed, no notice is requisite in order that either party should avail himself of his legal remedies.[3] Nor is notice to quit ever necessary unless the relation of landlord and tenant subsists.[4] Thus, if one in possession repudiates the relation of tenant to his landlord, or of vendee to his vendor, if he enters under a contract of purchase and sets up a hostile claim to title, no demand of possession or notice to quit is necessary.[5] So where the tenancy at will is a conditional limitation, and the event happens which determines the tenancy, no notice is requisite. As where the premises were let so long as the tenant kept a good school, and he failed to keep one.[6]

[1] 2 Flint, Real Prop. 220 ; People v. Rickert, 8 Cow. 226 ; Larkin v. Avery, 23 Conn. 304 ; Doe v. Bell, 5 T. R. 471 ; Schuyler v. Leggett, 2 Cow. 660 ; Prindle v. Anderson, 19 Wend. 391 ; Tress v. Savage, 4 Ellis & B. 36 ; Doe v. Moffatt, 15 Q. B. 257.

[2] Elliott v. Stone, 1 Gray, 571, where the tenant agreed to pay rent in advance, and failed to do so. Jackson v. Miller, 7 Cow. 747, where the defendant entered under contract to purchase, and failed to perform on his part. Chilton v. Niblett, 3 Humph. 404 ; Stone v. Sprague, 20 Barb. 509 ; Dolittle v. Eddy, 7 Barb. 74.

[3] Hall v. Burgess, 5 B. & C. 332, where the tenant quit at the end of the year, and the landlord before six months let the premises. In Thomas v. Cook, 2 B. & A. 119, where the tenant underlet, the landlord, by distraining on the undertenant, was held to have lost his claim on the tenant, though he had given no notice. Clemens v. Broomfield, 19 Mo. 118.

[4] Jackson v. Deyo, 3 Johns. 422 ; Williams v. Hensley, 1 A. K. Marsh. 181, where the tenant disclaimed and denied the landlord's title. Tuttle v. Reynolds, 1 Vt. 80 ; Ross v. Garrison, 1 Dana, 35 ; Larned v. Clarke, 8 Cush. 29.

[5] Ingraham v. Baldwin, 9 N. Y. 45, 46 ; Brown v. Keller, 32 Ill. 151.

[6] Ashley v. Warner, 11 Gray, 43; Bolton v. Landers, 27 Cal. 104 ; Smith v. Shaw, 16 Cal. 88 ; Elliott v. Stone, 1 Gray, 571 ; ante, pl. 39.

*SECTION II.　　　　[*382]

ESTATES FROM YEAR TO YEAR.

1. BECAUSE of the uncertainty of the rule requiring reasonable notice in order to determine a parol lease, and from the circumstance that rent was generally measured by the year, courts early adopted a rule which has been extensively followed in this country, that a general tenancy by a parol lease where rent is to be paid shall be considered as a lease for a year, which can only be determined by a notice for the time of at least six months, terminating at the expiration of the year. And if the tenant is allowed to hold without such notice into a second year, it will be considered as a holding for such second year, and so on. So that the common mode of designating such estates by parol is as estates from year to year, to continue till either party gives the other the requisite notice to determine it.[1] Where the tenancy is from year to year, or for an uncertain time, in Illinois sixty days' notice is sufficient to determine it. But if it be for less than a month,

---

[1] Smith, Land. & Ten. 21, 22; Wms. Real Prop. 326; 2 Prest. Abs. 25; Tud. Cas. 14; Lesley v. Randolph, 4 Rawle, 123; Right v. Darby, 1 T. R. 159, per Buller, J.; Ridgley v. Stillwell, 28 Mo. 400; Patton v. Axley, 5 Jones (N. C), 440. It is defined by Parke, B., as a "lease for a year certain, with a growing interest during every year thereafter springing out of the original contract and parcel of it." Oxley v. James, 13 M. & W. 214.

tiirty days is sufficient in tie absence of an express agreement upon tie subject.[1] In New York if a tenant enters under a parol lease, void as being within tie statute of frauds, tie landlord must give one monti's notice in order to determine it; iis tenancy tierefore is one from monti to monti, determinable by notice to quit.[2]

2. Tiis ciange of tenancies at will into estates from year to year was tie result of judicial legislation, as a measure of equity as well as sound policy, tiougi, as ias already been seen, numerous cases were still left of tenancies strictly at will;[3] and in Massaciusetts and Maine all parol leases, as we iave seen, still iave tiis ciaracter, and are determinable by operation of law in tie various ways already enumerated, altiougi a fixed term of notice to quit is prescribed by statute.[4]

3. An agreement to pay rent on tie part of tie tenant is regarded as an essential element of a tenancy from year to year, and tie times at wiici it is payable must iave reference to a yearly iolding, suci as by tie year, quarter, or some aliquot part of a year.[5]

4. It will be sufficient to establisi a tenancy from year to year, to siow an entry under a general letting, or a letting for an indefinite time, and eitier an agreement to pay [*383] rent * measured by tie year or its aliquot parts, or an actual payment of rent if none was originally fixed and agreed upon; and suci tenancy, once establisied, will continue until determined by notice to quit, or some otier sufficient legal cause.[6]   It ias accordingly been ield tiat

---

[1] Secor v. Pestana, 37 Ill. 525.

[2] People v. Darling, 47 N. Y. 666; 1 R. S. 745, §§ 7, 9; Reeder v. Sayre, 70 N. Y. 180, and see *post*, pl. 4.

[3] 4 Kent, Com. 115.

[4] *Ante*, *372 and notes; Iass. Pub. Stat., c. 120, § 3; Ellis v. Paige, 1 Pick. 43; Withers v. Larrabee, 48 Me. 570.

[5] Richardson v. Landgridge, 4 Taunt. 128; Tud. Cas. 14; Jackson v. Bradt, 2 Caines, 169; Doe v. Baker, 4 Dev. 220; Roe v. Lees, 2 W. Bl. 1173; Williams v. Deriar, 31 Mo. 13; Doidge v. Bowers, 2 I. & W. 365; Chamberlin v. Donahue, 45 Vt. 50; Rich v. Bolton, 46 Vt. 84.

[6] Lesley v. Randolph, 4 Rawle, 123, 129; Com. Land. & Ten. 7, 8; Squires v. Huff, 3 A. K. Iarsh. 17; Knight v. Benett, 3 Bing. 361; Hamerton v. Stead, 3 B. & C. 478, per Littledale, J.; Burton, Real Prop. 396, n.; Lockwood v.

w1en t1e 1iring is for a term w11c1 is wit1in the statute of frauds, and t1e lessee enters, it will be regarded as a tenancy from year to year.[1] But the landlord 1aving refused to give a lease, and 1aving denied the tenant's rig1t to occupy, who t1ereupon quitted, it was 1eld t1at he was not liable for rent w1ile 1e did so occupy.[2] A general tenancy in Indiana is one from year to year. It is ot1erwise, if made for t1e term of a single year. But t1e lessor could not determine the lease during t1e year for non-payment of rent, unless t1e terms of t1e 1iring contained a condition to t1at effect.[3] But aut1orizing one to go upon land and cut wood t1ereon, at an agreed price per cord, and 1is entering t1ereon and cutting and paying for t1e wood cut for several mont1s in succession, was 1eld not to be a tenancy from year to year, but strictly one at w:ll, nor was t1e contractor entitled to notice to quit.[4]

5. But w1ere the demise is for one year or ot1er term certain, no notice to quit is necessary,[5] t1oug1 if t1e tenant 1olds

---

Lockwood, 22 Conn. 425 ; Roe v. Lees, 2 W. Bl. 1173 ; Hall v. Wadsworth, 28 Vt. 412 ; Hunt v. Jorton, 18 Ill. 75 ; Ridgely v. Stillwell, 25 Mo. 570 ; Williams v. Deriar, 31 Mo. 13 ; Crommelin v. Thiess, 31 Ala. 412. Thus, where one without authority lets another's land, and the tenant pays rent to owner, it creates a tenancy from year to year. McDowell v. Simpson, 3 Watts, 129. Though rent is actually paid, however, it is not conclusive of the fact of a tenancy, — it may be eXplained by either payer or receiver. Doe v. Crago, 6 C. B. 90 ; Tud. Cas. 15 ; *contra*, Bishop v. Howard, 2 B. & C. 100.

[1] Schuyler v. Leggett, 2 Cow. 660 ; Thomas v. Nelson, 69 N. Y. 118 ; Thurber v. Dwyer, 10 R. I. 355 ; Shepherd v. Cummings, 1 Coldw. 354 ; Reeder v. Sayre, 70 N. Y. 180 ; Laughran v. Smith, 75 N. Y. 205.

[2] Greton v. Smith, 33 N. Y. 245 ; Lounsberry v. Snyder, 31 N. Y. 514.

[3] Brown v. Bragg, 22 Ind. 123.

[4] Kitchen v. Pridgen, 3 Jones (N. C.) 49. See Denton v. Strickland, 3 Jones (N. C.) 61 ; Funk v. Haldeman, 53 Penn. St. 229. So Colchester v. Brooke, 7 Q. B. 339, authority to dredge for oysters is a license only and no lease.

[5] Jackson v. McLeod, 12 Johns. 182 ; Cobb v. Stokes, 8 East, 358 ; Logan v. Herron, 8 S. & R. 459 ; Lesley v. Randolph, 4 Rawle, 126 ; Jessenger v. Armstrong, 1 T. R. 53 ; Right v. Darby, Id. 159. *Ante*, *380 and note. In some cases in New York a parol lease for one month, and thereafter for successive months, has been held a lease for fiXed terms, expiring each month without notice, People v. Schackno, 48 Barb. 551 ; Gibbons v. Dayton, 4 Hun, 451 ; People v. Goelet, 64 Barb. 476 ; and in others no notice has been required before bringing summary process, even in cases of tenancies from year to year, because not provided by the statute, Park v. Castle, 19 How. Pr. 33 ; Nichols v. Williams, 8 Cow. 13 ; but the right to notice has since been broadly affirmed in the latter class of tenancies, Reeder v. Sayre, 70 N. Y. 180 ; Laughran v Smith, 75 N. Y. 205.

over 1e may be 1eld at t1e election of t1e lessor as tenant for
rent at t1e rate originally reserved, and also by t1e payment
and receipt of rent or ot1er act expressly recognizing t1e ten.
ancy. Suc1 1olding over may be converted into a tenancy
from year to year, upon t1e same terms as t1e former 1old-
ing, including amount and times of payment of rent as far as
applicable to t1e situation of t1e parties.[1] But w1ere t1e military aut1ority of t1e country entered upon premises 1eld by a
lessee and occupied t1e same beyond t1e term of 1is lease, 1e
was not 1eld liable to 1is lessor for rent after t1e expiration
of 1is term.[2]

6. But merely suffering a tenant to 1old over wit1out any
act of assent on t1e part of t1e landlord, unless so long as to
raise a legal presumption of a new letting, will not c1ange t1e
1olding into a tenancy against t1e will of t1e lessor, or prevent
1is maintaining an action of trespass or ejectment against t1e
tenant as a tort feasor.[3]

[*384] *7. But trespass will not lie in favor of a lessor
against his tenant for merely 1olding over, until 1e
s1all 1ave entered and regained possession of t1e premises.
And suc1 would be t1e law before notice to quit given, in t1e

---

[1] Jackson v. McLeod, 12 Johns. 182 ; Barlow v. Wainwright, 22 Vt. 88 ; 4
Kent, Com. 112 ; Conway v. Starkweather, 1 Denio, 113 ; Bedford v. McElher-
ron, 2 S. & R. *49 ; 1oshier v. Reding, 12 Me. 478 ; Harkins v. Pope, 10 Ala.
493 ; Wms. Real Prop. 326, n. ; Bacon v. Brown, 9 Conn. 334 ; De Young v.
Buchanan, 10 Gill & J. 149 ; Whittemore v. 1oore, 9 Dana, 315 ; 1oore v. Beasley, 3 Ohio, 294 ; Jackson v. Salmon, 4 Wend. 327 ; Laguerenne v. Dougherty,
35 Penn. St. 45 ; Crommelin v. Thiess, 31 Ala. 418 ; Com. Land. & Ten. 354 ;
Brewer v. Knapp, 1 Pick. 332 ; Roe v. Ward, 1 H. Bl. 99. And this would be
true although the holding be by a sub-lessee of the tenant, if no new contract has
been made with lessor. Dimock v. Van Bergen, 12 Allen, 551. But whether
merely holding over after a term certain makes the tenant at sufferance a tenant
at will at the lessor's election is differently held in different States. The rule in
Conway v. Starkweather, *supra*, is denied in 1assachusetts, Edwards v. Hale,
9 Allen, 462, and elsewhere, but is sustained in most of the States. See *post*,
*393.

[2] Constant v. Abell, 36 Mo. 174 ; 14 Am. Law Reg. 443.

[3] Den v. Adams, 12 N. J. 99 ; Conway v. Starkweather, 1 Denio, 113 ; Hemphill v. Flynn, 2 Penn. St. 144 ; Tud. Cas. 17 ; Whiteacre v. Symonds, 10 East,
13. And the lessor has a right to hold a tenant at will as trespasser after due
notice to quit. Ellis v. Paige, 1 Pick. 43 ; Rising v. Stannard, 17 1ass. 282 ;
Danforth v. Sargeant, 14 1ass. 491 ; Vrooman v. McKaig, 4 1d. 450 ; Schuyler
v. Smith, 51 N. Y. 315.

case of a tenant at will who holds over after the determination of the estate by the death of the lessor.[1]

8. A tenancy from year to year, though indeterminate as to duration until notice given, has many of the qualities and incidents of a term for years,[2] and, when notice has been given, the term is regarded as for a definite period, expiring with the time of the notice. It would, among other things, go to the personal representatives of the tenant on his death.[3] It might be assigned.[4] The lessor might be liable to the tenant for trespass *quare clausum*, in the same manner as in case of an estate for years.[5] The lessor and tenant would have the same rights in respect to acts of strangers which they would have in a tenancy for years.[6] And their rights in respect to each other would be the same, in case of a holding over by such a tenant, as in case of an estate for years.[7] And the tenant would be liable for rent, if the premises burned down.[8] The same would be the law in those States where, though the doctrine of tenancy from year to year has not been adopted, a tenancy at will is to be determined by a notice to quit of a definite length of time.[9]

9. But such tenants are not bound to make substantial *repairs upon the premises, except by express [*385] stipulation to that effect.[10] And where a tenant from

---

[1] Co. Lit. 57 b ; 2 Bl. Com. 150 ; Turner v. Doe, 9 M. & W. 646, and note to Am. ed.

[2] Cattley v. Arnold, 1 Johns. & H. 651 ; Oxley v. James, 13 M. & W. 209.

[3] 2 Prest. Abs. 25 ; Doe v. Porter, 3 T. R. 13 ; Tud. Cas. 15 ; Cody v. Quarterman, 12 Ga. 386 ; Doe v. Wood, 14 M. & W. 682.

[4] Smith, Land. & Ten. 23 ; 2 Prest. Abs. 25 ; Botting v. Martin, 1 Camp. 317 ; Pleasant v. Benson, 14 East, 234. But in Hemphill r. Giles, 66 N. C. 512, the lessor's assignment was held to defeat the tenant's estate.

[5] Moore v. Boyd, 24 Me. 242. And this is true of tenancies at will in States where tenancies from year to year do not exist, Dickinson v. Goodspeed, 8 Cush. 119, where the tenant at will had trespass against the lessor for entering and cutting off a pump, before giving notice to quit ; and see Cunningham v. Holton, 55 Me. 33, 38 ; Same v. Horton, 57 Me. 422.

[6] Clark v. Smith, 25 Penn. St. 137 ; Howard v. Merriam, 5 Cush. 563 ; French v. Fuller, 23 Pick. 107 ; and see *ante*, *375.

[7] See cases cited above, p. *383, n.   [8] Izon v. Gorton, 5 Bing. N. C. 501.

[9] French v. Fuller, 23 Pick. 107 ; Howard v. Merriam, 5 Cush. 563.

[10] Gott v. Gandy, 2 Ellis & B. 845. But if the tenant holds over under a lease providing for such repair, he is presumed to have agreed to continue that

year to year erected a dwelling-house upon the premises, under a promise from the lessor to give him the estate, which he
failed to do, it was held that he might recover of the lessor for
such improvements.   But it would be otherwise in the case
of a vendee who should make erections on his own account,
though the vendor refuse to deliver a deed of the premises
according to his verbal agreement to sell and convey the
estate.[1]   The law upon the subject of repairs, as stated by
Mr. Platt, is as follows : " Independently of contract, a tenant
from year to year must keep the premises wind and water
tight, and make fair and tenantable repairs, as by putting
fences in order, or replacing windows or doors that are broken
during his occupation, but he is not liable for the mere wear
and tear of the premises, nor answerable if they are burned
down, nor bound to repair if they become ruinous by any
other accident, nor to replace doors and sashes worn out by
time, to put a new roof on, or make similar substantial repairs,
or what are called general repairs." [2]

10. The necessity of notice, in order to determine a tenancy
from year to year, applies as well to the tenant as the lessor,
the rule being the same as to both.[3]

11. When notice to quit has been given, it may be waived,
and the tenancy will in that case be re-established upon its
former footing.   This waiver may be shown in various ways,
such as by the payment and receipt of rent accruing subsequent to the expiration of the notice,[4] or by distraining for
such rent,[5] or giving a new notice to quit at a time subsequent
to the first.[6]   Though in all these cases it is a question of in-

---

obligation.   Richardson v. Gifford, 1 Ad. & E. 52 ; Doe v. Amey, 12 Ad. & E.
476, and see post, *391.

[1] Smith v. Smith, 28 N. J. L. 216 ; Gillet v. Maynard, 5 Johns. 85.

[2] 2 Platt on Leases, 182 ; Brown v. Newbold, 44 N. J. L. 266.

[3] Morehead v. Watkyns, 5 B. Mon. 228 ; Johnstone v. Huddlestone, 4 B. & C.
922 ; Hall v. Wadsworth, 28 Vt. 410.

[4] Prindle v. Anderson, 19 Wend. 391 ; Goodright v. Cordwent, 6 T. R. 219 ;
Collins v. Canty, 6 Cush. 415 ; Hoff v. Baum, 21 Cal. 120.   Where, after notice,
the landlord accepted the rent due at the time of notice, expressly reserving and
not waiving his right under the notice, it was held that the payment did not
affect the notice.   Kimball v. Rowland, 6 Gray, 224.

[5] Zouch v. Willingale, 1 H. Bl. 311.

[6] Doe v. Palmer, 16 East, 53.

tention, and even the receipt of rent may not be conclusive, but open to explanation.1

12. The mere demand of such rent by the landlord would not, of itself, be a waiver of such notice, but would be competent evidence for the jury to that effect.[2]

13. The tenant's liability for rent continues till he puts an end to the estate by notice, whether he continue to occupy the premises or not.[3]

14. If a tenant from year to year commit voluntary waste, he forfeits all right to notice to quit, as he thereby determines his estate.[4]

*15. The subject of notice, as a mode of determining [*386] estates at will and tenancies from year to year, is so important, that it should be presented distinctly by itself. In most respects the same rules apply, except in the matter of time, to notices, which are necessary to determine tenancies from year to year as to tenancies at will.[5] If the demise be by three, notice by two will not be sufficient to lay the foundation for summary proceedings to eject the tenant; all ought to join, each acting in reference to his own share.[6]

16. Such notice will be sufficient if by parol, unless required

---

[1] Doe v. Humphreys, 2 East, 237, a second notice proved not to be intended to waive the first. Messenger v. Armstrong, 1 T. R. 53 ; Doe v. Batten, Cowp. 243, where acceptance of rent was allowed to be explained, as not being intended as a waiver of notice. See also Kimball v. Rowland, 6 Gray, 224. But the doctrine of Doe v. Batten is denied in Croft v. Lumley, 5 Ellis & B. 648, 682, s. c. Ellis B. & E. 1069 ; Dendy v. Nicholl, 4 C. B. N. s. 376, 379 ; and acceptance of rent is conclusive evidence of intent to waive. See also Prindle v. Anderson, 19 Wend. 394 ; Goodright v. Cordwent, 6 T. R. 219 ; Jackson v. Sheldon, 5 Cow. 448.

[2] Blyth v. Dennett, 13 C. B. 178.

[3] Barlow v. Wainwright, 22 Vt. 88 ; Whitney v. Gordon, 1 Cush. 266 ; Hall v. Wadsworth, sup. ; Farson v. Goodale, 8 Allen, 203 ; Walker v. Furbush, 11 Cush. 366 ; Withers v. Larrabee, 48 Me. 573.

[4] Phillips v. Covert, 7 Johns. 1 ; Perry v. Carr, 44 N. H. 120.

[5] Nichols v. Williams, 8 Cow. 13 ; ante, p. *379. The dictum in this case, and Phillips v. Covert, supra, that the only difference between these tenancies is the right to notice before ejectment, while true of their origin, is not so as to their incidents. Ante, *384. The only point in issue was whether notice was required before summary process under the statute. Park v. Castle, 19 How. Pr. 33 ; Reeder v. Sayre, 70 N. Y. 180.

[6] Pickard v. Perley, 45 N. H. 195. Contra, Doe v. Summersett, 1 B. & Ad. 135 ; Alford v. Vickery, 1 Car. & M. 280 ; Doe v. Hughes, 7 M. & W. 139.

by agreement of the parties or some statute to be in writing.[1]
It must also be direct and express, and not in the alternative,
as to quit or do something else. Though where the notice
was accompanied with a declaration, that, if the tenant did
not quit, the lessor would insist on double rent, — the statutory penalty, — it was held to be a good one.[2]

17. Whether a longer or shorter time of notice is required, it must, in order to be binding, clearly indicate the
time when the tenancy is to expire, and, of course, must
be given a sufficient number of days before the time so
indicated.[3]

18. And the notice must be so made as to expire at the end
of the time during which the tenant may lawfully hold; if
from year to year, at the end of the year, or if from quarter
to quarter, month to month, and the like, it must expire at the
end of such quarter, month, and the like.[4] In New York, if
the tenancy be at will, a month's notice determines it, although
the time fixed for leaving the premises be one day anterior to
the full month, provided the landlord do not disturb the tenant
until one full month after the service of the notice.[5] Where
rent is payable monthly on the first day of the month, notice

[1] Tud. Cas. 16 ; Timmins v. Rowlinson, 3 Burr. 1607, s. c. 1 W. Bl. 533 ; Doe
v. Crick, 5 Esp. 196. And where the notice was oral, no objection was made to
its sufficiency on that account. Hanchet v. Whitney, 1 Vt. 311.

[2] Tud. Cas. 16 ; 2 Crabb, Real Prop. 429 ; Doe v. Jackson, Doug. 175 ; Doe
v. Goldwin, 2 Q. B. 143 ; Smith, Land. & Ten. 237. The same rule was adopted
in a recent case, where the tenant was required to pay an increased rent in advance. Ahearn v. Bellman, 4 Exch. Div. 201.

[3] Hanchet v. Whitney, 1 Vt. 311 ; Steward v. Harding, 2 Gray, 335 ; Currier
v. Barker, 2 Gray, 224. And it was held in the last case cited, that this principle applied where a landlord sought to put an end to a lease in writing by notice
to quit for non-payment of rent. A notice to quit "on the 11th of October next,
or when the tenant's tenancy might expire," was held too uncertain as to its expiration. Mills v. Goff, 14 M. & W. 72 ; Huyser v. Chase, 13 Mich. 102 ; Wood-
row v. Michael, 13 Mich. 190 ; Hultain v. Munigle, 6 Allen, 220.

[4] Comyn, Land. & Ten. 405 ; Prescott v. Elm, 7 Cush. 346 ; Godard v. So.
Car. R. R., 2 Rich. (S. C.) 346 ; Lloyd v. Cozens, 2 Ashm. 131 ; 2 Crabb, Real
Prop. 425 ; Hanchet v. Whitney, 1 Vt. 311 ; Doe v. Donovan, 1 Taunt. 555 ;
Doe v. Morphett, 7 Q. B. 577 ; Currier v. Barker, 2 Gray, 224 ; Baker v. Adams,
5 Cush. 99 ; Sanford v. Harvey, 11 Cush. 93 ; Oakes v. Monroe, 8 Cush. 282 ;
Johnson v. Stewart, 11 Gray, 181 ; Cunningham v. Holton, 55 Me. 33, 38 ; Same
v. Horton, 57 Me. 422. See post, pl. 24.

[5] Burns v. Bryant, 31 N. Y. 453.

on the first day of one month to quit on the first of the following month is sufficient.[1]

19. As a notice is technical, and fixes the time at which *the tenant is bound to quit and the landlord [*387] has a right to enter, and the time at which rent ceases, it is important to have a definite rule as to the time from which such notice is to be computed. Thus, if the tenant comes in at the middle of a quarter, and pays rent on the regular quarter-days, his year, in a tenancy from year to year, commences at the first regular quarter-day, and notice to quit must conform to that time.[2] And where different parts of the premises were entered on different days, the tenancy, for purposes of notice, is construed to begin on the day when the principal part of the estate was entered on, which is a question for the jury.[3] But a notice to quit a part only of premises leased together would be bad.[4] And during the pendency of notice to a tenant to quit, his rights are the same as if he held by a written lease, and he may have trespass *qu. cl. freg.* against his own landlord, while, for an injury to the freehold by a stranger, the landlord's remedy would be case instead of trespass.[5]

20. In the interpretation of notice, however, courts are not strict; the notice must be understood in order to be effective; but if the time is so indicated that the party notified will not

[1] Walker *v.* Sharpe, 14 Allen, 43. In this case the court applied literally the well-settled rule that the day to be named in the notice for quitting is the *rent day*, Baker *v.* Adams, 5 Cush. 99 ; Prescott *v.* Elm, 7 Cush. 346 ; although here the rent was payable in advance on the first day of the term. But the rent day is properly the last day of the term, Ackland *v.* Lutley, 9 Ad. & E. 879 ; and if the tenant is notified to quit on a later day, it will be after a new term has begun and too late, Fox *v.* Nathans, 32 Conn. 348 ; Thurber *v.* Dwyer, 10 R. I. 355 ; Doe *v.* Lea, 11 East, 310, where the notice held good on a lease from Michaelmas was to quit on Michaelmas. In Waters *v.* Young, 11 R. I. 1, and Steffens *v.* Earl, 40 N. J. 128, a contrary conclusion was reached, but in the former case its soundness was doubted and was based mainly on custom.

[2] Doe *v.* Johnson, 6 Esp. 10 ; Doe *v.* Stapleton, 3 Car. & P. 275 ; Sanhill *v.* Franklin, L. R. 10 C. P. 377.

[3] Doe *v.* Snowdon, 2 W. Bl. 1224 ; Doe *v.* Spence, 6 East, 120 ; Doe *v.* Watkins, 7 East, 551 ; Doe *v.* Howard, 11 East, 498 ; Doe *v.* Hughes, 7 M. & W 189.

[4] Doe *v.* Archer, 14 East, 245 ; Sanford *v.* Harvey, 11 Cush. 93.

[5] Dickinson *v.* Goodspeed, 8 Cush. 119 ; French *v.* Fuller, 23 Pick. 104.

be misled, it will be sufficient.[1] Nor will a misdescription of the place invalidate the notice, if the tenant be not thereby misled.[2]

21. And if the tenant states a day to the lessor's agent as the end of the term, and the lessor's notice conform to that, it will bind the tenant, though he was mistaken in respect to it.[3]

22. In respect to the service of the notice, it must be on the landlord's own tenant, and not a sub-tenant of his lessee.. The sub-lessee would be bound, so far as legal proceedings for possession of the premises are concerned, by notice to the landlord's lessee.[4] Where the premises let were a shop, and the lessee took a partner, but no new contract was made with the lessor, notice served upon the partner in the absence of the lessee and wife was held sufficient to determine the tenancy at will.[5] And it may either be personal, or, as a general rule, it may be left at the dwelling-house of the tenant [*388] with a * servant, though it may not be upon the premises.[6] But if merely left upon the premises, it will not be sufficient, unless it appear that it came to the hands of the tenant.[7]

23. The length of time required in order that a notice to quit should operate to determine a tenancy at will, answering to the English tenancy from year to year, varies in different States. By the English common law, from the time of Henry

---

[1] Smith, Land. & Ten. 237 ; Doe v. Morphett, 7 Q. B. 577 ; Sandford v. Harvey, 11 Cush. 93 ; Doe v. Kightley, 7 T. R. 63. In the latter case, notice in 1795 was given to quit at a time in 1795, already passed, being an obvious mistake for 1796. Doe v. Smith, 5 Ad. & E. 350 ; Doe v. Hughes, 7 M. & W. 139 ; Granger v. Brown, 11 Cush. 191.

[2] Doe d. Cox v. ——, 4 Esp. 185 ; Doe v. Wilkinson, 12 Ad. & E. 743.

[3] Doe v. Lambly, 2 Esp. 635.

[4] Pleasant v. Benson, 14 East, 234 ; Roe v. Wiggs, 2 Bos. & P., N. R. 330 ; Hatstat v. Packard, 7 Cush. 245 ; Schilling v. Holmes, 23 Cal. 231 ; Birdsall v. Phillips, 17 Wend. 464.

[5] Walker v. Sharpe, 103 Mass. 154.

[6] Smith, Land. & Ten. 240, and note ; Doe v. Dunbar, 1 Mood. & M. 10 ; Jones v. Marsh, 4 T. R. 464 ; Widger v. Browning, 2 Car. & P. 523 ; Tud. Cas. 17.

[7] Doe v. Lucas, 5 Esp. 153 ; Alford v. Vickery, 1 Car. & M. 280. In the latter case a notice was put under the tenant's door, but it was shown to have come to his hands before the six months previous to the expiration of the year.

CH. XI. § 2.]

VIII., it has been six months, and must expire at the end of the year.[1] The same rule is adopted in New York, North Carolina, Tennessee, Vermont, New Jersey, Illinois, and Kentucky.[2] In Pennsylvania, South Carolina, and New Hampshire, the term is three months, ending at the expiration of the year.[3]

24. It may be repeated, that in those cases which neither come within the notion of estates strictly at will, requiring no notice to determine them, nor strictly of estates from year to year, because, by implication, for some definite period less than a year, as for a quarter, a month, a week, and the like, the time of notice is measured, ordinarily, by the length of the term specified as the interval between the times of payment of rent and the notice must, if not regulated by statute, be equal to one of these intervals, and must end at the expiration thereof.[4]

*25. In Massachusetts, the subject of terminating [*389] an estate at will, by notice, is regulated by a statute, which requires the notice to be in writing, and if the tenancy be for an indefinite period, or longer than a quarter, or for a quarter, the notice is to be that of a quarter; if for a less period, or the rent is payable oftener than quarterly, the notice is to be equal to the interval of such payment.[5]

[1] Bessell v. Landsberg, 7 Q. B. 638 ; Doe v. Watts, 7 T. R. 83 ; 2 Flint. Real Prop. 219. But where the tenant gave notice of quitting, which was in proper form and time, and he actually had removed from the premises, it was held that his accidentally retaining the key two days beyond the proper time did not avoid the notice. Gray v. Bompas, 11 C. B. N. s. 520.

[2] Jackson v. Bryan, 1 Johns. 322, per Tompkins, J. ; 4 Kent, Com. 113 ; Den v. McIntosh, 4 Ired. 291 ; Trousdale v. Darnell, 6 Yerg. 431 ; Hanchett v. Whitney, 1 Vt. 315 ; Barlow v. Wainwright, 22 Vt. 88 ; Den v. Drake, 14 N. J. 523 ; Den v. Blair, 15 N. J. 181 ; Squires v. Huff, 3 A. K. Marsh, 17 ; Sullivan v. Enders, 3 Dana, 66 ; Morehead v. Watkyns, 5 B. Mon. 228 ; Hunt v. Morton, 18 Ill. 75.

[3] Logan v. Herron, 8 S. & R. 459 ; Lesley v. Randolph, 4 Rawle, 123 ; Lloyd v. Cozens, 2 Ashm. 131 ; Godard v. So. Car. R. R., 2 Rich. (S. C.) 346 ; Floyd v. Floyd, 4 Rich. (S. C.) 23 ; Currier v. Perley, 24 N. H. 219.

[4] Taylor, Land. & Ten. 50 ; Right v. Darby, 1 T. R. 159 ; Smith, Land. & Ten. 24 ; Doe v. Hazell, 1 Esp. 94 ; Sanford v. Harvey, 11 Cush. 93 ; Prescott v. Elm, 7 Cush. 346 ; Hollis v. Burns, 100 Penn. St. 206 ; Steffens v. Earl, 40 N. J. 128.

[5] Mass. Pub. Stat., c. 121, § 12 ; Howard v. Merriam, 5 Cush. 563. Where

26. But the distinction should be borne in mind between the notice required by the statutes of some of the States to determine an estate at will, and that which is required as preliminary to enforcing legal measures to expel the tenant. The former are alone referred to here.*

27. The effect of accepting rent, by the way of reviving a tenancy which has once been forfeited by failure to pay rent, or has been terminated, so far as giving notice may have that effect, seems to be this. If rent is in arrear under a tenancy at will, the landlord may terminate the tenancy by giving fourteen days' notice without any previous demand of the rent; and should he, after giving such notice, receive the rent so due, he would not thereby revive the lease, if at the time of receiving the same, he gives notice of his intent not to waive his right to claim the possession of the premises.[1] But if he accepts rent without any such notice of his intent, especially if he accepts rent accruing after the date of such notice, it is considered as a waiver of what he may have done towards terminating the tenancy at will.[2]

28. Another mode of determining estates at will, including estates from year to year, is by surrender, which is substan-

* NOTE. — There are in England, and in many of the States, summary methods provided by statute to enable a landlord to recover possession of leased premises, in some, if not all, of which a preliminary notice of a prescribed length of time must be given before commencing proceedings. But as the subject relates to the remedies of landlords rather than to the nature of estates at will, and the rights of landlords and tenants in respect to such estate, it is purposely omitted here. Stat. 1 & 2 Vict. c. 74 ; Taylor, Land. & Ten. § 728 a (7th ed.) and note ; Smith, Land. & Ten. 245, n., Morris' ed. ; Mass. Pub Stat. c. 175 ; Howard v. Merriam, 5 Cush. 563 ; Granger v. Brown, 11 Cush. 191 ; Sanford v. Harvey, 11 Cush. 93 ; Rooney v. Gillespie, 6 Allen, 74 ; Raynor v. Haggard, 18 Mich. 72 ; Dudley v. Lee, 39 Ill. 339 ; Alexander v. Carew, 13 Allen, 70. An eviction of lessee by summary proceedings does not affect his liability for past rent ; it only applies to what is future. Johnson v. Oppenheim, 55 N. Y. 294.

rent is in arrear a briefer notice of two weeks is provided for. But this applies to all tenancies, and need not expire with a rent day. Pub. Stat. c. 121, § 12.

[1] Kimball v. Rowland, 6 Gray, 224 ; Mass. Gen. Stat. 1860, c. 90, § 31.

[2] Tuttle v. Bean, 13 Met. 275 ; Collins v. Canty, 6 Cush. 415. See Norris v. Morrill, 43 N. H. 218, commenting on the above cases, and maintaining that merely accepting rent accrued before the termination of the tenancy is not a waiver of notice. It seems, after all, a mere question of intent. Farson v. Goodale, 8 Allen, 202. But see ante, *385 and note, that the intent will be conclusively implied from the act.

tially a yielding up of possession by the tenant to the lessor, or him who has the reversion, which may be legally inferred from the acts of the parties as well as their express words, such as abandoning the premises by the tenant, and the assuming possession thereof by the lessor.[1] But leaving the key with the lessor does not amount to a surrender, if he do not accept it as such.[2]

29. If, after a determination of a tenancy by notice, the lessee continues to hold the premises, and the landlord accepts rent for the same, it will be regarded as a renewal of the tenancy upon the former terms.[3]

30. If the tenancy is determined by notice, the lessor may, if he please, enter and take possession of the premises by force if necessary.[4] And where the written notice was directed to John, when the tenant's name was Thomas, but was handed to the tenant's wife at the dwelling-house in his absence, commanding the person to whom it was directed to quit the dwelling-house "you now hold under me," it was held to be sufficient; and the time of the notice having expired, and the lessee having failed to remove, the lessor entered in the absence of the lessee, and removed his goods, and fastened the door. It was held that the lessor was justified in so doing, although the goods were injured by remaining exposed to the weather.[5]

31. It remains to consider the effect of the statutes of frauds upon parol leases, as it will be found that these vary essentially in their provisions in respect to such leases. But it is

---

[1] Comyn, Land. & Ten. 337 ; Thomas v. Cook, 2 B. & Ald. 119 ; Nickells v. Atherstone, 10 Q. B. 944 ; Whitney v. Meyers, 1 Duer, 266 ; Smith, Land. & Ten. 231, n., Morris's ed.

[2] Withers v. Larrabee, 48 Me. 573 ; Cannan v. Hartley, 9 C. B. 635 ; Walker v. Furbush, 11 Cush. 366 ; Townsend v. Albers, 3 E. D. Smith, 560 ; *ante,* *351–354.

[3] Goodright v. Cordwent, 6 T. R. 219.

[4] Taunton v. Costar, 7 T. R. 431 ; Miner v. Stevens, 1 Cush. 482 ; Meader v. Stone, 7 Met. 147 ; Harvey v. Brydges, 14 M. & W. 437 ; Hyatt v. Wood, 4 Johns. 150 ; Overdeer v. Lewis, 1 Watts & S. 90. See *contra,* Newton v. Harland, 1 Mann. & G. 644, Coltman, J., dissenting. See this subject further discussed, *post,* c. 12, § 1, pl. 10 ; Mugford v. Richardson, 6 Allen, 76 ; Stevens v. Sampson, 59 Me. 568.

[5] Clark v. Keliher, 107 Mass. 406.

believed they all, with the exception of New York, agree in this, that if the agreement to let be executory, and not consummated by the lessee's taking possession, it cannot be enforced ; if it be by parol, the statute prohibits any action upon such a contract.[1]

32. If the lessee takes possession, the question arises whether by the statute of frauds the lease is binding as an agreement at common law, or the tenancy under it is a mere tenancy at will, or the lease, as such, is to be deemed void.

[*391]   *33. If the lease does not exceed three years from the time of *making*, it is by the English statute 29 Car. II. c. 3, §§ 1, 2, as valid and binding as if no such statute had been enacted.[2]   The same is the rule in Georgia, Indiana, Maryland, North Carolina, Pennsylvania, New Jersey, and South Carolina.   This term in Florida is two, and in the following States one year ; namely, Alabama, Arkansas, California, Connecticut, Delaware, Iowa, Kentucky, Michigan, Mississippi, New York, Nevada, Rhode Island, Tennessee, Texas, Virginia, and Wisconsin.   In Maine, Massachusetts, Missouri, New Hampshire, Ohio, and Vermont, all such leases create tenancies at will only.[3]

34. Although parol leases are, in the cases before enumerated, declared by these statutes mere estates at will, or in some cases void, yet if the lessee enters and occupies, and pays rent under them, he becomes a tenant from year to year, in those States where such tenancies are recognized, or a tenant at will in others, with the rights as to notice of such tenants.[4]

35. And in the cases embraced in the above section, the

[1] Browne, Stat. Frauds, § 37 ; Edge v. Strafford, 1 Tyrw. 293 ; Larkin v. Avery, 23 Conn. 304 ; Delano v. Montague, 4 Cush. 42 ; Young v. Dake, 5 N. Y. 463.

[2] Bolton v. Tomlin, 5 Ad. & E. 856 ; Rawlins v. Turner, 1 Ld. Raym. 736.

[3] Browne, Stat. Frauds, 501–532 ; Adams v. McKesson, 53 Penn. St. 83 ; Birckhead v. Cummings, 33 N. J. 44 ; Morrill v. Mackman, 24 Mich. 286 ; Lobdell v. Hall, 3 Nev. 517.

[4] Clayton v. Blakey, 8 T. R. 3 ; McDowell v. Simpson, 3 Watts, 129 ; People v. Rickhert, 8 Cow. 226 ; Blumenthal v. Bloomingdale, 100 N. Y. 561 ; Dumn v. Rothermel, 112 Penn. St. 272 ; Drake v. Newton, 23 N. J. 111 ; Lockwood v. Lockwood, 22 Conn. 425 ; 2 Smith, Lead. Cas. 76 n., Am. ed.

rights of the parties will be governed by the terms of the original letting, as agreed upon by the parties, so long as the holding continues.[1]

[1] Browne, Stat. Frauds, § 39 ; Schuyler *v.* Leggett, 2 Cow. 660 ; Barlow *v.* Wainwright, 22 Vt. 88 ; Doe *v.* Bell, 5 T. It. 471 ; Hollis *v.* Pool, 3 Met. 350 ; Currier *v.* Barker, 2 Gray, 224 ; Betz *v.* Delbert, 14 W. No. Cas. 360.

CHAPTER XII.

TENANCIES AT SUFFERANCE, LICENSES, ETC.

SECT. 1.   Tenancies at Sufferance.
SECT. 2.   License.

SECTION I.

TENANCIES AT SUFFERANCE.

1. What constitutes a tenant at sufferance.
2. Who is such tenant.
3. Tenancy at sufferance only grows out of agreement.
4, 5. Of the nature of such tenancy.
6. Tenant has no privity of estate, nor is liable to trespass or for rent.
7. Possession of such tenant not adverse to the owner.
8. When the owner may have trespass against him.
9. Effect of tenant's assigning, in making possession adverse.
10. Of the right of the owner to enter upon his tenant.
10 *a.* How far owner may use force to eject a tenant.
10 *b.* Same subject with cases cited.
11. Tenants not entitled to notice to quit.

1. WHEN a tenant has come rightfully into possession of lands by permission of the owner, and continues to [*393] occupy the * same, after the time for which, by such permission, he has a right to hold the same, he is said to be a tenant by sufferance.   In the language of the elementary writers, " he is one who comes in by right, and holds over without right." [1]   He holds without right, and yet is not a trespasser.[2]   Thus where the owner of land brought process of ejectment against the tenant, and a judgment was rendered that the tenant should remove by such a time or be expelled,

[1] 2 Bl. Com. 150 ; Co. Lit. 57 b ; Smith, Land. & Ten. 217; Doe *v.* Hull, 2 D. & R. 38 ; Russell *v.* Fabyan, 34 N. H. 218.
[2] Uridias *v.* Morrell, 25 Cal. 35.

it was held that trespass would not lie against him for retaining possession until the expiration of the time prescribed.[1] But to make one a tenant by sufferance in California and New York, there must be some laches on the part of the owner, in delaying to make entry upon his tenant after the expiration of his term. And in such case he must give his tenant a month's notice to quit before he can enter and remove him, or maintain ejectment against him.[2] But if he demands possession of his tenant who holds over, within a year from the termination of his lease, he may recover possession of his tenant by expelling him without first making a formal entry upon the premises.[3] But this permission must be that of a landlord to a tenant; if it be an occupancy as a mere matter of favor or accommodation, it would not be a tenancy at sufferance.

2. Under this class of occupants of land have been included tenants *per autre vie* after the death of the *cestui que vie*,[4] tenants for years whose terms have expired,[5] tenants at will whose estates have been determined by alienation or by death of the lessor,[6] or by the happening of some contingent event upon which the determination of an estate at will depended,[7] undertenants who hold after the expiration of the term of the original lessee,[8] a grantor who agrees to deliver possession by a certain day, and holds over.[9] In short, any one who continues in possession without agreement, after the determination of the particular estate by which he originally gained it.[10] And this, even though the original contract was a written lease which provided for the recovery of rent, *pro rata*, for

---

[1] Campbell v. Loader, 3 Hurlst. & C. 520.

[2] Boore v. Borrow, 28 Cal. 554 ; 2 N. Y. Rev. Stat. (6th ed.) 1126, § 7 ; Rowan v. Lytle, 11 Wend. 616 ; Smith v. Littlefield, 51 N. Y. 539. In Kentucky a tenant for a term of a year or more is at sufferance for ninety days after the term expires. Bendel v. Hall, 13 Bush, 232.

[3] Uridias v. Borrell, *sup.*   [4] Co. Lit. 57 b.

[5] Co. Lit. 57 b ; Jackson v. Parkhurst, 5 Johns. 128 ; 2 Bl. Com. 150.

[6] Co. Lit. 57 b ; Kinsley v. Ames, 2 Met. 29 ; Benedict v. Morse, 10 Met. 223.

[7] Creech v. Crockett, 5 Cush. 133 ; Elliott v. Stone, 1 Gray, 571.

[8] Simkin v. Ashurst, 1 Cr. M. & R. 261 ; Smith, Land. & Ten. 25.

[9] Hyatt v. Wood, 4 Johns. 150.

[10] Com. Dig. "Estate," I. 1 ; Burton, Real Prop. § 56 ; Livingston v. Tanner, 12 Barb. 481 ; 2 Flint. Real Prop. 222 ; Smith v. Littlefield, 51 N. Y. 543.

the time the tenant should hold after the expiration of the lease.[1] Thus, where the lessee underlet, and the tenancy between the original parties to the lease was determined by the original lessor, such sub-tenant became thereby a tenant at sufferance to the original lessor.[2] So where husband and wife conveyed land by deed, which deed was void as to the wife, it was held that, although it conveyed the husband's interest for life, the moment he died the purchaser became a tenant at sufferance to the wife. Nor could the tenant purchase in a new title from a third person and set it up against the wife's claim to recover, without first surrendering possession to her.[3] The following cases may serve to illustrate some of the foregoing propositions: B was tenant for life with a remainder to A, who, acting as his agent, leased the premises to C for three years, he knowing that he acted as agent. B died at the end of one year, and A conveyed the estate to the plaintiff, who sued C for possession. It was held that C's estate determined upon B's death, and that from that time he was tenant at sufferance, and the plaintiff recovered.[4] A, owning land, and being about to leave the country, requested B to take charge of it during his absence, and he let it to C. It was held that A's return determined the lease, and that C thereby became a tenant at sufferance.[5]

3. But in order to have a tenancy grow into one by sufferance, it must originally have been created by agreement of the parties, for where one was in, like a guardian, by act of the law, and held after his ward arrived at age, he was a tort feasor, intruder, abator, or trespasser, and not a tenant at sufferance.[6] It is held in New York and other States that a tenant who holds over after his term has expired may be treated by the lessor as a tenant from year to year or a trespasser, at his option, but that the tenant cannot elect in which capacity he shall be regarded.[7] In Massachusetts and Maine,

1 Edwards v. Hale, 9 Allen, 462.

2 Evans v. Reed, 5 Gray, 308.   3 Griffin v. Sheffield, 38 Miss. 390.

4 Page v. Wight, 14 Allen, 182.   5 Antoni v. Belknap, 102 Mass. 193.

7 Co. Lit. 57 b ; 2d Inst. 134 ; Merrill v. Bullock, 105 Mass. 491 ; Torrey v. Torrey, 14 N. Y. 430.

6 Conway v. Starkweather, 1 Denio, 113 ; Witt v. New York, 5 Rob. 248, s. c. 6 Id. 441; Vrooman v. McKaig, 4 Md. 450; Moore v. Beasley, 3 Ohio, 294;

however, a contrary rule prevails, and the tenant holding over remains at sufferance until he, as well as the landlord, have agreed to a new tenancy; though this agreement may be implied.[1] And the rule in England seems to be the same.[2]

4. The principle that regulates the relation of landlord and tenant, however, so far applies between them that a tenant at sufferance will not be admitted to question the title of his lessor in an action to recover possession of the land.[3]

5. And yet a holding by sufferance is rather like a tenancy between landlord and tenant than in fact such a tenancy, for it is defective in one of the elements of such a tenancy, namely, an agreement express or implied by which it is continued. The * moment the parties agree, the one to [*394] hold and the other to permit him to hold possession, it becomes a tenancy at will, or from year to year, and ceases to be one at sufferance.[4] Such would be the effect of paying and receiving rent for the time the tenant should hold over,[5] or suffering a distress,[6] and very slight circumstances will suffice to establish such an agreement.[7]

6. There is neither privity of contract nor of estate between the owner and tenant, for the tenant is not in by contract, nor has he any estate which he can transfer or transmit, or which can be enlarged by release. He has a mere naked possession without right of notice to quit. But though this possession is wrongful, he is, for technical reasons, not liable in trespass by reason thereof. His holding is by the laches of the owner, who may enter at any moment and put an end to the same. But until that has been done he cannot have trespass against

Schuyler v. Smith, 51 N. Y. 309 ; Bacon v. Brown, 9 Conn. 334 ; Hemphill v. Flynn, 2 Penn. St. 144 ; McGregor v. Rawle, 57 Penn. St. 184 ; Noel v. McCrory, 7 Coldw. 623 ; Ives v. Williams, 50 Mich. 100, 106 ; Tolle v. Orth, 75 Ind. 298.

[1] Edwards v. Hale, 9 Allen, 462 ; Eunnes v. Feely, 132 Mass. 346 ; Porter v. Hubbard, 134 Mass. 233, 238 ; Withers v. Larrabee, 48 Me. 570 ; Ackerman v. Lyman, 20 Wisc. 454 ; Russell v. Fabyan, 34 N. H. 218 ; Condon v. Barr, 47 N. J. 113.

[2] Ibbs v. Richardson, 9 Ad. & E. 849 ; Levy v. Lewis, 9 C. B. N. S. 872.

[3] Jackson v. M'Leod, 12 Johns. 182.

[4] Smith, Land. & Ten. 26 ; Watkins, Conv. 24.

[5] Smith, Land. & Ten. 219–221 ; Russell v. Fabyan, 34 N. H. 223 ; Emmons v. Scudder, 115 Mass. 367 ; Morris v. Niles, 12 Abb. Pr. R. 103.

[6] Panton v. Jones, 3 Camp. 372.   [7] Griffith v. Knisely, 75 Ill. 411.

the tenant for such occupation.[1] And where he has made such entry, he may treat the tenant as a trespasser in holding over, or any one holding under him.[2] But a tenant at sufferance cannot maintain trespass against lessor for making a peaceable entry upon the premises.[3] If, after the expiration of a tenant's term, his landlord bring a writ of entry at common law to recover possession, the judgment which he recovers embraces the mesne profits to which he will be entitled. But if he sues out the process of forcible entry and detainer, and thereby obtains possession of the premises, he may after that sue in trespass for mesne profits against the tenant.[4] Nor could he, at common law, recover rent as such for such possession, it being the owner's own laches in suffering him to retain it;[5] but he might recover in an action for use and occupation.[6] And the defect of the common law, in respect to its holding a tenant at sufferance exempt from rent, is obviated by the English statutes, 4 Geo. II. c. 28, and 11 Geo. II. c. 19, making him liable for double rent if he holds over after notice

---

[1] 2 Bl. Com. 150 ; Watkins, Conv. 24 ; Jackson v. Parkhurst, 5 Johns. 128 ; 4 Kent, Com. 117. " One tenant at sufferance cannot make another," per Lord Ellenborough, Thunder v. Belcher, 3 East, 451 ; Layman v. Throp, 11 Ind. 352.

[2] Curl v. Lowell, 19 Pick. 27 ; Butcher v. Butcher, 7 B. & C. 399 ; Hey v. Moorhouse, 6 Bing. N. C. 52.

[3] Esty v. Baker, 50 Me. 334.

[4] Sargent v. Smith, 12 Gray, 426 ; Raymond v. Andrews, 6 Cush. 265.

[5] 2 Bl. Com. 150, Chitty's note ; Sir Moil Finch's Case, 2 Leon. 143 ; Tud. Cas. 9. This point is noticed but left undecided by the court in Delano v. Montague, 4 Cush. 42. In Flood v. Flood, 1 Allen, 217, though the action was for use and occupation, it was said that *rent* was not recoverable ; and this is repeated in Cunningham v. Holton, 55 Me. 33, 38, though not in issue as the tenant had paid.

[6] Ibbs v. Richardson, 9 Ad. & E. 849 ; Levi v. Lewis, 6 C. B. N. s. 766. For the landlord may waive the tort and sue in assumpsit. Ib. ; Nat. Oil Ref. Co. v. Bush, 88 Penn. St. 335 ; Stockton's App., 64 Penn. St. 63. In Bonney v. Foss, 62 Me. 63, a tenant holding over was held liable, presumably as a tenant at sufferance. In Hogsett v. Ellis, 17 Mich. 351, 367-370, the authorities are carefully examined, and the distinction between rent and use and occupation pointed out. And now by statute in Massachusetts such tenant is liable. Pub. Stat. c. 121, §§ 3, 5. Although it is still doubtful if assumpsit for use and occupation lay prior thereto. Porter v. Hubbard, 134 Mass. 233, 238. But such action will not lie even under such a statute, where the occupant has never been in privity or his holding has been adverse. Hogsett v. Ellis, *supra; post*, p. 653, note 3.

to quit.[1] In Pennsylvania a landlord is allowed to recover against a tenant who holds over, without distinguishing whether the liability is for mesne profits or damages, or for use and occupation.[2] But generally no recovery can be had against an occupant, even under statutes giving an action against occupants, or tenants at sufferance, unless they originally held by some agreement with the plaintiff, or some other person with whom he is in privity. If the tenant denies the plaintiff's title, or that he holds under him, he must bring trespass or ejectment for mesne profits.[3] A tenant at sufferance is not entitled to emblements.[5] But to constitute a tenancy by sufferance, one must hold an estate less than a fee, and subordinate to a fee. If he hold by a title which does not answer these conditions, although it may have failed or come to an end, it would not render him a tenant at sufferance, or liable as such.[6]

7. While the owner cannot treat the tenant at sufferance as a trespasser, until he shall have gained possession of the premises by entry thereon,[7] the tenant cannot avail himself of his possession as being adverse to the owner for the purpose of barring his claim under the statute of limitations.[8] And the landlord may have case against such tenant for injuries

---

[1] Smith, Land. & Ten. 245. And similar statutes exist in New York, Delaware, South Carolina, and Arkansas. 1 Stat. at Large, 697 ; Rev. Stat. S. C., 1869, p. 435 ; Rev. Stat. 520.

[2] Stockton's Appeal, 64 Penn. St. 63.

[3] Knowles v. Hull, 99 Mass. 562 ; Merrill v. Bullock, 105 Mass. 491 ; Tinder v. Davis, 88 Ind. 99 ; Whitney v. Dart, 117 Mass. 513 ; Wills v. Wills, 34 Ind. 106 ; Chamberlain v. Dunahue, 45 Vt. 50 ; Marquette R. R. v. Harlow, 37 Mich. 554. But merely paying rent to the mortgagor or his assignee after entry by the mortgagee does not make an adverse holding as to the latter. Sucier v. Marsales, 133 Mass. 454.

[4] Schuyler v. Smith, 51 N. Y. 309, 314.

[5] Doe v. Turner, 7 M. & W. 226.   [6] Cook v. Norton, 48 Ill. 20.

[7] 2 Bl. Com. 150; Co. Lit. 57 b ; Rising v. Stannard, 17 Mass. 282 ; Newton v. Harland, 1 Mann. & G. 644 ; Trevillian v. Andrew, 5 Mod. 384.

[8] Watkins, Conv. 24, Morley & Coote's ed. ; Smith, Land. & Ten. 217 ; Doe v. Hull, 2 Dowl. & R. 38, per Abbott, C. J. ; 2 Smith, Lead. Cas. 5th Am. ed. 532 ; Tud. Cas. 8. By stat. 3 & 4 Wm. IV. c. 27, the limitation begins to run against the landlord from the time he might have entered. But this has not been followed, as is said, in any of the United States. Smith, Land. & Ten. 218, n., Morris's ed. ; Edwards v. Hale, 9 Allen, 464, 465 ; Colvin v. Warford, 20 Md. 396 ; Gwynn v. Jones, 2 Gill & J. 173.

done to the premises while retained by him, and before entry
made by the landlord.[1]

[*395]   *8. It seems to be immaterial that the owner should
make any formal declaration of the intent with which
he enters, if he actually regains his possession. He may then
have trespass against the tenant for holding adversely to him.[2]

9. But what has been said as to the possession of a tenant
at sufferance not being adverse to that of the owner, does not
apply to the case of one coming into possession as assignee or
representative of such tenant. As the latter can neither
assign nor transmit his tenancy at sufferance, whoever comes
in under him will hold adversely to the owner, and his possession may, under the statute of limitations, in process of
time, ripen into a good title, unless he shall have recognized
the title of the owner, and that he held under him.[3]

10. In a former chapter,[4] the right of the owner to enter
and regain possession of premises by force, after a tenancy at
will had been determined, was somewhat considered. The
question has been much discussed in England as well as this
country, in respect to entering thus upon a tenant at sufferance and expelling him. The question has principally grown
out of statute 5 Rich. II. c. 7, forbidding an entry to be made
" with strong hand or a multitude of people, but only in a
peaceable and easy manner ; " and the statute of 8 Hen. VI.
c. 9, by which damages and restitution were given to the freeholder disseised. Similar statutes have been passed in most or
all of the States.[5] Would the owner of land or tenements, who,
in recovering possession of the same from a tenant at sufferance,

[1] Russell *v.* Fabyan, 34 N. H. 218, 225.

[2] Dorrell *v.* Johnson, 17 Pick. 266 ; Butcher *v.* Butcher, 7 B. & C. 399 ; Hey
v. Moorehouse, 6 Bing. N. C. 52; Pearce *v.* Ferris, 10 N. Y. 280. This is not
intended to apply to cases where the statute requires the landlord to give formal
notice, in order to avail himself of the summary process for ejecting a tenant at
sufferance. Livingston *v.* Tanner, 12 Barb. 481.

[3] 2 Flint. Real Prop. 224 ; Smith, Land. & Ten. 217 ; Watkins, Conv. 25;
Nepean *v.* Doe, 2 M. & W. 911 ; Tud. Cas. 8 ; Fishar *v.* Prosser, Cowp. 217 ;
Reckhow *v.* Schanck, 43 N. Y. 448.

[4] *Ante*, p. *390.

[5] For what entry by force into premises in the possession of another would
not come within the meaning of " forcible entry," see Pike *v.* Witt, 104 Mass.
595.

should use so much violence as to subject him to indictment
for a breach of the peace, thereby become liable to the tenant
for thus ousting him ?   In 1840 it was stated by Erskine, J.,
that the question had never before been brought directly before *the court sitting in bench.[1]   It might [*396]
be added that it did not properly arise in that case,
as the entry was peaceable and the force used in expelling
was not excessive. The court in deciding the case, which was
trespass for assault, held that any force to the person of the
occupant made the entry an illegal one, *ab initio*, by relation.
The more modern doctrine of the English courts is clearly in
accordance with the opinion of Baron Parke, expressed in the
following terms : " I should have no difficulty in saying that
where a breach of the peace is committed by a freeholder who,
in order to get into possession of his land, assaults a person
wrongfully holding possession of it against his will, although
the freeholder may be responsible to the public in the shape of
an indictment for forcible entry, *he is not liable to the other
party*." [2]   And the law, as generally adopted in the United
States, may be assumed to be substantially as laid down by
Baron Parke. If the owner of land wrongfully held by another enter and expel the occupant, but makes use of
no more force than is reasonably necessary to *accom- [*397]
plish this, he will not be liable to an action of trespass
quare clausum, nor for assault and battery, nor for injury to
the occupant's goods, although, in order to effect such expulsion and removal, it becomes necessary to use so much force
and violence as to subject him to indictment at common law
for a breach of the peace, or under the statute for making for-

---

[1] Newton *v.* Harland, 1 Mann. & G. 644.

[2] Harvey *v.* Brydges, 14 M. & W. 442 ; Alderson and Platt, BB., concurred ;
see Taylor *v.* Cole, 3 T. R. 292 ; Taunton *v.* Costar, 7 T. R. 431 ; Butcher *v.*
Butcher, 7 B. & C. 399 ; Turner *v.* Maymott, 1 Bing. 159 ; Kavanagh *v.* Gudge,
7 Mann. & G. 316, preceding this case ; also Co. Lit. 257 a, Butler's note, 199 ;
and Pollen *v.* Brewer, 7 C. B. N. s. 371 ; Blades *v.* Higgs, 10 C. B. N. s. 713,
721 ; Davison *v.* Wilson, 11 Q. B. 890 ; Burling *v.* Read, Ib. 904 ; Davis *v.* Burell,
10 C. B. 821 ; Meriton *v.* Coombes, 1 Lowndes, M. & P. 510 ; Lows *v.* Telford,
1 App. Ca. 414, 426 ; which have followed and affirmed it. " The opinion in the
case of Newton *v.* Harland is alike adverse to the prior as well as the subsequent
decisions of the English courts on this question." Stearns *v.* Sampson, 59 Me.
568.

cible entry.[1] In accordance with the foregoing propositions, the cases cited below seem fully to sustain the doctrine, that trespass will not lie in favor of a tenant by sufferance against his landlord for entering and expelling him from the premises, assuming, of course, that he uses no unnecessary force or violence in so doing.[2]

10 *a.* Notwithstanding what has already been said upon the subject, the contrary rule has been so positively asserted by the courts of two of the States that it seems not uncalled for to briefly advert thereto. There has in England, since the cases of Hillary *v.* Gay and Newton *v.* Harland [3] were overruled, been no recurrence to the doctrine propounded by them, and it is unnecessary to do more than refer to the citations already made,[4] by which it will appear that, whatever may be the liability of the lessor to indictment for forcible entry or expulsion as a breach of the peace, he is under no liability to the occupant either in trespass *quare clausum* or for assault unless excessive force is used, and then only for the excess.[5] The uniform current of authority in the United States sustaining the same doctrine [6] is broken only by the decisions in Vermont and Illinois. In the former of these an action of trespass *quare clausum* was sustained in favor of a tenant at sufferance on the bare ground of the statutory prohibition of a forcible entry, irrespective of title;[7] though in an earlier case a possession gained by such entry had been held lawful.[8] The decision

---

[1] Hyatt *v.* Wood, 4 Johns. 150 ; Buldrow *v.* Jones, Rice (S. C.), 71 ; Ives *v.* Ives, 13 Johns. 235 ; Jackson *v.* Farmer, 9 Wend. 201 ; Jackson *v.* Morse, 16 Johns. 197 ; Beecher *v.* Parmele, 9 Vt. 352 ; Johnson *v.* Hannahan, 1 Strobh. 313 ; Overdeer *v.* Lewis, 1 Watts & S. 90 ; Sampson *v.* Henry, 13 Pick. 36, s. c. 11 Pick. 379 ; Meader *v.* Stone, 7 Met. 147 ; Miner *v.* Stevens, 1 Cush. 482 ; Lackey *v.* Holbrook, 11 Met. 458 ; Fifty Assoc. *v.* Howland, 5 Cush. 214.

[2] Taunton *v.* Costar, 7 T. R. 431 ; Moore *v.* Mason, 1 Allen, 406 ; Curtis *v.* Galvin, 1 Allen, 215 ; Mason *v.* Holt, 1 Allen, 46. See Todd *v.* Jackson, 26 N. J. 525 ; Krevet *v.* Meyer, 24 Mo. 107 ; Fuhr *v.* Dean, 26 Mo. 116, 118.

[3] Hillary *v.* Gay, 6 C. & P. 284 ; Newton *v.* Harland, 1 Mann. & G. 644.

[4] *Ante,* pl. 10 and notes.

[5] Ib. See also Sampson *v.* Henry, 13 Pick. 36 ; s. c. 11 Pick. 379.

[6] See in addition to cases cited, *post,* Killaree *v.* Jansen, 17 Penn. St. 467 ; Zell *v.* Raume, 31 Penn. St. 304.

[7] Dustin *v.* Cowdry, 23 Vt. 631 ; and see Whittaker *v.* Perry, 38 Vt. 107.

[8] Beecher *v.* Parmele, 9 Vt. 352 ; see also Yale *v.* Seely, 15 Vt. 221 ; Hodgeden *v.* Hubbard, 18 Vt. 504.

rested mainly on the authority of the two English cases above named,[1] and professed to recognize as conclusive whatever might be the English decisions on this point;[2] and might therefore be considered as no longer authority to the point, since those cases have been overruled.[3]   It is to be noticed further that the lease under which the tenant at sufferance had entered expressly justified his forcible removal ; and also that the court in commenting severely upon the confusion into which other tribunals were thought to have fallen between the statute of Richard II. which gave no damages, and that of Henry VI. which did, overlook the fact that by the latter only freeholders could recover.[4]   The illegality of mere force is denied in a later case, and it is held that if the tenant is not in possession the lessor may forcibly enter, and when in may forcibly resist the tenant's re-entry.[5]   In Illinois, though in one case the court held that " no case has been referred to, and it is believed that none exists, which holds that a trespasser, or a person in possession as a wrong-doer, can recover against the owner of the fee with right of possession," [6] yet in

---

[1] Hillary v. Gay, and Newton v. Harland.

[2] 23 Vt. 645.   " We have no disposition to add anything in regard to the true construction of the law as derived from the decisions of the courts in Westminster Hall.   And we think the decisions of the English courts as to the common law or the construction of ancient statutes are to be regarded of paramount authority."   Per Redfield, C. J.

[3] The court was not more fortunate in the American authorities upon which it relied.   The dictum in Sampson v. Henry, 11 Pick. 379, was controlled by an express decision to the contrary in s. c. 13 Pick. 36.   See also Low v. Elwell, 121 Mass. 309 ; and Moore v. Boyd, 24 Me. 242 ; Brock v. Berry, 31 Me. 293, if they had been cases of tenancy at sufferance — which they were not, see post, pl. 10 b — were overruled by Stearns v. Sampson, 59 Me. 568.

[4] Stat. Hen. VI., c. 9, § 6 ; Willard v. Warren, 17 Wend. 262 ; Cole v. Eagle, 8 B. & C. 409 ; Hawk. Pl. Cr. Bk. I., c. 64, §§ 15, 16 ; King v. Arden, 3 Bulstr. 71 ; Lover's Case, 1 Leon. 327 ; Rex v. Dormy, 1 Ld. Raym. 610.   The court, in referring to this statute as supporting an action by a tenant at sufferance, cite Lord Hale's note to 2 Fitzh. Nat. Brev. 248 H., to the effect that " he (the tenant) shall not maintain the action by the statute Richard II., *but may by the statute of* Hen. VI."   On recurring to that authority, it appears that there is no statement whatever that such action can be maintained ; that the reference to Hen. VI. is not to the statute at all, but to the 9 Hen. VI. fo. 19, pl. 12, which holds that no action can be maintained ; and that the words italicized do not appear at all in Lord Hale's note.

[5] Mussey v. Scott, 32 Vt. 82.   [6] Hoots v. Graham, 23 Ill. 84.

a more recent case[1] that court review the subject and many of
the cases above cited, and come to the conclusion, that " the
statutes of forcible entry and detainer should be construed as
taking away the previous common-law right of forcible entry
by the owner, and that such entry must therefore be held illegal in all forms of action." The doctrine of Wilder v. House[2]
depends mainly upon what is settled in Reeder v. Purdy,[3] and
the latter was decided chiefly upon the supposed exhaustive
inquiry in the case of Dustin v. Cowdry.[4] The Illinois doctrine, as stated in Reeder v. Purdy, is that, " in this State, it
has been constantly held that any entry is forcible, within the
meaning of the statute, that is made against the will of the
occupant; " and it is there assumed that even if a tenant were
at the end of the time to remove his family and furniture from
the premises, but refused to surrender the key, and claimed
possession, and the landlord were to force the door of the
vacant house, he might thereby render himself liable to his
tenant in nominal damages. In this respect the case is directly opposed to the Vermont case of Hussey v. Scott already
referred to,[5] although so much reliance is placed upon Dustin v. Cowdry. The later decisions[6] and dicta[7] still adhere
to the doctrine of Reeder v. Purdy, and carry it to the extreme
length of holding that the landlord or owner has no right of
forcible repossession even as against a trespasser.[8] It is to be
remarked, however, that a forcible expulsion has been recently
held to be authorized by a clause to that effect in the lease;[9]
which is hardly consistent with its being inherently a wrong;
and in another late case that the tenant's possession must be

---

[1] Reeder v. Purdy, 41 Ill. 279.   [2] 48 Ill. 280.

[3] Reeder v. Purdy, sup., and see Page v. De Puy, 40 Ill. 512; Phillips v.
Springfield, 39 Ill. 86.

[4] Dustin v. Cowdry, 23 Vt. 631.   [5] 32 Vt. 82.

[6] Reeder v. Purdy, 48 Ill. 261; Farwell v. Warren, 51 Ill. 467; Ill. R. R. v.
Cobb, 68 Ill. 53.

[7] Haskins v. Haskins, 67 Ill. 446, where title was not relied upon, but defendant abused the process he entered under; Chicago v. Wright, 32 Ill. 192; Huf-
talin v. Disner, 70 Ill. 205; Doty v. Burdick, 83 Ill. 473, where the process was
forcible entry and detainer; Dearlove v. Herrington, 70 Ill. 251, where the tenant's
term had not ended.

[8] Farwell v. Warren; Ill. R. R. v. Cobb; Doty v. Burdick, supra.

[9] Fabri v. Bryan, 80 Ill. 182.

more than temporary and be under a claim of right;[1] and again that where the tenant had no title he should not have trespass *quare clausum*, but only damages for the personal expulsion.[2]

10 *b*. But whatever may be the weight to be attached to these decisions in the jurisdictions where they were declared, they find no more support in the law of the other States than in that of the English courts. The weight of authority seems clearly to be in favor of the common-law right of the owner of land to recover by force possession of his premises of which another is wrongfully in possession, provided no more force is employed than becomes necessary to overcome the resistance made by the tenant to prevent his regaining such possession, especially if his entry is peaceable.[3] Thus in Maine, notwithstanding a dictum in earlier cases already referred to,[4] the court put the right of the owner of a dwelling-house who has gained entry into the same peaceably to expel a tenant wrongfully holding it as being " the same as where any person having entered a dwelling-house refuses to quit when requested." " Every man's house is his castle. But his neighbor's house where he has no right to be is not his castle." " The trespasser in his neighbor's castle must remove or be removed."[5] So in Kentucky it is held that the English statutes of forcible entry and detainer " have ever been so construed as not to affect the common-law right of justifying in an action of trespass *quare clausum* the forcible entry by pleading and proving a right of entry, and hence *liberum tenementum* has notwithstanding those statutes been always held to be an effectual plea to the action of trespass."[6] In New York the rule laid down in the emphatic language of Nelson, C. J., " statutes of forcible entry and detainer punish criminally the force and in some cases make restitution, but so far as civil remedy goes there is none whatever,"[7] has been consistently

---

[1] Ill. R. R. v. Cobb, 82 Ill. 183. [2] Comstock v. Brosseau, 65 Ill. 39.

[3] Sterling v. Warden, 51 N. H. 239, where the text is cited with approval.

[4] Moore v. Boyd, 24 Me. 242; Brock v. Berry, 31 Me. 293. In both these cases the tenancy was at will and not at sufferance, and tenant's possessory right had not been terminated.

[5] Stearns v. Sampson, 59 Me. 568.

[6] Trible v. Frame, 7 J. J. Marsh. 601. [7] Jackson v. Farmer, 9 Wend. 201.

adhered to.[1] In Massachusetts since the early cases of Sampson *v.* Henry and Meader *v.* Stone, already cited, which may be regarded as the leading cases in that State, the same rule has been enforced by repeated decisions,[2] and in a quite recent and very fully considered case it has in the broadest manner been held that the landlord may both forcibly enter and forcibly expel.[3]

11. A tenant at sufferance is not entitled to notice to quit before the summary process for his removal provided by statute, or an action of ejectment, is commenced, where the tenant holds over after the determination of his lease.[4] In Michigan, tenants at will and at sufferance are put on the same basis as to notice, in determining the tenancy, unless the tenancy at sufferance has become such by the determination of a tenancy by notice. But the court were divided on the point whether, after a sale and foreclosure of a mortgage, the mortgagor is entitled to notice before the purchaser can commence proceedings to remove him.[5]

---

[1] People *v.* Field, 52 Barb. 198 ; s. c. 1 Lans. 242.

[2] Mugford *v.* Richardson, 6 Allen, 76 ; Winter *v.* Stevens, 9 Allen, 526, 530 ; Merriam *v.* Willis, 10 Allen, 118 ; Pratt *v.* Farrar, Ib. 519, 521 ; Morrill *v.* De la Granja, 99 Mass. 383 ; Clark *v.* Keliher, 107 Mass. 406.

[3] Low *v.* Elwell, 121 Mass. 309, where the language of Comm'th *v.* Haley, 4 Allen, 318, is restricted ; Stone *v.* Lahey, 133 Mass. 426.

[4] Hollis *v.* Pool, 3 Met. 350 ; Mason *v.* Denison, 11 Wend. 612 ; Young *v.* Smith, 28 Mo. 65 ; Howard *v.* Carpenter, 22 Md. 25. The notice to quit referred to is the formal notice heretofore referred to in cases of tenancies at will or from year to year. They cannot, however, be treated as trespassers until they have been notified of the owner's demand for the premises. But for this purpose the briefest period is sufficient. Arnold *v.* Nash, 126 Mass. 397. In New York the statute requiring notice to terminate a tenancy "by sufferance," only applies where a tenant has held over for so long a time as to raise a presumption that he has the assent of the lessor so to do. Smith *v.* Littlefield, 51 N. Y. 543. But in Michigan it requires three months' notice to determine either estates at sufferance or will. Bennett *v.* Robinson, 27 Mich. 32.

[5] Allen *v.* Carpenter, 15 Mich. 34.

SECTION II.

LICENSE.

1. Of easements.
3. Licenses and easements, distinctions between.
2, 4, 5. Licenses executory and executed.
6. Executed licenses excuse acts done.
7, 8. What licenses revocable.
9. What operates to revoke a license.
10. May be revoked, if merely to do acts on licenser's land.
10 a. Instances of revocable licenses.
10 b. When equity restrains a revocation.
11. Easements created only by deed or prescription.
12. Not revocable if connected with property in chattels.
13. May be irrevocable if to affect licenser's easement only.
14, 15. Effect of revocation upon rights of the parties.

1. THE subjects of Easement and License are so nearly related to leases and tenancies of lands, in some of their characteristics, that it seems proper to notice this relation, since it is sometimes difficult to distinguish between them[1] An easement is always distinct from the occupation and enjoyment of the land itself, and in this respect differs altogether from the interest of a lessee. It is a liberty, privilege, or advantage in land, without profit, distinct from an ownership of the soil, and rests upon a grant by deed or writing, the existence and execution of which may be inferred by a length of enjoyment, to which is applied the term prescription.[2] It is an incorporeal * hereditament, susceptible of a [*398] permanent enjoyment by one man in another's land, such as that of way, or light, or air.[3]

2. A license is an authority to do a particular act or series of acts upon another's land, without possessing any estate therein.[4] A license to do a thing includes the doing what-

[1] Dolittle v. Eddy, 7 Barb. 74.

[2] 3 Kent, Com. 452; Gale & Whatley, Easements, 12; Dolittle v. Eddy, 7 Barb. 74; Morse v. Copeland, 2 Gray, 302; Blaisdell v. Railroad, 51 N. H. 485.

[3] Termes de la Ley, "Easement."

[4] Cook v. Stearns, 11 Mass. 533; Tayler v. Waters, 7 Taunt. 374; Mumford v. Whitney, 15 Wend. 380; Wolfe v. Frost, 4 Sandf. Ch. 72; Bridges v. Purcell, 1 Dev. & B. 496; Blaisdell v. Railroad, 51 N. H. 485. Hence, if the land is taken

ever is necessary to accomplish it, as, for example, to remove
a heavy object, the licensee may employ the necessary men
and means to do it.[1] But it does not relieve the licensee from
responsibility for acts done carelessly or unskilfully.[2] It may
be granted upon condition precedent; and upon the licensee's
failing to perform this his license will become inoperative
and of no effect.[3]

3. An easement implies an interest in the land which can
only be created as above stated, by writing, or, constructively,
its equivalent, — prescription. A license may be created by
parol, as it passes no interest in the land, though a permission
to use, occupy, or take the profits of land, is sometimes called
a license, but is more in the nature of a lease.[4] It matters
not whether the license be oral or in writing, in respect to its
being parol, if the paper giving it have no requisites of a grant.[5]
A license is often implied by the act of the owner of land:
" The publican, the miller, the broker, the banker, the wharf-
inger, the artisan, or any professional man whatever, licenses
the public to enter his place of business in order to attract
custom, but when the business is discontinued, the license is at
an end," per Gibson, C. J., illustrating the doctrine that when
one opens a way across his land from one public thoroughfare
to another, it would be regarded as a license to pass over it.[6]
So a familiar intercourse between families may be evidence
of a general license to pass over the land of each other for
the purpose of visiting.[7] And one has a license to enter a

by eminent domain, the licensee has no claim for damages. Clapp v. Boston, 133
Mass. 367.

[1] Sterling v. Warden, 51 N. H. 227.

[2] Selden v. Del. Canal Co., 29 N. Y. 640.

[3] Mumford v. Whitney, 15 Wend. 380 ; Pratt v. Ogden, 34 N. Y. 22.

[4] Wood v. Leadbitter, 13 M. & W. 838 ; 3 Kent, Com. 452 ; Gale & Whatley,
Ease. 20 ; King v. Horndon, 4 M. & S. 562 ; Dolittle v. Eddy, 7 Barb. 74 ;
Washb. Ease. 5 ; Ex parte Coburn, 1 Cow. 568 ; Wallis v. Harrison, 4 M. & W.
543 ; Thomas v. Sorrell, Vaughan, 351 ; Bailey v. Stephens, 12 C. B. N. s. 111 ;
Muskett v. Hill, 5 Bing. N. C. 694.

[5] Blaisdell v. Railroad, 51 N. H. 485 ; Dodge v. McClintock, 47 N. H. 383 ;
Wiseman v. Lucksinger, 84 N. Y. 31.

[6] Gowen v. Phila. Exch. Co., 5 W. & S. 141, 143 ; Kay v. Penn. R. R., 65
Penn. St. 273 ; Root v. Comm'th, 98 Penn. St. 170.

[7] Martin v. Houghton, 45 Barb. 258 ; Adams v. Freeman, 12 Johns. 408.

post-office at proper hours to inquire for and receive mail-matter.[1]

4. But it is proposed in this chapter to treat only of the subject of licenses. These are of two kinds, one called executory, where the act licensed to be done is yet to be performed, the other executed where it has been done. The distinction is an important one, as bearing upon the right of the licenser to revoke the license.

5. So long as it is executory, it may be revoked at the pleasure of the licenser, for, from its very nature, it is essentially different from a grant in respect to carrying with it the means of being enforced by legal or equitable process.[2] Where A and B mutually gave each other a license to do acts upon the other's land, it was deemed to be an executory one, even though one may have expended money upon the other's land, relying upon such license. And A may revoke the license on his part, even if B do not on his.[3] And where no time is fixed within which the license is to be exercised, it must be within a reasonable time.[4]

6. If it has been executed, it has the effect to relieve or excuse him who may have done the act from liability on account of the same, as well as from the consequences thereof, which may arise prior to a revocation of the license.[5] Thus, if one by license of another tears down an existing mill-dam, or digs and lays an aqueduct in the other's land, or cuts a tunnel in his land, by which the water of a stream is diverted, or cuts down * a tree in the other's land, and the like, [*399] no action will lie in favor of such land-owner, how-

---

[1] Sterling v. Warden, 51 N. H. 231.

[2] Cook v. Stearns, 11 Mass. 533 ; Rumford v. Whitney, 15 Wend. 380 ; Miller v. Aub. & S. R. R., 6 Hill, 61 ; Sterling v. Warden, 51 N. H. 227; Veghte v. Baritan Co., 19 N. J. Eq. 142, 154.

[3] Dodge v. McClintock, 47 N. H. 383 ; Houston v. Laffee, 46 N. H. 505.

[4] Hill v. Hill, 113 Mass. 103.

[5] Cook v. Stearns, 11 Mass. 533 ; Sampson v. Burnside, 13 N. H. 264 ; Hewlins v. Shippam, 5 B. & C. 221 ; Stevens v. Stevens, 11 Met. 251 ; Foot v. N. Haven & North. Co., 23 Conn. 214 ; Wood v. Leadbitter, 13 M. & W. 838 ; Byron v. Blakeman, 22 Barb. 336 ; Selden v. Del. Canal Co., 29 N. Y. 639. See Web v. Paternoster, Palmer, 71, a case of a license not revocable ; Barnes v. Barnes, 6 Vt. 388 ; Snowden v. Wilas, 19 Ind. 13 ; Pratt v. Ogden, 34 N. Y. 20.

ever much he may be injured by such act.[1] Nor does it make any difference that the license in such case is given by parol, since the statute of frauds does not apply to executed licenses like these.[2]

7. Questions of the most difficulty in respect to licenses arise, where the one who grants, seeks to revoke the license, after the party to whom it was given has enjoyed or exercised it, and especially where he has incurred expense thereby, as in erecting costly structures upon the land of the licenser, or upon his own land, affecting the land of the licenser. Many dicta and decisions upon this class of cases are to be found in the books. Thus, it is said, " A license under seal, provided it be a mere license, is as revocable as a license by parol," and " a license by parol, coupled with a grant, is as irrevocable as a license by deed, provided only that the grant is of a nature capable of being made by parol."[3] But even if the license be so granted as to be effectual, it will be strictly construed, and a license to build a dam upon the licenser's land does not carry a license to rebuild, if it is destroyed.[4]

8. If the parties, in case a license were revoked, would be left in the same condition as before it was given, the proposition seems to be a general one, that the licenser may revoke it at his pleasure. Such would be the case in respect to a license to fish in another's water, or to hunt in his park, or to use a carriage-way, and the like.[5]

9. A license is generally so much a matter of personal trust

---

[1] Prince v. Case, 10 Conn. 378 ; Fentiman v. Smith, 4 East, 107 ; Sampson v. Burnside, 13 N. H. 264 ; Kent v. Kent, 18 Pick. 569 ; Bridges v. Purcell, 1 Dev. & B. 496 ; Pratt v. Ogden, sup.

[2] Tayler v. Waters, 7 Taunt. 374 ; Woodbury v. Parshley, 7 N. H. 237 ; Walter v. Post, 6 Duer, 363. The authority of the two former cases is denied as to the irrevocability of such a license, post, pl. 10 a.

[3] Wood v. Leadbitter, 13 M. & W. 845, per Alderson, B. See also Jackson v. Babcock, 4 Johns. 418 ; Wood v. Manley, 11 Ad. & E. 34 ; Wallis v. Harrison, 4 M. & W. 538 ; Williamston, &c. R. R. v. Battle, 66 N. C. 545. See as to this post, pl. 12.

[4] Cowles v. Kidder, 24 N. H. 364 ; Carleton v. Redington, 21 N. H. 293 ; Wingard v. Tift, 24 Ga. 179. There is an able discussion of the subject of this section, especially so much of it as relates to flowing lands, by Judge Cooley of Michigan, in 2 Bench and Bar, N. S. 97–106.

[5] Sampson v. Burnside, 13 N. H. 264 ; Liggins v. Inge, 7 Bing. 682 ; Wood v. Leadbitter, 13 M. & W. 838.

and confidence that it does not extend to any one but the licensee. The death of either party will, of itself, revoke it. So would a transfer or alienation of the interest of the licenser or licensee in the subject-matter of the license.[1] Thus where one sold standing trees by parol, it was held to be a license to the vendee to enter and cut them. But he could not sell the trees standing to a third person and transfer his license to him, because it was in its nature personal.[2]

*10. Another class of cases where the license may [*400] be revoked is where the act licensed to be done is to be done upon the land of the licenser, and if granted by deed would amount to an easement therein. If such license be by parol, it may be revoked as to any act thereafter to be done, even though in order to enjoy it the licensee may have incurred expenses upon the premises of the licenser Thus where A, by B's license, laid an aqueduct across B's land, who then revoked it, and cut off the pipe that conducted the water, the court, as a court of equity, refused to interfere, because B had a right to revoke the license at his pleasure.[3] And in another case, the licensee not only had laid an aqueduct, but dug a well to supply it upon the land of the licenser, and was without remedy, though the licenser cut it off.[4] In another, the licensee, under a license to enter upon land, had expended money thereon and incurred expense on account of the same, and it was held revocable.[5]

. 10 a. The importance of the principle involved in the foregoing propositions in respect to the power of a licenser to revoke his license, even though the licensee, acting under

---

[1] Ruggles v. Lesure, 24 Pick. 187 ; Prince v. Case, 10 Conn. 375 ; Jackson v. Babcock, 4 Johns. 418; Emerson v. Fisk, 6 Me. 200 ; Cowles v. Kidder, 24 N. H. 364 ; Coleman v. Foster, 1 Hurlst. & N. 37 ; Wolfe v. Frost, 4 Sandf. Ch. 93; Wickham v. Hawker, 7 M. & W. 77 ; Duchess of Norfolk v. Wiseman, cited 7 M. & W. 77 ; Wallis v. Harrison, 4 M. & W. 538 ; Harris v. Gillingham, 6 N. H. 9; Carleton v. Redington, 21 N. H. 293 ; Snowden v. Wilas, 19 Ind. 13 ; Blaisdell v. Railroad, 51 N. H. 485.

[2] Howe v. Batchelder, 49 N. H. 204; Johnson v. Skillman, 29 Minn. 95.

[3] Owen v. Field, 12 Allen, 457 ; Selden v. Del. Canal Co., 29 N. Y. 639 ; Wiseman v. Lucksinger, 84 N. Y. 31 ; Eggleston v. N. Y. &c. R. R., 35 Barb. 162.

[4] Houston v. Laffee, 46 N. H. 507 ; Marston v. Gale, 24 N. H. 176.

[5] Hetfield v. Cent. R. R., 29 N. J. 571.

such license, may have incurred expense for which he can claim no remuneration, seems to render a review of some of the cases, where the question has been raised, proper by way of illustration. In one class of these, the licensee at a considerable expense cut a drain in the licenser's land, by which the water of a spring flowed to his own land, and, after enjoying it some years, the licenser revoked the license and stopped it. The licensee was held to be without remedy.[1] In another, the licenser gave the licensees permission to construct a culvert on their land, and thereby divert a current of water on to his land which they did at their own expense, and it was held to be revocable.[2] In another, the license was to build a dam, or part of it, on the licenser's land, for the purpose of working a mill belonging to the licensee.[3] And in another, the license was to flow the licenser's land for raising a head of water to work licensee's mill.[4] And in both, the licenses were held revocable, without remedy to the licensee for the expenses incurred. But in the case of Smith v. Goulding, cited above, it was held that the owner of the dam would not be liable in damages, after the license had been revoked, for keeping the same where it was until he had a reasonable time in which to remove it. In another class of cases the license has been to erect and maintain a house on the licenser's land, and, in some cases, the revocation has been before the building was completed, in others after it had been erected, and in both the builder was obliged to remove it without any right to claim compensation for loss.[5] A license to use a way

[1] Cocker v. Cowper, 1 Cr. M. & R. 418 ; Hewlins v. Shippam, 5 B. & C. 221 ; Sampson v. Burnside, 13 N. H. 264 ; Fentiman v. Smith, 4 East, 107.

[2] Foot v. N. Haven & North. Co., 23 Conn. 223.   See Mason v. Hill, 5 B. & Ad. 1.

[3] Mumford v. Whitney, 15 Wend. 380; Cook v. Stearns, 11 Mass. 533; Smith v. Goulding, 6 Cush. 155 ; Addison v. Hack, 2 Gill, 221 ; Cowles v. Kidder, 24 N. H. 364 ; Stevens v. Stevens, 11 Met. 251 ; Trammell v. Trammell, 11 Rich. 474.

[4] Hazleton v. Putnam, 3 Chand. (Wisc.) 117; Bridges v. Purcell, 1 Dev. & B. 492 ; Thompson v. Gregory, 4 Johns. 81 ; Carleton v. Redington, 21 N. H. 293 ; Hall v. Chaffee, 13 Vt. 150, 157 ; Woodward v. Seeley, 11 Ill. 157, 165 ; Clute v. Carr, 20 Wisc. 533.

[5] Jamieson v. Millemann, 3 Duer, 255; Prince v. Case, 10 Conn. 378; Jackson v. Babcock, 4 Johns. 418 ; Bachelder v. Wakefield, 8 Cush. 252 ; Harris v. Gillingham, 6 N. H. 9 ; Benedict v. Benedict, 5 Day, 464.

was held to be of the same character, although the licensee might have incurred expense upon the licenser's land in constructing a causeway for the purposes of the way.[1] So a license to cut trees on the licenser's land, though in writing, may be revoked.[2]   On the other hand, there is a class of cases where the courts of some of the States have been disposed to hold that a license, to the enjoyment of which it was necessary to expend money upon the licenser's land, could not be revoked without first reimbursing this expenditure, and doing what is equivalent to restoring the licensee *in statu quo*.[3]   But it is justly remarked in a case in New York,[4] that if the doctrine of the irrevocability of an executed license maintained in some jurisdictions [5] is law, a parol license executed or acted upon is sufficient to pass an incorporeal hereditament, thus not merely repealing the statute of frauds, but abolishing the rules of the common law that such an estate can only be conveyed by a deed.   And the court, in Jamieson *v.* Millemann, cited below, declare the case of Tayler *v.* Waters to be conclusively overruled by English and American cases. The case of Wood *v.* Leadbitter was this : The owner of land, on which was a stand for the spectators at a horse-race, sold a ticket to the plaintiff to enter and witness the race.   Before the race was over, without any misconduct on the part of the plaintiff, or tendering him back the admission fee, the owner ordered him to leave the premises, and afterwards removed him ; and it was held that his ticket was a mere license which was revocable.[6]   And the same doctrine of a right in the ven-

---

[1] *Ex parte* Coburn, 1 Cow. 568 ; Foster *v.* Browning, 4 R. I. 47 ; Dexter *v.* Hazen, 10 Johns. 246 ; Wallis *v.* Harrison, 4 M. & W. 538.

[2] Tillotson *v.* Preston, 7 Johns. 285 ; Giles *v.* Simonds, 15 Gray, 441.   But if coupled with a sale, *aliter* if executed and query if executory also. *Post*, pl. 12.

[3] Rhodes *v.* Otis, 33 Ala. 600 ; Addison *v.* Hack, 2 Gill, 221 ; Woodbury *v.* Parshley, 7 N. H. 237.

[4] Wolfe *v.* Frost, 4 Sandf. Ch. 90.

[5] See Tayler *v.* Waters, 7 Taunt. 384 ; Woodbury *v.* Parshley, *supra*.   And see the same doctrine laid down in Pennsylvania, Indiana, Iowa, Nebraska, and perhaps some other States, *post*, pl. 10 n, *ad fin.*

[6] Wood *v.* Leadbitter, 13 M. & W. 838 ; and see the same case for a criticism upon Tayler *v.* Waters, *sup.* ; Coleman *v.* Foster, 1 Hurlst. & N. 37.   To the above cases may be added, upon the general subject of revoking licenses, Fuhr *v.* Dean, 26 Mo. 119 ; Ford *v.* Whitlock, 27 Vt. 268 ; Hays *v.* Richardson, 1

dor of a ticket, to revoke the license it gives to witness an exhibition, was applied in case of a play at the theatre and at a concert. But in such a case, the purchaser would be entitled to damages in an action of assumpsit for a breach of contract. So where, by a parol license, one had gone on and excavated another's land for minerals, at great expense, and, while pursuing the business of mining, was forbidden by the owner, it was held that the latter might revoke the license, and the licensee would be without remedy.[1] In the case of Foster v. Browning,[2] Ames, C. J., remarks, that "in Maine,[3] New Hampshire, Pennsylvania, and Ohio, and perhaps in some other States, the exploded doctrine of some of the earlier English cases is still maintained at law, upon the equitable grounds of estoppel and part performance of a parol contract," and intimates that a court with full equity powers might, in some of those cases, give relief, where the same could not be had at common law. It will be accordingly found in a great number of cases, that in Pennsylvania the courts hold that an executed license, where the licensee has incurred expense, as in erecting a dam upon the licenser's land to operate a mill erected on his own, and the like, is not revocable.[4] The Pennsylvania doctrine rests upon the idea of estoppel, whereby equity treats an executed license as giving an absolute right, because the parties cannot be restored *in statu quo* if it is revoked. But it is limited to cases where something has been done under the license, and it is impossible to restore the licensee *in statu quo*. It would not be so if the licensee had simply paid a consideration for the license.[5] The Pennsylvania doctrine is substantially adopted in Iowa, Indiana, and Nevada. In one case the

Gill & J. 383; Morse v. Copeland, 2 Gray, 302; Williams v. Morris, 8 M. & W. 488.

[1] Desloge v. Pearce, 38 Mo. 599 ; McCrea v. Marsh, 12 Gray, 213 ; Burton v. Scherpf, 1 Allen, 134. See Adams v. Andrews, 15 Q. B. 296. In the case from 12 Gray, Wood v. Leadbitter is sustained, and Taylor v. Waters denied.

[2] 4 R. I. 52, 53.

[3] But see Pitman v. Poor, 38 Me. 237, *contra.*

[4] Rerick v. Kern, 14 S. & R. 267 ; Wheatley v. Chrisman, 24 Penn. St. 298 ; Strickler v. Todd, 10 S. & R. 74; Lacey v. Arnett, 33 Penn. St. 169; Campbell v. McCoy, 31 Penn. St. 263 ; Swartz v. Swartz, 4 Penn. St. 358.

[5] Huff v. McCauley, 53 Penn. St. 209 ; Wiseman v. Lucksinger, 84 N. Y. 31.

licensee had built a wall partly on the licenser's land.[1]   In another, the licensee had sunk shafts in licenser's land for mines.[2]   In another a railroad was built over that land.[3]   It was held that the license could not be revoked until compensation had been made for the expenses incurred.   But it might be revoked if no money had been expended by the licensee. Nor does a license to mine in another's land confer an exclusive right of property in the ore to be found therein.[4]

10 *b*. To pursue this subject in the light of later decisions, it would seem that courts of equity would restrain the revocation of a license, although the same may be done at common law, where the revocation would work a fraud, or it would construe the license as an agreement to give the right, and compel specific performance by deed as of a contract in part executed.[5]   The language of Bates, Ch., in a case in Delaware,[6] is this : " At law, a license can, under no circumstances, become irrevocable by estoppel, when the effect would be to create an interest in land."   " A mere license affecting lands is, at law, always revocable, even though granted for a valuable consideration, and although the licenser may have expended money under it."   But, as he states, in courts of equity, " equities in land, though not created by any deed, grant, or writing, but springing out of the acts and relations of the parties, are largely enforced."   " But this principle of equitable estoppel proceeds upon the ground of preventing fraud. Its effect, when applied, is to restrain a party from exercising his *legal* right."   And a recent case in New York, cited below, may serve to illustrate the present state of the law.   One having erected a mill-dam, by permission of the owners, across a stream of water, with a view of providing power thereby to work a mill which he erected on his own land, applied to an intermediate land-owner for permission to cut a canal through his land for the purpose of conducting the water from the dam

---

[1] Wickersham *v.* Orr, 9 Iowa, 260.   [2] Beatty *v.* Gregory, 17 Iowa, 114.

[3] Buchanan *v.* Logansport, 71 Ind. 265 ; and see Lee *v.* McLeod, 12 Nev. 280.

[4] Upton *v.* Brazier, 17 Iowa, 157; Snowden *v.* Wilas, 19 Ind. 14; 2 Am. Lead. Cas. 682 and cases.

[5] Veghte *v.* Raritan Co., 19 N. J. Eq. 142, 153 ; Williamston, &c. R. R. *v* Battle, 66 N. C. 546 (1872).

[6] Jackson Co. *v.* Phil. W. & B. R. R. 4 Del. Ch. 180.

to his mill, and obtained a license so to do.   He then mortgaged his land, but said nothing of the mill or privileges, and
the mortgage was foreclosed.   It was held that the mortgage
carried the mill and whatever privileges of water belonged to
it.   But, as the license to cut and maintain the canal was by
parol, it might be revoked at any time by the owner of the
land, although the mill had been run by means of the water
more than twenty-five years.   Hogeboom, J., was inclined to
adopt the Pennsylvania doctrine, and hold the license irrevocable ; but the court sustained the opposite doctrine, Johnson, J., denying that it came within the principle on which
equity acts.[1]   In Georgia it would be held in equity an irrevocable license.[2]   In Illinois, where the owner of a house, having
a wall adjacent to another's land, gave him license to erect a
wooden house on his own premises, and make use of the wall
for that purpose, and he did so, the court held the license was
irrevocable at law both as to the licensee and his grantee.[3]
But this case has been questioned in later cases in the same
State,[4] and the rule laid down in an early decision [5] reaffirmed that there is no equitable relief for one who has con
structed a dam under a license to flow another's land, upon
the revocation of the license by the latter.   The same doctrine
is held in Minnesota, where the revocation of the license to
flow destroyed the value of the mill erected by the licensee on
his own land and upon the faith of the grant of the license.[6]

11. The doctrine of the revocability of licenses rests upon
the familiar principle, that a freehold interest in lands can
only be created or conveyed by deed ; and, as before stated,
an easement in the land of another cannot be created, except
by deed, or what is equivalent, — prescription.[7]

---

[1] Babcock v. Utter, 1 Abbot, App. 27–60, in which the foregoing text is
referred to.   So Wiseman v. Lucksinger, 84 N. Y. 31.

[2] Cook v. Prigden, 45 Ga. 331.

[3] Russell v. Hubbard, 59 Ill. 337.

[4] Kamphouse v. Gaffner, 73 Ill. 453, 461 ; Tanner v. Volentine, 75 Ill. 624.

[5] Woodward v. Seeley, 11 Ill. 157.

[6] Johnson v. Skillman, 29 Minn. 95.   So in Maine, Pitman v. Poor, 38 Me.
237.

[7] Wood v. Leadbitter, 13 M. & W. 838, impugning the case of Tayler v. Waters, 7 Taunt. 374, and explaining Wood v. Manley, 11 Ad. & E. 34 ; Morse v.
Copeland, 2 Gray, 302 ; Stevens v. Stevens, 11 Met. 251 ; Foot v. N. Haven &

*12· But there are licenses which are irrevocable, [*401] though they relate to land and are by parol ; as where, for instance, the license is directly connected with the title to personal property which the licensee acquires from the licensor at the time the license is given, whereby the license is coupled with an interest. Thus, where one sells personal chattels on his own land, and, before a reasonable time to remove them, forbids the purchaser to enter and take them, it was held to be a license which he could not revoke within such reasonable time.[1] So, where A cut hay upon B's land upon shares, and stored it in B's barn upon the premises, by his permission, B could not revoke his license to A to come and divide it and carry off his share.[2] And, where one gave another license to cut trees on his land, at an agreed price, to be carried away, the vendor could not revoke the license to remove such of them as had been cut under it. But until cut the owner may revoke the license, and a conveyance of the land to a third party by deed would operate as such a revocation, as soon as known to the licensee, who would thereupon become a trespasser by afterwards cutting the trees.[3] So where the owner of land sold it, reserving the trees standing and down upon it, with a right, for three years, to cut and carry them away. It was held that all that he cuts in that time are personal property, and he may carry them away afterwards, but would thereby be liable in trespass *quare clausum* for going upon the land. And the same principle applies if one man's cattle are on another man's land without his permission.[4]

North. Co., 23 Conn. 223; Jamieson v. Millemann, 3 Duer, 255; Cook v. Stearns, 11 Mass. 533 ; Gale & Whatley. Ease. 19 ; Id. 45; Dolittle v. Eldy, 7 Barb. 74 ; Selden v. Del. Canal Co., 29 N. Y. 639 ; Clute v. Carr, 20 Wisc. 533.

[1] Whitmarsh v. Walker, 1 Met. 316 ; Nettleton v. Sikes, 8 Met. 34 ; Wood v. Manley, 11 Ad. & E. 34 ; Wood v. Leadbitter, 13 M. & W. 856 ; Am. ed. n.; Marshall v. Green, 1 C. P. Div. 35 ; Parsons v. Camp, 11 Conn. 525 ; Claflin v. Carpenter, 4 Met. 580, 583. But see Williams v. Morris, 8 M. & W. 488 ; Giles v. Simonds, 15 Gray, 442 ; Sterling v. Warden, 51 N. H. 227.

[2] White v. Elwell, 48 Me. 360.

[3] Drake v. Wells, 11 Allen, 143, 144; Giles v. Simonds, 15 Gray, 441; Coleman v. Foster, 1 Hurlst. & N. 37 and notes; Roffey v. Henderson, 17 Q. B. 586; Wescott v. Delano, 20 Wisc. 516, 517 ; but see Marshall v. Green, *supra ;* also *ante*, B. 1, ch. 1, pl. 8.   [4] Town v. Hazen, 51 N. H. 596.

13. The license may be irrevocable when executed, though it be given by parol, and affects the land of the licenser, if the act licensed be done on the licensee's land and its only effect be to impair or destroy an easement in the licenser's land, which that, as the dominant estate, has enjoyed in or out of the land of the licensee as the servient estate. Thus, where A gave B license to erect his house so near A's [*402] ancient house * as to obstruct his light and air, and B built accordingly, A could not revoke the license, though he was thereby deprived of these easements. But if in order to enjoy the license it is necessary to exercise a right of easement by using the licenser's land, it is a revocable one, as where in the case above cited, the licensee, in order to raise the pond for his mill, was obliged to flow back the water upon the licenser's land. In the one case, the licenser does an act, or, what is the same, authorizes it to be done, which extinguishes what he had before enjoyed in another's estate. In the other, in order to enjoy the license, the licensee must occupy the land of the licenser.* [1]

* NOTE. — By statute in Massachusetts, a mill-owner has a right to flow land of another under certain circumstances, being liable to pay damages therefor. It was held that where such land-owner, for a valuable consideration, consented to the mill-owner's flowing his land without further claim for damages, it could not be revoked. Seymour v. Carter, 2 Met. 520. The license in Morse v. Copeland, 2 Gray, 302, was to erect a dam upon the licensee's own land, which restricted the extent of the easement of flowing the same, belonging to the licenser, and held irrevocable after it had been executed. In Winter v. Brockwell, 8 East, 308, the license was to erect a sky-light on licensee's land, which obstructed the light and air from coming to licenser's house ; the license was held irrevocable after the sky-light had been erected. In Liggins v. Inge, 7 Bing. 682, the license was to lower the bank of a stream in the licensee's land, and erect a weir thereon, which diverted a portion of the water of the stream from the licenser's mill below. It was held that permitting this diversion to be made was in effect an abandonment of the natural flow of the stream ; and it having been done at the expense of the licensee on his own land, the license could not be revoked, nor the right thus abandoned resumed.

[1] Morse v. Copeland, 2 Gray, 302 ; Addison v. Hack, 2 Gill, 221 ; Dyer v. Sandford, 9 Met. 395 ; Liggins v. Inge, 7 Bing. 682 ; Hazleton v. Putnam, 3 Chand. (Wisc.) 124 ; Winter v. Brockwell, 8 East, 308 ; Hewlins v. Shippam, 5 B. & C. 221 ; Jamieson v. Millemann, 3 Duer, 255 ; Moore v. Rawson, 3 B. & C. 332 ; Foot v. N. Haven & North. Co., 23 Conn. 223; Gale & Whatley, Ease. 20 ; Cocker v. Cowper, per Parke, B., 1 Cr. M. & R. 420 ; Veghte v. Raritan Co., 19 N. J. Eq. 153.

14. Where, under a license which has been revoked, the licensee before such revocation has made improvements upon the licenser's land by labor or money expended thereon,
equity * will not allow the licenser to avail himself of [*403] these, without restoring the licensee to as good a situation as he stood in before he entered upon the execution of the license.[1]

15. And where, by such revocation, the structure erected by the licensee on the licenser's land acquires the character of personal property, as in case of a house erected under the license, the licensee has an interest in the same, and may remove the structure within a reasonable time. And to that extent the license would be irrevocable.[2] But whether the licenser, upon revoking the license, can compel the licensee to restore the premises to their original condition at his expense or not, depends upon the circumstances of the case.* [3]

---

* Note. — The subject of licenses is further treated of in Angell on Watercourses, c. 8, and 2 Am. Lead. Cas. 514–538, 1st ed.

---

[1] Hazleton v. Putnam, 3 Chand. (Wis.) 117 ; Story, Eq. Jur. § 1237 ; Angell, Watercourses, § 318 ; Short v. Taylor, cited 2 Eq. Cas. Abr. 522.

[2] Barnes v. Barnes, 6 Vt. 388 ; Wood v. Leadbitter, 13 M. & W. 856, Am. ed. n. ; Ashmun v. Williams, 8 Pick. 402.

[3] Prince v. Case, 10 Conn. 375 ; Stevens v. Stevens, 11 Met. 251.

1. AFTER treating of estates in respect to their quantity,
the next subject in the order of the work proposed is the

quality of these estates, or the manner in which the right of
enjoyment may be exercised, as either by one alone, as a tenancy in severalty, or by several under the names of joint-
tenants, coparceners, or tenants in common.[1] A tenancy in
severalty exists, as the term implies, where one has the right
to enjoy an estate separately by himself.[2] It is customary to
treat of joint-tenancy, coparcenary, and tenancy in common,
under separate heads. But the first two apply to so limited
an extent to estates in this country, and the three have so
many things in common, that it is proposed to discuss them
all in a single chapter.

2. A JOINT-TENANCY is defined to be " when several persons
have any subject of property jointly between them in equal
shares by purchase." " Each has the whole and every part
with the benefit of survivorship, unless the tenancy be severed."[3] In the quaint language of the law they hold, each
per my et per tout, the effect of which, technically considered,
is, that, for purposes of tenure and survivorship, each is the
holder of the whole. But for purposes of alienation, each has
only his own share.[4] And the shares of several joint-tenants,
as well as of tenants in common, are always presumed to be
equal.[5] If the grant of one parcel of land to two persons defines the share and interest which each is to take, it creates
an estate in common, and not a joint-tenancy.[6]

3. While, moreover, joint-tenants constitute but one person
in respect to the estate, as to the rest of the world,
between * themselves each is entitled to his share of [*407]
the rents and profits so long as he lives, but subject
to the right of the survivor or survivors to take the entire
estate upon his death, to the exclusion of his heirs or personal
representatives.[7]

[1] 1 Prest. Est. 22.
[2] 1 Prest. Est. 130 ; 2 Bl. Com. 179.   The term *entirety* as applied to estates,
it will be seen, is used to describe the interest of husband and wife as joint-owners
of an estate.
[3] 1 Prest. Est. 136 ; Co. Lit. 180 b.
[4] 1 Prest. Est. 136 ; Wms. Real Prop. 112 ; Co. Lit. 186 a.
[5] Shiels *v.* Stark, 14 Ga. 429.
[6] Craig *v.* Taylor, 6 B. Mon. 457 ; Penton *v.* Lord, 128 Mass. 466.
[7] Wms. Real Prop. 109 ; Lit. § 281.

4. There may be a joint-tenancy whether the estate be in fee, for life, for years, or at will,[1] and also of estates in re-mainder.[2] So there may be a joint-tenancy in an estate for life, though the reversion or remainder be in only one of the tenants; and if he who has the reversion in fee die first, his heir will be postponed as to his enjoyment of the estate until after the decease of the other joint-tenant.[3]

5. But a joint-tenancy can only be created by purchase or act of the parties, and not by descent or act of the law. It must, moreover, be created by one and the same act, deed, or devise, and joint disseisors may be joint-tenants.[4]

6. A joint-tenancy at common law must have a fourfold unity as it is called, namely, of interest, of title, of time, and of possession, — the interest being acquired by all, and by the same act or conveyance, commencing at the same time, and held by the same undivided possession.[5] But under the law of uses, as well as by will, the unity of time may be so far dispensed with as to allow two or more joint-tenants to take their shares at different times.[6]

7. The great distinctive characteristic of joint-tenancies among estates of which there is a joint-ownership is the right of survivorship, by which, though the estate is limited to them and their heirs, the survivor or survivors take the entire estate, to the exclusion of the heirs or representatives of the deceased co-tenant.[7] Two corporations, therefore, cannot be joint-ten-ants. If they jointly own land, they are tenants in common of the same.[8]

       8. By the common law, in England, if an estate is [*408]   *conveyed to two or more persons without indicating how the same is to be held, it will be understood to be in joint-tenancy, upon the feudal idea that the services due to the lord should be kept entire, though equity is inclined to

---

[1] 2 Bl. Com. 179 ; 2 Flint. Real Prop. 322.
[2] Co. Lit. 183 b.   [3] Lit. § 285.
[4] 2 Bl. Com. 180 ; Lit. §§ 277, 278 ; Putney v. Dresser, 2 Met. 583.
[5] 2 Bl. Com. 180.
[6] Wms. Real Prop. 112 ; 2 Prest. Abst. 67.
[7] Lit. § 280 ; 2 Bl. Com. 183.
[8] Dewitt v. San Francisco, 2 Cal. 289.

regard such estates as tenancies in common, especially where the parties have advanced money upon the estate.[1]

9. But the policy of the American law is opposed to the notion of survivorship, and therefore regards such estates as tenancies in common. In many of the States the rule of survivorship is abolished by statute, except in the case of joint trustees, or mortgagees, while in others all estates to two or more persons are taken to be tenancies in common, unless expressly declared to be joint tenancies by the deed or instrument creating them, with a similar exception of estates to joint-trustees or mortgagees. Thus the statute of Massachusetts makes conveyances or devises of estates to several, tenancies in common, unless expressly declared to be joint-tenancies, or, what is equivalent, except in cases of trusts, mortgages, or where the grantees or devisees are husband and wife.[2]

10. And the court of that State waive the question whether joint disseisors are tenants in common,[3] though they had previously treated them as joint-tenants, and held that, if either abandons, the other should have the entire estate.[4] But where the devise was to children, and the survivor or survivors of them, it was held to be an estate in joint-tenancy.[5] In Maryland a similar rule prevails as in Massachusetts, while in Ohio and Connecticut the estate of joint-tenancy does not exist.[6] *

* NOTE. — In the following States every estate granted or devised to two or more persons in their own right is construed to be a tenancy in common ; or survivorship is abolished ; or each joint-tenant's share descends, and is chargeable

[1] 2 Flint. Real Prop. 324; Rigden v. Vallier, 3 Atk. 734; Wms. Real Prop. 109, Rawle's note. It is said by Williams that the principal use of a joint-tenancy now in England is for the purpose of vesting estates in trustees, who are there invariably made joint-tenants. Wms. Real Prop. 111; Duncan v. Forrer, 6 Binn. 193.

[2] Pub. Stat. c. 126, § 5 ; Webster v. Vandeventer, 6 Gray, 428; Appleton v. Boyd, 7 Mass. 131; Jones v. Crane, 16 Gray, 308. But now, by statute, in Massachusetts, a conveyance to husband and wife does not create a joint-tenancy, unless it is expressed to be to the grantees or devisees jointly, or as joint-tenants, or in joint-tenancy, or to them and the survivor of them. Stat. 1885, c. 237.

[3] Fowler v. Thayer, 4 Cush. 111.

[4] Putney v. Dresser, 2 Met. 583 ; Allen v. Holton, 20 Pick. 458.

[5] Stimpson v. Batterman, 5 Cush. 153.

[6] Purdy v. Purdy, 3 Md. Ch. Dec. 547; Miles v. Fisher, 10 Ohio, 1; Walker, Am. Law, 292 ; Phelps v. Jepson, 1 Root, 48. For the statute laws of the several States on this subject, the reader is referred to the accompanying note.

[*409]   *11· Among the incidents of a joint-tenancy growing out of the identity of interest and title of the

with his debts, namely, Ɽassachusetts, Pub. Stat. c. 126, § 5[1]; Ɽaine, Rev. Stat.
1884, c. 73, § 7 ; New Hampshire, Gen. Stat. 1867, c. 121, § 14 ; Vermont, Gen.
Stat. 1863, c. 64, § 2 ; Rhode Island, Pub. Stat. 1882, c. 172, § 1 ; New Jersey, Rev. 1877, p. 167 ; New York, Rev. Stat. 1863, vol. 1, p. 676, vol. 3,
p. 14, § 44 ; Ɽichigan, Gen. Stat. 1882, §§ 5560, 5561 ; Ɽinnesota, Stat. 1878,
c. 45, § 44 ; Wisconsin, Rev. Stat. 1878, §§ 2068, 2069 ; Kentucky, Gen. Stat.
1873, pp. 531, 586 ; Tennessee, Stat. 1871, § 2010 ; Illinois, Rev. Stat. 1883,
c. 76, § 1 ; Delaware, Laws 1874, c. 86, § 1 ; Arkansas, Dig. 1874, § 3590 ; Mississippi, Rev. Code, 1880, § 1197 ; Ɽissouri, Gen. Stat. 1872, c. 140 ; Colorado,
Gen. Laws, 1877, c. 18, § 162 ; California, Hittell's Codes, 1876, § 6380 ; 7 Cal.
Rep. 347 ; Indiana, Rev. Stat. 1881, §§ 2922, 2923 ; Iowa, Rev. Code, 1880, § 1939
(husband and wife take as tenants in common, Hoffman *v.* Stigers, 28 Iowa,
302), Ɽaryland, Rev. Code, 1878, art. 45, § 3 ; Oregon, Gen. Laws, 1872, c. 6 ;
W. Virginia, Rev. Stat. 1878, c. 82, §§ 18, 19 ; Pennsylvania, Purd. Dig. 1872,
p. 815 ; Kennedy's Appeal, 60 Penn. St. 511, 516 ; North Carolina, Code 1883,
§§ 1326, 1502 ; Georgia, Code 1882, § 2300 ; Alabama Code, 1876, § 2191 ; Texas,
Rev. Stat. 1879, art. 1655.

In Ɽassachusetts, Ɽichigan, Wisconsin, Indiana, Ɽississippi, and Ɽinnesota,
joint-tenancies may exist as to mortgages, in case of devises or conveyances in
trust, and where, from the tenor of the instrument creating the estate, it is manifestly intended to create an estate in joint-tenancy. See the statutes above cited ;
also Nichols *v.* Denny, 37 Ɽiss. 59. The same provisions exist in Vermont and
West Virginia, except as to mortgages ; while in New Hampshire, New Jersey,
Ɽaryland, and Iowa, the only exception by statute is where the intent to create
a joint-tenancy is express on the face of the conveyance. In Ɽaine, when the
conveyance is by mortgage, or in trust, to two or more persons, with power to
appoint a successor in case one dies, it is construed a joint-tenancy. unless the
contrary is expressed, but otherwise is a tenancy in common. The only exceptions in New York, Illinois, Delaware, Ɽissouri, Arkansas, Colorado, and California, to the general rule above stated, where the joint-tenancy is not expressly
declared, arise in cases where estates are vested in executors or trustees. These
are held in joint-tenancy. In Virginia and Kentucky, the doctrine of survivorship is virtually abolished, as the share of each co-tenant, at his death, descends
to his heirs, or may be devised. Estates held by two or more as executors or trustees, and estates where the conveyance expresses the intention that the part of the
one dying shall go to the survivor, are excepted. Code, 1873, c. 112, §§ 18, 19 ;
Kentucky, Gen. Stat. 1873, c. 63, art. 1, § 13. The right of survivorship is abolished in Tennessee, Georgia, Texas, Florida, North Carolina, Alabama, and Pennsylvania. But, in Pennsylvania, there is an exception in case of estates in trustees ;
in North Carolina of estates in executors ; and the courts of Alabama hold that the
statute does not apply to trusts and estates held in *autre droit.* Parsons *v.* Boyd,
20 Ala. 112. In South Carolina, the right of survivorship is not recognized. 1
Brev. Dig. 435 ; but see Ball *v.* Deas, 2 Strobh. Eq. 24. In Rhode Island the
exception to the statute abolishing survivorship does not extend to devises or
conveyances to husband and wife, and only applies to devises or conveyances
where the instrument manifestly indicates an intention on the part of the devisor

_____
[1] See also Stat. 1885, c. 237.

several tenants *are these : that an entry or re-entry [*410]
made by one is deemed to be the entry of all, unless
clearly shown to be adverse towards his co-tenants; so livery
of seisin made to one is made to all ;[1] and the occupation by
one co-tenant is *prima facie* an occupation by all.[2] But, inasmuch as it is competent for them to sever their interests, each,
should he hold a separate and distinct portion of their common estate for the term of twenty years, would thereby acquire
an estate in severalty, unless such holding was by mutual
agreement.[3]

12. Upon the same principle of identity of interest, if one
joint-tenant purchases in an adverse title to the joint estate, or
acquires an older legal title, it will enure to the benefit of his
co-tenants, if they will contribute *pro rata* towards defraying
the expenses thereof.[4] And where a member of an existing
company purchases for the uses of the company, he cannot
sell it to the company at an enhanced price without disclosing
the facts ; the profits made belong to the company.[5] But one
co-tenant may purchase and become assignee of a mortgage
upon the common property, and hold as mortgagee against
his co-tenant.[6]

13. Another consequence is that a joint-tenant can neither
sue nor be sued alone in respect to their joint estate, if advantage of the omission to join his co-tenants be properly taken.[7]

14. The interest which a joint-tenant has as survivor is not
a new one acquired by him from his co-tenant, upon the latter's death; for his own interest is not changed in amount,
but only his co-tenant's is extinguished.[8]

or grantor to create an estate in joint-tenancy. So in Kentucky, Mississippi, and
West Virginia, survivorship in conveyances to husband and wife is abolished ;
while in Indiana and Wisconsin the joint character of such conveyances is expressly saved. And in Ohio, joint-tenancy, with a right of survivorship, never
existed. Sergeant *v.* Steinberger, 2 Ohio, 305 (1 Ohio, 423).

[1] Co. Lit. 49 b ; 2 Cruise, Dig. 377.
[2] Wiswall *v.* Wilkins, 5 Vt. 87 ; Small *v.* Clifford, 38 Me. 213.
[3] Taylor *v.* Cox, 2 B. Mon. 429 ; Drane *v.* Gregory, 3 B. Mon. 619.
[4] Picot *v.* Page, 26 Mo. 398 ; Gossam *v.* Donaldson, 18 B. Mon. 230 ; Brittin
v. Handy, 20 Ark. 381 ; *post*, p. *430 ; Brown *v.* Hogle, 30 Ill. 119.
[5] Densmore Co. *v.* Densmore, 64 Penn. St. 43.
[6] Blodgett *v.* Hildreth, 8 Allen, 188.
[7] Lit. § 311 ; Webster *v.* Vandeventer, 6 Gray, 428. [8] 2 Flint. Real Prop. 330.

15. No charge, therefore, like a rent, or a right of way, or a judgment, created by one co-tenant, can bind the es-
[*411] tate in the * hands of the survivor unless the charge be created by the one who becomes such survivor, or the creator of the charge releases his estate to a co-tenant, who, as releasee, accepts, with that part of the estate, the charge inhering therein by his own act.[1]

16. The relation, however, between joint-tenants is such, that, if either wastes the joint estate, the other may have an action of waste against him, by the statute of Westminster II. c. 22.[2] And in several of the States there are statutes giving joint-tenants actions of waste in similar cases.[3] If one of two joint-tenants flow the joint land, so as to appropriate it to himself, the other may have an action against him as for an ouster.[4]

17. Though thus united in their ownership, either tenant may convey his share to a co-tenant, or even to a stranger, who thereby becomes tenant in common with the other co-tenant. If the conveyance be by one of two joint-tenants to the other, the estate is turned into one in severalty. But if there be more than two, the purchaser remains joint-tenant with the others, as to their original shares, and tenant in common as

---

[1] Lit. § 286 ; Co. Lit. 185 b ; 2 Prest. Abst. 58 ; 65, 66 ; Tud. Cas. 724 ; Lord Abergaveny's Case, 6 Rep. 78.

[2] 2d Inst. 403 ; Shiels *v.* Stark, 14 Ga. 429.

[3] In Missouri, each tenant is liable to his co-tenant for the damage done, and to treble damages if the jury find that the act was wantonly committed. Stat. 1872, c. 85, § 46. A similar provision exists in Virginia. Code, 1873, c. 133. In Massachusetts each joint-tenant will be liable, without first giving thirty days' notice to his co-tenants in writing, to pay treble damages for waste committed on the premises. Pub. Stat. 1881, c. 179, § 7. A like provision exists in Maine. Rev. Stat. 1871, c. 95, § 5. In Rhode Island, if he commit waste without the consent of his co-tenant, he forfeits double the amount of the waste. Rev. Stat. 1872, c. 220, § 2. In New York, the co-tenant in such case may have the judgment for treble damages, and elect to recover these, or have partition of the estate, and have their amount set out to him from the defendant's share. Stat. 1863, vol. 2, p. 346. In New Jersey there is a similar statute, except that the damages are single. Rev. 1877, p. 1236. In California, such co-tenant may recover treble damages for waste done. Wood, Dig. 1858. In Michigan, the tenant committing waste is liable for double damages. Comp. Laws, 1871, c. 197, §§ 3, 6. In Wisconsin, the law is the same. Rev. Stat. 1858, c. 143. And see *post,* 723, 724.

[4] Jones *v.* Weathersbee, 4 Strobh. 50.

to the share acquired by purchase.[1] In conveying his interest to a stranger, * a joint-tenant, like a tenant in [*412] common, must do so by deed of grant with words of inheritance, if it is intended to pass an estate in fee. Whereas, in conveying to his co-tenant, a release is not only sufficient, but is the proper form of making such conveyance ; nor need there be any words of inheritance in the same, since the one to whom the conveyance is made is already seised of the estate as a whole, and it is only necessary to extinguish the right of his co-tenant in order to invest him with the exclusive ownership of the entire estate.[2] But a deed of grant from one joint-tenant to another would be effectual as a release in vesting the entire ownership in the grantee.[3] So, a mortgage by a joint-tenant of his share to a stranger would be effectual against survivorship, and may amount to a severance of the joint estate.[4]

18. But a devise by one joint-tenant of his share will be inoperative, inasmuch as the right of survivorship takes precedence of such devise. And so far does this principle prevail, that if such devisor be himself the survivor, he must republish his will after the survivorship has accrued, in order to give it effect.[5]

19. As a general proposition, estates given to two or more trustees will be held by them as joint-tenants, and will go to the survivor, nor will the heirs of any but the survivor be entitled to hold any interest in the joint estate.[6] And this will be found to apply in most of the States, even where the right of survivorship as to ordinary joint estates has been abolished by law.[7] Though it may be remarked that conveyances are

---

[1] Lit. §§ 292, 294, 304 ; 2 Prest. Abst. 61 ; Co. Lit. 273 b ; Tud. Cas. 724.

[2] Wms. Real Prop. 112, 113 ; 2 Prest. Abst. 61 ; Rector v. Waugh, 17 Mo. 13.

[3] Eustace v. Scawon, Cro. Jac. 696 ; Chester v. Willan, 2 Saund. 96.

[4] York v. Stone, 1 Salk. 158, s. c. 1 Eq. Cas. Abr. 293 ; Simpson v. Ammons, 1 Binn. 175.

[5] Duncan v. Forrer, 6 Binn. 193 ; 2 Prest. Abst. 67 ; Lit. § 287. In Co. Lit. 185 b, the rule of law is stated *jus accrescendi præfertur ultimæ voluntati.*

[6] Hill, Trust. 303, and Wharton's note of Am. cases ; Wms. Real Prop. 111 ; Rabe v. Fyler, 10 S. & M. 440 ; Webster v. Vandeventer, 6 Gray, 428 ; the case of an assignment of a mortgage to trustees.

[7] Parsons v. Boyd, 20 Ala. 112 ; Wms. Real Prop. 111, Rawle's note.

often made, in such cases, with an intention to create a joint-
tenancy, which fails, when technically considered, to
[*413] answer that end.   * Thus deeds and devises are often
made to two or more, and to the survivor of them and
his heirs, the effect of which is to make them joint-tenants
for life, with a contingent remainder in fee to the one who
survives.[1]

20. It may also be further remarked that it is a rule in
equity, that if an estate be conveyed to several in unequal
shares, in consequence of their having contributed unequally
towards the purchase, they become tenants in common, and
not joint-tenants.[2]

21. And another incidental remark which has been previously explained is, that there can be neither dower nor curtesy
of an estate held in joint-tenancy, the right of the survivor
taking precedence of that of the husband or the wife of the
deceased co-tenant.[3]

22. There are various ways of terminating joint-tenancies,
some of which have already been spoken of ; as by the estate
being wholly vested in one by survivorship, or being changed
into a tenancy in common, by alienation of his share by one of
the tenants.   So it might have been by a voluntary partition
of the estate among the co-tenants, each taking his part, to
be held thereafter in severalty without any right of survivorship.   But there was no compulsory process by the common
law to effect such partition, nor was it supplied until the
stat. 31 Hen. VIII. c. 1, and 32 Hen. VIII. c. 32.   The
subject of partition by process of law will be treated of in
the latter part of this chapter.   An illustration of the effect
of a partition is, that if there are two joint-tenants for life,
and partition be made between them, the reversioner, instead
of having to wait till the death of both before entering upon
any part of the estate, may enter and possess himself of the
part of either immediately upon his decease, and will hold
that in severalty.[4]

---

[1] Vick v. Edwards, 3 P. Wms. 372 ; Co. Lit. 191, Butler's note, 78 ; Ewing
v. Savary, 3 Bibb, 235 ; Watkins, Conv., White's ed. 208, n.

[2] Tud. Cas. 721 ; Burton, Real Prop. § 1524, n.

[3] Co. Lit. 37 b.   [4] 2 Flint. Real Prop. 334.

SECTION II.

COPARCENARY.

1. Estates in coparcenary defined.
2, 3. Distinction between coparceners and joint-tenants.
4. Of conveyance by coparceners.
5. Coparceners may devise their estates.
6. When heirs take as tenants in common.

1. OF estates in coparcenary, or, as commonly called, parcenary, little more need be said than to give some idea of their nature and incidents, because of their infrequency as subjects of reference in this country.   The term is applied to estates of which two or more persons form one heir, as is the case in England, where, in the absence of sons, several daughters together form the heir to the ancestor's estates ; or where several sons take as one heir by the custom of gavelkind.[1]

2. While joint-tenancies refer to persons, the idea of coparcenary refers to the estate.   The title to it is always by descent.   The respective shares may be unequal, as, for instance, one daughter and two grand-daughters, children of a deceased daughter, may take by the same act of descent.   As to strangers, the tenants' seisin is a joint one, but, as between themselves, each is seised of his or her own share, on whose death it goes to the heirs, and not by survivorship.[2]   The right of possession of coparceners is in common, and the possession of one is, in general, the possession of the others.[3]

3. And the relation of a tenant to the estate may be such, that he may be a parcener with himself, as, for instance, where one half of an estate descends to him from the father, and one half from the mother.   If, in such case, he die without lineal descendants, the half of the estate that came to him from his father descends to his father's heirs, while the other descends to the heirs of his mother.[4]

---

[1] 2 Bl. Com. 188.
[2] 2 Bl. Com. 188 ; Watkins, Conv. 143, Coventry's note ; Purcell v. Wilson, 4 Gratt. 16.
[3] I Prest. Est. 137 ; Manchester v. Doddrige, 3 Ind. 360 ; 2 Prest. Abst. 70.
[4] Watkins, Conv. 145, Coventry's note.

4. One parcener might convey his share to a third
[*415] person, * who would become thereby a tenant in common with the other parceners as to such share. But
to do this, a deed of feoffment, or grant with words of inheritance, was requisite in order to convey a fee. Whereas, by a
deed of release, one parcener might convey to his coparcener,
and a fee might be created without words of inheritance, since
he already has a seisin in fee of the estate by descent.[1] One
præcipe to recover the estate lay against them all.[2]

5. One parcener may dispose of his share by his last will,
nor will a devise thus made be affected by his subsequently
making a partition of the estate.[3] The name parcener is said
to have been derived from the power that either had to compel the other to make partition at common law,[4] a power still
incident to the estate, and which will be treated of hereafter.

6. But as in some of the States children and heirs take by
descent expressly as tenants in common, and as such is constructively the effect of a descent in most if not all the States,
the distinction of estates in coparcenary is of comparatively
little practical importance, and properly gives place to the
familiar form of joint estates in universal use, tenancy in
common.*

---

* NOTE. — In Maryland, children take the estates of parents in fee, as coparceners. Hoffar *v.* Dement, 5 Gill, 132.

---

[1] Co. Lit. 273 b, Rector *v.* Waugh, 17 Mo. 13 ; Watkins, Conv. 145, Coventry's note ; 1 Prest. Est. 138 ; Gilpin *v.* Hollingsworth, 3 Md. 190.

[2] Co. Lit. 174 a.   [3] 2 Prest. Abst. 72.

[4] Lit. § 241.

SECTION III.

TENANTS IN COMMON.

1. A TENANCY in common is where two or more hold possession of lands or tenements at the same time by several and distinct titles. The quantities of their estate may be different, their proportionate shares of the premises may be unequal, the modes of acquiring these titles may be unlike, and the only *unity between them be that [*416] of possession. Thus one may hold in fee, and another for life; one may acquire his title by purchase, and another by descent; one may hold a fifth, and another a twentieth, and the like.[1] And there may be a tenancy in common among several owners of a remainder.[2]

2. Each owner in respect to his share has all the rights, except that of sole possession, which a tenant in severalty would have; and if he wishes to convey his share to his co-tenant, he must do so by the same kind of deed that would be necessary to convey it to a stranger. A mere technical release would not, as in cases of joint-tenancy and coparcenary, have that effect.[3] He may manage his part of the

---

[1] 2 Bl. Com. 191; 1 Prest. Est. 139; Co. Lit. 189, 1; Lit. § 292; 2 Flint. Real Prop. 345.

[2] Coleman v. Lane, 26 Ga. 515.

[3] Co. Lit. 193 a, n. 80; 2 Flint. Real Prop. 349; 2 Prest. Abst. 77. For the rights of joint owners of a lake for sailing, fishing, and the like, see Menzies v. Macdonald, 36 E. L. & Eq. 20.

estate as he pleases, provided he does not injure his co-tenant in so doing.[1] But if he build buildings, or make improvements upon the common property, he may not charge them to his co-tenant, though, as will appear hereafter, sometimes partition of the estate is so made as to give him such improvements.[2] On the other hand, where one co-tenant cut timber upon the common estate, and sawed it into fencing materials at a mill upon the estate, and used it for constructing fences and making repairs upon the same, it was held that his co-tenant had no claim upon him for the property so taken and used.[3]

3. What would be necessary in a deed or will to constitute a tenancy in common, where several persons are grantees or devisees of an estate, is often a nice question of law, but it may be generally stated that, in this country, wherever two or more persons acquire the same estate by the same act, deed, or devise, and no indication is therein made to the contrary, they will hold as tenants in common.[4] Thus, where commissioners confirmed claims to the same land to two different persons, they took equal shares in common,[5] and the same would be the effect of two simultaneous conveyances to different persons.[6] So where two creditors made simultaneous levies on land, as they took at the same time with equal rights, they were held to be tenants in common in equal shares.[7] So if several persons take by descent.[8] If one joint-tenant convey his share of the estate to a stranger, the alienee and the other tenant become tenants in common, as has been before stated, and the same would be the effect if one who held in severalty

[1] Peabody v. Minot, 24 Pick. 329, 333.

[2] Thurston v. Dickinson, 2 Rich. Eq. 317 ; post, p. *427.

[3] Walker v. Humbert, 55 Penn. St. 408.

[4] Miller v. Miller, 16 Mass. 59 ; Gilman v. Morrill, 8 Vt. 74 ; Martin v. Smith, 5 Binn. 16 ; Partridge v. Colegate, 3 Har. & McH. 339 ; Briscoe v. McGee, 2 J. J. Marsh. 370 ; Wiswall v. Wilkins, 5 Vt. 87 ; Evans v. Brittain, 3 S. & R. 135 ; Hoffman v. Lyons, 5 Lea, 377.

[5] Challefoux v. Ducharme, 8 Wisc. 287.

[6] Young v. DeBruhl, 11 Rich. 638. See Clark v. Brown, 3 Allen, 509; Aldrich v. Martin, 4 R. I. 520, case of two mortgages.

[7] Shove v. Dow, 13 Mass. 529 ; Cutting v. Rockwood, 2 Pick. 443 ; Durant v. Johnson, 19 Pick. 544 ; Sigourney v. Eaton, 14 Pick. 414.

[8] Johnson v. Harris, 5 Hayw. (Tenn.) 113 ; 4 Kent, Com. 367.

were to convey one-half or any other share of his estate to another, without designating the part by metes and bounds, that
is, he would become tenant in common with his alienee.[1] So
if the owner of a parcel of land convey so many acres of it to
one, and so many to another, amounting together to the full
number of acres in the parcel, his grantees would take, as
tenants in common, the shares which their respective number
of acres bore to the entire parcel.[2] So where A granted one
acre of woodland, lying in common with his other woodland,
it was held to be such an aliquot part of his woodland in common as one acre would be to the whole woodland owned by the
grantor.[3] And, upon a similar principle, where a deed of a
given quantity of land, parcel of a larger tract, does not locate
it by its description, the purchaser becomes a tenant in common, *pro rata*, in the whole parcel.[4]

4. As has been heretofore stated, the husband or
wife of a * tenant in common of an estate of inherit- [*417]
ance is entitled to curtesy or dower out of the share
of such co-tenant.[5]

5. Although each tenant in common has so general a power
of alienation of his share, and may convey any aliquot portion
of his share, yet, as a general proposition, he may not convey
his share in any particular part of the estate so held by metes
and bounds, if objected to by his co-tenant,[6] though it would
be valid and effectual as against himself and all persons claiming under him. And the reason is, that such a conveyance
impairs the rights of his co-tenant in respect to partition.
Instead of giving him his share together in one parcel, by a
single partition, it would require him to have several, and to
take his share in as many distinct parcels. And, by analogy,
the same rule applies when the share of a tenant in common

---

[1] Lit. § 299 ; Adams v. Frothingham, 3 Mass. 352.

[2] Preston v. Robinson, 24 Vt. 583. See vol. 3, *622.

[3] Jewett v. Foster, 14 Gray, 496; Phillips v. Tudor, 10 Gray, 82 ; Battel v.
Smith, 14 Gray, 497 ; Gibbs v. Swift, 12 Cush. 393 ; Small v. Jenkins, 16 Gray,
158.

[4] Schenck r. Evoy, 24 Cal. 110 ; Jackson v. Livingston, 7 Wend. 136; Lick
v. O'Donnell, 3 Cal. 63 ; *post*, vol. 2, p. *622.

[5] 2 Flint. Real Prop. 347.

[6] Marks v. Sewall, 120 Mass. 174.

is set off to satisfy an execution against him.* ¹   The grant
of a specific portion of a larger joint estate, or the levy of an
execution on such portion, conveys no interest in common to
the grantee or creditor in the general estate.²   Thus, where
one tenant in common of a larger lot conveyed sixty-four rods
thereof, it was held to pass nothing, it being without bounds,
and not to be held in common with the lot generally.³   So in
a deed of one co-tenant's share of the common estate, a reservation of his share of the mines in the same, would be void.⁴
Nor can one of several joint owners of land dedicate it to the
public.⁵   Nor can he create an easement upon or over the
common estate.   Nor, if he owns land adjoining the common
estate, can he so use the latter in connection with the former
as to acquire an easement over the common estate in favor of
his private estate, though he might estop himself from claiming damages if the use is made by another.⁶   Where one has
conveyed a specific part of an estate, of which he is tenant in
common with others, the conveyance may be made good by
the other co-tenants releasing to him their interest in such
portion.   Or, if partition be made, the portion thus conveyed

---

* NOTE. — In Ohio and Maryland, a tenant in common may convey his share
in a particular part of the estate, and a levy may be made in the same manner.
Treon v. Emerick, 6 Ohio, 391 ; White v. Sayre, 2 Ohio, 110 ; Reinicker v.
Smith, 2 Har. & J. 421.

---

¹ Brown v. Bailey, 1 Met. 254 ; Peabody v. Minot, 24 Pick. 329 ; Bartlet v.
Harlow, 12 Mass. 348 ; Baldwin v. Whiting, 13 Mass. 57 ; Rising v. Stannard,
17 Mass. 282 ; Griswold v. Johnson, 5 Conn. 363 ; Duncan v. Sylvester, 24 Me.
482 ; Jewett v. Stockton, 3 Yerg. 492 ; Varnum v. Abbot, 12 Mass. 474 ;
Nichols v. Smith, 22 Pick. 316 ; Jeffers v. Radcliff, 10 N. H. 242 ; Staniford v.
Fullerton, 18 Me. 229 ; Smith v. Knight, 20 N. H. 9 ; Challefoux v. Ducharme,
4 Wise. 554 : Great Falls Co. v. Worster, 15 N. H. 412 ; Whitton v. Whitton, 38
N. H. 127 ; McKey v. Welch, 22 Tex. 390 ; Good v. Coombs, 28 Tex. 51 ; Blos-
som v. Brightman, 21 Pick. 283, 285 ; Primm v. Walker, 38 Mo. 97 ; but see
Barnhart v. Campbell, 50 Mo. 599.

² Soutter v. Porter, 27 Me. 405 ; Great Falls Co. v. Worster, 15 N. H. 412.

³ Phillips v. Tudor, 10 Gray, 82 ; post, vol. 3, p. *622.

⁴ Adam v. Briggs Iron Co., 7 Cush. 361.

⁵ Scott v. State, 1 Sneed, 629 ; Holcomb v. Coryell, 11 N. J. Eq. 548 ; Dorn
v. Dunham, 24 Tex. 376.   The same rule under the civil law, 1 Domat, Pt. 1,
B. 2, Tit. 5, § 2, art. 6.

⁶ Crippen v. Morss, 49 N. Y. 67.

falls to him as a part of all his property.[1] The court of Michigan hold that a conveyance by one co-tenant of a specific part of the land held in common with others would be good as to all persons except his co-tenants, and only voidable as to them where it works an injury to them, and cite cases from Virginia and New Jersey as sustaining the same doctrine.[2] But they hold unqualifiedly, that, if there are co-tenants of separate and distinct parcels of estate, it is competent for one of them to convey his interest in one of these to the exclusion of the others, or his creditor might levy his execution upon the debtor's interest in one or more of these as separate estates,[3] and refer to Peabody v. Minot,[4] as sustaining the same doctrine.

6. So distinct is the interest of one tenant in common from that of his co-tenant, that, if they join in making a lease, it is regarded as a demise by each of his own part.[5]

7. But their possession being common, and each having a right to occupy, not only will such possession, though held by one alone, be presumed not to be adverse to his co-tenant, but it is, ordinarily, held to be for the latter's benefit, so far as preserving his title thereto, the possession of one tenant in common being deemed to be the possession of all.[6] It was held to be a fraud in one co-tenant to suffer the common

---

[1] Johnson v. Stevens, 7 Cush. 431 ; Cox v. McMullin, 14 Gratt. 84 ; Cameron v. Thurmond, 56 Tex. 27 ; Boggess v. Meredith, 16 W. Va. 1 ; Barnhart v. Campbell, 50 Mo. 599. In other States the courts only recognize such grantee as a necessary party to a partition. Harlan v. Langham, 69 Penn. St. 238 ; Whitton v. Whitton, 38 N. H. 133.

[2] Campau v. Godfrey, 18 Mich. 39 ; Robinett v. Preston, 2 Robin. 273 ; McKee v. Barley, 11 Gratt. 340 ; Holcomb v. Coryell, 11 N. J. Eq. 548 ; and see preceding note. In California the same rule has been fully adopted. Gates v. Salmon, 35 Cal. 588 ; Sutter v. San Francisco, 36 Cal. 115.

[3] Butler v. Roys, 25 Mich. 53, 58.

[4] 24 Pick. 329.

[5] 2 Prest. Abst. 77 ; post, pl. 18. Cf. McKinley v. Peters, 111 Penn. St. 283.

[6] Co. Lit. 199 b ; Colburn v. Mason, 25 Me. 434 ; German v. Machin, 6 Paige, 288 ; Lloyd v. Gordon, 2 Har. & McH. 254 ; Brown v. Wood, 17 Mass. 68 ; Barnard v. Pope, 14 Mass. 434 ; Catlin v. Kidder, 7 Vt. 12 ; M'Clung v. Ross, 5 Wheat. 116 ; Allen v. Hall, 1 McCord, 131 ; Thomas v. Hatch, 3 Sumn. 170 ; Clymer v. Dawkins, 3 How. 674 ; Poage v. Chinn, 4 Dana, 50 ; Story v. Saunders, 8 Humph. 663 ; Thornton v. York B'k, 45 Me. 158.

property to be sold for taxes, and to purchase it in himself ;[1]
and if he do so, the tax title enures to the common
[*418] benefit.[2] Nor can one * co-tenant sue another to try
the title to the lands in question, unless he shall have
been disseised and kept out of possession by the defendant ;[3]
and inasmuch as one has an equal right with the other to hold
the papers or documents relating to the common estate, the
one out of possession of these cannot maintain any action
against the other for the recovery of them.[4]

8. But a tenant in common may be disseised by his co-
tenant's actually ousting or holding him out of possession
under a claim of an exclusive right of possession, and a denial
of the right of the tenant, but this must be known expressly
or by implication to the tenant.[5] One tenant in common may
maintain a process for forcible entry and detainer against another co-tenant who has evicted him from the premises.[6] But
it is difficult to determine by any fixed rule what constitutes
a disseisin, especially between tenants in common. The possession of one is the possession of all, unless by an actual
ouster or an exclusive pernancy of profits, against the will of
the others, one shall manifest an election to hold the land by
wrong, rather than by a common title.[7] And this would be

---

[1] Brown v. Hogle, 30 Ill. 119 ; Bender v. Stewart, 75 Ind. 88. So where the
possessory title was in several, and one of them bought in the legal fee. Bosko-
witz v. Davis, 12 Nev. 446.

[2] Flinn v. McKinley, 44 Iowa, 68 ; Austin v. Barrett, Ib. 488 ; Allen v. Poole,
54 Miss. 323 ; unless special circumstances exist to rebut the co-tenant's claim,
King v. Rowan, 10 Heisk. 675.

[3] Martin v. Quattlebam, 3 McCord, 205.

[4] Clowes v. Hawley, 12 Johns. 484.

[5] Bracket v. Norcross, 1 Me. 89 ; Doe v. Bird, 11 East, 49 ; Dexter v. Arnold, 3 Sumn. 152 ; Harpending v. Dutch Ch. 16 Pet. 455 ; Willison v. Watkins,
3 Pet. 52 ; Gray v. Givens, Riley, Ch. (S. C.) 41 ; Jackson v. Tibbits, 9 Cow.
241 ; M'Clung v. Ross, 5 Wheat. 116 ; Norris v. Sullivan, 47 Conn. 474 ; Culver
v. Rhodes, 87 N. Y. 348.

[6] Presbrey v. Presbrey, 13 Allen, 284. Cf. Byam v. Bickford, 140 Mass. 31.

[7] Munroe v. Luke, 1 Met. 459 ; Barnard v. Pope, sup. ; Small v. Clifford, 38
Me. 213 ; Corbin v. Cannon, 31 Miss. 570 ; Roberts v. Morgan, 30 Vt. 319 ; Forward v. Deetz, 32 Penn. St. 69 ; Hoffstetter v. Blattner, 8 Mo. 276 ; Meredith
v. Andres, 7 Ired. 5 ; Peck v. Ward, 18 Penn. St. 506 ; Abercrombie v. Baldwin,
15 Ala. 363 ; Johnson v. Swaine, Busbee (N. C.), 335 ; Brock v. Eastman, 28 Vt.
658 ; Owen v. Morton, 24 Cal. 377, 379 ; M'Clung v. Ross, 5 Wheat. 124.

true, so far as the exclusive occupation extended, although it be only a part of the entire common estate.[1] But mere separate occupancy, however long continued, would not affect the rights of the other co-tenants, unless intended to be in exclusion of these, with a view of thereby gaining an adverse right. Thus, where after the death of the father, the several children left the homestead one after another, except one, who continued to occupy and manage it from 1778 to 1822, it was held that such occupancy had nothing adverse in it, and gained no exclusive title for the occupant.[2] Among the acts which have been held to be evidence of a disseisin of one co-tenant by another, is the conveyance of the entire estate by deed to a third party, who enters and occupies the same under such deed.[3] So where one of two co-tenants devised the entire estate by a will to which the other was an attesting witness, and the devisee took possession, it was held to be a disseisin of the co-tenant.[4] And an open and exclusive possession may be so long continued as to be evidence of an original ouster. This was held in one case, where such occupation had been for thirty-six years without accounting for rents or profits. In another case, the holding had been for forty years, while in another twenty-one years were held sufficient.[5] So the flowing of the common land by one of the tenants in common may be equivalent to an ouster of his co-tenants.[6] And where the possession is sole, and under a claim adverse to the co-tenant, the Statute of Limitations begins to run as to all the land held in common by them.[7]

[1] Carpentier v. Webster, 27 Cal. 524, 560 ; Bennett v. Clemence, 6 Allen, 10.

[2] Campbell v. Campbell, 13 N. H. 483.

[3] Bogardus v. Trinity Ch., 4 Paige, 178 ; Bigelow v. Jones, 10 Pick. 161 ; Weisinger v. Murphy, 2 Head, 674 ; Thomas v. Pickering, 13 Me. 337 ; Burton v. Murphy, 2 Tayl. 259 ; Gill v. Fauntleroy, 8 B. Mon. 177 ; Higbee v. Rice, 5 Mass. 344, 352 ; Hinkley v. Greene, 52 Ill. 230 ; Culler v. Motzer, 13 S. & R. 356.   [4] Miller v. Miller, 60 Penn. St. 16, 22.

[5] Doe v. Prosser, Cowp. 217 ; Jackson v. Whitbeck, 6 Cow. 632 ; Frederick v. Gray, 10 S. & R. 182 ; Mehaffy v. Dobbs, 9 Watts, 363.

[6] Jones v. Weathersbee, 4 Strobh. 50 ; Great Falls Co. v. Worster, 15 N. H. 412.

[7] Hubbard v. Wood, 1 Sneed, 279. See Mehaffey v. Dobbs, 9 Watts, 363 ; Larman v. Huey, 13 B. Mon. 436 ; Black v. Lindsay, Busbee (N. C.), 467, where the holding had been but twenty years. Noble v. McFarland, 51 Ill. 230.

9. And where, by agreement of two tenants in common, one occupied a particular part of the common estate in severalty, as of a house, for instance, and the other entered upon it without his consent, it was held that he might have trespass *quare clausum fregit* against his co-tenant for making such entry.[1] If two co-tenants divide their estate, and each enters upon his allotted share and occupies it separately, and to the exclusion of the other, for the period of statute limitation, it will operate as a bar to the claim of either upon the other for the part so occupied by the latter.[2] And it has been held, that, if one co-tenant enters and actually [*419] * ousts the other tenant in common from the premises, the latter may have trespass *quare clausum fregit* for such ouster.[3] Where a railroad company were tenants in common of land with other owners, their co-tenants being a tenant for life and a reversioner in fee, and they purchased the life interest of the co-tenant and then laid their railroad across it, it was held that they had not, by so doing, so ousted the reversioner that, upon the death of the tenant for life, he could maintain ejectment against the railroad company. His only remedy was under the statute.[4] So if one co-tenant erect a building on the common land for his own special use, it is an act of ouster for which a co-tenant may have trespass, or may remove the building from the premises.[5] The rule, however, may be regarded as well-nigh imperative and universal, that one tenant in common may not have trespass *quare clausum* against another. It can never be done unless the party charged has done something inconsistent with the rights of the other co-tenant in the premises.[6] So long as both retain possession, neither can have this action against the other for any act done upon the premises, unless it amount to an unequivocal eviction from,[7] or destruction of, the property

---

[1] Keay *v.* Goodwin, 16 Mass. 1 ; *contra,* McPherson *v.* Seguine, 3 Dev. 153.

[2] Rider *v.* Maul, 46 Penn. St. 380.

[3] Erwin *v.* Olmsted, 7 Cow. 229 ; M'Gill *v.* Ash, 7 Penn. St. 397 ; Booth *v.* Adams, 11 Vt. 156 ; King *v.* Phillips, 1 Lans. 421.

[4] Austin *v.* Rutland, &c. R. R., 45 Vt. 215.

[5] Bennett *v.* Clemence, 6 Allen, 18 ; Stedman *v.* Smith, 8 Ellis & B. 1.

[6] Jones *v.* Chiles, 8 Dana, 163 ; McPherson *v.* Seguine, 3 Dev. 153 ; Lawton *v.* Adams, 29 Ga. 273.   [7] Filbert *v.* Hoff, 42 Penn. St. 97.

itself, **or** some part of it.[1] Trespass, however, lies to recover mesne profits, where one tenant has prevailed against another in a real action to recover his share of a common estate.[2] Mesne profits are only recoverable in England in trespass *quare clausum* after a judgment in ejectment. In this country, in several of the States, they form a part of the judgment recovered in actions for the recovery of the land ; and in Vermont and Massachusetts damages may also be recovered beyond these for acts done by the tenant while wrongfully in possession.[3] But mesne profits may not be recovered beyond six years or the limitation of an action of trespass.[4] Trespass or ejectment, at his election, lies in favor of one co-tenant against another who has actually expelled or ousted him from the premises. But not for merely taking the crops raised upon the common land.[5] Nor for cutting trees upon the common estate. Nor, generally, for an entry upon and enjoyment of the common property.[6]

10. Where a tenant, holding by a deed to him as a tenant in common, ousted his co-tenant, who brought ejectment for such ouster, it was held that the tenant could not set up in defence an adverse title in a stranger.[7]

11. If one co-tenant misuse or destroy the common property, his co-tenant may have an action against him for such misfeasance. But to render him liable as a tort feasor, he must do something more than exercise mere acts of ownership

---

[1] Bennet *v.* Bullock, 35 Penn. St. 364 ; Jewett *v.* Whitney, 43 Me. 242 ; Maddox *v.* Goddard, 15 Me. 218, the two last are cases of destroying mills. Silloway *v.* Brown, 12 Allen, 37 ; Co. Lit. 200 ; Stedman *v.* Smith, 8 Ellis & B. 1 ; Erwin *v.* Olmsted, 7 Cow. 229.

[2] Bennet *v.* Bullock, 35 Penn. St. 367 ; Goodtitle *v.* Tombs, 3 Wils. 118. See Marsh *v.* Hammond, 103 Mass. 150, for the rule of admeasuring the damages recoverable as mesne profits. Sears *v.* Sellew, 28 Iowa, 506, 507 ; Lane *v.* Harrold, 72 Penn. St. 267.

[3] Lippett *v.* Kelley, 46 Vt. 524, 525 ; Mass. Pub. Stat. c. 173, § 12.

[4] Hill *v.* Meyers, 46 Penn. St. 15.

[5] Murray *v.* Hall, 7 C. B. 441, 454 ; Silloway *v.* Brown, 12 Allen, 37. And in an action of ejectment the plaintiff may recover damages and mesne profits, while the defendant may recover for his betterments in such action. Backus *v.* Chapman, 111 Mass. 388.

[6] Hastings *v.* Hastings, 110 Mass. 285.

[7] Braintree *v.* Battles, 6 Vt. 395.

over it, or claim it as his own.[1] Thus, where one co-tenant of
a mill, while in the sole occupation of it, suffered it to be destroyed by his negligence, it was held that he was liable to the
other co-tenants for such destruction.[2] Such is the case where
one co-tenant of a mill erected a dam below the same on his
own private land, and flowed back upon the common mill to
its injury,[3] or authorized another to do this, or to divert the
waters of the stream from the common mill.[4] And where one
co-tenant of a well attempted to go down into it to examine if
it was clean, and the other prevented him, the latter had a
right of action for such obstruction.[5]

12. One tenant in common may have an action of waste
against his co-tenant, under the statute of Westminster II.
c. 22, for waste done on the premises, and by statute, or at
the common law, in the several States.[6] And so held in New
York, if, by the act complained of, the inheritance is permanently injured.[7] And if one co-tenant, while in possession of
the whole estate by consent of the others, threaten to commit
wilful waste, which would work an irremediable mischief,
chancery will interfere to enjoin him.[8]

13. If one tenant cut timber growing upon the common land,
and sell the same and convert it into money, the co-tenants
may recover of him their respective shares of the proceeds of
such sale.[9]

14. So in some cases, one tenant in common may recover from his co-tenant a share of the rents and profits of

[1] Martin v. Knowlys, 8 T. R. 146 ; Wilbraham v. Snow, 2 Saund. 47, n. f, g ;
Farr v. Smith, 9 Wend. 338 ; Co. Lit. 200 ; Hyde v. Stone, 9 Cow. 230 ; Fight-
master v. Beasly, 7 J. J. Marsh. 410 ; Gilbert v. Dickerson, 7 Wend. 449 ; Tubbs
v. Richardson, 6 Vt. 442 ; Harman v. Gartman, Harper, 430.

[2] Chesley v. Thompson, 3 N. H. 9.

[3] Odiorne v. Lyford, 9 N. H. 502 ; Hutchinson v. Chase, 39 Me. 508 ; Pills-
bury v. Moore, 44 Me. 154.

[4] Hines v. Robinson, 57 Me. 328.   [5] Newton v. Newton, 17 Pick. 201.

[6] Co. Lit. 200 b ; 4 Kent, Com. 369, n.; Matts v. Hawkins, 5 Taunt. 20. In
Missouri, Virginia, Maine, Massachusetts, Rhode Island, New Jersey, Michigan,
Wisconsin, and California, the law is the same as to waste by a tenant in com-
mon as by a joint-tenant, for which see the note at the end of this chapter.
Anders v. Meredith, 4 Dev. & B. 199 ; Shiels v. Stark, 14 Ga. 429.

[7] Elwell v. Burnside, 44 Barb. 454. See McCord v. Oakland Q. M. Co., 64
Cal. 134.

[8] Twort v. Twort, 16 Ves. 128, 132.   [9] Miller v. Miller, 7 Pick. 133.

the common *estate. But in order to charge a co- [*420]
tenant for such rents, he must either have been made
the bailiff of the other tenant, and then he would be liable at
common law, or he must have received more than his share of
the rents and profits of the estate, in which case he is liable
under the statute 4 Anne. c. 16.[1]   And this seems to be the
law generally in the United States.[2]   The same rule would
apply though the tenant who occupies the whole premises
were himself the lessee of one of the tenants in common, if
he had not attorned to the other co-tenants.[3]   If one tenant
in common sell hay, or grass growing upon the common estate,
he may recover therefor, although his co-tenant forbids the
purchaser to pay him.   It is a mode of occupying the estate
which he may exercise if he do not prevent his co-tenant from
occupying with him.[4]

15. One co-tenant may be liable to another for rent, or for
use and occupation under an express demise,[5] but there must
be something more than an occupancy of the estate by one
and a forbearance to occupy by the other.   The tenant who
merely occupies the estate does no more than he has a right
to do on his own account.[6]

[1] Co. Lit. 199 a, and Butler's note, 83 ; Peek v. Carpenter, 7 Gray, 283 ; Pico
v. Columbet, 12 Cal. 414 ; the stat. of Anne is not in force there.   Israel v.
Israel, 30 Md. 126.   Gregory v. Connolly, 7 U. C. Q. B. 500.

[2] Jones v. Harraden, 9 Mass. 540 ; Brigham v. Eveleth, 9 Mass. 538 ; Sargent
v. Parsons, 12 Mass. 149 ; Shiels v. Stark, 14 Ga. 429 ; Huff v. M'Donald, 22 Ga.
131 ; Shepard v. Richards, 2 Gray, 424 ; Gowen v. Shaw, 40 Me. 56 ; Dickinson
v. Williams, 11 Cush. 258 ; Munroe v. Luke, 1 Met. 459, 463 ; Izard v. Bodine,
11 N. J. Eq. 403 ; Webster v. Calef, 47 N. H. 289.

[3] Badger v. Holmes, 6 Gray, 118.　　　[4] Brown v. Wellington, 106 Mass. 318.

[5] Cowper v. Fletcher, 6 B. & S. 464 ; Leigh v. Dickeson, 12 Q. B. D. 194 ;
even after the lease expires, Ib. ; Bayley v. Bradley, 5 C. B. 696.

[6] Sargent v. Parsons, 12 Mass. 149 ; Calhoun v. Curtis, 4 Met. 413 ; Norris v.
Gould, 15 W. No. Cas. 187 ; Keisel v. Earnest, 21 Penn. St. 90 ; Kline v. Jacobs,
68 Penn. St. 57 ; Israel v. Israel, 30 Md. 120 ; Everts v. Beach, 31 Mich. 136 ;
Scott v. Guernsey, 60 Barb. 163 ; Balfour v. Balfour, 33 La. Ann. 297 ; Crow v.
Mark, 52 Ill. 332 ; Lyles v. Lyles, 1 Hill, Ch. (S. C.) 85 ; Volentine v. Johnson,
Id. 49.   In South Carolina, in equity, if one tenant occupies and cultivates and
derives profit from more than his share of the estate, he must account for net ex-
cess of profits.   Holt v. Robertson, McMullan, Ch. 475; Hancock v. Day, Id. 298;
Thompson v. Bostick, Id. 75; Edsall v. Merrill, 37 N. J. Eq. 114.   These cases
are disapproved in Pico v. Columbet, 12 Cal. 414; but a similar rule is adopted in
Mississippi in cases of partition.   Medford v. Frazier, 58 Miss. 241.

15 *a.* The court of Vermont consider this subject quite at
length, and point out the rules of the common law, and in what
respect that of Vermont differs.   By the common law, if one
co-tenant occupied the entire estate and took the profits, he
would not be liable to account therefor to his co-tenant.   By
the statute of 4 Anne, c. 16, account lies by one co-tenant
against another " *receiving* more than comes to his just share
and proportion."   It was held in the case cited below [1] that
the statute relates only to cases where one co-tenant receives
money or something else, where another person gives or pays
it, which the co-tenants are entitled to simply by reason of
their being tenants in common, and of which one receives and
keeps more than his just share, according to the proportion
of his interest as such tenant.   This includes cases of leasing
land at a rent, but it does not include occupation merely
without ousting the co-tenant, where no agreement to pay
has been made.   If one merely takes the grass growing and
sells it or uses it, he is not liable to the other tenant under
the statute.   " He is to account when he *receives*, not *takes*,
more than comes to his just share," citing the case below,[2]
and this seems to be the rule in some of the United States.[3]
But in Vermont, where one of several co-tenants of land converted it into a race-course, out of which he made a profit,
and to prepare it cut down and used trees growing upon it,
it was held he was liable to account both for the timber and
the profits of the race-course.[4]

16. In Massachusetts, however, it was held that where one
co-tenant was suffered to occupy the common property and to
plant and raise a crop thereon without objection by the other
tenant, the crop when severed became his individual property,
and that if the other took it when gathered, and carried it
away, or any part of it, he was thereby a trespasser.[5]   But had
the estate been divided between them before the crops were

---

[1] Henderson *v.* Eason, 17 Q. B. 701.   [2] McMahon *v.* Burchell, 2 Phillips, 134.

[3] Jones *v.* Massey, 14 S. C. 292; Jolly *v.* Bryan, 86 N. C. 457; Holmes *v.* Best,
58 Vt. 547.

[4] Hayden *v.* Merrill, 44 Vt. 336.   So in Tennessee, Tyner *v.* Fenner, 4 Lea,
469 ; and in Maine by statute, Richardson *v.* Richardson, 72 Me. 403.

[5] Calhoun *v.* Curtis, 4 Met. 413.

gathered, these would pass to the one to whose share the land on which they were growing was assigned, nor would the doctrine of emblements apply in such case in favor of the one who planted them, since a liability to have partition made is one of the incidents of such estates.[1] Where a claim does arise in favor of one tenant in common against another for occupying the common land, it is a personal one, and does not pass with the estate if such claimant grants his estate to another.[2]

*17. The law, independent of statute, as to the [*421] making of improvements or repairs upon common property, if either co-tenant is unwilling to join in the same, seems to be this: One tenant in common cannot go on and make improvements, erect buildings, and the like, on the common property, and make his co-tenant liable for any part of the same, nor has he a right to hold and use these to the exclusion of his co-tenants.[3] If the property is not susceptible of convenient partition, like a mill or a house, and requires repairs in order to its preservation, either tenant might have a writ at common law, *de reparatione facienda*, to compel his co-tenant to join in making such repairs.[4] But now it seems that such tenant may have a remedy by an action on the case against his co-tenant for refusing, if he shall have himself incurred the expense, after having first notified his co-tenant of such repairs being necessary, and requested him to join in making them.[5] The writ *de reparatione facienda*, is superseded, as to mills, by statute provisions upon the subject in Massachusetts.[6]

17 a. By the later decisions, however, the law upon these subjects seems to have been somewhat modified from what is above laid down in respect to the right which one tenant in

---

[1] Ibid.   [2] Hannan v. Osborn, 4 Paige, 336.

[3] Crest v. Jack, 3 Watts, 239 ; Taylor v. Baldwin, 10 Barb. 582 ; Stevens v. Thompson, 17 N. H. 109 ; Calvert v. Aldrich, 99 Mass. 74, 78 ; Converse v. Ferre, 11 Mass. 325.

[4] Co. Lit. 200 b ; Fitzh. N. B. 295 ; Doane v. Badger, 12 Mass. 65 ; Collin v. Heath, 6 Met. 79.

[5] Doane v. Badger, 12 Mass. 65, a case of a well and pump. Mumford v. Brown, 6 Cow. 475 ; Stevens v. Thompson, *sup.*

[6] Pub. Stat. c. 190, § 59; Carver v. Miller, 4 Mass. 559. As to buying the land at foreclosure, see Calkins v. Steinbach, 66 Cal. 117.

common has to make improvements and repairs upon the
common estate, and charge a part of it to his co-tenant.   The
court in Calvert *v.* Aldrich[1] review the cases, especially Doane
v. Badger, and, regarding the writ *de reparatione facienda* as
obsolete, they conclude that, " between tenants in common,
partition is the natural and usually the adequate remedy in
every case of controversy," and that, independent of any express agreement, neither in England nor this country " an
action at law of any kind has been sustained either for contribution or damages, after one has made needful repairs in which
the other refused to join," and approve of the law as laid down
in Converse *v.* Ferre, *sup.* The same rule prevails in England
unless the repairs are needed to prevent ruinous decay.[2]   In
New York it has been held, that, if a tenant in common of a
reversion erect buildings on the premises, he has no claim
in any form on account of the same against his co-tenant.[3]
In Maryland the court disallowed expenses incurred by one
co-tenant for improvements made, which " were not incurred
for the preservation of the property." [4]   In Pennsylvania, where
equitable remedies are sought through the forms of the common
law, one tenant may recover of his co-tenant for expenditures
which were necessary to the enjoyment of the property ; he
cannot for improvements made by him upon the same.[5]   And
there seems to be a remedy in equity for one co-tenant against
another to compel a contribution towards the repairs of the
common property when the same are necessary.[6]

18. From the nature of tenancies in common, a different
rule applies as to the joinder of the tenants in actions for the
recovery of the freehold, and for injuries affecting their possession.   As each has a separate and distinct freehold, if they
have been disseised and seek to recover the estate, they must
bring separate actions, and may not join.[7]   So in covenant

---

[1] 99 Mass. 78.   This, however, is directly opposed to the dicta of Wilde, J.,
in Coffin *v.* Heath.

[2] 6 Met. 79.   [3] Scott *v.* Guernsey, 48 N. Y. 106, 124.

[4] Israel *v.* Israel, 30 Md. 128.

[5] Dech's Appeal, 57 Penn. St. 472 ; Beaty *v.* Bordwell, 91 Penn. St. 438.

[6] Coffin *v.* Heath, 6 Met. 80 ; Story, 1 Eq. § 1236; Cheeseborough *v.* Green, 10
Conn. 318 ; *post*, vol. 2, *79, pl. 49.

[7] Lit. § 311 ; Co. Lit. 200 a ; Rehoboth *v.* Hunt, 1 Pick. 224 ; Brisco *v.* Mc-

broken upon covenants of warranty made to tenants in common, they must sue separately, and not jointly.[1] But tenants in common of a mortgage may sue upon it jointly or severally, if it secure separate and individual debts.[2] And if one tenant in common recover judgment for possession, in an action for the whole land, he can only recover damages *pro rata* according to his actual interest in the estate.[3] But as they have one possession, they must join in actions for injuries to this, as trespass *quare clausum fregit*, nuisance, and the like.[4] And if they make a joint demise of their common estate, reserving rent, the action to recover it must be joint.[5] For the reasons above stated, if one of several tenants in common bring an action for the recovery of land of which he has been disseised, and claim the entire estate instead of his proper undivided share, he will not * be nonsuited, but will have [*422] judgment for such share, in common, as he proves himself to be entitled to.[6] And in Vermont, one of two joint-tenants may recover the entire estate in an action of ejectment against one who has no title.[7] So one tenant in common may have trespass *quare clausum* against a stranger for entering

Gee, 2 J. J. Marsh. 370 ; Allen *v.* Gibson, 4 Rand. 468 ; Johnson *v.* Harris, 5 Hayw. 113 ; Hines *v.* Frantham, 27 Ala. 359 ; Hughes *v.* Holliday, 3 Greene, (Iowa) 30 ; Young *v.* Adams, 14 B. Mon. 127. But in Connecticut they may sue jointly or severally in such case. Hillhouse *v.* Nix, 1 Root, 246. So in Massachusetts by statute. Pub. Stat. c. 170, § 7. But if one fails to make title, judgment will be rendered against all. Chandler *v.* Simmons, 97 Mass. 508.

[1] Lamb *v.* Danforth, 59 Me. 324.

[2] Brown *v.* Bates, 55 Me. 522.   [3] Buller *v.* Boggs, 25 Cal. 187.

[4] Austin *v.* Hall, 13 Johns. 286 ; Decker *v.* Livingston, 15 Johns. 479 ; Gilmore *v.* Wilbur, 12 Pick. 120 ; Merrill *v.* Berkshire, 11 Pick. 269 ; Low *v.* Mumford, 14 Johns. 426 ; Doe *v.* Botts, 4 Bibb, 420 ; Winters *v.* McGhee, 3 Sneed, 128 ; Parke *v.* Kilham, 8 Cal. 77, case for diverting water ; Dupuy *v.* Strong, 37 N. Y. 372 ; Phillips *v.* Sherman, 61 Me. 548, case of flowing lands.

[5] Lit. § 316 ; Decker *v.* Livingston, 15 Johns. 479 ; Wall *v.* Hinds, 4 Gray, 256, 258 ; Wilkinson *v.* Hall, 1 Bing. N. C. 713 ; Co. Lit. 198 b ; *ante*, p. *417.

[6] M'Fadden *v.* Haley, 2 Bay, 457 ; Perry *v.* Walker, Id. 461 ; Watsou *v.* Hill, 1 McCord, 161 ; Dewey *v.* Brown, 2 Pick. 387 ; Somes *v.* Skinner, 3 Pick. 52. For the effect of one of several co-tenants paying off a charge or purchasing in an outstanding title affecting the common estate, see *post*, p. *430. In Illinois, demandant cannot recover a different estate from that sued for. He cannot recover a share where he sues for an entire estate. Winstanley *v.* Meacham, 58 Ill. 98, 99.

[7] Robinson *v.* Johnson, 36 Vt. 74 ; Chandler *v.* Spear, 22 Vt. 388.

upon and damaging the common property, and recover both
his own and his co-tenant's damage in such action.[1]

SECTION IV.

ESTATES IN PARTNERSHIP.

1. What constitutes estates in partnership.
2, 3. How far real is treated as personal estate, as to survivorship.
4. When partnership has the incidents of individual property.

1. THERE are other joint estates proper to be treated of here,
though not coming in all respects under any one of the foregoing classes, but rather partaking of the nature both of joint-
tenancies and tenancies in common. The first of these is an
ESTATE IN PARTNERSHIP. This is where real estate is purchased and held by two or more partners, out of partnership
funds for partnership purposes. But engaging in a single
transaction by several persons does not bring them so far into
the category of partners as to take away the common-law
jurisdiction of their affairs.[2] Independent of the rights of
creditors, such estate will be held by the owners as tenants in
common, with all the incidents of such estates.[3] Thus, where
one of two partners leased the land of the company under
seal, it only operated upon his share, since one partner cannot
convey another's interest in their real estate, unless specially
authorized. And if several join in a lease, each lets his own
share only, as by a distinct demise, though it may enure to the
benefit of the firm.[4] One reason for this would often be the
inequality of ownership or interest among the partners; and
another is, that, as partnership property, it partakes of the
character of stock in trade, held subject to the hazard of profit
or loss, to which the principle of *jus accrescendi* does not

---

[1] Bigelow v. Rising, 42 Vt. 678.   [2] Hurley v. Walton, 63 Ill. 260.

[3] Goodwin v. Richardson, 11 Mass. 469; Deloney v. Hutcheson, 2 Rand. 183;
Dyer v. Clark, 5 Met. 581; Cary, Part. 26; Gow, Part. 48; Lane v. Tyler, 49
Me. 252; Howard v. Priest, 5 Met. 582.

[4] Dillon v. Brown, 11 Gray, 180; Peek v. Fisher, 7 Cush. 386; Moderwell v.
Mullison, 21 Penn. St. 257.

apply.[1] These general principles have been applied in the American courts in a great variety of cases. Thus, real estate thus purchased is subject to the debts of the partnership, in preference to that of a private creditor of either partner.[2] Nor does it make any difference that the title is taken in the name of one partner. A trust results in favor of the partnership, as where the conveyance was to " S. L. & Co.," S. L. took the legal estate clothed with a trust for the company.[3] But if a partner purchase lands with partnership funds, and take the deed to himself, he may convey it to one ignorant of the source of his title, and if for a valuable consideration, his grantee will hold it against the creditors of the company as well as the copartners. And an obligatory promise to marry the grantor in such case would be deemed a valuable consideration if the marriage was prevented by the death of the grantor.[4] But though the legal title, where the conveyance is to the several partners, is in them as tenants in common, yet as to the beneficial interest it is held in trust, each holding his share in trust for the company until its accounts are settled, and the partnership debts are paid.[5] This is accomplished in equity by regarding such real estate as personal, enabling the surviving partner, if it is needed to pay company debts, to dispose of it and apply it accordingly.[6] And where the business of the partnership consisted of buying and selling lands, it was held that, on closing it, a court of chancery might cause the unsold lands to be sold, and the proceeds divided among the partners.[7] But in another case, a share of the

---

[1] Lake v. Craddock, 3 P. Wms. 158 ; Co. Lit. 182 a ; Tud. Cas. 721.

[2] Piatt v. Oliver, 3 McLean, 27 ; Hunter v. Martin, 2 Itieh. Law, 541 ; Marvin v. Trumbull, Wright, 386. But contra, Blake v. Nutter, 19 Me. 16.

[3] McGuire v. Ramsey, 4 Eng. (Ark.) 518 ; Moreau v. Safferans, 3 Sneed, 595 ; Hewitt v. Rankin, 41 Iowa, 35 ; Fowler v. Bailley, 14 Wisc. 125 ; King v. Weeks, 70 N. C. 372 ; Uhler v. Semple, 20 N. J. Eq. 288 ; Fairchild v. Fairchild, 64 N. Y. 471.　　　[4] Smith r. Allen, 5 Allen, 456.

[5] Howard v. Priest, 5 Met. 582, 585. See also Buchan v. Sumner, 2 Barb. Ch. 165 ; Galbraith v. Gedge, 16 B. Mon. 631 ; Smith v. Tarlton, 2 Barb. Ch. 336 ; Black v. Black, 15 Ga. 445 ; Lang v. Waring, 25 Ala. 625.

[6] Delmonico v. Guillaume, 2 Sandf. Ch. 366 ; Boyers v. Elliott, 7 Humph. 204 ; Boyce v. Coster, 4 Strobh. Eq. 25 ; Matlock v. Matlock, 5 Ind. 403 ; Arnold v. Wainwright, 6 Minn. 358.

[7] Olcott v. Wing, 4 McLean, 15.

surplus of unsold lands at the death of a partner went to his widow and heirs.[1] In order to subject real estate to the incidents of partnership assets, it must have been bought with partnership funds, for partnership purposes, though the deed may be made to the several partners, to hold to them and their heirs.[2] ·And the same can only be conveyed by a deed executed by those having the legal title.[3] And it may be added, if one partner leases the real estate of the partnership in his own name, it enures to the benefit of the firm.[4]

2. In England, however, courts of equity have recently been inclined to regard real estate thus held as personal, subject to the same rules of distribution as personal estate.[5] This doctrine was applied in the case cited below, where A and B purchased land on a joint speculation with their joint moneys, for the purpose of building upon and reselling at joint profit or loss. It was held to be a conversion *out and out ;* and upon one of them dying, his share in the real estate passed to his personal representatives.[6]

3. In this country, as formerly in England, the doctrine of survivorship is almost universally limited by the extent to which equity stamps the character of personalty upon such estates, and that is so far as and no farther than they are required to pay partnership debts. If, therefore, one of two partners owning real estate dies, the survivor has an [*423] equitable lien upon the * share of the deceased, which takes precedence of any claim for dower or of heirs, to have the same applied, if necessary, to the payment of the

---

[1] Dilworth *v.* Mayfield, 36 Miss. 40. See Ludlow *v.* Cooper, 4 Ohio St. 1 ; Whaling Co. *v.* Borden, 10 Cush. 458.

[2] Cox *v.* McBurney, 2 Sandf. 561 ; Lancaster Bank *v.* Myley, 13 Penn. St. 544 ; Deming *v.* Colt, 3 Sandf. 284 ; Coder *v.* Huling, 27 Penn. St. 84 ; Arnold *v.* Wainwright, 6 Minn. 370.

[3] Davis *v.* Christian, 15 Gratt. 11.

[4] Moderwell *v.* Mullison, 21 Penn. St. 257.

[5] Tud. Cas. 721. See also Rice *v.* Barnard, 20 Vt. 479 ; Lang *v.* Waring, 17 Ala. 145.

[6] Darby *v.* Darby, 3 Drewry, 495, in 1856 ; Essex *v.* Essex, 20 Beav. 442. See the comments on this case, 98 Mass. 114 ; 1 White & T. Cases in Equity (4th ed.), 192, 193, and cases there collected. The English rule is adopted in Kentucky. Cornwall *v.* Cornwall, 6 Bush, 372 ; Louisville Bank *v.* Hall, 8 Bush, 678. And see Pierce *v.* Trigg, 10 Leigh, 406.

outstanding debts of the partnership, or to reimburse the survivor if he shall have paid more than his share of the partnership indebtedness.[1] And if the surviving partner be himself insolvent, his assignees may avail themselves of the partnership real estate, if needed for the payment of the company debts, and to aid in this they may require the widow and heirs of the deceased to execute proper deeds of release.[2] In Tennessee and North Carolina this right of survivorship is secured by statute, and it has been, accordingly, held in the former State, that the survivor of a partnership may sell the entire partnership property as a surviving joint-tenant.[3] In Virginia and Maine the survivor of a partnership has no rights in respect to their real estate superior to any ordinary survivor of two or more tenants in common.[4] In Alabama, equity regards real estate owned by partners as the property of the firm, and will appropriate it in payment of the debts of the firm, whether it be in the possession of the surviving partner, or in that of his heirs; neither of them can have any beneficial interest in the real estate of the partnership until the debts of the firm are paid. But it was held, that if the surviving partner, for a valuable consideration, convey his interest in the real estate to a purchaser without notice that it is needed to pay partnership debts, he will hold it against the creditors of the firm. The surplus of partnership lands, after paying the partnership debts, has the qualities of real estate, and is disposed of accordingly.[5] And in Pennsylvania, partnership lands are no longer regarded as personalty than till the debts of the partnership are paid. Whatever remains has

---

[1] Burnside v. Merrick, 4 Met. 537; Dyer v. Clark, 5 Met. 562; Smith v. Jackson, 2 Edw. Ch. 28 ; Fairchild v. Fairchild, 64 N. Y. 471 ; Watkins, Conv. 167, 168 ; Howard v. Priest, 5 Met. 585 ; Buffum v. Buffum, 49 Me. 108 ; Loubat v. Nourse, 5 Fla. 350 ; Scruggs v. Blair, 44 Miss. 406.

[2] Winslow v. Chiffelle, Harper, Eq. 25 ; 2 Spence, Eq. Jur. 209 ; Story, Eq. Jur. §§ 674, 675 ; Delmonico v. Guillaume, 2 Sandf. Ch. 366 ; Willett v. Brown, 65 Mo. 138.

[3] Tennessee Code, 1858, § 2011 ; N. Carolina, Rev. Code, 1854, c. 43, § 2 ; M'Allister v. Montgomery, 3 Hayw. 96. But see Gaines v. Catron, 1 Humph. 514 ; Blake v. Nutter, 19 Me. 16.

[4] Deloney v. Hutcheson, 2 Rand. 183. But see Morris v. Morris, 4 Gratt. 293.

[5] Offutt v. Scott, 47 Ala. 105.

the properties of realty owned by the several partners. Neither of these can sell his interest in them as personalty.[1]

4. And, as would naturally be inferred from the premises above stated, whatever remains of such partnership real estate after the debts of the company shall have been discharged, is held in common, at once subject to dower or curtesy, and goes to heirs or devisees accordingly,[2] and is subject to partition.[3]

SECTION V.

JOINT MORTGAGES.

1, 2. Of mortgages to several to secure a joint debt.
  3. Of mortgages to several to secure separate debts.
  4. Effect of foreclosure on joint mortgages.

1. ANOTHER class of joint estates which has already been mentioned is that by JOINT MORTGAGES. In England [*424] and in *most of the States, the interest of a mortgagee in lands is regarded as an estate in lands, but so far partaking of the nature of the debt thereby secured,

, NOTE. — The following cases lately decided cover so many of the points stated in the several paragraphs of the foregoing section, and are so generally in accord with what is therein stated, that they are referred to in general terms, instead of citing them in detail, to sustain the several points upon which they bear. Lefevre's Appeal, 69 Penn. St. 122 ; Bopp v. Fox, 63 Ill. 540 ; Ebbert's Appeal, 70 Penn. St. 81 ; Wilcox v. Wilcox, 13 Allen, 252 ; Jones's Appeal, 70 Penn. St. 169 ; Shearer v. Shearer, 98 Mass. 107 ; Meily v. Wood, 71 Penn. St. 488 ; Foster's Appeal, 22 Am. L. Reg. 300, to which is appended an extended note, 307–310, collating the American cases upon the subject, and concluding "that the surplus proceeds of real estate of a partnership, after the creditors are satisfied, and the equities of the partners adjusted, are to be considered as realty, and that, on the death of a partner, his interest in such surplus goes to his heir, subject to the widow's dower, and not to his personal representatives."

---

[1] Foster's Appeal, 74 Penn. St. 398, 399.

[2] Burnside v. Merrick, 4 Met. 537 ; Howard v. Priest, 5 Met. 586 ; Buchan v. Sumner, 2 Barb. Ch. 163 ; Buckley v. Buckley, 11 Barb. 43 ; Tillinghast v. Chaplin, 4 R. I. 173 ; Dilworth v. Mayfield, 36 Miss. 40 ; Piper v. Smith, 1 Head, 93.

[3] Patterson v. Blake, 12 Ind. 436 ; Loubat v. Nourse, 5 Fla. 363·

that, for purposes of remedy and enforcement of the same, the doctrine of survivorship applies as well to the estate as the debt; and this extends to the assignment of a mortgage to two trustees.[1]

2. If, in such a case, either of the mortgagees dies, the survivors may proceed in their own name, and do whatever is necessary to foreclose the mortgage; and for that purpose they have a right to the possession of the mortgage and notes, without making the heir or personal representative of their co-mortgagee a party.[2]

3. But if the debts secured by the mortgage belong in severalty to the different mortgagees named, they become, in such case, tenants in common and not joint-tenants as to such estate, without the right of survivorship; and if, after the debt of one shall have been satisfied, the other dies, his representatives, and not the survivor or survivors, would be the only proper parties to proceedings to enforce the mortgage.[3]

4. As soon, however, as the mortgage is foreclosed, though the debt may have been a joint one, the mortgagees become tenants in common of the estate, the share of each being in proportion to his share of the debt.[4]

[1] Webster v. Vandeventer, 6 Gray, 428.

[2] Appleton v. Boyd, 7 Mass. 131 ; Kinsley v. Abbott, 19 Me. 430; Martin v. M'Reynolds, 6 Mich. 72 ; Cote v. Dequindre, Walker, Ch. 64.

[3] Burnett v. Pratt, 22 Pick. 557 ; 2 Dane, Abr. 226 ; Brown v. Bates, 55 Me. 522.

[4] Goodwin v. Richardson, 11 Mass. 469 ; Deloney v. Hutcheson, 2 Rand. 183 ; Donnels v. Edwards, 2 Pick. 617 ; Tud. Cas. 721 ; Pearce v. Savage, 45 Me. 90 ; Kinsley v. Abbott, 19 Me. 430.

SECTION VI.

ESTATES IN ENTIRETY.

1. Who are tenants by entirety, and how they hold.
2. Of the nature of survivorship as to such estates.
3. Effect of conveyance by husband.
3 *a*. Same subject, Stat. 32 Hen. VIII. c. 28, § 6.
4. When husband and wife may be tenants in common.
5. American law on the subject.

1. A STILL more peculiar joint estate is that which belongs to a husband and wife, where the same is conveyed to them as such. If a man and woman, tenants in common, marry, they still continue to hold in common.[1] But if the estate is [*425] conveyed * to them originally as husband and wife, they are neither tenants in common nor properly joint-tenants, though having the right of survivorship, but are what are called TENANTS BY ENTIRETY. While such estates have, like a joint-tenancy, the quality of survivorship, they differ from that in this essential respect, that neither can convey his or her interest so as to affect the right of survivorship in the other. They are not seised, in the eye of the law, of moieties, but of entireties.[2]

2. In such cases, the survivor does not take as a new acquisitiou, but under the original limitation, his estate being simply freed from participation by the other;[3] so that if, for

---

[1] 1 Prest. Est. 434 ; Co. Lit. 187 b ; Ames *v.* Norman, 4 Sneed, 683, 696 ; McDermott *v.* French, 15 N. J. Eq. 80 ; Babbit *v.* Scroggin, 1 Duv. 272.

[2] 1 Prest. Est. 131 ; 2 Flint. Real Prop. 527 ; Tud. Cas. 730 ; Shaw *v.* Hearsey, 5 Jass. 521 ; Fox *v.* Fletcher, 8 Jass. 274 ; Draper *v.* Jackson, 16 Jass. 480 ; Brownson *v.* Hull, 16 Vt. 309 ; Harding *v.* Springer, 14 Je. 407 ; Fairchild *v.* Chastelleux, 1 Penn. St. 176 ; Den *v.* Branson, 5 Ired. 426; Taul *v.* Campbell, 7 Yerg. 319 ; Cord, Mar. Women, § 107 ; Rogers *v.* Grider, 1 Dana, 242 ; Doe *v.* Howland, 8 Cow. 277; 2 Kent, Com. 132; Torrey *v.* Torrey, 14 N. Y. 430; Zorntlein *v.* Bram, 100 N. Y. 12; Ames *v.* Norman, 4 Sneed, 683; Wright *v.* Saddler, 20 N. Y. 320. See Gen. Stat. Vt. 1863, c. 64, § 3 ; Davis *v.* Clark, 26 Ind. 424 ; Ketchum *v.* Walsworth, 5 Wisc. 95 ; Babbit *v.* Scroggin, 1 Duv. 272 ; Wales *v.* Coffin, 13 Allen, 215 ; Lux *v.* Hoff, 47 Ill. 425 ; Jarriner *v.* Saunders, 10 Ill. 124 ; McCurdy *v.* Canning, 64 Penn. St. 39; Hemingway *v.* Scales, 42 Jiss. 1; Jarburg *v.* Cole, 49 Jd. 402 ; Hall *v.* Stephens, 65 Mo. 670; Fisher *v.* Provin, 25 Jich. 350.

[3] Watkins, Conv. 170; Tud. Cas. 730.

instance, the wife survives and then dies, her heirs would take to the exclusion of the heirs of the husband.[1] Nor can partition be made of the estate.[2]

3. If the husband convey the entire estate during coverture, and dies, his conveyance will not have affected her rights of survivorship to the entire estate. But if, in such case, the husband survive, his conveyance becomes as effective to pass the whole estate as it would have been had the husband been sole seised when he conveyed.[3] And during coverture, the husband has the entire control of the estate, and the same is liable to be seized by his creditors during his life.[4] But if husband's creditors levy upon the estate, it survives to the wife on the death of the husband, as if no such levy had been made.[5] And even where the husband mortgaged half the estate for the support of self and wife, and she joined in the deed releasing her dower and homestead, it was held to be of no avail to bar her right as survivor upon the death of the husband, since her release of dower conveyed nothing ; nor was she estopped by the mortgage, because, being a *feme covert*, she did not bind herself personally.[6]

3 *a*. Although the effect of a disseisin of the husband, or his conveyance of her estate upon a wife's interest in lands, has been referred to (p. * 141, *ante*), it seems proper to speak, in this connection, more at large upon the subject. By the common law, if a husband by fine or feoffment conveyed land in fee which he held in the right of his wife, including estates held in entirety, it worked a discontinuance of her estate, and, at his death, she or her heirs were driven to an action to recover it. To obviate this, the statute 32 Hen. VIII. c. 28, § 6, provided that such conveyance should not work a discontinuance, but that at the death of the husband, the wife or her heirs might enter upon the inheritance, without being driven to an action. This statute was once re-enacted, and still seems to be in force in New York. It is in force in Tennessee, in Massachusetts, and has been re-enacted in Ken-

---

[1] 1 Prest. Est. 132.   [2] Bennett v. Child, 19 Wisc. 362.
[3] 1 Prest. Est. 135 ; Ames v. Norman, 4 Sneed, 683.
[4] Barber v. Harris, 15 Wend. 615 ; Bennett v. Child, 19 Wisc. 362, 365.
[5] French v. Mehan, 56 Penn. St. 286.   [6] Pierce v. Chase, 108 Mass. 258.

tucky, and such is the effect of the statutes in New Jersey. In Tennessee, the wife has seven years after the husband's death in which to enter or bring her action. In Kentucky, she has twenty years. Nor has the tenant, in such case, any right to a notice to quit before proceedings are instituted to remove him. He is not even tenant at sufferance, as the relation of landlord and tenant did not subsist between him and the survivor.[1] If there be a divorce of the wife from the husband, she is restored to a moiety of the estate, during the lives of the two, with the right of survivorship upon his death. But such divorce cannot disturb a conveyance of the estate already made by the husband. So long as the husband lives, such conveyance will be good.[2]

4. It is always competent, however, to make husband and wife tenants in common, by proper words, in the deed or devise by which they take, indicating such an intention.[3] And if an estate be made to a husband and wife and a third person, the shares of each will depend upon the kind of estate the husband and wife take. If there is nothing to indicate a tenancy in common, they together would take one half by entirety, and the third person the other half, to be held in common;[4] whereas, if they take in common, then each is entitled to one third in common and undivided. And in the case supposed, if their connection with a third person [*426] was that of a joint-tenancy, and * he were to die, the husband and wife would, by their survivorship, take the whole estate by entirety.[5] Where a conveyance was to a husband and wife and their six children by name, it was held that the interest of the tenants was divisible into seven parts, of which the husband and wife held one by entirety, undivided and in common with the other six parts undivided, to which the several children were entitled.[6]

5. The law of this country is not, however, uniform as to

---

[1] Co. Lit. 326 a ; 2 Kent, Com. 133, and note ; Miller v. Miller, Meigs, 492, 493 ; Miller v. Shackleford, 4 Dana, 264, 277 ; Bruce v. Wood, 1 Met. 542.

[2] Ames v. Norman, 4 Sneed, 683.

[3] McDermott v. French, 15 N. J. Eq. 81.

[4] Hall v. Stephens, 65 Mo. 670 ; Hulet v. Inlow, 57 Ind. 412.

[5] 1 Prest. Est. 132 ; 2 Flint. Real Prop. 327.

[6] Barber v. Harris, 15 Wend. 615.

this doctrine of entirety. In Ohio, where there never was any joint-tenancy with a right of survivorship, it is held that a devise to a husband and wife and their heirs makes them tenants in common, and such is the effect of a conveyance to husband and wife of an equitable estate.[1] In Connecticut, a husband and wife, in such a case, are considered joint-tenants, and not tenants in entirety.[2] In Virginia, if an estate of inheritance is devised to husband and wife, upon the death of either, his or her share descends to heirs, subject to debts, rights of curtesy, or of dower, as the case may be.[3] In Rhode Island, such an estate in husband and wife is a tenancy in common, without the right of survivorship.[4] And the same is the law in Iowa, unless the contrary is expressed in the grant.[5] And while it has been generally held that the statutes abolishing joint-tenancies, or changing these into tenancies in common, do not apply to tenancies by entirety,[6] yet, by express provision,[7] or by implication from the statutes giving married women control of their own property, these have in several States been reduced to tenancies in common.[8] In Indiana, and perhaps in some other States, while tenancy by entirety is still held to exist, notwithstanding the married women's acts, the common-law incident of control of the joint property by the husband during coverture, or its alienability during the same period by his act, or liability for his debts, is denied.[9] In New York the continuance of this species of tenancy has

[1] Sergeant v. Steinberger, 2 Ohio, 305; Wilson v. Fleming, 13 Ohio, 68.

[2] Whittlesey v. Fuller, 11 Conn. 337, 341.

[3] Code, 1873, c. 112, 18, 19.

[4] Gen. Stat. 1872, e. 161, § 1.

[5] Hoffman v. Stigers, 28 Iowa, 302.

[6] Rogers v. Grider, 1 Dana, 242; Babbit v. Scroggin, 1 Duv. 272.

[7] Kentucky Gen. Stat. 1873, c. 52, art. 4, § 13; but this is not retrospective. Elliott v. Nichols, 4 Bush, 502.

[8] Clark v. Clark, 56 N. H. 105: Cooper v. Cooper, 76 Ill. 57, following the act of 1861, and distinguishing Lux v. Hoff, 47 Ill. 425, as prior to that statute; Mass. St. 1885, c. 237; Pray v. Stebbins, 141 Mass. 219.

[9] Arnold v. Arnold, 30 Ind. 305; Chandler v. Cheney, 37 Ind. 391, nothing passes by husband's deed; Davis v. Clark, 26 Ind. 424; Montgomery v. Hickman, 62 Ind. 598; Patton v. Rankin, 68 Ind. 245, or can be taken on execution by his creditors. So in New York and perhaps Mississippi, it is left undetermined whether the husband can alien his joint interest during coverture. Bertles v. Nunan, 92 N. Y. 152; McDuff v. Beauchamp, 50 Miss. 531.

been affirmed after some fluctuations of decision,[1] and the same rule has been laid down in Michigan, Mississippi, Arkansas, and Maryland, at least to the extent of the right of survivorship.[2] While in Pennsylvania, Missouri, New Jersey, and Wisconsin, the tenancy exists with all its common-law incidents.[3]

SECTION VII.

PARTITION.

1. AT common law no owner of any of these joint-estates, except parceners, had a right to have partition thereof made against the will of his co-tenant. The right of having partition in the excepted estates gave rise to the name of parcenary. And for this or some other reason, in some of the States it has been held that a parol partition of their estate between parceners, if followed by possession, is as good and effectual as if made by deed. It is apprehended that this is confined to

---

[1] In Goelet v. Gori, 31 Barb. 314 ; Farmer's Bk. v. Gregory, 49 Barb. 155; Miller v. Miller, 9 Abbot, Pr. N. s. 444 ; Freeman v. Barber, 3 Thomps. & C. 574; Beach v. Hollister, 3 Hun, 519, it was held still to exist ; but in Meeker v. Wright, 76 N. Y. 262, followed by Feely v. Buckley, 28 Hun, 451, it was declared inconsistent with the married women's statutes. But these latter cases have since been overruled in Bertles v. Nunan, 92 N. Y. 152 ; Zorntlein v. Bram, 100 N. Y. 12

[2] Fisher v. Provin, 25 Mich. 350; McDuff v. Beauchamp, 50 Miss. 531; Robinson v. Eagle, 29 Ark. 202 ; Marburg v. Cole, 49 Md. 402.

[3] Bates v. Seely, 46 Penn. St. 248 ; French v. Mehan, 56 Penn. St. 289 ; Washburn v. Burns, 34 N. J. 18 ; Hall v. Stephens, 65 Mo. 670 ; Bennett v. Child, 19 Wisc. 362.

States where coparcenary at common law is still retained, and would not extend to States where heirs take as tenants in common.[1] The statute 31 Hen. VIII. c. 1, and 32 Hen. VIII. c. 32, provided for a compulsory process of partition by a writ or action at common law.[2] This form of proceeding continued in England to be one of the forms by which partition could be effected, until the statute 3 & 4 Wm. IV. c. 27, by which it was abolished, and the statutes by which it was created have been *re-enacted in most of the States. But [*427] in England and this country it had become practically obsolete many years ago.[3]

2. There is still a power to compel partition which may be readily applied in both countries. In England it is done through chancery. The laws of the several States upon the subject will be found compiled at the close of this chapter. But in some form or other, the right of having partition made is incident to an ownership in joint-tenancy as well as to estates in common.[4] But it is competent for joint owners of land to have their estate so created as to prevent partition thereof being made except by mutual consent, as where several joined in purchasing an estate on which to erect and maintain a hotel, and had a clause inserted in the deed by which they acquired their title, prohibiting them from having partition thereof made. They were thereby estopped from maintaining a process for partition.[5] But where, by the terms of the grant of a parcel of land, it was to be occupied in common as a yard by the grantor and grantee and their heirs and assigns, it was held that partition of the premises might be made, giving to

---

[1] Coles v. Wooding, 2 Pat. & H. (Va.) 189, 197 , Wildey v. Bonney, 31 Miss. 644, 652.

[2] 2 Flint. Real Prop. 332 ; Story, Eq. Jur. § 647.

[3] 4 Kent, Com. 364 ; Champion v. Spencer, 1 Root, 147 ; Cook v. Allen, 2 Mass. 462 ; Witherspoon v. Dunlap, 1 McCord, 546 ; M'Kee v. Straub, 2 Binn. 1 ; Wms. Real Prop. 81, 115.

[4] Mitchell v. Starbuck, 10 Mass. 5 ; Witherspoon v. Dunlap, Harper, 390 ; Potter v. Wheeler, 13 Mass. 504 ; Ledbetter v. Gash, 8 Ired. 462 ; Hanbury v. Hussey, 5 E. L. & Eq. 81; Higginbottom v. Short, 25 Miss. 160 ; Holmes v. Holmes, 2 Jones, Eq. 334. See Coleman v. Coleman, 19 Penn. St. 100 ; Hoyt v. Kimball, 49 N. H. 322.

[5] Hunt v. Wright, 47 N. H. 399, 401 ; see also Fisher v. Dewerson, 3 Met. 546.

each an easement in the land of the other so as to serve the purposes of the grant.[1] But where one tenant in common owned one undivided part in his own right in common with another part of which he and others were trustees, it was held he could not have partition of the estate.[2]

3. This power of compelling partition has been exercised in England by chancery ever since the time of Elizabeth.[3] It may be done in chancery in several of the States, in most if not all of which there are also modes provided by statute for causing partitions to be made.[4] In New York a wife, owning land as tenant in common with her husband, may have a bill in equity for partition of the same.[5] The act of making partition through chancery is done by commissioners appointed for the purpose, who return their doings into court, and, in order to make it effectual, mutual conveyances to each other by the co-tenants are required.[6] And if it becomes necessary, in order to equalize the partition, the commissioners may require the payment of money by one co-tenant to another, called owelty of partition.[7] And if one co-tenant has made improvements upon the estate, equity may so divide it as to give these to the tenant who made them, although, at law, he would have no right of action to recover their value.[8] But under proceedings at law the commissioners cannot settle contested questions of title between the parties; such questions are to be settled at the original hearing : nor have they power to award that buildings standing upon the premises are the property of some one of the tenants in common, and to set the same to him as his own.[9] In Illinois, however, if one co-tenant make improvements upon the common estate, the

---

[1] Fisher v. Dewerson, sup.; Hoyt v. Kimball, 49 N. H. 322.

[2] Winthrop v. Minot, 9 Cush. 405.

[3] Story, Eq. Jur. § 647.

[4] Whitten v. Whitten, 36 N. H. 326 ; Patton v. Wagner, 19 Ark. 233 ; Bailey v. Sisson, 1 R. I. 233 ; Spitts v. Wells, 18 Mo. 468 ; Adam v. Ames Iron Co., 24 Conn. 230 ; Greenup v. Sewell, 18 Ill. 53. In Indiana the proceedings are in law, and not in equity. Wilbridge v. Case, 2 Carter (Ind.), 36.

[5] Moore v. Moore, 47 N. Y. 469.   [6] Story, Eq. Jur. § 650.

[7] Story, Eq. Jur. § 654.

[8] Green v. Putnam, 1 Barb. 500. See also Crafts v. Crafts, 13 Gray, 360; Thorn v. Thorn, 14 Iowa, 55 ; Robinson v. McDonald, 11 Tex. 385.

[9] Gourley v. Woodbury, 43 Vt. 89.

court directs the commissioners to set the improved part to him without charging him for such improvements.[1]

4. When partition was made upon proceedings at common law, it was done by a sheriff and jury, who set out to each his proper share, and this was binding upon the parties without the formality of mutual conveyances, as required when made in chancery.[2] But chancery did not act in case the title to the land was in dispute. It required the question of title to be first settled at law.[3]

5. Proceedings in partition, like real actions, generally are local, and must be had in the county in which the land lies which is the subject of division.[4] A petition for partition is a proceeding *in rem*.[5] In a writ of partition all the co-tenants must be named, and partition must be made amongst them, the share of each must be stated, and no partition can be made where any of the co-tenants are unknown, or their shares cannot be stated. But in Massachusetts one co-tenant can have his share set off, leaving the other co-tenants to have their shares set off by a new process, and this though the others are unknown. The essential thing in such a process is, that the petitioner should have an estate in possession in common with some other person. It is no objection to the proceeding that there is a contingent remainder in another in some portion of the estate. But a remainder-man cannot have partition, and if he has a share in possession, and one in remainder, he may have the first set off without affecting his right to the other share. As to the two he is regarded as a separate tenant. It is no objection to maintaining partition that the petitioner's share is subject to a mortgage if the mortgagor is in possession.[6] By the law of the same State, a tenant in common for life may have partition, and it is no

---

[1] Dean v. O'Meara, 47 Ill. 120 ; Kurtz v. Hibner, 55 Ill. 521. See a like doctrine in Kentucky. Borah v. Archers, 7 Dana, 177.

[2] Story, Eq. Jur. §§ 652, 654.

[3] 2 Daniels, Ch. (Perk. ed.) 1326, n.; 4 Kent, Com. 365 ; Hosford v. Merwin, 5 Barb. 51 ; McCall v. Carpenter, 18 How. 297 ; Shearer v. Winston, 33 Miss. 149 ; Tabler v. Wiseman, 2 Ohio St. 207 ; Obert v. Obert, 10 N. J. Eq. 98.

[4] Bonner, Petitioner, 4 Mass. 122 ; Brown v. McMullen, 1 Nott & McC. 252 ; Peabody v. Minot, 24 Pick. 333.

[5] Corwithe v. Griffing, 21 Barb. 9.   [6] Taylor v. Blake, 109 Mass. 513.

objection to the process that the petitioner holds his estate sub-
jcet to a condition if the same has not been broken.[1]

[*428]   * 6. It is not competent for a tenant in common to
enforce partition as to a part of the common estate.
He must go for a partition of the entire estate if he would
divide any part.[2]   And where the commissioners, in dividing
the land, laid an open passage-way through it, and then set off
the respective shares of the co-tenants, bounding them by this
passage-way, and giving to each an easement of way over the
open passage to be used by them in common, it was held to
be a good partition ; the share of each would be bounded by
the centre line of this way.[3]   But two or more of several
tenants in common may join in having their respective interests set off together from the other shares of their co-tenants.
Or one or more of the tenants may have their shares set off,
leaving the rest of the common estate undivided.[4] This would
be so, though the parties, other than the petitioners, are unknown.   The effect of a partition is like that of a judgment
in establishing the titles of the respective tenants.   It requires no deeds between the parties to make good the titles.[5]
A judgment in partition, settling and confirming the shares and
interests of the several parties, is equivalent to a conveyance,
and is to be construed by the same rules as ordinary conveyances.[6]   But where tenants in common covenanted that a
certain part of the premises should for ever remain to be occupied by them and their heirs and assigns as a yard, it was
no bar to having a partition of the premises, but the right to
this occupation in the nature of an easement will remain after
as before the partition.[7]   But if, in a deed to two persons, it
is recited at the close of the grant that the premises are " to
remain in common and undivided," such recital would not
prevent either of the parties from having partition by process

---

[1] Judkins v. Judkins, 109 Mass. 181.

[2] Duncan v. Sylvester, 16 Me. 388 ; Colton v. Smith, 11 Pick. 311 ; Bigelow
v. Littlefield, 52 Me. 24.

[3] Clark v. Parker, 106 Mass. 554.

[4] Ladd v. Perley, 18 N. H. 396 ; Abbott v. Berry, 46 N. H. 369.

[5] Hassett v. Ridgley, 49 Ill. 201.

[6] Hoffman v. Stigers, 28 Iowa, 302.

[7] Fisher v. Dewerson, 3 Met. 544 ; Hoyt v. Kimball, 49 N. H. 324.

of law.[1]　But a condition that partition should never be made of the premises granted would be good.[2]　By the statute 31 Henry VIII., none but tenants of the freehold who have estates of inheritance could have partition, and only against tenants of the freehold.　By that of 32 Henry VIII. tenants for life or years might have partition, but not to affect the reversioner or remainder-man.[3]　Where, during the pendency of proceedings for partition, one co-tenant mortgaged his interest, it was held that the mortgage attached to his property as soon as set out to the mortgagor, and the same rule would apply if the conveyance had been in fee.[4]　Within the rule above stated, a tenant by the curtesy initiate may have partition.[5]

7. There are some general rules and principles applicable to the partition of estates which may be stated in anticipation of the statute regulations of the several States, which will be found at the close of this chapter.　A petition for partition ordinarily lies only in favor of one who has a seisin and right of immediate possession,[6] and a disseisin or adverse possession negatives the community of possession upon which the right to partition depends.[7]　Partition is not a process to try questions of title if the petitioner is out of possession.　If therefore another than the petitioner is in adverse possession for however short a time, he cannot sustain the petition, so that one

---

[1] Spalding v. Woodward, 53 N. H. 573.

[2] Hunt v. Wright, 47 N. H. 396 ; post, vol. 2, *448.

[3] Co. Lit. 167 ; Mussey v. Sanborn, 15 Mass. 155 ; Austin v. Rutland R. R., 45 Vt. 215.

[4] Westervelt v. Half, 2 Sandf. Ch. 98 ; Baird v. Corwin, 17 Penn. St. 462.

[5] Biker v. Darke, 4 Edw. Ch. 668.

[6] Bonner v. Kennebeck Purch., 7 Mass. 475 ; Rickard v. Rickard, 13 Pick. 251 ; Wells v. Prince, 9 Mass. 508; Bradshaw v. Callaghan, 8 Johns. 558; Brownell v. Brownell, 19 Wend. 367 ; Barnard v. Pope, 14 Mass. 434 ; Miller v. Dennett, 6 N. H. 109 ; Call v. Barker, 12 Me. 320 ; Stevens v. Enders, 13 N. J. 271 ; Whitten v. Whitten, 36 N. H. 326 ; Maxwell v. Maxwell, 8 Ind. Eq. 25 ; Hunnewell v. Taylor, 6 Cush. 472 ; Foust v. Moorman, 2 Carter (Ind.), 17 ; Tabler v. Wiseman, 2 Ohio St. 207 ; Lambert v. Blumenthal, 26 Mo. 471 ; Brock v. Eastman, 28 Vt. 658.

[7] Clapp v. Bromagham, 9 Cow. 530 ; Thomas v. Garvan, 4 Dev. 223.　But in Massachusetts, it is held that a mere technical disseisin does not affect one tenant in common in maintaining partition, so long as he has a right to make an immediate entry.　Marshall v. Crehore, 13 Met. 462 ; Fisher v. Dewerson, 3 Met. 544.

co-tenant, by conveying the whole estate to a stranger, may compel his co-tenant to regain his seisin and possession before he can bring process for partition.[1] Thus, one claiming a share of an estate for an alleged breach of condition cannot have partition until he shall have regained his seisin by an entry upon the premises.[2] A judgment for partition, when executed, is conclusive evidence that the part set off to one petitioner was a part of the premises held by the parties in common, nor would it be open to a former co-tenant to set up an easement in the part thus set off, upon the ground that he had enjoyed it adversely before such partition was made.[3]

8. Partition, consequently, does not lie by tenants in common in reversion or remainder,[4] though in New York it may be made of an equitable estate,[5] and of a vested remainder by a statute of that State.[6] An outstanding right of dower in a widow, which has never been enforced, is no objection to a valid partition among those having the inheritance.[7] So the owners of an equity of redemption may have partition, if the mortgagee has not entered and taken possession under his mortgage.[8] But one co-tenant cannot have partition against another who holds a mortgage upon the whole estate, although it may not have been recorded.[9] But if partition has been made while there is an outstanding mortgage, attachment, or other lien upon the share of one of the co-tenants, it will conclude the one having such lien, and the same will attach to the part set off to the one against whom it exists.[10]

---

[1] Florence v. Hopkins, 46 N. Y. 184, 186.

[2] O'Dougherty v. Aldrich, 5 Denio, 385.   [3] Edson v. Bunsell, 12 Allen, 602.

[4] Culver v. Culver, 2 Root, 278 ; Ziegler v. Grim, 6 Watts, 106 ; Hodgkinson, Pet., 12 Pick. 374 ; Brown v. Brown, 8 N. H. 93 ; Robertson v. Robertson, 2 Swan, 197 ; Tabler v. Wiseman, 2 Ohio St. 207 ; Adam v. Ames Iron Co., 24 Conn. 230 ; Nichols v. Nichols, 28 Vt. 228 ; Hunnewell v. Taylor, 6 Cush. 472 ; Johnson v. Johnson, 7 Allen, 198.

[5] Hitchcock v. Skinner, 1 Hoffm. Ch. 21.

[6] Blakeley v. Calder, 15 N. Y. 617. So in Illinois and New Jersey. Scoville v. Hilliard, 48 Ill. 453 ; Hilliard v. Scoville, 52 Ill. 449; Smith v. Gaines, 38 N. J. Eq. 65.

[7] Bradshaw v. Callaghan, 8 Johns. 558 ; Motley v. Blake, 12 Mass. 280 ; Leonard v. Motley, 75 Me. 418.

[8] Call v. Barker, 12 Me. 320.

[9] Blodgett v. Hildreth, 8 Allen, 186; Fuller v. Bradley, 23 Pick. 9.

[10] Mass. Pub. Stat. c. 178, § 44.

But two mortgagees with simultaneous mortgages *can- [*429]
not have partition until after foreclosure of their
mortgages.[1]

8 a. To give validity and effect to a partition, all persons
interested should be made parties to the proceedings. Such
parties and none others would be bound by the judgment.
Thus, before the statute bound mortgagees and attaching
creditors of one co-tenant by a partition to which he is party,
and gave a lien upon his property when set out to him, such
mortgagee or attaching creditor was not bound by such partition commenced and perfected after the lien thus created
was instituted, unless he was made a party to the proceedings.[2] And a partition where one of the co-tenants is a
disseisor, or wrongfully claims a share of the estate, will
not affect the rights of the disseisee, although such co-ten-
nant is in possession of the premises, but when the disseisee regains his seisin he will be tenant in common with
the rightful co-tenant.[3]

9. It has been held in Massachusetts, that if the common
estate consists of several parcels, it is not required in making
partition that each parcel should be divided; the entire share
of one of the co-tenants may be set off in one of the parcels,
if the commissioners see fit.[4] The same rule applies in describing what is set off to a co-tenant upon partition made, as
in making a deed from one to another. Thus the assignment
of a *mill* to one carries with it the land on which it stands,
and the appurtenant easements necessary to its full enjoyment.[5]

10. In Vermont, the court refused to order a partition of an
ore bed, or of a mill, mill-pond, and mill-yard, which formed

[1] Ewer v. Hobbs, 5 Met. 1. *Contra*, Munroe v. Walbridge, 2 Aik. 410.

[2] Colton v. Smith, 11 Pick. 311 ; Munroe v. Luke, 19 Pick. 39 ; Mass. Pub.
Stat. c. 178, § 43 ; Cook v. Allen, 2 Mass. 462. See Purvis v. Wilson, 5 Jones
(N. C.), 22 ; Kester v. Stark, 19 Ill. 328 ; Burhans v. Burhans, 2 Barb. Ch. 398 ;
De Uprey v. De Uprey, 27 Cal. 332 ; Harlan v. Stout, 22 Ind. 488 ; Ross v. Cobb,
48 Ill. 114 ; Kilgour v. Crawford, 51 Ill. 249. Cf. Duke v. Hague, 15 W. No.
Cas. 353.

[3] Dorn v. Beasly, 7 Rich. Eq. 84 ; Foxcroft v. Barnes, 29 Me. 128 ; Argyle v.
Dwinel, 29 Me. 29. *Contra*, Mass. Pub. Stat. c. 178, § 35 ; Poster v. Abbot,
8 Met. 596.

[4] Hagar v. Wiswall, 10 Pick. 152. Cf. Hardin v. Lawrence, 40 N. J. Eq. 154.

[5] Munroe v. Stickney, 48 Me. 458.

one estate, because they were not subjects of partition.[1]   And
a partition made in New Hampshire, of a mill, by assigning to
the co-tenants the alternate use of it for specified periods, was
set aside as being unauthorized by law;[2] and such was held to
be the case in Massachusetts, until a statute made provision
for such a partition.[3]   The courts of California do not regard
the water flowing in a ditch designed for mining purposes as
a subject of partition by any mechanical division.   And the
only way in which the interests of such common owners can
be divided is by making sale of the same.[4]   But in New York,
where there were several mills upon the same stream, partition was made by assigning a mill and mill-dam to one, with a
privilege of flowing the land of the other above him, for the
purpose of raising the necessary head of water.[5]   In a case in
Maine, where the common property was a cotton factory, the
commissioners reported that it could not be divided, to be
used for the purposes for which it was constructed, but might
be for other uses, and the court required it to be done.[6]   In
some of the States, if the property is not susceptible of partition, the court may order it sold, and the proceeds divided.[7]
In Massachusetts, if the premises cannot be divided, they may
all be set to one, and he be required to pay the estimated value
of his co-tenant's share to him.[8]

11. In most of the States, in addition to the modes of effecting partition above mentioned, courts of probate jurisdiction
have the power to cause partition to be made among the heirs
or devisees of an estate which has come within the cognizance

[1] Conant v. Smith, 1 Aik. 67 ; Brown v. Turner, Id. 350.

[2] Crowell v. Woodbury, 52 N. H. 613.

[3] Miller v. Miller, 13 Pick. 237; Pub. Stat. c. 136, § 77 ; De Witt v. Harvey,
4 Gray, 486.

[4] McGillivray v. Evans, 27 Cal. 96.

[5] Hills v. Dey, 14 Wend. 204.   See, as to special partition of mines and other
indivisible hereditaments by means of resort to equity, Adam v. Briggs Iron Co.,
7 Cush. 361 ; Tyler v. Wilkinson, 4 Mason, 397 ; Belknap v. Trimble, 3 Paige,
577 ; De Witt v. Harvey, 4 Gray, 499 ; Story, Eq. Jur. § 656.   See also, as to
dividing water-power in New Hampshire, Morrill v. Morrill, 5 N. H. 134; and
Me. Stat. 1821, c. 37, § 2 ; Hanson v. Willard, 12 Me. 142.

[6] Wood v. Little, 35 Me. 107.

[7] Royston v. Royston, 13 Ga. 425 ; Higginbottom v. Short, 25 Miss. 160.

[8] King v. Reed, 11 Gray, 490.

of the court.[1] In such case no deed of release of their several proportions by one heir or devisee to another is required, as the adjudication of the court, accepting and affirming the doings of the commissioners appointed to make the partition, is binding and conclusive. The partition must be of the entire estate and not of a part only,[2] nor can it affect an alienee of one of the heirs * or devisees who acquires [*430] his title before proceedings are commenced, as such alienee is not a party to the proceedings of settling the estate in the probate court.[3]

12. No parol partition can be effectual unless accompanied by deeds from one co-tenant to the other, inasmuch as the statute of frauds applies to such cases.[4] But where two tenants in common made parol partition of land, it was held to be good and effectual against creditors and purchasers if it is followed by separate open and notorious possession. And such possession would be notice of an existing deed, though it had not been recorded.[5] But in one case in New York, the court gave practical effect to a partition made by co-tenants by parol between themselves, which was followed by a separate occupation by each tenant for several, though less than twenty years. One of these having made expensive improvements upon the part set to him, and another of the original co-tenants having sought to enforce a new partition, the court refused to allow this partition to be disturbed.[6] But in New Hampshire and Massachusetts there is a class of *quasi* corporations known as proprietors of common lands, which may make partition of their lands by a simple vote properly made and recorded without any deed.[7]

[1] Walton v. Willis, 1 Dall. 265 ; Witham v. Cutts, 4 Me. 31.

[2] Arms v. Lyman, 5 Pick. 210.

[3] Pond v. Poud, 13 Mass. 413 ; Cook v. Davenport, 17 Mass. 345.

[4] Porter v. Hill, 9 Mass. 34 ; Porter v. Perkins, 5 Mass. 232 ; Snively r. Luce, 1 Watts, 69 ; Gratz v. Gratz, 4 Rawle, 411 ; Gardiner Mg. Co. v. Heald, 5 Me. 384 ; Dow v. Jewell, 18 N. H. 354 ; Den v. Longstreet, 18 N. J. L. 414. But it is otherwise in Texas. Stuart v. Baker, 17 Tex. 420.

[5] Manly v. Pettee, 38 Ill. 128–132.

[6] Wood v. Fleet, 36 N. Y. 501. See also Conkling v. Brown, 57 Barb. 265.

[7] Coburn v. Ellenwood, 4 N. H. 99 ; Folger v. Mitchell, 3 Pick. 396 ; Adams v. Frothingham, 3 Mass. 352 ; Corbett v. Norcross, 35 N. H. 99 ; Rothwell v. Dewees, 2 Black, 613.

13. But although a parol partition between tenants in common may not, for the reasons stated, affect the legal title of
the several owners, where it is followed by a possession in
conformity with such partition it will so far bind the possession as to give to each co-tenant the rights and incidents of
an exclusive possession of his purparty.[1] Exclusive possession by one tenant in common of a particular part of the
estate, accompanied by a denial of his co-tenant's right of
possession in the part thus occupied, may grow into a legal
presumption of partition having been made.[2] And in some
cases the law will infer this from the mere sole and exclusive
occupation of such part, if continued a sufficient length of
time, — in Pennsylvania twenty-one years, and in Kentucky
twenty years.[3]

14. Although each of several tenants in common has a
several freehold in his share or part of the common inheritance, yet the interests of all are so far identical, and each is
so far regarded as acting for the others in regard to the estate,
that, if there were an outstanding adverse title to any part of
the estate, no one of them, before partition made, could, by
purchasing it in, use it against his co-tenants if they were
willing to contribute *pro rata* towards reimbursing him the
moneys he may have had to pay to acquire such title. Equity
would, in such case, restrain the use of such title adversely to
his co-tenants. In making such purchase, he would be considered as acting as trustee for his co-tenants, until they should
have disaffirmed the presumption by refusing to contribute.[4]
The rule of equity is thus stated in Britton v. Handy : " Equity
prohibits a purchase by parties placed in the situation of trust

[1] Jackson v. Harder, 4 Johns. 202, 212 ; Jackson v. Vosburgh, 9 Johns. 276 ;
Slice v. Derrick, 2 Rich. 627, 629 ; Piatt v. Hubbel, 5 Ohio, 243 ; Corbin v. Jackson, 14 Wend. 619 ; Keay v. Goodwin, 16 Mass. 1, 3 ; Rider v. Maul, 46 Penn. St.
376 ; Maul v. Rider, 51 Penn. St. 377. And see Hazen v. Barnett, 50 Mo. 507,
that it gives an equitable title. So Tomlin v. Hilyard, 43 Ill. 302.

[2] Lloyd v. Gordon, 2 Har. & McH. 254.

[3] Gregg v. Blackmore, 10 Watts, 192 ; Drane v. Gregory, 3 B. Mon. 619.

[4] Venable v. Beauchamp, 3 Dana, 321 ; Lee v. Fox, 6 Dana, 171 ; Thruston
v. Masterson, 9 Dana, 228 ; Owings v. M'Clain, 1 A. K. Marsh. 230 ; Van Horne
v. Fonda, 5 Johns. Ch. 407 ; 4 Kent, Com. 371 ; Titsworth v. Stout, 49 Ill.
78, 80.

or confidence with respect to the subject of the purchase, — no party can be permitted to purchase for his own benefit or interest, where he has a duty to perform which is inconsistent with the character of the purchase; and this has been applied to purchases of outstanding titles and incumbrances by joint-tenants, and, in some instances, by tenants in common."[1] And it has accordingly been held that one tenant cannot gain any advantage against his co-tenant by bidding in the common property, if sold for taxes;[2] though it has been said that, after the period of redemption from such sale has expired, either of the co-tenants may purchase the estate of the one who may have bid it off, without thereby creating any rights in his co-tenant.[3]

*15. But how far this principle shall be applied [*431] after partition made, depends upon the circumstances of the cases as they arise. Thus, supposing partition to be made by mutual deeds of release without fraud, and the title to some part of the premises fails, the loss, as a general proposition, falls on the party whose property is immediately affected by it.[4]

16. But by the statute 31 Henry VIII. it was expressly provided that tenants in common, between whom partition has been made by a writ of partition, may have the aid of each other " to deraign the warranty " as to the estate; that is, to avail himself of the benefit of the general warranty which had attached to the estate, by rendering it effectual for the protection of, or compensation for, the land which should

---

[1] Brittin v. Handy, 20 Ark. 381, 402. See also Jones v. Stanton, 11 Mo. 433; Flagg v. Mann, 2 Sumn. 486; Weaver v. Wible, 25 Penn. St. 270; Tisdale v. Tisdale, 2 Sneed, 596; Lloyd v. Lynch, 28 Penn. St. 419; Picot v. Page, 26 Mo. 398; Gossom v. Donaldson, 18 B. Mon. 230; ante, p. *410; Sullivan v. McLenans, 2 Iowa, 442. But see Wells v. Chapman, 4 Sandf. Ch. 312. The general doctrine above stated is fully sustained by the U. S. Court. Rothwell v. Dewees, 2 Black, 613, citing Farmer v. Samuel, 4 Littell, 187; Lee v. Fox, 6 Dana, 176; Butler v. Porter, 13 Mich. 292; Downer v. Smith, 38 Vt. 464; Titsworth v. Stout, 49 Ill. 80.

[2] Page v. Webster, 8 Mich. 263; Lloyd v. Lynch, 28 Penn. St. 419; Halsey v. Blood, 29 Penn. St. 319; Morgan v. Herrick, 21 Ill. 481.

[3] Reinboth v. Zerbe Run Imp. Co., 29 Penn. St. 139. See also Watkins v. Eaton, 30 Me. 529.

[4] Beardsley v. Knight, 10 Vt. 185; Weiser v. Weiser, 5 Watts, 279.

be adversely demanded or recovered.[1] This proposition may perhaps be made a little more intelligible by the analogy there is between the case of such tenant in common, and that of a tenant having the right to call "in aid" another to protect his title. Thus, for instance, if a tenant for life is sued in a writ of entry by some one claiming the inheritance, as he is not supposed to be cognizant of the full title, he properly calls upon the reversioner to aid him in making defence. So if one has purchased the inheritance, and his vendor has warranted the title, and he is sued, in such an action he may call upon, or, in technical terms, "vouch in," his warrantor to defend the title.[2] But as tenants in common, after partition made, are not considered as holding under each other, so that, if one is sued in respect to his title to his property, he can call the others in aid, or vouch them in to defend as warrantors, they are all considered as holding under the original general or paramount warrantor. And when either of them was sued in respect to his title, he might require the aid of his former co-tenants in calling upon their general or paramount warrantor to make good his warranty, or make compensation.[3]

[*432]   *17. Applying this common-law duty of co-tenants to aid each other in protecting what had been a common estate, even after partition made, the law holds it incompatible with their duty towards each other for either to become

---

1 Cowel, Interp. Verb. "Deraign," Norrice's Case, 6 Rep. 12 ; Allnatt, Part. 161, 163 ; 6 Dane, Abr. 5, where it is said the Stat. 31 Henry VIII. is a part of Massachusetts common law ; and so in Tennessee, 8 Humph. 285. "*De arraign*," applied to hindering or preventing battle when tenant waged it, is said to be derived from "*derismer*," signifying to *deny* or *refuse*. Barringt. Stat. 296, and note. In this sense it would seem to imply the making use of the warranty by way of estoppel, by calling in a party to whom it applied. But in a book called "Law French and Latin Dictionary," published in 1701, "by F. O." one definition of "deraign" is "to prove or make good." "A deraignment or proof."

2 Stearns, Real Act. 99, 131 ; Booth, Real Act. 60.

3 Norrice's Case, 6 Rep. 12 ; Allnatt, Part. 156–164 ; 1 Prest. Abs. 304 ; Sawyers *v.* Cator, 8 Humph. 256 ; Norris *v.* Harris, 9 Gill, 19 ; Dugan *v.* Hollins, 4 Md. Ch. 139 ; Co. Lit. 174 a. The reader, however, should bear in mind that the warranty here spoken of is the ancient warranty of the common law, which never practically obtained in the United States. 4 Kent, Com. 470.

the demandant in a suit to recover any portion of the land by a paramount title, and thus to place himself in antagonism to his co-tenants and their common warrantor.[1]

18. And where partition has been made by law, each partitioner becomes a warrantor to all the others to the extent of his share, so long as the privity of estate continues between them. And inasmuch as a warrantor cannot claim against his own warranty, no tenant after partition made can set up an adverse title to the portion of another, for the purpose of ousting him from the part which has been parted off to him.[2] When partition has been made, the tenant, to whom a part has been set out, is regarded in law as a purchaser for value of the same.[3]

19. If, after the partition has been made, one of the parties is evicted of his property by a paramount title, the partition as to him is defeated at his election, and he may enter upon the shares of the others as if none had been made, and have a new partition of the premises. But this right does not extend to the alienee of one of these tenants, because by such alienation the privity of estate between them and the holder of his share is destroyed. Nor can the alienee himself enter upon the shares of the other tenants in such a case and defeat the partition.[4] And if, in the case supposed, one co-tenant after partition is evicted by paramount title, he is not confined for his remedy to a new partition, but may rely upon his warranty and recover his recompense for his loss by an action thereon against his former co-tenants.* [5]

* NOTE. — In some of the States, as before stated, joint tenants and tenants * in common are prohibited by statute from committing waste [*433] upon the common inheritance. In *Massachusetts* and *Maine*, if a tenant commits waste without first giving thirty days' prior notice to his co-tenants in writing, he forfeits three times the amount of the damages that shall be occasioned thereby in a suit by one or more of the co-tenants. Mass. Gen. Stat.

---

[1] Venable *v.* Beauchamp, 3 Dana, 326.

[2] Co. Lit. 174 a ; Com. Dig. Parcener, C. 13 ; Venable *v.* Beauchamp, 3 Dana, 326.

[3] Campau *v.* Barnard, 25 Mich. 382.

[4] Co. Lit. 173 b; Id. 174 a; Com. Dig. Parcener, C. 13; Feather *v.* Strohoecker, 3 Penn. 505.

[5] Com. Dig. Parcener, C. 14.

1860, c. 138, § 7; Maine Rev. Stat. 1871, c. 95, § 5. In *Rhode Island*, if a tenant commit waste without the consent of his co-tenants, he forfeits double damages for the waste done. Gen. Stat. c. 220, § 2. In *New York*, the co-tenant in such a case may take judgment for treble damages, or he may have partition of the estate at his election, and the amount of such damage deducted from the defendant's share and added to his own. And the law is the same in *New Jersey*, except that single damages only can be recovered. In *Ohio*, one parcener may have an action of waste in a civil form against his coparceners. N. Y. Rev. Stat. vol. 2, p. 346 ; Nixon, Dig. of N. J. Stat. 1868, p. 1022 ; Ohio Rev. Stat. 1860, c. 81, § 15. In *Missouri*, a tenant in common is liable to his co-tenant in an action at law for doing waste upon the premises, and if wantonly done he may recover treble damages. Stat. 1872, vol. 2, c. 85, § 46. In *Virginia*, the law is the same in such cases as in Missouri. Code, 1873, c. 133, § 2. So in *Kentucky*, Gen. Stat. 1873, c. 66, art. 3, § 5. In *Minnesota*, the tenant committing waste is liable to forfeit his estate and pay treble damages to his co-tenant in certain cases. Stat. 1873, c. 43, § 27. And a similar law prevails in *Iowa* and *Indiana*. Iowa, Code, 1873, Tit. 20, § 3332 ; Ind. Rev. Stat. 1852, vol. 2, p. 174. In *Michigan* and *Wisconsin*, such tenant may have an action on the case for the waste, and recover double damages. Mich. Comp. Laws, 1871, vol. 2, c. 197, § 3; Wis. Rev. Stat. 1858, c. 143. In *California*, he may recover treble damages in an action for such waste. Wood, Dig. 1858.

NOTE. — In a large majority of the States, partition may be made by a summary and convenient method of petition to the courts of common law.

In *Massachusetts*, one or more of the persons holding lands as joint-tenants, coparceners, or tenants in common may apply by petition to the Superior or Supreme Court, held for the county in which the lands lie, for a partition of the same. The petition may be maintained by any person who has an estate in possession, but not by one who has only a remainder or reversion ; nor by any tenant for years, of whose term less than twenty years remain unexpired, as against a tenant of the freehold. Tenants for years, however, may have partition between themselves, though such partition shall not affect the premises when they revert to the respective landlords or reversioners. The petition sets forth the rights and titles of all persons interested who would be bound by the partition, whether they have an estate of inheritance for life or years, in possession, remainder, or reversion, and whether vested or contingent ; and if the petitioner holds an estate for life or years, the person entitled to the remainder or reversion is a party interested, and entitled to notice. Parties within the State are notified by serving upon them an attested copy of the petition and of the summons ; and parties absent from [*434] the State, or unknown, are notified by public * advertisement, and the court may allow them time to appear and answer. Where some of the parties are infants or insane persons, the court may assign guardians to such. If a person not named in the petition appears and defends, the petitioner may deny his title. If it appears that the petitioner is entitled to partition, an interlocutory judgment that partition be made is awarded, and commissioners are appointed to make it. If there are several petitioners, they may, at their election, have their shares set off together or in severalty. If a division cannot be made without damage to the owners, the whole estate, or the part incapable of division, may be set off to any one who will accept it, he paying a sum of money to make the partition just and equal; or the exclusive occupancy and enjoyment of the whole or part may be assigned to each of the parties alternately for certain specified times, in proportion to their respective interests. In such case the occupant for the time being is liable to his co-tenants for any injury to the premises occasioned by his misconduct, as if a tenant for years without express covenants ; and like such tenant he may recover damages for an injury by a stranger; and he and the other tenants may recover jointly for any further damages in like manner as lessors. Upon the return of the commissioners, the final judgment confirming their report is conclusive as to the rights of property, and possession of parties and privies to the judgment, including all who might have appeared and answered, except that an absent part-owner may apply for a new partition within three years. A stranger claiming in severalty is not bound by a judgment of partition : but if one who has not appeared and answered, claims the share assigned to or left for any of the supposed part-owners, he is bound by the judgment, so far as it respects the partition and assignment of the shares, like a party to the suit; but he may bring his action for the share claimed by him against the person to whom it was assigned or left. In case two or more respondents claim the same share, their respective claims may be left undecided, except so far as to determine which shall be admitted to appear ; and the share so claimed is left for whichever party is proved to be entitled to it in a suit between themselves subsequent to the partition. If it is decided in the suit for partition that either of the respondents is not entitled to the share that he claims, he is concluded by the judgment, so far as it respects the partition and assignment, but he may bring an action against the other claimant for his share. If any person who has not appeared and answered, claims an additional share as part-owner, he is bound by the partition, but may recover against each of the other tenants his proportion thereof. In case a share is left or assigned to a part-owner who is dead, his heir or devisee may claim the original share, though made a party to the petition. A party evicted of his share by paramount title may have a new partition of the residue. A person having a mortgage or other lien upon the share of a part-owner is concluded by the partition ; but his lien remains in full force upon the part assigned or left to such part-owner. If the petitioner recovers judgment in any process of partition in which the respondent claims any part of the premises as his own estate in fee, and it is proved that the latter held the same under a title which he believed to be good, * he is entitled to betterments as [*435] provided for tenants in real actions, and the petitioner must pay for them after deducting the rents, profits, and other damages for which the respondent is chargeable. So a party holding under partition is entitled to betterments in case of eviction. If, after a first partition, improvements have been made on any part of the premises which by the new partition is taken from the share of the party who made them, he is entitled to contribution, to be awarded by the commissioners. A lease of the whole or a part of the estate to be divided does not prevent or invalidate the partition ; nor is it prevented or invalidated by any of the tenants being trustee, attorney, or guardian of a co-tenant. In case of remainders or estates devised or limited to, or in trust for, persons not in being at the time of the application for partition, upon notice to the persons who may be parents of such persons, the court may appoint a person to appear as the next friend of such persons. The return of the commissioners is to be recorded in the registry of deeds for the county where the land lies. Partition may also be compelled by writ of partition at the common law. (Pub. Stat. c. 178, § 1.) Courts of probate may make partition of lands held in common by joint-tenants or tenants in common, where their respective shares are not in dispute, in the same way as such partition might be made among heirs or devisees of an estate of a deceased person.   And if the lands of which partition is to be made cannot be advantage-ously divided, the court may authorize the commissioners to make sale and con-veyance of the whole or any part of the same, and the proceeds to be distributed in such a manner as to make the partition equal.   Pub. Stat. 1881, c. 178.

In *Maine,* the petition is addressed to the Supreme Court held for the county where the land lies, and the proceedings under the petition are, in all the more important features, similar to those in Þassachusetts, as described above.   A writ of partition may also be had at common law.   Rev. Stat. 1857, c. 88.   And see Acts 1860, c. 180 ; Rev. Stat. 1871, c. 88 ; Rev. Stat. 1884, c. 88.

In *New Hampshire,* one or more persons having or holding real estate with others may have partition by applying by petition to the Superior Court in the county where the land lies.   Issues of fact may be made and tried as on a writ at common law.   Gen. Stat. 1867, c. 228.   The partition is made by a committee of three residents of the county.   It is provided that no partition shall be avoided by any conveyance after the entry of the petition, nor unless recorded before such entry ; nor by any mortgage or other lien upon the estate.   If any share be set off to any person other than the legal owner, such share enures to the benefit of the legal owner.   If there is no dispute about the title, the petition may be directed to the judge of probate.   If the property is not susceptible of division, a sale may be ordered by the Superior Court.   In other respects the mode of procedure is similar to that in Þassachusetts.   Comp. Stat. 1853, c. 219; Gen. Stat. 1867, c. 228 ; Gen. Laws, 1878, c. 247.

In *Vermont,* the petition is made to the county court, and three commissioners from the county are appointed to make the partition.   If the land cannot be con-veniently divided, and no one of the parties interested will consent to raise an assignment of it, and pay such sum as the commissioners direct, the court will order the commissioners to sell such estate, and execute conveyances which bind the owners, and all persons claiming under them.   No commissioner can become a purchaser at such sale.   No partition is avoided by any conveyance by a part-owner previous to the service of the petition, unless it be recorded, or it appear that the petitioner had knowledge of such conveyance.   If any share is set off to any person other than the legal owner, such share enures to the benefit of the legal owner.   A party without the State who had not a personal notice may avoid the partition within three years for sufficient cause, when a new partition is [*436] ordered.   Improvements * made after the first partition are allowed for.

The process does not abate by death of a party   Gen. Stat. 1860, c. 45 ; Rev. Laws, 1880, c. 70.   By the Public Acts, 1870, No. 69, provision is made for effecting partition of the waters of any mineral or medicinal spring which is owned by joint-tenants, tenants in common, or copartners, in such man-ner as commissioners shall judge just and equitable.

In *Rhode Island,* joint-tenants, tenants in common, and coparceners, actually seised of an estate for life or years, may have partition by writ of partition.   If the premises are situate in two or more counties, partition may be sued for by action at law, or by bill in equity in either county.   In suits in equity the Su-preme Court may, in their discretion, upon motion of any party, order the whole or any portion of the premises to be sold at auction by commissioners.   In actions at law, the court appoint one or more persons to make partition. The report of the commissioners and the judgment of the court thereon is recorded in the office of the clerk of the town. Rev. Stat. 1857, c. 208. Partition may be made at law by metes and bounds, or in equity by sale and division of proceeds, all persons in interest being made parties by actual notice or by publication, and their titles set forth, the court appointing persons to represent those having interests who are not in being ; and the purchaser takes a perfect title. Laws, 1866. Partition in ordinary cases may be effected upon petition, wherein are set forth the owners' names and the titles by which they claim, and creditors may, at the petitioner's election, be made parties to such proceedings. The mode of proceeding in the matter of pleas and answers is prescribed in the act. Upon the trial of an issue, the court renders judgment, and directs partition to be made by referees ; and if by their report it should appear that a partition would be injurious, the court may direct a sale of the whole or a part of the estate, and a partition of the rest. A judgment upon the final report of the referees, affirming the same, becomes a final and effectual partition. Rev. Stat. 1866, p. 538 ; Pub. Stat. 1882, c. 230.

In *Connecticut*, the Superior Court, as a court of equity, may, upon the petition of any person interested, order partition of any estate held in joint-tenancy, tenancy in common, or coparcenary ; and may appoint a committee for that purpose. When in the opinion of the court a sale will better promote the interest of all parties, they may appoint a committee to make a sale. The decree for partition and the proceedings under it must be recorded in the records of lands in the town where the estate lies. Gen. Stat. 1866, pp. 398, 416; Gen. Stat. 1875, p. 414, § 8, p. 480.

In *Nebraska*, all joint tenants and tenants in common are entitled to partition, and this is made by commissioners upon a petition to the court of the county where the land lies ; and these are appointed by the Probate Court. And the court may assign the whole to one of them, on payment by him to the others of the value of their shares, or may order a sale of a whole or a part if no division can be made conveniently of the land. Incumbrancers may be made parties at the option of the petitioners ; and the incumbrances are either to be paid off or a security given or sum invested to secure them. Gen. Stat. 1873, c. 17, §§ 292, 297 : Comp. Stat. 1881, pt. 1, tit. 3; pt. 2, tit. 26.

In *New York*, any joint tenant, or tenant in common, having an estate of inheritance for life or for years, may proceed in the Supreme Court, or the court of the county, or the mayor's court of a city or superior court of the city of New York for partition, or, if necessary, for a sale of the land. The proceeding is partly legal and partly equitable, but a jury trial is a matter of right, by suit at law in place of petition as formerly, and describes the premises and the rights and titles of parties, and is verified by affidavit. Every person interested may be made a party. In case any party or his interest is unknown, uncertain, or contingent, or the ownership depends upon an executory devise, or the remainder is contingent, it must be so stated. Creditors having liens need not be made parties. Such liens attach to the part set off to the debtor. The complainant may make persons having specific liens parties to the proceeding. Notice of the proceeding having been given, any party interested may appear and answer, and any person not named as a party therein may be admitted to appear. All issues are tried as in personal actions. The court appoint three commissioners to make the division. The final judgment upon their report is conclusive on all parties named therein, and all persons interested, who may be unknown, to whom notice was given by publication. But the judgment does not affect persons having claims to the *whole* of the premises, as tenants in dower, by the curtesy, or for life. If the commissioners report that the land cannot be divided without prejudice to the owners, the court may order a sale on such security as they shall prescribe. Before the order of sale, all holders of specific liens are to be made parties, and their incumbrances are first satisfied from the proceeds of the sale, and the residue is then distributed. The court in their discretion may order any estate in dower, by the curtesy, or for life, to be sold, or otherwise excepted from the sale; and in case of the sale of such interest, the court directs the payment of such sum in gross to the party, if he formally assent; otherwise an investment is made for his benefit, in amount proportioned to his interest. No commissioner or [*437] guardian to an infant party * can be a purchaser. The commissioners execute conveyances, which are recorded, and which are a bar to all parties named, and all unknown, if the required notice has been given, and to all having liens on any undivided share. The late court of chancery had the same power, upon petition or bill, to decree partitions and sales, as is given to the common-law courts. The Supreme Court may appoint a receiver of the rents or profits, pending proceedings for partition. Acts, 1863; Rev. Stat. 5th ed. vol. 3, pt. 3, tit. 3, c. 5, pp. 603–620; 1863, vol. 2, pp. 326–342; Rev. Stat. 7th ed. vol. 4, c. 14, tit. 1, art. 2; c. 3, tit. 3, art. 1; Croghan *v.* Livingston, 17 N. Y. 225; Hewlett *v.* Wood, 62 N. Y. 75.

In *Wisconsin*, one or more tenants in common, or coparcenary, or joint-tenants, may have partition by complaint in the circuit court for the county where the land lies. The action may be maintained by any such person who has an estate in possession, but not by one who has only an estate in remainder or reversion. The manner of procedure is the same as that in New York. Rev. Stat. 1858, c. 142; Rev. Stat. 1878, c. 184.

In *Michigan*, joint-tenants, and tenants in common, may have partition by a suit in the circuit court for the county by bill in equity. The suit may be maintained by any one who has an estate in possession, but not by one who has only an estate in remainder or reversion. If the bill is taken as confessed by any of the defendants, the court order a reference to a Master to take proof of the title of the complainants. Upon making a decree for partition, reference is made to a commissioner to inquire whether the premises can be divided without prejudice. Partition is made by three commissioners, who proceed in the same manner as the commissioners under the statutes of New York; and the bill in equity is in other respects conducted in the same manner as the suit by petition was in that State. Comp. Laws, 1857, vol. 2, c. 135. Persons having contingent interests which become certain after the filing of the bill may become parties. Laws, 1867; Comp. Laws, 1871, vol. 2, p. 196; Gen. Laws, 1882, c. 270. Partition is also had by petition in the probate court among heirs or devisees on petition of any of them. The partition is made by commissioners appointed by the court who may set off the whole to one if the property is insusceptible of division. Gen. Laws, 1882, c. 226.

In *Minnesota*, joint-tenants, and tenants in common, having an estate of inheritance, for life or for years, may have partition by an action in the district court of the proper county by complaint. After notice, if it be alleged in the complaint, and established by proof, that partition cannot be made without prejudice to the owner, the court order a sale, and for that purpose appoint one or more referees;

otherwise a partition is ordered to be made by three referees. The judgment upon their report is conclusive upon all parties named or interested who have been notified as required ; but it does not affect the claims of tenants in dower, by the curtesy, or for life, to the *whole* of the property. If there are general liens upon the property, the court order a reference to ascertain the amount and priority of the same ; and all liens are satisfied before any distribution to the part-owner. If the tenants do not consent to receive a sum in gross, the court order a just proportion to be invested for their benefit. Inchoate rights of dower and curtesy are estimated on the principle of annuities and survivorships. The sale is at auction in the same manner as on execution, and the conveyances are executed by the referees and recorded in the county where situated. Comp. Stat. 1859, c. 65. And the court may authorize the sale of all, or only a part, of the lands. Gen. Laws, 1864 ; Stat. 1873, vol. 2, c. 43, tit. 2 ; Stat. 1878, c. 74.

In *Illinois*, partition between joint-tenants, tenants in common, or in coparcenary, is made by petition to the circuit court of the county describing the premises, and all persons having a vested or contingent interest therein, and verified by affidavit. All persons interested, in possession or otherwise, or entitled to dower in the premises, must be made parties and notified by summons, or, if absent, • by publication. New parties may be admitted by way of [•438] interpleader. The court appoint three commissioners to make partition, or, if they find that this cannot be done without prejudice, to sell the same by order of court, and execute conveyances, which shall operate as a bar against all owners and all persons claiming under them. Comp. Stat. 1858, vol. 1, p. 160 ; Rev. Stat. 1874, c. 106.

In *Indiana*, joint-tenants, tenants in common, or coparcenary, may have partition by applying to the circuit court or court having proper jurisdiction of the county by petition. The proceeding is the same as in civil suits and if it appear to the court that partition ought to be made, the court award an interlocutory judgment to this effect, and appoint three commissioners to make partition. When the premises cannot be divided without damage to the owners, the court may order the whole or a part to be sold at public or private sale. The commissioners execute conveyances which are as effectual as if executed by the owners themselves. On the death of a party, the proceedings do not abate if his heirs are made parties. Upon showing sufficient cause, any person not served with summons may open the proceedings within one year, and also any person of unsound mind, or any infant whose guardian did not attend and approve such partition, may, within one year after the removal of his disability, have a review of such partition. Rev. Stat. 1852, vol. 2, p. 329, c. 13; and see Acts, 1859, c. 101; Sup. Rev. St. 1870, p. 363 ; Rev. Stat. 1881, §§ 1186–1209.

In *Ohio*, joint tenants, tenants in common, or in coparcenary, may have partition by applying by petition to the court of common pleas for the county, or, where the premises are situate in two or more counties, to the court of common pleas held for either of the counties. The court issue a writ of partition to the sheriff of the county, directing him to make partition by the oaths of three freeholders named by the court. If the freeholders are of opinion that the premises cannot be divided according to the writ without injury thereto, they return a just valuation of such estate to the court ; and if one or more of the parties elect to take the land at the appraisement, the same is adjudged to him or them, and, on payment of a proper proportion of the appraised value, the sheriff executes the conveyances. Otherwise the court order a sale by the sheriff, who executes a deed of the estate. A widow entitled to dower in the estate must be made a party, and dower must be assigned unless it is in an undivided interest only, or is already assigned, or the dowress elects to be endowed in the proceeds. Guardians of minor heirs, and guardians of idiots and insane persons, may act in their behalf in any partition. Williams's Rev. Stat. (1883), vol. 2, §§ 5754-5778.

In *Pennsylvania*, the Supreme Court and the county courts of common pleas grant writs of partition at the suit of joint-tenants, tenants in common, and co-parceners, by an inquest of seven men or a commission of three men. When the inquest, who are directed to make such partition, are of opinion that the lands cannot be divided without prejudice to the whole, they shall return to the court an appraisement ; whereupon the court may adjudge the same to one or more of the parties who may elect to take it at the valuation, and the sheriff shall execute the deed, which is to be recorded in the registry of deeds. In case none of the parties agree to take the land, it is sold by the sheriff at public auction. Where partition is made upon default of any party, he may, for good cause shown, obtain a reversal within a year thereafter. When equal partition cannot be made without prejudice to the whole, the inquest shall return a just valuation of the lands and tenements ; and if one or more of the parties shall elect to take the same at the appraised value, the court shall adjudge the same to him or them on payment to the other parties of their proportions of the appraised value ; whereupon the sheriff executes conveyances to the party or parties making such election, subject to a lien in favor of the others for the payment of their shares. In case none of the parties elect to take the land, the court may order a sale at public auction ; and the sheriff is empowered to execute deeds to the purchasers. The sheriff's inquisition and all orders of court in relation to partition are recorded. Purdon, Dig. 1861, pp. 770-775, 1872, pp. 1112-1119 ; Laws, 1874, p. 156.

[*439]   * In *New Jersey*, a coparcener, joint-tenant, or tenant in common, may make application for partition to the Supreme Court, or circuit court, or court of common pleas for the county. The court appoints three commissioners to divide the land into a definite number of shares. The shares are numbered, and an allotment made by ballot, at which, on the application of any party, a judge or justice shall attend. The proceedings are recorded in the clerk's office, and are as effectual to make a partition as if made on writs of partition at common law. Where one or more of the joint-tenants, &c., are minors, the orphans' court may order partition.

Any lien upon the undivided estate of any owner becomes a lien only on the share allotted to such owner. If a partition would be injurious, the court may order the commissioners to sell the whole at auction, and execute conveyances. This act does not extend to the partitioning of lands held in common by the general proprietors of the eastern or western divisions of the State. Joint-tenants, and tenants in common, may also be compelled to make partition, like coparceners at common law, by writ of partition in the court of chancery. A part of the lands may be sold, and the remainder divided, when the whole cannot be divided without prejudice. There may be partition among parties holding in reversion or remainder, by consent of the particular tenants ; or if partition cannot be made, the premises may be sold, and the particular tenants paid their proportion of the proceeds. If any of the parties are minors, the partition may be made by the Prerogative Court. Nixon, Dig. 1855, pp. 572-583 ; Laws, 1858, c. 50, and c. 223 ; Rev. Stat. 1875, pp. 555-573 ; Rev. 1877, 795-806.

In *Virginia*, tenants in common, joint-tenants, and coparceners, are compellable to make partition, and the court of equity of the county or corporation, wherein the estate or any part thereof is situate, has jurisdiction for such purpose. When partition cannot be conveniently made, the entire estate may be allotted to any party who will accept the same, and compensate the other parties in interest therefor ; or if the interest of the parties will be promoted thereby, the court may order a sale of the entire estate, or an allotment of part and sale of the residue, and make distribution of the proceeds of sale. Any two or more of the parties, if they so elect, may have their shares laid off together. If the name or share of any person interested be unknown, so much as is known in relation thereto must be stated in the bill. Any lessee of lands thus divided or sold still holds the same of him to whom such land is allotted or sold. Code, 1849, tit. 34, e. 124, p. 525, §§ 1-5 ; Code, 1873, p. 920, §§ 1-5.

In *Mississippi*, application for partition is made to the courts of chancery by petition, and partition is made by these courts by allotment in the same manner as in New Jersey, but they may in the first instance order a sale. Rev. Code, 1857, pp. 316-320 ; Rev. Code, 1871, c. 26 ; Rev. Code, 1880, c. 71.

In *Alabama*, partition is made in the same manner, on application to the probate court. Code, 1867, §§ 3105, 3119 ; Code, 1876, §§ 3497-3520.

* In *Georgia*, joint-tenants, tenants in common, and coparceners, may [*440] apply to the superior court of the county for a writ of partition. This may be contested, but if allowed the writ issues to five partitioners, who proceed to make partition; which being made, the court give final judgment which concludes all parties. Within one year after such judgment, or, in case of disability, within one year after its removal, a party interested may have the partition set aside for good cause shown ; when it is shown to the court that a division cannot be made without prejudice to the whole, they may order a sale thereof by persons appointed, who are to make conveyances binding on all parties. Parties interested but under disability have a year after the disability is removed to reopen the partition. Cobb, New Dig. 1851, vol. I, p. 581 ; Code, 1873, pp. 711-715 ; Code, 1882, §§ 3996-4007.

In *Arkansas*, partition between joint-tenants, tenants in common, and coparceners, is made by petition to the circuit court for the county. Partition may be had by owners of the fee, freehold, or for years, or by a dowress ; and whether it shall be had or not is tried as a suit at law. If allowed, it is made by commissioners, or, if this cannot be done without prejudice to the owners, the premises are ordered to be sold at auction, when the conveyances are executed by the commissioners and recorded. Partition or sale is not to be made contrary to the will of a testator. Ark. Dig. 1858, c. 122 ; Dig. 1874, c. 102.

In *Kentucky*, land held by joint-tenants, tenants in common, coparceners, or devisees, may be divided by commissioners appointed by the county court. The deeds of partition are executed by the commissioners and recorded. Rev. Stat. 1860, c. 57. And if partition would be injurious, the court on petition may order sale. Sup. Rev. Stat. 1866, p. 751. Joint-tenants may be compelled to make partition ; and if a joint-tenant dies, his part descends to heirs, &c., subject to debts, dower, curtesy, and distribution. Gen. Stat. 1873, c. 63.

In *Tennessee*, any person having an estate in common or otherwise with others in fee for life or years may have partition by bill or petition to the county, circuit, or chancery courts.   The bill or petition must set forth the parties and their titles, with a description of the property.   It is no objection that parties are infants or the premises incumbered by dower, curtesy, or mortgage rights.   No sale is made if the will directs otherwise.   Partition is made by three commissioners, and their report, when confirmed by the court, vests the title according to its terms, and such partition is conclusive upon all parties named and parties un. known to whom the required notice has been given by publication, but does not affect the claim of any one having a claim of dower or a life-estate in the whole of the premises.   The commissioners may divide the land into unequal shares, and charge the larger shares with the sums necessary to equalize all the shares.   If partition cannot be made without prejudice to the whole, the court may order a sale by the commissioners.   There is a lien upon the land for the purchase-money till the whole is paid.   Incumbrances upon the estate are paid before distribution of the proceeds of sale.   The court may order an investment of the shares of any persons under any disability.   Stat. 1871, §§ 3262–3322.

In *North Carolina*, tenants in common may have partition on petition to the superior courts, who appoint three commissioners to make partition, and if necessary they may make the shares unequal, and charge the more valuable of them with a sum of money sufficient to make an equitable division.   Such sums charged on minors are not payable till they are of age, but these sums bear interest, and the guardian is to pay them upon receiving assets.   A superior court may order a sale when partition would be injurious, and also when the land of joint-owners is required for public uses.   The proceeds belonging to any party under disability must be invested for his benefit.   Rev. Code, 1854, c. 82; Battles' Revisal, 1873, c. 84; Code, 1883, c. 47.

[*441]   * In *South Carolina*, joint-tenants, tenants in common, and coparceners, may apply to the court of common pleas for a writ of partition ; whereupon the court issue the writ to three or more persons, commanding them to make a division of the lands.   Division is made by allotment if not prejudicial.   The writ may also issue from the court of chancery.   Stat. at Large, vol. 3, p. 708 ; vol. 6, p. 412.   Judges of probate may direct partition where there is no dispute as to title.   If there is, it is referred to the circuit court for adjudication.   Rev. Stat. 1873, c. 114.

In *Florida*, joint tenants, tenants in common, and coparceners, may sue for partition of real estate by bill or petition, on the equity side of the circuit courts for the county or circuit in which the lands lie.   The court, if partition is decreed, appoint three commissioners to make the partition, and the final decree upon their report vests the title of the several portions in the respective parties.   If they report that the premises cannot be divided without prejudice to the owners, the court may order a sale and conveyance by the commissioners.   Thompson, Dig. 1847, p. 382; Dig. 1881, c. 160.

In *Texas*, it is provided that any joint owner of lands may compel partition by a petition to the district court of the county where the land lies ; and the court are to determine not only the several shares, but any questions as to title.   The partition is to be made by three commissioners, but no such partition shall prejudice those entitled to reversions or remainders.   If no fair partition can be made of the estate or any part thereof, a sale may be ordered.   After the partition, tenants shall hold of the landlords to whom the lands are allotted in severalty,

CH. XIII. § 7.]   JOINT ESTATES.   733

under the same rents and covenants, and the landlords shall warrant the several
parts unto the tenants, as they were bound by leases or grants respectively.   And
the decree of the court vests title without other conveyance.   Oldham & White,
Dig. 1859, p. 340, art. 1510 ; Paschal's Dig. 1866, pp. 790–792; Rev. Stat. 1879,
art. 3465–3583.

In *California*, joint-tenants, parceners, and tenants in common, may have partition on complaint, setting forth the parties and their titles.   After notice and
the requisite proofs being made the court order a partition of the whole or part,
and appoint three referees therefor.   The judgment of the court confirming their
partition is binding on all parties named, and on all unknown parties to whom
notice has been given by publication ; but such partition does not affect a tenant
for a term of less than ten years to the whole of the property.   When it is alleged
in the complaint, and established by proof, that a partition cannot be made without great prejudice, the court may order a sale of the land.   The proceeds of the
sale of incumbered property are applied to satisfy the liens of record before any
distribution is made to the part-owners.   If the lien is on the undivided share, it
remains a charge thereon after partition.   The sale is made on such terms as the
court direct, by the referees, who must not be interested in any purchase, and the
court will protect future and contingent interests.   If the sale is confirmed, the court
order the referees to execute conveyances, and take securities pursuant to such sale.
The conveyance must be recorded, and will be a bar against all persons named as
parties or notified by publication.   Wood, Dig. 1858, p. 202, art. 999–1036.   Co-
tenants having an estate for life or years, or of inheritance, may have a process for
partition, or for sale of all or a part of the lands according to their respective interests ; and no one having an unrecorded conveyance need be made a party.   Acts,
1866 ; Code, 1872, c. 4, §§ 752–801 ; Hittell, Code, 1876, §§ 10752–10801.

In *Missouri*, joint-tenants, tenants in common, and coparceners, of estates in
fee for life or years, may petition the circuit court of the county for a partition
of their lands, and for a sale thereof, if it shall appear that partition cannot be
made without prejudice to the owners.   The petition shall describe the premises,
and set forth the titles of all parties interested.   Every person having any vested
or contingent interest, whether in possession or otherwise, and every person entitled to dower in the premises, may be made a party.   The court appoint commissioners to make the partition, who are authorized at their discretion to divide the
land into lots, and lay out streets and alleys, and a map thereof shall be recorded.
The court may order any number of shares to be set off in one parcel.   If
their report is confirmed, the judgment thereon is * conclusive on all parties [*442]
to the proceedings.   The report and judgment must be recorded.   If the
commissioners report that partition is impracticable, the court may order a sale of
the whole premises by the sheriff of the county, who makes a deed, which is a bar
against all parties to the proceedings.   In the distribution of the proceeds, if any
of the parties are absent from the State, or unknown, the court must direct their
shares to be invested.   Any party claiming the money arising from such sales by
adverse title, on petition to the circuit court, may have his claim tried, and the
court will order payment to the party entitled.   No partition or sale of lands is to
be made contrary to the intention of any testator.   Guardians are authorized to act
for their wards in partition of lands, and the court may appoint a guardian for any
minor for the purpose of such division.   Gen. Stat. 1866, c. 152 ; Stat. 1872, c.
104 ; Rev. Stat. 1879, §§ 3339–3397.

In *Iowa*, joint-owners may have partition of real estate by petition in equity, setting forth the interests of the parties and describing the property. Lien holders may be made parties at the option of plaintiff or defendant. When all the shares of the parties have been settled, judgment is rendered confirming those shares, and directing partition accordingly. The court appoint referees to make the partition. If it appears to them that a partition cannot be made without great prejudice to the owners, and the court are satisfied with such report, they may order a sale of the premises. Provision is made for satisfying incumbrances upon the estate. The court, on confirming the sale, order the referees to execute conveyances, which on being recorded are valid against all subsequent purchasers, and also against all parties to the proceedings. When the referees deem a partition proper, the court, for good reasons shown, may direct particular portions of the land to be allotted to particular individuals. There may be partition of one part, and a sale of the other. The partition, when confirmed by the court, is conclusive on all parties in interest who have been notified by service or publication. The ascertained share of any absent owner shall be retained, or the proceeds invested for his benefit. Code, 1851, c. 117 ; Revision, 1860, c. 145 ; Code, 1873, tit. 20, c. 3 ; Rev. Code, 1880, §§ 3277–3306.

In *Kansas*, joint-tenants, tenants in common, and coparceners, may be compelled to make or suffer partition, on petition to the district court of the county, setting forth the title of the demandant, and describing the property and the other parties in interest. After notice, the court order partition by writ directed to commissioners to make partition as directed. If the freeholders are of opinion that partition cannot be made without injury to the property, they are required to make and return to the court a just valuation of the property. Whereupon, if the court approve the return, and any of the parties elect to take the property at the appraised value, the same is adjudged to such party on his paying to the other parties their proportion of the appraised value. In case the parties cannot agree, and no one elects to take the estate, the court may order a sale at auction by the sheriff, provided the sale be not for less than two-thirds the appraised value. The court has full power to make any order not inconsistent with the provisions of this article that may be necessary to make a just and equitable partition between the parties and to secure their respective rights. Comp. Laws, 1862, c. 162 ; Gen. Stat. 1868, c. 80, § 16.

In *Oregon*, partition may be had between tenants in common by suit in equity. If it is alleged in the complaint, and proved, that the property cannot be divided without prejudice to the owner, the court may order a sale, and for that purpose may appoint one or more referees. Otherwise, upon the requisite proof being made, it shall decree partition and appoint three referees, who make partition according to the rights of the parties as determined by the court, and make report of their proceedings to the court. Upon the report being confirmed, a decree is made that such partition be effectual for ever. The decree does not affect tenants for years or for life of the whole property. When a sale is made, the referees are required to report their proceedings to the court ; and if the sale is confirmed, the referees are ordered to execute conveyances. Code, 1862, pp. 109–119, c. 5, tit. 5 ; Comp. Laws, 1872, c. 5, pp. 198, 205.

In *Delaware*, writs for the partition of real estate held in joint-tenancy, or tenancy in common, may be issued by the superior court of the county. Upon judgment in partition, the court may, instead of awarding a writ of partition, appoint five judicious and impartial freeholders of the county to make the partition. Joint-tenants and tenants in common may also petition to the chancellor of the State for partition ; and upon decree that partition shall be made, he shall issue a commission to five freeholders for this purpose, and the final decree upon their return is conclusive upon all the parties. If from the return of the commissioners it appears that no partition has been made, the chancellor shall order the estate to be sold by a trustee ; and such sale having been approved, the trustee is ordered to execute a deed to the purchaser, who takes all the interest of the joint-owners, free from all incumbrances, except such as may be paramount. Rev. Code, 1852, c. 86 ; Rev. Code, 1874, c. 86.

In *Maryland*, joint-tenants, and tenants in common, may have partition by bill in the court of chancery, or on the equity side of the county court. If it *appears to the court that a sale will be most equitable for all con- [*443] cerned, the court may decree a sale on the terms and conditions usual in sales under decrees in chancery ;[1] and if it appears that there ought to be a specific division of the lands, such division is decreed accordingly. Code, 1860, p. 91, art. 19, § 99. Rev. Code, 1878, art. 66, § 13. Partition may also be had in the circuit court of the county among heirs of an intestate. Five commissioners are appointed, who after notice to parties in interest and non-residents shall divide the whole or so much as is susceptible of division without injury, and allot the shares. If not so susceptible, a right of election is given in order of priority to the heirs, on payment of the value of their shares to the others. If neither partition nor election takes place, a sale may be made and the proceeds after providing for liens be divided and invested till claimed. Deeds are to be made by the commissioners. Rev. Code, 1878, art. 47.

In *West Virginia*, tenants in common, &c., may have partition, the circuit courts of the counties having jurisdiction. Any two or more may have their shares set off together. If the estate cannot be conveniently divided, the court may allot it entire to one, he paying the others their proportional amounts, or may sell it, or allot a part and sell the remainder. Code, 1870, c. 79. Rev. Stat. 1878, c. 144.

In *Nevada*, partition is made by courts of equity. The court may order a sale when partition cannot be made without prejudice, or may appoint three referees to make partition, and in case of sale the referees execute the conveyances. The court may require compensation to be made by one party to another to equalize partition. Comp. Laws, 1873, pp. 373–382.

In *Colorado*, where any land is held in joint-tenancy, tenancy in common or coparcenary the petition is to the district court of the county where the major part of the premises is situate. The court appoint three commissioners to make the partition, or, if that would be prejudicial, to make sale of the premises. Courts of chancery may also have power to make partition, or to order sale upon a bill in equity for partition. Rev. Stat. 1868, c. 67 ; Gen. Laws, 1877, c. 74.

[1] Wilson v. Green, 63 Md. 547.

END OF VOL. I.

Lightning Source UK Ltd.
Milton Keynes UK
UKHW012310140219
337323UK00011B/358/P